DATE DUE

DEMCO 38-296

THE BORDEAUX ATLAS

& Encyclopaedia of Châteaux

THE BORDEAUX ATLAS

& ENCYCLOPAEDIA OF CHÂTEAUX

HUBRECHT DUIJKER

&

MICHAEL BROADBENT

St. Martin's Press ⚏ New York

Contents

LIST OF MAPS; ACKNOWLEDGMENTS   6

FOREWORD   7

INTRODUCTION   8

The Region & its Wines   12
Bordeaux in context   14
Zones, appellations and classifications   19
Bordeaux's environment   23
The Bordeaux trade and the
   château system   26

Médoc & Graves   30
Margaux by Michael Broadbent   36
   Directory of châteaux   40
St-Julien by Michael Broadbent   51
   Directory of châteaux   55
Pauillac by Michael Broadbent   61
   Directory of châteaux   67
St-Estèphe by Michael Broadbent   78
   Directory of châteaux   83
Moulis-en-Médoc & Listrac-Médoc   92
   Directory of châteaux   94
Haut-Médoc   103
   Directory of châteaux   106
Médoc   122
   Directory of châteaux   126
Pessac-Léognan by Michael Broadbent   138
   Directory of châteaux   143
Graves   153
   Directory of châteaux: Graves,
   Graves Supérieures & Cérons   155
Sauternes by Michael Broadbent   170
   Directory of châteaux: Sauternes, Barsac   176

The Bordeaux Atlas
& Encyclopaedia of Châteaux

A THOMAS DUNNE BOOK

Copyright © Segrave Foulkes
Publishers/Uitgeverij Het Spectrum
B.V. 1997

Text © Hubrecht Duijker 1997
Text © Michael Broadbent 1997
Maps and commissioned
photographs Copyright © Segrave
Foulkes Publishers/Uitgeverij Het
Spectrum B.V. 1997

Created by Segrave Foulkes
Publishers/Uitgeverij Het Spectrum B.V.

ISBN 0-312-18276-7

The authors and publishers will be
grateful for any information which will
assist them in keeping future editions
up to date. Although all reasonable care
has been taken in the production of this
book, neither the publishers nor the
authors can accept any liability for any
consequences arising from the use
thereof or from any information
contained therein.

First published in the United Kingdom
by Ebury Press, an imprint of Random
House U.K.

First U.S. edition

10 9 8 7 6 5 4 3 2 1

Between the Rivers & the Wider Appellations   190

Premières Côtes de Bordeaux; Cadillac; AC Bordeaux   194
Directory of châteaux   196

Loupiac & Ste-Croix-du-Mont   212
Directory of châteaux   214

Entre-Deux-Mers; ACs Bordeaux & Bordeaux Supérieur   219
Directory of châteaux: *also includes ACs Haut-Benauge, Ste-Foy & St-Macaire*   222
Directory of châteaux: *Graves de Vayres*   266

The Right Bank   268

St-Emilion *by Michael Broadbent*   274
Directory of châteaux   280

St-Emilion Satellites   311
Directory of châteaux   314

Pomerol *by Michael Broadbent*   326
Directory of châteaux   331

Lalande-de-Pomerol   341
Directory of châteaux   342

Fronsac & Canon-Fronsac   348
Directory of châteaux   351

Côtes de Castillon & Bordeaux-Côtes de Francs   360
Directory of châteaux   362

Bourg & Blaye   369
Directory of châteaux   372

CLASSIFICATIONS   389
INDEX & GAZETTEER, INDEX OF COMMUNES

The Bordeaux Atlas
& Encyclopaedia of Châteaux

Editors & contributors
Christopher Foulkes, Carrie Segrave
& Gabrielle Shaw MW

Assistant editor
Alison Franks

Database
Bart Drubbel, Peggy Brouwer

Art director
Eljay Yildirim, Thunderbolt
Partnership

Senior designer
Flora Awolaja

Photographers
Nick Barlow, Hubrecht Duijker,
Hendrick Holler/Rootstock,
Janet Price, Alan Williams

The maps
Cartographic editor
Eugene Fleury

Cartographic production
European Map Graphics

Cartographic research
Ben Eve, Andrew Thompson

The maps in this book were created
from commissioned field surveys,
information supplied by châteaux and
syndicats, and archive material. Aspects
have been verified, with grateful
acknowledgment, with the Institut
Géographique National maps (IGN
France, series 1:25,000 & 1:100,000)
for the Gironde, and also with aerial
photographs supplied by the IGN's
Service de la Documentation
Géographique (2 avenue Pasteur,
94160 St-Mandé). Reproduction of
the maps by any means must have the
express permission of the copyright
owners (*see opposite*).

6

LIST OF MAPS

Title	Map	Page
Western France: Bordeaux in context	*1*	11
The Gironde & its wine zones	*2 & 3*	18
Climate	*4 & 5*	24
Soils	*6*	25
Médoc & Graves key map	*7*	35
Margaux	*8*	44
Margaux: Ch Margaux & its neighbours	*9*	47
St-Julien	*10*	57
St-Julien: the Léoville châteaux	*11*	59
Pauillac	*12*	68
Pauillac: Ch Latour and the Pichons	*13*	73
Pauillac: Ch Lafite Rothschild & Ch Mouton Rothschild	*14*	75
St-Estèphe	*15*	85
St-Estèphe: Ch Cos d'Estournel & Ch Montrose	*16*	87
Moulis-en-Médoc & Listrac-Médoc	*17*	95
Haut-Médoc I: the south	*18*	109
Haut-Médoc II: the centre	*19*	113
Haut-Médoc III: the west and north	*20*	117
Médoc I: the south and centre	*21*	124
Médoc II: the north	*22*	126
Pessac-Léognan	*23*	144
Pessac-Léognan: Ch Haut-Brion & its neighbours	*24*	147
Graves I: the centre	*25*	158
Graves II: the south	*26*	166
Sauternes	*27*	180
Sauternes: Ch d'Yquem & its neighbours	*28*	185
Barsac	*29*	187
Between the Rivers key map	*30*	193
Premières Côtes de Bordeaux & Cadillac south; Loupiac & Ste-Croix-du-Mont	*31*	200
Premières Côtes de Bordeaux & Cadillac north	*32/33*	206
ACs Bordeaux & Bordeaux Supérieur north	*34*	226
Entre-Deux-Mers, Graves de Vayres, Entre-Deux-Mers Haut-Benauge, Bordeaux Haut-Benauge, Bordeaux, Bordeaux Supérieur	*35*	236
Entre-Deux-Mers, Ste-Foy Bordeaux, Côtes de Bordeaux St-Macaire, Bordeaux, Bordeaux Supérieur	*36*	252
The Right Bank key map	*37*	273
St-Emilion	*38*	282
St-Emilion: the *côte*	*39*	297
St-Emilion Satellites: Montagne-St-Emilion, Lussac-St-Emilion, Puisseguin-St-Emilion, St-Georges-St-Emilion	*40*	317
Pomerol	*41*	333
Pomerol: Ch Pétrus & its neighbours	*42*	337
Lalande-de-Pomerol	*43*	345
Fronsac & Canon-Fronsac	*44*	355
Côtes de Castillon & Côtes de Francs	*45*	365
Bourg & Blaye	*46*	371
Bourg & Blaye: the riverside châteaux	*47*	375

HOW TO USE THE MAPS

The Atlas is divided into three sections: Médoc and Graves, Between the Rivers and the Right Bank. The map on page 18 shows all the Bordeaux appellations. At the start of each section is a key map to the detailed maps within it: these are Map 7 on page 35, Map 30 on page 193 and Map 37 on page 273. To locate a specific area use the list on this page or turn to the relevant key map.

The maps vary in scale and detail. Senior appellations have larger-scale maps. Many of these show not only landscape detail, the locations of châteaux and vineyards, but also the land owned by important individual châteaux. (This is vineyard land owned, not necessarily in production.) Nine maps go into further detail and show especially complex and/or high-quality zones; on the appellation maps, the area covered by these maps is shown by a pale red box and a map number. Each map has a north point and a scale (most, but not all, are oriented with north to the top of the page). Châteaux are marked with a red square, other buildings in black. Contour lines are included, at an interval chosen for each map to give the clearest picture of the landscape. Thus on the smaller-scale maps not all contours are shown. In urban areas, detail is generalized to simplify the maps.

Each map has its number next to the title. References from the text are to these numbers. Most châteaux in the directory pages have a map reference (the exceptions are those estates without buildings: the wine is usually made at another estate belonging to the same owner). Thus Map 38/L C7 refers you to Map 38, left-hand page, grid reference C7. For the large-scale maps where individual châteaux are not marked, the map number alone is given, and the general location can be seen by looking up the commune.

Not all châteaux marked on the maps have entries in the directories: as many châteaux as possible have been marked, as an aid to visitors to the region, but as is explained in the Introduction, not all are covered in the text. To find a particular château, consult the relevant directory pages or the index.

NOTE ON CHÂTEAU NAMES

Spellings, abbreviations, hyphenations in château names in the directory pages have been taken from the labels of the bottles tasted.

AUTHORS' ACKNOWLEDGMENTS

Invaluable advice and help was freely given by many people in Bordeaux, in particular Philippe Casteja, President of the CIVB and his colleagues Fiona Morrison and Anne Marbot; Christian Lartigue of the INAO; Christian Moueix and his colleagues in Libourne; Charles and Pat Eve in Pauillac, Claude Pomares of Météo France and of course the many château owners, *régisseurs*, *syndicats viticoles* and others who provided map information, arranged tastings and answered endless questions.

The basic research for the maps was mainly undertaken by Ben Eve in Bordeaux. Additional work, in the region and in the archives, was carried out by Andrew Thompson, Gabrielle Shaw and others. Eugene Fleury, assisted by Pat Fleury, acted as editor and compiler of all the maps. European Map Graphics created the maps on computer.

The massive amount of information that the text contains had to be sorted, checked and re-checked, computer-coded and entered, edited and, when necessary, updated. Then came the photography, design, picture research, the complicated translation and production process in four languages and in four countries. In addition to those mentioned above and in the Introduction, the key players in making this Atlas were Flora Awolaja, Veronica Beattie, Joost Bloemsma, Peggy Brouwer, Claude Dovaz, Bart Drubbel, Claire Forgeot, Christopher Foulkes, Alison Franks, Léon Janssen, Raymond Kaye, Wolfgang Kissel, Beat Koelliker, Eva Meyer, Malcolm Saunders, Carrie Segrave, Gabrielle Shaw and Eljay Yildirim.

The work of all these people was long, hard and skilful – and the authors' gratitude is deep.

Foreword

The fundamental purpose of writing a wine book is to educate people about wine. No wine writer in the world has produced as many extraordinary books that have educated so many thousands about the pleasures of wine, its heritage, history and enduring popularity than Hubrecht Duijker, who has devoted much of his life to the task. More than a decade before I ever wrote a word as a professional wine writer, I was eagerly devouring his books, all of which have proved enormously beneficial and educational to me, and to friends to whom I have recommended his works.

All of Hubrecht Duijker's previous books have maintained a freshness and relevance to this day, and his newest book, the Bordeaux Atlas, may be his finest work to date. Bordeaux is the most important vineyard region in the world, offering in quality and quantity an extraordinary array of wines. The Bordeaux Atlas contains an astonishing amount of insight and information, leading the reader on a remarkable academic, visual and educational journey through the great, well-known estates, as well as the less prestigious and lesser-known. The illuminating prose, in addition to the finest maps I have ever seen on this hallowed wine region, will make this book a modern-day classic. It is a privilege for me to write this foreword and to recommend, without reservation, the Bordeaux Atlas and Encyclopaedia of Châteaux.

ROBERT M. PARKER, JR.
Monkton, Maryland
May 1997

Introduction

It was a Bordeaux that first made me realize just how fine, fascinating and delicious wine can be. My wife gave it to me on my birthday, in 1966: a Château Branaire (Duluc-Ducru) 1959. I still remember that first glass. This St-Julien had a bouquet smelling of violets, ripe fruit and all sorts of other notes that in those days I still found elusive; a complexity matched by the equally wonderful taste. It was a revelation. At once I understood how people could wax lyrical about wine, and even write about it. Red Bordeaux immediately became my benchmark for all other red wines. I started to read about the region and became more and more fascinated. At last, in September 1970 I made my first exploratory visit to Bordeaux. On that trip I discovered great wines. I also discovered that there was sometimes much more to be said about the great and famous estates than had so far appeared in print. The seed had been sown for my first book on Bordeaux, a work published in four languages and dealing with the best, mostly classified, estates of the Médoc, Graves, St-Emilion and Pomerol.

When on January 1, 1975, I got into my 2CV to make a tour of the 90 or so châteaux for that book, I was in fact making a start on this *Bordeaux Atlas & Encyclopaedia of Châteaux*. More than 20 years of close and happy investigation of this most fascinating of wine regions (with many a visit – for further books, for family holidays, for pleasure) have gone into it. The

region and the wines have continued to enthrall me – not least because in the course of the 1980s, all kinds of things began to change. Many of the châteaux acquired new owners; new estates were appearing; large-scale investment in modern cellar equipment was taking place; the phenomenon of second wines underwent dramatic expansion; many of the unclassified estates started making special *cuvées* – and the number of really good wines was growing throughout the area. And, at the same time, far more of these excellent, lesser-known wines were finding their way out onto the shelves of the world's wine-stores and super-markets. Bordeaux was taking on a new élan, a new vitality.

Out of all this arose the realization that a new book was needed for what is, after all, the largest fine-wine-producing region in the world, and the most enduringly popular. An up-to-date guide to the whole region, a reference source for the best wines and the best châteaux – but (a big 'but') at every level, not just the stratosphere. And with really useful maps, specially commissioned and breaking new ground by showing, first, the top appellations in sufficient detail to see where the individual châteaux' vineyards lie and second, the lesser-known areas not usually mapped at all – but the source of much first-rate everyday wine.

It was years before this concept of mine could be realized, but at last the green light came, late in 1994. Since then whole mountains of work have been got through. Tasting – both in the region and elsewhere in the world – recording, researching, collating the tons of information on what turned out to be more than 2,000 châteaux – upwards of 4,000 wines – was my responsibility. Meanwhile the erudite Michael Broadbent M.W. (whose enviable duty as the head, for the past 30 years, of the Wine Department of the international auctioneers Christie's has been to sample and assess the finest wines, from the finest cellars, of this century and the last) brought his depth of knowledge to writing introductory essays describing the eight most celebrated districts.

I spent many weeks over two years journeying through almost the entire region, tasting the wines both at individual estates and at the *syndicats viticoles*, who assembled bottles from their districts. However, it was physically impossible to taste all the wines myself; the number of them – in the thousands – ruled this out. A number of talented tasters therefore lent their aid.

Many wines from St-Emilion, Pomerol and neighbouring districts were expertly assessed by Cornelis van Leeuwen, Reader in Viniculture at the University of Bordeaux and technical consultant to Château Cheval Blanc. Ronald de Groot, publisher and editor-in-chief of the Dutch journal *PersWijn*, together with his panel of tasters, took on the range of

Bordeaux available on the Dutch market, and tasted further wines in the Premières Côtes de Bordeaux. Many bottles of Bordeaux, Bordeaux Supérieur and Entre-Deux-Mers that came in late were assessed by René Lambert of the Consortium Vinicole de Bordeaux et de la Gironde, whose tasting notes are published in various countries. Our combined, exhaustive tastings not only served to furnish an up-to-date impression of the wines, their character and quality, but also in making the selection.

Thus châteaux described are exclusively those whose wines have been tasted – and who supplied the information requested. (Strange to relate, there were producers who supplied their wines for tasting, but not the factual data – reminders by post, fax and telephone notwithstanding.) For each estate selected I have gathered, direct from the château and from other sources, useful and rarely published data such as the size of the vineyard, production (in cases), the vines planted, second wines, other estates under the same ownership.

Through this process, it has been possible for me to document each château and its wines, and to write my profiles of them. In addition to Michael Broadbent's essays, other introductory articles are by Christopher Foulkes (also the moving spirit behind the maps) and Gabrielle Shaw M.W.

Below: Château Latour, one of the top echelon of Médoc châteaux, the First Growths, surveys its vineyards

The other component is, of course, the maps. Four dozen entirely new maps have been made for the Atlas. The research for these was meticulously carried out from scratch: on the ground by foot, bicycle, motorbike and car, and in the archives. For the basic information on the shape of the land, rivers and contours use was made of, for example, very detailed, aerial-survey-based, German military maps of 1942-3 which our research uncovered in London. We have been given the exact positions for their vineyard plots by some 100 châteaux: the nine most detailed maps were made on the basis of these. They enable the Bordeaux enthusiast to see the precise boundaries of the legendary Château Pétrus, for example, and its relationship to neighbouring estates. The tiny two-hectare vineyard of Château Le Pin is revealed by the map to be split into three even smaller plots, two of which are sundered by a house and garden. In St-Julien the sheer size of the combined Léoville estates shows clearly, revealing quite how enormous the domaine was before the French Revolution. The intricate patchwork of the St-Emilion *côte* is at last made clear to see. Wherever possible the exact locations are given for the châteaux described, and a map reference provided.

My sincere thanks go to those who worked in Bordeaux, in London and in Utrecht to produce the maps and the book: their names are listed on page 6.

HUBRECHT DUIJKER
Abcoude, May 1997

If the essence of this book is who makes what where, the purpose of my essays introducing the senior appellations is to explain why Bordeaux and its wine is effective on so many levels, to attempt to describe the surprisingly variable landscapes depicted two-dimensionally in map form and to define the various styles and qualities of wine.

Red Bordeaux varies from decent, robust, good-value everyday wines, through a gamut of distinctive wines in a middle price bracket, up to the most supremely great, capable of appealing subtly, almost magically, to the eye, nose and palate – particularly when, after ageing in bottle, they have reached their peak of perfection. This book covers them all. There are the facts on and profiles of the great, the obscure and everything in between. Hubrecht Duijker explains how these were compiled. Let me add that no other work to my knowledge reveals so much about so many Bordeaux wines. What all these differing styles and qualities of red Bordeaux have in common is a singular ability to accompany food: to create anticipation, to whet the appetite, to set the gastric juices in motion, to please, to refresh and to aid the digestion. If this sounds either trite or obvious let me stress that by no means do all red wines have these capabilities. Indeed, many of the modern, easy, deep-coloured, full, fruity reds – pleasing enough to drink – do not perform well with food: certainly not to the same extent as claret. For the common denominator of a modest bourgeois growth and a renowned *premier cru* is mouth-cleansing tannin.

The dry and sweet white wines must not be neglected, and this book gives more detail than ever before published on a wide range of white-wine estates, again from the great to the rustic. But it is fair to admit that it is claret to which we return, both as scholars and hedonists, again and again....

The fascination of Bordeaux lies in its variety: the large areas of production, the astonishing number of individual producers, of 'châteaux', the variations of style due to soil, subsoil and microclimate, and of quality resulting from annual climatic variations. Then, finally, the effect of age and maturation.

The most fascinating aspect of red Bordeaux is the way it changes over its lifespan. Red Bordeaux of a good vintage should have a deep colour, virtually opaque when young, with a purple rim, then becoming less deep and changing colour from immature violet to mature mahogany red as it ages. It will have a good, positive, varietal aroma when young, a subtle bouquet developing as it matures; and on the palate a positive, slightly sweet entry (the sweetness of alcohol and ripe grapes) good 'body' or weight – not too heavy – with an attractive flavour, refreshing acidity and pleasantly mouth-drying tannin. In a poor vintage, the wine is initially, and becomes increasingly, paler, with a feeble, more watery rim. All the component parts are weaker, less satisfactory, unbalanced. These wines are destined for quick consumption, not for long keeping. As such they have their uses.

I trust that this combination of an exhaustive gazetteer of châteaux, pen portraits and tantalising and informative maps will enrich the interest of connoisseurs and entice the newcomer. Not just to know, to theorize, but to explore, taste and drink the wonderful wines of Bordeaux.

"Allez, vieux fous, allez apprendre à boire. On est savant quant on sait boire. Qui ne sait boire ne sait rien." (Boileau). "Off with you, old fools, and learn to drink. For he that knows how to drink is wise, and he that does not knows nothing!"

MICHAEL BROADBENT
London, May 1997

Bordeaux
1

200m

The Region
and its Wines

The majestic barrel cellars at Château Margaux provide a fitting nursery for the wine of one of Bordeaux's First Growths

To enjoy a bottle of Bordeaux it is not necessary to study the history of the region, nor to know anything much about the subsoil or the climate. Pleasure at every level, from the simple to the most subtle, is what Bordeaux offers. It is when one bottle reminds you of another, when comparisons and contrasts start to tease at the memory, that the region needs to come into focus. The largest part of this book is about the châteaux: where they are on the maps, what they do, how they do it, what their wines are like. The next few pages paint in the background: the history and habits, soils and weather, localities and legalities of Bordeaux as a region of France and a vineyard. This extraordinary setting created and supports the world's largest fine-wine-producing area – past, present, and as far into the future as we can reasonably see.

BORDEAUX IN CONTEXT

Bordeaux has such a long history of making and selling wine that the practice is almost subconscious. Outsiders conclude that among the Bordelais the knack of viticulture, and the habit of trade in wine, is inborn. This heritage is documented in a thousand charters and records, letters and notebooks. To read the correspondence of eighteenth-century château stewards and owners, or the diaries of the Lawton family of wine-brokers from the same period, is to enter a world centuries old – yet wholly familiar. The concerns are unchanged: will the weather be kind? Are the foreign buyers eager or coy? Will the last vintage be sold in time to make cellar-room for the next? The gossip at today's Bordeaux parties, or a château's welcome to a foreign buyer, could be transcribed direct from a source a hundred – or a thousand – years old.

Wine lovers find comfort in Bordeaux's history when the market in wine seems to go mad, with prices rising beyond reason; and when poor vintages succeed one another. It is easy to believe at such times that Bordeaux will never again be affordable, or obtainable. History reminds us that booms, slumps and extremes of weather are regular, if unpredictable. (The slumps, indeed, have lasted longer

Wine for sale: bottles in a restaurant window in Bordeaux entice the wine lover

than the booms, and châteaux and *chais* have spent more decades neglected than they have in being cosseted and cared for.) Wine-makers and merchants take solace from history too – but at perhaps rather different points in the cycle.

The history of wine in Bordeaux spans 2,000 years and has occupied many scholars. A brief survey may put the wines of today into the context of their past.

TWO MILLENNIA OF TRADE

The Romans dealt in cargoes of wine on the quaysides of the town that they knew as Burdigala, and in medieval times the great fleets of wine ships were the mainspring of the economy not just of Bordeaux, but of much of western France, England, Holland and the other northern lands. This trade is carried on today (if now by truck, not by sailing ship) with striking continuity of attitudes and concerns, practices and techniques. Latin texts tell us that traders transported wine from Burdigala's quays to Roman Britain, and doubtless elsewhere, but (so the historians postulate) this wine came from inland, from the Haut-Pays up-river. By the end of the Roman era vineyards were thriving around Bordeaux, and they have been there ever since. Winegrowing faltered in the Dark Ages, but revived during the early Middle Ages.

The gentle landscape of the Bourgeais, on the east bank of the Gironde, was one of the first vineyard areas

Bordeaux was not alone in France in having a thriving wine trade, but it was the only centre able to trade freely by sea – and by the Atlantic at that. Mediterranean wine regions such as the Rhône faced competition from Iberia, Italy and the Levant. Bordeaux had only the Rhine vineyards to contend with in serving the thirsty nations of the North.

In this contest the city gained, by dynastic accident, a splendid advantage. In the year 1152 Henry Plantagenet, the future Henry II of England, married the heiress of Aquitaine, Aliénor (to the English, Eleanor). Aquitaine was a separate duchy – but before this marriage Eleanor, one of the most colourful and liberated women of her day, had been Queen of France through her first marriage to Louis VII. The French kings never became reconciled to their loss.

Thus through a wedding much of western France came under English rule. Henry and Eleanor's son Richard, Duke of Aquitaine, became King Richard I and based himself for much of his reign at Bordeaux. His brother John, who succeeded him, made a deal with the burghers of Bordeaux: ships to aid his wars in return for lower taxes. Henceforward the wines of Bordeaux could compete with those shipped from rivals on the Loire and from La Rochelle.

The real turning-point in Bordeaux's fortunes was the year 1224, when the French king captured the port of La Rochelle. English trade subsequently depended even more on Bordeaux for the supplies of wine that it needed. The city's merchants prospered, and buttressed their prosperity by negotiating canny trading concessions at the expense of their inland rivals. The annual wine fleet, already a fixture of sea-borne trade, became a domestic matter, with Bordeaux wine filling the English royal cellars and many others. The amounts imported were huge: when Edward II married Isabella of France in the year 1308, he ordered 1,000 *tonneaux* of wine: the equivalent of 1.1 million bottles. England was not the only market – Scotland and Ireland took their share, as did the Low Countries, northern Germany and the Baltic lands – but it was the largest. In 1300 the wine fleet comprised 900 ships. Their total annual cargo, taking an average from the records of the 14th century, was around 83,000 *tonneaux* (more than 8 million cases). At least half – sometimes 80 per cent – went to Britain.

London and Bordeaux prospered together: the City of London's ancient guild of wine merchants, the Vintners' Company, descends directly from the medieval Merchant Wine Tunners of Gascony. Vineyards were planted by everyone from the Archbishop to the peasantry: the Bordeaux *vignoble* has been estimated at 100,000 hectares – about the same area as today. The vineyards expanded from the original Graves and Premières Côtes to take in parts of the southern Médoc and the St-Emilion area.

But the French kings were tireless in their efforts to regain Aquitaine. Wars and sieges ravaged the land, and in 1453 the final battle – at Castillon on the Dordogne – saw the triumph of France. The French king cautiously confirmed the trading privileges of the Bordeaux merchants, including their right to keep out wine from the Haut-Pays up-river until their own produce was sold. Indeed the kings went so far as to grant Bordeaux its own *parlement* – a law court whose members became a hereditary class of rich, but non-noble, citizens (known as the *noblesse de la robe*, as distinct from the *noblesse de l'épée*), a concession which gave Bordeaux a special character among French cities.

FROM CLAIRET TO CLARET: FINE WINE IS BORN

The Bordeaux wine of those days was rarely red. Some was white, but most was '*clairet*' – what the English later called claret. This was a very light red or rosé. Clairet was a wine to drink as soon as possible – as were most wines of the day. It did not keep, and each year's new wine displaced any surviving stocks of the old, which was marked down in price as the summer turned it to vinegar and the new vintage approached.

But at some time in the late 17th century, a discovery was made (or rather, a rediscovery: the Romans, as with so many aspects of civilization, got there first). Wine could improve with age. Much ink and scholarship has been spent in establishing exactly when this took place. Two innovations prompted it: the use of sulphur as a disinfectant to clean casks and utensils, and the glass bottle.

The revolution in wine nurture that resulted was the work of the Bordeaux merchants. They perfected the art of ageing claret in casks. Winemaking – the actual process of picking and fermenting – changed little between the Middle Ages and the 1960s. But in the cellars of the Chartrons, the merchant quarter of Bordeaux, a great leap forward was made in the early 18th century. Casks purified with sulphur could keep wine for long periods, providing they were well made and stoppered, topped up frequently and properly stored.

One step in quality led to another, and another, with the discovery that wine would gain from being fined and racked. Bottles and corks allowed wine to age even further – and to gain more from its ageing. However, most Bordeaux wine was bottled later in its life span than it would be today – after at least four years in cask – and this operation was almost invariably carried out by the customer, not by the producer. Barrel-ageing, under controlled conditions, was the key breakthrough.

In parallel with these changes in technique came a switch in the pattern of trade. England took to other drinks (sack, or sherry, from Spain was one) as well as claret, and quantities sold to England fell. The Dutch took their place, but they wanted white wine not red, and cheap white wine at that, for blending or distilling. The English market gradually turned to what we would call fine wine. Colonial trade, too, became important, as French colonies in the West Indies and elsewhere contributed their wealth and their thirsts.

Statistics from 1739-40 show who bought what. The UK (then including Ireland) took 7,500 *tonneaux* of Bordeaux at a total value of 4,110,000 *livres* while the other export markets together bought 36,600 *tonneaux*, but at a total of not a great deal more: 5,790,300 *livres*. England paid the highest per *tonneau* of 'grand wine': 1,500 *livres* (about £107) against 1,000 *livres* for Holland.

The UK market had come to concentrate on the top wines partly because of the high tax on French wine, then discriminated against due to wars. These taxes were levied at a flat rate of £55 per *tonneau*, making everyday wine impossibly dear. However the growth of a rich governing class – at once landowners and politicians – provided the market for quality wine. Behind the growth of this market was, as Nicholas Faith has observed, the revolutionary idea that one bottle of claret could be distinguished from another. This notion seems to have had its birth in London, among the pleasure-loving society of the late 17th century.

The demand for fine wine was answered by the Bordeaux *parlementaires*, whose riches from trade were translated into land-holdings. They founded dynasties whose names occur even today on label after label: Ségur, Pichon, Lalande; Brane, Larose, Lascombes. The Pontac family, owners of Haut-Brion, built up the first wine estate whose name was attached to the wine. Haut-Brion is mentioned in the writings of the English philosopher Locke (who visited the château in 1677 and was astonished at the obvious poverty of the gravel soil) and by the diarist Pepys, who enjoyed a bottle or two in London in 1663. Quite early in the 18th century the pattern of the Médoc was established: a flurry of land-draining (Dutch engineers were responsible) and buying led to the great estates which are now at the head of the 1855 Classification. Lafite's vineyard was new in 1680; in the same decade Margaux's was 188 acres – almost as large as today. Latour took a generation more to emerge, but by 1714 the four First Growths (even then so called) commanded prices of between 330-550 *livres* a *tonneau*,

Left: landscape in the Libournais. The agricultural richness of the Gironde attracted the Romans, medieval monks and princes – and everyone from philosophers to bankers since.

Pomerol and St-Emilion are rural, self-absorbed places

whereas a *tonneau* of plain, unidentified Médoc wine cost 310 *livres* or less, and ordinary wine around 100 *livres*.

THE MERCHANTS

While it became accepted that the wine of one estate might be better than another, the actual producers had little or no say in how their wine was sold. Indeed, they had no control over what happened to their wine at all. Château names could not be protected and mislabelling scandals regularly occurred. It was only with the acceptance of château-bottling between the two world wars that authenticity became achievable.

Once the new wine was in the cellars behind the Quai des Chartrons in Bordeaux, at about a year old, it was fair game. The merchants knew what their (mostly overseas) customers wanted, and they did not hesitate to 'amend' the wine so that they got it. This meant adding doses of strong, dark sweet 'southern' wine, or even brandy, to the sometimes rather austere claret. At the same period the Bordeaux merchants' colleagues in Oporto were developing port in a similar way. However, they found that Douro wine needed a dose of about 20% brandy: claret was never that much in need of aid.

This adulteration (as we now regard it) was the other side of the coin of the *chartronnais'* cellar skills. The châteaux owners hated it, but feared the loss of their markets if they failed to sell to the Bordeaux trade. Widespread château-bottling and stricter official control mean these creative cellar practices are history.

DISASTER AND RECOVERY

The pattern of trade was invariably shaken up by wars, weather and revolutions, but continuity not disruption is the main theme from 1700 to the late 19th century. The 1860s and 1870s saw a real-estate boom in Bordeaux, especially the Médoc, only paralleled over a century later. Many of the estates gained their châteaux and *chais* in this period, making Bordeaux a museum of 19th-century domestic and rural architecture.

But close behind this prosperity were problems: the oïdium disease and the phylloxera louse. In succession these scourges ravaged the vineyards, driving production down and, insidiously, sapping the reputation of fine wine. Financial crises, labour unrest, world war: troubles came hard upon each other.

The 1855 Classification, devised in a period of prosperity, gave the leading Médoc and Sauternes châteaux a status which perhaps helped to carry them through the wars and slumps, but the lesser estates, especially on the periphery, suffered from colonial competition, the high cost of eradicating phylloxera and the decline during the 1920s and '30s of overseas trade. It was not until the 1960s that prosperity truly returned to the Bordeaux vineyards, as is shown by the absence of any château-building in the 20th century until the flurry of investment during the 1980s.

This investment was built upon a second technical revolution. The use of temperature control equipment, and new insights into the biochemistry of fermentation, increasingly allowed control to replace custom and guesswork in winemaking. White wine especially has benefited, but the leap in the quality of ordinary claret is noticeable, as is its consistency over varying vintages.

Today white wines – the rejuvenated dry style and the recently-revived sweet wines of Sauternes – have an importance which begins to rival the reds. It is no longer accurate to talk about Bordeaux as if it is all claret. That said, the glamour that attaches to the great red-wine châteaux has led to several of them being bought by ambitious conglomerates, both French and foreign, and by rich individuals. The pattern of family ownership, so constant (if sometimes diffused by inheritance law) for three centuries at least, is breaking down. Bordeaux has always traded its wine, but even with distinctly un-French names like Smith, Lynch, Lawson, Becker, Barton, Kirwan laced firmly into its history, it has stayed somewhat isolated as a society. The ambition to own, or work on, a Bordeaux wine estate is attracting people to the region from all over the world, bringing a transfusion of cash and a sharing of wine expertise, changing the character and structure of the wine trade. These are exciting times.

Bordeaux
2/3

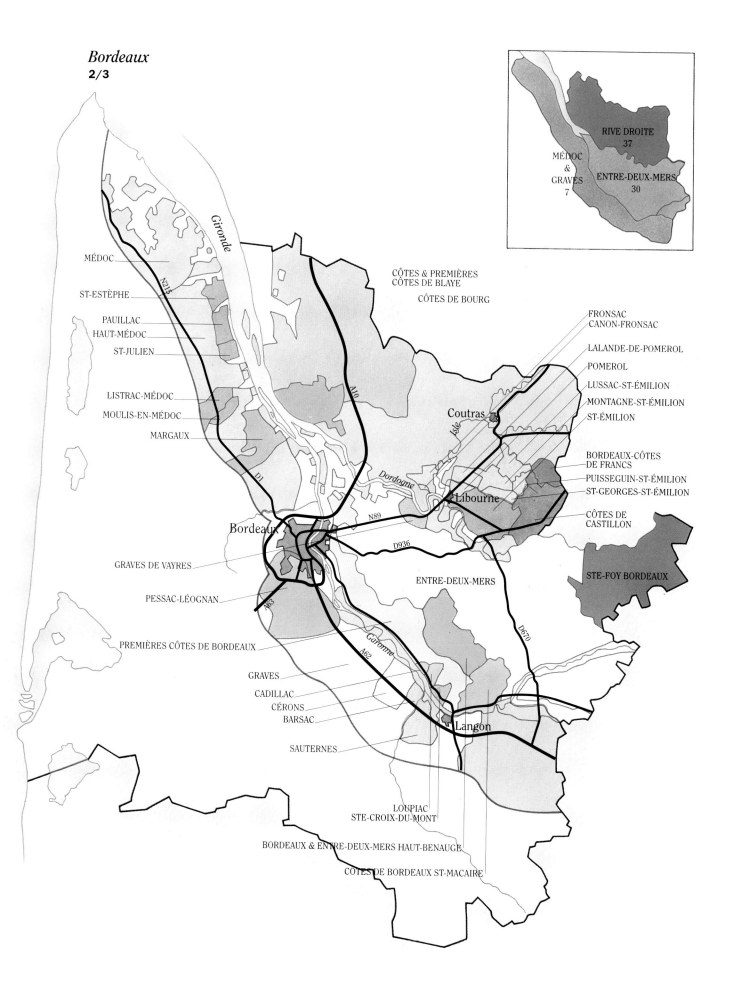

Gironde

RIVE DROITE
37

MÉDOC
&
GRAVES
7

ENTRE-DEUX-MERS
30

MÉDOC

ST-ESTÈPHE

PAUILLAC
HAUT-MÉDOC

ST-JULIEN

LISTRAC-MÉDOC

MOULIS-EN-MÉDOC

MARGAUX

N215

CÔTES & PREMIÈRES
CÔTES DE BLAYE

CÔTES DE BOURG

A10

FRONSAC
CANON-FRONSAC

LALANDE-DE-POMEROL

POMEROL

LUSSAC-ST-ÉMILION

MONTAGNE-ST-ÉMILION

ST-ÉMILION

Coutras

Isle

BORDEAUX-CÔTES
DE FRANCS

PUISSEGUIN-ST-ÉMILION

ST-GEORGES-ST-ÉMILION

CÔTES DE
CASTILLON

Dordogne

Libourne

D1

N89

Bordeaux

GRAVES DE VAYRES

PESSAC-LÉOGNAN

A63

D936

ENTRE-DEUX-MERS

STE-FOY BORDEAUX

D670

PREMIÈRES CÔTES DE BORDEAUX

GRAVES

CADILLAC

CÉRONS

BARSAC

Garonne

A62

Langon

SAUTERNES

LOUPIAC
STE-CROIX-DU-MONT

BORDEAUX & ENTRE-DEUX-MERS HAUT-BENAUGE

CÔTES DE BORDEAUX ST-MACAIRE

Zones, ACs and Classifications

The Gironde is a *département* of France, one of the country's governmental sub-divisions. Its boundaries are very similar to those of the medieval Sénéchaussée of Guyenne: the area under the control of the city of Bordeaux. The city is still the heart of the wine region, and the whole *vignoble* is usually called 'Bordeaux'.

THE BORDEAUX WINE ZONES

The two great rivers Dordogne and Garonne – and after their confluence the Gironde estuary – divide the region into three. This division is reflected in many ways, from wine styles to the organization of the wine trade, and it is used in this Atlas. The three main zones are the Médoc and Graves, on the Left Bank (of the Garonne/Gironde) – where are also found the sweet-wine enclaves of Sauternes and Barsac; the Right Bank (of the Dordogne/Gironde) or the Libournais, dominated by St-

Below: growing grapes and making wine requires much skilled manual work, such as hand-grafting

Emilion and Pomerol; and the area between the Dordogne and Garonne rivers, the Entre-Deux-Mers.

Wine from the Bordeaux region comes in a range of styles and under thousands of labels and there is nothing on many of them to show that the wine comes from Bordeaux. What does appear is one of the region's appellations, which legally pins the wine down as being from a specific area and attests that it conforms to specific rules governing its making.

THE APPELLATION SYSTEM

Appellation d'Origine Contrôlée is the legal basis for all quality French wine production. The appellation system, which the region shares with the rest of winemaking France, has its own personality in the Gironde. There are several hundred ACs in France – and Bordeaux has 57 of them. Some apply to a single type of wine, others to two, a few to several. There are two basic groups: generic and specific. In Bordeaux, generic ACs are used for wines which – in principle, if not in practice – can come from anywhere within the 115,000 hectares of the Bordeaux vineyard area. There are four generic appellations:

- Bordeaux (for red, dry white, rosé, clairet)
- Bordeaux Supérieur (for red and semi-sweet white)
- Crémant de Bordeaux (for sparkling wine made by the traditional method)
- Fine de Bordeaux (for a brandy)

The specific ACs relate to defined parcels of land and can vary enormously in size and style. For example one of Bordeaux's largest specific ACs, St-Emilion, covers over 7,000 hectares; its smallest, St-Georges-St-Emilion, less than 300. Some apply to a single style of wine (such as Pomerol or Pauillac), others apply to a variety of styles and colours (Graves, for instance, can be red or white). Appellations can overlap: the more specific apply to land within the more general. For example, AC Margaux overlies (in descending order) Haut-Médoc, Médoc and Bordeaux. The more strictly limited the production area, the more senior – and commercially valuable – the appellation. Châteaux with land in a senior AC will label their wine accordingly, if it meets the production criteria (see below). They may use a more junior AC for a second wine. Even in Pomerol, though, with its single-style AC, there is nothing to stop you growing Sauvignon Blanc and making a generic AC Bordeaux blanc – other than economic imperatives.

Rules governing AC wine production are laid down by Ministerial Decree and cover:

- **Area** Communes (or parts of communes) entitled to use the appellation (disallowing unsuitable land: see below).
- **Grape variety** or varieties For some ACs, maximum and/or minimum percentages are stipulated for certain varieties.
- **Production**, in both vineyard and cellar Covers planting density, pruning methods, fertilizing, equipment used, etc.
- **Alcohol level** by volume or in total Minimum sugar content of must before any additions, minimum and maximum degree of alcohol after fermentation.
- **Basic yield** per hectare This may be modified according to size and quality of the year's crop.
- **Labelling** Labels must conform to European Union legislation, which includes details such as alcohol level, volume of contents, print size, etc.

The AC can only be used if the conditions are met. Each year, the producer must make a harvest declaration and a request for approval, which is only granted after analysis of the wine. Without this certificate of approval, the wine cannot be sold.

APPELLATIONS ON THE MAP

Appellations seem simple: they are, *au fond*, areas of land. But as the maps in this Atlas show, they are seldom that clear-cut. They are rarely solid blocks of land, nor do their names tell the whole story. For example, St-Julien is both a commune and an AC, but in fact parts of the commune of St-Julien actually fall within the Pauillac AC boundary. The official decree may list a clutch of communes which make up an appellation, but only certain designated parts of those communes can actually grow grapes to make the relevant AC.

Each appellation is defined in terms of a geographical area and a delimited area. The geographical

area is the communes cited in the decree. The delimited area corresponds to parcels of land within the geographical area which have been recognized as suitable to produce the wine of the AC.

A commission of experts, chosen by the INAO, delimits these parcels. The commission is composed of geologists, soil experts and wine specialists. Generally, they omit land which is low-lying, badly drained, badly exposed, with sandy soil, on an impermeable subsoil, etc. Of course, parcels may be listed as suitable, but may not currently be planted with vines: they can be meadows, farmland and sometimes woods. The parcels also include buildings and roads which fall within them.

The surface area of parcels actually planted with vines and producing AC wine can thus be very different from the delimited area. First, not all the land classified AC is planted with vines. And second, not all the planted vineyards are using the main AC.

When vines are uprooted, the grower keeps the right to replant for a period of eight years, on the same parcel or on another parcel. At the end of eight years, if he has not replanted his vines he will lose his right to do so, but his parcel will remain classified AC.

It would be wrong to assume that all the best wines of Bordeaux are classified – they are not: the wines of Pomerol, for example, have never been classified, nor is it likely they ever will be. It is also wrong to assume that just because a wine is classified it carries an automatic guarantee of quality: even some of the very finest châteaux have been known to go through very poor periods – but without ever having to suffer the ignominy of losing their official status.

Each classification differs in its breadth and structure and the way in which it is drawn up. Some encompass little more than a handful of properties, others are much wider-reaching; some are hierarchical, others make no distinction of rank at all; some revise their list regularly, others have been in existence for well over a hundred years, with barely any changes. The one element they do have in common is that they only cover the *top* wine – or wines in the case of some of the red- and white-wine producing Graves châteaux – of the property; second and third wines do not form a part of the classification.

There are three different classifications for the leading Growths of Bordeaux:

THE 1855 CLASSIFICATION OF THE RED AND WHITE WINES OF THE GIRONDE

At the request of Napoléon III, the wines of the Gironde were classified for the Universal Exhibition in Paris in 1855. The Bordeaux Chamber of Commerce handed the task over to a group of leading brokers who came up with a list of suggestions, based on track record and market prices. Some of these properties had already enjoyed a good reputation for a century or more – and the terms 'First Growth' and 'Second Growth' were in common use. In many ways the 1855 Classification formalized an existing list. The result covers red wines from the Médoc (and Haut-Brion) and whites from Sauternes and Barsac – the wines traded internationally at the time. It is the most structured of all the systems, with five classes for the reds and two for the whites (with Yquem standing on its own as a *premier cru supérieur*). Since 1855, very few modifications have taken place – mainly changes of names as estates were divided. The only re-classification was the long-overdue elevation of Ch Mouton Rothschild from Second to First Growth in 1973. At the same time the continuing status of Ch Haut-Brion (the only non-Médocain red wine in the original classification) as First Growth was re-affirmed. Although a few wines are widely acknowledged to be under- or

On the maps in this book, the outlines of ACs are shown where two or more apply in the map area, and for the most important appellations. Thus the map of St-Julien shows the land which is in the delineated area. Actual vineyards are shown where they have been found to exist. Lesser areas, such as the northern Médoc, are mapped at a smaller scale. Here, all planted land has one AC, Médoc, so no appellation boundaries are shown.

CLASSIFICATIONS

A classification is very different to an AC. Whereas an AC relates to land, a classification belongs to a property or *cru* ('growth') – in effect a château. The most prestigious classified properties are the Growths of the Médoc, Graves, Sauternes, Barsac and St-Emilion, which total less than 200. Classifications are made (and amended) by commissions of outside experts, not by the châteaux themselves. Most of the classifications have various classes or ranks within them. The two categories of *crus bourgeois* and *crus artisans*, both relating to the Médoc, include several hundred lesser properties. They are growers' syndicates, not classifications. *Crus bourgeois*, as noted below, have various categories.

over-rated, the 1855 list remains remarkable overall for its accuracy today – which does not stop constant speculation about its revision.

THE 1959 CLASSIFICATION OF THE RED AND WHITE WINES OF THE GRAVES

These wines were classified relatively recently at the request of the Syndicate of the Defence of the Graves Appellation. There is no hierarchy to the classification, nor any fixed date in the future for revision. It is the only list where certain properties are classified for both their red and dry white wines. Ch Haut-Brion is the only Bordeaux property to belong to two classifications for its red wine: the Graves one and the 1855 Classification of the wines of the Gironde.

CLASSIFICATION OF ST-EMILION

This is the most complicated system of all, with membership being revised every ten years or so. The first classification took place in 1955 and became official in 1958 and has been revised three times since: 1969, 1986 and 1996. The next revision is due in 2006. There are two classes: *premiers grands crus classés*, which in the 1996 revision numbered 13, divided into 'A' (Ausone and Cheval Blanc) and 'B', and *grands crus classés*, which currently number 55. Growers must submit an application each time a revision is due and promotions and/or demotions do occur. The classification should not be confused with the AC St-Emilion Grand Cru, which can be applied for on an annual basis by any St-Emilion producer. Wines judged up to standard are awarded the appellation and can put '*grand cru*' on the label.

CRUS BOURGEOIS, CRUS ARTISANS

In addition to these three major classifications, there are two lesser categories for the wines of the Médoc:

1932 list of crus bourgeois   Between 1930 and 1932, under the authority of the Chamber of Agriculture of the Gironde and the Chamber of Commerce of Bordeaux, a group of *courtiers* were requested to draw up a list of châteaux in the Médoc deemed worthy of *cru bourgeois* status. The list recognized 444 properties split into three tiers: *crus bourgeois supérieurs exceptionnels*, *crus bourgeois supérieurs* and *crus bourgeois*. During the crisis years which followed, very little more was heard about them, but the growers' syndicate was reformed in 1962 and in 1966 and 1978 gave awards to wines in three categories: *crus grands bourgeois exceptionnels*, *crus grands bourgeois* and *crus bourgeois*. Such distinctions were subsequently banned from labels by the EU, so that the only mention which may now appear is that of *cru bourgeois*. The list of *crus bourgeois* today remains very similar to the original one, although about 50 châteaux have never applied for membership of today's syndicate. Nonetheless, they are entitled to use the term on the label. In this Atlas, you will see the words '*cru bourgeois*' when a château is actually on the 1996 Syndicate list.

The crus artisans   This term has been in use as a description for more than 150 years and is now being revived. A syndicate of growers, formed in 1989, currently numbers about 60 – although more than 300 châteaux could lay claim to the title – and in 1994 the EU ruled that *cru artisan* could appear on a label.

Gentle swellings of land, hardly hills, distinguish the top vineyards in St-Julien from the rest

BORDEAUX'S ENVIRONMENT

The Bordeaux region is well-nigh ideal for growing grapes for fine wine. The underlying geology, the soils and landforms, the climate all combine to create a superb environment. The many areas offer a succession of *terroirs* – unities of microclimate, soil and landforms – that vary subtly but which all provide what makes vines bear best. These are discussed in the Atlas. But the wider context is revealing. Geology and subsoils stay unchanged for millenia – though man has modified topsoil and drainage considerably in some places – but the climate, or weather pattern, does vary. Bordeaux has a thousand vintages to look back on, and knows that within the broad parameters of a temperate maritime climate, only the unexpected is constant. Variation in sun hours, temperature and rainfall, and the timing of all three, means that each vintage will be different – a factor which tries the patience and pockets of growers and winemakers, but excites the interest of wine lovers.

GEOLOGY AND SOILS

Dig deep enough beneath most Bordeaux vineyards and you will reach limestone or an associated rock. But, unlike many wine regions such as Burgundy and Champagne, the underlying geology is not central to the picture. In Bordeaux, more depends upon the local variations in landform and soil, and these stem from relatively recent geological time.

The limestone is most prominent in the landscapes of the Right Bank and Entre-Deux-Mers. In some places it becomes important: the St-Emilion *côte* is the most telling example, but the hills and slopes of Fronsac, Castillon, the St-Emilion satellites and Blaye are the limestone bones breaking through the surface. In other parts of St-Emilion and Pomerol gravel overlies the limestone, producing soils similar, but by no means identical, to the Médoc's.

GLACIERS AND GRAVEL

It takes a leap of imagination to see the influence of long-gone glaciers and rivers on present-day wine, but ice was perhaps the single most important factor in shaping Bordeaux. The glaciers fed ancient rivers, predecessors of the Garonne and Dordogne, with abundant melt-water and rock débris, and the rivers distributed the resulting gravel across Aquitaine. And, in the Médoc and Graves almost wholly, and elsewhere to a degree, gravel forms the best vineyards. These stones, varying in size from centimetre-wide pebbles to sizeable, rounded lumps, had their origin far away in the Pyrénées and Massif Central. Geologists can identify pebbles in a Médoc or Sauternes vineyard as coming from the highlands several hundred kilometres to the south and east. Today the precious gravel forms swelling dunes or slopes, known as *croupes*, which rise 10-30m above the surrounding landscape. The soil is not pure stones – there is a varying amount of clay – but especially after rain the surface of many a top vineyard looks like nothing so much as a shingle beach.

These gravel terraces are common: most of the valleys of south-west France are lined with them; but few are top-class vineyard sites. This is because they are normally covered by layers of silt, laid down by the rivers in more recent times. This makes for fine farmland, but an indifferent vineyard: the soil is too rich and the drainage is less ideal than on pure gravel. Only in the Bordelais are the gravel beds exposed, or denuded. A denuded gravel terrace, especially one where erosion by streams has cut small valleys between the *croupes*, offers the vine poor soil, good drainage and air circulation, and the depth to allow deep penetration by the roots.

The process by which these gravel beds were exposed, eroded, then divided up by streams took place over several hundred thousand years. A rise in sea level 12,000 years ago then altered the pattern further, making islands of some of the *croupes* of the northern Médoc: they only rejoined the mainland thanks to the work of drainage engineers over the last three centuries. Today the contrast between the gravel and the low-lying *palus* meadows is stark, not least because vines grow widely on the former and hardly at all on the latter. This is true right along the two rivers and along the Gironde. The rise in sea level left another legacy: underground drainage channels in the *croupes* which recall, in their pattern, a lower sea level. They are thus steeper than they need to be today, further improving the drainage.

The greatest vineyards of the Médoc and Graves – Haut-Brion and its neighbours, the four First Growths of the Médoc, the Sauternes *crus classés* – share very similar soils, an eclectic mix of gravels from varying places, but all laid down at the same time. Pioneers of quality wine, in the late Middle Ages and early modern times, spotted these sites and have nurtured them since. Good wine means high prices, which allows investment in drainage (all the great Médoc estates are extensively drained) and restricted yields. Thus quality can increase further still.

THE RIGHT BANK AND THE ENTRE-DEUX-MERS

To cross the Gironde or Garonne from south to north is to move into a very different landscape. At virtually every point, steep south- or southwest-facing hills line the northern river banks. The whole of the Right Bank area, and the Entre-Deux-Mers, is higher and far more varied in topography than the Médoc and Graves.

In places the underlying limestone breaks the surface as steep slopes, even cliffs. Behind are rolling hills and deep little valleys. The St-Emilion *côte*, a snaking slope, provides both superb vineyard sites and, in the limestone beneath, rock-cut cellars to house the wine. Most of the top châteaux of St-Emilion are on this slope or the limestone plateau behind it. The exceptions are mostly on beds of gravel which overlie the limestone. These were produced in the same way as in the Médoc and Graves, but the terrain was even then higher, and there was less scope for the gravel to form deep terraces. Some gravel in these districts is masked by later wind-blown soils. Pomerol has its gently-sloping plateau, created by several layers of gravel on top of the bedrock. Here the gravel is mixed with clay, and there are patches, such as the Pétrus vineyard, where the soil is virtually pure clay. But the gravel is underneath. Elsewhere on the Right Bank, in the Fronsac and Bourg hills, and those north and east of St-Emilion, it is site, rather than soil, that is the main factor for quality. The same is true of the slopes which form the Premières Côtes de Bordeaux.

It is perhaps no coincidence that the zones with the most formalized gradations of quality – Médoc, Graves, Sauternes, St-Emilion, Pomerol (though its

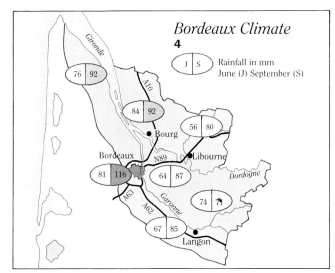

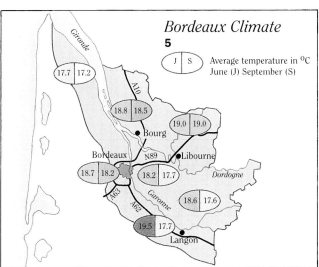

classification is unofficial) – are those where the soils and landforms contribute most to *terroir*. Elsewhere, other factors have a relatively greater role in wine quality.

CLIMATE

The whole of south-west France has an enviable climate; mild in winter, warm in summer, with adequate rain. The Gironde has one of the best. In other regions inland, there are greater extremes of both heat and cold. Further south, there is more rain. The broad parameters of Bordeaux's temperature and rainfall are shown in the table and on maps 5 and 6, but the distribution of rain and warmth through the growing season can be too subtle for the statistical averages, and it is these variations that affect quality. If there is warm, damp weather in the spring, the flowering of the vines may be affected. Rain in summer, especially if it coincides with warmth, can induce rot in the developing grape bunches. Rain in September and October can dilute a crop by promoting vine growth, leading to plump but flavourless grapes. In all, growers fear rain more than its absence, rain in summer far more than rain in winter, and cold

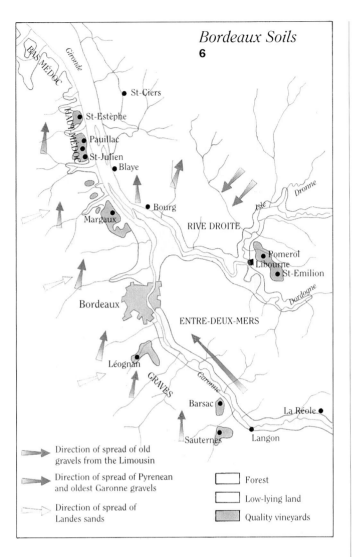

Bordeaux Soils
6

St-Ciers

St-Estèphe

Pauillac

St-Julien

Blaye

Bourg

Margaux

RIVE DROITE

Pomerol
Libourne
St-Emilion

Bordeaux

ENTRE-DEUX-MERS

Léognan

GRAVES

Barsac

La Réole

Sauternes

Langon

Direction of spread of old gravels from the Limousin

Direction of spread of Pyrenean and oldest Garonne gravels

Direction of spread of Landes sands

Forest

Low-lying land

Quality vineyards

more than heat. Frost in spring, as in April 1991, is the most feared disaster: it can wipe out the year's growth by killing nascent vine buds. Only summer hail, which is very localized, can do as much damage. The years 1982 and 1992, with their contrasting wine character and quality (rich and long-lived; slight and short-lived), are interesting when compared with the averages:

Average figures for Mérignac (west of Bordeaux city)

	Average 1987-96	1982	1992
June temperature (°C)	19.7	19.2	17.7
July temperature (°C)	21.4	21.7	21.4
August temperature (°C)	21.8	19.0	21.8
September temperature (°C)	18.1	19.1	17.3
Average for 12 months (°C)	13.8	13.6	13.4
June rainfall (mm)	81	76	167
July rainfall (mm)	58	52	73
August rainfall (mm)	63	76	248
September rainfall (mm)	116	86	96
Rainfall for year (mm)	993	1158	1231

June and September are crucial: the first for the flowering, the second for ripening and the start of the

harvest. Both were appreciably warmer in 1982 than 1992. There was more than average rainfall in both years, but in 1982 June, July and September were below average. In 1992 June and August were very wet – August had four times the average. Combined with the warmth, this was enough to kill hopes of a top-quality vintage. If there is more than 130 mm of rain in July and August, problems can be expected.

LOCAL CLIMATES

Much is made in Bordeaux of micro-, or local, climates. There is good evidence that riverside properties in the Médoc have a more benign climate than those only a kilometre or so further west, away from the Gironde. Latour's site in Pauillac is notoriously freer from frost and hail than some of its neighbours'. The same is true of the renowned Sauternes châteaux. However, the well-known Bordeaux boast 'yes, it rained, but only on the vines of my neighbours' is wonderfully familiar.

Many châteaux keep weather records, but detailed official observations are made by Météo France at sites across the Gironde. These reveal small but significant variations. The north-west – the Médoc – is wettest, with an average 20% more rain at Lesparre than at Sauveterre in the east of Entre-Deux-Mers. Sauternes is less prone to autumn rain than the Médoc. Taking annual averages, Lesparre is the coolest site, with Mérignac and Plassac, near Blaye, the warmest: however, thus averaged the difference is, interestingly, about 6% or less than one degree centigrade.

GRAPES, TERROIRS AND CLIMATE

The variations between one part of the Gironde and another may be subtle, but they are real enough to influence the choice of grape varieties. Soil and climate in St-Emilion and Pomerol do not favour Cabernet Sauvignon to the same extent as do the conditions in the Médoc. This is true on average, but in some years – the warm ones – Cabernet Sauvignon does better than usual, changing the character of the wine.

A careful proprietor will match varieties to his vineyard: Cabernets on well-drained land, Merlot where it is a little damper. Most Bordeaux red-wine châteaux grow two, three or more varieties as this provides not only a palette of flavours to blend with, but also insurance against the failure of one grape. Merlot has problems in cool, wet springs, Cabernet Sauvignon dislikes a damp summer. (Bordeaux people talk about 'a Cabernet vintage' as a shorthand for a style of wine.) Each year is different, as is each appellation, each property – and a good year for Pauillac may be an indifferent one in St-Emilion or even Margaux. Which is what makes Bordeaux so engrossing.

THE BORDEAUX TRADE AND THE CHÂTEAU SYSTEM

Most lovers of Bordeaux wine remain unaware of the complex and often frenzied activity which goes into getting a bottle of Château X onto table Y – perhaps right around the world. This activity is seen at its most extreme during a successful *en primeur* campaign, when the Bordeaux wine trade resembles nothing more than a stock exchange in a bull market. The wine lover may, however, get a clue to what is involved if they ask their local supplier to track down a specific wine, especially if it has something like 'Bel Air' or 'La Tour' in the name – the Bordeaux equivalent of Smith or Brown. It rapidly becomes clear that there are several thousand châteaux, and further layers of detail emerge when second wines and brands are considered. At the centre of this web of complexity are the Bordeaux merchants.

The Bordeaux wine trade is huge, complicated and – to its members at least – endlessly fascinating. Some see it as a dinosaur, way overdue for a complete overhaul; to most, it's an intricate piece of machinery which has proved its efficacy time and again. When you look at the sheer volume of wine produced, the plethora of styles, names, appellations and classifications, plus the enormous diversity and number of people involved (including many a colourful individual), this polarisation of opinion is not surprising.

The Quai des Chartrons in Bordeaux is today a rather run-down dockside quarter. But its eighteenth-century houses were built for a flourishing community of wine merchants – the *chartronnais*.

Bordeaux represents an extremely important part of the French economy. Second among wine regions only to Champagne in terms of turnover, Bordeaux produces a massive fifty-five million cases in an average vintage. Like Champagne, Bordeaux wines come in a wide range of styles, but whereas the Champagne region has only one major appellation, Bordeaux boasts no less than fifty-seven. Even the one instantly recognizable and almost ubiquitous word on a Bordeaux label, 'château' – a seemingly straightforward and original concept – is not in itself a cast-iron guarantee of quality.

The business can be seen as a board game. There are three pieces on the table – the technical, financial and commercial elements – and two major players, the vineyard owners and the merchants. Until fairly recently the game was reasonably clear-cut, with each player acknowledging from experience their strengths and weaknesses and mutual dependence. It is less clear now: probably more changes have occurred since the early 1980s than at any other period in the lengthy history of the Bordeaux trade.

Historically, the power was firmly with the merchant, or *négociant-éleveur*, to give him his correct title. Many of the leading firms in Bordeaux were founded during the 18th and 19th centuries by Dutch, German, English and Irish traders. Despite revolution, wars and blockades, they prospered as Bordeaux wine merchants beside their French competitors and colleagues. This foreign influence is still clear today in some of Bordeaux's best-known names – Barton, Beyerman, Johnston, Lynch, Mähler-Besse, Sichel, to name just a few.

Until the twentieth century, it was the merchant who bought the crude young wine from the ill-equipped château owner, took it into his cellars on the once-magnificent Quai des Chartrons, blended, matured and shipped the wine abroad (usually in bulk but occasionally in bottle) to the expanding markets he had carefully nurtured in the Netherlands, Belgium, Germany and the United Kingdom. In 1875 the volume of wine exported from the port of Bordeaux was an astonishing 1.5 million hectolitres (equivalent to more than 16 million cases), of which only a little over 100,000 hectolitres was actually shipped in bottle (as opposed to cask). Now, in a typical year, the amount exported is 1.8 million hectolitres, about a third of the region's production.

The château owner, isolated from the world outside – and even from the city of Bordeaux if, say, he lived at the far end of the Médoc – occupied himself with tending his vines. Phylloxera and oïdium were the dual catalysts for change to this simple existence. As a result of these two vine destroyers the Bordeaux vineyards of the nineteenth century were devastated; severe wine shortages led to rampant fraud and top château owners decided that, in order to protect their reputations, they had to take much greater control over wine production. Thus in the 1920s château-bottling began, although it did not actually become the rule for even classed Growths until the 1960s.

EN PRIMEUR SELLING AND THE BORDEAUX CYCLE

Another traditional part of the *négociant's* role has been that of financier, notably via his stockholding of wines. The onset of high interest rates due to the oil crisis in the early 1970s made this increasingly untenable; a timely innovation was *en primeur* selling – which means the customers pay early – although it was not until the 1982 vintage that it really took off. With the exception of a few bad years since, the *en primeur* market has proved to be an excellent way of generating cash-flow for *négociant* and château-owner alike. The advantage to the consumer is that he buys at opening prices and is often able to get hold of wines – not just classed Growths but *crus bourgeois* and even *petits châteaux* – which may well not re-appear on the marketplace.

The problems with *en primeur* begin when the market gets overheated (the selling of the 1995s and 1996s being an example) and a customer's willingness to pay almost any price for a leading or fashionable wine can show the Bordeaux trade at its least attractive and, potentially, its most explosive.

In a normal campaign, top châteaux release a good percentage of their crop onto the market in a first release or *tranche*. The *négociant* adds a flat commission (around 10 per cent), and offers the wine to his loyal and long-standing customers. A *deuxième tranche* comes out a few weeks later, at a slightly higher price. This scenario, however, differs considerably in an overheated marketplace: less wine is released by the châteaux in the first *tranche* – just enough to test the market – and the second *tranche* is inevitably much dearer. The *négociant* faces a strong temptation to hold onto the first release in the hope of selling it at a far higher price just a few weeks later. His traditional customers go thirsty in the face of the fierce scramble for this scarce and desirable vintage.

As you drive today along the D2 road through the Médoc, past all the elegant edifices and state-of-the-art cellars, it is all too easy to believe that Bordeaux has known only success. Nothing could be further from the truth; right up until the 1970s whole generations of château-owners (including some with extremely grand wines) were barely able to scrape a living as one poor vintage succeeded another and demand for the wines slumped. Even now, the older and wiser heads – producer and merchant alike – are well aware of the cyclical nature of Bordeaux's prosperity.

THE CHÂTEAU SYSTEM

There are two types of wine produced in Bordeaux: those that are the product of a single estate and those that are not. The former includes all wines with the word 'château' on the label – from a First Growth Médoc like Latour, right down to a modest Bordeaux AC from one of the region's more obscure districts. Legally these wines must be the product of grapes grown on specific plots of a single property which are then vinified, matured and bottled separately – usually at the château where they are grown, but this could equally well take place at another château or even at a cooperative.

In some cases, a 'château' exists in name only (although it must be a name which can be found on the local map – like a *lieu-dit* for example) and there is no actual building. Château-labelled wines from one appellation might even be produced in the cellars of a château in a neighbouring appellation. The important point is that the grapes must be grown in the AC indicated on the label, and kept separate.

Cooperatives, mostly founded during the crisis years of the 1930s, form a very important part of the Bordeaux trade: there are 57 in the Gironde and the vast Entre-Deux-Mers region alone has 20 of them.

Above: as grapes arrive at Château Latour they are tipped into a hopper which feeds the crusher-destemmer

Above: pumps are used to pass the new wine through an aerating tank

Bordeaux's oldest cooperative, established in 1932, is that of St-Emilion. Many are extremely well run, and in addition to making the various wines for their members, are also responsible for marketing them. These cooperatives will have a list of their own château-labelled wines – but these will be *petits châteaux* rather than classed Growths (although the St-Emilion cooperative, for example, vinifies a Grand Cru Classé, Ch Berliquet).

THE MARQUES

The second category of wines includes all Bordeaux's branded wines, which are blends produced by a *négociant* or cooperative. They are created by using a range of wine sources (and often vintages) and they do not specify a château of origin. Brands may use a specific appellation, or the generic ACs Bordeaux or Bordeaux Supérieur. They may carry the buyer's own label ('house claret') or one of Bordeaux's leading 30 *marques*, which are known worldwide. These top brands are the modern-day continuation of the traditional role of the *négociant-éleveur*, and (at best) are truly representative in style and consistent in quality and flavour.

There has been a recent resurgence in *négociant* brands in an attempt to make Bordeaux more consumer-friendly and easier to find on a supermarket shelf among the confusing array of château-bottled wines. Modern, well-made brands like bestsellers Mouton-Cadet, Sirius, Michel Lynch and Maître d'Estournel are designed to satisfy the modern requirement for wines of dependable quality. Perhaps it is also the *négociant* realizing that in future he may not be able to rely on a string of fine vintages or the best châteaux to provide a good part of his bread and butter, especially as some château-owners are taking an ever greater interest in all aspects of their wines – technical, financial and commercial – thereby potentially cutting out the *négociant* altogether.

THE BORDEAUX TRADE TODAY

Today, there are some 400 *négociants* in Bordeaux, but only half of them fulfil the traditional role of *négociant-éleveur* – and of these only around 30 are major players, responsible for about four-fifths of trade turnover. Some so-called *négociants* who appeared on the *en primeur* scene in the 1980s were little more than commission agents with a telephone in one hand and a fax in the other – but no heavy overheads like large amounts of stock. These fly-by-nights helped give the Bordeaux merchant a bad name, and did little to enhance the historically often uneasy relationship between the château-owner and the *négociant*.

After centuries with the majority of estates in family ownership, an increasing number of star properties – Pichon-Longueville, for example, or Canon in St-Emilion – are being bought up by outside concerns and large conglomerates. These groups often acquire several châteaux, spread throughout Bordeaux or perhaps just concentrated in the Médoc. Some such companies find little need to use the full *négociant* network: either they already have their own international distribution system, or can easily link up with one. This gives them several advantages over the old system of selling their wine via the open marketplace: they can control the price internationally, they know exactly where their wines are going and who their eventual clients are, they get involved with the sales and promotion of their wines and they can regulate the amount of stock released onto each market.

These châteaux, however, make up a mere fraction of the Bordeaux trade: most of the *crus classés* and *crus bourgeois*, as well as the innumerable smaller, less prestigious châteaux, have neither the means, experience nor manpower to market their own wines. For many a merchant, the core of his business comes from his own range of unclassified château wines, which he will have sought out with the help of a *courtier* or commission agent, who acts as a go-between between himself and the château. The rest of a merchant's business will usually stem from his own wine brands and (perhaps) some spirits. Only a handful of prestigious merchants rely almost exclusively on classed Growths for their bread and butter.

Each firm operates differently. Some are château-owners in their own right; the firm of Sichel, for example, is a shareholder in Third Growth Château Palmer. A few have invested in wineries, so that instead of depending on a grower's wine, they are actually able to buy grapes and create added value by making a better wine

Above: stainless steel vats have replaced oak vats or concrete tanks for fermentation and storage at many châteaux: they allow rapid cooling of the fermenting wine and are easy to clean

themselves. Other firms own a number of lesser properties, as well as several brand names (which may be internationally known).

In addition to actual ownership, many merchants have the exclusive rights to market certain properties. Such agreements can go back many decades; they continue either because it suits both parties or merely out of habit. Other châteaux are linked to a handful of merchants, each of whom may only have the right to sell the wines in specific countries, whereas some use several

négociants in order to increase sales and distribution, and to prevent too great a financial loss if something goes wrong. As some merchants concentrate on the French market, selling either to the traditional café/restaurant/hotel sector or, increasingly, to the super- and hyper-markets and the mail order firms, many wines never find their way abroad.

Tradition and lack of availability may also be a restricting factor: in Belgium, for example, you will find Pomerols that are not found anywhere else. This is because Pomerols have been drunk there for a very long time – well before they became fashionable elsewhere. The expertise of the finest Bordeaux merchants, however, remains firmly with exports: selling to some of the 150-odd countries in which Bordeaux wines can be found, and opening up and creating new markets. From experience they understand each market intimately, whether wines are bought on price or taste, fashion or status, and they have an established list of customers who regularly receive lists and offers, backed up by samples and regular visits.

These customers are usually retail or wholesale wine merchants, dealing with the public either directly or at one remove. Some major customers such as supermarket groups bypass the *négoce* and deal directly with cooperatives and large producers, specifying exactly what they want. At the other end of the scale, many small châteaux (and an increasing number of large ones) sell wine direct to the public. You may find a scrawled, chalked price-list on the *chai* door, or a multi-lingual hostess and an audio-visual presentation, but the message is the same: buy some wine, please.

Dinosaur it may be, but the trade works; and until Bordeaux discovers another way of successfully selling some 50 million cases a year across the globe, it is difficult to imagine any major upheaval taking place.

Below: the wine goes into 'new oak' – the trade, and writers', shorthand for the 225-litre *barriques* used for maturing wine. The shape and size are traditional, but they also have been proved to allow just the right ratio of wine to oak.

Médoc & Graves

For 120 kilometres, or 75 miles, the left banks of the River Garonne and the Gironde estuary are lined by vineyard districts – the virtually continuous strip broken only by the city of Bordeaux. To the north of the city stretches the Médoc; to the south, the Graves. West of both is the great sheltering forest of Les Landes. In the Graves, it forms part of the landscape as well as a frontier: the vines are in patches and tongues of land, often edged by trees. The wider Médoc and Graves are largely unknown, and uninteresting, to all but foresters and nudists, surfers and hunters. But the eastern shore lays claim to the attention of the rest of the world, for it is here, in a narrow strip between forest and water, that the vineyards lie, and small signposts point unassumingly to 'Margaux', 'Latour', 'Mouton Rothschild'....

There are few better examples of the self-confidence that returned to the Médoc in the 1980s than the flamboyant new *chai* at Château Pichon-Longueville in Pauillac

MÉDOC & GRAVES

The Médoc and Graves are the hinterland of the city of Bordeaux – a wide sweep which stretches westwards to the Atlantic Ocean, north to the Gironde's mouth and south to beyond Langon. It is almost flat, remote and (apart from the vineyards) fairly poor. Trees – including some enormous conifers – far outnumber vines, and Europe's biggest sand-dunes guard windswept beaches and shelter brackish lagoons. Long straight roads through the forests link quiet little towns, rather drab villages and, on the sea and lake shores, holiday resorts and camp-sites that pulse with life in July and August and are deserted for the other ten months.

The two areas have much in common in grapes and wines, subsoil and climate. There are important and distinct variations, but the Médoc and Graves are closer to each other in most respects than either is to the Right Bank vineyards of St-Emilion or Pomerol. In the past the whole Left Bank vineyard was often called the Graves – the name coming from the outcrops of gravel soil which provide the best vineyard sites. Until the early eighteenth century there were fewer vines in the Médoc

than today, and certainly fewer (with some renowned exceptions) large estates. The Graves, though, provided wine for popes and archbishops in the Middle Ages. Being close to the city helped: the Médoc was by contrast a long wagon-ride, or an uncertain boat-trip, away.

Both areas make red wines, using Cabernets Sauvignon and Franc, Merlot and varying (but always small) proportions of Petit Verdot and Malbec. The Graves area overall puts less stress on Cabernet Sauvignon, giving Merlot and Cabernet Franc more attention than does the Médoc. (The exception is Pessac-Léognan, the high-quality appellation in the northern Graves.) The balance of red grape varieties is changing in both areas, however, as more Merlot is planted to soften the minor wines. In both Médoc and Graves there is an important distinction to be made between the *vins de garde* – oak-aged, built to last – and the wines designed for earlier drinking.

White wines are made in the Graves appellation roughly in the ratio of one bottle of white to every two of red. (Again, there is less white made in Pessac-Léognan.)

Left: what matters about a vineyard in the Médoc or Graves can be seen between the rows: the glint of gravel

The grapes used are Sauvignon Blanc and Sémillon in varying proportions plus, in some cases, a small percentage of Muscadelle. White wines are made in the Médoc from the same grapes, but in very small amounts at a mere handful of châteaux. The Médoc appellations are for red wines, so whites are labelled as AC Bordeaux.

READING THE LANDSCAPE: TERROIR AND QUALITY

The Médoc and Graves are about gravel. It is on the well-drained *croupes* – banks or dunes of gravel that form the almost imperceptible rises in the ground, too low to be called hills – that the vines grow best. This insight allows the landscape to be read and understood, both on the ground and from the maps. As the visitor drives through the wine villages, he or she becomes attuned to the flatness – and begins to notice those points where the road rises, if only 10 or 20 metres, for it is here that the vines begin. Examples are the southern approach to St-Julien where, after crossing a low plain, the D2 road bends left and climbs past Château Beychevelle. The same sequence can be observed on the frontier between Pauillac and St-Estèphe, where the Cos d'Estournel *chais* and vineyards rise abruptly above the waterlogged cow-pastures of the valley of the Jalle du Breuil. In both cases the difference in height is tiny: from 4-16 metres above sea level. Indeed, the Breuil valley, which regularly floods, can hardly be said to be above sea level at all.

In the Graves the pattern is not so apparent, and the exploring visitor will find that the ample trees obscure the views – but the gravel is here. Indeed the *croupes* are higher, reaching 50 metres in one or two instances. These great beds of gravel in places form the soil itself: they have been laid bare by wind and water, and dissected by little streams. The Eau Blanche and Bourran brooks have carved steep gulleys between the vines of Châteaux Carbonnieux and Haut-Bailly, Bouscaut and Smith Haut-Lafitte. The gravel is smaller, or finer, than the coarser type found in the great Médoc vineyards – though significantly the soils of Haut-Brion and Sauternes, and parts of St-Emilion, consist of these coarser pebbles. The origins of this vital gravel are explored in the pages on geology and soils (see page 23).

THE APPELLATION PATTERN

Map 7 shows all the Médoc and Graves appellations. The Médoc has a linear pattern, easy to understand if not quite so clear on the ground (everyone gets lost in St-Estèphe). The Graves is more random, and exploration more time-consuming, though a signposted *circuit touristique* attempts to provide a route. The Médoc is both a geographical area and an appellation. To confuse the picture further, the actual Médoc appellation is only one of a hierarchy of ACs which applies to the Médoc area. These ACs can be viewed as a pyramid. At its base are the generic Bordeaux and Bordeaux Supérieur ACs, which may be used throughout the whole of the Médoc vineyard (and of course throughout Bordeaux). They rarely are: the Médoc is almost totally red-wine country and virtually the entire vineyard area is covered by more elevated appellations, from AC Médoc upwards. The main exceptions are small areas of *palus* or low-lying land along the river bank, and on islands in the Gironde. The tiny quantities of dry white and rosé made in the Médoc are only entitled to the generic Bordeaux appellation, irrespective of quality.

The next two tiers in the pyramid are still quite general: Médoc and Haut-Médoc. The Médoc AC covers most of the vineyard area, while Haut-Médoc is restricted to the 29 communes in the southern half of the peninsula. Then come the six specific appellations: the two junior ones of Moulis-en-Médoc and Listrac-Médoc, and the four senior ones: Margaux, St-Julien, Pauillac and St-Estèphe. The total Médoc vineyard land planted is roughly 14,500 hectares, of which the six specific appellations account for some 6,000, the Haut-Médoc 4,200 and the Médoc about 4,700.

Working north from Bordeaux, and having passed through a zone of Haut-Médoc vineyards, the first of the senior ACs is Margaux, which includes land in five communes. To its west the Haut-Médoc land continues until, with Moulis, the position is reversed: here the eastern riverside land is confined to the Haut-Médoc level, while Moulis and its neighbour Listrac have their own ACs. Again, gravel is the key: these two 'inland' communes are on *croupes* where the overlying sand has been worn, or blown, clear. The riverside Haut-Médoc communes of Lamarque, Arcins and Cussac are lower-lying than their northern and southern neighbours, and thus have less land worthy of top status.

St-Julien comes next, approached via a theatrically-placed bridge and a rising bend which takes you past several famous names up onto a plateau, through the hamlet of Beychevelle and on across a shallow valley to St-Julien itself. This is the heart of the Léoville estate (see map 11) which runs on north to the Pauillac boundary, formed by another brook, the Ruisseau de Juillac, which drains the southern edge of Latour. Other serious St-Julien estates lie over to the left.

Pauillac has two main concentrations of vineyards, on a pair of *croupes* to the south and north of the town. The dividing line is a stream just beyond the town's northern edge. To the south are Latour and the two Pichons; the northern plateau, home to Mouton and Lafite, ends with an abrupt descent by the D2, with Lafite on view to the left, then a bridge before the climb to Cos.

St-Estèphe is less clear-cut – it is more of a rolling plateau. The riverside has a neat line of gravel slopes: Montrose and Calon-Ségur take advantage of them. St-Estèphe tapers off with a final hillock of gravel; then comes the Haut-Médoc land of St-Seurin-de-Cadourne.

The Haut-Médoc AC has been running parallel with the riverside greats, over to the west, ever since the latitude of St-Julien. Now it takes over for a final flourish before the AC Médoc (once known as the Bas-Médoc) begins with the communes of St-Yzans, by the river, and St-Germain-d'Esteuil, further west. Until the northern end of the Médoc, the vines are now grouped on the patches of gravel amid marshes and former marshes. The D2 takes you on to Le-Verdon-sur-Mer (for the ferry) and the Pointe de Grave, for the Atlantic breezes.

The history of the Graves is clear in the location

start in earnest in the south-western suburbs.

A glance at maps 25 and 26 shows that there is plenty of AC land not planted in the Graves. The INAO has excluded the river valleys and areas covered by sand, but large tracts remain the empire of pines rather than grapes. This in part reflects a decline in the Graves which followed the disasters of oïdium and phylloxera and which has only recently started to reverse itself.

Unlike the Médoc, the pattern of appellations is straightforward. There is one AC, Graves, for red, dry white and (as Graves Supérieures) semi-sweet white. A few vineyards in the Garonne valley have the Bordeaux AC. To the north, the best communes of the Graves have the right to an additional AC, Pessac-Léognan. This is for red and dry white wine. The Graves area has three enclaves for renowned sweet white wines. These are the small appellation of Cérons and the far larger and adjoining Sauternes and Barsac ACs. Many vineyards in Cérons produce red and white (both dry and semi-sweet) Graves despite their right to yield Cérons. In Sauternes and Barsac, a few vineyards make dry white and red wines (which have to be labelled as AC Bordeaux). Taking the Pessac-Léognan and Graves ACs together, the area planted for red wines is roughly 3,000 hectares, with 1,200 for dry whites, 400 for medium-sweet Graves Supérieures and nearly 3,000 for the sweet whites wines (Sauternes, Barsac and Cérons). The whole Graves area is thus less than half the size of the Médoc. Even in prestigious Pessac-Léognan, vineyards are patchy: in Pessac, now a suburb of Bordeaux, only the most famous have survived. The main road to Arcachon, the N250, and a railway bisect Haut-Brion and its sister châteaux (see map 24), and houses line every boundary of this enclave. There are few other vines north of the Bordeaux *rocade* or ring road: the only other *cru classé* is Pape-Clément, also just north of the N250 but further west. The heartland of the Pessac-Léognan AC is the commune of Léognan, to the south. The D651 road goes through the village centre

Above: a fisherman's hut on the Gironde at Pauillac

of great estates such as Haut-Brion and Pape-Clément. Once close to the city, they now lie within it: islands of vines amid the streets and houses. The Graves appellation runs – on paper – from just north of the city round through its western suburbs and down to beyond Langon to the south-east. In fact there are very few vines to the west and north of Bordeaux, and the vineyards

and then passes estates such as Malartic-Lagravière and de Fieuzal. Domaine de Chevalier and a few other estates are off to the west, many others, like Carbonnieux and Haut-Bailly, to the east.

Further south, the Graves AC takes over, with châteaux scattered throughout an increasingly wooded region. The Sauternes and Barsac appellations are more densely planted, and a further area of Graves land can be found east of Langon around St-Pierre-de-Mons.

Médoc & Graves
7

8   Margaux
9   Margaux
10   St-Julien
11   St-Julien
12   Pauillac
13   Pauillac
14   Pauillac
15   St-Estèphe
16   St-Estèphe
17   Moulis-en-Médoc & Listrac-Médoc
18   Haut-Médoc I
19   Haut-Médoc II
20   Haut-Médoc III
21   Médoc I:
22   Médoc II
23   Pessac-Léognan
24   Pessac-Léognan
25   Graves I
26   Graves II
27   Sauternes
28   Sauternes
29   Barsac

Bordeaux

MARGAUX

MICHAEL BROADBENT

Margaux is one of the best-known and surely one of the most evocative names in wine. It epitomizes elegance; there is a distinct femininity about it. Unusually – for there is no 'Château Graves' or 'Château Pomerol' – the appellation's name is also that of the First Growth château which, in itself, personifies the wine at its supreme best. The Margaux appellation has a wonderful image, its wines a flying start.

MARGAUX, THE DISTRICT

Rather like Sauternes, which incorporates in its name five communes, there are four other parishes or communes entitled to use the name Margaux on their wines, subject to certain INAO regulations: Soussans to its north, Arsac, Cantenac and Labarde to its south. The five form what I think of as the 'greater Margaux' district. Margaux is the first of the Big Four Médoc appellations (Margaux, St-Julien, Pauillac, St-Estèphe) which stretch up from just north of the outer suburbs of Bordeaux along the Left Bank, a point more or less level with the junction of the rivers Garonne and Dordogne where they merge to become the Gironde estuary.

Although not strictly speaking Margaux, the two Haut-Médoc communes Ludon and Macau that one passes through going north from Bordeaux on the D2 act as the overture; they are also home to the first of the classified growths along the *route du vin* of the Médoc: Château La Lagune on the right-hand side of the road and, a little further along on the left, the white fences bordering the estate of Château Cantemerle.

To be truthful, the Médoc countryside is rather flat and featureless; the villages very humdrum, almost entirely devoid of architectural merit – which instead is lavished on some truly magnificent châteaux. Even the most superficial glimpse of the vineyard of La Lagune reveals the gentle, almost sensuous, slope of vines, swelling up from the road and then down out of sight on the far side, overlooking the river.

This, for me, encapsulates what the top vineyards of the Médoc are all about and why (unlike Pomerol for example) they are not in unbroken stretches, one leading to another. For it is only on these subtly raised outcrops of gravel soil that the best, the classified-growth, vines are planted: they combine aspect – to take advantage of the sun's rays – good drainage, perfect soil and subsoil. They are sufficiently close to the broad Gironde to benefit from the microclimate yet sufficiently distanced and raised above the lower, rich and marshy *palus*, on which vines might grow – but not produce grapes of quality.

MARGAUX AND ITS CHÂTEAUX

The entire rather diffuse area is roughly divided into two, a strip adjacent to Labarde and a large concentration of vineyards around the village of Margaux itself. Dominating the district is, of course, Château Margaux. Hubrecht Duijker gives us the vital statistics and the taste of the wine, so perhaps I can flesh it out architecturally, and more personally.

Without question it is the most handsome, stately, colonnaded mansion in the whole of the Gironde. Its main facade has been endlessly photographed, illustrated and, frankly, gawped at. Few have had the privilege of entering its portals, the interior lovingly restored in Empire style (the French equivalent of the Regency period); no expense spared, and all with great taste. More frequently visited but less often pictured is the great first-year *chai*, the most handsome in Bordeaux: row upon row of stern Doric columns

The classical portico at Château Margaux is the most-photographed view in the Médoc, but it still has the power to impress

supporting a high roof above avenues of new, purple-stained *barriques* nursing the precious young wine.

Wine does not make itself. The management team is all-important, and what I like about Margaux is the brilliant triumvirate headed by the most attractive and perceptive Président, Corinne Mentzelopoulos, the daughter of the French-Greek supermarket tycoon who purchased the château in 1977 from the Ginestet family. At her right hand is the charming, enthusiastic and highly competent managing director, Paul Pontallier, and, at the blunt end, the vastly experienced *maître de chai* M. Grandjou. A winning team making superb wines. But Château Margaux always has made superb wines. The AM/PM story – *ante* and *post* Mentzelopoulos – is unfair on the Ginestets, who did in fact run the property extremely well until the very unfortunate financial debacle in the mid-1970s (out of which my old friend the late Pierre Ginestet emerged honourably).

Two centuries before this, Margaux was, after Lafite, considered the finest château in Bordeaux. With Lafite, it was the first vineyard ever to be mentioned by name in a Christie wine auction catalogue, in February 1788. Château Margaux 1784 was both highly rated and very expensive. Thomas Jefferson, then American envoy (ambassador) in Paris, in a letter to a friend writes: "It is of the best vintage which has happened in nine years, and is one of the four vineyards which are admitted to possess exclusively the first reputation. I may safely assure you therefore that, according to the taste of this country [France] and of England that there cannot be a bottle of better Bordeaux produced in France. It cost me at Bordeaux three Livres a bottle, ready bottled and packed. This is very dear....."

The twin Second-Growth châteaux Rauzan-Ségla and Rauzan-Gassies are virtually back-to-back, sharing adjoining vineyards. In Jefferson's day Madame Rauzan's wine was considered far and away the top of the Second Growths, just below Château Margaux and the other three Firsts. Gassies, after under-performing for years, has at last in the 1995 produced a wine worthy of

Looking north over the vineyards of Margaux, with Château Palmer in the centre

its name. Ségla has long had the better reputation; now, with Chanel money investing heavily and, as Président, the former managing director of Latour, the next millennium should with luck see it achieving its original status. And, as if in anticipation, the spelling has now reverted from Rausan- to Rauzan-Ségla.

The beautiful, moated d'Issan, the only pre-17th-century château in the area, is well worth a visit. Prieuré-Lichine, until recently owned by the son of the late Alexis Lichine – a wonderful, larger-than-life character – caters for visitors seven days a week. Unhappily not lived in, and barely furnished, is the strikingly attractive Palmer, its elegant tiled turrets and very French facade epitomizing the femininity and charm of Margaux.

Not all the châteaux of Margaux are grand, though some decidedly verge on the pretentious (Cantenac-Brown reminding me, somehow, of a large Victorian girls' school). Very much lived-in, and modest in appearance, is Château d'Angludet – of classed-growth standard despite not making the grade in 1855 – which now flourishes under the ownership of the French-based branch of the Sichel family. This unusually widespread district is worth exploring before continuing the journey to St-Julien and Pauillac. But first, the wine.

Margaux, the wine

Margaux's wines tend to split into two broad styles, depending on the château and on the vintage. One is feminine and fragrant, as epitomized by Château Margaux itself – famously in vintages like 1949 and 1953 – the other firmer, with more backbone, such as the 1966 Rausan-Ségla. Nearer our own time, vintages with charm include 1985; those of the more sturdy persuasion the 1988 and 1990. But above all 'fragrance' is the operative word – of bouquet and of taste. Yet fragrance in tandem with the firm tannic structure which is part and parcel of the best wines of the Médoc: tannin to preserve,

tannin to refresh. Having said this, there is a wider range of styles (and, in particular, of quality) in Margaux than in the more compact St-Julien and Pauillac.

History and geography

In common with the rest of the Médoc, Margaux's history as a wine region did not begin until Dutch engineers were brought in to drain the land. This left pockets of relatively high pebbly areas – gentle swells only just visible to the casual eye – amid very much more obvious stretches of low, rather marshy, land, unfit for vine-growing. This is why history and geography are more closely related in the Médoc, as exemplified by Margaux. The geography differs, however, from St-Julien and the districts to the north in that here the Ice-Age gravel emanates from the Pyrénées and not from the Dordogne. Margaux gravel is peculiarly rich in quartz pebbles, which when polished become semi-precious stones. What is neither known nor understood these days is that the whole of the Médoc, in particular the southerly portion stretching up from the suburbs of Bordeaux, was originally termed 'the Graves'. The expansion of the city itself effectively divided this north end of the Graves from the south, with only the southern part retaining its name and identity. Moreover, it was not until early in the 18th century that the vineyards started to produce wines of note, though by the 1770s they had achieved that reputation and status, led principally by Château Margaux, that is taken for granted today.

Vintages

For a fairly large, important and relatively diffuse district (compared, for example, to the compact districts of St-Julien and Pomerol), it is both difficult and unfair to generalize. It is a fact of life that the weather – which, after all, is largely responsible for the overall quality, weight and style of a vintage – can vary from district to district in a given year. Storms are sometimes quite localized, not to mention the unpredictable hail that can cut a swathe across individual vineyards.

The conditions in 1983, for example, were rated more satisfactory in Margaux than other districts of the Médoc and even, it is said, better in that year than the otherwise more renowned 1982 (though unlike some other 'authorities' I find the 1982 vintage of Château Margaux as good as, possibly superior to, 1983).

Best, perhaps, to take Château Margaux itself as a vintage yardstick, for it has, unlike some other First Growths, performed fairly consistently. I have already made reference to the outstanding 1784, recorded by Jefferson. But throughout the 19th century the quality and style of Château Margaux was as consistent as weather permitted, some great vintages just occasionally seen in the salesroom (and tasted by me at other times) being the 1847 and 1848, the 1864 and 1865 (though the latter two were 'over the hill'), 1868 and 1869, the magnificent 1870 and lovely 1875, and the surprisingly attractive faded old ladies 1888 and 1889 – mildew years – from the Glamis Castle cellars.

Continuing with Château Margaux, the 1893 was excellent and the twin vintages 1899 and 1900 outstanding. 1905 was very good, 1906, 1908 and 1911 fairly good; then on to the classic 1920, 1924, magnificent 1926, good 1928 and superb 1929. The château's 1934, first drunk with pheasant cooked in chocolate sauce(!), was one of the best wines of that vintage – as was the 1937 and, jumping a decade, the 1950. The post-war pattern saw Château Margaux performing excellently: 1945, 1947, the glorious 1949 and 1953, a good 1955, excellent 1959 and 1961; good 1962, a so-so 1964, firm 1966 – and then perhaps better than most throughout the uneven decade of the 1970s. The Mentzelopoulos vintages of Château Margaux are brilliant but often

hard, somewhat unyielding but undoubtedly well made. All this emphasis on the great First Growths does not mean that the other classed Growths did not follow the leader – though, to be frank, some of even the *deuxièmes crus* châteaux had off-periods. Performing well up until 1929 were Brane Cantenac, notably the 1893, 1898, 1899 and wonderful 1900, the 1905 and 1920; Rausan-Ségla and to a lesser extent Cantenac Brown. The 1930s were dismal for most, though Ségla made a good 1934. Not all recovered fully after the Second World War. Brane Cantenac became idiosyncratic, Ségla was good enough, but Rauzan-Gassies, as previously noted, was way below par.

Château Palmer gained its palm with its 1961, one of the most magnificent wines of that great vintage. The 1966 was – still is – stylish, and the generally thin and sharp 1967 is now surprisingly good. Palmer's 1970 is good, but its wines pretty dismal thereafter until 1976. Then the attractive 1978 and, in the decade of the 1980s, Palmer is more or less as good as its peers – though not, in my opinion, wholly justifying its 'super-second' sobriquet, the 1982 being a case in point. Amongst the *bourgeois* Growths, d'Angludet stands out: Peter Sichel's nurturing brings out the best from its mineral-loaded vineyard soil, the 1989 being particularly delicious.

Hubrecht Duijker lists many more, and spells out those that, like Dauzac, have had a 'face-lift' following a change of ownerships and updating of equipment.

Great Margaux vintages since 1940:
1945, 1947, 1949, 1953, 1955, 1959, 1961, 1983, 1989, 1990.
Good Margaux vintages since 1940:
1943, 1950, 1966, 1970, 1971, 1975, 1982, 1985, 1988, 1993.

PERSONAL FAVOURITES
In addition to Château Margaux itself, d'Angludet, Palmer, Rauzan-Ségla.

THE APPELLATION

MARGAUX (red)

Location: *Margaux, the southernmost of the four great Médoc appellations, lies on the left bank of the Gironde. It is just under 25 km from the city centre to the village of Margaux itself. To the north-west are the appellations of Moulis-en-Médoc and Listrac-Médoc. Immediately to the west and south is the Haut-Médoc.*
Area of AC: *1,847 ha*
Area under vine: *1,348 ha*
Communes: *Arsac, Cantenac, Labarde, Margaux, Soussans; excluding low-lying areas: some land has the Haut-Médoc and Bordeaux appellations (see map 8)*

Average annual production: *630,000 cases*
Classed growths: *21, of which 10 are in Margaux, 8 in Cantenac, 2 in Labarde and 1 in Arsac (1 premier cru, 5 deuxièmes crus, 10 troisièmes crus, 4 quatrièmes crus and 2 cinquièmes crus)*
Others: *25 crus bourgeois, 38 others*
Cooperatives: *None*
Main grape varieties: *Cabernet Sauvignon*
Others: *Cabernet Franc, Merlot, Petit Verdot, Malbec*
Main soil types: *Fine and gravelly; pebbly in Arsac, with sand in Labarde. Overall thin top soils; clay and sand in alluvial areas.*

APPELLATION MARGAUX

Ch d'Angludet — map 8/R I3

owner: Famille Sichel **area:** 32 ha **cases:** 14,500 **grape % R:** CS 58% MER 35% CF 5% PV 2% **second wine:** La Ferme d'Angludet **other wines:** Le Clairet d'Angludet *(Bordeaux Clairet)* **other châteaux owned:** Ch Palmer *(Margaux)*; Domaine du Reverend *(Corbières)*; Domaine du Trillot *(Corbières)*
33460 Cantenac tel: 05 57 88 71 41
fax: 05 57 88 72 52

This centuries-old estate lies near the point where three communes of the Margaux appellation, Arsac, Cantenac and Labarde, meet. The landscape here is one of low hills, and is less dominated by the vine than elsewhere in the area. In front of this low, white château with its dark-green shutters stretches rolling parkland, with an ornamental lake where swans swim. The British wine merchant Peter Sichel bought the estate in 1961, when it had gone to rack and ruin and was producing almost no wine (just 11 casks in the first year). Under Sichel's management, however, the estate began to flourish once more. Today the wine is among the best from Cantenac – just as it was before the French Revolution. It has as a rule a lively colour and a polished, balanced taste with generous, ripe berry fruit, fine integrated tannins, a judicious measure of oak (the wine spends about a year in barrels of which 25-33% are new), and a stylish charm. Besides its first and second wines d'Angludet produces a light Bordeaux Clairet.

Ch d'Arsac — map 8/L M7

owner: Philippe Raoux **area:** 80 ha **cases:** 44,000 **grape % R:** CS 60% MER 40% **second wines:** Ch Le Monteil *(Haut-Médoc)*; Ruban Blue du Château d'Arsac *(Haut-Médoc)* **other wines:** Crémant de Bordeaux
33460 Arsac tel: 05 56 58 83 90
fax: 05 56 58 83 08

This is a notable château in more than one respect. In its 19th-century *cuvier* and *chai* classical forms mix with modern materials and vivid colours – bright blue among them. Exhibitions of modern art are regularly held here. D'Arsac made the headlines on 6 September 1993 when the French authorities decided that the estate could be transferred

Below: Ch d'Arsac

Above: Ch d'Angludet

from Haut-Médoc to the Margaux appellation. The owner, Philippe Raoux, had submitted the application immediately after taking over in 1986. But d'Arsac is remarkable above all for the standard of its wine. Despite the relatively young vines, this has refinement and charm, with autumnal aromas, ripe black currants and cherries, spiciness, plus vanilla oak (25% of the *barriques* for maturing are new). More of the Raoux family's production (not related to d'Arsac) is made into a series of Crémants de Bordeaux by the firm of A. Chamvermeil.

Ch les Barraillots — map 8/L F10

owner: Michel Brunet **area:** 5 ha **cases:** 2,500 **grape % R:** CS 50% MER 40% CF 5% PV 5%
33460 Margaux tel: 05 57 88 74 19
fax: 05 57 88 36 66

Skilfully made, fairly solid, somewhat rustic *cru artisan*, with 18-24 months' ageing in mostly used casks; of decent quality.

Ch Bel-Air Marquis d'Aligre — map 8/L F7

owner: Pierre & Jean-Pierre Boyer **area:** 17 ha **cases:** 4,500 **grape % R:** CS 30% MER 30% CF 20% PV 10% MAL 10% **second wine:** Ch Bel Air-Marquis de Pomereu
33460 Soussans tel: 05 56 88 70 70

From old vines in an isolated vineyard the publicity-shy Boyer family produces a Margaux that is particularly dark-toned – bayleaf, licorice root, bitter chocolate – with slight fruit, and often with roundness rather than breeding. It spends at least a year and a half in barrel, but this can be extended to more than two years. No artificial fertilizers or weedkillers are used on this estate.

Ch Boyd-Cantenac — map 8/R H3

3ème cru
owner: Pierre Guillemet **area:** 18 ha **cases:** 8,000 **grape % R:** CS 67% MER 20% CF 7% PV 6% **other châteaux owned:** Ch Pouget *(Margaux)*
33460 Cantenac tel: 05 57 88 30 58

This wine estate dates from 1754, but boasts no château. For decades after it was acquired by the Guillemets in 1932, the Boyd-Cantenac harvest was mingled with the grapes from Ch Pouget, which the family already owned. During

that time the wines were of course identical. Not until the 1970s were separate Boyd-Cantenac *cuvées* created. A real division only came about in 1983, when Pierre Guillemet built Boyd-Cantenac its own *cuvier* and *chai*. The wine made and nurtured here for 18 months in casks of which 25% are new, seldom reaches the standard of a *troisième cru classé*. It is not a really subtle Margaux, but quite firm and traditionally styled, with solid tannins, considerable fruit and spicy oak.

Ch Brane-Cantenac — map 8/R H2

2ème cru
owner: Henri Lurton **area:** 85 ha **cases:** 38,000 **grape % R:** CS 70% MER 20% CF 10% **second wines:** Le Baron de Brane; Ch Notton
33460 Cantenac tel: 05 57 88 70 20
fax: 05 57 88 72 51

In 1838 Baron Hector de Brane published an open letter in *Le Producteur* announcing that Ch Gorse-Gui would henceforth be called Brane-Cantenac. The baron had altered so much there over the previous four years that, in his opinion, this was almost an entirely new

◆
Quantities

Figures are as supplied by the châteaux.

Area of vineyard: given in hectares, abbreviated to ha. Châteaux are asked to specify vineyards in production, and to exclude from their answers those owned but unplanted, and to advise when extensions are planned.

Production: given in cases of 12 bottles, each of 0.75 litres. A case is thus 9 litres. A hectolitre is 100 litres or just over 11 cases.

Yield per hectare: to obtain this, multiply the 'cases' figure by 9, to give litres, then divide by 100, to give hectolitres. Then divide the result by the area in hectares.

property. Besides, he wrote, the name of Brane was certainly not inferior to that of Gorse. The wine was already aromatic, fine and delicate. When a gentle west wind brought the first scents of spring to Cantenac, people would say, 'Baron de Brane is racking his wines'. In its present form this Margaux is generally a likeable lightweight, not especially concentrated or nuanced, and sometimes even rather thin. However, more full-bodied, exciting wines do occur – as in 1989; and under Henri Lurton's direction efforts are being made to improve the quality of the grapes, through vine replanting and putting in a drainage system. Because of the delicate character of the wine, barrel maturation is limited to six months, although this is in *barriques* of which a third to a half are new.

Ch Cantenac-Brown
map 8/L G10

3ème cru

owner: AXA Millésimes *area:* 52 ha *cases:* 26,000 *grape % R:* CS 65% MER 25% CF 10% *second wine:* Ch Canuet *other wines:* Ch Brown-Lamartine (*AC Bordeaux Supérieur*) *other châteaux owned:* include Ch Suduiraut (*Sauternes*); Ch Pichon-Longueville (*Pauillac*); Ch Petit Village (*Pomerol*)
33460 Margaux tel: 05 56 73 24 20
fax: 05 57 88 81 90

In 1987 this estate was bought by the insurance firm Compagnie du Midi after outbidding AXA, another such company. Two years later, however, the two concerns merged and the Margaux property was put under AXA Millésimes. Both owners have spent tens of millions of francs renovating and improving the vineyard, cellars and château. The wine spends 15 months in cask, and it was decided to replace half of these with new ones each year. Sometimes the wine is marked by a surplus of rather tough tannins, especially in the lesser years. But vintages have also been brought out with smooth, velvety tannins and plenty of succulent, luscious fruit, enriched with toasty oak – wines without perhaps the utmost in concentration or finesse, but certainly delicious to drink. The estate was called Ch Cantenac until 1826, after which the wine merchant John Lewis Brown attached his name to it. The château itself, a notable structure in Victorian style, was built by Armand Lalande in the second half of the 19th century.

Ch Charmant
map 8/L D9

owner: SCEA René Renon *area:* 5 ha *cases:* 2,200 *grape % R:* MER 50% CS 45% PV 5% *second wine:* Clos Charmant *other châteaux owned:* Ch La Galiane (*Margaux*)
33460 Margaux tel: 05 57 88 35 27
fax: 05 57 88 70 59

After spending at least 18 months in almost exclusively used *barriques*, this wine is at once quite smooth and solidly built, but without great depth or refinement.

Ch Le Coteau
map 8/L L9

owner: Claude Léglise *area:* 9.1 ha *cases:* 6,500 *grape % R:* CS 65% MER 25% CF 7% PV 3% *second wine:* Ch Laroque
33460 Arsac tel: 05 56 58 82 30

This is generally a quite accessible Margaux with berry fruit, supple tannins and reasonable oak – after 18 months in casks of which a third are new for each vintage.

Ch Dauzac
map 8/R I7

5ème cru

owner: MAIF *area:* 45 ha *cases:* 22,700 *grape % R:* CS 58% MER 37% CF 5% *second wine:* Ch Labarde Dauzac *other wines:* Ch Labarde (*Haut-Médoc*)
33460 Labarde tel: 05 57 88 32 10
fax: 05 57 88 96 00

Due to family problems, this estate slipped into oblivion during the 1970s. The tide turned, however, with the arrival of Félix Chatelier in 1978. This new owner built a modern *cuvier*, and a cellar complete with humidifiers for the barrels. The vineyard was enlarged as well. In 1989 Dauzac passed into the hands of the MAIF insurance company and two banks. They continued the investment, and put André Lurton in as manager just before the 1992 harvest. As a result the already satisfactory quality of the wine, with its elegant, firm taste, balanced and reasonably complex, was further improved – especially from the 1993 onwards. Dauzac wine today has an average structure and a gentle taste. It is stylishly equipped with fruit and charred oak (half the casks are new), its foundation provided by good tannins, firmer in some years than in others.

◆
Crus Bourgeois

Only one area – the Médoc – has a recognized list of *crus bourgeois*. The ranking procedure is described on page 34 and the full list is given in the appendix which precedes the index. The *crus bourgeois* are in appellations Médoc, Haut-Médoc and the 'village' ACs: Margaux, St-Julien, Pauillac, St-Estèphe, Listrac and Moulis. In this Atlas the châteaux which belong to the Syndicat of Crus Bourgeois have the words *cru bourgeois* printed after their name. Other châteaux use the term on labels: these were among the *crus bourgeois* on the list that was compiled in the 1930s.

The term *cru bourgeois* is in use in other areas, including Sauternes, but unofficially, and thus not on labels.

Below: Ch Brane-Cantenac

Ch Desmirail
map 8/R G4

3ème cru

owner: Denis Lurton *area:* 30 ha *cases:* 13,000 *grape % R:* CS 80% MER 15% CF 5% *second wine:* Ch Fontarney
33460 Cantenac tel: 05 57 88 34 33
fax: 05 57 88 72 51

In the 18th century wine from this château (named after Jean Desmirail) enjoyed an excellent reputation and was sold at the same price as, for example, Ch d'Issan. The estate was included in the 1855 classification. This illustrious past could not prevent the break-up of the property in 1938 due to financial problems. The château and a part of the vineyard went to the Zuger family, and is known today as Ch Marquis d'Alesme Becker. Another portion was taken over by Ch Palmer, which also acquired the rights to the Ch Desmirail name – and for a time made it a second wine. The Lurtons bought some of the land, and it was Lucien Lurton who through purchase and exchange managed to revive Desmirail in 1980. The former Port Aubin in Cantenac was chosen as its château. Desmirail wine is supple, likeable and fairly quick-developing; seldom rich or very concentrated, but seductive, with fruit and spicy vanilla oak as well. About 30-50% of the barrels are new; the time spent in them can vary greatly.

Ch Deyrem Valentin
map 8/L C9

cru bourgeois

owner: Jean Sorge *area:* 12 ha *cases:* 6,000 *grape % R:* CS 51% MER 45% MAL 2% PV 2% *second wines:* Ch Valentin; Ch Soussans
33460 Soussans tel: 05 57 88 35 70
fax: 05 57 88 36 84

Not a spectacular Margaux, but certainly a likeable one, and fairly straightforward; it often has somewhat dry tannins. The owner, whose grandfather bought Deyrem Valentin in 1928, uses casks of which about a third are new.

Ch Durfort-Vivens
map 8/R F1

2ème cru

owner: Gonzague Lurton *area:* 30 ha *cases:* 13,000 *grape % R:* CS 65% CF 15% MER 20% *second wines:* Second de Durfort; Domaine de Cure-Bourse
33460 Margaux tel: 05 57 83 10 61
fax: 05 57 83 10 11

After some drastic work at the beginning of the 1990s, Durfort-Vivens looks like a château once again, rather than a *chai* with a semicircular turret attached. The casks are in fact housed in a separate cellar by the road to Avensan. At the same time the quality of the wine has been worked on, for this Margaux used not to justify its *deuxième cru* status. But today the wine offers considerable, usually jammy, fruit, with a sometimes excessive dose of oak and vanilla from 12-18 months in wood (30-50% new casks). Powerful tannins still remain, although these are less astringent than formerly.

Ch Ferrière   map 8/R E1
3ème cru
owner: Claire Villars/Famille Merlaut *area:* 10 ha
cases: 5,000 *grape % R:* cs 75% mer 20% pv 5%
second wine: Les Remparts de Ferrière *other châteaux owned:* Ch Chasse-Spleen *(Moulis-en-Médoc)*; Ch Haut-Bages Libéral *(Pauillac)*; Ch La Gurgue *(Margaux)*; Ch Citran *(Haut-Médoc)*
33460 Margaux tel: 05 56 58 02 37
fax: 05 56 58 05 70
In extent and production this is the smallest *cru classé* of the Médoc. The heart of the estate consists of a walled plot in the Margaux commune; the simple château is also here. It takes its name from Jean Ferrière, who became mayor of Bordeaux in 1795. His descendants ran the vineyard until 1915, after which it fell into decay. Revival came in 1960 when Alexis Lichine began to lease and work the vineyard. But its star only really started to shine in 1992 after the owner, Jean Merlaut, entrusted the management to his niece Claire Villars. Since then the wine has been an at once delicate and intense-tasting, silky middleweight that comes across expressively through its oak – 50% of the *barriques* are new – and its fruit: black currants, plums and cherries.

Ch La Galiane   map 8/L C8
owner: SCEA René Renon *area:* 5 ha *cases:* 2,500
grape % R: mer 50% cs 45% pv 5% *other châteaux owned:* Ch Charmant
33460 Soussans tel: 05 57 88 35 27
fax: 05 57 88 70 59
Amiable, balanced, usually aromatic Margaux of average quality. Maturing lasts at least 18 months, with at most 10% of the casks new. The unremarkable château is said to have been named after one Galian, a 15th-century English military commander.

Ch Giscours   map 8/R J5
3ème cru
owner: Eric Albada Jelgersma *area:* 80.5 ha *cases:* 42,000 *grape % R:* cs 55% mer 35% cf 5% pv 5%
second wine: La Sirène de Giscours *other châteaux owned:* Ch Rose la Biche *(Haut-Médoc)*; Ch La Houringue *(Haut-Médoc)*
33460 Labarde tel: 05 57 97 09 09
fax: 05 57 97 09 00
In the mid-19th century a Parisian banker had a new château built here in Renaissance style, so as to be able to receive the Empress Eugénie in a fitting manner. Giscours had then existed as a wine estate for about three centuries. 100 years after the château was built it was acquired by Pierre Tari. The whole property, covering about 300 ha, was in a very bad state: of the 80 ha of vineyard, only 7 ha were planted. The Tari family brought Giscours back up to standard, but by around 1990 they themselves were having financial problems, which did the

Above: Ch Durfort-Vivens, pictured before the early-'90s renovations

quality of the wine no good. In 1995 the Dutchman Eric Albada Jelgersma took over the estate and embarked on a rigorous quality policy. He recruited a talented winemaker, developed an intensive programme both of replanting and new planting, ordered more fermentation tanks, enlarged the *chai* and bought new barrels (50-60% new for each harvest). His first vintage, the 1995, was an immediate and spectacular success. The very concentrated wine, rich in fruit and noble oak, called up memories of great past years. Giscours is back at the top.

Ch La Gurgue   map 8/R E1
cru bourgeois
owner: Claire Villars/Famille Merlaut *area:* 12 ha
cases: 6,000 *grape % R:* cs 65% mer 35% *other châteaux owned:* Ch Chasse-Spleen *(Moulis-en-Médoc)*; Ch Citran *(Haut-Médoc)*; Ch Haut-Bages Libéral *(Pauillac)*; Ch Ferrière *(Margaux)*
33460 Margaux tel: 05 57 88 76 65
fax: 05 88 76 37 87
Through the work of the talented Bernadette Villars – whose death unfortunately came too soon – and her daughter Claire who succeeded

Below: Ch Desmirail

her, this has become one of the best of Margaux's *crus bourgeois*. The wine is cask-matured for at least a year (25% of the *barriques* are new), and combines elegance with concentration, flavour with finesse. And in addition to its oak and its polished tannins, this Margaux has a delicious fruitiness: blackcurrants, blackberries, bilberries.

Ch Haut Breton Larigaudière
map 8/L C7
cru bourgeois
owner: Jacques de Schepper *area:* 13 ha *cases:* 7,000 *grape % R:* cs 59% mer 35% pv 4% cf 2%
second wines: Ch Castelbruck; Ch du Courneau *other châteaux owned:* Ch Tour Baladoz *(St-Emilion)*; Ch Les Charmilles *(AC Bordeaux)*
33460 Soussans tel: 05 57 88 94 17
fax: 05 57 88 39 14
This château, by the main road in Soussans, also boasts a pleasant restaurant. A very creditable Margaux is produced that nearly always has considerable fruit (red currants, cherries), as well as a good amount of wood with its associated aromas: caramel, vanilla, mocha, spices. With 60-80% of the barrels being new, oak can sometimes be a little too dominant, with the finish tending to dryness as a result.

Ch d'Issan   map 8/R F3
3ème cru
owner: Emmanuel Cruse *area:* 52 ha *cases:* 27,000 *grape % R:* cs 75% mer 25% *second wine:* Ch de Candale *(Haut-Médoc)*
33460 Cantenac tel: 05 57 88 35 91
fax: 05 57 88 74 24
The Latin words *Regum Mensis Arisque Deorum* ('for the table of men and the altar of the gods') appear over the gate and on the labels of this château. It owes the motto to Emperor Franz Joseph of Austria, who preferred d'Issan to all other red Bordeaux. Still today d'Issan wine cannot be denied a certain nobility. It is usually a little introvert in taste, a delicate, sometimes almost subtle Margaux with a fine interlacing of red and black berry fruits with oak: the wine spends 18 months in *barriques*, a third of them new. The tannins mostly stay restrained. The château stands near its undulating, partly walled vineyard, secure

behind its encircling moat. It dates from the 17th century, and in the years since 1945 has been restored with great care and taste by the Cruse family.

Ch Kirwan
map 8/R H3
3ème cru
owner: Jean-Henri Schÿler *area:* 35 ha *cases:* 15,500 *grape % R:* CS 40% MER 30% CF 20% PV 10% *second wines:* Les Charmes de Kirwan; Private Réserve *other wines:* Domaine de Lassalle, Rosé Private *(Bordeaux) other châteaux owned:* Ch Fourcas-Hosten *(Listrac-Médoc)*
33460 Cantenac tel: 05 57 88 71 42
fax: 05 57 88 77 62
This 18th-century estate named after an Irish owner stands near a railway line and is surrounded by its elegant park, rich in flowers and stately trees. It was laid out in the 19th century by the botanist Camille Godard. The Schÿler family of wine merchants has owned this fine estate since 1926; but early in 1994 the GAN insurance group became – indirectly – a joint owner. The group immediately engaged the winemaker from Ch Clinet in Pomerol for the *assemblage* and maturing of the 1993 vintage. This was one of the best Margaux of the year – and subsequent harvests continued the success. Characteristics now are a dark colour, an intense aroma – lots of black fruit, creamy vanilla, toast and violets – and an elegant, well-concentrated, harmonious taste with silky tannins. The proportion of new casks varies from 25-40%, and maturing generally lasts 18 months.

Ch Labégorce
map 8/L D9
cru bourgeois
owner: Hubert Perrodo *area:* 33 ha *cases:* 13,400 *grape % R:* CS 60% MER 35% CF 5% *second wine:* Ch La Mouline de Labégorce *(Haut-Médoc) other wines:* Ch La Mouline de Labégorce Rosé *(Bordeaux)*
33460 Margaux tel: 05 57 88 71 32
fax: 05 57 88 35 01
This château is the finest and most important building in the little hamlet of la Bégorce, between Soussans and Margaux, where Ch Labégorce Zédé is also to be found. The two presumably derive their names from the same owner, an abbot called Gorce. The Labégorce château was completed at the beginning of the 19th century, designed in Louis XVI style by the celebrated architect Corcelles. After the Perrodo

family took over in 1989 the building was thoroughly refurbished. At least as drastic was the work of renewal and enlargement in cellars and vineyard. The effects of all this gradually began to be noticeable in the wine, although in the mid-1990s this was still often somewhat lacking in substance and personality. However, considerable toasted oak was already present and, to a lesser extent, berry fruit. The wine matures for 12-15 months in *barriques* of which a third are new. Worth following.

Ch Labégorce Zédé
map 8/L D9
cru bourgeois
owner: Famille Thienpont *area:* 27.5 ha *cases:* 14,000 *grape % R:* CS 50% MER 35% CF 10% PV 5% *second wine:* Domaine Zédé *other wines:* Z de Zédé *(Bordeaux) other châteaux owned:* include Vieux Château Certan *(Pomerol)*; Ch Le Pin *(Pomerol)*
33460 Soussans tel: 05 57 88 71 31
fax: 05 57 88 72 54
This vineyard, separated from the Labégorce estate in 1795, came to Pierre Zédé in 1840. (One of his five children was Gustave Zédé, who

Above: Ch Giscours

Below: Ch Labégorce

designed the first French submarine.) The Zédés remained owners of the estate until 1931. It had various proprietors after that, until the Flemish Thienpont family, owner of properties that include Vieux Château Certan in Pomerol, acquired it in 1979. The dedicated, gifted Luc Thienpont became the manager. He took the estate into the top ranks of the *crus bourgeois* with a Margaux of great class and character. It is generally distinguished by breeding, a relatively firm structure, masses of fruit, beautiful oak (40% of the *barriques* are new), and good tannins. In 1988 the Thienponts created a vineyard, now 9 ha in area, from which Z de Zédé is produced: a delicious Bordeaux AC wine from 60% Merlot grapes, and similarly aged in cask.

Ch Larruau
map 8/R E1
cru bourgeois
owner: SCE Vignobles Bernard Château *area:* 10 ha *cases:* 5,500 *grape % R:* CS 55% MER 45% *other wines:* Cru de l'Espérance *(Haut-Médoc)*
33460 Margaux tel: 05 57 88 35 50
Excellent but not very well-known Margaux of extremely reliable quality. Eighteen months in wood (30% new barrels) means that the wine usually has spicy oak, with vanilla as well. Bouquet and taste have finesse, fruit and adequate tannins. The château stands in Margaux's main street; until 1970 it was called Ch Dubignon-Talbot.

Ch Lascombes
map 8/L E10
2ème cru
owner: Bass *area:* 83 ha *cases:* 40,000 *grape % R:* CS 55% MER 40% PV 5% *second wine:* Ch Segonnes
33460 Margaux tel: 05 57 88 70 66
fax: 05 57 88 72 17
When the well-known oenologist Patrick Léon was still responsible for this château he remarked, 'I always have the greatest difficulty in understanding Lascombes. It is a wine that changes an awful lot with time. For example, it improves in colour in bottle, so it is difficult to judge it properly in its early days.' It is a fact that this Margaux used to require time before it showed its true class, and blossomed out and away from a youth sometimes dominated by its oak (half the casks being new) and angular tannins. Usually only Lascombes from lesser years could be drunk early. Nowadays it is made to be somewhat more supple, as well as a little fleshier, and has gained in depth, aroma and complexity. However, it still gains from bottle-age. For a long time a *deuxième cru classé* standard was not attained, but this is coming into view again. The château dates from 1904. From 1952 to 1971 it belonged to Alexis Lichine. Both he and Bass, now the owners, have invested heavily in this Margaux estate.

Ch Malescot St-Exupéry
map 8/R F1
3ème cru
owner: Roger Zuger *area:* 31 ha *cases:* 18,500 *grape % R:* CS 50% MER 35% CF 10% PV 5% *second wines:* Dame de Malescot; Ch Loyac *other wines:* Domaine du Balardin *(Bordeaux Supérieur)*
33460 Margaux tel: 05 57 88 70 68
fax: 05 57 88 35 80
Two owners gave their names to this château: Simon Malescot, counsellor to the king at the end of the 17th century; and Jean-Baptiste de St-Exupéry, the count who bought the estate in 1827 and added the Loyac property to it. The château was built about three decades later by a

44

MARGAUX

8

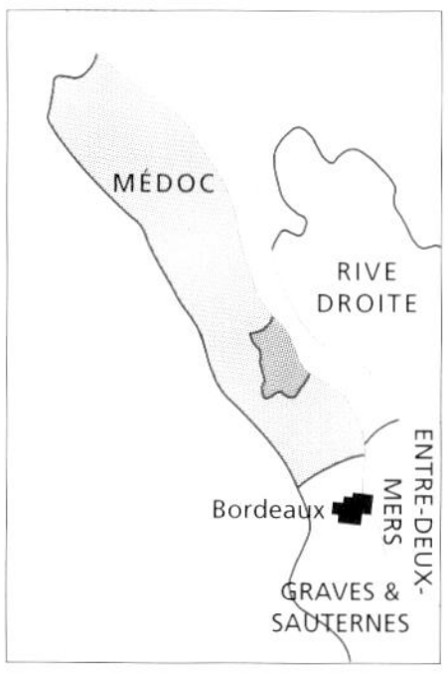

MÉDOC

RIVE
DROITE

Bordeaux

ENTRE-DEUX-MERS

GRAVES & SAUTERNES

Desmirail
Durfort-Vivens
Brane-Cantenac
Lascombes
Margaux
Rauzan-Gassies
Rauzan-Ségla
Palmer
d'Issan
Kirwan
Giscours
Other vineyards
Woods
AC Margaux
AC Haut-Médoc
AC Bordeaux
Commune boundary
Canton boundary
Contour line

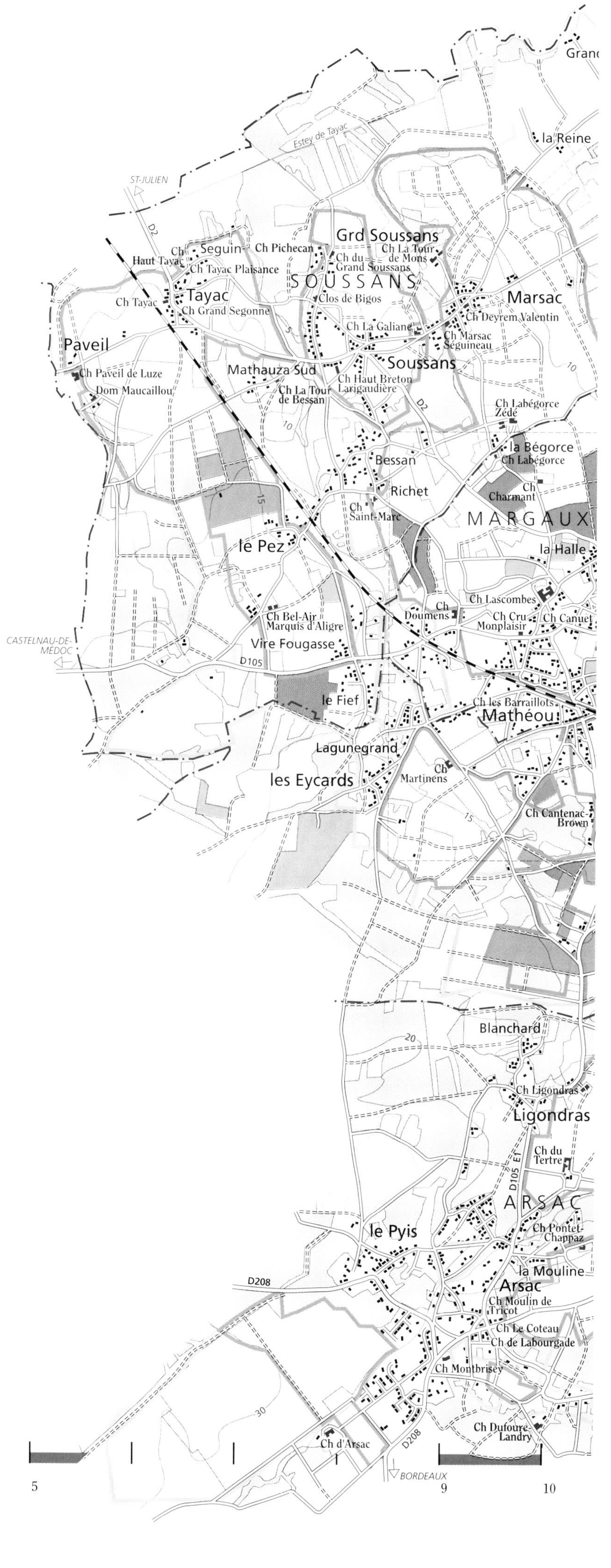

ST-JULIEN

Estey de Tayac

la Reine

Grd Soussans
Ch La Tour
de Mons
Ch du
Grand Soussans

Seguin
Ch Pichecan
Ch
Haut Tayac
Ch Tayac Plaisance

SOUSSANS

Marsac

Tayac
Ch Tayac
Ch Grand Segonne
Clos de Bigos
Ch La Galiane
Ch Deyrem Valentin
Ch Marsac
Séguineau

Paveil
Ch Paveil de Luze
Dom Maucaillou
Mathauza Sud
Ch Haut Breton
Larigaudière
Soussans
Ch Labégorce
Zédé

Ch La Tour
de Bessan
la Bégorce
Ch Labégorce

Bessan
Ch
Charmant

Richet
Ch
Saint-Marc
MARGAUX

le Pez
la Halle

Ch Lascombes
Ch
Doumens
Ch Cru
Monplaisir
Ch Canuet

Ch Bel-Air
Marquis d'Aligre
Vire Fougasse

CASTELNAU-DE-MÉDOC

D105

le Fief
Ch les Barraillots
Mathéou

Lagunegrand

les Eycards
Ch
Martinens

Ch Cantenac-
Brown

Blanchard

Ch Ligondras
Ligondras

Ch du
Tertre

ARSAC

le Pyis
Ch Pontet-
Chappaz

la Mouline
Arsac
Ch Moulin de
Tricot
D208
Ch Le Coteau
Ch de Labourgade

Ch Montbrisey

Ch d'Arsac
Ch Dufouré
Landry

BORDEAUX

1 2 3 4 5 9 10

d Meyre

Fumadelle

La Gironde

Ile du Nord

Ile des Vaches

N

1:35,700

0   1   2km

9

Port d'Issan

Ch Margaux

D105

Ch La Gurgue
Ch Ferrière
Ch Marquis d'Alesme Becker
Ch Larruau
Ch Malescot St-Exupery
Ch Durfort-
Vivens   Margaux
Ch Marquis de Terme
Ch Palmer
Ch Rauzan
Gassies   Ch
Vincent   Ch
Issan   Montbrun
Ch Rauzan-Ségla

Ch Pontac
Lynch

Ch
d'Issan

la Maquadune-Eau

D2

Ch Prieuré-
Lichine

Grange Neuve

CANTENAC

D105 E11

Ninotte

Cantenac

Ch Desmirail

Ch Kirwan

Ch Brane-Cantenac

Ch Boyd-
Cantenac

Jean Faure

le Mail

La Gironde

Ch Pouget

Ch Siran

Benqueyre

Pont de Labarde

la Bastide

Ch
Dauzac

Gassion

D209   MACAU

Ch
d'Angludet

Labarde

LABARDE

D2

Ferme
Suzanne

Ch Giscours

BORDEAUX

Cantelaude

Ch Monbrison

A
B
C
D
E
F
G
H
I
J
K
L
M

1   2   3   4   5   6   7   8   9   10

certain Fourcade and his son-in-law. The Zuger family took over the property, then in deplorable condition, in 1955 and put the motto *semper ad altum* ('ever higher') into practice. Margaux from Malescot performs well in the good or the great years. Besides plenty of colour it then has fine, blackcurranty fruit, elegant tannins, a reasonable texture and spicy oak from its 25% of new barrels. Though this is not an outstandingly concentrated wine, its maturing potential stretches easily to 10 or 15 years. In lighter years, however, the wine may contend with unripe fruit, herbaceous aromas, a lack of depth and too much tannin – and then it can fall somewhat short of its *troisième cru classé* status.

Ch Margaux   map 8/R E2
1er cru
owner: Familles Agnelli, Mentzelopoulos **area:** 90 ha **cases:** 33,000 **grape % R:** CS 75% MER 20% PV 3% CF 2% **grape % W:** SAUV B 100% **second wine:** Pavillon Rouge du Château Margaux **other wines:** Pavillon Blanc du Château Margaux *(Bordeaux)*
33460 Margaux tel: 05 57 88 70 28
fax: 05 57 88 31 32
The essence of this wine can be summed up in two words: elegant strength. For in its aroma and its taste, finesse and concentration are brilliantly combined. On the one hand it presents the silky elegance characteristic of its appellation, and on the other an intense, multi-dimensional fruitiness coupled with the best possible oak aromas, an often charming touch of spring blossom, and a long, reverberating finish with mature tannins. This is the Margaux of all Margaux, and quite often it is one of the greatest and most refined of the world's red wines. That the château has achieved such superior quality is in large part due to the Mentzelopoulos family. This *premier cru classé* had somewhat declined when André Mentzelopoulos took over in 1978 – but right from that vintage Ch Margaux was back at the top. After André's death in 1980 his work was energetically continued by his wife Laura and their daughter Corinne, with a talented team in support. The château itself has the air of a palace. A long and splendid drive leads up to broad steps and a four-column portico, while another flight of steps at the rear gives a view over a large park. The winery buildings are partly above, partly below ground and include spectacular vaulted barrel cellars. Besides its *grand vin* (all new casks), Ch Margaux produces an excellent second wine in Pavillon Rouge (half the barrels new), and a high-quality floral and fruity white Bordeaux, Pavillon Blanc du Ch Margaux. This white has been produced since the First World War, and is made entirely from Sauvignon Blanc grown at Vire Fougasse on the the west side of the commune.

Ch Marquis d'Alesme Becker
map 8/R E1
3ème cru
owner: Jean-Claude Zuger **area:** 10 ha **cases:** 5,250 **grape % R:** CS 30% CF 30% MER 30% PV 10% **second wine:** Marquise d'Alesme
33460 Margaux tel: 05 57 88 70 27
fax: 05 57 88 73 78
This attractive château, set at right-angles to the main street in Margaux, is the former Desmirail (which see), built in 1859. Its park borders on the Ch Margaux vineyard. After investing in a modern *cuvier* and new *chai* in

Above: Ch Kirwan

1979 the owner, Jean-Claude Zuger, was able to raise the standard of the wine – but the level of a *troisième cru classé* has not as yet been reached. The Margaux made here generally has colour, firmness and tannin, but often does not quite have enough fruit, charm or finesse. Its oak comes from a year's maturing in 20% new barrels.

Ch Marquis de Terme   map 8/R F1
4ème cru
owner: Famille Sénéclauze **area:** 35 ha **cases:** 13,000 **grape % R:** CS 55% MER 35% PV 7% CF 3% **other wines:** Ch des Gondats *(Bordeaux Supérieur)*
33460 Margaux tel: 05 57 88 30 01
fax: 05 57 88 32 51
In 1762 Pierre de Rausan's great-niece married François de Péguilhan de Larboust, Marquis de Terme, her dowry being a family estate not far from Ch Margaux. The coat of arms of the marquis is still to be seen on the front of the white château. The Margaux from Marquis de Terme usually displays a deep colour, and since the beginning of the 1980s it has had a firm profile, generally with ripe fruit, and spicy oak from the 18 months the wine spends in *barriques* (30-50% of them are new each year), and a long aftertaste with good tannins. An excellent Bordeaux Supérieur, Château des Gondats, is also produced, partly from a separate vineyard.

Ch Marsac Séguineau   map 8/L C9
cru bourgeois
owner: Société Civile du Château Marsac Séguineau/Mestrezat **area:** 10.2 ha **cases:** 4,130 **grape % R:** MER 65% CS 23% CF 12% **second wine:** Ch Gravières de Marsac **other châteaux owned:** Ch de Rayne Vigneau *(Sauternes)*; Ch Tourteau Chollet *(Graves)*; Ch Blaignan *(Médoc)*; Ch Lamothe Bergeron *(Haut-Médoc)*; Ch Grand-Puy Ducasse *(Pauillac)*
33460 Soussans tel: 05 56 01 30 10
fax: 05 56 79 23 57
Pleasant, supple and lively wine with reasonable concentration and, in good years, ripe soft fruit (notes of berries and cherries). It requires only a little patience. The estate was created in 1886 by the Comte de Robieu, who added vineyard plots to the *cru bourgeois* Ch Séguineau-Deyres near Marsac.

Ch Martinens   map 8/L G9
cru bourgeois
owner: Jean-Pierre Seynat Dulos **area:** 31 ha **cases:** 14,000 **grape % R:** MER 40% CS 30% PV 20% CF 10% **second wine:** Ch Guyney **other wines:** Ch Bois du Monteil, Ch Corneillan *(Haut-Médoc)*
33460 Cantenac tel: 05 57 88 71 37
According to the records this estate came into being through three unmarried sisters from England called White, who had the château built in 1767. The vineyard, almost entirely replanted since 1960, has a relatively large amount of Petit Verdot, but Merlot is the most important grape. Artificial fertilizers are not used. The wine has a fairly low acidity, supple roundness and some agreeable fruit. This is a fairly generous kind of Margaux. About a quarter of the casks are new each year. The same team makes two Haut-Médocs from another vineyard, Ch Bois du Montail and its second wine Ch Corneillan.

Ch Monbrison   map 8/R L1
cru bourgeois
owner: E.M. Davis & Fils **area:** 13.2 ha **cases:** 6,500 **grape % R:** CS 50% MER 30% CF 15% PV 5% **second wine:** Bouquet de Monbrison **other châteaux owned:** Ch Cordet *(Margaux)*
33460 Arsac tel: 05 56 58 80 04
fax: 05 56 58 85 33
One of the most outstanding winemakers of the Médoc, the 35-year-old Jean Luc Vonderheyden, died in 1992. He had succeeded in raising this family property above its *cru bourgeois* status, producing wines of *cru classé* level. It was not for nothing that Monbrison twice won the Coupe des Crus Bourgeois. Luxurious blackcurrant fruit, smoky oak and a superb

◆
Finding a second wine
To locate a second wine or any other wine not listed in the appellation's Directory pages, consult the index, where all château names are listed. Not all second wines use the appellation of the château's *grand vin*.

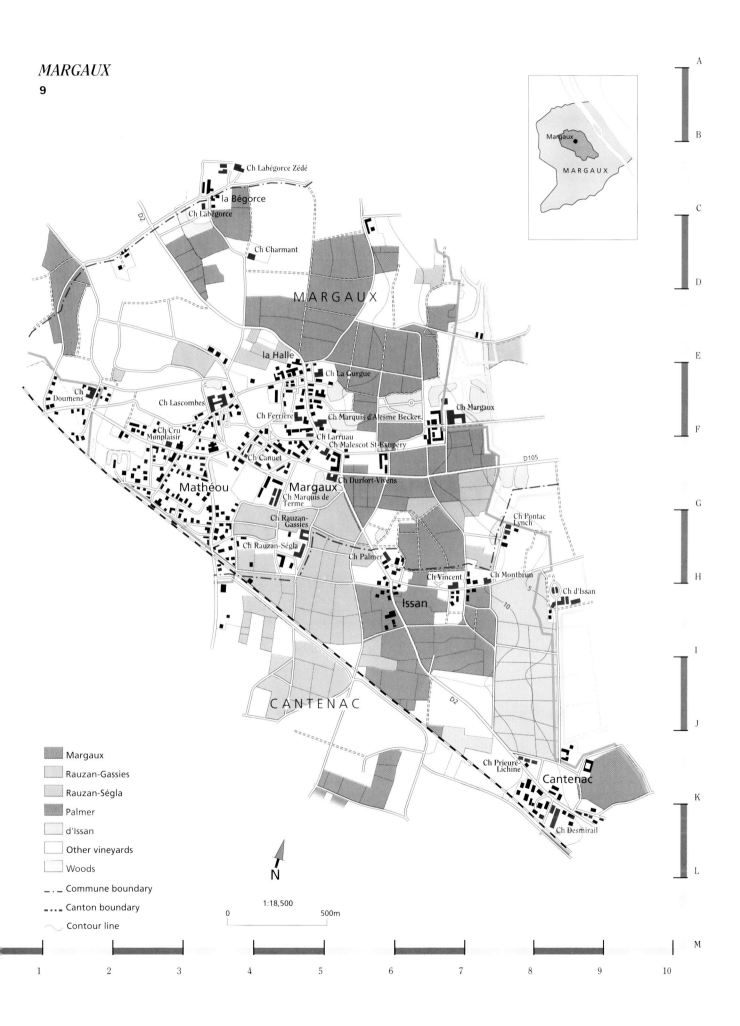

MARGAUX

9

MARGAUX

Ch Labégorce Zédé

la Bégorce

Ch Labégorce

Ch Charmant

la Halle

Ch La Gurgue

Ch
Doumens

Ch Margaux

Ch Lascombes

Ch Ferrière

Ch Marquis d'Alesme Becker

Ch Cru
Monplaisir

Ch Larruau

Ch Malescot St-Exupéry

Ch Canuet

Mathéou

Margaux

Ch Durfort-Vivens

Ch Marquis de
Terme

Ch Pontac
Lynch

Ch Rauzan-
Gassies

Ch Rauzan-Ségla

Ch Palmer

Ch Vincent

Ch Montbrun

Ch d'Issan

Issan

D105

D2

CANTENAC

Ch Prieuré-
Lichine

Cantenac

Ch Desmirail

Margaux

Rauzan-Gassies

Rauzan-Ségla

Palmer

d'Issan

Other vineyards

Woods

_ . _ Commune boundary

. . . Canton boundary

Contour line

N

1:18,500

0   500m

Margaux

MARGAUX

A

B

C

D

E

F

G

H

I

J

K

L

M

1   2   3   4   5   6   7   8   9   10

concentration were among the characteristics
of this Margaux. Despite great dedication and
effort, Monbrison has not yet been able to attain
its former class. The vintages so far tried have
tasted tougher, less intense, and did not
convince. What remains is the relatively high
proportion of new casks, which can rise from 30
to 60%.

Ch Moulin de Tricot   map 8/L L9
owner: Claude & Viviane Rey *area:* 2 ha *cases:*
1,000 *grape % R:* cs 70% mer 30%
33460 Arsac tel: 05 56 58 83 55
Not great, either in quantity or quality, but a
likeable, competently made and matured *cru
artisan.*

Ch Palmer   map 8/R F2
3ème cru
owner: Familles Mähler-Besse, Sichel *area:* 45 ha
cases: 20,000 *grape % R:* cs 55% mer 40% cf 5%
second wine: La Réserve du Général *other
châteaux owned:* include Ch d`Arche *(Haut-Médoc);*
Ch d'Angludet *(Margaux);* Ch Alfa Bernarde
(Premières Côtes de Bordeaux); Ch Bouguey *(St-
Emilion)*
33460 Cantenac tel: 05 57 88 72 72
fax: 05 57 88 37 16
In 1814 a British officer, Major-General Palmer,
decided to settle in Bordeaux, where he bought
Ch de Gascq (then called Domaine d'Issan) and
numerous vineyard plots. Nearly four decades
later Palmer landed in financial difficulties and
was obliged to sell his property to a family of
bankers. They built an elegant château with
pointed towers, but the economic crisis of the
1930s left these owners short of money in their
turn. On the initiative of Henry Mähler-Besse,
the Margaux property was taken over by the
Ginestet, Miailhe, Mähler-Besse and Sichel
families, variously wine merchants, growers and
brokers. Of these there now remain the Mähler-
Besses with about a two-thirds share, and the
Sichels with one-third, plus a few more shares
held by various individuals. Ever since the
1960s the Palmer wines have been among the
very best from Margaux. After stringent
selection and 18-24 months in *barriques,* a
third of them new, what emerges is an
exquisite, gratifying wine which immediately
seduces with its fine, nuanced bouquet where
mellow fruit predominates. Its taste is generally

Below: Ch Lascombes

characterized by the same distinguished,
smooth fruit, a firm elegance and rounded,
mature tannins; while noble, toasted oak makes
a stylish setting for the whole.

Ch Paveil de Luze   map 8/L C5
cru bourgeois
owner: Geoffroy de Luze *area:* 27 ha *cases:*
15,000 *grape % R:* cs 60% mer 35% cf 5% *second
wine:* l'Enclos du Banneret
33460 Soussans tel: 05 57 88 30 03
fax: 05 56 39 94 57
This wine is an accessible, easy, not very intense
Margaux, with modest fruit as well as spicy
notes, bayleaf and licorice. A third of the
maturing casks are new. Soon ready for
drinking. The de Luze family has owned this
estate since 1862. The name 'Paveil' is derived
from *pavillon.*

Ch Pontac Lynch   map 8/R F3
owner: Famille Bondon *area:* 10 ha *cases:* 5,000
grape % R: mer 45% cs 25% cf 20% pv 10% *second
wine:* Ch Pontac-Phénix *(Haut-Médoc)*
33460 Cantenac tel: 05 57 88 30 04
fax: 05 57 88 32 63
Wine estate with an enviable position between
Chx Margaux and d'Issan; it took shape in 1720
through the efforts of the aristocrat Arnaud de
Pontac. The château, ivy-covered and guarded
by large dogs, is the birthplace of a seldom
striking but always very correct wine. This is
matured for a year in oak, a third of the barrels
being new. It usually has a deep colour, a
discreet fruitiness and sufficient tannin for
about five years' development.

Ch Pontet-Chappaz   map 8/L L10
cru bourgeois
owner: Vignobles Rocher-Cap de Rive *area:* 7 ha
cases: 4,750 *grape % R:* cs 57% mer 33% cf 10%
second wine: Ch Tricot d'Arsac *other châteaux
owned:* include Ch Cap d'Or *(St-Georges-St-Emilion)*
33460 Arsac tel: 05 57 40 08 88
fax: 05 57 40 19 93
Dark-red, sometimes even opaque wine,
reasonably elegant in structure and with an
aroma in which licorice, bayleaf, leather and
oak tones can be recognized, together with a
touch of black fruit. A third of the casks used
for maturing are new, and the time in them
varies from 10-12 months.

Above: Ch Malescot St-Exupéry

Ch Pouget   map 8/R H3
4ème cru
owner: Pierre Guillemet *area:* 10 ha *cases:* 4,500
grape % R: cs 66% mer 30% cf 4% *second wine:* Ch
La Tour Massac *other châteaux owned:* Ch Boyd
Cantenac *(Margaux)*
33460 Cantenac tel: 05 57 88 30 58
It is said that centuries ago this estate belonged
to the monks of the priory at Cantenac. They
served their wine to Cardinal Richelieu, who
was plagued by fatigue and stomach complaints.
Restored by it, he introduced Pouget wine to
the court of Louis XIII. Ch Pouget has had a
rather obscure existence in the 20th century,
for its wine has been sold exclusively by one
firm, mainly to private buyers in France.
Besides this, for decades it very closely
resembled Ch Boyd-Cantenac wine (which see);
only since 1983 has it been totally distinct. Its
quality is seldom impressive. Often it is an
angular, foursquare sort of Margaux, with not
much fruit and sometimes rather bitter, dry
tannins. It tastes at its best after about 10 years.

Ch Prieuré-Lichine   map 8/R G3
4ème cru
owner: Sacha Lichine *area:* 68 ha *cases:* 35,000,
white: 500 *grape % R:* cs 52% mer 39% pv 5% cf 4%
grape % W: sauv 75% sem 25% *second wine:* Ch de
Clairefont *other wines:* Blanc du Château Prieuré-
Lichine *(Bordeaux),* Bordeaux rosé, Le Haut-Médoc
du Prieuré.
33460 Cantenac tel: 05 57 88 36 28
fax: 05 57 88 78 93
The American Alexis Lichine, who bought the
estate in 1951, made it into one of the most
hospitable *crus* of the Médoc. Large billboards
announce that visitors are welcome all year
round, seven days a week. The reception area is
Californian in style, and besides the various
aspects of wine, the château has a 16th-century
priory to offer and a collection of cast-iron
firebacks. The wine had usually been fairly
elegant and harmonious, with sufficient – but
not excessive – tannins and reasonable fruit.
However, under the direction of Sacha Lichine,
who took over after his father's death in 1988,
the wine has gradually acquired more
substance, depth, fruit, and new oak (50-65% of
the casks now), as well as more backbone and

Above: the second-year cellar at Ch Margaux

class. The definitive breakthrough came with the 1994 vintage – although the 1992 and 1993 were already impressive. Since 1992 a white Bordeaux has been made from 1.6 ha: the Blanc du Ch Prieuré-Lichine is 75% Sauvignon grapes, the rest being Sémillon. This expressive wine is fermented in new oak.

Ch Rauzan-Gassies   map 8/R F1
2ème cru
owner: Jean-Michel Quié *area:* 28 ha *cases:* 12,500 *grape % R:* cs 65% mer 20% cf 15% *other châteaux owned:* Ch Croizet-Bages *(Pauillac)*; Ch Bel-Orme Tronquoy de Lalande *(Haut-Médoc)*
33460 Margaux tel: 05 57 88 71 88
fax: 05 57 88 37 49
This château is no more than a simple dwelling, with its cellars next to those of Rauzan-Ségla. The two properties were part of the estate founded by Pierre de Rausan in 1661. They were split up at the time of the French Revolution. The Quié family has been running Rauzan-Gassies since 1946, and until the beginning of the 1990s mostly made dark-coloured, harsh and rather empty wines, lacking in fruit, class and charm. Only with the installation of a modern *cuvier* in 1992, and the arrival of a quality-oriented *régisseur* (who also works for the other two Quié châteaux), has the wine started to taste more agreeable and to offer more fruit – but much has still to be done before the standard of a *deuxième cru classé* is reached.

Ch Rauzan-Ségla   map 8/R F1
2ème cru
owner: Chanel *area:* 45 ha *cases:* 23,500 *grape % R:* cs 63% mer 35% cf 2% *second wine:* Ségla *other châteaux owned:* Ch Canon *(St-Emilion)*
33460 Margaux tel: 05 57 88 82 10
fax: 05 57 88 34 54
The château at Rauzan-Ségla (spelled Rausan until the 1990s) was built in 1904 by the Cruses. This family of wine merchants bought the property in 1866, and were to own it for 90 years. After a period of substandard performance the estate began to merit attention once more with its 1983 vintage. Considerable improvements were carried through in the vineyard and cellars. The quality policy was continued by the perfumes and fashion group

Chanel, which took over Rauzan-Ségla in April 1994, and entrusted the former director of Ch Latour with the running of it. The wine from that year was glorious, and surpassed within its appellation only by Ch Margaux: massive colour, toasty oak (50-60% new casks), silky yet deep tannins, elegant structure and a delicious aroma of fruit, with a touch of violets. Since then the wine has maintained that standard, and it is very worthy of its status as a *deuxième cru classé.*

◆
Finding a château
When the name is known To locate a château from its name alone, use the index/gazetteer, which will provide a page and a map reference. When the name and the appellation are known consult the Directory pages of the relevant chapter. **When the commune is known**, but not the appellation: consult the index by commune, which lists châteaux in the Atlas under the commune name.

Below: Ch Palmer

Ch Saint-Marc   map 8/L E8
owner: Marc Faure *area:* 7 ha *cases:* 4,000 *grape % R:* cs 50% mer 50%
33460 Soussans tel: 05 57 88 30 67
Wine matured, to a modest degree, in cask. It has a solid taste with considerable tannin, without great refinement or nuance. This carefully made, traditional Margaux deserves to be laid down for several years.

Ch Siran   map 8/R H6
owner: Famille Miailhe *area:* 25 ha *cases:* 11,000 *grape % R:* cs 50% mer 30% pv 12% cf 8% *second wine:* Ch Bellegarde *other wines:* La Bastide de Siran *(Haut-Médoc) other châteaux owned:* Ch Saint-Jacques *(Bordeaux Supérieur)*
33460 Labarde tel: 05 57 88 34 04
fax: 05 57 88 70 05
The name probably goes back to a certain Guilhem de Siran, who in 1428 took the oath of allegiance to an abbot in the south of the Médoc. For a long time afterwards the estate was known as St-Suran. The forebears of the present owner acquired it in 1848. The château itself, a modest building from the early 19th century, is at its most beautiful in September, for then it is surrounded by thousands of cyclamens in bloom. It is open every day to visitors and has Chinese porcelain, shells and modern art among its exhibits, plus an old cooper's workshop. Siran's wine offered more breeding in the past than at present; then it was of *cru classé* quality. In the good years the wine still has distinction, yet lacks that extra bit of depth and complexity to generate great enthusiasm – and the tannin can sometimes be somewhat tough. Vintages from 1981 onward are stored in a bomb-proof shelter. Other wines are Ch Bellegarde (the second wine, a Margaux), La Bastide de Siran from a single hectare (Haut-Médoc), and Ch Saint-Jacques, a creditable wine from 13 ha of low-lying ground (a Bordeaux Supérieur).

Ch Tayac   map 8/L C6
cru bourgeois
owner: GFA Château Tayac *area:* 37 ha *cases:* 20,000 *grape % R:* cs 65% mer 30% pv 5% *second wines:* Ch Grand Soussans; Ch Tayac la Rauza; Ch Labory de Tayac *other châteaux owned:* Domaine du Pont Rouge *(Bordeaux Supérieur)*
33460 Soussans tel: 05 57 88 33 06
Usually this Margaux is more firm than fine, with considerable charred wood in both

Above: Ch Rauzan-Ségla

Above: Ch du Tertre

bouquet and taste, from new *barriques* (a third of the total). Smooth berry fruit and a generally solid colour complete this quite pleasant whole, which is meant for bottle-ageing.

Ch Tayac Plaisance
map 8/L B6

owner: Paul Bajeux *area:* 2.2 ha *cases:* 1,000 *grape % R:* CS 50% MER 35% CF 10% PV 5%

33460 Soussans tel: 05 57 88 36 83
fax: 05 57 88 36 83

Small family estate run by a builder. The wine is sturdy, rich in tannin, and tends to the rustic. Its Petit Verdot content comes from the oldest vines in Soussans.

Ch du Tertre
map 8/L K10

5ème cru

owner: Famille Capbern-Gasqueton *area:* 50 ha *cases:* 20,000 *grape % R:* CS 85% MER 10% CF 5%

second wines: Les Hauts du Tertre; Margaux Réserve *other châteaux owned:* Ch Capbern Gasqueton *(St-Estèphe)*; Ch Calon-Ségur *(St-Estèphe)*

33460 Arsac tel: 05 56 59 30 08
fax: 05 56 59 71 51

Château set on a hill *(tertre)* surrounded by vines. The origins of the estate probably go back to the 12th century. Among later owners have been the counts of Ségur and the entrepreneur Mitchell who in the 18th century built the first glass-making factory at Bordeaux. Interest in du Tertre wine revived at the end of the 1970s after a complete overhaul of the winemaking installations and the vineyard. It is matured in the classic way, with two years in casks of which 30-50% are new each year. This Margaux therefore has plenty of oak and its associated aromas, with tannins that can vary from quite hard and firm to reasonably supple and round. In addition the wine often has an undertone of jammy berry fruit.

Ch La Tour de Bessan
map 8/L C7

owner: SC Les Grands Crus Réunis/Marie-Laure Lurton-Roux *area:* 17 ha *cases:* 8,300 *grape % R:* CF 58% CS 28% MER 14% *other châteaux owned:* Ch de Villegeorge *(Haut-Médoc)*; Ch Duplessis *(Moulis)*

33460 Soussans tel: 05 57 88 83 33
fax: 05 57 88 72 51

This Soussans château, with its predominance of Cabernet Franc, offers a charming, fragrant,

smooth Margaux with considerable fruit and not much oak. The estate took its name from an ancient tower, all that remains of a castle built around 1280.

Ch La Tour de Mons
map 8/L B8

cru bourgeois

owner: Grands Crus Investissements *area:* 35 ha *cases:* 18,000 *grape % R:* CS 45% MER 40% CF 10% PV 5% *second wine:* Ch Richeterre

33460 Soussans tel: 05 57 88 33 03
fax: 05 57 88 32 46

The owners of this estate can trace their family ancestry back to Pierre de Mons, of Belgian origin, who acquired it in 1615. Of the château that stood here then, built in the 15th century on the foundations of a 13th-century fortress, only a few fragments of wall, part of a tower and a chapel remain, for it burned down in 1895. In quality the wine of this well-known château is no longer among the leading *crus bourgeois*, as it was in the 1960s, but is still well up in the field. Although sufficient body, fruit and tannin are present in the taste, the whole is still somewhat angular, with less dimensions than wines from various other *crus bourgeois*. However, a modest improvement in quality is being shown in recent vintages. This could be due in part to the modern fermentation equipment that has now been installed, and the gradually increasing proportion of new barrels

used for maturing the wine – from one-fifth previously to the present one-quarter to one-third.

Ch de Tressan/La Bessane
map 8

owner: SARL Cantegraves/Martine Cazeneuve *area:* 3 ha *cases:* 1,200 *grape % R:* PV 70% CS 10% MAL 10% MER 10% *other châteaux owned:* Ch Paloumey *(Haut-Médoc)*; Ch La Garricq *(Moulis-en-Médoc)*

33290 Ludon tel: 05 57 88 00 66
fax: 05 57 88 00 67

That the Petit Verdot variety yields a wine rich in colour, firm and with a good deal of tannin can be fully confirmed by this Margaux, for it comes from a small vineyard near Ch Prieuré-Lichine which boasts 70% of Petit Verdot vines. The present owners took over Ch de Tressan in 1993 and have now renamed it Ch La Bessane.

Ch les Vimières Le Tronquéra
map 12

owner: Jacques Boissenot *area:* 0.46 ha *cases:* 250 *grape % R:* MER 100% *other châteaux owned:* Ch Les Vimières *(Haut-Médoc)*

33460 Lamarque tel: 05 56 58 91 74
fax: 05 56 58 98 36

This château produces tiny amounts of a pure Merlot wine, beautifully supported by oak (a third of the casks are new each vintage), and dark-toned in its aroma. A Margaux of a high standard.

◆
Grape varieties: synonyms and oddities

Local variants and synonyms have traditionally been, and sometimes still are, used for some of the Bordeaux grapes. Some of these names are given official status in the appellation decrees. Synonyms include:

Bouchet St-Emilion name for Cabernet Franc
Côt or Cot Synonym for Malbec
Pressac St-Emilion name for Malbec

There are also some minor varieties which figure in the appellation decrees but are obscure or seldom grown:

Carmenère Red grape considered the equal of Cabernet Sauvignon in the Médoc in the early 19th century. Susceptible to disease, therefore now very rare; though still legal in all Médoc ACs and in the Premières Côtes.

Merlot Blanc May be a mutation of Merlot, or a separate variety. Little is grown.

Ondenc A virtually vanished white grape, still permitted for the Bordeaux AC.

Mauzac White variety still important further east; all but gone from Bordeaux, but legal as a *cépage accessoire* in Entre-Deux-Mers.

Sauvignon Gris White variety described by some growers as an old clone, now reintroduced. Fresh, aromatic wine.

St-Julien

MICHAEL BROADBENT

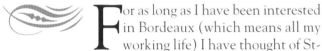

For as long as I have been interested in Bordeaux (which means all my working life) I have thought of St-Julien – the district and its wines – as the 'fulcrum', the home for me of the archetypal 'Englishman's claret'. Geographically and stylistically it holds a sort of midway position in the Médoc. To the south lies the 'greater Margaux' district with its diffuse types and, at its best, feminine qualities. On its northern boundary is trim, compact Pauillac with its intense, deep-coloured wines; beyond Pauillac, the most northerly, more extensive district of St-Estèphe, with its rustic – I nearly said rough and ready – reds. Moreover, the wines of St-Julien can never be confused with the Right-Bank Pomerols and the sweeter, more alcoholic St-Emilions.

The wines of St-Julien are gentlemanly and somewhat understated. And, as if to prove they have no need to show off, this neat little district does not include a single First Growth; yet no other in the whole of the Médoc contains so many classed Growths.

ST-JULIEN WINES AND THEIR INFLUENCES

How can one, in words, convey the look, smell and taste of a typical St-Julien, (if indeed there is such a thing), and what are the causes? Let's deal with the causes first: the climate it shares of course with the rest of the Médoc, though perhaps with pockets, with microclimates. The variables really start with the soil, subsoil, aspect and, crucially, drainage. The principal block of vineyards is on one broad *croupe* – a slightly, though distinctly, raised outcrop of gravel, the result of millennia of pebbles swept down the Garonne and Dordogne. The slopes and interspersed *jalles* (tiny streams) provide perfect drainage, producing wines with finesse. Away from the river the soil is richer, as is the wine produced –

exemplified by the generous, fruity Gruaud-Larose. The choice of vine varieties is a matter of local tradition and individual judgment but, unlike Pauillac, it is not such a pronounced and dramatic Cabernet Sauvignon area. The variables comprise a combination of sound finance, experienced estate management and winemaking skills. If, therefore, I was to sum up an ideal St-Julien it would have depth of colour but not the dense opacity of a great Pauillac or, for that matter, Pomerol. Its initial varietal aroma less dramatic, its bottle-age bouquet harmonious, subtle, perhaps cedar-like; on the palate perfectly balanced, middle weight, with silky texture, assimilated fruit and a clean, dry finish. The perfect beverage, the perfect claret.

In my opening paragraphs I suggested a style and character of wine which, in effect, shuns excesses. It is lower-keyed, less dramatic than, for example, Pauillac – its aim being harmony, balance, perfect weight, length. Yet the best St-Juliens, from good vintages, have remarkable staying power.

Importantly there is more consistency of style and reliability of quality than the wines of any other district. I well recall the exquisitely balanced 1900 Léoville Las Cases from the cellars of Glamis Castle which acted as a prelude to the magnum of celebrated 1870 Lafite at a pre-sale dinner at Christie's in 1971 – so good that we all thought it would upstage the Lafite. It didn't; merely bowing gracefully and respectfully while holding its own.

Whereas Las Cases has ploughed a steady furrow, particularly under the firm management of M. Alain Delon and his father, Léoville Poyferré has had its ups and downs. From the middle of the 19th century it was held in great esteem, culminating in the superb 1929 – reputed to be one of, if not the, best wine of that lovely vintage. Its vineyard site is one of the finest in the whole

Right: The *portail cour d'honneur* at
Léoville Las Cases

of the Médoc and, under new management, will I am sure revert to its former glory. Léoville Barton also had a reputation similar to that of Poyferré in those *fin de siècle* years. During the long reign of Ronald Barton, the *grand seigneur* of the Médoc, the wine was uniformly good but, in my opinion, rather too uncompromising; not severe exactly, nor yet masculine, but perhaps lacking a little flexibility and charm. His nephew, Anthony, the latest of the long line of Bartons, has made some necessary improvements and this innately gentlemanly wine has shaken off its old tweeds and become more beguiling.

THE LAND AND THE CHÂTEAUX

The heart of St-Julien is a solid block of vineyards, 3.5 km by 4 km wide, the north-east quarter dominated by the large walled vineyard of Léoville Las Cases, its gently sloping rows of vines not only with a superb view of the Gironde but also those of its neighbouring First-Growth Château Latour – a mere ditch being the dividing line.

The châteaux are on the whole handsome rather than grand; most reflecting the dependability and style of the wine produced. They and their vineyards either have a desirable river view – notably Ducru-Beaucaillou and Beychevelle – or stand somewhat aloof, a little to the west, at the centre of the district: for example Talbot and, on its southern flank, Gruaud-Larose.

Beychevelle is the most exquisite château in the Médoc, if not the whole of Bordeaux. Built in 1757 in the *chartreuse* style, with single-storey principal rooms flanked by two-storey pavilions and enclosing wings set at right-angles to form a U-shape, its delicacy and fine proportions are matched only by its view over the Gironde. Ducru-Beaucaillou, the home of the greatly respected Jean-Eugène Borie, is a more stolid, monumental version, also with a superb commanding view. Beneath the main rooms are the cellars. (I always wonder what it must be like to sleep here, with the gentle fumes of the wine rising from the slumbering yet ever active *barriques* beneath. Soundly I am sure.)

Another handsome and very much lived-in château is Langoa Barton, the home of Anthony Barton. Anthony can boast (but doesn't) that his family can trace their ownership back to the early decades of the 18th century, now the longest unbroken family succession of any major château in the Médoc. Both house and garden have a distinctly aristocratic feel, with that unselfconscious elegance, quality and style of an English stately home in miniature. Confusingly, Langoa is also the 'home' of château-less Léoville Barton, which is made in the Langoa *cuvier*. Equally mystifying – if one is not aware that the original Léoville estate, once reputed to be the biggest in the Médoc, was subdivided – is the non-existence of actual, proper 'châteaux' at Léoville Las Cases and Léoville Poyferré, which boast merely *chais*, cask cellars and modest offices.

One thinks of Gruaud-Larose and Talbot as twins, partly because of the long connections with the Cordier family which owned both. Both were – still are – immaculately kept. The late M. Jean Cordier lived at Château Talbot, his wife at a similarly handsome town house in Bordeaux. I recall visiting both châteaux one autumn to find at each a gardener with broom in hand

patiently sweeping leaves off the neat gravel carriageways. Another world. Gruaud-Larose – not lived in but used for entertaining – is a very handsome, classically designed two-storey 18th-century mansion with (when I last visited it) period furniture, and beautifully maintained *chais* and cellars housing a considerable stock of old vintages.

Of the other major châteaux, Lagrange is architecturally rather dull, with an unusual and disproportionate square tower. Branaire (Branaire-Ducru, before that Branaire-Duluc-Ducru) is rather similar but smaller: within pistol-shot of Beychevelle and

unoccupied for many years; the new owners, probably wisely, are concentrating on improving the winemaking and cellar facilities. Château St-Pierre (Bontemps et Sevaistre, to give the rest of its former name in full) has been recently transformed from a rather plain farmhouse to a handsome mansion, standing in a park.

Among the relatively few *bourgeois* châteaux, Gloria (virtually the creation of the late M. Henri Martin, a notable character and a former director of Latour) is an extremely plain building gazing longingly across the vineyards towards the altogether more majestic Ducru-Beaucaillou. Equally plain, indeed

The *cuvier* at Léoville Las Cases

nondescript, are the small villages of St-Julien and Beychevelle, both straddling the *route du vin*, the D2.

VINTAGES

In addition to the 1900 Léoville Las Cases and 1929 Poyferré already mentioned, the most exquisite St-Julien I ever tasted – first in London in 1971 and, more recently, at the château – is the 1948 Léoville Barton, a wine of exceptional fragrance, delicacy and vivacity, quite the best of all the red Bordeaux of this challenging vintage.

Of the 1945s I rate Poyferré the best, followed closely by Gruaud-Larose, the latter coming into its own in 1949 and 1953, both superb. 1952 St-Juliens were rather severe but 1953 was the perfect Médoc vintage, Las Cases and Léoville Barton both on top of their form, the latter particularly magnificent in 1959. 1961 was of course great throughout Bordeaux, Ducru-Beaucaillou and Gruaud-Larose, despite their contrasting styles, topping the bill with Las Cases. 1962 (an underrated vintage) was however not wholly successful in St-Julien – but, yet again, Las Cases was first rate; 1964 was less successful. 1966 was more suited to the St-Julien style and that year's Léoville Barton I describe as 'text-book'.

The 1970 vintage – a prolific one in which all the grape varieties ripened fully – was initially excellent in St-Julien; but then many of the wines went through a long closed-up period from which not all have emerged triumphant. Ducru-Beaucaillou's 1970 vintage is a notable exception: superb, at its peak, now. 1971s, '72s, '73s and '74s were all disappointing; and even in the much-heralded 1975 there were some failures – though Gruaud-Larose triumphed once again. 1976 St-Juliens were easier and more charming; 1978s initially attractive but tiring now; 1979s unflatteringly tannic and austere, lacking fruit; 1981s better: Las Cases the top St-Julien that year; 1982s (most untypical for St-Julien) rich chunky wines. The combination of St-Julien and 1983 is almost ideal: good, straightforward, undemonstrative, drinking well; but in 1985 they really come into their own – Gruaud-Larose, Léoville Barton and Las Cases superb. To a certain extent the 1986s remind me of 1952s, lacking a little charm but with promise of a better future – though for a long and potentially interesting life I would put my money on 1988s. 1989 witnessed the re-emergence of Léoville Poyferré which, in common with Léoville Barton, Ducru and Gruaud-Larose, produced a lovely fruity wine. The most recent classically balanced St-Julien vintage is 1990. As always, time will tell.

Great St-Julien vintages: *1870, 1899, 1900, 1926, 1928, 1929, 1945, 1949, 1953, 1959, 1961, 1966, 1982, 1985, 1990*
Good St-Julien vintages: *1918, 1920, 1924, 1934, 1947, 1948, 1952, 1955, 1962, 1964, 1968, 1970, 1971, 1975 but variable, 1976, 1978 also variable, 1981, 1983, 1986, 1988, 1989*

PERSONAL FAVOURITES

My personal favourites, in alphabetical order: Beychevelle, Branaire, Ducru-Beaucaillou, Gruaud-Larose, the Léovilles Barton, Las Cases, Poyferré, and Talbot.

THE APPELLATION

ST-JULIEN

Location: *In the heart of the Médoc, between the appellations of Margaux and Pauillac, just over 40 km north-west of Bordeaux. St-Laurent is to the west (with the Haut-Médoc AC); while to the south lies Cussac-Fort-Médoc, again Haut-Médoc. The northern border is with Pauillac.*
Area of AC: *893 ha*
Area under vine: *880 ha*
Communes: *St-Julien, plus small, precisely defined parcels of Cussac and St-Laurent. Some land on the northern edge has the Pauillac AC: see map. The commune is 5km north to south and a little less east to west.*

Average annual production: *485,000 cases*
Classed growths: *11 (5 deuxièmes crus, 2 troisièmes crus, 4 quatrièmes crus)*
Others: *8 crus bourgeois, 11 others*
Cooperatives: *None*
Main grape varieties: *Cabernet Sauvignon*
Others: *Merlot, Cabernet Franc and a small proportion of Petit Verdot*
Main soil types: *Relatively gravelly, especially in the centre; contains slightly more clay than Margaux.*

APPELLATION ST-JULIEN

Ch Beychevelle   map 10 I8
4ème cru
owner: GMF **area:** 85 ha **cases:** 46,500 **grape % R:**
CS 60% MER 28% CF 8% PV 4% **second wine:** Amiral
de Beychevelle **other wines:** Brulières de
Beychevelle (Haut-Médoc) **other châteaux owned:**
Ch Beaumont (Haut-Médoc)
33250 St-Julien-Beychevelle tel: 05 56 73 20 70
fax: 05 56 73 20 71

For Jean-Louis de Nogaret de La Valette, first
duke of Epernon and governor of Guyenne,
1587 was a memorable year. He was made
Amiral de France and married, receiving the Ch
du Médoc as his wife's dowry. This subsequently
acquired the name Beychevelle, said in
romantic legend to be a corruption of the
French expression *baisse voile*, 'lower sail' – a
command given to ships sailing past the
château as a salute to the admiral. The estate
passed through many hands until in 1757 the
Marquis de Brassier rebuilt it in the sumptuous
yet elegant style of that time. Beychevelle
remains an architectural gem, harmonious in
proportion, with a cedar centuries old at the
front and a fine formal park at the rear. From
1983 the Garantie Mutuelle des Fonctionnaires
group (GMF) invested a great deal in
Beychevelle. This policy was continued after
GMF linked up with the Japanese Suntory
concern in 1989,to form Grands Millésimes de
France, the present owner. The wine often
presents a lot of charred wood, which is apt to
dominate at first – 60% of the casks for the 20
months' ageing are new. In quality this is
certainly a *quatrième cru classé*, although in
finesse and concentration it is seldom above
average. The wine is elegant, with generally
firm tannins, candied fruit (cherry, currants),
sometimes paprika and often a hint of spices.

Ch Branaire   map 10 I7
4ème cru
owner: Patrick Maroteaux **area:** 52 ha **cases:**
27,000 **grape % R:** CS 70% MER 22% CF 5% PV 3%
second wine: Ch Duluc (St-Julien) **other châteaux
owned:** Ch La Rose de France (Haut-Médoc)
33250 St-Julien-Beychevelle tel: 05 56 59 25 86
The wine is an alluring, very characteristic St-
Julien, generally with a good balance between
fruit, oak and moderate tannins. In mature
form its bouquet has fruity as well as floral
elements, and the elegant taste a silky
smoothness. The château lies opposite
Beychevelle and got its name from Jean-
Baptiste Braneyre, the first owner. Along with
the Ducru-Beaucaillou estate Branaire was
detached from Beychevelle in 1680. A family
group under the guidance of former banker
Patrick Maroteaux bought Ch Branaire in 1988
and has subsequently invested tens of millions
of francs in the vineyard, a magnificent, ultra-
modern *cuvier*, a remarkable *chai* – where at
least 35% of the barrels are new each year – and
a total renovation of the château.

Ch La Bridane   map 10 E7
cru bourgeois
owner: GFA Pierre Saintout **area:** 15 ha **cases:**
3,500 **grape % R:** MER 38% CF 30% CS 30% PV 2%
second wine: Ch Moulin de la Bridane **other
châteaux owned:** Domaine de Cartujac (Haut-
Médoc)
33250 St-Julien-Beychevelle tel: 05 56 59 91 70
fax: 05 56 59 46 13

Above: the Langoa Barton and Léoville Barton wines are made at the Langoa château

A respectable St-Julien, a frequent prize-winner
that in successful vintages is fairly substantial,
with a good amount of tannin. Spicy, toasted
oak – a third of the casks are new – forest
scents and berry fruit determine its aroma.

Domaine Castaing   map 10 H6
owner: Jean-Jacques Cazeau **area:** 1.2 ha **cases:**
600 **grape % R:** CS 50% MER 40% CF 5% PV 5% **other
châteaux owned:** Domaine de Pey-Baron (Haut-
Médoc)
33250 St-Julien-Beychevelle tel: 05 56 59 25 60
Small estate built up since 1922, from land
bought from Branaire, Gloria and Léoville-
Barton. Refined, clean, harmonious wine that
offers both fruit – blackcurrant – and oak, a
third of the *barriques* being new.

Ch Ducru-Beaucaillou   map 10 H8
2ème cru
owner: Jean-Eugène Borie **area:** 50 ha **cases:**
19,000 **grape % R:** CS 65% MER 25% CF 5% PV 5%
second wine: La Croix **other châteaux owned:** Ch
Ducluzeau (Listrac-Médoc); Ch Grand-Puy-Lacoste
(Pauillac); Ch Haut-Batailley (Pauillac); Ch Lalande-
Borie (St-Julien)
33250 St-Julien-Beychevelle tel: 05 56 59 05 20
fax: 05 56 59 27 37

Below: Ch Beychevelle

Above : Ch Ducru-Beaucaillou

Left: Ch Gruaud-Larose

Above: Ch Lagrange

Property named after its very gravelly vineyard (*beaux cailloux*), and Bertrand Ducru, who became its owner in 1795. Here a classic, long-lasting, exquisite wine is made that for decades has ranked among the best of Bordeaux. The Borie family, owners since 1941, make this St-Julien in the traditional way and mature it for at least 18 months in casks of which 40-60% are new. The wine, combining colour, strength, fruit and finesse in an exceptionally harmonious whole, always requires at least a decade's patience. The château itself is also impressive; a wide main building between two square towers. These were added in 1880 by the *négociants* the Johnstons, the then owners. It was here, in the Johnstons' time, that Bordeaux mixture (*bouillie bordelaise*), the remedy for mildew still in use today, was accidentally discovered.

Ch du Glana map 10 H7
cru bourgeois
owner: GFA Vignobles Meffre **area:** 42 ha **cases:** 20,000 **grape % R:** cs 60% mer 35% cf 5% **second wine:** Ch Sirène **other châteaux owned:** Ch Lalande (*St-Julien*); Ch Canteloup (*St-Estèphe*); Ch La Commanderie (*St-Estèphe*); Ch Plantey (*Pauillac*)
33250 St-Julien-Beychevelle tel: 05 56 59 06 47 fax: 04 90 65 03 73
The standard wine is a fairly generous, supple St-Julien, usually with ripe fruit but without great depth or distinction. The Cuvée Vieilles

Vignes produced by *négociants* Dourthe Frères is of a considerably higher standard. This not only has more concentration and smoky oak, but also flavoursome blackcurrant fruit. This special *cuvée* demonstrates that the du Glana vineyard does have a sound potential. It comprises plots bought first from Ch St-Pierre, and later also from Ch Lagrange.

Ch Gloria map 10 H7
owner: Françoise Triaud **area:** 48 ha **cases:** 20,000 **grape % R:** cs 65% mer 25% cf 5% pv 5% **second wine:** Ch Peymartin **other châteaux owned:** Ch Saint-Pierre (*St-Julien*); Ch Haut-Beychevelle Gloria (*St-Julien*); Ch Bel Air (*Haut-Médoc*)
33250 St-Julien-Beychevelle tel: 05 56 59 08 18 fax: 05 56 59 16 18
Ch Gloria is the creation of the late and legendary Henri Martin, descendant of a family of coopers. During his lifetime he managed to acquire the land – bought in small parcels from *crus classés* – to replace the vineyard his father had sold. The wine has a likeable character and in taste is usually generous, with smooth fruit.

◆
About St-Julien
The Maison du Vin is at the Mairie in St-Julien-Beychevelle, 33750 St-Julien-Beychevelle, which is in the south of the appellation. Tel: 05 56 59 08 11.

◆
Grape varieties
Main and other permitted varieties for each appellation are given in the appellation fact box at the end of the relevant introduction. For châteaux in this Atlas, percentages of grapes grown are given as supplied by the château.

Abbreviations: cf Cabernet Franc, col Colombard, cs Cabernet Sauvignon, mal Malbec, mer Merlot, musc Muscadelle, pv Petit Verdot, sauv b Sauvignon Blanc, sém Sémillon

---

It is rounded, very accessible, yet firm and with restrained tannins. About a third of the casks for ageing are new.

Ch Gruaud-Larose map 10 I5
2ème cru
owner: Alcatel-Alsthom **area:** 82 ha **cases:** 45,800 **grape % R:** cs 60% mer 30% cf 7% pv 3% **second wine:** Sarget de Gruaud-Larose **other châteaux owned:** Ch Malescasse (*Haut-Médoc*)
33250 St-Julien-Beychevelle tel: 05 56 73 15 20 fax: 05 56 59 64 72
Aristocratic is the right word to describe both the perfectly maintained 1875 château, and the St-Julien made there. This comes across as distinguished rather than exuberant, as classic and rich in tannin rather than accessible and supple. It is also a wine that normally only begins to unfold after years, if not decades. As a counterbalance to the tannin Gruaud-Larose generally has ample fruit, together with oak from 18 months' ageing (30% new *barriques*), and also slightly spicy elements. A massive programme of rebuilding and renovation has taken place since the Alcatel-Alsthom group acquired the estate from Cordier in 1993.

Ch Haut-Beychevelle Gloria
map 10 H7
owner: Françoise Triaud **area:** 5 ha **cases:** 2,000 **grape % R:** cs 65% mer 25% cf 5% pv 5% **other châteaux owned:** Ch Gloria (*St-Julien*); Ch Saint-Pierre (*St-Julien*); Ch Bel Air (*Haut-Médoc*)
33250 St-Julien-Beychevelle tel: 05 56 59 08 18 fax: 05 56 59 16 18
Wine estate founded by Henri Martin's father (*see* Ch Gloria). The vines grow quite close to those of Ch Gloria and the mixture of grapes is identical. The wine matures in oak (20% of the barrels are new each year); the result is balanced and well made. A pleasant wine, though not one that boasts ample tannins, nor great concentration.

Ch Hortevie map 10 H7
owner: Henri Pradère **area:** 3.5 ha **cases:** 1,500 **grape % R:** cs 70% mer 25% pv 5% **other châteaux owned:** Ch Terrey-Gros-Cailloux (*St-Julien*)
33250 St-Julien-Beychevelle tel: 05 56 59 06 27 fax: 05 56 59 29 32
Concentrated St-Julien: stylish and mouthfilling, with nuances of both oak and ripe fruit.

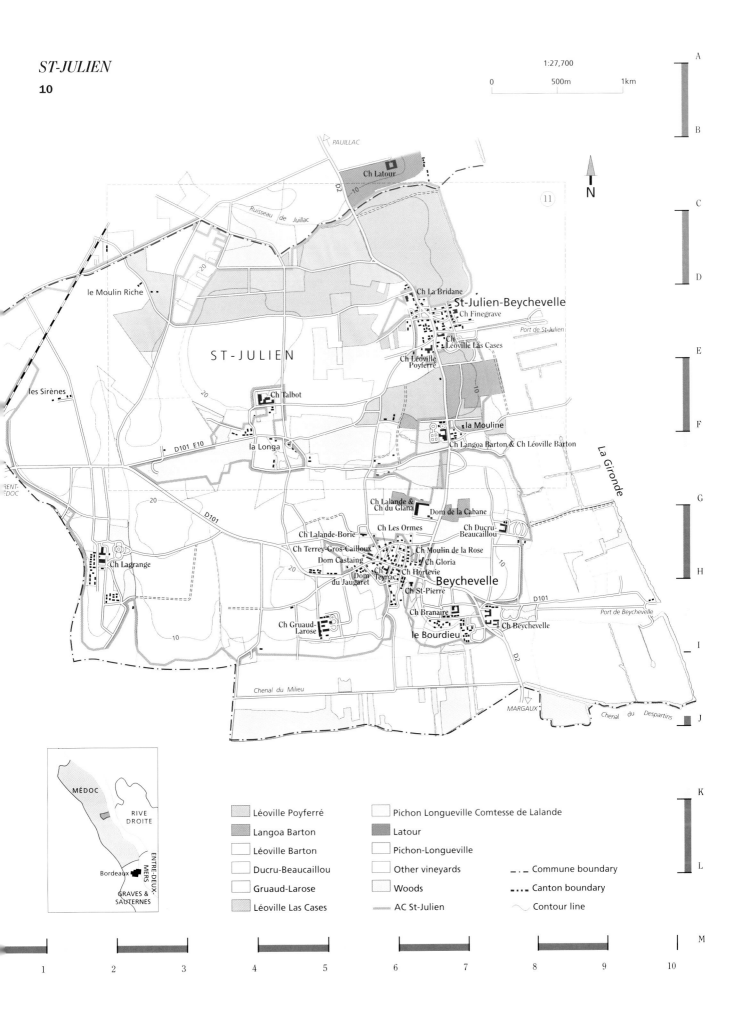

ST-JULIEN

10

1:27,700

0   500m   1km

PAUILLAC

Ch Latour

N

le Moulin Riche

Ch La Bridane

St-Julien-Beychevelle

Ch Finegrave

Port de St-Julien

Ch Léoville Las Cases

Ch Léoville Poyferré

ST-JULIEN

les Sirènes

Ch Talbot

la Mouline

Ch Langoa Barton & Ch Léoville Barton

D101 E10

la Longa

La Gironde

Ch Lalande & Ch du Glana

Dom de la Cabane

Ch Les Ormes

Ch Ducru-Beaucaillou

Ch Lalande-Borie

D101

Ch Terrey-Gros-Cailloux

Ch Moulin de la Rose

Dom Castaing

Ch Gloria

Ch Lagrange

Dom du Jaugaret

Ch Teynac

Ch Hortevie

Beychevelle

Ch St-Pierre

D101

Ch Branaire

Port de Beychevelle

Ch Gruaud-Larose

le Bourdieu

Ch Beychevelle

D2

Chenal du Milieu

MARGAUX

Chenal du Despartins

MÉDOC

RIVE DROITE

ENTRE-DEUX-MERS

Bordeaux

GRAVES & SAUTERNES

Léoville Poyferré	Pichon Longueville Comtesse de Lalande	
Langoa Barton	Latour	
Léoville Barton	Pichon-Longueville	
Ducru-Beaucaillou	Other vineyards	
Gruaud-Larose	Woods	
Léoville Las Cases	AC St-Julien	Commune boundary
		Canton boundary
		Contour line

Above: Ch Langoa Barton

Domaine du Jaugaret   map 10 H6

owner: Héritiers Fillastre **area:** 1.3 ha **cases:** 450
grape % R: CS 70% MER 25% MAL 5%
**33250 St-Julien-Beychevelle tel: 05 56 59 09 71
fax: 05 56 59 09 71**
Fermented in wooden vats. It is dominated by
flavours of berry fruit, seldom tastes very full,
and tends towards the rustic. Matured for 24-34
months in *barriques*, 20% of them new.

Ch Lagrange   map 10 H2
3ème cru

owner: Sté Suntory **area:** 113 ha **cases:** 52,000
grape % R: CS 66% MER 27% PV 7% **second wine:**
Les Fiefs de Lagrange
**33250 St-Julien-Beychevelle tel: 05 56 59 23 63
fax: 05 56 59 26 09**
Things began to happen at this château when
new owners arrived after the 1983 vintage. A
small army of workers was hired: first to
provide the vineyard – largely lying waste –
with a drainage system, then to plant all of it
with vines. In addition an entirely new *cuvier*
and *chai* were erected, the whole interior of the
château was rebuilt, and a long-vanished
watchtower was replaced on the site where it
had once stood – the architect reconstructed it
from an old engraving. The wine, too, was
restored to its *troisième cru classé* level. The
Franco-Japanese management introduced a very
stringent selection; as a rule at least half of the
vintage is sold as Les Fiefs de Lagrange, the
second wine. For the *grand vin* new casks
amounting to 60% of the total are bought in;
the wine spends 18 months in them. As a result
this St-Julien is notably successful, even in less-
good years. After 5-10 years' ageing its qualities
include an expansive bouquet, with toasted oak,
vanilla, licorice and jammy fruit; a fleshy,
sensual, beautifully concentrated and nuanced
taste; a fine, balanced finish.

Ch Lalande   map 10 H7

owner: Gabriel Meffre **area:** 32 ha **cases:** 15,000
grape % R: CS 55% MER 35% CF 5% PV 5% **second
wine:** Marquis de Lalande **other châteaux owned:**
Ch du Glana *(St-Julien)*; Ch Canteloup *(St-Estèphe)*;
Ch La Commanderie *(St-Estèphe)*; Ch Plantey
(Pauillac)
**33250 St-Julien-Beychevelle tel: 05 56 59 06 47
fax: 04 90 65 03 73**

Above: Ch Léoville Las Cases

This property came into being in 1964 when the
present owner bought a plot from Ch Lagrange.
In the good years, power is the most important
attribute of this St-Julien. Generally the wine
rather lacks charm, and also fruit. Yet the
plateau on which the estate's vineyard lies, with
all its gravel, has unmistakeable potential for
quality.

Ch Lalande-Borie   map 10 H6

owner: Jean-Eugène Borie **area:** 18 ha **cases:**
8,000 **grape % R:** CS 65% MER 25% CF 10% **other
châteaux owned:** Ch Ducru-Beaucaillou *(St-Julien)*;
Ch Ducluzeau *(Listrac-Médoc)*; Ch Haut-Batailley
(Pauillac); Ch Grand-Puy-Lacoste *(Pauillac)*
**33250 St-Julien-Beychevelle tel: 05 56 59 05 20
fax: 05 56 59 27 37**
Alluring, well-structured wine with ripe fruit
and a lively taste. Lalande-Borie gives much
satisfaction even when young, after the 16
months it spends in cask. The estate has existed
since 1970; it was created out of land bought
from a *troisième cru*.

Below: Ch Saint-Pierre

Ch Langoa Barton   map 10 G7
3ème cru

owner: Anthony Barton **area:** 20 ha **cases:** 8,300
grape % R: CS 71% MER 21% CF 8% **second wine:**
Lady Langoa **other châteaux owned:** Ch Léoville
Barton *(St-Julien)*
**33250 St-Julien tel: 05 56 59 06 05
fax: 05 56 59 14 29**
The château stands near the road between the
hamlet of Beychevelle and the centre of St-
Julien village. It was built by Bernard de Pontet
in 1758 over a vaulted, semi-underground cellar
and has stood up well to the ravages of time.
Since 1821 Langoa Barton has belonged to the
Barton family, originally from Ireland. They also
produce the Ch Léoville Barton wine here – but
the two clarets are kept strictly separate, as is
apparent from their very different personalities.
Langoa Barton is the more graceful wine of the
two. It can be dense in colour, with a vital
elegance and fruit, especially red and black
currants, a touch of spice, and the noble aromas
of new oak – half of the barrels are replaced
each year. After about five years from the
vintage Langoa Barton is already showing great
charm, but as a rule it can easily go on for
another decade after that.

Ch Léoville Barton   map 10 G7
2ème cru

owner: Anthony Barton **area:** 48 ha **cases:** 25,000
grape % R: CS 72% MER 20% CF 8% **second wine:**
Lady Langoa **other châteaux owned:** Ch Langoa
Barton *(St-Julien)*
**33250 St-Julien-Beychevelle tel: 05 56 59 06 05
fax: 05 56 59 14 29**
In 1826, five years after the acquisition of Ch
Langoa, Hugh Barton bought a part of the
Léoville estate. He named it Ch Léoville Barton,
even though this *deuxième cru* has no château
of its own; the wine is made at Ch Langoa
Barton. In the 1980s and 1990s, under Anthony
Barton's management, the estate returned
permanently to exemplary form. It is a St-Julien
with concentration and complexity; with
marvellous fruit (blackcurrant, bilberry,
blackberry); with noble oak, 50% of casks being

ST-JULIEN
11

Léoville Poyferré
Léoville Barton
Léoville Las Cases
Other vineyards
Woods
—·— Commune boundary
—··· Canton boundary
⌒ Contour line

ST-JULIEN

le Moulin Riche

Ch La Bridane

St-Julien-Beychevelle
Ch Finegrave
Port de St-Julien

Ch Léoville Poyferré
Ch Léoville Las Cases

le Tasta
la Mouline
Ch Langoa Barton &
Ch Léoville Barton

la Longa

N

1:19,200
0   500m

new; with plenty of style and tannin. Like Langoa Barton, it is still fermented in wooden vats. The two wines are given completely separate treatment; they are blended only for Lady Langoa, the second wine.

Ch Léoville Las Cases   map 10 E7
2ème cru
owner: SC du Château Léoville Las Cases (Familles Delon & Las Cases) **area:** 97 ha **cases:** 45,000 **grape % R:** cs 65% cf 13% mer 19% pv 3% **second wines:** Clos du Marquis; Ch du Grand Parc; Domaine de Bigarnon **other châteaux owned:** Ch Potensac *(Médoc)*
33250 St-Julien-Beychevelle tel: 05 56 59 25 26 fax: 05 56 59 18 33
The wine from this estate, the largest of the three Léovilles, is nothing less than monumental. In terms of power and class it belongs at the top not only of its appellation, but of all Bordeaux. Its colour is intense and its perfume becomes richly nuanced with a great amount of smoky oak (from at least 18 months in *barriques*, 60-90% of them new) and abundant fruit – blackcurrant, blackberry. The same elements occur in the superbly concentrated taste, which also displays spices, minerals, pencil shavings, chocolate, a suggestion of mint, licorice and other nuances, all balancing firm, deep and mature tannins. The wine is produced to perfectionist standards, and even in good years half or more of the vintage can be consigned to the second wine, Clos du Marquis. The Las Cases château

consists of various buildings on either side of the main street in St-Julien. The largest of the vineyard plots is walled; it lies directly north of the village itself, and stretches to the Pauillac boundary.

Ch Léoville Poyferré   map 10 E7
2ème cru
owner: Domaines Cuvelier **area:** 80 ha **cases:** 38,000 **grape % R:** cs 65% mer 25% pv 8% cf 2% **second wines:** Ch Moulin Riche; Pavillon des Connétables **other châteaux owned:** Ch Le Crock *(St-Estèphe)*
33250 St-Julien-Beychevelle tel: 05 56 59 08 30 fax: 05 56 59 60 09
An enlarged and modernized cellar complex, with its main entrance almost opposite that of Ch Léoville Las Cases, forms the birthplace of this third of the Léoville wines. There was a period when the wine from this château did not merit its *deuxième cru* status, but phased investments – the first series in 1979, the second in 1994 – have led to a gradual improvement. Today the wine most definitely displays noble oak, from the 50-75% of new barrels. The colour is usually dark and the taste rich in extract, with ample jammy red and black berry fruit. Equally characteristic are the solid, slightly angular tannins that give many vintages their grip, backbone and ageing potential. This is a St-Julien made for the future: even if from a lesser vintage, a Léoville Poyferré wine needs to be laid down for six to eight years to allow the oak and the tannin to

◆
Map numbers

Map 2, in the opening pages of the Atlas, shows the areas of all the Bordeaux appellations. To find a map for a specific appellation, turn to the regional key maps:

Maps of the Médoc & Graves appellations
For a key map showing all the appellations in this zone, with the outlines of the maps in this Atlas, consult Map 7.

Maps of the appellations between the rivers
For a key map showing all the appellations in this zone, with the outlines of the maps in this Atlas, consult Map 30.

Maps of the Right Bank appellations
For a key map showing all the appellations in this zone, such as St-Emilion and Pomerol, with the outlines of the maps in this Atlas, consult Map 37.

Above: Ch Moulin de la Rose

Above: Ch Talbot

integrate with the other elements. The domaine is named after one of its owners in the first half of the 19th century, Baron Jean-Marie de Poyferré de Céres.

Ch Moulin de la Rose   map 10 H7
cru bourgeois
owner: Guy Delon **area:** 4.65 ha **cases:** 2,500
grape % R: CS 62% MER 28% PV 5% CF 5% **other châteaux owned:** Ch Ségur de Cabanac (St-Estèphe)
33250 St-Julien-Beychevelle tel: 05 56 59 08 45 fax: 05 56 59 73 94
Attractive wine with varied expressions of breadcrust, cedarwood, jammy fruit – blackcurrant, blackberry – and supple tannins. It matures in casks of which a third are new. The small vineyard is in little plots scattered around *cru classé* territory.

Ch Saint-Pierre   map 10 I7
4ème cru
owner: Françoise Triaud **area:** 17 ha **cases:** 9,000
grape % R: CS 70% MER 20% CF 10% **other châteaux owned:** Ch Gloria (St-Julien); Ch Bel Air (Haut-Médoc); Ch Haut-Beychevelle Gloria (St-Julien)
33250 St-Julien-Beychevelle tel: 05 56 59 08 18 fax: 05 56 59 16 18

Below: Ch Terrey-Gros-Cailloux

This château derives its name from the Baron de Saint-Pierre who bought the estate, then called Ch Serançan, in 1767. After the baron's death in 1832 the property was divided up. 90 years later the Van den Bussche family from Antwerp reunited the two parts, but without the château itself. Through a complicated deal a part of the St-Pierre vineyard was acquired by Henri Martin in 1981 and joined to the château. Subsequently this 17th-century building was entirely restored. After Martin's death his successor and son-in-law, Jean-Louis Triaud, built a futuristic and controversial *chai*. This is used for both Ch St-Pierre and Ch Gloria. The St-Pierre wine characteristically has a substantial, creamy taste with facets of ripe blackcurrants, plums and figs. Spicy and earthy aspects – fungi – are not lacking; nor fine, toasty oak, for the wine spends a year or longer in oak (50-75% new casks). It displays charm when young, but can also age excellently.

Ch Talbot   map 10 F5
4ème cru
owner: Lorraine Rustmann-Cordier, Nancy Bignon-Cordier **area:** 107 ha **cases:** 56,000, white 3,300
grape % R: CS 66% MER 24% PV 5% CF 3% MAL 2%
grape % W: SAUV B 100% **second wines:** Connétable

Talbot; Moulin de T. **other wines:** Ch Talbot Caillou Blanc (AC Bordeaux blanc)
33250 St-Julien-Beychevelle tel: 05 56 73 21 50 fax: 05 56 73 21 51
This estate, named after John Talbot, Earl of Shrewsbury, who fell at Castillon in 1453, is the largest in St-Julien and has belonged to the Cordier family since 1917. The wine has enjoyed a good reputation for some decades: it is very reliable, even in lesser years. Rather tough tannins and a somewhat limited refinement used to be its characteristics; in the course of the 1980s and 1990s, however, wines with more fruit and more finesse have been appearing more often. With this St-Julien there is only rarely a very great concentration, but it always has good oak – from 18 months spent in barrels of which half are new – and as a rule this is nicely integrated with the fruit. A white Bordeaux, Caillou Blanc, is produced at Talbot from 5 ha of vineyard. A pure Sauvignon wine, this often has the class and character of a Pessac-Léognan.

Ch Terrey-Gros-Cailloux   map 10 H6
cru bourgeois
owner: Henri Pradère **area:** 15 ha **cases:** 9,000
grape % R: CS 70% MER 25% PV 5% **second wine:** Ch Le Castagney **other châteaux owned:** Ch Hortevie (St-Julien)
33250 St-Julien-Beychevelle tel: 05 56 59 06 27 fax: 05 56 59 29 32
A wine that belongs among the best of the St-Julien *crus bourgeois*. Generally its aroma is expressive of undergrowth, leather, autumn woodlands, jammy fruit, charred oak; and its taste is smooth, with elegance and the same nuances as the bouquet. The owner gives it 20 months in wood: one-third of the casks are new each year.

PAUILLAC

MICHAEL BROADBENT

If St-Julien represents the calm, self-confident, somewhat intellectual centre of the Médoc, Pauillac provides the drama, the excitement, the big guns – to mix metaphors. Whereas the approach to St-Julien from the south is surprisingly attenuated, crossing marshy meadows and *jalles* (rather muddy, often rather smelly, small creeks or brooks), one slips from St-Julien into Pauillac almost without noticing – the vineyards of Léoville Las Cases within jumping distance of those of Latour on the river side of the D2; the vines almost indistinguishable from those of the Pichons to the left of that road. As if to prove the point, a block of some sixteen hectares of land within the St-Julien commune is actually entitled to the appellation Pauillac, because it is part of a Pauillac château's vineyard.

The commune of Pauillac is in fact divided into two quite different areas: roughly equal in size but entirely different in appearance and producing somewhat different styles of wine. Pauillac, the largest town of the four major Médoc districts, acts like a hinge in a folding door, north and south of which are the two panels containing the major vineyard sections.

Dominating the area to the south of the town is Château Latour, its vines on a well-drained *croupe* overlooking the river; next to it are the two *deuxième cru* Pichons: Pichon-Longueville (formerly Longueville Baron) and Pichon Longueville Comtesse de Lalande. Here the river is the dominant feature: Latour looks down at it across its *palus* cow-pastures, and the Pichons are only a field further away.

Following the main road up through the village of St-Lambert, next comes the hamlet of Bages, the home of the popular and attractive Lynch-Bages and of Croizet-Bages. Skirting Pauillac on the inland side one crosses a railway line, then the road curves steeply up to the northern section – the highest part of the Pauillac *vignoble* and home of the two other *premiers crus*, Lafite Rothschild and Mouton Rothschild, with the shared Carruades plateau behind and the equally well situated Château Pontet-Canet nearby. The land here is higher, the river more distant than in the south.

These two parts of the commune look different, and the wines have a different character – to the extent that in certain vintages those of St-Julien and south Pauillac are not dissimilar, whereas the higher, more northerly vineyard wines have a more distinctive and dramatic bouquet and flavour.

Pauillac itself is a small town for which I have always had a soft spot – particularly the long straight riverside avenue, one side flanked by undistinguished houses, restaurants and one château, Grand-Puy-Ducasse, all facing the normally placid grey-green river, with a jetty and small marina. At this point, the Gironde is surprisingly wide – some five kilometres (over three miles) across from left bank to right. The atmosphere, somehow, always reminds me of a sleepy Venezuelan oil port, with the tide out. Happily the Shell oil refinery at the northern edge of the town is no longer in operation; the fumes from its tall thin chimneys, once clearly visible from Lafite a mere kilometre away, have ceased polluting the air and adding, one feared – despite the prevailing wind being in the opposite direction – an unwelcome element to the flavour of the grapes.

THE CHÂTEAUX, THE VINEYARDS AND THE WINES

Lafite, its wine certainly known in the 17th century and well established by the middle of the 18th, was one of the four First Growths noted by Thomas Jefferson during his visit to Bordeaux in May 1787. Indeed he placed orders

Once a busy trading port, Pauillac's harbour now shelters yachts and fishing boats

for Lafite, for Château Margaux and other wine on the spot, insisting on his wine being bottled at the château as he did not trust wine merchants!

He also instructed his agent in Bordeaux to *etiquetté* – identify – the bottles. As this was in the days before labelling, when wine was shipped packed 50 bottles or more to a hamper and not in clearly branded 12-bottle boxes, Jefferson solved the problem of mixed shipments by having the bottles of wine for everyday consumption identified by scratching with a diamond point the initial letter of the wine, for example F for Frontignan. When it came to the – even then – very expensive First Growths, his agent saw to it that the full name of the wine and the vintage was wheel-engraved on each bottle. Moreover, in 1791, when buying wine for himself and the President, George Washington, he gave orders for the initials TJ and GW to be added so that the bottles could be sorted on arrival in Philadelphia.

French historians credit the English aristocracy with the creation of the First-Growth market. Lafite was, from the start, considered the first of the Firsts, being the cornerstone of many a lordly cellar. Then, as now, the best wines were usually kept for special occasions which is why, when owners died, Lafite often remained unconsumed, the heirs consigning the wine to auction as 'the property of Noblemen deceas'd'. Moreover, as now, it attracted appreciative buyers. Indeed 'Lafete' (*sic*) was the first specific vineyard name to appear in a Christie auction catalogue, in February 1788.

The château itself, dating from the 17th century, looks like a grand old rambling farmhouse. It has a rather ugly tower, an attractive pepperpot turret and handsome terrace. But the interior affords a complete contrast; small salons, a domestically sized dining room and bedrooms all richly decorated in *fin de siècle* or High Victorian style, with damask walls and upholstery, dotted with Rothschild portraits. A warm, lived-in – when family and friends descend from Paris – period piece.

My own memories of Lafite include a Sunday luncheon at which boiled eggs, nestling in a large flat wickerwork tray, were proffered by a white-gloved servant. Toast 'soldiers' dunked in the soft yoke were accompanied by Lafite of the 1912 vintage! One's fellow guests were always distinguished and multi-lingual. After lunch a fast 20-minute drive in Eric de Rothschild's Volvo, and a long brisk walk along the beach, studiously ignoring topless Swedish holidaymakers; and after an equally delightful supper climbing into a very high, very old-fashioned, very comfortable canopied bed.

To be more down to earth, it does not need a trained or very perceptive eye to appreciate the great swelling curve of vines – convex, sensuous, sloping down towards the road: a dramatic exposure of gravel, perfectly drained. It is this, the ideal vineyard site, and not just Rothschild wealth, that makes Lafite Lafite – that and, of course, suitable weather conditions during the growing season, plus scrupulous winemaking. And the wine? Lafite at its best has a femininity and charm quite unlike

Mouton and Latour, yet still with the ability to keep for an extraordinary length of time. I have had the privilege of tasting wines from the château cellars dating back to the 1799 – faded but still drinkable – and vintages of the pre-phylloxera period that were still deep, rich, superb. More important than the sheer ability to keep is the almost miraculous way in which the wine, with bottle-age, develops nuances and facets which tantalize and dazzle like a kaleidoscope. Lafite is not necessarily an obvious wine: certainly not for those who are impressed solely by deep colour and lots of conspicuous fruit. Lafite needs time and air. It is often misleadingly lighter in colour and style. Thomas Jefferson, following his visit to Bordeaux in May 1787, observed that "Of Red Wines there are four vineyards of first quality, viz. 1. Chateau Margau...., 2. La Tour de Ségur [Latour]....., 3. Hout Brion [Haut-Brion]....., 4. Chateau de la Fite". He adds that "the wines of the first three are not in perfection til four years old. Those [of] de la Fite, being somewhat lighter are good at three years". He mentions the size of each vineyard, average production and prices of various vintages. The point, however, is that even then Lafite was considered a lighter style of wine. And yet, and yet: its almost unique ageing capability and development was of course unknown even to the percipient Jefferson.

Lafite was purchased by Baron James Rothschild, the richest man in France, at auction in 1868 for the astonishing sum of 4.4 million (old) francs. His cousin Nathaniel had bought Mouton (admittedly not a First Growth) 15 years earlier for just over 1.1 million francs. Two years later Mouton missed being classified as a *premier cru* – probably with justification, for nothing much happened at or to Mouton until the early 1920s.

Mouton is quite rightly associated with Baron Philippe de Rothschild, a man of tremendous energy and foresight who, on being put in charge of the somewhat neglected family property in 1922 at the tender age of 20, proceeded vigorously with a series of innovations ranging from mandatory château-bottling to 'designer labels', the first very original and stylish label by the artist Carlu pre-dating the more familiar post-war labels by 20 years. (It is not realized that most claret was shipped *en barrique* to England, the Low Countries and Scandinavia for bottling: even Margaux and Cheval-Blanc were still being bottled in England by respectable wine merchants as recently as the 1952 and 1962 vintages respectively.) But Baron Philippe's avowed ambition, fiercely opposed by his Rothschild cousins, to make Mouton a First Growth, was finally realized in 1973 – though for many years, judged by price alone, it had been on level-pegging with its great rival Lafite.

The château itself is a modest 19th-century house encircled by trees and sheltered, as it were, on three sides by *chais*. The first-year cellar is a spectacular sight with long, regimented parallel rows of casks leading the eye to an illuminated coat of arms on the far end wall.

Unique to Mouton – indeed in Bordeaux – is the superb museum, lovingly and painstakingly created over the years by Baron Philippe and his adored American wife, Pauline, its rare collection devoted to wine themes, the exhibits presented and lit with exquisite taste. Perhaps I should add that entrance to both cellars and museum – particularly the latter – is restricted. Introductions or at least an advance call is essential.

Mouton the wine: the first word this conjures up is dramatic. If Pauillac is the natural home of the Cabernet Sauvignon grape, Mouton represents its apotheosis. The percentage of Cabernet is high and, adding to this the wine's annual cradle of 100 per cent new oak *barriques*, the result is an almost exotically rich spiciness. In a lesser wine one would be tempted to use the word flashy. A total contrast to its neighbour Lafite, Mouton is more open, more obvious, with an immediacy and appeal that is easy to appreciate and hard to resist. Yet quality is there – great quality, as well as sheer brilliance.

Latour, making up the triumvirate of Pauillac's First Growths, and ahead of Mouton in precedence, has, again, a totally contrasting character and style. As we saw earlier, its geographical position is completely different, right on the St-Julien border, its elevation lower, its vines – had they eyes – with a magnificent and close view of the Gironde. The château itself is a neat, attractive, but by no means imposing mid-19th century house, its interior quite clearly in the taste of a fashionable English decorator, the result of British ownership from 1962 until its sale to a wealthy French businessman in 1993; doubtless there will be changes. But the château has never been lived in, merely used by visiting proprietors – a century of de Beaumonts followed by the directors of Pearsons and Harveys of Bristol – and used by them too for entertaining VIPs. The *tour* of Latour is an attractive free-standing tower, circular, three-storied, with a domed roof: more a large dovecot than a fortified watch tower. Along a short pebbly path are the *chais*, the presses, and the stainless steel fermentation tanks – the first to be introduced in the Médoc, they caused considerable consternation at the time. This was in the early 1960s, and for a First-Growth château to turn its back on the use of large traditional oak vats was considered very risky. (It is worth mentioning that wooden vats for fermentation are still in use at Château Margaux.)

Winemaking requires experience and skill. But this is not what makes fine wine. Everyone, in the New World as well as the old, concedes that first and foremost it is the quality of grapes that counts. In Bordeaux, given this basic quality and suitability of Cabernet and other related vine varieties, it is the vineyard site – its soil, subsoil, aspect and drainage – that differentiates the great from the good and the good from the mediocre. To make one simple and incontrovertible point: the same grapes grown on the rich low-lying riverside meadows or *palus* – or, alternatively, on unsuitable soil in the hinterland – transported to and handled by the staff of a *premier cru* winery would not result in good, let alone fine, wine. In short, what makes Latour Latour is the site and the distinctive quality of grapes produced.

How different is the wine of Latour to Lafite and Mouton? Summing up, Latour has a greater solidity and immense staying-power. Deep, often opaque, holding its vivid purple longer than most, it is packed with fruit and all the essential component parts, in particular tannin. Latour in a good vintage is slower to mature, needs longer in bottle. The 1970 and 1961 vintages are still, in the mid-1990s, not fully mature; the 1945 has reached its plateau of maturity and with the 1928, a notoriously hard and tannic vintage, it took literally half a century for Latour to become drinkable. But also, thanks mainly to its well-drained vineyard, Latour is known for its ability to produce remarkable wines in terrible years.

From the First Growths to the two best-known Seconds (both neighbours of Latour), the Pichons. This is not the place to explain how the Pichon Longueville property was divided; suffice it to say that the portion belonging to the Comtesse de Lalande was eventually acquired by the Miailhe family and is now owned and run with great gusto and flair by a daughter, now in her early seventies, Mme. May-Eliane de Lencquesaing (recently, I am delighted to note, awarded the coveted *Légion d'Honneur*). The Pichon Longueville Comtesse de Lalande château, full of the original 19th-century furniture, is opulent in a cosy, lived-in way; and the wine seems to reflect its character and that of its owner. It is full of fruit and flavour, consistently attractive.

For many years the Pichon Lalande estate outshone its once-related baronial rival, whose rather cold, unlived-in, turreted château (in appearance not unlike Palmer) faces it across the road. Now under the ownership of AXA, France's biggest insurance company, and on their behalf overlorded by Jean-Michel Cazes of

Lynch-Bages, it has taken on new life. A vastly impressive new winery has been built, the monumental blank walls of which can hardly be missed as one drives past. Undoubtedly the wine has improved enormously and in recent vintages has equalled, and on occasion has even overtaken, Lalande. They say that competition is healthy, and May-Eliane de Lencquesaing can more than hold her own! However it is perhaps unfortunate that AXA's Pichon-Longueville has dropped its additional title Baron – helpful for identification, but, unintentionally I am sure, seeming somewhat presumptuous, giving the impression that Pichon Lalande is the former Baron's second wine or subsidiary. I can understand, and indeed supported, Mme. de Lencquesaing's objections; but wine, like water, finds its own level. Mention of Michel Cazes brings me to one of the best-known and most popular of Pauillac's 12 Fifth Growths, Château Lynch-Bages. Once referred to as the poor man's Mouton, mainly on account of the brilliance of its Cabernet Sauvignon character and flavour, it was for generations a great favourite amongst the traditional middle-class British claret lovers and one of the mainstays of the old 'carriage trade' wine merchants: Lafite for the aristocrats, Lynch-Bages for the comfortably off. The château – very much a family home – and its vineyards are well away from the St-Julien border, on the plateau above the hamlet of Bages. Its new, large, custom-built *chai* is on the main road from Pauillac that curls gently round towards St-Laurent and then (as the N 215) speeds, straight but dangerous, towards Bordeaux. Set back on the opposite side of this initially west-bound road is Grand-Puy-Lacoste, the most underrated of the Fifth Growths despite, for as long as one can recall, making the most uncompromisingly correct 'copybook' Pauillac; a wine which perhaps makes too few concessions to be really popular but, in my opinion, is the epitome of a claret-lover's claret. The château itself is handsome, the back half very domesticated, occupied by Xavier, one of Jean-Eugène Borie's sons, his wife and three children.

Not far away, a little further down the road towards St-Laurent, is another Borie-owned vineyard property, Haut-Batailley – and behind this, almost back-tracking to St-Julien, is its twin, Batailley. The wine of Haut-Batailley has an understated charm and elegance; Batailley is softer, fuller, and consistently rounded and fruity but less refined. As one might gather from their names, it used to be one vineyard. The château itself belongs to Batailley and is a fairly large, solidly prosperous-looking house, its style reflecting the dependable and conventional wine produced.

Of the several other – all more or less attractive and characterful – Pauillacs, mention must be made of Mouton's next-door *cinquième cru* vineyard, originally called d'Armailhacq. After its purchase in 1934 its name changed to Mouton Baron Philippe; later, to honour his wife, Baronne Philippe. Following the death of his beloved Pauline, Baron Philippe wanted to change the name yet again: to Mouton Baronne Pauline, but was eventually persuaded against this, mainly on the grounds of confusion! The present proprietor, Philippe's daughter, the Baroness Philippine de Rothschild, has changed the name again, back to the original, but with a slightly simplified spelling: Château d'Armailhac. Whatever its name, the wine has always had charm and a lightness of style, very much to the taste of Baron Philippe who preferred it as a drink to his somewhat more hefty and distinctly more opulent Mouton-Rothschild.

Another large and important property, a close neighbour of Mouton and occupying the highest *croupe* in the region, some thirty metres above the level of the Gironde, is Pontet-Canet – for generations one of the best-known and most popular of all the Médocs

traditionally shipped to England. Owned by the once-powerful Cruse family, the merchant princes of Bordeaux, the wine was never bottled at the château but always in their labyrinthine cellars on the Quai des Chartrons. Frankly, the wine under-performed for a fairly long period, but the château, owned for some time by the Tesseron family (Guy Tesseron being Emmanuel Cruse's son-in-law), is now once more producing wine that reflects the excellence of the vineyard site.

Space prevents me from mentioning every one of the châteaux listed by Hubrecht Duijker in the Pauillac gazetteer , but all are worth exploring.

If Bordeaux is the mecca of all who appreciate fine wine, the holiest 'city' must be Pauillac with its three First Growth shrines; the pilgrim stopping en route at Château Margaux having, of course, first genuflected at the venerable Haut-Brion. But of the latter, more anon.

VINTAGES

If Lafite dominates the surviving old vintages, in particular the high-water-marks of the 19th century, it is because of the sheer quality of the wine and because of fashion. Judging by the catalogues in Christie's archives – a unique collection from 1766 to the present day – the

The patient process of fining wine with egg white in a Pauillac *chai*

most favoured claret was Lafite; Latour and Mouton scarcely appear. So the great vintages are almost solely represented by Lafite. The roll-call is as follows: 1811, reputed to be the best of the century (but alas, not tasted), 1825, 1844, 1846 and 1848 – the last two both astonishing, still deep, rich, lovely to drink – 1858 now fading, 1864 equalling 1811 in reputation and, at its best, still magnificent, the 1865 and 1870 both remarkably dependable still, full-bodied, perfectly balanced; the exquisite 1875, considered too light for the English market but which lasted extraordinarily well, and finally the 1899, the first of the 'heavenly twins': more delicate and feminine than the opulent 1900.

The 1920, 1924 and 1926 Lafites were, and still can be, marvellous; but the other famous twin vintages, 1928 and 1929, are well below standard. In common with almost all the other top Bordeaux, 1945 was magnificent and is still, at its best, lovely; 1947 and 1949 excellent, though now variable; 1953 exquisite (my favourite Lafite) and 1959 magnificent – better than the much-vaunted 1961 vintage. Some very disappointing wines were made in the 1970s, but there has been a renaissance in the 1980s: the 1985 and 1989 being particularly good.

Mouton, as discussed, was far less frequently seen in the 19th century, though I have tasted a good 1858 and 1869, and a magnificent 1870. But Mouton really flowered under Baron Philippe: his 1924, and his 1929 in particular, were superb. Thirty years ago the first great star of the saleroom was a jeroboam of Mouton 1929. This vintage can still give much pleasure. But undoubtedly the greatest of all Moutons is the incomparable 1945, unmatched in beauty and depth of colour, opulence of bouquet, glorious mouthfilling flavour – and price. The 1947 is very good, the 1949 exquisite: Baron Philippe's favourite; one of the best 1952s, 1953 excellent, 1959 magnificent, as is the 1961. More consistent than Lafite in the 1960s and 1970s and, in keeping with the others, making wonderful wine in the 1980s: the 1986 being the best wine of that vintage.

Latour, though taking a long time fully to mature and capable of remarkable longevity, was never as highly regarded as Lafite, and old vintages are rare. Of the pre-phylloxera vintages tasted 1865 stands out, as does the 1870 and 1875. 1899 was excellent, 1900 should be; but its best period was in the 1920s: the 1920, 1924, 1926, 1928 – a monumental wine – and the 1929 all first rate. 1934 was good, 1945 magnificent: one of the best ever and perfect now; 1947 and 1949 good, 1952 and 1955 very good – better even than the 1953. 1959 Latour is massive, as is the 1961, 1966, 1970 (better than Lafite or Mouton) and with greater consistency in the 1970s. Recent years up to standard – but few are ready.

Of the other classed growths, Pontet-Canet made one of the finest of all 1929s, Lynch-Bages was attractive and successful in the 1950s and 1960s (and, it should be added, since then), Grand-Puy-Lacoste predictably excellent in 1945, 1949 and 1953; the 1959 and 1961 slow to evolve, still with potential – as is the archetypal 1966. Pichon-Lalande has given immense pleasure, particularly the 1966, and even recent vintages are gloriously drinkable because of their soft fruitiness.

To summarize, on reflection (and from my notes) it is a matter of horses for courses: the First Growths for long keeping and greatest potential, the Second, Fourth and Fifth for a 10- to 20-year span depending on vintage.

Great Pauillac vintages: *1811, 1825, 1844, 1846, 1848, 1858, 1864, 1865, 1870, 1875, 1893, 1899, 1900, 1920, 1924, 1926, 1928, 1929, 1945, 1947, 1949, 1953, 1959, 1961, 1982, 1985, 1989, 1990.*

Good Pauillac vintages: *1832, 1869, 1874, 1878, 1898, 1904, 1906, 1918, 1919, 1921, 1934, 1943, 1952, 1955, 1962, 1970, 1975, 1976, 1978, 1981, 1983, 1986, 1988.*

PERSONAL FAVOURITES

In alphabetical order Batailley, Grand-Puy-Lacoste, Haut-Batailley, Lafite, Latour, Lynch-Bages, Mouton Rothschild and the two Pichons.

THE APPELLATION

PAUILLAC (red)

Location: *On the left bank of the Gironde. The town of Pauillac is 42 km to the north-north-west of the centre of Bordeaux. Immediately to the south is St-Julien; to the north, across the Jalle du Breuil, is St-Estèphe.*
Area of AC: *1,452 ha*
Area under vine: *1,200 ha*
Communes: *Pauillac. Precisely defined parcels of: Cissac, St-Julien, St-Estèphe, St-Sauveur. The commune is just under 7 km between the borders of St-Julien and St-Estèphe and 3.5 km from the riverside to the western boundary.*
Average annual production: *630,000 cases*
Classed growths: *18 (3 premiers crus, 2 deuxièmes crus, no troisième, 1 quatrième and 12 cinquièmes crus)*
Others: *16 crus bourgeois, 7 others*
Cooperatives: *1 (c. 80 members)*
Main grape varieties: *Cabernet Sauvignon, Merlot*
Others: *Cabernet Franc, Petit Verdot*
Main soil types: *Deep gravel*

APPELLATION PAUILLAC

Ch d'Armailhac
map 12/L G7

5ème cru
owner: Philippine de Rothschild **area:** 49 ha **cases:**
22,000 **grape % R:** cs 49% mer 26% cf 23% pv 2%
other châteaux owned: include Ch Clerc Milon
(Pauillac); Ch Mouton Rothschild *(Pauillac)*
33250 Pauillac tel: 05 56 59 22 22
fax: 05 56 73 20 44

This *cinquième cru classé* was bought in 1934
by Baron Philippe de Rothschild, who had taken
on the management of neighbouring Ch
Mouton Rothschild a decade earlier. Thus these
two properties were in the same ownership
once more, as they had been under the
Armailhacq family, who ran what was then a
single estate from the end of the 17th century
until the French Revolution. Under the
Rothschild regime – which still continues –
there have been several changes of name. In
1956 Ch Mouton d'Armailhacq became Ch
Mouton Baron Philippe; then Ch Mouton
Baronne Philippe in 1975, in honour of
Baroness Pauline, his late wife. Then in 1989,
on the initiative of the Baroness Philippine de
Rothschild, who had succeeded on her father's
death, it became Ch d'Armailhac once more
(but without the 'q'). From this château – a
large but half-completed country mansion of
around 1825 – a charming, not to say seductive
wine emerges, often with juicy ripe fruit
(including blackcurrants, black cherry), dark
tones such as chocolate, supple but also firm
tannins, an average structure, and smoky, spicy
oak. About a third of the *barriques* in which the
wine spends 15-18 months are new.

Ch Batailley
map 12/R H7

5ème cru
owner: Emile Castéja **area:** 55 ha **cases:** 22,000
grape % R: cs 70% mer 25% cf 3% pv 2% **second
wine:** Plaisance St. Lambert **other châteaux
owned:** Ch Haut-Bages Monpelou *(Pauillac)*; Ch
Lynch-Moussas *(Pauillac)*; Ch Beau-Site *(St-
Estèphe)*; Ch du Domaine de l'Eglise *(Pomerol)*; Ch
Bergat *(St-Emilion)*; Ch Trotte Vieille *(St-Emilion)*
33250 Pauillac tel: 05 56 00 00 70
fax: 05 56 52 29 54

A château on the road to St-Laurent that is said
to derive its name from a *bataille* fought here
between the French and English six centuries
ago. Behind the building, its park boasts a great
collection of trees – some from such distant
lands as India, China, Mexico and the United
States: the designer who landscaped this park
also worked for Napoleon III. Batailley's wine is
characteristically a well-structured Pauillac
supported by tannins and much new oak (from
50% of the casks). Quite meaty as a rule, its
concentration is not overdone: Batailley's wine
offers both flavours of spices and berry fruit. Its
classification as a *cinquième cru* is fully
justified.

Ch La Bécasse
map 12/R E3

owner: Georges & Roland Fonteneau **area:** 4.2 ha
cases: 2,200 **grape % R:** cs 55% mer 36% cf 9%
33250 Pauillac tel: 05 56 59 07 14
fax: 05 56 59 18 44

For an unclassified Pauillac this is generally a
very successful wine: solid colour, a dark, fruity
aroma (licorice, bayleaf, leather, pencil
shavings), and a lively, firm taste in which these
same elements occur. No lack of oak, either,
since 30-40% of the barrels for the 18-month

Above: Ch Bellegrave Van der Voort

maturing period are new. This estate, founded
in 1966, was established by the *régisseur* from
Ch Ducru-Beaucaillou in St-Julien.

Ch Bellegrave Van der Voort
map 12/R D5

owner: Famille Van der Voort **area:** 2.3 ha **cases:**
1,500 **grape % R:** cs 80% mer 15% mal 3% pv 2%
33250 Pauillac tel: 05 56 59 21 97

An estate closed off from the outside world by a
high fence, and which receives no visitors. The
château is a building with two wings and a
pointed tower to one side. Built in about 1850,
since 1901 it has belonged to the Van der
Voorts, a family of Dutch origin. In the top
years a classic wine for keeping is made here,
sturdy and without great complexity. Wine from
the lesser vintages is ready for drinking sooner.

Ch Belle Rose
map 12/L E6

owner: Famille Jugla **area:** 7.4 ha **cases:** 4,000
grape % R: cs 75% mer 20% cf 5% **other châteaux
owned:** Ch Pédesclaux *(Pauillac)*; Ch Grand-Duroc-
Milon *(Pauillac)*
33250 Pauillac tel: 05 56 59 22 59
fax: 05 56 59 22 59

Estate linked to Ch Pédesclaux, but its wine is
vinified separately. This select Pauillac is quite
meaty in good years, with firm tannins and a
reasonable amount of fruit. A third of the casks
for ageing are replaced each year. The Jugla
family, which owns two other Pauillac châteaux,
has been running Belle Rose since 1960.

Ch Bernadotte
map 20

cru bourgeois
owner: Curt Eklund **area:** 8 ha **cases:** 4,000 **grape
% R:** cs 63% mer 35% cf 1% pv 1% **other châteaux
owned:** Ch Fournas Bernadotte *(Haut-Médoc)*; Ch
Proche-Pontet *(Haut-Médoc)*
33250 Pauillac tel: 05 56 59 57 04
fax: 05 56 59 54 84

Wine matured exclusively in new *barriques* for
at least a year, yet not dominated by oak; its
tannin is seldom tough either, but is nicely
integrated. This Pauillac combines
concentration with elegance, often has ripe
fruit and is duly expansive in the mouth. The
owner plans to extend the vineyard by 10 ha.

Ch Clerc Milon
map 12/L G5

5ème cru
owner: Philippine de Rothschild **area:** 32 ha **cases:**
16,000 **grape % R:** cs 50% mer 34% cf 13% pv 3%
other châteaux owned: include Ch d'Armailhac
(Pauillac); Ch Mouton Rothschild *(Pauillac)*
33250 Pauillac tel: 05 56 59 22 22
fax: 05 56 73 20 44

A château that is no more than a simple house
in the hamlet of Mousset. Baroness Philippine
de Rothschild's staff refer to it as *'notre château
bourguignon'* – since its size is so modest. The
cuvier is modern, however, and a third of the
maturing casks are new each year. The wine
used to be more muscular than refined, but
since the 1980s its character has undergone a
change. The Merlot – about a third of the vines
– has become more manifest, the fruit richer
and riper, the tannin smoother. In this Pauillac,
reserve has given way to sensuality – and it has
also gained in complexity. When Baron Philippe
de Rothschild bought the property in 1970 it
was called Ch Clerc Milon-Mondon; in the 19th
century simply Ch Clerc.

Below: Ch Clerc Milon

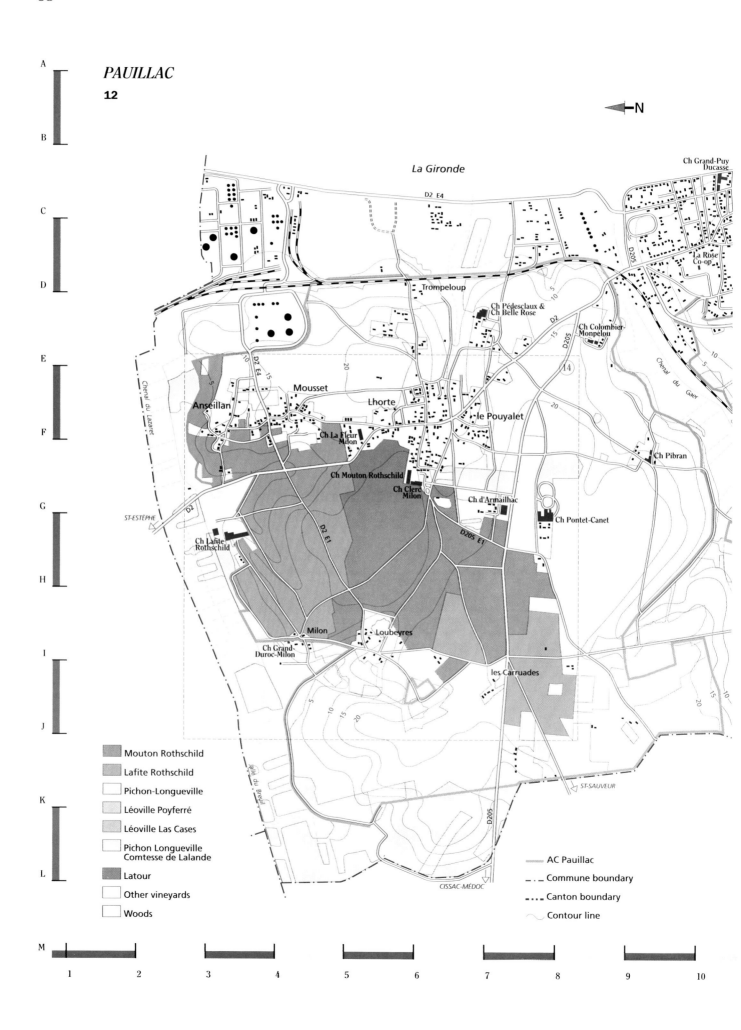

PAUILLAC

12

N

La Gironde

D2 E4

Ch Grand-Puy
Ducasse

La Rose
Co-op

Trompeloup

Ch Pédesclaux &
Ch Belle Rose

Ch Colombier-
Monpelou

Mousset

Anseillan

Lhorte

le Pouyalet

Ch La Fleur
Milon

Ch Pibran

Ch Mouton Rothschild

Ch Clerc
Milon

Ch d'Armailhac

ST-ESTÈPHE

Ch Pontet-Canet

Ch Lafite
Rothschild

Milon

Loubeyres

Ch Grand-
Duroc-Milon

les Carruades

ST-SAUVEUR

CISSAC-MÉDOC

Mouton Rothschild

Lafite Rothschild

Pichon-Longueville

Léoville Poyferré

Léoville Las Cases

Pichon Longueville
Comtesse de Lalande

Latour

Other vineyards

Woods

AC Pauillac

Commune boundary

Canton boundary

Contour line

| 1 | 2 | 3 | 4 | 5 | 6 | 7 | 8 | 9 | 10 |

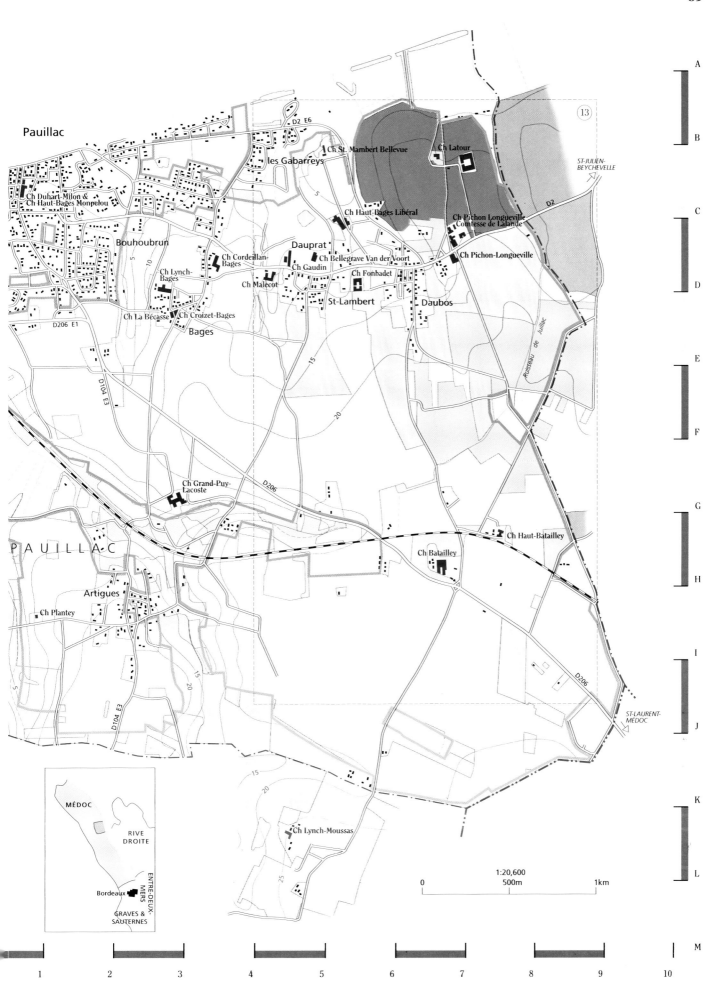

Pauillac

les Gabarreys

Ch Duhart-Milon &
Ch Haut-Bages Monpelou

Bouhoubrun

Ch Cordeillan-
Bages

Ch Lynch-
Bages

Ch Malecot

Ch La Bécasse   Ch Croizet-Bages

Bages

Ch St. Mambert Bellevue

Ch Latour

Ch Haut-Bages Libéral

Ch Pichon Longueville
Comtesse de Lalande

Dauprat

Ch Bellegrave Van der Voort

Ch Gaudin

Ch Pichon-Longueville

Ch Fonbadet

St-Lambert

Daubos

D2 E6

D2

ST-JULIEN-
BEYCHEVELLE

Ruisseau de Juillac

D206 E1

D104 E3

D206

Ch Grand-Puy-
Lacoste

PAUILLAC

Ch Haut-Batailley

Ch Batailley

Artigues

Ch Plantey

D104 E3

D206

ST-LAURENT-
MÉDOC

MÉDOC

RIVE
DROITE

ENTRE-DEUX-
MERS

Bordeaux

GRAVES &
SAUTERNES

Ch Lynch-Moussas

1:20,600

0   500m   1km

A

B

C

D

E

F

G

H

I

J

K

L

M

1   2   3   4   5   6   7   8   9   10

Ch Colombier-Monpelou   map 12/L E8
cru bourgeois
owner: Bernard Jugla **area:** 25 ha **cases:** 10,000
grape % R: cs 65% mer 25% cf 10% **second wine:**
Ch Grand Canyon
33250 Pauillac tel: 05 56 59 01 48
fax: 05 56 59 12 01
This château, owned by the Jugla family since
1970, has a reception area adorned with
barriques and diplomas. Here a Pauillac can be
tasted that at its best is quite complete, with a
meaty, decently fruity taste; but a wine without
any great depth, or refinement of nuance. This
respectable *cru bourgeois* matures for some 15
months in oak, of which 30% are new barrels.
The second wine here, Ch Grand Canyon,
comes from an organically cultivated plot.

Ch Cordeillan-Bages   map 12/R D4
owner: Jean-Michel Cazes **area:** 2 ha **cases:** 1,000
grape % R: cs 60% mer 30% mal 5% pv 5% **other
châteaux owned:** Ch Lynch-Bages *(Pauillac)*; Villa
Bel Air *(Graves)*; Ch Les Ormes de Pez *(St-Estèphe)*
33250 Pauillac tel: 05 56 59 24 24
fax: 05 56 59 01 89
Wine made by the Ch Lynch-Bages team. It has
an often opaque depth of colour, glorious and
juicy fruit aromas, good firm tannins, chocolate
and other dark notes, and is attractively set off
by its oak. This estate is linked to a luxurious
hotel-restaurant of the same name.

Ch Croizet-Bages   map 12/R E3
5ème cru
owner: Jean-Michel Quié **area:** 25 ha **cases:**
11,000 **grape % R:** mer 40% cs 40% cf 20% **other
châteaux owned:** Ch Bel Orme Tronquoy de Lalande
(Haut-Médoc); Ch Rauzan-Gassies *(Margaux)*
33250 Pauillac tel: 05 56 59 01 62
fax: 05 56 59 23 39
Until 1994 the track record of this *cinquième
cru classé* was exceptionally dismal. For decades
this estate in Bages produced meagre wines
lacking any class. However, a new technical
director for this and the other Quié properties
has begun to chart a fresh course, with the
result that since 1994 the wine has displayed a
little more fruit, more charm. Subsequent steps
should be aimed at more body, more
concentration – and more new oak than the
present 20%. Worth watching.

Below: Ch Cordeillan-Bages

Ch Duhart-Milon   map 12/R C1
4ème cru
owner: Domaines Barons de Rothschild **area:** 65 ha
cases: 28,000 **grape % R:** cs 65% mer 30% cf 5%
second wine: Moulin de Duhart **other châteaux
owned:** include Ch Lafite Rothschild *(Pauillac)*; Ch
l'Evangile *(Pomerol)*; Ch Rieussec *(Sauternes)*
33250 Pauillac tel: 05 56 73 18 18
fax: 05 56 59 26 83
This wine is at its best and most attractive when
the Merlot grapes have fully ripened, for
otherwise the tannins, the acidity and the
herbaceous tones get the better of its more
agreeable aspects. The vineyard borders on Ch
Lafite Rothschild and has the same owners;
something of the latter wine's refined elegance
is nearly always present in Duhart-Milon,
together with spicy notes of oak, vanilla and
tobacco. The cellars stand near the quay at
Pauillac. Of the *barriques* used here, 33-40%
are new each vintage.

Ch La Fleur Milon   map 12/L F5
cru bourgeois
owner: Héritiers Gimenez **area:** 13 ha **cases:** 7,200
grape % R: cs 65% mer 25% cf 5% pv 5% **second
wine:** Chantecler Milon
33250 Pauillac tel: 05 56 59 29 01
fax: 05 56 59 23 22
After spending an average 20 months in casks of
which a third are new, the Pauillac made here is
of the rich-in-tannin type. But soft, jammy fruit
and animal aromas are also present as a rule,
and the total impression is therefore not too
rustic. The estate is run by the family of André
Gimenez, who bought La Fleur Milon in 1958
when the vineyard covered just 3 ha. This
enterprising winegrower built the *chai* single-
handed.

Ch Fonbadet   map 12/R D6
cru bourgeois
owner: SCEA Domaines Peyronie **area:** 16 ha
cases: 6,600 **grape % R:** cs 60% mer 20% cf 15%
pv & mal 5% **other châteaux owned:** Ch Tour du Roc
Milon *(Pauillac)*; Ch Montgrand-Milon *(Pauillac)*; Ch
Padarnac *(Pauillac)*; Ch Haut-Pauillac *(Pauillac)*
33250 Pauillac tel: 05 56 59 02 11
fax: 05 56 59 22 61
Just as the low, white Fonbadet château is
hidden from view by trees, so the personality of

Above: Ch Grand-Puy-Lacoste

Below: Ch La Fleur Milon

its wine may remain long concealed by a wall of
tannin. For this is a deep-coloured, substantial,
classic wine, harsh at first and usually calling
for years of patience. This Pauillac, full of
character, is certainly not an endearingly
friendly or easily accessible wine, but behind its
tannins there are eventually fruity aspects to
discover (blackcurrant, blackberry, prune and
fig), as well as woodland aromas and elements
of tobacco and oak – 25% of the casks are new.
Vines over 50 years old contribute to the
quality. A number of other Pauillacs are vinified
at this château, all showing kinship to the
Fonbadet wine. They are Ch Haut-Pauillac
(from 2.5 ha), Ch Montgrand (3 ha), Ch
Padarnac (2 ha), Ch Pauillac (1.75 ha) and Ch
Tour du Roc Milon (3 ha).

◆
About Pauillac
The Maison du Vin et de Tourisme, 33250
Pauillac, is in a modern, circular building
at the southern end of the town's
waterfront. Tel: 05 56 73 19 02.

Finding a château
To locate a château from its name use the
index/gazetteer, which will provide a page
and a map reference. When the name and
appellation are known, consult the
Directory pages of the relevant chapter.
When the commune is known, but not the
appellation, consult the index by
commune.

Above: Ch Lafite Rothschild

Ch Grand-Duroc-Milon   map 12/L I4

owner: Famille Jugla *area:* 8 ha *cases:* 4,000 *grape % R:* CS 60% MER 28% CF 12% *other châteaux owned:* Ch Pédesclaux *(Pauillac)*; Ch Belle Rose *(Pauillac)*
33250 Pauillac tel: 05 56 59 22 59
Pauillac of at best a reasonable quality. Its most engaging feature is an aroma clearly characterized by blackcurrant.

Ch Grand-Puy Ducasse   map 12/L C10

5ème cru
owner: SC de Grand-Puy Ducasse/Mestrezat *area:* 39.8 ha *cases:* 14,700 *grape % R:* CS 61% MER 39% *second wine:* Ch Artigues Arnaud *other châteaux owned:* Ch de Rayne Vigneau *(Sauternes)*; Ch Tourteau Chollet *(Graves)*; Ch Blaignan *(Médoc)*; Ch Marsac Séguineau *(Margaux)*; Ch Lamothe Bergeron *(Haut-Médoc)*
33250 Pauillac tel: 05 56 01 30 10
fax: 05 56 79 23 57
Since acquiring this property in 1971 the firm of Mestrezat has invested a great deal in it, step by step. The vineyard has been quadrupled in size, there is a new *cuvier*, an air-conditioned *chai* has been built, the proportion of new casks has risen to 30%, and the white, 19th-century château on the quay at Pauillac received a facelift. Then in 1992 mechanical picking was abandoned to facilitate selection of the best grapes; as a result up to 60% of the fruit may be rejected for the *grand vin* and used instead for the second wine. Today this Pauillac combines much candied fruit with cedarwood, bitter chocolate and spices, and is further characterized by firm but not tough tannins, a supple roundness and average structure. Grand-Puy Ducasse generally benefits from 5-10 years' bottle-age.

Ch Grand-Puy-Lacoste   map 12/R G3

5ème cru
owner: Famille Borie *area:* 50 ha *cases:* 18,000 *grape % R:* CS 75% MER 25% *second wine:* Lacoste-Borie *other châteaux owned:* Ch Ducluzeau *(Listrac-Médoc)*; Ch Haut-Batailley *(Pauillac)*; Ch Lalande-Borie *(St-Julien)*; Ch Ducru-Beaucaillou *(St-Julien)*
33250 Pauillac tel: 05 56 59 06 66
fax: 05 56 59 27 37

Very old – probably early 16th-century – wine estate with a château built partly in 1737, partly in 1850. This stands beside its vineyard, which extends over a splendid gravel bank south-west of Pauillac. The epicurean Raymond Dupin ran Grand-Puy-Lacoste from 1932 to 1987, and endowed the wine with a fine reputation. The Borie family, of Ch Ducru-Beaucaillou in St-Julien and other estates, have subsequently built on this, with the result that this Pauillac has in the interim risen above its *cinquième cru classé* status. Its facets usually include a rich, polished, duly concentrated taste with noble tannins, splendid fruit – particularly blackcurrant, and often cherry and plum as well – restrained oak and vanilla notes, plus discreet earthy, spicy elements.

Ch Haut-Bages Libéral   map 12/R D6

5ème cru
owner: Claire Villars/Famille Merlaut *area:* 29 ha *cases:* 14,000 *grape % R:* CS 80% MER 17% PV 3% *second wine:* La Chapelle de Bages *other châteaux owned:* Ch Chasse-Spleen *(Moulis-en-Médoc)*; Ch La Gurgue *(Margaux)*; Ch Ferrière *(Margaux)*; Ch Citran *(Haut-Médoc)*
33250 Pauillac tel: 05 56 58 02 37
fax: 05 56 58 05 70
Named after the Libéral family of wine brokers, this estate was acquired by the Cruse family in 1960. The property was then in a neglected condition. The Cruses invested much money and energy in a complete renovation, and also built a modern *cuvier*. New owners came forward in 1983: the Bernard Taillan group and the Paribas bank. They delegated the management first to Bernadette Villars, and after her death to her daughter Claire. Wine from Ch Haut-Bages Libéral generally has no problem in maintaining its position among the *cinquièmes crus*. It is a fairly elegant, but seldom really full-bodied or super-concentrated Pauillac, with a tannin content that is at least average, and a lively, juicy taste in which black berry fruit and spicy, vanilla oak (a third of the casks are new for each vintage) are the most important elements. The somewhat unremarkable, rectangular château was built around the year 1850.

Below: Ch Haut-Bages Libéral

◆
Crus Bourgeois

Only one area – the Médoc – has a recognized list of *crus bourgeois*. The ranking procedure is described on page 34 and the full list is given in the appendix at the end of the book. The *crus bourgeois* are in appellations Médoc, Haut-Médoc and the 'village' ACs such as Pauillac. The term *cru bourgeois* is in use in other areas of Bordeaux, but unofficially, and thus not on labels.

◆
Finding a second wine

To locate a second wine or any other wine not listed in the appellation's Directory pages, consult the index, where all château names are listed. Not all second wines use the appellation of the château's *grand vin*.

Above: the tower and *chai* at Ch Latour

Ch Haut-Bages Monpelou   map 12/R C1
cru bourgeois
owner: Héritiers Castéja-Borie **area:** 15 ha **cases:** 8,200 **grape % R:** CS 34% CF 33% MER 33% **other châteaux owned:** Ch du Domaine de l'Eglise *(Pomerol)*; Ch Bergat *(St-Emilion)*; Ch Trotte Vieille *(St-Emilion)*; Ch Beau-Site *(St-Estèphe)*; Ch Lynch-Moussac *(Pauillac)*; Ch Batailley *(Pauillac)*
33250 Pauillac tel: 05 56 00 00 70
fax: 05 56 52 29 54
Estate split from Ch Duhart-Milon in 1948. Its wine is seldom spectacular, but can provide pleasure with its succulent, ripe blackcurrant and reasonable oak from one-third new *barriques*. It could almost be a lighter version of Ch Batailley, which has the same owners.

Ch Haut-Batailley   map 12/R H8
5ème cru
owner: Madame des Brest-Borie, Famille Borie **area:** 22 ha **cases:** 10,000 **grape % R:** CS 65% MER 25% CF 10% **second wine:** Ch La Tour d'Aspic **other châteaux owned:** Ch Ducluzeau *(Listrac-Médoc)*; Ch Grand-Puy-Lacoste *(Pauillac)*; Ch Lalande-Borie *(St-Julien)*; Ch Ducru-Beaucaillon *(St-Julien)*
33250 Pauillac tel: 05 56 59 05 20
fax: 05 56 59 27 37
In 1949 the poet Biarnez wrote 'we must make great wines, not great buildings.' This certainly fits Haut-Batailley, for this *cinquième cru classé* has just a vineyard and winery, and no château. In among the vines, however, there is a solitary, slender tower, the Tour d'Aspic, with its image of Our Lady of Lourdes. The estate, separated from Ch Batailley in 1942, is run by the Borie family of St-Julien (and Ducru-Beaucaillou and other properties). It can hardly be coincidental that Haut-Batailley is a Pauillac with the same structure, and likeableness, as a St-Julien – albeit more tightly wrapped in tannin.

Ch Lafite Rothschild   map 12/L H3
1er cru
owner: Domaines Barons de Rothschild **area:** 94 ha **cases:** 20,000 **grape % R:** CS 70% MER 20% CF 10% **second wine:** Carruades de Château Lafite **other châteaux owned:** include Ch Rieussec *(Sauternes)*; Ch l'Evangile *(Pomerol)*; Ch Duhart-Milon *(Pauillac)*
33250 Pauillac tel: 05 56 73 18 18
fax: 05 56 59 26 83

Anyone seeing this château from the road will be able to discern little difference between the present building and what is depicted in the old print used on the discreetly-styled label. It still looks exactly as it did long ago, with its two wings at an angle, its pepperpot turret in the corner, the two towers to the sides, and the raised park with its low surrounding wall. Even the *salons* breathe the atmosphere of the past. Yet a great deal has changed at Lafite in recent decades – although mainly in the cellars. The fermenting vats of Bosnian oak have been replaced by stainless steel, and an extraordinary circular *chai* was completed in 1989. The wine is moved to this temple-like edifice for its second period in cask, after spending 12 months in the first-year cellar. The total time in cask is 18-24 months, and only new *barriques* are used. There have also been changes in management. In 1975 Eric de Rothschild took over from Elie, his uncle. The wine from that year showed that a relatively weak period for Lafite Rothschild of about a decade was now over. Since then this *premier cru classé* has shone again in all its glory. The wine has a grace more likely to be associated with Margaux

Below: Ch Lynch-Bages

than with Pauillac, and a style that is pure aristocrat. Nature and man have combined brilliantly to create, in wine terms, the delicate, rich complexity of a Mozart piano concerto. A wine with perfect harmony in its clean, ripe berry fruit, its cedarwood, pencil shavings, mellow spices and beautifully integrated fine tannins. Time adds the finishing touches of a silky structure and a never-ending finish.

Ch Latour   map 12/R C8
1er cru
owner: François Pinault **area:** 65 ha **cases:** 34,000 **grape % R:** CS 80% MER 15% CF 4% PV 1% **second wine:** Les Forts de Latour **other wine:** Pauillac
33250 Pauillac tel: 05 56 73 19 80
fax: 05 56 73 19 81
From the extraordinary archives that survive at this renowned château it appears that the estate derives its name ('the Tower') from a 14th-century fortification, the Tour de St Maubert. This was captured by the English in 1378. After the latter had left Aquitaine in 1453, following the decisive battle at Castillon, the French totally destroyed the fort. The tower that now stands near the château dates from 1625 and was originally a *pigeonnier*; it was probably built with stones from the demolished stronghold. After many generations of French owners, Latour once again passed into English hands – this time peacefully – in 1962. After this there came a comprehensive investment programme. Stainless-steel fermentation tanks arrived, with a drainage system for the vineyard, and comfortable bungalows for the staff. Today Ch Latour has become French once more: the Allied Lyons group sold the estate in July 1993 to François Pinault. About three-quarters of this vineyard just south of Pauillac occupies an

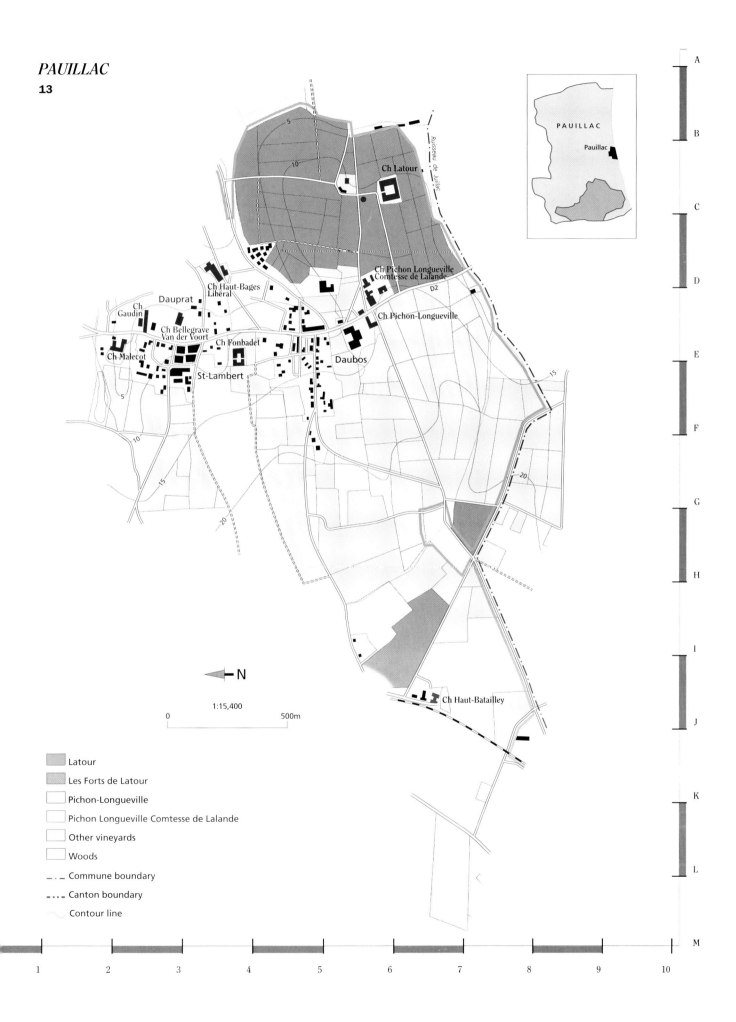

PAUILLAC

13

PAUILLAC

Pauillac

Ch Latour

Ruisseau de Juillac

Ch Pichon Longueville
Comtesse de Lalande

D2

Ch Haut-Bages
Libéral

Dauprat

Ch
Gaudin

Ch Bellegrave
Van der Voort

Ch Fonbadet

Ch Pichon-Longueville

Ch Malecot

Daubos

St-Lambert

N

1:15,400

0   500m

Ch Haut-Batailley

Latour

Les Forts de Latour

Pichon-Longueville

Pichon Longueville Comtesse de Lalande

Other vineyards

Woods

_ . _ Commune boundary

_ _ _ Canton boundary

Contour line

A B C D E F G H I J K L M

1 2 3 4 5 6 7 8 9 10

Above: Ch Lynch-Moussas

impressively high (for this imperceptibly undulating area) gravel bank around the château. The Cabernet Sauvignon, with 80% of the vines, is the dominant grape. Latour wine can only be described in superlatives. It is a majestic creation combining substantial ripe tannins with a concentrated, muscular and at the same time brilliantly variegated taste. Frequent nuances are of ripe blackcurrants (often abundantly present, sometimes together with black cherry), roasted nuts, leather, licorice and bayleaf – and the best imaginable oak, with creamy vanilla. The colour is nearly always very dark, and the finish lasts for minutes on end. In lesser years, too, the wine generally offers very high quality – and then it is often unequalled by any other Bordeaux. Of its kind the second wine, Les Forts de Latour, is also among the best from the region. In short, Latour is a bastion of towering quality.

Ch Lynch-Bages   map 12/R D3
5ème cru
owner: Jean-Michel Cazes **area:** 90 ha **cases:** 46,000, white: 2,000 **grape % R:** CS 75% CF 10% MER 15% **grape % W:** SAUV B 40% SEM 40% MUSC 20% **second wine:** Ch Haut-Bages Averous **other wines:** Blanc de Lynch-Bages (Bordeaux Blanc) **other châteaux owned:** Villa Bel Air (Graves); Ch Cordeillan-Bages (Pauillac); Ch les Ormes de Pez (St-Estèphe)
33250 Pauillac tel: 05 56 73 24 00
fax: 05 56 59 26 42
The white, foursquare château of Lynch-Bages with its spacious winery buildings stands on the Bages plateau, just south of Pauillac and north of the hamlet of St-Lambert. The property acquired its name in 1750 when Thomas Lynch married the daughter of the owner of the Domaine de Bages. The Lynch family, of Irish descent, were to own the estate for 75 years. Their name is linked to several other Bordeaux estates. Since 1934 Lynch-Bages has belonged to the Cazes family, who make impressively good wines, particularly with Jean-Michel Cazes in charge. Lynch-Bages has *cinquième cru classé* status, but its wines can usually match Third and sometimes even Second Growths

with no problem at all – including in price. They are characterized by their richness – rich in colour, in extract, in concentration, in taste, and in beautifully integrated tannins. Oak (from 15 months in *barriques*, of which half are new each year) is always gratifyingly present, as well as layers of soft black fruit, and a touch of mint. After 5-10 years in bottle this almost sumptuous Pauillac starts to become velvety – and then it is wholly irresistible. In 1987 Jean-Michel Cazes planted 4.5 ha with three white varieties, Sauvignon, Sémillon, and a smaller amount of Muscadelle. Since 1990 Blanc de Lynch-Bages has been produced from these vines, a captivatingly fruity and floral white Bordeaux fermented in new casks.

Ch Lynch-Moussas   map 12/R L5
5ème cru
owner: Emile Castéja **area:** 35 ha **cases:** 15,000 **grape % R:** CS 60% MER 40% **second wine:** Ch Haut-Madrac **other châteaux owned:** Ch Batailley (Pauillac); Ch Haut-Bages Monpelou (Pauillac); Ch Beau-Site (St-Estèphe); Ch du Domaine de l'Eglise (Pomerol); Ch Bergat (St-Emilion); Ch Trotte Vieille (St-Emilion)
33250 Pauillac tel: 05 56 59 57 14
Wines from this estate, which is surrounded by forest in the south-west of the appellation, can vary greatly from year to year. One vintage can be meagre, another light, short and fairly green, the next richly coloured, full-bodied and respectably concentrated (1990 and 1994 were vintages of this kind). The better bottles nearly always offer a combination of stewed fruit flavours, woodland aromas, toasty oak (50% of the casks are new), and strong tannins. The château dates from 1850, and along with the vineyard and cellars it has been wholly renovated since 1969 by Emile Castéja.

Ch Mouton Rothschild   map 12/L G5
1er cru
owner: Philippine de Rothschild **area:** 79 ha **cases:** 32,500, white 1,200 **grape % R:** CS 76% MER 13% CF 9% PV 2% **grape % W:** SEM 48% SAUV 38% MUSC 14% **second wine:** Le Petit Mouton de Mouton Rothschild, Le Second Vin de Mouton Rothschild

(1993) **other wines:** Aile d'Argent (Bordeaux Blanc) **other châteaux owned:** include Ch Clerc Milon (Pauillac); Ch d'Armailhac (Pauillac)
33250 Pauillac tel: 05 56 59 22 22
fax: 05 56 73 20 44
This is the most often described and most visited of all the Bordeaux châteaux. Baron Philippe de Rothschild, who had a great interest in literature and the theatre, took over the management of the estate at the age of 20, and achieved publicity for it in brilliant fashion. Two years after his arrival Philippe decided that henceforth all the wine would be bottled on the estate – a revolutionary step for those days. From the 1934 vintage onward the exact number of bottles produced was stated on the labels. And from 1945 he had the upper part of the labels designed by a different, often famous, artist each year; among them were Bacon, Chagall, Cocteau, Henry Moore and Andy Warhol. At least as spectacular was the opening in 1962 of a private museum full of splendid *objets d'art* with wine connections. Hundreds of thousands of people have now visited it. The Baron also acquired two other châteaux, d'Armailhac and Clerc-Milon, and created an extremely successful branded wine, Mouton-Cadet. Despite all these activities, Mouton Rothschild was by no means forgotten. With a wholehearted commitment the Baron and his staff succeeded in making this one of the world's best wines – in the good years at least. A *grand* Mouton like this has a sumptuous and intense fruitiness with blackcurrant and cherry, a richly rounded structure, deep, ripe tannins, and some striking aspects of oak, with charred notes, cedar, coffee, cocoa, tobacco from the 100% new casks. Often, too, there are all kinds of subtle nuances, such as spices, leather and flowers. The Baron, who died in 1988 and was succeeded by his daughter Philippine, was justifiably successful in 1973 in getting his Mouton Rothschild promoted from second to first *cru classé* – the only château to achieve this since 1855. The estate now also produces a very expensive white wine, the Aile d'Argent. This is an aromatic Bordeaux, reasonably nuanced and clearly supported by its oak.

Below: at Ch Mouton Rothschild

PAUILLAC

Pauillac

Anseillan

Mousset

Ch La Fleur
Milon

Pouyalet

Ch Mouton Rothschild

Ch Clerc Milon

Ch Lafite
Rothschild

Ch d'Armailhac

Milon

Loubeyres

les Carruades

Chenal du Lazaret

Jale du Breuil

LAFITE

D2 E4

D2

D2 E1

D205 E1

D205

Mouton Rothschild

Lafite Rothschild

Other vineyards

Woods

Commune boundary

Canton boundary

Contour line

N

1:13,000

0   500m

Ch Pédesclaux
map 12/L E6

5ème cru

owner: Famille Jugla **area:** 20 ha **cases:** 9,000
grape % R: cs 65% mer 25% cf 8% pv 2% **second wine:** Ch Haut Padarnac **other châteaux owned:** Ch Grand-Duroc-Milon *(Pauillac)*, Ch Belle Rose *(Pauillac)*
33250 Pauillac tel: 05 56 59 22 59
fax: 05 56 59 22 59

For years this estate has been waiting for its breakthrough in quality to come: for decades it has been performing below its *cinquième cru classé* status. Improvements in working practice were carried through in the 1980s, with new fermentation tanks of stainless steel, and the proportion of new casks up to 40%. However, these efforts have led to only a slight rise in quality. All this does not alter the fact that Pédesclaux can be an agreeable Pauillac, particularly when this reasonably powerful wine has undergone 5-10 years' maturing in bottle.

Ch Pey la Rose

owner: Denis Jugla **area:** 6 ha **cases:** 2,500 **grape % R:** cs 60% mer 30% cf 10% **other châteaux owned:** Ch Puy la Rose *(Pauillac)*
33250 Pauillac tel: 05 56 57 01 48
fax: 05 56 59 12 01

Decent *cru bourgeois* showing links with Ch Colombier-Monpelou and Ch Puy la Rose. Matured for 18 months in wood, a third new.

Ch Pibran
map 12/L G9

cru bourgeois

owner: AXA Millésimes **area:** 9.5 ha **cases:** 4,000
grape % R: cs 60% mer 25% cf 10% pv 5% **other châteaux owned:** include Ch Pichon-Longueville *(Pauillac)*
33250 Pauillac tel: 05 56 73 24 20
fax: 05 56 73 17 28

A *cru bourgeois* vinified at Ch Pichon-Longueville; it acquired star status after being taken over by AXA Millésimes. In good years this wine often achieves the level of a *cru classé*: dark colour, a lot of oak, toast and vanilla, solid tannins, low acidity, a mouthfilling structure, and delightful, blackcurrant-style fruit. The vineyard stretches across a well-

Above: Ch Pichon Longueville Comtesse de Lalande

drained gravel bank and borders the estates of Châteaux Lynch-Bages, Mouton Rothschild and Pontet-Cantet.

Ch Pichon-Longueville
map 12/R D7

2ème cru

owner: AXA Millésimes **area:** 50 ha **cases:** 24,500
grape % R: cs 75% mer 25% **second wine:** Les Tourelles de Longueville **other châteaux owned:** include Ch Pibran *(Pauillac)*; Ch Suduiraut *(Sauternes)*; Ch La Fleur Pourret *(St-Emilion)*; Ch Petit Figeac *(St-Emilion)*; Ch Petit Village *(Pomerol)*; Ch Cantenac-Brown *(Margaux)*
33250 Pauillac tel: 05 56 73 24 20
fax: 05 56 73 17 28

When Baron Jacques de Pichon de Longueville, first *président* of the Bordeaux parliament, married Thérèse de Rausan in 1694 the dowry she brought was a large estate at St-Lambert, near Pauillac. This inheritance was eventually divided up in 1850. Baron Raoul received two-fifths of the land, and on it a year later he built a château in a mixture of styles, flanked by pointed towers. It was given the official name of Ch Longueville au Baron de Pichon-Longueville. In 1987, after it had belonged to the Bouteiller family for 54 years, the property was bought by Axa Millésimes. In order to have the obsolete winery here brought up to date, *gérant* Jean-Michel Cazes (of Ch Lynch-Bages and elsewhere) arranged a competition for four teams of architects. What resulted from this was a spectacular, symmetrical design, very modern but also with elements that call ancient Egypt to mind. It dominates the D2 road at St-Lambert, just opposite the unassuming entrance to Latour. The complex was ready in 1992, but the wine had already shown a considerable improvement in quality by then. A *deuxième cru classé* level was convincingly

Below: Ch Pichon-Longueville

reached for the first time in decades. Today
Pichon-Longueville is usually an intensely
coloured Pauillac, rich in extract, meaty and
sinewy. It is very classic in character, with
spices, sultry and smoky oak (60% of the casks
for the 15 months' maturing are new each
year), pencil shavings, thick layers of ripe black
fruit, and firm tannins.

Ch Pichon Longueville Comtesse de Lalande   map 12/R D7

2ème cru

owner: May-Eliane de Lencquesaing **area:** 75 ha
cases: 36,000 **grape % R:** cs 45% mer 35% cf 12%
pv 8% **second wines:** Réserve de la Comtesse;
Domaine des Gartieux
33250 Pauillac tel: 05 56 59 19 40
fax. 05 56 59 26 56

In 1818 Marie-Laure de Pichon de Longueville
married Comte Henri de Lalande. As a dowry
she had some land from the Pichon estate in St-
Lambert, and here the couple built a château in
1840. The division of the Pichon land a decade
later led in stages to the Comtesse de Lalande
estate making its own wine. The estate lacked
direction for a period in the 20th century, but
then passed to May-Eliane de Lencquesaing in
1978. With great energy she subsequently
brought a new lustre to the faded reputation of
the Pichon Longueville Comtesse de Lalande
estate. She invested in a new *chai*, after the
existing one had been enlarged, built an ultra-
modern *cuvier*, constructed new housing for
the employees, and restored both the château
and its park. In addition, the proportion of new
barriques was increased to 50%, and
winemaking improvements implemented. As a
result the Pauillac produced here is one of the
best of the *deuxième crus*. It is typically silky
and rounded, with an alluring, elegant taste
whose nuances include jammy fruit, spices,
cedar, fine and integrated tannins, and creamy,
toasty oak.

Ch Plantey   map 12/R I1

cru bourgeois
owner: Gabriel Meffre **area:** 26 ha **cases:** 15,000
grape % R: cs 55% cf 5% mer 40% **second wine:** Ch
Artigues **other châteaux owned:** Ch du Glana (St-
Julien); Ch Lalande (St-Julien); Ch Canteloup (St-
Estèphe); Ch La Commanderie (St-Estèphe)
33250 Pauillac tel: 05 56 59 06 47
fax: 04 90 65 03 73

A vineyard in one block, close to those of Ch
d'Armailhac and Ch Pontet-Canet. Here Gabriel
Meffre has been in charge since 1958. The wine
is firm and mouthfilling in taste, smoothly
rounded, with solid tannins and ripe fruit. It
spends a year maturing in used barrels.

Ch Pontet-Canet   map 12/L H7

5ème cru
owner: Famille Tesseron **area:** 78 ha **cases:** 45,000
grape % R: cs 63% mer 32% cf 5% **second wine:**
Les Hauts de Pontet **other châteaux owned:** Ch
Lafon-Rochet (St-Estèphe)
33250 Pauillac tel: 05 56 59 04 04
fax: 05 56 59 26 63

'Tough tannins', 'dour', 'introvert', 'austere' are
notes that are often applied to wine from this
estate – although less frequently today than in
the past, since the proportion of Cabernet
Sauvignon in the vineyard, which used to be
75%, has gradually been brought down to 63%
– in favour of the Merlot. Besides its tannin-
defined structure, this Pauillac has other

Above: Ch Pontet-Canet

elements to offer in good years: tobacco, mint,
fruit, spicy oak (40% of the casks are new and
maturing lasts 18 months), ink, licorice and tar.
In this way, and after sufficient bottle-ageing,
an exceptionally enjoyable wine emerges. The
origin of this property goes back to 1725 when
Jean-François Pontet, governor of the Médoc,
gave his name to the estate of Canet he had
acquired.

◆

Second wines

An increasing number of châteaux select
only the best wine for bottling and sale
under their main label, and use a second
name for wine from young vines and
less-than-perfect vats.

The proportion declared as the '*grand vin*'
varies with the vintage, and some estates
are more perfectionist than others. In
some years, top estates may downgrade
half or more of the production to the
second label. In dire years, they may not
market the wine under a château label at
all, but sell it anonymously into the trade
for blending.

A few châteaux have a third label for wine
that does not meet their second wine's
standards.

Some châteaux regularly sell a part of their
production to a *négociant*, who then
bottles it under a different château name.
This wine can be of the same standard as
the château's *grand vin*, or at second wine
level. On occasions it is better than the
château's wine.

Where possible, the text tells if this is so.

Ch Puy la Rose

owner: Denis Jugla **area:** 8 ha **cases:** 3,500 **grape
% R:** cs 65% mer 30% cf 5% **other châteaux owned:**
Ch Pey la Rose (Pauillac)
33250 Pauillac tel: 05 56 59 01 48
fax: 05 56 59 12 01

Not an exciting Pauillac, but certainly a sound
one of average quality. It is produced from vines
around 30 years old, and a third of the
maturing casks are new. In character the wine
shows its family ties with Châteaux Colombier-
Monpelou and Pey la Rose.

Ch St Mambert Bellevue   map 12/R C6

owner: Domingo Reyes **area:** 0.5 ha **cases:** 270
grape % R: cs 50% cf 40% mer 10%
33250 Pauillac tel: 05 56 59 22 72

Tiny estate bordering those of the two Pichons
and Latour. Until 1993 the wine was vinified by
the Pauillac cooperative. Maturing lasts 18
months, mainly in used *barriques* from Latour.
The first estate-made vintages have been very
promising.

Ch La Tourette   map 20K9

owner: AGF **area:** 3 ha **cases:** 1,800 **grape % R:** cs
60% mer 30% cf 10% **other châteaux owned:**
include Ch Larose-Trintaudon (Haut-Médoc)
33112 St-Laurent-Médoc tel: 05 56 59 41 72
fax: 05 56 59 93 22

One plot belonging to the Haut-Médoc estate
Ch Larose-Trintaudon lies in Pauillac. The wine
from it bears the name Ch La Tourette, and has
been made since 1986. It is a likeable wine, with
plenty of fruit and good oak structure from the
annual quota of 50% new casks.

St-Estèphe

Michael Broadbent

Our next port of call is St-Estèphe, the most northerly of the major appellations of the Haut-Médoc. It is also by far the largest, in area and production, yet contains the fewest classed growths.

The most usual point of entry is almost dramatic. It certainly starts off well: continuing north from Pauillac along the road which dips almost reverentially past Lafite, crossing a small stream and curling steeply up again, we reach an escarpment topped with an astonishingly original building of mixed Arabian/Oriental style. This turns out to be the *chai* of Cos d'Estournel, one of St Estèphe's two very distinguished Second Growths. There is no 'château' as such, which is why the labels of some vintages, with apparent inconsistency, omit the prefix. Immediately behind it to the north is a relatively high gravel plateau, ideally suited for Cabernet Sauvignon. Yet, despite its proximity to Pauillac, Cos produces a wine of different style, at its best with some of the delicacy – an adjective not usually appropriate to the wines of St-Estèphe – of Lafite. Fairly near, to the north, is Montrose, a homely but handsome château, overlooking its vineyard as it dips down towards the river. I always think of Montrose as the 'Latour' of St-Estèphe: deep, firm, tannic, long-lasting wine.

St-Estèphe itself is a not unattractive village, sited in the north of the appellation on high ground overlooking the Gironde. The village centre is dominated by the church with its high tower and steeple – the latter not only proclaiming its importance but easily identifiable to passing ships, for the estuary is, and always has been, an important sea-lane. Whether one is standing on the terrace of Beychevelle or Ducru, gazing from the window of the drawing-room at Latour, or merely sauntering along the river front at Pauillac, one is constantly surprised at the number – and the size – of the ships that glide smoothly up to the docks of Bordeaux, or back past the Pointe de Grave to the open sea. What one forgets, for it is lost in the distant past, is that the Gironde, and its feeder rivers the Garonne and the Dordogne, for centuries afforded the most convenient and cheapest transport of wines in cask: first from the estates to the offices and cellars of the *négociants* lining the Quai des Chartrons and Quai de Bacalan, and then on to their importing agents in London, Bristol, Antwerp and the rest of the wine-drinking world.

Up and down the Médoc, each commune, each village – sometimes each château – had its own port. The barrels were carted down to the jetties by the river's edge and rolled on to small sailing barges for transportation to Bordeaux. Until well into the 19th century the life and commerce of the Médoc was dependent on the river and, to this day, it is noticeable that the main facade of each château faces the river. The châteaux could thus be recognized (and, of course, admired) from the Gironde – the 'high road' for people as well as wine. From the little ports, now mainly silted up, the proprietors, visitors and *courtiers* (brokers) stepped ashore to visit châteaux and cellars. The advent of the railway put the boatmen out of business. Steel rails formed a commercial spine along the whole length of the Médoc, reaching Pauillac in 1870 and the northern tip, the Pointe de Grave, in 1902.

Away from the river, villages and châteaux were – still are – connected by a mass of minor roads, some merely muddy tracks. Driving around St-Estèphe, trying to locate châteaux, I am constantly reminded of a line from a poem by G K Chesterton: "when the rolling English drunkard built the rolling English road". His French counterpart was plainly just as hazily at work in this part of the Médoc.

Above: The creeks and inlets of the
Gironde shelter fishing boats

Left: Château Cos d'Estournel seen from
the south

Page 79: The village of St-Estèphe is
dominated by its church

THE CHÂTEAUX, THE VINEYARDS, THE VINTAGES

Unquestionably the two top wines of St-Estèphe are, as already mentioned, Cos (pronounced Koss, not Kó) and Montrose. The latter, lived in and run by the Charmolüe family, has always been a favourite of mine. Over the years, I have admired its consistent style, perhaps rather four-square, tough when young, and needing a good deal of bottle-ageing. But like Latour (though not on quite the same monumental scale), it develops a smoothness and serenity hard to envisage when first tasted in cask.

Montrose 1947 and 1949, if well-kept, are still magnificent, a joy; 1959 and 1961 vast, both benefiting from further cellaring. Alas, the secret is out: the 1990 vintage received the plaudits, and highest possible score, of America's most influential wine critic: as a result the price soared well above its class and beyond the pocket of most level-headed, long-term lovers of Bordeaux. This hitherto stolid and dependable wine now enjoys 'star' status. A pity. We shall see.

Cos d'Estournel, owned and (very much hands-on) run by the highly respected Prats family, used to make wine somewhat more amenable than Montrose. Their experiments – with casks, with winemaking, possibly with varietal juggling – reminds me a little of the endlessly questing Robert Mondavi. Happily the reputation of Bruno Prats is such that Cos has certainly more than justified its *deuxième cru* status, though not, in my opinion, sufficient to warrant upgrading. It is regarded as a 'super second' – an abhorrent term!

The *troisième cru* Calon-Ségur is a far older property – its origins date back to the 12th century – with an impressive old château settled comfortably in a slight dip of land in the heart of the commune. At one time it shared the popularity, among British claret lovers, of Pontet-Canet, Lynch-Bages and Talbot: certainly one of the main stock-in-trade, middle-class clarets of the traditional British wine merchant. It owed its attraction partly to its style, partly to the people who managed the property and exclusively shipped the wine. Calon-Ségur is owned by two old Bordeaux families, the Gasquetons and the Peyrelongues. Philippe Gasqueton, who lives at Calon, inherited in 1962 from his uncle, who had really put the wine firmly on the map. It also helped that Bertrand Peyrelongue was much liked by the English trade, and I well remember, in the mid-1950s, Bertrand sailing up the Thames in his yacht. This he moored near the Tower of London, and invited his wine-trade friends on board to taste samples and to put back a bottle or two. A stylish way to sell claret! Calon-Ségur later went into something of a decline – triggered, I sometimes think, by the washed-out 1964 vintage (mind you, the harvest at Lynch-Bages, even at Lafite and Mouton, was spoiled by the torrential rain mid-*vendange*), but recent vintages have seen a welcome return to form. It makes up in balance and firm fruit what it lacks in elegance – after all it is St-Estèphe – and keeps well.

The only other Classed Growths of the appellation are the *quatrième cru* Lafon-Rochet, and the *cinquième* Cos Labory, the former on the edge of the plateau, near Cos d'Estournel, and even nearer to Lafite which is on the opposite side of the Jalle du Breuil. I have often found the wine of Lafon-Rochet, owned by the Tesseron family of Pontet-Canet, to be hard and unsympathetic. Cos Labory is a smallish property immediately opposite *the* Cos. It makes agreeable wine. Of the several dozen *bourgeois* properties, the châteaux Meyney and Phélan-Ségur, both well sited overlooking the Gironde between Montrose and the village of St-Estèphe, make competent wines, as do Houissant, de Pez and les Ormes de Pez – but Hubrecht Duijker lists the best. In style, the lesser wines of St-Estèphe are deep-coloured, full of fruit, often in the past overladen with tannin – at best mouthfillingly fruity, at worst coarse.

Just north of the village of St-Estèphe a *jalle*, the Chenal de Calon, drains the vineyards of Calon-Ségur and divides the broad plateau of St-Estèphe from an outlying hill. On this rise or mound – which reaches all of 19 metres in height – are a collection of *crus bourgeois*, including le Boscq and Beau-Site.

BEYOND ST-ESTÈPHE

North again is a wider plain, another *jalle* – and the end of St-Estèphe. The commune of St-Seurin-de-Cadourne is in the Haut-Médoc appellation, discussed in detail on pages 103-121. Among my favourites in St-Seurin are three châteaux owned by the Miailhe family, (Jean Miailhe is May-Eliane de Lencquesaing's cousin): Coufran, which uses a high percentage of Merlot (the fleshiness of that grape countering any tendency to severity in its wine); Verdignan, which is under the same ownership: and – recently gaining a special reputation – Soudars. The winemaker at all three châteaux is Jean's son. There the Haut-Médoc suddenly comes to an abrupt halt. But not the vines. Onwards to the north lies the spreading vineyards of the Médoc (formerly known as the Bas-Médoc) appellation – again with a chapter to themselves starting on page 122.

PERSONAL FAVOURITES

Among the St-Estèphe Classed Growths my favourites are Montrose and Cos d'Estournal, followed closely, in certain vintages, by Calon-Ségur. Dependable *bourgeois* growths including de Pez, (and just outside the appellation, in Haut-Médoc) Coufran and Verdignan.

THE APPELLATION

ST-ESTÈPHE (red)

Location: On the left bank of the Gironde, the most northerly of the four principal wine appellations of the Médoc. Its southern border, along the Jalle du Breuil, is with Pauillac, the northern one with the Haut-Médoc commune of St-Seurin-de-Cadourne. The southern edge of St-Estèphe is 45 km from the centre of the city of Bordeaux.
Area of AC: 1,519 ha
Area under vine: 1,378 ha
Communes: St-Estèphe. Largest of the 'great four' Médoc communes, 5.5 km north-south; 5 km from the river to neighbouring Vertheuil and Cissac.

Average annual production: 761,000 cases
Classed growths: 5 (2 deuxièmes crus, 1 troisième, 1 quatrième, 1 cinquième)
Others: 43 crus bourgeois, 25 others
Cooperatives: 1 (c. 100 members)
Main grape varieties: Cabernet Sauvignon, Merlot
Others: Cabernet Franc, Petit Verdot
Main soil types: Very varied: gravel ridges, mixed with sand; some clay and a limestone subsoil

Appellation St-Estèphe

Ch Andron Blanquet   map 15 J5
cru bourgeois

owner: SCE Domaines Audoy **area:** 16 ha **cases:** 10,000 **grape % R:** CS 40% CF 30% MER 30% **second wine:** Ch Saint Roch **other châteaux owned:** Ch Cos Labory (St-Estèphe)

33180 St-Estèphe tel: 05 56 59 30 22

fax: 05 56 59 73 52

With its often angular, sometimes rather rustic tannins, this wine is not everyone's favourite; but after four or five years the fruit – blackcurrant, plum, blackberry – generally begins to break through nicely. It is matured for a year in oak (a fifth at most are new barrels). Since 1971 the estate, which is in the south of the commune, has belonged to the Audoy family of the adjoining Ch Cos Labory.

Ch Beau-Site   map 15 D5
cru bourgeois

owner: Emile Castéja **area:** 34 ha **cases:** 17,500 **grape % R:** CS 60% MER 34% CF 5% PV 1% **second wine:** Pavillons de Saint-Estèphe **other châteaux owned:** Ch Batailley (Pauillac); Ch Haut-Bages Monpelou (Pauillac); Ch Lynch-Moussac (Pauillac); Ch du Domaine de l'Eglise (Pomerol); Ch Bergat (St-Emilion); Ch Trotte Vieille (St-Emilion)

33250 St-Estèphe tel: 05 56 59 30 50

The wide, wrought-iron gates to Beau-Site are more impressive than the château itself, which was originally just a subsidiary building of a larger estate. The wine is fairly meaty, with firm, supple tannins – at its best if from a sunny year, when it has plenty of berry fruit and adequate concentration; then, too, the toast aromas of the oak (50% of the casks are new) are nicely in balance with the other elements.

Ch Beau-Site Haut-Vignoble
map 15 D5
cru bourgeois

owner: Jean-Louis Braquessac **area:** 15 ha **cases:** 7,500 **grape % R:** CS 69% MER 22% CF 4% PV 5%

33180 St-Estèphe tel: 05 56 59 30 40

fax: 05 56 59 39 13

◆

Finding a second wine
To locate a second wine or any other wine not listed in the appellation's Directory pages, consult the index, where all château names are listed. Not all second wines use the appellation of the château's grand vin.

◆

Classed growths
Recognized classifications are listed at the end of the Atlas. Châteaux profiled in the Atlas which appear on one of these lists have their classification and rank noted immediately below the château name.

◆

Maps of the Médoc & Graves appellations
For a key map showing all the appellations in this zone, with the outlines of the maps in this Atlas, consult Map 7.

Above: Ch La Commanderie

Estate that has belonged to the same family for over a century. Some three-quarters of its 20 plots are on gravel *croupes*. The wine spends a year in used casks and is normally a fairly slender St-Estèphe, characterized by tough tannins and modest in its fruit and personality.

Ch Bel-Air Ortet   map 15 F7
owner: Marcel & Christian Quancard **area:** 2 ha **cases:** 1,000 **grape % R:** CS 75% MER 25% **other châteaux owned:** include Ch Cossieu-Coutelin (St-Estèphe); Ch Faget (St-Estèphe); Ch de Terrefort-Quancard (Bordeaux Supérieur); Ch Tour St Joseph (Haut-Médoc); Ch Haut-Logat (Haut-Médoc); Ch de Paillet-Quancard (Premières Côtes de Bordeaux)

33250 St-Estèphe tel: 05 56 33 80 60

fax: 05 56 33 80 70

Sound, flawless wine made in a powerful, compact style. Plenty of charred oak (one-third new barrels) but not a great deal of fruit. The modest vineyard is on one of the highest parts of St-Estèphe; its vines average 45 years old.

Ch Le Boscq   map 15 C6
owner: UFG/Groupe CVBG **area:** 16.6 ha **cases:** 11,000 **grape % R:** MER 40% CS 30% CF 20% PV 10% **other châteaux owned:** include Ch Belgrave (Haut-Médoc)

33250 St-Estèphe tel: 05 56 35 53 00

fax: 05 56 35 53 29

This deep-coloured, sinewy wine, rich in tannin and containing fruit, has improved in quality since the '95 vintage. In that year the estate was taken over by UFG, owners of Château Bellegrave in Haut-Médoc, and leased to CVBG (Dourthe Kressmann). Just before that vintage, considerable improvements were made in the cellar and new casks were bought for maturing; the intention is to do this each year.

Ch Calon-Ségur   map 15 D6
3ème cru

owner: Famille Capbern Gasqueton **area:** 74 ha **cases:** 30,000 **grape % R:** CS 65% MER 20% CF 15% **second wines:** Saint-Estèphe de Calon la Chapelle; Mademoiselle de Calon; Ch Marquis de Calon **other châteaux owned:** Ch Capbern Gasqueton (St-Estèphe); Ch du Tertre (Margaux)

33180 St-Estèphe tel: 05 56 59 30 08

fax: 05 56 59 71 51

In Roman times *calon* meant 'wood', and the small boats in which it was transported were called *calones*. This same name was given to the parish from which St-Estèphe was later to develop. This estate developed out of the Domaine de Calon, where wine was probably made as early as the 13th century. The present château was built at the end of the 16th century on the site of a fort – about 150 years before St-Estèphe got its church. The most famous owner of this estate was Marquis Alexandre de Ségur, the 18th-century president of the Bordeaux *parlement*. He owned Lafite, Latour and Mouton, but he preferred Calon. 'I make wine at Lafite and Latour, but my heart is at Calon' is apparently what he used to say. A heart still appears on the Ch Calon-Ségur label. In lesser vintages this *troisième cru classé* sometimes lacks depth, body and maturing potential; in the great and the good years, however, a classic, concentrated St-Estèphe appears. Reserved at first, it possesses spicy fruit, woodland scents, well-integrated tannins and considerable oak. Maturing in *barriques* – 40% of them new – lasts a long time here: 22 months as a rule.

Ch Capbern Gasqueton   map 15 E8
cru bourgeois

owner: Famille Capbern Gasqueton **area:** 20 ha **cases:** 8,000 **grape % R:** CS 65% MER 20% CF 15% **second wine:** Capbern Grand Village **other châteaux owned:** Ch Calon-Ségur (St-Estèphe); Ch du Tertre (Margaux)

33180 St-Estèphe tel: 05 56 59 30 08

fax: 05 56 59 71 51

The château is a grey, unassuming building behind the church at St-Estèphe; a barrel-cellar runs the whole length of it. The Capbern Gasqueton family has owned the property since 1730. The wine is usually rich in colour and tannin: even when from less-abundant vintages, it needs to mature for at least five years. Berry fruit, licorice and oak then manifest themselves. The average time in wood is 20 months, and 20% of the *barriques* are new each year.

Ch Chambert-Marbuzet
map 15 J8

cru bourgeois

owner: Henri Duboscq **area:** 7 ha **cases:** 3,750
grape % R: CS 70% MER 30% **other châteaux owned:**
Ch Haut-Marbuzet (St-Estèphe); Ch Mac Carthy (St-Estèphe); Ch Tour de Marbuzet (St-Estèphe)
33180 St-Estèphe tel: 05 56 59 30 54
fax: 05 56 59 70 87

This St-Estèphe usually develops quite quickly:
there is often a dashing bouquet to it, and its
quite elegant taste has jammy fruit, supple
tannins and considerable oak. For the 18-20
months it matures, the wine spends half its
time in new casks, half in wooden vats. The
Duboscq family acquired the estate in 1962.

Ch Clauzet
map 15 H5

owner: Max Boisseau **area:** 6 ha **cases:** 3,000
grape % R: CS 60% MER 40%
33180 St-Estèphe tel: 05 56 59 34 16

In most vintages this is a decently mouthfilling,
firm wine characterized to a reasonable extent
by oak from the 25% of new barrels. The estate
was established at the end of the 19th century
by the man who gave it his name. The château
also dates from that period.

Ch La Commanderie
map 15 I5

cru bourgeois

owner: Gabriel Meffre **area:** 20 ha **cases:** 9,000
grape % R: CS 50% MER 45% CF 5% **other châteaux
owned:** Ch Canteloup (St-Estèphe); Ch Plantey
(Pauillac); Ch Lalande (St-Julien); Ch du Glana (St-Julien)
33180 St-Estèphe tel: 05 56 59 06 47
fax: 04 90 65 03 73

This St-Estèphe certainly has merit. At its best
it has an agreeable aroma (rich spice, bayleaf,
coffee, caramel, jammy fruit) and is reasonably
powerful in flavour – sometimes with a touch of
acidity, but rounded by the 20% new casks. The
château dates from after the French Revolution
and was built where the Knights Templar once
had a *commanderie*.

Ch Cos d'Estournel
map 15 K7

2ème cru

owner: Domaines Prats **area:** 64 ha **cases:** 36,000
grape % R: CS 60% MER 38% CF 2% **second wine:**
Les Pagodes de Cos **other châteaux owned:** Ch
Marbuzet (St-Estèphe)

Below: Ch Cos d'Estournel

33180 St-Estèphe tel: 05 56 73 15 50
fax: 05 56 59 72 59

In 1811 Louis Gaspard d'Estournel set out to
produce wine of the very best quality in the
hamlet of Cos. He was a dealer in Arab horses,
which were shipped to and from the Far East –
accompanied, eventually, by some bottles of the
Estournel wine. Part of the consignment came
back however – and these bottles, far from
suffering, appeared to have developed
remarkably well. The enterprising grower
therefore decided that in future all his wine
would make a sea voyage. To emphasize this
connection with the Far East he started to build
a château in the form of an Oriental temple,
complete with pagoda towers. D'Estournel
repeatedly went bankrupt, but after 20 years it
was finally finished. It is the most bizarrely
striking building in all Bordeaux, and this
extraordinary structure today yields an equally
extraordinary wine. After a first step in that
direction in 1978, Cos d'Estournel went right to
the top with its 1982 and later vintages. This is
due to the energetic, expert management of
director and co-owner Bruno Prats, who has
carried through fundamental improvements
and invested on a large scale. The wine is
practically always deeply concentrated in its
colour and taste, with the finest possible
tannins and an admirable framework of new oak
(from the 50-100% of virgin *barriques*); the
rich, vigorous taste holds nuances of ample and
very ripe fruit (black cherry, blackcurrant), plus
chocolate, coffee and spices.

Ch Cos Labory
map 15 K6

5ème cru

owner: SCE Domaines Audoy **area:** 18 ha **cases:**
8,500 **grape % R:** CS 50% MER 30% CF 15% PV 5%
second wine: Charme Labory **other châteaux
owned:** Ch Andron Blanquet (St-Estèphe)
33180 St-Estèphe tel: 05 56 59 30 22
fax: 05 56 59 73 52

This estate was once called Ch Cos Gaston, but
the name was changed in the first half of the
19th century when François Labory acquired it.
(When he died in 1845, the estate was for seven
years the property of Louis Gaspard
d'Estournel, of neighbouring Cos d'Estournel.)
Since 1990 the wine has been back on form
after a relatively weak period. Its broad taste
tends to creaminess, and offers solid tannins as

---

well as considerable body. There is no lack of
fruit – blackcurrant, plum, cherry can be noted
– and the oak is of good quality, from the 30-
50% of new casks.

Ch Coussieu-Coutelin

owner: Marcel & Christian Quancard **area:** 2 ha
cases: 1,000 **grape % R:** CS 75% MER 25% **other
châteaux owned:** include Ch Bel-Air Ortet (St-
Estèphe); Ch Faget (St-Estèphe); Ch de Terrefort
Quancard (Bordeaux Supérieur); Ch de Paillet
Quancard (Premières Côtes de Bordeaux)
33180 St-Estèphe tel: 05 56 33 80 60
fax: 05 56 33 80 70

Modest property that has belonged to the
Quancard family since 1977. The wine is
nurtured for a year or longer in barrels of
which a third are new, so that it has some oak
and vanilla. In its structure it is one of the more
elegant St-Estèphes, and often boasts
considerable charm.

Ch Coutelin-Merville
map 15 I3

cru bourgeois

owner: G. Estager & Fils **area:** 20 ha **cases:**
12,000 **grape % R:** MER 44% CF 26% CS 26% PV 4%
second wine: Ch Merville
33180 St-Estèphe tel: 05 56 59 32 10

Estate on the western edge of the appellation
that was separated from Ch Hanteillan, Haut-
Médoc, in 1972; Merlot is the grape most grown
here. The wine used to be quite mediocre, but
has improved in standard since the end of the
1980s. It is reasonably full-tasting, with supple
tannins, a pleasing, toasty aroma of oak (after a
year in wood: at least 20% new barrels), and
with sufficient fruit.

Ch Le Crock
map 15 J7

cru bourgeois

owner: Domaines Cuvelier **area:** 33 ha **cases:**
17,500 **grape % R:** CS 60% MER 25% CF 10% PV 5%
second wine: Ch la Croix St-Estèphe **other
châteaux owned:** Ch Léoville Poyferré (St-Julien)
33180 St-Estèphe tel: 05 56 86 49 25
fax: 05 56 86 57 18

In 1992 Le Crock won *la coupe*: it was awarded
the Coupe des Crus Bourgeois for its 1986,
1988 and 1989 vintages. The St-Estèphe
produced here is indeed a wine of distinction in
the classic mode, generally characterized by
plenty of colour, a muscular mouthful rich in

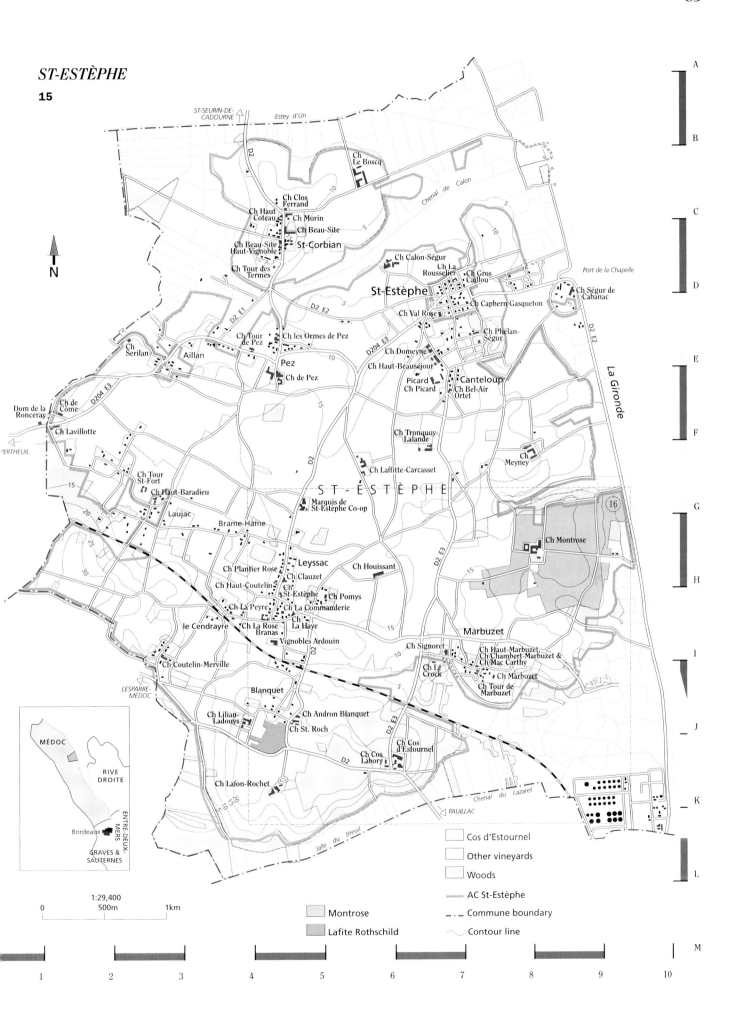

Above: Ch La Haye

Above: Ch Lilian-Ladouys

tannin, fruit notes that vary with the vintage, and oak from casks of which a third are new. The imposing château was built around 1820 and is set in an extensive park, with palm trees and a small lake fed by a natural spring.

Ch Domeyne   map 15 E7
cru bourgeois
owner: Famille Franchini **area:** 7.2 ha **cases:** 4,000
grape % R: cs 60% mer 35% cf 5% **other châteaux
owned:** Ch Haut-Vignoble du Parc (Haut-Médoc)
33180 St-Estèphe tel: 05 56 59 72 29
fax: 05 56 59 72 21
Fairly rustic St-Estèphe from a well-equipped estate; the château is in St-Estèphe village. Maturing lasts for 18 months in wood (20-30% new casks), and gives the wine spicy tones of oak, while the aroma shows some fruit and bayleaf. Numerous medals are confirmation of the sound quality. Wine from Ch Haut Vignoble du Parc is also made here, a cru bourgeois grown on 8.81 ha in Vertheuil, Haut-Médoc.

Ch Haut-Baradieu   map 15 G3
cru bourgeois
owner: Jean Anney **area:** 15 ha **cases:** 6,600 **grape
% R:** mer 50% cs 50% **other châteaux owned:** Ch
Comtesse du Parc (Haut-Médoc); Ch Tour des
Termes (St-Estèphe)
33180 St-Estèphe tel: 05 56 59 32 89
fax: 05 56 59 73 74
For decades wine from this estate was identical with that from Ch Tour de Termes, but since 1979 the two have been vinified separately. Ch Haut-Baradieu is the simpler of the pair: a decent, but in no way remarkable, St-Estèphe given a short spell in used casks.

Ch Haut-Beauséjour   map 15 E7
cru bourgeois
owner: SC du Domaine Picard-Beauséjour/Louis
Roederer **area:** 18.7 ha **cases:** 10,000 **grape % R:**
mer 52% cs 40% pv 5% mal 3% **other châteaux
owned:** Ch de Pez (St-Estèphe)
33180 St-Estèphe tel: 05 56 59 30 26
fax: 05 56 59 39 25
In 1992 Jean-Claude Rouzaud, managing director of the Champagne firm of Louis Roederer, discovered a neglected château with, he thought, great potential for quality – and decided to buy it. It had always worked with two

names, Beauséjour and Picard, both with cru bourgeois status. Rouzaud, however, chose to proceed with the new name of Haut-Beauséjour. A charter of quality was drawn up for the cultivation of the vineyard, and the cellars underwent total renewal and refurbishment. The first vintage to appear was the 1993 – the 1992 did not come up to standard. This St-Estèphe is characterized by deep colour, rounded tannins and a lively taste in which black fruit and flattering oak (from at least a year in barriques of which 33-40% are new) go together harmoniously.

Ch Haut Coteau   map 15 C5
cru bourgeois
owner: Arlette Brousseau **area:** 11 ha **cases:** 5,500
grape % R: cs 34% mer 33% cf 33% **second wine:**
Ch des Nougueys **other châteaux owned:** Ch
Brousseau Haut Vignoble (Haut-Médoc)
33180 St-Estèphe tel: 05 56 59 39 84
fax: 05 56 59 39 09

◆
About St-Estèphe
The Maison du Vin is in the village of St-Estèphe itself, towards the north of the appellation. Tel 05 56 59 30 59.

◆
Classed growths
Recognized classifications are listed at the end of the Atlas which appear on one of these lists have their classification and rank noted immediately below the château name.

◆
Crus Bourgeois
Only one area – the Médoc – has a recognized list of crus bourgeois. The ranking procedure is described on page 34 and the full list is given in an appendix. The crus bourgeois are in appellations Médoc, Haut-Médoc and the 'village' ACs such as St-Estèphe. The term cru bourgeois is in use in other areas, but unofficially, and thus not on labels.

Wine fermented in stainless steel, then nurtured for 12-15 months in wood – about a third of the casks being new. Not a really complex St-Estèphe, but it usually has a decent concentration that benefits from maturing. The estate was created in 1908, and from 1935 to 1988 it was connected to the local cooperative.

Ch Haut-Coutelin   map 15 H5
owner: Claude Clerté **area:** 5.48 ha **cases:** 2,750
grape % R: cs 75% mer 25%
33180 St-Estèphe tel: 05 56 32 82 44
fax: 05 56 40 33 45
Property run by an enthusiastic ocean sailor that yields a decently substantial wine. It bears the stamp of its Cabernet Sauvignon, with berry fruit and tannin, matures for 18 months in used casks, and has won numerous medals at wine shows.

Ch Haut-Marbuzet   map 15 J8
cru bourgeois
owner: Henri Duboscq **area:** 50 ha **cases:** 25,000
grape % R: cs 50% mer 40% cf 10% **second wine:**
La Rose MacCarthy **other châteaux owned:** Ch Mac
Carthy (St-Estèphe); Ch Tour de Marbuzet (St-
Estèphe); Ch Chambert-Marbuzet (St-Estèphe)
33180 St-Estèphe tel: 05 56 59 30 54
fax: 05 56 59 70 87
A famous property, made great since 1952 by Hervé Duboscq and his son Henri. Their wine appears resplendent on the tables of celebrities, and on the menus of top restaurants. Haut-Marbuzet is not a cru classé, but is nearly always among the best three or four St-Estèphes of the year. It spends 18 months exclusively in new casks, so oak is noticeably there in its aroma. Other trademarks are an expansive taste of considerable distinction, a rich, sensual charm, ripe tannins and concentrated fruit. Haut-Marbuzet generally offers the greatest enjoyment 10-15 years after the vintage.

Ch La Haye   map 15 I5
cru bourgeois
owner: Georges Lecallier **area:** 10 ha **cases:** 4,170
grape % R: cs 50% mer 42% cf 8%
33180 St-Estèphe tel: 05 56 59 32 18
A rising star among the St-Estèphe crus bourgeois. In recent years the wine has excelled

ST-ESTÈPHE

16

St-Estèphe

ST-ESTÈPHE

La Gironde

Ch Montrose

Marbuzet

Ch Signoret

Ch Haut-Marbuzet & Ch Chambert-Marbuzet
Ch Marbuzet
Ch Mac Carthy

Ch Le Crock

Ch Tour de Marbuzet

Blanquet

Ch Andron
Blanquet

Ch Cos
d'Estournel

Ch St. Roch

Ch Cos
Labory

D2

D2 E2

D2 E3

Cos d'Estournel

Montrose

Lafite Rothschild

Other vineyards

Woods

Commune boundary

Canton boundary

Contour line

N

1:17,500

0   500m

with its very attractive, rich and succulent fruit, its full-bodied, long-lasting taste and its well-knit tannins. A further dimension is added to this enticing wine by oak from the 25-33% new casks. The vineyard dates from 1557: according to tradition the château was a hunting lodge where Diane de Poitiers and Henri II used to meet. A monogram of their initials adorns the château's label.

Ch Houissant   map 15 H6

owner: Jean Ardouin **area:** 28 ha **cases:** 19,000 **grape % R:** CS 70% MER 25% PV 5% **second wine:** Ch Tour Pomys **other châteaux owned:** Ch Leyssac (St-Estèphe)

33180 St-Estèphe tel: 05 56 59 32 21
fax: 05 56 59 73 41

Fairly light-footed, fruity St-Estèphe, with notes of bayleaf and spices, and a slightly bitter touch. Before bottling, this pleasant wine matures for 6-12 months in used barrels.

Ch Laffitte-Carcasset   map 15 G6

owner: Philippe de Padirac **area:** 42 ha **cases:** 26,100 **grape % R:** CS 60% MER 40% **second wine:** Ch la Vicomtesse **other wines:** Ch Haut la Gravière (Haut-Médoc)

33180 St-Estèphe tel: 05 56 59 34 32
fax: 05 56 59 35 75

Nowadays a wine that is better than just correct, with considerable depth, fruit and tannin. A third of the casks for maturing are new each year. The good quality is partly due to strict selection: on average less than 60% of the year's production is used for the first wine here.

Ch Lafon-Rochet   map 15 K5

4ème cru

owner: Guy Tesseron **area:** 40 ha **cases:** 22,500 **grape % R:** CS 56% MER 40% CF 4% **second wine:** Numéro 2 du Château Lafon-Rochet **other châteaux owned:** Ch Pontet-Canet (Pauillac)

33180 St-Estèphe tel: 05 56 59 32 06
fax: 05 56 59 72 43

When Guy Tesseron bought this property on the southern edge of the appellation in 1959, the vineyard was neglected, the château in ruins. Both have since been entirely restored – Tesseron in fact building an entirely new château in chartreuse style. For re-planting, a high proportion of Cabernet Sauvignon was

Below: Ch Marbuzet

Above: Ch Meyney

chosen in the first instance – 70%. However, this yielded too harsh a wine with too much tannin, and the percentage was gradually reduced to the present 56%. The wine still has a relatively large measure of tannin, but its structure is less angular. In good years this St-Estèphe has rather more than average concentration, is meatily rounded, with elements of toasted oak from 16-18 months in cask (40% new barrels), dark tones of leather, tar and bayleaf, and the classic berry fruit of Cabernet and Merlot.

Ch Lavillotte   map 15 F2

cru bourgeois

owner: SCEA des Domaines Pedro **area:** 12 ha **cases:** 4,500 **grape % R:** CS 72% MER 25% PV 3% **second wine:** Ch Aillan **other châteaux owned:** Ch Le Meynieu (Haut-Médoc); Domaine de la Ronceray (St-Estèphe)

33180 St-Estèphe tel: 05 56 41 98 17
fax: 05 56 41 98 89

Normally this is a complete St-Estèphe, furnished with black fruit, considerable oak – from 20 months in wood of which 40% are new casks – and well-measured tannins. The vineyard had practically disappeared when Jacques Pedro bought it in 1962, but it has been totally replanted since.

Ch Lilian-Ladouys   map 15 J4

cru bourgeois

owner: Christian Thiéblot **area:** 48 ha **cases:** 28,000 **grape % R:** CS 58% MER 37% CF 5% **second wine:** La Devise de Lilian

33180 St-Estèphe tel: 05 56 59 71 96
fax: 05 56 59 35 97

In May 1989 Christian Thiéblot, from the world of computers, was tipped off that this cru bourgeois in St-Estèphe was for sale, an estate that went back to the 16th century. Thiéblot proceeded to buy it and within a year also managed to acquire a few dozen hectares more, all planted with old vines. In addition, the neglected château flanked by its two round towers was painstakingly restored, and a whole new cellar installation was built. Thiéblot decided to add the name of his hard-working wife Lilian to that of the reborn estate. Even in 1989, their first vintage, an impressively good wine was made. And most vintages since then

Above: Ch Montrose

have likewise impressed. This St-Estèphe is characterized by fine fruit (blackcurrant, cherry, prune), very flattering oak, with vanilla and toast notes from a year in new barriques, integrated, supple tannins and a velvety structure.

Ch Mac Carthy   map 15 J8

cru bourgeois

owner: Henri Duboscq **area:** 7 ha **cases:** 3,750 **grape % R:** CS 50% MER 50% **other châteaux owned:** Ch Tour de Marbuzet (St-Estèphe); Ch Chambert-Marbuzet (St-Estèphe); Ch Haut-Marbuzet (St-Estèphe)

33180 St-Estèphe tel: 05 56 59 30 54
fax: 05 56 59 70 87

A wine of a fairly generous, accessible character aged in used casks from Ch Haut-Marbuzet (which has the same owner). Often there is plummy fruit apparent in its aroma. The château is named after a family of Irish origin who went to France in the 18th century. One Mac Carthy of that era was the director of the Bordeaux chamber of commerce, and a street in the city is named after him. The present owner acquired the estate in 1988.

Ch Marbuzet   map 15 J8

cru bourgeois

owner: Domaines Prats **area:** 7 ha **cases:** 4,000 **grape % R:** CS 46% MER 42% PV 12% **other châteaux owned:** Ch Cos d'Estournel (St-Estèphe)

33180 St-Estèphe tel: 05 56 73 15 50
fax: 05 56 59 72 59

It is alleged that a well-to-do wine merchant had this château built for his mistress at the beginning of the 20th century. Its design is based on that of Ch de Rastignac, which also served as the model for the White House in Washington. Although Marbuzet has its own vineyard, the wine from it was blended with the lesser cuvées from Cos d'Estournel: in fact the name Ch Marbuzet used to serve for d'Estournel's second wine. Starting with the 1994 vintage, however, Ch Marbuzet wine is now vinified separately, nurtured for a year in used barriques from Cos d'Estournel and bottled separately. The wine is rounded and combines fruit and elegance in a pleasing and balanced manner, without an enormous amount of tannin.

Ch Meyney map 15 G8
cru bourgeois

owner: Domaines Cordier **area:** 49 ha **cases:** 29,200 **grape % R:** CS 70% MER 24% CF 4% PV 2% **second wine:** Prieur de Meyney **other châteaux owned:** include Ch Clos des Jacobins (St-Emilion); Ch Tanesse (Bordeaux); Ch Plagnac (Médoc); Ch Le Gardera (Bordeaux Supérieur)

33250 St-Estèphe tel: 05 56 59 30 01
fax: 05 56 59 39 89

Meyney's wine is nearly always among the best crus bourgeois in both the good and the lesser years. This is due not only to a superbly sited vineyard on a hill close to the Gironde, but also to the meticulous way the wine is made by Domaines Cordier. This includes an average 15 months spent in barriques, a third of them new. What distinguishes this St-Estèphe is its classic character, its depth and concentration, its firm, sound tannins. Besides oak notes, aroma and taste offer jammy red and black fruits, and also earthy aspects. The château is a former monastery, founded in 1662.

Ch Montrose map 15 H9
2ème cru

owner: Jean-Louis Charmolüe **area:** 68 ha **cases:** 27,000 **grape % R:** CS 65% MER 25% CF 10% **second wine:** La Dame de Montrose

33180 St-Estèphe tel: 05 56 59 30 12
fax: 05 56 59 38 48

Since the vintage of 1989 this estate has been one of the shining lights of Bordeaux. The wine of Montrose is nothing less than monumental: a colour dense as ink, a bouquet that is compact and at the same time richly faceted, and an expansive, muscular, very complex taste that lingers for minutes on end. Its aroma is at once spicy and very fruity, its oak of a high standard from 19 months in casks of which a third are new. Usually this St-Estèphe also shows a great wealth of ripe tannins, which means that it has to be laid down for at least 10 years. The château, a charming manor house, stands proudly with its chai on an extensive gravel slope not far from and overlooking the Gironde. It has belonged to the Charmolüe family since 1896. Its most famous owner in the 19th century was Mathieu Dolfuss, a very progressive character who, for example, let his workers share in the profits as well as paying their medical bills for them.

Ch Morin map 15 C5
cru bourgeois

owner: Maxime & Marguerite Sidaine **area:** 10 ha **cases:** 6,000 **grape % R:** MER 50% CS 48% PV 2%

33180 St-Estèphe tel: 05 56 59 30 53

This vineyard, founded in 1738, has now belonged to the same family for about two centuries. The wine is a somewhat old-fashioned kind of St-Estèphe, not really fine or concentrated, but not unpleasing. In its aroma and taste there can, for example, be dried fruit, plum, coffee and bayleaf – as well as aspects of old oak (since new casks are seldom if ever used for the 18 months of nurture).

Ch les Ormes de Pez map 15 E5
cru bourgeois

owner: Jean-Michel Cazes **area:** 32 ha **cases:** 15,000 **grape % R:** CS 55% MER 35% CF 10% **other châteaux owned:** Villa Bel Air (Graves); Ch Cordeillan-Bages (Pauillac); Ch Lynch-Bages (Pauillac)

33250 St-Estèphe tel: 05 56 73 24 00
fax: 05 56 59 26 42

In the wide range of crus bourgeois, this château is today among the best. The wine is characterized by an opaque colour and a generous taste that oozes fruit – blackcurrant, black cherry, plum, fig. Oak is discreetly present, from 15 months in used casks, and its tannins are ripe. This château won the Coupe des Crus Bourgeois for its vintages of 1989, 1990 and 1991 taken together. Since 1928 the property has belonged to the Cazes family of Ch Lynch-Bages, etc. The Lynch-Bages team also makes the wine here.

Ch La Peyre map 15 I4
owner: René Rabiller **area:** 7 ha **cases:** 3,800 **grape % R:** MER 50% CS 50% **second wine:** Ch Clos du Moulin

33180 St-Estèphe tel: 05 56 59 32 51
fax: 05 56 59 70 09

Estate that broke away from the local cooperative in 1994. It makes a supple, rounded, reasonably meaty and decently fruity wine. This is matured in casks of which a third are new. From 1989 to 1994 the owners also made a small amount of Haut-Médoc under the same name. They intend to enlarge the size of the vineyard by 5 ha.

Below: Ch les Ormes de Pez

Ch de Pez map 15 F5
owner: SC de Château de Pez/Louis Roederer **area:** 24 ha **cases:** 12,000 **grape % R:** CS 70% CF 15% MER 15% **second wine:** Ch La Salle de Pez **other châteaux owned:** Ch Haut-Beauséjour (St-Estèphe)

33180 St-Estèphe tel: 05 56 59 30 26

The origins of this château can be traced back to 1452, but it was only in 1749 that the first vines were planted. This came about through the illustrious Pontac family, then also the owners of Ch Haut-Brion and Ch Margaux. The wine is a refined, balanced, quite rounded St-Estèphe, in most years with decent concentration, low acidity, spicy fruit and oak from the 25% of new casks. Since 1995 the estate has belonged to Champagne Louis Roederer.

Ch Phélan-Ségur map 15 E8
cru bourgeois

owner: Xavier Gardinier **area:** 66 ha **cases:** 33,000 **grape % R:** CS 60% MER 30% CF 10% **second wine:** Frank Phélan

33180 St-Estèphe tel: 05 56 59 30 09
fax: 05 56 59 30 04

◆
Quantities

Figures are as supplied by the châteaux.

Area of vineyard: given in hectares, abbreviated to ha. Châteaux are asked to specify vineyards in production, and to exclude from their answers those owned but unplanted, and to advise when extensions are planned.

Production: given in cases of 12 bottles, each of 0.75 litres. A case is thus 9 litres. A hectolitre is 100 litres or just over 11 cases.

Yield per hectare: this can be obtained by multiplying the 'cases' figure by 9, to give litres, then dividing by 100, to give hectolitres. Then divide the result by the area in hectares.

The Phélan-Ségur estate came into being at the beginning of the 19th century, when the progressive Frank Phélan joined two properties together: Clos de Garamey and Ch Ségur. The Gardinier family took over this *cru bourgeois* in 1985, but they were very soon faced with three unsaleable vintages. A pesticide used in the vineyard had irreparably contaminated the 1983, 1984 and 1985. From 1986 onward Phélan-Ségur has produced a very good, well-matured wine with an attractive aroma. In good vintages this is meaty and lingering; among its nuances are jammy berry fruit and notes of cherry, as well as toast and vanilla from 15 months in *barriques*, 30% of them new. Supple tannins complete the picture. Investments made by the Gardiniers since taking over in 1985 have included a complete renovation of the 1820 château.

Ch Pomys
map 15 I6

cru bourgeois

owner: François Arnaud **area:** 10 ha **cases:** 7,500
grape % R: CS 50% MER 30% CF 20% **second wine:**
Le Blason de Pomys **other châteaux owned:** Ch
Saint-Estèphe *(St-Estèphe)*
33180 St-Estèphe tel: 05 56 59 32 26
fax: 05 56 59 35 24

In the 19th century this was one of the largest of St-Estèphe's estates, but frequent changes of ownership greatly reduced the size of the vineyard. In 1951, the year the Arnaud family took over, practically nothing was left. Gradually the Arnauds extended the vineyard once more, and then in 1991 a three-star hotel was opened in the stately château. The wine made here is a classic, firmly built St-Estèphe – mouthfilling, rounded and nicely provided with candied fruit and oak aromas. Maturing lasts 18 months in cask, a quarter of them new year.

Domaine de la Ronceray
map 15 F1

owner: SCEA des Domaines Pedro **area:** 3 ha
cases: 1,000 **grape % R:** CS 70% MER 30% **other
châteaux owned:** Ch Le Meynieu *(Haut-Médoc)*; Ch
Lavillotte *(St-Estèphe)*
33180 St-Estèphe tel: 05 56 41 98 17
fax: 05 56 41 98 89

Tobacco, leather, cedarwood, a slight bitter touch and good tannins are found in this wine made in classic style. It gets 20 months in cask.

Below: Ch Pomys

Above: Ch Saint Estèphe

Ch Saint Estèphe
map 15 I5

cru bourgeois

owner: François Arnaud **area:** 10 ha **cases:** 5,000
grape % R: CS 55% MER 30% CF 10% MAL 3% PV 2%
other châteaux owned: Ch Pomys *(St-Estèphe)*
33180 St-Estèphe tel: 05 56 59 32 26
fax: 05 56 59 35 24

A well-filled-out, generally powerful wine – not really rich in nuances, but with fruit and oak (from the 25% of new barrels). Very suitable for ageing in good years. The estate dates from 1870.

Ch Ségur de Cabanac
map 15 D9

cru bourgeois

owner: Guy Delon **area:** 6.3 ha **cases:** 3,000 **grape
% R:** CS 60% MER 30% PV 5% CF 5% **other châteaux
owned:** Ch Moulin de la Rose *(St-Julien)*
33180 St-Estèphe tel: 05 56 59 70 10
fax: 05 56 59 73 94

Guy Delon bought this estate in 1985, the year he took leave of Ch Phélan-Ségur. The wine has a fairly expansive, yet also rather angular profile, filled with soft fruit, firm tannins and the vanilla notes of oak: Delon's wine goes into casks, 30% of them new, for 20 months.

Ch Tour de Marbuzet
map 15 J8

cru bourgeois

owner: Henri Duboscq **area:** 7 ha **cases:** 3,750
grape % R: CS 40% MER 40% CF 20% **other châteaux
owned:** Ch Mac Carthy *(St-Estèphe)*; Ch Chambert-
Marbuzet *(St-Estèphe)*; Ch Haut-Marbuzet *(St-
Estèphe)*
33180 St-Estèphe tel: 05 56 59 30 54
fax: 05 56 59 70 87

This wine has a rather old-fashioned character. Tannin is clearly perceptible, and tends to dryness, while the fruit is juicy and often spicy as well. From each vintage 75% is matured in used wooden vats, the rest in new *barriques*. Since 1981 the estate has belonged to the Duboscq family, and the wine has improved; but it remains quite a way behind the same owner's Ch Haut-Marbuzet – including in price.

Ch Tour de Pez
map 15 E4

cru bourgeois

owner: Famille Bouchara **area:** 23 ha **cases:**
12,300 **grape % R:** CS 45% MER 40% CF 10% PV 5%
second wines: Ch Les Hauts de Pez; Ch l'Héreteyre
other châteaux owned: Ch du Caillou *(Graves)*
33180 St-Estèphe tel: 05 56 59 31 60
fax: 05 56 59 71 12

◆
Grape varieties

Main and other permitted varieties for each appellation are given in the appellation fact box at the end of the relevant introduction. For châteaux, percentages of grapes grown are given as supplied by the château.

The abbreviations used are:
CF Cabernet Franc,
COL Colombard, CS Cabernet Sauvignon,
MAL Malbec, MER Merlot, MUSC Muscadelle,
PV Petit Verdot, SAUV B Sauvignon Blanc,
SEM Sémillon

◆
Finding a second wine

To locate a second wine, consult the index which lists all châteaux in the Atlas.

Above: Ch Tour de Marbuzet

Above: Ch Tour des Termes

Since 1989 this estate's star has been strongly in the ascendant after total renovation and refurbishment by a new owner. The high standard is in part thanks to rigorous selection: until well into the 1990s less than a third of the vintage went out with the Tour de Pez label. The wine has a firm elegance, jammy fruit (blackcurrant, plum, fig), a good concentration, substantial tannins, and oak notes from a year and a half to two years in wood, of which new casks form a third.

Ch Tour des Termes   map 15 D5
cru bourgeois
owner: Jean Anney *area:* 16 ha *cases:* 7,500 *grape % R:* MER 50% CS 40% CF 5% PV 5% *second wine:* Ch St Corbian *other châteaux owned:* Ch Comtesse du Parc *(Haut-Médoc)*; Ch Haut-Baradieu *(St-Estèphe)*
**33180 St-Estèphe tel: 05 56 59 32 89
fax: 05 56 59 73 74**
The name comes from a medieval tower – still standing – on a site thought once to have held Roman baths. The château, a low, balconied building, has belonged to the Anney family since the 1930s. They make a decently concentrated wine here: spicy, fruity (jammy

Below: Ch Tronquoy-Lalande

currant, blackberry, cherry notes are apparent), and a slight mineral note. As a rule this St-Estèphe is agreeably drinkable after five years. Its touch of oak comes from an average 16 months in *barriques*, and a third of these are new each vintage.

Ch Tour Saint-Fort   map 15 G3
owner: SCA Laujac (J.L. Laffort) *area:* 10 ha *cases:* 5,500 *grape % R:* CS 53% MER 38% PV 5% CF 4% *second wine:* Baron d'Estours *other châteaux owned:* Ch Barreyre *(Premières Côtes de Bordeaux)*
**33180 St-Estèphe tel: 05 56 59 38 19
fax: 05 56 13 05 54**
Wine estate completely overhauled at the beginning of the 1990s; its 'château' consists of a massive white *chai* and *cuvier* block in the middle of the vines. The property was originally called Ch Tour St-Estèphe, but the name was changed to Tour Saint-Fort in 1992. The wine that has resulted from the investment is a balanced, mouthfilling creation, and its aroma holds nuances that include cedarwood and blackcurrant. It spends up to 18 months in cask (one-third new oak each year). Its tannins are supple. This is a château worth watching.

Ch Tronquoy-Lalande   map 15 G7
cru bourgeois
owner: Arlette Castéja-Texier *area:* 17 ha *cases:* 7,000 *grape % R:* MER 45% CS 45% PV 10% *second wine:* Tronquoy de Sainte-Anne
33180 St-Estèphe tel: 05 56 59 30 24
The attractive château, a *chartreuse* with the later addition of square corner towers, hardly suggests that in 1969 it was a total ruin. The present owner restored it lovingly with her husband, who died in 1973. A substantially-built St-Estèphe with adequate oak is made here – full of flavour, reasonably succulent, its range of fruit notes including plum, prune, cherry, blackcurrant. Earthy and spicy elements may also appear, and a hint of tobacco.

Ch Vieux Coutelin   map 15 I5
owner: SA/Vignobles Rocher-Cap de Rive *area:* 6 ha *cases:* 3,300 *grape % R:* CS 75% MER 25% *second wine:* Chevalier Coutelin *other châteaux owned:* include Ch Cap d'Or *(St-Georges-St-Emilion)*
**33250 St-Estèphe tel: 05 57 40 08 88
fax: 05 57 40 19 93**
Prune and other dark fruit characterize the aroma of this sound St-Estèphe. Sometimes there is a herbaceous touch – and always some oak, for it spends 10-12 months in cask.

MOULIS-EN-MÉDOC AND LISTRAC-MÉDOC

Well to the west of the D2 *route des châteaux* – that temptress which leads you enticingly past so many of the great names of the Left Bank – lie the Haut-Médoc's two junior village appellations, Moulis-en-Médoc and Listrac-Médoc. These two communes sit almost exactly halfway up the Haut-Médoc, with a band of its vineyards separating them from Margaux to the south-east and St-Julien to the north-east. Unlike the four great Médoc names whose vineyards sweep down to the Gironde and possessively straddle the D2, Moulis and Listrac are relatively discreet, well hidden inland among the forests which close in more completely the further west you go.

Nor are their wines especially well-known, although they were fashionable in the eighteenth century and a few of the top names like Chasse-Spleen and Fourcas-Hosten have long enjoyed a good reputation. Neither district had any châteaux in the 1855 Classification – not because they were refused, but because they were not particularly interested in participating. However, some of the better wines were at *cru classé* level even then, and today, though this is essentially *cru bourgeois* country, some wines rival the 1855 châteaux.

Well-draining gravel is the *raison d'être* of these two appellations. Go much further west into the forests and you encounter soils of pure sand, making quality wine impossible. Here, however, the gravel layers – very similar to those which provide sites for the great riverside

The rose garden
at Château Clarke

classed growths – form attractive ridges with well-drained, gentle slopes on which the grapes flourish. An added advantage is that on this land, slightly higher in altitude and far removed from the humid influence of the river, rot is less of a problem and harvesting can take place later, when the grapes have had a better chance of ripening.

MOULIS-EN-MÉDOC

This is the smallest of the Médoc appellations. It produces slightly less wine than Listrac and well under half that of St-Estèphe, the largest of the four great Médoc names. Vineyards cover almost the entire surface area of the commune, nearly all enjoying the Moulis-en-Médoc appellation – though a tiny area of vines (roughly one per cent of the total) has the right to the neighbouring Listrac name, while somewhat more land has the Haut-Médoc AC. The commune is long and narrow in shape, running in a band from north-east to south-west. The vineyards are all in the north-east, straddling the D5 road which runs through the village of Grand-Poujeaux – where nearly every building is a wine château – on through the (even smaller) hamlet of Moulis-en-Médoc itself, to the junction with the N215 at Bouqueran.

There are just under 40 properties here making their own wine, most of which are classified as *crus bourgeois*. Cabernet Sauvignon is the main grape, ideally suited to the gravel soil – although some estates do have a

The village of Listrac, with the church spire rising in the distance

higher percentage of Merlot. At least one château – La Garricq – uses a lot of Petit Verdot (20 per cent as opposed to the usual 5-10 per cent grown in this appellation).

The style of wines in Moulis aspires to combine some of the subtlety of Margaux with the power of a St-Julien. They have finesse plus generous body, and can take 7-10 years to reach maturity. Many are quite tannic in youth, especially those where a high percentage of new oak has been used – a fashion which is increasing here as the reputation of these wines grows.

LISTRAC-MÉDOC

To the north of Moulis and surrounded by forest, this commune boasts the highest point of the Médoc, a spot beside the N215 road which attains 43 metres: the height is crowned by an observation tower to keep watch for forest fires. The commune takes in a block of mostly vineyard land astride the N215, plus wide swathes of forest to the west. Listrac is slightly larger than its neighbouring appellation but still produces less wine than St-Julien, the smallest of the top four Médoc appellations. There are some 29 *crus bourgeois* here. The local cooperative is important too, and is responsible for roughly a quarter of total production.

These are well-structured wines, perhaps without quite as much staying-power or concentration as a top Moulis, but nonetheless with a good tannic framework and quite full, meaty flavours. They begin to drink well some five years after the vintage.

THE APPELLATIONS

LISTRAC-MÉDOC (red)

Location: *About 33 km north-west of Bordeaux, with Margaux to the south-east and St-Julien to the north-east. To its immediate south is Moulis; immediately north and east is Haut-Médoc land. There are no vineyards to its west, nor in the western portion of the commune.*
Area of AC: *1,368 ha*
Area under vine: *700 ha*
Communes: *Listrac, plus precisely defined parcels of Moulis-en-Médoc*
Average annual production: *290,000 cases*
Classed growths: *None*
Others: *29 crus bourgeois, 12 others*
Cooperatives: *1 (c. 60 members)*
Main grape varieties: *Cabernet Sauvignon, Merlot*
Others: *Cabernet Franc, Petit Verdot*
Main soil types: *Gravel, clay-limestone*

MOULIS-EN-MÉDOC (red)

Location: *About 30 km north-west of Bordeaux. To the south-east lies Margaux, separated from Moulis by Haut-Médoc vineyards. Immediately to the north is Listrac-Médoc, then more Haut-Médoc land before the next senior Médoc appellation, St-Julien, some 12 km north-east.*
Area of AC: *1,078 ha*
Area under vine: *575 ha*
Communes: *Moulis-en-Médoc, plus precisely defined parcels of Arcins, Castelnau-de-Médoc, Lamarque and Listrac-Médoc*
Average annual production: *275,000 cases*
Classed growths: *None*
Others: *31 crus bourgeois, 13 others*
Cooperatives: *None*
Main grape varieties: *Cabernet Sauvignon, Merlot*
Others: *Cabernet Franc, Petit Verdot*
Main soil types: *Sand and gravel, clay, limestone*

APPELLATION LISTRAC-MÉDOC

Ch Bibian Tigana
map 17 F5

owner: Jean Tigana **area:** 24 ha **cases:** 10,000
grape % R: MER 60% CS 35% PV 5% **second wine:** Ch
Pierre Bibian
33480 Listrac-Médoc tel: 05 56 58 05 47
fax: 05 56 58 06 86

After he became fascinated by wine – thanks to
the cellarmaster at Ch Ducru-Beaucaillou in St-
Julien – the celebrated French soccer player
Jean Tigana bought the badly neglected Ch
Pierre Bibian in Listrac. The estate cost him
around 6 million francs; restoring the vineyard,
cellars and château almost three times as
much. The wine from this reborn property, now
called Ch Bibian Tigana, is notable for its firm,
sometimes rather dry tannins, its earthy aroma
with its hint of licorice, its plummy fruit and
generally good concentration. Only 10% of the
maturing barrels for this Listrac are new.

Ch Cap Léon Veyrin
map 17 B5

cru bourgeois
owner: Alain Meyre **area:** 30 ha **cases:** 15,000
grape % R: MER 55% CS 40% PV 5% **second wine:** Ch
Julien (Haut-Médoc)
33480 Listrac-Médoc tel: 05 56 58 07 28
fax: 05 56 58 07 50

A vineyard created in 1910, out by itself in the
north of the appellation. The château is
hospitable (you can stay there), has a small
museum of cellar and cooperage tools, and
cherishes a series of vintages going back to
1929. The wine is usually a deep-coloured,
meaty one; rich in extract and made in
traditional style. Among its nuances are black
fruit and restrained oak – from maturing for a
year in casks of which 20% are new. Apart from
an occasional vintage – such as 1990 with its
tart, appley tannins – Ch Cap Léon Veyrin
displays a consistent, very correct quality. This
is emphasized by the various medals won.

Ch Clarke
map 17 G6

cru bourgeois
owner: Baron Edmond de Rothschild/Compagnie
Vinicole des Barons de Rothschild **area:** 55 ha
cases: 29,500, white 900 **grape % R:** CS 48% MER
42% CF 8% PV 2% **grape % W:** SAUV 50% SEM 30%
MUSC 20% **second wine:** Les Granges des Domaines
Edmond de Rothschild (Haut-Médoc) **other**

Below: Ch Cap Léon Veyrin

Above: Ch Clarke

châteaux owned: Ch Peyre-Lebade (Listrac-Médoc);
Ch Malmaison (Moulis-en-Médoc) **other wines:** Le
Merle Blanc (Bordeaux blanc)
33480 Listrac-Médoc tel: 05 56 58 38 00
fax: 05 56 58 26 46

Baron Edmond de Rothschild, entrepreneur and
joint-owner of Ch Lafite Rothschild, decided in
1973 to buy a vineyard of his own in the Médoc.
His choice fell on Ch Clarke. This estate (named
after the Irish family who owned it for two
centuries from 1750) existed only in name by
the 1970s – for the previous owner had
uprooted the whole vineyard. Planting and the
laying out of a drainage system began in 1974.
It was to be 10 years before all the work had
been carried out. One investment made for
every vintage is in new *barriques*: 40-60% of
the stock. Partly because of this high
proportion of new wood, Ch Clarke is always a
polished wine, with creamy vanilla. In addition
there's the seductive fruit of cherry,
blackcurrant and plum – sometimes it is almost
sweet. The tannins are supple, and the wine has
a certain finesse. Le Merle Blanc, a floral, fresh
Bordeaux also marked by oak, comes from 2 ha
of Sauvignon, Sémillon and Muscadelle.

Clos des Demoiselles
map 17 H4

owner: Jacques de Pourquery **area:** 3.5 ha **cases:**
1,800 **grape % R:** CS 60% MER 40% **other châteaux
owned:** Ch Branas Grand Poujeaux (Moulis-en-
Médoc)
33480 Listrac-Médoc tel: 05 56 58 05 12
fax: 05 56 58 02 44

Estate on comparatively high ground in Listrac,
close to the fire tower south of the village. It
produces a good-value, generally excellent wine.
This offers a dark colour and a stimulating,
succulent, full taste with candied black fruit,
powerful tannins, the rarely-overdone influence
of oak (25% of the casks are new, and the
maturing period is 18 months), and a sound
balance. Unfortunately the quantity is very
limited – just 1,800 cases a year.

Ch Ducluzeau
map 17 H2

owner: Madame Jean-Eugène Borie/Famille Borie
area: 4.5 ha **cases:** 2,500 **grape % R:** MER 90% CS
10% **other châteaux owned:** Ch Grand-Puy-Lacoste
(Pauillac); Ch Haut-Batailley (Pauillac); Ch Ducru-
Beaucaillou (St-Julien); Ch Lalande-Borie (St-Julien)
33480 Listrac-Médoc tel: 05 56 59 05 20
fax: 05 56 59 27 37

An honest – and often delicious – wine with a
reasonably firm constitution. It is made from
90% Merlot and as a result is rounded, with
earthy notes, bayleaf and rich black fruit.
Usually it begins to show its charms after about
five years. Matured in used casks only, for 14
months. This wine has been back on the market
under its own name since 1976, after years of
being produced by the Listrac cooperative.

Ch Fonréaud
map 17 H4

cru bourgeois
owner: Héritiers Chanfreau **area:** 30 ha **cases:**
18,500 **grape % R:** CS 63% MER 35% PV 2% **second
wine:** Ch Fontaine Royale **other wines:** Le Cygne de
Château Fonréaud (Bordeaux blanc) **other châteaux
owned:** Ch Lestage (Listrac-Médoc); Ch Caroline
(Moulis-en-Médoc); Ch Chemin Royal (Moulis-en-
Médoc)
33480 Listrac-Médoc tel: 05 56 58 02 43
fax: 05 56 58 04 33

The name Fonréaud is said to come from
fontaine royale: in the 11th century a king of
England is said to have discovered a spring
here. The prominent château, near the D2 road,
was built in 1855 and since 1962 has belonged
to the Chanfreau family. The wine is a classic
Listrac of sound average structure and quality,
containing a good deal of tannin. Its fruit –
blackcurrant – is complemented by spicy oak, a
third of the barrels being new for each vintage.
Ch Fonréaud sometimes shows great

◆
About Listrac
The Syndicat Viticole de Listrac-Médoc is at
the Mairie, 33480 Listrac-Médoc.
Tel 05 56 58 03 16.

◆
Rosé and clairet
When an estate also produces a rosé
and/or clairet, the production has been
added to that of the red wine in the
statistics for the château.

MOULIS & LISTRAC

17

N

1:45,500

0   1   2km

MÉDOC

RIVE
DROITE

Bordeaux

ENTRE-DEUX-
MERS

GRAVES &
SAUTERNES

Ch Cap Léon Veyrin

Donissan

Ch Donissan
Ch l'Ermitage
Ch Reverdi

Couhenne

Ch
La Lauzette

Ch
Bellegrave

ST-LAURENT-
ET-BENON

Ch Fourcas
Loubaney

Ch La Bécade

Ch
Gobinaud

Ch Lafon

Ch Fourcas
Dupré

le Fourcas

L I S T R A C - M É D O C

Ch Peyredon Lagravette

Ch Maucaillou &
Dom de Maucaillou

LAMARQUE

Ch Sansarot-
Dupré

le Tris

Ch Haut Brugas

Médrac
Ch Galland

D5. E2

Ch La Closerie du Grand Poujeaux
Ch Bel-Air Lagrave &
Ch Haut-Franquet

Ch Poujeaux

la Potence

Ch
Liounier

Ch du Fourcas
Ch Fourcas Hosten
Ch Bibian Tigana

Grand-Poujeaux
Ch Tour-Granins

Ch Lestage-Darquier

Ch Franquet Grand Poujeaux
Ch Granins Grand Poujeaux

Ch Gressier Grand Poujeaux
Ch Branas Grand Poujeaux

Libardac

Ch Vieux Moulin &
Grand Listrac Co-op

Ch Peyre-
Lebade

Ch Dutruch
Grand Poujeaux

Ch Chasse-
Spleen

Listrac-Médoc

Ch Rose
Ste-Croix

D208

Ruisseau de Larrayaut

D5

Ch Sémeillan Mazeau &
Ch Decorde

Ch Lestage

Ch Malmaison

Ch
Clarke

M O U L I S - E N - M É D O C

Ch Sémeillan

Ch Anthonic

Ch Fonréaud, Ch Caroline &
Ch Chemin Royal

Clos des
Démoiselles

Ch La Garricq

Ch Brillette

Ruisseau du Pont d'Eysson

Estey du Houguey

Jalle de Tiquetorte

Ch Lalande

Ch
Ducluzeau

Moulis-en-Médoc

Clos de la Rose de Graves
le Petit-Poujeaux

Ch Mayne Lalande &
Ch Myon de l'Enclos

Ch Ruat Petit Poujeaux

Ch La Mouline

Ch Duplessis
Hauchecorne

Ch Biston-
Brillette

Ch Citran

Barbat

Ch Moulin
à Vent

Ch Bouqueyran

la Jallette

Ch Semonlon

Bouqueyran

Ch Lacour
Bouqueyran

Ch Moulis

Barreau

A V E N S A N

Ch Mauvesin

le Pont

Primat
Dom de Primat

Ch Pomeys

MARGAUX

Ch de Villegeorge

D105

Ch Tour Carrelot

le Haut

agorce Bernadas
mbert

Avensan

Castelnau-de-Médoc

Ch
Meyre

D105

BORDEAUX

D207

N215   D1

SALAUNES

Villeranque

ARSAC

Vineyards

Woods

Commune boundary

AC Moulis-en-Médoc

Canton boundary

AC Listrac Médoc

Contour line

1   2   3   4   5   6   7   8   9   10

A

B

C

D

E

F

G

H

I

J

K

L

M

Above: Ch Fonréaud

fluctuations in quality: in the lesser years the wine can taste rather thin and herbaceous. Le Cygne, a lively, engaging and enjoyable white Bordeaux which is fermented in cask, is produced here from 2 ha.

Ch du Fourcas
map 17 E4

owner: SCA du Château du Fourcas *area:* 30 ha
cases: 16,500 *grape % R:* MER 50% CS 40% PV 10%
second wine: Ch Moulin du Bourg; Ch Hautegrave-Tris *other wines:* Bordeaux Clairet
33480 Listrac-Médoc tel: 05 56 58 03 84
fax: 05 56 58 01 20
Since the beginning of the 1990s the wine made here has been one of Listrac's rising stars. It characteristically tastes creamy and stylish, with smooth fruit (black cherry, bilberry) and integrated tannins, plus a fine framework from its maturing, which lasts a year or longer in casks of which half are new. The estate was formed by combining Chx Fourcas and Moulin du Bourg, both of them among the oldest in this commune.

Ch Fourcas Dupré
map 17 D4

cru bourgeois
owner: Patrice Pagès *area:* 44 ha *cases:* 20,000
grape % R: CS 50% MER 38% CF 10% PV 2% *second wine:* Ch Bellevue Laffont
33480 Listrac-Médoc tel: 05 56 58 01 07
fax: 05 56 58 02 27
From the map made by Belleyme, geographer to Louis XV, it appears that there was already a vineyard on the site of Fourcas Dupré; the estate is therefore at least two centuries old. Since 1967 it has been run with drive and energy by the Pagès family. They make an expressive and attractive wine, in good years duly replete with notes of red and black fruit, mint, spice, supple tannins and smooth, toasty oak – from a year spent in barrels of which 20-25% are new.

Ch Fourcas Hosten
map 17 F4

cru bourgeois
owners: B de Rivoyre, P Pagès & H Schÿler *area:* 43 ha *cases:* 20,000 *grape % R:* CS 50% MER 40% CF 10% *second wine:* Chartreuse d'Hosten *other châteaux owned:* Ch Fourcas Dupré (*Listrac-Médoc*); Ch Kirwan (*Margaux*)
33480 Listrac-Médoc tel: 05 56 58 01 15
fax: 05 56 58 06 73

The château is a wide, low *chartreuse* of 1810, set on a small hill in the centre of the village of Listrac, close to the Romanesque church. A fine park in English style has been laid out on the slope, and hundreds of cyclamen bloom there in autumn. The vineyard comprises two large plots on different types of soil: one gravel, the other clay. When young, the wine often tastes rather austere; but in the course of time the tannins and the oak (from a year in *barriques*, 20% of them new) retreat somewhat in favour of refined berry, plum and fruit notes. This Listrac seldom shows great concentration: its structure tends rather to the athletic and elegant.

Ch Fourcas Loubaney
map 17 C4

cru bourgeois
owner: Altus Finances (Crédit Lyonnais) *area:* 46 ha
cases: 23,000 *grape % R:* CS 60% MER 30% PV 10%
second wines: Ch La Bécade; Ch Moulin de Laborde; Ch La Fleur-Bécade; La Closerie de Fourcas-Loubaney
33480 Listrac-Médoc tel: 05 56 58 03 83
fax: 05 56 58 06 30
An estate considerably enlarged since 1989: its original 4 ha is now 46 ha, and this is to be increased to 50. This expansion has been brought about by the addition of two other

Below: Ch Fourcas Dupré

Above: Ch Gobinaud

châteaux: Moulin de Laborde and La Bécade. These two names are used for superior second wines – there are also regular second wines: La Closerie de Fourcas Loubaney and Ch La Fleur Bécade. Only 20% of the total production is sold as Ch Fourcas Loubaney, so the selection is rigorous. For a Listrac this wine has a notably smooth, creamy, rounded taste. Soft, succulent fruit is often abundantly present in blackcurrant and ripe cherry form, as well as the toast-and-vanilla elements of the new oak – half the casks – in which it matures for 18 months. This Fourcas has the standard of a *cru classé*, and the Ch Moulin de Laborde and Ch La Bécade are certainly not to be overlooked.

Ch Gobinaud
map 17 C7

owner: Fréres Gobinaud *area:* 10 ha *cases:* 4,500
grape % R: CS 40% MER 40% CF 10% PV 10% *second wine:* Domaine de Capdeville; Ch Les Marcieuse
33480 Listrac-Médoc tel: 05 56 58 03 36
For many generations, since the early 19th century, the Gobinauds have been making wine up on the Marcieux plateau in Listrac. The present owners – two brothers – work to produce a sound, full-bodied, *cru artisan* Listrac with fruit, firm tannins, and a slightly rustic touch of oak.

Above: Ch Lalande

Above: Ch Mayne Lalande

Ch Lafon   map 17 D7
cru bourgeois
owner: Jean-Pierre Théron *area:* 12.9 ha *cases:*
7,200 *grape % R:* CS 55% MER 45% *second wine:*
Ch Les Hauts Marcieux *other châteaux owned:* Ch
de Portets (*Graves*)
33480 Listrac-Médoc tel: 05 56 58 01 09
fax: 05 56 67 33 47
Sound Listrac, generally with adequate
amounts of fruit and a firm structure, as well as
tannin and spicy notes. Oak-ageing is applied
only in the great vintages. The château stands
in a small, isolated hamlet surrounded by
woods a few kilometres from Listrac.

Ch Lalande   map 17 H2
cru bourgeois
owner: EARL Darriet Lescoutra *area:* 10 ha *cases:*
6,000 *grape % R:* MER 60% CS 30% PV 10%
33480 Listrac-Médoc tel: 05 56 58 19 45
fax: 05 56 58 15 62
Rather rustic wine with a lot of tannin that
sometimes spends up to 21 months maturing:
currently 30% of the casks are new each year.
The estate usually has various older vintages in
stock, from up to 8 or 10 years back.

Ch La Lauzette   map 17 C7
owner: Jean-Louis Declercq *area:* 13 ha *cases:*
7,000 *grape % R:* CS 47% MER 46% PV 5% CF 2%
second wine: Galets de Couhenne
33480 Listrac-Médoc tel: 05 56 58 02 40
In 1981 the Belgian Jean-Louis Declercq bought
the Ch Bellegrave vineyard in Listrac – but
some years later, and for not altogether
comprehensible reasons, he was obliged to
relinquish the use of that name. With the help
of the *cru bourgeois* syndicate and others, the
new name of Ch La Lauzette was finally chosen,
and used from the 1993 vintage. The wine is a
concentrated, firmly structured Listrac, nearly
always generously provided with tannins. In its
aroma there is often toast (the wine spends 18
months in *barriques,* 40% of them new), spice
and berry fruit. This wine represents one of the
sure and certain values of this appellation.

Ch Lestage   map 17 G5
cru bourgeois
owner: Hérities Chanfreau *area:* 44 ha *cases:*
12,500 *grape % R:* MER 52% CS 46% PV 2% *second*

wine: La Dame de Coeur du Château Lestage *other*
châteaux owned: Ch Fonréaud (*Listrac-Médoc*); Ch
Caroline (*Moulis-en-Médoc*); Ch Chemin Royal
(*Moulis-en-Médoc*)
33480 Listrac-Médoc tel: 05 56 58 02 43
fax: 05 56 58 04 33
The château, a superb example of 19th-century
architecture from the time of Napoléon III, is
more outstanding than its wine. This is made in
a fairly accessible, fruity style, firm and meaty.
A third of the maturing casks are new each year.

Ch Liounier   map 17 F2
cru bourgeois
owner: EARL Bosq & fils *area:* 25 ha *cases:*
15,000 *grape % R:* CS 50% MER 40% PV 10% *second*
wine: Ch Cantegric *other wines:* Bordeaux Clairet
33480 Listrac-Médoc tel: 05 56 58 04 38
fax: 05 56 58 01 21
Vineyard spread over many plots where a
somewhat old-fashioned, but soundly
constructed, Listrac is produced, a wine that
can often rather lack fruit and charm. It tastes
best after considerable bottle-age. It is matured
in wood, and 20% of the barrels are new.
Besides its red wines Liounier also makes a
Bordeaux Clairet.

Domaine de Maucaillou   map 17 D9
cru bourgeois
owner: Philippe Dourthe *area:* 4 ha *cases:* 2,200
grape % R: MER 90% CS 10% *other châteaux owned:*
Ch Maucaillou Felletin (*Haut-Médoc*); Ch Duplessis-
Fabre (*Moulis-en-Médoc*); Ch Maucaillou (*Moulis-en-
Médoc*)
33480 Listrac-Médoc tel: 05 56 58 01 23
fax: 05 56 58 00 88
Wine vinified by the team from Ch Maucaillou
in Moulis. It is a Listrac dominated by its
Merlot, with licorice, spices, bayleaf, a little
pepper, animal scents, oak and an average
concentration. The estate's first vintage
appeared in 1988.

Ch Mayne Lalande   map 17 H2
cru bourgeois
owner: Bernard Lartigue *area:* 16 ha *cases:* 8,200
grape % R: MER 45% CS 45% CF 5% PV 5% *second*
wine: Ch Malbec Lartigue *other châteaux owned:*
Ch Myon de l'Enclos (*Moulis-en-Médoc*)
33480 Listrac-Médoc tel: 05 56 58 27 63
fax: 05 56 58 22 41

In 1973 Bernard Lartigue decided to become a
winegrower. Together with his wife he gradually
expanded this small family vineyard, which had
been sending its grapes to the cooperative, and
launched the first wine of his own in 1982. This
was very positively received, and the same has
held good for the subsequent vintages. Two
versions of Ch Mayne Lalande have emerged:
the standard one matures for 18 months in
wood (30% of the casks are new), and is a
concentrated, powerful, full-bodied wine with a
good balance between its fruity, earthy and
tannin aspects. Still more classic in both style
and nurture is the special *cuvée* labelled Grande
Réserve, with its long, lingering finish –
Lartigue ages this wine in barrel for an amazing
three years.

Ch Peyredon Lagravette   map 17 E8
cru bourgeois
owner: Paul Hostein *area:* 7 ha *cases:* 3,500
grape % R: CS 65% MER 35% *second wine:* Ch
Cazeau Vieil
33480 Listrac-Médoc tel: 05 56 58 05 55
fax: 05 56 58 05 50
This is a most reliable wine, made with great
respect for tradition. It has an agreeable
personality and practically always a
mouthfilling, generous taste. Maturing at this

Locating a château on a map
To locate a château from its entry in the
Atlas, note the map number and the
letter/number grid reference given next to
the château name. Maps are listed on
pages 6 & 7. The grid reference locates
the château within a 2cm square. Grid
numbers are also given in the
index/gazetteer.

Finding a second wine
To locate a second wine or any other wine
not listed in the appellation's Directory
pages, consult the index. Not all second
wines use the same appellation as the
château's *grand vin.*

Above: Ch Peyre-Lebade

Above: Ch Sémeillan Mazeau

estate lasts 18 months – 25% of the casks are
new – and brings out berry fruit and toast
aromas in the wine. The tannins are firm, but
not aggressive. The château and its cellars were
built in 1868.

Ch Peyre-Lebade   map 17 F6
cru bourgeois
owner: Compagnie Vinicole des Barons de
Rothschild **area:** 56 ha **cases:** 32,000 **grape % R:**
MER 58% CS 37% CF 5% **second wine:** Les Granges
des Domaines Rothschild (Haut-Médoc) **other
châteaux owned:** Ch Malmaison (Moulis-en-Médoc);
Ch Clarke (Listrac-Médoc)
**33480 Listrac-Médoc tel: 05 56 58 38 00
fax: 05 56 58 26 46**
Baron Edmond de Rothschild, of (among other
estates) Ch Clarke, acquired Ch Peyre-Lebade in
1979. The first five years of Baron Edmond's
ownership were marked by great activity, with
the laying out of a new drainage system, the
complete replanting of 55 ha of vineyard, the
construction of a new *cuvier* and *chai*, and the
restoration of the other buildings. At first the
wine was sold as a generic Haut-Médoc: only
with the 1988 vintage was it deemed good
enough to carry the château name and the
Listrac-Médoc appellation. The wine is deep in
colour, quite aromatic, rounded and boasts
supple tannins and spicy candied fruit; but
there is no great complexity to it. The oak
aspects come from the 14-16 months it spends
ageing in one-year-old *barriques*. As the
vineyard matures the wine may gain in depth
and interest.

Ch Reverdi   map 17 C5
cru bourgeois
owner: Christian Thomas **area:** 25 ha **cases:**
14,500 **grape % R:** CS 50% MER 50% **second wine:**
Ch Croix de Laborde; Ch l'Ermitage
**33480 Listrac-Médoc tel: 05 56 58 02 25
fax: 05 56 58 06 56**
This Listrac used to taste rather dour, but since
the 1986 vintage it has gained greater charm
and quality. Ch Reverdi is now an agreeable,
very correct wine in classic style that after five
years achieves a smooth and also powerful taste,
with elements of cedar, tobacco, spicy oak from
the 15% of new casks, and fruit such as prune.
In the less successful vintages the tannins may
be somewhat dry.

Ch Rose Ste-Croix   map 17 F4
owner: Philippe Porcheron **area:** 13 ha **cases:**
5,500 **grape % R:** MER 60% CS 37% PV 3% **second
wine:** Ch Bellevue Lagravette (Haut-Médoc)
**33480 Moulis-en-Médoc tel: 05 56 58 14 24
fax: 05 56 58 14 24**
A straightforward Listrac of decent quality and
traditional character that benefits from bottle-
age. The grapes are carefully selected,
fermentation takes place in stainless-steel tanks
and maturing lasts for two years, in casks of
which 30% are new. The owners also run an
inn, with rooms and a simple restaurant, and a
wine shop.

Ch Sansarot-Dupré   map 17 E4
cru bourgeois
owner: Yves Raymond **area:** 14 ha **cases:** 6,000,
white 1,000 **grape % R:** MER 65% CS 30% CF 5%
grape % W: SEM 55% SAUV 40% MUSC 5% **second
wine:** Ch Pérac **other wines:** Bordeaux blanc
**33480 Listrac-Médoc tel: 05 56 58 03 02
fax: 05 56 58 07 64**
The Domaine de Sansarot was mentioned as
long ago as 1735, but it only became a wine
estate some 110 years later. Then Adolphe
Dupré renovated the *Directoire*-style château
and laid out an attractive park. The Raymond
family acquired Ch Sansarot-Dupré in 1875 and
have been there ever since. The present owner,
a qualified oenologist, makes a dependable wine
full of candied fruit, integrated tannins, forest
aromas and oak; it has grip and at the same
time a certain grace. Its quality has been
reliable down the years. A fairly generous,
meaty white wine is also made here: a smooth,
expressive Bordeaux fermented in cask.

Ch Sémeillan Mazeau   map 17 G3
cru bourgeois
owner: GFA familial Sémeillan Mazeau **area:** 17 ha
cases: 8,333 **grape % R:** MER 50% CS 50% **second
wine:** Ch Decorde
**33480 Listrac-Médoc tel: 05 56 58 01 12
fax: 05 56 58 01 57**
A wine that has won many medals. This Listrac
is full of flavour, with berry and cherry fruit,
licorice, spice, woodland notes and vanilla –
plus good tannins and a sound average
structure. Its maturing lasts a year in barrels of
which 20% are new.

Above: Ch Sansarot-Dupré

Ch Vieux Moulin   map 17 F4
owner: Fort-Dufau **area:** 6 ha **cases:** 3,000 **grape %
R:** CS 47% MER 38% PV 15%
**33480 Listrac-Médoc tel: 05 56 58 03 19
fax: 05 56 58 07 22**
This is the most interesting of the château
wines vinified by the cooperative at Listrac.
Since the 1986 vintage it has been matured for
a year in used barrels. Tannin, spice and black
fruit are usually among its features. It has won
several gold medals.

APPELLATION MOULIS-EN-MÉDOC

Ch Anthonic
map 17 G7

cru bourgeois

owner: Pierre Cordonnier **area:** 21.5 ha **cases:**
10,000 **grape % R:** CS 50% MER 45% PV 5% **second**
wine: Le Malinay

33480 Moulis-en-Médoc tel: 05 56 58 34 60

fax: 05 56 58 06 22

In good years the wine is a full-bodied,
complete Moulis with firm, ripe tannins, quite
toasty oak from 18 months in *barriques* (a
quarter to a third of them new), considerable
fruit and decent concentration. Ch Anthonic is
not, perhaps, at the pinnacle of finesse, but it is
a sound and pleasing wine. The estate has had
other names since it was founded in the late
18th century: Ch Puy de Menjon, Ch Graves de
Gueytignan, and Ch Le Malinay (now used for
the second wine).

Ch Bel-Air Lagrave
map 17 B9

cru bourgeois

owner: Jean-Paul Bacquey **area:** 8 ha **cases:** 3,000
grape % R: CS 65% MER 30% PV 5% **second wines:**
Ch Peyvigneau; Le Dauphin de Bel-Air Lagrave **other**
châteaux owned: Ch La Closerie du Grand Poujeaux
(Moulis-en-Médoc); Ch Haut-Franquet *(Moulis-en-
Médoc)*

33480 Moulis-en-Médoc tel: 05 56 58 01 89

fax: 05 56 58 05 21

Licorice, bayleaf, black fruit, oak and ripe,
rounded tannins are characteristic of this
competently made Moulis. The owner tries to
pick the grapes as late as possible, and ages the
wine for 15 20 months in casks of which 25-
50% are new. This château has belonged to the
same family for around 150 years. The vineyard
is to be extended by 4 ha.

Ch Biston-Brillette
map 17 H7

cru bourgeois

owner: Michel Barbarin **area:** 21.5 ha **cases:** 9,000
grape % R: CS 55% MER 40% PV 5% **second wine:** Ch
Graveyron

33480 Moulis-en-Médoc tel: 05 56 58 22 86

fax: 05 56 58 13 16

Vineyard divided off in 1930 from Ch Brillette.
It was created at the beginning of the 19th
century by a certain M. Biston. This is a very
reliable wine, not least because of the stringent
selection process: in 1992, for example, only

55% of the total crop was given the Biston-
Brillette label. This Moulis is made in a fairly
classic style – fragrant, elegant, with a firm core
and good tannins, plus ripe blackcurrant and
flattering smoky oak from a 15-month stay in
wood (about a third of the barrels are new), and
a fine balance.

Ch Branas Grand Poujeaux
map 17 F9

owner: Jacques de Pourquery **area:** 6 ha **cases:**
3,500 **grape % R:** CS 50% MER 45% PV 5% **other**
châteaux owned: Clos des Demoiselles *(Listrac-
Médoc)*

33480 Moulis-en-Médoc tel: 05 56 58 03 07

Exemplary wine – dark-coloured, athletic in
build, expressive – with jammy berry fruit,
integrated tannins, bayleaf, low acidity and
restrained oak. Half the production spends 18
months in *barriques* of which 25% are new, and
the other half in tanks.

Ch Brillette
map 17 G7

cru bourgeois

owner: Jean-Louis Flageul **area:** 36 ha **cases:**
15,000 **grape % R:** CS 50% MER 40% PV 5% CF 5%
second wine: Ch Berthault Brillette

33480 Moulis-en-Médoc tel: 05 56 58 22 09

fax: 05 56 58 12 26

By about 1960 only 3 ha of this vineyard was
still producting, but since then the property has
been thoroughly overhauled and renewed by
successive owners. At its best Ch Brillette is a
rounded, fairly supple, succulent wine with
power and fruit (blackcurrant, cherry), made
from 40% Merlot. In less-good years, however,
the wine can lack body and be rather
herbaceous. The spicy oak tones result from 12
months in wood: a third of casks are new.

Ch Caroline
map 17 H4

cru bourgeois

owner: Famille Chanfreau **area:** 7 ha **cases:** 2,500
grape % R: MER 55% CS 45% **other châteaux owned:**
Ch Lestage *(Listrac-Médoc)*; Ch Chemin Royal
(Moulis-en-Médoc); Ch Fonréaud *(Listrac-Médoc)*

33480 Moulis-en-Médoc tel: 05 56 58 02 43

fax: 05 56 58 04 33

This wine appears under two labels – the
owner's and that of the *négociants* Robert
Giraud. Ch Caroline used to carry the Listrac

appellation, as it was then a second label of Ch
Lestage; that is where it is still made. In quality
it is a wine without great depth, at times rather
angular and lacking in charm, but sometimes
quite supple and pleasingly fruity.

Ch Chasse-Spleen
map 17 F9

cru bourgeois

owner: Claire Villars/Famille Merlaut **area:** 75 ha
cases: 37,000; white 600 **grape % R:** CS 65% MER
30% PV 5% **grape % W:** SEM 70% SAUV 30% **second**
wines: L'Oratoire de Chasse-Spleen; L'Ermitage de
Chasse Spleen *(Haut-Médoc)* **other wines:** Bordeaux
blanc **other châteaux owned:** Ch La Gurgue
(Margaux); Ch Ferrière *(Margaux)*; Ch Haut-Bages
Libéral *(Pauillac)*; Ch Citran *(Haut-Médoc)*

33480 Moulis-en-Médoc tel: 05 56 58 02 37

fax: 05 56 58 05 70

The name of this property may perhaps have
originated with Lord Byron. After a visit in 1821
he is said to have dubbed the wine a 'dispeller of
melancholy'. Wine had already been made here
for a very long time – probably since the 12th
century. The present château was built between
1840 and 1870. In quality Chasse-Spleen wine is
among the best *crus bourgeois*; not infrequently
it is even of *cru classé* standard. It is a wine in
the classic tradition and therefore has a good
deal of tannin, a considerable ageing potential
(up to 20 years for successful vintages),
blackcurrant and black cherry for fruit, good
concentration, oak tones – vanilla, spice and
tobacco. This Moulis, full of character and
sometimes masterly, is matured for 14-18
months in *barriques*, one in three of them new.
Since 1993 Chasse-Spleen has also produced a
fine, elegant, dry white Bordeaux, fermented in
new casks, from a 1.66 ha plot .

◆
Other châteaux owned

The Directory entries in these pages show
other wine estates owned (especially in the
Bordeaux region) by the proprietor of the
château (when this information is
available).

Below: Ch Biston-Brillette

Below: Ch Chasse-Spleen

Ch Chemin Royal   map 17 H4
cru bourgeois
owner: Héritiers Chanfreau **area:** 10 ha **cases:**
4,200 **grape % R:** MER 65% CS 35% **other châteaux
owned:** Ch Fonréaud *(Listrac-Médoc)*; Ch Caroline
(Moulis-en-Médoc); Ch Lestage *(Listrac-Médoc)*
**33480 Moulis-en-Médoc tel: 05 56 58 02 43
fax: 05 56 58 04 33**
Estate in the same ownership as Ch Fonréaud
in Listrac-Médoc. It produces a fairly open, not
especially full-bodied wine with sometimes
rather rustic tannins. Fruit – particularly black
varieties – is usually discernible.

Ch La Closerie du Grand Poujeaux
map 17 E9
cru bourgeois
owner: Jean-Paul Bacquey **area:** 8 ha **cases:** 3,000
grape % R: CS 65% MER 30% PV 5% **second wine:** Ch
Le Bergieu **other châteaux owned:** Ch Haut-
Franquet *(Moulis-en-Médoc)*; Ch Bel-Air Lagrave
(Moulis-en-Médoc)
**33480 Moulis-en-Médoc tel: 05 56 58 01 89
fax: 05 56 58 05 21**
Jean-Paul Bacquey bought this vineyard in 1984
and here he makes a Moulis of good quality,
suitable for laying down and with considerable
tannin. Its aroma – with blackcurrant as one
aspect – is given extra dimension (notes of
vanilla and breadcrust) by its average 18
months in wood. A quarter to a half of the
barrels are new.

Ch Duplessis Hauchecorne   map 17 H6
cru bourgeois
owner: SC Les Grands Crus Réunis/Marie-Laure
Lurton-Roux **area:** 18 ha **cases:** 8,700 **grape % R:**
MER 60% CS 27% CF 10% PV 3% **second wine:** La
Licorne de Duplessis **other châteaux owned:** Ch de
Villegeorge *(Haut-Médoc)*; Ch La Tour de Bessan
(Margaux)
**33480 Moulis-en-Médoc tel: 05 57 88 70 20
fax: 05 57 88 72 51**
This property originated as a hunting estate for
the family of Armand du Plessis – Cardinal
Richelieu. It was split up about 200 years ago,
so there are two Duplessis châteaux in Moulis
(the other one, Duplessis-Fabre, has since 1989
belonged to Philippe Dourthe of Ch
Maucaillou). Lucien Lurton became part-owner
of Duplessis Hauchecorne in 1960; sole
proprietor in 1983. His daughter Marie-Laure
now runs it. The wine possesses an elegant

firmness, aspects of both candied and dried
fruit, firm, ripe tannins, earthy tones and
integrated oak, from a maximum 18 months in
barriques of which 20% are new.

Ch Dutruch Grand Poujeaux
map 17 F9
cru bourgeois
owner: François Cordonnier **area:** 25 ha **cases:**
13,500 **grape % R:** CS 50% MER 40% PV 10% **second
wine:** Ch La Gravière Grand Poujeaux
**33480 Moulis-en-Médoc tel: 05 56 58 02 55
fax: 05 56 58 06 22**
Until the mid-19th century this estate at the
hamlet of Grand Poujeaux belonged to the
Dutruch family. The château itself dates from
1863. Autumnal woodland scents are often
combined in the wine with a dash of spice and
ripe black fruit. Vanilla and oak are not lacking
either: the wine matures for 18 months in
barriques, 25% of them new. Firm tannins
complete the whole picture. This is a sound,
classic Moulis.

Ch Franquet Grand Poujeaux
map 17 E8
cru bourgeois
owner: Famille Lambert **area:** 8 ha **cases:** 3,500
grape % R: MER 50% CS 40% PV 8% MAL 2% **second
wine:** Ch Clos de Lacaussade; Ch Moulin de
Poujeaux
**33480 Moulis-en-Médoc tel: 05 56 59 04 94
fax: 05 56 59 09 97**
This wine is an example of a traditionally made,
traditionally matured Moulis. At its best it
possesses a reasonably full-bodied taste
supported by firm tannins, and has in particular
earthy, dark tones to its aroma: mushroom,
licorice, bayleaf, spice. Fruit is generally more
discreetly present. A quarter of the casks in
which the wine spends 12-18 months are new.
For the rest the wine quality can vary greatly
from vintage to vintage – and may not always
be satisfactory.

Ch Galland   map 17 E8
cru bourgeois
owner: Jacques Brochet **area:** 8.5 ha **cases:** 3,000
grape % R: CS 55% MER 45% **second wine:** Ch Haut-
Paradie *(Haut-Médoc)*
**33480 Moulis-en-Médoc tel: 05 56 58 03 24
fax: 05 56 58 16 25**
This wine reappeared in 1988, after many years
when the owner neither sold it himself nor used

Above: Ch Dutruch Grand Poujeaux

the Ch Galland name. In that year Jacques
Brochet bought the estate and decided to
market his wine. This is a Moulis that has won
some awards – supple, meaty, with spicy oak
from the 30% of new *barriques*, a pleasing
amount of fruit and adequate tannins.

Ch La Garricq
owner: SARL Cantegraves/Martine Cazeneuve **area:**
3 ha **cases:** 1,250 **grape % R:** CS 50% MER 30% PV
20% **other châteaux owned:** Ch Paloumey *(Haut-
Médoc)*; Ch La Bessane *(Margaux)*
**33290 Ludon tel: 05 57 87 00 66
fax: 05 57 88 00 67**
Traditionally produced and nurtured Moulis –
that is a year in barrels, a fifth of them new –
made from hand-picked and selected grapes of
which 20% are Petit Verdot. It is an agreeable
kind of wine, supple and open, with a pleasing
amount of fruit. (The estate has in the past been
called Ch Graves de Guitignan Brillette and Ch
de Tressan.)

Ch Granins Grand Poujeaux   map 17 E9
owner: Guillaume Batailley **area:** 8 ha **cases:** 4,500
grape % R: MER 40% CS 40% PV 15% MAL 5% **second
wine:** Ch Granins
**33480 Moulis-en-Médoc tel: 05 56 58 02 99
fax: 05 56 58 05 82**
A wine well armed with silky tannins, classic in
style, but seldom really compact or
concentrated. Its 15-month spell in casks, a
quarter of them new, gives it spicy oak and
vanilla, as well as dark animal aromas. When
the present owner's family took over the estate
in 1944 it was called Ch La Tour Granins;
however, after a law case with Ch Latour in
Pauillac it became Ch Tour Granins and then,
in 1983, Granins Grand Poujeaux. The estate
also uses just Ch Granins as the name for
exactly the same quality of wine.

Ch Gressier Grand Poujeaux
map 17 E9
owner: Bertrand de Marcellus **area:** 22 ha **cases:**
11,000 **grape % R:** CS 60% MER 30% CF 10%
33480 Moulis-en-Médoc tel: 05 56 58 02 51
In fine years this is a powerful wine, rich in
colour and extract, traditional in style. Tannins
are very much present, along with spices and
berry fruit. Time in wood is kept to nine
months, and a third of the barrels are new. The

estate has been owned by the same family since 1760. It was once much bigger, but was divided under the terms of a will in 1820. The other part became Ch Chasse-Spleen.

Ch Haut-Franquet
map 17 E9
cru bourgeois
owner: Jean-Paul Bacquey **area:** 5 ha **cases:** 1,600 **grape % R:** CS 65% MER 30% PV 5% **second wine:** Ch Maleterre **other châteaux owned:** Ch La Closerie du Grand Poujeaux *(Moulis-en-Médoc)*; Ch Bel-Air Lagrave *(Moulis-en-Médoc)*
33480 Moulis-en-Médoc tel: 05 56 58 01 89 fax: 05 56 58 05 21
Somewhat rustic wine, with modest fruit. As at Jean-Paul Bacquey's other Moulis properties, a quarter to a half of the maturing casks are replaced annually. The owner hopes to have doubled the vineyard area before the year 2005.

Ch Lagorce Bernadas
map 17 K1
owner: Martine Vallette **area:** 2 ha **cases:** 600 **grape % R:** CS 55% MER 40% PV 5% **second wine:** Ch Hountic **other châteaux owned:** Ch Roque-Peyre *(Bergerac, Montravel)*
33480 Moulis-en-Médoc tel: 05 53 24 77 98 fax: 05 53 61 36 87
Tiny amounts of rather dour, old-fashioned wine with aromas of black fruit and woodland. Spends up to two years in barrels, a third new.

Below: Ch Maucaillou

Ch Lestage-Darquier
map 17 E9
owner: François Bernard **area:** 8 ha **cases:** 4,000 **grape % R:** CS 50% MER 45% CF 5%:
33480 Moulis-en-Médoc tel: 05 56 58 18 16 fax: 05 56 58 38 42
This is perhaps not the most engaging Moulis, given its often strong tannins and fairly inaccessible personality. But it is a wine with substance and potential for ageing. Its oak-maturing (in one-third new casks) is limited to 8-12 months.

Ch Malmaison
map 17 G6
cru bourgeois
owner: Compagnie Vinicole des Barons de Rothschild **area:** 24 ha **cases:** 13,300 **grape % R:** MER 55% CS 45% **second wine:** Les Granges des Domaines Rothschild **other châteaux owned:** Ch Peyre-Lebade *(Listrac-Médoc)*; Ch Clarke *(Listrac-Médoc)*
33480 Moulis-en-Médoc tel: 05 56 58 38 00 fax: 05 56 58 26 46
Estate bordering on Ch Clarke (Listrac-Médoc) that had all but disappeared in the early 1970s: one single vine-planted hectare remained. Then Baron Edmond de Rothschild bought Ch Malmaison in 1973 and, with his wife Nadine, restored it to new life within four years. The wine is distinguished by its smooth berry fruit (cherry, plum) a sound structure and supple tannins, and rounded by the 55% of Merlot grapes. The refined notes of oak and vanilla come from a year in wood, with 30% of the barrels replaced annually.

Ch Maucaillou
map 17 D9
cru bourgeois
owner: Philippe Dourthe **area:** 62 ha **cases:** 35,000 **grape % R:** CS 48% MER 35% CF 10% PV 7% **second wine:** Ch Cap-de-Haut-Maucaillou *(Haut-Médoc)* **other châteaux owned:** Domaine de Maucaillou *(Listrac-Médoc)*; Ch Maucaillou Felletin *(Haut-Médoc)*; Ch Duplessis-Fabre *(Moulis-en-Médoc)*
33480 Moulis-en-Médoc tel: 05 56 58 01 23 fax: 05 56 58 00 88
This is the most important attraction for visitors to Moulis, for opposite the fancifully styled 1875 château stands the Musée des Arts et Métiers de la Vigne et du Vin. The traditional craft aspects of winemaking are attractively displayed. The Maucaillou vineyard has grown from 55 to 62 ha since 1984, with a further 3 ha

◆
Classed growths
Recognized classifications are listed at the end of the Atlas. Châteaux profiled in the Atlas which appear on one of these lists have their classification and rank noted immediately below the château name.

◆
Crus Bourgeois
Only one area – the Médoc – has a recognized list of *crus bourgeois*. The ranking procedure is described on page 34 and the full list is given in an appendix. The *crus bourgeois* are in appellations Médoc, Haut-Médoc and the 'village' ACs such as Moulis-en-Médoc and Listrac-Médoc, where they are especially common.

The term *cru bourgeois* is in use in other areas, but unofficially, and thus does not appear on labels.

Above: Ch Moulin à Vent

Below: Ch Mauvesin

Above: Ch La Mouline

Above: Ch Poujeaux

planned. The wine is distinguished less by its concentration than its stylish character, its tempting, ripe fruit, and its creamy oak notes of toast and vanilla (after 18 months in cask, 45-60% of them new). This nuanced wine is usually ready for drinking quite soon.

Ch Mauvesin
map 17 J4

owner: Vicomte A. de Baritault du Carpia/Société Viticole de France **area:** 60 ha **cases:** 30,000 **grape % R:** CS 48% MER 36% CF 10% PV 6% **second wine:** Ch La Montagne de Mauvesin (Haut-Médoc)
33480 Castelnau-de-Médoc tel: 05 56 67 23 89 fax: 05 56 67 08 38
Very correct but unremarkable Moulis from one of the larger properties. This generally accessible wine spends an average 10 months in wood (25% new barrels). As part of the estate lies in Castelnau, the whole vintage used to be sold as Haut-Médoc.

Ch Moulin à Vent
map 17 I4

cru bourgeois
owner: Dominique & Marie-Hélène Hessel **area:** 25 ha **cases:** 10,000 **grape % R:** CS 65% MER 30% PV 5% **second wine:** Ch Moulin de Saint Vincent **other châteaux owned:** Ch Tour Blanche (Médoc)
33480 Moulis-en-Médoc tel: 05 56 58 15 79 fax: 05 56 58 12 05
This wine estate dating from 1820 lies on the Moulis–Listrac boundary, by the busy D1 road. The present owner has been gradually restoring it since 1977. At its best the wine is a straightforward, good Moulis, usually firm, with black fruit, a slight fatness and supple tannins. Ch Moulin à Vent tends not to have great concentration or refinement, and in the lesser years it can lack some substance and conviction. Each year 20-25% of the maturing casks are replaced.

Ch La Mouline
map 17 H4

owner: Jean-Louis Coubris **area:** 25 ha **cases:** 10,000 **grape % R:** CS 50% MER 45% CF 3% PV 2% **second wine:** Domaine de Lagorce du Château La Mouline **other wines:** Ch Tour du Palais (Haut-Médoc)
33480 Moulis-en-Médoc tel: 05 56 17 13 17 fax: 05 56 17 13 18
This wine is usually accessible, characterized by a lot of new oak (80%) and well provided with fruit. The estate is equipped to perfection, and

the barrels for maturing the wine are stacked one row above the other on metal racks, in the Californian manner.

Ch Myon de l'Enclos
map 17 H2

owner: Bernard Lartigue **area:** 3 ha **cases:** 1,300 **grape % R:** CS 80% MER 20% **other châteaux owned:** Ch Mayne-Lalande (Listrac-Médoc)
33480 Moulis-en-Médoc tel: 05 56 58 27 63 fax: 05 56 58 22 41
Both aroma and character of the Moulis from this little property are very much determined by Cabernet Sauvignon and its associated tannins. Its years spent in oak – 20% of the barrels are new – is not enough: to become agreeable the wine then needs to age in bottle for several times as long as that.

Ch Pomeys
map 17 J3

owner: Jean-François Barennes **area:** 8 ha **cases:** 3,000 **grape % R:** CS 67% MER 33%
33480 Moulis-en-Médoc tel: 05 56 58 37 62
For seven generations, since 1826, this estate has been run by the same family. The wine, which some find reminiscent of a Margaux, has an elegant structure and a dark-toned aroma – often with some berry fruit and a hint of violets. A long, patient wait is not a requirement. A third of the maturing casks are renewed each year.

Ch Poujeaux
map 17 E9

cru bourgeois
owner: Indivision Theil **area:** 52 ha **cases:** 25,000 **grape % R:** CS 50% MER 40% CF 5% PV 5% **second wine:** La Salle de Poujeaux **other châteaux owned:** Ch Arnauld (Haut-Médoc)
33480 Moulis-en-Médoc tel: 05 56 58 02 96 fax: 05 56 58 01 25
This is often one of the best wines – if not indeed the very best – of the Moulis-en-Médoc appellation. Its indisputable refinement (Baron Elie de Rothschild once mistook the 1953 for his own Lafite Rothschild) goes with an expansive taste, rich in nuance and with velvety tannins. Since the second half of the 1980s the wine has been becoming somewhat more accessible than before, but without any loss of quality. This is also apparent from the times that it has won the Coupe des Crus Bourgeois. This wine estate came into being in the 16th century as an offshoot of Ch Latour in Pauillac,

and was made great by the Theil family, who have been running Poujeaux since 1921. The present generation has gradually raised the proportion of new maturing *barriques* from 25% to the present 50%.

Ch Ruat Petit Poujeaux
map 17 H6

owner: Pierre Goffre-Viaud **area:** 15 ha **cases:** 8,000 **grape % R:** MER 50% CS 35% CF 15% **second wine:** Ch Ruat
33480 Moulis-en-Médoc tel: 05 56 58 25 15 fax: 05 56 58 15 90
A not very complex Moulis, old-fashioned in style and with a taste in which there may be creamy elements, a slightly bitter touch, firm tannins, some fruit and a little oak, from just six months in used casks.

HAUT-MÉDOC

The Haut-Médoc appellation occupies the middle ground: above it in status are the named commune vineyards such as St-Julien, below is the wide area of northern land covered by the more humble Médoc AC. Haut-Médoc vineyards can and do border on those of their more expensive neighbours: only an invisible commune boundary – a mere administrative or historical accident – divides the vines of Château Lagrange, with its St-Julien appellation, from those of Château Camensac, also a Classed Growth but with just Haut-Médoc on its label.

The Haut-Médoc begins at the Jalle de Blanquefort, the small stream a few kilometres north of the city of Bordeaux which also marks the most northern tip of the Graves appellation. From there the Haut-Médoc stretches northwards for some 60 kilometres. Beyond St-Estèphe it meets its lesser cousin, the area formerly known as the Bas-Médoc that is now just the greater part of the AC Médoc, at the Chenal de la Maréchale. To the east it is bordered initially by the Garonne river; further downstream by the Gironde estuary. (Not all of the riverside land comes within the Haut-Médoc appellation: some parcels are only entitled to the generic Bordeaux AC; some is not entitled to be used for vine-growing at all.) To the west the Haut-Médoc extends for several kilometres, well into the forested areas which straddle the N215 north of Castelnau-de-Médoc.

The Haut-Médoc vineyard was legally defined in 1935, when it was split off from the rest of the Médoc. In fact many wines from this area had been well known

Roses are a traditional partner to the vines in Médoc vineyards

since the late eighteenth century, when the Médoc was thriving commercially and the waterways saw a constant flow of traffic. Today, the Haut-Médoc AC covers several hundred châteaux; some are still very well known throughout the world, and many offer a good alternative to their more illustrious cousins lucky enough to be in one of the top six communes. Indeed, five of the châteaux included in the 1855 Classification have the appellation Haut-Médoc. It is very interesting to take a close look at the Haut-Médoc AC and the land that it covers, and to understand the (on occasion) fine line which prevented these wines having a more elevated status.

THE COMMUNES
The Haut-Médoc appellation covers a total of 29 communes, although the best-known châteaux are concentrated in roughly half of these. If you take the D2 out of Bordeaux you will pass through almost endless suburbs, three of which are the southernmost communes entitled to produce Haut-Médoc wines: Blanquefort, Parempuyre and Le Taillan-Médoc. Old maps show that these were once well-stocked with vines: the pattern now is of the snaking avenues of garden girt villas (a recent French passion) and the orderly grids of warehouse estates.

A little further up the road, and you pass Le Pian-Médoc to your left and Ludon-Médoc to your right. Ludon boasts one Classed Growth: the *troisième cru classé* La Lagune, the foremost of the handful of top-ranking châteaux that are not in one of the four great Médoc appellations. Just above Ludon, to the east of the D2 and

Many of the Cru Bourgeois châteaux have invested heavily in new oak

very close to the river is the next commune of note, Macau, which has Fifth Growth Château Cantemerle.

Next comes a gap, for the next five communes are entitled to the Margaux appellation (see page 36). The Haut-Médoc takes up again with Avensan, west of Margaux and just south of the separate appellation of Moulis-en-Médoc.

Then you have Arcins, Lamarque, Cussac-Fort-Médoc and, almost directly west of St-Julien, St-Laurent-Médoc. There are more than 30 highly-rated Haut-Médoc properties in these four communes, including three Classed Growths in St-Laurent: Châteaux Belgrave and Camensac, both of them Fifth Growths, and La Tour Carnet, a Fourth Growth.

The final cluster of highly-rated properties appear in four more communes: to the west of Pauillac and St-Estèphe lie St-Sauveur, Cissac-Médoc and Vertheuil;

and then the most northern Haut-Médoc commune, St-Seurin-de-Cadourne, almost directly above St-Estèphe. These four communes together account for some forty-odd Haut-Médoc properties of note.

STATUS AND TERROIR

With the exception of the five Classed-Growth Haut-Médocs, many of these wines are ranked as *crus bourgeois*. This whole subject is complicated: there have been two attempts to list and codify the *bourgeoisie* of the Médoc, both in the 20th century, though the term goes back to at least as far as 1853 and is probably older. In 1932 a committee of *courtiers* published a list, conferring the status on 490 Médoc châteaux. The list was revised in the 1960s when the newly-formed Syndicat des Crus Bourgeois issued a somewhat shorter version: over 100 estates had vanished in the preceding 30 years of war and depression. The Syndicat's list was revised again in 1978, and the term takes its legitimacy from a French government decree of 1972, which provides for three ranks: in descending order there are Cru Bourgeois Exceptionnel, Grand Bourgeois and plain Bourgeois. Current EU law does not allow these levels to be used on labels, although the Syndicat does lay down different quality criteria: a Grand Bourgeois must age its wines in *barriques*, an Exceptionnel must be in one of the top communes of the Médoc, from Ludon in the south to St-Estèphe in the north. To add to the confusion not all the surviving 1932 *crus bourgeois* have joined the Syndicat – yet some still use the term *cru bourgeois* on their labels. There is also a waiting-list of châteaux which wish to join the Syndicat, but the process is held up by the EU. In the directory pages which follow, châteaux on the current list issued by the Syndicat have *cru bourgeois* after their names.

The reason for the lesser status of the Haut-Médoc châteaux is essentially the type of soil. The *raison d'être* of the top appellations of the Médoc is the prevalence of gravel outcrops. The four leading appellations of Margaux, St-Julien, Pauillac and St-Estèphe all lie very close to the river where these deposits are at their most abundant. This same type of soil was important in establishing the Haut-Médoc appellation, but the sites, though good, were not judged quite as good as for the specific appellations. A glance at the maps shows that the vines, as ever in the Médoc, occupy the higher ground, away from the damp soil of the river plain and the valleys of the *jalles* and drainage channels.

PRODUCTION AND WINES

The total production of Haut-Médoc wines comes from some 4,200 hectares, averaging some 2,000,000 cases annually – slightly less than that of wines from the Médoc appellation. Of the almost 400 producers, just under half belong to one of five cooperatives.

As with all Médoc appellations, the Haut-Médoc AC applies to red wines only. It is more difficult to define a typical Haut-Médoc style than for any of the other appellations, since there are many possible variables. The grapes may have been grown on a fairly light soil like that to the south of Margaux, or on one of the heavier ones which are found in the northern section, bordering St-Estèphe. The dominant grape variety could be either Cabernet Sauvignon or Merlot, depending on location and producer's preference. The degree to which the wine has been influenced by new oak maturation will again depend on the winemaker. However, leaving aside the Classed Growths, these are some of the best-known wines from the Médoc. Some are excellent value because they are relatively inexpensive. Others, although quite expensive, can still represent value because in quality they often approach a good Classed Growth – and even surpass some of the lesser ones. They are also worth buying 'en primeur' in a fine and even good vintage, offering an alternative to more highly-priced wines from senior appellations. A good Haut-Médoc from a really fine vintage will easily last a decade, maybe even two.

Cissac-Médoc's village church viewed from Château Cissac

THE APPELLATION

HAUT-MÉDOC (red)

Location: *The southern two-thirds of the Médoc peninsula, to the north of the city of Bordeaux, between the Landes forests to the west and the Gironde estuary to the east. To the south it is limited by the Jalle de Blanquefort, to the north by the Chenal de la Maréchale, beyond which begins the Médoc AC.*
Area of AC: 8,759 ha
Area under vine: 4,200 ha
Communes: *South to north: Blanquefort, Le Taillan-Médoc, Parempuyre, Ludon-Médoc, le Pian-Médoc, Macau, Arsac, Castelnau-de-Médoc, Avensan, Arcins, Lamarque, Cussac-Fort-Médoc, St-Laurent-Médoc, St-Sauveur, Cissac-Médoc, Vertheuil, St-Seurin-de-*

Cadourne. In addition, the communes with their own ACs, such as St-Julien, are also entitled to the Haut-Médoc AC.
Average annual production: 2,000,000 cases
Classed growths: 5: *Ludon has a troisième cru, Château La Lagune; St-Laurent-Médoc has a quatrième cru, Château La Tour Carnet and two cinquièmes, Châteaux Belgrave and Camensac; Macau has one cinquième cru, Château Cantemerle.*
Others: 140 crus bourgeois, 116 others
Cooperatives: 5 (c. 170 members)
Main grape varieties: *Cabernet Sauvignon, Cabernet Franc, Merlot*
Others: *Malbec, Petit Verdot*
Main soil types: Gravel

APPELLATION HAUT–MÉDOC

Ch d'Agassac
map 18 F7

cru bourgeois

owner: Groupama **area:** 35 ha **cases:** 10,000 **grape % R:** CS 60% MER 40% **second wine:** Le Grand Verger d'Agassac

33290 Ludon tel: 05 56 59 30 08

This château is one of the oldest buildings in the Médoc: a true castle, dating from the 13th century, flanked by pointed towers and with a moat. For hundreds of years the *seigneurs* of Agassac lived here. The Capbern-Gasqueton family bought this stronghold in the early 1960s; they nursed a vineyard on the extensive estate to prosperity. In 1996 d'Agassac was taken over by the Groupama company. The wine is a dark-toned, properly concentrated, complete Haut-Médoc with firmness, tannin and character.

Ch Aney
map 19 F6

cru bourgeois

owner: Raimond père & fils **area:** 30 ha **cases:** 16,000 **grape % R:** CS 65% MER 25% CF 7% PV 3% **other wines:** Ch d'Arnaussan *(Bordeaux Supérieur)*

33460 Cussac-Fort-Médoc tel: 05 56 58 94 89 fax: 05 56 58 98 15

This vineyard was named after the man who created it around 1850. His son-in-law built an elegant château here on the D2 road in 1880. A balanced wine is produced, usually with soft fruit (mainly plum) notes: a Haut-Médoc that matures to smoothness quite quickly. A third of the maturing casks are replaced each year.

Ch d'Arche
map 18 E7

cru bourgeois

owner: Société des Grands Vignobles de la Gironde/Mähler-Besse **area:** 9.1 ha **cases:** 5,000 **grape % R:** CS 50% MER 40% CF 10% **second wine:** Ch Egmont **other châteaux owned:** include Ch Palmer *(Margaux)*; Ch Alfa Bernarde *(Premières Côtes de Blaye)*; Ch La Couronne *(St-Emilion)*; Ch Bouquey *(St-Emilion)*; Ch Biré *(Bordeaux Supérieur)*

33290 Ludon tel: 05 56 56 04 30 fax: 05 56 56 04 59

Château almost opposite the church at Ludon that for decades now has been producing a good, reliable, quite classic Haut-Médoc. It has adequate tannins, an elegant firmness and also plenty of fruit – cherry, raspberry, blackcurrant. Oak frames it all, from 10-18 months spent maturing in barrels of which a quarter are new for each vintage.

Ch d'Arcins
map 19 K7

owner: SC du Château d'Arcins/Castel Frères **area:** 96.5 ha **cases:** 58,000 **grape % R:** CS 60% MER 40% **second wine:** Ch Tour du Mayne **other châteaux owned:** include Ch Barreyres *(Haut-Médoc)*; Ch Ferrande *(Graves)*

33460 Arcins tel: 05 56 52 91 29 fax: 05 57 88 50 26

An 18th-century château, with vast cellars, near a bend in the D2 road through Arcins. At great expense it has been very sympathetically renovated by Castel Frères, and the firm has also considerably enlarged the vineyard. Arcins' wine is an attractive Haut-Médoc, conveying impressions of juicy, spicy fruit – especially blackcurrants – a touch of mint and sometimes a herbaceous element. All this presents itself elegantly, and is supported by oak and supple tannins. About a third of the barrels in which the wine spends a year are new.

Ch Arnauld
map 19 K7

cru bourgeois

owner: SCEA Theil-Roggy **area:** 27 ha **cases:** 10,000 **grape % R:** CS 60% MER 40% **second wine:** Ch Clairbore **other châteaux owned:** Ch Poujeaux *(Moulis-en-Médoc)*

33460 Arcins tel: 05 57 88 50 34 fax: 05 57 88 50 35

Through marriages the Theil brothers of Ch Poujeaux, Moulis, have been involved with this estate since 1976 – with a spectacular improvement in quality of the wine as a result. Arnauld is an absolutely sound Haut-Médoc: lively, elegant, with juicy fruit, earthy aromas and toasty oak (one-third new barrels). As a rule it is splendidly drinkable after about five years.

Ch d'Aurilhac
map 21/R J6

cru bourgeois

owner: Erik Nieuwaal **area:** 16 ha **cases:** 9,500 **grape % R:** CS 67% MER 27% CF 3% PV 3% **other wines:** Ch La Fagotte

33180 St-Seurin-de-Cadourne tel: 05 56 59 35 32

For no less than 40 years the present owner's father-in-law planted this land, up on the northern edge of the appellation, with clover and corn to build up the fertility of the soil. The first vines went in at the end of the 1980s. The wine is made with care in excellently equipped cellars, and remains for 18 months in *barriques* of which half are new. Usually characterized by ripe fruit, elements of oak and a pleasing taste, as the vines get older this Haut-Médoc begins to gain in depth and substance (the 1993 vintage won a gold medal). Ch La Fagotte is produced at this same estate: a more accessible, faster-maturing wine made from 60% Merlot, 40% Cabernet Sauvignon (1,000 cases).

Ch Balac
map 20 K6

cru bourgeois

owner: Luc Touchais **area:** 15 ha **cases:** 7,500 **grape % R:** CS 40% CF 30% MER 30% **second wine:** Ch Le Colombier

33112 St-Laurent-Médoc tel: 05 56 59 41 76 fax: 05 56 59 93 90

Very old property, isolated in the woods west of Pauillac, that has known some illustrious owners. In the 18th century one of them had the famous architect Victor Louis carry out work on the château – but there was little of this glorious past left to see when the Touchais family bought the estate in 1964. The château was a ruin and the vineyard had vanished. Little by little, Luc Touchais restored the building and laid out a vineyard. Since 1986 this has been yielding an honourable, quite fragrant, balanced wine with blackcurrant, oak and tannin. There has been a superior version since 1988: Cuvée Sélection Limitée, briefly matured in new casks.

Ch Barateau
map 20 H7

cru bourgeois

owner: Patrick Leroy **area:** 24 ha **cases:** 10,000 **grape % R:** CS 50% MER 40% CF 5% PV 5% **second wine:** Les Vignes de Saint Sauveur

33112 St-Laurent-Médoc tel: 05 56 59 42 07

The standard wine is a fairly supple, quick-developing Haut-Médoc, with an agreeable roundness. There is more concentration and oak to be found in the rather rare Cuvée Prestige. The château dates from 1820, but the vineyard was already here in the 18th century.

◆

Second wines

An increasing number of châteaux select only the best wine for bottling and sale under their main label, and use a second name for wine from young vines and less-than-perfect vats. The proportion declared as the 'grand vin' varies with the vintage, and some estates are more perfectionist than others. In some years, top estates may downgrade half or more of the crop. In dire years, they may not sell the wine under a château label at all, but sell it anonymously into the trade for blending.

A few château have a third label for wine that does not meet second-wine standards.

Some châteaux routinely sell a part of their production to a *négociant*, who then bottles it under a different château name. This wine can be of the same standard as the château's *grand vin*, or at second wine level. On occasions it is better than the château's wine.

Below: Ch Arnauld

Above: Ch d'Agassac

Above: Ch Dalac

Ch Barreyres   map 19 J9
cru bourgeois
owner: SC de Château Barreyres/Castel Fréres
area: 109 ha *cases:* 68,100 *grape % R:* CS 60%
MER 40% *second wine:* Ch Tour Bellevue *other
wines:* Ch Fougey *(Bordeaux)* *other châteaux
owned:* include Ch d'Arcins *(Haut-Médoc)*; Ch
Ferrande *(Graves)*
**33460 Arcins tel: 05 56 58 91 29
fax: 05 57 88 50 26**
This extensive estate on the eastern edge of
Arcins was bought by the Castel brothers in
1973, along with Ch d'Arcins: since then a
whole new cellar complex has been built. The
wine generally has fruit such as cherry, with
some bayleaf as well. It is made in an
uncomplicated, supple, accessible style.

Ch Beaumont   map 20 G5
cru bourgeois
owner: Grands Millésimes de France *area:* 105 ha
cases: 45,000 *grape % R:* CS 62% MER 30% CF 5%
PV 3% *second wines:* Ch d'Arvigny; Les Tours de
Beaumont *other châteaux owned:* Ch Beychevelle
(St-Julien)
**33460 Cussac-Fort-Médoc tel: 05 56 58 92 29
fax: 05 56 58 90 94**
Since it was created in 1824 this estate has had
a dozen owners. The present incumbents, since
December 1986, have been Grands Millésimes
de France, a joint venture between Garantie
Mutuelle des Fonctionnaires and the Japanese
Suntory group. The wine is normally a smooth,
flavoursome Haut-Médoc, with sweet fruit and
spices but without any sharp acidity. Toasted
oak comes through clearly from a year in
barriques, a third of them new. The 1854
château was built in Renaissance style.

Ch Bel Air   map 20 E7
cru bourgeois
owner: Françoise Triaud *area:* 37 ha *cases:* 20,000
grape % R: CS 65% MER 35% *other châteaux owned:*
include Ch Gloria *(St-Julien)*
**33460 Cussac-Fort-Médoc tel: 05 56 59 08 18
fax: 05 56 59 16 18**
Since 1980 a good, supple, attractive wine, well
endowed with fresh fruit and creamy oak, has
been made here by the same team as at Ch
Gloria and Ch St-Pierre (St-Julien).

Ch Belgrave   map 20 L10
5ème cru
owner: GFA du Château Belgrave/Groupe CVBG.
area: 53 ha *cases:* 29,000 *grape % R:* CS 40% MER
35% CF 20% PV 5% *second wine:* Diane de Belgrave
other châteaux owned: include Ch Teyssier
(Montagne-St-Emilion/Puisseguin-St-Emilion); Ch de
la Tour *(Bordeaux)*; Ch La Garde *(Pessac-Léognan)*;
Ch le Boscq *(St-Estèphe)*
**33112 St-Laurent-Médoc tel: 05 56 59 40 20
fax: 05 56 59 40 20**
The *cinquième cru classé* on the borders of St-
Julien is managed by the CVBG firm (including
Dourthe). Since being taken over in 1979 it has
undergone a complete overhaul and renovation,
both in the cellars and in the vineyard. This has
been greatly to the good of the wine quality.
From being poor, this Haut-Médoc has
blossomed into an agreeable, balanced and also
relatively consistent wine – not really deep or
complex, but certainly pleasing with its jammy
fruit (blackcurrant, plum), spicy, vanilla oak
(half the casks are new), and adequate tannins.

Ch Bel Orme Tronquoy de Lalande
cru bourgeois   map 21/R J9
owner: Jean-Michel Quié *area:* 28 ha *cases:*
11,000 *grape % R:* MER 50% CS 40% CF 10% *other
châteaux owned:* Ch Croizet-Bages *(Pauillac)*; Ch
Rauzan-Gassies *(Margaux)*
**33180 St-Seurin-de-Cadourne tel: 05 56 59 31 09
fax: 05 56 59 72 83**
After years of making a rather tough wine,
lacking meat and depth, since 1994 this estate
has reached a higher standard. Its Haut-Médoc
now offers more fruit and charm, although it is
still without great refinement since its
structure remains so solid. It is to be hoped
that progress continues, and that eventually the
most will be made of this vineyard's potential.
The château bears the hallmark of the architect
Victor Louis, and has stylishly furnished *salons*.

Ch Bernones   map 19 F7
owner: Famille Ruton *area:* 16 ha *cases:* 8,600
grape % R: MER 52% CS 28% CF 18% PV 1% MAL 1%
other châteaux owned: include Ch Mauras
(Sauternes)
**33460 Cussac-Fort-Médoc tel: 05 56 67 23 89
fax: 05 56 67 08 38**

A correct Haut-Médoc of average quality. It
ferments in stainless-steel tanks and matures in
oak (25% new casks). In the 19th century
practically the whole of each Bernones vintage
was reserved for the royal courts of Europe.

Ch Le Bourdieu Vertheuil   map 20 D6
cru bourgeois
owner: André Richard *area:* 55 ha *cases:* 27,000
grape % R: CS 50% MER 30% CF 15% PV 5% *second
wines:* Ch Picourneau; Ch Victoria
**33180 Vertheuil tel: 05 56 41 98 01
fax: 05 56 41 99 32**
The Cuvée Prestige here is worth discovering: a
mouthfilling, complete Haut-Médoc with rich
fruit and a noble, toasty aroma of oak. In its
shadow, in good years, a firm, nicely lasting
standard wine is made. Visitors to the château
can see the remains of the abbey of Vertheuil.

◆
About Haut-Médoc
Information about Haut-Médoc wines and
châteaux can be had from the Maison du
Vin et de Tourisme de Médoc, 33250
Pauillac, which deals with all the Médoc
appellations. Tel 05 56 59 03 08.
Mairies in individual villages can also
supply details.

Ch du Breuil   map 20 F7
cru bourgeois
owner: Danielle Vialard *area:* 20 ha *cases:* 10,000
grape % R: MER 34% CS 28% CF 23% PV 11% MAL 4%
second wine: Ch Moulin du Breuil *other châteaux
owned:* Ch Cissac *(Haut-Médoc)*; Ch Tour du Mirai
(Haut-Médoc)
**33250 Cissac-Médoc tel: 05 56 59 58 13
fax: 05 56 59 55 67**
The original château is a romantic ruined fort,
hidden down a track in the woods. It belonged
to the English kings during the Hundred Years
War. In the 18th century a house was built
beside it, the present château. The Vialard
family, of Ch Cissac and other properties, took
over in 1987. In good years, with its ripe fruit,

smooth texture and supple tannins, Ch du Breuil is an accessible, seductive Haut-Médoc. At least 25% of the barrels are new and maturing lasts 18 months.

Ch Cambon la Pelouse
map 18 C6

cru bourgeois
owner: SCEA Carrère Fils **area:** 60 ha **cases:** 30,000 **grape % R:** MER 50% CS 30% CF 20% **second wine:** Ch Trois Moulins
33460 Macau tel: 05 57 88 40 32
fax: 05 57 88 19 12

The vineyard, half of it planted with Merlot, stretches out over a low, gravelly hill between the châteaux of Cantemerle and Giscours. Normally the wine made here is reasonably substantial, slightly spicy, perhaps somewhat one-dimensional; it benefits from bottle-age. It is oak-matured in 80% new barrels.

Ch Camensac
map 20 M9

5ème cru
owner: GFA du Château Camensac/Familles Forner & Merlaut **area:** 65 ha **cases:** 29,500 **grape % R:** CS 60% MER 25% CF 15% **second wine:** La Closerie de Camensac
33112 St-Laurent-Médoc tel: 05 56 59 41 69
fax: 05 56 59 41 73

The Forner family acquired this totally neglected estate in 1964, and in the decades since they have given both property and wine back their former lustre. This is not perhaps the most distinguished Haut-Médoc, the most full of character, but in good years it offers sufficient body, roundness, backbone, supple tannins, fruit and oak (from its 18 months in barrel, one-third of them new). The origins of this white château, a *chartreuse* standing among pines, date back to the 18th century.

Ch Cantemerle
map 18 D6

5ème cru
owner: SMABTP **area:** 67 ha **cases:** 35,000 **grape % R:** MER 40% CS 35% CF 20% PV 5% **second wine:** Baron Villeneuve de Cantemerle **other châteaux owned:** include Ch Le Jurat *(St-Emilion)*; Ch Haut Corbin *(St-Emilion)*
33460 Macau tel: 05 57 97 02 82
fax: 05 57 97 02 84

Below: Ch Beaumont
Right: Ch Bel Orme Tronquoy de Lalande

The château, built in various styles and set in a wooded park, is said to derive its name from the 'singing' of the Merle, a great cannon the French fired at the English during the Hundred Years War. Since autumn 1990 the estate has belonged to the SMABTP (a French insurance company) and its wine has been made under the supervision of Cordier. This *cinquième cru classé* has quite an elegant (but seldom really deep or concentrated) taste, with fresh berry fruit, spiciness and firm, sometimes rather angular or bitter tannins. Restrained oak is supplied by the barrel-ageing, in casks of which one-third are new.

Ch Cap de Haut
map 19 H8

cru bourgeois
owner: Pierre Gilles Gromand d'Evry **area:** 13 ha **cases:** 6,500 **grape % R:** CS 46% MER 25% CF 24% PV 5% **second wine:** Réserve du Marquis de Sorans **other châteaux owned:** Ch de Lamarque *(Haut-Médoc)*
33460 Lamarque tel: 05 56 58 90 03
fax: 05 56 58 93 43

Quite a firm-tasting *cru bourgeois*, its style stiff rather than creamy. Besides its berry fruit – sometimes with herbaceous elements as well – the wine has spicy oak from 6-10 months' maturing in casks, 30% of them new. On average, the quality is correct.

Ch Caronne Ste Gemme
map 19 D2

cru bourgeois
owner: SCE des Vignobles Nony-Borie **area:** 45 ha **cases:** 19,500 **grape % R:** CS 63% MER 35% PV 2% **second wine:** Ch Lagrave-Genestra; Ch Labat
33112 St-Laurent-Médoc tel: 05 56 81 29 44
fax: 05 56 51 71 51

Isolated estate on the southern border of St-Laurent, surrounding a distinguished *chartreuse* with a great stone terrace. The St James's Spring wine ('Caronne' comes from the Latin *carona* – which means small spring – and Ste Gemme is a corruption of St James or Jaime) spends about 15 months in casks of which 20% are new. It offers a quite stylish taste and is dark-toned – notes of bayleaf and leather – rather than fruity, the whole contained by fairly firm tannins.

Ch du Cartillon
map 19 H7

cru bourgeois
owner: Robert Giraud **area:** 45 ha **cases:** 22,500 **grape % R:** MER 30% CS 30% CF 10% PV 10% **second**

wine: Moulin du Cartillon **other châteaux owned:** include Ch Timberlay *(Bordeaux Supérieur)*; Ch Villemaurine *(St-Emilion)*
33460 Lamarque tel: 05 57 43 01 44
fax: 05 57 43 08 75

In the spring of 1995 work went on with a will to complete the refurbishing of this château for the imminent Vinexpo. The 18th-century building looks out on an expanse of traditionally-planted vineyard. The Haut-Médoc made here is classic in character, with solid tannins, berry fruit, some oak and vanilla – 25% new casks – and sometimes some spicy notes.

◆
Crus Bourgeois

Only one area – the Médoc – has a recognized list of *crus bourgeois*. The ranking procedure is described on page 34 and the full list is given in an appendix. The *crus bourgeois* are in appellations Médoc, Haut-Médoc and the 'village' ACs such as St-Julien. The term *cru bourgeois* is in use in other areas, but unofficially, and thus not on labels.

Domaine de Cartujac
map 20 M6

owner: GFA Pierre Saintout **area:** 7 ha **cases:** 2,700 **grape % R:** CS 50% MER 50% **other châteaux owned:** Ch du Périer *(Médoc)*; Ch La Bridane *(St-Julien)*
33112 St-Laurent-Médoc tel: 05 56 59 91 70
fax: 05 56 59 46 13

Reliable, elegantly firm Haut-Médoc with an agreeable amount of red and black fruit and a due measure of oak (25% of the barrels are new) and sufficient tannins.

Domaine Chalet de Germignan
map 18 J2

owner: EARL Graveyron Monlun **area:** 6 ha **cases:** 3,500 **grape % R:** MER 40% CF 30% PV 5% MAL 2% **second wine:** Ch de Germignan
33320 Le Taillan-Médoc tel: 05 56 05 01 39
fax: 05 56 95 87 34

Somewhat rustic wine, a respectable mouthful with plenty of Merlot, from a modest estate just north of Germignan, near Le Taillan. The larger part of the domaine's harvest is sold through *négociants* under the name Ch de Germignan.

HAUT-MÉDOC I
18

RIVE DROITE

• Libourne

Bordeaux

ENTRE-DEUX-
MERS

GRAVES &
SAUTERNES

• Langon

MARGAUX

Ch Larrieu
Terrefort

Macau

Ch
Barreyre

Ch Cambon
la Pelouse

Ch Maucamps

Ch Guittot-
Felloneau

M A C A U

Ch Cantemerle

Ch La Houringue

Cru Larrouquey

Dom
Grand Lafont

Ch de Gironville

Ch La Providence

Ch
Paloumey

Ch
d'Arche

Ludon-Médoc

Paloumey

Ch
La Lagune

Ch Lemoine-
Lafon-Rochet

les Lauriers

Ch Moulin de Soubeyran

L U D O N - M É D O C

LE PIAN-MÉDOC

Ch de Malleret

Ch d'Agassac

Chenal du Despartins

Sénéjac

Chenal de St-Aubin

Ch Sénéjac

**Le Pian-
Médoc**

D211

La Jalle de Ludon

Ch Ségur

P A R E M P U Y R E

Rau de l'Artigue

CASTELNAU-DE-
MÉDOC

Bertranot

Ch Bellegrave
de Poujeaux

le Poujeau

Jalle d'Olive

Parempuyre

Rau de l'Aygue

Louens

les Airials

Ch Clément
Pichon

Ch Maurian
de Prade

le Neurin

Jalle de la Lande

Ch Grand
Clapeau Olivier

B L A N Q U E F O R T

Caychac

Ch Saint Ahon

Ch
Dillon

**Zone Industrielle
de Blanquefort**

Port des Michels

LE TAILLAN-MÉDOC

Dom Chalet
de Germignan

Blanquefort

Bois de
Bordeaux

**Le Taillan-
Médoc**

Ch du Taillan

Ch
Magnol

Jalle du Taillan

Jalle de Canteret

N215

Jalle du Sable

BORDEAUX

BORDEAUX

N215

N

Vineyards		
Woods		– · – Commune boundary
—— AC Haut-Médoc		– · · · Canton boundary
—— AC Bordeaux		⌒ Contour line

1:71,500

0   1   2km

Above: Ch Le Bourdieu Vertheuil

Above: Ch du Breuil

Ch Chano   map 20 E6
owner: Ferrié-Parys *area:* 3.5 ha *cases:* 1,500
grape % R: CS 60% MER 35% PV 5%
33250 Cissac-Médoc tel: 05 56 73 94 04
fax: 05 56 59 50 70
Home of a pleasant Haut-Médoc – a juicy
mouthful with good tannins, reasonable power
and agreeable impressions of bayleaf and
vanilla. The first vintage was the 1993. Matured
in 50% new barrels. The vineyard is to be
almost doubled in area.

Ch Charmail   map 21/R K9
cru bourgeois
owner: Roger Sèze *area:* 22 ha *cases:* 12,300
grape % R: MER 50% CF 20% CS 30% *second wine:*
Ch Saint-Seurin *other châteaux owned:* Ch Mayne-
Vieil *(Fronsac)*
33180 St-Seurin-de-Cadourne tel: 05 56 59 70 63
fax: 05 56 59 39 20
Strikingly good wines have been made here
since 1990, rich in extract and with a good
depth of taste. They usually have ripe
blackcurrant fruit, a supple, fleshy structure,
and show a range of nuances from their one
year in *barriques*, a quarter of which are new:
toast, coffee, herbs, creamy vanilla.

Ch Cissac   map 20 F6
cru bourgeois
owner: Louis Vialard *area:* 50 ha *cases:* 25,000
grape % R: CS 75% MER 20% PV 5% *second wine:*
Reflets du Château Cissac *other châteaux owned:*
Ch du Breuil *(Haut-Médoc)*; Ch Tour du Mirail *(Haut-
Médoc)*
33250 Cissac-Médoc tel: 05 56 59 58 13
fax: 05 56 59 55 67
The Cissac style is that of a fairly classic, quite
robust Haut-Médoc, sometimes a little austere
but also full of character. Generally the wine
has depth, length, good tannins, and the
nuances of berry and cherry fruit, spice and
leather. Maturing lasts 18 months in cask (25-
50% new). The Vialard family acquired Cissac in
1885. The château, attributed to the famous
architect Victor Louis, dates from 1769 and may
stand on the site of a villa that belonged to the
Roman poet Cissus – the village of Cissac is
named after him. The Vialard family also look
after the commercial interests of the local
cooperative and bottle its wines.

Ch Citran   map 17 H8
cru bourgeois
owner: Groupe Bernard Taillan/Famille Merlaut
area: 90 ha *cases:* 45,000 *grape % R:* CS 58% MER
42% *second wine:* Moulins de Citran *other wines:*
Moulins de Citran *(Bordeaux Rosé)* *other châteaux*
owned: Ch Chasse-Spleen *(Moulis-en-Médoc)*, Ch
Ferrière *(Margaux)*; Ch La Gurgue *(Margaux)*
33480 Avensan tel: 05 56 58 21 01
fax: 05 56 58 12 19
Now owned by the family which controls Ch
Chasse-Spleen among other estates, for nearly
10 years from 1987 Citran belonged to the
Japanese real estate company Touko-Haus. In a
spectacular and most admirable way the firm
took this estate to the top of the *crus bourgeois*.
Artificial fertilizers, weedkillers and grape-
picking machines were barred from the
vineyard, which was given a new drainage
system. The hand-picked bunches are now also
hand-sorted and there is an ultra-modern
cuvier. The annual 40-50% of new *barriques*
come from four different coopers (ageing lasts
16 months). After surprisingly good wines in
1987 and 1988, Citran achieved a definitive
breakthrough with the 1989 and subsequent
vintages. The taste is rich and mouthfilling; a
delicious combination of voluptuous fruit, a
velvety spiciness, creamy vanilla, toasty oak and
integrated tannins. Besides its similarly fine
second wine, Citran also makes an exquisite
Bordeaux rosé.

Ch Clément Pichon   map 18 H7
cru bourgeois
owner: Clément Fayat *area:* 25 ha *cases:* 15,000
grape % R: MER 40% CS 35% CF 25% *second wine:*
La Motte de Clément Pichon *other châteaux*
owned: Ch Prieurs de la Commanderie *(Pomerol)*;
Ch La Dominique *(St-Emilion)*
33290 Parempuyre tel: 05 56 35 23 79
fax: 05 56 35 85 23
This château, on the northern outskirts of the
city, is one of the most attractive in the Médoc,
if not in all Bordeaux. It was built in 1881 in a
richly detailed style with Gothic, Renaissance
and Baroque features, and stands in the middle
of a delightful park replete with pools, trees and
statuary. The interior, too, is impressive in its
splendour. Since 1976 it has belonged to the
industrialist and wine grower Clément Fayat,

who has replanted the whole vineyard and
refurbished the winery. This appealing wine is
generally smooth and rounded, with supple
fruit (plum, cherry, black and red currants),
dark earthy aromas and vanilla oak from 16-18
months in cask, 25-50% of these being new.

Ch Colome Peylande   map 19 E6
owner: Nicole Dedieu-Benoit *area:* 4.5 ha *cases:*
2,000 *grape % R:* CS 60% MER 40%
33460 Cussac-Fort-Médoc tel: 05 56 58 93 08
This modest family concern has been bottling
its own wine since 1987. It is a classic Haut-
Médoc, somewhat austere and with firm tannins
at first – but with fruit to keep the balance.
Aged in used casks.

Ch Comtesse du Parc   map 20 C8
owner: Jean Anney *area:* 6 ha *cases:* 2,500 *grape*
% R: MER 50% CS 50% *other châteaux owned:* Ch
Baradieu *(St-Estèphe)*; Ch Tour des Termes *(St-
Estèphe)*
33180 Vertheuil tel: 05 56 59 32 89
fax: 05 56 59 73 74
Decent, although not very expressive Haut-
Médoc with reasonable fruit and not much oak.
Soon ready to drink as a rule.

Below: Ch Cambon la Pelouse

Above: Ch Cantemerle

Above: Ch Charmail

Ch Coufran   map 21/R H9
cru bourgeois
owner: Famille Miailhe **area:** 75 ha **cases:** 40,000 **grape % R:** MER 85% CS 15% **second wine:** Ch La Rose Maréchale **other châteaux owned:** Ch Verdignan (Haut-Médoc)
33180 St-Seurin-de-Cadourne tel: 05 56 59 31 02
fax: 05 56 81 32 35
This estate has a remarkably high proportion of Merlot in its vineyard 85%. From this comes a rather untypical Haut-Médoc, generally with more roundness than breeding, and not intended for very long maturing. At the same time it is a wine with juicy, jammy fruit and discreet elements of oak, toast and vanilla – 25% of the *barriques* are new. Its quality presents a consistent profile. The tastefully restored white château dates from the end of the 18th century.

Ch Dasvin-Bel-Air   map 18 C7
cru bourgeois
owner: Indivision Tessandier **area:** 13 ha **cases:** 10,000 **grape % R:** CS 60% MER 30% CF 10% **other châteaux owned:** include Ch Maucamps (Haut-Médoc); Ch Lescalle (Bordeaux Supérieur); Ch Barreyre (Bordeaux Supérieur); Ch Laronde Desormes (Bordeaux); Ch Moulin Noir (Lussac-St-Emilion/Montagne-St-Emilion)
33460 Macau tel: 05 57 88 07 64
fax: 05 57 88 07 00
This estate has plots both on the highest gravel soils of Blanquefort and in Macau, near Ch Cantemerle. Its wine is made at Ch Maucamps, Macau, and usually has a very creditable quality: a reasonably full-bodied structure, some fruit and vanilla; seldom really austere.

Ch Decorde   map 17 G3
cru bourgeois
owner: SCE Mazeau **area:** 15 ha **cases:** 8,300 **grape % R:** MER 50% CS 50%.
33480 Listrac tel: 05 57 43 01 44
fax: 05 57 43 08 75
This wine, distributed by Robert Giraud, generally offers an accessible, supple taste – not especially complex but provided with oak from the 20% of new casks each year – good tannins, spices and juicy, jammy fruit, including plum. The Ch Decorde vineyard was laid out in the 18th century.

Ch Devise d'Ardilley   map 20 L7
owner: Hervé Godin **area:** 8 ha **cases:** 3,500 **grape % R:** CS 40% CF 20% MER 30% PV 10%
33112 St-Laurent-Médoc tel: 05 56 59 40 87
fax: 05 56 59 92 65
The tennis coach Hervé Godin took over this estate in 1992 when it covered 5 ha. He invested in extra maturing casks – a sixth of them new for each vintage – and right from the start made a superb Haut-Médoc. The wine has colour, power, tannin, concentration and a lot of black fruit. The vineyard will extend over 10-12 ha before the 21st century begins.

Ch Dillon   map 18 I5
owner: Lycée Viticole de Bordeaux-Blanquefort **area:** 35 ha **cases:** 17,500 **grape % R:** MER 48% CS 44% CF 5% PV 2% CARMENÈRE 1% **second wine:** Ch Breillan **other châteaux owned:** Ch Linas (Bordeaux)
33290 Blanquefort tel: 05 56 95 39 94
fax: 05 56 95 36 75
Following the sale of this estate – named after an 18th-century owner – to an educational institute, a *lycée agricole* was set up here. This has its own vineyard from which a dry white Bordeaux is made, as well as a decent Haut-Médoc. The latter is not a particularly distinctive wine, but it has a generally supple taste, with reasonable concentration, a good length and a pleasing amount of fruit. In the *chai* the casks, a third of them new, are watched over by huge sculptures of noses, the work of Erik Dietman.

Ch d'Esteau   map 20 H5
owner: Serge Playa **area:** 3.6 ha **cases:** 2,000 **grape % R:** CS 60% MER 30% CF 10%
33250 St-Sauveur tel: 05 56 59 57 02
This small estate, soon to grow by 1.5 ha, yields a pleasant wine. Without claiming greatness, it offers fresh berry fruit and some spicy oak. About 40% of the *barriques* are new each year.

Ch La Fon Du Berger   map 19 J8
owner: Gerard Bougés **area:** 11 ha **cases:** 6,000 **grape % R:** CS 60% MER 30% CF 5% PV 5% **second wine:** Ch Plantey de Lieujean
33250 St-Sauveur tel: 05 56 59 51 43
fax: 05 56 73 90 61
The wine is a firm Haut-Médoc supported by tannin and classically nurtured, with 14 months

in casks of which 20% are new. After planting the vines here in 1983 the owner worked with the local cooperative up to the 1987 vintage. Since 1988 he has vinified the grapes himself. The wine is in the *cru artisan* category.

Ch Fontesteau   map 20 G5
cru bourgeois
owner: Dominique Fouin & Jean Renaud **area:** 22 ha **cases:** 10,000 **grape % R:** CS 40% MER 30% CF 25% PV 5% **second wines:** Messire de Fontesteau; Ch Croix de Moussas **other wines:** Messire de Fontesteau (Bordeaux Clairet)
33250 St-Sauveur tel: 05 56 59 52 76
fax: 05 56 59 57 89
An isolated estate in the middle of a wood; it derives its name from the springs (*fontaines d'eau*) on its land. The château was once a hunting lodge. Up against the front of the unremarkable building there stands a tower from 1277, and the lower sections of two other towers are to be found round the back. As a rule it takes about five years before this fairly light wine begins to lose its rather tough and sometimes dry tannins, and smooth, ripe fruit (blackberry, blackcurrants), together with a hint of vanilla, starts to break through. The Cuvée Vinésimes tastes rather more full-bodied, powerful and intense.

Ch Fort de Vauban   map 19 H7
cru bourgeois
owner: André Noleau **area:** 12 ha **cases:** 6,050 **grape % R:** MER 60% CS 30% PV 10% **second wine:** Les Treilles de Vauban (Bordeaux Supérieur)
33460 Cussac-Fort-Médoc tel: 05 56 58 93 38
An estate worked in *artisanale* mode; it still has some plots of very old vines. The wine matures for two years in tanks and casks; its style is traditional, tending to the rustic. It ages well, as is clear from the old vintages still available at the château. Buyers can choose between two labels, one with a drawing of the Marquis de Vauban, the other with a photo of the fort. A dry white Bordeaux, a pure Sauvignon, is produced under the name Clos Lisot.

◆ Châteaux in a commune

To find out which châteaux are in a certain commune, which may be useful in a large appellation such as Haut-Médoc, or in zones such as the Entre-Deux-Mers where several appellations can apply, consult the index of châteaux by commune at the end of the book.

This lists the châteaux in this Atlas, arranged alphabetically by commune, with a page number.

Ch Fournas Bernadotte   map 19 I8
cru bourgeois
owner: Curt Eklund **area:** 20.2 ha **cases:** 12,950 **grape % R:** CS 62% MER 26% PV 1% CF 1% **other châteaux owned:** Ch Bernadotte (Pauillac); Ch Proche-Pontet (Haut-Médoc)
33250 St-Sauveur tel: 05 56 59 57 04
fax: 05 56 59 54 84
Clean, attractive, fragrant Haut-Médoc. In its elegant taste nuances of noble oak and a touch of fresh berry fruit can be found. The name

Bernadotte comes from the family of the Napoleonic period whose connections include the Swedish royal house.

Ch de Gironville
map **18 D6**

cru bourgeois
owner: SC de la Gironville/Familles Fouin & Raoult
area: 12 ha **cases:** 6,000 **grape % R:** CS 58% MER
34% PV 8% **second wine:** Ch Duc de Gironville
33460 Macau tel: 05 57 88 19 79
fax: 05 57 88 41 79

The 18th-century château was built where a huge Roman villa once stood, and later a mighty fortress called Gironville. In the 19th century the wine produced here enjoyed a great reputation, but in 1929 the whole vineyard was uprooted except for one small plot. There was no replanting until 1987. The wine lacks some depth and backbone as yet, but gives a good deal of pleasure, especially when young. Besides its smooth fruit there are elements of oak present: this Haut-Médoc is aged for 14 months in 20-30% new barrels. Worth following.

Ch Grand Clapeau Olivier
map **18 H4**

cru bourgeois
owner: Pierre Baudinière **area:** 26 ha **cases:**
15,000 **grape % R:** CS 55% MER 35% CF 5% PV 5%
33290 Blanquefort tel: 05 56 95 00 89
fax: 05 56 95 35 92

Not really full-bodied, but nevertheless a fairly classic Haut-Médoc, quite taut from its tannins, with blackcurrant from the Cabernets, juiciness from the Merlot and oak notes from 18-24 months in cask. This property is one of the best-known in Blanquefort, with a vineyard that lies on the highest gravel bed in the locality.

Ch Grandis
map **21/R J9**

cru bourgeois
owner: François-Joseph Vergez **area:** 9.2 ha **cases:**
3,000 **grape % R:** CS 50% MER 30% CF 20% **second
wine:** Ch Maurac-Major
33180 St-Seurin-de-Cadourne tel: 05 56 59 31 16
fax: 05 56 59 39 85

An estate to be increased by about 30%; its wine is not grandiose, nor very complex, but is has firmness, juicy berry fruit balanced with spicy oak (a third of the barrels are new), and strong, sometimes rather dry tannins. The name comes from a Dutch engineer who came to the Médoc in the 17th century to drain the marshes.

Below: Ch Cissac

Above: Ch Coufran

Domaine Grand Lafont
map **18 D7**

owner: André-Marc Lavanceau **area:** 4 ha **cases:**
1,300 **grape % R:** CS 50% MER 35% CF 10% PV 5%
33290 Ludon-Médoc tel: 05 57 88 44 31

Wines from this modest estate have received awards nearly every year since 1975, although their character can vary from vintage to vintage. Sometimes this Haut-Médoc is rather rustic in taste, with spicy oak as well as some berry fruit; sometimes it is rich and rounded, with remarkable depths – as happened in 1991 and 1993. Maturing in barrel lasts at least 22 months. The Grand Lafont vineyard lies close to that of Ch La Lagune.

Ch Grand Moulin
map **21/R J7**

owner: Robert Gonzalvez **area:** 18 ha **cases:**
10,000 **grape % R:** CS 50% MER 45% CF 5% **second
wine:** Ch Mouliney
33180 St-Seurin-de-Cadourne tel: 05 56 59 35 95
fax: 05 56 59 35 44

Juicy, supple-tasting wine without any great rigour, or hard tannins. It is fairly rounded and agreeable, but rather short of complexity and depth. Grand Moulin Is aged for a short time in used barrels. The same wine is also sold as Ch La Mothe.

Ch Hanteillan
map **20 E8**

cru bourgeois
owner: Catherine Blasco **area:** 82 ha **cases:**
45,000 **grape % R:** CS 52% MER 39% CF 5% PV 4%
second wines: Ch Laborde; Ch Blagnac
33250 Cissac-Médoc tel: 05 56 59 35 31
fax: 05 56 59 31 51

As early as 1179 this estate was mentioned as belonging to the abbey of Vertheuil. However, as the 20th century proceeded the château fell into ruin, the vineyard into neglect. At last, in 1972 new owners took over and a total rehabilitation began. The estate has since been transformed – the old château has been demolished and replaced by a new building. The park has been laid out anew, the winery has been modernized, and the vineyard area has grown from 10 ha to 82. Characteristically the wine possesses a feminine grace, the attractive fruitiness of berries and currants, an oak aroma suggesting toast and chocolate (a third of the barrels being new each year) and a fine balance.

Ch Haut-Bellevue
map **19 I8**

owner: Alain Roses **area:** 10 ha **cases:** 5,200
grape % R: MER 55% CS 45% **second wine:** Ch
Bellevue Canteranne
33460 Lamarque tel: 05 56 58 91 64
fax: 05 57 88 50 64

Unfiltered wine, mostly Merlot, that offers integrated tannins, spicy oak, and berries as its fruit. It is consistent in quality and often wins medals. Since 1991 the owner has had at his disposal stainless-steel fermentation tanks and a newly-built barrel-cellar.

Ch Haut du Puy

owner: Famille Pelletier **area:** 6 ha **cases:** 3,000
grape % R: CS 60% MER 40%
33250 Cissac-Médoc tel: 05 56 59 58 13
fax: 05 56 59 55 67

Wine with a not unpleasing taste, vinified by the Cissac cooperative and bottled by Louis Vialard of Ch Cissac. Although it possesses little depth, it does have a touch of cherry, blackcurrants and spices, with also a hint of bitterness and sometimes freshness. The wine does not come into contact with wood.

Ch Haut-Gouat
map **20 C5**

cru bourgeois
owner: Nicole Lepine **area:** 4.5 ha **cases:** 1,500
grape % R: MER 50% CS 50% **other châteaux owned:**
Ch Cassan d'Esteuil *(Médoc)*
33180 Vertheuil tel: 05 56 41 97 98
fax: 05 56 41 98 53

Firm, traditionally made wine with the potential to age in bottle. It spends 18-24 months in casks which have been used for one previous vintage.

Ch Haut-Logat
map **20 F6**

cru bourgeois
owner: Marcel & Christian Quancard **area:** 20 ha
cases: 10,000 **grape % R:** CS 60% MER 30% CF 10%
second wine: Ch La Croix Margantot **other
châteaux owned:** include Ch de Terrefort-Quancard
(Bordeaux Supérieur); Ch de Paillet-Quancard
(Premières Côtes de Bordeaux); Ch Tour St-Joseph
(Haut-Médoc)
33250 Cissac-Médoc tel: 05 56 33 80 60

Succulent, quite lively Haut-Médoc with elements of jammy fruit – especially plum – spice, oak (30% of the casks are new each year) and reasonably firm, but not tough, tannins. This is simply a good-tasting, well-made wine.

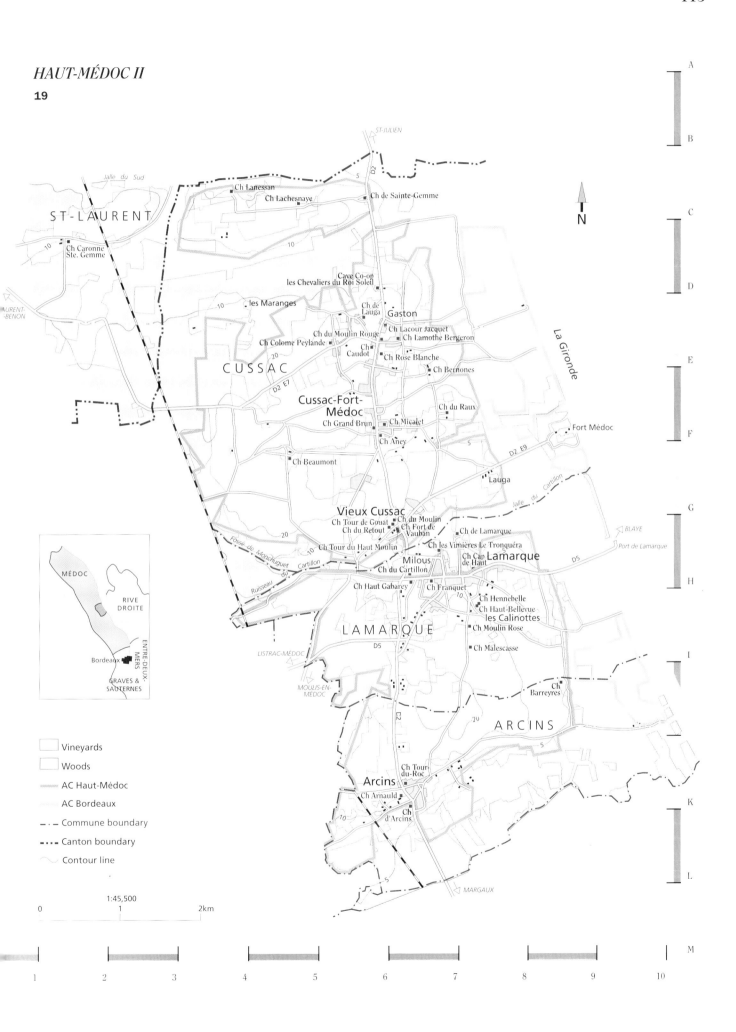

ST-JULIEN

ST-LAURENT

Jalle du Sud

Ch Lanessan
Ch Lachesnaye
Ch de Sainte-Gemme

Ch Caronne
Ste. Gemme

AURENT-
-BENON

10

10

Cave Co-op
les Chevaliers du Roi Soleil

les Maranges

Ch de
Lauga

Gaston

Ch du Moulin Rouge

Ch Lacour Jacquet
Ch Lamothe Bergeron

Ch Colome Peylande

Ch
Caudot

Ch Rose Blanche

CUSSAC

Ch Bernones

D2 E7

Cussac-Fort-
Médoc

Ch du Raux

Ch Micalet

Ch Grand Brun

Fort Médoc

Ch Aney

5

D2 E9

Ch Beaumont

Lauga

La Gironde

Jalle du Cartillon

Vieux Cussac

Ch Tour de Gouat
Ch du Retout

Ch du Moulin
Ch Fort de
Vauban

Ch de Lamarque

BLAYE

Ch Tour du Haut Moulin

Ch les Vimières Le Tronquéra

Port de Lamarque

Fossé de Monchuquet

Milous

Ch Cap
de Haut

Lamarque

D5

Ruisseau du Cartillon

Ch du Cartillon

Ch Haut Gabarey

Ch Franquet

Ch Hennebelle
Ch Haut-Bellevue
les Calinottes

Ch Moulin Rose

LAMARQUE

D5

Ch Malescasse

LISTRAC-MÉDOC

Ch
Barreyres

MOULIS-EN-
MÉDOC

D2

ARCINS

20

5

Ch Tour-
du-Roc

Arcins

Ch Arnauld

Ch
d'Arcins

10

5

MARGAUX

MÉDOC

RIVE
DROITE

Bordeaux

ENTRE-DEUX-
MERS

GRAVES &
SAUTERNES

☐ Vineyards

☐ Woods

Ξ AC Haut-Médoc

Ξ AC Bordeaux

–·–· Commune boundary

▪▪▪ Canton boundary

〰 Contour line

1:45,500

0   1   2km

Above: Ch Hanteillan

Above: Ch de Lamarque

Ch La Houringue
map **18 D5**

owner: Eric Albada Jelgersma **area:** 28 ha **cases:** 16,000 **grape % R:** MER 47% CS 43% CF 5% PV 5% **other châteaux owned:** Ch Rose la Biche (Haut-Médoc); Ch Giscours (Margaux)
33460 Macau tel: 05 57 97 09 09
fax: 05 57 97 09 00

Wine made by the team from Ch Giscours, Margaux. It usually has a quite firm structure with berry fruit, supple tannins and smoothly spicy oak. Some 70% of it goes into *barriques*, almost half of these being new.

Ch du Junca
map **20 G7**

owner: Serge Tiffon **area:** 14 ha **cases:** 7,000 **grape % R:** CS 70% MER 30% **second wine:** Ch Haut Carras
33250 St-Sauveur-de-Médoc tel: 05 56 59 56 35

Solidly built Haut-Médoc which usually displays a good dose of berry fruits in its aroma, together with vanilla oak elements: 25% of the casks are new; maturing in them lasts a year. Until the early 1980s a cooperative made the du Junca wine.

◆

Grape varieties

Main and other permitted varieties for each appellation are given in the appellation fact box at the end of the relevant introduction. For châteaux, percentages of grapes grown are given as supplied by the château.

The abbreviations used are:
CF Cabernet Franc,
COL Colombard, CS Cabernet Sauvignon,
MAL Malbec, MER Merlot, MUSC Muscadelle,
PV Petit Verdot, SAUV B Sauvignon Blanc,
SEM Sémillon

◆

Maps of the Médoc & Graves appellations

For a key map showing all the appellations in this zone, with the outlines of the maps in this Atlas, consult Map 7.

Ch Lachesnaye
map **19 C5**

cru bourgeois

owner: GFA des Domaines Bouteiller **area:** 20 ha **cases:** 10,000 **grape % R:** MER 50% CS 50% **other châteaux owned:** Ch Lanessan (Haut-Médoc); Ch de Sainte Gemme (Haut-Médoc)
33460 Cussac-Fort-Médoc tel: 05 56 58 94 80
fax: 05 56 58 93 10

Anyone taking the road up to Ch Lanessan will pass this property. It was therefore logical for the Bouteiller family, Lanessan's owners, to buy this neighbouring estate – which they did in 1961. All the vines had disappeared by then, but gradually the Lachesnaye vineyard has been replanted: eventually it will cover 22 ha. The wine is both elegant and firm, a little reserved in character, with modest notes of black and red fruit, oak from a year in used barrels, and sometimes a little licorice and bayleaf. Like Lanessan, the château is in English Stuart style.

Ch Lacour Jacquet
map **19 E6**

owner: GAEC Lartigue **area:** 12.8 ha **cases:** 6,500 **grape % R:** MER 50% CS 50%
33460 Cussac-Fort-Médoc tel: 05 56 58 91 55

The Merlot that accounts for half the vines here can distinctly be tasted in this quite rounded, mouthfilling and usually dark-toned wine. One-third of the barrels in which it matures for 18 months before bottling are new.

Ch La Lagune
map **18 E6**

3ème cru

owner: Jean-Michel & Alain Ducellier **area:** 72 ha **cases:** 37,000 **grape % R:** CS 60% MER 20% CF 10% PV 10% **second wine:** Ch Ludon Pomiès Agassac ; Le Moulin de Ludon **other firms owned:** Champagne Ayala; Champagne Montebello
33290 Ludon-Médoc tel: 05 57 88 44 07
fax: 05 57 88 05 37

This *chartreuse*, from 1715, boasts a double flight of steps at the front, and a wide terrace at the back from which to view the vineyard. Despite its classification in 1855 the estate underwent difficult times in the first half of the 20th century. Georges Brunet was its rescuer; he bought the totally neglected La Lagune in 1954 and built it up again. Since then the wine has proved exceptionally reliable. It is a great, complete Haut-Médoc – substantial without being overwhelming, full of appealing oak

nuances such as fresh toast from the 80% of new casks, with candied plum and berry fruit, earthy, spicy tones, some bayleaf as well... and every component is usually beautifully balanced.

Ch de Lamarque
map **19 H7**

cru bourgeois

owner: Pierre-Gilles Gromand d'Evry **area:** 50 ha **cases:** 24,000 **grape % R:** CS 46% MER 25% CF 24% PV 5% **second wines:** Donjon de Lamarque; Reservé de Marquis d'Evry **other châteaux owned:** Ch Cap de Haut (Haut-Médoc)
33460 Lamarque tel: 05 56 58 90 03
fax: 05 56 58 93 43

This castle is a splendidly preserved medieval stronghold, reached by way of a tree-lined drive. It boasts a variety of towers, walls and battlements, a fine courtyard and richly furnished rooms. The oldest parts, including cellars and chapel, go back to the 11th and 12th centuries. The castle acquired its present form in the 14th century. The only subsequent rebuilding took place in the 17th century. Ch de Lamarque wine is a fairly solid, full-bodied Haut-Médoc, matured for at least a year in *barriques* of which 30% are new. After a few years' bottle-age to soften the tannins, the wine takes on a velvety taste in which spicy oak and blackcurrants generally play a leading part.

Ch Lamothe Bergeron
map **19 E7**

cru bourgeois

owner: SC de Grand-Puy Ducasse (Mestrezat) **area:** 66 ha **cases:** 30,000 **grape % R:** CS 52% MER 34% CF 14% **second wine:** Ch Romefort **other châteaux owned:** Ch Tourteau Chollet (Graves); Ch Marsac Seguineau (Margaux); Ch Blaignan (Médoc); Ch de Rayne Vigneau (Sauternes); Ch Grand-Puy Ducasse (Pauillac)
33460 Cussac-Fort-Médoc tel: 05 56 01 30 10
fax: 05 56 79 23 57

Balanced, elegant, firm wine with a deep colour and fresh fruit – all the various berries can be tasted. It has good oak, being matured for 16-18 months (a quarter of the casks are new each vintage), and displays supple tannins and a lively character. The château dates from 1868; it replaced an earlier castle on this mound (*motte* or *mothe* in French), sited halfway between the Cussac village church and the banks of the Gironde.

Ch Lamothe-Cissac map **20 F6**
cru bourgeois
owner: Domaines Fabre *area:* 33 ha *cases:* 18,300
grape % R: CS 70% MER 26% PV 4% *second wine:* Ch
Fonsèche *other châteaux owned:* Ch La Tonnelle
(Haut-Médoc); Ch Landat *(Haut-Médoc)*
33250 Cissac-Médoc tel: 05 56 59 58 16
fax: 05 56 59 57 97
This is a Belle-Epoque-style château of 1912.
Remains of a Roman villa have been found on
the estate, which may mean that winemaking
has a particularly long history here. Today's
wine is generally an unremarkable Haut-Médoc.
Its average quality, however, seems to be
improving – and in some years, for example
1990, the outcome is actually a fine, thoroughly
fruity wine, with elements of tobacco, bayleaf,
cedar and vanilla. 20% of the barrels are
replaced by new ones each year. The potential is
clearly there.

Ch Landat map **20 E6**
cru bourgeois
owner: Domaines Fabre *area:* 20 ha *cases:* 11,000
grape % R: CS 75% MER 20% PV 5% *second wine:* Ch
Labastide *other châteaux owned:* Ch Lamothe-
Cissac *(Haut-Médoc)*; Ch La Tonnelle *(Haut-Médoc)*
33250 Cissac-Médoc tel: 05 56 59 58 16
fax: 05 56 59 57 97
Fairly angular, slender wine with notes of an
autumn wood, spices, berry fruit and oak. A
fifth of the casks for maturing are new. The
Vieilles Vignes *cuvée* has more oak to it. The
vineyard stretches into two communes, Cissac
and Verteuil.

Ch Lanessan map **19 C4**
owner: GFA des Domaines Bouteiller *area:* 40 ha
cases: 20,000 *grape % R:* CS 75% MER 20% CF 3%
PV 2% *other châteaux owned:* Ch de Sainte Gemme
(Haut-Médoc); Ch Lachesnaye *(Haut-Médoc)*
33460 Cussac-Fort-Médoc tel: 05 56 58 94 80
fax: 05 56 58 93 10
In the first half of the 19th century the writer
Jullien placed Lanessan among the wines that
in 1855 were to be classified as *quatrièmes crus
classés*. Alas, the estate did not appear, due to
the carelessness, or complacency, of the owner
at that time, Louis Delbos: he submitted no
bottles for sampling. André Delbos, owner from
1867 to 1909, had a different attitude. In 1878
he built an entirely new château in English
Stuart style, installed what for those days was a
very modern *cuvier*, and also used the estate as
a base for his hobby: horses and carriages. This
is why Ch Lanessan still has stables, a saddlery
and a collection of coaches; together they make
up the Musée du Cheval. Lanessan remains a
superior Haut-Médoc – rich in tannin,
muscular, concentrated, dark-coloured. And in
good years it also has spices, herbs, cedarwood
and ample fruit – berries and prunes. Ageing
can last from 18-30 months, mostly in used
barriques.

Ch Larose-Trintaudon map **20 K9**
cru bourgeois
owner: AGF *area:* 172 ha *cases:* 100,000 *grape %
R:* CS 60% MER 30% CF 10% *second wine:* Ch Larose
Saint-Laurent *other châteaux owned:* Ch La Fleur
Saint Georges *(Lalande-de-Pomerol)*; Ch La Tourette
(Pauillac)
33112 St-Laurent-Médoc tel: 05 56 59 41 72
fax: 05 56 59 92 22
When the Forner brothers, who up till then
produced *vins de table* in the South of France,

Above: Ch Lamothe-Cissac

bought this château in 1965 not a single vine
remained. A year later, with the expert help of
the renowned Professor Emile Peynaud and
others, an extensive replanting programme was
started – and from it emerged the biggest
vineyard in the Médoc. It covers no less than
172 ha and is good for 100,000 cases annually. A
new cellar complex had of course to be built to
process the huge quantities of wine. The first
commercial vintage came in 1975. Some 11
years later, in October 1986, the Forners sold
the estate to the AGF insurance company,
which made further investments here. The
château with its notable tower was also
refurbished. This reliable wine is
characteristically a quite supple, smooth Haut-
Médoc from the outset: elegant, pleasantly
fruity and with toasty oak. Each year AGF
replaces 30-35% of the 2,700 *barriques*.

Ch Larrivaux Vicomtesse de Carheil
map **20 E7**
cru bourgeois
owner: Famille Carlsberg *area:* 23.90 ha *cases:*
12,000 *grape % R:* CS 43% MER 37% PV 13% CF 7%
second wine: Ch Le Borderon
33250 Cissac-Médoc tel: 05 56 59 58 15
fax: 05 56 02 73 31

Below: Ch Lanessan

Vineyard just east of the village of Cissac, that
for three centuries has been handed down from
daughter to daughter within the same family.
This is a decent, middle-range wine, not really
full-bodied or complex, but with pleasing fruit –
berries especially, sometimes a hint of plum and
cherry – and with little oak.

Ch de Lauga map **19 E6**
owner: Christian Brun *area:* 4 ha *cases:* 1,250
grape % R: CS 50% MER 40% CF 5% PV 5%
33460 Cussac-Fort-Médoc tel: 05 56 58 92 83
fax: 05 56 58 92 83
It was a family of coopers who established this
cru artisan more than five generations ago.
Needless to say good *barriques* – a third of
them new – are still used, giving a slight aroma
of toast, with a touch of aniseed. Appetizing
fresh fruit is another feature of this engaging
wine. The vineyard is to grow by 1.5 ha.

Ch Lemoine-Lafon-Rochet map **18 E7**
cru bourgeois
owner: Famille Sabourin *area:* 8 ha *cases:* 4,600
grape % R: CS 75% MER 25% *other châteaux owned:*
Ch Crusquet-Sabourin *(1èr Côtes de Blaye)*; Ch
Cône-Taillasson-Sabourin *(1èr Côtes de Blaye)*
33290 Ludon-Médoc tel: 05 57 42 15 27
fax: 05 57 42 05 47
Vineyard on the Ludon plateau, bordering Ch
La Lagune. The wine often has elements of
cedar and angular tannins; its fruit is somewhat
restrained. It spends 18 months in mainly used
casks. Of average, unremarkable quality.

Ch Lestage Simon map **21/R J8**
cru bourgeois
owner: Charles Simon *area:* 40 ha *cases:* 16,000
grape % R: MER 68% CS 22% CF 10% *second wine:*
Ch Troupian
33180 St-Seurin-de-Cadourne tel: 05 56 59 31 83
fax: 05 56 59 70 56
Perfectly equipped and maintained estate; its
wine appears on the menus of many a top-class
restaurant, and is often an award-winner. It
offers a taste rich in extract and alcohol, juicy,
reasonably expansive and well concentrated.
The tannins are likely to be ripe, and the aroma
to contain elements of black cherry (a lot of
Merlot is used), blackberry, strawberry and
raspberry. No lack of oak, either, with a third of
the casks renewed each year. The wine is not
perhaps the last word in finesse, but it does
show class – and is simply a delight to drink.

Ch Lieujean
map 20 I8

cru bourgeois
owner: Dovile Lieujean/Famille Penot **area:** 66 ha
cases: 34,000; white 750 **grape % R:** CS 64% MER
30% PV 6% **grape % W:** SAUV B 100% **second wine:**
Fief de Cantelande **other wine:** Bordeaux blanc
other châteaux owned: Ch La Grave (Haut-Médoc);
Ch Bell Ille (Bordeaux Supérieur); Ch La Terrasse
(Bordeaux Supérieur); Ch Calmeilh (Bordeaux
Supérieur)
33250 St-Sauveur tel: 05 56 59 57 23
fax: 05 56 59 50 81
Lieujean's calibre was demonstrated by the
quarter-final place once achieved in the Coupe
des Crus Bourgeois. This Haut-Médoc generally
has the tannins and the staying-power of a
Pauillac, with elements of charred oak from the
20-30% of new barrels, some fruit and spices.
About 1.5 ha is planted with Sauvignon Blanc,
from which a small amount of dry white
Bordeaux is made. The history of the estate
goes back to the 15th century, but Lieujean
only turned its hand to wine in 1868. Part of
the Haut-Médoc production is often sold as Ch
Haut-Laborde, exclusively through a négociant.

Ch Liversan
map 20 H7

cru bourgeois
owner: Prince Guy de Polignac **area:** 50 ha **cases:**
27,000 **grape % R:** CS 49% MER 38% CF 10% PV 3%
second wines: Les Charmes de Liversan; Ch
Fonpigueyre
33250 St-Sauveur tel: 05 56 41 50 18
fax: 05 56 41 54 65
The original château here survives only as an
overgrown ruin. The building that now goes by
the name of Ch Liversan is in fact Ch
Fonpigueyre (a second wine carries that name).
A great deal was invested in this estate in the
1980s, with favourable results for the wine. This
Haut-Médoc possesses tannins that are at once
firm and supple, and in the silky, not overly
expressive taste, elements of oak, spice and fruit
are wont to blend harmoniously.

Ch Magnol
map 18 K6

cru bourgeois
owner: Barton & Guestier **area:** 17 ha **cases:** 8,000
grape % R: CS 50% MER 50%
33290 Blanquefort tel: 05 56 95 48 00
fax: 05 56 95 48 01

Below: Ch Larose-Trintaudon

Attractive, quite meaty Haut-Médoc with
creamy vanilla, berry fruit and smooth, well-knit
tannins. The château is a chartreuse with a fine
courtyard and reception rooms in the wings.
Since 1968 it has belonged to Barton & Guestier.

Ch Malescasse
map 19 I8

cru bourgeois
owner: Alcatel Alsthom **area:** 37 ha **cases:** 16,700
grape % R: CS 46% MER 44% CF 10% **second wine:**
La Closerie de Malescasse **other châteaux owned:**
Ch Gruaud-Larose (St-Julien)
33460 Lamarque tel: 05 56 58 90 09
fax: 05 56 58 97 89
Château that sits at the highest point in
Lamarque; in June 1992 the Tesseron family, of
Ch Pontet-Canet, Pauillac, and other properties,
sold it to the telecommunications giant Alcatel
Alsthom. Alcatel built a new cuvier with
stainless-steel fermentation tanks, plus a new
chai; they bought barriques – 25% of them are
new each year – and made other improvements.
Since the 1992 vintage the results have been
there to taste. From being creditable the wine is
now close to excellence: plenty of colour, a firm
elegance, a creamy structure, aromatic, ripe
fruit, good oak and fine tannins. The first wine
spends 14 months in oak; the second 9.

Ch de Malleret
map 18 F5

cru bourgeois
owner: Bertrand du Vivier **area:** 31 ha **cases:**
19,000 **grape % R:** CS 60% MER 30% PV 5% CF 5%
second wine: Ch Barthez
33290 Le Pian-Médoc tel: 05 56 35 05 36
fax: 05 56 35 05 36
This estate is a whole world of its own. It covers
400 ha, with meadows, wheatfields, woodland
and vineyard. Horses are also bred here. The
monumental château is 19th-century. In good
years the wine is fairly flavoursome, respectably
mouthfilling but never heavy: smooth in its
fruit (a lot of berries) and spices, and with a
measure of oak. To mature the wine goes into
barriques, at least 20% new, for 12-14 months.

Ch Maucaillou Felletin
cru bourgeois
owner: Philippe Dourthe **area:** 6.7 ha **cases:** 4,000
grape % R: CS 60% MER 24% CF 16% **other châteaux
owned:** include Ch Maucaillou (Moulis-en-Médoc)

33480 Lamarque tel: 05 56 58 01 23
fax: 05 56 58 00 88
Philippe Dourthe bought Ch Felletin in 1972;
he added Maucaillou to the name in 1990, from
his property in Moulis. The wine is a very
creditable cru bourgeois, given 18 months in
barrels of which half to three-quarters are new.
It has an agreeable, generally fresh fruitiness, a
succulent taste, and good tannins.

Ch Maucamps
map 18 C7

owner: Indivision Tessandier **area:** 19 ha **cases:**
7,750 **grape % R:** CS 55% MER 40% PV 5% **second
wine:** Clos de May **other châteaux owned:** include
Ch Dasvin Belair (Haut-Médoc); Ch Moulin Noir
(Montagne-St-Emilion/Lussac-St-Emilion); Ch
Barreyre (Bordeaux Supérieur); Ch Lescalle
(Bordeaux Supérieur)
33460 Macau tel: 05 57 88 07 64
fax: 05 57 88 07 00
Estate that believes in traditional methods, and
one where the quality of the wine has been
improving greatly since the end of the 1980s.
Maucamps now yields a decently made wine
with fruit, a good measure of oak (from 12-16
months in casks of which at least a quarter are
new), agreeable tannins, style and finesse.
Visitors are only shown round the cellars, since
the 18th-century château itself functions today
as a rest home.

Ch Maurian de Prade
map 18 H5

cru bourgeois
owner: Jean-Pierre Cantelaube **area:** 6 ha **cases:**
3,000 **grape % R:** CS 40% CF 40% MER 20% **second
wine:** Ch Maurian
33290 Le Pian-Médoc tel: 05 56 79 36 20
At its best this is a reasonably firm, quite juicy
Haut-Médoc with plum and fig for its fruit, a
pleasantly bitter touch and a reasonable length.
Not matured in wood.

Ch Métria
map 17

owner: Christian Braquessac **area:** 17 ha **cases:**
8,500 **grape % R:** CS 50% MER 35% PV 15% **second
wines:** Ch d'Avensan; Ch Detey **other wines:** Ch
Tour Carelot (Haut-Médoc)
33480 Avensan tel: 05 56 58 71 39
fax: 05 56 58 19 97
Métria, created in 1985, launched its first
vintage in 1989. The Braquessac family sells
part of the production as Ch Tour Carelot.
There are also second wines: Ch d'Avensan and,
for cubitainers only, Ch Detey. The grand vin
contains a strikingly high percentage of Petit
Verdot and is a carefully made, elegant Haut-
Médoc. It matures for a year in oak (one-third
new casks), and has more substance, depth and
length than the Ch Tour Carelot.

Ch le Meynieu
map 20 D7

cru bourgeois
owner: SCEA des Domaines Pedro **area:** 15 ha
cases: 7,000 **grape % R:** CS 62% MER 30% CF 8%
second wine: Ch la Gravière **other châteaux owned:**
Ch de la Ronceray, Ch Lavillotte (St-Estèphe)
33180 Vertheuil tel: 05 56 41 98 17
fax: 05 56 41 98 89
The Pedro family put the accent more on
maturation than on vinification; so after three
months in tank the wine spends 20 months in
barrels, 30-40% of them new. Besides plentiful
oak, the wine nearly always has a spiciness, ripe
berry fruit and backbone, but in lighter years
oak and tannin can sometimes dominate. The
grey, unremarkable château is 19th-century.

HAUT-MÉDOC III

20

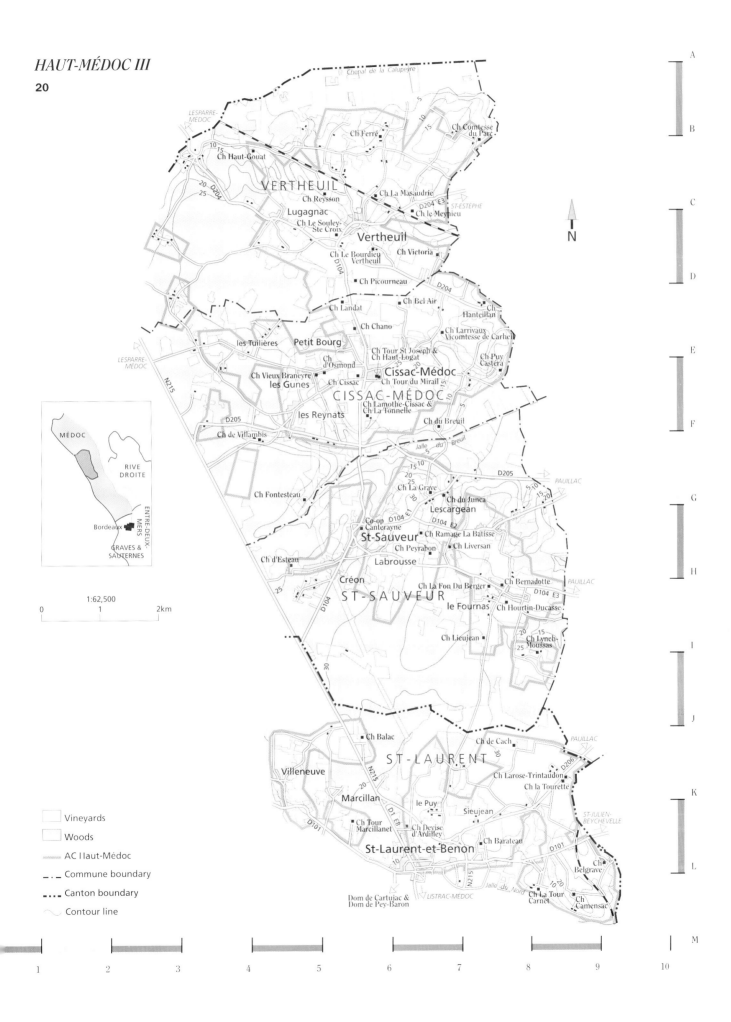

MÉDOC

RIVE
DROITE

ENTRE-DEUX-
MERS

Bordeaux

GRAVES-
SAUTERNES

1:62,500

0   1   2km

Vineyards

Woods

AC Haut-Médoc

Commune boundary

Canton boundary

Contour line

Ch Meyre
map 17 K6

cru bourgeois
owner: Colette Lenôtre *area:* 15.6 ha *cases:* 9,200
grape % R: MER 40% CS 36% CF 17% PV 7% *second wine:* Ch La Douve de Romefort *other châteaux owned:* l'Enclos Maucaillou *(Margaux)*
33480 Avensan tel: 05 56 58 10 77
fax: 05 56 58 13 20
In 1990 this château, which lies between its vineyard and a forest, was taken over by Colette Lenôtre, wife of the Parisian restaurateur Gaston Lenôtre. In the cellars with their modern equipment a graceful, quite fragrant wine emerges. It is still perhaps a little two-dimensional, but it is based on ripe fruit, good tannins and good oak – it matures for up to 18 months in *barriques*, 30% new. Worth watching.

Ch Micalet
map 19 F6

owner: Denis Fedieu *area:* 4.5 ha *cases:* 2,000
grape % R: MER 55% CS 40% CF 5%
33460 Cussac-Fort-Médoc tel: 05 56 58 95 48
Hand-picked grapes, macerated for three weeks, matured 18 months in mainly used casks, clarified with fresh egg white – methods are traditional at this *cru artisan*. The wine has a dark colour and a fairly firm, long, lingering taste, with fruit as well as oak. The vineyard area is to be increased by 2 ha. The château dates from 1850. From 1950 to 1970 the total grape harvest was taken to a cooperative.

Ch du Moulin Rouge
map 19 E6

cru bourgeois
owner: Famille Pelon-Ribeiro *area:* 15 ha *cases:* 8,500 *grape % R:* MER 50% CS 40% CF 10%
33460 Cussac-Fort-Médoc tel: 05 56 58 91 13
fax: 05 56 58 93 68
If the sun collaborates, wine from Moulin Rouge – named after an 18th-century mill on the estate – is a powerful, gutsy Haut-Médoc, full of character and rich in fruit (cherry, plum, berries), with some licorice and bayleaf. A third of the prodution spends 18 months in oak; around 20-33% of the barrels are new.

Ch d'Osmond
map 20 F6

owner: Philippe Tressol *area:* 6.3 ha *cases:* 3,000
grape % R: CS 50% MER 35% CF 8% PV 7% *second wine:* Domaine des Ardilleys
33250 Cissac-Médoc tel: 05 56 59 59 17
Talented winemaker Philippe Tressol created this estate in 1987 and makes an excellent *cru artisan*. This has fine oak tones with a hint of breadcrusts – 20% of the casks are of new wood. It has a firmly structured taste, generous in the great years and approachable rather than reserved. The wine will undoubtedly gain in depth as the vines get older.

Ch Paloumey
map 18 D5

owner: Martine Cazeneuve *area:* 18 ha *cases:* 10,000 *grape % R:* CS 55% MER 40% CF 5% *second wine:* Les Ailes de Paloumey *other châteaux owned:* Ch La Garricq *(Moulis)*; Ch La Bessane *(Margaux)*
33290 Ludon-Médoc tel: 05 57 88 00 66
fax: 05 57 88 00 67
Although this estate won international medals with its wines in the 19th century, it disappeared completely from the scene halfway through the 20th. Even the vineyard had been uprooted. Paloumey came to life again in 1990 after Martine Cazeneuve took over. The first vintages to appear were very promising, displaying considerable oak (25% of the

Above: Ch Lestage Simon

barriques being new), decent fruit and tannin. More depth can be expected as the vines' average age increases.

Domaine de Pey-Baron
map 20 M6

owner: Jacques André Rey *area:* 0.73 ha *cases:* 350 *grape % R:* CS 62% MER 26% PV 9% CF 3%
33112 St-Laurent-Médoc tel: 05 56 59 44 71
Tiny estate that even in less-good years can produce deep, powerful wines – though they can be dominated by acidity and hard tannins at the cost of the fruit. Five months in wood.

Ch Peyrabon
map 20 H7

cru bourgeois
owner: Jacques Babeau *area:* 53 ha *cases:* 27,500
grape % R: CS 50% MER 27% CF 23% *second wines:* Ch Lapiey; Ch Pierbone *other wines:* Ch La Fleur Peyrabon *(Pauillac)*
33250 St. Sauveur tel: 05 56 59 57 10 fax: 05 56 59 59 45
The great hall at this stately château boasts a painting of musical instruments, created specially for a concert that Queen Victoria attended here. Oak can sometimes rather dominate the wine, at least in the early years. For the rest Ch Peyrabon is a respectable, not over-refined or nuanced Haut-Médoc that leaves impressions of its earthy, dark and spicy elements.

Ch Pontoise Cabarrus
map 21/R K9

cru bourgeois
owner: Famille Tereygeol *area:* 30 ha *cases:* 18,500 *grape % R:* CS 55% MER 35% PV 5% CF 5% *second wine:* Ch Les Hauts de Plaisance
33180 St-Seurin-de-Cadourne tel: 05 56 59 34 92
fax: 05 56 59 72 42
The two capital Ns with the imperial crown on the label of this wine are due to the enormously rich Comte de Cabarrus, a witness at Napoleon's marriage to Joséphine. The count's daughter was Thérésa de Cabarrus, a controversial figure

◆
Finding a second wine
To locate a second wine, consult the index which lists all châteaux in the Atlas.

during the Revolution. The wine is sound in quality and generally has a fair degree of substance, juicy berry fruit, spicy but restrained oak (the wine is partly aged in casks of which one-sixth are new), and integrated tannins.

Domaine de Primat
map 17 J8

owner: Jean-Jack Duvigneau *area:* 1 ha *cases:* 400
grape % R: CS 50% MER 50%
33480 Avensan tel: 05 56 58 20 24
Simple, well-crafted Haut-Médoc of decent quality. Aged in barrels of which 25% are new.

Ch Proche-Pontet
map 19 I8

owner: Curt Eklund *area:* 6 ha *cases:* 3,750 *grape % R:* CS 62% MER 36% CF 1% PV 1% *other châteaux owned:* Ch Bernadotte *(Pauillac)*; Ch Fournas Bernadotte *(Haut-Médoc)*
33250 St-Sauveur tel: 05 56 59 57 04
fax: 05 56 59 54 84
Firm wine, with considerable tannin in most years. The aroma has elements of blackcurrant jam, blackberry, bayleaf and spicy oak from used casks. Made at Ch Fournas Bernadotte.

Ch Puy Castéra
map 20 F8

cru bourgeois
owner: SCE Château Puy Castéra/Famille Marès *area:* 25 ha *cases:* 16,000 *grape % R:* CS 58% MER 29% CF 10% MAL 2% PV 1% *second wine:* Ch Holden *other châteaux owned:* Mas de Bressades *(Costières de Nîmes)*
33250 Cissac-Médoc tel: 05 56 59 58 80
fax: 05 56 59 54 57
A property entirely overhauled since 1973. The wine is reasonably classic in style, but without much depth or concentration. Smooth fruit makes an accessible. A year's oak-maturing takes place in casks of which a quarter are new. A steady medal-winner.

Ch Ramage La Batisse
map 20 H7

cru bourgeois
owner: MACIF *area:* 56 ha *cases:* 28,000 *grape % R:* CS 45% MER 45% CF 5% PV 5% *second wine:* Ch Tourteran *other châteaux owned:* Ch de Belcier *(Côtes de Castillon)*
33250 St-Sauveur tel: 05 56 59 57 24
fax: 05 56 59 54 14
The wine made here stands out from many other Haut-Médocs; for one thing, half the

Below: Ch le Meynieu

Above: Ch Sénéjac

Above: Ch La Tour Carnet

barriques are new each year. Fine elements of spicy oak and ample vanilla are therefore present in bouquet and taste. Other nuances often include jammy fruit (berries, plum, fig) and smooth, ripe tannins. The château producing this generous wine is a cool, white, 18th-century *chartreuse*. Since 1986 Ch Ramage la Batisse has been owned by the MACIF company.

Ch du Raux   map 19 F7
owner: SCI du Raux/Famille Bernard *area:* 15.7 ha
cases: 8,000 *grape % R:* CS 50% MER 50% *second wine:* L'Enclos de Château du Raux
33460 Cussac-Fort-Médoc tel: 05 56 58 91 07
From this vineyard, which is to be increased by 3 ha, comes a dark-toned wine with spicy licorice and berries, usually firmly contained in its tannin. It matures in mainly used casks for 12-18 months. A reliable buy in lesser years.

Ch Reysson   map 20 C6
cru bourgeois
owner: SARL du Château Reysson/Mercian Corporation *area:* 67 ha *cases:* 32,000 *grape % R:* CS 56% MER 44% *second wine:* Ch de l'Abbaye
33180 Vertheuil tel: 05 56 01 30 10
fax: 05 56 79 23 57
This estate, named after a long-vanished medieval castle, has known swings in fortune. Reysson began its revival as a wine estate when the firm of Mestrezat-Preller acquired it in 1972. That company is still involved, despite the take-over by the Japanese Mercian Corporation in 1988. Matured in barrels of which 25% are new, the wine is a supple, quite accessible and easy style of Haut-Médoc.

Ch Saint Ahon   map 18 I5
cru bourgeois
owner: Bernard de Colbert *area:* 31 ha *cases:* 15,800 *grape % R:* CS 60% MER 28% CF 10% PV 2% *second wine:* Ch Colbert Cannet *other châteaux owned:* Ch de Brézé *(Saumur)*
33290 Blanquefort tel: 05 56 35 06 45
fax: 05 56 35 87 16
At the beginning of the 19th century a fine country house was built here on the foundations of a much older château – and then rebuilt in Renaissance style in 1875. It looks out over a garden and the winery buildings at the front, and over a wooded park at the back.

◆
Map numbers
Map 2, in the opening pages of the Atlas, shows the areas of all the Bordeaux appellations. To find a map for a specific appellation, turn to the regional key maps: the Médoc's is Map 7.

Key areas of the main appellations have maps showing individual château vineyards. These cover the four top Médoc appellations and their counterparts elsewhere in Bordeaux.

In its excellently-equipped cellars, the wine is made with great care and a feeling for tradition. It is nurtured for a year in oak: a third of the *barriques* are new. The result, in the better vintages, is a most successful Haut-Médoc that, after a few years' bottle-age, is creamy to the taste with flavoursome ripe tannins, coffee and tobacco notes, and sufficient fruit.

Ch de Sainte-Gemme   map 19 C6
owner: GFA des Domaines Bouteiller *area:* 5 ha *cases:* 3,000 *grape % R:* CS 50% MER 50% *other châteaux owned:* Ch Lachesnaye *(Haut-Médoc)*; Ch Lanessan *(Haut-Médoc)*
33460 Cussac-Fort-Médoc tel: 05 56 58 94 80
fax: 05 56 58 93 10
Although the Bouteiller family of neighbouring Ch Lanessan (and others) have owned this property since 1962, it was not until 1981 that its grapes were vinified separately. In good years the wine has breeding, considerable substance, a smooth spiciness (partly from the oak of the used *barriques*) and a combination of fresh and dried fruit. In lesser years bitter tannins may be dominant. No more than a decent Haut-Médoc so far, it could still improve – in quantity, too: the vineyard has a potential area of 25 ha.

Ch Saint Paul   map21/R K9
owner: SC du Château Saint Paul/Famille Boucher *area:* 20 ha *cases:* 10,000 *grape % R:* CS 55% CF 40% MER 5% *second wines:* Ch Terre Brune de St. Paul; Ch Antogan
33180 St-Seurin-de-Cadourne tel: 05 56 59 34 72
fax: 05 56 02 42 92

Wine estate founded in 1979, with plots from two St-Estèphe châteaux, Le Boscq and Morin. A *cuvier* with stainless-steel vats was built then. Tannin, red and black fruits, spices and oak (25% of the casks are new) are characteristics of this wine. It usually benefits from at least five years' bottle-age.

Ch Ségur   map 18 F7
cru bourgeois
owner: Jean-Pierre Grazioli *area:* 38 ha *cases:* 16,600 *grape % R:* MER 42% CS 35% CF 17% PV 6% *second wines:* Ch Ségur Fillon; Domaine Boisgrand
33290 Parempuyre tel: 05 56 35 28 25
fax: 05 56 35 82 32
This estate takes its name from a count who built a château on this site – at that time an island, the Ile d'Arès – and planted vines. This was in the early 17th century, and the Ségurs remained owners of the property until the French Revolution, when it was confiscated by the state and publicly auctioned. Its recent history rests with the Graziolis, who have owned Ch Ségur since 1959 and have completely restored the neglected vineyard. Jean-Pierre Grazioli, the present owner, has gradually been able to improve the quality of the wine. He has invested in up-to-date cellar equipment and in barrels; a third of these are new annually, and maturing lasts a year. This Haut-Médoc is at its best in vintages when both the Merlot and the Cabernet grapes ripen fully, for then the generally elegant, firm and supple taste acquires rather more breeding and depth than usual, with an agreeable aroma of soft black fruits.

Ch Semonlon   map 17 F2
owner: Glaxei Dumora *area:* 5 ha *cases:* 850 *grape % R:* MER 60% CS 40% *other châteaux owned:* Domaine La Rose Maucaillou *(Margaux)*
33480 Avensan tel: 05 56 58 21 29
fax: 05 57 88 78 14
This is an Haut-Médoc of merit. Semonlon offers considerable oak, with roundness and earthy elements. It is matured in barrels of which half are new.

Ch Sénéjac   map 18 F2
cru bourgeois
owner: Comte Charles de Guigne *area:* 28 ha *cases:* 11,500 *grape % R:* CS 60% MER 25% CF 14% PV 1% *second wine:* Artigue de Sénéjac *other wines:* Blanc de Senejac *(Bordeaux)*
33290 Le Pian-Médoc tel: 05 56 70 20 11
fax: 05 56 70 23 91
On returning in 1973 from America, where he was born, Comte Charles de Guigné decided to breathe new life into this old family estate. He won a gold medal with his 1974 vintage, but Sénéjac's star only really began to shine after the arrival of a New Zealand winemaker, Jenny Bailey-Dobson. From the mid-1980s to the mid-1990s, during her incumbency, the installations were also completely modernized. The Haut-Médoc from this property is at once expressive, fleshy and elegant, with a good flavour of fruit, refined tannins and integrated oak: 20-25% of the barrels in which the wine matures for a maximum 18 months are new each year. At this fine-looking château two white Bordeaux are also produced. The Blanc de Sénéjac, a mouthfilling wine of character, is the more interesting, with its floral aroma and toasty oak elements. It is fermented in new barrels and production reaches just 2,800 bottles a year.

Ch Senilhac
map 21/R J6

cru bourgeois

owner: SCEA Grassin *area:* 20 ha *cases:* 10,000
grape % R: cs 54% mer 31% cf 12% pv 3% *second wine:* Ch Dilhac

**33180 St-Seurin-de-Cadourne tel: 05 56 59 31 41
fax: 05 56 59 39 19**

Starting with the 1981 vintage the wine has been made at the château rather than at a cooperative; and the vineyard has grown from 12 ha to 20. Fermented in stainless steel and partly matured in used *barriques*, this is Haut-Médoc of a pleasant, accessible kind, reasonably full-bodied but seldom exciting.

Ch Sociando-Mallet
map 21/R K10

cru bourgeois

owner: Jean Gautreau *area:* 45 ha *cases:* 22,500
grape % R: mer cs 60% 30% cf 8% pv 2% *second wines:* La Demoiselle de Sociando-Mallet; Ch Lartigue de Bronchon; Ch Bonneau-Livran

**33180 St-Seurin-de-Cadourne tel: 05 56 59 36 57
fax: 05 56 59 70 88**

This is an enviably placed estate. The château has an unhindered view of the Gironde; the soil of its gently-sloping vineyard contains a lot of gravel, and is often compared to that of the famous Ch Montrose in St-Estèphe. Despite the excellent location, this was a badly neglected estate in 1969: the vineyard covered only 6 ha, and cows were kept in some of the winery buildings. The winegrower and merchant Jean Gautreau acquired Sociando-Mallet in that year, and since then has made the most of its potential. The Haut-Médoc produced here has the stature of a *cru classé* – and is one of the very best *crus bourgeois*. The wine characteristically offers splendid depth, concentration and complexity, with undeniable finesse, delightful fruit, integrated tannins; also spicy, smoky, noble oak and creamy vanilla. A high proportion of new *barriques* – 70-90% – are used for ageing the wine over 12-15 months. The château, more of a country house in character, takes its name from two former owners.

Ch Soudars
map 21/R I9

cru bourgeois

owner: Eric Miailhe *area:* 22 ha *cases:* 14,000
grape % R: mer 54% cs 45% cf 1% *second wine:* Ch Marquis de Cadourne

**33180 St-Seurin-de-Cadourne tel: 05 56 59 36 09
fax: 05 56 59 72 39**

This estate was created in the course of the 1970s; the first vintage appeared in 1981. The wine is a good, middle-of-the-range *cru bourgeois* that develops comparatively quickly, tends to be slender rather than fat, is well-balanced, and often has nuances of berry fruit (black and red currants, strawberry, cherry), leather, spices and smoky oak – one-third of the casks being new.

Ch Le Souley-Ste Croix
map 20 B6

cru bourgeois

owner: Jean Riffaud *area:* 22 ha *cases:* 13,000
grape % R: cs 60% mer 40%

**33180 Vertheuil tel: 05 56 41 98 54
fax: 05 56 41 95 36**

Decent Haut-Médoc that due to its tannins lingers well – at times rather drily – and has a somewhat rustic character. It would benefit from just a little more body, fruit and dimension. One-third of the casks in which it spends eight months are new. The estate is 17th

century and apparently once enjoyed something of a reputation for its hundred-year-old vines. The château was a ruin when the present owners bought it in 1950.

Ch du Taillan
map 18 K3

cru bourgeois

owner: Héritiers H.F. Cruse *area:* 30 ha *cases:* 12,800; white 1,800 *grape % R:* cs 50% mer 40% cf 10% *grape % W:* sauv b 100% *second wine:* Ch La Vie *other wines:* Ch La Dame Blanche *(Bordeaux blanc)*

**33320 Le Taillan-Médoc tel: 05 56 95 14 07
fax: 05 56 35 87 49**

The château is an imposing 18th-century structure, in the middle of a large park dotted with statues. A cellar here has been declared a historic monument: it was probably built to serve a monastery some three centuries ago. The wine it shelters is a generous, clean and elegant Haut-Médoc with a smooth fruitiness and restrained tannins. White grape varieties are grown on a separate plot, from which comes Ch La Dame Blanche. This smooth and fresh, congenial dry white Bordeaux, made from 100% Sauvignon, is named after a Moorish princess who wore clothes of white. She is said to return when the morning mist hangs over the land.

Ch La Tonnelle
map 20 F6

cru bourgeois

owner: Domaines Fabre *area:* 25 ha *cases:* 15,000
grape % R: cs 70% mer 26% pv 4% *second wine:* Ch Le Chêne *other châteaux owned:* Ch Lamothe-Cissac *(Haut-Médoc)*; Ch Landat *(Haut-Médoc)*

**33250 Cissac-Médoc tel: 05 56 59 58 16
fax: 05 56 59 57 97**

A correct Haut-Médoc, but one somewhat limited in its structure, concentration, and nuances. There is generally a decent amount of fruit– fermentation is in stainless steel at controlled temperature – and a small measure of oak, after six months' maturation in cask (10% new barrels).

Ch Tour Bellegrave
map 19

owner: Guy Pinet *area:* 4.3 ha *cases:* 2,000 *grape % R:* cs 50% mer 45% pv 5%

33460 Arcins tel: 05 56 58 90 45

Not a really fine or lingering wine, but a very pleasantly drinkable one nonetheless. In the generally supple, elegant taste there are balanced notes of fruit (cherry; red and black currants) and slightly toasty oak, together with some spice.

Below: Ch Tour-du-Roc

Ch La Tour Carnet
map 20 M9

4ème cru

owner: Marie-Claire Pelegrin *area:* 42 ha *cases:* 19,000 *grape % R:* cs 53% mer 33% cf 10% pv 4% *second wine:* Les Douves de Carnet

**33112 St-Laurent-Médoc tel: 05 56 73 30 90
fax: 05 56 59 48 54**

To take the long driveway to this château is to travel far back in time, for in origin this is a 13th-century castle, ringed by a moat. The gatehouse dates from that early period, as does the ground floor of the main building. Other parts were built later, chiefly in the 17th and 18th centuries. Since 1979 an extensive investment programme has taken place, directed by Marie-Claire Pelegrin, whose parents bought the neglected estate in 1962. The winemaking equipment has been modernized and the vineyard area increased by a third. It is mainly in the great vintages that this wine rises above the average. Then it is a complete Haut-Médoc with a quite full-bodied taste, agreeable, well founded on tannin and oak (about 30% of the *barriques* are new for each vintage), and with berry fruit. Average or less-good years usually produce a lighter, shorter-finishing wine – but one that is clearly still skilfully made.

Ch Tour du Haut Moulin
map 19 H7

cru bourgeois

owner: Béatrice & Lionel Poitou *area:* 30 ha *cases:* 20,000 *grape % R:* mer 50% cs 45% pv 5%

**33460 Cussac-Fort-Médoc tel: 05 56 58 91 10
fax: 05 56 58 99 30**

Classically modelled, very reliable Haut-Médoc. Its tannins are solid and of good quality, and the wine comes across with elements of oak like aniseed and vanilla, woodland scents and ripe fruit, including berries and cherry. A third of the casks are new each year, and the wine matures for 18 months. The château name comes from a tall, old windmill that once stood on a plot in the vineyard.

Ch Tour du Mirail
map 20 F6

cru bourgeois

owner: D. Vialard *area:* 18 ha *cases:* 10,000 *grape % R:* cs 75% mer 20% pv 5% *other châteaux owned:* Ch du Breuil *(Haut-Médoc)*; Ch Cissac *(Haut-Médoc)*

**33250 Cissac-Médoc tel: 05 56 59 58 13
fax: 05 56 59 55 67**

Fairly simple, accessible wine from a good stable. It has fruit, charm and a hint of spicy oak and is soon ready to drink.

Ch Tour-du-Roc — map 19 K7
owner: Philippe Robert *area:* 12 ha *cases:* 5,200
grape % R: CS 50% MER 45% PV 5% *second wine:* Ch
Fontanelle
33460 Arcins tel: 05 56 58 90 25
fax: 05 56 58 94 41
Château opposite the church at Arcins where a
pleasant, quick-maturing and reasonably
nuanced wine is made, with a dark-toned,
earthy aroma. The oak – a third of the casks are
new – adds spicy elements. No weedkillers are
used in the vineyard.

Ch Tour Marcillanet — map 20 L6
cru bourgeois
owner: Marc Ponsar *area:* 11 ha *cases:* 7,100
grape % R: CS 55% MER 35% CF 10% *second wine:*
Ch Goulefaisan
33112 St-Laurent-Médoc tel: 05 56 59 92 94
The Tour Marcillante estate is situated halfway
between St-Laurent and the hamlet of Marcillan
to the north-west. As the name suggests, a
tower from the 14th century does indeed flank
the château. Blackcurrant determines the
aroma of the wine as a rule, and spicy and
earthy elements are frequently found as well.
Maturing in *barriques* lasts for twelve months,
20% of them new.

Ch Tour St Joseph — map 20 F6
cru bourgeois
owner: Marcel & Christian Quancard *area:* 10 ha
cases: 5,000 *grape % R:* CS 75% MER 25% *other
châteaux owned:* include Ch de Terrefort-Quancard
(*Bordeaux Supérieur*); Ch de Paillet-Quancard
(*Premières Côtes de Bordeaux*); Ch Haut-Logat
(*Haut-Médoc*)
33250 Cissac tel: 05 56 33 80 60
fax: 05 56 33 80 70
This estate, which was known as Cru Latour St
Joseph at the beginning of the 20th century,
stretches out over the highest part of Cissac. A
classic Haut-Médoc is made here – a wine with
plenty of colour, a foundation of tannin, spice,
oak (a third of its barrels are new each year),
berry fruit, leather and bayleaf. It has won
numerous medals.

Ch Le Trale — map 21/R K1
owner: GFA Le Trale/Famille Gabas *area:* 18 ha
cases: 9,500 *grape % R:* CS 40% MER 40% CF 20%
second wines: Ch Croix de Cabaleyran; Ch Maurac
33250 St-Seurin-de-Cadourne tel: 05 57 88 07 64
fax: 05 57 88 07 00
A Haut-Médoc with personality; as a rule it
boasts considerable fruit and also tannin. Its
aroma is dark-toned; the oaky elements are due
to 12-16 months' maturation – one-fifth of the
casks are new.

Domaine du Vatican — map 20
owner: Marcelle Verdier *area:* 1 ha *cases:* 458
grape % R: MER 70% CS 30%
33180 St-Estèphe tel: 05 56 73 94 32
For its simple *cru artisan* status this is a good
wine, offering fruit, firmness and suppleness –
often along with a deep colour. The Domaine du
Vatican estate is in Cissac, but its owner lives in
St-Estèphe.

Ch Verdignan — map 21/R I9
cru bourgeois
owner: Famille Miailhe *area:* 90 ha *cases:* 40,000
grape % R: CS 50% MER 45% CF 5% *second wine:* Ch
Plantey de la Croix *other châteaux owned:* Ch
Coufran (*Haut-Médoc*)

33180 St-Seurin-de-Cadourne tel: 05 56 59 31 02
fax: 05 56 81 32 35
This is the oldest wine estate in St-Seurin-de-
Cadourne and its château, which bears a vague
resemblance to Lafite Rothschild, one of the
most attractive in the district. The wine, too,
has quality. It is stylish, balanced and lively,
quite elegant and often displays both juicy, ripe
fruit (berries and plums) and earthy tones. Each
year 25% of the barrels are new.

Ch Verdus — map 21/R K9
cru bourgeois
owner: Alain Dailledouze *area:* 8.5 ha *cases:* 3,000
grape % R: CS 65% MER 32% PV 3% *second wines:*
Ch Bardis; Colombier de Bardis
33180 St-Seurin-de-Cadourne tel: 05 56 59 71 10
fax: 05 56 59 73 71
This château is a former fortress and dates from
the 16th century. Among its features are a small
collection of winemaking tools and the
impressive dovecot from Bardis, one of the
finest in the *département*. The wine, a *cru
bourgeois*, has a reasonably firm, not especially
complex taste with an agreeable creaminess,
good fruit, supple tannins, and some spices.

Ch Vieux Braneyre — map 20 F5
owner: Ludwig Cooreman *area:* 11.5 ha *cases:*
6,500 *grape % R:* CS 70% MER 15% CF 10% PV 5%
second wine: Les Demoiselles de Braneyre
33250 Cissac tel: 05 56 59 54 03
fax: 05 56 59 59 46
Estate created around 1750 that has had
Belgian owners since 1993. They have fitted out
a new barrel *chai* for the 18 months' wood-
ageing – about a third of the *barriques* are
replaced each year. In addition the vineyard has
been enlarged: there are plans to increase the
whole estate to 26.5 ha. What has continued is
the accommodation – five bedrooms – for
visitors. Today the wine is among the better
Haut-Médocs. It possesses breeding, structure,
good oak, and berry fruit. Its quality is,
however, surpassed by the *cuvée prestige*, La
Mouline du Ch Vieux Braneyre.

Ch de Villambis — map 20 G5
cru bourgeois
owner: ADAPEI de la Gironde *area:* 12 ha *cases:*
5,000 *grape % R:* CS 55% MER 40% CF 5% *second
wine:* Ch l'Aôst
33250 Cissac-Médoc tel: 05 56 59 58 02
fax: 05 56 59 58 67
Handicapped people work at this estate,
through the Centre d'Aide par le Travail. They
make a respectably long-lived Haut-Médoc,
somewhat slender and of an average quality. A
fresh berry note is often there in its aroma, and
a modest dose of oak. The estate dates from the
18th century.

Ch de Villegeorge — map 17 K9
owner: SC Les Grands Crus Réunis/Marie-Laure
Lurton-Roux *area:* 15 ha *cases:* 2,700 *grape % R:*
MER 60% CS 30% CF 10% *other châteaux owned:* Ch
Duplessis (*Moulis*); Ch La Tour de Bessan (*Margaux*)
33480 Avensan tel: 05 57 88 70 20
fax: 05 57 88 72 51
In 1936 wine from this estate was classed by
brokers as a *cru bourgeois exceptionnel*. Today's
Villegeorge vintages are not only exceptional in
quality, but in character – the wine has a
strikingly smooth, almost lush roundness, with
in particular dark animal tones in a fine setting
of oak (about 20% of the casks are new), and

Above: Ch Verdignan

black fruit – blackcurrants, blackberries,
cherries. This wine's special personality is partly
due to the high proportion of Merlot grapes. De
Villegeorge, very run down then, was bought by
Lucien Lurton in 1973. He overhauled and
renovated it all, then gave it to his daughter
Marie-Laure. The fact that Lurton made de
Villegeorge prosper was a small miracle, for in
the 1970s most vintages were being severely
reduced by night frosts.

MÉDOC

Somewhere beyond St-Estèphe – to be precise, where a bridge takes the ever-more-rural D2 road across a ditch called the Chenal de la Maréchale – the Haut-Médoc ends and the mere Médoc begins. Formerly referred to as the Bas-Médoc – for its location downstream rather than anything else – this name was modified in 1936 at the producers' instigation. So now we have to make do with just 'Médoc' for the land stretching from the northern edge of St-Seurin-de-Cadourne as far north and northwest as Lesparre-Médoc and St-Vivien-de-Médoc.

This is confusing, since of course all vineyard land within the Médoc is in theory entitled to this appellation. Production is actually very concentrated: if you are lucky enough to have the right to one of the higher appellations (and your wine meets its production criteria) it would be illogical to use a lesser one. Most AC Médoc wine, therefore, is produced in this tract to the north of the Haut-Médoc. The main town is Lesparre-Médoc, which lies a few kilometres to the north-west of St-Estèphe, at the junction of the N215 and D204 (a continuation of the *route du Médoc*).

Sunflowers in the Médoc: grown for their oil, not for their beauty

TERROIR AND GRAPE VARIETIES

This is a land of marshy pastures and streams dividing patches of higher land, some virtually islands. Wine production here is far more recent than in the rest of the Médoc, which is due both to its relative isolation and the local geography. Inevitably, because of the enormous size of the appellation, the diversity of soil types is quite wide: as with St-Estèphe further south, in places it is quite heavy and poorly-drained, and thus not ideally suited to grape production; but gravel outcrops, with good drainage and heat retention, can also be found. As in St-Estèphe, the Merlot grape is becoming increasingly important. Wines from Médoc AC land made with a high percentage of Cabernet Sauvignon can seem too rough and even coarse; Merlot helps to fill them out and soften them, making them more approachable at a young age. Cabernet Sauvignon is still very important though, and some Cabernet Franc is also grown.

PRODUCTION

This is essentially an area of small wine producers plus a few large estates, and production of the best wines is concentrated in a handful of communes. Those communes on the west side of the appellation, closest to the N215 road, are the least important; this land is near to the forest, where the soil is too light and sandy to make for wines of any particular note. Thus Queyrac, Gaillan and even Lesparre itself are not especially known for quality wine.

On the south side, towards the boundary with the Haut-Médoc, three communes – St-Germain-d'Esteuil, Ordonnac and St-Yzans-de-Médoc – are home to some good châteaux. Slightly further north, on either side of the D103E, are further important wine-producing communes: Blaignan, Civrac, Bégadan and St-Christoly-Médoc. Further north again are the last two significant communes: Valeyrac, on the edge of the Gironde, and Jau-Dignac-et-Loirac, which is almost equidistant from the N215 and the Garonne.

Vineyards and tower at Château La Tour de By

Unlike the Haut-Médoc, there are no classified growths, but there are well over a hundred *crus bourgeois* and also a number of *crus artisans*, a class attempting a renaissance. Cooperatives are very important too: five in total, with four of them grouped to form the Union UniMédoc. Production from the cooperatives accounts for around one-third of the total of somewhere between two-and-a-half and three million cases a year.

THE WINES

Although it is impossible to make any sweeping generalisations because of its enormous size, the Médoc has made great strides forward recently to improve the quality of its wines. There are hundreds of châteaux here and the best are very aware that they offer an extremely affordable, good-value alternative to the more elevated Médoc appellations. Hence the increased plantings of Merlot, better vinification techniques and discreet use of new oak, imbuing the best of these wines with finesse and breeding, and making them capable of ageing well in bottle. These are the wines to seek out. There are, however, two other broad styles of Médoc wines: those which are decidedly lean and slender, lacking in sufficient weight or body and of very little interest; the second is the coarser, old-fashioned style, with earthy overtones and too little fruit – both of these are best avoided. Many *négociants* offer a Médoc AC wine as part of their portfolio: these can be good if from reliable firms.

THE APPELLATION

MÉDOC (red)

Location: *The northern third of the Médoc vineyard, north of the Haut-Médoc, bordered by the Landes forests to the west and the Gironde estuary to the east, with the southern edge 52 km from the centre of Bordeaux.*
Area of AC: *10,476 ha*
Area under vine: *4,700 ha*
Communes: *From south to north: St-Germain-d'Esteuil, Ordonnac, St-Yzans-de-Médoc, Blaignan, Lesparre-Médoc, Gaillanen-Médoc, Prignac-en-Médoc, Couquèques, Civrac-en-Médoc, St-Christoly-Médoc, Bégadan, Queyrac, Valeyrac, Vensac, Jau-Dignac-et-Loirac, St-Vivien-de-Médoc. In addition, communes entitled to the Haut-Médoc*

AC, and the individual ACs, can also use the Médoc AC.
Average annual production: *2,500,000 cases*
Classed growths: *None*
Others: *127 crus bourgeois, 113 others*
Cooperatives: *5 (c. 460 members)*
Main grape varieties: *Cabernet Sauvignon, Cabernet Franc, Merlot*
Others: *Malbec, Petit Verdot*
Main soil types: *Very diverse: vineyard land includes gravel and clay-limestone; other land is alluvial and recent aeolian (wind-blown sand) deposits.*

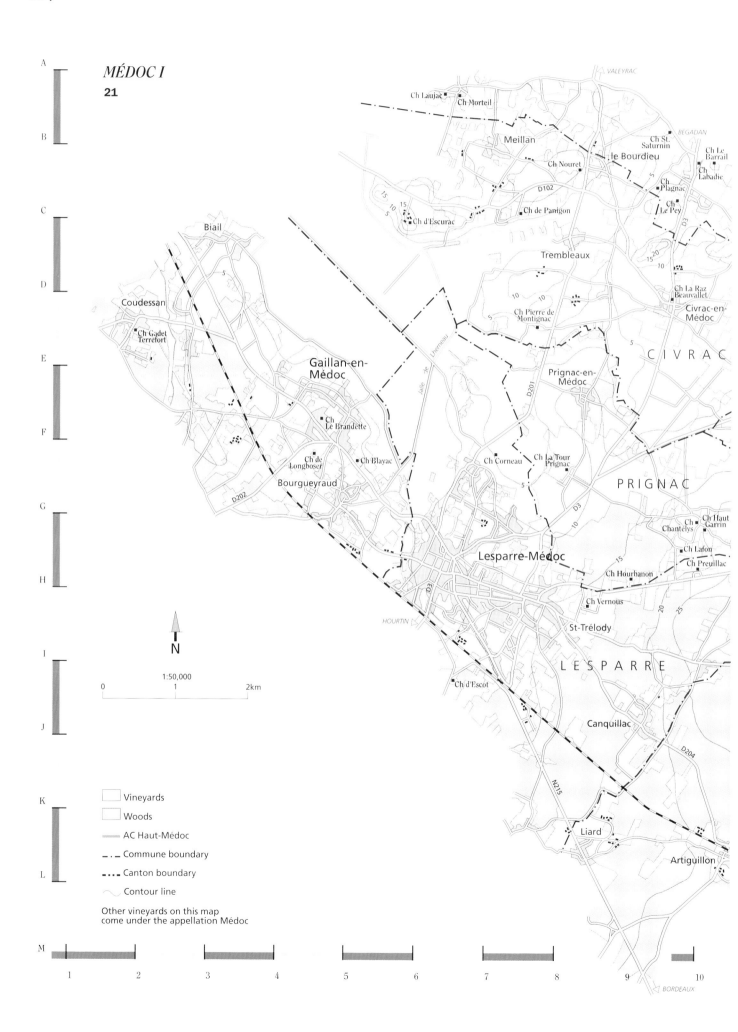

MÉDOC I

21

VALEYRAC

Ch Laujac Ch Morteil

BEGADAN

Meillan
Ch St. Saturnin
le Bourdieu
Ch Le Barrail
Ch Nouret
Ch Labadie
D102
Ch Plagnac
Ch de Panigon
Ch Le Pey
Ch d'Escurac

Biail

Trembleaux
Ch La Raz Beauvallet
Civrac-en-Médoc

Coudessan
Ch Pierre de Montignac
CIVRAC

Ch Gadet Terrefort
Gaillan-en-Médoc
Prignac-en-Médoc
D201

Ch Le Brandette
Ch Corneau
Ch La Tour Prignac
PRIGNAC

Ch de Longboser
Ch Blayac
Bourgueyraud
D202
D3

Ch Haut Garrin
Chantelys
Ch Lafon
Lesparre-Médoc
Ch Preuillac
Ch Hourbanon
D31

Ch Vernous

HOURTIN
St-Trélody
LESPARRE

Ch d'Escot

Canquillac
D204

N215

Liard

Artiguillon

Legend:

☐ Vineyards

☐ Woods

━━ AC Haut-Médoc

—·—· Commune boundary

···· Canton boundary

Contour line

Other vineyards on this map
come under the appellation Médoc

N

1:50,000

0   1   2km

BORDEAUX

A B C D E F G H I J K L M

1 2 3 4 5 6 7 8 9 10

VALEYRAC

Ch La Tour
Seran

Ch La Tour
St. Bonnet
Ch St. Bonnet

le Boscq
Ch Le Boscq
Ch St-Christoly
Ch Haut Canteloup
Ch Cantegric
Ch Haut Lignon
du Perrier
Ch Les Grands Chênes &
Ch Les Vieux Chênes
Clos de la Grange-Vieille
Ch Tour Blanche
Ch Le Chalet
Ch Moulin de
Castillon &
Clos de Moulin
Ch St-Christophe

St-Christoly-
Médoc

BEGADAN
Ch Le Breuil
Renaissance

le Breuil
Ch
La Gorre
Vieux
Château Landon

D103

ST-CHRISTOLY

Couquèques
Ch Les Moines
Ch Les
Ormes Sorbet

Ch Mazails

Ch La Chandellière les Petites
Granges
Ch
Bournac

COUQUÈQUES

Ch Haut-
Maurac
Queyzans
Ch des Brousteras

Ch Les
Granges d'Or

D103 E5

Ch La
Gorce

Ch
Sigognac

ST-YZANS

La Gironde

Ch des
Tourelles
BLAIGNAN
Caussan
Ch La France
Ch Caussan
Ch La Grave
Ch-Pontet
Ch Lalande
d'Auvion
Ch Tour
Haut-Caussan
Ch Blaignan
Ch Haut
Griviere
Blaignan
Ch Ramafort

Ch l'Estorelle
Ch Haut Plantey
Ch Clair
Moulin
Ch La Ribaud
Ch Bois de Roc
Ch Les Tuileries
Ch Le Longa
St-Yzans-de-Médoc

Ch Loudenne

Ch La
Mothe

Peyressan

D2

Ch La
Cardonne
D203

Ch Taffard
de Blaignan

ORDONNAC

Chenal de la Marechale

Ch Potensac
Ch des
Belles-Graves
Potensac
Ch de la Croix
Ch Peymartin
Ordonnac

Coufran
Cadourne

Plautignan

Ch Soudars

Lussan

l'Hôpital
Ch Marcat
Ch La Rose
St. Germain
Ch La Rose
d'Esteuil

Marque
Ch Lamothe-
Grand Moulin
Ch Troupian
Ch Grand Moulin
Ch La Fagotte &
Ch d'Aurilhac
Ch Sénilhac
Ch Muret

Ch Verdignan

Lestage
Ch Tour des Graves
Ch Lestage-Simon

Ch Bel Orme
Tronquoy de Lalande
St-Seurin-de-Cadourne
Ch Bonneau Listran
Ch Haut-Brégat
Ch Grandis
Ch Pontoise Cabarrus

Ch Castera

Boyentran

La Pardise Co-op
Ch Sociando-Mallet
Ch Charmail
Ch Verdus

St-Germain-
d'Esteuil

Ch Livran

Ch Doyac
Ch Le Trale
Ch Moulin de Blanchon
Ch St. Paul

ST-GERMAIN-D'ESTEUIL

Miqueu

ST-ESTEPHE

Ch
Hauterive

PAUILLAC

MÉDOC
RIVE
DROITE
ENTRE-DEUX-
MERS
Bordeaux
GRAVES &
SAUTERNES

A
B
C
D
E
F
G
H
I
J
K
L
M

1 2 3 4 5 6 7 8 9 10

APPELLATION MÉDOC

Ch l'Argenteyre   Map 22/R I5
owner: Philippe & Filles Reich **area:** 19 ha **cases:** 9,000 **grape % R:** CS 55% MER 40% PV 5% **second wine:** Ch Grand Courbian
33340 Bégadan tel: 05 56 41 52 34
A fairly new estate; its first vintage in 1992. This does not mean that the vineyard is planted solely with young vines – those used for Ch l'Argenteyre have an average age of 25. The wine, aged for a year in casks of which a third are new, is clean-tasting and elegant in structure.

Ch Bellegrave   Map 22/R G7
cru bourgeois
owner: Christian Caussèque **area:** 15 ha **cases:** 7,500 **grape % R:** CS 60% MER 35% CF 5%
33340 Valeyrac tel: 05 56 41 53 82
fax: 05 56 41 50 10
The *cuvée spéciale*, matured for an average of 18 months in mainly used barrels, is worth discovering: a Médoc with solid tannins, spices, earthy notes and some fruit. As the name suggests, most of the vines grow in gravel soil.

Ch Bellerive   Map 22/R G9
cru bourgeois
owner: Guy Perrin **area:** 13 ha **cases:** 5,000 **grape % R:** MER 60% CS 30% CF 10%
33340 Valeyrac tel: 05 56 41 52 13
Merlot is the predominant grape in the vineyard, to an extent unusual for the Médoc. In good years the wine – aged mostly in used *barriques* – has a touch of aniseed in its aroma, a juicy, reasonably fleshy taste, a slight roundness, and a finish that is sometimes almost dry, with considerable tannin. Of at least average quality.

Ch Bellevue   Map 22/R G8
cru bourgeois
owner: Yves Lassalle **area:** 23 ha **cases:** 12,500 **grape % R:** MER 50% CS 45% CF 5% **second wine:** Ch la Magnotte
33340 Valeyrac tel: 05 56 41 52 17
fax: 05 56 41 36 64
Generally this is a fairly firm, mouthfilling Médoc containing a lot of Merlot, and with supple tannin, some fruit – black cherry, blackcurrant and other berries – plus discreet hints of tobacco, coffee, leather and spices. About one-seventh of the casks in which the wine matures for eight months are new. All picking is still done by hand at this estate.

Ch le Bernet   Map 22/R J8
owner: SARL Degas **area:** 12.7 ha **cases:** 6,300 **grape % R:** CS 55% MER 45%
33340 Bégadan tel: 05 56 41 50 13
fax: 05 56 41 50 78
Fairly reserved, clean, slender Médoc that can usually be drunk quite young. Its vinification takes place at the Bégadan cooperative.

Ch Blaignan   Map 21/R G3
cru bourgeois
owner: Société Civile du Château Taffard (Mestrezat) **area:** 75 ha **cases:** 37,500 **grape % R:** CS 60% MER 40% **other châteaux owned:** Ch Tourteau Chollet (Graves); Ch Marsac Seguineau (Margaux); Ch Lamothe Bergeron (Haut-Médoc); Ch de Rayne Vigneau (Sauternes); Ch Grand-Puy Ducasse (Pauillac)
33340 Blaignan tel: 05 56 01 30 10
fax: 05 56 79 23 57
This extensive vineyard is the biggest in the Blaignan commune. Ch Blaignan's history goes back to the 16th century. More recently, it has since 1973 belonged to the house of Mestrezat. The wine is not oak-aged; it generally displays good tannins and berry fruit. In lesser years herbaceous aromas may occur, combined with a somewhat dry aftertaste. Ready for drinking after three to five years.

Ch Blayac   Map 21/L G5
owner: Jean Birot **area:** 20 ha **cases:** 12,500 **grape % R:** CS 60% MER 40% **second wine:** Ch Font Bonnet
33340 Gaillan-en-Médoc tel: 05 56 41 03 11
An average Médoc, fermented in stainless steel; it does not come into contact with oak. The same wine is also bottled with the Ch Font Bonnet label.

Ch Bois de Roc   Map 21/R F6
owner: Philippe Cazenave **area:** 17 ha **cases:** 8,200 **grape % R:** CS 40% MER 40% CF 15% PV 3% CARMENÈRE 2% **second wine:** Ch Letaillanet
33340 St-Yzans-de-Médoc tel: 05 56 09 09 79
fax: 05 56 09 06 29
One of the bigger – and better – *crus artisans*. A decent wine, oak-matured (half the casks are new), with reasonable fruit, a hint of spice and adequate tannins. A notable grape in this vineyard is the old Carmenère variety. The château boasts a collection of wind-chimes.

Ch Le Boscq   Map 21/R B6
cru bourgeois
owner: Jean-Michel Lapalu **area:** 27 ha **cases:** 16,000 **grape % R:** CS 70% MER 20% CF 10% **other châteaux owned:** Ch Patache d'Aux (Médoc); Ch Lacombe Noaillac (Médoc)
33340 St-Christoly-Médoc tel: 05 56 41 50 18
fax: 05 56 41 54 65
Le Boscq's wine is made at Ch Patache d'Aux, which is under the same ownership. There are two versions: the standard, not aged in wood, is firm and full of character in a fairly rustic style. The Cuvée Vieilles Vignes, first made in 1989, usually spends a year in barrel (a fifth are new), and offers a medley of spicy, jammy fruit with animal aromas and more rounded tannins: a tempting Médoc.

Ch Le Bourdieu   Map 22/R H8
cru bourgeois
owner: Guy Bailly **area:** 28 ha **cases:** 18,000 **grape % R:** CS 60% MER 40% **second wine:** Ch Bois-Cardon
33340 Valeyrac tel: 05 56 41 58 52
fax: 05 56 41 36 09
The stately château shown on the label was built around 1830. Its wine is an attractive Médoc with forest aromas, berry fruit, decent concentration, sometimes also toasty oak – with a touch of roasted coffee-beans as well. The vineyard is to be enlarged to 32 ha.

◆
Finding a second wine
To locate a second wine or any other wine not listed in the appellation's Directory pages, consult the index, where all château names are listed. Not all second wines use the appellation of the château's *grand vin*.

MÉDOC II

22

RIVE
DROITE

MÉDOC

Bordeaux

ENTRE-DEUX-
MERS

GRAVES &
SAUTERNES

Ch Listran

la Hourcade

Ch La
Hourcade

Ch Haut-
Gravat   Jau   Semensan

Dignac

Méric   Ch St-Aubin

JAU-DIGNAC-
ET-LOIRAC   le Centre

Noaillac   Ch René
Georges

Ch Lacombe   Boussan
Noaillac

Ch Noaillac   Ch Sestignan

Ch Laulan Ducos   Sestignan

Ch Haut   Loirac
Brisey

Ch Jeanton

La Matte de Valeyrac

Janton

Ch Bellegrave   La Gironde

Ch Haut-   Valeyrac
Grignon

Ch
Bellevue   Villeneuve

Sipian   Ch Bellerive

Ch   la Rivière
Roquegrave

Ch   la Verdasse
Sipian

Ch Le Bourdieu   Troussas

Larnac   Ch Lousteauneuf

VALEYRAC   Ch Beau
Rivage de By

Ch Le Temple

Ch Rose du   Ch Lassus   Condissas   Ch La Tour
Pont   Courbian   de By

la Hontaine   Ch Le Tréhon   Ch du   Ch Vieux   Ch La Clare   By
Monthil   Robin

QUEYRAC   Ch   Ch Rollan
l'Argenteyre   Ch La   de By

Garron   Reysse   Ch Greysac   Ch de By

Ch La Font   BÉGADAN
Neuve

Queyrac   Ch le Bernet   Bégadanet

Ch des
Cabans

Ch Patache
d'Aux

Ch Carcanieux   CIVRAC

Lescapon

Queyzac

les
Ourmes

N

☐ Vineyards

☐ Woods

—·— Commune boundary

▪▪▪ Canton boundary

〜 Contour line

All vineyards on this map
are in annellation Médoc

1:66,500

0   1   2   3km

Above: Ch Le Boscq

Ch Bournac   Map 21/R E2
cru bourgeois
owner: Bruno Secret *area:* 13 ha *cases:* 8,200
grape % R: CS 65% MER 35%
33340 Civrac-en-Médoc tel: 05 56 41 51 24
fax: 05 56 41 51 24
Fairly rustic Médoc that sometimes rather lacks
charm, although the quality seems to be
improving a little. Maturing lasts a year and
takes place in casks of which 20-25% are new.

Ch Le Bouscat   Map 20 L8
owner: Roger Parfait *area:* 0.43 ha *cases:* 500
grape % R: CS 65% MER 35%
33112 St-Laurent-Médoc tel: 05 56 59 48 80
Reliable *barrique*-aged Médoc (one-fifth new
wood). Mainly sold to private buyers in France.

Ch Le Breuil Renaissance   Map 21/R C2
owner: Philippe Bérard *area:* 25 ha *cases:* 12,500
grape % R: MER 50% CS 50% *second wine:* Ch
Haut-Bana
33340 Bégadan tel: 05 56 41 50 67
 fax: 05 56 41 36 77
In 1990 Philippe Bérard decided to detach this
estate – acquired by his family 70 years earlier –
from the cooperative in Bégadan and to make
his own wine. Right from the start success
rewarded his efforts: vintages were quickly sold
out, and usually attracted medals. The wine
possesses an agreeable, slightly spicy fruitiness,
a reasonably rounded taste (from a lot of
Merlot), a hint of oak and supple tannins.

Ch Brie-Caillou   Map 21
cru bourgeois
owner: SA Vignobles Rocher-Cap de Rive *area:* 10
ha *cases:* 5,000 *grape % R:* CS 64% MER 35% CF 1%
second wine: Ch L'Ormeau *other châteaux owned:*
include Ch Cap d'Or *(St-Georges-St-Emilion)*
33340 St-Germain-d'Esteuil tel: 05 57 40 08 88
fax: 05 57 40 19 93
Somewhat slender Médoc, often rather austere,
with some berry fruit in its aroma and taste. It
goes into cask for 10-12 months.

Ch des Brousteras   Map 21/R E7
cru bourgeois
owner: Frères Renouil *area:* 25 ha *cases:* 15,500
grape % R: MER 50% CS 40% CF 10% *second wine:*
Domaine de Lebrevigne

33340 St-Yzans-de-Médoc tel: 05 56 09 05 44
fax: 05 56 09 04 21
A Médoc that has attracted a string of awards:
elegant in structure, with a fresh fruit aroma
(and some earthy tones), plus a solid foundation
of tannin. It is matured in the classic way in
barriques, of which a fifth are new.

Ch de By   Map 22/R I10
cru bourgeois
owner: J.-C. Baudon *area:* 11 ha *cases:* 5,000
grape % R: MER 40% CS 30% PV 20% CF 10% *second
wine:* Ch Hautes Graves de By
33340 Bégadan tel 05 56 41 51 53
fax: 05 56 41 38 72
Sturdy, deep-coloured wine of sound quality,
but of somewhat modest finesse. It benefits
from a few years in bottle. In the *chai* this
Médoc is given 12 months' ageing in mainly
(90%) used casks.

Ch des Cabans   Map 22/R J8
cru bourgeois
owner: Jean-Marie Aberne *area:* 10.5 ha *cases:*
6,400 *grape % R:* CS 68% MER 28% CF 2% PV 2%
second wine: Ch Haut Picot
33340 Bégadan tel: 05 56 41 57 62
fax: 05 56 41 57 62
The wine produced here is at its best in sunny
years, when the Cabernets (70% of the vines)
ripen fully and give out a mellow fruitiness, and
the tannins are not too tough. A fifth of the
barrels in which the wine spends 16 months are
new. The estate lies next to the local
cooperative.

Ch Cantegric   Map 21/R C6
owner: Feugas-Joany *area:* 5.5 ha *cases:* 2,500
grape % R: CS 60% MER 40%
33340 St-Christoly-Médoc tel: 05 56 41 57 00
Modest family estate, worked by three
successive generations. Slender, impeccable
Médoc with smooth fruit and some spicy oak –
40% of casks are new each year. A small plot in
this vineyard has some 150-year-old Merlot
vines that were untouched by phylloxera.

Ch Carcanieux   Map 22/R J3
cru bourgeois
owner: Defforey *area:* 36 ha *cases:* 15,000 *grape
% R:* CS 60% MER 25% CF 15% *second wine:* Ch Les
Lattes

Below: Ch Le Bourdieu

33340 Queyrac tel: 05 56 59 84 23
 fax: 05 56 59 86 60
From 1981 to 1990 Carcanieux produced a
number of very successful vintages – utterly
sound, balanced, with good fruit, firm tannins,
and supported by their oak. Ther early '90s
yielded pleasant but unremarkable wines (the
whole 1991 vintage was declassified). The 1995
was the first to regain a high standard.

Ch La Cardonne   Map 21/R H1
cru bourgeois
owner: Domaines CGR *area:* 70 ha *cases:* 35,000
grape % R: MER 50% CS 45% CF 5% *second wine:* Ch
Cardus *other châteaux owned:* Ch Grivière *(Médoc)*;
Ch Ramafort *(Médoc)*
33340 Blaignan tel: 05 56 73 31 51
fax: 05 56 73 31 52
Once part of the Domaines Barons de
Rothschild, this estate became independent at
the beginning of the 1990s, along with two
other *crus bourgeois*. The wine quality
benefited: La Cardonne remains among the
really fine AC Médoc châteaux, and now also
offers considerable substance and a taste in
which there can be elements of blackcurrant,
plum, cocoa, tobacco and oak (a third of the
casks are new). The wine generally develops
quite quickly. Worth following.

Ch Castera   Map 21/R J3
cru bourgeois
owner: SNC Château Castera/Deugro *area:* 50 ha
cases: 27,000 *grape % R:* CS 45% MER 45% CF 7%
PV 3% *second wine:* Ch Bourbon La Chapelle
33340 St-Germain-d'Esteuil tel: 05 56 09 03 10
fax: 05 56 09 03 00

◆

Finding a château

To locate a château from its name alone,
use the index/gazetteer, which will provide
a page and a map reference. When the
name and appellation are known consult
the Directory pages of the relevant
chapter.
When the commune is known, but not the
appellation, consult the index by
commune, which lists châteaux in the
Atlas under the commune name.

Above: Ch La Clare

Above: Ch Castera

The original castle here was a fortress taken in the 14th century by the Black Prince; only a square tower remains. Later the château had some famous owners, including the Arsac and Montaigne families. The estate, which used to produce white wine as well, covers 185 ha – of these 50 are vineyard. In a good year these yield a tasty Médoc, reasonably elegant, with the flavour of black berry fruits as well as some oak and vanilla (a third of the barrels are new).

Ch La Chandellière Map 21/R E2
cru bourgeois
owner: Hubert & Didier Secret *area:* 18 ha *cases:* 12,000 *grape % R:* CS 66% MER 34% *second wine:* Ch Vieux Pignon
33340 Civrac-en-Médoc tel: 05 56 41 53 51
fax: 05 56 41 53 51
La Chandellière was created in 1980, and today its wine is a pleasing Médoc, juicy and accessible, with fresh fruit and firmness, together with tannin (sometimes a bit tough). It is also aged in *barriques*, a third of them new.

Ch Chantélys Map 21/L H10
cru bourgeois
owner: Christine Courrian-Braquessac *area:* 11 ha *cases:* 5,500 *grape % R:* CS 65% MER 30% PV 5% *second wine:* Ch Gauthier *other châteaux owned:* Ch Bel Air *(St-Estèphe)*
33340 Prignac-en-Médoc tel: 05 56 09 00 16
fax: 05 56 58 17 20
This property, which is due to expand by 4 ha, belongs to a niece of Philippe Courrian of Ch Tour Haut-Caussan. The wine has a certain class, and in good years has a juicy roundness, black fruit, oak suggesting aniseed and spices (a quarter of the casks are new), and a long finish.

Ch La Clare Map 22/L I9
cru bourgeois
owner: Paul de Rozières *area:* 27 ha *cases:* 13,500 *grape % R:* CS 57% MER 36% CF 7% *second wines:* Ch Laveline; Ch du Gentilhomme
33340 Bégadan tel: 05 56 41 50 61
A Médoc of a good standard and very consistent quality. It has a hearty, generally lively taste with bayleaf, blackcurrant and cherry. Despite the tannins always present (but seldom harsh), its structure is fairly elegant. The Réserve du Château is created only in the very best years; this wine matures exclusively in new oak.

Ch de la Croix Map 21/R H4
cru bourgeois
owner: SCF du Château de la Croix/Famille Francisco *area:* 20 ha *cases:* 14,000 *grape % R:* CS 50% MER 45% CF 4% PV 1% *second wines:* Ch Roc-Taillade, Ch Terre Rouge
33340 Ordonnac tel: 05 56 09 04 14
fax: 05 56 09 01 32
A Médoc that is fairly classic in style, and therefore made for keeping. Berry fruit is seldom lacking, and oak and vanilla add extra dimensions. The same wine – known as Domaine de la Croix until the 1980s – is sold by *négociants* as Ch Roc-Taillade or Ch Terre Rouge.

Ch David Map 22/L G9
cru bourgeois
owner: Henry Coutreau *area:* 10 ha *cases:* 5,000 *grape % R:* CS 60% MER 30% CF 5% PV 5%
33590 Vensac tel: 05 56 09 44 62
fax: 05 56 09 46 62
When young, this rather rustic wine is apt to be somewhat austere thanks to its tannins, but after a decade's ageing it comes into its own. Maturing lasts for 18-24 months, and takes place in barrels of which 30% are new. A fourth generation of the owner's family now works on the estate.

Ch d'Escol Map 21/L J6
owner: Famille Rouy *area:* 18.8 ha *cases:* 10,000 *grape % R:* CS 75% MER 24% PV 1% *second wine:* Ch Priverat
33340 Lesparre-Médoc tel: 05 56 41 06 92
fax: 05 56 41 82 42
This is one of the better wines from Lesparre; it normally shows a good balance, with considerable fruit (berries, cherries), a slight bitter note, spicy elements and fine oak from the roughly 30% of new casks. One round and two square towers flank the white château.

Ch d'Escurac Map 21/L D5
cru bourgeois
owner: SCFED Landureau *area:* 14 ha *cases:* 7,000 *grape % R:* CS 50% MER 40% CF 10% *second wine:* Ch la Chapelle d'Escurac *other châteaux owned:* Ch Haut-Myles *(Médoc)*
33340 Civrac-en-Médoc tel: 05 56 44 50 81
fax: 05 56 41 36 48

An 11th-century chapel has been fitted out as a mini-museum here; and in the 18th-century cellar a modern *cuvier* has been installed since d'Escurac left a cooperative in 1990. The wine spends at least a year in cask (25-30% new wood), but the oak elements are counter-balanced by considerable fruit. Ample tannin gives this unfiltered Médoc the potential for ageing.

Ch La Font Neuve Map 22/R I5
owner: Gérard Cazelles *area:* 2.2 ha *cases:* 1,100 *grape % R:* CS 60% MER 40% *second wine:* Ch La Saumey
33340 Bégadan tel: 05 56 41 88 14
Simple, decent *cru artisan*. Of the modest quantity produced, the greater part has so far gone into the trade. No new barrels are used.

Ch La France Map 21/R F1
owner: Michel Querre *area:* 20 ha *cases:* 10,000 *grape % R:* MER 50% CS 50% *second wine:* Ch Tour Saint Vincent *other châteaux owned:* Ch Patris *(St-Emilion)*; Ch Brun Despagne *(Bordeaux Supérieur)*
33340 Blaignan tel: 05 57 55 51 60
fax: 05 57 55 51 61
Congenial *cru bourgeois*, usually fairly rounded and accessible, with a reasonable amount of fruit and discreet oak.

Ch Gadet Terrefort Map 22/L E1
owner: Christian Bernard *area:* 6 ha *cases:* 3,000 *grape % R:* CS 70% MER 30%
33340 Gaillan-en-Médoc tel: 05 56 41 70 88
fax: 05 56 41 21 42
This is usually quite a lively Médoc of consistent quality: a *cru artisan* with ripe fruit and reasonable oak.

Ch La Gorce
Map 21/R F4

cru bourgeois

owner: Henri Fabre *area:* 37 ha *cases:* 23,000
grape % R: CS 50% MER 45% CF 5% *second wine:* Ch
Canteloup
**33340 Blaignan tel: 05 56 09 01 22
fax: 05 56 09 03 27**

The vineyard of this estate 7 km north of St-
Estèphe stretches out around an 1821
chartreuse, graced with a small roof turret. The
wine is of a reliable quality and usually a juicy
taste, on the slender side, in which berry fruit,
herbaceous notes and a hint of licorice can be
found. Maturing – 20% of the casks are new –
lasts just six months.

Ch La Gorre
Map 21/R C2

cru bourgeois

owner: Michel Laforgue *area:* 13 ha *cases:* 7,500
grape % R: CS 50% MER 45% PV 5% *second wines:*
Ch Haut-Peyrillat, Ch La Croix Landon *other
châteaux owned:* Ch Le Peyrat *(Médoc)*
**33340 Bégadan tel: 05 56 41 52 62
fax: 05 56 41 35 83**

In general this is a solidly-built, decent Médoc,
at once powerful and elegant. The tannin gives
it a long finish, and in its aroma such elements
as blackcurrant, prune, tobacco and earthy
forest notes can be distinguished. It is matured
for a maximum 18 months in barrel (25% new).
Part of the vintage goes to the firm of Dourthe,
which sells the wine as Ch La Croix Landon.

Ch Les Grands Chênes
Map 21/R C6

cru bourgeois

owner: Jacqueline Gauzy *area:* 7 ha *cases:* 3,500
grape % R: CS 65% MER 30% CF 5% *second wine:* Ch
Le Chêne Noir
**33340 St-Christoly-Médoc tel: 05 56 41 53 12
fax: 05 56 41 35 69**

Since Mme Jacqueline Gauzy-Darricade took
over the management here in 1981, wine from
this estate has been much praised. It is a Médoc
made with expertise and passion: elegant and
firm, with marvellous fruit and good oak (a
third of the *barriques* are new), plus beautifully
integrated, smooth tannins. Even in lesser years
this is a Médoc to rely upon. There is also a
Cuvée Prestige, matured entirely in new
barriques: the oak tends to dominate at first.

Clos de la Grange-Vieille
Map 21/R C6

owner: G. Pillault-Monfoulet/R Monfoulet *area:* 1.5
ha *cases:* 830 *grape % R:* CS 66% MER 34% *other
châteaux owned:* Ch Saint-Benoît *(Médoc)*
33340 St-Christoly-Médoc tel: 05 56 41 38 26
Choice Médoc, usually with generous tannin
and with berry fruit. Mostly used casks. Very
small production.

Ch Greysac
Map 22/R I10

cru bourgeois

owner: Domaine Codem/Exor *area:* 60 ha *cases:*
40,000; white 600 *grape % R:* CS 45% MER 38% CF
15% PV 2% *grape % W:* SAUV B 80% MUSC 20%
second wine: Domaine de By *other wines:*
Bordeaux blanc *other châteaux owned:* Ch des
Bertins *(Médoc)*; Ch du Monthil *(Médoc)*
**33340 Bégadan tel: 05 56 73 26 56
fax: 05 56 73 26 58**

From the mid-1970s until well into the 1980s
Greysac was an undemanding Médoc, meant for
drinking within four or five years of its vintage.
However, a new owner has now given the wine
more substance and more complexity. Greysac
often shows aspects of oak from the 15% of new

Above: Ch La Gorce

barrels, spices, bayleaf and blackcurrant. A
rising star. The estate also makes some 600
cases a year of dry white Bordeaux.

Ch Grivière
Map 21/R G2

cru bourgeois

owner: Domaines CGR *area:* 25 ha *cases:* 12,500
grape % R: MER 55% CS 40% CF 5% *second wine:* Ch
Le Vivier *other châteaux owned:* Ch La Cardonne
(Médoc); Ch Ramafort *(Médoc)*
**33340 Blaignan tel: 05 56 73 31 51
fax: 05 56 73 31 52**

Until now an agreeable, reasonably supple wine
of a fairly modest character, intended for
drinking young. Well balanced, correctly made
and matured (a third of the casks are new each
year). New owners have now made considerable
investments, which could mean that the wine
will gain in intensity, depth and class.

Ch Haut Brisey
Map 22/R G3

cru bourgeois

owner: Christian Denis *area:* 15 ha *cases:* 7,500
grape % R: CS 70% MER 30% *second wine:* Ch
Nausicaa
**33590 Jau-Dignac-et-Loirac tel: 05 56 09 56 77
fax: 05 56 73 98 36**

Wholly new property, created since 1983.
Despite the relatively young vines, the wine is

Below: Ch Greysac

already showing distinct merits – which can
only increase. In its bouquet elements of
blackcurrant, sweet pepper and animal aromas
blend with those of spicy oak (one-tenth are
new casks). Still lacks some depth and
concentration.

Ch Hauterive
Map 21/R L3

cru bourgeois

owner: Vignobles Rocher-Cap de Rive *area:* 72 ha
cases: 50,000 *grape % R:* CS 70% MER 30% *second
wines:* Letourt; Marquis de Brassane *other
châteaux owned:* include Ch Cap d'Or *(St-Georges-
St-Emilion)*
**33340 St-Germain-d'Esteuil tel: 05 57 40 08 88
fax: 05 57 40 19 93**

This vineyard has been increased by 15 ha since
the beginning of the 1980s. An exceptionally
sound Médoc is made: a quite supple wine
boasting spicy oak from its 10 months in
barriques, with juice, freshness, and smooth
berry fruit. The estate was formed in the mid-
19th century.

Ch Haut-Gravat
Map 22/R E3

owner: Alain Lanneau *area:* 8 ha *cases:* 4,000
grape % R: CS 34% CF 33% MER 33% *second wine:*
Ch Le Tretin
**33590 Jau-Dignac-et-Loirac tel: 05 56 09 41 20
fax: 05 56 73 98 06**

Hospitable family estate, where visitors are
welcome seven days a week; it has gradually
been extended in recent years and its
equipment is modern. In 1989 oak-ageing (15%
of the barrels are new) was also introduced. The
wine is a very decent, reasonably fruity Médoc,
with a firm tannin setting.

Ch Haut-Grignon
Map 22/R G7

owner: Léa Ducos, Jean-Denis Ducos *area:* 9.4 ha
cases: 4,000 *grape % R:* CS 70% MER 30% *second
wine:* Ch Fauconnin
**33340 Valeyrac tel: 05 56 41 58 76
fax: 05 56 41 35 12**

Estate built up by a former vineyard manager of
Baron Philippe de Rothschild in 1980, partly by
buying plots with old vines, partly by new
planting. Fermented in stainless-steel tanks and
matured in cask – half of which are always one
to two years old – this wine is a worthy, supple
Médoc. Haut-Grignon's labels display its
makers' signs of the zodiac.

Ch Haut-Maurac
Map 21/R E7

cru bourgeois

owner: Manizan *area:* 30 ha *cases:* 16,000 *grape % R:* CS 53% MER 45% MAL 2% *second wine:* Ch Quintaine Mazails

33340 St-Yzans-de-Médoc tel: 05 56 09 05 37 fax: 05 56 09 00 90

Of the various wines made here, that with the Ch Haut-Maurac Bellecourt label has the best and most consistent quality. This is made from selected grapes and is aged for 9-12 months in cask, a third of them new – about twice as long as for the not always successful Ch Haut-Maurac. Besides some berry fruit and oak, the wine's aroma is marked by licorice, bayleaf and spices.

Ch Haut Plantey
Map 21/R F6

owner: André Salabaras *area:* 6.5 ha *cases:* 2,750 *grape % R:* CS 50% MER 50%

33340 Civrac-en-Médoc tel: 05 56 41 58 99

A reasonably rounded Médoc – at least in good years – with some fruit, and at times a hint of sweet pepper. No oak to it. In lesser years this middle-rank wine may rather lack substance.

Ch Hourbanon
Map 21/L H9

cru bourgeois

owner: Delayat *area:* 10 ha *cases:* 5,000 *grape % R:* CS 60% MER 35% CF 5%

33340 Prignac-en-Médoc tel: 05 56 41 02 88 fax: 05 56 41 24 33

Average Médoc without great depth or personality. It usually has just a little fruit (cherry, raspberry) as well as angular tannins and some oak from its 14-18 months in *barriques*, a quarter of them new.

Ch La Hourcade
Map 22/R E3

owner: Gino & Florent Cecchini *area:* 14 ha *cases:* 7,000 *grape % R:* CS 70% MER 30% *second wine:* Ch Les Médulli

33590 Jau-Dignac-et-Loirac tel: 05 56 09 53 61

Enthusiastically-run family estate, with continuing investment in both cellars and vineyard. The planted area is due to be expanded to 21 ha. At its best the wine has considerable fruit, dark tones, a really firm structure, good tannins, and some spicy oak from 15 months in cask, a fifth of them being new. The resulting wine can sometimes be a little rough when young , but adequate bottle-age brings more polish.

Below: Ch Lacombe Noaillac

Above: Ch Livran

Ch Jeanton
Map 22/R F7

owner: Paul Borderon *area:* 5 ha *cases:* 2,500 *grape % R:* MER 60% CS 40%

33340 Valeyrac tel: 05 56 41 50 50

This *cru artisan* yields an agreeable, fairly slender Médoc that lingers nicely and has a decent amount of fruit. Maturing lasts a year on average, in barrels of which a fifth are new.

Ch Labadie
Map 21/L C10

cru bourgeois

owner: Yves Bibey *area:* 40 ha *cases:* 20,500 *grape % R:* MER 54% CS 45% PV 1% *second wine:* Ch Pontet-Barrail

33340 Bégadan tel: 05 56 41 55 58 fax: 05 56 41 39 47

Reliable estate where even in the lesser years the wine is of a more than acceptable standard. A firm taste with juicy red and black berry fruit, freshness, a certain suppleness early on from a preponderance of Merlot, and a discreet impression of oak and vanilla – from 12-15 months' maturing in one-third new barrels. The greater part of each vintage is bottled not under the château label, but for the Bordeaux trade.

Ch Lacombe Noaillac
Map 22/R F3

cru bourgeois

owner: Jean-Michel Lapalu *area:* 28 ha *cases:* 20,000 *grape % R:* CS 58% MER 32% CF 6% PV 4% *second wine:* Ch les Traverses *other châteaux owned:* Ch Patache d'Aux *(Médoc)*; Ch Le Boscq *(Médoc)*

33590 Jau-Dignac-et-Loirac tel: 05 56 09 42 55 fax: 05 56 09 58 49

An estate entirely reorganized since 1979, spreading out from a château built in 1835. Part of the vineyard consists of an 18-metre high gravel *croupe*, which is planted with Cabernet Sauvignon. The wine is perhaps not the last word in concentration, but is generally well made with balanced doses of fruit (especially blackcurrant), tannin and oak from its eight months in mainly used barrels.

Ch Laffitte Laujac
Map 21/L B6

cru bourgeois

owner: SC Château Laujac/Famille Cruse *area:* 15 ha *cases:* 8,000 *grape % R:* MER 60% CS 20% CF 20% *other châteaux owned:* Ch Laujac *(Médoc)*

33340 Bégadan tel: 05 56 41 50 12

Above: Ch Loudenne

◆

Châteaux in a commune

To find out which châteaux are in a certain commune, which may be useful in a large appellation like Médoc, consult the index of châteaux by commune at the end of the book. This lists the châteaux in this Atlas, arranged alphabetically commune by commune, with a page number.

◆

Maps covering AC Médoc

The main areas using the Médoc appellation, those in the north of the peninsula, are shown on maps 21 & 22. Other parts of the Médoc are entitled to, and use, the Haut-Médoc AC or one of the commune-based appellations such as St-Julien

---

Vineyard replanted after the frost of 1956. Vinification takes place at Ch Laujac, but the wine tastes rounder, more supple, than the Laujac wines. This is due both to the soil (clay and limestone rather than gravel), and to a predominance of Merlot. The two wines are given the same nurture: 18 months' maturing in casks of which 25% are new.

Ch Lafon
Map 21/L H9

cru bourgeois

owner: Rémy Fauchey *area:* 15 ha *cases:* 7,400 *grape % R:* CS 55% MER 30% CF 9% PV 6% *second wine:* Ch Fontaine de l'Aubier

33340 Prignac-en-Médoc tel: 05 56 09 02 17 fax: 05 56 09 04 96

Smartly maintained and carefully managed estate producing a classic, often medal-winning Médoc: a wine with plenty of colour, solid tannins, meat and berry fruit. A third of the casks in which the wine spends a year are new.

Ch Lalande d'Auvion
Map 21/R G2

cru bourgeois

owner: Christian Bénillan *area:* 20 ha *cases:* 12,000 *grape % R:* MER 60% CS 40% *second wine:* Ch Bénillan

33340 Blaignan tel: 05 56 09 05 52

Vineyard made up of two large plots, now cultivated by a fifth generation of the family that owns it. The wine has a preponderance of Merlot, and usually a fairly supple, rounded taste, with smooth, jammy fruit and a discreet hint of oak. There are plans to increase the planted area by 5 ha.

Ch Lalande de Gravelongue Map 22/R F3
owner: Gerard & Josette Castrice-Wastyne *area:* 2.9 ha *cases:* 1,600 *grape % R:* MER 35% PV 25% MAL 15% CF 15% CS 10%
33590 Jau-Dignac-et-Loirac tel: 05 56 09 47 66
Classical methods of winemaking are carried to the extreme here: grapes spend as a rule not just a few weeks but up to six months in the vats. The wine is then matured in *barriques* of which half are new. The result is a richly-coloured wine, powerful, aromatic, tending to rusticity - and with a character entirely its own.

Ch Lassus Map 22/R I9
owner: Patrick Chaumont *area:* 22 ha *cases:* 13,000 *grape % R:* MER 58% CS 35% CF 5% PV 2%
second wine: Ch Le Reysse
33340 Bégadan tel: 05 56 41 50 79
Vinified and bottled by the Bégadan cooperative. The standard version is of limited sublety, though with fairly supple tannins; this Médoc is sold via the Bordeaux trade. Since the '95 vintage, however, there has been another *cuvée* – this is cask-matured at the château for 16 months (some new barrels). The owner sells this wine direct; the label shows the cellar entrance.

Ch Laujac Map 21/L B6
cru bourgeois
owner: SC Château Laujac/Famille Cruse *area:* 27 ha *cases:* 14,000 *grape % R:* CS 60% MER 30% CF 5% PV 5% *other châteaux owned:* Ch Lafitte Laujac (*Médoc*)
**33340 Bégadan tel: 05 56 41 50 12
fax: 05 56 41 36 65**
This château dates from 1810 and is half the size originally planned. It is attractive, nevertheless. That Laujac was once a much bigger property can clearly be seen from the winery buildings: at the beginning of the 20th century the vineyard covered 140 ha, and the total estate 323 ha. The wine produced here is a clean, elegant Médoc with berry fruit; given its

Below: Ch Mazails

Above: Ch Les Ormes Sorbet

generous dose of tannin, it usually needs to mature in bottle for 9-10 years.

Ch Laulan Ducos Map 22/R G3
owner: Francis Ducos *area:* 20 ha *cases:* 11,600 *grape % R:* CS 70% MER 30% *second wines:* Ch Graves de Laulan; Ch Moulin de Ferregrave; Ch les Maurandes
**33590 Jau-Dignac-et-Loirac tel: 05 56 09 42 37
fax: 05 56 09 48 40**
In 1460 this estate formed part of the Loirac *seigneurie*. From that date, it belonged to the same family until 1911, when it passed to the great-grandfather of the present owner. He makes a stylish, comparatively supple Médoc: well balanced, with some fruit, tobacco and coffee notes. The Cuvée Prestige has more concentration, more power, a sometimes almost lush spiciness, ripe fruit and good, reasonably rounded tannins.

Ch Listran Map 22/R E4
cru bourgeois
owner: Arnaud & Noël Crété *area:* 22 ha *cases:* 12,000 *grape % R:* CS 60% MER 30% CF 5% PV 5%
second wine: Ch Larose St-Genès
**33590 Jau-Dignac-et-Loirac tel: 05 56 09 48 59
fax: 05 56 09 58 70**

Above: Ch Patache d'Aux

This vineyard, on an estate that also raises cattle, disappeared from the scene for a while but was wholly replanted in the 1980s: the first vintage released as Ch Listran came in 1988. Sometimes the wine can taste dry and hard, but in other years has a certain charm, with suppleness and fresh fruit (blackcurrant, blackberry). It is given about 12 months in casks, of which a third are new each year.

Ch Livran Map 21/R K2
cru bourgeois
owner: Famille Godfrin *area:* 48 ha *cases:* 25,000 *grape % R:* MER 50% CS 35% CF 15% *second wine:* Ch La Rose Garamey
**33340 St-Germain-d'Esteuil tel: 05 56 09 02 05
fax: 05 56 09 03 90**
The long history of this notable ivy-covered château goes back to 1310. At one point it was owned by the brother of Pope Clement V, and in the past Livran wine enjoyed a considerable reputation. But despite its modern winemaking the Godfrin family has for a long time been unable to manage more than a correct Médoc at best. It lacks body, depth and length, and does not last well. Better times must be hoped for.

Ch Loudenne Map 21/R G9
cru bourgeois
owner: W. & A. Gilbey *area:* 48 ha *cases:* 27,500; white 7,500 *grape % R:* CS 50% MER 42% CF 6% MAL 1% PV 1% *grape % W:* SAUV B 62% SEM 38% *second wine:* Ch l'Estagne *other wines:* Bordeaux blanc
**33340 St-Yzans-de-Médoc tel: 05 56 73 17 80
fax: 05 56 09 02 87**
When the brothers Walter and Alfred Gilbey, London wine and spirit merchants, bought this estate in 1875 it was mainly because of its situation close to the Gironde. They saw it as the perfect place for shipping out great quantities of wine. A large cellar complex was therefore built, as well as a cooper's shop and a dock. The vineyard was extended at the same time. Today Ch Loudenne, now part of the company which succeeded Gilbey's, is still run in a go-ahead, but also hospitable, way – and a respected wine school has been established at the charming pink-coloured château. The Loudenne Médoc possesses style, an elegant firmness and a fairly lively taste, often with nuances of fruit (blackcurrant, blackberry), bayleaf and leather, bitter chocolate, and good

Above: Ch St-Aubin

tannins and oak from a minimum of one year in *barriques* of which a fifth are new. An engaging, clean, fresh and fruity white Bordeaux is produced from a separate 14-ha plot. This stimulating wine is composed of 62% Sauvignon and 38% Sémillon. A small proportion of it is matured in new casks. From 1995 onwards the white wine has been barrel-fermented, with a further six months' cask-ageing.

Ch Lousteauneuf   Map 22/R H7
cru bourgeois
owner: Bruno Segond *area:* 20 ha *cases:* 11,800
grape % R: CS 65% MER 30% CF 5%
33340 Valeyrac tel: 05 56 41 52 11
fax: 05 56 41 52 11
A property about a century old, taken over in 1962 by the Segond family, who since then have gradually been enlarging the vineyard; it will eventually be increased to 24 ha. The greater part of the crop goes into the trade in bulk – only the Cuvée Art et Tradition is bottled at the château. This comes from old vines and is given at least a year in wood (one-third new barrels). It is a most pleasant *cru bourgeois* wine: full of character, reasonably fruity (including cherry and blackcurrant), quite firm, with sometimes a touch of sweet pepper in bouquet and taste.

Ch Mazails   Map 21/R D8
cru bourgeois
owner: Philippe Chacun *area:* 18.8 ha *cases:* 9,500
grape % R: CS 70% MER 20% MAL 10%
33340 St-Yzans-de-Médoc tel: 05 56 09 00 62
fax: 05 56 09 06 02
Nicely situated château with wine that is quite full-bodied in style. Its substantial flavour often has some fruit such as blackcurrant and cherry, but otherwise there is no great complexity.

Ch Les Moines   Map 21/R D4
cru bourgeois
owner: Claude Pourreau *area:* 30 ha *cases:* 19,000
grape % R: CS 75% MER 25% *second wine:* Ch Moulin de Brion
33340 Lesparre tel: 05 56 41 38 06
fax: 05 56 41 37 81

A Médoc that is rarely either slender or fat, and often has a solid colour and an aroma in which berry fruit and darker tones combine. Before bottling it spends 10 months in cask (25-35% new oak). The same wine is also sold as Ch Moulin de Brion.

Ch du Monthil   Map 22/R I7
cru bourgeois
owner: Domaine Codem/Exor *area:* 20 ha *cases:* 10,000 *grape % R:* CS 50% MER 40% CF 5% PV 5%
second wine: Ch Croix de Monthil *other châteaux owned:* Ch Greysac *(Médoc)*; Ch des Bertins *(Médoc)*
33340 Bégadan tel: 05 56 73 26 56
fax: 05 56 73 26 58
Very characteristic Médoc – and therefore possessing fresh berry fruit, elegance and considerable tannin. Aged in wooden vats.

Ch Moulin de Bel Air   Map 21
cru bourgeois
owner: G. Dartiguenave *area:* 8 ha *cases:* 4,400
grape % R: MER 50% CS 50%
St-Yzans-de-Médoc tel: 05 56 09 05 31
fax: 05 56 09 02 43
Firm, quite classic wine, often with considerable concentration even in the lesser years. Not at the pinnacle of finesse, but a good, lingering Médoc with personality.

Ch Noaillac   Map 22/R F2
cru bourgeois
owner: Xavier Pagès *area:* 41 ha *cases:* 20,500
grape % R: CS 55% MER 40% PV 5% *second wines:* Ch la Rose Noaillac; Les Palombes de Noaillac
33590 Jau-Dignac-et-Loirac tel: 05 56 09 52 20
fax: 05 56 09 58 75
The prestigious three-star Parisian restaurant Taillevent has carried wine from this château under its own label, which is a distinct compliment. Characteristics are an often velvety taste with supple tannins and smooth, ripe fruit. The Pagès family, of Ch La Tour de By and elsewhere, has owned the estate since 1983.

Ch Nouret   Map 21/L C8
owner: SCEA Château Noure/Famille Duhau *area:* 6 ha *cases:* 3,000 *grape % R:* CS 50% MER 50%
second wine: Ch Duhau-Laplace
33340 Civrac-en-Médoc tel: 05 56 41 50 40
fax: 05 56 41 50 40

A modest-sized vineyard for the Médoc, with stainless-steel fermentation tanks and a *chai* where the wine spends 15 months resting in oak, a third of the casks being new. Its bouquet has woodland aromas, spices including bayleaf, some blackcurrant and a hint of vanilla.

Ch Les Ormes Sorbet   Map 21/R D4
cru bourgeois
owner: Jean Boivert *area:* 21 ha *cases:* 10,000
grape % R: CS 65% MER 30% PV 5% *second wine:* Ch de Conques
33340 Couquèques tel: 05 56 41 53 78
fax: 05 56 41 38 42
This estate was created in 1764. Recent investment in the vineyard (it has 10% more Cabernet Sauvignon now) and the cellars, combined with most zealous management, have made Les Ormes Sorbet one of the stars of the district. The wine nearly always has a delicious fruitiness, with notes of fresh toast and vanilla – a third of the barrels are new, and maturing lasts 20 months. Other nuances are often those of bitter chocolate and refined tannins.

Ch de Panigon   Map 21/L C7
cru bourgeois
owner: J.K. & J.R. Leveilley *area:* 50 ha *cases:* 25,000 *grape % R:* CS 45% MER 45% PV 10% *second wine:* Ch Les Hautes Gravilles de Panigon
33340 Civrac-en-Médoc tel: 05 56 41 37 00
fax: 05 45 63 24 56
Estate run by a former Parisian restaurateur and totally renovated since the beginning of the 1980s. In great years the wine has reasonable strength and concentration, but in average and less-good ones it can sometimes lack substance and intensity. It seldom brims over with fruit; spicy notes are usually dominant. Maturing lasts 6-12 months; a third of the casks are new.

Ch Patache d'Aux   Map 22/R J8
cru bourgeois
owner: SC du Ch Patache d'Aux/Famille Lapalu *area:* 43 ha *cases:* 25,000 *grape % R:* CS 70% MER 20% CF 7% PV 3% *second wine:* Le Relais de Patache d'Aux *other châteaux owned:* Ch Le Boscq *(Médoc)*; Ch Lacombe Noaillac *(Médoc)*
33340 Bégadan tel: 05 56 41 50 18
fax: 05 56 41 54 65
Château in the village of Bégadan that once belonged to the Chevaliers d'Aux, then after the

Above: Ch Le Temple

French Revolution served as a stopping-place for *pataches* (stagecoaches). Now only the cellars function as a wine château; the actual Patache d'Aux mansion has been separated from the estate and has become a holiday centre. The wine is dominated by the Cabernet Sauvignon. It has backbone, average structure, blackcurrant – sometimes also strawberry and cherry – as fruit, spice, oak (about 25-35% new barrels), and supple tannins. The whole is generally very attractive.

Ch du Périer   Map 21/R C6
cru bourgeois
owner: Bruno Saintout *area:* 7 ha *cases:* 2,412 *grape % R:* CS 50% MER 50% *second wine:* Ch Hautesserre *other châteaux owned:* Ch La Bridane *(St-Julien)*; Domaine de Cartujac *(Haut-Médoc)*
33340 St-Christoly-Médoc tel: 05 56 41 58 32
The vineyard here is made up of three kinds of soil: gravel, sand with gravel, and sand with clay. The Merlot and Cabernet vines that grow on them yield a well-structured, dependable Médoc that has gone on winning medals since 1990. When young the wine may taste somewhat harsh, but it has the potential for maturing. It receives a year in *barriques*, and a quarter of these are new.

Ch Le Pey   Map 21/L C9
owner: Claude Compagnet *area:* 38 ha *cases:* 19,000 *grape % R:* MER 50% CS 50% *second wine:* Ch Pey Barrail
33340 Bégadan tel: 05 56 41 57 75
fax: 05 56 41 53 22

◆
Finding a château
When the name is known: to locate a château from its name alone, use the index/gazetteer, which will provide a page and a map reference. When the name and appellation are known, consult the Directory pages of the relevant chapter. When the commune is known, but not the appellation, consult the index by commune, which lists châteaux mentioned in the Atlas under the commune name

After 12 months in oak (a third new casks) this wine not only displays oak, but also jammy black fruit, spices and fairly solid tannins.

Ch Pierre de Montignac   Map 21/L E7
owner: Famille Sallette *area:* 11 ha *cases:* 5,500 *grape % R:* CS 55% MER 35% CF 5% PV 5% *second wine:* Ch Clos de Montignac
33340 Civrac-en-Médoc tel: 05 56 41 58 93
Still a young vineyard, with vines planted in the 1980s and its first vintage in 1993. Some 30% of the maturing-casks are new. Worth watching.

Ch La Pigotte Terre Feu   Map 21
owner: Pierre Freche *area:* 14 ha *cases:* 7,000 *grape % R:* MER 50% CS 50%
33340 Blaignan tel: 05 56 09 07 80
This is usually one of the better *crus artisans*, with a good deal of fruit and a lively, really full-bodied taste. No wood is used.

Ch Plagnac   Map 21/L C9
cru bourgeois
owner: Domaines Cordier *area:* 31 ha *cases:* 19,600 *grape % R:* CS 70% MER 30% *second wine:* Haut de Plaignac *other châteaux owned:* include Ch Clos des Jacobins *(St-Emilion)*
33340 Bégadan tel: 05 56 41 54 34
fax: 05 56 41 59 02
At this vineyard, owned by Cordier since 1972, a genuine, usually pleasantly fruity Médoc is made: it boasts considerable concentration and a smooth, somewhat earthy spiciness. Matured for a year in *barriques* and *foudres*, it is not intended for long keeping.

Ch Pontet   Map 21/R G2
cru bourgeois
owner: Christian Quancard *area:* 11 ha *cases:* 5,100 *grape % R:* MER 50% CS 40% CF 10% *second wines:* Ch Vieux Prézat, Ch Pontet-Coussan *other châteaux owned:* include Ch Haut-Logat *(Haut-Médoc)*; Ch Tour St-Joseph *(Haut-Médoc)*; Ch de Terrefort-Quancard *(Bordeaux Supérieur)*
33340 Blaignan tel: 05 56 20 71 03
fax: 05 56 20 11 30
The wine makes no claims to greatness, but is a pleasant, supple Médoc that spends an average 18 months in casks of which a third are new. Owned by the Quancard family, who also run the house of Cheval Quancard. Exactly the same quality of Médoc is sold under the name Ch Vieux Prezat.

Ch Potensac   Map 21/R H3
cru bourgeois
owner: Jean-Hubert Delon & Geneviève d'Alton *area:* 51 ha *cases:* 25,000 *grape % R:* CS 60% MER 25% CF 15% *second wines:* Ch Lassalle; Ch Gallais-Bellevue; Ch Goudy La Cardonne *other châteaux owned:* Ch Léoville Las Cases *(St-Julien)*
33340 Ordonnac tel: 05 56 59 25 26
fax: 05 56 59 18 33
Médoc produced by the team from Ch Léoville Las Cases, St-Julien: very reliable and totally classic. Not a gentle wine, for it usually requires a wait of at least 5-10 years for it to lose its initial reserve. Among its features are a deep colour, ripe, intense fruit (especially blackcurrant), notes of spice and cedarwood, a meaty taste and a good basis of oak (from a maximum of 20% new casks, and 12-16 months' maturing); also, as a rule, a long finish. The former church in the hamlet of Potensac is used to store the bottles.

Ch Preuillac   Map 21/L H10
cru bourgeois
owner: Mmes Bouët & Demars *area:* 30 ha *cases:* 17,000 *grape % R:* CS 50% MER 50%
33340 Lesparre tel: 05 56 09 00 29
fax: 05 56 09 00 34
A fairly slender Médoc is produced from hand-picked grapes here, in a splendid traditional cellar with wooden vats. The wine is rather introvert, but besides its fresh, fruity aspects there are herbaceous and spicy elements.

Ch Ramafort   Map 21/R G2
cru bourgeois
owner: Domaines CGR *area:* 23.7 ha *cases:* 12,000 *grape % R:* CS 50% MER 50% *other châteaux owned:* Ch La Cardonne *(Médoc)*; Ch Grivière *(Médoc)*
33340 Blaignan tel: 05 56 73 31 51
fax: 05 56 73 31 52
The Ramafort name first appeared with the 1994 vintage. Before that the estate was called Ch Romefort, a name that until 1990 was used for La Cardonne's second wine. For a long time the Ramafort vineyard formed part of La Cardonne, but at last regained its original identity. The wine has good fruit, some firmness, and is reasonably classic in character. It ages for a year in barrels of which a third are new. The château goes back to the 13th century.

Below: Ch Tour Blanche

Above: Ch La Tour de By

Ch René Georges   Map 22/R F4

owner: Guillaume Poitevin *area:* 19 ha *cases:* 10,000 *grape % R:* CS 60% MER 35% PV 5% *second wine:* Ch Lamothe Pontac

33590 Jau-Dignac-et-Loirac tel: 05 56 09 45 32 fax: 05 56 09 45 32

Quite lively wine that spends 16 months in cask, a third of them new, and normally has a brisk flavour with juicy berry fruit and some oak. It benefits from a few years' bottle age. The present owner created the estate by putting together small plots around the commune of Jau-Dignac-et-Loirac which he obtained from his parents and parents-in-law.

Ch Rollan de By   Map 22/R I10

cru bourgeois

owner: Jean Guyon *area:* 14 ha *cases:* 7,000 *grape % R:* MER 70% CS 25% PV 5% *second wine:* Ch Fleur de By

33340 Bégadan tel: 05 56 41 58 59 fax: 05 56 41 37 82

In 1989 Jean Guyon, son of a Burgundian father and a mother from Champagne, fulfilled a long-held dream by acquiring his own château in the Médoc. This was Rollan de By, then with 2 ha, which Guyon has boosted to 14 ha. He built a new cellar complex – with fermentation tanks of his own design – and decided to mature the wine for a year in casks of which half would be new. The wine is already enjoying an excellent reputation, even when it is from a less-than-bountiful year. The aroma of this Médoc includes a great deal of new oak, together with vanilla and blackcurrant, and the taste has a supple foundation of integrated tannins.

Ch Roquegrave   Map 22/R H9

owner: Joannon & Lleu *area:* 30 ha *cases:* 17,000 *grape % R:* CS 63% MER 34% PV 3%

33340 Valeyrac tel: 05 56 41 52 02 fax: 05 56 41 50 53

There is a fine view across the Gironde from Roquegrave's hill, one of the highest points in Valeyrac: this is always a good sign for a Médoc vineyard, spelling good drainage. The taste of the wine made here tends to be full-bodied and firm, often with a somewhat herbaceous aroma and some black fruit. It lasts well in bottle. Barrel-ageing is practiced only to a modest degree here.

◆
Crossing the Gironde

Visiting the northern Médoc by road is made easier by the Le Verdon–Royan ferry, which crosses the mouth of the estuary. From Royan it is about 30km to the A10 *autoroute* at Saintes. The nearest bridge is just north of Bordeaux.

Ch Rose du Pont   Map 22/R I5

owner: Pierre Lambert *area:* 1.25 ha *cases:* 700 *grape % R:* CS 48% MER 42% CF 10%

33340 Bégadan tel: 05 56 41 36 04

Small estate dating from 1902, and making its own wine once more since 1987. It produces a richly coloured, substantial Médoc that's improved by keeping.

Ch La Rose St Germain   Map 21/R I2

owner: Bernard Broussard *area:* 7.5 ha *cases:* 2,000 *grape % R:* MER 55% CS 40% CF 5% *second wine:* Ch Pey de Lalo

33340 St-Germain-d'Esteuil tel: 05 56 41 00 94

The Médoc made here, with its discreet oak, used to be mainly sold to the trade in bulk. But given its decent quality, the proportion now bottled on the estate has been increasing steadily.

Ch Saint-Aubin   Map 22/R F10

cru bourgeois

owner: Charles Fernandez de Pastro *area:* 11 ha *cases:* 6,500 *grape % R:* CS 45% MER 37% CF 18% *second wine:* Ch Saint Pierre en l'Isle

33590 Jau-Dignac-et-Loirac tel: 05 56 73 98 08 fax: 05 56 58 35 46

The château stands on what was an island until Dutch engineers carried out their drainage work in Louis XIV's time. Earlier there was a monastery on this site (its name is used for Saint-Aubin's second wine). The Médoc made here is perhaps not the finest or the most concentrated, but with plenty of substance and fresh fruit – partly from a relatively high proportion of Cabernet Franc – it's a satisfying wine. Oak is rather in the background here. There are plans for an additional 4 ha of vines.

Ch Saint-Benoît   Map 21

owner: R. Monfoulet *area:* 6 ha *cases:* 2,500 *grape % R:* CS 55% MER 45% *other châteaux owned:* Ch de la Grange-Veille (*Médoc*)

33340 St-Yzans-de-Médoc tel: 05 56 09 05 05 fax: 05 56 09 01 92

Given a moderately good vintage, this is a successful, quite light and gently fruity Médoc with a sufficiency of tannin. It is efficiently produced by the cooperative at St-Yzans-du-Médoc.

Ch Saint Bonnet   Map 21/R B5

cru bourgeois

owner: Gérard Solivérès *area:* 52 ha *cases:* 30,000 *grape % R:* MER 50% CS 50% *second wine:* Ch du Moulin

33340 St-Christoly-Médoc tel: 05 56 41 53 24 fax: 05 56 41 52 51

In most years this is a dark-coloured Médoc of consistent quality. It is given a year in oak and can mature well, although it is not usually really harsh in taste when young.

Ch Saint-Christoly   Map 21/R B6

owner: Heraud Hervé *area:* 25 ha *cases:* 12,500 *grape % R:* MER 50% CS 40% CF 5% PV 5% *second wine:* Ch La Rose Saint-Bonnet

33340 St-Christoly-de-Blaye tel: 05 56 41 52 95

A usually deep-coloured Médoc that is ready for drinking quite quickly: within about five years of the vintage as a rule. Its aroma holds notes of red and black fruit, and its character is firm rather than fine. The greater part of each vintage goes in bulk to *négociants*. The wine that the owner bottles spends two years in oak, a quarter of the casks being new. In the coming years the vineyard is to be extended by 10 ha.

Ch Saint-Christophe   Map 21/R C7

owner: Jean-Patrick Gillet *area:* 27 ha *cases:* 13,500 *grape % R:* CS 55% MER 35% CF 5% PV 5%

33340 St-Christoly-Médoc tel: 05 56 41 57 22 fax: 05 56 41 59 95

After its time in *barriques* of which a third are new, the wine's bouquet often has a hint of fresh toast, which greatly enhances it. The taste is firm in its tannin, with fresh, spicy fruit.

Ch Sestignan   Map 22/R F3

cru bourgeois

owner: Bertrand de Rozières *area:* 19.5 ha *cases:* 12,000 *grape % R:* CS 60% MER 25% CF 13% MAL 1% PV 1% *second wine:* Ch Gravelongue

33590 Jau-Dignac-et-Loirac tel: 05 56 09 43 06 fax: 05 56 09 55 85

A quite stimulating, elegant Médoc with flavours of fresh fruit – blackcurrant – and sometimes sweet pepper. The vineyard was almost doubled in size during the 1980s. The château dates back at least to the 18th century.

Ch Sigognac   Map 21/R E5

cru bourgeois

owner: Colette Bonny *area:* 47 ha *cases:* 25,000 *grape % R:* MER 34% CS 33% CF 33% *second wine:* Ch La Croix du Chevalier

33340 St-Yzans-de-Médoc tel: 05 56 09 05 04 fax: 05 56 09 00 65

This château, just north of St-Yzans-de-Médoc, is on the site of a Roman villa. After the great frost of 1956 only a few hectares of vines survived: replanting took 12 years. This is nearly always quite a slender, elegant wine, generally fragrant, and in its engaging taste there is an undertone of berry fruit with some oak from a year in wood (15% new casks).

Ch Sipian   Map 22/R H7

cru bourgeois

owner: Nicole Méhaye *area:* 17 ha *cases:* 8,300 *grape % R:* CS 40% MER 50% PV 10% *second wines:* Ch du Verdun; Les Grands Cèdres de Sipian

33340 Valeyrac tel: 05 56 41 56 05 fax: 05 56 41 35 36

Charming – but seldom really full-bodied or powerful – Médoc that does not usually demand much patience. Merlot is its most important grape, and a decent amount of Petit Verdot gives the wine some extra colour and backbone. Toasty oak (from the 40% of new barrels) imparts some extra dimensions.

Ch Taffard de Blaignan   Map 21/R H3

cru bourgeois

owner: Henri Cadillac *area:* 18 ha *cases:* 11,250 *grape % R:* MER 50% CS 50% *second wine:* Ch Les Terrasses de Taffar

33140 Ordonnac tel: 05 56 09 00 00 fax: 05 56 09 04 28

Above: Ch Tour Haut-Caussan

The owner of Taffard de Blaignan, Henri Cadillac, makes a respectable Médoc which goes into *barriques* – a third of them new – to mature for a year. The wine generally has an accessible, lively, elegant taste with vanilla, spice, licorice, bayleaf, fruit (blackcurrant, black cherry) and sometimes sweet pepper.

Ch de Taste   Map 22/L G9
cru bourgeois
owner: Jean-François Blanc *area:* 13.5 ha *cases:* 6,800 *grape % R:* CS 60% MER 35% CF 5% *second wine:* Ch Comtesse de Gombault
33590 Vensac tel: 05 56 09 44 45
fax: 05 56 09 48 96
Château by the church square at Vensac, with an estate that dates back to the 14th century. Here a reliable, typical, and therefore elegant Médoc is produced, with finesse and a consistent quality. The wine matures for 15 months in one-year-old barrels.

Ch Le Temple   Map 22/R H7
cru bourgeois
owner: Denis & Jean-Pierre Bergey *area:* 24 ha *cases:* 13,000 *grape % R:* CS 60% MER 35% PV 5% *second wines:* Ch Breuilh; Ch Balirac
33340 Valeyrac tel: 05 56 41 53 62
fax: 05 56 41 57 35
The château derives its name from the Templars, who had a hospice for pilgrims on this site some six centuries ago. Later a castle with four towers was built here on the same hill; but that, too, has vanished. The present estate took shape at the beginning of the 20th century. The best wine is the Cuvée Prestige, a rounded, almost creamy Médoc, usually fruity without being highly concentrated. This balanced wine is matured in new casks and also shows good tannins. The rather lighter and more supple standard Médoc has less oak, 20% at most of the barrels being new.

Ch Tour Blanche   Map 21/R C6
cru bourgeois
owner: Dominique Hessel *area:* 36 ha *cases:* 13,000 *grape % R:* MER 45% CS 40% CF 10% PV 5% *second wine:* Ch Guiraud Peyrebrune *other châteaux owned:* Ch Moulin à Vent *(Moulis-en-Médoc)*
33340 St-Christoly-Médoc tel: 05 56 58 15 79
fax: 05 56 58 12 05

It was a notary named Merlet who at the beginning of the 20th century created this estate, near the ruins of a medieval English fort – of which part of a tower remains. From 1970 to 1980 the estate belonged to the *négociant* firm of Barton & Guestier; after that it came into the hands of the present owner. Originally the name was Ch *La* Tour Blanche, but Ch Latour in Pauillac insisted that the 'La' should be dropped, starting from the 1991 vintage. The wine has a friendly personality, with juicy fruit (plums, currants) and a respectably long finish. The ageing of this pleasant, slightly superficial Médoc lasts just six months. Land from châteaux Les Maurines and Laforest was added to the estate in 1983 and 1986 respectively.

Ch La Tour de By   Map 22/R I3
cru bourgeois
owner: Cailloux, Lapalu, Pagès *area:* 73 ha *cases:* 42,000 *grape % R:* CS 65% MER 30% CF 3% PV 2% *second wines:* Ch Moulin de la Roque; Ch La Roque de By; Cailloux de By
33340 Bégadan tel: 05 56 41 50 03
fax: 05 53 41 36 10
In both quantity and quality, Ch La Tour de By is one of the most important *crus bourgeois* of the Médoc. The *tour* is the former lighthouse at the hamlet of By. The tower, now awash with vines, was built on the foundations of a windmill, while the actual château is a stately building of 1876 and affords a view out over the Gironde. From the extensive gravelly vineyard a most reliable, vigorous wine is produced, juicy and meaty, full of fruit (blackcurrant, blackberry, cherry, plum), with a pinch of spice and integrated, toasted oak. It is in wood for a year – a fifth of the casks are new – in an air-conditioned *chai*. Until the early 1980s the wine was apt to taste rather hard, but since then it has been made fruitier and more supple.

Ch Tour Haut-Caussan   Map 21/R G2
cru bourgeois
owner: Philippe Courrian *area:* 17 ha *cases:* 8,000 *grape % R:* MER 50% CS 50% *second wine:* Ch La Landotte *other châteaux owned:* Ch Cascadais *(Corbières)*
33340 Blaignan tel: 05 56 09 00 77
fax: 05 56 09 06 24
Under the dynamic management of the Courrians – a family who have lived in Blaignan

Below: Ch La Tour St Bonnet

since 1634 – this has become the best estate in the Médoc appellation. The Courrians make the most of the real potential of this district: the wine is almost in a class of its own. What is striking is its deep colour, its concentration, its often expansive taste, its supple, beautifully integrated tannins, its enormous length and its immaculate balance. It is a complex wine, with toasty oak (a third of the casks being new), black and red currant fruit, and spicy notes. In the centre of the vineyard there stands a 1734 windmill; brilliantly restored in 1981, it can even be used once more for milling wheat.

Ch La Tour St Bonnet   Map 21/R B4
cru bourgeois
owner: GFA Tour Saint-Bonnet/Famille Lafon *area:* 40 ha *cases:* 20,000 *grape % R:* CS 45% MER 45% MAL 5% PV 5% *second wine:* Ch la Fuie-St Bonnet
33340 St-Christoly-Médoc tel: 05 56 41 53 03
fax: 05 56 41 53 03
In good years this is a compact, reasonably concentrated Médoc, rich in extract and ripe, blackcurrant-style fruit. In a lesser year, however, the finish can show some hard, dry tannins although the taste is fairly smooth and accessible. All in all, wine from La Tour St Bonnet can vary considerably from year to year.

Ch Le Tréhon   Map 22/R I6
owner: Alain Monge *area:* 37 ha *cases:* 16,500 *grape % R:* CS 42% MER 30% CF 12% PV 12% MAL 4%
33340 Lesparre tel: 05 56 41 52 71
fax: 05 56 41 36 07
Although the standard wine from this property has little distinction, its Cuvée Fûts Neufs possesses real quality. It is quite a fleshy wine, characterized by spicy oak, vanilla and stewed fruit, supported by solid tannins. This *cuvée* would nevertheless benefit from more refinement and concentration.

Ch Les Tuileries   Map 21/R F6
cru bourgeois
owner: Jean-Luc Dartiguenave *area:* 20 ha *cases:* 10,000 *grape % R:* MER 60% CS 40% *second wines:* Ch Terre Blanche; Ch de Moulin de Bel Air
33340 St-Yzans-de-Médoc tel: 05 56 09 05 31
fax: 05 56 09 02 43
This wine estate was established about a century and a half ago by a family of coopers and cellarmasters. Besides the generously-

Quantities

Figures are as supplied by the châteaux.

Area of vineyard: given in hectares, abbreviated to ha. Châteaux are asked to specify vineyards in production, to exclude from their answers those owned but unplanted, and to advise when extensions are planned: this is sometimes noted in the text.

Production: given in cases of 12 bottles, each of 0.75 litres. A case is thus 9 litres. A hectolitre, an alternative measure of production, is 100 litres or just over 11 cases. Production figures represent an average-sized vintage.

Yield: from the area and production figures, the yield can be deduced: convert production to hectolitres by multiplying the 'cases' figure by 9, to give litres, then divide by 100, to give production in hectolitres per hectare (hl/ha).

Grape varieties: synonyms and oddities

Local variants and synonyms have traditionally been, and sometimes still are, used for some of the Bordeaux grapes. Some of these names are given official status in the appellation decrees. Synonyms include:

Bouchet St-Emilion name for Cabernet Franc

Côt or Cot Synonym for Malbec

Pressac St-Emilion name for Malbec

There are also some minor varieties which figure in the appellation decrees but are obscure or seldom grown.

Carmenère Red grape considered the equal of Cabernet Sauvignon in the Médoc in the early 19th century. Susceptible to disease, therefore now very rare; though still legal in all Médoc ACs and in the Premières Côtes.

Merlot Blanc May be a mutation of Merlot, or a separate variety. Little is grown.

Ondenc A virtually vanished white grape, still permitted for the Bordeaux AC.

Mauzac White variety still important further east; all but gone from Bordeaux, but still legal as a *cépage accessoire* in Entre-Deux-Mers.

Sauvignon Gris White variety described by some growers as an old clone, now reintroduced. Grown in the eastern Entre-Deux-Mers. Fresh, aromatically fruity wine.

Some varieties are quite common, but are less discussed than the 'major' ones. Chief among these is:

Ugni Blanc Permitted for white AC Bordeaux, in Entre-Deux-Mers and Crémant de Bordeaux as a *cépage accessoire* up to a maximum of 30%. Widely planted, especially in the north, adjoining Cognac, where it is the dominant vine.

Above: Ch Vieux Robin

proportioned reception room for formal occasions, there is also a small Musée de la Tonnellerie. Of the wines made here the Cuvée Prestige is the most interesting: vanilla, oak (a third of the casks are new), ripe – at times lush – berry fruit, sometimes a hint of chocolate, and an elegantly firm constitution.

Ch Vernous
Map 21/L I8

cru bourgeois
owner: André Lallier *area:* 21 ha *cases:* 13,000
grape % R: CS 70% MER 23% CF 7% *second wine:* La Marche de Vernous *other firms owned:* include Champagne Deutz; Delas Frères (Rhône)
33340 Lesparre tel: 05 56 41 13 57
fax: 05 56 41 21 12
André Lallier, managing director of Champagne Deutz, took over this château at the end of the 1980s. He has invested in an ultra-modern *cuvier* and a totally new *chai* for maturing the wine: 10-12 months in barrels of which 20% are new. These improvements were ready in 1991. The result is a wine of agreeable personality, with sensible measures of oak and smooth fruit, and elements of coffee, spices, leather, tobacco. Worth following.

Vieux Château Landon
Map 21/R C2

cru bourgeois
owner: Philippe Gillet *area:* 36 ha *cases:* 22,200
grape % R: CS 70% MER 25% MAL 5% *second wine:* Ch Les Dernèdes
33340 Bégadan tel: 05 56 41 50 42
fax: 05 56 41 57 10
At this estate, nearly 400 years old, the wine is treated with great care. This is apparent, for example, from the spotless *chai*, ornamented with sculptures, where a third of the barrels are new. The Médoc is an accessible wine, but one with sufficient tannin to mature for some years. Its fruit suggests jam (plum, cherry, red and blackcurrants), accompanied by spices and touches of coffee and cocoa.

Ch Les Vieux Chênes
Map 21/R C6

owner: Cédric Chamaison *area:* 1.75 ha *cases:* 900
grape % R: MER 40% CS 35% CF 15% PV 10%
33340 Valeyrac tel: 05 56 41 55 93
Micro-estate (to be enlarged by 1 ha), with 1994 its first vintage. The wine is fermented in stainless steel and matured in new *barriques*, a half of them new. A good-quality Médoc is the

result. The vines are 25 years old: formerly the grapes were taken to a cooperative.

Ch Vieux Robin
Map 22/R I9

cru bourgeois
owner: Didier & Maryse Roba *area:* 18 ha *cases:* 8,000 *grape % R:* CS 60% MER 35% CF 2% PV 3%
second wine: Ch Lalande Robin
33340 Bégadan tel: 05 56 41 50 64
fax: 05 56 41 37 85
A new generation of owners – the fifth – has pushed this estate to the top in the Médoc. The Cuvée Bois de Lunier, named after a plot in the vineyard, is an absolutely enchanting wine, elegant and firm, concentrated (in the lesser years as well), enticingly fruity, supported by new oak and generally dark in colour. The standard wine, too, has considerable merits: it is a sound Médoc without aggressiveness, and with earthy, spicy aspects. A permanent collection of modern paintings, often connected with wine, is exhibited at the château.

PESSAC-LÉOGNAN

MICHAEL BROADBENT

Graves is the cradle of the wines of Bordeaux. Wine was made here when the Médoc was a marsh. It is a large area which – on the appellation map, if not in actual vineyards – curls around the top (northern) edge of the city and sidles down the western side past Mérignac airport. Mérignac is nowadays the principal entry to the Gironde *département* – apart from those who speed down the autoroutes or (the wise ones) ride the smooth TGVs of the sophisticated railway system. For many centuries before, the gateway was of course the sea.

Then, beyond the suburbs, the Graves spreads south over a broad, undulating countryside – modest valleys rather than hills, fairly well wooded, with masses of small hamlets (few of which have any pretence to beauty or importance). Eventually it does a bit more curling – this time embracing the sweet-wine districts of Cérons, Barsac and Sauternes. With the exception of these, the river Garonne forms its eastern border.

The principal difference between the Graves and the Médoc, Pomerol and St-Emilion is that here both red *and* white wine is made. Approximately one-third of the Graves, at the upper, northern end, produces the best wine, and for this reason the two principal communes or parishes Pessac and Léognan managed – as recently as 1987 – to create for themselves a new appellation. Pessac-Léognan embraces Talence, like Pessac itself buried in the south-west suburbs of the City, plus Villenave d'Ornon, Mérignac and Gradignan, which have few vines; and the more important Martillac. The communes of St-Médard-d'Eyrans and Cadaujac, to the east, complete the list. Which does tend to leave the rest – the southern part – of the Graves rather out in the cold.

Let's tour the district. Driving from the centre of Bordeaux, take the main road south-west towards Arcachon, cross the inner ring road, and continue westward through a busy, rather ugly, built-up area. The main road climbs almost imperceptibly until the by-now practiced eye will notice on the right hand side an unmistakeable *croupe*: an exposed, sensuously convex site covered with vines. We have arrived at Pessac – itself in the heart of the outer suburbs of Bordeaux. The vineyard is that of Haut-Brion.

HAUT-BRION AND LA MISSION

First Haut-Brion. The château itself, as depicted on the wine's labels, is in a dip, somewhat hidden from the main road. Equally extraordinary, on the opposite side of the very same main road yet in the parish of Talence, lies the other leading Graves vineyard, La Mission Haut-Brion; its rather stolid château, with a chapel at one end, clearly visible through the tall iron gates.

Each of these châteaux warrants a chapter to itself – Haut-Brion being particularly rich, historically and architecturally. But what seems an eccentricity – two great vineyards in a built-up suburb – was not always so. It is just that the city, like all cities, has expanded and spread, overrunning several other old-established vineyards. Only these two, and Château Pape Clément a little further up the road, are important enough to have survived, remaining isolated amidst housing estates, shopping areas and the university campus. Indeed, Pape Clément can claim an even more ancient history, its vineyard having been planted early in the 14th century.

Haut-Brion, its château and even the fame of its wine, dates back to the 16th century. Its reputation was firmly established by the mid-17th century, by virtue of the wealthy and very enterprising Pontac family: to promote their wine they even had their own tavern with a slightly anglicized name, 'Pontack's Head', in the City

Above: Château Haut-Brion

Left: Vineyards in Pessac-Léognan

of London. When most wine was sold generically, virtually the only recorded individual vineyard name was Haut-Brion, made famous (to his later readers) by Samuel Pepys who in his diary, on 10 April 1663, wrote the now immortal words "To the Royall Oake Taverne in Lumbard-street... and here drank a sort of French wine called Ho Bryan, that hath a good and most perticular taste that I never met with". A century later, Thomas Jefferson wrote from Paris in 1788 to John Bondfield, his agent in Bordeaux: "I will also ask a favor of you to purchase for me from Monsieur le Comte de Fumelle 125 bottles of his vin d'Hautbrion of 1784".

Bondfield replied that "The Comte has only four hhds [hogsheads] of 1784 on hand. I offer'd him six hundred Livres for one of them which he refused. I am to have the first two cases of the first hhd he draws off. It is urging too much to pay three Livres in Bordeaux for a Bottle of Bordeaux wine, but so great has been the demand for that Vintage that holders obtain that exorbitant price...". Nothing changes.

The next milestone was the 1855 classification: Haut-Brion was the only château outside the Médoc to be included. It was ranked as a First Growth. Strangely enough it was not, after Pepys' day, tremendously popular in England; certainly never on a par with Lafite and Margaux. I suggest this is partly because of its very distinctive style and taste, partly because of the tendency for English wine merchants and their customers in the 19th century to stick, rather unenterprisingly, to their habitual favourite and well-tried Médocs.

Above: Château Olivier

Facing page: Gravel in a Pessac vineyard

The older vintages of Haut-Brion haven't survived very well, though I recall a superb 1926 from the Dillon family cellars. The 1928s and 1929s were very odd – stewed and overblown. It was a dismal period and in 1935 the American banking family, the Dillons, came to the rescue, buying the property. Ten years later Haut-Brion produced a great 1945 followed by a succession of very consistent, well-made wines.

La Mission Haut-Brion has come full circle. Up until the early 17th century it was part of the Haut-Brion estate, at which period it was bequeathed by a member of the family to a priestly order who, at the end of that century, built a chapel consecrated to Notre Dame de La Mission. In the mid- to late-19th century the house and chapel were restored in a rather dull, heavy-handed way, very respectable wines continuing to be made until, in 1918, the estate came into the hands of Frédéric Woltner. His two sons, Henri and Fernand, took control in 1921. For over half a century they improved the quality and style out of all recognition. The 1928 and, in particular, the 1929 were magnificent, as were the superb post-war vintages, notably 1945, 1947, the glorious 1949, the 1952 (one of the best red Bordeaux of that year), 1953; then 1955 and 1959, both magnificent, and 1961 immensely impressive.

These two brilliant and innovative brothers died in the mid-1970s, Fernand's daughter and son-in-law continuing to run the estate. In 1983 they sold out – happily not to an insurance company or an acquisitive conglomerate but to the neighbouring Dillons. Any worries that La Mission would become a sort of 'number two' to Haut-Brion were quickly dispelled; in any case the peculiarly strong soil, the slightly different aspect of the vineyard (not forgetting the railway cutting on its southern flank, whose embankment has for over a century provided unique drainage) conspire to produce a wine of a quite distinctive character.

What, might one ask, is the difference between the wines of Haut-Brion and La Mission? During the latter part of the Woltners' reign there was a school of thought, or rather of taste, that rated La Mission more highly; it caused considerable controversy, well aired in *Decanter* magazine. Though an admirer of La Mission, I think it is a more obvious wine than Haut-Brion. The latter warrants its First Growth status not least because of its finesse, its harmony, subtlety, length, its elegance and its consistency. La Mission at its best is strikingly deep in colour, mouthfilling, intense, more masculine; sometimes a little too aggressive, verging on the excessive, with noticeably high volatile acidity in otherwise good vintages like 1970.

One thing the wines of both these châteaux have in common is a very distinctive earthy character, a curious tobacco-like flavour and end taste. Another situation they share is that they, like most other and lesser châteaux in the Graves, produce a white wine. Both are superb, dry, capable of – indeed needing – bottle-ageing. Haut-Brion *blanc* has a great reputation and, because of this and the very small quantity made, it is both scarce and highly priced. My personal preference is for the white wine made at La Mission. This wine, Laville Haut-Brion, is from a six-hectare vineyard (double the area of Haut-Brion's white vines) and has, from 1928, been superb. The early post-war vintages are still holding well: the 1945 *crème de tête*, with its golden sheen, its orange-blossom bouquet, is opulent, rich yet dry; the 1947 good, 1949 fragrant; then some excellent wines throughout the 1960s and 1970s – particularly the fabulous 1971. Most recently, the 1989 Laville, one of the greatest dry white wines I have ever encountered.

Last but not least, Haut-Brion and La Mission have in common one of Bordeaux's most respected technical managers: the 'king of cloning' Jean Delmas.

OTHER CHÂTEAUX IN PESSAC-LÉOGNAN

It is easy to get carried away by Haut-Brion and La Mission. Pape Clément, already briefly mentioned, has been through some disappointing years: 'under-performing' is the popular expression. However, although I try not to dwell too much on personalities, the present proprietors have made great strides – their manager Bernard Pujol, appointed in 1985, being responsible for making wine worthy of its ancient and distinguished past and, crucially, taking advantage of its excellent, slightly elevated, vineyard site.

Continuing up the road from Haut-Brion and past Pape Clément one reaches the *rocade*. Turning south, peel off this outer ring road at Gradignan and drive on south into the heart of the Léognan half of the appellation. In appearance, distinctly unspectacular – just a tract of woods and small, plain villages – Léognan itself a bit straggly but not unattractive. A short distance beyond is one of the gems of the district (indeed of Bordeaux), Domaine de Chevalier. A modest one-storey château sits at the end of a drive flanked by vines: no slopes here, but good deep gravel soil. Claud Ricard, an accomplished pianist, put this domaine on the map, producing supremely elegant red and white wines. Then I am afraid that a not unusual situation arose, with family shareholders wishing to pull out, resulting in the sale of the domaine. The new proprietor, Olivier Bernard, has invested heavily, extending the vineyard and building an impressive new *cuverie* with an arena of stainless steel tanks. These, to some extent, diminish Chevalier's previous hands-on boutique winery image – though the likeable and enthusiastic Bernard, who wisely retained M. Ricard as joint administrator, pursues the latter's ideals with great determination.

Another of my favourite Graves is Château Haut-Bailly (not to be confused with Haut-Batailley in Pauillac). I well recall at a dinner in London to celebrate the 90th birthday of André Simon, the founder of the Wine and Food Society, drinking the then century-old Haut-Bailly in magnums. André, typically, informed the guests that in 1877 the vineyard of Château Haut-Bailly was not only far larger than at present but was awarded a gold medal for the best-run property in the Gironde. It is unusual, for Graves, in producing only red wine: soft, mildly earthy, of subtle fruit style, which develops early but matures well.

Smith Haut Lafitte is enjoying a new lease of life, a fortune having recently been spent on vineyard, *chai* and château by the very dashing and enthusiastic Cathiards. They make a fashionably crisp, refreshing, dry white, dominated by Sauvignon Blanc and bearing the tell-tale spicy, clove-like taste of expensive new oak *barriques*; also a fruity, leaner but elegant style of red.

As if to make up for the unexciting scenery, there are a surprising number of beautiful and historic châteaux in the Graves, the best-known for wine being Carbonnieux, its medieval, turreted 14th-century château strongly resembling Yquem though not as prominently sited. Here the Perrin family makes an easy to drink, quick-maturing red and a good deal of light, refreshing, dry white, much in evidence in French restaurants. Which reminds me to draw attention to the

great advantage – to the proprietors – of the châteaux in the Graves producing both red and white wine. The latter, which can be marketed and consumed quickly, provides a useful cash flow. Very handy for the already wealthy Perrins, for Carbonnieux is the biggest producer of dry white wine of all the classified growths.

Another most historic châteaux is Olivier, dating from the 11th century – moated, architecturally ravishing, a gem with both early fortress and later, elegant château. Although not (as some say) the birthplace of the Black Prince, it was certainly in use as a royal hunting lodge; it is worth mentioning here that the Black Prince's son – later to be King Richard II – was born in the area and baptised in Bordeaux. The Olivier wines have never reached the stature of the château itself, though quite recently great improvements have been made with both the whites and the reds. A further *monument classique* is La Brède, also moated, calm, beautiful, mellow and famed as the home of the great philosopher Montesquieu: it is still owned by his descendents. The wine, however, is not exceptional.

Other well-made reds and whites are produced at Châteaux Bouscaut, Couhins-Lurton, Malartic-Lagravière and de Fieuzal – the latter greatly improved by Denis Dubourbieu, whose influence on Bordeaux winemaking, particularly white Graves, has been notable. Malartic-Lagravière and de Fieuzal are close to Chevalier on the south-east side of Pessac-Léognan. To the east of Léognan are Bouscaut and the splendid, impressive La Louvière, the latter making excellent red and white wines under the ubiquitous Lurtons. To the south of the village of Martillac are Châteaux La Garde and La Tour Martillac, whose whites have greatly improved under Dubourdieu's influence.

SOUTHERN GRAVES
Just as the Haut-Médoc has at its northern end the (Bas-) Médoc, a fairly large *vignoble* producing sound but on the whole unremarkable wine, so, stretching roughly to forty kilometres south of the Pessac-Léognan border, the greater (or rather, in quality terms, lesser) Graves region contains innumerable villages and vineyards churning out quantities of wine of varying quality. The main differences between the two regions are that the southern Graves produces white wines as well as red, and that it curls round the highly important sweet wine district of Sauternes. This appellation has a chapter of its own (see page 170).

Of the more notable, interesting and reliable châteaux in Graves I would include Archambeau, owned by Jean-Philippe Dubourdieu, Cabannieux (not to be confused with Carbonnieux), Chantegrive, Cheret-Pitres, Ferrande; also La Grave and Landiras, both run by an innovative winemaker, Peter Vinding-Diers, who produces an interesting 100-per-cent Sémillon dry white at Château Landiras, his home; Magence, Millet; Montalivet (jointly owned by Dubourdieu and Pierre Coste, another formidably influential winemaker); last but not least, Rahoul and Respide.

I will round up the Pessac-Léognan/Graves region by adding that only a generation ago the vines – apart from the top *crus classés* already mentioned – yielded pretty dismal wines: undistinguished reds and thoroughly stodgy and unattractive whites. The latter were notorious for their too-yellow colour, sulphur-laden noses and boring, zestless, often flabby taste. The past 10-15 years have seen a marked improvement – partly as a result of outside criticism, probably more because of the beneficial influence and examples set by a handful of growers versed in oenology, particularly those I've named.

The reds, by and large, offer the best value of all. My tip, if in a good restaurant in Paris or Bordeaux and seriously put off by inflated wine prices, is to buy a minor red Graves. They have two advantages: their names are largely unfamiliar and unfashionable – with prices to match – and, for some unaccountable reason, they tend to develop early: mature enough to drink even at three or four years of age. As for the whites, they have been enlivened, perforce due to a more demanding market and certainly the more intelligent approach to modern winemakings: cleaner grapes, colder fermentation, use of steel tanks, avoidance of oxidation. If I have one serious criticism, it is that some producers have concentrated too much on Sauvignon Blanc – producing a crisp, acidic, international style which can as easily pall in

fashion as the old flat oxidised Graves did in taste – and the over-use of new oak. In my opinion, Sauvignon Blanc and new oak are not wholly compatible. But overall, Graves is good news. Bordeaux red and white at its pleasing, fit-for-table, good-value best.

VINTAGES

Great Pessac-Léognan dry white vintages: *1928, 1929, 1937, 1945, 1949, 1955, 1959 (but only those of top châteaux, perfectly stored), 1971, 1975, 1983, 1985, 1989, 1990.*

Good Pessac-Léognan dry white vintages: *1947, 1952, 1953, 1961, 1962, 1966, 1970, 1976, 1978, 1982, 1986, 1988, 1994.*

Below: Château La Mission Haut-Brion seen from Château Haut-Brion

---

THE APPELLATION

PESSAC-LÉOGNAN (red & dry white)

Location: On the left bank of the Garonne, the appellation covers a major, northern, part of the Graves. The Pessac-Léognan AC covers the 10 northern communes, but (as map 23 shows) only parts of these communes: there are wide areas of woods, wider areas of suburbs.
Area of AC: 4,641 ha (of which 1,700 ha are plantable)
Area under vine: 1,200 ha
Communes: Cadaujac, Canéjan, Gradignan, Léognan, Martillac, Mérignac, Pessac, Saint-Médard d'Eyrans, Talence, Villenave d'Ornon
Average annual production: 556,000 cases (80% red; 20% white)
Classed growths: 16 crus classés des Graves. Pessac-Léognan does not have its own classification system, but all the classified Graves properties are located here (6 are classified for both red and white wines, 7 just for reds and 3 for whites only). In addition, Château Haut-Brion is the only non-Médoc property to have been included in the 1855 classification of the wines of the Gironde.

Others: 44
Cooperatives: None
Main grape varieties:
Red: Cabernet Sauvignon, Merlot, Cabernet Franc
White: Sauvignon, Sémillon
Others:
Red: Petit Verdot, Malbec
White: Muscadelle
Main soil types: Deep gravel beds with some lighter, sandier topsoils

APPELLATION PESSAC-LÉOGNAN

Ch Bardins　　　Map 23/R C4
owner: Yves de Bernardy de Sigoyer *area:* 7.1 ha
cases: 3,150; W 220 *grape % R:* cf 42% mer 32%
cs 15% mal 11% *grape % W:* sem 34% sauv b 33%
musc 33% *second wine:* Ch Bardey
33140 Cadaujac tel: 05 56 30 75 85
fax: 05 56 30 04 99
This estate covers 33 ha, of which about one-
fifth is planted with vines. Its red wine has a
high percentage of Cabernet Franc and a
supple, smoothly fruity taste, with some oak. A
tiny amount of white is also made; this is
usually matured for nine months in wood, half
the casks being new. In the grounds of the
château itself (a real one: originally an
aristocrat's seat), stands a picturesque old mill.

Ch Baret　　　Map 23/R B1
owner: Héritiers Ballande *area:* 20 ha *cases:*
6,500; W 2,500 *grape % R:* cs 70% mer 25% cf 5%
grape % W: sauv b 55% sem 45%
33140 Villenave-d'Ornon tel: 05 56 00 00 70
The château's park and vineyard form a green
oasis in the built-up suburb of Villenave
d'Ornon. The château, which was partly
damaged by fire, dates from the early 18th
century. The Baret red offers reliable quality, as
well as ageing potential; dark, gamey notes are
more strongly present than fruit in the aroma.
The white is fermented in new casks and is, at
its best, quite an elegant creation in which the
freshness of the Sauvignon predominates at
first. Handled exclusively by Borie Manoux.

Ch Bouscaut　　　Map 23/R E4
cru classé blanc & rouge
owner: Sophie Lurton *area:* 45 ha *cases:* 23,000;
W 4,400 *grape % R:* mer 45% cs 40% cf 15% *grape
% W:* sem 70% sauv b 30% *second wine:* Ch Valoux;
Domaine de la Marianotte
33140 Cadaujac tel: 05 57 96 01 26
fax: 05 57 96 01 27
Bouscaut was totally overhauled under the
direction of Jean-Bernard Delmas (of Haut-
Brion) after its purchase in 1968 by an
American group. At the end of 1979 Lucien
Lurton acquired this splendid estate, and
carried through further improvements in
cellars and vineyard, and in the vinification. He
then gave it all to his daughter Sophie in 1992.
Red Bouscaut is an often firmly-structured,
serious wine with considerable substance,
reasonable fruit and the distinct presence of
oak. When young, this Pessac-Léognan usually
tastes hard and sometimes even bitter; bottle-
ageing increases its charm. The white version
offers impressions of flowers and fruit,
freshness, spicy oak and – like the red – limited
refinement. It, too, develops well in bottle.

Ch Brown　　　Map 23/L
owner: Bernard Barthe *area:* 25 ha *cases:* 9,500;
W 1,500 *grape % R:* cf 60% mer 40% *grape % W:*
sem 45% sauv b 45% musc 10% *second wine:* Le
Colombier de Château Brown
33850 Léognan tel: 05 56 87 08 10
fax: 05 56 87 87 34
Since Bernard Barthe took over in 1994, Ch
Brown has been thoroughly updated and a new
chai built – investments that have benefited the
quality of the wine. The red is rather less one-
dimensional than it was, and now boasts
engaging nuances of jammy fruit, coffee,
caramel and leather, along with oak and vanilla.

Above: Ch Brown

It is usually just right for drinking after four or
five years. Since 1994, the white wine has been
fermented in new casks and often has a lychee-
like fruitiness, and a floral note in its bouquet.
The château's name comes from John Lewis
Brown, the 19th-century English wine
merchant who also became the owner of
Cantenac-Brown in Margaux.

Ch Cantelys　　　Map 23/R J2
owner: GFA Malice/Daniel Cathiard *area:* 15 ha
cases: 3,000; W 1,000 *grape % R:* mer 50% cs
50% *grape % W:* sauv b 50% sem 50% *other
châteaux owned:* Ch Smith Haut Lafitte (Pessac-
Léognan)
33650 Martillac tel: 05 57 83 11 22
fax: 05 57 83 11 21
Daniel Cathiard from nearby Ch Smith Haut
Lafitte has leased Cantelys since 1994, and the
Smith Haut Lafitte team makes the wine. The
red is an engaging wine with considerable fruit
(cherry, raspberry) and reasonable oak (14
months' maturation, a fifth of the barrels being
new). White Cantelys, half of it from new casks,
has rather more facets: an elegant, complex
wine with a good balance between oak, fruit
(apple, grapefruit, pear, pineapple) and acidity.

Ch Carbonnieux　　　Map 23/R E1
cru classé blanc & rouge
owner: SC des Grandes Graves/Famille Perrin *area:*
90 ha *cases:* 22,000; W 22,000 *grape % R:* cs
60% mer 30% cf 7% mal 2% pv 1% *grape % W:* sauv
b 60% sem 38% musc 2% *second wine:* Ch La Tour
Léognan *other châteaux owned:* Ch Haut-Vigneau
(Pessac-Léognan); Ch le Sartre (Pessac-Léognan);
Ch Le Pape (Pessac-Léognan)
33850 Léognan tel: 05 56 87 08 28
fax: 05 56 87 52 18
The origins of this wine estate, today the
biggest in Pessac-Léognan, date back to the
12th century. In 1741 it was acquired by
Benedictine monks, who with early marketing
flair used to ship the white wine to the teetotal
Turkish court at Constantinople as *'eau
minérale de Carbonnieux en Guienne'*. The
Perrin family, returning to France from Algeria,
bought the totally neglected estate in 1956 and
made it prosperous again. A modern cellar
complex has been built alongside the château

with its atmospheric inner courtyard. Some of
the white Carbonnieux ferments in new barrels,
and it generally has a stylish, balanced taste of
minerally fruit (citrus, apple), floral hints and
an agreeable undertone of toasty oak. The red is
often characterized by a firm elegance, spicy
oak, red and black currant fruit and an
accessible character, without any really great
concentration.

Ch Les Carmes Haut-Brion　　　Map 24
owner: Famille Chantecaille *area:* 4.5 ha *cases:*
1,800 *grape % R:* mer 50% cf 40% cs 10% *second
wine:* Le Clos des Carmes
33600 Pessac tel: 05 56 51 49 43
fax: 05 56 93 10 71
Small wine estate in the middle of urban
Pessac. The charming château stands in a tree-
shaded park that borders the partly enclosed
vineyard. Only red wine is produced here, fairly
classic in character and usually demanding
patience – especially for good years such as
1990 and '94. Once mature, this attractive wine
is characterized by refined oak fragrance, dark
tones such as cocoa, and mellow fruit. This
estate, too, has monastic roots: for three
centuries it belonged to the Carmelites.

◆
About Pessac-Léognan
Information about Pessac-Léognan wines
can be obtained from the Syndicat Viticole
at 1 Cours de XXX Juillet, 33000
Bordeaux. Tel 05 56 00 22 99.
◆
Grape varieties
Main and other permitted varieties for each
appellation are given in the appellation fact
box at the end of the relevant introduction.
For châteaux, percentages of grapes grown
are given as supplied by the château.
Abbreviations: cf Cabernet Franc,
col Colombard, cs Cabernet Sauvignon,
mal Malbec, mer Merlot, musc Muscadelle,
pv Petit Verdot, sauv b Sauvignon Blanc,
sem Semillon

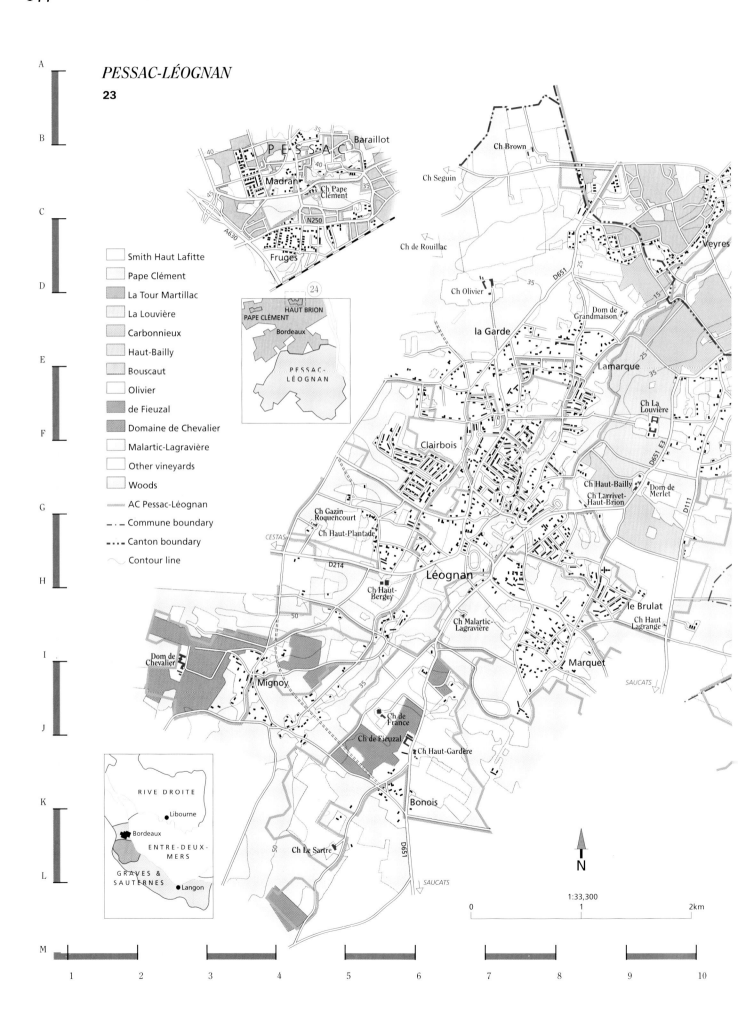

PESSAC-LÉOGNAN

23

Smith Haut Lafitte

Pape Clément

La Tour Martillac

La Louvière

Carbonnieux

Haut-Bailly

Bouscaut

Olivier

de Fieuzal

Domaine de Chevalier

Malartic-Lagravière

Other vineyards

Woods

—— AC Pessac-Léognan

– · – Commune boundary

– · · Canton boundary

～ Contour line

PESSAC

Baraillot

Ch Brown

Ch Seguin

Madran

Ch Pape Clément

N250

Fruges

Ch de Rouillac

Veyres

24

HAUT BRION

PAPE CLÉMENT

Bordeaux

PESSAC-LÉOGNAN

Ch Olivier

Dom de Grandmaison

la Garde

Lamarque

Ch La Louvière

Clairbois

Ch Haut-Bailly

Dom de Merlet

Ch Larrivet-Haut-Brion

Ch Gazin Roquencourt

CESTAS

Ch Haut-Plantade

D214

Léognan

le Brulat

Ch Haut Lagrange

Ch Haut-Bergey

Ch Malartic-Lagravière

Marquet

SAUCATS

Dom de Chevalier

Mignoy

Ch de France

Ch de Fieuzal

Ch Haut-Gardère

Bonois

RIVE DROITE

Libourne

Bordeaux

ENTRE-DEUX-MERS

GRAVES & SAUTERNES

Langon

Ch Le Sartre

SAUCATS

1:33,300

0   1   2km

N

Ch Pontac Monplaisir
Ch Baret

Couhins

Ch
Trigan
la Gamarde
Ch Couhins

Ch Bardins

Cadaujac

D111

La Garonne

Ch Couhins-
Lurton

BORDEAUX

A62

D108

VILLE-
NAVE

CADAUJAC

D111

les
Brousteys

Ile de la Lande

Ch Bouscaut

Ch Carbonnieux

Dussole

15

N113

10

5

D108

Brousley
Conilh

Ch
e Pape
Ch Le Thil
Comte Clary
Ch Smith
Haut Lafitte

Ch Malleprat

D108

A62

Ch de
Rochemorin
Ch Lafargue

50

D109

D214

15

le Breyra

Martillac

Ch Ferran

Ch d'Eyrans

M A R T I L L A C

Ch La Tour Martillac

Ch La Garde

ST-MÉDARD-
D'EYRANS

Ch Lespault

Dom de la Solitude
Ch Haut-
Nouchet

25

N113

Ch Haut-Vigneau

TOULOUSE

Clos Marsalette

35

50

D109

Ch de Cruzeau

LA BRÈDE

LANGON

Ch Le
Bruilleau

1   2   3   4   9   10

Above: Ch Les Carmes Haut-Brion

Above: Domaine de Chevalier

Domaine de Chevalier   Map 23/L I2
cru classé blanc & rouge
owner: Olivier Bernard *area:* 35 ha *cases:* 10,000;
W 1,500 *grape % R:* CS 65% MER 30% CF 5% *grape
% W:* SAUV B 70% SEM 30% *second wine:* l'Esprit de
Chevalier *other châteaux owned:* Domaine de la
Solitude *(Pessac-Léognan)*
33850 Léognan tel: 05 56 64 16 16
fax: 05 56 64 18 18
Set in the middle of woods, and often a prey to
night frosts, this domaine yields one of the
world's great dry white wines – one that can be
regarded as the epitome of finesse. What is
more, this wine will generally age for 10-20
years without losing class or vitality. Such years
as 1983, '85, '86 and '90 are a few examples of
Chevalier longevity, all offering a splendid
wealth of nuance. The red, too, is impressive: a
classic wine for laying down: aristocratic,
gracious, subtle, with fruit and oak impeccably
balanced. White Domaine de Chevalier ferments
in cask (35% new barrels); the red in stainless
steel in a spectacular circular hall.

Ch Couhins   Map 23/R C3
cru classé blanc
owner: INRA *area:* 8.5 ha *cases:* 5,500; W 1,000
grape % R: CS 48% MER 39% CF 12% PV 1% *grape %
W:* SAUV B 82% SEM 18%
33140 Villenave-d'Ornon tel: 05 56 30 77 61
fax: 05 56 30 70 49
Almost the whole production from this estate
goes to staff at the Institut National de la
Recherche Agronomique (INRA), which
government establishment has owned the
château since 1968 and carries out research
there. Since the 1983 vintage, Couhins wines
have been vinified on the estate. This is done in
the traditional way for the red, resulting in a
classic wine with a good deal of tannin. The
white, mostly Sauvignon, lacks complexity, yet
has a certain refinement and distinction.

Ch Couhins-Lurton   Map 23/R C2
cru classé blanc
owner: André Lurton *area:* 5.5 ha *cases:* 2,100
grape % W: SAUV B 100% *second wine:* Ch Cantebau
other châteaux owned: Ch de Rochemorin *(Pessac-
Léognan)*; Ch de Cruzeau *(Pessac-Léognan)*; Ch La
Louvière *(Pessac-Léognan)* ;Ch Bonnet *(Bordeaux &
Entre-Deux-Mers)*

33140 Villenave-d'Ornon tel: 05 57 25 58 58
fax: 05 57 74 98 59
The white wine created here is sometimes so
rich, mouthfilling, aromatic and complex that it
is hard to imagine that this Pessac-Léognan
comes solely from Sauvignon grapes. The secret
lies in the very gravelly soil, the ripeness of the
grapes – selectively gathered in successive
pickings – and careful vinification in casks of
which half are new. No malolactic fermentation
occurs, so that this stylish wine keeps its
freshness. It will easily mature in bottle for 4-5
years.

Ch de Cruzeau   Map 23/R M6
owner: André Lurton *area:* 81 ha *cases:* 30,000; W
19,000 *grape % R:* CS 55% MER 43% CF 2% *grape %
W:* SAUV B 85% SEM 15% *second wine:* Ch de
Quentin *other châteaux owned:* Ch Couhins-Lurton
(Pessac-Léognan); Ch La Louvière *(Pessac-Léognan)*;
Ch de Rochemorin *(Pessac-Léognan)*; Ch Bonnet
(Bordeaux & Entre-Deux-Mers)
33650 St-Médard-d'Eyrans tel: 05 57 25 58 58
fax: 05 57 74 98 59
Estate on the border of Martillac and St-
Médard-d'Eyrans, wholly restored since 1973 by
André Lurton. This vineyard, one of the biggest
in Pessac-Léognan, has a great deal of gravel
and gives an alluring red wine with strength,
mature tannins, suppleness and much fruit –
notes of plum, fig, raspberry, blackcurrant,
cherry. The white tastes light-footed, fresh and
lively: Sauvignon predominates, resulting in
aromatic impressions of gooseberry and
asparagus, sometimes with grapefruit and a
certain herbaceousness.

Ch d'Eyrans   Map 23/R J10
owner: Famille de Sèze *area:* 11 ha *cases:* 5,000
grape % R: MER 50% CS 50% *other châteaux owned:*
Ch Bastian *(Bordeaux)*
33650 St-Médard-d'Eyrans tel: 05 56 65 51 59
fax: 05 56 65 43 78
This estate is the source of a not particularly
expressive, usually quick-maturing red wine. It
rather lacks depth but can be pleasing, with
subtle suggestions of coffee, spices, caramel and
green peppercorns. The château has belonged
to the same family since 1796; after the Second
World War they replanted the previously-
uprooted vineyard with Cabernet Sauvignon
and Merlot vines.

Ch Ferran   Map 23/R K6
owner: Hervé Beraud-Sudreau *area:* 15 ha *cases:*
5,200; W 2,700 *grape % R:* MER 60% CF 20% CS
20% *grape % W:* SEM 60% SAUV B 40% *second wine:*
Ch de Belloc
33650 Martillac tel: 05 56 72 78 73
This stately home took its name from Robert de
Ferrand, a lawyer at Bordeaux's pre-
Revolutionary *parlement*, and was also once
owned by the philosopher Montesquieu.
Splendid pines grace the surrounding park. The
red here is rather old-fashioned in style, firm
and with reasonable fruit: nothing very exalted,
but reliable. White Ferran is usually quite
firmly structured, with some fat, reasonable
fruit, low acidity and hints of oak. All in all a
fairly classic white Graves, very correct but not
really exciting.

◆
Classed growths
Recognized classifications are listed at the
end of the Atlas. Châteaux profiled in the
Atlas which appear on one of these lists
have their classification and rank noted
immediately below the château name.

In Pessac-Léognan the classification of the
Graves applies. This covers both red and
white wines. Some châteaux have classed-
Growth status for one, some for both. All
the Graves classed Growths are in the
Pessac-Léognan area.

◆
Locating a château on a map
To locate a château from its entry in the
Atlas, note the map number and the
letter/number grid reference given next to
the château name. Maps are listed on
pages 6 & 7. The grid reference locates
the château within a 2cm square. Grid
numbers are also given in the
index/gazetteer.

Maps 23 and 24 cover the Pessac-
Léognan appellation.

Bordeaux

PESSAC-
LÉOGNAN

Ch Les Carmes
Haut-Brion

Berliquet

Cordier

Jean

Ch Picque-
Caillou

Avenue

Verthamon

20

25

BORDEAUX
CENTRE

Jaures

Jean

Ch La Misson
Haut-Brion

Ch Haut-Brion

Echoppes

Avenue

N250

P   E   S   S   A   C

Rue   Peybouquey

T   A   L   E   N   C   E

Ch La Tour
Haut-Brion

Rue   de   Candau

30

25

Avenue   Vieille   Tour

20

Haut-Brion

Haut-Brion Blanc

Les Carmes Haut-Brion

La Tour Haut-Brion

Laville Haut-Brion

La Mission Haut-Brion

Other vineyards

Woods

Canton boundary

Contour line

N

1:14,700

0   500m

A

B

C

D

E

F

G

H

I

J

K

L

M

1   2   3   4   5   6   7   8   9   10

Above: Ch de Fieuzal

Ch de Fieuzal
Map 23/L K5

cru classé rouge

owner: SA Château de Fieuzal/Gérard Gribelin *area:* 45 ha *cases:* 12,000; W 3,000 *grape % R:* CS 60% MER 30% PV 5% CF 5% *grape % W:* SEM 50% SAUV B 50% *second wine:* l'Abeille de Fieuzal *other châteaux owned:* Ch Haut-Gardère (Pessac-Léognan); Ch Le Bonnat (Graves)

33850 Léognan tel: 05 56 64 77 86
fax: 05 56 64 18 88

Thanks to Swedish-born Erik Bocké, who resurrected Fieuzal after World War II, the château's red wine secured admission to the Graves *crus classés* in the 1959 classification. Gérard Gribelin, the new owner's son-in-law, took over management of the estate in 1974, continuing in the same spirit and adding to its stature in his own perfectionist way. The vineyard was enlarged, a real château built, the cellars modernized, and both the red and white wines further improved. Fieuzal red has plenty of taste, with delicious, ripe fruit, impressions of noble oak – toast and vanilla as well – and a rich finish with civilized tannins. The white is at least equally impressive. Its fragrance and taste form a brilliant combination, full of character, with a cornucopia of fruits (apple, gooseberry, lemon, pear, peach), and discreet toasty oak. Since 1994 Fructivie, an insurance company belonging to a French bank, has owned Ch Fieuzal; however Gribelin remains at the helm.

Ch de France
Map 23/L J5

owner: Bernard Thomassin *area:* 32 ha *cases:* 13,500; W 1,400 *grape % R:* CS 55% MER 40% CF 5% *grape % W:* SAUV B 65% SEM 30% MUSC 5% *second wines:* Ch Coquillas; Ganga Cata; Le Bec en Sabot

33850 Léognan tel: 05 56 64 75 39
fax: 05 56 64 72 13

The grapes here grow on the highest of Léognan's four gravel terraces. Since 1971 the Ch de France estate has belonged to Bernard Romassin, who has made continual investments in the vineyard and cellars, not to mention the château itself. In 1984 the estate was admitted to the Union des Grands Crus de Bordeaux. The red wine here comes over as supple and agreeably rounded, with good fruit, pleasing oak overtones and a fine balance. The white – 1988

was its first year – forms a pleasant combination of oak with various fruits, citrus and tropical. Oak usually dominates at first.

Ch La Garde
Map 23/R K5

owner: Dourthe Frères/Groupe CVBG *area:* 45 ha *cases:* 16,000; W 1,300 *grape % R:* CS 65% MER 35% *grape % W:* SAUV B 100% *second wine:* Ch Naudin Larchey *other châteaux owned:* include Ch Belgrave (Haut-Médoc); Ch Teyssier (Montagne-St-Emilion) (Puisseguin-St-Emilion); Ch de la Tour (Bordeaux)

33650 Martillac tel: 05 56 72 71 07
fax: 05 56 72 66 36

Dourthe Frères, a firm belonging to the CVBG group, took over La Garde in 1990 and has since invested a great deal in it. The quality of the wines has consequently made a considerable leap forward. Greatest production is of the red Réserve du Château, made from the best grapes and matured for 12-20 months: 35% of the casks used are new. The wine has class and personality, fruit suggestive of blackcurrant, considerable oak and a fine finish. The ordinary red offers rather more fruit and less oak: it is a very palatable, juicy creation. White La Garde is produced only as Réserve du Château, a soft, gently fresh wine that smells and tastes of vanilla, fruit (pear, pineapple) and spices, with a certain fullness to it and a good finish.

Ch Gazin Roquencourt
Map 23/L H4

owner: Jean-Marie Michotte *area:* 14 ha *cases:* 6,500 *grape % R:* CS 70% MER 20% CF 10% *second wine:* Les Granges de Gazin

33850 Léognan tel: 05 56 64 77 89
fax: 05 56 64 77 89

An estate totally replanted since 1973, with a high percentage of Cabernet Sauvignon: 70% (initially as much as 80%). Cabernet Sauvignon characteristics are clearly present, with red and black berry fruit, tannin, a deep colour. The wine generally requires ageing. The château dates from 1663.

Domaine de Grandmaison
Map 23/L E8

owner: Jean Bouquier *area:* 18 ha *cases:* 7,000; W 1,900 *grape % R:* CS 60% MER 40% *grape % W:* SAUV B 60% SEM 30% MUSC 10%

33850 Léognan tel: 05 56 64 75 37
fax: 05 56 64 55 24

Château and vineyard lie on the west bank of l'Eau Blanche, the little stream that divides Léognan in two. The vines here grow in a variety of soils. The firm, at times almost sultry, red wine generally develops quite quickly – plum, cherry and other fruits can be present in the taste. The white is fresh and lively, sometimes with a hint of green apple and grapefruit, as well as a touch of oak.

Clos Grivet
Map 23/R

owner: Christian & Sylvie Auny *area:* 0.5 ha *cases:* 250 *grape % R:* CS 70% MER 30% *other châteaux owned:* Ch Le Chec (Graves)

33650 Martillac tel: 05 56 20 31 94
fax: 05 56 20 31 94

Tiny property with the same owners as Ch Le Chec, Graves. A firm red wine with subtle nuances and ageing potential. It is matured for 18 months in oak, half of the casks are new.

◆
Quantities

Figures are as supplied by the châteaux.

Area of vineyard: given in hectares, abbreviated to ha. Châteaux are asked to specify vineyards in production, and to exclude from their answers those owned but unplanted, and to advise when extensions are planned.

Production: given in cases of 12 bottles, each of 0.75 litres. A case is thus 9 litres. A hectolitre is 100 litres or just over 11 cases.

Yield per hectare: to obtain this, multiply the 'cases' figure by 9, to give litres, then divide by 100, to give hectolitres. Then divide the result by the area in hectares.

◆
Finding a second wine

To locate a second wine or any other wine not listed in the appellation's Directory pages, consult the index, where all château names are listed.

Below: Ch Haut-Brion

Ch Haut-Bailly   Map 23/L G9
cru classé rouge
owner: GFA Héritiers Sanders **area:** 28 ha **cases:**
14,800 **grape % R:** cs 65% mer 25% cf 10% **second
wine:** La Parde de Haut-Bailly **other châteaux
owned:** Ch de Courbon (Graves); Ch du Mayne
(Sauternes)
33850 Léognan tel: 05 56 64 75 11
fax: 05 56 64 53 60
Since 1982 Haut-Bailly has been back on top
form, after a difficult period in the 1970s. A
velvety taste is very characteristic of its
exclusively red wine, complemented by ripe
fruit and a stylish, restrained oak framework
(with 14 months in barrels of which half are
new). This Pessac-Léognan already displays
charm in its youth, yet has enough backbone to
last for years. Since 1955 Haut-Bailly has
belonged to the Sanders family; their
improvements include a new *chai* and a double
cuvier with stainless-steel tanks. Château and
vineyard are set on high, gravelly ground just
east of Léognan village.

Ch Haut-Bergey   Map 23/L
owner: Sylviane Garcin-Cathiard **area:** 18 ha **cases:**
8,500; W 500 **grape % R:** cs 70% mer 30% **grape %
W:** sauv b 70% sem 30% **second wine:** Ch Ponteilh-
Monplaisir **other châteaux owned:** Clos de l'Eglise
(Pomerol)
33850 Léognan tel: 05 56 64 05 22
fax: 05 56 64 06 98
Haut-Bergey, in origin a 15th-century country
retreat, was taken over in 1991 by Sylviane
Garcin-Cathiard, sister of Daniel Cathiard (of
Ch Smith Haut Lafitte). She has spent some
FF22 million on modernizing the cellars and
renovating the château. Production here
consists chiefly of red wine of distinct merits,
characterized by good tannins, dark notes of
coffee, tobacco and caramel; a pinch of spices,
some fruit and a fairly elegant structure. Oak is
strongly evident in the white, whose exotic fruit
is backed by a fresh acidity. Worth watching.

Ch Haut-Brion   Map 24
1er cru, 1855 & 1973; cru classé rouge, Graves
owner: Domaine Clarence Dillon **area:** 45.9 ha
cases: 16,000; W 800 **grape % R:** cs 45% mer 37%
cf 18% **grape % W:** sem 63% sauv b 37% **second
wine:** Le Bahans de Ch Haut-Brion **other châteaux
owned:** Ch Laville Haut-Brion (Pessac-Léognan); Ch
La Tour Haut-Brion (Pessac-Léognan); Ch La Mission
Haut-Brion (Pessac-Léognan)
33600 Pessac tel: 05 56 00 29 30
fax: 05 56 98 75 14
On 23 April 1525 Jean de Pontac married
Jeanne de Belon. Part of Jeanne's dowry was the
vineyard at Haut-Brion, a hamlet in Pessac.
Eight years later Jean de Pontac also succeeded
in buying the buildings at Haut-Brion. Such
were the origins, in 1533, of Bordeaux's first
grand cru. The vineyard consists of a gravel
bank that, according to the experts, closely
resembles the one at Ch Latour in Pauillac.
This soil, so excellent for growing vines, has for
centuries given an outstanding red wine – the
only non-Médoc property included in the 1855
classification, where it is placed among the
premiers crus classés. (Haut-Brion is also a *cru
classé* in the 1959 Graves classification.) Right
from the start this wine gives an impression of
a gracious generosity; in great years, such as
1990, this tends almost to lavishness. In
addition there are aromas of cooked, almost
caramelized, fruits, cocoa, freshly-toasted bread,

Above: Ch Haut-Bailly

mild oak – all creating a most harmonious
whole. The second wine here, Le Bahans de Ch
Haut-Brion, can be drunk sooner, and
delightfully combines ripe fruit, oak and a
satiny suppleness. There is also a white Haut-
Brion, a wine full of character with almost the
structure of a red, and verging on generosity.
Barriques are 100% new each year for both the
red and the white Haut-Brion.

Ch Haut-Gardère   Map 23/L K6
owner: SA Château de Fieuzal/Gérard Gribelin **area:**
25 ha **cases:** 10,500; W 2,700 **grape % R:** cs 55%
mer 40% cf 5% **grape % W:** sauv b 55% sem 35%
musc 10% **other châteaux owned:** Ch de Fieuzal
(Pessac-Léognan); Ch Le Bonnat (Graves)
33850 Léognan tel: 05 56 64 77 86
fax: 05 56 64 18 88
Estate situated near Ch de Fieuzal. It enjoyed
an excellent reputation up to the Second World
War, but declined thereafter: the vines were
even replaced by conifers. At last, in 1979, the
vines were replanted and Haut-Gardère began
to flourish as a wine estate once more. This
took place under the management of Jacques
and Bernadette Lesineau; then in 1995 they
sold the château to the Banque Populaire. The
red wine is generally notable for its very
agreeable, subtly-shaded taste in which smoky
oak, ripe fruit and fine tannins can be
discerned. Since 1987 Haut-Gardère has also
made a white wine. This is fermented in new
wood. It offers a solid taste, with plenty of oak
on the nose – as well as toast, vanilla and nuts –
and a gentle fruitiness.

Ch Haut Lagrange   Map 23/L I9
owner: Francis Boutemy **area:** 14.3 ha **cases:**
6,000; W 1,700 **grape % R:** cs 50% mer 45% cf 5%
grape % W: sauv b 55% sem 45% **other châteaux
owned:** Clos Marsalette (Pessac-Léognan)
33850 Léognan tel: 05 56 64 09 93
fax: 05 56 64 10 08
A relatively recent arrival – for although wine
was being made at this château back in 1764,
the present vineyard plantings only date from
1989. Despite this the red wine has substance
and strength, with firm tannins and sufficient
fruit, suggestive of blackcurrant. The white
offers a hint of vanilla, mellow fruit, and a
stimulating freshness. A third of the white wine
is fermented in wood.

Ch Haut-Nouchet   Map 23/R L5
owner: Louis Lurton **area:** 38 ha **cases:** 13,000; W
3,000 **grape % R:** cs 72% mer 28% **grape % W:**
sauv b 78% sem 22% **second wine:** Domaine du
Milan **other châteaux owned:** Ch Doisy-Dubroca
(Sauternes)
33560 Martillac tel: 05 57 83 10 10
fax: 05 57 83 10 11
Under the management first of Lucien Lurton,
and then his son Louis, Haut-Nouchet has
undergone a total regeneration. The vineyard,
lying waste, was swiftly replanted. Their white
wine was the first to appear: complex in aroma
and taste, with tropical fruit, a hint of honey,
discreet oak and the freshness of Sauvignon.
The red is fairly generous and amiable in taste,
without great depth – but this could be due in
part to the relatively young vines.

Ch Haut-Plantade   Map 23/L H5
owner: Alain Plantade **area:** 5.1 ha **cases:** 1,750;
W 450 **grape % R:** cs 65% mer 33% cf 2% **grape %
W:** sem 50% sauv b 50%
33850 Léognan tel: 05 56 64 07 09
fax: 05 56 64 02 24
An estate of modest size, and spread over seven
different plots; but in terms of quality well
worth discovering – as is apparent from a series
of awards and good reviews. The red wine is
fairly classic in character, with a reasonable
amount of fruit and concentration, plus oak and
firm, sometimes rather hard, tannins. It is often
attractive in the lighter years, when the fruit is
more to the fore. Since 1995 the château has
also produced a white Pessac-Léognan.

Ch Haut-Vigneau   Map 23/R
owner: GFA du Ch Haut Vigneau/Famille Perrin
area: 12 ha **cases:** 6,000 **grape % R:** cs 70% mer
30% **other châteaux owned:** Ch Carbonnieux
(Pessac-Léognan); Ch Le Pape (Pessac-Léognan);
Ch le Sartre (Pessac-Léognan)
33650 Martillac tel: 05 56 87 08 28
fax: 05 56 87 52 18
In existence since the mid-1980s, this estate
comprises a single vineyard in one piece, which
is to be increased to 18 ha. Early vintages were
rather light in taste, lacking in both backbone
and fruit. However, the potential quality is
there – and Ch Haut-Vigneau belongs to
committed winemakers: the Perrin family of
Ch Carbonnieux.

Ch Lafargue   Map 23/R J3
owner: Jean-Pierre Leymarie **area:** 19.9 ha **cases:**
7,500; W 1,500 **grape % R:** cs 40% mer 40% cf
20% **grape % W:** sauv b 70% sem 30% **second wine:**
Ch Haut de Domy
33650 Martillac tel: 05 56 72 72 30
fax: 05 56 72 64 61
Estate west of the village of Martillac. The red
wine here can be pleasant, if sometimes rather
lacking in length and depth. Tobacco and other
such dark notes are usually more strongly
present than fruit. The white can be short on
charm and freshness.

Ch Larrivet-Haut-Brion   Map 23/L G8
owner: Andros **area:** 45.3 ha **cases:** 17,000; W
5,000 **grape % R:** cs 55% mer 45% **grape % W:**
sauv b 60% sem 35% musc 5% **second wine:**
Domaine de Larrivet
33850 Léognan tel: 05 56 64 75 51
fax: 05 56 64 53 47
Although wines from the Larrivet-Haut-Brion
estate are not right in the Pessac-Léognan front

rank, they do represent sound, established value. The red tastes agreeable and elegant, with oak and vanilla, nice fruit (black cherry, plum) and good tannins. The white wine has a style all its own: flowery, with subtle fruit (pear, apple, melon, lemon), and at the same time balanced and fresh, with not too much oak and good length. This vineyard – which was formerly known as Haut-Brion-Larrivet – is owned by one of the country's biggest jam manufacturers.

Ch Laville Haut-Brion Map 24
cru classé blanc
owner: Domaine Clarence Dillon *area:* 3.7 ha;
cases: W 1,100 *grape % W:* SEM 70% SAUV B 30%
other châteaux owned: Ch La Tour Haut-Brion
(Pessac-Léognan); Ch La Mission Haut-Brion
(Pessac-Léognan); Ch Haut-Brion *(Pessac-Léognan)*
33400 Talence tel: 05 56 00 29 30
fax: 05 56 98 75 14
The very expensive, rare white wine (12,000 bottles a year) from this estate has incredible vitality – this Pessac-Léognan can still be glorious after 15-20 years. Characteristically it is very complex and aromatic: the senses are treated to impressions of pear, peach, coconut and vanilla. Sauvignon dominates until four or five years after the vintage, then the Sémillon suddenly breaks through and changes the wine considerably: it begins to resemble a dry version of Sauternes. Laville Haut-Brion does not have its own château; it is vinified at La Mission Haut-Brion.

Ch Lespault Map 23/R L2
owner: Jean-Claude Bolleau/Domaines Kressmann
area: 7 ha *cases:* 2,500; W 1,000 *grape % R:* MER
70% CS 25% MAL 5% *grape % W:* SAUV B 75% SEM
25% *other châteaux owned:* Ch La Tour Martillac
(Pessac-Léognan); Ch de Gorce *(Premières Côtes de Bordeaux)*
33650 Martillac tel: 05 56 72 71 21
fax: 05 56 72 64 03
This vineyard is one of Martillac's oldest, and is run by the Kressmann family of La Tour Martillac. The red is a dark-toned, fairly substantial wine for keeping, with a vanilla oak aroma. The white is reasonably expressive without being very subtly nuanced.

Ch La Louvière Map 23/L F9
owner: André Lurton *area:* 50 ha *cases:* 17,500; W
6,800 *grape % R:* CS 64% MER 30% CF 3% PV 3%
grape % W: SAUV B 85% SEM 15% *second wine:* L de
Louvière *other châteaux owned:* Ch Couhins-Lurton
(Pessac-Léognan); Ch de Cruzeau *(Pessac-Léognan);*
Ch de Rochemorin *(Pessac-Léognan);* Ch Bonnet
(Bordeaux & Entre-Deux-Mers)
33850 Léognan tel: 05 57 25 58 58
fax: 05 57 74 98 59
Victor Louis, renowned architect of the Grand Théâtre of Bordeaux, is also credited with the design for La Louvière. The château building, in all its distinction, went up in 1795, and from it there are views out over a splendid park. The wines made here are equally distinguished: they are among the best from the Pessac-Léognan appellation. This is *grâce à* André Lurton, who bought the neglected estate in 1965 and has restored it, in his perfectionist way, to all its former splendour. Red La Louvière combines concentration, fruit, body, depth and finesse into a delicious whole. The white – which is rich, aromatic and stylish – offers the same class, and matures excellently.

Above: Ch Malartic-Lagravière

Ch Malartic-Lagravière Map 23/L I6
cru classé blanc & rouge
owner: Alfred Alexandre Bonnie *area:* 19 ha *cases:*
6,000; W 1,500 *grape % R:* CS 50% MER 25% CF
25% *grape % W:* SAUV B 85% SEM 15% *second wine:*
Le Sillage de Malartic
33850 Léognan tel: 05 56 64 75 08
fax: 05 56 64 53 66
Château and *chai* stand at the lower end of their gently sloping vineyard. A red wine is produced here that is seldom really full-bodied, meaty or sensationally fruity – yet it has a certain distinction and ageing potential. The white, usually crisply fresh, is strongly characterized by the Sauvignon and often has a long finish; its bouquet can give subdued impressions of blossom, honey and peach. From 1990 until early 1997 the estate belonged to the champagne firm Laurent-Perrier, which instigated certain improvements: these include more stringent grape selection.

Clos Marsalette Map 23/L
owner: Boutemy-Von Neipperg *area:* 2.6 ha *cases:*
1,000; W 325 *grape % R:* CS 50% MER 50% *grape %
W:* SAUV B 50% SEM 50% *other châteaux owned:*
include Ch Haut Lagrange *(Pessac-Léognan);* Ch
Canon La Gaffelière *(St-Emilion)*
33850 Léognan tel: 05 56 64 09 93
fax: 05 56 64 10 08
Relatively recent small estate owned by two families: Neipperg of Canon La Gaffelière in St-Emilion and Boutemy of Haut-Lagrange in Pessac-Léognan, where the wine is made. The first red wine vintages had an attractive, racy taste with good fruit and reasonably ripe tannins: a promising start. The white-wine vines here were planted in 1993, and fermentation will be in new wood.

Domaine de Merlet Map 23/L G9
owner: Indivision Tauzin *area:* 2.5 ha *cases:* 1,000
grape % R: CS 75% MER 25% *other wines:* Bordeaux
Rosé
33850 Léognan tel: 05 56 64 77 73
De Merlet lies opposite Haut-Bailly. It was in total decline at the beginning of the 20th century, but since 1989 three young members of the Tauzin family have been energetically restoring it. Their Herculean efforts have resulted in a very decent red wine with

Cabernet Sauvignon predominating. A pleasant Bordeaux rosé is also made here.

Ch La Mission Haut-Brion Map 24
cru classé rouge
owner: Domaine Clarence Dillon *area:* 20.9 ha
cases: 7,500 *grape % R:* CS 48% MER 45% CF 7%
second wine: La Chapelle de La Mission Haut-Brion
other châteaux owned: Ch La Tour Haut-Brion
(Pessac-Léognan); Ch Laville Haut-Brion *(Pessac-Léognan);* Ch Haut-Brion *(Pessac-Léognan)*
33400 Talence tel: 05 56 00 29 30
fax: 05 56 98 75 14
After being split off from Haut-Brion, this property was acquired by the Prêcheurs de la Mission, a religious order. The fathers enlarged the vineyard and built a chapel that still stands. Haut-Brion took over La Mission once more in 1983 – but the two estates have kept their separate identities, so the wine here has its own style. The colour is usually dense and the taste generally has much energy as well as strength – with blackcurrant, fine oak and plenty of substance. The bouquet of a mature La Mission often tends towards forest-floor and truffles. This wine is treated as a *premier cru;* thus all the *barriques* are new for each vintage.

Ch Olivier Map 23/L D7
cru classé blanc & rouge
owner: Jean-Jacques de Bethmann *area:* 45 ha
cases: 13,000; W 10,000 *grape % R:* CS 65% MER
35% *grape % W:* SEM 65% SAUV B 30% MUSC 5%
second wine: Réserve d'O du Château Olivier
33850 Léognan tel: 05 56 64 73 31
fax: 05 56 64 54 23
Here 'château' means 'château'. Olivier is a partly-medieval castle, ringed by a moat, with a rich history – the Black Prince came hunting here in the 14th century. After a leasing arrangement with the *négociant* firm of Eschenauer had been ended, the de Bethmann family took over the operation themselves, in 1982. Since then considerable improvements have been made, and these are reflected in the wines. The Olivier white is the star: a nicely nuanced, balanced vitality, wine with ripe fruit, freshness and good oak. Red Olivier shows steady improvement in quality. In ordinary years the structure is somewhat slender – but in great years, such as 1989 and '90, the wine is fuller in taste, with a lot of fruit to it, noble tannin, dark notes, spices and considerable oak.

Ch Le Pape Map 23/R G1
owner: GFA Château le Pape/Famille Perrin *area:* 5
ha *cases:* 2,500 *grape % R:* MER 90% CS 10% *other
châteaux owned:* Ch Carbonnieux *(Pessac-Léognan);* Ch Haut-Vigneau *(Pessac-Léognan);* Ch le
Sartre *(Pessac-Léognan)*
33850 Léognan tel: 05 56 87 08 28
fax: 05 56 87 52 18
Balanced, fairly supple, elegant red wine: dark in bouquet, with adequate doses of oak and tannin, but without great depth or refinement. The 18th-century château stands on one of the highest points in Léognan.

Ch Pape Clément Map 23/L C4
cru classé rouge
owner: Léo Montagne & Bernard Magrez *area:* 32.5
ha *cases:* 13,300; W 900 *grape % R:* CS 60% MER
40% *grape % W:* SAUV B 45% SEM 45% MUSC 10%
second wine: Le Clementin du Ch Pape Clément
33600 Pessac tel: 05 56 07 04 11
fax: 05 56 07 36 70

After Archbishop Bertrand de Got had been elected Pope Clément V in 1305, the wine estate which he had established acquired the name Pape Clément. It lies in Pessac, stretching out over what is, for this urbanized district, a wide plateau, which boasts three types of soil. From 1979 the quality of the red declined somewhat, but from the beginning of 1985 Ch Pape Clément was altogether back in shape. The taste is meaty, generous, sensual; with a beautiful and intense fruity bouquet, satiny tannins and noble oak (50-90% of the barrels are new each year). The white wine – for decades only 100-150 cases a year; now 900 – has a fine acidity, fresh fruit, subtle oak, and much more class than before.

Ch Picque Caillou   Map 24
owner: SCI Château Picque Caillou/Famille Denis **area:** 19.5 ha **cases:** 10,300; W 450 **grape % R:** cs 35% mer 35% cf 30% **grape % W:** sem 50% sauv b 50% **second wine:** Ch Chênevert **other wines:** Ch Petit Caillou Blanc (AC Pessac-Léognan)
33700 Mérignac tel: 05 56 47 37 98
fax: 05 56 47 17 72
This is the most important wine estate left in Mérignac, nowadays more famous for Bordeaux's airport. Since 1993, thanks to the arrival of a new team, the red wine has had more élan than formerly. Its taste offers decent oak (about 12 months' maturing in casks, a third of them new), and an agreeable fruitiness. A white wine, Petit Caillou Blanc, is also made – the quantity being well-nigh secret.

Ch Pontac Monplaisir   Map 23/R
owner: Jean Maufras **area:** 15 ha **cases:** 4,700; W 4,700 **grape % R:** mer 60% cs 40% **grape % W:** sauv b 55% sem 45% **second wine:** Ch Limbourg; Domaine de la Grâce d'Ornon
33140 Villenave-d'Ornon tel: 05 56 87 35 10
fax: 05 56 87 35 10
Once a 16th-century hunting lodge belonging to Comte Jacques de Pontac, lord of 'Monplesir'. From 1955, Jean Maufras embarked on the restoration of the estate. The white is rounded and supple, with pleasing oak; a hint of apricot may also be present. The red wine, quite powerful and full-bodied, is somewhat rustic and angular, with tobacco, mocha and spices.

Below: Ch de Rochemorin

Ch de Rochemorin   Map 23/R I3
owner: André Lurton **area:** 85 ha **cases:** 28,000; W 10,500 **grape % R:** cs 60% mer 40% **grape % W:** sauv b 90% sem 10% **second wine:** Ch Coucheroy **other châteaux owned:** Ch Couhins-Lurton (Pessac-Léognan); Ch de Cruzeau (Pessac-Léognan); Ch La Louvière (Pessac-Léognan); Ch Bonnet (Bordeaux & Entre-Deux-Mers)
33650 Martillac tel: 05 57 25 58 58
fax: 05 57 74 98 59
Wines from this château were mentioned by the philosopher Montesquieu, and by 19th-century writers. Today they still collect good reviews, for they are of a good – even flawless – quality. Bouquet and taste generally offer a whole palette of impressions – ripe fruit, tobacco,

◆
Grape varieties: synonyms and oddities
Local variants and synonyms have traditionally been, and sometimes still are, used for some Bordeaux grapes.
Some synonyms are: **Bouchet** St-Emilion name for Cabernet Franc, **Côt or Cot** Synonym for Malbec, **Pressac** St-Emilion name for Malbec
There are also some minor varieties which figure in the appellation decrees but are obscure or seldom grown:
Carmenère Red grape considered the equal of Cabernet Sauvignon in the Médoc in the early 19th century. Susceptible to disease, therefore now very rare; though still legal in all Médoc ACs and in the Premières Côtes.
Merlot Blanc May be a mutation of Merlot, or a separate variety. Little is grown.
Ondenc A virtually vanished white grape, still permitted for the Bordeaux AC.
Mauzac White variety still important further east; all but gone from Bordeaux, but still a legal cépage accessoire in Entre-Deux-Mers.
Sauvignon Gris White variety described by some growers as an old clone, now grown in the eastern Entre-Deux-Mers.

vanilla, rounded tannins – attractively concentrated, with a sometimes creamily-textured, accessible character. The white, too, has many merits: gently fresh but with a sufficient acidity, as well as a sound balance between fruit and smoky oak. This estate has been re-created out of nothing since 1973 by André Lurton.

Ch de Rouillac   Map 23/L D6
owner: Pierre Sarthou **area:** 10 ha **cases:** 5,000 **grape % R:** cs 80% mer 20% **second wine:** Ch de Cassiot
33610 Canéjan tel: 05 56 89 09 11
fax: 05 56 89 67 23
One of the last surviving wine estates in Canéjan. The château's modern installations produce a good, somewhat austere red, a wine which benefits from bottle-age. The Sarthou family live in the château and have plans to double the size of the vineyard.

Ch le Sartre   Map 23/L L4
owner: GFA du Château le Sartre/Famille Perrin **area:** 22 ha **cases:** 8,000; W 2,500 **grape % R:** cs 70% mer 30% **grape % W:** sauv b 80% sem 20% **other châteaux owned:** Ch Carbonnieux (Pessac-Léognan); Ch Haut-Vigneau (Pessac-Léognan); Ch Le Pape (Pessac-Léognan)
33850 Léognan tel: 05 56 87 08 28 fax:
05 56 87 52 18
An isolated estate, surrounded by woods. The vineyard (having vanished) was replanted by Anthony Perrin of Ch Carbonnieux; the Perrins bought le Sartre in 1981. The red wine is not perhaps the last word in refinement, but usually has a structured taste with tannin and fruit (notes of cherry, blackcurrant, plum). The white version sometimes has rather pronounced oak, and a pure, fairly straightforward taste with slight elements of flowers and fruit.

Ch Seguin   Map 23/L C6
owner: SC Domaine de Seguin/Familles Boutet & Darriet **area:** 23.7 ha **cases:** 9,500; W 2,000 **grape % R:** cs 60% mer 40% **grape % W:** sem 50% sauv b 50%
33610 Canéjan tel: 05 56 75 02 43
fax: 05 56 89 35 41
Between 1944 and 1987 this once-renowned vineyard lay untended. It was then replanted, with 1991 being the first vintage. So far the red has been rather old-fashioned in style, although not too austere in taste. Reasonable, black cherry fruit and a fresh acidity are also discernible. Maturation in cask is kept to 7-8 months (a third of the casks are new). The white wine is simple stuff, and lacks depth as well as concentration and charm.

Ch Smith Haut Lafitte   Map 23/R F3
cru classé rouge
owner: Daniel Cathiard **area:** 55 ha **cases:** 23,000; W 2,200 **grape % R:** cs 55% mer 35% cf 10% **grape % W:** sauv b 100% **second wines:** Les Hauts de Smith; Ch de Maujan **other wines:** Les Hauts de Smith Rosé (AC Bordeaux) **other châteaux owned:** Ch Cantelys (Pessac-Léognan)
33650 Martillac tel: 05 56 30 72 30
fax: 05 56 30 96 26
The négociant firm of Eschenauer, the previous owners, invested a great deal in this estate. This policy has continued even more impressively under Daniel Cathiard, who bought it in 1990. Together with his wife, he has enlarged and improved the château; and

Above: Ch Smith Haut Lafitte

while the most modern cellar equipment has been installed, they have also returned to such traditional, labour-intensive methods as picking by hand and clarifying with fresh egg white. All these efforts have made Smith Haut Lafitte one of the rising stars of its appellation. The white wine, made entirely from Sauvignon grapes and fermented in new wood, is marked by an often exuberant yet gentle fruitiness (notes of pineapple, melon, fig, mango, peach), great purity and charm, with oak harmoniously present. In the red, too, the oak is not too dominant. The wine has an elegant structure, with a firm core and a fine undertone of fruit; its other nuances sometimes include cocoa and spices.

Domaine de la Solitude   Map 23/R L2
owner: Communauté de la Sainte Famille/Olivier Bernard *area:* 25 ha *cases:* 10,000; W 2,000 *grape % R:* MER 35% CF 35% CS 30% *grape % W:* SAUV B 50% SEM 50% *other wines:* Domaine de Chevalier *(AC Pessac-Léognan)*
33650 Martillac tel: 05 56 72 74 74
fax: 05 56 72 74 74

Below: Ch La Tour Martillac

This estate belongs to La Sainte Famille, a religious order founded in 1920. In 1993 they handed the management of the vineyard over to the Bernard family of Domaine de Chevalier, who drastically modernized the cellar installations. The first white-wine vintage was immediately successful: a marvellous, vital wine with fine fruit, especially citrus, that is well supported by oak. After 14 months in barrel the red shows a pleasant combination of earthy and fruity elements, with good tannins.

Ch Le Thil Comte Clary   Map 23/R F2
owner: Barons de Laitre *area:* 10.7 ha *cases:* 4,200; W 1,600 *grape % R:* MER 66% CS 34% *grape % W:* SAUV B 50% SEM 50%
33850 Léognan tel: 05 56 30 01 02
fax: 05 56 30 04 32
This château, in the middle of a great park, belongs to a family with distant connections to various European royal houses – among them those of Denmark, Norway and Sweden. Wines from this estate have clearly progressed in recent years. The red has jammy fruit (blackberry, cherry) and oak in its mellow, almost rich taste. Tropical fruits – pineapple, mango – are present in the bouquet and taste of the delicious, cask-fermented white.

Ch La Tour Haut-Brion   Map 24
cru classé rouge
owner: Domaine Clarence Dillon *area:* 4.9 ha *cases:* 2,500 *grape % R:* CS 42% CF 35% MER 23% *other châteaux owned:* Ch Laville Haut-Brion *(Pessac-Léognan)*; Ch La Mission Haut-Brion *(Pessac-Léognan)*; Ch Haut-Brion *(Pessac-Léognan)*
33400 Talence tel: 05 56 00 29 30
fax: 05 56 98 75 14
The high proportion of the two Cabernet grapes gives this wine a different personality to the reds from the two other Domaine Clarence Dillon estates, Haut-Brion and La Mission-Haut-Brion. In the La Tour Haut-Brion bouquet there are, in particular, elements of blackcurrant, cedarwood and pencil shavings. As a rule this wine will easily keep its vitality for 10-15 years. Nowadays the château itself serves as a rest home – the wine is made at La Mission.

Ch La Tour Martillac   Map 23/R K5
cru classé blanc & rouge
owner: Domaines Kressmann *area:* 36 ha *cases:* 15,000; W 5,000 *grape % R:* CS 59% MER 35% MAL 6% *grape % W:* SEM 60% SAUV B 35% MUSC 5% *second wine:* Ch La Grave Martillac *other châteaux owned:* Ch de Gorce *(Premières Côtes de Bordeaux)*; Ch Lespault *(Pessac-Léognan)*
33650 Martillac tel: 05 56 72 71 21
fax: 05 56 72 64 03
The tower that gives its name to this estate just outside Martillac is all that remains of a 12th-century fortification: today's château is a low, inconspicuous building. The quality of the wine has improved further since a new generation of the Kressmann family, owners since 1929, took over the management. What is unchanged is the ageing potential of Pessac-Léognan red, for tannin and oak are there in plenty. Nowadays the wine also has considerable fruit, especially red and black currant. The complex white, too, demands some patience; generally it takes five or six years before it opens up, loses its initial dourness, and the oak integrates beautifully with the fruit in it.

GRAVES

The Graves is the vineyard area to the south of the city of Bordeaux, mirroring the Médoc to the north. The large, rectangular sweep of the Graves appellation, some 55 kilometres long and 10 wide, begins (in law if not fact) just north of the city, where its border is the Jalle de Blanquefort – the small stream which also marks the southern frontier of the Haut-Médoc. Skirting the city on its western flank, the Graves appellation stretches away southeast-wards to just beyond Langon. To the east is the Garonne river, to the west and south-west the pine forests of Les Landes; both play a part in this area's particularly favourable microclimate: temperate and mild, with some (hopefully) well-timed humidity – especially in the south. It is interesting to note that the Graves is often the first major area of Bordeaux to begin picking its grapes – sometimes even as soon as late August.

The backbone of the Graves is the A61: join the Toulouse-bound autoroute from the *rocade* ring road, and you will find yourself among some of Bordeaux's finest vineyards: from those lying incongruously surrounded by the concrete apartment blocks of the city's suburbs to those in the densely forested, somewhat wild landscape that takes over further south. Unlike the other great Left Bank area, the Médoc, where vineyards consistently dominate the barren landscape, in the Graves their presence is often more discreet and well-hidden. Big though the area is, the vineyards are not continuous.

The famous wine-based apéritif has its home in the Graves

Suburbs in the north, and forests in the centre and south, account for large tracts.

THE APPELLATIONS

The broad Graves vineyard zone covers more than forty communes, and there are several layers of appellations within its geographical boundaries. The first is formed by the generic Bordeaux and Bordeaux Supérieur ACs, which apply throughout (though they are only used for some riverside land). The next layer is Graves (for reds and dry whites) and Graves Supérieures (semi-sweet whites). On top of these two broad layers are four other appellations which apply to specific communes. In the north, around the city of Bordeaux, ten communes are entitled to the appellation Pessac-Léognan, created in 1987 to distinguish most of the finest red and dry white wines of the area. These are covered in a separate chapter on page 138. The other three lie much further south, where the microclimate favours the development of noble rot. These are the sweet white wine enclaves of Cérons (which covers the communes of Cérons, Illats and Podensac, and is included in this chapter), Barsac and Sauternes (see page 170). The five communes in the Barsac and Sauternes appellation are not entitled to use the Graves appellations for their non-*liquoreux* white wines – only the lower Bordeaux or Bordeaux Supérieur ACs may be used.

The Graves is Bordeaux's oldest vineyard area. Vines have been grown here for more than 2,000 years and the wines already had a reputation in the Middle Ages – long before the Médoc rose to prominence. Its name stems from the gravel outcrops found throughout the area, but most prevalent closest to Bordeaux. The 'gravel' comes in differing colours, shapes and sizes, and its origins vary too – but, as in the Médoc, it affords excellent drainage and retains the heat well, making it ideally suited to the production of top-quality grapes. However the Graves has had a fairly chequered history, especially in the recent past; it is only in the last ten to fifteen years that it has succeeded in re-establishing its reputation for wines worthy of the name. Before that it had become known mainly for the production of semi-sweet wines under the Graves Supérieures appellation, which were particularly popular in Holland.

GRAPE VARIETIES AND WINES

Today, this is one of Bordeaux's most dynamic areas: although some semi-sweet white wines are still produced (roughly a tenth of total production), this area is now far better known for its reds and dry whites. Cabernet Sauvignon is the dominant variety for the reds, followed by Merlot. Red Graves, which makes up more than 50 per cent of the total production, has a very distinctive character, sometimes referred to as smoky or slightly earthy, which becomes tobacco-like with age. It is rare to find any youthful *médocain* austerity in these wines, in spite of the fact that they have the same major grape variety in common. The biggest revolution, however, has occurred in the quality of the Graves dry white wines. Produced mainly from Sémillon, with Sauvignon Blanc and sometimes a little Muscadelle, state-of-the-art technology and discreet use of new oak have altered these wines completely – even those of fairly modest origin. Graves whites are now aromatic, fresh and well made; some of them have a distinctly exotic edge, with tropical fruit and a New World tang. The best are now both fermented and aged in new oak, and last well in bottle. They can be fascinating at ten years old.

Currently, some 3,100 hectares produce Graves wines, although this is likely to continue to diminish somewhat as the Pessac-Léognan appellation grows. Since its creation in 1987 this AC has been steadily using more and more Graves land.

The sweet white wine enclave of Cérons produces a style of wine that, while lighter than that of its neighbour Barsac, is more concentrated and has more individuality than a semi-sweet Graves Supérieures. Very little Cérons is actually produced – under 30,000 cases a year. The Cérons châteaux are included in the A-Z directory which follows, since all of them also – and often mainly – make dry white and red Graves wines.

CLASSIFICATIONS

Sixteen properties form the *crus classés des Graves*; all of them are located in Pessac-Léognan. (When the classification was made in 1959, Pessac-Léognan did not exist.) Some châteaux are classified for both their red and white wines (Domaine de Chevalier for example), others for one or the other (Château Haut-Brion's red wine is *classé*, its white is not). The Graves is very much an area of small growers – around 420 in total – and many estates are under five hectares. Less than five per cent have more than twenty-five hectares. Surprisingly, there is no cooperative.

$\diamond\diamond\diamond$ **THE APPELLATIONS** $\diamond\diamond\diamond$

GRAVES (red and dry white)
GRAVES SUPÉRIEURES (semi-sweet white)
Location: *A large area on the left bank of the Garonne, mostly south of the city of Bordeaux. The northern boundary is with the Médoc, north of the city, but there are very few vineyards until south of Bordeaux. Here, the 10-commune Pessac-Léognan AC overlies the Graves AC. Sauternes and Barsac, to the south, form enclaves in the Graves. The southern edge of the AC is 45 km from the centre of Bordeaux.*
Area of AC: *9,090 ha*
Area under vine: *Graves 3,100 ha, Graves Supérieures 400 ha*
Communes (producing): *Arbanats, Ayguemorte-les-Graves, Bègles, Labrède, Beautiran, Budos, Cabanac-et-Villagrains, Castres, Cérons, Cestas, Guillos, Illats, Isle-St-Georges, Landiras, Langon, Léogeats, Mazères, Podensac, Portets, Pujols-sur-Ciron, Roaillan, St-Pardon-de-Conques, St-Selve, St-Morillon, St-Michel-de-Rieufret, St-Pierre-de-Mons, Saucats, Toulenne, Virelade plus the 10 Pessac-Léognan communes.*
Average annual production: *Graves 1,900,000 cases (67% red; 33% white), Graves Supérieures 160,000 cases*
Classed growths: *The 16 crus classés des Graves are in Pessac-Léognan*

Others: *Graves 420, Graves Supérieures 40*
Cooperatives: *None*
Main grape varieties: *Graves red: Merlot; Graves white: Sémillon; Graves Supérieures: Sémillon*
Others: *Graves red: Cabernet Sauvignon, Cabernet Franc; Graves white & Graves Supérieures: Sauvignon, Muscadelle*
Main soil types: *Gravel*

CÉRONS (sweet white)
Location: *Overlaps the Graves some 35km south-east of Bordeaux*
Area of AC: *2,089 ha*
Area under vine: *115 ha*
Communes: *Cérons, Illats, Podensac*
Average annual production: *30,000 cases*
Classed growths: *None*   **Others:** *38*
Cooperatives: *None*
Main grape varieties: *Sémillon, Sauvignon*   **Others:** *Muscadelle*
Main soil types: *Gravel over limestone*

APPELLATIONS GRAVES, GRAVES SUPÉRIEURES & CÉRONS

Ch d'Archambeau Map 26/L G6
owner: Jean-Philippe Dubourdieu **area:** 30 ha
cases: 6,500; W 6,000 **grape % R:** MER 45% CS
40% CF 15% **grape % W:** SEM 50% SAUV B 50%
second wine: Ch Mourlet
33720 Illats tel: 05 56 62 51 46
fax: 05 56 62 47 98
This château and its vineyard are up on the
Illats plateau, which borders the vast forests of
Les Landes. Its white wine is matured in barrel
and has, besides its oak, elements of fruit
(gooseberry, lychee, grapefruit), a hint of spice
and a taste that verges on the rich. The red has
elegance, a succulent suppleness and a dark
aroma that also contains fruit – a wine with
charm. A powerful, sweet Cérons is also made.

Ch d'Ardennes Map 26/L G6
owner: François Dubrey **area:** 62 ha **cases:** 20,000;
W 10,000 **grape % R:** MER 45% CS 40% CF 10% PV
5% **grape % W:** SEM 65% SAUV B 30% MUSC 5%
second wine: Ch La Tuilerie
33720 Illats tcl: 05 56 62 53 80
fax: 05 56 62 43 67
This is a comparatively extensive property,
surrounded by pines, between Illats and
Landiras. Very good wines are produced here.
With almost one-third of the casks being new,
after 10-12 months in them the red wine has
toast and oak in its aroma, along with fine
tannins, black fruit and some bayleaf. Its taste is
supple and meaty, its structure firm. The white
Graves has rather less oak, after its eight
months in cask. It fills the mouth generously
and succulently with elements that include
licorice and spices.

Ch d'Arricaud Map 26/L H6
owner: A. & J. Bouyx **area:** 25 ha **cases:** 6,500; W
5,500 **grape % R:** MER 55% CS 45% **grape % W:** SEM
60% SAUV B 30% MUSC 10% **second wine:** Ch de
Portail
33720 Landiras tel: 05 56 62 51 29
fax: 05 56 62 41 47
D'Arricaud, on its gravel hill, boasts a delightful
view over the Garonne valley. The château was
built in 1783, by the Speaker of the Bordeaux
parlement. The semi-sweet Graves Supérieures
is generally excellent, and the slender, fresh dry
white is particularly marked by its licorice and
spice. The quality and character of the red wine
can vary greatly from year to year: from stalky
and dour to supple and almost smooth, usually
with little fruit. Earthy and spicy elements are
nearly always present.

Ch Beauregard Ducasse Map 26/R J6
owner: GFA de Gaillote **area:** 35 ha **cases:** 12,000;
W 5,000 **grape % R:** CS 55% MER 35% CF 10% **grape
% W:** SEM 60% SAUV B 30% MUSC 10% **second wines:**
Ch Lagupeau; Ch Ducasse **other châteaux owned:**
include Domaine de Cabirol (AC Bordeaux); Ch
d'Armajan Les Ormes (Sauternes)
33210 Mazères tel: 05 56 76 18 97
fax: 05 56 63 21 55
The best wines here are the special *cuvées*. The
red Albert Duran is full of character: quite rich,
with substance, a distinctly dark-noted bouquet
and decent fruit. Vanilla, plus tropical and
citrus fruits, characterize the white Albertine
Payri, a stylish, reasonably subtle wine with
appetizing acidity. The ordinary wines, too, have
merit. The château is at 112 m above sea level –
the highest point in the southern Graves.

Above: Ch d'Arricaud

Ch Belon Map 25/L I4
owner: Jean Dépiot **area:** 30 ha **cases:** 7,500; W
3,500 **grape % R:** CS 65% MER 35% **grape % W:** SEM
60% SAUV B 40% **other wines:** Crémant de Bordeaux
33650 St-Morillon tel: 05 56 20 30 35
fax: 05 56 78 44 76
This estate has belonged to the same family for
about four centuries. Their red ferments in
stainless steel and matures for six months in
cask. It is an agreeable straightforward wine,
with the predominant Cabernet Sauvignon
clearly showing. White Belon has a fairly
pronounced bouquet and taste: spices dominate,
backed up by fruit (sometimes tropical) and
adequate acidity.

Ch Berger Map 25/R
owner: SCA Château Berger/Famille Berger **area:**
7.1 ha **cases:** 1,450; W 1,200 **grape % R:** CS 50%
MER 50% **grape % W:** SEM 85% MUSC 15% **second
wine:** Ch de Gueydon (Bordeaux Supérieur) **other
wines:** Cérons, Bordeaux rouge, Bordeaux Clairet
33640 Portets tel: 05 56 67 28 98
fax: 05 56 67 04 88
A modest property – but to be enlarged by 4 ha
– where Emile Berger has been producing
superior wines since 1987. The white Graves,
fermented in cask, is at once fine and complex;
the red Graves, with a year in cask, is rounded
and has elegance as well as spicy black fruit;
and Le Clairet du Ch Berger, a Bordeaux, is
simply delicious.

Ch Bichon Cassignols Map 25/L E5
owner: Jean-François Lespinasse **area:** 12 ha
cases: 4,000; W 2,700 **grape % R:** MER 60% CS
40% **grape % W:** SEM 75% SAUV B 25% **second wine:**
Ch La Creste
33650 La Brède tel: 05 56 20 28 20
fax: 05 56 20 20 08
An estate that since 1981 has been extended and
modernized. Situated on the north side of La
Brède, it lies on a plateau of sand and gravel.
The Merlot comes across strongly in the red
wine, through its dark, animal tones, supple
tannins, its roundness and its berry fruit. The
white wine is a classic dry Graves, reasonably
full, smooth and fresh, with plenty of fruit and
an attractive balance.

Ch La Blancherie Map 25/L F5
owner: Françoise Braud-Coussié **area:** 9 ha **cases:**
4,000 **grape % R:** CS 70% MER 30%
33650 La Brède tel: 05 56 20 20 39
fax: 05 56 20 35 01
The history of this estate goes back to the 17th
century. During the French Revolution its
owners were guillotined; their ghosts are said to
return at night to taste the wine. The white is
reasonably aromatic, with fresh fruit from the
Sauvignon and the rounded quality of the
Sémillon. A similar correctness is displayed by
the red – which confusingly enough is sold
under the name of Ch La Blancherie-Peyret.
This sometimes rather slender wine with its
berry fruit spends 18 months in cask.

Ch Le Bonnat Map 25/L I10
owner: SA Château de Fieuzal/Gérard Gribelin **area:**
31 ha **cases:** 8,750; W 7,500 **grape % R:** MER 50%
CS 50% **grape % W:** SEM 60% SAUV B 35% MUSC 5%
other châteaux owned: Ch de Fieuzal (Pessac-
Léognan); Ch Haut-Gardère (Pessac-Léognan)
33650 St-Selve tel: 05 56 64 77 86
fax: 05 56 64 18 88
Leased since 1987 by the owners of Ch de
Fieuzal (Pessac-Léognan). The wines are made
expertly and with great care. Even in lesser
years the red has substance and vitality in due
measure, with ripe, dark fruit and good tannins.
The white has style: it is smoothly aromatic,
with oak and vanilla as well as flower and fruit
elements, and has an agreeable length and a
pleasing roundness.

Ch Le Bourdillot   Map 25/R E4

owner: Patrice Haverlan **area:** 9 ha **cases:** 1,200;
W 200 **grape % R:** MER 60% CS 40% **grape % W:** SEM
80% SAUV B 20% **second wine:** Ch Pontet Caillou
other châteaux owned: Domaine des Lucques
(Graves); Ch Monet (Sauternes)
33720 Virelade tel: 05 56 67 11 32
fax: 05 56 67 11 32
The white wine is given first-class care here:
fermentation in new barrels is followed by 10
months' ageing. Bouquet and taste offer toasted
oak in plenty, with banana and other exotic
fruit – totally delightful. The red, too, shows
real quality, with its refined bouquet of oak (12
months in cask, a quarter of them new) and
fruit (blackcurrant, blackberry, cherry), and a
taste that combines grace and concentration.

Clos Bourgelat   Map 26/L C8

owner: Dominique Lafosse **area:** 14 ha **cases:**
4,700; W 2,700 **grape % R:** MER 50% CS 50% **grape
% W:** SEM 80% SAUV B 20% **other wines:** Cérons,
Sauternes, AC Bordeaux
33720 Cérons tel: 05 56 27 01 73
fax: 05 56 27 13 72
This property lies in a quiet part of Cérons, and
has been there since 1732. For a long time the
vineyard at this former hunting lodge of the
Duc d'Epernon was planted with white grapes
only, but black varieties were introduced from
1948. These give a firm wine, rich in tannin.
Fruit and a touch of licorice, as well as spice,
are to be tasted in the dry white Graves; while
the Cérons is among the best from this
appellation and, if from a good year, keeps well.

Ch Brondelle   Map 26/R G6

owner: Vignobles Belloc-Rochet **area:** 42 ha **cases:**
12,000; W 6,000 **grape % R:** CS 50% MER 40% CF
10% **grape % W:** SEM 50% SAUV B 40% MUSC 10%
second wine: Ch La Croix Saint Pey **other châteaux
owned:** Ch La Rose Sarron (Graves)
33210 Langon tel: 05 56 62 38 14
fax: 05 56 62 23 14
This has been a wine estate since the beginning
of the 19th century; before that it formed part
of the *seigneurie* of the Ch de Roquetaillade.
The vineyard, on gravel soil, was almost totally
replanted in 1968 and is now in full production.
The standard white is a firm, complete wine
with pleasing nuances – but the oak-fermented
Cuvée Anaïs has even more class. This is a
minor masterpiece, in which exotic fruit and
toasted, smoky oak are beautifully integrated.
Sometimes Sauternesque elements such as
apricot and honey are also there. Cuvée Damien
is the comparable red, with a lot of oak and
good concentration. The standard red has a
strikingly delicious, almost jammy fruit aroma.

Ch Cabannieux   Map 25/R F3

owner: Régine Didignac-Barrière **area:** 20 ha **cases:**
6,000; W 2,500 **grape % R:** MER 50% CS 45% CF 5%
grape % W: SEM 80% SAUV B 20% **second wines:** Ch
Haut Migot; Ch de Curcier
33640 Portets tel: 05 56 67 22 01
fax: 05 56 67 32 54
This long-established vineyard is on a well-
drained spot in the highest part of Portets. The
red wine is the more important, in quantity and
quality. It is not a thrilling wine, but certainly a
very decent one; with a touch of oak, a hint of
both blackcurrant and paprika, and good
balance and length. The white is sometimes
rather old-fashioned and short on fruit, but
with some oak and herbs in its taste.

Above: Ch Cabannieux

Ch du Caillou   Map 26/L D9

owner: SA Château du Caillou/Francis Bellet &
Philippe Desset **area:** 7.5 ha **cases:** 200; W 2,500
grape % R: CS 100% **grape % W:** SAUV B 75% SEM
25% **other wines:** Cérons, Bordeaux Clairet
33720 Cérons tel: 05 56 27 17 60
fax: 05 56 27 00 31
Du Caillou is a small property producing a
quartet of wines, mainly for the French market.
The white Graves Cuvée Saint-Cricq, with its
generous fruit and noble oak, fermented in new
casks, is the most interesting wine. The
standard white Graves has rather less oak, but
there are flowers and fruit. Honey and other
sweet flavours are manifest in the Cérons, a
Sémillon wine given a year in barrel. Finally
there is a Bordeaux Clairet, wholly from
Cabernet Sauvignon.

Ch de Callac   Map 26/L F7

owner: Philippe Rivière **area:** 21 ha **cases:** 7,500;
W 3,500 **grape % R:** CS 50% MER 50% **grape % W:**
SEM 60% SAUV B 40% **other châteaux owned:** Ch
Saint Michel (Sauternes); Clos des Menuts (St-
Emilion); Ch Haut Piquat (Lussac-St-Emilion); Ch de
Beaulieu (Montagne-St-Emilion); Ch de Lavagnac
(Bordeaux Supérieur)

Below: Ch de Cérons

33720 Illats tel: 05 57 55 59 59
fax: 05 57 55 59 51
Since this estate was modernized in 1988, its
most interesting wine has been the white
Graves: fermented in new casks; its floral and
fruity aspects combine with all manner of oak
aromas. The white wine spends six months in
barrel; the red matures for twice as long in
barriques of which a third are new. The result is
an agreeable, quite elegant red Graves, with
reasonable fruit.

Ch Camarset   Map 25/L

owner: Christian Auney **area:** 3 ha **cases:** 300; W
300 **grape % R:** MER 50% CS 30% CF 20% **grape %
W:** SEM 50% SAUV B 42% MUSC 8%
33650 St-Morillon tel: 05 56 20 31 94
fax: 05 56 20 31 94
Tiny estate of only 3 ha, where the quality of
both the fruity white wine and the red, which is
characterized by oak, shows continuing
improvement.

Ch Camus   Map 26/R F7

owner: Jean-Luc Larriaut **area:** 9.5 ha **cases:**
3,000; W 1,200 **grape % R:** CS 70% MER 30% **grape
% W:** SEM 60% SAUV B 40% **second wine:** Ch Le Bos
33210 Langon tel: 05 56 63 13 29
fax: 05 56 63 11 57
The unpretentious château is complemented by
a very handsome *chai.* Since the 1980s the wine
from this estate has been steadily improving.
The red Ch Camus characteristically boasts a
fairly firm structure, though supple and with
quite a lot of fruit. The wine is given a year's
maturing in barrel. New casks are used for
fermenting the dry white wine: this is an
expressive Graves, fresh and with fruit, with oak
in due balance. The estate also makes a semi-
sweet white wine.

Ch Carbon d'Artigues   Map 26/L G5

owner: Michel Bonnot **area:** 12 ha **cases:** 4,500; W
1,500 **grape % R:** MER 50% CF 40% CS 10% **grape %
W:** SEM 80% SAUV B 20% **other châteaux owned:** Ch
La Passonne (Loupiac & Premières Côtes de
Bordeaux)
33720 Landiras tel: 05 56 62 53 24
fax: 05 56 62 53 24
Traditional, quite tannic red Graves with an
almost dry finish. It needs time to develop – and
to a degree this is also true of the good, classic

Above: Ch de Chantegrive

white Graves, which is dominated by the somewhat spicy aroma of the Sémillon.

Ch du Castéra   Map 25/R F6
owner: M. & C. Subernie *area:* 5.5 ha *cases:* 800; W 400 *grape % R:* MER 42% CF 30% CS 22% *grape % W:* SEM 59% MUSC 22% SAUV B 19% *second wine:* Domaine des Gonbères *(Bordeaux Supérieur)*
33640 Arbanats tel: 05 56 67 13 24
There is no great finesse to the red wine, which is meaty, with a dark-toned aroma, tannin and modest fruit. The white is fairly traditional in character, and contains a relatively high proportion of the simple Muscadelle grape.

Ch de Cérons   Map 26/L B9
owner: Jean Perromat *area:* 10 ha; *cases:* W 3,300 *grape % W:* SEM 70% SAUV B 30% *second wine:* Ch de Calvimont *other châteaux owned:* Ch du Mayne *(Graves)*; Domaine de Terrefort *(Bordeaux Supérieur)*; Ch Prost *(Sauternes)*; Ch du Vieux Moulin *(Loupiac)*
33720 Cérons tel: 05 56 27 01 13
fax: 05 56 27 22 17
The entrance gate to this château and its walled vineyard is opposite the Romanesque church at Cérons. Here an exemplary syrupy wine is produced, one of the best from the Cérons appellation. In its fairly sweet aroma and taste there are often elements of spice, oak, honey and fresh fruit. It is also a wine that will mature for decades. If nature does not allow a Cérons to be made, then a dry white wine is produced under the name Ch Calvimont.

Ch de Chantegrive   Map 25/R H7
owner: Henri J.M. Lévêque *area:* 92 ha *cases:* 25,000; W 20,800 *grape % R:* CS 50% MER 40% CF 10% *grape % W:* SEM 55% SAUV B 35% MUSC 10% *second wines:* Ch Bon Dieu des Vignes; Ch Mayne Lévêque; Ch Moulin de Mare *other châteaux owned:* Ch du Mayne d'Anice *(Graves)*
33720 Podensac tel: 05 56 27 17 38
fax: 05 56 27 29 42
Extensive model estate with vineyards in Podensac, Illats and Virelade. The large cellar has room for some 800 *barriques*. Some of these are used for the white Cuvée Caroline. Oak – not obtrusive – keeps company in this rich-tasting wine with licorice, ripe fruit (pear, citrus) and honey, all wrapped round a firm core. The standard white tastes lighter and

fresher, with juicy fruit, and is meant for drinking young. The everyday red, with some oak as well as berry and cherry-style fruit, seldom has a really full-bodied taste. The Cuvée Edouard offers more strength, subtle nuance and class. When nature allows – as in 1990 – Chantegrive makes a sweet Cérons.

Ch Le Chec   Map 25/L F6
owner: Christian Sylvie Auney *area:* 6 ha *cases:* 1,700; W 750 *grape % R:* MER 40% CS 40% CF 10% MAL 10% *grape % W:* SEM 50% SAUV B 35% MUSC 15% *other wines:* Ch Le Chec *(Pessac-Léognan)* *other châteaux owned:* Clos Grivet *(Pessac-Léognan)*
33650 La Brède tel: 05 56 20 31 94
fax: 05 56 20 31 94
Le Chec is on the border of the Graves and Pessac-Léognan appellations. More red than white wine is made; the red has a somewhat rustic character with appreciable oak (it spends 14-16 months in cask) and tannin. The white Graves is fairly rounded in the mouth, with discreet nuances, including those of oak.

Ch Cheret-Pitres   Map 25/R C5
owner: Caroline Dulugat *area:* 13.8 ha *cases:* 7,800 *grape % R:* MER 60% CS 40% *other wines:* AC Bordeaux
33640 Portets tel: 05 56 67 27 76
fax: 05 56 67 27 76
This white château stands between Portets and the Garonne; the Dulugat family saved it from ruin in 1956. Only red wine is produced here: the Graves often has a somewhat smoky, dark aroma, berry fruit and a supple, rather quickly-evolving taste. The second red wine is a Bordeaux.

Ch La Croix   Map 26/R F7
owner: René Espagnet *area:* 11.5 ha *cases:* 4,500; W 1,600 *grape % R:* CS 60% MER 20% CF 20% *grape % W:* SEM 60% SAUV B 40% *second wine:* Ch Gueydon
33210 Langon tel: 05 56 63 29 36
fax: 05 56 76 27 30
The red Graves made here, with its taste of ripe red and black currants, is quite pleasing – but is somewhat lacking in substance and intensity. Slightly vegetal elements, with fruit (quince, lychee) and some spice, characterize the château's white wine. The Espagnet family has owned Ch La Croix since 1932.

Ch Duc d'Arnauton   Map 29/J5
owner: SCEA Domaines Bernard *area:* 16 ha *cases:* 2,900; W 4,800 *grape % R:* MER 51% CS 43% CF 6% *grape % W:* SEM 62% SAUV 28% MUSC 10% *other châteaux owned:* Ch Gravas *(Sauternes)*
33720 Barsac tel 05 56 27 15 20
fax 05 56 27 29 83
The d'Arnauton Graves Supérieures is among the better wines of this appellation. But then the Bernard family know how to make a sweet white wine: they also own Ch Gravas in Barsac. Their Graves Supérieures even suggests a minor Sauternes, and is matured in oak. The estate also makes an above-average dry white Graves, and a red. Both come from plots in Landiras and Pujols-sur-Ciron.

Ch Duverger   Map 26/L J5
owner: Yannick Zausa *area:* 20 ha *cases:* 4,500; W 4,500 *grape % R:* MER 70% CS 25% CF 5% *grape % W:* SEM 100%
33720 Budos tel: 05 56 62 43 45
fax: 05 56 62 43 40
From his gently sloping vineyard in Budos, Yannick Zausa makes a succulent red wine in which bayleaves and other dark tones combine with spicy oak. Sémillon is the sole grape for the appetizingly fresh white, with its aroma and taste tending to spice and licorice, with a flowery element.

Ch de l'Emigré   Map 26/L C9
owner: Gérard & Pierre Despujols *area:* 10.5 ha *cases:* 1,000; W 3,200 *grape % R:* MER 60% CS 30% CF 10% *grape % W:* SEM 34% SAUV B 33% MUSC 33% *second wine:* Ch de Valdor *other wines:* Burdigala *(Crémant de Bordeaux)* *other châteaux owned:* Ch Coulac *(Ste-Croix-du-Mont)*
33720 Cérons tel: 05 56 27 01 64
fax: 05 56 27 13 70
The present château dates from the 19th century, but the vineyard goes back to the 18th. The red wine has a fair amount of fruit, combined with oak, vanilla and tannin. The white, on the other hand, tastes rather flat and lacks personality.

Ch Fernon   Map 26/R F6
owner: Jacques Girard de Langlade *area:* 11.2 ha *cases:* 2,850; W 1,425 *grape % R:* CS 38% MER 35% CF 15% MAL 12% *grape % W:* SEM 60% SAUV B 40%
33210 Langon fax: 05 56 76 21 23
Estate just south of Langon, and not far from the hospital. Decent but seldom remarkable Graves, red and white, are produced here, and also a Graves Supérieures. In the 19th century Ch Fernon wines were served at the table of Prince Jérome Bonaparte.

◆
Grape varieties

Main and other permitted varieties for each appellation are given in the appellation fact box at the end of the relevant introduction. For châteaux, percentages of grapes grown are given as supplied by the château.

The abbreviations used are: CF Cabernet Franc, COL Colombard, CS Cabernet Sauvignon, MAL Malbec, MER Merlot, MUSC Muscadelle, PV Petit Verdot, SAUV B Sauvignon Blanc, SEM Sémillon.

Vineyards

Woods

━━━ AC Graves

━━━ AC Cérons

━·━·━ Commune boundary

▪▪▪▪ Canton boundary

〜 Contour line

BORDEAUX

ST-MÉDARD

MARTILLAC

Ch Haut-Lamothe

Ch de Haut-Calens

Ch St-Gêrome

Ch Tour de Calens

B E A U T I R A N

la Prade

Ch Lusseau

Ch Le Tuquet

Ch Grand Bourdieu

Civrac

C A S T R E S

Ch Chanteloiseau

Dom Le Haut-Reynaut

Ch Bichon Cassignols

Dom de Cassignols

La Brède

Ch Ricotte

Moras

Dom de Couquereau

Dom de Beaucaillou

Eyquem

Ch La Brède

Ch La Blancherie

Ch Le Chec

Clos du Pape

Dom du Reys

St-Selve

Ch du Grand Bos

la Lisière

Ninon

Ch des Fougères

Ch Lassalle

Pinchot

Esclauzets

Ch Gales

L A   B R È D E

Ch Magneau

Ch Méric

S T - S E L V E

SAUCATS

Joaquim

Lacanau

Ch Haut-Selve

Larnavey

S A U C A T S

le Son

St-Morillon

Lagouargey

Jeansotte

Ch Le Bonnat

Ch Belon

Villa Bel-Air

Ch Plantat

S T - M O R I L L O N

RIVE DROITE

● Libourne

■ Bordeaux

ENTRE-DEUX-
MERS

GRAVES &
SAUTERNES

● Langon

Ch Limagère ■

Dom
Calens ■

D214

Ch Peyreyre ■

La Garonne

Ch Cheret-
Pitres ■

Castres-
Gironde

Beautiran
Nadon

Ch de
Portets ■

Portets

Ch Lagueloup ■

Dom Perin
de Naudine ■
Clos Le
Perichere ■

Darroubin
Dom des Lucques ■

Ch de
Sansaric ■

Ch
Ferrande ■

Ch
Pessan ■

Ch Mirail &
Clos Lamothe ■

Ch Pommarède ■

Ch Le Bourdillot
Vieux Ch Gaubert ■

Ch Millet ■
Ch Jean Gervais ■

Ch Pommarède
de Haut ■

Ch Rahoul ■
Dom La Grave ■
Ch de l'Hospital ■

Ch des
Gravières ■

Ch Pingoy ■

GIRONDE

Ch La Vieille France ■

Ch du
Grand Abord ■
Dom
Haut Corneau ■
le Cournau

Ch Graveyron ■

Ch Guérin-
Jacquet ■

Chaye

Ch
Tour
Bicheau ■

Ch Girafle ■

Ch Cabannieux ■

Ch Crabitey ■

N113

Carros

Ch des Places ■

PORTETS

Ch
Bequin ■

Ch du
Castéra ■

Arbanats

Ch Doms ■

Teychon

Ch
Lagrange ■

D115

Ch Tourteau-
Cholet ■

ARBANATS

Virelade

l'Ailley

Ch La Fleur
Jonquet ■

Dom
de Lugey ■

Nodoy

A62

Ch Virelade ■

Ch Mayne
d'Anice ■

Ch Maure ■
Ch Mayne d'Imbert ■

Podensac

D109

Ch de
Chantegrive ■

Ch de Matives ■

le Moulin

VIRELADE

D117 E1

PODENSAC

Graouères

Ch Larrouquey ■

N113

CÉRONS

D115

D214

ILLATS

St-Michel-
de-Rieufret

D117

ST-MICHEL-
DE-RIEUFRET

N

1:55,500

0   1   2   3km

Ch Ferrande
Map 25/R D2

owner: Castel Frères *area:* 43 ha *cases:* 18,500; W 4,450 *grape % R:* MER 34% CS 33% CF 33% *grape % W:* SEM 65% SAUV B 35% *second wine:* Ch Guillon *other châteaux owned:* Ch d'Arcins *(Haut-Médoc)*; Ch Barreyres *(Haut-Médoc)*; Ch du Bousquet *(Côtes de Bourg)*; Ch de Goëlane *(Bordeaux Supérieur & Entre-Deux-Mers)*; Ch Mirefleurs *(Bordeaux & Bordeaux Supérieur)*; Ch Latour Camblanes *(Premières Côtes de Bordeaux)*; Ch Tour Prignac *(Médoc)*
33640 Castres tel: 05 56 67 05 86
fax: 05 56 67 04 99

Fine, well-maintained château that is a member of the Union des Grands Crus, and has been producing reliable wines for some decades now. The red usually has a sound, generous, elegant and accessible taste, with both oak and fruit (plum, fig). Smooth citrus is often present in the similarly elegant white Graves.

Ch La Fleur Jonquet
Map 25/R H4

owner: J.M. & L. Lataste *area:* 4.5 ha *cases:* 1,550; W 600 *grape % R:* MER 70% CS 30% *grape % W:* SEM 60% SAUV B 35% MUSC 5% *second wine:* J de Jonquet *other wines:* Rosé de Jonquet *(Bordeaux rosé)*
33640 Portets tel: 05 56 17 08 18

Estate of less than 5 ha. The red wine ferments in stainless steel and concrete, the white in new casks. The white displays the vanilla and almond aromas of the oak, and has breeding and a certain finesse. The red has good doses of oak, tannin and lush black fruit.

Clos Floridène
Map 26/L H8

owner: Denis & Florence Dubourdieu *area:* 17.7 ha *cases:* 2,900; W 5,000 *grape % R:* CS 80% MER 20% *grape % W:* SEM 60% SAUV B 35% MUSC 5% *second wine:* Le Second de Floridène *other châteaux owned:* Ch Reynon *(Bordeaux & Premières Côtes de Bordeaux)*
33210 Pujols sur Ciron tel: 05 56 62 96 51
fax: 05 56 62 14 89

'Floridène' was coined from the first names of the owners, Florence and Denis Dubourdieu. This vineyard, which has been undergoing renewal since 1982, is on land very similar to Barsac's; but the white produced here is distinctly dry. It is fermented in wood (one-third new barrels); it has allure in its purity, its

Below: Ch Ferrande

Above: Ch du Grand Bos

stimulating acidity and its delightful fruit, with oak to make up the balance. Fruit – black and red currants – characterizes both bouquet and taste of the elegant, well-balanced red wine.

Ch des Fougères
Map 25/L F5

owner: Henry de Secondat Baron de Montesquieu/Nicole Tari *area:* 8.5 ha; *cases:* 3,000 *grape % W:* SAUV B 50% SEM 50% *other châteaux owned:* Ch Nairac *(Sauternes)*
33650 La Brède tel: 05 56 27 16 16
fax: 05 56 27 26 50

Small but steadily-growing vineyard, where 1991 was the first harvest for the present owner, Nicole Tari (also of Ch Nairac in Barsac). The wine – white only – ferments and matures in casks of which a fifth are replaced annually. In bouquet and taste, elements of oak blend expressively with flowery notes and fresh, exotic and citrus fruits. The origins of the château itself go back to the beginning of the 16th century.

Ch du Gaillat
Map 26/R E6

owner: Famille Coste *area:* 11 ha *cases:* 5,000 *grape % R:* CS 65% MER 30% MAL 5%
33210 Langon tel: 05 56 63 50 77
fax: 05 56 62 20 96

Today this vineyard yields only red wine, where once it was exclusively white. The changeover took place between 1968 and 1972 when the Coste family, Gaillat's owners since the 19th century, replanted with black grapes. The wine usually has a dark aroma – calling to mind prune, bayleaves, coffee and caramel. The succulent, usually fairly quick-developing taste is built on a framework of oak and ripe tannins.

Ch du Grand Abord
Map 25/R E4

owner: Marc & Colette Dugoua *area:* 20 ha *cases:* 8,300; W 2,300 *grape % R:* MER 90% CS 10% *grape % W:* SEM 80% SAUV B 20% *other wines:* Bordeaux blanc
33640 Portets tel: 05 56 67 22 79
fax: 05 56 67 22 23

This estate used to lie along the bank of the Garonne, but today it adjoins the *route nationale* that crosses Portets. Thanks to its 90% of Merlot the red wine has a succulent, meaty taste with considerable substance and a strong undertone of fruit (prune among it), with oak providing an elegant setting for it all.

Grand Abord's white often has a mineral freshness to its taste, with citrus fruit and other subtle nuances.

Ch du Grand Bos
Map 25/L F10

owner: André Vincent *area:* 11 ha *cases:* 4,500; W 450 *grape % R:* CS 45% MER 45% PV 8% CF 2% *grape % W:* SEM 57% SAUV B 29% MUSC 14% *second wine:* Ch Plégat-La Gravière
33640 Castres tel: 05 56 67 39 20
fax: 05 56 67 16 77

After making excellent wine at Ch La Haye in St-Estèphe, André Vincent moved to Castres, closer to Bordeaux. Here he has revived an 18th-century vineyard, partly with new plantings, partly by incorporating plots of old vines. The first harvest was in 1992. The red wine, with its fruit (red and black currants) and a good structure supported by tannin, has roundness and potential for ageing. His white Graves – just one-tenth of the production – has a floral aroma with spice and modest oak. This estate is worth following.

Ch Grand Bourdieu
Map 25/L E9

owner: Dominique Haverlan *area:* 6 ha *cases:* 2,500; W 1,650 *grape % R:* MER 70% CS 30% *grape % W:* SEM 80% SAUV B 20% *other châteaux owned:* include Vieux Château Gaubert *(Graves)*
33640 Portets tel: 05 56 67 52 76
fax: 05 56 67 52 76

Makes red and white wines of mainstream quality – and reasonable price. Exactly the same wines are sold as Ch Civrac-Lagrange, a label mainly intended for the supermarkets. The Cuvée Prestige has more class, being selected from the best red and white Graves. The red is matured for a year in cask, a fifth of them new. The proportion of new barrels rises to half for the white Grand Bourdieu, which is also fermented in oak. Since 1985 this estate has been run by Dominique Haverlan.

Ch de Gravaillas
Map 26/L C8

owner: SC Les Vignobles des Moulins à Vent *area:* 17 ha *cases:* 3,200; W 4,500 *grape % R:* CS 65% MER 35% *grape % W:* SEM 60% SAUV B 35% MUSC 5% *second wine:* Ch des Magens *other wines:* Cérons *other châteaux owned:* Ch de Condrine *(Graves)* *(Cérons)*; Ch Haut-Mayne *(Graves)*
33720 Cérons tel: 05 56 27 08 53
fax: 05 56 27 05 82

Traditional wines, white and red, are made here. Power, an almost rich taste, and the potential to mature typifies the dry white Graves. The sweet version is sold as Cérons. For the 14- to 16-month maturing of the red wine, 25-30% of the barrels are new each year.

Domaine La Grave — Map 25/R E4
owner: Peter Vinding-Diers **area:** 6 ha **cases:** 1,000; W 2,000 **grape % R:** cs 50% mer 50% **grape % W:** sem 100% **second wine:** Domaine La Grave (AC Bordeaux) **other châteaux owned:** Ch de Landiras (Graves); Notre Dame de Landiras (Premières Côtes de Bordeaux)
33640 Portets tel: 05 56 62 44 70
fax: 05 56 62 43 78
Since 1980 this estate, formerly called Ch La Borderie, has been directed by the talented Danish-born grower Peter Vinding-Diers. Both the white and the red wine command attention for their ripe, elegant fruit, unmistakeable finesse, noble oak and flawless balance. They are made and nurtured in the cellars at Ch de Landiras.

Ch Graveyron — Map 25/R E4
owner: GAEC H. Cante & Fils **area:** 10 ha **cases:** 3,000; W 1,400 **grape % R:** mer 70% cs 30% **grape % W:** sem 60% musc 25% sauv b 15% **second wine:** Ch Mondiet **other wines:** AC Bordeaux
33640 Portets tel: 05 56 67 23 69
The estate has belonged to nine generations of the Cante family, who have doubled the size of the vineyard since 1985. The red wines always have a lot of Merlot, and tannin too, making them supple yet with backbone. Only the Cuvée Tradition undergoes oak-ageing (one-third new wood), for 12 months. This adds to the stature of the wine. The standard white tastes fresh, round, and gives discreet impressions of flowers and fruit. Oak characterizes the white Cuvée Tradition.

Ch des Gravières — Map 25/R E4
owner: Bernard Labuzan & Fils **area:** 38 ha **cases:** 18,500; W 1,200 **grape % R:** mer 80% cs 20% **grape % W:** sem 100% **second wine:** Ch du Barrailh **other wines:** Ch la Grave Singalier (AC Bordeaux Supérieur)
33640 Portets tel: 05 56 67 15 70
fax: 05 56 67 07 50

Below: Ch Guérin-Jacquet

Superbly equipped family property with its own laboratory for analysis in the *chai*. The red wine, 80% Merlot, is rounded, dark-toned, reasonably fruity and often quite firm. It is bottled after a year in cask. The white, which makes up less than a tenth of production, is a pure, not too exciting Sémillon.

Ch Guérin-Jacquet — Map 25/R E4
owner: Thierry Boulanger **area:** 9 ha **cases:** 3,000; W 85 **grape % R:** mer 70% cs 20% cf 10% **grape % W:** sauv b 65% sem 35%
33640 Portets tel: 05 56 67 26 47
fax: 05 56 67 30 09
The white wine here is worth discovering. It blends spicy oak, firmness and fruit into a splendid whole. The red tastes supple, but can sometimes rather lack concentration – besides having a curious aroma that does not appeal to everyone.

Domaine du Hauret Lalande — Map 26/L
owner: Jean & Frédéric Lalande **area:** 5.5 ha **cases:** 600; W 2,100 **grape % R:** cs 100% **grape % W:** sem 100% **other wines:** Cérons **other châteaux owned:** Ch Piada (Sauternes)
33720 Illats tel: 05 56 27 16 13
fax: 05 56 27 26 30
Small estate created in 1988, with vines an average of 35 years old. The white Graves from here is fresh, clean and pleasantly fruity. It is fermented partly in barrel, partly in stainless steel. A small amount of Cérons is also produced, and a fairly recent appearance (1995) is a red Graves.

Ch de Haut-Calens — Map 25/L C10
owner: EARL Vignobles Albert Yung **area:** 20 ha **cases:** 9,000 **grape % R:** mer 50% cs 50% **second wine:** Ch Belle-Croix **other wines:** Ch Croix de Calens (Bordeaux Supérieur)
33640 Beautiran tel: 05 56 67 05 25
fax: 05 56 67 24 91
Albert Yung bought this estate in 1980 and replanted it half with Cabernet Sauvignon, half with Merlot. Later a modern *cuverie* was built. The red wine at times lacks some 'bite' and breeding; but it can give pleasure, particularly when young, thanks to its accessible, dark-toned taste with fruit, spice and smoky elements. The history of this château goes back to the early 18th century.

Ch Haut-Lamothe — Map 25/L C10
owner: Lucien Yung **area:** 20 ha **cases:** 10,000 **grape % R:** cs 70% mer 30% **other wines:** Ch de la Limagère (Bordeaux Supérieur)
33640 Beautiran tel: 05 56 67 05 71
fax: 05 56 67 52 62
Fairly simple red wine that is not aged in wood, but spends an average two years in tanks and achieves a correct quality. Of the 20 ha here, 12 produce Ch La Limagère, a Bordeaux Supérieur.

Ch Haut-Mayne — Map 26/L C8
owner: SCA Château Haut-Mayne/Michel Boyer **area:** 12 ha **cases:** 2,500; W 3,600 **grape % R:** cf 50% cs 50% **grape % W:** sem 80% sauv b 20% **second wine:** Ch Caulet **other wines:** Cérons **other châteaux owned:** include Ch de Lucques (Sauternes); Ch du Cros (Loupiac)
33720 Cérons tel: 05 56 62 99 31
Fruit – including blackcurrant, strawberry – is to be found in the red Graves, a pure Cabernet wine of which 35-60% is matured in new casks. This wine displays charm when still young, but

can easily be kept for five to ten years. The fragrant, mellow white has succulent fruit and unmistakeable style.

Ch Haut-Mayne — Map 26/L C8
owner: SC Les Vignobles des Moulins à Vent **area:** 9 ha **cases:** 3,000; W 2,500 **grape % R:** cs 55% mer 45% **grape % W:** sem 60% sauv b 35% musc 5% **other châteaux owned:** Ch de Gravaillas (Graves); Ch de Condrine (Graves)
33720 Cérons tel: 05 56 27 08 53
fax: 05 56 27 05 82
Having two châteaux in Cérons with the name Haut-Mayne is confusing: this one is the smaller in area. Its wines are of a decent quality. Fresh fruit characterizes the white Graves; twice as much of this is produced as of the barrel-aged red.

Ch Haut-Selve — Map 25
owner: Jean-Jacques Lesgourgues **area:** 42 ha **cases:** 15,500; W 11,500 **grape % R:** cs 58% mer 42% **grape % W:** sem 57% sauv b 43% **other châteaux owned:** Ch Cadillac-Branda (Bordeaux Supérieur); Ch de Laubade (Bas-Armagnac)
33650 St-Selve tel: 05 57 58 23 05
fax: 05 57 58 23 09
Estate created out of nothing in the early 1990s. It was all laid out with perfection as the aim – including the design of the château. The first vintage was 1996. This estate is certainly worth watching.

Clos du Hez — Map 26
owner: Philippe & Jacques Guignard **area:** 6.5 ha **cases:** 250; W 1,250 **grape % R:** mer 50% cs 50% **grape % W:** sem 85% musc 10% sauv b 5% **other châteaux owned:** Ch de Roquetaillade La Grange (Graves); Ch Lamothe Guignard (Sauternes); Ch de Rolland (Sauternes)
33210 Pujols-sur-Ciron fax: 05 56 76 69 05
Here the white Graves in particular deserves attention: a rich, lively taste with gentle fruit, and sometimes floral notes as well.

Ch de l'Hospital — Map 25/R D2
owner: Marcel Disch **area:** 10 ha **cases:** 6,000; W 1,300 **grape % R:** mer 63% cs 18% cf 15% mal 2% **grape % W:** sem 65% sauv b 34% musc 3% **second wines:** Ch Thibaut-Ducasse (Bordeaux Supérieur & Bordeaux rosé)
33640 Portets tel: 05 56 67 54 73
fax: 05 56 67 09 93
The origins of this wine estate go back to the early 18th century, when it was the country house of Jacques de l'Hospital, adviser to the king. The present building, set in parkland, is in Louis XVI style; since 1989 it has belonged to the Swiss Marcel Disch, who has been making delightful wines here. The red generally boasts plenty of oak, toast and vanilla as well as fruit; also coffee and caramel. The white wine is a distinguished Graves of considerable complexity: mellow oak, vanilla, floral notes, fine spice and fresh fruit.

◆
Maps of the Graves appellations
The Graves appellation is covered by Maps 25 and 26. The Pessac-Léognan appellation is on Maps 23 and 24. Cérons is on map 26. For a key map showing all the ACs in this zone, see Map 7.

Above: Ch de l'Hospital

Above: Ch de Landiras

Ch Jean Gervais   Map 25/R E4

owner: SCE Counilh & Fils *area:* 54 ha *cases:* 20,000; W 7,500 *grape % R:* MER 60% CS 40% *grape % W:* SEM 85% SAUV B 10% MUSC 5% *second wines:* Ch Puyjalon; Ch Tour de Cluchon *other wines:* Bordeaux Supérieur *other châteaux owned:* Ch Lanette *(Graves, Bordeaux Supérieur & Cérons)* **33640 Portets tel: 05 56 67 18 61 fax: 05 56 67 32 43**
The wine-growing Counilh family have been active in Portets for five generations. At first their wine was sold anonymously in cask, but in 1928 the then owner started to bottle his wine himself. M Counilh chose his son's two christian names, Jean and Gervais, as his trademark. The château, so named later, is near the *route nationale* and produces a nice supple red wine, with dark aromas and reasonable tannin. The white Graves has a somewhat reserved character, and in taste it often provides quite a mellow mouthful.

Ch Lagrange   Map 25/R F6

owner: GFA du Château Lagrange *area:* 14 ha *cases:* 4,000; W 1,500 *grape % R:* MER 70% CS 30% *grape % W:* SEM 50% SAUV B 50% *other wines:* Domaine de Teychon *(AC Bordeaux)* **33640 Arbanats tel: 05 56 67 21 35 fax: 05 56 67 23 91**
The red Graves from this estate is made mostly from Merlot. It matures in *barriques* of which 15% are new for each vintage and 30% one year old. The oak comes through as vanilla elements – while the wine also shows fruit: blackcurrant, blackberry. It is a quite rounded, reliable Graves. The Ch Lagrange white is fairly traditional in character.

Clos Lamothe   Map 25/R D4

owner: J. & L. Rouanet *area:* 10.5 ha *cases:* 5,450; W 500 *grape % R:* MER 100% *grape % W:* SEM 100% *second wine:* Ch Lamothe Chaveau *other wines:* Bordeaux Supérieur, Bordeaux Rosé **33640 Portets tel: 05 56 67 23 12 fax: 05 56 67 23 12**
An estate selling mostly to private buyers, not through the wine trade. It makes a powerful, black-fruited red Graves exclusively from Merlot. The mellow white from here is made solely from Sémillon, and it has a lot of spice in its taste.

Ch Lamouroux/Grand Enclos du Château de Cérons   Map 26/L C9

owner: Olivier Lataste *area:* 26 ha *cases:* 6,500; W 1,000 *grape % R:* MER 50% CS 50% *grape % W:* SEM 70% SAUV B 30% *other wines:* Cuvée de l'Enclos *(Bordeaux rosé)* **33720 Cérons tel: 05 56 27 01 53 fax: 05 56 27 08 86**
The emphasis here is laid very strongly on white wine. In terms of quantity, the dry white Graves comes first: an engaging regular version, and a barrel-aged wine offering more subtleties. Under the name 'Grand Enclos du Château de Cérons' (the Enclos is the walled vineyards of the original Cérons estate) is produced a very good cask-matured Cérons – beautifully sweet and full of fruit. This wine is one of the best of its appellation.

Ch de Landiras   Map 26/L G3

owner: Peter Vinding-Diers *area:* 20 ha *cases:* 2,000; W 7,000 *grape % R:* CS 80% MER 20% *grape % W:* SEM 80% SAUV GRIS 20% *other châteaux owned:* include Notre Dame de Landiras *(Premières Côtes de Bordeaux)*; Domaine La Grave *(Graves)* **33720 Landiras tel: 05 56 62 44 70 fax: 05 56 62 43 78**

Below: Ch Lamouroux/Grand Enclos du Château de Cérons

An estate that dates back to when Bordeaux belonged to the English crown. Until the French Revolution the estate covered 6,000 ha. At present there are 2,000 ha, of which eventually about 40 will yield the red and white Graves. Of the château itself, dating from 1377, only ruins remain – but even these are impressive. Today, part of the orangery is lived in. The stylish white wine often has a taste that verges on sweet, with elements of ripe tropical fruit and spices, as well as some oak. It is fermented in cask. The red Graves displays a good balance between its fruit, dark notes and oak aromas.

Ch Léhoul   Map 26/R F6

owner: GAEC Fonta & Fils *area:* 9 ha *cases:* 3,300; W 700 *grape % R:* CS 45% MER 45% MAL 5% CF 5% *grape % W:* SEM 60% SAUV B 40% *second wine:* Pavillon du Château Léhoul **33210 Langon tel: 05 56 63 17 74 fax: 05 56 63 06 06**
A tenth of production here consists of a sweet Graves Supérieures, a white wine of superb quality that spends 6-12 months in barrel. The dry white, too, has class and character, and gets 6-8 months in cask. Léhoul's main business, though, is in the red, which the Fonta family

assembles from four grape varieties: it is elegantly firm, with ripe, red and black berry fruit, and spends 8-14 months in wood.

Domaine des Lucques   Map 25/R D4
owner: Patrice Haverlan *area:* 11 ha *cases:* 2,200; W 2,500 *grape % R:* MER 60% CS 40% *grape % W:* SEM 80% SAUV B 20% *second wine:* Ch La Rose Coulon *other wines:* AC Bordeaux *other châteaux owned:* Ch de Bourdillot *(Graves)*; Ch Monet *(Sauternes)*
33640 Portets tel: 05 56 67 11 32
fax: 05 56 67 11 32
Decent red wine with reasonable fruit, oak and breadth. In good form in sunny years in particular, as exemplified by the impressive 1986. The white is quite lively, with good fruit and roundness from the Semillon.

Ch Ludeman La Côte   Map 26/R E6
owner: GAEC Chalopin Lambrot *area:* 16 ha *cases:* 5,000; W 3,500 *grape % R:* CS 70% MER 30% *grape % W:* SEM 65% SAUV B 30% MUSC 5% *second wine:* Clos les Majureaux
33210 Langon tel: 05 56 63 07 15
fax: 05 56 63 48 17
With its high Cabernet Sauvignon content the red wine usually calls for a few years of patience, and it generally displays considerable black fruit. The white, too, is usually fruity, with an agreeable liveliness.

Ch Magence   Map 26/R E8
owner: Guillaut de Suduiraut *area:* 37 ha *cases:* 10,000; W 7,500 *grape % R:* CS 43% MER 34% CF 23% *grape % W:* SAUV B 66% SEM 34% *second wines:* Ch Maragnac; Ch Magence-Maragnac; Ch Brannens
33210 St-Pierre-de-Mons tel: 05 56 63 07 05
fax: 05 56 62 21 60
A Roman villa once stood on this site, and later in its history Magence was a barony. The red Graves has some refinement, soft tannins, supple fruit (such as ripe strawberry), and a certain creaminess. It is not matured in cask. The dry white wine has a refreshing character, with fresh fruit – there is a lot of Sauvignon in it. The estate sometimes also makes a surprisingly rich, almost Sauternesque Graves Supérieures: this is sold under the name of Ch Magence-Maragnac.

Ch Magneau   Map 25/L G5
owner: Famille Ardurats *area:* 40 ha *cases:* 7,000; W 12,000 *grape % R:* MER 50% CS 45% CF 5% *grape % W:* SAUV B 45% SEM 40% MUSC 15% *second wines:* Ch Guirauton; Ch Coustaut
33650 Labrède tel: 05 56 20 20 57
fax: 05 56 20 39 95
Five minutes' drive from the famous Ch La Brède are the Ch Magneau cellars and residence, a small complex of white-painted buildings with red-brown shutters and doors. The red wine created here has a mouth-filling but never heavy taste, in which smooth fruit and oak and tobacco notes blend into a satisfying whole. The standard white Magneau needs to be drunk young; its taste is firm, broad and succulent, with lively fruit from the Sauvignon and licorice from the Sémillon. The Cuvée Julien is a more serious, more powerful and longer-living wine, where toasted oak emphatically provides the framework and fruit is quite dominant. This unfiltered white wine spends 10 months in cask: half of the barrels are bought new each year.

Above: Ch Mayne d'Imbert

Ch du Maine   Map 26/R G7
owner: J.-P. Duprat *area:* 12.2 ha *cases:* 4,500 *grape % R:* MER 55% CS 27% CF 10% MAL 8% *second wine:* Ch Du Maine-Barail
33210 Langon tel: 05 56 62 23 40
fax: 05 56 76 20 48
A conscientious estate – it demoted its entire 1984 vintage to second-wine status – where four red grape varieties are grown. Maturing the red wine takes 18-24 months in *barriques*, a quarter of them new. The result: a rather powerful, mouth-filling Graves with aromas that include bay, coffee, caramel and spice, as well as fruits such as blackcurrant.

Ch de Mauves   Map 25/R I8
owner: Bernard Bouche & Fils *area:* 22 ha *cases:* 11,000; W 500 *grape % R:* CS 70% MER 30% *grape % W:* SEM 100%
33720 Podensac tel: 05 56 27 17 05
fax: 05 56 27 24 19
An inconspicuous building around the corner from the Maison des Graves, by the railway line in Podensac. The red wine has the slightly smoky aroma characteristic of Graves and, given its tannin, a potential for ageing. It sees no oak. The white Graves is a pure Sémillon, fermented at low temperature, with discreet spice and fruit.

◆
Quantities

Figures are as supplied by the châteaux.

Area of vineyard: given in hectares, abbreviated to ha. Châteaux are asked to specify vineyards in production, and to exclude from their answers those owned but unplanted.

Production: given in cases of 12 bottles, each of 0.75 litres. A case is thus 9 litres. A hectolitre is 100 litres: just over 11 cases.

Yield per hectare: to obtain this, multiply the 'cases' figure by 9, to give litres, then divide by 100, to give hectolitres. Then divide by the area in hectares.

Ch du Mayne   Map 26/R G7
owner: Jean Perromat *area:* 14 ha *cases:* 5,000; W 5,000 *grape % R:* CS 90% MER 10% *grape % W:* SAUV B 60% SEM 35% MUSC 5% *second wine:* Ch Ferbos *other châteaux owned:* Domaine de Terrefort *(Bordeaux Supérieur)*; Ch Prost *(Sauternes)*; Ch du Vieux Moulin *(Loupiac)*; Ch de Cérons *(Graves & Cérons)*
33720 Cérons tel: 05 56 27 01 13
fax: 05 56 27 22 17
Supple, ripe berry fruit characterizes the red Graves, a wine made with 90% Cabernet Sauvignon. Usually it is only bottled after two to three years; just 10% of the volume goes into oak. The white Graves is typical of its kind: smoothly fresh, rounded, and with a little ripe fruit that includes peach. Since the 1990 vintage it has been briefly aged in cask.

Ch Mayne de Coutureau
owner: F. & G. Bord-Daile *area:* 3 ha *cases:* 900; W 600 *grape % R:* MER 50% CF 25% CS 25% *grape % W:* SEM 70% SAUV B 30% *other wines:* Ch La Prioulette *(Premières Côtes de Bordeaux)*
33490 St-Maixant tel: 05 56 62 01 97
fax: 05 56 76 70 79
Spice, licorice and some oak in the white wine indicate the dominance of Sémillon – 70%, in fact – and barrel fermentation. The red is also quite traditional in character.

Ch Mayne d'Imbert   Map 25/R I8
owner: SCEA Vignobles H. & G. Bouche *area:* 25 ha *cases:* 8,000; W 2,000 *grape % R:* CS 60% MER 30% CF 10% *grape % W:* SEM 85% SAUV B 15% *second wine:* Ch Haut Saint Vincent
33720 Podensac tel: 05 56 27 18 17
fax: 05 56 27 21 16
This belongs to the family who own Ch de Mauves. Nuances of various fruits, black and red, combine with earthy tones and supple tannins to give an excellent red Graves of a fairly traditional kind. In good years it is given 12-18 months' maturing in cask. The white is not an exuberant wine, but is fresh and clean.

Ch Millet   Map 25/R E5
owner: EARL Les Domaines de la Mette *area:* 78 ha *cases:* 29,000; W 7,930 *grape % R:* MER 70% CS 30% *grape % W:* SEM 65% SAUV B 35% *second wine:* Ch du Hautmont; Ch Prieuré les Tours; Ch des Lucques *other wines:* Ch Morton *(Bordeaux Supérieur)* Ch Clos Renon *(Bordeaux Supérieur)* *other châteaux owned:* Ch Lapeyrouse *(Graves)*
33640 Portets tel: 05 56 67 18 18
fax: 05 56 67 53 66
Splendidly preserved and furnished small château dating from 1882 – built by the original owner for his mistress. Today this building and its cellars form the heart of an extensive, successful wine estate (which is to be enlarged to more than 100 ha in the coming years). The red wine usually has a ripe, juicy style with smooth tannins, coffee and spice – no great depth to it, but some toasted oak is present. The white Ch. Millet now has more fruit and distinction than before; the wine spends half a year in wood.

Ch Mongenan   Map 25/R E5
owner: Suzanne Faivre-Mangou *area:* 6.4 ha *cases:* 1,400; W 500 *grape % R:* MER 60% CF 20% MAL 20% *grape % W:* SEM 80% SAUV B 15% MUSC 5% *second wine:* Domaine de Vergnes
33640 Portets tel: 05 56 67 18 11
fax: 05 56 67 23 88

Above: Ch Mongenan

At this charming château, built in Louis XV style, the botanical garden boasts more than a thousand types of roses and other plants, and an eight-roomed museum has been set up. This gives a picture of France during the reign of Louis XVI. Good wine is produced here: an engaging, supple red Graves enhanced by oak, and a smooth white.

Ch Le Pavillon de Boyrein Map 26/R H3
owner: SCEA Vignobles Pierre Bonnet *area:* 25 ha *cases:* 10,000; W 2,000 *grape % R:* MER 70% CS 30% *grape % W:* SEM 65% SAUV B 35% *second wine:* Ch les Lauriers de Boyrein *other châteaux owned:* Ch de Respide *(Graves)*
33210 Roaillan tel: 05 56 63 24 24
fax: 05 56 62 31 59
The vines here grow on a clay and gravel plateau bordering the forests of Les Landes. About 80% of production is red: a well-structured Graves with succulent ripe fruit and sufficient tannins to develop for some years in bottle. It spends 6-12 months in barrels of which one-third are new. In the lively white wine, fresh gooseberry fruit from the Sauvignon is often more dominant than the percentage of this variety might suggest.

Domaine Perin de Naudine Map 25
owner: Jean Cesselin *area:* 5 ha *cases:* 2,000 *grape % R:* MER 50% CS 30% CF 20%
33640 Castres tel: 05 56 67 06 65
Around this charming country home lies a small vineyard yielding agreeable, dark-red wine that can be drunk quite early. In contrast to earlier practice here this is now oak-aged, in *barriques* of which one-fifth are new.

Ch Pessan Map 25/R D4
owner: Mme E. Bitot/Jean Médeville & Fils *area:* 12 ha *cases:* 5,500; W 1,200 *grape % R:* CS 45% MER 40% CF 15% *grape % W:* SAUV B 70% SEM 30% *other châteaux owned:* include Ch Fayau *(Cadillac & Premières Côtes de Bordeaux)*
33640 Portets tel: 05 57 98 08 08
An ancient estate – a watchtower built by Henri IV still stands – worked by Jean Médeville & Fils of Cadillac. They make reasonably full-bodied and powerful red wine, with spice notes, some tobacco and a modest dose of fruit. The white, with a lot of Sauvignon, is of a springtime lightness and is meant for drinking young.

Ch Plantat Map 25/L J5
owner: Christian & Irène Labarrède *area:* 10 ha *cases:* 2,500; W 1,000 *grape % R:* MER 50% CS 45% CF 5% *grape % W:* SEM 50% SAUV B 45% MUSC 5%
33650 St-Morillon tel: 05 56 78 40 77
fax: 05 56 20 34 90
This estate, created in 1861, was bought in 1984 by Christian and Irène Labarrède, who have been energetically renovating it. Both their red and white regularly win awards. Neither is particularly complex, but these are wines of good quality, and characteristic of their appellation. Their fruity white Graves is generally just a little better than the red. Cuvée de la Pucelle is a wood-matured version.

Ch Pont de Brion Map 26/R E7
owner: A. & P. Molinari *area:* 20 ha *cases:* 7,200; W 3,600 *grape % R:* CS 55% MER 45% *grape % W:* SEM 70% SAUV B 30% *second wine:* Ch Ludeman les Cèdres
33210 Langon tel: 05 56 63 09 52
fax: 05 56 63 13 47
In contrast to most other Graves estates, half or even two-thirds of the wine made here is sold under the second label, Ch Ludeman les Cèdres.

Below: Ch de Portets

The *grand vin* therefore very definitely represents the best. White Pont de Brion comes from vines with an average age of 45 years, and is fermented in new barrels. It is a fine, balanced wine with nuances of fresh tropical fruit, mint, nuts, spice and vanilla, with oak discreetly present. The red wine has an agreeable personality. Its smoky oak aroma is due to the 12-18 months in *barriques,* a third of them new. An outstanding medium-sweet Graves Supérieures white is occasionally made.

Ch de Portets Map 25/R D3
owner: Jean-Pierre Théron *area:* 38.2 ha *cases:* 17,300; W 2,100 *grape % R:* MER 50% CS 45% CF 5% *grape % W:* SEM 60% SAUV B 30% MUSC 10% *second wine:* Barons du Château de Portets *other wines:* Ch Tour Baron de Gascq *(Bordeaux Supérieur) other wines:* Ch Port du Roy *(Bordeaux Supérieur) other châteaux owned:* Ch Lafon *(Listrac-Médoc)*
33640 Portets tel: 05 56 67 12 30
fax: 05 56 67 33 47
This château with its large park, its statues, its wrought-iron gates and its balustrade has had a rich history. It stands on the foundations of both a Roman villa and a medieval castle, has been lived in by 15 barons all told, and in 1808 received a visit from Napoléon on his way back from Spain. Here an attractive, reasonably fruity, harmonious wine is made, which is nurtured for a year in barrels of which 30% are new. The standard rises further with the white Graves, with its citrus and tropical fruit: a wine that also has spicy oak as a result of being fermented partly (60%) in new casks.

◆
Finding a château

To locate a château from its name alone, use the index/gazetteer, which will provide a page and a map reference. When the name and appellation are known consult the Directory pages of the relevant chapter. When the commune is known, but not the appellation, consult the index by commune, which lists châteaux in the Atlas under the commune name.

Above: Ch Rahoul

Above: Ch Respide-Médeville

Ch Pouyanne Map 26/L J5

owner: Elie Zausa ***area:*** 50 ha ***cases:*** 15,000; W 8,000 ***grape % R:*** MAL 50% CS 35% CF 15% ***grape % W:*** SEM 100% ***second wines:*** Ch Margès; Ch Bousquet

33720 Budos tel: 05 56 62 51 73

fax: 05 56 62 59 18

Quite generous, supple red that matures mainly in cask and makes pleasant drinking quite early. In the tasting room, with its rustic décor, a white wine made purely from Sémillon is also served; it is not, though, as good as the red.

Ch Rahoul Map 25/R E4

owner: Alain Thiénot ***area:*** 20 ha ***cases:*** 10,000; W 1,700 ***grape % R:*** MER 50% CS 50% ***grape % W:*** SEM 100% ***second wine:*** Ch la Garance ***other châteaux owned:*** include Ch Haut-Gros-Caillou (*St-Emilion*); Ch de Ricaud (*Premières Côtes de Bordeaux*)

33640 Portets tel: 05 56 67 01 12

fax: 05 56 67 02 88

This château, near the road into Portets from the north, takes its name from Guillaume de Rahoul, who built it in 1646. The white wine made here is a distinguished one, and among the best of Graves. Pure Sémillon, it ferments in cask and has a polished taste combining ripe fruit, vanilla, a hint of honey, weight and sufficient acidity. It usually shows its true class only after four to five years. Since 1989 the red has been on form once more: a creamy, juicy, sometimes almost velvety taste with good fruit (cherry, blackberry, blackcurrant), not too much oak, and impeccable balance.

Ch de Respide Map 26/R F7

owner: SCEA Vignobles Pierre Bonnet ***area:*** 35 ha ***cases:*** 12,000; W 6,000 ***grape % R:*** MER 65% CS 35% ***grape % W:*** SEM 65% SAUV B 35% ***second wine:*** Ch Maine Bonnet ***other châteaux owned:*** Ch Pavillon de Boyrein (*Graves*)

33210 Roaillan tel: 05 56 63 24 24

fax: 05 56 62 31 59

An imposing château, once home to one of Louis XIV's ministers, in a parkland setting of ancient trees. Its vineyard is Langon's biggest, and yields twice as much red as white wine. A fairly expansive taste, with a supple roundness and a dark Merlot bouquet, is characteristic of the red Graves. It matures for 12 months in barrel and offers great enjoyment after four to five years. White Respide is balanced, with a pleasant acidity, spice and nuances of fruit – tropical, as well as gooseberry, apple and pear.

Ch Respide-Médeville Map 26/R D4

owner: Christian & Andrée Médeville ***area:*** 13 ha ***cases:*** 3,500; W 2,500 ***grape % R:*** MER 50% CS 50% ***grape % W:*** SAUV B 50% SEM 38% MUSC 12% ***second wine:*** Dame de Respide ***other châteaux owned:*** Ch Les Justices (*Sauternes*); Ch Gilette (*Sauternes*)

33210 Toulenne tel: 05 56 76 28 44

fax: 05 56 76 28 44

This graceful, well-restored 19th-century château is the birthplace of excellent wines. The white usually has little acidity, but easily keeps its vitality for four or five years. In its bouquet and taste there are elements of smoky oak (it ferments in cask), honey, flowers and exotic fruit. The Sauvignon dominates at first, but in due time the Sémillon aroma starts to burgeon. Besides its fruit the red wine offers notes of bay, tobacco and spicy oak. This successful Graves is matured in *barriques* for 12-15 months.

Domaine du Reys Map 25/L F8

owner: Groupe Pouey ***area:*** 8 ha ***cases:*** 3,400; W 1,000 ***grape % R:*** MER 70% CS 30% ***grape % W:*** SEM 65% SAUV B 35%

33650 St-Selve tel: 05 56 78 49 10

fax: 05 56 78 49 11

The present owner took over this estate in 1993, and in the same year constructed modern facilities for fermenting and maturing the wines. Oak and fruit combine distinctively in the red Graves, and the white displays fruity and floral elements as well as a gentle acidity.

Ch de Roquetaillade Map 26/R J4

owner: Vicomte de Baritault du Carpia ***area:*** 15 ha ***cases:*** 800; W 2,500 ***grape % R:*** MER 50% CS 50% ***grape % W:*** SAUV B 50% SEM 50%

33210 Mazères tel: 05 56 76 14 16

fax: 05 56 76 14 61

Roquetaillade, on its hill, forms a unique example of French architecture of the feudal period: it consists of the remains of two adjoining strongholds, the 12th-century Château Vieux and the 14th-century Château Neuf. The family that has owned this monument for the last 600 years now manages a wine estate here as well. The vines are still fairly young, which explains why the wines rather lack depth. The white tastes reasonably vital and fresh; the red – which is not matured in oak – has a supple fruitiness.

Ch de Roquetaillade La Grange Map 26/R J4

owner: P. & S. Guignard ***area:*** 43 ha ***cases:*** 13,000; W 7,000 ***grape % R:*** MER 50% CS 25% CF 20% MAL 5% ***grape % W:*** SEM 70% SAUV B 20% MUSC 10% ***second wines:*** Ch de Roquetaillade le Bernet; Ch de Carolle ***other châteaux owned:*** Ch de Rolland (*Sauternes*); Ch Lamothe Guignard (*Sauternes*); Clos du Hez (*Graves*)

33210 Mazères tel: 05 56 76 14 23

fax: 05 56 62 30 62

This property was separated from the rest of the Ch de Roquetaillade estate in 1962. An attractive, somewhat slender red wine boasts both finesse and creaminess, as well as notes of fruit (blackcurrant, raspberry) and oak. The white is seldom absolutely bone-dry: it is a classic Graves – rounded, with spice, mellow fruit and adequate acidity. Both wines are matured in cask: the red for 15 months, the white for seven. A quarter of the *barriques* are replaced each year.

Ch Saint-Agrèves Map 26/L G5

owner: Marie-Christiane Landry ***area:*** 15 ha ***cases:*** 6,000; W 1,200 ***grape % R:*** MER 34% CF 33% CS 33% ***grape % W:*** SEM 34% SAUV B 33% MUSC 33% ***second wine:*** Ch Victoria

33720 Landiras tel: 05 56 62 50 85

This estate has belonged to the same family since the 18th century; the present generation has been able to enlarge the vineyard. The red wine lingers nicely and has a quite firm, accessible taste with ripe, dark fruit. Oak is there, but does not dominate. Spice and licorice notes give the firm white a fairly striking, rather robust character.

◆

Finding a second wine

To locate a second wine, consult the index which lists all the châteaux mentioned in this Atlas.

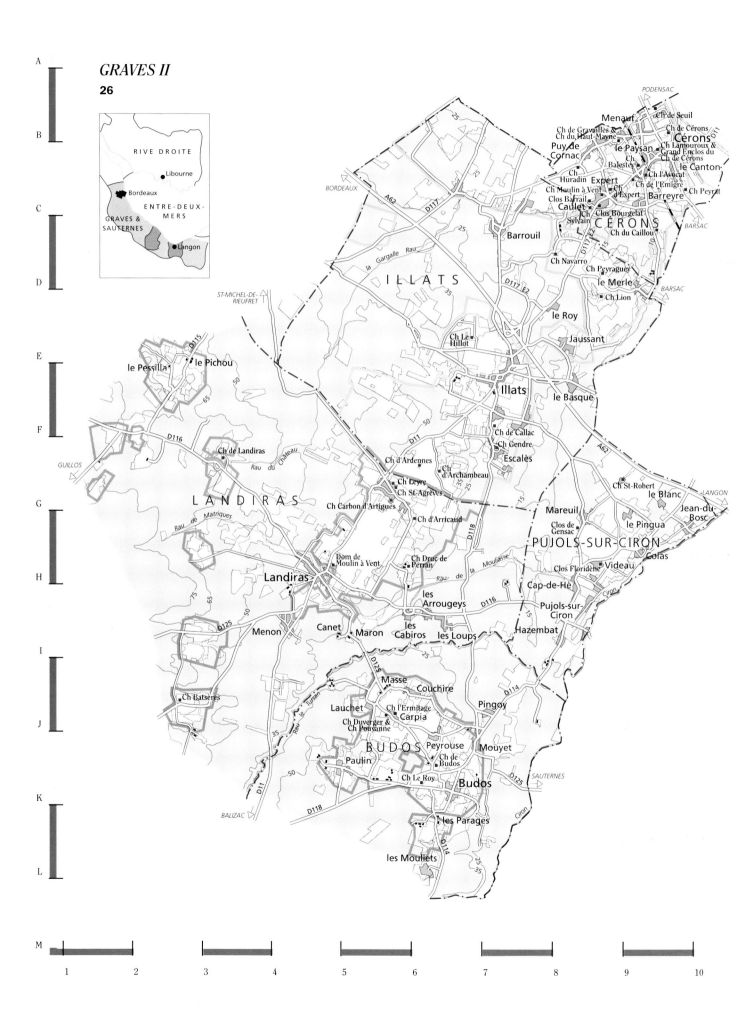

GRAVES II

26

RIVE DROITE

Libourne

Bordeaux

ENTRE-DEUX-
MERS

GRAVES &
SAUTERNES

Langon

PODENSAC

Menaut · Ch de Seuil
Ch de Gravailles & · Ch de Cérons
Ch du Haut-Mayne · Cérons
Puy de · le Paysan · Ch Lamouroux &
Cornac · Grand Enclos du
Ch · Ch de Cérons
Balestey · le Canton
Ch · Ch l'Avocat
Huradin · Expert · Ch d'Emigré
Ch Moulin à Vent · Ch · Ch Peyrat
Clos Barrail · d'Expert · Barreyre
Caulet · Ch · Clos Bourgelat
Ch · CÉRONS
Sylvain · Ch du Caillou
Barrouil · BARSAC

BORDEAUX
A62
D117
25
la Gargalle Rau
Ch Navarro
25
D117 E2
Ch Peyraguey
le Merle · BARSAC
Ch Lion

I L L A T S

ST-MICHEL-DE-
RIEUFRET
25
35
le Roy

D115
Jaussant
le Pessilla · le Pichou
50
Ch Le
65
Hillot
le Basque

GUILLOS
D116
50
Illats
Ch de Callac
D11
Ch Gendre
Escalès
A62
Ch de Landiras
Rau du Château
Ch d'Ardennes
25
Ch St-Robert
L A N D I R A S · Ch · le Blanc
Ch Leyre · d'Archambeau · LANGON
Ch St-Agrèves · Mareuil · Jean-du-
Ch Carbon d'Artigues · 15 · Bosc
Rau de Matriques · Clos de · le Pingua
75 · Gensac · Colas
Ch d'Arricaud · PUJOLS-SUR-CIRON
Clos Floridène · Videau
Dom de · Rau · de · la · Mouliasse · Cap-de-Hè
Moulin à Vent · Ch Druc de · 15 · Ciron
Landiras · Perran · Pujols-sur-
les Arrougeys · Ciron
D116
75 · Hazembat
65 · 50
D125 · les
Menon · Canet · Maron · Cabiros · les Loups
25

D125
Masse · Couchire
Ch Batsères
Lauchet · Ch l'Ermitage · Pingoy
D114
Ch Duverger & · Carpia
Ch Pouyanne
35 · Rau de Tursan · B U D O S · Peyrouse · Mouyet
Ch de
Paulin · Budos
SAUTERNES
50 · Ch Le Roy · Budos
D125
D11 · D118
BALIZAC
les Parages
Ciron
D114
les Mouliets
25
35

M
1   2   3   4   5   6   7   8   9   10

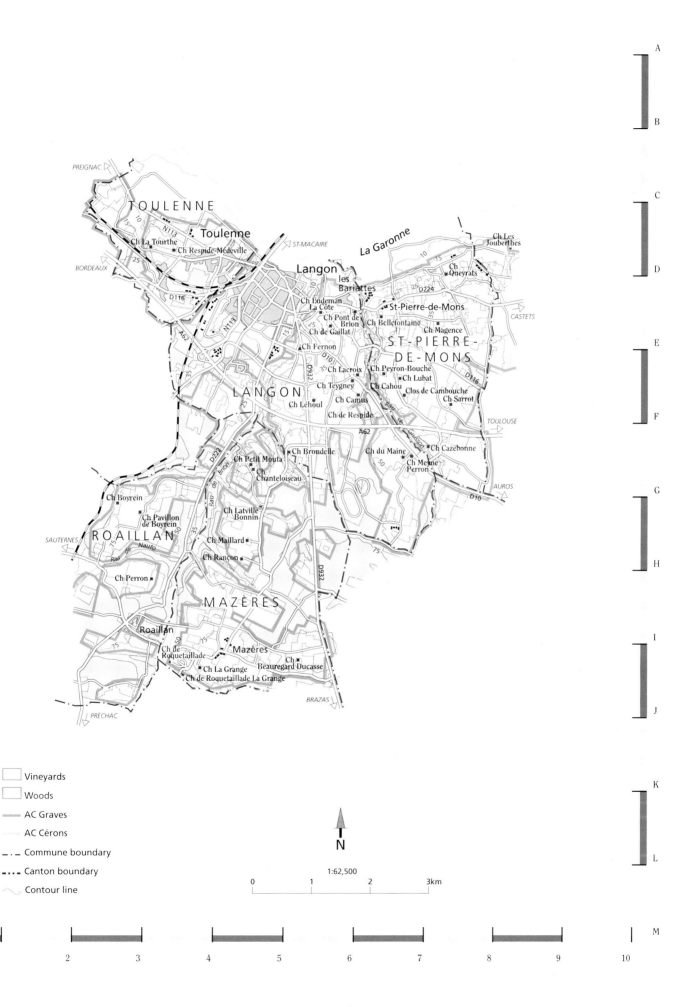

A
B
C
D
E
F
G
H
I
J

PREIGNAC

TOULENNE

Toulenne

N113

Ch La Tourthe

Ch Respide-Médeville

BORDEAUX

D116

ST-MACAIRE

La Garonne

Langon

les Bariattes

Ch Les Jouberthes

Ch Queyrats

D224

St-Pierre-de-Mons

Ch Bellefontaine

Ch Ludeman La Côte

Ch Pont de Brion

Ch de Gaillat

Ch Fernon

Ch Lacroix

Ch Peyron-Bouché

Ch Lubat

Ch Magence

CASTETS

ST-PIERRE-DE-MONS

N113

A62

D932

D10

LANGON

Ch Teygney

Ch Cahou

Ch Camus

Clos de Cambouche

Ch Sarrot

Ch Léhoul

Ch de Respide

A62

TOULOUSE

D116

D222

Ch Petit Mouta

Ch Brondelle

Ch du Maine

Ch Cazebonne

Ch Meyne Perron

Ch Chanteloiseau

AUROS

Ch Boyrein

D10

Ch Pavillon de Boyrein

ROAILLAN

Ch Latville Bonnin

SAUTERNES

Rau de Nauto

Ch Maillard

Ch Rançon

D932

Ch Perron

MAZÈRES

Roaillan

Ch de Roquetaillade

Mazères

Ch La Grange

Ch Beauregard Ducasse

Ch de Roquetaillade La Grange

BRAZAS

PRÉCHAC

Vineyards

Woods

AC Graves

AC Cérons

Commune boundary

Canton boundary

Contour line

N

1:62,500

0   1   2   3km

K
L
M

1   2   3   4   5   6   7   8   9   10

Above: Ch de Roquetaillade

Above: Ch de Roquetaillade La Grange

Ch St-Jean-des-Graves   Map 30 K4
owner: Jean Gérard David *area:* 20 ha *cases:*
4,100; W 2,500 *grape % R:* MER 70% CF 30%
grape % W: SAUV B 50% SEM 50% *other châteaux
owned:* Ch Liot *(Sauternes)*
33210 Pujols-sur-Ciron tel: 05 56 27 15 31
fax: 05 56 27 14 42
Pujols-sur-Ciron, where this estate is situated,
lies between Sauternes and Barsac and has
roughly the same soil. Its owner also has Ch
Liot in Barsac. The red Graves is well made: its
aroma is dark-toned, and the 14 months in cask
give it some spicy, aniseedy oak; berry fruit can
also be tasted. The white has a fairly firm and
almost generous taste, with discreet nuances
and sound balance.

Ch Saint-Robert   Map 26/L G9
owner: Crédit Foncier de France *area:* 33 ha
cases: 10,000; W 5,000 *grape % R:* MER 38%
CS 33% CF 29% *grape % W:* SAUV B 60% SEM 40%
other châteaux owned: Ch Beauregard *(Pomerol)*;
Ch de Barbe Blanche *(Lussac-St-Emilion)*; Ch Bosta-
Lamontagne *(Sauternes)*
33210 Pujols-sur-Ciron tel: 05 56 63 27 66
fax: 05 56 76 87 03

The history of this property goes back at least to
1686, but Saint-Robert only began to flourish as
a wine estate in the 19th century, under the
Poncet-Deville family. Crédit Foncier, which
also runs other Bordeaux châteaux, bought
Saint-Robert in 1879. The ordinary red Graves
is exceptionally reliable, and displays an elegant,
attractive taste with fruit and oak. The stops are
pulled out even further with the Cuvée Poncet-
Deville, a most recommendable wine with
generous amounts of new oak, toast and vanilla,
together with red berry fruits and good body.
The white Cuvée Poncet-Deville is fermented in
new barrels. Noble toasted oak is emphatically
there, and the stylish taste of this wine also
offers lively fruit.

Ch de Sansaric   Map 25/R D2
owner: Dominique Abadie *area:* 7 ha *cases:* 3,400
grape % R: MER 50% CF 25% CS 25%
33640 Portets tel: 05 56 67 03 17
fax: 05 56 67 59 53
This walled estate produces exclusively red
Graves. In the 1630s it was a royal hunting
lodge, belonging to Louis XIII. A classic,
elegantly firm wine, with dark tones to its
bouquet and a long finish, all with an
undertone of mellow, ripe fruit. It is made in
stainless-steel fermentation tanks and aged in
barrels, a quarter of them new.

Ch du Seuil   Map 26/L B9
owner: Trevor Robert Watts *area:* 12.5 ha *cases:*
2,500; W 1,000 *grape % R:* CS 60% MER 40% *grape
% W:* SEM 80% SAUV B 20% *second wine:* Domaine
du Seuil *(AC Bordeaux blanc)* *other wines:* Domaine
du Seuil *(Premières Côtes de Bordeaux)*
33720 Cérons tel: 05 56 27 11 56
fax: 05 56 27 28 79
In 1988 this estate was bought by a Welsh
couple; with great enthusiasm they have carried
out many improvements, and have built an
entirely new *cuvier*. The 19th-century château –
reckoned in 1930 to be the best in Cérons – has
once again acquired great lustre. Cabernet
Sauvignon dominates in the red Graves: an
elegant, balanced wine with an agreeable
fruitiness and well-integrated oak. The white
Graves, fermented in new casks, is a harmonious
mix of smoky oak, spice, citrus and honey.

Ch Tour Bicheau   Map 25/R E4
owner: Hugues Daubas *area:* 20 ha *cases:* 10,000;
W 2,000 *grape % R:* MER 50% CS 40% CF *grape %
W:* SAUV B 60% SEM 40%
33640 Portets tel: 05 56 67 37 75
fax: 05 56 67 37 75
A soundly-made red wine, fermented in
stainless steel and matured in large oaken
casks. It is usually somewhat slender, with
modest measures of spices and ripe black fruit.
The white is mainly Sauvignon and tastes fresh,
with spicy fruit. The château can be recognized
by a small square tower at one of its corners.

Ch Tour de Calens   Map 25/L D9
owner: Bernard Doublet *area:* 6 ha *cases:* 1,500;
W 400 *grape % R:* CS 63% MER 28% CF 9% *grape %
W:* SEM 72% SAUV B 28% *other wines:* Ch Vignol
(AC Bordeaux & Entre-Deux-Mers)
33640 Beautiran tel: 05 57 24 12 93
fax: 05 57 24 12 83
In good years the red Graves has the potential
to mature, while in lesser vintages it tastes more
supple. Berry fruit is always present, and Merlot
complements this with darker notes. A third of
the casks in which the wine spends a year are
new. A Graves full of flavour: expressive, with a
smooth freshness and a certain refinement.

◆
Grape varieties: synonyms and oddities
Local variants and synonyms have traditionally
been, and sometimes still are, used for some
Bordeaux grapes. Some synonyms are given
official status in the appellation decrees.
Synonyms include: **Bouchet** St-Emilion name
for Cabernet Franc, **Côt or Cot** Synonym for
Malbec, **Pressac** St-Emilion name for Malbec.

There are also some minor varieties which
figure in the appellation decrees but are
obscure or seldom grown.
Carmenère Red grape considered the equal of
Cabernet Sauvignon in the Médoc in the early
19th century. Susceptible to disease,
therefore now very rare; though still legal in all
Médoc ACs and in the Premières Côtes.
Merlot Blanc May be a mutation of Merlot,
or a separate variety. Little is grown.

Ondenc A virtually vanished white grape, still
permitted for the Bordeaux AC.
Mauzac White variety still important further
east; all but gone from Bordeaux, but still a
legal *cépage accessoire* in Entre-Deux-Mers.
Sauvignon Gris White variety described by
some growers as an old clone, now
reintroduced. Grown in the eastern Entre-Deux-
Mers. Fresh, aromatically fruity wine.

Some varieties are quite common, but are
less discussed than the 'major' ones.
Chief among these is:
Ugni Blanc Permitted for white AC Bordeaux,
in Entre-Deux-Mers and Crémant de Bordeaux
as a *cépage accessoire* up to a maximum of
30%. Widely planted, especially in the north,
adjoining Cognac, where it dominates.

Ch Le Tuquet
Map 25/L D9

owner: Paul Ragon *area:* 52 ha *cases:* 15,000; W 6,500 *grape % R:* CS 50% MER 45% MAL 5% *grape % W:* SEM 80% SAUV B 20% *second wines:* Ch de Bellefont; Ch Rocher du Tuquet; Ch Couloumey-le Tuquet

33640 Beautiran tel: 05 56 20 21 23
fax: 05 56 20 21 83

This château by the *route nationale* was built around 1730, and renovated in 1765 under the auspices of Victor Louis, that famous architect of the Grand Théâtre in Bordeaux. Serious, slightly spicy red wine of reasonable strength, modest fruit, and sometimes a touch of bitterness. There is a version bottled by the firm of Armand Moueix, which has a little more depth, richness and fruit. The appetizing white Graves is usually of simple good quality, marked by succulent licorice and spices (Sémillon is the predominant grape here), as well as by a touch of honey. Oaky elements characterize the Cuvée Spéciale.

Ch La Vieille France
Map 25/R E3

owner: Michel Dugoua *area:* 24 ha *cases:* 10,500; W 2,500 *grape % R:* MER 80% CS 20% *grape % W:* SEM 75% SAUV B 25% *second wine:* Ch Cadet La Vieille France

33640 Portets tel: 05 56 67 19 11
fax: 05 56 67 17 54

The top of the range here is the Cuvée Marie, fermented in new casks. After six months in wood this white Graves offers an elegantly firm, nuanced, lively taste, with citrus fruit and a flattering aroma of oak, toast and vanilla. The standard version also has its merits, but is rather more neutral. Features of the red Graves, made from 80% Merlot, are a supple, sometimes almost fat taste, with elements of spicy, smoky oak after a year in cask (a third of the barrels are new), and aspects of leather and of bayleaf. The origins of the estate go back to the 18th century.

Vieux Château Gaubert
Map 25/R E4

owner: Dominique Haverlan *area:* 16 ha *cases:* 6,000; W 2,000 *grape % R:* CS 50% MER 45% CF 5% *grape % W:* SEM 60% SAUV B 30% MUSC 10% *other châteaux owned:* include Ch Grand Bourdieu (Graves)

33640 Portets tel: 05 56 67 52 76
fax: 05 56 67 52 76

Below: Ch du Seuil

Above: Ch Le Tuquet

This château is what remains of a once-beautiful building, designed in 1796 around a country house from earlier that century. Today it is an historic monument. Dominique Haverlan bought the property in 1988, and the wines made here are delicious: the red generally has a very sound, fleshy, black-fruited taste, with mature tannins and creamy oak (it spends 18 months in cask). The white wine, fermented in barrel, has a whole complex of nuances, vibrant with fruit and toast.

Villa Bel Air
Map 25/L I8

owner: Jean-Michel Cazes *area:* 46 ha *cases:* 12,000; W 10,000 *grape % R:* CS 50% MER 40% CF 10% *grape % W:* SAUV B 42% SEM 42% MUSC 16% *other châteaux owned:* Ch Lynch-Bages *(Pauillac);* Ch Cordeillan-Bages *(Pauillac);* Ch les Ormes de Pez *(St-Estèphe);*

33650 St-Morillon tel: 05 56 20 29 35
fax: 05 56 78 44 80

The team from Lynch-Bages and the other Cazes properties also makes the wine here. The red is full-bodied and juicy in the mouth, with oak, fruit, and a touch of spice and minerals. Since the 1993 vintage the white has shown refinement, noble oak with a little vanilla, reasonable body, fruit rather suggesting pear, and also spice. The building itself is a fine example of a classic *'chartreuse'* country villa, a low dwelling with pediment and sculptures.

Ch Virelade
Map 25/R H7

owner: G. de Bengy de Puyvallée *area:* 28.2 ha *grape % R:* CS 60% MER 25% CF 10% MAL 5%

33720 Virelade tel: 05 56 27 18 38

Traditional winemaking rules at this publicity-shy estate: the red is thus given almost three years in cask (a third are new barrels). Once bottled, the rare, deep-coloured wine has an almost velvety taste and an aroma that is characterized by spicy oak. The château, which boasts a 9th-century tower, is set in a large walled park where small deer roam freely. The *chai* is elsewhere in the commune.

SAUTERNES

MICHAEL BROADBENT

Sauternes is the name of a commune, a village, a wine and also a district – the most renowned district for the making of sweet wine in the world. It embraces a concentration of châteaux large and small – some ancient and very grand, others modest farms – all devoted to making white wines which manage (at their best and weather permitting) to combine extraordinary richness and finesse. The name Sauternes is, quite simply, synonymous with sweet wine.

SAUTERNES, ITS COMMUNES AND ITS WHEREABOUTS

The little hamlet of Sauternes is situated forty kilometres south-east of the city of Bordeaux. Five communes or parishes are entitled to the Sauternes appellation. In addition to Sauternes itself, its neighbours are Bommes, Fargues, Preignac and Barsac – the latter a fairly big commune, somewhat 'semi-detached' and proud of its own name and distinctive style of wine. Indeed, it has its own appellation – but can also use that of Sauternes.

Leaving aside the slightly lower-lying Barsac on the northern flank, the actual Sauternes district is relatively small and compact, consisting of an area of low hills dotted with a dozen or so little, and surprisingly rural, villages interspersed with châteaux. These include de Fargues' impressively ruined castle, owned by the Lur Saluces family; substantial 18th-century farmhouses such as Suduiraut; the beautiful and historic de Malle; the stately, classic Filhot. Crowning them all stands the turreted, medieval Château d'Yquem itself, occupying a commanding view of its own vineyard slopes and the far banks of the river Garonne which, indirectly, has such an influence on the wine.

In area, Sauternes is not dissimilar to Pomerol, but in looks it is a total contrast. It is now a relatively speedy drive from the city of Bordeaux on the *autoroute* heading towards Toulouse, but when I pull off the road at Langon or the previous exit, I always have the feeling that I have entered another world. Though not all that far south of the city, Sauternes has an indefinably rustic air.

A glance at the map reminds one that the southern part of the Graves district encloses Sauternes on three sides like a snare; the fourth side, to the east of the old main road, is the Garonne, flowing graciously northwards to join the Dordogne a little way downstream from the *quais* of Bordeaux to swell into its tidal estuary, the Gironde. Isolated in the south, peaceful Sauternes seems light years away.

THE WINE: WHAT MAKES SAUTERNES SPECIAL?

Why, might one ask, is this area of France so peculiarly suited to making sweet white wine, and how does it occur? The basic combination of climate, soil, grape variety and winemaking applies to all wines in all regions. The peculiarity of Sauternes is the microclimate and the proximity of the river Garonne.

There are several ways of making sweet wine – apart from simply adding sugar. One is to put grape brandy or a neutral spirit into the fermenting must or grape juice. The result is to inhibit the action of the yeasts, thus stopping the fermentation: this leaves a proportion of unfermented natural grape sugar in the wine. This method is used elsewhere in France – for example in parts of the Midi to make *vin doux naturel*; it is also the method used in the making of port wine. There are other ways of inhibiting the fermentation, but the most natural is to leave the grapes on the vine to maximize their ripeness and concentrate their sugary juices, allowing the fermentation to grind to a halt due to excess sugar, without any manipulation or additives.

The Sauternes landscape is rural and remote: the hilly contours offer more pronounced vineyard slopes than elsewhere in the Graves region.

The first essential is a suitable climate. Warm summers, early autumn sun and heat to ripen the grapes – the longer and least interrupted the ripening process, the higher the level of sugar. In a good year, after early and successful flowering, with the benefit of summer heat and a warm sunny autumn, the grapes in Sauternes can achieve a maximum sugar content. These carefully selected and fully ripened grapes are then ready to start their fermentation.

However, once the alcoholic content rises above that of normal 'table' wine to around 14 per cent, the yeasts can no longer cope, which leaves some of the grape juice unfermented. The resulting wine is sweet – naturally sweet.

But there is one more natural 'active ingredient', and this is where the local microclimate and the River Garonne and its tributary, the Ciron, play a crucial role. Under ideal conditions the mid- to late-autumn sun-ripened grapes attract fungal spores induced by the early morning mists which arise where the rivers meet. Known, appropriately, as *pourriture noble* ('noble rot'), the *botrytis cinerea* fungus settles on the skins, its intrusive tentacles reducing the water content of the grape. This has the effect of concentrating the flesh and the natural grape-sugar content, enriching the remaining juice. These shrivelled, overripe and botrytis-affected grapes are fermented – the fermentation is sluggish and lengthy – and this results not only in wine of great sweetness and intensity, but with a flavour of exceptional beauty, subtlety and extra nuances.

Sadly, the ideal set of conditions – hot summer, warm ripening autumn and botrytis – does not occur every year. Sometimes, as in 1970, the heat and the ripening result in very sweet grapes but the mists are not there to produce botrytis. In other years (1993 for example), the summer was so poor, the autumn so wet that the grapes were insufficiently ripe and the resulting rot was anything but 'noble'.

The shape of the land makes a difference too. From the position of Château d'Yquem on the map one can imagine the long, even, well-drained and sun-catching slopes of vines, and the relative proximity of the river. This, and the immense care taken, accounts for the supreme quality of Yquem.

Trees border a Sauternes vineyard: this is a gentle countryside, in contrast to the more austere Médoc

THE GRAPES AND THE TASTE OF SAUTERNES

So the business of the vineyard proprietor in Sauternes is in the lap of the gods climatically; and over and above the climate, the extra care harvesting and the relatively tiny amount of juice left in these overripe, shrunken grapes results in a small-volume, high-cost wine.

What grapes are used in Sauternes and what are their characteristics? The two principal (indeed basic) varieties are Sémillon and Sauvignon Blanc – both white of course. Proportions vary either side of 75:25. A third grape, used either sparingly or not at all, is the Muscadelle.

The golden-hued Sémillon, a dependable workhorse of a grape, is neither early-ripening nor aromatic; happily, however, it is not particularly susceptible to rot yet manages to succumb to *botrytis cinerea* with ease. Sémillon is the understated yet major component of Sauternes; it provides the wine with a sort of serious solidity, good for ageing.

Sauvignon Blanc is a variety that needs no introduction. Alone, this grape provides the lovely acidic fragrant zest of Sancerre and Pouilly-Fumé in the Loire and, increasingly ubiquitous, is responsible for the somewhat exaggerated, scented, Sauvignons of New Zealand and elsewhere. But as the somewhat unlikely bedfellow of Sémillon, its character adds to Sauternes that vital fragrance and vivacity without which the relatively dour Sémillon would pall. A mere two to five per cent of Muscadelle can give a Sauternes an additional grapy floweriness – reminding one of the Muscat variety but apparently unrelated.

Interestingly, the individual smell, flavour and basic characteristics of the three grape varieties can be detected by an experienced taster when a Sauternes is young: the waxy solidity and texture of the Sémillon, the mouthwatering, gooseberry-like acidity of the Sauvignon Blanc, and the light grapiness of Muscadelle. However, as the wine matures in bottle, the component parts harmonise and – as in the case of all really fine mature wines – the individual varietal smells and tastes should not be apparent.

The growing season in Sauternes follows the same pattern as elsewhere: the budding period, the risk of spring frosts, the importance of the flowering, of a judicious mixture of sun, warmth and beneficial light rain through the summer, and a benign, warm early autumn. It is the final ripening period of the Sémillon and Sauvignon Blanc that is crucial in Sauternes.

With or without the much-desired *botrytis cinerea*, the grapes can rarely be picked in one *tri*. On the contrary, in certain years the team of experienced pickers will be sent out day after day to comb the vineyard, selecting only the most perfectly ripe bunches – sometimes just individual berries. This is an extremely painstaking and costly business. No wonder the finest Sauternes of a good vintage is expensive.

THE IMPORTANCE OF VINTAGES AND THE AGEING CAPACITY OF SAUTERNES

To own a château and its vineyard in Sauternes needs a great deal of money, the long-term outlook of a patient farmer and extremely calm nerves. It really is a risky business, ever dependent on unpredictable weather conditions and a fickle market-place.

It seems that weather patterns and the market move in cycles. Is it a coincidence that, not infrequently, both go together? For example, the good weather and prosperity of the 1920s, the atrocious winter and the slump of the early 1930s. Nearer to our time, the relatively stable and healthy wine market and good vintages of the 1980s, and the rain (for *vignerons*) and relative recession of 1991, 1992 and 1993. Perhaps this is stretching things too far.

The situation with the great sweet wines of the Rhine and Mosel, those famous Trockenbeerenauslesen made from individually-picked overripe grapes affected with *botrytis cinerea*, known in Germany as *edelfäule*, is different. The owner of a great estate in the Rheingau will pick his grapes in stages, depending on the weather. All being well his early-picked grapes will make a pleasantly refreshing wine, relatively inexpensive, for early drinking. Those that are riper, with a higher sugar-content, he will classify as Spätlese; the next stage is Auslese and – weather continuing to permit – he will leave on the vine some grapes to ripen even further. These individually picked grapes are classified as Beerenauslese and have a high degree of natural sugar. Finally, and only in certain years, conditions will be ripe for the formation of botrytis-affected *edelfäule*, and a few bottles of 'TBA' will be produced – the 'trocken' in Trockenbeerenauslesen means 'dried' or shrivelled –

sheer nectar, and sold at a commensurately high price. In short, the commercial side of the German vineyard is quite differently organized. And the owner can choose, weather permitting, what level of wine(s) to make.

In Sauternes the château proprietor has no option. It is all or nothing; 'Sauternes' or nothing. There is no such thing as a dry Sauternes. For though certain proprietors in the Sauternes district can and do make a dry wine – at Yquem it is called 'Y' (pronounced ee-grec in French); others, like Rieussec ('R') and Guiraud ('G') also use their initials, while some just add 'sec' to the name of the château – none of their dry wines are entitled to the appellation 'Sauternes'.

Around him, in the vineyards of the Graves, or in those across the river in the Entre-Deux-Mers, the early-picked Sémillon and Sauvignon Blanc will provide his neighbouring château owners with a fairly dependable supply of dry white wine.

Unlike most white wine, which is made to be drunk young and fresh, Sauternes is not only capable of keeping in bottle but distinctly benefits from bottle-age. Ten to fifteen years could be considered average, but the really convincing answer to the question of the ideal age lies in the individual performance of individual wines, the track-record of châteaux. In this respect Château d'Yquem holds pride of place. All the good post-war vintages are – if they have been kept well – still marvellous to drink; those made in the inter-war years can still be excellent, and bottles of pre-World War I and 19th-century vintages of Yquem have also survived. At a remarkable great wine dinner in Oslo my host served 1893 Yquem with *pâté de foie gras*. The wine had a bouquet like nectar, honeyed. It was a lovely amber-gold colour; still sweet, with glorious flavour and excellent acidity. The dinner ended with an immaculate bottle of the famous Yquem 1921: pure gold, the scent of almond and orange blossom, a flavour of *crème brûlée*. How can mere words describe perfection?

BRIEF HISTORY OF SAUTERNES

I have left the history until towards the end. Illogical, but to start with a string of dates and facts is a bit deadening. In any case no one really knows exactly when the dry white wine of Sauternes became the sweet white as we know it today.

The history of Yquem is, in effect, the history of Sauternes. Yquem was certainly famed as a wine by the mid- to late-seventeenth century and well established in the eighteenth century. Thomas Jefferson, while American envoy (ambassador) in Paris, exchanged correspondence with 'Mr Diquem' (*sic*), ordering a quantity for his own use. In May 1787 Jefferson visited Bordeaux, making precise notes of all the top wines, listing meticulously the First Growths, ordering on the spot and insisting on bottling at the château – because, as he said, he did not trust wine merchants. And, coincidentally, the other end of Jefferson's transaction is also well documented: in the archives of Yquem are copies of the original invoices referring to his purchases. The wine at that time was almost certainly rich, if not sweet. Long time the property of the Sauvage family, Yquem came to the Lur Saluces in 1785 through marriage. It has been in the hands of the family ever since, and only late in 1996 did the first rumours trickle out of a possible sale to LVMH.

It is quite probable that the beneficial effects of botrytis were fortuitous. Leaving aside the ages of antiquity – for we know little about the actual taste of Greek and Roman wines – Hungary can fairly claim to have understood and used over-ripe, botrytized grapes as far back as the mid-seventeenth century. At Schloss Johannisberg on the Rhine they can be very precise: in the autumn of 1775, according to their records, the messenger bringing instructions to start picking was delayed. The over-ripe grapes developed an unwelcome rot which, when fermented, produced a wine of singular richness. However at Yquem the precise date is not known. What is recorded is that the Grand Duke of Constantine, the brother of the Czar of Russia and a man inordinately fond of sweet wines, was so impressed with the 1847 that he purchased a cask for 20,000 Francs, an astonishing price at that time.

VINTAGES

When it comes to the older vintages, the state of development and drinkability will depend on the provenance: specifically the cellar conditions in which the bottles have been kept, the state of the cork and the level of the wine in the bottle. Having said this, Sauternes corks tend to be the least troublesome of all, retaining their moisture and flexibility better than most; the natural richness, almost oiliness, of the wine acting as a sort of air-deterring lubricant.

Venerable classic Sauternes vintages: 1811, 1825, 1847 (reputed to be the greatest of all), *1864, 1865, 1869, 1875, 1878, 1893, 1896, 1899, 1900, 1904, 1906, 1909.*

The inter-war years: 1921, arguably the greatest white wine vintage so far this century; *1926, 1928, 1929, 1934; 1937* (outstanding).

The 1940s to 1970s: 1943, 1945, 1947, 1949, 1953, 1955, 1959, 1961 (not as great as the reds), *1962* (better than *1961*), *1967, 1971, 1975, 1976.*

The 1980s to date: 1983 and *1986; 1988, 1989* and *1990.* Regarding the last three, it is very rare to have two really top-class Sauternes vintages in a row; to have three, one after the other, is historically unprecedented. Unhappily the early part of the 1990s has not been successful, due entirely to poor weather conditions, excessive rain and rot: 1991 not good, 1992 poor (Yquem declassified its wine). 1993 was atrocious. Thankfully the 1994s are quite good and 1995 has promise.

The perfect Sauternes vintages for drinking now are 1976, 1975, 1971, 1967 and those of the 1950s listed above The top châteaux of the great post-war trio of 1945, 1947 and 1949 are still beautiful; the 1937, 1929, 1928 and 1921 can be sublime. Bottles older than that can be a revelation – and somewhat of a risk.

An important note about colour. Some Sauternes are as pale as any dry white wine when young: yellow-tinged, perhaps with a touch of youthful lime green; but most Sauternes of good, rich yet immature vintages tend to be yellow with a touch of gold. Unlike red wines, which lose colour and become paler with age, Sauternes do the opposite: they deepen – first more golden, then amber. When extremely old they can be quite a dark amber brown. At the same time the fruity aromas of a good young Sauternes develop and change with bottle-age, becoming richer, more harmonious, more complex, with strong overtones of honey. On the palate there is a tendency to dry out, though many old wines retain some of their pristine sweetness to a remarkable degree.

Acidity – the essential natural tartaric acid element of all wine – performs an important dual function in relation to Sauternes. It acts as a preservative and also provides a foil for the wine's natural sugar content. Without adequate counterbalancing acidity, the sweetness of Sauternes would pall.

WHEN AND WITH WHAT TO DRINK SAUTERNES

Sauternes is sweet. It is therefore often categorized under the heading 'dessert wine'; worse still referred to, colloquially, as a 'pudding wine' – even, more vulgarly, as a 'sticky'. Not surprisingly, it is served more frequently than not with a dessert or sweet pudding. Nothing can be more disastrous. The effect of most sweet desserts, unless something like the mildest of apple flans, is to make the Sauternes taste dry. I am afraid that even in the best circles, among otherwise knowledgeable wine enthusiasts and at some of the greatest of French restaurants, a really fine Sauternes is served alongside an inappropriately sweet dish. It happens so often that I despair. When faced with the inevitable I at least try to persuade my fellow guests to taste the Sauternes before having a mouthful of the pudding. And then to taste it again afterwards. They are like two different wines.

I ask you: what is the point of the proprietor of a top château in Sauternes, with great labour, at great cost and risk, making an inimitably superb sweet wine if the consumer after one mouthful destroys its richness and flavour, turning it into something rather duller and distinctly dry?

So when, and with what, do you drink your lovely Sauternes? The classic accompaniment is at the start of a meal with *foie gras*, the richness and sweetness of the wine matching the richness and fat of the *foie gras*. The problem here, however, is that the combination is doubly rich and tends to blunt the appetite for the courses to follow. The other place for Sauternes is at the end of the meal – not with the dessert, but with cheese. Most mild cheeses go well with sweet wines, but strong creamy cheeses like a ripe brie or camembert can, in my opinion, spoil its taste. The traditional cheese to accompany Yquem is Roquefort, but beware: an equivalent blue cheese – Stilton in particular – can be too pungent and salty and will overpower the wine.

The French drink the lighter Barsacs, even a rich Sauternes, as an apéritif. Another alternative is to drink it with a ripe nectarine. Better still, with no other accompaniment than an appreciative friend.

PERSONAL FAVOURITES

All the major châteaux are described below by Hubrecht Duijker so I will be selective – which of course is always unfair to those I omit.

Unquestionably the greatest of all Sauternes is Yquem. Following this, and in my opinion highly dependable, is Climens: the 1971, 1937 and 1929 all as fine as it is possible to be. In certain vintages, Suduiraut is outstanding: for example the 1976, better still the 1975; the 1967 being almost on a par with Yquem.

Rieussec can also be excellent but has had a rather chequered career. The wines made in the mid-1970s – 1975 and 1976 in particular – have an almost alarmingly deep golden colour, but are rich and lovely. The 1983 is excellent.

The trouble about a personal rating of châteaux is that they have not necessarily performed well or made the same style of wine in even comparable vintages. Rayne-Vigneau was superb prior to World War I and has been making lovely wine recently. Lafaurie-Peyraguey went through a period of making pale, greenish, light in style, rather 'grassy' wines. Coutet has had its ups and downs. Filhot often disappoints, but it is, despite the grandeur of the château, only a Second Growth. To be more detailed requires a reprint of The Great Vintage Wine Book II: I recommend it for detailed tasting notes!

Sémillon grapes attacked by noble rot
in a Sauternes vineyard

THE APPELLATIONS

SAUTERNES and BARSAC (sweet white)

Location: *South-east of Bordeaux, 40 km from the city centre to the heart of the district, its eastern flank borders the N113, beyond which are Bordeaux AC vineyards and the left bank of the river Garonne*
Area of ACs: *Sauternes c. 2,082 ha; Barsac c. 863 ha*
Area under vine: *Sauternes 1,600 ha, Barsac 400 ha*
Communes: *Sauternes, Bommes, Fargues, Preignac and Barsac. Barsac is entitled to, and uses, its own appellation as well as AC Sauternes.*
Average annual production: *Sauternes 310,000 cases, Barsac 140,500*

Classed growths: *26 (1 premier cru supérieur – Ch d'Yquem, uniquely classified in 1855 – 11 premiers crus, 14 deuxièmes crus*
Others: *Over 200, including a number of unofficial crus bourgeois*
Cooperatives: *None*
Main grape varieties: *Sémillon, Sauvignon Blanc*
Others: *Muscadelle as a minor blending variety*
Main soil types: *Gravel over limestone, the limestone most notably in Barsac; also clay and sand*

176

APPELLATIONS SAUTERNES & BARSAC

Ch d'Arche
map 27/R K3
2ème cru; AC Sauternes
owner: Pierre Perromat **area:** 29 ha **cases:** 3,000
grape % W: SEM 70% SAUV 29% MUSC 1% **second wine:** Cru de Braneyre
33210 Sauternes tel: 05 56 76 66 55
The château stands resplendent on a hill above the village of Sauternes, and is one of the district's oldest wine estates – the main building dates from 1530. The property takes its name from the Comte d'Arche, who owned it in the 18th century. A period of disappointing quality ended in 1980, when Pierre Perromat leased the estate and began to apply stricter standards. Today the wine is in the ranks of *deuxièmes crus*, through its power, ample fruit, considerable body, and an initially dominant dose of oak.

Ch Cru d'Arche Pugneau
map 27/L H10
AC Sauternes
owner: Jean-Pierre & Jean Francis Daney
area: 11 ha **cases:** 1,000 **grape % W:** SEM 70% SAUV B 25% MUSC 5%
33210 Preignac tel: 05 56 63 24 84
fax: 05 56 63 39 69
This dynamically-run estate, dating from the 19th century, has been owned by the Daney family since 1923. After fermenting in oak the wine matures in barrel for at least 20 months; sometimes up to 36 months. In good years the taste is elegant with a subtle aroma – jammy fruit, spicy oak, a hint of coffee – and a good balance between sweetness and acidity.

Ch d'Argilas le Pape
map 27/L H8
AC Sauternes
owner: Yvon Breignaud **area:** 3.5 ha **cases:** 800
grape % W: SEM 80% SAUV B 10% MUSC 10%
33210 Preignac tel: 05 56 63 50 08
fax: 05 56 63 50 08
A Sauternes of very acceptable quality, oak-aged for a year in barrels of which one-tenth are new. The estate was created in the mid-1970s and sells the its entire production directly to private buyers.

Ch d'Armajan des Ormes
map 27/L E4
AC Sauternes
owner: Michel Perromat **area:** 13.5 ha **cases:** 2,000 **grape % W:** SEM 70% SAUV B 25% MUSC 5%
second wine: Ch des Ormes **other châteaux owned:** Ch Beauregard Ducasse (*Graves*); Domaine de Cabirol (*Bordeaux*)
33210 Preignac tel: 05 56 63 22 17
fax: 05 56 63 21 55
The wine from this fine and stately château is not exceptionally rich or complex, but generally has enough fruit and substance to give pleasure, with a touch of aniseedy oak. Matured for 12 months in cask (30% new wood). In exceptional years a Crème de Tête is also produced here; it goes into new *barriques* for its ageing.

Domaine de Barjuneau Chauvin
map 28/R M5
AC Sauternes
owner: Philippe Fouquet **area:** 11 ha **cases:** 2,700
grape % W: SEM 89% SAUV B 8% MUSC 3% **other châteaux owned:** Domaine de Terrier (*Premières Côtes de Bordeaux*)
33210 Sauternes tel: 05 56 76 64 96
fax: 05 56 76 69 47

Above: Ch d'Armajan des Ormes

◆
About Sauternes & Barsac
Information about Sauternes wines can be obtained from the Syndicat Viticole de Sauternes which is in the centre of the village of Sauternes at 13, place de la Mairie, 33210 Sauternes.
Tel 05 56 76 60 37.

Somewhat bitter-sweet Sauternes, with plentiful oak, sometimes mint notes, modest fruit – apricot, pear – and often around 14% alcohol.

Ch Cru Barréjats
map 29 J3
AC Sauternes
owner: SCEA Barréjats/Philippe Andurand & Mireille Daret **area:** 2.5 ha **cases:** 850 **grape % W:** SEM 85% SAUV B 10% MUSC 5% **second wine:** Accabailles de Barréjats
33210 Pujols-sur-Ciron tel: 05 56 76 69 06
fax: 05 56 76 69 06

Below: Ch Caillou

Tiny, fairly new estate near Ch Climens, run with great care and passion. The first harvest was in 1990. The wine usually has a refined opulence although the oak – 100% new casks are used – is apt at first to dominate the lush fruit and honey aromas.

Ch Bastor-Lamontagne
map 27 G8
AC Sauternes
owner: Crédit Foncier de France **area:** 50 ha **cases:** 12,000 **grape % W:** SEM 78% SAUV B 17% MUSC 5%
second wine: Les Remparts de Bastor **other châteaux owned:** Ch de Barbe Blanche (*Lussac-St-Emilion*); Ch Beauregard (*Pomerol*); Ch Saint Robert (*Graves*)
33210 Preignac tel: 05 56 63 27 66
fax: 05 56 76 87 03
Bastor-Lamontagne, which once belonged to the kings of France, was bought by Crédit Foncier in 1936. They follow a strict quality policy, with the result that today the wine can compete with the appellation's *crus classés*. In good years such as 1989 and '90 this Sauternes has a beautiful golden colour and a concentrated, firm taste, with sun-soaked sweet fruit, and the *rôti* bouquet of noble rot.

Ch Bêchereau
map 27/L L9
AC Sauternes
owner: Eliane Deloubes **area:** 11 ha **cases:** 2,000
grape % W: SEM 75% SAUV B 20% MUSC 5% **other châteaux owned:** Ch La Capère (*Graves*); Domaine Terrefort (*Graves*)
33210 Bommes tel: 05 56 76 61 73
fax: 05 56 76 67 84
Un vrai château, with courtyard, tower, and an impressive rock cellar. Various wines are produced here. About half the vineyard yields a modest, pure Sauternes that matures for 12 months in cask, half of them new. A simple dry white Graves is sold as Domaine Terrefort, and the lean, darkly-fruited red Graves bears the label Ch la Capère.

Ch La Bouade
map 29 E6
AC Barsac
owner: Héritiers Pauly **area:** 18 ha **cases:** 4,000
grape % W: SEM 90% SAUV B 10% **second wine:** Clos Mercier **other châteaux owned:** Ch Clos Haut-Peyraguey (*Sauternes*)

33720 Barsac tel: 05 56 27 30 53
fax: 05 56 27 30 53
Medium-sized, little-known property producing a worthwhile, powerful Barsac. The oak in this wine is discreet.

Ch Broustet
map 29 H6
2ème cru; AC Barsac
owner: Didier Laulan *area:* 16 ha *cases:* 2,000
grape % W: SEM 63% SAUV B 25% MUSC 12% *second wine:* Ch de Ségur *other châteaux owned:* Ch Saint-Marc *(Sauternes)*
33720 Barsac tel: 05 56 27 16 87
fax: 05 56 27 05 93
The Fournier family bought Broustet in 1885, not for its wine but as a storage area for the next-door cooperage. Vines were not planted until 1900. The Fourniers left Broustet in the early 1990s, having sold to the Laulan family of Ch Saint-Marc. In a successful year the wine is of an average intensity, elegantly fresh, with echoes of tropical fruit, honey and fresh toast.

Ch Caillou
map 29 J3
2ème cru; AC Sauternes
owner: M.J. & J.B. Bravo *area:* 13 ha *cases:* 4,500
grape % W: SEM 90% SAUV B 10% *second wine:* Ch Haut Mayne *other wines:* Graves Rouge du Château Caillou *(AC Graves)*, Cru du Clocher *(Bordeaux Supérieur)*, Bordeaux rosé *other châteaux owned:* Ch Petit Mayne *(Sauternes)*
33720 Barsac tel: 05 56 27 16 38
fax: 05 56 27 09 60
'A bit theatrical' is how the Bravo family describes their slender little château which, with its two towers, is one of Barsac's most striking buildings. At its purchase in 1909 the vineyard amounted to 3 ha; now it has 13. The wine is full of character, seldom very complex or exuberant, but well made and always endowed with honeyed fruit – apricot, orange, pear. Usually a few years' patience is needed for it to open out fully. The Private Cuvée, launched in 1981, is somewhat richer. Half a hectare here is planted with Merlot, which yields the earthy, dark-toned Graves Rouge du Château Caillou. At least as interesting is the Bordeaux Supérieur Cru du Clocher, a well-made wine blend of 95% Merlot and 5% Cabernet, grown on 1.07 ha. A minuscule quantity of Bordeaux rosé is also made.

◆ Classed growths
Recognized classifications are listed at the end of the Atlas. Châteaux profiled in the Atlas which appear on one of these lists have their classification and rank noted immediately below the château name.

◆ Crus Bourgeois
Only one area – the Médoc – has a recognized list of *crus bourgeois*. The ranking procedure is described on page 34 and the full list is given in an appendix. The *crus bourgeois* are in appellations Médoc, Haut-Médoc and the 'village' ACs such as St-Estèphe. The term *cru bourgeois* is in use in other areas, but unofficially,

---

Domaine de Carbonnieu
map 27/L K8
AC Sauternes
owner: Alain Charrier *area:* 10.75 ha *cases:* 2,800
grape % W: SEM 80% SAUV B 10% MUSC 10%
33210 Bommes tel: 05 56 76 64 48
Quite lively, balanced Sauternes, not usually very opulent, with slight *rôti* to it; apricot and other fruit are there, with some almond and oak. A pleasing wine from a family that has been running this estate for some 200 years.

Cru Claverie/Domaine du Petit de l'Eglise
map 27/R B3
AC Sauternes
owner: Claude Saint-Marc *area:* 20 ha *cases:* 4,500 *grape % W:* SEM 70% SAUV B 25% MUSC 5%
second wine: Clos Fontaine *other wines:* Clos Fontaine *(AC Bordeaux rouge)*
33210 Langon tel: 05 56 62 24 78
fax: 05 56 76 86 68
Estate by the railway. In good years its wine is characterized by candied, raisiny fruit, is duly sweet, and with a touch of *pourriture noble*.

Ch Climens
Map 29 K4
1er cru; AC Barsac
owner: Brigitte & Bérénice Lurton *area:* 29 ha *cases:* 3,900 *grape % W:* SEM 100% *second wine:* Les Cyprès de Climens *other châteaux owned:* Ch de Camarsac *(AC Bordeaux)*
33720 Barsac tel: 05 56 27 15 33
fax: 05 56 27 21 04

Above: Ch Climens

Left: Ch Coutet

The first vines were planted here at the end of the 16th century, since when Climens has belonged to only four families. The present owners are the Lurtons. The château stands on the highest part of Barsac and yields a wine that is among the very best from this commune. It owes its class not least to rigorous selection: no Climens appeared in 1984, '87, '92 or '93. Even in better years, some of the vintage is sold as a second wine. Wine from years such as 1988, '89 and '90 comprises a glorious symphony of intense *rôti* tones, luscious fruit – apricot, citrus, peach, pear – toasted oak and honey. But in less-great years the wine can still surprise you, as was the case with the 1991 vintage. The wine is cask-fermented (one-third new barrels), and usually matures in *barriques* for two years.

Ch Closiot
map 29 K7
AC Sauternes
owner: Françoise Soizeau *area:* 8 ha *cases:* 1,300
grape % W: SEM 95% SAUV B 3% MUSC 2% *second wine:* Ch Camperos
33720 Barsac tel: 05 56 27 05 92
fax: 05 56 27 11 06
This former inn for pilgrims *en route* to Santiago de Compostela has been a wine estate since 1895. When nature cooperates, the wine has a certain freshness, with a fairly full-bodied, sound *rôti* taste in which apricot is clearly discernible.

Ch Coutet
map 29 J6
1er cru; AC Barsac
owner: Marcel & Bertrand Baly *area:* 38.5 ha *cases:* 5,500 *grape % W:* SEM 75% SAUV B 23% MUSC 2% *second wine:* La Chartreuse de Château Coutet *other châteaux owned:* Ch Reverdon *(Graves)*
33720 Barsac tel: 05 56 27 15 46
fax: 05 56 27 02 20
The oldest part of this château is a square 13th-century tower, and there is a chapel built a century later. The historical link with the Filhot family, its owners up to the French Revolution, can be seen from the label, which closely resembles the Ch Filhot design. The most spectacular Coutet wine is the Cuvée Madame, a monumental Sauternes that produces an

explosion of sensations – of bouquet, taste, and aftertaste lasting for minutes on end: pure perfection. The pity is that this wine is made only in exceptional years, and then just for a limited clientele. The first vintage was in 1943. Happily, ordinary Coutet offers considerable quality: fine elements of exotic, honeyed fruit, a touch of spices and vanilla with other nuances of oak. The wine is at once rich and elegant, firm and refined.

Ch du Coy
map 27 I3

AC Sauternes

owner: Roger Biarnès **area:** 7 ha **cases:** 1,416 **grape % W:** SEM 80% SAUV B 10% MUSC 10% **other châteaux owned:** Ch de Navarro *(Graves)*; Ch Suau *(Barsac)*

33210 Sauternes tel: 05 56 27 20 27

fax: 05 56 27 26 53

Pleasant, accessible wine with fruit, floral elements and a little honey, plus spicy oak. In the same ownership as Ch Suau.

Ch Cru Peyraguey
map 27/L I9

AC Sauternes

owner: Hubert C. Mussotte **area:** 7 ha **cases:** 1,200 **grape % W:** SEM 80% SAUV B 20%

33210 Preignac tel: 05 56 44 43 48

They work traditionally and in earnest on this two-centuries-old family estate. Thus the wine is fermented in *barriques*, a fifth of them new. Wine from a good year tastes full-bodied, almost fat, with power, candied tropical fruit and low acidity.

Ch Doisy-Daëne
map 29 J5

2ème cru; AC Barsac

owner: Pierre & Denis Dubourdieu **area:** 15 ha **cases:** 6,500 **grape % W:** SEM 100% **other wines:** Bordeaux blanc **other châteaux owned:** Ch Montalivet *(Graves)*; Ch Cantegril *(Sauternes)*

33720 Barsac tel: 05 56 27 15 84

fax: 05 56 27 18 99

Pure Sémillon with a fine sweetness, fruit (apricot, peach, mango, orange-peel) and a reasonable intensity. This wine will usually mature beautifully – for decades even – becoming more expressive with the years. A special *cuvée* appeared in 1990 called l'Extravagance: a sensational Barsac, very concentrated – but, at just 100 cases, sadly rare. The dry white Bordeaux (70% Sauvignon Blanc,

Below: Ch Doisy-Daëne

Above: Ch Doisy-Védrines

30% Sémillon) from this château is also worth seeking out. The estate takes the second part of its name from the Englishman who bought it when the Doisy estate was split up in the 19th century.

Ch Doisy-Dubroca
map 29 J5

2ème cru; AC Barsac

owner: Louis Lurton **area:** 3.3 ha **cases:** 600 **grape % W:** SEM 100% **other châteaux owned:** Ch Haut-Nouchet *(Pessac-Léognan)*

33720 Barsac tel: 05 57 83 10 10

fax: 05 57 83 10 11

By far the smallest of the three Doisys; the 'château' is just an inconspicuous, empty country house. The wine is made at Ch Climens, where it ferments in *barriques*, a third of them new. It offers a nice balance between sweetness and acidity. Besides its vanilla and spices, fruit – apricot, lemon, orange – is often evident. Dubroca is less rich than Climens, but in great years such as 1989 shows its kinship.

Ch Doisy-Védrines
map 29 L6

2ème cru; AC Sauternes

owner: Pierre Castéja **area:** 27 ha **cases:** 2,200 **grape % W:** SEM 80% SAUV B 15% MUSC 5%

33720 Barsac tel: 05 56 27 15 13

fax: 05 56 27 26 76

The building dates from the 16th century, and the round tower here is said to be the remains of a windmill. Jean-Baptiste Védrines, a judge, became the owner through marriage in 1704. Pierre Castéja and his wife have been here since 1946. Theirs is an exceptionally reliable Sauternes, improved in quality during the 1980s through investments in the cellar. The wine has a bouquet of tropical fruit in a context of oak, honey and sufficient acidity. At this, the biggest of the three Doisy châteaux, they work with a low yield and between three and nine grape pickings.

Ch Dudon
map 27 I6

AC Sauternes

owner: Evelyne Allien **area:** 10.4 ha **cases:** 2,500 **grape % W:** SEM 83% SAUV B 15% MUSC 2% **second wine:** Ch Gallies

33720 Barsac tel: 05 56 27 29 38

fax: 05 56 27 29 38

A walled vineyard: the château is an old Carthusian monastery, bracketed by two towers,

◆
About Barsac

For information about Barsac contact the Syndicat Viticole de Barsac at rue du 11 Novembre, BP6, 33720 Barsac. Tel 05 56 27 08 73. The Office Viticole in the centre of Barsac sells local wines.

◆
Quantities

Figures are as supplied by the châteaux.

Area of vineyard: given in hectares, abbreviated to ha. Châteaux are asked to specify vineyards in production, and to exclude from their answers those owned but unplanted, and to advise when extensions are planned.

Production: given in cases of 12 bottles, each of 0.75 litres. A case is thus 9 litres. A hectolitre is 100 litres or just over 11 cases.

Yield per hectare: to obtain this, multiply the 'cases' figure by 9, to give litres, then divide by 100, to give hectolitres. Then divide the result by the area in hectares.

with a small wine museum in its cellars. The wine has at best a correct quality, with more power than refinement, and can sometimes be disappointing. Careful choice of vintages is called for.

Ch l'Ermitage
map 27/L F4

AC Sauternes

owner: GFA Château l'Ermitage/Famille Crampes **area:** 10.5 ha **cases:** 2,600 **grape % W:** SEM 85% MUSC 10% SAUV B 5% **second wine:** Ch Guilhem de Rey **other châteaux owned:** Ch Gayon *(AC Bordeaux)*

33210 Preignac tel: 05 56 76 12 74

fax: 05 56 76 12 75

There has been total renovation at Ch l'Ermitage since the estate changed hands in 1991. A golden wine, with floral elements and a firm foundation of oak. A reliable Sauternes, even in lesser years.

Ch de Fargues   map 27/R D4
AC Sauternes
owner: Comte Alexandre de Lur Saluces *area:* 15
ha *cases:* 3,000 *grape % W:* SEM 80% SAUV B 20%
second wine: Guilhem de Fargues *(AC Bordeaux
blanc)* *other châteaux owned:* Ch d' Yquem
(Sauternes)
33210 Fargues tel: 05 57 98 04 20
fax: 05 57 98 04 21
The Fargues *seigneurie* came to the Lur Saluces
family through marriage. That was in 1472 –
about three centuries before the same thing
happened with Ch d'Yquem. Behind the present
château, a long, low building, are the ruins of
an older, much larger, castle. The vineyard lies
at the eastern edge of the Sauternes district,
and the grapes generally ripen 10 days later
than at d'Yquem   with therefore a greater risk
of rain and poor harvests. The Ch de Fargues
wine ferments and matures in casks from
d'Yquem. It could be regarded as a lesser
version of d'Yquem, but it is an exquisite wine
nonetheless, and in no way inferior to the
better *crus classés*. It begins gradually to show
its true class only after four to five years.

Ch Farluret   map 29 L5
AC Sauternes
owner: R. Lamothe & Fils *area:* 8 ha *cases:* 2,000
grape % W: SEM 90% MUSC 5% SAUV B 5% *second
wine:* Ch Grand Jauga *other châteaux owned:* Ch
Haut-Bergeron *(Sauternes)*
33720 Barsac tel: 05 56 63 24 76
fax: 05 56 63 23 31
Estate right in the south of Barsac, where a
sound, tasty Sauternes is produced by the Ch
Haut-Bergeron team. It ferments in stainless
steel and ages for two years in 80% new oak.

Ch Filhot   map 27/R K6
2ème cru; AC Sauternes
owner: Comte Henri de Vaucelles *area:* 60 ha
cases: 12,000 *grape % W:* SEM 50% SAUV B 45%
MUSC 5% *other wines:* Ch Pineau du Rey *(Bordeaux
blanc)*
33210 Sauternes tel: 05 56 76 61 09
fax: 05 56 76 67 91
This grand and extensive estate boasts a palatial
château set amid rolling, English-style
parkland. It has a rich history, and for more
than a century has been owned by the Lur
Saluces family of d'Yquem. In contrast to other

Above: Ch Guiraud

great Sauternes, Filhot does not come into
contact with oak. In style the wine is elegant
rather than generous, not exaggeratedly sweet,
and with a lively taste. Its fruit suggests apricot,
with pineapple and pear notes. Its balance is
usually faultless. A really great year for Filhot
was 1990. Sometimes a Crème de Tête is also
produced – aromatic, concentrated, with
botrytis much in evidence.

Ch Gilette   map 27/L D4
AC Sauternes
owner: Christian Médeville *area:* 4.5 ha *cases:* 500
grape % W: SEM 90% SAUV B 8% MUSC 2% *other
châteaux owned:* Ch Les Justices *(Sauternes)*; Ch
Respide-Médeville *(Graves)*
33210 Preignac tel: 05 56 76 28 44
fax: 05 56 76 28 44
Gilette does things its own way: the wine ages
for at least 15 years in concrete vats before
being bottled. What at last reaches the glass is
golden-amber in colour, with a creamy, very
concentrated, deeply-fruited taste, fragrant and
sometimes almost exotic. The greatest years
have 'Crème de Tête' on the label. The same
owners are also very committed to their regular
Sauternes – a sort of junior version of Gilette –
Ch Les Justices (which see).

Ch Gravas   map 29 J5
AC Sauternes
owner: SCEA Domaines Bernard *area:* 11 ha *cases:*
2,800 *grape % W:* SEM 80% SAUV B 10% MUSC 10%
second wine: Ch Simon Carretey *other châteaux
owned:* Ch Duc d'Arnauton *(Graves)*
33720 Barsac tel: 05 56 27 15 20
fax: 05 56 27 29 83
One of the better Barsac *bourgeois*, mouthfilling, with a long finish, honeyed and showing
fruit as well as spicy oak; it has two years in
barrel (one-third new). Sometimes a Cuvée
Spéciale is also made, honeyed and rich.
'Gravas' comes from *graves*, a reference to the
gravel soil here. The Bernard family has been
running this vineyard since 1850.

Ch Guiraud   map 27/R J4
1er cru; AC Sauternes
owner: Famille Narby *area:* 100 ha *cases:* 16,000
grape % W: SEM 65% SAUV B 35% *second wine:* Le
Dauphin du Château Guiraud *other wines:* "G"
Château Guiraud *(Bordeaux blanc)*
33210 Sauternes tel: 05 56 76 61 01
fax: 05 56 76 67 52
The vineyard, on one of the hills above the
village of Sauternes, took shape at the end of
the 19th century. The Maxwell family spent a
fortune then, providing the château with a
second storey, building a hunting lodge and
installing their own water-tower. After a difficult
period in the 1970s the estate passed to
Canadian owners, who brought to it a new *élan*.
The first successful new-style Guiraud was the
1983 vintage. In its best years, Guiraud is
balanced and full-bodied, with a wonderful
blend of succulent apricot, honey and
beautifully integrated, toasted oak – 45 to 50%
of the wood is new. Examples of such years are
1986, '88, '89, and the splendid 1990. When
young, Guiraud wines can be rather reserved
to begin with; long bottle-ageing usually
brings its reward.

Below: Ch de Fargues

◆
Finding a second wine

To locate a second wine, consult the index
which lists all châteaux in the Atlas.

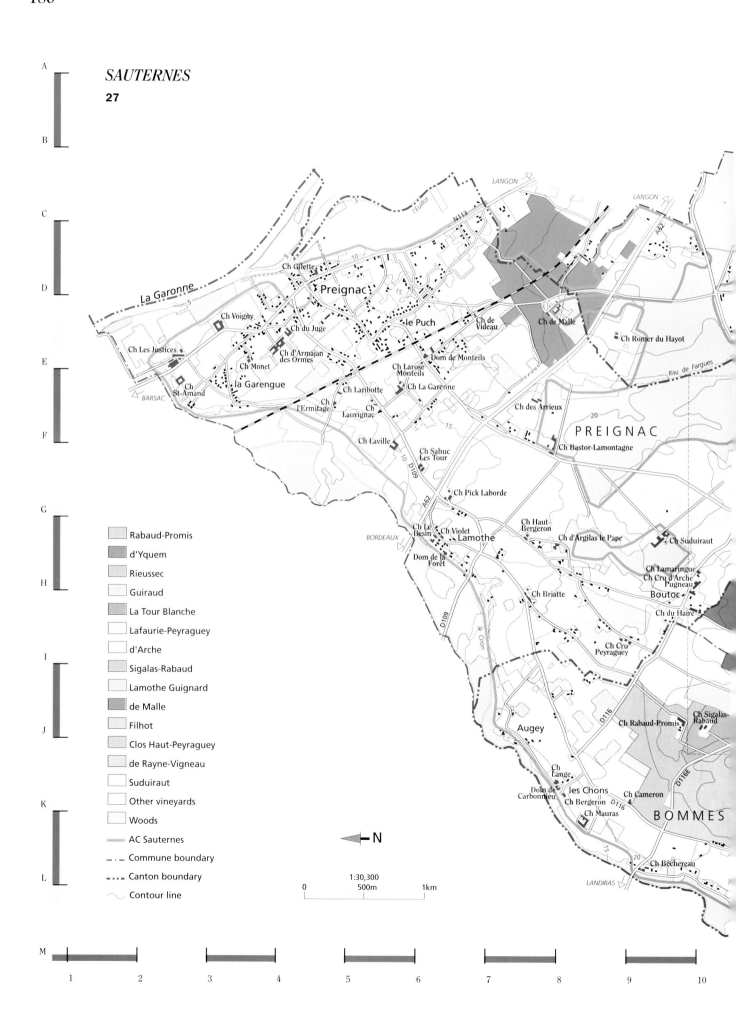

SAUTERNES

27

Rabaud-Promis
d'Yquem
Rieussec
Guiraud
La Tour Blanche
Lafaurie-Peyraguey
d'Arche
Sigalas-Rabaud
Lamothe Guignard
de Malle
Filhot
Clos Haut-Peyraguey
de Rayne-Vigneau
Suduiraut
Other vineyards
Woods
AC Sauternes
Commune boundary
Canton boundary
Contour line

N

1:30,300

0   500m   1km

Cru Claverie/
Dom du Petit de l'Eglise

Clos Fontaine

Ch Barbier

RIVE DROITE

• Libourne

Bordeaux

ENTRE-DEUX-
MERS

GRAVES &
SAUTERNES

• Langon

le Grison

Ch de Fargues

Mounic

Fargues

Ch Peillon
Claverie

la Tuilerie

les Claveries

28

Ch Haut-
Claverie

Ch Rieussec

Dom de
Quincarnon

Arrançon

FARGUES

Ch Lafon-
Larose • Ch Lafon

Ch d'Yquem

Ch du Coy

Brouquet

PRÉCHAC

Ch Raymond-Lafon

Ch Guiraud

Caplane

Nautet

Ch Lafaurie-
Peyraguey

Ch Haut-
Caplane

Clos Haut-
Peyraguey

Ch
Caplane

Sauternes

Ch de Rayne-
Vigneau

Ch Filhot

Ch d'Arche

Ch Haut
Bommes

Ch Lamothe
Guignard

Ch La Rivière

Ch Lamothe

SAUTERNES

Ch La Tour
Blanche

Ch
Lamourette

Bommes

Dom de
Barjuneau Chauvin

Ch de Commarque

A

B

C

D

E

F

G

H

I

J

K

L

M

1   2   3   4   5   6   7   8   9   10

Above: Ch Guiteronde du Hayot

Ch Guiteronde du Hayot　map 29 J3
AC Sauternes
owner: André du Hayot *area:* 45 ha *cases:* 10,000
grape % W: SEM 70% SAUV B 20% MUSC 10% *second wines:* Ch Brassens-Guiteronde; Ch Camperos *other châteaux owned:* Ch de Pebayle (Graves); Ch Romer du Hayot (Sauternes)
33720 Barsac tel: 05 56 27 15 37
fax: 05 56 27 04 24
Commercial wine, correct but without any very distinct personality or much depth. Oak is modestly present.

Ch Haut-Bergeron　map 27/L H7
AC Sauternes
owner: R. Lamothe & Fils *area:* 25 ha *cases:* 5,500
grape % W: SEM 90% MUSC 5% SAUV B 5% *second wine:* Ch Fontebride *other châteaux owned:* Ch Farluret (Sauternes)
33210 Preignac tel: 05 56 63 24 76
fax: 05 56 63 23 31
Vines on average 60 years old, careful picking, a most meticulous vinification and 18 months' oak-ageing (60-80% new barrels) make Haut-Bergeron the equal of wines with more prestigious names. Its bouquet often comprises a cocktail of over-ripe fruit – apricot, nectarine, peach – and the unctuous, almost honey-sweet taste with its elements of butter, vanilla and spicy oak lingers long in the mouth.

Ch Haut-Claverie　map 27/R F5
AC Sauternes
owner: SCEA Sendrey Frères & Fils *area:* 12.5 ha *cases:* 3,000 *grape % W:* SEM 85% SAUV B 12% MUSC 3% *other châteaux owned:* Ch la Mourasse (Graves)
33210 Fargues tel: 05 56 63 43 09
fax: 05 56 63 51 16
Haut-Claverie – now Château, formerly Domaine – is on a hill facing Ch de Fargues. A good straightforward Sauternes is produced here, with fruit and honey in its usually sinewy taste. The *rôti* aroma is very obviously present in some years; only modestly so in others. Part of the vintage goes in cask to a wine merchant.

Clos Haut-Peyraguey　map 27/R K2
1er cru; AC Sauternes
owner: Héritiers Pauly *area:* 23 ha *cases:* 3,500
grape % W: SEM 83% SAUV B 15% MUSC 2% *second wine:* Ch Haut-Bommes

The Sauternes classification
The Sauternes classification dates from 1855 and has not been altered. Ch d'Yquem was placed alone in the top rank as *Premier Cru Supérieur*. Nine châteaux were rated as *Premiers Crus*, and eleven as *Deuxièmes Crus*. Division of properties has raised these numbers to eleven *Premiers Crus* and fourteen *Deuxièmes Crus*. The classified châteaux can be identified in these pages by the terms 1er cru and 2ème cru on the line beneath the château name.

Ten of the classed growths are in Barsac. Like other Barsac estates, they can use either AC Barsac or AC Sauternes

33210 Bommes tel: 05 56 76 61 53
fax: 05 56 76 69 65
This estate was split off from Ch Lafaurie-Peyraguey in 1878. The plain and simple little château is graced by a central turret. The Sauternes, however, is certainly not simple. Generally its style is elegant and fresh, with fine fruit – pineapple, apricot, peach, lemon. This wine becomes luxurious in superb years such as 1990. Characteristic of Clos Haut-Peyraguey is the time it needs to develop: at least six to ten years as a rule.

Ch Les Justices　map 27/L E2
AC Sauternes
owner: Christian Médeville *area:* 14 ha *cases:* red 3,000; white 2,000 *grape % R:* MER 55% CS 45%
grape % W: SEM 88% SAUV B 8% MUSC 4% *other wines:* Domaine des Justices (AC Bordeaux) *other châteaux owned:* Ch Respide-Médeville (Graves); Ch Gilette (Sauternes)
33210 Preignac tel: 05 56 76 28 44
fax: 05 56 76 28 44
A most carefully made wine that may be regarded as a junior version of Ch Gilette, from the same owner. In good years it is a reasonably rich Sauternes with not only elements of spicy oak, but also honeyed fruit, an elegant

Below: Ch Lafaurie-Peyraguey

structure and the aroma from *pourriture noble*. It spends 12-18 months in oak. Creditable dry white and red Bordeaux are produced under the name Domaine des Justices. The red version is also aged in cask, for a maximum 12 months.

Ch Lafaurie-Peyraguey　map 27/R J1
1er cru; AC Sauternes
owner: Domaines Cordier *area:* 40 ha *cases:* 7,500
grape % W: SEM 90% MUSC 5% SAUV B 5% *second wine:* La Chapelle de Lafaurie *other châteaux owned:* include Ch Clos des Jacobins (St-Emilion)
33210 Bommes tel: 05 56 76 60 54
fax: 05 56 76 61 89
This château was built as a real fortress in the 13th century, complete with towers and battlements – and some of these survive. The Cordier family became the owners in 1917; Domaines Cordier still run this *premier cru*. Since the 1980s, when the vineyard was enlarged by 4.5 ha through the acquisition of Ch d'Arche-Vimeney, the wine has been on brilliant form. It is a distinguished, complete, classic Sauternes, very honeyed – with usually a nice freshness as well – rich tropical fruit and noble oak. In the lesser years, too, the wine can show surprising class.

Ch Lafon　map 27/R I2
AC Sauternes
owner: Jean-Pierre Dufour *area:* 6 ha *cases:* 1,500
grape % W: SEM 90% SAUV B 10%
33210 Sauternes tel: 05 56 63 30 82
By far the greater part of production is nurtured by the firm of Dourthe, giving a wine tasting better than that from the château itself. It is an elegant, delicious Sauternes, often having a fine complexity, with raisin, orange, banana and mango fruit.

Ch Lamothe　map 27/R L4
2ème cru; AC Sauternes
owner: Guy Despujols *area:* 7.5 ha *cases:* 1,250
grape % W: SEM 85% SAUV B 10% MUSC 5% *second wine:* Les Tourelles de Lamothe
33210 Sauternes tel: 05 56 76 67 89
fax: 05 56 76 63 77
The remains of a small Merovingian fort behind Ch Lamothe show that the region once knew less peaceful times. Lamothe and neighbouring Lamothe-Guignard formed a single estate until the end of the 19th century. Under the dynamic management of Guy Despujols, whose family bought Lamothe in 1961, the wine has improved in quality. He carefully guards its particular pure fruit personality: it does not as a rule spend time in cask. It is usually reasonably substantial, with average concentration and an attractive flowers-and-fruit bouquet. The wine gains in richness in great years such as 1989 and 1990. Guy Despujols runs a tasting and sales centre in nearby Sauternes village, next to the Auberge des Vignes.

Ch Lamothe Guignard　map 27/R L4
2ème cru; AC Sauternes
owner: Philippe & Jacques Guignard *area:* 17 ha *cases:* 2,700 *grape % W:* SEM 90% SAUV B 5% MUSC 5% *other châteaux owned:* Le Clos du Hez (Graves); Ch de Rolland (Barsac) (Sauternes); Ch de Roquetaillade La Grange (Graves)
33210 Sauternes tel: 05 56 76 60 28
fax: 05 56 76 69 05
Since 1981 this, the larger of the two Lamothes, has been run by Jacques and Philippe Guignard.

They have carried through essential changes
that have led to a remarkable improvement in
the wine. In good years it shows depth,
generosity and a considerable bouquet,
luxuriously blending honeyed exotic and citrus
fruits together with a slight touch of oak and
vanilla. Oak-ageing lasts 12-15 months; 30% at
most of the *barriques* are replaced annually.

Ch Lamourette
map 27/R M1
AC Sauternes
owner: Anne-Marie Léglise *area:* 12 ha *cases:*
2,000, white 1,500 *grape % R:* MER 100% *grape %
W:* SEM 90% MUSC 6% SAUV B 4% *other wines:* Ch
Grava-Lacoste *(Graves)*
33210 Bommes tel: 05 56 76 63 58
fax: 05 56 76 60 85
Since 1860 this estate has been passed down
from mother to daughter. The present owner,
Anne-Marie Léglise, runs Lamourette in a way
that is expert as well as loving, and the wines of
her little-known château can be of a striking
quality. The hallmark is a floral fragrance, a
rich, full taste, and the constitution for long
cellaring. Ch Grava-Lacoste, the red Graves
made entirely from Merlot, also has great
charm.

Ch Lange
map 27/L K8
AC Sauternes
owner: Bernard Réglat *area:* 12.5 ha *cases:* 3,000
grape % W: SEM 98% MUSC 2% *second wine:* Ch du
Mayne *other châteaux owned:* Ch La Gravelière
(Graves)
33210 Bommes tel: 05 56 62 98 63
fax: 05 56 62 17 98
An engaging Sauternes: slightly *rôti*, quite
sweet but with balancing acidity; reasonably
full, but seldom really rich. This wine spends
eight months in oak. It has won awards from
time to time.

Ch Laribotte
map 27/L F4
AC Sauternes
owner: Jean-Pierre Lamiteau *area:* 16 ha *cases:*
3,500 *grape % W:* SEM 90% SAUV B 8% MUSC 2%
33210 Preignac tel: 05 56 63 27 88
fax: 05 56 62 24 80
Characteristically this is a fairly light, supple,
harmonious wine with subtle flowers and fruit.
Sometimes this estate brings out a Cuvée
Spéciale, with more concentration and *rôti*.

Ch Latrezotte
map 29 L5
AC Sauternes
owner: Horst Glock *area:* 8.5 ha *cases:* 1,000
grape % W: SEM 70% SAUV B 15% MUSC 15% *other
wine:* Graves Supérieures
33720 Barsac tel: 05 56 27 16 50
This property lies in the south of Barsac, on the
La Pinesse plateau. Its wine is made with great
care: three pickings as a rule, barrel
fermentation and at least a year in oak. Its taste
forms a marvellous whole of sun-soaked fruit,
with sweetness and acidity well-balanced.

Ch Laville
map 27/L G5
AC Sauternes
owner: Yvette & Claude Barbe *area:* 13 ha *cases:*
3,000 *grape % W:* SEM 80% SAUV B 15% MUSC 5%
second wine: Ch Delmond *other châteaux owned:*
Ch Mouras *(Graves)*, Ch Mahon-Laville *(AC Bordeaux)*
33210 Preignac tel: 05 56 63 28 14
fax: 05 56 63 16 28
An impressive estate, with a walled vineyard
around its 17th-century château. The

Above: Ch de Malle

Sauvignon (15% of the vines) shows clearly in
the wine's freshness and elegance. Eighteen
months' maturing in casks, 30 to 50% of them
new, makes the wine more structured, with the
aromas of oak. Honey and fruit notes – peach,
apricot – are discernible, too. Can also be
successful in lesser years.

Ch Liot
map 29 K4
AC Sauternes
owner: Jean-Gérard David *area:* 20 ha *cases:* 5,500
grape % W: SEM 85% SAUV B 10% MUSC 5% *second
wine:* Ch du Levant *other châteaux owned:* Ch
Saint Jean des Graves *(Graves)*
33720 Barsac tel: 05 56 27 15 31
fax: 05 56 27 14 42
One of Barsac's more reliable *bourgeois*. Like
neighbouring Climens, château and vineyard
are in the highest part of Barsac, and low walls
protect the vines. This is a wine of quiet
character: fresh and sweet, with ripe fruit –
apricot, apple, pear, lemon – balanced by its
framework of oak.

Ch de Malle
map 27/L E8
2ème cru; AC Sauternes
owner: Comtesse de Bournazel *area:* 50 ha *cases:*
red 9,000; white 5,200 *grape % R:* CS 60%, MER
40% *grape % W:* SEM 75% SAUV B 25% *second wine:*
Ch de Sainte-Hélène *other wines:* Ch Tours de Malle
(Graves); Chevalier de Malle *(Bordeaux blanc);*
Ch de Cardaillan *(Graves);* M de Malle *(Graves
blanc)*
33210 Preignac tel: 05 56 62 36 86
fax: 05 56 76 82 40
This château with its pepperpot towers was
built in the 17th century by Jacques de Malle.
The only listed historic monument in the
Sauternes, it is open to visitors, who can enjoy
antique furniture and *objets d'art* which include
Europe's biggest collection of silhouettes. These
are lifesize figures cut out of wood, used in the
18th century for theatrical presentations and as
fire-screens. De Malle's wine is seldom overtly
brilliant or sumptuous, but certainly has
charm, with elements of tropical fruit, almond
and elegant oak. In great Sauternes vintages,
such as 1988 and 1990, it is more substantial,
with greater depth. The estate also produces a
portfolio of other wines, one of the most
successful among them being the red Graves,
Ch de Cardaillan.

Ch Mauras
map 27/L L8
AC Sauternes
owner: Société Viticole de France *area:* 14 ha
cases: 9,330 *grape % W:* SEM 67% SAUV B 30% MUSC
3% *other châteaux owned:* Ch Bernones *(Haut-
Médoc);* Ch Mauvesin *(Moulis-en-Médoc);* Ch Vieira
(Bordeaux Supérieur); Ch du Crava *(Bordeaux
Supérieur)*
33210 Bommes tel: 05 56 67 23 89
fax: 05 56 67 08 38
The stone château, among the most attractive
in Bommes, looks out over a vineyard with 30%
Sauvignon – a relatively high proportion for
Sauternes. The wine is meant for drinking
young and has a light, fresh and fruity style
with no oak.

Ch du Mayne
map 29 H7
AC Barsac
owner: Héritiers Sanders *area:* 8 ha *cases:* 2,000
grape % W: SEM 60% SAUV B 40% *second wine:* Ch
Mayne Pompon *other châteaux owned:* Ch Haut-
Bailly *(Pessac-Léognan);* Ch de Courbon *(Graves)*
33720 Barsac tel: 05 56 27 16 07
fax: 05 56 27 16 02
Walled estate with a park half the size of its
vineyard. Since 1937 it has belonged to the
Sanders family, of Flemish origin, who also run
Ch Haut-Bailly in Pessac-Léognan. The wine has
fine fruit, a sensible dose of oak, a stimulating
character and unmistakeable finesse.

◆
Special cuvées

In great years some Sauternes châteaux
produce a special wine, selected from the
best that the vintage yields. These are
known as *crème de tête* or *tête de cuvée*.
They sometimes represent the wine from a
specific picking or pickings of the ripest,
most botrytis-affected grapes. The wine will
be richer, more intense that the château's
standard offering – and even more
expensive. They may have special names,
rather like second wines, or can just be
labelled *tête de cuvée*.

Ch Ménota
map 29 H6

AC Sauternes

owner: SCEA du Château Ménota/Famille Labat
area: 30 ha *cases:* 8,300 *grape % W:* SAUV B 30%
SEM 60% MUSC 10% *second wine:* Ch Menate *other*
châteaux owned: Clos Saint Georges de
Montgarède *(Graves)*
33720 Barsac tel: 05 56 27 15 80
fax: 05 56 27 00 79

Not an opulent or subtly-nuanced wine, but
quite an expressive one with suggestions of
grapefruit, lime and lemon. It ages well. The
entrance to this property is a gateway in an old
castellated wall.

Ch Monet
map 27/L E3

AC Sauternes

owner: Patrice Haverlan *area:* 2.1 ha *cases:* 400
grape % W: SEM 95% SAUV B 5% *other châteaux*
owned: Domaine des Lucques *(Graves)*; Ch Le
Bourdillot *(Graves)*
33640 Portets tel: 05 56 67 11 32
fax: 05 56 67 11 32

Small estate belonging to a renowned grower in
the Graves district. At its best the wine is fat,
almost unctuous, with lovely aromas of *rôti* and
vanilla-like oak.

Ch Mont-Joye
map 29 H4

AC Sauternes

owner: Franck Glaunès *area:* 20 ha *cases:* 4,000
grape % W: SEM 70% SAUV B 15% MUSC 15% *second*
wines: Ch Jacques le Haut; Ch Mercier *other*
châteaux owned: Domaine du Pas Saint-Georges
(AC Bordeaux)
33720 Barsac tel: 05 56 71 12 73
fax: 05 56 71 12 41

Not a great wine, and less *liquoreux* than many
other Sauternes. Nevertheless in better years it
can have a pleasing balance of fruit and honey,
as well as spicy oak.

Ch Myrat
map 29 I4

2ème cru; AC Sauternes

owner: Jacques de Pontac *area:* 22 ha *cases:*
4,000 *grape % W:* SEM 86% SAUV B 10% MUSC 4%
other châteaux owned: Ch Peychaud *(Bordeaux*
Supérieur)
33720 Barsac tel: 05 56 27 15 06
fax: 05 56 27 11 75

In 1976 the Myrat vineyard was uprooted, and it
looked as if this *deuxième cru* would disappear
for good. However, after the death of their
father in 1988, the brothers Jacques and Xavier
de Pontac decided to replant the whole
vineyard: this took some 140,000 vines. The
first Sauternes was harvested in 1991 – with a
yield of only 3 hl per hectare thanks to night
frosts. This and the subsequent, mostly difficult,
vintages have produced wines still rather
lacking in breadth and structure – but
judicious doses of fruit and oak are there. The
vines will have to age somewhat before the
miracle of Myrat is complete.

Ch Nairac
map 29 F7

2ème cru; AC Barsac

owner: Nicole Tari *area:* 17 ha *cases:* 1,800 *grape*
% W: SEM 88% SAUV B 9% MUSC 3% *other châteaux*
owned: Ch des Fougères *(Graves)*
33720 Barsac tel: 05 56 27 16 16
fax: 05 56 27 26 50

It was probably a pupil of the noted architect
Victor Louis who in 1776 was commissioned by
the Protestant Nairac family to design this
stately château. Since 1972 the vineyard, which

Above: Ch Nairac

is near the road into Barsac from the north, has
been managed in perfectionist style by Nicole
Tari, nowadays with the help of her son Nicolas
Heeter-Tari. The wine is very pure in taste,
lively and elegant, with a satisfying richness,
fruit (banana, apricot, pear, pineapple) and a
good dose of oak. After fermenting in wood, half
to all of it new, the wine matures in cask for
between 18 to 36 months.

Ch Pascaud-Villefranche
map 29 K7

AC Sauternes

owner: Pierre Pascaud *area:* 7.9 ha *cases:* 2,000
grape % W: SEM 75% SAUV B 20% MUSC 5%
33720 Barsac tel: 05 56 27 16 09

Expertly made, fresh and fruity wine with a
sufficient sweetness. The estate has belonged to
the same family for more than a century.

Ch Pernaud
map 29 K7

AC Sauternes

owner: Arlette Regelspeger *area:* 15.8 ha *cases:*
3,500 *grape % W:* SEM 80% SAUV B 15% MUSC 5%
second wine: Ch Pey-Arnaud
33720 Barsac tel: 05 56 27 26 52
fax: 05 56 27 32 08

Vineyard in a single block that once belonged to
Laurent Sauvage d'Yquem and his successors,
the Lur Saluces brothers. A Sauternes in the
apéritif style is produced here, fresh and light,
with some oak and not much *rôti*.

◆

Dry white & red wines

Only sweet white wines are entitled to the
Sauternes AC. Those dry white and red
wines made in the district have to use the
Bordeaux AC: they are not permitted to be
Graves – unlike neighbouring Cérons where
both dry Graves and sweet Cérons can be
made by the same château.

◆

Maps of the Médoc & Graves
appellations

For a key map showing all the appellations
in this zone, with the outlines of the maps
in this Atlas, consult Map 7.

Above: Ch Piada

Ch Piada
map 29 J7

AC Barsac

owner: Jean Lalande *area:* 9.5 ha *cases:* 2,500
grape % W: SEM 100% *second wine:* Clos du Roy
other wines: Ch Piada-Lalanda *(Bordeaux rouge)*
other châteaux owned: Domaine du Hauret-Lalande
(Graves)
33720 Barsac tel: 05 56 27 16 13
fax: 05 56 27 26 30

Piada first appears in the records in 1274, and
for a long time it formed part of Ch Coutet. At
the end of the 19th century, however, the estate
regained its independence. Pickers here usually
pass four to eight times along the rows,
harvesting only grapes much affected by
botrytis. The juice is then fermented in
barriques of which a fifth to a quarter are new;
the wine then spends 12 months in wood. All
these efforts result in a generally superior
Barsac that delightfully and luxuriously
combines apricot, honey, fine oak and other
nuances.

Ch Piot-David
map 29 J7

AC Sauternes

owner: Jean-Luc David *area:* 6.8 ha *cases:* 1,700
grape % W: SEM 80% SAUV B 20% *second wine:* Ch
Bourdon *other châteaux owned:* Ch Poncet
(Premières Côtes de Bordeaux)
33720 Barsac tel: 05 56 62 97 30
fax: 05 56 62 66 76

For Barsac this is a rather broad, almost
corpulent wine, which boasts elements of oak,
caramel, almond and rich, exotic fruit. The
1990 vintage was one of Ch Piot-David's
successful years.

Ch Prost
map 29 F7

AC Sauternes

owner: Jean Perromat & Fils *area:* 15 ha *cases:*
3,500 *grape % W:* SEM 65% SAUV B 20% MUSC 15%
other châteaux owned: Ch de Cérons *(Cérons)*; Ch
du Mayne *(Graves)*; Ch du Vieux Moulin *(Loupiac)*;
Domaine de Terrefort *(Bordeaux Supérieur)*
33720 Barsac tel: 05 56 27 01 13
fax: 05 56 27 22 17

Supple wine which is, at its best, of average
quality and reasonable fruit – often with a note
of freshness that is contributed by the
vineyard's fairly high proportion – 20% – of
Sauvignon vines.

SAUTERNES
28

Ch Lafon-Larose
Ch Raymond-Lafon
Ch Lafon
Clos Haut-Peyraguey
Ch d'Yquem
Caplane
Ch du Coy
la Carrade
Pouteau
Ch Rieussec
le Pape
Cosse

SAUTERNES
● Sauternes

N

1:14,000
0   500m

d'Yquem
Clos Haut-Peyraguey
Rieussec
Other vineyards
Woods
— · — Commune boundary
▪▪▪ Canton boundary
Contour line

Ch Rabaud-Promis   map 27/L J9

1er cru; AC Sauternes

owner: Philippe Dejean *area:* 33 ha *cases:* 5,000
grape % W: SEM 80% SAUV B 18% MUSC 2% *second wines:* Domaine de l'Estrémade; Ch Bequet

33210 Bommes tel: 05 56 76 67 38
fax: 05 56 76 63 10

Château set on a hill; part of this estate was sold by Henri de Sigalas to Adrien Promis in 1903. After a series of poor performances Rabaud-Promis returned to the ranks of the *premiers crus* with the 1983 harvest, and was brilliant once more from 1986. This was thanks to Philippe Dejean's direction; now freshness and vitality provide the wine with ageing potential, and honeyed fruit – pear, lemon, pineapple, coconut – gives it a seductive charm.

Ch Raymond-Lafon   map 27/R I1

AC Sauternes

owner: Famille Meslier *area:* 18 ha *cases:* 2,000
grape % W: SEM 80% SAUV B 20% *second wine:* Ch Lafon-Laroze

33210 Sauternes tel: 05 56 63 21 02
fax: 05 56 63 19 58

This rather English-looking château, at the foot of the d'Yquem hill, was named after the man who built it in 1850. The wine, too, is close to d'Yquem, for it is made with the same perfectionism. This is hardly surprising, for Pierre Meslier, who bought Raymond-Lafon in 1972, was for years the *régisseur* at d'Yquem. Thus fermentation takes place in new casks. Three years' maturing, also in barrel, follows. The estate has not been given a classification, but the wine is on a par with the very best *premiers crus*: a golden colour, satisfyingly rich bouquet, and a complex, rich taste that is suffused with fruit – grapefruit, pineapple, prune, banana and candied lemon.

Ch de Rayne-Vigneau   map 27/R K1

1er cru; AC Sauternes

owner: SC du Château de Rayne Vigneau (Mestrezat) *area:* 79 ha *cases:* 20,000 *grape % W:* SEM 75% SAUV B 23% MUSC 2% *second wine:* Clos l'Abeilley *other wines:* Le Sec de Rayne Vigneau *(Bordeaux blanc);* Gemme de Rayne Vigneau *(Bordeaux blanc) other châteaux owned:* Ch Tourteau Chollet *(Graves);* Ch Marsac Seguineau *(Margaux);* Ch Lamothe Bergeron *(Haut-Médoc);* Ch Blaignan *(Médoc);* Ch Grand-Puy Ducasse *(Pauillac)*

33210 Bommes tel: 05 56 01 30 10
fax: 05 56 79 23 57

The fame of Rayne-Vigneau, then called Vigneau-Pontac, was established in 1867 when it took the *grand prix* at the Paris world exhibition. That glory faded in the course of the present century, but since 1986 the quality of the wine has been gradually restored. Its fairly high percentage of Sauvignon contributes to making this a rather less rich Sauternes; but it does have the freshness of tropical and citrus fruit, as well as floral notes, and sometimes a touch of mint. The oak, too, is unmistakeable, from 18 months in barrels of which half are new. The vineyard stretches over an impressive hill, crowned by the (empty) château and park.

Ch Rieussec   map 27/R G3

1er cru; AC Sauternes

owner: Domaines Barons de Rothschild *area:* 75 ha *cases:* 10,000 *grape % W:* SEM 90% SAUV B 7% MUSC 3% *second wine:* Ch Mayne des Carmes *other wines:* 'R' de Rieussec *(Bordeaux blanc) other châteaux owned:* include Ch l'Evangile *(Pomerol);* Ch Duhart-Milon *(Pauillac);* Ch Lafite Rothschild *(Pauillac)*

33210 Fargues tel: 05 56 73 18 18
fax: 05 56 59 26 83

This château and its vineyard are on the second-highest hill in the Sauternes area (d'Yquem's is loftiest). The grapes here ripen just a little earlier than in the rest of the district, and are less often hit by night frosts. The estate flourished under Albert Vuillier, who acquired it in 1971. His management aimed at quality, and this approach has been continued by Domaines Barons de Rothschild, who have been the owners since 1985. Rieussec is a great, classic Sauternes: a golden-coloured, very concentrated, multi-dimensional wine, generous in fruit – dried apricot, succulent ripe pear, honeyed pineapple, dates and currants. It ferments in tanks but matures for 18 to 30 months in new *barriques*. In great years a very

---

◆

Finding a second wine

To locate a second wine, consult the index which lists all châteaux in the Atlas.

---

small amount of Crème de Tête – a special cuvée that tastes even more intense than ordinary Rieussec – is made. Ch Rieussec also produces an engaging dry white Bordeaux, called by its initial: 'R' de Rieussec.

Ch La Rivière   map 27/R L1

AC Sauternes

owner: Guillaume Réglat *area:* 3.5 ha *cases:* 600 *grape % W:* SEM 98% MUSC 2% *other châteaux owned:* Ch Cousteau *(Premières Côtes de Bordeaux);* Ch Gravelière *(Graves)*

33210 Bommes tel: 05 56 62 98 63
fax: 05 56 62 17 98

An estate which grows no Sauvignon: it is almost entirely Sémillon. It makes a succulent, firm wine, usually with limited *rôti*. There are plans to double the size of the vineyard here.

Ch de Rolland   map 29 I9

AC Barsac

owner: J. & P. Guignard *area:* 28 ha *cases:* 8,500 *grape % W:* SEM 80% SAUV B 15% MUSC 5% *other wines:* Le Graves Sec du Château de Rolland; Bordeaux sec *other châteaux owned:* Ch Lamothe Guignard *(Sauternes);* Ch de Roquetaillade La Grange *(Graves);* Clos du Hez *(Graves)*

33720 Barsac tel: 05 56 27 15 02
fax: 05 56 27 28 58

In good years this is a reasonably full wine, its aroma and taste offering notes of honey, oak and fruit, without any great complexity. The château, which stands beside the River Ciron, has become a small, comfortable hotel .

Ch Romer du Hayot   map 27/L E8

2ème cru; AC Sauternes

owner: André du Hayot *area:* 16 ha *cases:* 4,200 *grape % W:* SEM 70% SAUV B 25% MUSC 5% *second wine:* Ch Andoyse du Hayot *other châteaux owned:* Ch Guiteronde du Hayot *(Sauternes);* Ch de Peybayle *(Graves)*

33210 Fargues tel: 05 56 27 15 37
fax: 05 56 27 04 24

The wine is made at Ch Guiteronde; the grapes, however, come from the original Romer du Hayot vineyard, which lies beside the *autoroute*, and is surrounded on the other three sides by woods. As a rule the wine quite clearly does not reach *cru classé* level. Only in really great vintages does this Sauternes become anything more than a lightweight.

Below: Ch Raymond-Lafon

Below: Ch Rieussec

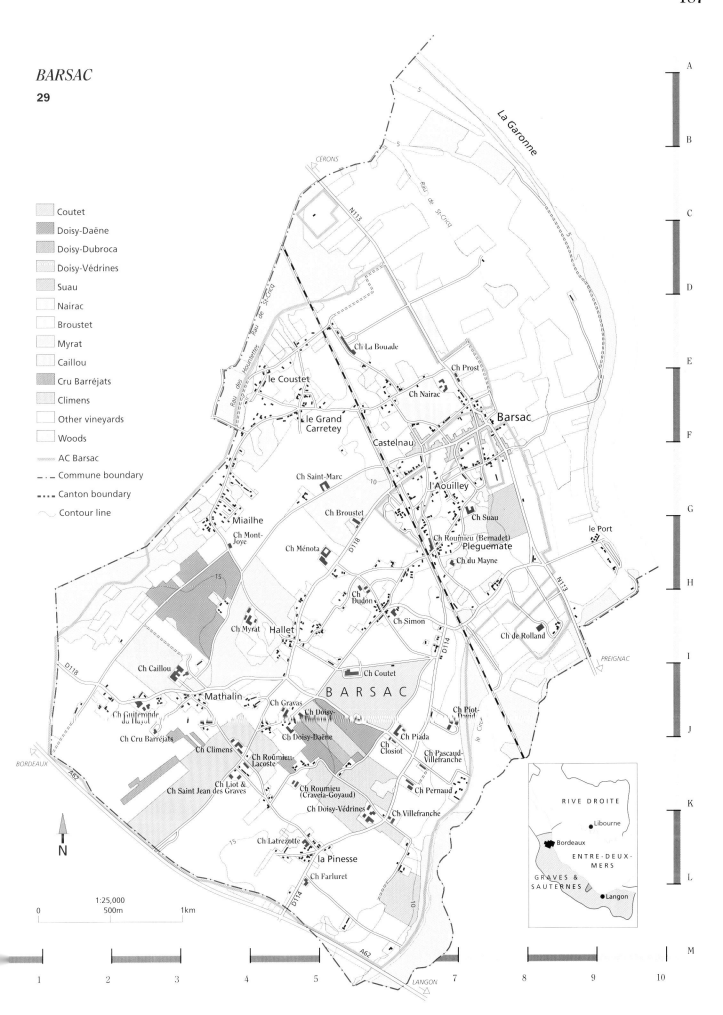

BARSAC
29

Coutet
Doisy-Daëne
Doisy-Dubroca
Doisy-Védrines
Suau
Nairac
Broustet
Myrat
Caillou
Cru Barréjats
Climens
Other vineyards
Woods

AC Barsac
Commune boundary
Canton boundary
Contour line

La Garonne

CÉRONS

N113

Rau de St-Crica

Rau des Hountettes

Rau de St-Crica

Ch La Bouade
Ch Prost
le Coustet
Ch Nairac
le Grand
Carretey
Barsac
Castelnau
Ch Saint-Marc
l'Aouilley
Ch Broustet
Miailhe
Ch Suau
Ch Mont-
Joye
Ch Roumieu (Bernadet)
Ch Ménota
Pleguemate
le Port
D118
Ch du Mayne
15
Ch Dudon
Ch Myrat
Hallet
Ch Simon
Ch de Rolland
D118
Ch Caillou
D114
Mathalin
Ch Coutet
B A R S A C
Ch Gravas
PREIGNAC
Ch Guiteronde
du Hayot
Ch Doisy-
Ch Piot-
David
Ch Cru Barréjats
Ch Doisy-Daëne
Ch Piada
le Crica
Ch Climens
Ch Closiot
Ch Roumieu-
Lacoste
Ch Pascaud-
Villefranche
Ch Liot &
Ch Saint Jean des Graves
Ch Roumieu
(Craveia-Goyaud)
Ch Pernaud
Ch Doisy-Védrines
Ch Villefranche
15
Ch Latrezotte
la Pinesse
Ch Farluret
10
D114
A62
LANGON

BORDEAUX

A62

1:25,000
0   500m   1km

N

RIVE DROITE
Libourne
Bordeaux
ENTRE-DEUX-
MERS
GRAVES &
SAUTERNES
Langon

Ch Roumieu
map 29

AC Sauternes

owner: Catherine Craveia-Goyaud *area:* 17 ha
cases: 3,500 *grape % W:* SEM 89% SAUV B 10%
MUSC 1%
33720 Barsac tel: 05 56 27 21 01
fax: 05 56 27 01 55
A traditionally-matured Barsac: after its
fermentation in cask there follows at least two,
and sometimes even three, years in wood. This
wine will usually age well. Mme Catherine
Craveia-Goyaud is the owner.

Ch Roumieu
map 29

AC Sauternes

owner: Olivier Bernadet *area:* 11 ha *cases:* 3,000
grape % W: SEM 80% MUSC 5% SAUV B 15%
other wines: Bordeaux blanc
33720 Barsac tel: 05 56 27 16 76
fax: 05 56 27 05 97
Exactly the same name as the above château –
but a different label, a different owner (Olivier
Bernadet), and a different wine. Its aroma is
often of candied fruit and raisins, with a hint of
fresh fruit and a touch of oak; the taste is
consistent with the nose. The vineyard has
rather more Sauvignon than the other Roumieu
and the wine spends less time – a year – in cask.

Ch Roûmieu-Lacoste
map 29 K4

AC Barsac

owner: Hervé Dubourdieu *area:* 12 ha *cases:* 2,000
grape % W: SEM 90% SAUV B 5% MUSC 5% *second
wine:* Ch Ducasse *other châteaux owned:* Ch
Graville Lacoste *(Graves)*
33720 Barsac tel: 05 56 27 16 29
fax: 05 56 27 02 65
A creamy, firm, and in richer years a sometimes
almost syrupy wine. Jammy tropical fruit
accompanies considerable oak notes. No great
finesse here, but certainly a sound wine. The
Dubourdieu family has been running this estate
since around 1900. From vines in nearby
Pujols-sur-Ciron the same team makes a
beautiful cask-fermented white Graves, sold as
Ch Graville-Lacoste or as Ch Les Fleurs de
Graville.

Ch Saint-Amand
map 27/L F2

AC Sauternes

owner: Anne-Mary Facchetti-Ricard *area:* 20 ha
cases: 4,800 *grape % W:* SEM 85% SAUV B 14%
MUSC 1% *second wine:* Ch de la Chartreuse *other
wines:* Ch Rocard *(Bordeaux Supérieur)*
33210 Preignac tel: 05 56 76 84 89
fax: 05 56 76 24 87
Wine estate close to the Ciron whose medieval
origins are shown by the remains of a chapel
dedicated to St Amand, patron saint of brewers.
The wine is a classic, reasonably rich Sauternes
with jammy fruit, plus slight floral and mineral
elements. Its quality has proved very consistent
down the years. The firm of Sichel sells the
same wine as Ch de la Chartreuse.

Ch Saint-Marc
map 29 G6

AC Barsac

owner: Didier Laulan *area:* 17 ha *cases:* 3,000
grape % W: SEM 85% SAUV B 12% MUSC 3% *second
wine:* Ch Bessan *other wines:* Le Lion de Saint
Marc *(Bordeaux blanc) other châteaux owned:* Ch
Broustet *(Sauternes)*
33720 Barsac tel: 05 56 27 16 87
fax: 05 56 27 05 93
Former hunting lodge that has belonged to four
generations of the Laulan family. The wine

produced here is at once elegant and powerful;
its bouquet has honeyed fruit and a dash of
spices. The grapes are selected – there are from
three to five separate pickings – and are then
fermented plot by plot. The standard wine may
rather lack richness and complexity, but the
Cuvée Spéciale – alas produced only rarely –
can be opulent in taste.

Ch St-Michel
map 29 I2

AC Sauternes

owner: Philippe Rivière *area:* 1.8 ha *cases:* 450
grape % W: SEM 80% SAUV B 20% *other châteaux
owned:* include Clos des Menuts *(St-Emilion)*
33720 Barsac tel: 05 57 55 59 59
fax: 05 57 55 59 51
Tiny property that produces an engaging
Sauternes, matured for a year in *barriques* of
which a third are new.

Ch Sigalas-Rabaud
map 27/L J10

1er cru; AC Sauternes

owner: Héritiers de la Marquise de Lambert des
Granges/Domaines Cordier *area:* 14 ha *cases:*
2,800 *grape % W:* SEM 98% SAUV B 2% *other
châteaux owned:* include Ch Lafaurie-Peyraguey
(Sauternes); Ch Clos des Jacobins *(St-Emilion)*
33210 Bommes tel: 05 56 76 60 54
fax: 05 56 76 61 89
That this once formed part of a much larger
estate is betrayed by the size of the cellar. This
was the original *chai* of Ch Rabaud, which was
divided into Chx Rabaud-Promis and Sigalas-
Rabaud in 1903. The wine does not perhaps
have the sumptuousness of some other
premiers crus, but does possess class, balance
and a fine blend of fruit (apricot, pear, coconut,
peach), honey and spices. Since the start of the
1994 harvest the estate has been managed by
Domaines Cordier, of Ch Lafaurie-Peyraguey –
resulting in even better quality. The wine now
ferments in casks of which one-third are new
each year.

Ch Simon
map 29 I7

AC Barsac

owner: Jean Hugues Dufour *area:* 40 ha *cases:* red
8,000, white 7,500 *grape % R:* MER 46% CS 38% CF
16% *grape % W:* SEM 90% SAUV B 7% MUSC 3%
second wine: Ch Piaut *other wines:* Ch Simon
(Graves) other wines: Domaine de la Riquette *(AC
Bordeaux)*

33720 Barsac tel: 05 56 27 15 35
fax: 05 56 27 24 79
In great years such as 1990, the Dufour family
makes an exquisite Sauternes, rich in *rôti*,
splendid in its bouquet (honey, sweet fruit of all
kinds), firm in its oak. The same class is not
achieved in ordinary years, but even then the
wine seldom disappoints. Sauternes is only one
of the wines made here, for 23 of the 40 ha yield
red and white Bordeaux, as well as red and
white Graves.

Ch Suau
map 29 G8

2ème cru; AC Barsac

owner: Roger Biarnès *area:* 8 ha *cases:* 1,580
grape % W: SEM 80% SAUV B 10% MUSC 10% *other
châteaux owned:* Ch de Navarro *(Graves)*; Ch du
Coy *(Sauternes)*
33210 Barsac tel: 05 56 27 20 27
fax: 05 56 27 26 53
This property owes its name to Elie de Suau,
adviser to Louis XIV. Since 1967 the modest
château itself has not formed part of the estate:
the wine is made at Ch de Navarro in Illats,
which has the same owner. Generally the wine
is a fairly lean Sauternes, somewhat lacking in
length, depth and concentration. There is the
potential here for better quality – which has

◆
Grape varieties

Main and other permitted varieties for each
appellation are given in the appellation fact
box at the end of the relevant introduction.
For châteaux, percentages of grapes grown
are given as supplied by the château.

Abbreviations: CF Cabernet Franc,
COL Colombard, CS Cabernet Sauvignon,
MAL Malbec, MER Merlot, MUSC Muscadelle,
PV Petit Verdot, SAUV B Sauvignon Blanc,
SÉM Sémillon
◆

Finding a château

To locate a château from its name alone,
use the index/gazetteer, which will provide
a page and a map reference.

Below: Ch Roumieu

Above: Ch Suduiraut

Above: Ch d'Yquem

been demonstrated in great years such as 1989 and '90, when the wine made striking gains in richness and dimension. At present half the *barriques* for maturing the wine (this lasts for about 18 months) are replaced each year.

Ch Suduiraut · map 27/L H9
1er cru; AC Sauternes
owner: AXA Millésimes *area:* 87 ha *cases:* 10,000 *grape % W:* SEM 80% SAUV B 20% *second wine:* Castelnau de Suduiraut *other châteaux owned:* include Ch Petit Village *(Pomerol)*; Ch Cantenac-Brown *(Margaux)*; Ch Pichon-Longueville *(Pauillac)*
33210 Preignac tel: 05 56 73 24 20
fax: 05 56 73 17 28

Only one wing of the original building remains: the château was destroyed in the 16th century by the Duc d'Epernon. It was the Suduiraut family who restored style to the estate; in the 17th and 18th centuries they built a new château, replanted the vineyard, and had a park laid out by Le Nôtre. Since 1992 the estate has belonged to the AXA insurance company (which made no wine in 1991, '92 or '93). The wine has a truly golden colour, an expansive bouquet of lush fruit, flowers, and toasted oak; in the taste there is plenty of power and alcohol and, again, ample honey-drenched fruit. It could well be that under AXA control the Suduiraut style will be further refined. The wine ferments in tanks and matures for 18-24 months in cask.

Ch La Tour Blanche · map 27/R L3
1er cru; AC Sauternes
owner: Ministère de l'Agriculture *area:* 34 ha *cases:* 6,250 *grape % W:* SEM 77% SAUV B 20% MUSC 3% *second wine:* Mademoiselle de St Marc *other wines:* Cru du Cinquet *(Bordeaux rouge)*; Osiris *(Bordeaux blanc)*; Isis *(Bordeaux blanc)*
33210 Bommes tel: 05 57 98 02 70
fax: 05 57 98 02 78

La Tour Blanche labels bear the words 'Donation Osiris', for in 1909 a Monsieur Osiris bequeathed the estate to the Institut Pasteur, on condition that an educational establishment should be set up here. This duly happened: one year later the Ecole de Viticulture et Oenologie opened its doors, and consequently the wine is

made here under the direction of the school. For quite a time the quality of this Sauternes did not correspond to its *premier cru* status; this changed with the arrival of a new director in 1983. Since then La Tour Blanche has been back at the top. The wine is characterized by its stylish opulence, with a great deal of exotic, almost syrupy fruit in its bouquet and its taste, a splendid *rôti* aroma, and ageing potential. It is fermented in new *barriques*, followed by 12-24 months in cask.

Ch Villefranche · map 29 L7
AC Sauternes
owner: Henri Guinabert *area:* 17 ha *cases:* 3,000 *grape % W:* SEM 85% MUSC 5% SAUV B 10% *second wine:* Ch Lapinesse *other wines:* Villefranche *(Graves)*; Domaine des Mingets *(Bordeaux rouge)*
33720 Barsac tel: 05 56 27 16 39
fax: 05 56 27 33 02

Very decent wine, with the elegance characteristic of Barsac. The Guinabert family has owned this château for around 350 years.

Ch d'Yquem · map 27/R I2 & 28
1er cru supérieur; AC Sauternes
owner: Comte Alexandre de Lur Saluces *area:* 113 ha *cases:* 7,920 *grape % W:* SEM 80% SAUV B 20% *other wines:* Y (Ygrec) *(AC Bordeaux blanc)* *other châteaux owned:* include Ch de Fargues
33210 Sauternes tel: 05 57 98 07 07
fax: 05 57 98 07 08

For generations now this château has represented the very summit of Sauternes. In the 1855 classification its wine was ranked above all others and awarded the honorary title *premier cru supérieur,* a status still justified today. The château, a partly 16th-, partly 17th-century structure with towers and a large inner courtyard, majestically surmounts the hill over which its vineyard spreads. This hill possesses its own microclimate, with in autumn a little more mist in the mornings, more warmth from the afternoon sun. For the grape harvest d'Yquem brings in a whole army of pickers, about 150 of them, who go through the vineyard from four to six times searching only for grapes affected by botrytis. After

fermentation – taking two to six weeks in new casks – the wine undergoes an extremely long ageing period in oak, usually three and a half years. In terms of pure class, style and luxury, the bottled wine is well-nigh perfect: a creation that allows description only in superlatives. You taste the very essence of the grape. A Dutch painter once described the colour of d'Yquem as 'Rembrandt's yellow, a colour whose secret we have lost'. And André Simon regarded this Sauternes as 'distilled dew and honey with the fragrance of all the fresh wild flowers of the field greeting the dawn'. For more than a quarter of a century Ch d'Yquem has been brilliantly directed by Comte Alexandre de Lur Saluces, whose family has owned the estate since 1785. In some years he also makes a dry wine full of character, the very costly 'Y'.

Between the
Rivers and the Wider
Appellations

Entre-Deux-Mers is the convenient middle slice of Bordeaux, between the Médoc and Graves and the Right Bank. But the wider appellations of Bordeaux make the pattern less tidy than it looks on the map. All of the Gironde *vignoble* is entitled to make wine using the generic Bordeaux and Bordeaux Supérieur ACs; much of this generic wine is however made in the geographic area of the Entre-Deux-Mers. There is a further concentration north and west of St-Emilion, and another east of Graves, where (along with low-lying riverside land in Médoc and Graves – even islands in the Gironde) these are the only ACs. The Atlas covers all Bordeaux and Bordeaux Supérieur wines in this section, as well as those of the very varied appellations specific to the lands that lie in the angle between the Garonne and Dordogne rivers.

The landscapes of the Entre-Deux-Mers districts captivate with their rural charm. Unlike the Médoc or Pomerol, here woods and meadows punctuate the vineyards.

Between the Rivers

The land north of the Garonne and south of the Dordogne is today something of an understated quiet passage in the Bordeaux symphony. The noisy stars of the Médoc, Graves and the Libournais drown out its gentler music.

It was not always so: at various times in Bordeaux's long history these vineyards have held a higher place. The Premières Côtes, especially those villages close to the city, were a valued source of red wines in medieval days. The Archbishops of Bordeaux held vineyards there, as did the Kings of England. The *liquoreux* wines from the slopes further south – Cadillac, Loupiac, Ste-Croix-du-Mont – were 19th-century rivals of Sauternes. However, during the first half of the 20th century too many undistinguished wines lowered the reputation of the whole area. The last three decades have seen a revival of some of the more specific appellations, with the sweet whites rescued from virtual extinction and the reds of the Premières Côtes finding new markets as Bordeaux's grander ACs increased their prices. The heart of the area, that pretty landscape of deep valleys and woods, is now yielding much-improved dry white wines instead of dull semi-sweet ones.

A pattern of landscapes and appellations

The western edge of the region is lined with hills – in some places riverside cliffs – from which there are splendid views across the flat Graves beyond the Garonne. This is the Premières Côtes de Bordeaux AC, which has provided fine sites for both vineyards and country homes for many centuries. The southern half of this belt of hills has long specialized in sweet white wines, and today has the appellations of Cadillac, Loupiac and Ste-Croix-du-Mont. To the north and north-east spreads the heart of the Entre-Deux-Mers appellation, a land of hills and woods rolling on to the Dordogne. Vines are a part of this landscape, but not dominant.

Entre-Deux-Mers and other wines

The name Entre-Deux-Mers applies both to the whole area – from river to river – and to an appellation. The appellation covers a large part – but by no means all – of this area. What is more, it is for dry white wine only. Inevitably, confusion occurs: many winelovers identify the entire area as a dry white zone and no more.

In truth, the Entre-Deux-Mers AC is just one appellation among many in this area, which also boasts specific ones for dry, semi-sweet and sweet whites as well as reds. The Premières Côtes de Bordeaux covers both red and semi-sweet white wines, whereas the Côtes de Bordeaux St-Macaire appellation is for semi-sweet white only. Red wines, as well as dry whites, can be produced in the gravelly vineyards of the Graves de Vayres, while Ste-Foy Bordeaux makes red, dry and semi-sweet whites. In a large tract in the west, overlapping ACs make it possible for a château to use, say, the appellation Cadillac for its sweet white wine, Premières Côtes for semi-sweet white and red, and Bordeaux Blanc Sec for dry white – which brings us to what might be called the AC Bordeaux factor.

Bordeaux and Bordeaux Supérieur

While the wine geography of the Entre-Deux-Mers region is made complex by the many ACs, it is made positively confusing by the Bordeaux appellation. This AC is the base of the Bordeaux pyramid, and it extends across most of the Gironde *département*. In the AC Entre-Deux-Mers, all red wines made (and there are many) must be called Bordeaux or Bordeaux Supérieur. Reds made in the sweet white districts of Ste-Croix-du-Mont and Loupiac also carry the generic appellations. In fact, between the rivers there is vastly more red Bordeaux and Bordeaux Supérieur produced than white Entre-Deux-Mers. However, there is nothing on the label to show where in the Gironde an AC Bordeaux or Bordeaux Supérieur comes from – except the name of the château and, in its address in the small print, the commune. Many of the châteaux that make these wines – wherever they are – also make wines under other appellations.

In the Atlas, therefore, to avoid duplication, the two main chapters in this Between the Rivers section together cover the generic appellations as well: the Premières Côtes and Cadillac chapter which follows covers Bordeaux and Bordeaux Supérieur AC wines made within its boundaries, while the Entre-Deux-Mers, appellations Bordeaux and Bordeaux Supérieur chapter includes hundreds of other châteaux which use these generic Bordeaux appellations, be they in the Entre-Deux-Mers area or outside it (this chapter, too, covers ACs Côtes-de-Bordeaux St-Macaire, Ste-Foy Bordeaux and Graves de Vayres.

To help identify where a wine comes from, three maps (nos 34, 35, 36) show the Entre-Deux-Mers and the major Bordeaux AC districts, with communes and appellation boundaries. From the communes, which are listed beside the maps, one can discover whereabouts the wine is made. Every château in the A-Z directories has its commune named in the address.

ENTRE-DEUX-MERS
30

31   Premières Côtes de Bordeaux &
        Cadillac; Loupiac & Ste-Croix-du-Mont
32/33 Premières Côtes de Bordeaux & Cadillac
35   Entre-Deux-Mers, Graves de Vayres,
        Entre-Deux-Mers Haut-Benauge,
        Bordeaux Haut-Benauge, Bordeaux,
        Bordeaux Supérieur
36   Entre-Deux-Mers, Ste-Foy Bordeaux,
        Côtes de Bordeaux St-Macaire,
        Bordeaux, Bordeaux Supérieur

Premières Côtes de Bordeaux; Cadillac; ac Bordeaux

Within the vast sweep of the Entre-Deux-Mers region lies the extensive appellation of the Premières Côtes de Bordeaux which, in turn, holds two enclaves, Loupiac and Ste-Croix-du-Mont, and the overlying AC of Cadillac. Loupiac and Ste-Croix-du-Mont are dealt with in the next chapter; here we are concerned with the Premières Côtes de Bordeaux and Cadillac.

The Premières Côtes is a narrow, elongated strip of land, quite hilly, clinging to the river Garonne's northern bank and running beside the A10/D10 roads. From just beyond Carbon-Blanc in the north-west (an unattractive industrial zone off the A10 on the outskirts of the

The old castle of Langoiran looms above the vineyards

city of Bordeaux), it stretches for some 60 kilometres in a south-easterly direction, ending near the bridge that crosses the Garonne to the town of Langon. Should you continue further east along the N113, you will arrive in the appellation of Côtes de Bordeaux St-Macaire. Rarely does the narrow band of the Premières Côtes extend more than five kilometres inland, where it is bordered by the vast Entre-Deux-Mers appellation (and its enclave, Haut-Benauge).

This is some of the most attractive and diverse countryside in the whole of the Entre-Deux-Mers – indeed, in all of the wider Bordeaux region. It becomes increasingly so the further south you go, away from the outskirts of Bordeaux, into rolling hills and deep little valleys – a delightful contrast to the unremitting, fairly flat landscape of the Graves or Médoc. Many have been seduced by this area – François Mauriac and Toulouse-Lautrec were just two who took up residence here – and the countryside is dotted with appealing villages complete with ancient churches, as well as fortified towns like Cadillac (whose showpiece château boasts some magnificently ornate fireplaces) and Rions.

Some of the better vineyards are located just east of the D10, where slopes and cliffs rise sharply away from the road. Vineyards here are set on the hillsides, and stretch up onto the plateau above. The soil is mainly chalky, providing good natural drainage, and is sometimes mixed with clay. Many of the vineyards enjoy a south-easterly exposure, which allows the vines to reach maximum ripeness in a good year.

As with some of the other appellations of the Entre-Deux-Mers, the Premières Côtes has had a somewhat chequered winemaking history. The vineyard achieved fame in medieval times but in the first half of the 20th century the area was known primarily for the production of rather unpleasant semi-sweet white wines which offered little competition to those of neighbouring Loupiac or Ste-Croix-du-Mont – never mind Sauternes. However, the notorious spring frost of 1956 hit this area very badly: many of the vines were killed off and had to be uprooted. But thanks to the foresight of a few leading producers, when the vineyards came to be replanted it was with red, rather than white, varieties. For several years thereafter, the Premières Côtes de Bordeaux became known as a producer of relatively inexpensive red wines – but using the generic Bordeaux or Bordeaux Supérieur AC, rather than the one specific to the area. It is only in the last 20 years or so that the area has re-established its individuality and that the Premières Côtes de Bordeaux appellation has once again been widely used by producers.

It is these red wines of the Premières Côtes de Bordeaux that have really gained the area its recent reputation, and which are produced in far larger quantites – roughly five times as much red as semi-sweet white. The reds can be very good, and certain producers also make special *cuvées*, which have benefited from some contact with new oak. Although red Premières Côtes are made throughout the appellation, production is concentrated in the north-western section, closer to Bordeaux. The most favoured variety is Merlot, followed by Cabernet Sauvignon, and the combination of *terroir* and grape varieties produces wines which have lively fruit, are quite round and supple, with soft, ripe tannins, but which also have some backbone and will age well – especially the special *cuvées* from the appellation's leading producers. At their best, these wines can be very elegant, with a certain finesse.

The Premières Côtes possesses two cooperatives, one at Langoiran and the other at Quinsac – the commune of Quinsac in particular is known as the Clairet capital of Bordeaux.

Today vineyards in the Premières Côtes cover a total area of some 12,300 hectares, spread across 37 communes. However, around a quarter of this land continues to produce wines under the various generic Bordeaux appellations (as elsewhere in the Entre-Deux-Mers, an individual producer may make as many as ten wines or more – most, for example, make a dry white AC Bordeaux – and the Premières Côtes de Bordeaux has something of a reputation for its Bordeaux Rosé and Bordeaux Clairet). Of the remaining vineyard land, almost 3,000 hectares are given over to Premières Côtes de Bordeaux red and 700-odd hectares are devoted to the production of semi-sweet and sweet white wines, mainly under the Premières Côtes appellation, and, to a much lesser extent, Cadillac.

CADILLAC

Cadillac is an appellation created in 1973 solely for the production of sweet white wines, mainly from Sémillon but with some Sauvignon and a little Muscadelle. In the southern half of the Premières Côtes, between Baurech and Saint-Maixant, lie 22 communes which were deemed to be particularly well-suited to sweet white wine production and were given this more restricted appellation. As the maps show, this section lies very close to the Garonne river whose proximity aids the development of *pourriture noble*. Noble rot is a legal requirement in the production of this wine (it is actually written into the AC rules), but of course it cannot always be relied upon. This may in part explain why so little Cadillac is produced today – roughly 250 hectares are registered – as most producers prefer to make a semi-sweet white wine under the more general Premières Côtes de Bordeaux appellation, plus one or more of the many other ACs permitted in this area. However, a good Cadillac (of which there are only a few) can resemble a Loupiac or Ste-Croix-du-Mont, though it will often be slightly lighter in style, with less of the influence of noble rot. Only a Cadillac from an exceptional year should be kept for any length of time.

THE APPELLATIONS

PREMIÈRES CÔTES DE BORDEAUX
(red and semi-sweet white)
CADILLAC *(sweet white)*

Location: *Right bank of the Garonne. Cadillac covers 22 communes within the Premières Côtes area.*
Area of ACs: *12,303 ha*
Area under vine: *3,320 ha; Cadillac 250 ha*
Communes: *(22 Cadillac communes indicated *)Bassens, Baurech*, Béguey*, Bouliac, Cadillac*, Cambes, Camblanes, Capian*, Carbon-Blanc, Cardan*, Carignan, Cénac, Cenon, Donzac*, Floirac, Gabarnac*, Haux*, Langoiran*, Laroque*, Latresne, Lestiac*, Lormont, Monprimblanc*, Omet*, Paillet*, Quinsac, Rions*,*

St-Caprais-de-Bordeaux, Ste-Eulalie, St-Germain-de-Graves*, St-Maixant*, Semens*, Tabanac*, Le Tourne*, Verdelais*, Villenave-de-Rions*, Yvrac
Average annual production: *2,000,000 cases (83% red; 17% white); Cadillac: 60,000 cases*
Producers: *300; Cadillac 50*
Cooperatives: *2 (c. 105 members); Cadillac 1 (c. 40 members)*
Main grape varieties: *Red: Merlot. White: Sémillon.*
Others: *Red: Cabernet Sauvignon, Cabernet Franc, Malbec. White: Sauvignon, Muscadelle.*
Main soil types: *Gravel on the plateaux, clay-limestone on the slopes and fine silicious gravel at the base of the scarp.*

Appellations Premières Côtes de Bordeaux; Cadillac; AC Bordeaux

Ch Anniche
map 32/R G6

owner: SCEA Vignobles Michel Pion **area:** 56 ha
cases: 29,000, white 8,500 **grape % R:** cs 40%
mer 30% cf 20% mal 10% **grape % W:** sem 70%
sauv b 20% musc 10% **other wines:** Ch Haut-
Roquefort *(Cadillac)*, Bordeaux blanc; Ch Lalande
Méric *(Bordeaux rosé)*
33550 Haux tel: 05 56 23 05 15
fax: 05 56 23 35 64
Nearly half this vineyard, 24 ha, produces
Premières Côtes de Bordeaux. This wine, not
matured in cask, comes across with pleasing
fruitiness – blackcurrant, cherry – and with
dark notes as well, including cocoa. From 5 ha
planted with around 80% Sémillon and 20%
Sauvignon comes a slightly sweet, fresh and
somewhat spicy Cadillac called Ch Haut-
Roquefort. Other wines from this estate are a
red AC Bordeaux (from 15 ha) and dry white AC
Bordeaux (9 ha), both sold as Ch Anniche; and
an agreeable Bordeaux rosé (9 ha) which is
made solely from Cabernet Sauvignon and bears
the name Ch Lalande Méric.

Ch Balot
map 31/R K2

owner: Yvan Réglat **area:** 49 ha **cases:** 14,400,
white 11,000 **grape % R:** mer 60% cs 20% cf 20%
grape % W: sem 80% sauv b 20% **second wines:**
Clos Terrefort *(Bordeaux Supérieur)*; Ch Beau Site
Monprimblanc **other wines:** Bordeaux blanc;
Cadillac **other châteaux owned:** Cru Champon
(Loupiac)
33410 Monprimblanc tel: 05 56 62 98 96
fax: 05 56 62 19 48
There are two red Premières Côtes wines here:
a standard and a barrel-aged version. The first is
usually nicely fruity and meant for quick
consumption; the *cuvée bois* has rather more
tannin and intensity, and so demands some
years' patience. A decent Loupiac and a Cadillac
are also made at this estate, as well as a red
Bordeaux Supérieur.

Ch Barreyre
map 32/R H8

owner: SCA F.L. Gilles Fabères & J.L. Laffort **area:**
12.3 ha **cases:** 6,800 **grape % R:** mer 52% cs 24%
cf 24% **second wine:** Ch Saint-Romans **other wines:**
Bordeaux Clairet **other châteaux owned:** Ch Tour
Saint Fort *(St-Estèphe)*
33550 Langoiran tel: 05 56 67 02 03
fax: 05 56 67 59 07
Both inside and out, the *chai* where the Cuvée
Spéciale matures in cask is one of the most
beautiful in the region: modern art is regularly
exhibited here. In good years this wine is
fragrant, supple and rounded, with aromatic
elements of spices, fruit (berries, prune) and
oak, including vanilla. The standard wine, of
lighter structure, is also fruity and agreeable.
Barreyre also makes a salmon-coloured
Bordeaux Clairet, which° tastes brisk and
refreshing.

Domaine de Bavolier
map 32/L J6

owner: Pierre & Geneviève Lambert **area:** 30 ha
cases: 1,200 **grape % R:** mer 60% cf 20% cs 19%
mal 1% **other wines:** Clos Maugey *(Bordeaux rosé)*
33360 Camblanes-et-Meynac tel: 05 56 20 76 72
fax: 05 56 20 17 37
The red Premières Côtes tends to have a slightly
herbaceous taste, with some rather harsh
tannin as well, but this is a wine which displays
more charm when drunk with food. No oak is
used for this wine.

Above: Ch Barreyre

Right: Ch de Birot

Clos Bellevue
map 31/R I2

owner: Patrick Gillet **area:** 10 ha **cases:** 5,000
grape % R: mer 70% cs 30% **other châteaux owned:**
Ch Le Tarey *(Loupiac)*; Cru du Pin Copies *(Ste-Croix-
du-Mont)*
33410 Loupiac tel: 05 56 62 99 99
fax: 05 56 62 65 33
Of the various wines – including a Loupiac –
that this grower produces, the red Premières
Côtes is the most interesting, with its jammy
red fruit in a supple setting.

Ch la Bertrande
map 31/R G2

owner: Anne-Marie Gillet **area:** 20 ha **cases:** 7,300,
white 8,200 **grape % R:** mer 50% cf 26% mal 24%
grape % W: sem 76% sauv b 24% **second wine:** Ch
du Biscarets **other wines:** Cadillac; AC Bordeaux;
Chevalier de Reignac *(Bordeaux rosé)*
33410 Omet tel: 05 56 62 19 64
fax: 05 56 76 90 55
This property, in existence for about 200 years,
is set on one of the highest points in the
département. The château is a low white
building, pinnacled turrets at either end, with
an entrance shaded by two centuries-old cedars.
Six different appellations are represented in its
range of wines, which includes a red Premières
Côtes – a very decent, reasonably concentrated
one – and a Cadillac. When nature has helped

◆
Grape varieties

Main and other permitted varieties for each
appellation are given in the appellation fact
box at the end of the relevant introduction.
For châteaux, percentages of grapes grown
are given as supplied by the château.

Abbreviations: cf Cabernet Franc,
col Colombard, cs Cabernet Sauvignon,
mal Malbec, mer Merlot, musc Muscadelle,
pv Petit Verdot, sauv b Sauvignon Blanc,
sém Sémillon

with some *pourriture noble*, this is a delicious
wine giving impressions of candied fruit,
tropical fruit and raisins. It has great ageing
potential.

Ch du Biac
map 32/R K6

owner: Paul-Louis Ducatez **area:** 10.2 ha **cases:**
3,750, white 2,000 **grape % R:** mer 50% cs 25% cf
25% **grape % W:** sem 90% sauv b 10% **other wines:**
Bordeaux blanc
33550 Langoiran tel: 05 56 67 19 98
Impeccably maintained estate producing a
somewhat rustic red wine, not without its
merits. Its bouquet often has something of
thyme in particular, plus bayleaves and a hint of
vanilla. A semi-sweet white Premières Côtes is
also made, and a dry white AC Bordeaux.

Ch de Birot
map 31/L J8

owner: Fournier-Castéja **area:** 23 ha **cases:** 5,000,
white 2,800 **grape % R:** mer 50% cs 25% cf 25%
grape % W: sem 58% sauv b 35% musc 7% **other
wines:** Bordeaux blanc
33410 Béguey tel: 05 56 52 29 70
fax: 05 57 24 68 00
This is an alluring château, a beautiful building
from the second half of the 18th century, set on
a hill. Since 1989 it has belonged to Eric

Fournier and his wife, *née* Castéja. The Premières Côtes red is generally an opaque wine; firm, with plenty of substance, spicy oak and a good undertone of fruit – blackberry, blackcurrant. It is matured for 6-12 months in cask. Besides this red there is a dry white AC Bordeaux: a serious wine, reminiscent of a Graves, and briefly aged in barrels.

Clos Bourbon
map 31/R I4

owner: Michel Boyer **area:** 14 ha **cases:** 5,500, white 700 **grape % R:** MER 60% CF 30% CS 10% **grape % W:** SEM 50% SAUV B 25% MUSC 25% **second wine:** Galop d'Essai du Clos Bourbon **other châteaux owned:** Ch du Cros (*Loupiac*); Ch Haut-Mayno (*Graves*); Ch de Lucquot (*Graves*)
33550 Paillet tel: 05 56 72 11 58
fax: 05 56 62 12 59

In 1994 this estate was acquired by Michel Boyer (of Ch du Cros in Loupiac), who then entrusted the running of it to his daughter Catherine and son-in-law Thibaut d'Halluin. Their red Premières Côtes is a well-structured wine with a seductive aroma that holds both fruity and floral elements. It goes into casks to mature for a year. More than half of the production is made up of Galop d'Essai du Clos Bourbon, the attractive second wine.

Domaine de Bouteilley
map 32/R D7

owner: Jean Guillot **area:** 30 ha **cases:** 20,000 **grape % R:** MER 50% CF 35% CS 15% **second wine:** Ch Peyrarey (*AC Bordeaux*) **other châteaux owned:** Ch Cap de Fer (*Bordeaux Supérieur*); Ch Grand Jour (*Premières Côtes de Bordeaux*); Ch Maillard (*AC Bordeaux*)
33370 Yvrac tel: 05 56 06 68 42
fax: 05 56 31 62 90

The same family has been making wine here since the beginning of the 17th century, although not in the same way: today's *cuvier* is ultra-modern. Attractive red wine, fairly elegant, with both dark and fruity elements. It develops more power and body in sunny years.

Ch Brethous
map 32/L I5

owner: François & Denise Verdier **area:** 13.5 ha **cases:** 4,600 **grape % R:** MER 50% CF 25% CS 15% MAL 10% **other wines:** Bordeaux Clairet
33360 Camblanes-et-Meynac tel: 05 56 20 77 75
fax: 05 56 20 08 45

Charming property with a small 18th-century *chartreuse* and a vaulted *chai*. There is also a beautiful view from here. About a fifth of the vintage is given 10 months' oak in one-third new barrels. The resultant Cuvée Prestige is a mouthfilling Premières Côtes, with creaminess,

tannin and rich fruit (plum, fig, candied cherries). The sometimes slightly bitter standard wine tastes a little bit drier and less fruity. There is a fresh, clean Bordeaux Clairet.

Ch du Broustaret
map 31/L G9

owner: SCEA Guillot de Suduiraut **area:** 6.5 ha **cases:** 2,900 **grape % R:** CS 60% MER 28% CF 12% **second wine:** Domaine de la Grèche **other wines:** Bordeaux Clairet
33410 Rions tel: 05 56 76 93 15
fax: 05 56 76 93 73

Winegrowing is not the only activity on this estate. Cattle are grazed, corn is grown and rooms are let. Since 1994 the wine has been fermented in a new *cuverie* with stainless steel tanks. The red wine is fairly fleshy and also has fruit – but sometimes, in its early youth, tough tannins too. However, these disappear gradually as it matures in cask, and after a couple of years in bottle. Worth following.

Ch de Caillavet
map 31/L E4

owner: Maaf Assurances **area:** 65 ha **cases:** 30,000, white 8,500 **grape % R:** CS 55% MER 44% CF 1% **grape % W:** SEM 62% SAUV B 38% **second wine:** Ch Haut-Morin **other wines:** AC Bordeaux; Crémant de Bordeaux
33550 Capian tel: 05 56 72 30 02
fax: 05 56 72 13 23

Extensive vineyard that is the birthplace of half a dozen different wines, among them a Crémant de Bordeaux. From the best plots and the oldest vines there comes a quite full-bodied, powerful wine with a good length. In it the Cabernet Sauvignon can be clearly discerned (berry fruits and paprika), plus spiciness and smooth vanilla. A bust of Anatole France by Antoine Bourdelle stands in the château courtyard.

Ch Camail
map 32/R J3

owner: François Masson Regnault **area:** 9 ha **cases:** 4,000, white 1,050 **grape % R:** MER 75% CS 15% CF 10% **grape % W:** SEM 75% SAUV B 15% MUSC 10% **second wine:** Ch Lalande Camail **other wines:** Cadillac; Bordeaux blanc; Bordeaux rosé; Crémant de Bordeaux **other châteaux owned:** Ch de Pic (*Premières Côtes de Bordeaux*)
33550 Tabanac tel: 05 56 67 07 51
fax: 05 56 67 21 22

Estate on the Tabanac plateau that was acquired by François Masson Regnault of Ch de Pic. Despite the rather modest acreage, five different wines are made at Ch Camail: the most interesting is the red Premières Côtes, a fragrant, lively wine with colour and power. Also worth discovering are the Cadillac and the dry white AC Bordeaux (barrel-fermented in new oak), as well as the limited quantity of Crémant de Bordeaux.

Ch Canteloup
map 32/L 54

owner: GAEC Vignobles Latorse **area:** 17 ha **cases:** 11,000 **grape % R:** MER 60% CF 20% CS 20% **other wines:** Cuvée Spéciale (*AC Bordeaux*) **other châteaux owned:** Clos Saint Vincent (*St Emilion*); Vieux Château Lamothe (*AC Bordeaux*); Ch Gabaron (*AC Bordeaux*); Ch Haut-Riot (*AC Bordeaux*)
33880 St-Caprais-de-Bordeaux tel: 05 56 23 92 76
fax: 05 56 23 61 65

Vignobles Latorse has the little town of La Sauve as its headquarters, but its 150 ha of estates are distributed over various districts, as far away as St-Emilion. A star of its portfolio of wines is the red Cuvée Prestige from Ch Canteloup, Premières Côtes. This has ample oak, with 18 months in new *barriques*, and also considerable fruit – cherry, plum, blackberry.

Ch Carignan
map 32/L E4

owner: GFA Philippe Pieraerts **area:** 43 ha **cases:** 28,000 **grape % R:** MER 52% CS 30% CF 18% **second wine:** Ch Léon
33360 Carignan-de-Bordeaux tel: 05 56 21 21 30
fax: 05 56 78 36 65

Carignan's large, devotedly maintained castle was built by one of Joan of Arc's comrades, the Sire de Xaintrailles, in the 15th century. A generous, well-structured red wine here; with spicy, curranty fruit and earthy, dark notes. Also a hint of oak, from 15-18 months in casks of which one-third are new. Has the alcohol and backbone to develop in bottle.

Ch Carsin
map 31/L H7

owner: Juha Berglund **area:** 40 ha **cases:** 5,000, white 14,500 **grape % R:** MER 50% CF 30% CS 20% **grape % W:** SEM 65% SAUV B 25% SAUV GRIS 10% **second wine:** Domaine de l'Esclade **other wines:** Bordeaux blanc

Below: Ch de Caillavet

33410 Rions tel: 05 56 76 93 06
fax: 05 56 62 64 80
Juha Berglund, a Finn, bought Ch Carsin in 1990, and just before the 1991 harvest a whole new cellar installation was imported from Australia. The first vintages were also supervised by an Australian winemaker: the New World has descended on the Premières Côtes de Bordeaux. The red wine is of remarkably good quality, even in the poorer years. It possesses fruit, oak – from a year in cask – and some depth and balance. The white AC Bordeaux wines are at least as notable: the standard version offers vibrant fresh fruit and very discreet oak after three months in barrel; and in the Cuvée Prestige the sumptuous fruit keeps balanced company with toasted oak, from fermentation in cask, followed by 6-8 months' maturing. Also worth discovering is the delicious semi-sweet white Premières Côtes, in which oak and fruit are beautifully combined.

Ch Cayla — map 31/L H7
owner: Patrick Doche **area:** 20 ha **cases:** 11,500, white 1,500 **grape % R:** MER 50% CS 35% CF 15% **grape % W:** SEM 100% **other wines:** Bordeaux blanc; Cadillac
33410 Rions tel: 05 56 62 15 40
fax: 05 56 62 16 45
In the red Premières Côtes a suggestion of jammy soft fruits can be made out, and in the generous white there are aspects of peach as well as flowers. This white wine comes from very old Sémillon vines. The château is of 16th- and 17th-century origins.

Domaine de Chastelet — map 32/L J7
owner: Pierre Estansan & Albert Barrachina **area:** 8.1 ha **cases:** 2,250 **grape % R:** MER 45% CF 25% CS 25% MAL 3% PV 2% **other wines:** Bordeaux Clairet
33360 Quinsac tel: 05 56 72 61 96
fax: 05 56 72 45 63
Estate tucked away in a little hidden valley. Chastelet was an early exponent of cask-ageing, for the father and grandfather of one of the present owners were coopers. Besides oak, the red Premières Côtes contains elements of ripe fruit, tobacco and chocolate; because of its tannin the wine generally benefits from a few years' bottle-age.

Clos Chaumont — map 32/R G5
owner: Pieter & Dorien Verbeek **area:** 8 ha **cases:** 2,300, white 1,600 **grape % R:** MER 60% CS 30% CF 5% MAL 5% **grape % W:** SEM 70% SAUV B 25% MUSC 5% **second wine:** Collin du Pin (Bordeaux blanc; Bordeaux Supérieur; Bordeaux rosé **other wines:** Cadillac; Bordeaux blanc
33550 Haux tel: 05 56 23 37 23
fax: 05 56 23 30 54
Estate bought by the Dutch timber merchant Pieter Verbeek in 1990, then thoroughly overhauled and renovated. The first wine was

Maps of the area
The Premières Côtes de Bordeaux and Cadillac appellations are covered by Maps 31 and 32. Map 31 also covers the enclaves of Ste-Croix-de-Mont and Loupiac. To locate these areas in their wider setting see map 30, which shows the zone between the rivers Garonne and Dordogne.

Above: Ch La Chèze

produced in 1993. The vineyard, which is to be increased to 14 ha, yields six different wines. The fine red Premières Côtes de Bordeaux, supported by good oak from the 30-50% of new casks, is the only one with this appellation. The white Clos Chaumont, fermented in *barriques* (some of them new), is characterized by spicy oak and citrus fruit, and is marketed in two styles: as a dry Bordeaux, and as a sweet Cadillac – with just 500 bottles a year of the latter. Worth following.

Ch de Chelivette — map 32/R C6
owner: Jean-Louis Boulière **area:** 10 ha **cases:** 5,500 **grape % R:** MER 55% CS 30% CF 15% **second wine:** Ch du Colombier (Bordeaux Supérieur); Cru du Manoir **other wines:** Bordeaux Supérieur, Bordeaux blanc
33560 Ste-Eulalie tel: 05 56 06 11 79
fax: 05 56 38 01 97
A 16th century wine estate, with a château, a chapel and a very fine dovecote tower from that period. An old telegraph tower of 1791 also stands in the grounds. An excellent red Premières Côtes de Bordeaux is made here, a wine with delightful nuances (fruit, cedarwood, bayleaves), power and finesse. Since 1988 the owner, Jean-Louis Boulière, has been allowing this wine to mature for a year in barrels of which half are new.

Ch La Chèze — map 31/L D3
owner: Claire & Jean-Pierre Sancier **area:** 8.3 ha **cases:** 3,000, white 400 **grape % R:** MER 45% CS 37% CF 18% **grape % W:** SAUV B 100% **other wine:** Bordeaux blanc
33550 Capian tel: 05 56 72 30 63
fax: 05 56 72 11 77
The *maison noble* of La Chèze was built in the 16th century by a gentleman of that name, and it is the oldest house in the commune of Capian. Since 1986 Ch La Chèze has been reborn as a wine estate, thanks to the engineer Jean-Pierre Sancier and his wife Claire, a mathematics professor, who have planted a vineyard here once more. They make a lively, fresh, likeable red Premières Côtes de Bordeaux, and a rather stronger Cuvée Réservée which requires more time: up to 12 months' maturing in casks of which one in six is new. Another wine produced is a dry white AC Bordeaux, entirely from Sauvignon Blanc.

Ch Cluzel — map 32/L F1
owner: Famille Rechenmann **area:** 9 ha **cases:** 3,750 **grape % R:** MER 60% CS 30% CF 7% MAL 3% **second wine:** Les Hauts de Cluzel
33270 Bouliac tel: 05 56 20 52 12
fax: 05 56 20 59 13
Cluzel generally yields a quite full-bodied, powerful wine, with firm tannins and not a lot of fruit. In the 15th century this estate belonged to the archbishop of Bordeaux, but the two wings that are the oldest parts of the present château date from the 16th.

Ch la Clyde — map 32/R K4
owner: Philippe Cathala **area:** 16 ha **cases:** 5,000, white 1,500 **grape % R:** MER 60% CS 22% CF 15% MAL 3% **grape % W:** SAUV B 50% SEM 50% **second wine:** Ch Tour-Camail **other wines:** Bordeaux rosé; Bordeaux blanc; Bordeaux rouge **other châteaux owned:** Ch Capon (Premières Côtes de Bordeaux)
33550 Tabanac tel: 05 56 67 56 84
fax: 05 56 67 12 06
The red wines from this property are more striking than its grey château. They are rich in colour, juicy, quite lively, elegantly clean and firm. The Cuvée Garde de la Clyde undergoes a year and a half of oak-ageing, and has rather more concentration than the straightforward Premières Côtes. There is also a white *moelleux*, which is only better than correct in warm years. Dry white and rosé AC Bordeaux are two other, usually likeable, creations.

Ch La Croix-Bouey — map 31/R L8
owner: Maxime Bouey **area:** 16 ha **cases:** 8,100, white 1,300 **grape % R:** MER 50% CS 50% **grape % W:** SEM 80% SAUV B 10% MUSC 10% **other wines:** Premières Côtes de Bordeaux; Bordeaux blanc; Bordeaux rosé; Bordeaux rouge
33490 St-Maixant tel: 05 56 76 87 75
fax: 05 56 72 62 29
Property on a sloping site, close to the Verdelais roadside cross. It has modern equipment and its grape-picking is mechanized. It yields mainly red wine. A small part of this comprises a fairly moderate Premières Côtes, which is spicy and sometimes slightly peppery, with licorice, and now and again a touch of herbaceousness. The white version can taste slightly of honey, with opulent ripe fruit and a firm structure.

Ch Dudon — map 32/R K1
owner: Jean Merlaut **area:** 24.4 ha **cases:** 8,000, white 900 **grape % R:** MER 40% CF 30% CS 30% **grape % W:** SEM 80% SAUV B 20% **second wine:** Remparts de Dudon (Bordeaux) **other wine:** Bordeaux blanc
33880 Baurech tel: 05 56 21 31 51
fax: 05 56 21 33 95
It was Jean-Baptiste Dudon, the royalist attorney at the Bordeaux *parlement*, who built the present *chartreuse* here. Earlier a castle had stood on this same site, so the red Cuvée Jean-Baptiste Dudon matures for a year in a 16th-century cellar. A third of the barrels are new. The wine offers colour, body, berry fruit and length, without being particularly expressive. Other wines from this estate are also worth dfiscovering; a number have won medals.

Ch Duplessy — map 32/L H5
owner: Robert Briguet-Lamarre **area:** 11 ha **cases:** 5,000 **grape % R:** MER 50% CS 25% CF 20% MAL 3% PV 2% **second wine:** Chevalier de Lamalétie
33360 Cénac tel: 05 56 48 06 06
fax: 05 56 51 95 32

Members of the Duplessy family were senators at the Bordeaux *parlement* in the 17th century; they built this beautiful, well-kept château. The cask-aged red wine is fragrant, and it usually benefits from ageing because of its tannins; fruity and floral elements give it charm.

Ch de l'Eglise
map 32/R K7

owner: Indivision Penaud **area:** 12 ha **cases:** 1,300, white 1,500 **grape % R:** MER 50% CS 50% **grape % W:** SEM 95% SAUV B 5% **other wines:** Domaine de Beauchamps *(Bordeaux rosé)*
33550 Langoiran tel: 05 56 67 14 43
White Premières Côtes is the speciality here, and also represents a considerable percentage of the production; 5 ha are planted with white grapes. Maturing in *barriques* gives the wine a good dose of oak in its perfume, in addition to discreet tropical fruit notes. There is a substantial core of alcohol, and a semi-sweet taste. The fruity red wine is of average quality. This estate should not be confused with the much larger – 50 ha – Ch de l'Eglise in St-Germain-de-Graves.

Ch Fayau
map 31/L H5

owner: Jean Médeville & fils **area:** 36 ha **cases:** 13,500, white 4,500 **grape % R:** CS 40% MER 35% CF 25% **grape % W:** SAUV B 50% SEM 40% MUSC 10% **other wines:** Cadillac; Bordeaux blanc; Bordeaux Supérieur; Bordeaux Clairet; Ch du Juge *(Bordeaux blanc);* Clos des Capucins *(Bordeaux blanc)* **other châteaux owned:** include Ch Pessan *(Graves);* Ch Greteau-Médeville *(Bordeaux Supérieur);* Ch Boyrein *(Graves);* Ch Barbier *(Sauternes)*
33410 Cadillac tel: 05 57 98 08 08
fax: 05 56 62 18 22
The Médeville family of coopers bought this estate in 1826 and have been in possession ever since. The château itself seems insignificant beside the extensive cellar buildings. Fayau functions as the headquarters for the properties run by the Médevilles: together these cover 100 ha. Fayau itself represents about a third of that area and yields a variety of wines. One of these is a fine, sweet and fresh Cadillac, mainly from Sémillon grapes. Clos des Capucins is a pleasant dry white AC Bordeaux. The quality of the red Premières Côtes is rather above average: as a rule it tastes agreeably creamy after four to five years, with a nice amount of fruit, plus spices, caramel, and some dark tones. The Cuvée Jean Médeville is a special selection.

Ch La Forêt
map 32/L J7

owner: Geneviève Camus **area:** 7 ha **cases:** 3,000 **grape % R:** MER 65% CS 35%
33880 Cambes tel: 05 56 21 31 25
Estate that originated in the 12th century, as a monastery. Communion wine was the first made here, by the monks. The U-shaped building, restored in 1979, still boasts a chapel. Fruit and vanilla oak contend for dominance in the best red wine. The oak usually wins – there is 12-18 months in casks, a third of them new. After a few years' bottle-age this Premières Côtes acquires more balance and charm.

Ch Frère
map 32/R H7

owner: Peter & Fleming Jørgensen **area:** 4 ha **cases:** 1,500 **grape % R:** MER 50% CS 40% CF 10% **other châteaux owned:** Domaine des Trois Clochers *(Premières Côtes de Bordeaux);* Ch Saint-Pierre *(AC Bordeaux);* Ch Gourran *(Premières Côtes de Bordeaux);* Ch de Haux *(Premières Côtes de Bordeaux)*

Above: Ch La Forêt

33550 Haux tel: 05 56 23 35 07
fax: 05 56 23 25 29
The Frère estate is linked with Ch de Haux. The red wine here, nurtured in new casks, is outstanding: great concentration, noble tannins, toast-like oak and jammy fruit – figs and plums among them. The vineyard area is to be increased by 10ha.

Ch Galland-Dast
map 32/L J8

owner: GFA Petit-Galland **area:** 2.6 ha **cases:** 1,250 **grape % R:** MER 70% CS 15% CF 15%
33880 Cambes tel: 05 56 20 87 54
Charming, supple red wine, dominated by Merlot; it remains in oak for a maximum 18 months. A third of the casks are new.

Ch Gassies
map 32/L H2

owner: Jean Egreteaud **area:** 7.5 ha **cases:** 4,500 **grape % R:** MER 60% CS 25% CF 15%
33360 Latresne tel: 05 56 44 60 10
fax: 05 56 36 76 32
The gracious château recalls the 18th century, but the cellar equipment is of our time: it is

Below: Ch du Grand Moëys

stainless steel that gleams here. Balance and fruit (blackcurrant, cherry) characterize the red wine, which also has nuances of undergrowth and spicy oak. A third of the barrels in which the 12 months' maturing takes place are new.

Ch Génisson
map 31/R G6

owner: SC Arrivet & Cauboue **area:** 18 ha **cases:** 4,900, white 2,000 **grape % R:** MER 40% CS 40% CF 10% MAL 10% **grape % W:** SEM 95% SAUV B 5% **second wine:** Ch St Jacques
33490 St-Germain-de-Grave tel: 05 56 76 41 01
fax: 05 56 76 45 39
About two centuries – and ten generations – unite Génisson and its owners. In the cellars of the 18th/19th-century château a usually slender red wine is made, accessible and fruity, with some spices, bayleaf and sometimes a touch of paprika. There is no cask-ageing. The white Premières Côtes is decent but unremarkable.

Ch La Gontrie
map 32/L J9

owner: Jean-Louis Rives **area:** 14 ha **cases:** 7,000 **grape % R:** MER 60% CF 20% CS 20% **other wine:** Bordeaux Clairet
33880 St-Caprais-de-Bordeaux tel: 05 56 21 34 21
fax: 05 56 21 30 15
Wine estate laid out in 1984; turkeys, geese, guinea fowl and chickens are also raised here. It follows that only organic manure is used in the vineyard. La Gontrie's red wine is given 8-12 months in *barriques*, and offers agreeable impressions of red and black berry fruits, together with some dark aromas. The other wine is a Bordeaux Clairet.

Ch de Gorce
map 32/L K6

owner: Société Fermière des Domaines Kressmann **area:** 7.5 ha **cases:** 4,000 **grape % R:** MER 70% CS 15% CF 10% MAL 5% **other châteaux owned:** Ch La Tour Martillac, Ch Lespault *(both Pessac-Léognan)*
33360 Quinsac tel: 05 56 72 71 21
fax: 05 56 72 64 03
The wine here is made by the team from Ch La Tour Martillac in Pessac-Léognan – partly explaining why its quality has been improving since 1990. The Cuvée Sélectionnée is matured for at least 10 months in one-year-old casks.

PREMIÈRES CÔTES DE BORDEAUX, CADILLAC, LOUPIAC & STE-CROIX-DU-MONT
31

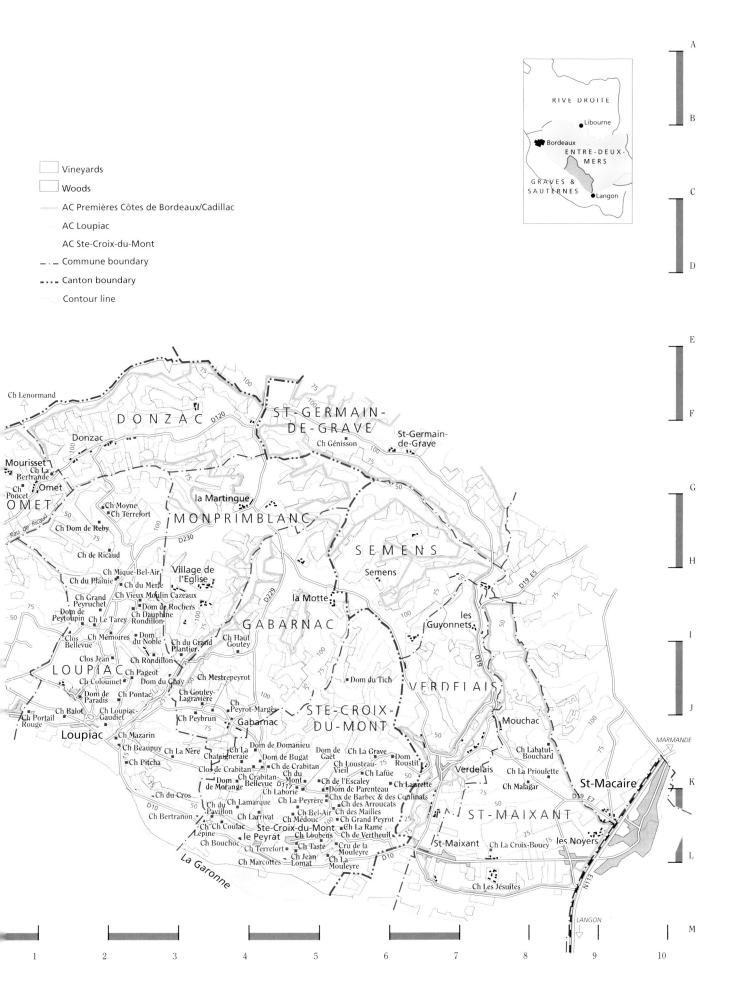

Vineyards

Woods

AC Premières Côtes de Bordeaux/Cadillac

AC Loupiac

AC Ste-Croix-du-Mont

_ . _ Commune boundary

···· Canton boundary

Contour line

RIVE DROITE

Libourne

Bordeaux

ENTRE-DEUX-
MERS

GRAVES &
SAUTERNES

Langon

Ch Lenormand

D O N Z A C

Donzac

Mourisset
Ch La
Bertrande
Ch
Poncet   Omet
O M E T
Ch Moyne
Ch Terrefort
Rau de Ricaud
Ch Dom de Reby

Ch de Ricaud

Ch Mique-Bel-Air
Ch du Plainie
Ch du Merle
Ch Grand
Peyruchet   Ch Vieux Moulin Cazeaux
Dom de   Dom de Rochers
Peytoupin   Ch Dauphine
Ch Le Tarey   Rondillon
Clos   Ch Mémoires   Dom
Bellevue   du Noble
Clos Jean   Ch Rondillon
L O U P I A C   Ch Pageot
Ch Coloumet   Ch du Chay
Dom de   Ch Pontac
Paradis
Ch Balot   Ch Loupiac-
Ch Portail   Gaudiet
Rouge
L o u p i a c   Ch Mazarin
Ch Beaupuy   Ch La Nère
Ch Pitcha   Ch La
Chataigneraie
Clos de Crabitan
Ch Crabitan-
Dom   Bellevue
de Morange
Ch du Cros   Ch Lamarque
Ch Laborie
Ch Bertranon   Ch du   Ch Larrivat
Pavillon   Ch Médouc
Ch Ch Coulac   Ste-Croix-du-Mont
Lépine   le Peyrat
Ch Bouchoc   Ch Loubens
Ch Terrefort   Ch Taste
Ch Marcottes   Ch Jean
Lomat

S T - G E R M A I N -
D E - G R A V E
St-Germain-
de-Grave
Ch Génisson

la Martingue

M O N P R I M B L A N C

S E M E N S
Semens

Village de
l'Eglise
la Motte
G A B A R N A C
Ch Haut
Goutey
les
Guyonnets
Ch du Grand
Plantier
Ch Mestrepeyrot
Dom du Tich
Ch Goutey-
Lagravière
V E R D E L A I S
Ch
Peyrot-Marges   S T E - C R O I X -
Ch Peybrun   D U - M O N T
Gabarnac   Mouchac
Dom de Domanieu
Dom de   Ch La Grave   Ch Labatut-
Dom de Bugat   Gaët   Bouchard
Ch de   Ch Lousteau-   Verdelais
Crabitan   Vieil   Ch La Prioulette
Mont   Ch du   Ch Lafüe
Ch La Peyrère   D117   Ch de l'Escaley   Ch Malagar
Chx de Barbec & des Confinats   Ch Lanrette
Dom de Parenteau
Ch Bel-Air   Ch des Arroucats   St-Macaire
Ch des Mailles
Ch Grand Peyrot   S T - M A I X A N T
Ch La Rame
Ch de Vertheuil
Cru de la
Mouleyre   St-Maixant   Ch La Croix-Bouey   les Noyers
Ch La
Mouleyre
Ch Les Jésuites

La Garonne

MARMANDE

LANGON

Ch Gourran
map 32/R J8

owner: Kaare Thal-Jantzen *area:* 6.5 ha *cases:* 3,200 *grape % R:* MER 45% CS 40% CF 15% *other wine:* Bordeaux Clairet *other châteaux owned:* Ch de Haux *(Premières Côtes de Bordeaux)*; Ch Frère *(Premières Côtes de Bordeaux)*; Domaine des Trois Clochers *(Premières Côtes de Bordeaux)*; Ch Saint-Pierre *(Bordeaux)*

33550 Langoiran tel: 05 56 23 35 07

fax: 05 56 23 25 29

The label gives two dates: that of the vintage and 1773, the year the estate came into being. The red wine is exemplary, thanks to all its fruit (including cherry, blackcurrant, prune), spiciness and licorice, its body, good tannins and vanilla. It has 10-12 months in *barriques*, a quarter of them new. The wine here is made under the supervision of the team from Ch de Haux.

Ch Grand Jour
map 32/R D7

owner: Jean Guillot *area:* 7 ha *cases:* 4,500 *grape % R:* MER 50% CF 35% CS 15% *other châteaux owned:* Domaine de Bouteilley *(Premières Côtes de Bordeaux)*; Ch Maillard *(AC Bordeaux)*; Ch Cap de Fer *(Bordeaux Supérieur)*

33370 Yvrac tel: 05 56 06 68 42

fax: 05 56 31 62 90

This vineyard forms an enclave within Domaine de Bouteilley, and since 1974 has been entirely reconstructed. It yields a supple, quite elegant red wine with discreet, jammy fruit. There is no oak-ageing.

Ch du Grand Moëys
map 31/L D1

owner: Bömers & Fils *area:* 86 ha *cases:* 30,000, white 10,000 *grape % R:* MER 45% CS 34% CF 21% *grape % W:* SEM 48% SAUV B 45% MUSC 7% *second wines:* Ch du Piras; Domaine de la Gatine; Domaine des Joualles; Clos de la Garenne *other wines:* Bordeaux blanc

33550 Capian tel: 05 57 97 04 44

fax: 05 57 97 04 60

Small, curious-looking neo-Gothic castle, complete with ornamental crenellations and two corner towers. It stands in a 170-ha estate, and since 1989 has belonged to a family of German wine merchants committed to quality. About half the estate is planted with vines. The red Premières Côtes from these has a decent amount of oak (half the casks are new, half one year old; the wine matures for 12-18 months), together with bayleaves, spices and ripe red and black currants. Its quality, certainly from around 1993, has been more than creditable. There are two versions of the dry white AC Bordeaux: a stimulatingly fresh standard wine, and a more serious one fermented in new barrels.

Ch du Grand Plantier
map 31/R J4

owner: GAEC des Vignobles Albucher *area:* 20 ha *cases:* 3,600, white 5,500 *grape % R:* MER 85% CF 10% CS 5% *grape % W:* SEM 85% MUSC 15% *other wines:* Bordeaux rosé; Bordeaux blanc; Ste-Croix-du-Mont; Loupiac

33410 Monprimblanc tel: 05 56 62 99 03

fax: 05 56 76 91 35

Produces seven different wines, among them a standard Loupiac and an attractive, complex cask-aged variant. The red Premières Côtes offers an average quality: it is soon ready for drinking as a rule, has no austere side to it, and in its aroma often has something of caramel and spices. The atmospheric barrel-cellar has impressive timber beams.

◆

Quantities

Figures are as supplied by the châteaux.

Area of vineyard: given in hectares, abbreviated to ha. Châteaux are asked to specify vineyards in production, to exclude from their answers those owned but unplanted, and to advise when extensions are planned.

Production: given in cases of 12 bottles, each of 0.75 litres. A case is thus 9 litres. A hectolitre is 100 litres or just over 11 cases.

Yield per hectare: to obtain this, multiply the 'cases' figure by 9, to give litres, then divide by 100, to give hectolitres. Then divide the result by the area in hectares.

Ch La Grange Clinet
map 32/R J1

owner: Michel Haury *area:* 23 ha *cases:* 12,500 *grape % R:* MER 52% CS 33% CF 15% *second wine:* Ch Grand Claret

33880 St-Caprais-de-Bordeaux tel: 05 56 78 70 88

fax: 05 56 21 33 23

Estate nearly 100 m up. In the early 1980s the present owners replanted the entire vineyard, under the direction of Professor Peynaud. Pleasant red wine – not among the high-fliers nor really generous, but having adequate fruit. The Cabernets often confer a hint of paprika and at times slightly bitter tannins.

Ch Grimont
map 32/L L5

owner: SCEA Pierre Yung & Fils *area:* 25 ha *cases:* 15,200 *grape % R:* MER 60% CS 35% CF 5% *other wines:* Ch Tour Saint Paul *(Bordeaux Supérieur; Bordeaux Clairet)* *other châteaux owned:* Ch Sissan *(Premières Côtes de Bordeaux)*

33360 Quinsac tel: 05 56 20 86 18

fax: 05 56 20 82 50

The red Prestige is the top wine at this château, which dates from the end of the 17th century. It represents around a fifth of the total harvest and is given a year to mature in oak (25% new barrels). The oak tends to be rather dominant – and sometimes remains so, in the taste and in the somewhat dry finish. There is more fruit in the standard red wine.

Ch Haut Goutey
map 31/R J4

owner: Françoise Duperrieu *area:* 2.5 ha *cases:* 1,710 *grape % R:* MER 60% CS 30% CF 10% *other châteaux owned:* Ch La Gravière *(Ste-Croix-du-Mont)*

33410 Gabarnac tel: 05 56 62 19 75

fax: 05 56 76 91 32

The vineyard here is tiny, but its area is to be tripled in the coming years. Of its two red wines, the *élevé en fût de chêne* is the more interesting. This is aged for a year, and half the casks are new. Its character tends towards the rustic, with some bitter notes and excess tannins – but a juiciness and a touch of fruit are also there. The château is large and impressive, and dates from 1870.

Ch Haut-Greyzeau
map 32/R D6

owner: Rolland Pestoury *area:* 6 ha *cases:* 1,650 *grape % R:* MER 50% CS 30% CF 15% MAL 5%

33370 Yvrac tel: 05 56 06 75 51

fax: 05 56 06 75 51

Above: Ch Jonchet

This property owes its name to the little Greyzeau stream, which flows into the Garonne. The red wine is a pleasant composition of berry fruit, tannin and spices. It usually merits keeping for some years.

Ch Haut Mouleyre
map 31/L G7

owner: Michel Fourcassies *area:* 8 ha *cases:* 4,400, white 1,300 *grape % R:* MER 85% CS 15% *grape % W:* SEM 100% *second wine:* Ch de Coqs *(AC Bordeaux)* *other wines:* Bordeaux Supérieur *other châteaux owned:* Ch Dublanc Puy-Domine *(Sauternes)*; Ch Haut Mouleyre *(Bordeaux Supérieur)*; Ch Laubès *(AC Bordeaux)*; Ch Le Bos *(Entre-Deux-Mers Haut-Benauge)*

33410 Cardan tel: 05 56 23 93 77

fax: 05 56 23 46 44

Red Premières Côtes de Bordeaux suitable for laying down. As well as its tannin it has fruit and spicy oak with vanilla, the result of a year maturing in cask. Of the whites the Cadillac is the most interesting: a firm, quite generous wine with a hint of honey.

Ch Haut Rian
map 31/L I5

owner: Michel Dietrich *area:* 76 ha *cases:* 18,000, white 23,100 *grape % R:* MER 50% CS 40% CF 10% *grape % W:* SEM 70% SAUV B 30% *other wines:* Cadillac; Entre-Deux-Mers; Bordeaux blanc; Bordeaux rosé

33410 Rions tel: 05 56 76 95 01

fax: 05 56 76 93 51

Michel and Isabelle Dietrich established themselves at this 200-year-old wine estate in 1988. Using modern technology they make various wines, including a very correct red Premières Côtes de Bordeaux. The estate enjoys a good reputation in particular for its Entre-Deux-Mers, a wine dominated by Sémillon and sometimes slightly sparkling, with some mint, fruit (apple, pear, grapefruit), and a fresh finish.

Ch Les Hauts de Palette
map 31/L J9

owner: SCEA des Frères Yung *area:* 11 ha *cases:* 3,300 *grape % R:* MER 50% CS 45% CF 5% *second wine:* Ch de Palette *other wines:* Ch Lapeyrere *(Bordeaux rouge)* *other châteaux owned:* Ch Haut-Mondain *(Bordeaux)*; Ch du Barrail *(Bordeaux)*

33410 Béguey tel: 05 56 62 94 85

fax: 05 56 62 18 11

An impeccable Cuvée de Prestige here offers a good balance between ripe fruit, oak and other

Above: Ch Labatut-Bouchard

elements. It matures for 12 months; a quarter of the barrels are new. The red Premières Côtes, not oak-aged, is sold as Ch de Palette. The château, dating from 1740, is in Béguey commune, about 600 m from the Cadillac castle.

Ch de Haux   map 32/R H7
owner: Peter & Fleming Jørgensen *area:* 28 ha
cases: 16,000 *grape % R:* CS 45% MER 42% CF 13%
other wines: Bordeaux blanc; Bordeaux Clairet)
other châteaux owned: Ch Frère *(Premières Côtes de Bordeaux)*; Domaine des Trois Clochers *(Premières Côtes de Bordeaux)*; Gourran *(Premières Côtes de Bordeaux)*; Saint-Pierre *(Bordeaux)*
33550 Haux tel: 05 56 23 35 07
fax: 05 56 23 25 29
The flagship of the properties run by Peter and Fleming Jørgensen. These Danish wine merchants have not only renovated the stately château (financing this by a share issue), but have also enlarged the vineyard. This expansion is to continue and the area will be more than doubled. The red Premières Côtes is usually one of the richest and most concentrated from the district, with a very full-bodied taste, plenty of fruit, and fine, mature tannins. It is bottled after 10-15 months in casks, of which a fifth are new. The dry white AC Bordeaux and the fruity Clairet are also splendid.

Ch Henry de France   map 32/L K7
owner: Jean Costes *area:* 4 ha *cases:* 1,900 *grape % R:* MER 60% CS 20% CF 15% MAL 5% *other wines:* Bordeaux rosé
33880 Cambes tel: 05 56 08 31 43
fax: 05 57 22 17 10
Estate named after the 'good' King Henri IV of France, making somewhat old-fashioned red wines. On average about half of the production consists of the firm Cuvée Prestige with its ample tannins. This wine matures for two years, one in tank and one in barrels.

Ch Les Jésuites   map 31/R M8
owner: Guy Lucmaret *area:* 5 ha *cases:* 3,300
grape % R: MER 60% CS 20% CF 20% *other wines:* Bordeaux rosé
33490 St-Maixant tel: 05 56 63 17 97
fax: 05 56 63 17 46
Before the French Revolution this vineyard was the property of the Jesuit monastery at St-Macaire, hence the name. The present

'agrobiologically-cultivated' vineyard yields a fairly firm, often rather austere wine, which can be a little dusty in its finish. Besides paprika and spices there is aa touch of elderberry.

Ch Jonchet   map 32/L J8
owner: Philippe Rullaud *area:* 7 ha *cases:* 3,350
grape % R: MER 56% CS 37% MAL 7% *other wines:* Bordeaux Clairet
33880 Cambes tel: 05 56 21 34 16
fax: 05 56 78 75 32
Since 1990 Jonchet has been run by a former army photographer. His military precision extends to winemaking, for his red Premières Côtes is always immaculate. Its substantial structure is underpinned by red fruit and a pinch of spices – and, in the Prestige de Jonchet, good oak as well. The property is named after Daniel Jonchet, who built the château in the 17th century.

Ch du Juge   map 31/L I9
owner: Chantal Dupleich *area:* 30 ha *cases:* 5,000, white 12,000 *grape % R:* MER 60% CS 40% *grape % W:* SEM 70% SAUV B 30% *second wine:* Ch de la Closerie *other wines:* Cadillac; Bordeaux blanc
33410 Cadillac tel: 05 56 62 17 77
fax: 05 56 62 17 59

Below: Ch Lagarosse

A third of this vineyard yields black grapes. From these an exceptionally pleasant red Premières Côtes is made, a wine with smooth tannins, an accessible taste, some attractive ripe fruit (plum, cherry), and a hint of bayleaf. There is still more charm and class in the dry white AC Bordeaux; from the glass leap the intense aromas of candied lemon, grapefruit, pineapple, melon. Skin contact, selected yeast cells and other modern techniques contribute to this wine. Also very fine is the cask-matured Cadillac, an exemplary wine of its kind. Comparable qualities can be found under the Ch de la Closerie label.

Ch Labatut-Bouchard   map 31/R K9
owner: SCEA des Vignobles Bouchard *area:* 50 ha
cases: 13,000, white 6,500 *grape % R:* CS 60% MER 40% *grape % W:* SAUV B 50% SEM 50% *second wine:* Ch Fayon *other wines:* Bordeaux blanc; Cadillac
other châteaux owned: Ch Mont-Célestin *(Premières Côtes de Bordeaux)*
33490 St-Maixant tel: 05 56 62 02 44
fax: 05 56 62 09 46
This hilltop estate has a good name for the dependable quality of its white wines. Its dry AC Bordeaux, solely from Sauvignon, is marked by a lively taste of fruit – gooseberry, pear, tropical. Its Cadillac has a fat, opulent, slightly honeyed taste in which there can also be fresh mango and passion fruit. The red Premières Côtes is simpler: rather lacking in fruit and depth, even in sunny years, it is meant for early drinking.

Ch Lagarosse   map 32/RJ3
owner: Gérard Laurencin *area:* 32 ha *cases:* 15,500, white 2,000 *grape % R:* MER 80% CS 10% CF 10% *grape % W:* SEM 70% SAUV B 30% *second wine:* Ch Douley *other wine:* Bordeaux blanc
33550 Tabanac tel: 05 56 67 13 31
fax: 05 56 67 12 64
The aristocratic ambience of this château, built in 1840 in a forerunner of the Napoleon III

> ◆
> ### About the red wines of the Premières Côtes
> For information about the red wines of the Premières Côtes contact the Syndicat at the place de l'Eglise, 33360 Quinsac. Telephone 05 56 20 85 84.

style, is largely reflected in the red wine. This is well provided with oak and has an alluring jammy fruitiness (plum, blackcurrant, fig, cherry) and a firm elegance.

Ch Lagorce
map 32/R I6

owner: Marcel Baudier **area:** 22 ha **cases:** 9,000, white 3,500 **grape % R:** MER 50% CS 50% **grape % W:** SEM 40% SAUV B 30% MUSC 30% **other wines:** Bordeaux blanc; Bordeaux rosé
33550 Haux tel: 05 56 67 01 52
Of the wines made here, the red Premières Côtes is the most important. This has a generous character, and its aroma largely conveys ripe fruit such as blackcurrant. The dry white AC Bordeaux, slightly floral with some gooseberry, is also of a decent standard.

Ch Lamothe de Haux
map 32/R H5

owner: Fabrice Neel **area:** 60 ha **cases:** 21,000, white 13,500 **grape % R:** MER 60% CS 30% CF 10% **grape % W:** SEM 40% SAUV B 30% MUSC 30% **other wines:** Cadillac; Bordeaux blanc; Bordeaux Clairet **other châteaux owned:** Ch Manos (Premières Côtes de Bordeaux); Ch Sauvage (Premières Côtes de Bordeaux)
33550 Haux tel: 05 56 23 05 07
fax: 05 56 23 24 49
The foundations of this fine château are 16th century, but it acquired its present exterior in the 19th. Below the building there are stone quarries where the wine matures. The red Première Cuvée spends about 12 months there in barrel (one cask in five is new). Thanks to the oak the wine has a seductive creaminess, usually complemented by tannins, fruit, licorice and bayleaf. The Cuvée Tradition tastes rather more supple. The dry white AC Bordeaux is a well-made, decent wine, firm and rounded, with pineapple, pear and apple notes.

Ch Langoiran
map 32/R K7

owner: Philippe & Francis Neeser **area:** 24 ha **cases:** 11,500 **grape % R:** MER 65% CF 20% CS 15% **other wines:** Cadillac; Bordeaux rosé
33550 Langoiran tel: 05 56 67 08 55
fax: 05 56 67 32 87
On a hill just south of Langoiran itself are the impressive ruins of Château Langoiran, which date back to the 12th century and which can be visited. Below the castle walls stands a 19th-century *chartreuse*, the heart of a wine estate. The cellars are underground, and can be entered by way of a former chapel. Since the beginning of the 1990s the wines here have gained more class. Ch Langoiran is a Premières Côtes with berry fruit and supple backbone. Ch Tour de Langoiran is a selection, made with 85% Merlot, that spends a year in cask: spicy, gutsy, dark-toned, a pleasant touch of bitterness, with fruity aromas.

Ch Laroche
map 32/R K1

owner: Martine & Julien Palau **area:** 25 ha **cases:** 11,400, white 1,500 **grape % R:** MER 50% CS 30% CF 20% **grape % W:** SEM 90% SAUV B 10% **other wines:** Bordeaux blanc; Bordeaux rosé **other châteaux owned:** Ch Pontet Teyssier (St-Emilion)
33880 Baurech tel: 05 56 21 31 03
fax: 05 56 21 36 58
The current owners bought this estate in 1976 and have since enlarged it by about a half. Around the fine château, set on a hill and with a notable 16th-century tower, there lies a very carefully tended vineyard, where generally excellent wines are produced. The best is the Ch

Above: Ch Malagar

Laroche Belair, a special *cuvée* matured for a year in barrels of which a third are new. This red offers more concentration than the also successful standard wine, with finesse allied to fine, firm tannins, oaky aromas, animal scents, red and black fruit, liquorice and bayleaves. The fragrant dry white Bordeaux is also of a good standard.

Ch Latour Camblanes
map 32/L I5

owner: SC du Ch Latour Camblanes **area:** 29 ha **cases:** 17,000 **grape % R:** CS 50% MER 50%
33360 Camblanes-et-Meynac tel: 05 56 20 71 40
fax: 05 56 95 12 44
Fairly full-bodied and powerful wine that would, however, benefit from just a little more fruit. The view from this château is splendid.

Ch Lenormand
map 31/R F1

owner: Janine & Jean-Michel Menguin **area:** 15 ha **cases:** 16,000 **grape % R:** MER 50% CF 30% CS 20% **other châteaux owned:** Ch Les Vieilles Tuileries (AC Bordeaux; Entre-Deux-Mers Haut-Benauge); Ch Haut Reygnac (AC Bordeaux)
33550 Villenave-de-Rions tel: 05 56 23 61 70
fax: 05 56 23 49 79
Although the name indicates a Norman origin, the present owner's father came from the Pyrénées. There is no great depth to the red wine made here, but it does have a very pleasant taste with jam-like berry fruit and a brisk, refreshing crispness. To this, the Cuvée Prestige adds smoky oak and vanilla.

Ch de Lestiac
map 32/R K7

owner: Gonfrier frères **area:** 10 ha **cases:** 5,000 **grape % R:** MER 60% CS 40% **second wine:** Ch Haut Lestiac (Bordeaux Supérieur) **other châteaux owned:** Ch Baracan (Premières Côtes de Bordeaux); Ch de Marsan (Premières Côtes de Bordeaux); Ch du Grand Bern (Bordeaux Supérieur);
33550 Lestiac tel: 05 72 14 38
fax: 05 72 72 10 38
Accessible, supple and quite full-bodied wine, rested for an average one year in casks of which a third are new. Among its nuances there are often elements of chocolate and animal scents.

Ch Lézongars
map 31/L G4

owner: SC du Château Lézongars/Famille Loncan **area:** 45 ha **cases:** 20,800, white 3,500 **grape % R:** CS 60% MER 40% **grape % W:** SAUV B 80% SEM 20% **second wine:** Ch de Prieuré **other wines:** Bordeaux blanc **other châteaux owned:** Ch de Prieuré (Premières Côtes de Bordeaux); Ch Reine Carbonnieu (Sauternes)
33550 Villenave-de-Rions tel: 05 56 72 18 06
fax: 05 56 72 31 44

◆
Appellations in this chapter
The ACs covered here are Premières Côtes de Bordeaux and Cadillac. Also included are wines using the ACs Bordeaux and Bordeaux Supérieur where the châteaux are in this area.

Ste-Croix-du-Mont and Loupiac have their own chapter, which follows this. AC Entre-Deux-Mers and associated appellations are covered in another chapter.

The château was formerly a hunting lodge belonging to the Lézongars family. Earlier, it was called the Ch de Roque. A beautiful park surrounds it, and the long view it offers sometimes stretches to the Pyrénées. The standard red wine is not that full-bodied or meaty, but certainly very acceptable. Rather more depth is encountered in the *cuvée*, with its nine months in cask and its elements of smoke and vanilla thanks to the oak.

Ch Ligassonne
map 32/R K7

owner: Indivision Bordenave **area:** 12 ha **cases:** 6,000 **grape % R:** MER 50% CS 30% CF 20%
33550 Langoiran tel: 05 56 67 36 01
Well-made red wine which has smooth tannins and notes of coffee and caramel, but is not rich in fruit. The lesser vintages are quite soon ready for drinking, but it has considerable tannin in the sunnier years. The estate name is said to derive from *lien*, 'bond' or 'link', which the owners think of as a reference to the commitment of the winegrower to his land.

Ch Macalan
map 32/R C5

owner: Jean-Jacques Hias **area:** 5 ha **cases:** 1,670, white 50 **grape % R:** MER 70% CS 15% CF 15% **grape % W:** SEM 100% **other wines:** Bordeaux blanc; Bordeaux rosé
33560 Ste-Eulalie tel: 05 56 38 92 41
fax: 05 56 38 92 41
Despite its modest size this estate yields three wines. Both in quantity and quality the red Premières Côtes de Bordeaux is the most important, with its bayleaf, licorice, black fruit, firm constitution and discreet oak.

Ch Malagar
map 31/R K8

owner: Domaines Cordier **area:** 14 ha **cases:** 3,900, white 3,625 **grape % R:** CS 50% MER 50% **grape % W:** SEM 60% SAUV B 40% **other châteaux owned:** Ch Clos des Jacobins (St-Emilion)
33490 St-Maixant tel: 05 56 95 53 00
fax: 05 56 59 39 89
François Mauriac, Nobel prize winner for literature in 1952, lived and worked here. He said that he hoped to view eternity from its terrace – without blinking too much. The château not only functions as a museum and monument, but also as a wine estate. Domaines Cordier own the vineyard. The red wine is a success: plenty of fruit, meaty, with mature tannins and generous in its oak. The white Premières Côtes also merits praise; the dry white is a flavoursome AC Bordeaux, matured in wood, with fruit and breeding. Wine from Ch Malagar was served at the dinner marking the 90th anniversary of the Nobel prize – and deservedly so.

Ch de Malherbes   map 32/L G3

owner: Jacques Fritz *area:* 12 ha *cases:* 6,500, white 500 *grape % R:* MER 66% CF 20% CS 13% MAL 1% *W:* SEM 55% SAUV B 45% *second wine:* Ch de Rambal *other wines:* Bordeaux blanc
33360 Latresne tel: 05 56 20 78 36

In the 14th century the owner was Guilhem de Malherbe, a Norman by origin. Since then the estate has had many changes of both proprietor and appearance: the buildings were drastically altered in the course of the 19th century. The present owner, Jacques Fritz, has his wine made by the Quinsac cooperative, of which he has been chairman. He then matures it himself with six months in cask, and bottles it. This red wine tastes reasonably full-bodied and fruity, while tannin makes its presence felt.

Ch Manos   map 32/L G6

owner: Pierre Niotout/Fabrice Neel *area:* 8.6 ha *cases:* 1,200, white 2,500 *grape % R:* MER 40% CS 30% CF 25% MAL 5% *grape % W:* SEM 70% SAUV B 15% MUSC 15% *other wines:* Cadillac; Bordeaux blanc *other châteaux owned:* Ch Lamothe de Haux *(Premières Côtes de Bordeaux),* Ch Sauvage *(Premières Côtes de Bordeaux)*
33550 Haux tel: 05 56 23 05 18
fax: 05 56 23 24 49

Pierre Niotout, one of the owners, worked at Ch Coutet in Barsac and learned there how a fine sweet white wine should be made. That knowledge is put into practice at Ch Manos, where Cadillac is the speciality. The ordinary version is a refined wine, with elements of candied tropical fruit and spices but not tasting exaggeratedly sweet. From time to time a Réserve is also made, fermented in new barrels. This wine is richly sweet, if not honeyed, and beautifully concentrated.

Ch de Marsan   map 32/R K8

owner: Paul Gonfrier *area:* 30 ha *cases:* 7,000, white 6,500 *grape % R:* MER 50% CS 40% CF 10% *grape %W:* SEM 70% SAUV B 30% *second wine:* Ch Lagarère *(Bordeaux Supérieur) other wines:* Ch Baragan *(Premières Côtes de Bordeaux);* Ch du Grand Bern *(Bordeaux Supérieur);* Ch de Lestiac *(Premières Côtes de Bordeaux);* Bordeaux blanc; Cadillac; Bordeaux Clairet

33550 Lestiac-sur-Garonne tel: 05 56 72 14 38
fax: 05 56 72 10 38

The red Premières Côtes de Bordeaux here is an expansive wine rather than one with great depth. Woodland scents, vanilla (from maturing in *barriques,* about a third of them new), and berry fruit are generally to be detected in the aroma. The château also produces an exquisite Bordeaux Clairet, with a flavour that is full of jammy fruit.

Ch Martindoit   map 32/R H7

owner: David Thomas *area:* 7.1 ha *cases:* 3,000, white 500 *grape % R:* MER 65% CS 35% *grape % W:* SEM 50% MUSC 50% *other wines:* Cadillac *other châteaux owned:* Ch Bauduc *(AC Bordeaux)*
33550 Capian tel: 05 56 23 23 58
fax: 05 56 23 06 05

Besides the better-than-correct red Premières Côtes, with its nine months in wood, a small amount of Cadillac is also made here. This is often excellent – particularly when (as in 1990) *pourriture noble* occurs. In such years is made an amazingly rich wine in which all the sweet essence of the grape is delightfully present.

Ch Mathereau   map 32/R C6

owner: Philippe Boulière *area:* 15 ha *cases:* 5,000, white 100 *grape % R:* MER 60% CF 35% CS 5% *grape % W:* SAUV B 40% SEM 40% MUSC 20% *second wine:* Domaine de Cantelaudette *(Bordeaux rouge) other wines:* Bordeaux blanc; Bordeaux rosé
33360 Ste-Eulalie tel: 05 56 06 05 56
fax: 05 56 38 02 01

A red Premières Côtes de Bordeaux which calls for some patience, and which shows fruity and slightly herbaceous elements, sometimes cocoa, plus restrained oak: it matures for 12 months in casks of which a third are new. The château, an 18th-century *chartreuse,* has belonged to the same family since 1908.

Ch Melin   map 32/R J2

owner: Claude Modet *area:* 32 ha *cases:* 15,000, white 2,800 *grape % R:* MER 70% CS 30% *grape % W:* SEM 50% SAUV B 50% *second wines:* Ch Constantin; Ch Melin Cadet Courreau *(Bordeaux rouge) other wines:* Bordeaux blanc, Bordeaux Clairet

33880 Baurech tel: 05 56 21 34 71
fax: 05 56 21 37 72

Ch Melin is a Premières Côtes de Bordeaux of calibre: powerful, with good tannins, considerable fruit, slight oak, agreeable juiciness and balance. The Clairet made here is delicious too. Ch Melin also makes a white AC Bordeaux with the name of Cuvée Osmose Sec, fermented and aged in cask, plus several other wines.

Ch Mestrepeyrot   map 31/R K4

owner: Vignobles Chassagnol *area:* 12.4 ha *cases:* 6,300, white 2,000 *grape % R:* MER 60% CS 20% CF 20% *grape % W:* SEM 80% SAUV B 10% MUSC 10% *second wine:* Domaine de Labatut *(Bordeaux blanc) other wine:* Cadillac *other châteaux owned:* Ch La Grave Saint Roch *(Graves);* Ch Peyrot-Marges *(Loupiac)*
33410 Gabarnac tel: 05 56 62 98 00

The red Cuvée Prestige here is a fairly elegant wine in which impressions of red berry fruit (currants in particular), chocolate and vanilla, together with oak, can be found. The semi-sweet Premières Côtes de Bordeaux is generally one of the better wines of the appellation; a Cuvée Prestige version of this white is made in better years only. Besides these the owners make ten or so other wines.

Ch de la Meulière   map 32/L F6

owner: Jacques Fourès *area:* 23 ha *cases:* 13,000, *grape % R:* MER 38% CS 33% CF 29% *other châteaux owned:* Ch Ogier de Gourgue *(Premières Côtes de Bordeaux);* Ch Gazin *(Pessac-Léognan);* Ch Saint-Genès *(Bordeaux Supérieur)*
33360 Cénac tel: 05 56 20 64 38
fax: 05 56 20 11 98

Distinguished red Premières Côtes de Bordeaux with jammy berry fruit and cocoa; the usually generous dose of tannin means it needs to be given time to mature in bottle. It spends on average a year in barrel (25% of which new each vintage). The winegrower and oenologist Jacques Fourès has been chairman of the Premières Côtes de Bordeaux association; he also invented the Cru-Over, a system for keeping wine in good condition once the bottle has been opened.

Below: Ch Ogier de Gourgue

Below: Ch de Paillet-Quancard

PREMIÈRES CÔTES DE BORDEAUX & CADILLAC

32

Vineyards

Woods

AC Premières Côtes de Bordeaux-Cadillac

AC Premières Côtes de Bordeaux

Commune boundary

Canton boundary

Contour line

Above: Ch Le Parvis de Dom Tapiau

Above: Ch Plaisance

Ch Montjouan
map 32/L G1

owner: Anne-Marie Le Barazer *area:* 8 ha *cases:* 4,000 *grape % R:* MER 60% CS 30% CF 10% *second wine:* Ch Delord *other wines:* Bordeaux blanc
33270 Bouliac tel: 05 56 20 52 18
fax: 05 56 20 90 31
From vines with an average age of 25 years, the lady owner here makes an elegant red wine, supple, dark-toned and meant for drinking quite early. Its oak aroma comes from spending 12 months in casks, a quarter of them new.

Ch Ogier de Gourgue
map 32/L J9

owner: Jacques Fourès *area:* 4.7 ha *cases:* 3,200 *grape % R:* MER 70% CS 30% *other châteaux owned:* Ch Gazin *(Pessac-Léognan)*; Ch Saint-Genès *(Bordeaux Supérieur)*; Ch de la Meulière *(Premières Côtes de Bordeaux)*
33880 Saint-Caprais tel: 05 56 78 70 99
fax: 05 56 20 11 98
Once the property of a statesman of Louis XIV's time and now run by Jacques Fourès of Ch de la Meulière. The càsk-aged red wine does not rank as great, but is clean-tasting and pleasant, with fresh fruit and a hint of pepper besides its oak.

Ch de Paillet-Quancard
map 31/L I4

owner: Cheval Quancard *area:* 40 ha *cases:* 20,000 *grape % R:* MER 60% CS 30% CF 10% *second wine:* Ch de Sadran-Quancard; Ch des Lannes *(Bordeaux Supérieur)* *other châteaux owned:* include Ch de Terrefort-Quancard *(Bordeaux Supérieur)*
33550 Paillet tel: 05 56 33 80 60
fax: 05 56 33 80 70
There is a good view of this château from the D10 road, so it is much photographed. It dates from the 18th century, and since 1970 it has belonged to the Cheval Quancard firm, which has carried out a lot of restoration work. The red wine, a frequent award winner, offers a markedly dark aroma (prunes, tobacco, chocolate), with smooth fruit, and a soft fleshiness. Since the 1992 vintage there has been no maturing in cask.

Ch Le Parvis de Dom Tapiau
map 32/L I5

owner: Olivier Reumau *area:* 6 ha *cases:* 2,750 *grape % R:* MER 34% CF 33% CS 33% *other wines:* Clairet d'Une Nuit *(Bordeaux Clairet)*

◆
Grape varieties
Some traditional names are given official status in the appellation decrees:
Bouchet St-Emilion name for Cabernet Franc, **Côt or Cot** Synonym for Malbec, **Pressac** St-Emilion name for Malbec

Some minor varieties figure in the decrees:
Carmenère Red grape of quality, liable to disease, therefore now very rare; though still legal in the Premières Côtes.
Merlot Blanc May be a mutation of Merlot, or a separate variety. Little is grown.
Mauzac White variety still important further east; still a legal *cépage accessoire* in Entre-Deux-Mers.
Sauvignon Gris White variety recently returned to favour, especially in the eastern Entre-Deux-Mers. Fresh, aromatically fruity wine.

33360 Camblanes-et-Meynac tel: 05 56 20 15 62
fax: 05 56 20 08 19
Small wine estate beside an 18th-century château. Full-bodied, firm red wine, velvety after a few years, with mature tannins and agreeable fruit. There is spicy oak here as well, from a year in barrel. Reliable in lesser vintages.

Ch Pascot
map 32/L H2

owner: Nicole Doermann *area:* 4 ha *cases:* 2,300 *grape % R:* MER 55% CS 40% MAL 5%
33360 Latresne tel: 05 56 20 78 19
fax: 05 56 20 78 19
A sound red wine is made here, agreeably framed in spicy oak. It matures for a year (25% new barrels are used). The first vintage made by the present lady owner was the 1991.

Ch du Payre/Clos du Monastère de Broussey
map 31/L G6

owner: SCEA Vignobles Arnaud & Marcuzzi *area:* 32 ha *cases:* 13,000, white 3,400 *grape % R:* MER 50% CS 30% CF 20% *grape % W:* SEM 60% SAUV B 40% *second wine:* Domaine de la Fontanille *(Bordeaux rouge)* *other wines:* Domaine du Vic *(Cadillac)*; Bordeaux blanc; Bordeaux rouge; Bordeaux rosé

33410 Cardan tel: 05 56 62 60 91
fax: 05 56 62 67 05
A property using two names, where all grapes are mechanically picked except those intended for the Cadillac. The red Premières Côtes de Bordeaux comes across as supple and slightly fruity, without great depth or concentration. The Cadillac tastes elegant, slightly sweet and with the licorice-and-spice aroma of its Sémillon.

Ch Peybrun
map 31/R J4

owner: Catherine de Loze *area:* 15 ha *cases:* 2,000, white 4,500 *grape % R:* MER 60% CS 40% *grape % W:* SEM 70% SAUV B 20% MUSC 10% *second wine:* Ch Valentin *other wines:* Premières Côtes de Bordeaux; Loupiac
33410 Gabarnac tel: 05 56 96 10 84
One of the very few estates in the two appellations producing more Cadillac than Premières Côtes de Bordeaux. The Cadillac is of superior quality: stylish, nicely sweet (without being heavy or ungainly), and it often comes with a fine *rôti* aroma. The pickers go through the vineyard a number of times to harvest the grapes for this wine, and for the luscious Loupiac (only 500 cases per year). The relatively rare red Premières Côtes is also good: its usually firm constitution is complemented by notes of black and red fruits. The same family has been running this vineyard for around four centuries.

Ch du Peyrat
map 31/L C5

owner: Lambert Frères *area:* 99 ha *cases:* 45,000, white 18,000 *grape % R:* CS 45% MER 41% CF 14% *grape % W:* SEM 63% SAUV B 22% MUSC 15% *second wine:* Ch de Lucat *other wines:* Bordeaux blanc; Bordeaux rosé
33550 Capian tel: 05 56 23 95 03
fax: 05 56 23 49 72
The present château was rebuilt in the 1930s after a fire, but the history of this wine estate goes back much further. It certainly existed in the 17th century, for Henri de Navarre slept here. Power and elegance are well combined in the red wine, and nuances of cherry, plum, raspberry and tannins are ample: this is an attractive Premières Côtes de Bordeaux. Dry white and rosé AC Bordeaux also figure in the estate's range.

Ch La Peyruche
map 32/R J6

owner: GFA du Château La Peyruche *area:* 19.5 ha
cases: 7,600, white 3,200 *grape % R:* MER 61%
CS 27% CF 12% *grape % W:* SEM 80% SAUV B 20%
other wines: Cadillac; Bordeaux blanc
33550 Langoiran tel: 05 56 67 36 01
fax: 05 56 67 20 61
A château in the hills behind Langoiran
producing a small range of different wines. The
red Premières Côtes de Bordeaux matures for
10 months in oak and has reasonable fruit. It is
a very decent wine, as is the lively, fragrant
white Bordeaux Sec with its citrus fruit.

Ch de Pic
map 32/R J5

owner: François Masson Regnault *area:* 28 ha
cases: 18,000, white 2,000 *grape % R:* MER 55%
CS 40% CF 5% *grape % W:* SEM 70% SAUV B 25%
MUSC 5% *second wine:* Ch Tour de Pic *other wines:*
Bordeaux blanc *other châteaux owned:* Ch Camail
(Premières Côtes de Bordeaux)
33550 Le Tourne tel: 05 56 67 07 51
fax: 05 56 67 21 22
There is no certainty as to the exact origins of
this château, but one of the towers definitely
dates from the 14th century. The barrel-cellar is
of more recent date – 1990. The red Cuvée
Tradition spends 12-14 months in this *chai*: it is
a Premières Côtes striking for its thick, rich,
jammy taste (black cherry, plum) and its noble
tannins. The standard red is more supple,
reasonably fruity, with some licorice and spices.
In less-good years, too, this is a highly
attractive wine. The Cuvée Tradition version of
the dry white AC Bordeaux is fermented in new
casks and then matured for six months.

Ch Plaisance
map 31/L D3

owner: Patrick Bayle *area:* 25 ha *cases:* 11,000,
white 1,000 *grape % R:* MER 50% CS 40% CF 10%
grape % W: SEM 100% *second wine:* Ch Florestan;
Ch de l'Esplanade *other wines:* Bordeaux blanc
33550 Capian tel: 05 56 72 15 06
fax: 05 56 72 13 40
This château takes pride in maturing its red
Cuvée Tradition *à l'ancienne*: in new casks, with
no filtering and clarified with fresh egg white.
Fruit is very pronounced in this wine – plum,
cherry, currant – along with noble wood and
smooth tannins. It is a mouthfilling, firm
Premières Côtes, and usually well balanced.
Another special wine is the Cuvée Alex, which

undergoes the same treatment, but comes
exclusively from old vines. Moreover, the barrels
used have heavier charring. The standard red is
more accessible, but is well made and with fine
fruit. The white Cuvée Tradition, a dry white AC
Bordeaux, certainly deserves notice as well. It
comes from 35-year-old Sémillon vines and is
vinified in new wood. Its full taste is sometimes
slightly honeyed, and it will readily mature for
five or more years. The white Cuvée Alex has an
even stronger wood aroma.

Ch de Plassan
map 32/R J4

owner: Jean Brianceau *area:* 33 ha *cases:* 9,000,
white 5,700 *grape % R:* MER 45% CS 35% CF 15%
MAL 5% *grape % W:* SEM 50% SAUV B 40% MUSC 10%
second wine: Ch Lamothe *other wines:* Bordeaux
blanc; Bordeaux Clairet
33550 Tabanac tel: 05 56 67 53 16
fax: 05 56 67 26 28
The château has an aristocratic allure. It went
up not long after the French Revolution and
was commissioned by the Clauzel family, back
from exile in Martinique. Its red wine, too, has
allure. In bouquet and taste it is substantial and
fruity (blackcurrant, blackberry), and fills the
mouth expansively with ripe tannins and spicy
oak. Other wines made here are a dry white AC
Bordeaux (Cuvée Spéciale Fût), full of
character, and a Clairet.

Ch Poncet
map 31/R G1

owner: Jean-Luc David *area:* 38 ha *cases:* 8,300,
white 14,000 *grape % R:* MER 75% CS 25% *grape %
W:* SEM 50% SAUV B 25% MUSC 25% *second wine:* Ch
de Vigneau *other wines:* Ch Poncet *(Cadillac;
Bordeaux blanc) other châteaux owned:* Ch Piot-
David *(Sauternes)*
33410 Omet tel: 05 56 62 97 30
fax: 05 56 62 66 76
The red Premières Côtes de Bordeaux is not bad
– perhaps a little rustic, but showing attractive
fruity and floral elements. The real star is the
Cadillac, which is hardly surprising since the
same owner also makes Sauternes at Ch Piot-
David. The golden-yellow wine is aromatic and
freshly fruity, with a sound balance.

Ch La Prioulette
map 31/R K9

owner: François Bord *area:* 13 ha *cases:* 6,500,
white 1,100 *grape % R:* MER 60% CS 20% CF 20%
grape % W: SEM 70% SAUV B 30% *second wine:* Ch

au Cypres *other wines:* Bordeaux blanc; Bordeaux
rouge *other châteaux owned:* Ch Mayne de
Coutureau *(Graves)*
33490 St-Maixant tel: 05 56 62 01 97
fax: 05 56 76 70 79
From this hilltop château you look down on Ch
Malagar, formerly owned by the author François
Mauriac. The Prioulette red is solidly built, with
a slightly animal aroma, a limited dose of fruit,
and sometimes a little dusty bitterness. The
quality can vary considerably according to
vintage. Its two years in cask is a relatively long
spell for the appellation. Among other wines
made are a semi-sweet white Premières Côtes,
with a suggestion of citrus fruit.

Ch Puy Bardens
map 32/L K8

owner: GFA Lamiable *area:* 17 ha *cases:* 8,500,
grape % R: MER 45% CS 45% CF 10% *second wine:*
Les Graves de Matiou
33880 Cambes tel: 05 56 21 31 14
fax: 05 56 21 86 40
The original modest *chartreuse* here was rebuilt
in 1864 into a small ornamental castle, with
two octagonal towers adorning its front. The
red Premières Côtes produced here is a
mouthfilling wine: it is compact, with both ripe
fruit and vanilla, as well as dark notes of
bayleaf, licorice, cocoa, spice and tannin. The
Merlot is clearly dominant. This wine is given
12 months in oak, about a third of the barrels
being new.

Ch Renon
map 32/R J4

owner: Jacques Boucherie *area:* 11 ha *cases:*
3,300, white 2,900 *grape % R:* MER 60% CS 40%
grape % W: SAUV B 70% SEM 30% *other wines:*
Cadillac; Bordeaux blanc; Bordeaux Clairet
33550 Tabanac tel: 05 56 67 13 59
fax: 05 56 67 14 90
An estate dating from the 11th century which
in 1583 acquired its name from Jean de Renon.
Among the subsequent owners have been the
Lur Saluces family of Ch d'Yquem. The present
talented owner, Jacques Boucherie, makes seven
wines, among them the amazing cask-aged
white AC Bordeaux Cuvée Marie-Claire, and a
reasonably rich Cadillac. Down through the
years the red Premières Côtes de Bordeaux has
shown an immaculate quality: vigorous,
elegant, with berry fruit, mellow vanilla and
solid tannins.

Ch Reynon
map 31/L I8

owner: Denis & Florence Dubourdieu *area:* 38 ha
cases: 9,500, white 11,000 *grape % R:* MER 60% CS
40% *grape % W:* SEM 50% SAUV B 45% MUSC 5%
second wine: Le Second de Reynon *other wines:*
Bordeaux blanc *other châteaux owned:* Clos
Floridène *(Graves)*
33410 Béguey tel: 05 56 62 96 51
fax: 05 56 62 14 89
This is the residence of Denis Dubourdieu, the
brilliant professor who has contributed so much
to better vinification of the dry white wines
here in Bordeaux. The classical foursquare
château stands on a hill above Béguey, with a
good-sized cellar complex adjoining. Every one
of the wines made here is delicious. Thus the
red Premières Côtes de Bordeaux has colour,
backbone, toasted oak and juicy, ripe fruit with
a hint of cocoa. The dry white wines have the
Bordeaux appellation: Sémillon is the dominant
grape in the standard wine; Sauvignon from old
vines determines the splendid, fruity aroma of
the Ch Reynon Vieilles Vignes.

Below: Ch Puy Bardens

Above: Ch Reynon

Ch de Ricaud
map 31/R H2

owner: Alain Thiénot *area:* 75 ha *cases:* 35,000, white 5,600 *grape % R:* MER 50% CS 50% *grape % W:* SEM 80% SAUV B 20% *second wine:* Ch Garreau (Bordeaux Supérieur) *other wines:* Hauts de Ricaud (Loupiac); Bordeaux Supérieur; Bordeaux blanc; Bordeaux rosé *other châteaux owned:* include Ch Haut-Gros-Caillou (St-Emilion); Ch Rahoul (Graves)
33410 Loupiac tel: 05 56 62 66 16
fax: 05 56 76 93 30
Against the backdrop of an old castle a correct, fairly straightforward red Premières Côtes de Bordeaux is produced, with berry fruit and oak in exemplary balance. More notable is the Loupiac: this gets a year's oak-ageing (a quarter of the barrels are new), giving distinct oak in the perfume and taste. It also has finesse, and gentle hints of candied fruits and honey. The Ch de Ricaud Bordeaux rosé, too, can be very successful.

Ch Roquebert
map 32/L L7

owner: Christian & Philippe Neys *area:* 15 ha *cases:* 6,650 *grape % R:* MER 50% CS 30% CF 15% MAL 5% *other wines:* Bordeaux Clairet
33360 Quinsac tel: 05 56 87 60 01
fax: 05 56 87 60 01
Quinsac is, as it were, the Clairet capital, so this light red wine is well to the fore at Ch Roquebert – and is in fact of considerable merit. The red Cuvée Spéciale (Premières Côtes de Bordeaux) tastes quite different; it is rather rustic and angular in style, with at the same time power and sometimes rather dry tannins. The fruitier and more supple standard wine is more accessible.

Ch Roquebrune
map 32/L G5

owner: SCE Vidal *area:* 20 ha *cases:* 10,200, white 700 *grape % R:* CS 65% MER 35% *grape % W:* SAUV B 100% *other wines:* Bordeaux blanc *other châteaux owned:* Ch Cursol (AC Bordeaux); Ch de Brice (Bordeaux Supérieur)
33360 Cénac tel: 05 56 20 70 75
fax: 05 56 20 11 99

Since 1962 this vineyard has been enlarged from 3 ha to its present size, and the Vidal family restored the 17th-century barrel-cellar. Here the Grand Roquebrune du Ch Roquebrune matures for a year: a red wine with more substance and depth than the fresh, sometimes rather slender standard Premières Côtes de Bordeaux.

Clos Sainte-Anne
map 31/L F4

owner: Francis Courselle *area:* 6 ha *cases:* 2,000, white 1,250 *grape % R:* MER 80% CS 20% *grape % W:* SAUV B 60% SEM 40% *other wines:* Cadillac *other châteaux owned:* Ch Thieuley (AC Bordeaux)
33550 Capian tel: 05 56 23 00 01
fax: 05 56 23 34 37
This property is run by the well-known winemaker Francis Courselle from the Entre-Deux-Mers. It yields an excellently-made red wine, fairly rich and strong, with a balanced taste in which black fruit from the Merlot goes splendidly with notes of smoky oak, bayleaf and spices.

Below: Ch de Ricaud

Ch Sainte-Catherine
map 31/L G3

owner: Famille de Coster *area:* 40 ha *cases:* 8,200, white 11,000 *grape % R:* CS 50% MER 50% *grape % W:* SEM 80% MUSC 15% SAUV B 5% *second wine:* Catherine de France *other wines:* Bordeaux blanc; Bordeaux rouge; Bordeaux rosé; Crémant de Bordeaux
33550 Paillet tel: 05 56 72 11 64
fax: 05 56 72 13 62
Old property with a chapel, once a refuge for pilgrims. A red wine of substance and breeding is produced here, in which the Cabernet Sauvignon sets the tone, with ripe berry fruit, a hint of paprika, and oak making its presence felt. Oak is also harmoniously present in the semi-sweet white, a fresh, fruity wine fermented in new casks.

Ch Saint-Ourens
map 32/R J8

owner: Michel Maës *area:* 4.1 ha *cases:* 1,670, white 900 *grape % R:* MER 34% CF 33% CS 33% *grape % W:* SEM 80% SAUV B 20% *other wines:* Bordeaux blanc; Bordeaux Clairet
33550 Langoiran tel: 05 56 67 39 45
fax: 05 56 67 37 56
In 1968 this very modest vineyard covered just 2 ha. It was then acquired by a restaurateur; he extended it to its present area of about 4 ha. The agricultural engineer Michel Maes, its owner since 1990, hopes to add another 1.2 ha. The red Premières Côtes de Bordeaux made here contains a lot of Cabernet, which shows through in the notes of mint and a red and black fruit cocktail in its aroma. Somewhat slender, at present this is a wine of average quality.

Ch Le Sens
map 32/L G5

owner: Francine & Francis Courrèges *area:* 10 ha *cases:* 3,300 *grape % R:* MER 55% CS 30% CF 15% *other châteaux owned:* Ch Margoton (Premières Côtes de Bordeaux); Ch La Joffrière (Premières Côtes de Bordeaux)
33880 Saint-Caprais tel: 05 56 21 32 87
fax: 05 56 21 37 18
In the cellar of this château, built between 1900 and 1930, the oenologist Francis Courrèges can offer his visitors various wines to sample. One of these is the aromatic red Premières Côtes de Bordeaux with its seductive fruit (black cherry, tropical). Ch Le Sens also produces a more solid, oak-aged *cuvée*.

Above: Ch Sainte-Catherine

Above: Ch Suau

Ch Sissan
map 32/L H8

owner: SCEA Pierre Yung & Fils *area:* 20 ha *cases:* 12,500 *grape % R:* MER 55% CS 35% CF 10% *other châteaux owned:* Ch Grimont *(Premières Côtes de Bordeaux)*

33360 Camblanes-et-Meynac tel: 05 56 20 00 98

Wine estate in existence since 1980, belonging to the Vignobles Yung concern. The red wine is not unpleasing with its fruit (blackcurrant) and its cedary oak, but sometimes it shows a slight lack of depth. However, the quality seems to be improving; this château could be worth following.

Ch Suau
map 31/L F5

owner: Monique Aldebert *area:* 59 ha *cases:* 28,100, white 5,000 *grape % R:* CS 40% MER 35% CF 25% *grape % W:* SEM 40% SAUV B 30% MUSC 30% *second wine:* Ch Maubert *other wines:* Bordeaux blanc; Bordeaux rosé

33550 Capian tel: 05 56 72 19 06
fax: 05 56 72 12 43

Wholly renovated estate, where the 15th-century château with its round towers stands in parkland among ancient trees. The Duc d'Epernon used to come here hunting game, but today it is wine that is sought – for it is very good, particularly the red Cuvée Prestige. Blackberry, black cherry and blackcurrant fruit, plus bayleaf, cocoa, some oak and powerful tannins, are all there to stir the senses. There is, too, a Prestige variant which the lady owner ferments in new oak: an exquisite wine that is a match for a good Graves.

Ch Tanesse
map 32/R K7

owner: Domaines Cordier *area:* 40 ha *cases:* 10,830, white 13,300 *grape % R:* CS 55% MER 40% CF 5% *grape % W:* SAUV B 60% SEM 40% *second wine:* Ch Haut-Mardan *other wines:* Bordeaux blanc *other châteaux owned:* include Ch Clos des Jacobins *(St-Emilion)*

33550 Langoiran tel: 05 56 67 00 51
fax: 05 56 67 58 81

Here the wines are matured in large vats rather than the smaller *barriques*: the red Premières Côtes for twelve months, the dry white AC Bordeaux for four. The influence of the wood is noticeable. Thus the red wine has a touch of vanilla: its style is fruity and elegant, with sufficient texture as well. A creamy agreeable

aftertaste, nicely juicy. The château was built in the 19th century.

Domaine des Trois Clochers
map 32/R H7

owner: Peter & Fleming Jørgensen *area:* 5 ha *cases:* 1,800, white 300 *grape % R:* CS 40% MER 35% CF 25% *grape % W:* SEM 60% SAUV B 30% MUSC 10% *other wines:* Bordeaux blanc; Bordeaux Clairet *other châteaux owned:* Ch Saint-Pierre *(Bordeaux)*; Ch de Haux *(Premières Côtes de Bordeaux)*; Ch Gourran *(Premières Côtes de Bordeaux)*; Ch Frère *(Premières Côtes de Bordeaux)*

33550 Haux tel: 05 56 23 35 07
fax: 05 56 23 25 29

Small vineyard, supervised by the team from Ch de Haux. In good years the red Premières Côtes here is very fine: rich and expansive, with freshness, good tannins, the fruit of black currants and cherries, vanilla (a fifth of the casks are new, and the wine spends 6-10 months in them). A dry white AC Bordeaux is also produced. The planted area of this domaine is to be increased.

◆
ACs Bordeaux & Bordeaux Supérieur

These are the basic generic ACs that cover the entire Bordeaux *vignoble*. In practice, however, since a large proportion of these wines come from the wider Entre-Deux-Mers area, wherever they come from they are covered in that chapter – or in this, the Premières Côtes de Bordeaux chapter, if the château is in this zone.

◆
Neighbouring appellations

The Premières Côtes de Bordeaux and Cadillac are bordered to the north-east by the Entre-Deux-Mers appellation. The Haut-Benauge zone, which is a sub-district of the Entre-Deux-Mers AC, lies to the east of the southern part of the Premières Côtes.

Some low-lying land along the Garonne valley can only use the generic Bordeaux appellations.

Ch Vieille Tour
map 31/L H8

owner: Arlette Gouin *area:* 26.5 ha *cases:* 12,500, white 7,600 *grape % R:* MER 70% CS 20% CF 10% *grape % W:* SEM 60% SAUV B 20% MUSC 20% *other wines:* Bordeaux rosé; Bordeaux blanc; Bordeaux rouge

33410 Laroque tel: 05 56 62 61 21
fax: 05 56 76 94 18

Family property where seven wines are made. The oak-aged red and white Premières Côtes are both very decent. They are matured for nine months in barrels of which most are new.

LOUPIAC AND STE-CROIX-DU-MONT

These two small sweet white wine appellations are located on the southern side of the Entre-Deux-Mers. They sit as enclaves within the south-eastern half of the Premières Côtes de Bordeaux AC and both share a landscape of quite steep hills and charming valleys, a world away from the plains of the Graves just opposite. Immediately to the north-west is Cadillac, a third sweet white wine-producing zone, which is discussed in the previous chapter. To the south Loupiac and Ste-Croix-du-Mont are limited by the D10 road, just beyond which runs the Garonne river, which has an influential role in determining the microclimate of these two appellations. As in Sauternes, growers hope for a mild, misty autumn to encourage noble rot. The main grape variety for these sweet wines is Sémillon, followed by Sauvignon and Muscadelle. Although some red wine is also produced here, this is only entitled to the basic Bordeaux or Bordeaux Supérieur appellation.

LOUPIAC

This is the smaller and more north-westerly of the two appellations. It faces Barsac across the River Garonne. The soil types are generally quite similar to that of Ste-Croix-du-Mont: clay-limestone with some clay-gravel. In good years (and especially in those properties which lie closest to the river) noble rot does occur: these wines can be fairly rich with good ageing potential. However,

The golden hues of Loupiac

most Loupiacs are on the lighter side, and less full and weighty than those of neighbouring Ste-Croix, although decidedly better than anything else from this side of the river other than a leading Cadillac. Annual production averages 140,000 cases.

STE-CROIX-DU-MONT

Immediately south-east of Loupiac, a further five kilometres upstream from Bordeaux, is the commune of Ste-Croix-du-Mont. Topography and soil types are similar – steep limestone hills with some clay on the plateau behind them. Across the Garonne river lies Sauternes and indeed, in a good year, the wines from this area are often considered to be a type of junior Sauternes – not quite as rich or concentrated, but *pourriture noble* plays its part and the best wines can be rich, weighty and mouthfilling with some ageing potential. These are generally considered the best of all the area's sweet wines, and the longest-lived. They also cost considerably less than their more famous neighbours across the river. Average production here is slightly higher than that in Loupiac – around the 165,000 case mark.

Both zones also have châteaux making dry white and red wines using the Bordeaux and Bordeaux Supérieur generic appellations. Several properties in neighbouring communes which lie within the Premières Côtes area also have vineyards in Loupiac or Ste-Croix-du-Mont and include these among their range of wines.

Wide views are a feature of the vineyards of Ste-Croix-du-Mont

THE APPELLATIONS

LOUPIAC (*sweet white*)

Location: *On the right bank of the Garonne, on the southern side of the Entre-Deux-Mers. Approximately 40 km south-east of Bordeaux, 12 from Langon. To the north-west, north and east it is surrounded by the Premières Côtes de Bordeaux and Cadillac. To the south-east is Ste-Croix-du-Mont. Beyond the D10 and the river is land covered by the straight Bordeaux AC.*
Area of AC: *758 ha*
Area under vine: *350 ha*
Communes: *Loupiac*
Average annual production: *140,000 cases*
Classed growths: *None*
Others: *70*
Cooperatives: *None*
Main grape varieties: *Sémillon, Sauvignon*
Others: *Muscadelle*
Main soil types: *Clay-limestone, clay-gravel*

STE-CROIX-DU-MONT (*sweet white*)

Location: *On the right bank of the Garonne, on the southern side of the Entre-Deux-Mers. Approximately 42 km south-east of Bordeaux, 10 from Langon. To the north-west is Loupiac, to the north and east the Premières Côtes de Bordeaux. Immediately to the south of the D10 is the river and riverside land covered by the straight Bordeaux and Bordeaux Supérieur ACs.*
Area of AC: *770 ha*
Area under vine: *440 ha*
Communes: *Ste-Croix-du-Mont*
Average annual production: *165,000 cases*
Classed growths: *None*
Others: *90*
Cooperatives: *None*
Main grape varieties: *Sémillon, Sauvignon*
Others: *Muscadelle*
Main soil types: *Clay-limestone, clay-gravel*

APPELLATION LOUPIAC

Domaine du Chaÿ
map 31/R J3

owner: J. Tourré **area:** 10 ha **cases:** white 4,000 **grape % W:** SEM 80% MUSC 10% SAUV B 10% **second wine:** Ch Fortin **other châteaux owned:** Ch de Toulet *(AC Bordeaux; Entre-Deux-Mers)*; Ch Les Gaillardes *(Graves)*
33410 Loupiac tel: 05 56 62 99 45
fax: 05 56 27 01 24
This is often a quite sweet, opulent Loupiac, frequently with a touch of tropical fruit in its firm, supple taste. The wine is not oak-aged.

Ch du Cros
map 31/R L3

owner: Vignobles Michel Boyer **area:** 43 ha **cases:** white 15,500 **grape % W:** SEM 70% SAUV B 20% MUSC 10% **second wines:** Ch Ségur du Cros; Fleur de Cros; Ch des Roches **other wines:** Bordeaux rouge & blanc **other châteaux owned:** Clos Bourbon *(Premières Côtes de Bordeaux)*; Ch Lepine *(Ste-Croix-du-Mont)*; Ch Haut-Mayne *(Graves)*; Ch de Lucques *(Sauternes)*
33410 Loupiac tel: 05 56 62 99 31
fax: 05 56 62 12 59
The present château stands close to the tree-surrounded remains of a 14th-century stronghold. This in its turn was built on the foundations of a 13th-century castle. The Loupiac made here is generally among the better examples of the appellation. Characteristically it boasts a fine perfume – blossom, candied apricot, a touch of vanilla, a hint of honey – and a well-structured, fresh and elegant taste that is sufficiently sweet. Its time in cask is geared to the quality of the harvest. Lesser years are given nine months, in 20% new barrels; the best years 18 months in 60–100% new wood. The estate also produces an outstanding, expressive dry white Bordeaux, Le Cros Bois et Tradition.

Ch Cru Champon
map 31

owner: Yvan Réglat **area:** 4 ha **cases:** white 1,600 **grape % W:** SEM 85% SAUV B 10% MUSC 5% **other châteaux owned:** Ch Balot *(Premières Côtes de Bordeaux)*; Ch Jean du Roy *(Cadillac)*
33410 Loupiac tel: 05 56 62 98 96
fax: 05 56 62 19 48
A clean, fruity, freshly sweet Loupiac is made here and given about eight months' maturing in casks of which 25% are new.

Ch Dauphiné Rondillon
map 31/R I3

owner: G. Darriet **area:** 18.5 ha **cases:** white 7,000 **grape % W:** SEM 80% SAUV B 15% MUSC 5% **second wine:** Ch de Rouquette **other châteaux owned:** Ch Les Tourelles *(Premières Côtes de Bordeaux)*; Ch Moutin *(Graves)*
33410 Loupiac tel: 05 56 62 61 75
Carefully made Loupiac that in good vintages presents a mixture of citrus and exotic fruit, with a balanced, mouthfilling taste.

Ch Grand Peyruchet
map 31/R I1

owner: M. Gillet & B. Queyrens **area:** 9 ha **cases:** white 2,000 **grape % W:** SEM 100% **second wine:** Ch du Moulin **other châteaux owned:** Domaine du Moulin *(Premières Côtes de Bordeaux)*; Ch Peyruchet *(Premières Côtes de Bordeaux)*
33410 Loupiac tel: 05 56 62 62 71
fax: 05 56 76 92 09
In this wine the *rôti* aroma is clearly and agreeably present in good vintages, as in the 1990 for example. In more ordinary years it is a quite expansive, pleasing, but not especially

finely nuanced or exciting Loupiac. The time in wood lasts six to nine months. The wine is made at Ch Peyruchet, a property whose modern equipment produces mainly Premières Côtes de Bordeaux and Bordeaux.

Clos Jean
map 31/R J3

owner: Lionel Bord **area:** 16 ha **cases:** 4,500, white 10,800 **grape % R:** MER 90% MAL 10% **grape % W:** SEM 80% SAUV B 20% **second wines:** Ch Jean Fontenille; Ch Loustalot **other wines:** AC Bordeaux **other châteaux owned:** Ch Rondillon *(Loupiac)*
33410 Loupiac tel: 05 56 62 99 83
fax: 05 56 62 93 55
For five generations the Bord family has been making Loupiac from the high ground on which Clos Jean lies. Their experience generally produces a delicious wine, expressive and fine-boned. Its aroma has elements of raisin, tropical fruit, spices, a very light touch of oak. The white Bordeaux, too, is worth discovering: where Sémillon is dominant in the Loupiac, in this Clos Jean dry white Sauvignon is pre-eminent

Ch Loupiac-Gaudiet
map 31/R K2

owner: Marc Ducau **area:** 27 ha **cases:** white 8,000 **grape % W:** SEM 80% SAUV B 20% **second wines:** Ch Sterlines; Ch Martillac **other wines:** Ch Desclan *(AC Bordeaux)*; Ch Rosier *(AC Bordeaux)*
33410 Loupiac tel: 05 56 62 99 88
fax: 05 56 62 60 13
This château, a *chartreuse* flanked by two pavilions and set among the plane trees of its park, has been the home of the Ducau family for four generations. Floral notes and spicy fruit (apricot, peach, banana), are usually characteristic of both bouquet and taste of this wine – a most reliable, graceful, fresh Loupiac, deliberately given no ageing in wood.

Ch Mazarin
map 31/R K3

owner: Louis Courbin & Jean-Yves Arnaud **area:** 21 ha **cases:** 5,000, white 4,000 **grape % R:** MER 60% CS 30% CF 10% **grape % W:** SEM 70% SAUV B 20% MUSC 10% **other wines:** Domaine de la Croix *(AC Bordeaux)*; Ch Frappe-Peyrot *(AC Bordeaux)*
33410 Loupiac tel: 05 56 20 23 52

Below: Clos Jean

Above: Ch Dauphiné Rondillon

That Mazarin's Loupiac spends about a year in *barriques,* 25% of which are new, is clearly evident: vanilla and oak aromas generously complement the fruit of this elegant wine.

Ch Mémoires
map 31/R L8

owner: Jean-François Menard **area:** 42 ha **cases:** 15,700, white 10,500 **grape % R:** MER 60% CS 35% CF 5% **grape % W:** SEM 70% SAUV B 15% MUSC 15% **other wines:** Cadillac; Bordeaux rouge & blanc
33490 St-Maixant tel: 05 56 62 06 43
fax: 05 56 62 04 32
Loupiac, Cadillac, Red Premières Côtes de Bordeaux, red and white Bordeaux: the wines from this estate come in many styles. The Loupiac is the most memorable. It is matured for about a year, sometimes even in exclusively new casks. The standard version has an average, by no means remarkable quality. The Sélection des Grains Nobles, only sporadically produced, is of a considerably higher standard and better balanced. This wine – 1990 was its first year – offers fine oak, a lot of vanilla, a very reasonable

Above: Ch Loupiac Gaudiet

Above: Ch Mazarin

richness, depth, concentration and, because of its freshness, refinement as well.

Ch du Merle
map 31/R I3

owner: Viviane Fouquet *area:* 6.5 ha *cases:* white 1,000 *grape % W:* SEM 70% SAUV B 20% MUSC 10% *second wine:* Domaine du Moulin Vieux; Bordeaux
33410 Loupiac tel: 05 56 62 94 35
fax: 05 56 62 94 35
Family estate working to traditional standards where the grape pickers comb the vineyard at least three times. Tropical fruit and apricot often characterize the fresh, slightly honeyed taste. A brief maturing in wood only takes place with the better vintages.

Ch La Nère
map 31/R K3

owner: Yves Dulac *area:* 14 ha *cases:* white 6,100 *grape % W:* SEM 90% SAUV B 10% *other châteaux owned:* Ch Chanteloiseau (*Premières Côtes de Bordeaux*); Domaine Roustit (*Ste-Croix-du-Mont*)
33410 Loupiac tel: 05 56 62 03 20
fax: 05 56 76 71 49
Decent, fairly straightforward and often pleasantly fruity Loupiac. It is made mainly from Sémillon grapes and does not come into contact with wood.

Domaine du Noble
map 31/R I3

owner: Patrick Dejean *area:* 11 ha *cases:* white 4,300 *grape % W:* SEM 85% SAUV B 15% *second wine:* Ch du Gascon
33410 Loupiac tel: 05 56 62 99 36
Wine estate adorning a hilltop, with a marvellous view over the Garonne valley; it justifies its name, for it produces one of the best and most noble of Loupiacs. Even in lesser years the wine has a notable richness and finesse to it. Its aroma often has gentle fresh fruit notes – apricots, peaches – as well as honey, almonds and oak. Maturing lasts 10-18 months, depending on the vintage, and at least 25% of the barrels are new.

Ch Les Rocques
map 31/R L4

owner: Alain & Viviane Fertal *area:* 3.8 ha *cases:* white 1,000 *grape % W:* SEM 85% SAUV B 12% MUSC 3% *other châteaux owned:* Ch du Pavillon (*Ste-Croix-du-Mont; Bordeaux*)
33410 Loupiac tel: 05 56 62 01 04

fax: 05 56 62 00 92
This is in most years a fresh wine somewhat short of sweetness or opulence. It could be a lighter version of Ch du Pavillon in Ste-Croix-du-Mont – which has the same owner.

Ch Rondillon
map 31/R J3

owner: François Bord *area:* 10 ha *cases:* white 3,500 *grape % W:* SEM 80% SAUV B 15% MUSC 5% *second wines:* Ch Loustalot; Ch Rondillon Loubat; Ch Jean Fontenille *other wines:* AC Bordeaux; Ch Mingot (*AC Bordeaux*) *other châteaux owned:* Clos Jean (*Loupiac*)
33410 Loupiac tel: 05 56 62 99 83
fax: 05 56 62 93 55
Wine akin to that from Clos Jean, which has the same owners and methods. It is seldom highly concentrated, but does have lively nuances. Sometimes, too, there is a fine *rôti* aroma – as in 1994, when 80% of the grapes were affected by *pourriture noble*. The Bord family bought the estate in 1970, having previously leased it.

Below Domaine du Noble

Ch Le Tarey
map 31/R I2

owner: Patrick Gillet *area:* 7.5 ha *cases:* white 3,000 *grape % W:* SEM 90% SAUV B 5% MUSC 5% *other châteaux owned:* Clos Bellevue (*Premières Côtes*); Cru du Pin Copies (*Ste-Croix-du-Mont*)
33410 Loupiac tel: 05 56 62 99 99
fax: 05 56 62 65 33
A reasonably sweet, but not really refined Loupiac in which elements of tropical fruit, lime blossom and sometimes almond can be found. No ageing in cask.

Ch Terrefort
map 31/R H2

owner: François Peyrondet *area:* 13 ha *cases:* 2,800, white 3,200 *grape % R:* MER 60% CS 40% *grape % W:* SEM 80% SAUV B 10% MUSC 10% *second wine:* Bois de Roche *other wines:* Ch Ternefat (*Bordeaux rouge*)
33410 Loupiac tel: 05 56 62 61 28
fax: 05 56 62 19 42
Fresh, very decent, although seldom unctuously sweet Loupiac. In good vintages only, it has a short spell of three-six months in used barrels.

Ch Vieux Moulin Cazeaux
map 31/R I3

owner: Suzanne Perromat *area:* 12 ha *cases:* white 4,500 *grape % W:* SEM 75% SAUV B 20% MUSC 5% *other châteaux owned:* Domaine de Terrefort (*Bordeaux Supérieur*); Ch du Mayne (*Graves*); Ch de Cérons (*Cérons*); Ch Prost (*Sauternes*)
33410 Loupiac tel: 05 56 27 01 13
fax: 05 56 27 22 17
At this estate, on high ground, the pickers often go through the vines four or five times. Also traditional is the average two years' cask-ageing in 20% new oak. The wine is satisfactorily, but not extremely, sweet – and definitely has style. Its nuances are often of citrus and other Mediterranean fruits, plus spicy oak.

◆
About Loupiac
For information about the wines contact the Syndicat viticole at the Chambre d'Agriculture, 22 chemin le Vergey, 33410 Cadillac. Tel 05 56 62 67 18.

APPELLATION STE-CROIX-DU-MONT

Ch des Arroucats
map 31/R L6

owner: Annie Lapouge **area:** 17 ha **cases:** white 3,000 **grape % W:** SEM 50% MUSC 30% SAUV B 20% **second wines:** Ch Bougan; Ch d'Orleac **other wines:** Bordeaux blanc **other châteaux owned:** Domaine du Merle (Premières Côtes de Bordeaux)
33410 Ste-Croix-du-Mont tel: 05 56 62 07 37 fax: 05 56 62 13 14

A wine seldom affected by *pourriture noble*, fairly sweet and quite lively, with a touch of candied fruit and floral elements in its aroma. Maturing in cask in most vintages lasts approximately six months. The estate has also used a label with the name Domaine des Arroucats, and the firm Edmond Coste in Langon takes part of the vintage, bottling it as Cru des Arroucats.

Ch Bel-Air
map 31/R L5

owner: Michel Méric **area:** 12 ha **cases:** white 4,000 **grape % W:** SEM 87% SAUV B 13%
33410 Ste-Croix-du-Mont tel: 05 56 62 01 19 fax: 05 56 62 09 33

The exotic fruit and spice aroma of Sémillon clearly comes through in this generally firm, fairly full-bodied Ste-Croix-du-Mont. The wine is not matured in wood.

Ch Coulac
map 31/R L4

owner: Gérard Despujols **area:** 16 ha **cases:** white 5,000 **grape % W:** SEM 80% SAUV B 10% MUSC 10% **other wines:** Burdigala (Crémant de Bordeaux) **other châteaux owned:** Ch de l'Emigré (Graves)
33410 Ste-Croix-du-Mont tel: 05 56 27 01 64 fax: 05 56 27 13 70

Acacia, almond, and just slightly peppery fruit can be found in this generally very correct wine. Its oak notes are due to one to two years in barrels of which a third are new.

Ch des Coulinats
map 31/R L6

owner: Camille Brun **area:** 16 ha **cases:** 1,750, white 6,100 **grape % R:** MER 50% CS 50% **grape % W:** SEM 90% MUSC 5% SAUV B 5% **other wines:** Ch de Berbec (Bordeaux rouge; Premières Côtes de Bordeaux; Cadillac)
33410 Ste-Croix-du-Mont tel: 05 56 62 10 60

Family estate now some 200 years old where, to increase its aromas, the wine is often kept on its lees for a long time. It is only bottled after 4-5 years in tanks. Features of this exemplary Ste-Croix-du-Mont are its substantial structure, its candied tropical fruits, a hint of caramel and the potential for long maturing. The château cellar still holds vintages from decades ago.

Ch Crabitan-Bellevue
map 31/R K5

owner: GFA B. Solane & Fils **area:** 33 ha **cases:** 3,800, white 14,400 **grape % R:** MER 70% CS 25% CF 5% **grape % W:** SEM 85% SAUV B 8% MUSC 7% **second wine:** Clos de Crabitan **other wines:** Premières Côtes de Bordeaux; Bordeaux rouge, blanc & rosé
33410 Ste-Croix-du-Mont tel: 05 56 62 01 53 fax: 05 56 76 72 09

The Solane family, originally coopers, created this estate in 1870. Besides the clean, elegant and fresh standard sweet wine, a remarkable Cuvée Spéciale is produced here in the great years. This wine, usually oak-matured for 11-12 months (one-third new casks), can reach an alcohol content of 15%, as in 1990, and combines vanilla oak with apricot and peach nectar. This hilltop château – hence the 'Bellevue' name – also produces various other

Top: Ch des Arroucats

Above: Ch Crabitan-Bellevue

wines. One of the most interesting is the red Bordeaux Cuvée Spéciale – more or less fruity, concentrated and matured in wood.

Ch de l'Escaley
map 31/R K5

owner: GFA du Ch de l'Escaley/Famille Saint-Marc **area:** 8 ha **cases:** white 1,080 **grape % W:** SEM 85% SAUV B 10% MUSC 5% **second wine:** Ch Bertrand
33410 Ste-Croix-du-Mont tel: 05 56 62 06 12

There are many old vines here, and the grapes are picked as late as possible. The wine – or some of it – goes into cask for between two to four years. This Ste-Croix-du-Mont will age in bottle superbly – as is shown by the vintages the owner has in stock. Apricot, peach, grapefruit and pineapple are among the aromas that can occur in its clean, generous taste.

♦

About Ste-Croix-du-Mont

For information about the wines of Ste-Croix-du-Mont contact the Syndicat viticole at the Chambre d'Agriculture, 22 chemin le Vergey, 33410 Cadillac. Tel 05 56 62 67 18.

Ch Goutey-Lagravière
map 31/R J4

owner: Françoise Duperrieu **area:** 2.2 ha **cases:** white 970 **grape % W:** SEM 95% SAUV B 5% **other châteaux owned:** Ch Haut-Goutey (Premières Côtes de Bordeaux; Cadillac)
33410 Ste-Croix-du-Mont tel: 05 56 62 08 85 fax: 05 56 76 91 32

Very modest production of a decent, firm, correctly sweet wine; however, it rather tends to be somewhat lacking in its concentration, substance and richness. Not oak-aged.

Ch La Grave
map 31/R K6

owner: Jean-Marie Tinon **area:** 23 ha **cases:** 3,500, white 5,500 **grape % R:** MER 55% CS 45% **grape % W:** SEM 90% SAUV B 10% **other wines:** Bordeaux rouge & blanc **other châteaux owned:** Ch Grand Peyrot (Ste-Croix-du-Mont)
33410 Ste-Croix-du-Mont tel: 05 56 62 01 65 fax: 05 56 62 00 04

This wine estate enjoys a solid reputation for its Ste-Croix-du-Mont – nearly always a firm, rounded, properly sweet and aromatic creation that also has a hint of oak. A comparable wine, albeit from rather older vines, is the Ch Grand Peyrot. Red and dry white Bordeaux are also produced here.

Ch Laborie
map 31/R L6

owner: Roland Danies-Sauvestre **area:** 12 ha **cases:** white 4,400 **grape % W:** SEM 80% SAUV B 20% **second wines:** Ch Grolet; Ch Laton **other châteaux owned:** Ch Bramepan (Ste-Croix-du-Mont); Ch Terrefort (Premières Côtes de Bordeaux); Ch Vieux Mourlane (Premières Côtes de Bordeaux)
33410 Ste-Croix-du-Mont tel: 05 56 62 01 52

A good year means a reasonably rich, balanced Ste-Croix-du-Mont from this 1879 château. It has no contact with wood.

Ch Lamarque
map 31/R L4

owner: Bernard Darroman **area:** 22 ha **cases:** 3,000, white 5,000 **grape % R:** MER 60% CS 40% **grape % W:** SEM 85% SAUV B 15% **second wine:** Ch La Perguerie **other wines:** Bordeaux rouge
33410 Ste-Croix-du-Mont tel: 05 56 62 01 21 fax: 05 56 76 72 10

The vineyard belonging to this château on a hill began life in 1640: it contains many old vines. Their average age is 45 years, and one two-hectare plot even has some century-old vines.

The Darroman family has run Lamarque since 1950 and makes an elegant style of Ste-Croix-du-Mont, reserved rather than exuberant. The wine spends about a year in cask and offers some discreet fruit – pineapple, apricot, grapefruit – and a hint of almond.

Ch Lepine
map 31/R L4

owner: Vignobles M. Boyer *area:* 2.7 ha *cases:* white 1,000 *grape % W:* SEM 60% SAUV B 40% *other châteaux owned:* include Ch du Cros *(Loupiac)* **33410 Ste-Croix-du-Mont tel: 05 56 62 99 31 fax: 05 56 62 12 59**
Wine aged in tanks, quite straightforward in taste and seldom richly sweet. Develops relatively quickly.

Ch Loubens
map 31/R L5

owner: Arnaud de Sèze *area:* 21 ha *cases:* white 8,500 *grape % W:* SEM 97% SAUV B 3% *second wine:* Ch des Tours *other wines:* Fleuron Blanc *(AC Bordeaux)*; Ch Le Grand Pré *(AC Bordeaux)* *other châteaux owned:* Ch Terfort *(Ste-Croix-du-Mont)* **33410 Ste-Croix-du-Mont tel: 05 56 62 01 25 fax: 05 56 76 71 65**
The history of this estate goes back to the early 17th century, when it belonged to Pierre de Lancre. Counsellor to Henri IV – *'le feu roi'* Henri-le-Grand – de Lancre was commissioned by the king to write treatises on witches and wizards, with the result that more than 500 witchcraft suspects went to the stake. The king also visited Loubens. In the 19th century the château was rebuilt, acquiring its seven underground cellars. The Loubens Ste-Croix-du-Mont is generally the best of its appellation. The wine ages for three years in tank, and it is normally given a further year in bottle. Its aroma has elements of ripe fruit (peach, apricot, banana), mild spices and, to a greater or lesser degree, *pourriture noble*. As a rule this stylish sweet wine will easily age for 15 years.

Ch Lousteau-Vieil
map 31/R L6

owner: R. Sessacq *area:* 12 ha *cases:* white 4,400 *grape % W:* SEM 75% SAUV B 15% MUSC 10% *other châteaux owned:* Clos La Maurasse *(Graves)*; Ch Lamaringue *(Sauternes)* **33410 Ste-Croix-du-Mont tel: 05 56 62 01 15 fax: 05 56 62 01 68**

Below: Ch La Grave

Above: Ch du Pavillon

Aniseed and other spices, from both the Sémillon and the oak (the casks are mainly used ones) are nearly always present in the bouquet and taste of this Ste-Croix-du-Mont. Fruit – raisins, citrus, tropical – and an adequate sweetness are seldom lacking either. All this adds up to an attractive whole – a wine of quality that has attracted a long series of bronze, silver and gold medals. At 118 m, the château is at the highest point of this commune; its first recorded owner, during the French Revolution, was the local mayor. Since 1843 it has belonged to the Sessacq family.

Ch des Mailles
map 31/R L6

owner: Daniel Larrieu *area:* 17 ha *cases:* 700, white 6,400 *grape % R:* MER 60% CF 35% CS 5% *grape % W:* SEM 80% SAUV B 10% MUSC 10% *second wine:* Domaine du Haut Mayne *other wines:* Bordeaux Supérieur; Bordeaux blanc, rosé & rouge **33410 Ste-Croix-du-Mont tel: 05 56 62 01 20 fax: 05 56 76 71 99**
While the standard, quite decent Ste-Croix-du-Mont is reasonably sweet and fruity, des Mailles' Réserve Personnelle is of significantly higher quality. It pleases the senses with a fine, creamy sweetness, spicy fruit, a touch of almond and slight toasted notes from the wood. Normally some of this wine is fermented in cask – after which, as with the standard version, there follows about a year in oak. The first Réserve Personnelle vintage was the 1990.

Ch Médouc
map 31/R L5

owner: Philippe Gaussem *area:* 6.5 ha *cases:* white 2,000 *grape % W:* SEM 90% SAUV B 10% *second wine:* Ch Les Charmilles *other wines:* Ch Médoc *(Bordeaux rouge)* *other châteaux owned:* Ch Tucau *(Sauternes)* **33410 Ste-Croix-du-Mont tel: 05 56 62 08 23 fax: 05 56 62 08 23**
There is often pineapple in the aroma of this Ste-Croix-du-Mont – a fine, quite generous wine, full of character, which is not oak-aged.

Ch du Mont
map 31/R K5

owner: Paul Chouvac *area:* 20 ha *cases:* 3,000, white 3,000 *grape % R:* MER 50% CS 30% CF 20% *grape % W:* SEM 80% SAUV B 10% MUSC 10% *second wine:* Ch de l'If *other wines:* Bordeaux blanc & rouge; Crémant de Bordeaux; Graves **33410 Ste-Croix-du-Mont tel: 05 56 62 01 72 fax: 05 56 62 07 58**
The quality of the wine here is usually good even in the less-than-great years. The taste is honeyed, almost syrupy, with nuances of Mediterranean fruits and oak. Of the casks this Ste-Croix-du-Mont matures in, a third are new

◆
Map numbers
Map 2, in the opening pages of the Atlas, shows the areas of all the Bordeaux appellations. To find a map for a specific appellation, turn to the regional key map.
◆
Maps of the appellations between the rivers
For a key map showing all the appellations in this zone, with the outlines of the maps in this Atlas, consult Map 30.

Above: Ch Loubens

Left: Ch Lousteau-Vieil

both bouquet and taste – the wine has 8-10 months in wood, and 20-25% of the barrels are new. The Loupiac, from old Sémillon vines, generally offers more opulence, more fruit (apricot, peach, mango), and more complexity.

Ch La Rame

map 31/R L6

owner: Yves Armand *area:* 20 ha *cases:* white 4,000 *grape % W:* SEM 75% SAUV B 25%
33410 Ste-Croix-du-Mont tel: 05 56 62 01 50 fax: 05 56 62 01 94
Lime blossom, candied apricot, banana, peach nectar, fresh pineapple, rôti tones, honey, vanilla, oak, spice – these are the kind of impressions that La Rame's Réserve du Château can subtly convey. This wine is among the best from Ste-Croix-du-Mont; it has style and balance as well as those subtle nuances. It spends from 18-24 months in *barriques*, a third of them new. The Armand family have owned the estate since 1956, and have given it the kind of lustre it had in the 19th century.

Domaine Roustit

map 31/R K7

owner: Jean Séraphon *area:* 3.5 ha *cases:* white 1,250 *grape % W:* SEM 90% SAUV B 10% *other châteaux owned:* Ch Chanteloiseau *(Premières Côtes de Bordeaux)*; Ch La Nère *(Loupiac)*
33410 Ste-Croix-du-Mont tel: 05 56 62 03 08 fax: 05 56 76 71 49
Decent Ste-Croix-du-Mont, strongly characterized by the Sémillon grape. It is matured entirely in stainless steel.

each year. Ch du Mont also produces no fewer than eight other wines, among them a red and a white Graves, and a Crémant de Bordeaux rosé.

Ch du Pavillon

map 31/R L4

owner: Viviane & Alain Fertac *area:* 4 ha *cases:* 2,000, white 1,200 *grape % R:* MER 80% CS 20% *grape % W:* SEM 85% SAUV B 12% MUSC 3% *other wines:* Bordeaux rouge *other châteaux owned:* Ch Les Rocques *(Loupiac)*
33410 Ste-Croix-du-Mont tel: 05 56 62 01 04 fax: 05 56 62 00 92
The owners here are proud that the terrace of their 18th-century château affords one of the best views in the region. The vineyard, partly on · a slope, delivers a Ste-Croix-du-Mont of generally sound quality: firm, reasonably sweet, with some freshness – sometimes with a slightly bitter or herbaceous touch. The only ageing is in tank. The good red Bordeaux is elegant and plummy.

Ch La Peyrère

map 31/R L6

owner: Jean-Pierre Dupuy *area:* 10 ha *cases:* white 4,000 *grape % W:* SEM 85% SAUV B 10% MUSC 5% *second wine:* Ch Daubrin *other wines:* Bordeaux *other châteaux owned:* Ch Rouquette *(Sauternes)*

33410 Ste-Croix-du-Mont tel: 05 56 62 01 82 fax: 05 56 76 70 80
The château is an austere-looking white building just north of the village centre. A wine is made here that is only modestly sweet, but has nuances of spice, oak (from eight months in barrel), and citrus fruit.

Ch Peyrot-Marges

map 31/R J4

owner: Famille Chassagnol *area:* 7.6 ha *cases:* white 3,050 *grape % W:* SEM 80% SAUV B 10% MUSC 10% *other wines:* Loupiac *other châteaux owned:* Ch La Grave Saint Roch *(Graves)*; Ch Mestrepeyrot *(Premières Côtes de Bordeaux)*; Domaine de Labatut *(AC Bordeaux)*
33410 Gabarnac tel: 05 56 62 98 00 fax: 05 56 62 93 23
At this property both a Ste-Croix-du-Mont and a Loupiac are produced: 2,300 and 750 cases a year respectively. The former wine is mostly quite slender, and richer in alcohol than in sweetness. Spicy oak adds some dimension to

Below: Ch La Rame

◆
Quantities
Figures are as supplied by the châteaux.

Area of vineyard: given in hectares, abbreviated to ha. Châteaux are asked to specify vineyards in production, and to exclude land owned but unplanted.

Production: given in cases of 12 bottles, each of 0.75 litres. A case is thus 9 litres. A hectolitre is 100 litres or just over 11 cases.

Yield per hectare: to obtain this, multiply the 'cases' figure by 9, to give litres, then divide by 100, to give hectolitres. Then divide by the area in hectares.

Entre-Deux-Mers; ACs Bordeaux and Bordeaux Supérieur

The main approach to the city of Bordeaux from the north, the A10 autoroute, crosses the River Dordogne and then, just before reaching the city, the Garonne. These rivers are the two '*mers*' of the Entre-Deux-Mers (literally 'between two seas'), an enormous, roughly triangular tract of land which fans out to your left and stretches eastwards to the *départemental* boundary. Note, if you travel this route, the signpost to Floirac: this is where phylloxera first struck in the Gironde in 1866. Today it is a suburb of Bordeaux.

The Entre-Deux-Mers is easily the most confusing part of the Bordeaux *vignoble*: first the name, which is both that of a vast geographical area as well as the largest specific appellation within that area; second, the profusion of wine types made here – red, *clairet* (light red), rosé, dry white, semi- and fully-sweet white – and the various ACs which apply, both generic and specific. It is not unheard of for a single small producer to make as many as ten different AC wines – a concept which is totally alien to a producer in Pomerol or the Médoc, for example. Bordeaux has a total of 57 different appellations; the Entre-Deux-Mers uses more than 20 of them. The geographical area as a whole is covered by the generic Bordeaux and Bordeaux Supérieur ACs, which, although not exclusive to the

Rural life in Entre-Deux-Mers

area (see below) certainly make up an important part of its production. Then it is overlaid with various specific appellations: apart from the vast Entre-Deux-Mers AC (including its enclave Haut-Benauge), a number of smaller ones are dotted around its edges: of these, Ste-Foy Bordeaux, the Côtes de Bordeaux St-Macaire and Graves de Vayres (the latter with its own château list on page 266) are covered here; For the Premières Côtes de Bordeaux and Cadillac see the separate chapter on page 194; for Loupiac and Ste-Croix-du-Mont see page 212.

Bordeaux & Bordeaux Supérieur

In principle, wines for these non-specific appellations can come from any of the 100,000-odd hectares of the whole Bordeaux AC *vignoble*. In practice, these wines are produced from roughly half this hectarage spread right across the Bordeaux region. Production, however, is mainly concentrated in certain large tracts of land (apart from the Entre-Deux-Mers itself, the zones between the Libournais and the Blayais, and to the south of the Graves, are important) and whereas some of these areas are only entitled to these generic ACs, in others overlapping occurs. A good example is the land covered by the Entre-Deux-Mers AC: this AC is for dry white wine only, yet much red wine is also produced here – but

Entre-deux-mers; Appellations Bordeaux & Bordeaux Supérieur

Above: Ch d'Abzac

Ch Abbaye de St Ferme
map 36

Bordeaux
owner: Arnaud de Raignac & Patrick Valette **area:** 6
ha **cases:** white 3,000 **grape % W:** SAUV B 40% SEM
40% MUSC 20% **other châteaux owned:** include Ch
Pavie *(St-Emilion)*
33580 Sauveterre-de-Guyenne tel: 05 57 55 43 43
fax: 05 57 24 63 99
At this well-preserved 12th-century abbey,
Arnaud de Raignac and Patrick Valette make a
complex, aromatic white wine. This is
fermented in new *barriques*, then aged in them
for eight months. The high average age of the
vines – 40 years – helps to give the wine depth.

Ch d'Abzac
map 34

Bordeaux Supérieur
owner: Jean-Louis d'Anglade **area:** 9 ha **cases:**
5,000 **grape % R:** MER 70% CF 30%
33230 Abzac tel: 05 57 49 32 82
fax: 05 57 49 29 73
This low-built château around its square
courtyard dates back to the second half of the
17th century, though it probably stands on the
site of a medieval fortress. Here industrialist
Jean-Louis d'Anglade produces a quite rounded
Bordeaux Supérieur, dominated by the Merlot
grape. This rather earthy, but also softly fruity
wine, with plum and cherry notes, often has
animal and bayleaf elements as well. It matures
for two years in stainless steel before bottling.

Ch Alexandre
map 35

Bordeaux Supérieur, Entre-Deux-Mers Haut-Benauge
owner: Michel Pernette **area:** 20 ha **cases:** 10,000,
white 2,500 **grape % R:** MER 40% CS 40% CF 20%
grape % W: SAUV B 100%
33760 Targon tel: 05 56 23 45 27
fax: 05 56 23 64 32
In good years the Bordeaux Supérieur here has
a relatively firm structure, ripe tannins and
high quality. The Entre-Deux-Mers Haut-
Benauge, made solely from Sauvignon Blanc
grapes, is brisk and engaging.

Ch Allegret

Bordeaux
owner: Jean-Bernard Rivaud **area:** 15 ha **cases:**
6,000, white 2,500 **grape % R:** MER 40% CS 30%
CF 30% **grape % W:** SEM 70% SAUV B 20% MUSC 10%

◆
Grape varieties
Main and other permitted varieties for each
appellation are given in the appellation fact
box at the end of the relevant introduction.
For châteaux, percentages of grapes grown
are given as supplied by the château.

Abbreviations: CF Cabernet Franc,
COL Colombard, CS Cabernet Sauvignon,
MAL Malbec, MER Merlot, MUSC Muscadelle,
PV Petit Verdot, SAUV B Sauvignon Blanc,
SÉM Sémillon.

33670 La Sauve Majeure tel: 05 56 23 22 48
fax: 05 56 23 22 48
The red Bordeaux often has an aroma of
blackcurrants. It is of average quality, which
also goes for the white version.

Ch Des Arras
map 34

AC Bordeaux, Bordeaux Supérieur
owner: J.M.A. Rozier **area:** 28 ha **cases:** 21,000,
white 830 **grape % R:** MER 60% CS 30% CF 10%
grape % W: SEM 50% UGNI BLANC 20% MUSC 20% SAUV
B 10% **other wines:** Bordeaux rosé
33240 St-Gervais tel: 05 57 43 00 35
fax: 05 57 43 58 25
This château, beautifully situated on a slope
above the Dordogne, developed out of a 15th-
century fortification. It acquired its present
form, including its double flight of entrance
steps, in the 17th century. The two wings were
added in 1795. The red, white and rosé made
here are usually reliable. The white is relatively
the weakest, while the best quality is to be
found in the red Réserve JR, which is matured
for 10 months in cask.

Ch Les Arromans
map 35

Bordeaux, Entre-Deux-Mers
owner: Jean Duffau **area:** 30 ha **cases:** 17,000,
white 2,200 **grape % R:** MER 80% CS 10% CF 10%
grape % W: SEM 50% SAUV B 50% **other wines:**
Bordeaux rosé
33420 Moulon tel: 05 57 84 50 87
fax: 05 57 84 52 84

An estate geared to quality: its best wine is the
Cuvée Prestige red Bordeaux, which is aged in
barriques (25% of them new). This is usually a
mouthfilling wine, characterized by oak and
vanilla. The standard red Bordeaux is also
agreeable, with considerable red fruit and
sufficient tannins. The rosé is somewhat neutral
in character. In the Entre-Deux-Mers the
freshness of the Sauvignon is generally the
most conspicuous element.

Ch De l'Aubrade
map 36

Bordeaux Supérieur, Bordeaux, Entre-Deux-Mers
owner: Paulette & Jean-Pierre Lobre **area:** 40 ha
cases: 12,000, white 11,000 **grape % R:** CF 60% CS
30% MER 10% **grape % W:** SAUV B 35% SEM 35% MUSC
30% **second wine:** Ch Jamin *(Bordeaux; Entre-Deux-
Mers; Bordeaux rosé)*
33580 Rimons tel: 05 56 71 55 10
fax: 05 56 71 61 94
Half the production here is of white wines
(Bordeaux Sec, Entre-Deux-Mers), half of red
(Bordeaux Supérieur, Bordeaux). The Bordeaux
Supérieur usually displays a succulent, pleasing
taste with vanilla oak, ripe fruit and a touch of
spice. The red Bordeaux is not matured in cask,
but is nevertheless attractive and balanced.
Fruit is abundantly present in both the stylish,
stimulating white wines; the Bordeaux Sec has
just a little more Sauvignon than the Entre-
Deux-Mers. In the fresh rosé, a pure Cabernet
Franc wine, there is plenty of jammy fruit.

Ch de Balan
map 36

Bordeaux
owner: Michel Jéans & Mme Darnauzan **area:** 24 ha
cases: 14,500 **grape % R:** MER 34% CS 33% CF 33%
33490 Ste-Foy-la-Longue tel: 05 56 76 43 41
Correct, firm red Bordeaux principally sold in
bulk. Not cask-aged.

Ch de Balestard
map 35

Bordeaux Supérieur, Entre-Deux-Mers
owner: Jean-Charles Castex **area:** 9.5 ha **cases:**
4,200, white 1,000 **grape % R:** MER 60% CS 40%
grape % W: SEM 70% SAUV B 30% **second wine:**
Lalande de Balestard *(Bordeaux, Entre-Deux-Mers)*
33750 St-Quentin-de-Baron tel: 05 57 24 28 09
fax: 05 57 24 18 76
The former winemaker at Ch de Sours has been
producing his own wines here since 1990. The
red in particular is impressive, especially in the
top vintages: an expansive, meaty, velvety taste
with integrated tannins and a variety of fruit,
including bilberry, blackberry and prune.

Ch Ballan-Larquette
map 36

Bordeaux, Bordeaux Supérieur
owner: Vignobles Chaigne & Fils **area:** 12.1 ha
cases: 7,500 **grape % R:** CS 56% MER 23% CF 21%
other wines: Clairet de Ballan *(Bordeaux Clairet)*
other châteaux owned: Ch Peynaud *(Bordeaux
blanc & rouge; Bordeaux Supérieur)*; Domaine de
Ricaud *(Entre-Deux-Mers Haut-Benauge; Bordeaux
blanc)*
33540 St-Laurent-du-Bois tel: 05 56 76 46 02
fax: 05 56 76 40 90
Successive generations of the families owning
this estate have moved step by step from mixed
farming in the 1930s to wine growing
exclusively today. The first estate bottling took
place in 1975. The red Bordeaux chiefly displays
fruit and tannin, with a hint of bayleaf. The
Clairet de Ballan is a pleasant summer wine.

Ch Le Barail Beaulien   map 35
Bordeaux Supérieur
owner: Michel Porte **area:** 4.9 ha **cases:** 1,300, white 500 **grape % R:** cs 42% cf 37% mer 21% **grape % W:** sem 100% **other wines:** Crémant de Bordeaux
33670 Le Pout tel: 05 56 23 03 78
This estate was created in 1992. It has a modern *cuvier* and matures its Bordeaux Supérieur for six months in barrels, of which a third are new. The wine produced here is of better than average quality. A Crémant de Bordeaux is also made. A further 2 ha of vineyard are being planted with Merlot.

Ch Barbazan   map 36
Bordeaux
owner: Huguette Bayle **area:** 18 ha **cases:** 10,000 **grape % R:** cf 65% mer 35%
33350 Flaujagues tel: 05 57 40 08 06
fax: 05 57 40 06 10
Wine vinified and bottled by the Juillac & Flaujagues cooperative. The quality is very reliable: a well-filled-out taste, with spicy fruit, and a deep colour.

Ch La Bardonne   map 34
Bordeaux
owner: Vignobles Alain Faure **area:** 10 ha **cases:** 3,500, white 2,000 **grape % R:** mer 60% cs 40% **grape % W:** sauv b 90% sem 10% **other châteaux owned:** Ch Fontarabie (*Premières Côtes de Blaye*); Ch Belair-Coubet (*Côtes de Bourg*)
33620 Lapouyade tel: 05 57 64 90 06
fax: 05 57 64 90 61
Elegant red Bordeaux, and a fresh white with a lot of Sauvignon. A dry rosé is the third wine made here.

Ch Baron Bertin   map 35
Bordeaux Supérieur
owner: Vignobles Garzaro **area:** 12 ha **cases:** 5,000, white 2,200 **grape % R:** mer 60% cf 20% cs 20% **grape % W:** sem 70% sauv b 30% **second wine:** Ch Baron La Mouline **other châteaux owned:** include Vieux Château Perron (*Pomerol*); Ch Prévost (*Bordeaux, Entre-Deux-Mers*); Ch Le Prieur (*Bordeaux Supérieur, Entre-Deux-Mers*)
33750 Baron tel: 05 56 30 16 16
fax: 05 56 30 12 63

Both the Bordeaux Supérieur and the Bordeaux Sec are matured in cask, for 12 months and 6 months respectively. The barrels come from an estate in Pomerol in the same ownership, where they have been used for one vintage. The red is very substantial in taste, but does not require a long wait. The white is supple and round, with smooth fruit and a hint of licorice.

Ch du Barrail   map 35
Bordeaux
owner: Charles Yung **area:** 60 ha **cases:** 25,000, white 7,500 **grape % R:** cs 50% mer 40% cf 5% pv 5% **grape % W:** sem 80% ugni blanc 20% **second wine:** Ch Haut-Mondain **other châteaux owned:** include Ch Lapeyrère (*Bordeaux*); Ch Les Hauts de Palette (*Premières Côtes de Bordeaux*)
33410 Mourens tel: 05 56 62 94 85
fax: 05 56 62 18 11
Somewhat rustic red Bordeaux characterized by tannin. A small amount of the wine is given oak ageing.

Ch Barrail de Guillon   map 27
Bordeaux Supérieur
owner: Jean-Michel Billot **area:** 8 ha **cases:** 2,000 **grape % R:** mer 70% cs 25% cf 5%
33230 Fargues tel: 05 57 49 05 36
fax: 05 57 49 09 08
Well-equipped estate yielding a reasonably concentrated Bordeaux Supérieur. The wine is not oak-aged, but it has sufficient tannins and red and black fruit.

Ch Barreyre   map 18
Bordeaux Supérieur
owner: SCF du Ch Barreyre/Famille Tessandier **area:** 9 ha **cases:** 3,750 **grape % R:** mer 50% cs 40% pv 10% **other châteaux owned:** include Ch Dasvin-Bel-Air (*Haut-Médoc*); Ch Maucamps (*Haut-Médoc*); Ch du Moulin Noir (*Lussac-St-Emilion; Montagne-St-Emilion*); Ch Lescalle (*Bordeaux Supérieur*)
33460 Macau tel: 05 57 88 07 64
fax: 05 57 88 07 00
Château close to the river-bank at Macau in the Médoc, a *chartreuse* built in 1774 by Nicolas Barreyre. Since the 1988 vintage the wine has been oak-matured for a year, mainly in used casks. Characteristically it is a succulent, clean

Bordeaux Supérieur with berry fruit, licorice and adequate tannins. Its quality lies just above the average.

Ch Bastian   map 36
Bordeaux
owner: Stéphane Savigneux **area:** 7 ha **cases:** 3,000 **grape % R:** mer 50% cf 30% cs 20%
33124 Auros tel: 05 56 65 51 59
fax: 05 56 65 43 78
Vineyard dating from 1988 – therefore with relatively young vines – where a supple, slender and at the same time charming red Bordeaux is made. It is given a short spell (six months) in oak, of which 10% are new barrels.

Ch Bauduc   map 35
Bordeaux, Bordeaux Supérieur
owner: David Thomas **area:** 20 ha **cases:** 7,000, white 5,500 **grape % R:** mer 65% cs 35% **grape % W:** sem 60% sauv b 40% **other châteaux owned:** Ch Martindoit (*Premières Côtes de Bordeaux*)
33670 Créon tel: 05 56 23 23 58
fax: 05 56 23 06 05
The main wines produced at this white château, flanked by twin towers, are red Bordeaux Supérieur and white Bordeaux Sec. Both have won many awards. After spending six months in cask (a third of them new barrels), the stylish tannins of the Bordeaux Supérieur are combined with the aromas of brushwood, leather and black fruits. The standard white wine is lively, elegant and clean, with an

---

◆
Map numbers
Map 2, in the opening pages of the Atlas, shows the areas of all the Bordeaux appellations. To find a map for a specific appellation, turn to the regional key maps:
◆
Maps of the appellations between the rivers
For a key map showing all the appellations in this zone, with the outlines of the maps in this Atlas, consult Map 30.

Below: Ch Barreyre

Below: Cellar at Ch Bauduc

agreeable acidity and notes of gooseberry and asparagus. A superior version is sold as Les Trois Hectares: a pure Sémillon, fermented in new oak. This wine drips with fruit – peach, melon – has a generous, almost honeyed composition, and fills the mouth expansively.

Ch Beaufresque   map 34
Bordeaux Supérieur
owner: Pierre Cramail **area:** 6 ha **cases:** 3,500
grape % R: MER 90% CS 10%
33350 Ste-Terre tel: 05 57 40 20 50
fax: 05 57 40 13 90
This comparatively modest family estate yields a generally fragrant Bordeaux Supérieur, rounded and with ripe fruit and good tannins. Casks are not used here.

Ch de Beaulieu   map 34
Bordeaux Supérieur
owner: Jacques Rabanier **area:** 14 ha **cases:** 7,500
grape % R: MER 65% CF 30% CS 5%
33230 Abzac tel: 05 57 69 63 50
fax: 05 57 69 77 76
In good years this is a muscular Bordeaux Supérieur with a firm foundation of tannins. It is not matured in cask. The Rabanier family has been running this estate since the 19th century.

Ch de Beaulieu   map 36
Bordeaux, Entre-Deux-Mers
owner: Famille Bonneau **area:** 22 ha **cases:** 6,250, white 3,000 **grape % R:** CS 39% MER 31% CF 30%
grape % W: SEM 34% SAUV B 33% MUSC 33%
33540 Sauveterre-de-Guyenne tel: 05 56 64 52 21
Besides a light, undemanding, sometimes rather appley Entre-Deux-Mers this château delivers a quite fruity, firm red Bordeaux, which has sufficient tannin to age for some years. These two wines are vinified by two different cooperatives, the Union St-Vincent and Cellier de la Bastide respectively. The château has belonged to the Bonneau family since the 18th century.

Ch Beaulieu Bergey   map 36
Bordeaux
owner: SCEA Vignobles Michel Bergey **area:** 36 ha **cases:** 16,000, white 4,000 **grape % R:** MER 45% CS 40% CF 15% **grape % W:** SEM 60% SAUV B 40% **other wines:** Ch Haut Desarnaud (Bordeaux Supérieur); Ch Les Rocs de Damis (Bordeaux rosé); Ch des Rocs (Bordeaux Supérieur); Ch de Damis (Côtes de Bordeaux St-Macaire) **other châteaux owned:** Ch de la Barde (St-Emilion)
33490 Ste-Foy-la-Longue tel: 05 56 76 41 42
fax: 05 56 76 46 42
Very expertly managed and welcoming family estate that has, for example, marked out walks through the vineyards for its visitors. The red

---

◆
Finding a château

To locate a château from its name alone, use the index/gazetteer, which will provide a page and a map reference. When the name and appellation are known consult the Directory pages of the relevant chapter. When the commune is known, but not the appellation, consult the index by commune, which lists châteaux in the Atlas under the commune name.

Bordeaux generally has plenty of colour and a substantial, meaty taste in which oak is modestly apparent. This wine is nurtured for a year in barrel (20% new wood). This property also makes Ch des Rocs, a dry white Bordeaux purely from Sauvignon grapes; a rosé, Ch Les Rocs de Damis; Ch de Damis, a semi-sweet Côtes de Bordeaux St-Macaire; and Ch Haut Desarnaud, a semi-sweet white wine.

Ch de Beauregard-Ducourt   map 35
Bordeaux, Entre-Deux-Mers
owner: Vignobles Ducourt **area:** 61 ha **cases:** 22,500, white 13,500 **grape % R:** CS 45% MER 34% CF 19% MAL 2% **grape % W:** SEM 63% SAUV B 34% MUSC 3% **other châteaux owned:** include Ch La Rose St-Germain (Bordeaux)
33760 Targon tel: 05 56 23 93 53
fax: 05 56 23 48 78
Quantity and quality go hand in hand at this important estate. With the aid of modern technology the Ducourt family make an energetic, fairly meaty, pleasingly fruity red Bordeaux that is already very enjoyable when still young. The quite lively, pale-pink rosé should in fact be drunk young, which also holds good for the very correct, refreshing Bordeaux Sec and the not too expressive Entre-Deux-Mers.

Ch de Beau Rivage Laguens   map 32
Bordeaux Supérieur
owner: René Laguens **area:** 62 ha **cases:** 31,500
grape % R: MER 40% CS 30% CF 30% **second wine:** Ch Pressac **other wines:** Ch Haut Lafitte (Bordeaux rosé) **other châteaux owned:** Ch Lafitte Laguens (Premières Côtes de Bordeaux)
33880 Baurech tel: 05 56 52 14 70
fax: 05 56 01 04 29
The Laguens family has owned this estate since the beginning of the 20th century. In the large cellars near the château – recognizable by the massive square corner tower with its pointed roof – a dark-coloured, well-structured Bordeaux Supérieur is made. As this wine spends eight months in cask it has some oak, licorice and cocoa to add to its fruit.

Ch Beauval   map 35
Bordeaux
owner: E. & J. Alphand **area:** 73 ha **cases:** 46,800, white 1,200 **grape % R:** MER 50% CS 45% CF 5% **grape % W:** SEM 70% SAUV B 20% MUSC 10% **other wines:** Bordeaux rosé
33450 St-Sulpice-et-Cameyrac tel: 05 56 72 96 20
fax: 05 56 72 46 89
The red Bordeaux from this 18th-century *chartreuse* is of a correct but unremarkable quality. There is a perceptible hint of oak from its eight months in cask. Beauval has attacked the French gift market with personalized labels bearing the name of giver or receiver.

Ch Béchereau   map 34
Bordeaux Supérieur
owner: Jean-Michel Bertrand **area:** 25 ha **cases:** 15,100 **grape % R:** MER 60% CF 20% CS 20% **other wines:** Ch Béchereau (Montagne-St-Emilion; Lalande-de-Pomerol)
33570 Les Artigues-de-Lussac tel: 05 57 24 31 22
fax: 05 57 24 34 59
Besides its reasonably complex Bordeaux Supérieur, and a Montagne-St-Emilion of better than average quality, this well-placed vineyard also makes an engaging Lalande-de-Pomerol. None of these wines is aged in cask.

Above: Spring vineyards in Créon

Ch Bel Air   map 35
Bordeaux, Entre-Deux-Mers
owner: Jean Louis Despagne **area:** 40 ha **cases:** 8,000, white 21,000 **grape % R:** MER 58% CS 42% **grape % W:** SEM 57% SAUV B 22% MUSC 21% **other wines:** Bordeaux Clairet **other châteaux owned:** Ch Rauzan Despagne (Bordeaux); Ch Tour de Mirambeau (Bordeaux)
33420 Naujan-et-Postiac tel: 05 57 84 55 08
fax: 05 57 84 57 31
The owner, Jean Louis Despagne, prefers to call this estate Ch Bel Air Perponcher, to distinguish it from all the other Bel Airs in Bordeaux. The estate is the oldest and largest in its *commune*; Despagne and his family have owned it since 1990. White Bordeaux, their main wine, generally offers tropical fruit – and remarkable depth for this kind of wine. The best version is the cask-matured Cuvée Passion – with the name Perponcher on the label. There is style, too, in the red Bordeaux, a delightful mouthful of ripe fruit and discreet oak. Nor are the Entre-Deux-Mers or the Clairet at all disappointing.

Ch Bel Air   map 36
Bordeaux, Entre-Deux-Mers
owner: Philippe Moysson **area:** 50 ha **cases:** 25,000, white 2,000 **grape % R:** MER 50% CS 25% CF 25% **grape % W:** SEM 50% SAUV B 25% MUSC 25% **second wine:** Ch Teyssier
33450 Blasimon tel: 05 57 84 10 74
fax: 05 57 84 00 51
At this estate, still expanding its vineyard towards its ultimate goal of 60 ha, three black grape varieties form the basis of a balanced, complete red Bordeaux, matured for a year in *barriques* of which 30% are new. Three white grapes produce an often delicious, rounded and fruity Entre-Deux-Mers. Both of these wines have frequently won awards.

Ch Bel-Air l'Espérance
map 35

Bordeaux
owner: Marie-Claire Percier **area:** 18 ha **cases:** 5,000, white 6,000 **grape % R:** MER 70% CS 20% CF 10% **grape % W:** SAUV B 40% SEM 40% UGNI BLANC 20%
33760 Targon tel: 05 56 23 57 10
Practically all the wine goes to *négociants* who also bottle it. Experience shows that the quality can vary somewhat according to the firm involved. At its best the red Bordeaux has an elegant, supple taste with jammy fruit, as well as some darker aromas.

Ch Belle-Garde
map 35

Bordeaux
owner: Eric Duffau **area:** 21 ha **cases:** 8,500, white 670 **grape % R:** MER 80% CS 20% **grape % W:** SAUV B 50% SEM 50%
33420 Génissac tel: 05 57 24 49 12
fax: 05 57 24 41 28
Delicious red wines are made here, strongly reflecting their Merlot content. The ordinary version has plenty of character and elegance, but the standard rises by leaps and bounds with the Cuvée Elevée en Fût de Chêne. This aromatic, firm Bordeaux with its supple tannins often contains elements of eucalyptus, menthol, black fruit – and oak, for it spends a year in casks, of which a third are new. Ch Belle-Garde's white Bordeaux offers a lively taste with exotic fruit.

Ch Belle Ile
map 8

Bordeaux Supérieur
owner: Société Dovile **area:** 100 ha **cases:** 55,000 **grape % R:** CS 40% MER 40% CF 10% PV 5% MAL 5%
second wines: Ch La Terrasse; Ch Valrose; Ch La Rose Laurent **other wines:** Ch Calmeilh *(Bordeaux Supérieur)* **other châteaux owned:** Ch Lieujan *(Haut-Médoc)*

33750 Gauriac tel: 05 56 59 57 23
fax: 05 56 59 50 81
Since the end of the 1980s an extensive vineyard has once again been developed on the long, narrow island in the Gironde that stretches between the wine districts of Margaux and Côtes de Bourg. The first Ch Belle Ile vines were planted in 1720, on the north of the island (Ile Verte). In the 19th century estates also prospered in the central area (Ile du Nord), and in the south (Ile Cazeau); these were the Ch Calmeilh and Ch Carmeilh. The whole area is now run as a single property. Of the six château names in use, Ch Belle Ile represents the highest quality. It is as a rule a fruity Bordeaux Supérieur (berries, cherry, raspberry), supple, elegant and nicely framed in oak. It is matured for a year in barrels, 25-30% of them new.

Ch Bellevue Jos
map 35

Bordeaux
owner: Jacques Pessotto **area:** 3.2 ha **cases:** 2,000 **grape % R:** MER 50% CS 26% CF 24%
33420 Grézillac tel: 05 57 84 60 36
Gradually enlarged between 1979 and 1987, but still a very modest-sized estate. The first vintage bottled here, the 1990, was assessed most favourably by a French consumer publication. The wine matures for a year in cask and combines spicy oak elements with forest scents and a dash of fruit.

◆
About Entre-Deux-Mers

The Syndicat Viticole de l'Entre-deux-Mers is at 4, rue de l'Abbaye, 33670 La Sauve. Telephone 05 57 34 32 12.

The appellation Bordeaux-Haut-Benauge has its own Syndicat: telephone 05 56 23 93 61.

Côtes de Bordeaux St-Macaire has a separate Syndicat: the telephone number is 05 56 76 41 42.

The Syndicat Viticole Régionale for ACs Bordeaux and Bordeaux Supérieur is at the Maison de la Qualité, 33750 Beychac-et-Caillau. Telephone 05 56 72 90 99. They also cover Crémant de Bordeaux.

Ch Bellevue La Mongie
map 35

Bordeaux, Bordeaux Supérieur
owner: Michel Boyer **area:** 20.5 ha **cases:** 11,600 **grape % R:** MER 70% CF 15% CS 15% **other wines:** Bordeaux Clairet
33420 Génissac tel: 05 57 24 48 43
fax: 05 57 24 48 43
The Bordeaux Supérieur spends a year in oak, of which a third are new barrels. There is often vanilla and a touch of caramel in its aroma, and the taste contains a reasonable amount of extract, with sometimes slightly bitter tannins in the fairly short finish. A little more balance would be welcome. The standard Bordeaux is simpler, quite mouthfilling, supple and aromatic. Also made is an agreeable, harmonious Clairet with a delicate fragrance.

Ch de Bertin
map 35

Bordeaux Supérieur, Entre-Deux-Mers Haut-Benauge, Bordeaux Haut-Benauge
owner: Françoise Ferran **area:** 18 ha **cases:** 6,800,

white 3,200 **grape % R:** CS 60% MER 35% CF 5% **grape % W:** SAUV B 50% MUSC 45% SEM 5% **other wines:** Ch Cantelon la Sablière *(Bordeaux)* **other wines:** Ch Jossème *(Bordeaux)*
33760 Cantois tel: 05 56 23 61 02
fax: 05 56 23 94 77
The wines bottled at the château itself form a small part of the production – but are certainly worth discovering: for example the delightful, expressive Entre-Deux-Mers Haut-Benauge. Another successful item in the range is the Ch Cantelon La Sablière, a red Bordeaux given at least a year in cask. The wine has jammy fruit and, through its tannin, backbone as well. A small amount of semi-sweet Bordeaux Haut-Benauge is made for the aficionados.

Ch Bétoule
map 34

Bordeaux Supérieur
owner: SCA Domaine de la Rogère **area:** 5.2 ha **cases:** 2,600 **grape % R:** CS 60% MER 30% CF 10% **second wine:** Ch Barrail de Franc **other châteaux owned:** Domaine de la Rogère *(Côtes de Bergerac)*
33660 Gours tel: 05 58 80 78 43
Partly because of its relatively high Cabernet Sauvignon content this Bordeaux Supérieur will often age for 5-10 years without problem. The estate lies close to the border with the Dordogne *département*, where the owner runs another wine property.

Ch Biarnès
map 35

Bordeaux Supérieur, Bordeaux, Entre-Deux-Mers
owner: Eric Bourseaud **area:** 25 ha **cases:** 9,500, white 4,000 **grape % R:** MER 65% CF 35% **grape % W:** SEM 100% **other wines:** Bordeaux rosé
33670 St-Genès-de-Lombaud tel: 05 56 23 00 60
fax: 05 57 34 31 20
Smoky oak and related elements – chocolate and cocoa – are present in the fairly fruity red Bordeaux Supérieur. The small amount bottled by the producer is nurtured for a year in *barriques*, 30% of them new.

Ch Biré
map 18

Bordeaux Supérieur
owner: Société des Grands Vignobles de la Gironde/Mähler Besse **area:** 9.1 ha **cases:** 5,500 **grape % R:** MER 50% CS 40% CF 10% **other châteaux owned:** include Ch d'Arche *(Haut-Médoc)*
33460 Macau tel: 05 56 56 04 30
fax: 05 56 56 04 59
Elegant, agreeable and succulent wine, well balanced, and usually with fresh fruit (berries, cherry). Its time in *barriques*, 16% of them new, lasts 10-18 months. Mähler-Besse has exclusive rights.

Domaine de Birot
map 34

Bordeaux Supérieur
owner: François Landais **area:** 15 ha **cases:** 7,000, white 1,500 **grape % R:** MER 60% CF 30% CS 10% **grape % W:** SEM 70% MUSC 30% **other wines:** Ch La Caderie *(Bordeaux Supérieur; Bordeaux blanc, rosé & mousseux)*
33910 St-Martin-du-Bois tel: 05 5? 49 41 32
The lady who bought this estate in 1956 had to replant it entirely, for all the vines had gone. In 1973 the first bottled wine was sold. Her grandson, the present owner, has run Domaine de Birot since 1991 – making a cask-aged Cuvée Spéciale that year for the first time. Like the standard wine, this has a very correct quality and requires little patience. Red Ch La Caderie is made of 100% Merlot and ages 18 months in barrels, of which a quarter are new.

A

B

C

D

E

F

G

H

I

J

K

L

M

1 2 3 4 5 6 7 8 9 10

RIVE DROITE

MÉDOC

Libourne

Bordeaux

ENTRE-DEUX-MERS

GRAVES &
SAUTERNES

BLAYE

BOURG

Lapouyade

Tizac-de-Lapouyade

Maransin

Bayas

Guîtres

Peujard

Gauriaguet

St-Ciers-d'Abzac

D10

St-Martin-de-Laye

Sablons

St-Laurent-d'Arce

Virsac

Aubie-et-Espessas

Salignac

St-Genès-de-Fronsac

Périssac

St-Martin-du-Bois

Bonzac

St-Denis-de-Pile

Prignac-et-Marcamps

St-Gervais

Salignac

Mouillac

Galgon

Savignac-de-l'Isle

St-André-de-Cubzac

St-André-de-Cubzac

Vérac

Galgon

Saye

l'Isle

La Lande-de-Fronsac

Villegouge

D18

Cubzac-les-Ponts

Tarnès

Les
Billaux

LALANDE-DE-POMEROL

St-Romain-la-Virvée

Cadillac-en-Fronsadais

D670

Asques

Lugon-et-l'île-du-Carney

Dordogne

FRONSAC/
CANON-FRONSAC

Libourne

A10

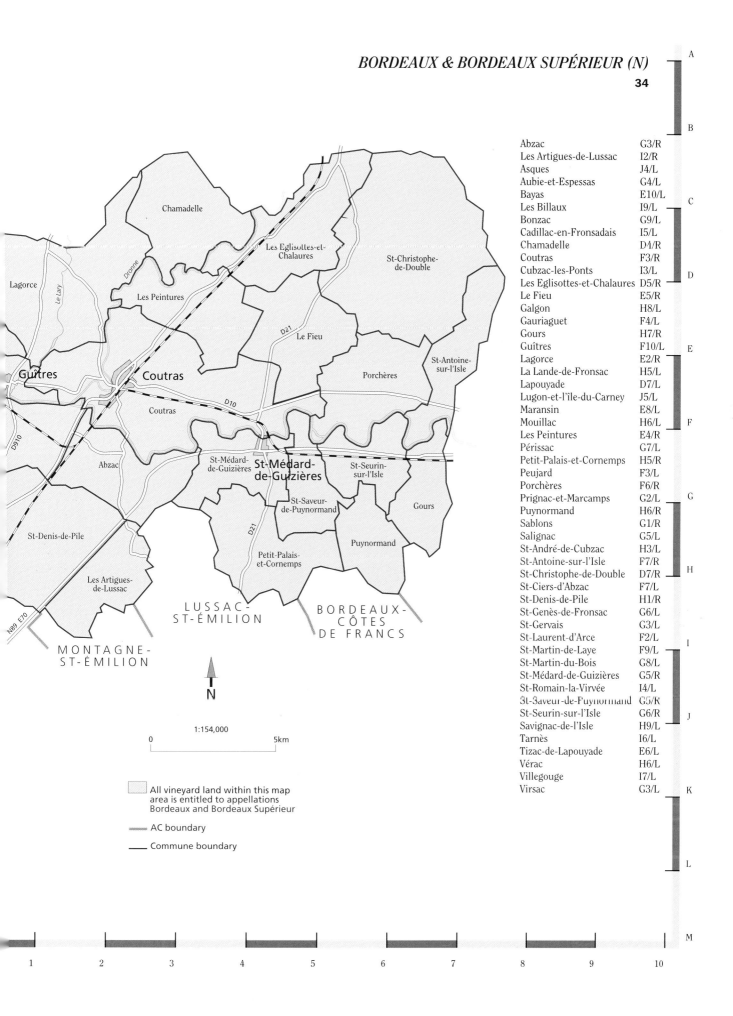

Abzac	G3/R
Les Artigues-de-Lussac	I2/R
Asques	J4/L
Aubie-et-Espessas	G4/L
Bayas	E10/L
Les Billaux	I9/L
Bonzac	G9/L
Cadillac-en-Fronsadais	I5/L
Chamadelle	D4/R
Coutras	F3/R
Cubzac-les-Ponts	I3/L
Les Eglisottes-et-Chalaures	D5/R
Le Fieu	E5/R
Galgon	H8/L
Gauriaguet	F4/L
Gours	H7/R
Guîtres	F10/L
Lagorce	E2/R
La Lande-de-Fronsac	H5/L
Lapouyade	D7/L
Lugon-et-l'île-du-Carney	J5/L
Maransin	E8/L
Mouillac	H6/L
Les Peintures	E4/R
Périssac	G7/L
Petit-Palais-et-Cornemps	H5/R
Peujard	F3/L
Porchères	F6/R
Prignac-et-Marcamps	G2/L
Puynormand	H6/R
Sablons	G1/R
Salignac	G5/L
St-André-de-Cubzac	H3/L
St-Antoine-sur-l'Isle	F7/R
St-Christophe-de-Double	D7/R
St-Ciers-d'Abzac	F7/L
St-Denis-de-Pile	H1/R
St-Genès-de-Fronsac	G6/L
St-Gervais	G3/L
St-Laurent-d'Arce	F2/L
St-Martin-de-Laye	F9/L
St-Martin-du-Bois	G8/L
St-Médard-de-Guizières	G5/R
St-Romain-la-Virvée	I4/L
St-Saveur-de-Puynormand	G5/R
St-Seurin-sur-l'Isle	G6/R
Savignac-de-l'Isle	H9/L
Tarnès	I6/L
Tizac-de-Lapouyade	E6/L
Vérac	H6/L
Villegouge	I7/L
Virsac	G3/L

Above: Ch Bonnet

Domaine des Bizelles map 34

Bordeaux Supérieur
owner: Alain Hue *area:* 6 ha *cases:* 3,000 *grape %
R:* MER 70% CS 20% CF 10% *other châteaux owned:*
Ch Pichot Chenevelle *(Lalande-de-Pomerol)*
33910 Savignac-de-l'Isle tel: 05 57 84 23 94
fax: 05 57 84 20 95
Reasonably rounded Bordeaux Supérieur of
average quality. No contact with oak. Has won
bronze medals.

Ch Blanchet map 36

Bordeaux Supérieur
owner: Yves Broquin *area:* 8 ha *cases:* 4,200 *grape
% R:* MER 50% CS 30% CF 20% *second wine:* Ch Haut
Rouargue
33790 Massugas tel: 05 56 61 40 19
Vineyard reborn in 1987 with modern
equipment. However, traditional values are also
honoured here, such as hand-picking the
grapes, and ageing the wine for 6-12 months in
barriques. In the aroma of the Bordeaux
Supérieur, old oak sometimes rather detracts
from the good quality of the wine itself.

Ch La Blanquerie map 36

Bordeaux Supérieur, Entre-Deux-Mers
owner: Serge & Jean-Louis Rougier *area:* 36 ha
cases: 14,700, white 6,000 *grape % R:* MER 67% CS
33% *grape % W:* SAUV B 54% SEM 29% MERLOT BLANC
14% MUSC 3% *second wine:* Ch Vieux Gabiran *other
wines:* Bordeaux rosé
33350 Mérignas tel: 05 57 84 10 35
fax: 05 57 84 00 85
Organically cultivated vineyard yielding a
reliable, supple Bordeaux Supérieur with berry
fruit, as well as a good, really fruity Entre-Deux-
Mers, and a rosé. The estate has an 18th-
century dovecot.

Ch de Blassan map 34

Bordeaux Supérieur
owner: Guy Cenni *area:* 31 ha *cases:* 16,500, white
1,500 *grape % R:* MER 75% CS 15% CF 10% *grape %
W:* SAUV B 85% SEM 15%
33240 Lugon tel: 05 57 84 40 91
fax: 05 57 84 82 93
Property on a plateau north of Lugon that
specializes in Bordeaux Supérieur. There is a
standard, quite fruity version, and a more
serious variant matured for about a year in oak.

The latter tastes fairly meaty and has firm
tannins. The two other wines here are a very
fresh, quite light Bordeaux Sec, and a pleasingly
fruity, lingering Bordeaux rosé.

Ch Le Bocage map 34

Bordeaux Supérieur
owner: Philippe Giraud *area:* 18 ha *cases:* 12,000
grape % R: MER 100% *other wines:* Bordeaux rosé
other châteaux owned: include Ch Timberlay
(Bordeaux Supérieur)
33240 Cadillac-en-Fronsadais tel: 05 57 43 01 44
fax: 05 57 43 08 75
Both the red Bordeaux Supérieur and the
Bordeaux rosé are pure Merlot wines. The rosé
tastes light and attractive; the red is
characterized by sometimes rather rustic
tannins, spiciness, a discreet dose of fruit,
vanilla – and some oak from a year in casks (a
third are new). The Giraud family have been the
owners since 1973. The château is a 19th-
century *chartreuse.*

Ch Bois-Malot map 35

Bordeaux Supérieur, Entre-Deux-Mers
owner: Meynard & Fils *area:* 11 ha *cases:* 5,200,
white 2,800 *grape % R:* CS 70% MER 30% *grape %
W:* SAUV B 50% SEM 40% MUSC 10% *other châteaux
owned:* Ch des Valentons Canteloup *(Bordeaux
Supérieur)*
33450 St-Loubès tel: 05 56 38 94 18
fax: 05 56 38 92 47
Oak is usually clearly perceptible in the
Bordeaux Supérieur Cuvée Tradition. The
Meynard family mature this elegantly firm,
rounded wine with its berry fruit for a year; half
the *barriques* are new. The white Entre-Deux-
Mers at times tastes somewhat rough, but is
otherwise correct.

Ch Bois Noir map 34

Bordeaux Supérieur
owner: Cyrille Grégoire *area:* 25 ha *cases:* 12,500
grape % R: MER 80% CS 20% *second wine:* Ch Vieux
Dominique *other wines:* Clairet du Château Bois
Noir
33230 Maransin tel: 05 57 49 41 09
fax: 05 57 49 49 43
Despite the name, woodland scents are only
modestly apparent in the aroma of Bois Noir, a
Bordeaux Supérieur of quality. Red and black
fruits are more noticeable, while oak and vanilla

are also present in the reasonably full-bodied
yet elegant taste. The wine matures for 8-12
months in cask of which 25% are new. The
Bordeaux Clairet, too, is to be recommended.

Ch de Bonhoste map 36

Bordeaux, Bordeaux Supérieur
owner: Bernard Fournier *area:* 24 ha *cases:* 8,200,
white 4,100 *grape % R:* MER 70% CS 20% CF 10%
grape % W: SEM 50% SAUV B 30% MUSC 10% UGNI
BLANC 10% *other wines:* Bordeaux rosé *other
châteaux owned:* Ch La Grave de Pujols *(Bordeaux);*
Ch La Moulière *(Bergerac)*
33420 St-Jean-de-Blaignac tel: 05 57 84 12 18
fax: 05 57 84 15 36
The people at this hospitable wine estate with
its underground cellars (in a former quarry) are
both expert and strongly motivated. The result
is a range of very successful wines. The best of
the reds is the oak-aged Bordeaux Supérieur,
which has both fruit and supple tannins, and in
most years considerable body. The rosé is fruity
and subtly nuanced. The Bordeaux Sec, made
from four grape varieties, is an expressive white
with a generous amount of fruit.

Ch Bon Jouan map 36

Bordeaux, Bordeaux Supérieur
owner: Nadine Saint-Jean *area:* 13.5 ha *cases:*
7,800, white 2,000 *grape % R:* CS 40% MER 35% CF
25% *grape % W:* SAUV B 50% MUSC 40% SEM 10%
other wines: Crémant de Bordeaux
33790 Pellegrue tel: 05 56 61 34 73
fax: 05 56 61 34 73
In some vintages the Bordeaux Supérieur here
is rather angular and slightly bitter in taste, but
in other years fruity aromas, as of blackcurrant,
come to the fore. The white Bordeaux Sec is apt
to have a pleasing aroma, with flowers and fruit,
along with a fairly straightforward taste with an
emphatic acidity.

Ch Bonnet map 35

Bordeaux, Entre-Deux-Mers
owner: André Lurton *area:* 225 ha *cases:* 75,000,
white 50,000 *grape % R:* CS 50% MER 50% *grape %
W:* SEM 45% SAUV B 45% MUSC 10% *second wines:*
Ch Guibon; Ch Goumin *other wines:* Bordeaux
Clairet *other châteaux owned:* Ch Couhins-Lurton
(Pessac-Léognan); Ch Rochemorin *(Pessac-
Léognan);* Ch de Cruzeau *(Pessac-Léognan);* Ch La
Louvière *(Pessac-Léognan)*
33420 Grézillac tel: 05 57 25 58 58
fax: 05 57 74 98 59
In all respects this is an impressive estate. Its
vineyard covers no less than 225 ha; the
château, dating from 1788, with its attractive

◆
Neighbouring appellations
The south-western side of the Entre-Deux-
Mers area has the ACs Premières Côtes de
Bordeaux, Cadillac, Loupiac and Ste-Croix-
du-Mont. These have chapters of their own
beginning on page 194.
◆
Graves de Vayres
This AC is for red and white wines made in
a small area beside the Dordogne. It is
described on p221, and its châteaux are
profiled on pp266-7.

small tower and stylish park is a feast for the eyes; and both its red and its white wines are among the very best of their *appellations*. The red Bordeaux tastes succulent, supple, pure, quite powerful (even in lesser years), and has berry fruit and cherry. All in all pure perfection. There is also a Réserve that spends a year in *barriques*, 15% of these being new; this wine offers rather more extract, greater dimension. In addition, the Lurton family makes two versions of Entre-Deux-Mers. The standard one possesses a recognizable style of its own: expansive, succulent, with citrus and exotic fruits, along with a hint of asparagus. The Réserve is fermented, and spends five months maturing, in cask. In this way the buttery, vanilla aspects of the oak come to accompany the fruity notes, and the wine is somewhat richer in substance. The least-known of the wines made is the somewhat neutral Bordeaux Clairet.

Domaine de Bordenave
map 36

Bordeaux
owner: Frédéric Carreyre *area:* 27 ha *cases:* 13,900, white 1,550 *grape % R:* MER 70% CS 30% *grape % W:* SEM 40% MUSC 40% SAUV B 20% *second wine:* Ch de Marjolaine *other châteaux owned:* Ch Fourneau du Roc *(St-Estèphe)*; Ch Grand-Marceaux *(Médoc)*
33490 Caudrot tel: 05 56 62 83 96
fax: 05 56 62 73 10
The most interesting wine here is the fairly slender, supple red Bordeaux, an agreeable lunchtime bottle. It is not oak-aged.

Ch Le Bory Rollet
map 36

Bordeaux
owner: Vignobles Rollet *area:* 16.8 ha *cases:* 7,000, white 2,000 *grape % R:* MER 66% CF 34% *grape % W:* SEM 51% SAUV B 27% MUSC 18% UGNI BLANC 4% *other châteaux owned:* include Ch Rollet Sauviac *(Entre-Deux-Mers; Bordeaux)*; Ch La Fourquerie *(Côtes de Castillon)*; Ch Fourney *(St-Emilion)*; Ch Vieux Guinot *(St-Emilion)*
33890 Juillac tel: 05 57 47 15 13
fax: 05 57 47 10 50
From this estate – one of nine belonging to Vignobles Rollet – comes well-made supple Bordeaux, often with both fruity and herbaceous elements. The white tastes fresh, but sometimes lacks a bit of fruit.

Below: Ch Brande-Bergère

Ch Le Bos
map 35

Bordeaux, Entre-Deux-Mers Haut-Benauge
owner: Michel Fourcassies *area:* 12 ha *cases:* 4,600, white 4,600 *grape % R:* CS 100% *grape % W:* SAUV B 40% SEM 30% MUSC 30% *second wine:* Ch de Coqs *other wines:* Comtesse de Laubès *(Crémant de Bordeaux)*; Bordeaux rosé *other châteaux owned:* Ch Dublanc Puy-Domine *(Sauternes)*; Ch Haut Mouleyre *(Premières Côtes de Bordeaux)*; Ch Laubès *(Bordeaux)*
33760 Escoussans tel: 05 56 23 93 77
fax: 05 56 23 46 44
Both the red and the rosé Bordeaux generally rise above the merely correct, and both are made exclusively from Cabernet Sauvignon. Of an even higher standard is the white Entre-Deux-Mers Haut-Benauge, an aromatic, smoothly fresh wine with succulent tropical fruit.

Ch Bosquet
map 36

Bordeaux Supérieur
owner: Magoli & Serge Ley *area:* 14 ha *cases:* 7,500 *grape % R:* MER 50% CS 30% CF 20% *second wine:* Ch La Fleur Frimont *other wines:* Bordeaux rosé
33190 Gironde-sur-Dropt tel: 05 56 61 06 75
fax: 05 56 61 18 61
The tannins in this cask-matured Bordeaux Supérieur can be somewhat hard at times, without refinement. The wine therefore remains stuck at an average quality. The château used to be called Beauséjour, but was renamed Bosquet by repatriates from Algeria, after a French marshal who served in that country.

Ch Bossuet
map 34

Bordeaux Supérieur
owner: SARL Dubost *area:* 8 ha *cases:* 3,400 *grape % R:* MER 60% CF 20% CS 20% *second wine:* Ch Graves de Bossuet *other châteaux owned:* Ch Pâquerette *(Bordeaux blanc)*; Ch La Vallière *(Lalande-de-Pomerol)*; Ch Lafleur du Roy *(Pomerol)*
33500 St-Denis-de-Pile tel: 05 57 51 74 57
fax: 05 57 25 99 95
An unexaggerated oak aroma, licorice and aniseed, a firm core, impressive tannins: this is a serious, traditional kind of Bordeaux Supérieur. The well-situated gravel-soil vineyard and 18 months in *barriques* determine its character.

Ch La Botte
map 46

Bordeaux
owner: René Blanchard *area:* 15 ha *cases:* 6,000, white 2,700 *grape % R:* MER 80% CS 15% CF 5% *grape % W:* SAUV B 60% UGNI BLANC 25% COL 10% SEM 5% *other wines:* Bordeaux rosé; Crémant de Bordeaux; Cru Cazeaux la Botte *(Premières Côtes de Blaye)*
33390 Campugnan tel: 05 57 58 90 03
fax: 05 57 58 97 89
This estate, created shortly after the French Revolution, produces a relatively generous red Bordeaux in sunny years. Some of it is selected to spend a year in oak, and the resulting special *cuvée* has won various medals. The same holds good for the fresh Premières Côtes de Blaye, the Crémant de Bordeaux and the distilled Bordeaux *fine*.

Ch du Bouilh
map 34

Bordeaux Supérieur
owner: Indivision de Feuilhade de Chauvin *area:* 45 ha *cases:* 21,250 *grape % R:* MER 51% CS 30% CF 15% MAL 2% PV 2% *second wines:* Ch Tour-Clanet; Ch Moulin de la Tonnelle; Domaine de la Garosse
33240 St-André-de-Cubzac tel: 05 57 43 01 45
fax: 05 57 43 91 96
Although the château designed by Victor Louis was never completed, this mansion is one of the most impressive in the *département*, with a park full of ancient trees. The cellars of this 18th-century building have traditional equipment, with wooden fermentation vats. Wood is also used for the maturing barrels – 20% of them new – in which the Bordeaux Supérieur spends eight months. The wine tastes quite supple, reasonably firm, and generally has enough tannin to develop for some years in bottle. The names Domaine de la Garosse and Ch Moulin de la Tonnelle are used for wines of virtually the same quality.

Domaine de Bouillerot
map 36

Bordeaux, Bordeaux Supérieur
owner: Thierry Bos *area:* 7 ha *cases:* 4,000, white 350 *grape % R:* MER 65% CS 15% CF 10% MAL 10% *grape % W:* SEM 50% SAUV B 50% *other wines:* Bordeaux rosé
33190 Gironde-sur-Dropt tel: 05 56 71 46 04
fax: 05 56 71 46 04
The present generation of Domaine de Bouillerot's owners – the family arrived in 1935 – is making a distinguished Cuvée Passion, a Bordeaux Supérieur matured for a year in cask. This wine offers a fairly expansive taste, sufficient tannins, earthy tones, fruit – all of it beautifully balanced. The standard red, rosé and dry white Bordeaux also have both character and quality. There are plans to add 3 ha to the size of the vineyard.

Ch Bourdicotte
map 36

Bordeaux, Entre-Deux-Mers
owner: Vignobles Rocher–Cap de Rive *area:* 70 ha *cases:* 19,750, white 30,000 *grape % R:* MER 80% CS 20% *grape % W:* SAUV B 80% SEM 20% *second wine:* Moulin de Pillardot *other châteaux owned:* include Ch Cap d'Or *(St-Georges-St-Emilion)*
33790 Cazaugitat tel: 05 57 40 08 88
fax: 05 57 40 19 93
Enjoyable, agreeably fruity red Bordeaux and a markedly fresh Entre-Deux-Mers. The better qualities come in a heavy bottle with just the name Bourdicotte on the label, without 'Château'. These special *cuvées* spend three months maturing in oak.

Above: Ch de Castelneau

Ch La Bourguette
map 36

Bordeaux, Bordeaux Supérieur

owner: Jean-François Lepetit *area:* 18 ha *cases:*
5,000, white 3,000 *grape % R:* CF 40% MER 35% CS
25% *grape % W:* SAUV B 60% SEM 30% MUSC 10%
33220 St-Philippe-du-Seignal tel: 05 57 46 34 86
fax: 05 57 46 07 83
While the Bordeaux Sec here varies in quality,
the Bordeaux Supérieur can be regarded as
reliable. It is a reasonably substantial wine with
berry fruit, spicy oak, licorice and good tannins.
Once a hunting-lodge, the estate has existed for
some 800 years.

Ch Le Bouscat
map 35

Bordeaux

owner: Pierre Barthe *area:* 19 ha *cases:* 7,000,
white 4,000 *grape % R:* MER 53% CS 27% CF 20%
grape % W: SAUV B 51% SEM 49%
33760 Lugasson tel: 05 57 84 13 22
fax: 05 57 84 12 67
Wines made by the Rauzan cooperative: a quite
full-bodied red Bordeaux with ripe fruit, and an
attractive fresh white.

Ch Boutillon
map 36

Bordeaux Supérieur

owner: SCEA Filippi-Gillet *area:* 15 ha *cases:* 8,000
grape % R: MER 40% CS 40% CF 20% *other wines:*
Bordeaux rosé
33540 Mesterrieux tel: 05 56 71 41 47
fax: 05 56 71 32 27
The Bordeaux Supérieur made here does not
quite live up to the style of the distinguished
white château. At its best it is a creditable,
rounded wine, with black and red fruit notes;
but sometimes it also has some volatile acidity.
The rosé deserves a sympathetic reception.

Ch les Bouzigues
map 36

Bordeaux, Bordeaux Supérieur

owner: Karl-Heinz Krawczyk *area:* 4.6 ha *cases:*
2,500, white 300 *grape % R:* MER 50% CS 40% CF
10% *grape % W:* SEM 50% SAUV B 45% UGNI BLANC 5%
other properties owned: Fattoria Vadiavolo (*Chianti
Putto*)
33580 Ste-Gemme tel: 05 56 61 80 77
fax: 05 56 61 68 11
A young German has bought this three-
centuries-old estate with just one aim in view:
to make one of the best Bordeaux wines. He

seems to have succeeded. His Réserve is a red,
broad-shouldered Bordeaux, splendidly
supported by plenty of oak (50% of the casks
being new), with ripe fruit and an
unmistakeable distinction. Three white wines
are being produced; the most interesting is the
Réserve Blanc, a pure Sauvignon.

Ch Brande-Bergère
map 34

Bordeaux Supérieur

owner: GFA Doussoux *area:* 5.6 ha *cases:* 3,000
grape % R: MER 50% CF 30% CS 20% *other wines:*
Bordeaux rosé
33230 Les Eglisottes-et-Chalaures tel:
05 57 69 36 00
This wine estate took shape in the first half of
the 19th century. The vineyard was laid out
then and the ruined château, a 1780 *chartreuse*,
was restored. The owner also added a pair of
pointed turrets. Since the end of the 1980s this
hilltop estate has built up a solid reputation
with its Bordeaux Supérieur. The cask-aged
cuvée is particularly noteworthy, with its filled-
out structure, good tannins, candied fruit and
spices; the ordinary version is not to be
despised, either.

Ch Bran de Compostelle
map 35

Bordeaux

owner: Eric Barrat *area:* 12 ha *cases:* 7,000, white
600 *grape % R:* MER 63% CS 31% CF 6% *grape % W:*
SAUV B 50% SEM 50% *other wines:* Bordeaux
Supérieur *other châteaux owned:* Ch Driholle
(*Bordeaux*)
33760 Frontenac tel: 05 56 23 98 50
In 1993 the present owner produced his first
wines from this 800-year-old vineyard – and
straight away won a silver medal with his red
Bordeaux. Rather greater depth is present in
the Bordeaux Supérieur, a wine with
considerable tannin; this spends a year in
barriques, 25% of them new. The white
Bordeaux, a rounded, fruity Sauvignon wine,
offers a similar good standard.

Domaine de la Brandille
map 34

Bordeaux Supérieur

owner: Daniel Lagenèbre *area:* 5 ha *cases:* 2,000
grape % R: MER 80% CF 20%
33910 St-Denis-de-Pile tel: 05 57 74 21 06
A Bordeaux Supérieur that still perhaps lacks
some depth – the vines are young – but is

nevertheless tempting with its soft, fruity
fragrance and taste. It matures for a year in oak.

Ch Briot
map 35

Bordeaux

owner: Philippe Ducourt/Vignobles Ducourt *area:*
40 ha *cases:* 21,000, white 6,500 *grape % R:* CS
44% MER 29% CF 27% *grape % W:* SEM 100% *other
châteaux owned:* include Ch La Rose St-Germain
(*Bordeaux*)
33760 Cessac tel: 05 56 23 93 53
fax: 05 56 23 48 78
Although Briot's dry white Bordeaux is correct
in quality but does not have so very much fruit,
this element is well and truly present in the red
wine, which can be drunk quite young. The
vineyard has been considerably enlarged since
the beginning of the 1990s.

Ch de Brondeau
map 35

Bordeaux Supérieur

owner: Jean-Baptiste Lafond *area:* 10 ha *cases:*
5,000 *grape % R:* MER 65% CF 35% *other châteaux
owned:* Clos du Clocher (*Pomerol*)
33500 Arveyres tel: 05 57 51 62 17
fax: 05 57 51 28 28
Generally this is a very good-tasting Bordeaux
Supérieur, due to its almost jam-like fruit, good
concentration and rich tannins. It is matured
for six months in used casks from the Pomerol
estate of Clos du Clocher.

Ch Brown-Lamartine
map 8

Bordeaux Supérieur

owner: Axa Millésimes *area:* 11 ha *cases:* 5,800
grape % R: CS 80% MER 20% *other châteaux owned:*
include Ch Cantenac-Brown (*Margaux*)
33460 Cantenac tel: 05 57 88 81 81
fax: 05 57 88 81 90
A Bordeaux Supérieur with a high Cabernet
Sauvignon content, made by the team from Ch
Cantenac-Brown in Margaux. The wine is
solidly packed with generally ripe tannins, and
has a taste that is elegantly firm, clean, and that
offers fruit too. It spends a year in barrels.

Ch du Bru
map 36

Bordeaux, Bordeaux Supérieur, Ste-Foy Bordeaux

owner: Guy & Josette Duchant *area:* 30 ha *cases:*
5,700, white 2,800 *grape % R:* MER 50% CF 30% CS
20% *grape % W:* SAUV B 100% *other wines:*
Bordeaux Clairet; Crémant de Bordeaux
33220 St-Avit-St-Nazaire tel: 05 57 46 12 71
fax: 05 57 46 10 64
This property not far from Ste-Foy-la-Grande
has belonged to the same family since the 19th
century. It is run with enthusiasm, quality

◆
Quantities

Figures are as supplied by the châteaux.

Area of vineyard: given in hectares,
abbreviated to ha. Châteaux are asked to
specify planted vineyards in production.

Production: given in cases of 12 bottles,
each of 0.75 litres: a case is thus 9 litres.
A hectolitre is 100 litres or just over 11
cases.

Yield per hectare: to obtain this, multiply
the 'cases' figure by 9, to give litres, divide
by 100, to give hectolitres, then divide
the result by the area in hectares.

being very much the aim, and the result is a portfolio of excellent wines. There are nine or so of these, and one of the highlights of the range is the Bordeaux Supérieur matured in new casks: a Cuvée Réservée with a mouthfilling, solid taste full of firm tannins and a fine toast-and-vanilla aroma. The standard Bordeaux Supérieur is also aged in *barriques* – mainly used ones – and has nuances to it as well as real quality. The likeable red Bordeaux has rather less tannin. Of the whites the Ste-Foy Bordeaux, matured in oak and with Sauvignon its main grape, deserves the most attention. However, the standard dry white, the Bordeaux Clairet and the Crémant Rosé are by no means to be ignored.

Ch Brun Despagne — map 35
Bordeaux Supérieur
owner: Geneviève Querre **area:** 12.6 ha **cases:** 8,000 **grape % R:** MER 70% CS 30% **other châteaux owned:** Ch Patris (St-Emilion); Ch La France (Médoc)
33420 Génissac tel: 05 57 55 51 60
fax: 05 57 55 51 61
This vineyard has many old vines, and the owner can only guess at their identity; the percentages quoted are only estimates. At the top of the range is the Héritage, a *cuvée* matured for a year in used casks. It is as a rule a compact Bordeaux Supérieur with considerable oak and other nuances, and its development calls for patience.

Ch Burayre — map 35
Bordeaux Supérieur
owner: Didier Boudot **area:** 3.4 ha **cases:** 1,700 **grape % R:** MER 83% CF 12% MAL 5%
33500 Arveyres tel: 05 57 74 50 04
A small yield of a sound wine, dark in its aroma. No oak is used.

Ch Butte de Cazevert — map 35
Bordeaux
owner: J.F. Dufaget **area:** 20 ha **cases:** 9,500, white 3,200 **grape % R:** MER 50% CS 30% CF 20% **grape % W:** SAUV B 70% MUSC 22% SEM 8% **second wine:** Ch Moulin du Prieur
33420 Naujan-et-Postiac tel: 05 57 84 57 03
fax: 05 57 74 97 14
Wine estate spread out on one of the highest hills in Entre-Deux-Mers. It yields a supple, fruity red Bordeaux, a lively rosé, and a white characterized by Sauvignon. Casks are not used.

Ch des Cabannes — map 35
Bordeaux, Entre-Deux-Mers
owner: P. Baratin **area:** 23 ha **cases:** 10,500, white 3,500 **grape % R:** CF 35% CS 35% MER 30% **grape % W:** SEM 80% SAUV B 10% MUSC 10% **other wines:** Bordeaux Clairet
33760 Targon tel: 05 56 23 90 25
A range of wines are made at Ch des Cabannes; all are of standard quality.

Ch Cablanc — map 36
Bordeaux
owner: Jean-Lou Debart **area:** 50 ha **cases:** 30,000 **grape % R:** MER 60% CS 20% CF 20% **second wine:** Les Murailles de Château Cablanc **other châteaux owned:** Ch La Roche de Broue (Bordeaux)
33350 St-Pey-de-Castets tel: 05 57 40 52 20
fax: 05 57 40 72 65
There is a *cuvée* of red Bordeaux here that is matured for a year in barrel. This is a wine with a good deal of tannin, which is improved by a period in bottle.

Above: Ch Cazeau

Ch Cadillac-Branda — map 34
Bordeaux Supérieur
owner: Jean-Jacques Lesgourgues **area:** 75 ha **cases:** 35,000, white 7,500 **grape % R:** MER 80% CS 20% **grape % W:** SEM 50% SAUV B 50% **other châteaux owned:** Ch Haut-Selve (Graves); Ch de Laubade (Bas-Armagnac)
33240 Cadillac-en-Fronsadais tel: 05 57 58 23 05
fax: 05 57 58 23 09
This estate, dating from 1502, was taken over in 1991 by an Armagnac producer, Jean-Jacques Lesgourgues. This collector of contemporary art aims to make wines of the best quality at this extensive holding. The standard red, white and rosé Bordeaux, sold as Cadillac-Branda, are of considerable merit. The quality improves still further with the Bordeaux Supérieur, labelled Ch Cadillac Lesgourgues. This is an excellent wine in its category, firm, expansive, succulent – and it has depth. A year in oak gives it spicy, vanilla tones together with toast and coffee.

Domaine des Cailloux — map 35
Bordeaux Supérieur, Bordeaux, Entre-Deux-Mers
owner: Nicole Dupuy & Benoît Maulun **area:** 35 ha **cases:** 12,000, white 8,000 **grape % R:** MER 63% CS 23% CF 14% **grape % W:** SEM 50% SAUV B 40% MUSC 10% **other wines:** Bordeaux rosé; Crémant de Bordeaux
33760 Romagne tel: 05 56 23 60 17
fax: 05 56 23 32 05
A great range of wines is made at this estate – some marketed under the name Ch Vieux l'Estage. The red Supérieur is usually ready for drinking after some two years, and combines reasonable firmness with jammy fruit. The dry white Bordeaux is a pure Sauvignon. There is also a white moelleux, a firm rosé, three sparkling wines and an Entre-Deux-Mers. This last offers the best quality: it is aromatic, with peach, apricot, apple and citrus fruit, juicy and lively. The château bottles a considerable amount in both half-bottles and large sizes.

Domaine du Calvaire — map 34
Bordeaux
owner: Serge Coudroy **area:** 15 ha **cases:** 8,000 **grape % R:** MER 70% CS 30% **other wines:** Ch Croix de Chouteau (Lussac-St-Emilion); Ch Borie de l'Anglais (Puisseguin-St-Emilion); Ch Le Bernat (Puisseguin-St-Emilion)

33570 Petit-Palais-et-Cornemps
tel: 05 57 74 67 73 fax: 05 57 74 56 05
Balanced, pleasing Bordeaux with aspects in its bouquet and taste of both black fruit and animal tones. Adequate tannins make up the whole. The wine does not come into contact with wood.

Ch de Camarsac — map 35
Bordeaux, Entre-Deux-Mers
owner: Bérénice & Lucien Lurton **area:** 58 ha **cases:** 32,500, white 500 **grape % R:** CS 60% MER 30% CF 10% **grape % W:** SAUV B 50% SEM 50% **other châteaux owned:** include Ch Climens (Barsac)
33750 Camarsac tel: 05 56 27 15 33
fax: 05 56 30 12 92
Camarsac's castle has had its ups and downs. It needed rebuilding at the beginning of the 14th century: England's Black Prince saw to that. Destroyed again in 1377, it was rebuilt once more at the start of the 15th. Thereafter various owners made various alterations – fundamental ones in 1859. Then in 1972 Lucien Lurton bought the estate, and since 1992 it has been run by his daughter Bérénice. Behind the rather medieval labels there lurk wines made in a modern style. The standard red Bordeaux drips with fruit and is elegant in structure. The *sélection* matured in oak, offers somewhat more volume and depth. The generous, softly fruity Entre-Deux-Mers is also – briefly – aged in cask.

Ch Canada — map 34
Bordeaux Supérieur
owner: Demoiselles Falloux/Quancard Frères **area:** 9 ha **cases:** 4,300, white 600 **grape % R:** MER 70% CS 30% **grape % W:** SAUV B 45% SEM 45% MUSC 10% **other châteaux owned:** include Ch de Terrefort-Quancard (Bordeaux Supérieur)
33240 Cubzac-les-Ponts tel: 05 57 43 08 69
fax: 05 57 43 59 87
Supple, attractive Bordeaux Supérieur, with berry and cherry fruit. It is given about six months in barrel. Since 1972 the estate has been rented by the Quancard family.

Ch Candelley — map 36
Bordeaux Supérieur, Entre-Deux-Mers
owner: Henry Devillaire **area:** 21 ha **cases:** 7,000, white 6,000 **grape % R:** CS 50% MER 40% CF 10% **grape % W:** MUSC 40% SEM 40% SAUV B 20% **second wine:** Ch Goffreteau

33790 St-Antoine-du-Queret tel: 05 56 61 31 46 fax: 05 56 61 37 37

At this estate an engineer from the Paris region, trained also in viticulture, makes wines that include an honourable Bordeaux Supérieur and a fresh Entre-Deux-Mers with succulent fruit. Both wines are very successfully exported.

Ch Canet   map 35

Bordeaux, Entre-Deux-Mers

owner: Bernard Large *area:* 44 ha *cases:* 10,000, white 11,000 *grape % R:* MER 60% CF 30% CS 10% *grape % W:* SEM 50% SAUV B 30% MUSC 20% *second wine:* Ch Large-Malartic *other wines:* Bordeaux rosé **33420 Guillac tel: 05 57 84 57 87 fax: 05 57 74 94 94**

Out of respect for nature neither artificial fertilizers nor weedkillers are used on this property. The resultant wines are of a generally good standard. The red Bordeaux is rounded, slightly fruity and easy to like, the rosé has character, and the Entre-Deux-Mers combines elements of gooseberry and other fruit with a touch of herbaceousness; it also has style, and reasonable structure.

Ch Canteloudette   map 35

Bordeaux, Entre-Deux-Mers

owner: GAEC Pelotin *area:* 29 ha *cases:* 8,000, white 8,500 *grape % R:* CS 54% MER 35% CF 11% *grape % W:* SEM 70% SAUV B 17% MUSC 13% **33760 Lugasson tel: 05 57 84 13 22 fax: 05 57 84 12 67**

Very decent red Bordeaux, meant for drinking young, and a balanced, fruity, fresh Entre-Deux-Mers. Both wines are vinified by the cooperative at Rauzan.

Ch La Capelle   map 35

Bordeaux, Bordeaux Supérieur

owner: Jean-Raymond & Jean-Dominique Feyzeau *area:* 39 ha *cases:* 25,000, white 300 *grape % R:* MER 56% CF 36% CS 8% *grape % W:* SEM 75% SAUV B 25% *second wines:* Ch Lestey Noir; Domaine de Damazac *other wines:* Bordeaux rosé **33500 Arveyres tel: 05 57 51 09 35 fax: 05 57 51 86 27**

The standard Bordeaux Supérieur generally manages to taste both meaty and fairly fine at the same time. The cask-aged version is richer, with more nuances: vanilla, eucalyptus, ripe black fruit. The maturing lasts at least a year. In small vintages, such as 1991, the estate does not make the two wines – just the Cuvée Capella, which does not go into wood.

Ch de Cappes   map 36

Bordeaux

owner: Patrick Boulin *area:* 15 ha *cases:* 6,000, white 2,000 *grape % R:* CS 40% CF 30% MER 30% *grape % W:* SAUV B 50% MUSC 40% SEM 10% *other wines:* Bordeaux Supérieur; Côtes de Bordeaux St-Macaire **33490 St-André-du-Bois tel: 05 56 76 40 88 fax: 05 56 76 46 15**

Notes of aniseed and spices can often be found in the best wine from this estate, the Bordeaux Supérieur. This spends from 6-12 months in *barriques*. For those who love semi-sweet whites a slightly spicy Côtes de Bordeaux St-Macaire is made.

Ch du Carpia   map 36

Bordeaux, Bordeaux Supérieur

owner: Famille de Baritault du Carpia *area:* 20 ha *cases:* 8,000, white 3,100 *grape % R:* CS 60%

MER 40% *grape % W:* SAUV B 50% SEM 30% SAUV GRIS 20%

33210 Castillon-de-Castets tel: 05 56 61 19 80 fax: 05 56 71 24 38

An accessible red Bordeaux, dominated by blackcurrant and given a short time in barrel is made here, along with a white in which the fairly rare Sauvignon Gris grape is used. This estate has been in the same family since 1641.

Ch de Castelneau   map 35

Bordeaux, Entre-Deux-Mers

owner: Vicomte & Vicomtesse Loïc de Roquefeuil *area:* 20 ha *cases:* 6,000, white 5,000 *grape % R:* MER 34% CS 33% CF 33% *grape % W:* SEM 50% SAUV B 40% MUSC 10% *second wines:* Ch de Seignouret; Ch Les Marches de Castelneau *other wines:* Bordeaux Supérieur; Bordeaux Clairet **33670 St-Léon tel: 05 56 23 47 01 fax: 05 56 23 46 31**

The château in this case is a real castle, almost medieval in appearance, its main building flanked by two round towers. The Entre-Deux-Mers here is particularly remarkable: both fermented and then matured for about eight months in cask, it boasts an aroma of exotic fruits with a floral note to it as well, plus restrained tones of oak and a good balance. It comes from old Sémillon vines. There is, too, a standard Entre-Deux-Mers – also to be recommended, along with the quite substantial Bordeaux Supérieur.

Ch Castel Vieilh La Salle   map 35

Bordeaux

owner: Jean-Marie Jaumain *area:* 6 ha *cases:* 3,000 *grape % R:* MER 50% CF 25% CS 25% **33540 Castelvieil tel: 05 56 61 96 16**

An attractive, spicy and fruity red Bordeaux from an organically-worked vineyard. The château dates from the 12th century.

Ch Castenet-Greffier   map 36

Bordeaux, Entre-Deux-Mers

owner: François Greffier *area:* 25 ha *cases:* 9,600, white 2,000 *grape % R:* MER 60% CS 30% CF 10% *grape % W:* SAUV B 70% SEM 30% *second wine:* Ch Les Grenons *other wines:* Bordeaux rosé; Ch Haut-Castenet; La Rose Castenet *(Bordeaux rosé)* **33790 Auriolles tel: 05 56 61 40 67 fax: 05 56 61 38 82**

This estate was bought in 1986 by François Greffier, an experienced winemaker of perfectionist disposition. He produces exemplary wines, among them a well-constructed Bordeaux Supérieur, Ch Haut-Castenet, that spends a year in *barriques*, a fruity rosé (La Rose Castenet), and a clean, elegant and smoothly fresh Entre-Deux-Mers in which a touch of citrus can often be detected.

Ch Cazalis   map 36

Bordeaux, Bordeaux Supérieur

owner: SCEA Domaine de Cazalis/Claude Billot *area:* 26 ha *cases:* 15,200 *grape % R:* MER 70% CS 15% CF 15% *second wine:* Les Moulins de Château Cazalis *other wines:* La Tonnelle de Cazalis *(Bordeaux rosé)* **33350 Pujols-sur-Dordogne tel: 05 57 40 72 72 fax: 05 57 40 72 00**

The Cuvée CL, a Bordeaux Supérieur, is produced here just in good years; it contains rather more Merlot than the standard wine. This CL generally has a somewhat earthy, woodland aroma; its constitution is firm, with good tannins but no oak. The owner, Claude

Billot, is also strictly selective for his standard Ch Cazalis. Thus no wine appeared under this name in 1991, 1992 or 1993.

Ch Cazeau   map 35

Bordeaux, Bordeaux Supérieur

owner: SCI Domaines de Cazeau & Perey/Famille Martin *area:* 200 ha *cases:* 125,000 *grape % R:* MER 34% CS 33% CF 33% *second wine:* Ch Giraudot **33540 Gornac tel: 05 56 71 50 76 fax: 05 56 71 87 70**

Honest, fruity and at least reasonably concentrated Bordeaux Supérieur that receives just a little ageing in cask. Since 1986 it has won numerous medals. In 1940 part of the Belgian government found refuge at this château, a beautiful *chartreuse*.

Ch de Cazenove   map 8

Bordeaux Supérieur

owner: Willemijn de Cazenove-van Essen *area:* 7 ha *cases:* 4,000 *grape % R:* MER 80% CS 15% CF 5% **33460 Macau tel: 05 57 88 79 98 fax: 05 57 88 79 98**

This estate, formerly called Domaine de la Maqueline, lies between the Dauzac and Siran châteaux in Margaux, to which it used to belong. Willemijn de Cazenove-van Essen, who is Dutch, and her children replanted the vanished vineyard themselves, and produced their first vintage in 1991. This wine, a Bordeaux Supérieur matured for 12 months in oak, improved in quality from the 1994 vintage onward – for that was the first year it was made from Merlot grapes only.

Ch Chabiran   map 34

Bordeaux Supérieur

owner: Famille Carayon *area:* 17 ha *cases:* 8,000 *grape % R:* MER 80% CF 20% *other wines:* Ch Pétrarque *(Fronsac)* *other châteaux owned:* Ch La Croix St-André *(Lalande-de-Pomerol)* **33133 Galgon tel: 05 57 51 08 36 fax: 05 57 25 93 44**

The greater part of the production goes to make a full-bodied, well-upholstered Bordeaux Supérieur with woodland and animal notes in its aroma. In addition a small amount of Fronsac is made under the name Ch Pétrarque.

Ch Chanteloiseau   map 31

Bordeaux

owner: Jean Séraphon *area:* 26 ha *cases:* 17,000 *grape % R:* MER 60% CS 20% CF 20% *other châteaux owned:* Ch La Nère *(Loupiac)*; Domaine Roustit *(Ste-Croix-du-Mont)* **33490 Verdelais tel: 05 56 62 02 08 fax: 05 56 76 71 49**

Certainly an acceptable Bordeaux, although not a remarkable one, with a dark aroma.

Ch des Chapelains   map 36

Bordeaux, Ste-Foy Bordeaux

owner: Pierre Charlot *area:* 35 ha *cases:* 17,500, white 5,500 *grape % R:* MER 47% CS 43% CF 10% *grape % W:* SAUV B 56% SEM 36% MUSC 8% *other wines:* Bordeaux Clairet **33220 St-André-et-Appelles tel: 05 57 41 21 74 fax: 05 57 41 27 42**

The same family has been running this estate since the 17th century. The present generation, in the person of Pierre Charlot, decided that from the 1991 vintage onwards the vinification and bottling, hitherto done by a cooperative, should now be carried out at the château. The Bordeaux Blanc, of which they produce most, is a wine of abundant aroma – with fruit in particular – and a succulent, supple taste. The white Ste-Foy Bordeaux, which can be regarded as a superior version, has eight months in oak: clean, complex, with much fat – not exuberant but offering a good deal of class. There are also red versions of these two wines, with the more than worthwhile Ste-Foy Bordeaux bottled after a year in *barriques*, 25% of them new. Quality also characterizes the Bordeaux Clairet.

Ch La Chapelle Maillard map 36
Bordeaux, Bordeaux Supérieur, Ste-Foy Bordeaux
owner: Jean-Luc Devert *area:* 12 ha *cases:* 3,800, white 2,500 *grape % R:* CF 50% MER 30% CS 20% *grape % W:* SAUV B 40% SEM 30% MUSC 30% *other wines:* Bordeaux Clairet; Crémant de Bordeaux
33220 St-Quentin-de-Caplong tel: 05 57 41 26 13 fax: 05 57 41 25 99
Jean-Luc Devert bought this château, then very run down, in 1984 and has since built it up again. He has earned respect at home and abroad for the results. The best is the red Ste-Foy Bordeaux, a wine that spends 14 months in cask, has an often opaque colour and a delightful, meaty taste with ripe berry fruit and a sensible measure of oak. The standard red, a Bordeaux Supérieur, is a little lighter and more supple. Another, generally delicious, wine is the Bordeaux Clairet; and the Crémant makes a festive aperitif. The vineyard has been organically worked since 1993.

Ch Chapelle Maracan map 36
Bordeaux Supérieur, Bordeaux, Entre-Deux-Mers
owner: Jean-Louis Terras *area:* 20 ha *cases:* 4,900, white 4,500 *grape % R:* MER 60% CF 20% CS 20% *grape % W:* SEM 50% MUSC 40% SAUV B 10% *second wine:* Ch Maracan
33350 Mouliets-et-Villemartin tel: 05 57 40 56 73 fax: 05 57 40 57 89
A very traditional Bordeaux Supérieur, solely from Merlot grapes, which are not de-stalked. After fermentation there follows 8-10 months in barrels of which a third are new. The Entre-Deux-Mers is rather simple in taste, and more spicy than fruity.

Domaine des Chapelles map 34
Bordeaux Supérieur
owner: SCE des Vignobles Lacroix *area:* 22 ha *cases:* 13,000 *grape % R:* MER 70% CS 20% CF 10%

33570 Les Artigues-de-Lussac tel: 05 57 55 50 40 fax: 05 57 74 57 43
In this reasonably lively, if not especially deep or intense Bordeaux Supérieur, there is often a distinct black fruit note.

Ch Les Charmettes map 34
Bordeaux Supérieur
owner: Jean-Louis Trocard *area:* 20 ha *cases:* 12,000 *grape % R:* MER 70% CF 15% CS 15% *other châteaux owned:* include Ch Trocard (*Bordeaux Supérieur*)
33570 Les Artigues-de-Lussac tel: 05 57 24 31 16 fax: 05 57 24 33 87
Made by the same team as Ch Trocard, but this is a different Bordeaux Supérieur nonetheless – lighter, more accessible and supple. Not oak-aged.

Ch Les Charmilles map 18
Bordeaux Supérieur
owner: Jacques de Schepper *area:* 7 ha *cases:* 4,000 *grape % R:* MER 60% CS 40% *other châteaux owned:* Ch Tour Baladoz (*St-Emilion*); Ch Haut Breton Larigaudière (*Margaux*)
33460 Macau tel: 05 57 88 94 17 fax: 05 57 88 39 14

◆
Grape varieties
Some traditional names are given official status in the appellation decrees:
Bouchet St-Emilion name for Cabernet Franc, **Côt or Cot** Synonym for Malbec, **Pressac** St-Emilion name for Malbec

Some minor varieties figure in the decrees:
Carmenère Red grape of quality, liable to disease, therefore now very rare; though still legal in the Premières Côtes.
Merlot Blanc May be a mutation of Merlot, or a separate variety. Little is grown.
Mauzac White variety still important further east; still a legal *cépage accessoire* in Entre-Deux-Mers.

Sauvignon Gris White variety recently returned to favour, especially in the eastern Entre-Deux-Mers. Fresh, aromatically fruity wine.

A respectably mouthfilling Bordeaux Supérieur originating from the Médoc, with bayleaf and black fruit in its aroma, and also a touch of spicy oak from a year in cask.

Ch du Charron map 35
Bordeaux
owner: G. César *area:* 33.3 ha *cases:* 15,500, white 4,200 *grape % R:* MER 55% CS 43% CF 2% *grape % W:* SEM 60% SAUV B 23% MUSC 17%
33420 Rauzan tel: 05 57 84 13 22 fax: 05 57 84 12 67
Berry fruit and a fairly meaty taste are distinguishing features of the clean red Bordeaux; the white is quite rounded to the taste. The Rauzan cooperative makes the wine.

Ch La Chassière map 34
Bordeaux Supérieur
owner: SCEA des Domaines Wery *area:* 8.5 ha *cases:* 4,250 *grape % R:* MER 40% CF 30% CS 30% *second wine:* Clos de Laborde *other wines:* Rosé de l'Illot (*Bordeaux rosé*) *other châteaux owned:* Clos Pimpineuilh (*St-Emilion*)
33240 Cadillac-en-Fronsadais tel: 05 57 58 21 15
Estate run by an oenologist and his brothers. They have owned it since 1986 and have steadily enlarged it – with another 2.5 ha of vineyards planned. The La Chassière wines include a substantial, sound Bordeaux Supérieur, given a year in wood.

Domaine de Cheval Blanc
map 34
Bordeaux
owner: Robert Giraud *area:* 9 ha *cases:* 5,000 *grape % R:* MER 60% CS 40% *other châteaux owned:* include Ch Timberlay (*Bordeaux Supérieur*)
33240 St-André-de-Cubzac tel: 05 57 43 01 44 fax: 05 57 43 08 75
The fruit is not very prominent in this red Bordeaux, but it is there – as are a reasonably powerful flavour and some spiciness.

Domaine de Cheval-Blanc Signé
map 35
Bordeaux
owner: Alain Signé *area:* 12 ha *cases:* 3,500, white 4,000 *grape % R:* MER 34% CS 33% CF 33% *grape % W:* SEM 60% SAUV B 25% MUSC 15% *other châteaux owned:* Ch Petit-Moulin (*Bordeaux*)
33760 Arbis tel: 05 56 23 93 22 fax: 05 56 23 45 75
Clean, quite stimulating white Bordeaux with gooseberry fruit, and a red that is nowadays rather elegant, supple and pleasingly fruity. The same family has owned this domaine for some 150 years.

Domaine de la Colombine map 34
Bordeaux
owner: Jean-Louis Rabiller *area:* 5 ha *cases:* 3,000 *grape % R:* MER 70% CS 20% CF 10%
33570 Les Artigues-de-Lussac tel: 05 57 55 50 40 fax: 05 57 74 57 43
Nice, rather simple red Bordeaux that develops fairly quickly; it is vinified by the Puisseguin- and Lussac-St-Emilion cooperative.

Ch des Combes map 35
Bordeaux
owner: GFA du Hourc/Vignobles Ducourt *area:* 19 ha *cases:* 5,000, white 6,000 *grape % R:* CS 76% MER 19% CF 5% *grape % W:* SEM 50% SAUV B 36% MUSC 10% UGNI BLANC 4% *other châteaux owned:* include Ch La Rose St-Germain (*Bordeaux*)

Below: Ch La Commanderie de Queyret

◆

Appellations in this chapter

Apart from ACs Bordeaux and Bordeaux Supérieur, all the other ACs covered here are in the wider Entre-Deux-Mers region. As well as the white-wine Entre-Deux-Mers AC these are Entre-Deux-Mers Haut-Benauge and Bordeaux Haut-Benauge, Ste-Foy Bordeaux and Côtes de Bordeaux St-Macaire.
See page 221 for full details.

◆

Bordeaux & Bordeaux Supérieur

These are the basic generic ACs that cover the entire Bordeaux *vignoble*. In practice, however, since many of these wines come from the wider Entre-Deux-Mers area, wherever they come from they are covered here – or in the Premières Côtes de Bordeaux chapter if the estate is in that zone.

**33420 Ladaux tel: 05 56 23 93 53
fax: 05 56 23 48 78**
In the heart of the Haut-Benauge district of Entre-Deux-Mers is the hamlet of Hourc, close to Ladaux. On the site of the former village bakehouse there now stands the modern *cuvier* belonging to this estate. Here the Ducourt family produces a quite energetic, delightfully fruity red Bordeaux, as well as a lively, succulent Bordeaux Sec.

Ch la Commanderie   map 35
Bordeaux, Entre-Deux-Mers
owner: Michel Raffin *area:* 35 ha *cases:* 8,000, white 5,500 *grape % R:* cs 50% mer 30% cf 20% *grape % W:* sauv b 50% musc 40% sem 10% *second wine:* Ch Le Grand Queyron *other wines:* Bordeaux rosé
33760 Martres tel: 05 56 71 54 62
Decent Bordeaux AC wines; red, white and rosé. All are fairly elegant and possess a reasonable amount of fruit.

Ch La Commanderie de Queyret
map 36
Bordeaux Supérieur, Bordeaux, Entre-Deux-Mers
owner: Claude Comin *area:* 102 ha *cases:* 40,000, white 18,000 *grape % R:* mer 60% cs 30% cf 10% *grape % W:* sem 40% sauv b 40% musc 20% *second wines:* Ch Tour-Chapoux; Ch Haut-Toutifaut *other wines:* Bordeaux rosé
**33790 St-Antoine-du-Queret tel: 05 56 61 31 98
fax: 05 56 61 34 22**
This former *commanderie* of the Knights Templar was established in the 13th century. Before it there spreads a small park complete with trees, lawns and pond. At the back there lies an immense vineyard, broken by copses and groves, which stretches to the horizon. Despite the very considerable volume produced, the wines are of good, sound quality. For example, there's a charming, quick-developing red Bordeaux. And a limited *cuvée*, which spends 10 months in cask, is made under the Bordeaux Supérieur AC. This is a generously full-bodied, balanced wine. The Entre-Deux-Mers tastes fruity, lively and reasonably firm; the Bordeaux Sec is a clean, agreeable Sauvignon, and the Bordeaux Rosé, too, is quite fruity.

Clos des Confréries   map 35
Bordeaux
owner: EARL René Lafon *area:* 39 ha *cases:* 21,000, white 500 *grape % R:* mer 66% cf 17% cs 17% *grape % W:* sauv b 50% sem 45% musc 5% *other wines:* Ch Colin Lamothe *(Graves de Vayres)*
**33750 St-Germain-du-Puch tel: 05 57 24 52 53
fax: 05 57 24 05 74**
Quite a generous Bordeaux that can be drunk within a few years. The Merlot makes it rounded, and gives it an aroma of concentrated black fruit, such as plum and cherry. The same estate also offers a respectable red Graves de Vayres – Ch Colin Lamothe, which is matured in cask for a year.

Ch Le Conseiller   map 34
Bordeaux, Bordeaux Supérieur
owner: Vignobles Liotard *area:* 23 ha *cases:* 15,000 *grape % R:* mer 50% cf 40% cs 10% *second wine:* Domaine de La Fleur-Carney *other wines:* Bordeaux rosé *other châteaux owned:* Ch de la Grange Chapelle *(Bordeaux Supérieur)*
**33240 Lugon tel: 05 57 84 44 56
fax: 05 57 84 45 02**
The red Bordeaux is the most interesting wine here, and forms the bulk of the production. Ripe fruit and integrated tannins often give it a velvety aspect. With rather more new wood – 15% of casks at present – the standard could improve further.

Ch de Cornemps   map 34
Bordeaux Supérieur
owner: Henri-Louis Fagard *area:* 30 ha *cases:* 17,500 *grape % R:* mer 60% cs 40% *second wine:* Ch Bois Redon *other wines:* Lussac-St-Emilion; Bordeaux rosé
**33570 Petit-Palais-et-Cornemps tel:
05 57 69 73 19
fax: 05 57 69 73 75**
The *chais* at this estate stand near an ancient chapel on a high hill, affording a panoramic view. In the Bordeaux Supérieur there are normally flavours of jammy fruits, including blackberry and cherry, supple tannins, roundness, and some toasted elements from the oak – at least in the Cuvée Prestige, which is nurtured for a year in casks of which a third are new. Ch de Cornemps also makes a standard Bordeaux Supérieur, a Lussac-St-Emilion, and a Bordeaux Rosé.

Below: Ch du Clos Delord

Ch Côtes des Caris   map 36
Bordeaux, Bordeaux Supérieur, Ste-Foy Bordeaux
owner: Christian Guichand *area:* 13.5 ha *cases:* 4,000, white 3,000 *grape % R:* mer 50% cs 30% cf 20% *grape % W:* sauv b 60% sem 20% musc 20% *second wine:* Ch Les Coteaux Verts
**33220 St-André-et-Appelles tel: 05 57 46 16 25
fax: 05 57 46 47 63**
Since the 1994 vintage this estate has labelled its former Cuvée Prestige as a red Ste-Foy Bordeaux. This wine spends six months in cask and in its aroma there are, besides oak, earthy tones, forest scents and some fruit. It is a usually firm wine that will generally keep its vitality for a good five years. There is also a semi-sweet white Ste-Foy Bordeaux, from Sémillon and Muscadelle grapes. Artificial fertilizer and other chemicals are not used in the vineyard.

Ch Couronneau   map 36
Bordeaux, Bordeaux Supérieur
owner: Christophe Piat *area:* 23 ha *cases:* 10,000, white 1,500 *grape % R:* mer 60% cs 25% cf 15% *grape % W:* sauv b 34% musc 33% sem 33%
**33220 Ligueux tel: 05 57 41 26 55
fax: 05 57 41 26 55**
When this castle was originally built is not known; it probably dates from the 15th century. It has been extensively rebuilt more than once – in 1940 one owner gave it a Swiss look, with a lot of woodwork. In 1994, after standing empty for five years, the former stronghold was bought by Christophe Piat. He started on a total renovation – and also began to make wine, in a modern *cuvier*. The Bordeaux Supérieur is given a year in oak, the white Bordeaux half a year. The first vintages from the revived Couronneau have shown that this estate is worth watching.

Ch du Courros   map 36
Bordeaux, Bordeaux Supérieur
owner: GFA du Courros/Famille Durand *area:* 25 ha *cases:* 11,000, white 3,000 *grape % R:* mer 50% cs 35% cf 15% *grape % W:* sem 55% musc 30% sauv b 15% *second wine:* Ch La Salle du Courros
**33420 St-Vincent-de-Pertignas tel: 05 57 84 11 89
fax: 05 57 84 01 58**
This château, mentioned in local archives as early as 1229, makes a Bordeaux Supérieur that combines supple tannins and fruit, including

7 7 7 77

blackcurrant, in an engaging manner. There is no maturing in wood, but the wine does spend 20 months in tank.

Ch Coursou — map 36
Bordeaux, Bordeaux Supérieur
owner: GFA Dupas **area:** 25 ha **cases:** 11,500, white 3,000 **grape % R:** MER 34% CF 33% CS 33% **grape % W:** SEM 60% SAUV B 35% MUSC 5% **other wines:** Bordeaux rosé
33890 Pessac-sur-Dordogne tel: 05 57 47 40 27
fax: 05 57 47 47 10
For years now Coursou, on its hill, its entrance marked by an old stone cross, has been organically cultivated. Quality can vary greatly from vintage to vintage, from disappointing to very good. At its best the Bordeaux Supérieur is a firm, characterful product with herbs and spices as well as fruit – blackcurrant and cherry. Rounded tannins and a slightly bitter touch generally complete the picture. The white definitely has to be drunk young – which also holds good for the rosé, from Cabernet grapes. Exactly the same wines are sometimes sold as Ch La Tour de Beaupoil.

Domaine de Courteillac — map 36
Bordeaux, Bordeaux Supérieur
owner: Stéphane Asséo **area:** 17 ha **cases:** 5,600, white 900 **grape % R:** MER 65% CF 15% CS 15% MAL 5% **grape % W:** SEM 50% SAUV B 25% MUSC 25% **second wine:** Domaine La Fleur de Courteillac **other wines:** Ch Guillot-Clauzel (Pomerol); Ch Robin (Côtes de Castillon) **other châteaux owned:** Ch Fleur Cardinale (St-Emilion)
33350 Ruch tel: 05 57 40 55 65
fax: 05 57 40 58 07
Passionate and talented winemaker Stéphane Asséo has performed wonders since the beginning of the 1960s, having taken over what was then a totally derelict vineyard. With great attention to detail he makes a first-rate Bordeaux Supérieur, a wine with concentration, a good deal of fruit (plum, blackcurrant, blackberry, bilberry), ripe smooth tannins, a touch of spice, and fine oak – maturing lasts 10-14 months; up to 25% of the barrels are new, the rest not long in use. The white Bordeaux, Cuvée Antholien, fermented in new casks, is at least as splendid. This aromatic composition offers freshness, elegance, and also a touch of vanilla oak along with both citrus and tropical fruit.

Ch Courtey — map 36
Bordeaux, Bordeaux Supérieur
owner: GFA Courtey/Françoise Ligou & Norbert Depaire **area:** 9 ha **cases:** 3,500, white 1,200 **grape % R:** MER 50% CS 33% CF 17% **grape % W:** SAUV B 55% SEM 45% **second wine:** Ch Jauguet **other wines:** Côtes de Bordeaux St-Macaire
33490 St-Martial tel: 05 56 76 42 56
All the wines here are aged in wood: the richly coloured, classic Bordeaux Supérieur for at least 12 months, the Bordeaux Sec white (made solely from Sauvignon) and the semi-sweet Bordeaux St-Macaire both for a maximum 8 months.

Ch La Courtiade Peyvergès — map 36
Bordeaux Supérieur, Bordeaux, Entre-Deux-Mers
owner: Jean-Pierre Peyvergès **area:** 30 ha **cases:** 11,000, white 5,000 **grape % R:** CF 40% MER 30% CS 30% **grape % W:** SEM 50% SAUV B 40% MUSC 10% **second wine:** Ch Haut Tucot (Bordeaux) **other wines:** Bordeaux rosé

33190 Casseuil tel: 05 56 71 10 46
fax: 05 56 71 16 31
This diligent château is one of the rare properties where, besides a traditional red Bordeaux Supérieur, a white *moelleux* version and even a rosé can be tasted. Charlemagne apparently had the estate as a summer residence.

Ch de Crain — map 35
Bordeaux Supérieur, Entre-Deux-Mers
owner: Michel Fougère **area:** 32 ha **cases:** 12,500, white 7,000 **grape % R:** MER 50% CF 29% CS 21% **grape % W:** SEM 41% SAUV B 36% MUSC 23% **second wine:** Ch Noulet
33750 Baron tel: 05 57 24 50 66
fax: 05 45 25 03 73
In the distant past this property was owned by the abbey of La Sauve. The white château acquired its present form in 1845, through a wine merchant who restored it according to the tastes of that period: the main structure is flanked by two square towers with imitation loopholes. Across the three-sided courtyard there stands a very large *chai*. The Bordeaux Supérieur, winner of many awards, usually has prunes in its aroma and taste, and a firm core to it. The Entre-Deux-Mers offers at least equal quality, being reasonably lively and with a little tropical fruit.

Ch La Croix de Roche — map 34
Bordeaux, Bordeaux Supérieur
owner: François Maurin **area:** 20 ha **cases:** 11,000, white 200 **grape % R:** MER 80% CF 15% CS 5% **grape % W:** SEM 100% **second wine:** Ch La Croix de Roche **other wines:** Bordeaux rosé **other châteaux owned:** Ch du Prévot (Bordeaux Côtes de Francs); Ch Grand Place (Bergerac)
33133 Galgon tel: 05 57 84 35 52
fax: 05 57 84 31 39
Estate that has gradually grown since 1948, and acquired stainless-steel tanks in 1994. The standard red Bordeaux is a fairly light, acceptable wine. The Bordeaux Supérieur is more complete and complex in taste, and usually has the potential to mature.

Ch Croix Grand Barail — map 34
Bordeaux, Bordeaux Supérieur
owner: Roland Lhuillier **area:** 22 ha **cases:** 12,000 **grape % R:** MER 60% CF 20% CS 20% **second wine:** Ch La Barauderie
33230 Maransin tel: 05 57 49 40 37
Until about 1980 only white *vin de table* was produced at this estate. The present owner, however, has replanted so as to make red Bordeaux and Bordeaux Supérieur. The latter wine in particular is worthy of note. No cask-ageing is used.

Ch Dallau — map 34
Bordeaux Supérieur
owner: Vignobles Bertin **area:** 30.5 ha **cases:** 16,500 **grape % R:** MER 43% CS 29% CF 28% **second wine:** Domaine de Picardan **other châteaux owned:** Clos l'Hermitage (Lalande-de-Pomerol); Ch Cardinal (St-Emilion)
33910 St-Denis-de-Pile tel: 05 57 84 21 17
fax: 05 57 84 29 44
The Bordeaux Supérieur made here is by no means outstanding, but it is a fairly quick-developing, very correct wine with fruity – and sometimes also slightly herbaceous elements. The estate has belonged to the same family since 1742.

Ch Damase — map 34
Bordeaux Supérieur
owner: Xavier Milhade **area:** 10.9 ha **cases:** 5,800 **grape % R:** MER 93% CS 7% **second wine:** Ch Les Hauts de Savignac **other châteaux owned:** Ch Recougne (Bordeaux Supérieur); Ch Sergant (Lalande-de-Pomerol); Ch Lyonnat (Lussac-St-Emilion)
33910 Savignac-de-l'Isle tel: 05 57 74 21 71
Practically all the vines here are Merlot, giving the wine, a Bordeaux Supérieur, firmness as well as candied black and red fruit, spices and licorice. Oak is present, too, from a year in barrels of which a third are new.

Ch Degas — map 35
Bordeaux
owner: Marie-Josée Degas **area:** 10 ha **cases:** 5,500 **grape % R:** MER 70% CS 20% CF 8% MAL 2% **other châteaux owned:** Ch Haut-Gayat (Graves de Vayres); Ch Capmartin (Bordeaux, Bordeaux Supérieur); Ch Les Conquêtes (Bordeaux, Bordeaux Supérieur); Ch de la Souloire (Bordeaux, Bordeaux Supérieur)
33750 St-Germain-du-Puch tel: 05 57 24 52 32
fax: 05 57 24 03 72
Reliable red Bordeaux presented in a heavy bottle. Generally quite lively in taste; its aroma is dominated by Merlot, with bayleaf, leather, and black fruit.

Ch du Clos Delord — map 35
Bordeaux, Bordeaux Supérieur
owner: Jean-Pierre Soubie **area:** 30 ha **cases:** 20,000 **grape % R:** MER 34% CF 33% CS 33% **other châteaux owned:** Ch de Lisennes (Bordeaux, Bordeaux Supérieur)
33370 Tresses tel: 05 57 34 13 03
fax: 05 57 34 05 36
Reliable, well-rounded Bordeaux Supérieur offering a blend of forest scents and fruit in its aroma. The owners – there have been three generations of the family at this estate – give the wine 6-12 months in oak. Wine has been made at this property since the 13th century. It derives its name from Etienne Delord, an apothecary who acquired the château in 1811.

Clos Desclaux — map 32
Bordeaux Supérieur
owner: Frédéric & Jean-Marie Gassoit **area:** 4 ha **cases:** 2,000 **grape % R:** MER 50% CF 30% MAL 20% **second wine:** Ch Lauzac-Desclaux
33360 Latresne tel: 05 56 20 63 64
fax: 05 56 20 83 84
Small but still-growing estate, mainly equipped with stainless-steel fermentation tanks. The wine has adequate body, even in modest years. Its meaty taste is agreeably supported by oak.

◆
One château, many wines
In this zone many châteaux make a range of wines, frequently under more than one appellation. These may be of differing colours and styles, with anything from a red wine to a sparkling Crémant de Bordeaux under the same château name.

The main ACs in use are given beneath the château name. However, the range made may vary from vintage to vintage.

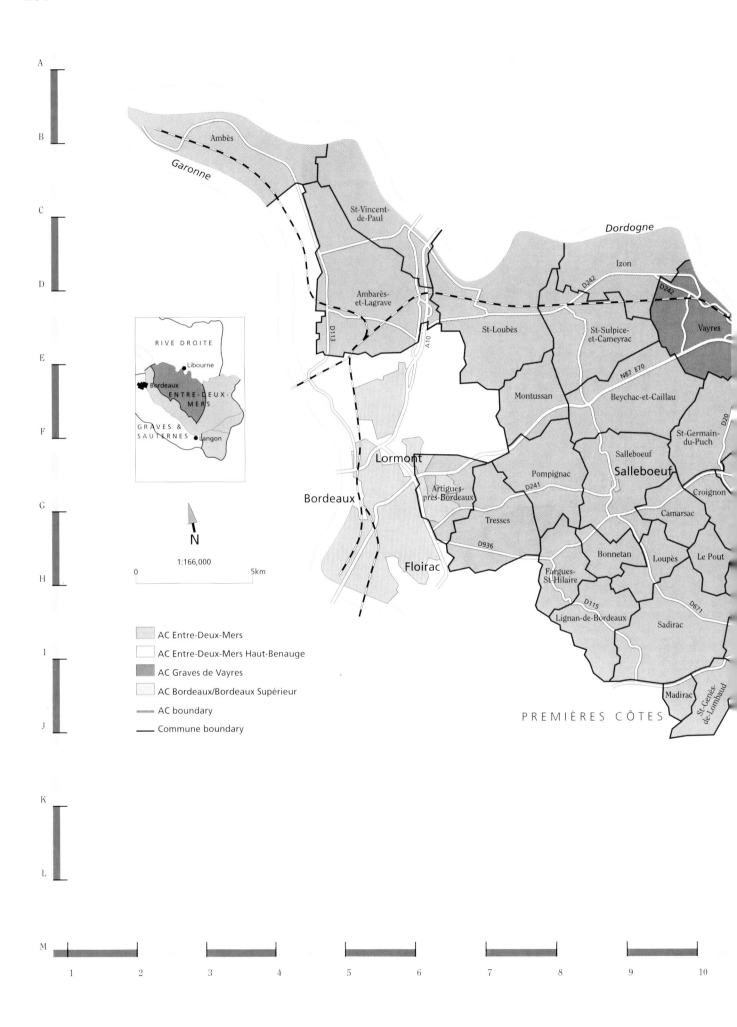

A
B
C
D
E
F
G
H
I
J
K
L
M

1 2 3 4 5 6 7 8 9 10

Ambès

Garonne

St-Vincent-
de-Paul

Dordogne

Izon

D242

D242

Ambarès-
et-Lagrave

D113

A10

St-Loubès

St-Sulpice-
et-Cameyrac

Vayres

N87 E70

Montussan

Beychac-et-Caillau

D20

St-Germain-
du-Puch

Salleboeuf

Salleboeuf

Lormont

Pompignac

D241

Croignon

Bordeaux

Artigues-
près-Bordeaux

Camarsac

Tresses

D936

Bonnetan

Loupès

Le Pout

Floirac

Fargues-
St-Hilaire

Lignan-de-Bordeaux

D115

Sadirac

D671

Madirac

St-Genès-
de-Lombaud

PREMIÈRES CÔTES

RIVE DROITE

Libourne

Bordeaux

ENTRE-DEUX-
MERS

GRAVES &
SAUTERNES

Langon

N

1:166,000

0   5km

AC Entre-Deux-Mers

AC Entre-Deux-Mers Haut-Benauge

AC Graves de Vayres

AC Bordeaux/Bordeaux Supérieur

AC boundary

Commune boundary

ENTRE-DEUX-MERS, BORDEAUX & BORDEAUX SUPÉRIEUR

35

Ambarès-et-Lagrave	E5/L	Camiac-et-St-Denis	H2/R
Ambès	C3/L	Cantois	K5/R
Arbis	L5/R	Castelviel	K7/R
Artigues-près-Bordeaux	G6/L	Cessac	I6/R
Arveyres	E2/R	Coirac	K6/R
Baigneaux	I5/R	Courpiac	H5/R
Baron	G1/R	Créon	I1/R
Bellebat	I5/R	Croignon	G10/L
Bellefond	H6/R	Cursan	H1/R
Beychac-et-Caillau	F9/L	Daignac	H4/R
Blésignac	H4/R	Dardenac	H4/R
Bonnetan	H8/L	Daubèze	J7/R
Branne	F5/R	Escoussans	L4/R
Cabara	F5/R	Espiet	H3/R
Cadarsac	F2/R	Faleyras	H4/R
Camarsac	H9/L	Fargues-St-Hilaire	H8/L
		Frontenac	I7/R
		Génissac	F3/R
		Gornac	L7/R
		Grézillac	G4/R
		Guillac	G4/R
		Izon	D8/L
		Jugazan	G6/R
		Ladaux	K5/R
		Lignan-de-Bordeaux	I8/L
		Loupès	H9/L
		Lugaignac	G5/R
		Lugasson	H6/R
		Madirac	J9/L
		Martres	J6/R
		Montignac	J5/R
		Montussan	F7/L
		Moulon	F4/R
		Mourens	L6/R
		Naujan-et-Postiac	G5/R
		Nérigean	F2/R
		Pompignac	G7/L
		Le Pout	H10/L
		Rauzan	G7/R
		Romagne	H5/R
		Sadirac	I9/L
		Salleboeuf	G8/L
		St-Aubin-de-Branne	F5/R
		St-Brice	J7/R
		St-Genès-de-Lombaud	J10/L
		St-Genis-du-Bois	J6/R
		St-Germain-du-Puch	F10/L
		St-Léon	I3/R
		St-Loubès	E7/L
		St-Pierre-de-Bat	L5/R
		St-Quentin-de-Baron	G2/R
		St-Sulpice-et-Cameyrac	E8/L
		St-Vincent-de-Paul	D5/L
		La Sauve	I2/R
		Soulignac	K4/R
		Targon	J4/R
		Tizac-de-Curton	G3/R
		Tresses	H7/L
		Vayres	E10/L

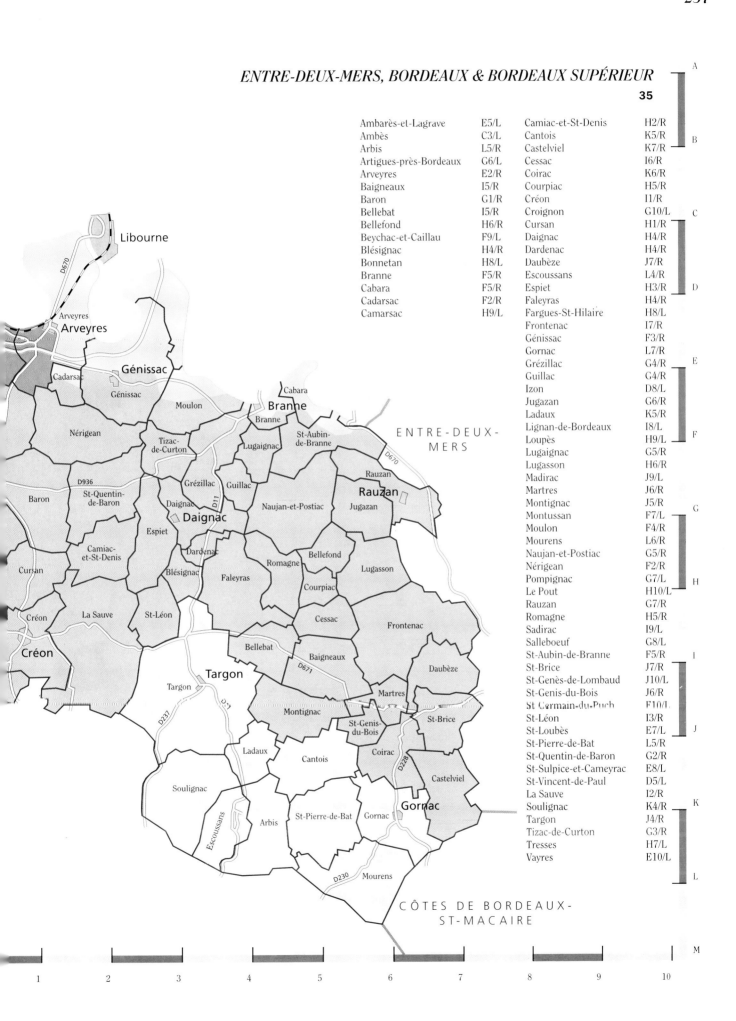

CÔTES DE BORDEAUX-
ST-MACAIRE

Ch La Dominante
map 34

Bordeaux Supérieur
owner: Laurent & Gérard Turpeau *area:* 16 ha
cases: 8,000 *grape % R:* MER 60% CS 40%
33910 St-Denis-de-Pile tel: 05 57 84 22 35
fax: 05 57 84 25 44
Quite lush and expansive in taste, this slightly
spicy Bordeaux Supérieur; no great depth, but
engaging.

Ch Dubois Claverie
map 36

Bordeaux, Ste-Foy Bordeaux
owner: Frédéric Dubois *area:* 17.5 ha *cases:*
8,000, white 3,450 *grape % R:* CS 44% MER 38%
CF 18% *grape % W:* SEM 50% SAUV B 50% *second
wine:* Ch Monteil
33220 Caplong tel: 05 57 41 23 11
Dubois Claverie is a family property dating from
1869; the house and cellars stand almost
opposite the churchyard at Caplong. Its red
Bordeaux is a traditional, somewhat rustic wine
with a reasonable amount of fruit. One of the
whites, the *moelleux*, bears the Ste-Foy
Bordeaux appellation. Barrels are not used at
this estate.

Ch Ducla
map 36

Bordeaux, Entre-Deux-Mers
owner: Domaines Mau *area:* 85 ha *cases:* 27,500,
white 21,200 *grape % R:* MER 50% CF 25% CS 25%
grape % W: SAUV B 40% SEM 40% MUSC 15% SAUV GRIS
5% *second wine:* Ch La Forêt Saint-Hilaire *other
wines:* Bordeaux rosé
33190 St-Exupéry tel: 05 56 71 02 27
fax: 05 56 61 09 02
It is said that Englishmen came to sample this
wine during the Hundred Years' War. The estate
is still worth a visit, for here the Yvon Mau firm
makes delightful wines. The ordinary red
Bordeaux often has a rich taste full of character,
with succulent fruit. There is greater depth and
complexity with the Coeur de Cuvée, which has
18 months in cask. There is also a fresh
Bordeaux Rosé and a couple of Entre-Deux-
Mers: the crisp standard wine, and the
Expérience, luxuriously fermented in cask.
Tropical fruit and a judicious dose of oak are
among the features of this fine wine.

Ch L'Enclos
map 36

Bordeaux, Bordeaux Supérieur, Ste-Foy Bordeaux
owner: Xavier de Pianelli *area:* 10 ha *cases:* 4,500,
white 500 *grape % R:* MER 50% CS 30% CF 10% MAL
10% *grape % W:* SEM 50% SAUV B 50%
33220 Ste-Foy-la-Grande tel: 05 57 46 55 97
With great enthusiasm the bridge-builder
Xavier de Pianelli and his wife Arnelle took over
this estate in December 1990. There were no
vines left in the vineyard near the fine château
itself, so it was replanted between 1991 and
1994. Meanwhile the Pianellis made wine from
a 4-ha plot on a slope a little further away. In
addition they built a modern *cuvier* and a barrel
chai. The red Ste-Foy Bordeaux, matured in
wood, has more class than most Bordeaux
Supérieurs. And the white Ste-Foy Bordeaux
moelleux is recommended by the makers as an
accompaniment to asparagus with a hollandaise
sauce. The dry white Bordeaux, too, is very
flavoursome, and made partly from 30-year-old
Sauvignon vines.

Ch L'Escart
map 35

Bordeaux, Bordeaux Supérieur
owner: Francis Testa *area:* 16.7 ha *cases:* 9,500,
white 450 *grape % R:* MER 43% CS 42% CF 7%

Above: Ch Ducla

MAL 6% PV 2% *grape % W:* SEM 40% SAUV B 20%
MUSC 20% MERLOT BLANC 20% *second wine:* Comte
de L'Escart
33450 St-Loubès tel: 05 56 77 53 19
fax: 05 56 77 68 59
After a year-long stay in wood the Bordeaux
Supérieur here offers some vanilla as well as its
fruit and powerful, ripe tannins. This wine will
often age for 10 years without any problem.
The second wine made here is a fairly simple
Bordeaux Sec.

Ch de Faise
map 34

Bordeaux Supérieur
owner: Daniel Devaud *area:* 10 ha *cases:* 5,000
grape % R: MER 70% CS 15% CF 15% *second wine:*
Domaine de Monrepos *other châteaux owned:* Ch
La Haute Claymore *(Lussac-St-Emilion);* Ch Grand
Barrailh *(Montagne-St-Emilion)*
33570 Les Artigues-de-Lussac tel: 05 57 24 31 39
fax: 05 57 24 34 17
The history of this wine estate goes back to
1137, at which time it formed part of the land
belonging to the Cistercian abbey of Faise,
founded in that year. The Bordeaux Supérieur
made here is reasonably energetic, with black
fruit and toast in its aroma – and it has won
many awards.

Below: Ch La Favière

Ch Les Faures
map 36

Bordeaux
owner: Jacky Certain *area:* 22 ha *cases:* 10,000,
white 3,000 *grape % R:* CS 60% MER 25% CF 15%
grape % W: SAUV B 60% SEM 30% MUSC 10%
33190 Camiran tel: 05 56 71 41 86
fax: 05 56 71 32 76
Only a tiny part of the production is matured
(for six to eight months in barrel) and bottled at
the château itself. It is a quite slender,
sympathetic red Bordeaux.

Ch Favereau
map 36

Bordeaux
owner: Bernard Tabouy *area:* 62 ha *cases:* 32,500
grape % R: MER 34% CF 33% CS 33%
33790 Pellegrue tel: 05 56 61 35 41
More than 99% of the vintage is sold in bulk
and thus anonymously. Only a very small
amount of this wine, which is of a good average
quality, is offered at the château itself. A fine
view over Pellegrue.

Ch La Favière
map 34

Bordeaux Supérieur
owner: GFA Domaine de la Cabanne *area:* 21 ha
cases: 11,000 *grape % R:* MER 60% CF 30% CS 10%
second wine: Ch Haut-Barry
33660 St-Seurin-sur-l'Isle tel: 05 57 49 72 03
fax: 05 57 49 64 89
The château is a beautiful house from the end
of the 19th century; the wine a very good
Bordeaux Supérieur that needs to mature for
about five years. Woodland scents determine its
aroma. It spends two years in *cuves*.

Domaine Florimond-La-Brède
map 46

Bordeaux, Bordeaux Supérieur
owner: Monique & Marie-Hélène Marinier *area:* 30
ha *cases:* 24,000, white 2,000 *grape % R:* MER
75% CS 20% MAL 5% *grape % W:* SEM 30% MUSC 30%
SAUV B 20% UGNI BLANC 10% COL 10% *second wine:*
Ch Florimond *other wines:* La Petite Chardonne
(Côtes de Bourg); Ch Haut-Chardon *(Bordeaux);* Ch
Haut-Peyredoule *(Bordeaux Supérieur; Premières
Côtes de Blaye)*
33390 Berson tel: 05 57 64 39 07
fax: 05 57 64 23 27
Five names are in use at this estate for different
qualities of wine. The second-largest production
here is a Bordeaux Supérieur, characterized by

Merlot: properly concentrated, yet also showing a measure of finesse. The property is run by two daughters of the late Louis Marinier, a personality who did much for the Bordeaux Supérieur *syndicat*.

Ch Fonchereau
map 35

Bordeaux Supérieur, Bordeaux, Entre-Deux-Mers
owner: Madame Vinot-Postry *area:* 28 ha *cases:*
18,000, white 2,000 *grape % R:* MER 67% CS 15% CF
15% MAL 3% *grape % W:* SEM 50% SAUV B 30% MUSC
20% *second wine:* Ch Sauvetat (*Bordeaux Supérieur*)
33450 Montussan tel: 05 56 72 96 12
fax: 05 56 72 44 91
An estate rich in history, with a château that abuts a tower of 16th-century origin. In the best vintages a sometimes impressively fine Bordeaux Supérieur is made: concentrated, meaty, with nuances and smooth tannins. In more average years the wine is still apt to be successful and firmly structured. The Entre-Deux-Mers generally tastes clean and succulently fresh.

Ch Fondarzac
map 35

Entre-Deux-Mers, Bordeaux
owner: Jean-Claude Barthe *area:* 56.7 ha *cases:*
19,000, white 19,500 *grape % R:* MER 50% CS 25%
CF 25% *grape % W:* SEM 40% SAUV B 40% MUSC 20%
other wines: Bordeaux Clairet
33420 Naujan-et-Postiac tel: 05 57 84 55 04
fax: 05 57 84 60 23
The Entre-Deux-Mers is made here almost in the Alsace style: soft and spicy, quite expansive, slightly fruity (citrus notes in particular). Jean-Claude Barthe also makes a not especially notable red Bordeaux, and a fresh, quite light Bordeaux Clairet. Exactly the same wines are also sold under the name Ch Darzac.

Ch Fonfroide
map 36

Bordeaux, Entre-Deux-Mers
owner: Famille Dutheillet de Lamothe *area:* 53 ha
cases: 30,000, white 5,000 *grape % R:* MER 60% CS
20% CF 20% *grape % W:* SEM 58% SAUV B 30% MUSC
12%
33890 Coubeyrac tel: 05 56 68 81 82
fax: 05 56 20 94 47
This estate has belonged to the same family since 1646, but vinification is now supervised by the firm of Ginestet. The accent is very much

Below: Ch Fonchereau

Above: Ch La France

on red Bordeaux: six times as much is made as of the fruity Entre-Deux-Mers. The red wine offers grip, concentration, good tannins, and a discreet, flattering aroma of oak from three to six months in cask.

Ch de Fontenille
map 35

Bordeaux, Entre-Deux-Mers
owner: Stéphane Defraine *area:* 25 ha *cases:*
12,500, white 2,000 *grape % R:* MER 50% CF 35% CS
15% *grape % W:* SEM 40% SAUV B 30% MUSC 30%
other wines: Bordeaux Clairet
33670 La Sauve Majeure tel: 05 56 23 03 26
fax: 05 56 23 30 03
Belgian-born Stéphane Defraine bought this château in 1988 and since then has given it a solid reputation. He harvests late and selects stringently. At the top of the range is his red Cuvée Prestige, given 10 months in casks of which 50% are new. This Bordeaux Supérieur offers integrated tannins, jammy red and black currant fruit, and a mouthfilling taste. The ordinary red Bordeaux, the Clairet, and the Entre-Deux-Mers (aromatic, partly because of long skin-contact) afford great enjoyment too.

Ch Fosselongue
map 35

Bordeaux, Entre-Deux-Mers
owner: André Bernard *area:* 15 ha *cases:* 6,000,
white 4,000 *grape % R:* MER 50% CF 40% MAL 10%
grape % W: SAUV B 60% SEM 30% MUSC 10% *other wines:* Bordeaux rosé; Crémant de Bordeaux
33750 Beychac-et-Caillau tel: 05 57 24 51 96
Generation after generation of the same family have made wine here since 1780. The range now comprises seven wines, with the red Bordeaux Cuvée Prestige boasting the best quality. This spends a year in *barriques*, of which half are replaced annually. It is a complete wine, with an aroma that includes candied black fruit.

Ch La France
map 35

Bordeaux Supérieur, Entre-Deux-Mers
owner: La France Assurances *area:* 80 ha *cases:*
33,500, white 6,500 *grape % R:* MER 60% CF 20% CS
20% *grape % W:* SEM 80% SAUV B 15% MUSC 5%
second wine: Ch Quinsac
33750 Beychac-et-Caillau tel: 05 57 24 51 10
fax: 05 57 24 01 76
The stylish, perfectly maintained, symmetrical château is probably built on the site of a Roman

villa. Since 1988 it has belonged to an insurance company, which has invested a great deal in the *cuvier* and *chai*. The Bordeaux Supérieur is made in a firm style: plenty of smooth tannin, ripe fruit, a long finish, a hint of oak and a good balance. The supple Entre-Deux-Mers is at once fruity and floral.

Ch Franc La Cour
map 36

Bordeaux, Ste-Foy Bordeaux
owner: Claudine & Guy Binninger *area:* 15 ha
cases: 6,600, white 3,300 *grape % R:* MER 50% CS
40% CF 10% *grape % W:* SEM 95% MUSC 5%
33220 La Roquille tel: 05 57 41 26 93
fax: 05 57 41 23 64
An estate reborn since 1989; it has been winning various awards for its wines. Best of the range is the Ste-Foy Bordeaux, a delicious, fruity red wine with supple tannins. In contrast to other similar wines, it is not as yet oak-aged.

Ch La Freynelle
map 35

Bordeaux, Entre-Deux-Mers
owner: Véronique Barthe *area:* 75 ha *cases:*
29,000, white 15,500 *grape % R:* MER 50% CS 50%
grape % W: SAUV B 60% SEM 30% MUSC 10% *second wine:* Ch Poncet *other wines:* Bordeaux Clairet; Crémant de Bordeaux
33420 Daignac tel: 05 56 23 90 83
fax: 05 56 23 45 71
Until well into the 1980s this vineyard's crop was sold in bulk. The oenologist Véronique Barthe put an end to this by bottling a series of very successful wines. Examples are the extremely agreeable, satiny red Bordeaux, the fruity, flowery Bordeaux Clairet, the succulent, slightly spicy, refined Entre-Deux-Mers, the Bordeaux Sec – again with plenty of fruit, – and two special *cuvées*. Spices, licorice and other nuances characterize the white Bordeaux Cuvée Emotion, fermented in cask; and the red version is a quite full-bodied, creamy wine which gains dimension and depth from its 10-12 months in oak. The Crémant rosé makes a delicious aperitif.

Ch de Frimont
map 36

Bordeaux, Bordeaux Supérieur
owner: Jocelyne & Jean-François Degregorio
area: 9 ha *cases:* 5,200 *grape % R:* CS 50%
MER 30% CF 20%
33190 Girode-sur-Dropt tel: 05 56 61 23 89

The Bordeaux Supérieur is the best of the three wines made at Ch de Frimont: firm tannins, a notable oak aroma from 15 months in barrel, and ripe berry fruit.

Ch Frontenac   map 36
Bordeaux, Bordeaux Supérieur
owner: Roger Mesange *area:* 33 ha *cases:* 16,500, white 6,500 *grape % R:* MER 40% CF 30% CS 30% *grape % W:* SEM 70% SAUV B 30% *second wine:* Ch Haut-Pineuilh
33220 Pineuilh tel: 05 57 46 16 59
fax: 05 57 46 16 59
Somewhat rustic red Bordeaux, and Bordeaux Supérieur, with strong tannins and an aroma with woodland, animal and fruity elements. No ageing in cask.

Ch de Fussignac   map 34
Bordeaux, Bordeaux Supérieur
owner: Jean-François Carrille *area:* 14 ha *cases:* 6,000, white 1,500 *grape % R:* MER 70% CS 25% CF 5% *grape % W:* UGNI BLANC 50% SEM 20% SAUV B 20% MUSC 10% *second wine:* Ch Fussignac Le Cofour *other châteaux owned:* include Ch Boutisse (St-Emilion); Ch Cardinal Villemaurine (St-Emilion); Ch Caillou les Martins (Lussac-St-Emilion)
33570 Petit-Palais-et-Cornemps tel:
05 57 24 74 46
fax: 05 57 24 64 40
Estate situated on a hill, renovated since 1983, where a generally pleasing, supple Bordeaux Supérieur is made. This is given some time in wood – an average of six months. However, there are vintages when the wine lacks some substance and class.

Ch La Gaborie   map 35
Bordeaux Supérieur, Bordeaux, Entre-Deux-Mers
owner: Jean-Hubert Laville *area:* 15 ha *cases:* 6,700, white 2,000 *grape % R:* MER 40% CS 40% CF 20% *grape % W:* SEM 50% SAUV B 40% MUSC 10% *other châteaux owned:* Ch Lacombe (Bordeaux); Ch du Mont Carlau (Bordeaux); Ch des Tuquets (Bordeaux)
33760 Ladaux tel: 05 56 71 53 56
fax: 05 56 71 53 42
The well-made Entre-Deux-Mers is meant for drinking young. The Bordeaux Supérieur benefits from some years' maturing to bring its initially rather tough tannins into better balance with the other elements.

Domaine du Galet   map 34
Bordeaux Supérieur
owner: Vignobles J. Janoueix *area:* 12 ha *cases:* 4,400 *grape % R:* MER 70% CF 20% CS 10% *other châteaux owned:* include Ch Haut-Sarpe (St-Emilion)
33500 Libourne tel: 05 57 51 41 86
Wine estate in the Libourne *commune* taking its name from the large stones the English used to bring in as ballast in their ships. Here a supple, honest Bordeaux Supérieur is made, meant for early drinking. Some well-known Paris restaurants have it on their wine lists.

Ch Gamage   map 36
Bordeaux Supérieur, Entre-Deux-Mers
owner: Famille Moulinet *area:* 34 ha *cases:* 17,000, white 2,300 *grape % R:* MER 70% CF 15% CS 15% *grape % W:* SEM 60% SAUV B 30% MUSC 10% *second wine:* Ch Dartigue
33350 St-Pey-de-Castets tel: 05 57 40 52 02
fax: 05 57 40 53 77
The Cuvée Spéciale here, matured for a year in cask, deserves attention. This red Bordeaux

Supérieur offers more grip, more plum-like fruit, is rounder than the supple standard version and, of course, it has its flattering oak. The Entre-Deux-Mers tastes clean and refreshing.

Ch Gantonet   map 36
Bordeaux, Bordeaux Supérieur
owner: André Richard *area:* 70 ha *cases:* 40,000, white 5,000 *grape % R:* MER 50% CF 25% CS 20% MAL 5% *grape % W:* SAUV B 50% SEM 40% MUSC 10% *second wines:* Ch Guillot; Ch Cap Blanc; Ch Moulin de Laborde *other wines:* Bordeaux Clairet
33350 Ste-Radegonde tel: 05 57 40 53 83
fax: 05 57 40 58 95
In the Bordeaux Sec from this extensive property the Sauvignon sets the tone, with gooseberry and a hint of herbaceousness. A pleasant Bordeaux Clairet is also made here, and a reasonably fruity Bordeaux Supérieur which has six months in oak.

Ch Le Gardera   map 32
Bordeaux Supérieur
owner: Domaines Cordier *area:* 35 ha *cases:* 22,500 *grape % R:* MER 60% CS 35% CF 5% *second wine:* Galeteau *other wines:* Bordeaux rosé *other châteaux owned:* include Ch Clos des Jacobins (St-Emilion)
33550 Langoiran tel: 05 56 67 00 51
fax: 05 56 67 58 81
Expertly made Bordeaux Supérieur that today is among the best from this appellation. Firm in taste, with some spice and rich, fine tannins, not an enormous amount of fruit, and a good balance. Domaines Cordier give it a year in oak. Another product is a creditable Bordeaux Rosé made from half Merlot, half Cabernet Franc.

Ch Gaury Balette   map 36
Bordeaux Supérieur, Bordeaux, Entre-Deux-Mers
owner: Bernard Yon *area:* 30 ha *cases:* 17,000, white 1,500 *grape % R:* MER 50% CS 48% PV 2% *grape % W:* SAUV B 70% SEM 30% *second wine:* Ch Les Hauts de Perey
33540 Mauriac tel: 05 57 40 52 82
fax: 05 57 40 51 71
Dynamically run property making an ample range of wines. A red that compels admiration is the Comte Auguste, a Bordeaux Supérieur matured for six months in *barriques*. This is produced only in good years and has a seductive

Below: Ch Le Gardera

aroma and a lively, nuanced taste. The Entre-Deux-Mers is the best white wine: fruity, lively and with a fine finish.

Ch Gauthier   map 46
Bordeaux Supérieur
owner: Michel Massé *area:* 10 ha *cases:* 4,000 *grape % R:* CS 70% MER 30%
33920 Civrac-de-Blaye tel: 05 57 68 81 01
fax: 05 57 68 83 17
The tannins in this Bordeaux Supérieur can be rather rough at times, but its constitution is good and there is often black fruit in the aroma. The wine, which is not cask-aged, is made by the cooperative at Pugnac.

Ch Le Gay   map 35
Bordeaux
owner: Claude Boursaud *area:* 20 ha *cases:* 7,000, white 4,500 *grape % R:* MER 54% CS 46% *grape % W:* SEM 43% COL 22% UGNI BLANC 12% MUSC 12% SAUV B 11%
33370 Artigues-près-Bordeaux tel: 05 56 86 36 77
The wines here may not be stupendous, but they do offer decent quality: supple, softly fruity red Bordeaux; amiable white characterized by spice. The estate dates from 1922.

Ch Les Gazelles   map 34
Bordeaux Supérieur
owner: Claude Merlet *area:* 4.5 ha *cases:* 3,000 *grape % R:* MER 70% CF 15% CS 15% *other châteaux owned:* Ch Les Gazelles (Lalande-de-Pomerol)
33910 St-Denis-de-Pile tel: 05 57 74 23 87
fax: 05 57 74 23 87
Delightfully fruity (blackberry, cherry, raspberry) and often velvety Bordeaux Supérieur from a vineyard that has roughly tripled in size in less than 10 years.

Ch Georges de Guestres   map 36
Bordeaux Supérieur
owner: Paule & Michel Dubois *area:* 3 ha *cases:* 1,700 *grape % R:* MER 80% CF 20% *other châteaux owned:* Ch La Ganne (Pomerol)
33500 Les Billaux tel: 05 57 51 18 24
fax: 05 57 51 62 20
Decent, supple Bordeaux Supérieur with earthy tones and forest scents. Has a year in wood.

Ch Grand Bireau   map 35
Bordeaux
owner: Michel Barthe *area:* 35 ha *cases:* 12,500, white 6,500 *grape % R:* MER 50% CS 30% CF 20% *grape % W:* SEM 50% SAUV B 40% MUSC 10% *second wine:* Ch Reléou
33420 Naujan-et-Postiac tel: 05 57 84 55 23
fax: 05 57 84 57 37
Since 1978 a great deal has been invested in this estate of 18th-century origin. The Barthe family makes an often meaty red Bordeaux from mechanically picked grapes, a dark-coloured wine with licorice, bayleaf and oak aromas from 16 months in cask in its nicely lingering taste. The white version is positively exhilarating in style, slightly mineral and with some citrus fruit. In effect, the same qualities are offered under the name Ch Reléou.

Ch Le Grand Chemin   map 34
Bordeaux Supérieur
owner: Jean-Yves Bourseau *area:* 16 ha *cases:* 9,000, white 350 *grape % R:* MER 80% CS 15% MAL 3% CF 2% *grape % W:* SAUV B 80% SEM 20% *second wine:* Ch Saint Mathieu *other wines:*

Bordeaux Clairet; Crémant de Bordeaux
**33240 Virsac tel: 05 57 43 29 32
fax: 05 57 43 39 57**
Property formed out of a number of plots in 1987, for which Jean-Yves and Christiane Bourseau have built a *cuvier* and *chai*. Apart from tiny amounts of white wine (sometimes processed into a Crémant) and of Clairet, this is a red-wine estate. The best wine is the Bordeaux Supérieur, which generally requires some years in bottle after its 6-9 months spent maturing in oak. Often there is some fruit in its bouquet and taste, spice, and sometimes herbaceous elements as well.

Ch Grand Clauset　　　　map 35
Bordeaux
owner: Patrick Carteyron *area:* 7 ha *cases:* 3,000 *grape % R:* MER 80% CF 15% CS 5% *other châteaux owned:* Ch Penin *(Bordeaux, Bordeaux Supérieur)*
**33420 Génissac tel: 05 57 24 46 98
fax: 05 57 24 41 99**
The soil here is different from that at the same owner's Ch Penin – clay and chalk rather than gravel. This makes the Grand Clauset wine more supple and less complex. An open style of Bordeaux, it has aspects of black fruit (prune), bayleaf and animal scents.

Ch Grand Donnezac　　　　map 36
Bordeaux
owner: Didier Merit *area:* 44 ha *cases:* 21,500, white 2,200 *grape % R:* MER 52% CF 25% CS 23% *grape % W:* SAUV B 68% SEM 25% MUSC 7%
**33420 St-Vincent-de-Pertignas
tel: 05 57 84 13 22
fax: 05 57 84 12 67**
Decent-quality wines made at the Rauzan cooperative. The red has a foundation of firm tannins and plummy fruit. In the white, the aroma speaks of the fresh, gooseberry notes of Sauvignon.

Ch de la Grande Chapelle　　　　map 34
Bordeaux, Bordeaux Supérieur
owner: Vignobles Liotard *area:* 20 ha *cases:* 10,500, white 1,200 *grape % R:* MER 60% CF 30% CS 10% *grape % W:* SEM 80% SAUV B 20% *second wine:* Ch La Freychère *other châteaux owned:* Ch Le Conseiller *(Bordeaux Supérieur)*
**33240 Lugon tel: 05 57 84 41 52
fax: 05 57 84 45 02**
A velvety taste, integrated tannins, fine quality: the Bordeaux Supérieur from this estate usually develops these aspects after about five years. Oak – from a year in barrel – and earthy tones are often more strongly present than fruit. The estate also produces a pleasing Bordeaux Sec. The vineyard, which is to be increased by 7 ha, spreads out around a chapel mentioned as early as the year 1171.

Ch Les Grandes Bornes　　　　map 36
Bordeaux Supérieur
owner: Alain Bernard *area:* 37.5 ha *cases:* 19,500 *grape % R:* MER 50% CF 30% CS 20% *second wine:* Ch Haut-Marmont
**33350 Mouliets-et-Villemartin
tel: 05 57 40 09 03**
The Bernard family have owned this estate since 1862. Between 1972 and 1986 the vineyard was replanted and the cellar complex modernized. The Grandes Bornes wine, a Bordeaux Supérieur, generally tastes quite firm, with a slightly bitter touch, some spice and a very acceptable quality.

Ch du Grand Ferrand　　　　map 36
Bordeaux Supérieur, Bordeaux, Entre-Deux-Mers
owner: Vignobles Rocher-Cap de Rive *area:* 42 ha *cases:* 20,000, white 29,000 *grape % R:* MER 80% CS 20% *grape % W:* SAUV B 80% SEM 20% *second wines:* Ch Ventouse; Ch Joffre *other châteaux owned:* include Ch Cap d'Or *(St-Georges-St-Emilion)*
**33540 Sauveterre-de-Guyenne tel: 05 57 40 08 88
fax: 05 57 40 14 93**
Here the generally well-balanced Bordeaux Sec, based on Sauvignon Blanc, is the most pleasing wine – and the largest in terms of production. It usually has an agreeable nose of tropical and citrus fruit, and a clean taste, at once supple and fresh.

Ch Grand-Jean　　　　map 35
Bordeaux, Entre-Deux-Mers
owner: Michel Dulon *area:* 75 ha *cases:* 25,000, white 25,000 *grape % R:* CS 70% MER 25% CF 5% *grape % W:* SEM 80% SAUV B 10% MUSC 10% *other wines:* Ch Le Templey *(Bordeaux blanc & rouge)*
**33760 Soulignac tel: 05 56 23 69 16
fax: 05 57 34 41 29**
Estate of considerable size; half its production is of white Entre-Deux-Mers, and half of red Bordeaux. Since 1993 the quality of the wine has shown steady improvement. The Bordeaux is now matured for about 10 months in *barriques*, so that its aroma of black and red berry fruit is accompanied by creamy tones of oak and vanilla. The same wines are also sold under the name Ch Le Templey.

Ch Grand Monteil　　　　map 35
Bordeaux Supérieur, Entre-Deux-Mers
owner: Famille Techenet *area:* 110 ha *cases:* 50,000, white 8,500 *grape % R:* MER 50% CS 40% CF 10% *grape % W:* SAUV B 50% SEM 50% *second wine:* Ch Lafite Monteil *other wines:* Bordeaux rosé
**33370 Salleboeuf tel: 05 56 21 29 70
fax: 05 56 78 39 91**
The *chai* here bears the signature of the most famous owner that this large wine estate ever had – the engineer Alexandre Gustave Eiffel, who also built a bridge across the Dordogne. The Bordeaux Supérieur matures for six months in this above-ground cellar. It is a wine to be recommended, well provided with tannin. Of at least an equal standard are the Bordeaux Rosé, with a lot of red fruit, and the Entre-Deux-Mers.

Below: Ch Grand Monteil

Ch Au Grand Paris　　　　map 36
Bordeaux
owner: GAEC des Trois Paris/Familles Langel & Castenet *area:* 29 ha *cases:* 10,000, white 7,000 *grape % R:* MER 52% CS 38% CF 10% *grape % W:* SEM 43% SAUV B 41% MUSC 16% *second wine:* Ch Malène
**33790 Cazaugitat tel: 05 56 71 80 94
fax: 05 56 71 62 15**
Estate with up-to-date equipment producing wines that include an agreeable, slightly fruity red Bordeaux of average quality. The château stands on the site of a 15th-century monastery which had a small vineyard.

Ch du Grand Puch　　　　map 35
Bordeaux Supérieur
owner: André Weber *area:* 85 ha *cases:* 50,000 *grape % R:* MER 50% CF 25% CS 25% *second wine:* Ch Saint Germain
33750 St-Germain-du-Puch tel: 05 57 24 51 03
The history and architecture of this estate are more intriguing than its wine, an ordinarily good Bordeaux Supérieur, not oak-aged. The very striking castle dates back to the 13th century, and it is amazingly well preserved. Since 1962 practically the whole of the vintage has been handled exclusively by the firm of Calvet.

Ch Les Grands Jays　　　　map 34
Bordeaux Supérieur
owner: Jean Boireau *area:* 22 ha *cases:* 12,000 *grape % R:* MER 80% CS 20% *other châteaux owned:* Ch Grand Lavergne *(Bordeaux Supérieur)*; Ch Haut Milon *(Lussac-St-Emilion)*
**33570 Les Artigues-de-Lussac tel: 05 57 24 32 08
fax: 05 57 24 33 24**
The standard Bordeaux Supérieur is a medal-winning, charming wine, rounded in the mouth and made chiefly from Merlot. It is not oak-matured – unlike the *cuvée* from old vines, made in limited quantities, which first appeared in 1992, or the Ch Haut Milon, a Lussac-St-Emilion, produced by the same grower.

Ch Le Grand Verdus　　　　map 35
Bordeaux Supérieur
owner: Ph. & A. Le Grix de la Salle *area:* 80 ha *cases:* 50,000 *grape % R:* MER 40% CS 40% CF 20% *second wine:* Ch la Rode *other wines:* Rosé du Grand Verdus *(Bordeaux rosé)*
**33670 Sadirac tel: 05 56 30 64 22
fax: 05 56 23 71 37**

The Grand Verdus vineyard already covers 80 ha, but is to grow by a further 20 ha in the coming years. This is undoubtedly feasible since the wine is so much in demand – a reflection of its high average quality. The Cuvée Tradition is a wine in which fruit and tannin are always to be found in pleasing measure. The Cuvée Réservée, made in very limited quantities and given eight months in cask, has rather more depth and lots of oak. The château itself is an imposing 16th-century fortified manor house, its peaceful, enclosed inner courtyard shaded by trees.

Ch Grand Village   map 34
Bordeaux, Bordeaux Supérieur
owner: Sylvie & Jacques Guinaudeau **area:** 17 ha **cases:** 8,000, white 800 **grape % R:** MER 50% CF 40% CS 10% **grape % W:** SAUV B 50% SEM 50% **second wine:** Beau Village **other wines:** Cuvée Florys (Bordeaux rosé) **other châteaux owned:** Ch Lafleur (Pomerol)
33240 Mouillac tel: 05 57 84 44 03
An estate run with dedication that has been making wine since the 15th century, and today produces a classy Bordeaux Supérieur: deep red, richly fruity, with integrated tannins, fine concentration and subtle oak from six months in barrel. The owners reject an average 25% of each vintage – not even using it for the second wine. The white Ch Grand Village also spends time in wood, and besides its fruit – which includes pineapple – it has vanilla and a long finish. The rosé Cuvée Florys tends to be delicious too.

Domaine de la Grange Brûlée
map 35
Bordeaux Supérieur
owner: Vignobles Landeau **area:** 10 ha **cases:** 4,500 **grape % R:** MER 50% CS 30% CF 20% **second wines:** Domaine de Mondion; Ch Papin **other wines:** Bordeaux rosé
33440 St-Vincent-de-Paul tel: 05 56 77 11 17
The rounded, agreeable and reasonably fruity rosé is sometimes rather better than the Bordeaux Supérieur red, which often has a touch of undergrowth and dead leaves in its aroma and taste. Only the red wine goes into *barriques* – for one year. The vineyard is being enlarged to 15 ha.

Domaine de la Grange du Roy
map 36
Bordeaux
owner: Bernard Bouillon **area:** 5 ha **cases:** 1,600 **grape % R:** MER 50% CS 30% CF 20%
33350 Pujols-sur-Dordogne
tel: 05 57 40 50 71
Traditional, decent red Bordeaux that spends two years in cask and is made from organically grown grapes.

Ch des Granges   map 35
Bordeaux Supérieur, Bordeaux, Entre-Deux-Mers
owner: René Faucher **area:** 16 ha **cases:** 7,500, white 1,000 **grape % R:** CF 70% MER 25% CS 5% **grape % W:** SAUV B 60% SEM 35% MUSC 5% **second wine:** Ch Lestillon
33420 Rauzan tel: 05 57 84 13 29
fax: 05 57 84 01 79
Since the 1950s this estate has grown from 6 to 32 ha. It was split in two under the terms of a will in 1988. An oenologist runs des Granges, and among its wines are a good Supérieur and a lovely, fragrant Entre-Deux-Mers.

Ch du Grava   map 32
Bordeaux Supérieur
owner: Société Viticole de France **area:** 45 ha **cases:** 32,000 **grape % R:** CS 42% MER 38% CF 20% **other châteaux owned:** Ch Bernones (Haut-Médoc); Ch Viera (Bordeaux Supérieur); Ch Mauvesin (Moulis-en-Médoc); Ch Mauras (Sauternes)
33550 Haux tel: 05 56 67 23 89
fax: 05 56 67 08 38
Oak-ageing is not applied at Ch du Grava – partly to enable the very correctly made Bordeaux Supérieur to retain its berry fruit. The vineyard is in one solid block, and forms part of a 75-ha estate that stretches across three communes.

Domaine de Grava   map 31
Bordeaux
owner: Jean Fonteyreaud **area:** 14 ha **cases:** 8,000 **grape % R:** MER 65% CS 15% CF 15% MAL 5% **other châteaux owned:** Domaine du Tich (Ste-Croix-du-Mont)
33490 Verdelais tel: 05 56 62 05 42
fax: 05 56 62 01 71
Modest red Bordeaux, offering some berry fruit, which goes into cask for half a year. The same producer also makes Domaine du Tich, a Ste-Croix-du-Mont.

Domaine de la Grave   map 35
Bordeaux, Bordeaux Supérieur
owner: François Roche **area:** 12 ha **cases:** 5,700, white 1,000 **grape % R:** MER 75% CS 15% CF 10% **grape % W:** SEM 35% MUSC 35% SAUV B 30% **second wine:** Domaine de Roquebert
33750 Beychac-et-Caillau tel: 05 56 72 41 28
fax: 05 56 72 41 28
From this property, with its picturesque 18th-century house adorned by a delightful open belfry, come a red Bordeaux Supérieur and also two white Bordeaux. The red Supérieur is

---

◆
Maps of the area
The main areas that produce Bordeaux and Bordeaux Supérieur, and the various Entre-Deux-Mers appellations in this chapter, are covered by Maps 34, 35 & 36.

Below: Ch Grossombre

matured in cask for a maximum of one year and its tannins are usually very evident – and also sometimes a little hard.

Ch La Grave   map 34
Bordeaux Supérieur
owner: Louis Decazes **area:** 8 ha **cases:** 4,000 **grape % R:** MER 50% CF 25% CS 25%
33910 Bonzac tel: 05 57 84 22 03
fax: 05 57 84 41 06
The standard Bordeaux Supérieur here can sometimes be rather light and unexceptional, but the Cuvée Réservée Duc Decazes is worth discovering. Behind its considerable oak, from a year in barrel, there lurks a supple, quite rounded taste with elements of berry fruit, spice and earthy tones. The neo-Gothic château has belonged to the same family since the 18th century; one Decazes was a minister under Louis XVIII.

Ch La Gravelière   map 36
Bordeaux, Bordeaux Supérieur
owner: GFA René Mayon **area:** 20 ha **cases:** 11,000 **grape % R:** CS 60% MER 40%
33490 Le Pian-sur-Garonne tel: 05 56 81 59 03
fax: 05 56 01 25 39
Consistently good Bordeaux Supérieur, characterized by blackcurrant fruit, and made from hand-picked grapes. A further 4 ha are being planted.

Ch Graveyron La France   map 34
Bordeaux Supérieur
owner: Jean-Claude Simon **area:** 20 ha **cases:** 11,000 **grape % R:** MER 80% CS 20%
33126 Fronsac tel: 05 57 51 45 02
fax: 05 57 25 27 41
Quite generous Bordeaux Supérieur characterized by its Merlot, from a property in Fronsac that has undergone renewal and renovation since 1973. The wine spends a year in concrete *cuves*.

Ch Greteau   map 36
Bordeaux, Bordeaux Supérieur
owner: Jean Médeville & Fils **area:** 9 ha **cases:** 4,000, white 1,200 **grape % R:** MER 40% CS 35% CF 25% **grape % W:** SAUV B 50% SEM 40% MUSC 10% **other châteaux owned:** include Ch Fayau (Premières Côtes de Bordeaux; Cadillac); Ch du Juge (Bordeaux Supérieur; Cadillac)

Above: Ch d'Haurets

33410 Cadillac tel: 05 58 98 08 08
fax: 05 56 62 18 22
Jean Médeville added Ch Greteau to his
portfolio in 1953. It produces an accessible
Bordeaux Supérieur soon ready for drinking,
and a decent Bordeaux Sec. The firm of Dubos
Frères offers practically the same wines with
the label Ch Greteau-Médeville.

Ch Grossombre   map 35
Bordeaux, Entre-Deux-Mers
owner: Béatrice Lurton *area:* 35 ha *cases:* 9,500,
white 12,000 *grape % R:* CS 67% MER 33% *grape %
W:* SEM 50% SAUV B 30% MUSC 20% *other wines:*
Bordeaux rosé
33420 Dardenac tel: 05 57 25 88 58
fax: 05 57 74 98 59
This estate derives its name from a centuries-
old oak that used to stand in front of the
château itself , which is a charming *chartreuse*.
Since 1989 Grossombre has belonged to
Béatrice Lurton. The Entre-Deux-Mers is a
clean, aromatic wine, with exotic and
gooseberry fruit, and is exceptionally pleasing.
The red Bordeaux, matured for a year in casks
of which 20% are new, is also a satisfying bottle.
Meaty and lively, it has considerable berry fruit.
The château also makes an absolutely delicious
Bordeaux Rosé – fragrant and full of jammy
red fruit.

Ch de Guérin   map 35
Bordeaux
owner: Léon Jaumain *area:* 9 ha *cases:* 2,900,
white 2,500 *grape % R:* MER 60% CS 30% CF 10%
grape % W: SEM 65% MUSC 30% SAUV B 5% *second
wine:* Ch Clos de Guérin
33540 Castelvieil tel: 05 56 61 97 58
Tannin gives backbone to the Bordeaux from
this carefully managed vineyard, and a
potential maturing time of four to five years.
This is a well-made wine, as is the fresh
Bordeaux Sec.

Ch Guichot   map 36
Bordeaux Supérieur, Entre-Deux-Mers
owner: Gaston Founé *area:* 16 ha *cases:* 13,500,
white 2,500 *grape % R:* MER 40% CS 40% CF 20%
grape % W: SEM 50% SAUV B 25% MUSC 25% *other
wines:* Bordeaux rosé
33790 St-Antoine-du-Queret tel: 05 56 61 36 99
fax: 05 56 61 36 99

Although Guichot's Entre-Deux-Mers and
Bordeaux Rosé have their merits, it is the
Bordeaux Supérieur that flies the flag here. It
has an elegant firmness, and six months in cask
give this wine the aroma of a blend of berry
fruit and oak.

Ch La Hargue   map 35
Bordeaux
owner: Vignobles Ducourt *area:* 34 ha *cases:*
8,500, white 10,500 *grape % R:* MER 77% CS 23%
grape % W: SAUV B 54% SEM 24% MUSC 15% UGNI
BLANC 7% *other wines:* Bordeaux rosé *other
châteaux owned:* include Ch La Rose St-Germain
(Bordeaux)
33760 Ladaux tel: 05 56 23 93 53
fax: 05 56 23 48 78
At this Ducourt estate a pleasing, clean white
Bordeaux with gooseberry fruit is made, and a
quite elegant and lively red Bordeaux which
soon becomes supple and is not without fruit.
The third wine is a fragrant rosé.

Ch de Hartes   map 35
Bordeaux
owner: P. & M. Mazeau-Hautbois *area:* 15 ha
cases: 10,000 *grape % R:* CF 70% CS 30% *other
châteaux owned:* Ch Toutigeac *(Bordeaux)*
33760 Targon tel: 05 56 23 90 95
fax: 05 56 23 67 21
A modern red Bordeaux with a taste full of
succulent berry fruit and suppleness. It is made
with a notably high proportion of Cabernet
Franc.

Ch d'Haurets   map 35
Bordeaux
owner: Philippe Ducourt *area:* 34 ha *cases:*
10,000, white 9,000 *grape % R:* CS 43% CF 29% MER
28% *grape % W:* MUSC 49% SAUV B 35% SEM 16%
other wines: Bordeaux rosé *other châteaux owned:*
include Ch La Rose St-Germain *(Bordeaux)*
33760 Ladaux tel: 05 56 23 93 53
fax: 05 56 23 48 78
The name is derived from a Celtic word for
forest, but long rows of vines now surround the
château, a delightful 18th-century chartreuse.
The vineyard yields rather more red than white
wine. The red Bordeaux is elegantly firm, with
vitality and a good deal of fruit; the softly fresh
white Sauvignon combines fruit with spices.
The rosé made here is also very commendable.

Ch Haut Bastor   map 35
Bordeaux
owner: Pascal Maurin *area:* 76 ha *cases:* 23,000,
white 27,500 *grape % R:* MER 50% CS 30% CF 20%
grape % W: SEM 40% SAUV B 25% MUSC 25% UGNI
BLANC 10% *second wines:* Ch Croix de Terrefort; Ch
Les Tourelles *other wines:* Bordeaux rosé
33540 St-Brice tel: 05 56 71 54 18
fax: 05 56 71 50 22
The most interesting of the five wines here is
the red Bordeaux Cuvée des Deux Moulins, aged
for four months in barrels of which a quarter
are new. This red Bordeaux has a reasonably
mouthfilling taste with both berry fruit and
animal tones; and supple tannins are not
lacking. The wine is named after the remains of
two 19th-century windmills on the estate.

Ch Haut-Boisron   map 46
Bordeaux
owner: Bernard Gourtade *area:* 10 ha *cases:*
4,200, white 2,700 *grape % R:* MER 80% CS 20%
grape % W: SAUV B 71% UGNI BLANC 29% *other wines:*
Blayais; Bordeaux rosé *other châteaux owned:* Ch
Godineau *(Côtes de Bourg)*
33860 Reignac tel: 05 57 32 48 83
Although this property lies in the Blaye district,
it yields mainly Bordeaux wine. The red,
matured for 10-12 months in oak, generally is
very acceptable, albeit rather light. The cask-
aged Blanc Sec, however, is not really a success.

Ch Haut Bourdieu   map 34
Bordeaux Supérieur
owner: Nicole Mallard *area:* 15 ha *cases:* 8,500
grape % R: MER 60% CS 30% CF 10% *second wine:*
Clos du Tertre de La Veine *(Bordeaux)*
33240 St-Laurent-d'Arce tel: 05 57 43 33 16
This is usually a Bordeaux Supérieur with good
concentration, ripe tannins and a better-than-
average quality. It has four months in oak. The
estate dates from the end of the 19th century.

Domaine du Haut Cantelaudette
map 35
Bordeaux, Bordeaux Supérieur
owner: Pierre & Colette Réau *area:* 1.4 ha *cases:*
1,050 *grape % R:* MER 80% CF 20% *other wines:* La
Roseé de Bacchus *(Bordeaux rosé)*
33450 St-Loubès tel: 05 56 06 79 30
In good and great wine years a red Bordeaux
Supérieur is made here. This is colourful,
meaty, and aged in oak for six months. In lesser
vintages the straight Bordeaux appellation is
chosen, and the wine tastes more supple.

Ch Haut Cantonnet   map 36
Bordeaux, Bordeaux Supérieur
owner: Jean-Paul Rigal *area:* 5.5 ha *cases:* 3,500
grape % R: CF 40% CS 40% MER 20% *other châteaux
owned:* Domaine du Cantonnet *(Bergerac)*
33220 St-Avit-St-Nazaire tel: 05 53 27 88 63
fax: 05 53 23 77 11
A vineyard almost wholly replanted since 1974.
Besides a standard Bordeaux it also supplies a
cuvée nurtured in the traditional way in oak
casks, and called Ch Haut Lespinasse. Maturing
lasts from 8-12 months, and the *barriques* are
replaced by new ones every other year.

Ch Haut-Colas-Nouet   map 34
Bordeaux Supérieur
owner: SCE J.-P. & J.-C. Quet *area:* 16 ha *cases:*
9,000 *grape % R:* MER 60% CS 25% CF 15% *second
wine:* Ch La Fleur Baudron *other châteaux owned:*
Ch Petit-Faurie-Quet *(St-Emilion)*

33570 Les Artigues-de-Lussac tel: 05 57 24 37 88 fax: 05 57 24 34 10
An appealing Bordeaux Supérieur: rounded, with fruit and enough backbone to develop for some years in bottle. Not aged in cask. The vineyard is being extended by 4 ha.

Ch Haute Brande   map 36
Bordeaux Supérieur, Bordeaux, Entre-Deux-Mers
owner: R. Boudigue & Fils *area:* 40 ha *cases:* 10,500, white 9,000 *grape % R:* MER 70% CS 20% CF 10% *grape % W:* SAUV B 50% SEM 30% MUSC 20%
33580 Rimons tel: 05 56 61 60 55 fax: 05 56 61 89 07
This estate is the source of a complete, well-fruited, quite meaty red Bordeaux, a somewhat licorice-like Bordeaux Supérieur, and a Bordeaux Supérieur Cuvée Prestige in which ripe fruit is combined with pleasing tones of oak and vanilla. The white wine is a correct Entre-Deux-Mers.

Ch Haut-Favereau   map 36
Bordeaux
owner: Michel Galineau *area:* 25 ha *cases:* 9,500, white 6,500 *grape % R:* MER 40% CF 32% CS 28% *grape % W:* SAUV B 80% SEM 16% MUSC 4% *second wine:* Bois de Favereau *other wines:* Crémant de Bordeaux; Bordeaux rosé; Ch Bellevue Favereau *(Entre-Deux-Mers)*
33790 Pellegrue tel: 05 56 61 32 49
Of the range of five wines made here, the red Bordeaux is particularly worth discovering. This, with its 11 months in oak, often boasts a meaty taste with notes of spice and vanilla. It generally benefits greatly from a few years in bottle.

Ch Haut-Garriga   map 35
Bordeaux, Entre-Deux-Mers
owner: Claude Barreau *area:* 65 ha *cases:* 31,000, white 10,000 *grape % R:* MER 65% CF 20% CS 15% *grape % W:* SEM 60% SAUV B 30% MUSC 10% *second wines:* Ch Coutreau; Domaine du Moulin de Jos *other wines:* Bordeaux rosé
33420 Grézillac tel: 05 57 74 90 06 fax: 05 57 74 96 03
The many medals alone show that successful wines are made at this estate, which dates from 1890. The red Bordeaux is generally supple, well put together, and temptingly fruity. A prickle of carbon dioxide, as well as citrus notes, can be perceptible in the Entre-Deux-Mers. The rosé is at once suitably fruity and mouthfilling. Only a small part of the total production is bottled at the château.

Ch Haut-Graveyron   map 35
Bordeaux, Bordeaux Supérieur
owner: J.-L. Roumage *area:* 15 ha *cases:* 8,000 *grape % R:* MER 90% CS 10% *other châteaux owned:* Ch Lestrille *(Bordeaux)*
33750 St-Germain-du-Puch tel: 05 57 24 51 02 fax: 05 57 24 04 58
A remarkable, generous Bordeaux Supérieur with black fruit and other nuances, made almost exclusively from Merlot.

◆
Graves de Vayres
This AC is for red and white wines made in a small area beside the Dordogne. It is described on page 221, and its châteaux are profiled on pages 266-7.

Ch Haut-Guérin   map 35
Bordeaux
owner: Marc Caminade *area:* 30 ha *cases:* 12,500 *grape % R:* MER 80% CF 10% CS 10% *second wine:* Ch Belliquet
33420 Génissac tel: 05 57 24 48 37 fax: 05 57 24 40 58
Attractive, expertly made red Bordeaux, elegant rather than powerful, and with pleasing tannins. The estate, built up gradually since 1968, extends over a well-exposed plateau above the Dordogne.

Ch Haut Guillebot   map 35
Bordeaux, Bordeaux Supérieur, Entre-Deux-Mers
owner: Eveline Renier *area:* 53 ha *cases:* 17,500, white 16,500 *grape % R:* MER 50% CS 25% CF 20% MAL 5% *grape % W:* SEM 60% SAUV B 35% MUSC 5% *second wines:* Ch Martinot; Ch Montet
33420 Lugaignac tel: 05 57 84 53 92 fax: 05 57 84 62 73
Perfectly equipped property, run by women for several generations. The red Bordeaux and the Bordeaux Supérieur are quite light wines as a rule, with an agreeable mixture of black fruit and forest scents in their aroma. These reds are matured in tank only. Wood is used for the white Bordeaux: a *cuvée spéciale*, made from 90% Sémillon, of which 20% is fermented in new casks. It is quite a full-bodied wine, with spices and a hint of tropical fruit; the oak does not dominate. As a rule, the Entre-Deux-Mers also tastes good.

Ch Haut Mallet   map 35
Bordeaux, Bordeaux Supérieur, Bordeaux Haut-Benauge, Entre-Deux-Mers
owner: Patrick Boudon *area:* 25 ha *cases:* 9,500, white 15,000 *grape % R:* CS 55% MER 28% CF 17% *grape % W:* SEM 37% MUSC 26% SAUV B 24% UGNI BLANC 13% *second wines:* Domaine du Bourdieu; Domaine Sainte Anne *other wines:* Bordeaux rosé; Le Bourdieu *(Crémant de Bordeaux)*
33760 Soulignac tel: 05 56 23 65 60 fax: 05 56 23 45 58
This estate has existed since 1920, and since 1963 it has been cultivated organically. Stars of its range are the red Bordeaux Supérieur and the white Bordeaux Haut Benauge. The red matures in oak – 25% new barrels – the white is fermented in all new ones. It often takes around five years before the tannin in the red is in balance with its fruit, and with the animal and other aromas. The white wine, made in limited quantities, presents a complex of toasty impressions and exotic candied fruit. The wines of one of the château's second brands, Domaine du Bourdieu, frequently display surprisingly good quality.

Ch Haut Maurin   map 31
Bordeaux Supérieur, Bordeaux, Entre-Deux-Mers
owner: Jean Sanfourche *area:* 38 ha *cases:* 10,000, white 6,000 *grape % R:* MER 50% CS 50% *grape % W:* SEM 70% SAUV B 30% *second wine:* Ch Maurin des Mottes *(Bordeaux)* *other wines:* Domaine de Maurin *(Premières Côtes de Bordeaux; Bordeaux; Entre-Deux-Mers; Bordeaux rosé)*
33410 Donzac tel: 05 56 62 97 43 fax: 05 56 62 16 87
Beautifully situated estate, with a view of the imposing Benauge castle. Its Bordeaux Supérieur is usually ready for drinking quite soon; this wine often has elements of dried leaves and tobacco. The white Sauvignon here is not unpleasing, with a fresh acidity. Those

who like semi-sweet white wine will be agreeably surprised by the Premières Côtes de Bordeaux. A number of wines from Haut Maurin are also sold under the Domaine de Maurin name.

Ch Haut-Mazières   map 35
Bordeaux
owner: Christian Vazelle *area:* 22 ha *cases:* 9,500, white 3,000 *grape % R:* MER 65% CS 30% CF 5% *grape % W:* SEM 56% SAUV B 31% MUSC 13%
33420 Rauzan tel: 05 57 84 13 22 fax: 05 57 84 12 67
These wines are made and nurtured with care by the Union de Producteurs, the cooperative at Rauzan. The red Bordeaux in fact spends a year in wood (25% new barrels). Depending on the vintage, it is reasonable to good in structure and concentration, with earthy aspects, a fair amount of fruit, and an at least acceptable quality. The only minus point is the sometimes rather bitter aftertaste. The white tastes fresh without being meagre; here, too, the finish can be a trifle bitter.

Ch Haut-Meillac   map 34
Bordeaux, Bordeaux Supérieur
owner: Jean-Paul Grelaud *area:* 10 ha *cases:* 4,500, white 1,200 *grape % R:* MER 40% CF 40% CS 16% MAL 4% *grape % W:* SEM 82% UGNI BLANC 8% MUSC 6% SAUV B 4% *other wines:* Bordeaux rosé & mousseux
33660 Gours tel: 05 57 49 75 08 fax: 05 57 49 64 13
The Bordeaux Supérieur is an attractive, fairly firm wine in which the Merlot seems rather more dominant than its percentage of the vines might suggest. The white Bordeaux is very dry and reasonably expressive: here the Sémillon sets the tone.

Ch Haut-Mourleaux   map 36
Bordeaux
owner: Anthony Kröner *area:* 5.8 ha *cases:* 1,700, white 1,700 *grape % R:* MER 82% CF 18% *grape % W:* SEM 85% SAUV B 8% MUSC 7%
33220 Les Lèves-et-Thoumeyragues tel: 05 57 41 29 15
Simple white Bordeaux, and a supple red soon ready for drinking. The red is rather short of grip and fruit, but it does have six months in wood.

Ch Haut Nadeau   map 36
Bordeaux Supérieur, Bordeaux, Entre-Deux-Mers
owner: Mauricette Audouit *area:* 13 ha *cases:* 5,000, white 2,600 *grape % R:* MER 80% CS 20% *grape % W:* SAUV B 56% SEM 22% MUSC 13% MERLOT BLANC 5% UGNI BLANC 4% *second wine:* Ch d'Estève
33760 Targon tel: 05 56 23 49 15 fax: 05 57 34 40 18
A steadily growing vineyard where a simply good-tasting Bordeaux Supérieur is produced – elegant, with succulent fruit including blackberry, and with a hint of oak: 10% of the vintage goes into cask for a year. The Entre-Deux-Mers is as a rule a delicious wine, made from five grape varieties. The estate has been vinifying and bottling its own wines since 1985.

Ch Haut Pougnan   map 35
Bordeaux, Bordeaux Supérieur
owner: J. Guéridon *area:* 40 ha *cases:* 10,000, white 10,000 *grape % R:* MER 50% CS 40% CF 10% *grape % W:* SAUV B 80% SEM 15% MUSC 5% *other wines:* Bordeaux rosé

**33670 St-Genès-de-Lombaud tel: 05 56 23 06 00
fax: 05 57 95 99 84**
This estate, formed halfway through the 19th
century, enjoys a good reputation in particular
for its Bordeaux Sec, made from Sauvignon
Blanc. This wine is fermented at low
temperature, sometimes contains a little carbon
dioxide, is lively, aromatic and nicely fruity. The
red Bordeaux is of average quality, and there is
a stimulating rosé.

Ch Haut Reygnac   map 35
Bordeaux, Bordeaux Haut-Benauge
owner: Jean-Michel Menguin **area:** 20 ha **cases:**
6,000, white 5,000 **grape % R:** CS 60% CF 20% MER
20% **grape % W:** SEM 50% SAUV B 40% MUSC 10%
other châteaux owned: Ch Lenormand (Premières
Côtes de Bordeaux); Ch Les Vieilles Tuileries
(Bordeaux, Entre-Deux-Mers)
**33760 Arbis tel: 05 56 23 61 70
fax: 05 56 23 49 79**
The most interesting wine here is a white
Bordeaux Haut-Benauge produced by up-to-date
techniques. A generous dose of spicy oak, with
an undertone of citrus and tropical fruit.

Ch Haut-Rigaleau   map 36
Bordeaux, Bordeaux Supérieur
owner: Henri Verhaeghe **area:** 19 ha **cases:** 10,500
grape % R: MER 60% CF 20% CS 20% **second wine:**
Ch Negre Pey (Bordeaux) **other wines:** Bordeaux
rosé
**33790 Massugas tel: 05 56 61 33 09
fax: 05 56 61 33 94**
The character of the Bordeaux Supérieur here
can be described as classic: a considerable dose
of tannin and oak (it spends at least 18 months
in mainly used casks), plus some berry fruit.
The estate also offers self-catering holidays (gîte
rurale) with a swimming pool.

Ch Haut Saint Pey   map 36
Bordeaux, Bordeaux Supérieur
owner: Philippe Nauze **area:** 12 ha **cases:** 7,500
grape % R: MER 75% CS 25%
**33350 St-Pey-de-Castets tel: 05 57 84 10 28
fax: 05 57 84 15 60**
In 1986 the oenologist Philippe Nauze decided
to detach his estate from a cooperative and to
do his own vinification. This he does with verve
and talent, as is shown by his Bordeaux (and
Bordeaux Supérieur). Rich in personality and in

tannin, this wine lingers long in the mouth and
will mature extremely well. Some of the wine
spends time in wood.

Ch Haut-Saint-Romain   map 34
Bordeaux, Bordeaux Supérieur
owner: Alain Montion **area:** 15.5 ha **cases:** 10,500
grape % R: MER 70% CS 30% **other wines:** Bordeaux
rosé
**33240 St-Romain-la-Virvée tel: 05 57 58 22 77
fax: 05 57 58 20 87**
At the weekend that falls around 8 May, St-
Romain-la-Virvée puts on an exhibition of local
wine, cheese and spirits. One of the wines that
can be tasted there is the Bordeaux Supérieur
from this château, with its firm tannins and
jammy fruit; it spends 12 months in wood.

Ch Haut-Sorillon   map 34
Bordeaux Supérieur
owner: Vignobles Rousseau **area:** 32 ha **cases:**
18,000 **grape % R:** MER 50% CS 25% CF 25% **second
wine:** Ch Croix des Bommes **other wines:** Ch Vieux
Grenet (Bordeaux); Ch Haut-Barry (Bordeaux blanc);
Bordeaux rosé **other châteaux owned:** Ch des
Rochers (Lussac-St-Emilion); Ch La Borderie-
Mondésir (Lalande-de-Pomerol)
**33230 Abzac tel: 05 57 49 06 10
fax: 05 57 49 38 96**
Because of its solid tannins the lively Bordeaux
Supérieur can benefit from four to five years in
bottle. An attractive, fruity rosé is also made
here. In 15 years the present owner has more
than doubled the area of his estate.

Ch L'Heyrisson   map 35
Bordeaux, Entre-Deux-Mers
owner: P. & H. Julia **area:** 23 ha **cases:** 15,600,
white 850 **grape % R:** MER 80% CF 20% **grape % W:**
SEM 84% UGNI BLANC 10% MUSC 6%
**33420 Rauzan tel: 05 57 84 13 22
fax: 05 57 84 12 67**
Red Bordeaux made by the Rauzan cooperative,
rather muscular with in particular elements of
black fruit and spices. The dry white wine, sold
as Bordeaux Sec or Entre-Deux-Mers, has very
decent quality and freshness.

Ch L'Hoste-Blanc   map 35
Bordeaux, Bordeaux Supérieur
owner: Michel Baylet **area:** 18 ha **cases:** 6,500,
white 2,500 **grape % R:** MER 50% CS 40% CF 10%

grape % W: SEM 70% SAUV B 30% **other châteaux
owned:** Ch Landereau (Bordeaux Supérieur, Entre-
Deux-Mers)
**33670 Sadirac tel: 05 56 30 64 28
fax: 05 56 30 63 90**
The star from this estate is the white Bordeaux,
fermented and matured for six months in wood.
This elegant wine has firmness, toasty oak and
succulent fruit. The red Bordeaux Supérieur
spends a year in barrels of which 25% are new,
and its quality is good to very good. Spicy fruit
characterizes its aroma.

Ch Hostens-Picant   map 36
AC Ste-Foy Bordeaux
owner: Yves & Nadine Picant **area:** 40 ha **cases:**
13,000, white 7,500 **grape % R:** MER 60% CS 22% CF
16% MAL 2% **grape % W:** SEM 50% SAUV B 40% MUSC
10% **second wine:** Ch de Grangeneuve (Bordeaux)
**33220 Les Lèves-et-Thoumeyragues tel:
05 57 46 38 11
fax: 05 57 46 26 23**
This is the largest – and the foremost – private
producer of Ste-Foy Bordeaux. The estate was
taken over in 1986 by Yves and Nadine Picant
who, after a number of experiments, decided to
leave the cooperative and do their own
vinification. Modern fermentation facilities were
put in, and they built the biggest cask cellar in
the appellation. This is in the middle of the
vineyard – at some distance from the château
itself, from which the view is splendid. The red
Ste-Foy Bordeaux is a lively, stylish wine with
refined oak and vanilla elements (from 12
months in barrels, of which 30% are new), and
candied fruit. The white Cuvée des Demoiselles,
fermented in new casks, has smoky, toasted oak,
a clean acidity, some spice and succulent fruit;
in quality it comes close to a good white Graves
or Pessac-Léognan.

Ch des Huguets   map 34
Bordeaux Supérieur
owner: EARL Vignobles Paul Bordes **area:** 10 ha
cases: 5,000 **grape % R:** MER 60% CF 20% CS 20%
other châteaux owned: Ch de Bordes (Lussac-St-
Emilion); Ch Lafaurie (Puisseguin-St-Emilion)
**33570 Les Artigues-de-Lussac tel: 05 57 24 33 66
fax: 05 57 24 30 42**
Quite lively, slightly spicy Bordeaux Supérieur
with a firm core and a quality ranging from
correct to good.

Domaine de l'Ile Margaux   map 8
Bordeaux Supérieur
owner: Louis & Jean-François Nègre **area:** 14 ha
cases: 7,500 **grape % R:** MER 50% CS 40% PV 10%
**33460 Margaux tel: 05 57 88 30 46
fax: 05 57 88 35 87**
This property can only be reached by boat, for it
stretches over an island in the Gironde near
Margaux. A smooth, firm Bordeaux Supérieur
comes from quite rich soil – no manure needed
– with many old vines. It is matured in wood for
a year (at least 20% new casks) and so has
considerable oak in its aroma.

Below: Ch La Jalgue

Ch de Jabastas
map 35

Bordeaux
owner: Jean-Marie Nadau **area:** 10 ha **cases:** 5,750
grape % R: MER 67% CS 33% **other wines:** Bordeaux
rosé
33450 Izon tel: 05 57 25 08 25
fax: 05 57 74 13 86
Supple, rounded Bordeaux that particularly
charms with its fruit; it is meant for early
drinking. More patience is needed for the cask-
aged Cuvée Prestige, where the fruit is clearly
complemented by tannin. The owner of Ch de
Jabastas qualified as an oenologist in 1989.

Ch La Jalgue
map 36

Bordeaux, Entre-Deux-Mers
owner: GFA Géromin **area:** 50 ha **cases:** 23,000,
white 7,000 **grape % R:** MER 40% CF 30% CS 30%
grape % W: SEM 50% SAUV B 40% MUSC 10% **other
châteaux owned:** Ch Tudin (Bordeaux)
33890 Coubeyrac tel: 05 57 47 45 86
As the Vatican records show, it was a religious
fraternity that developed this vineyard in the
19th century. The present owner trained in
winemaking both in Burgundy and Bordeaux.
On quite a large scale he makes a very
acceptable Bordeaux red, and an absolutely dry,
clean Entre-Deux-Mers offering fruit and a
slight bitter touch.

Ch Jamin
map 36

Bordeaux, Entre-Deux-Mers
owner: Paulette & Jean-Pierre Lobre **area:** 40 ha
cases: 11,000, white 11,500 **grape % R:** CF 60% CS
30% MER 10% **grape % W:** SAUV B 35% SEM 35% MUSC
30% **second wine:** Ch de L'Aubrade **other wines:**
Bordeaux rosé
33580 Rimons tel: 05 56 71 55 10
fax: 05 56 71 61 94
Gooseberry Sauvignon fruit characterizes the
clean, supple Entre-Deux-Mers – the most
attractive wine from this estate.

Ch de Jayle
map 36

Bordeaux
owner: Vignobles Pellé **area:** 52 ha **cases:** 24,000,
white 2,500 **grape % R:** MER 50% CS 50% **grape %
W:** SEM 50% SAUV B 45% MUSC 5% **second wine:** Ch
Les Ancres
33490 St-Martin-de-Sescas tel: 05 56 62 80 07
fax: 05 56 62 71 60
In 1991, after Denis Pellé had added the
vineyards he already ran to that of Ch de Jayle,
a great deal was invested in new cellar
equipment which meets the highest technical
requirements. As a result the red Bordeaux,
with its agreeable, supple tannins and berry
fruit, has since 1993 gained in concentration,
substance and quality.

Ch Jean Mathieu
map 34

Bordeaux Supérieur
owner: Christian Brasseur **area:** 3 ha **cases:** 1,000
grape % R: MER 70% CF 30% **other châteaux owned:**
Ch La Paillette (Bordeaux Supérieur)
33500 Libourne tel: 05 57 51 17 31
fax: 05 57 51 33 75
This barrel-matured Bordeaux Supérieur is
often characterized for years on end by hard
tannins, which sometimes makes 10 years'
bottle-ageing necessary – always in the hope
that the wine will still have sufficient fruit to
survive the experience. Perhaps Ch Jean
Mathieu's wine is therefore preferable from the
lesser vintages, when it tastes more supple and
accessible.

Domaine de Jeantieu
map 36

Bordeaux, Côtes de Bordeaux St-Macaire
owner: Joel Castagnet **area:** 17 ha **cases:** 7,700,
white 1,500 **grape % R:** MER 40% CS 40% CF 20%
grape % W: SEM 60% MUSC 30% SAUV B 10% **other
wines:** Bordeaux rosé
33490 St-André-du-Bois tel: 05 56 76 44 73
Of the four wines made here only the semi-
sweet white Côtes de Bordeaux St-Macaire
undergoes oak-maturing. The most important
in terms of quantity is the red Bordeaux, a
slightly introvert wine with smooth berry fruit.

Ch Joinin
map 35

Bordeaux
owner: Brigitte Mestreguilhem **area:** 14 ha **cases:**
8,500 **grape % R:** MER 80% CF 10% CS 10% **second
wine:** Ch Cabos **other châteaux owned:** Ch Pipeau
(St-Emilion)
33420 Rauzan tel: 05 57 24 72 95
fax: 05 57 24 71 25
Since the 1992 vintage, the red Bordeaux here
has been vinified by the owners themselves
rather than by a cooperative. Even in light years
this is a well-structured wine. Succulent fruit
and adequate tannins make it eminently
drinkable.

Ch des Joualles
map 36

Bordeaux Supérieur
owner: SC Vignobles Freylon **area:** 28 ha **cases:**
18,000 **grape % R:** MER 60% CF 20% CS 20% **second
wine:** Ch La Fleur des Joualles **other châteaux
owned:** Ch Lassègue (St-Emilion)
33350 Ruch tel: 05 57 24 72 83
fax: 05 57 74 48 88
Estate with a generally successful Bordeaux
Supérieur – a wine with earthy, black-fruited
and forest notes, plus firm tannins. A small part
of the production, 2,500 cases, goes out with
the name Clos Grangeotte-Freylon. This shows
its kinship to Ch des Joualles, although as a
rule rather more Cabernet Franc is used.

Ch Joumes-Fillon
map 36

Bordeaux, Bordeaux Supérieur, Côtes de Bordeaux
St-Macaire
owner: M. Joumes **area:** 44 ha **cases:** 17,500,
white 6,500 **grape % R:** CS 40% MER 30% CF 30%
grape % W: SEM 55% MUSC 20% SAUV B 15% UGNI
BLANC 10%
33540 St-Laurent-du-Bois tel: 05 56 76 41 84
fax: 05 56 76 45 32
The red Bordeaux and the Bordeaux Supérieur
are average for these appellations, whereas the
semi-sweet white Côtes de Bordeaux St-Macaire
is among its front-runners. Clos de Fillon is a
red, barrel-aged Bordeaux.

Ch La Joye
map 34

Bordeaux Supérieur
owner: Jean-Paul Froger **area:** 16.5 ha **cases:**
9,000 **grape % R:** MER 70% CS 20% CF 10% **second
wine:** Ch Croix Beaurivage
33240 St-André-de-Cubzac tel: 05 57 43 18 93
fax: 05 57 43 40 09
It is usually some years before this Bordeaux
Supérieur opens up, but then it lives up to its
name and joy is what it gives.

Ch Justa
map 31

Bordeaux
owner: M. Mas **area:** 19 ha **cases:** 10,000, white
2,100 **grape % R:** MER 50% CF 30% CS 20% **grape %
W:** SEM 90% SAUV B 10% **second wines:** Ch Gaillardon
Ch La Croisière **other wines:** Bordeaux Clairet

Above: The medieval fortress of Benauge

33410 Cadillac tel: 05 56 52 53 06
fax: 05 56 44 81 01
Although this château lies in Cadillac, the wines
that *négociant* Michel Mas produces have the
Bordeaux appellation. The red is attractive,
often with blackcurrant in its bouquet, and an
agreeable taste with average concentration. The
Bordeaux Sec tends to be rather neutral. The
Bordeaux Clairet on the other hand is a clean,
pleasant wine: fresh, fruity and balanced.

Ch Labatut
map 36

Bordeaux Supérieur
owner: GFA Leclerc **area:** 30 ha **cases:** 17,000
grape % R: CF 55% CS 30% MER 15% **other châteaux
owned:** Ch Lagnet (Bordeaux Supérieur); Ch
Roques-Mauriac (Bordeaux Supérieur)
33350 Doulezon tel: 05 57 40 51 84
fax: 05 57 40 55 48
Bordeaux Supérieur with a friendly personality:
no stubborn tannins, but the supple fruit of
blackcurrant and raspberry. A fifth of the
production is matured in wood. A great deal has
been invested in this estate since it became, in
1971, the property of the Leclercs, the French
super- and hypermarket family.

Ch de Laborde
map 35

Bordeaux
owner: Alain Duc **area:** 35 ha **cases:** 11,000, white
8,500 **grape % R:** MER 90% CS 10% **grape % W:**
SAUV B 100%
33420 Daignac tel: 05 57 24 24 08
fax: 05 57 24 18 91
The white wine is a clean, stimulating Bordeaux
from Sauvignon Blanc only, while the red with
its 90% Merlot content is creamily rounded and
has rich black fruit. The wines are made by the
cooperative at Espiet, which ages a very small
proportion (5%) of the red for nine months in
casks of which a third are new.

Ch Labourdette
map 36

Bordeaux Supérieur, Bordeaux, Entre-Deux-Mers
owner: Bernard Gauthier **area:** 63 ha **cases:**
17,000, white 14,000 **grape % R:** MER 40% CS 40%
MAL 10% CF 10% **grape % W:** SEM 55% SAUV B 33%
COL 6% UGNI BLANC 6% **second wine:** Ch Grand
Perreau
33540 St-Sulpice-de-Pommiers tel: 05 56 71 50 18
fax: 05 56 71 62 45

A red Bordeaux that has won some gold medals, and goes into barrel for six months. Its taste is supple, usually with considerable fruit. The same wines are also labelled Ch Tour de Buch.

Ch Lacombe　　　map 35
Bordeaux, Bordeaux Haut-Benauge
owner: Jean-Hubert Laville *area:* 23 ha *cases:* 8,300, white 2,000 *grape % R:* MER 40% CS 40% CF 20% *grape % W:* SEM 55% SAUV B 40% MUSC 5%
second wine: Moulin Saint Hubert *other châteaux owned:* Ch La Gaborie; Ch du Mont Carlau; Ch des Tuquets *(all Bordeaux, Entre-Deux-Mers)*
33540 Gornac tel: 05 56 71 53 56
fax: 05 56 71 89 42
Dynamically run property that stretches across the Gornac plateau in Haut-Benauge, where 16th-century windmills still stand. The red wine – labelled Bordeaux Haut-Benauge – is a classic, matured for no less than 18-24 months in cask. The white, which is called La Petite Culotte, is particularly special in its category, a Bordeaux Haut-Benauge fermented in new *barriques*, and

Below : Ch Laquet Doulezon

combining spicy oak and vanilla with elements of dried tropical fruit and citrus.

Ch Lafont-Fourcat　　　map 36
Bordeaux
owner: Paul-Marie Morillon *area:* 6 ha *cases:* 2,400, white 200 *grape % R:* MER 90% CS 5% MAL 5% *grape % W:* MUSC 100%
33350 Pujols-sur-Dordogne tel: 05 57 40 52 09
The most notable wine is an all-Muscadelle Bordeaux Sec white (just 200 cases a year), which after eight months in wood has a generous structure and a pleasing complexity. The red and rosé Bordeaux are attractive, fruity and well made. The red has 14 months in oak.

Ch Lagarenne　　　map 34
Bordeaux Supérieur
owner: SCEA A. & D. Merveillaut *area:* 19 ha *cases:* 10,500 *grape % R:* MER 60% CF 25% CS 10% MAL 5% *second wines:* Ch des Moines; Domaine du Moine *other wines:* Rosé des Moines *(Vin de Table)* *other châteaux owned:* Ch Beau Soleil *(Vin de Table)*

33240 La Lande-de-Fronsac tel: 05 57 58 14 00
fax: 05 57 43 43 19
Not a spectacular Bordeaux Supérieur, but certainly a decent one, relatively light as a rule; only a small proportion of it is barrel-aged. The vineyard is to be considerably extended.

Ch de Lage　　　map 35
Bordeaux, Entre-Deux-Mers
owner: Bernard Pelleter & Yves Raffin *area:* 62.5 ha *cases:* 22,000, white 10,000 *grape % R:* MER 54% CF 25% CS 21% *grape % W:* SEM 63% SAUV B 32% MUSC 5% *second wine:* Ch Liotin *other wines:* Bordeaux rosé
33540 Daubèze tel: 05 56 71 54 57
fax: 05 56 71 57 51
Fresh, clean, correct Entre-Deux-Mers and a light, clean red Bordeaux, reasonably fruity and meant for drinking young. As with the similarly engaging rosé, Calvet does the bottling.

Ch Lagnet　　　map 36
Bordeaux Supérieur
owner: GFA Leclerc *area:* 30 ha *cases:* 16,000 *grape % R:* CF 53% MER 27% CS 20% *other châteaux owned:* Ch Roques-Mauriac *(Bordeaux Supérieur)*; Ch Labatut *(Bordeaux Supérieur)*
33350 Doulezon tel: 05 57 40 51 84
fax: 05 57 40 55 48
Although the beautifully maintained château, set among lawns, rosebeds and old trees and complete with swimming pool, is fairly large, the cellar complex covers a much bigger area. The wine made in these *chais* is an elegant red Bordeaux Supérieur, generally with temptingly smooth fruitiness and supple tannins.

Ch Lagrange　　　map 35
Bordeaux, Entre-Deux-Mers
owner: GFA Lacoste *area:* 3 ha *cases:* white 1,000 *grape % W:* SAUV B 75% SEM 25%
33550 Capian tel: 05 56 72 15 96
fax: 05 56 72 31 41
An estate at present making exclusively white wines – Bordeaux Sec and Entre-Deux-Mers. They are left for five months on their lees, so that they can 'feed' and acquire plenty of aroma. The Bordeaux Sec is 70% Sauvignon, the Entre-Deux-Mers 50% – both are full of character. The vineyard will be enlarged by 10 ha. Worth watching.

Ch Lagrange les Tours　　　map 34
Bordeaux Supérieur
owner: Muriel Laval *area:* 21 ha *cases:* 12,000 *grape % R:* MER 70% CS 25% CF 5% *second wine:* Les Ormes de Lagrange
33240 Cubzac-les-Ponts tel: 05 46 04 65 60
fax: 05 46 04 63 88
It is hard to imagine that around 1965 this property had only one hectare of vines, and that cows grazed on the rest of the land. From 1975 the vineyard area was gradually increased, and in 1993 a further 12 ha were bought. The Bordeaux Supérieur from Lagrange les Tours has an agreeable scent of red and black fruits, and is quite elegant. There are plans to start maturing the wine in barrel.

Ch Lagrave Paran　　　map 36
Bordeaux, Bordeaux Supérieur
owner: Famille Lafon *area:* 16.5 ha *cases:* 5,500, white 2,800 *grape % R:* CS 50% MER 40% CF 10% *grape % W:* SEM 60% SAUV B 30% MUSC 10% *second wine:* Ch Cyprien
33490 St-André-du-Bois tel: 05 56 76 40 45

An estate well equipped with new technology, Lagrave Paran has grown from around 6 ha to 16.5 ha in ten years. The red Bordeaux Supérieur, a frequent award-winner, is put into *barriques* for a year; it combines ripe fruit with smooth tannins and an elegant structure. Cask-ageing is not applied to the red Bordeaux but this, too, is a graceful, attractive wine. The white Bordeaux is also pleasurable.

Domaine de Lahon   map 35
Bordeaux Supérieur
owner: Jean-Paul Normandin *area:* 10 ha *cases:* 5,000 *grape % R:* MER 80% MAL 10% CS 5% CF 5%
33450 St-Loubès tel: 05 56 20 45 93
Sound Bordeaux Supérieur, from time to time a medal-winner; given its solid tannins it generally calls for several years' patient waiting. Not aged in wood.

Ch Lamarche   map 44
Bordeaux Supérieur
owner: Eric Julien/Vignobles Germain *area:* 21 ha *cases:* 12,000 *grape % R:* MER 80% CS 20% *other châteaux owned:* include Ch La Marche-Canon (Canon-Fronsac)
33126 Fronsac tel: 05 57 42 66 66
fax: 05 57 64 36 20
Although the ordinary Bordeaux Supérieur has plenty of merit, with fruit and supple tannins, the standard rises considerably with the Lutet. This *cuvée*, nurtured for at least a year in cask, is aromatic and thoroughly full-bodied, with much oak in its aroma. The estate is in the Fronsac district, and the wine is made at Ch La Marche-Canon.

Ch Lamothe   map 35
Bordeaux, Bordeaux Supérieur
owner: Christophe & Bernard Vincent *area:* 67 ha *cases:* 34,000, white 11,700 *grape % R:* MER 50% CS 35% CF 15% *grape % W:* SAUV B 50% SEM 37% MUSC 13% *other wines:* Bordeaux rosé *other châteaux owned:* Ch Ringerd (Bordeaux)
33760 Montignac tel: 05 56 23 76 55
fax: 05 56 23 97 72
A conscientiously worked estate, which has been in the same family for four generations, where after picking the grapes are sorted by hand. The best wines are sold under the Ch Lamothe-Vincent name. These are a red and a dry white Bordeaux, both of which are matured in wood. The red tastes agreeably supple, and the white is strongly characterized by Sauvignon Blanc. Ch Lamothe's rosé can also be delightful.

Ch Lamothe-Gaillard   map 34
Bordeaux, Bordeaux Supérieur
owner: Claire & Daniel Lafoi *area:* 28 ha *cases:* 23,400, white 2,750 *grape % R:* MER 40% CF 40% CS 20% *grape % W:* SAUV B 95% SEM 4% UGNI BLANC 1% *second wine:* Ch Lamothe-Barrau *other wines:* Bordeaux Clairet & rosé; Crémant de Bordeaux
33910 St-Ciers-d'Abzac tel: 05 57 49 46 46
fax: 05 57 69 03 90
'Excellent' is frequently the right adjective for Lamothe-Gaillard's Bordeaux Supérieur wood-matured *cuvée* – this spends 15 months in cask. It is a well-nuanced wine that lingers in the mouth, with ripe fruit and vanilla. The standard Bordeaux Supérieur is rounded and engaging in taste. There is also a standard version of the Bordeaux Sec – less characterized by Sauvignon than the label might suggest – and a *cuvée* that has four months in cask.

Ch La Lande de Taleyran   map 35
Bordeaux, Bordeaux Supérieur
owner: Jacques Burliga & Philippe Archambaud *area:* 14 ha *cases:* 7,000, white 500 *grape % R:* MER 65% CS 25% CF 10% *grape % W:* SAUV B 50% SEM 40% MUSC 10% *other wines:* Bordeaux Clairet *other châteaux owned:* Ch de Jos (Bordeaux Supérieur); Ch Polin (Bordeaux Supérieur)
33750 Beychac-et-Caillau tel: 05 56 72 98 93
fax: 05 56 72 81 94
Estate established in 1984, with its winery buildings grouped around a former church. The red wine is clean-tasting and has an agreeable amount of fruit, but often rather lacks depth and substance. The white bears the mark of Sauvignon Blanc, but has no strongly defined personality.

Ch Landereau   map 35
Bordeaux Supérieur, Entre-Deux-Mers
owner: Michel Baylet *area:* 63 ha *cases:* 26,300, white 5,500 *grape % R:* MER 50% CS 30% CF 15% MAL 5% *grape % W:* SEM 50% SAUV B 40% MUSC 10% *second wine:* Ch Puy-Marceau *other wines:* Bordeaux Clairet; Brut de Landereau (Crémant de Bordeaux) *other châteaux owned:* Ch L'Hoste-Blanc (Bordeaux Supérieur, Entre-Deux-Mers)
33670 Sadirac tel: 05 56 30 64 28
fax: 05 56 30 63 90
The Bordeaux Supérieur from here is a sound, competently made red wine, quite substantial, with some oak (a proportion goes into cask for a year), and reasonably fruity. The Entre-Deux-Mers and the Bordeaux Clairet can at times be somewhat disappointing. The Baylet family bought Ch Landereau, then very neglected, in 1959. They have since equipped it to perfection and extended the vineyard considerably (and a further 6 ha will be added).

Ch Laronde Desormes   map 18
Bordeaux
owner: SC Laronde Desormes/Famille Tessandier *area:* 7.5 ha *cases:* 3,500 *grape % R:* CS 40% MER 40% CF 10% PV 10% *other châteaux owned:* include Ch Maucamps (Haut-Médoc)
33460 Macau tel: 05 57 88 07 64
fax: 05 57 88 07 00
This property in Macau, in the Médoc, is run by the team from Ch Maucamps in Haut-Médoc. Even in the less-good years the wine, a red Bordeaux, has plenty of colour. Its taste is

Below: Ch Latour-Laguens

succulent, reasonably firm and just a little fat, and besides licorice and bayleaf it also offers an undertone of fruit, including blackberry.

Ch Larroque   map 36
Bordeaux
owner: M.C. Boyer de la Giroday *area:* 76 ha *cases:* 30,000, white 12,000 *grape % R:* CS 48% MER 28% CF 23% MAL 1% *grape % W:* SAUV B 73% SEM 23% MUSC 4%
33210 Coimères tel: 05 56 23 93 53
fax: 05 56 23 48 78
Edward III of England apparently granted permission for a castle to be built here. It belonged to the De La Roque family and was originally called Ch de la Tour. Parts of it were later destroyed, but it was largely rebuilt in the 19th century. In 1866 the estate was much larger than it is now – it covered 400 ha. The red Bordeaux matures for nearly a year in wood: spicy, with supple tannins, and nicely framed by its oak. Gooseberry from the Sauvignon Blanc characterizes the clean, pleasing Bordeaux Sec . Vinification is by Vignobles Ducourt.

Ch Lartigue   map 35
Bordeaux
owner: Patrick Trabut-Cussac *area:* 21 ha *cases:* 9,500, white 2,500 *grape % R:* CS 32% MER 29% CF 25% MAL 14% *grape % W:* SAUV B 100% *second wine:* Ch Pelet
33370 Loupès tel: 05 56 68 36 56
fax: 05 56 68 36 57
Fairly elegant red Bordeaux, discreet in its bouquet, with delicate tannins. The wine is ready for drinking within five years. The greater part of the vintage goes to the trade in bulk.

Ch Lassime   map 36
Bordeaux Supérieur, Bordeaux, Entre-Deux-Mers
owner: SCEA Vignobles Elisabeth & Guy Claisse *area:* 16.5 ha *cases:* 7,000, white 2,750 *grape % R:* MER 40% CS 30% CF 30% *grape % W:* SEM 60% SAUV B 30% MUSC 10% *second wine:* Ch Le Chataignier
33540 Landerrouet-sur-Ségur tel: 05 56 71 49 43
fax: 05 56 71 31 76
The former journalist Guy Claisse and his wife, a professor of biology, bought this estate in 1988. They have enlarged it, built a modern *chai*, and have chosen quality as the criterion. Their finest red wine is the Bordeaux Supérieur Cuvée Olivia. This spends about a year in cask – there is a good measure of oak, considerable fruit, and a substantial structure. Fresh fruit characterizes the fairly slender, immaculate Entre-Deux-Mers.

Ch Latour-Laguens   map 36
Bordeaux Supérieur, Entre-Deux-Mers
owner: Raymond Laguens *area:* 28 ha *cases:* 13,500, white 2,200 *grape % R:* MER 53% CS 30% CF 12% MAL 5% *grape % W:* SAUV B 60% MUSC 30% Merlot Blanc 10%
33540 St-Martin-du-Puy tel: 05 56 71 53 15
fax: 05 56 71 60 86
From a Latin inscription on one of the walls of this château, graced by a fine, square keep, it appears that a castle has stood here since 774. Centuries later Henri IV had a meal here and enjoyed the local wine. Today Ch Latour-Laguens produces a quite complete Bordeaux Supérieur, firm, with good tannins and a touch of spicy oak. The wine generally has to mature for four to five years. The Entre-Deux-Mers, on the other hand, is not very distinguished.

Above: Ch Laville

Domaine de Laubertrie   map 34
Bordeaux
owner: Bernard Pontallier **area:** 15 ha **cases:**
4,500, white 1,200 **grape % R:** MER 55% CF 45%
grape % W: SAUV B 55% SEM 23% MUSC 22%
33240 Salignac tel: 05 57 43 24 73
fax: 05 57 43 49 25
Wild cherry and blackcurrant are often found in
the aroma of Laubertrie's supple red Bordeaux.
The Cuvée Spéciale, with four months in wood,
offers rather more concentration. The Bordeaux
Sec is a rounded white, fairly fat in the mouth.
The estate, which dates from the end of the
14th century, is managed by the fifth
generation of the family that own it today.

Ch Laubès   map 35
Bordeaux
owner: Michel Fourcassies **area:** 10 ha **cases:**
5,000, white 1,600 **grape % R:** MER 80% CS 20%
grape % W: SAUV B 50% Sauvignon Gris 50% **second
wine:** Ch de Coqs **other wines:** Comtesse de
Laubès (Crémant de Bordeaux) **other châteaux
owned:** Ch Dublanc Puy-Domine (Sauternes); Ch
Haut Mouleyre (Premières Côtes de Bordeaux); Ch
Le Bos (Bordeaux)
33760 Escoussans tel: 05 56 23 93 77
fax: 05 56 23 46 44
The vines here grow on the often steep south-
and southwest-facing slopes of the Oeille valley.
The white Bordeaux derives its character very
much from the Sauvignons, and offers a crisply
dry, fruity taste. A supple elegance typifies the
red wine. A pleasing Crémant de Bordeaux
called Comtesse de Laubès is produced jointly
by all the Michel Fourcassies estates.

Ch Launay   map 36
Bordeaux Supérieur, Bordeaux, Entre-Deux-Mers
owner: Marthe Greffier **area:** 62 ha **cases:** 10,000,
white 30,000 **grape % R:** MER 50% CF 25% CS 25%
grape % W: SAUV B 50% MUSC 25% SEM 25% **second
wines:** Ch Dubory (Entre-Deux-Mers); Ch Bridoire
(Entre-Deux-Mers; Bordeaux Supérieur) **other wines:**
Champ de la Rose (Bordeaux rosé); Ch Bridoire-
Bellevue (Bordeaux rouge)
33790 Soussac tel: 05 56 61 31 44
fax: 05 56 61 39 76
The Entre-Deux-Mers is a fresh, fruity, balanced
wine with an aroma determined in particular by
Sauvignon. It is reliable and commercial in

quality. A quarter of Launay's production is a
decent red Bordeaux, sold as Ch Bridoire-
Bellevue.

Ch Lauzac-Desclaux   map 32
Bordeaux Supérieur
owner: Jean-Marie Gassiot **area:** 4 ha **cases:** 2,000
grape % R: MER 70% CS 20% CF 10%
33360 Latresne tel: 05 56 20 63 64
fax: 05 56 20 63 64
A Bordeaux Supérieur fairly rich in tannin, with
a little fruit and reliable even in the lesser
vintages. Requires a few years' patience.

Ch Laville   map 35
Bordeaux Supérieur
owner: Alain Faye **area:** 26 ha **cases:** 15,500 **grape
% R:** MER 65% CS 30% CF 5% **second wine:** Ch
Moulin de Raymond (Bordeaux) **other wines:** Clairet
du Ch Laville (Bordeaux Clairet)
33450 St-Sulpice-et-Cameyrac tel: 05 56 30 84 19
fax: 05 56 30 81 45
This château is easily recognizable, for it stands
in the centre of St-Sulpice-et-Cameyrac and its
flat roof is surmounted by a small square tower
with a high spire. The owners of this 17th-
century building make a lively Clairet and
various qualities of red wine. At the highest

Below: Ch de Lisennes

level is the Les Granges De La Pierre Plantée
with its ample oak: it is matured for six months
in new barriques. The other Bordeaux
Supérieur, called Ch Laville, spends a year in
cask (25% new barrels), has a respectable
amount of tannin, and generally lingers long in
the mouth.

Ch Lescalle   map 18
Bordeaux Supérieur
owner: EARL Lescalle/Famille Tessandier **area:** 30
ha **cases:** 18,000 **grape % R:** MER 65% CS 15% CF
10% PV 10% **second wine:** Ch Terrefort (Bordeaux)
other châteaux owned: include Ch Maucamps
(Haut-Médoc)
33460 Macau tel: 05 57 88 07 64
fax: 05 57 88 07 00
The wine made here is a copybook example of a
good Bordeaux Supérieur: deep red in colour,
black and red fruits in its bouquet, plus vanilla,
and a full-fruited, elegantly firm taste with
restrained tannins and a noble touch of oak
from a year in wood (25% new casks). The
château, built in 1875, is splendidly sited near
the Garonne. The vineyard lay fallow for almost
30 years until it was replanted in 1983.

Ch Lestrille   map 35
Bordeaux, Bordeaux Supérieur, Entre-Deux-Mers
owner: J.-L. Roumage **area:** 12 ha **cases:** 4,800
grape % R: MER 70% CS 20% CF 10% **second wine:**
Ch Haut Graveyron (Bordeaux) **other wines:**
Bordeaux rosé; Crémant de Bordeaux
33750 St-Germain-du-Puch tel: 05 57 24 51 02
fax: 05 57 24 04 58
High standards are maintained at this property.
This is obvious even from the range marketed
as Ch Lestrille – the label for the second quality
of wine here. The red Bordeaux is fruity, with
animal aspects as well; the Entre-Deux-Mers,

◆
Finding a château
To locate a château from its name alone,
use the index/gazetteer.
When the name and appellation are known
consult the Directory pages of the
relevant chapter.

too, tastes agreeably fresh. The name Ch Lestrille Capmartin is used for the best wines: the red is fairly expansive in the mouth, generally with more oak than fruit from its year in cask. The white version also matures in *barriques* and is a subtly shaded, quite rich and full wine, with an aroma very much determined by oak. The Roumage family created this estate in 1918.

Ch de La Lezardière   map 35
Bordeaux, Entre-Deux-Mers
owner: Nicolas Thillet **area:** 22 ha **cases:** 8,000, white 6,000 **grape % R:** MER 90% CS 10% **grape % W:** SEM 70% SAUV B 30%
33420 Espiet tel: 05 57 24 24 08
fax: 05 57 24 18 91
The cooperative at Espiet is responsible for the wines from this château. The Entre-Deux-Mers is clean and smoothly fresh, with an attractive aroma of tropical and Mediterranean fruit, and a certain finesse. Berry fruit is normally clear in both aroma and taste of the red Bordeaux, a fairly slender wine of a good standard; 5% of it spends nine months in wood, and a third of the barrels are replaced every year.

Ch Linas   map 18
Bordeaux
owner: Lycée Viticole de Bordeaux-Blanquefort **area:** 5 ha **cases:** white 1,750 **grape % W:** SAUV B 95% SEM 3% MUSC 2% **other châteaux owned:** Ch Dillon *(Haut-Médoc)*
33290 Blanquefort tel: 05 56 95 39 94
fax: 05 56 95 36 75
This white Bordeaux produced by the pupils and staff of the Lycée Viticole at Blanquefort is lively, fruity and fairly slender.

Ch Lion Beaulieu   map 35
Bordeaux
owner: GFA de Lyon/Joël Elissalde **area:** 10 ha **cases:** 4,500, white 2,500 **grape % R:** MER 60% CS 40% **grape % W:** SEM 70% SAUV B 15% MUSC 15%
33420 Naujan-et-Postiac tel: 05 57 84 55 08
fax: 05 57 84 57 31
Charming, fruity red and white Bordeaux, vinified with the assistance of Jean-Louis Despagne, of Ch Tour de Mirambeau. The red spends 6-9 months in wood.

Ch de Lisennes   map 35
Bordeaux, Bordeaux Supérieur, Bordeaux Clairet, Entre-Deux-Mers
owner: Jean-Pierre Soubie **area:** 50 ha **cases:** 33,000 **grape % R:** MER 34% CF 33% CS 33% **other wines:** Bordeaux Clairet **other châteaux owned:** Ch du Clos Delord *(Bordeaux Supérieur)*
33370 Tresses tel: 05 57 34 13 03
fax: 05 57 34 05 36
Visitors who pass through the magnificent wrought-iron gates are received in a long, low *chartreuse*. Various red wines can be tasted here, as well as a pleasant Clairet and an Entre-Deux-Mers (which carries the Lisennes brand name). The standard Bordeaux and Bordeaux Supérieur can sometimes taste rather hard, with immature tannins, and need to age for at least five years. Even more patience is required as a rule for the Bordeaux Supérieur Cuvée Prestige, a firmly constituted wine that has 6-12 months in cask. As a considerable proportion of the *barriques* may be new – this varies from vintage to vintage – oak is strongly dominant at first. the Cuvée de l'Artiste is a Bordeaux made for early drinking.

Above: Ch. Maledan

Ch Le Livey   map 36
Bordeaux, Bordeaux Supérieur
owner: René Vannetelle **area:** 15 ha **cases:** 7,000, white 700 **grape % R:** MER 50% CS 30% CF 20% **grape % W:** SAUV B 40% SEM 40% MUSC 20% **second wine:** Ch La Tastère **other wines:** Bordeaux rosé
33490 St-Pierre-d'Aurillac tel: 05 56 63 30 58
fax: 05 56 63 52 76
This vineyard is the property of the man who for years managed the *cru classé* Ch Lascombes in Margaux. In the top vintages the best of the red wine is kept separate and subsequently undergoes 18 months in oak. This is the Carte Noire, a first-class Bordeaux Supérieur – full of character. The ordinary Bordeaux Supérieur, the Carte Blanche, is also of a high standard, with plenty of berry fruit; only its depth and length are somewhat less.

Ch Loiseau   map 34
Bordeaux, Bordeaux Supérieur
owner: Pierre Goujon **area:** 30 ha **cases:** 19,000, white 500 **grape % R:** MER 60% CS 39% PV 1% **grape % W:** SAUV B 70% SEM 30% **second wine:** Clos de Loiseau **other wines:** Bordeaux rosé **other châteaux owned:** Grand Barail *(Fronsac)*

Below: Ch Malromé

33240 La Lande-de-Fronsac tel: 05 57 58 14 02
fax: 05 57 58 15 46
The wine from this 18th-century château west of the Fronsac district has a sometimes smoky aspect, a decent amount of fruit and a certain refinement; the Merlot grape gives it roundness. It has two years in tank before bottling.

Ch Lorient   map 35
Bordeaux Supérieur
owner: Hilarion de Domingo **area:** 9 ha **cases:** 5,500 **grape % R:** MER 60% CS 30% MAL 10%
33450 St-Loubès tel: 05 56 20 41 12
Good, aromatic Bordeaux Supérieur with black fruit, bayleaf and earthy tones. Oak can also be detected, from a year in cask (one-third of the *barriques* are new each year). The towers at this château are 19th-century embellishments, but the building is of much earlier origin.

Ch Le Luc-Regula   map 36
Bordeaux Supérieur
owner: Rolande Mignard **area:** 5.5 ha **cases:** 3,000 **grape % R:** CS 45% MER 35% CF 15% PV 5%
33190 La Réole tel: 05 56 61 25 43
fax: 05 56 61 08 13
The château acquired its present form at the beginning of the 19th century, after being destroyed in 1789 for the last of many times. Woodland scents, berry fruit and integrated tannins characterize the standard Bordeaux Supérieur, while the Cuvée du Bois Sacrée also boasts the aromas of toast, plus oak and vanilla – for this wine is barrel-aged for 12-16 months.

◆

Bordeaux & Bordeaux Supérieur

These are the basic generic ACs that cover the entire Bordeaux *vignoble*. In practice, however, since many of these wines come from the wider Entre-Deux-Mers area, wherever they come from they are covered here – or the Premières Côtes de Bordeaux chapter if the estate is in that zone.

The Syndicat Viticole Régionale for ACs Bordeaux and Bordeaux Supérieur is at the Maison de la Qualité, 33750 Beychac-et-Caillau. Telephone 05 56 72 90 99.

Ch de Lugagnac
map 36

Bordeaux Supérieur

owner: Mylène & Maurice Bon **area:** 49.7 ha **cases:** 22,000 **grape % R:** MER 50% CS 40% CF 10% **second wine:** Ch La Croix Lugagnac **other wines:** Bordeaux rosé

33790 Pellegrue tel: 05 56 61 30 60

fax: 05 56 61 38 48

A fine château – of 13th-century origins, but rebuilt twice later – and fine wine. It is an often generous, firm, and eventually velvety Bordeaux Supérieur with good tannins – and reliable down the years. It is not aged in oak.

Ch de Lyne

Bordeaux

owner: Denis Barraud **area:** 15 ha **cases:** 9,000 **grape % R:** MER 90% CS 5% CF 5% **other wines:** Bordeaux Clairet **other châteaux owned:** Ch de La Cour d'Argent (Bordeaux); Ch Les Gravières (St-Emilion); Ch Haut-Renaissance (St-Emilion)

33350 Ste-Terre tel: 05 57 84 54 73

fax: 05 57 74 94 52

As a rule this is a delicious, fruity and slightly spicy red Bordeaux, very generous in character, with an agreeable measure of oak and vanilla. After the wine has spent a year in tank it goes into casks, about 30% of them new, for six months. The château, sited west of Castillon and south of St-Emilion, also makes a pleasing Bordeaux Clairet.

Ch Madran
map 36

Bordeaux Supérieur

owner: Bernard Tessandier/SCEA La Pommerie **area:** 10.5 ha **cases:** 5,500 **grape % R:** MER 60% CS 40% **second wine:** Ch La Pommerie

33440 St-Louis-de-Montferrand tel: 05 56 77 43 63

fax: 05 56 77 43 31

This Bordeaux Supérieur, made in the area north of Bordeaux on the east bank of the Garonne, is no high flyer, but a decent, supple, reasonably fruity wine that quite soon gives satisfaction.

Ch Maillard
map 32

Bordeaux

owner: GFA Guillot-Grelier **area:** 10 ha **cases:** 6,000 **grape % R:** MER 50% CS 30% CF 20% **other châteaux owned:** Ch Cap de Fer (Bordeaux Supérieur); Domaine de Bouteilley (Premières Côtes de Bordeaux); Ch Grand Jour (Premières Côtes de Bordeaux)

33370 Yvrac tel: 05 56 06 68 42

fax: 05 56 31 62 90

Reasonably lively red Bordeaux, supple, often with some freshness to it. Of good average quality.

Ch Le Maine Martin
map 35

Bordeaux Supérieur

owner: GFA de Frégent/Alain Cailley **area:** 25 ha **cases:** 14,000 **grape % R:** MER 65% CF 20% CS 15% **second wines:** Domaine de la Chapelle; Domaine de Frégent (Bordeaux) **other châteaux owned:** Ch Toulouze (Graves de Vayres)

33450 St-Sulpice-et-Cameyrac tel: 05 56 30 85 47

fax: 05 56 30 87 29

Documents from the 18th century show that this estate has belonged to the same family for many generations. One landmark was the devastating frost of 1956, after which they totally replanted their vineyard. The wine, a Bordeaux Supérieur, is not exuberant in character, but offers reasonable fruit and a touch of spice.

Above: Ch Martet

Ch Maison Noble Saint-Martin
map 36

Bordeaux, Bordeaux Supérieur, Entre-Deux-Mers

owner: Roger Pupovac **area:** 12 ha **cases:** 4,100, white 3,100 **grape % R:** MER 50% CS 30% CF 20% **grape % W:** SAUV B 50% SEM 30% MUSC 20% **other wines:** Bordeaux rosé

33540 St-Martin-du-Puy tel: 05 56 71 86 53

fax: 05 56 71 86 12

At this 14th-century château, on the site of an even earlier fortress, there are cellars with the most modern equipment. The range consists of a fruity Bordeaux rosé, a stimulating Entre-Deux-Mers and a good Bordeaux Supérieur with a pleasing amount of fruit – blackberry and prune. Picking is still done by hand.

Ch Majureau-Sercillan
map 34

Bordeaux Supérieur

owner: Alain Vironneau **area:** 20 ha **cases:** 8,300, white 3,000 **grape % R:** MER 50% CS 25% CF 25% **grape % W:** SAUV B 60% SEM 30% MUSC 10% **second wine:** Ch Sercillan

33240 Salignac tel: 05 57 43 00 25

fax: 05 57 43 91 34

In the atmospheric *chai* with its slanting wooden ceiling lie the barrels, a third of them new, in which the Bordeaux Supérieur matures for a year. It is a sound wine in which oak, tannin, fruit and other nuances are harmoniously balanced – or at least become so after some years' rest in bottle.

Ch Maledan
map 35

Bordeaux Supérieur

owner: Famille Brunot-Héraud **area:** 10 ha **cases:** 5,000 **grape % R:** MER 75% CS 25% **other châteaux owned:** Ch Cantenac (St-Emilion); Ch Piganeau (St-Emilion); Ch Tour de Grenet (Lussac-St-Emilion)

33370 Loupès tel: 05 57 51 38 46

fax: 05 57 51 38 46

◆
Finding a second wine

Second wines are wines of the same colour and style as a château's main product, but of a junior status. To locate a second wine, consult the index.

A Bordeaux Supérieur not matured in cask and strongly characterized by Merlot (with black fruit and bayleaf notes); it often makes an agreeable table companion within two to three years. The château is a former hunting-lodge dating from before the French Revolution.

Ch Malromé
map 36

Bordeaux Supérieur, Côtes de Bordeaux St-Macaire

owner: SCP Brumaire **area:** 20 ha **cases:** 8,000, white 500 **grape % R:** MER 50% CS 40% CF 10% **grape % W:** SEM 100%

33490 St-André-du-Bois tel: 05 56 76 44 92

fax: 05 56 76 46 18

In this 14th-century castle, rebuilt at the end of the 16th, the celebrated painter Henri de Toulouse-Lautrec lived and worked; the estate belonged to his mother. The artist died here and is buried in nearby Verdelais. The château functions as a museum, a hotel, as a venue for receptions and as a wine estate – just as it did in the 19th century. The emphasis is on red wine; this is a not always impeccable, sometimes rather lean Bordeaux Supérieur with a striking label in the artist's style. The quality rises with the barrel-aged *cuvée* Comtesse Adèle. Among the other wines is a semi-sweet white Côtes de Bordeaux St-Macaire, aged for 18 months in wood.

Ch Les Mangons
map 36

AC Ste-Foy Bordeaux

owner: Michel Comps **area:** 17 ha **cases:** 9,000, white 1,000 **grape % R:** CS 50% MER 40% CF 10% **grape % W:** SEM 60% SAUV B 40% **second wine:** Ch Les Ardilles **other wines:** Bordeaux rosé

33220 Ste-Foy-la-Grande tel: 05 57 46 17 27

The most important offering here is the red Ste-Foy Bordeaux, an accessible, quite expressive wine with red and black fruit in its aroma, and some bayleaf. From the 1995 vintage onwards it has been matured in *barriques*, a third of them new. The property takes its name from a family who settled here soon after the battle of Castillon in 1453, and remained in ownership until the early 19th century.

Ch Marac
map 36

Bordeaux, Bordeaux Supérieur

owner: Alain Bonville **area:** 18.5 ha **cases:** 9,700, white 1,400 **grape % R:** MER 60% CF 25% CS 15% **grape % W:** SAUV B 60% SEM 40% **second wine:** Ch Larode-Bonvil (Bordeaux) **other wines:** Bordeaux rosé **other châteaux owned:** Ch Les Bordes (Montagne-St-Emilion); Ch Haut-Saint-Georges (St-Georges-St-Emilion); Ch Peyroutas (St-Emilion)

33350 Pujols-sur-Dordogne tel: 05 57 40 53 21

fax: 05 57 74 90 04

Here the Bordeaux Supérieur is deliberately vinified and nurtured in stainless-steel tanks 'for the best possible expression of the *terroir* and grapes'. It is a usually aromatic wine with ripe fruit and good, powerful tannins. Exotic fruit (from the Sauvignon Blanc) generally determines the aroma and taste of the white Bordeaux, and the rosé displays crisp fresh fruit.

Ch Marcisseau
map 34

Bordeaux

owner: Sylvain Prugnoli **area:** 5 ha **cases:** 7,000 **grape % R:** MER 70% CF 15% CS 15%

33350 Ste-Terre tel: 05 57 40 23 03

Sylvain Prugnoli bottles his red Bordeaux after it has spent 18 months in concrete *cuves* and has been lightly filtered. The wine is usually of

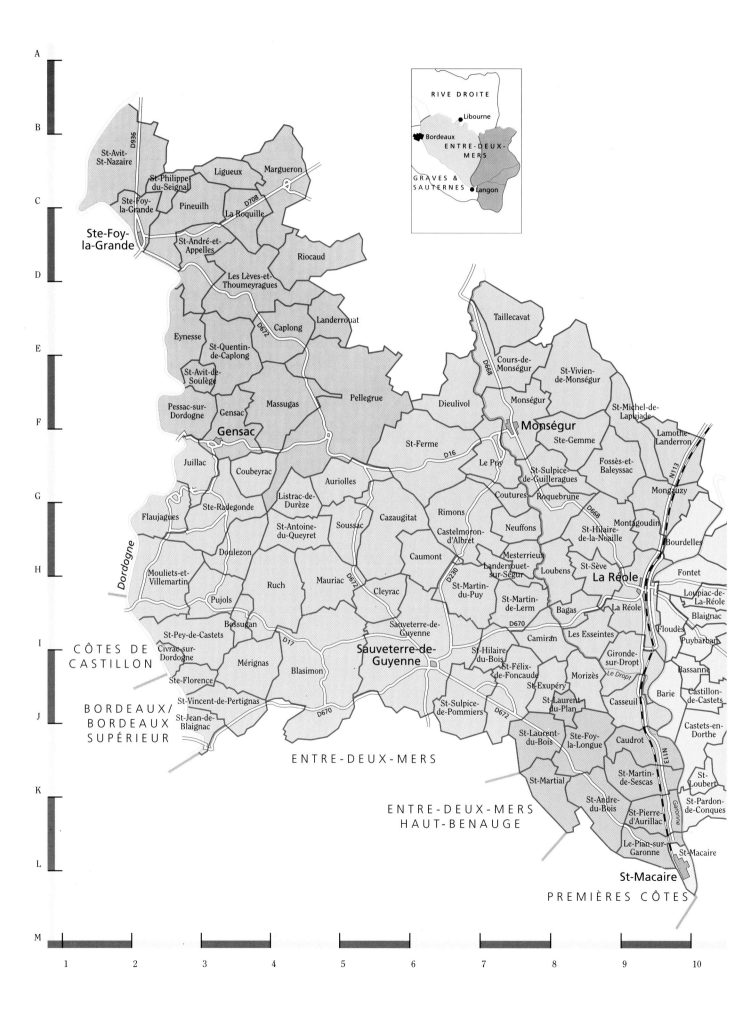

A
B
C
D
E
F
G
H
I
J
K
L
M

1 2 3 4 5 6 7 8 9 10

RIVE DROITE
Libourne
Bordeaux
ENTRE-DEUX-MERS
GRAVES &
SAUTERNES
Langon

St-Avit-
St-Nazaire
D936
St-Philippe-
du-Seignal
Ligueux
Margueron
Ste-Foy-
la-Grande
Pineuilh
La Roquille
D708
Ste-Foy-
la-Grande
St-André-et-
Appelles
Riocaud
Les Lèves-et-
Thoumeyragues
Eynesse
Caplong
Landerrouat
D672
St-Quentin-
de-Caplong
St-Avit-de-
Soulège
Pessac-sur-
Dordogne
Massugas
Pellegrue
Gensac
Gensac
Juillac
Coubeyrac
Auriolles
Listrac-de-
Durèze
Ste-Radegonde
Soussac
Cazaugitat
Flaujagues
St-Antoine-
du-Queyret
Dordogne
Doulezon
Mouliets-et-
Villemartin
Ruch
Mauriac
D672
Cleyrac
Pujols
Bossugan
St-Pey-de-Castets
Civrac-sur-
Dordogne
D17
Mérignas
Blasimon
D670
Ste-Florence
St-Vincent-de-Pertignas
St-Jean-de-
Blaignac
Sauveterre-de-
Guyenne
Sauveterre-de-
Guyenne

CÔTES DE
CASTILLON

BORDEAUX/
BORDEAUX
SUPÉRIEUR

ENTRE-DEUX-MERS

ENTRE-DEUX-MERS
HAUT-BENAUGE

Taillecavat
Cours-de-
Monségur
D668
St-Vivien-
de-Monségur
Dieulivol
Monségur
Monségur
St-Michel-de-
Lapujade
St-Ferme
D16
Ste-Gemme
Lamothe-
Landerron
N113
Le Puy
St-Sulpice-
de-Guilleragues
Fossès-et-
Baleyssac
Coutures
Roquebrune
Mongauzy
D668
Rimons
Neuffons
Montagoudin
Castelmoron-
d'Albret
Mesterrieux
St-Hilaire-
de-la-Noaille
Bourdelles
Caumont
Landerrouet-
sur-Ségur
Loubens
St-Sève
La Réole
D230
St-Martin-
du-Puy
Fontet
St-Martin-
de-Lerm
Bagas
La Réole
Loupiac-de-
La-Réole
Camiran
Les Esseintes
Blaignac
St-Hilaire-
du-Bois
D670
Floudès
Puybarban
St-Félix-
de-Foncaude
Gironde-
sur-Drop
Le Drop
Bassanne
Morizès
Barie
St-Exupéry
Casseuil
Castillon-
de-Castets
St-Sulpice-
de-Pommiers
St-Laurent-
du-Plan
Castets-en-
Dorthe
D672
St-Laurent-
du-Bois
Ste-Foy-
la-Longue
Caudrot
St-
Loubert
St-Martial
St-Martin-
de-Sescas
St-Pardon-
de-Conques
St-André-
du-Bois
St-Pierre-
d'Aurillac
Garonne
N113
Le-Pian-sur-
Garonne
St-Macaire

St-Macaire

PREMIÈRES CÔTES

ENTRE-DEUX-MERS, BORDEAUX & BORDEAUX SUPÉRIEUR

36

Aillas	I3/R	Mongauzy	G9/L
Auriolles	G4/L	Monségur	F7/L
Auros	K2/R	Montagoudin	H9/L
Bagas	I8/L	Morizès	J8/L
Barie	J9/L	Mouliets-et-Villemartin	I2/L
Bassanne	J10/L	Neuffons	H7/L
Berthez	J3/R	Noaillac	H2/R
Bieujac	K1/R	Pellegrue	F5/L
Birac	K5/R	Pessac-sur-Dordogne	F2/L
Blaignac	I10/L	Le-Pian-sur-Garonne	L9/L
Blasimon	J4/L	Pineuilh	D2/L
Bossugan	I3/L	Pondaurat	I1/R
Bourdelles	H9/L	Pujols	I3/L
Brannens	K1/R	Le Puy	G7/L
Brouqueyran	K2/R	Puybarban	I10/L
Camiran	I7/L	La Réole	I9/L
Caplong	E4/L	Rimons	H6/L
Casseuil	J9/L	Riocaud	D4/L
Castelmoron-d'Albret	H6/L	Roquebrune	H8/L
Castets-en-Dorthe	K10/L	La Roquille	D3/L
Castillon-de-Castets	J10/L	Ruch	I4/L
Caudrot	K9/L	Sauveterre-de-Guyenne	J6/L
Caumont	H6/L	Savignac	J2/R
Cauvignac	I4/R	Sendets	J4/R
Cazats	L3/R	Sigalens	H3/R
Cazaugitat	H5/L	Soussac	H5/L
Civrac-sur-Dordogne	J2/L	St-André-du-Bois	L8/L
Cleyrac	I5/L	St-André-et-Appelles	D2/L
Coimères	L2/R	St-Antoine-du-Queyret	H4/L
Coubeyrac	G3/L	St-Avit-de-Soulège	F2/L
Cours-de-Monségur	F7/L	St-Avit-St-Nazaire	C1/L
Cours-les-Bains	H5/R	St-Exupéry	J7/L
Coutures	G7/L	St-Félix-de-Foncaude	J7/L
Dieulivol	F6/L	St-Ferme	G6/L
Doulezon	H3/L	Ste-Florence	J2/L
Les Esseintes	I8/L	Ste-Foy-la-Grande	D2/L
Eynesse	E2/L	Ste Foy la Longue	K8/L
Flaujagues	H2/L	Ste-Gemme	G8/L
Floudès	I9/L	St-Hilaire-de-la-Noaille	H8/L
Fontet	I9/L	St-Hilaire-du-Bois	I7/L
Fossès-et-Baleyssac	G8/L	St-Jean-de-Blaignac	J2/L
Gajac	J4/R	St-Laurent-du-Bois	K7/L
Gans	J3/R	St-Laurent-du-Plan	J8/L
Gensac	G3/L	St-Loubert	K10/L
Gironde-sur-Dropt	J9/L	St-Macaire	L9/L
Grignols	H4/R	St-Martial	K7/L
Hure	H1/R	St-Martin-de-Lerm	I7/L
Juillac	G2/L	St-Martin-de-Sescas	K9/L
Labescau	J3/R	St-Martin-du-Puy	I6/L
Lados	K3/R	St-Michel-de-Lapujade	F9/L
Lamothe-Landerron	G9/L	St-Pardon-de-Conques	L10/L
Landerrouat	E4/L	St-Pey-de-Castets	I2/L
Landerrouet-sur-Ségur	H7/L	St-Philippe-du-Seignal	C2/L
Les Lèves-et-Thoumeyragues	E3/L	St-Pierre-d'Aurillac	L9/L
Ligueux	C3/L	St-Quentin-de-Caplong	E3/L
Listrac-de-Durèze	G4/L	Ste-Radegonde	G3/L
Loubens	H8/L	St-Sève	H8/L
Loupiac-de-La-Réole	I10/L	St-Sulpice-de-Guilleragues	G7/L
Margueron	C4/L	St-Sulpice-de-Pommiers	J6/L
Masseilles	I5/R	St-Vincent-de-Pertignas	J3/L
Massugas	F4/L	St-Vivien-de-Monségur	F8/L
Mauriac	I4/L	Taillecavat	E7/L
Mérignas	J3/L		
Mesterrieux	H7/L		

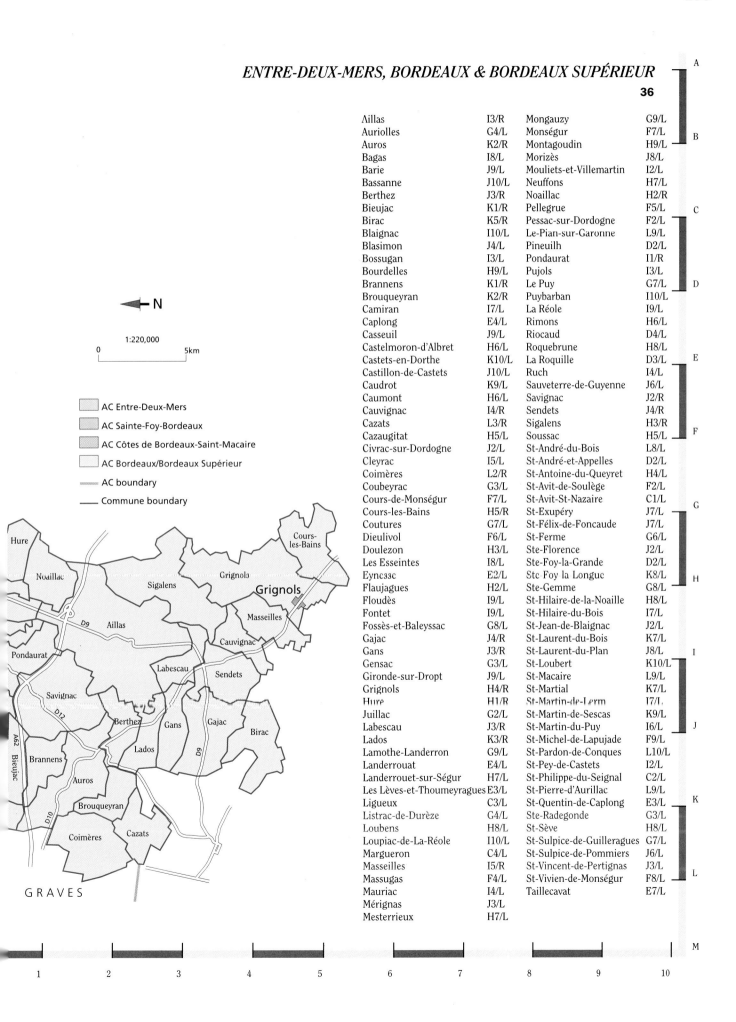

← N

1:220,000

0   5km

☐ AC Entre-Deux-Mers

☐ AC Sainte-Foy-Bordeaux

☐ AC Côtes de Bordeaux-Saint-Macaire

☐ AC Bordeaux/Bordeaux Supérieur

⌇⌇⌇ AC boundary

—— Commune boundary

Hure

Noaillac

Sigalens

Grignola

Grignols

Cours-les-Bains

Masseilles

Aillas

Cauvignac

Pondaurat

Labescau

Sendets

Savignac

Berthez

Gans

Gajac

Birac

Brannens

Lados

Auros

Brouqueyran

Coimères

Cazats

Bieujac

GRAVES

respectable quality, and has an undertone of ripe blackcurrant, but no especially pronounced personality. Ch Marcisseau is sited close to the Dordogne, south of St-Emilion.

Ch Marot   map 36
Bordeaux
owner: Claude Bonnet *area:* 21 ha *cases:* 13,000
grape % R: MER 50% CS 40% CF 10% *other wines:*
Bordeaux rosé
33790 Soussac tel: 05 56 61 32 65
Honest, sometimes rather stiff red Bordeaux, with no oak ageing; also a fairly fruity rosé.

Ch Martet   map 36
Bordeaux Supérieur, Ste-Foy Bordeaux
owner: SCEA Ch Martet/Patrick de Coninck *area:*
21 ha *cases:* 10,000, white 2,500 *grape % R:* MER
70% CF 15% CS 15% *grape % W:* SEM 100% *other
wines:* Bordeaux Clairet
33220 Eynesse tel: 05 57 41 00 49
fax: 05 57 41 00 49
This château is an old *chartreuse* dating from 1530; pilgrims to Santiago de Compostela used to find shelter here. In 1992 the winery buildings were wholly renovated and modernized. A choice, aromatic red Ste-Foy Bordeaux, Les Hauts de Martet, is made here from hand-picked grapes. With a year in cask, 25% of them new, this wine has elements of jammy fruit and sufficient tannins, as well as spicy notes of oak. Also worth discovering is the dry white wine, made purely from Sémillon.

Ch Martinon   map 35
Bordeaux Supérieur, Entre-Deux-Mers
owner: Famille Trolliet *area:* 44 ha *cases:* 10,000,
white 13,000 *grape % R:* MER 60% CS 30% CF 10%
grape % W: SEM 65% SAUV B 20% MUSC 15% *second
wines:* Ch Laurès; Ch Ninon
33540 Gornac tel: 05 56 61 97 09
fax: 05 56 61 96 23
The Trolliet family spare no effort to produce good wines. Their Entre-Deux-Mers has a lively, refreshing taste, with fruit and elegance. Ageing in barrel for 6-10 months is used for the Bordeaux Supérieur, and in the better vintages this is a reasonably full wine with spicy fruit and good tannins.

Ch Martouret   map 35
Bordeaux Supérieur, Bordeaux, Entre-Deux-Mers
owner: Dominique Lurton *area:* 40 ha *cases:*
22,000, white 2,300 *grape % R:* MER 50% CS 50%
grape % W: SAUV B 50% SEM 50% *other châteaux
owned:* Ch Reynier (*Bordeaux Supérieur, Bordeaux,
Entre-Deux-Mers*)
33750 Nérigean tel: 05 57 24 50 02
fax: 05 57 24 03 30
The red wines are often no more than fairly fruity. A fresh taste frequently characterizes the standard Bordeaux, while the Bordeaux Supérieur is rather more firmly structured and also has a year in wood. The Entre-Deux-Mers, with spicy fruit and an adequate acidity, is usually at least correct in quality.

Ch Mauros   map 35
Bordeaux
owner: André Barreau *area:* 30 ha *cases:* 13,000,
white 4,000 *grape % R:* MER 65% CF 26% CS 9%
grape % W: SEM 70% SAUV B 19% UGNI BLANC 9% MUSC
2% *other wines:* Ch Haut-Germineau; Bordeaux
mousseux
33420 Guillac tel: 05 57 84 50 31
fax: 05 57 84 54 27

There have been positive developments here since 1994, when a third generation in the person of Maryse Barreau took over the management. The small amount of wine bottled by the estate itself consists of highly rated red and white Bordeaux, and a sparkling wine matured for eight months.

Ch Le Mayne   map 36
Bordeaux Supérieur
owner: SCEA Ch Le Mayne/Daniel Amar *area:* 70
ha *cases:* 45,000 *grape % R:* MER 40% CS 30% CF
25% MAL 5% *other châteaux owned:* Ch La Grave
Béchade (*Côtes de Duras*)
33220 St-Quentin-de-Caplong tel: 05 57 41 00 05
fax: 05 53 83 82 14
Despite the considerable quantities it produces, this estate manages to make an excellent Bordeaux Supérieur which fills the mouth agreeably even in lesser vintages. No oak.

Ch Méaume   map 34
Bordeaux Supérieur
owner: Alan Johnson-Hill *area:* 28 ha *cases:*
13,000 *grape % R:* MER 75% CF 15% CS 10% *other
wines:* Bordeaux rosé
33230 Maransin tel: 05 57 49 41 04
fax: 05 57 69 02 70
The Johnson-Hills, a British couple, bought this totally neglected property in 1980. With great energy they restored and modernized it. Thus a modern *cuvier* with stainless-steel tanks was built, as well as a *chai* to give the Bordeaux Supérieur a year in casks, 50% of them new. They also decided to use organic fertilizers and no weedkillers. These efforts resulted in an exquisite red wine, rich in fragrance and taste, with bayleaf, spice, blackberry jam, black cherry, elements of toast and soft tannins.

Ch Meillac   map 34
Bordeaux Supérieur
owner: Claude Bertrand *area:* 6.3 ha *cases:* 3,000
grape % R: MER 75% CF 15% CS 10%
33240 St-Romain-la-Virvée tel: 05 57 58 20 58
Immaculately maintained vineyard, with its *chai* at right angles to the château, and the remains of a windmill in between. Besides the standard, quite fruity, pleasing Bordeaux Supérieur a Cuvée Prestige is also made. This matures in new barrels for 13 months and is much graced by creamy oak aroma; licorice and other nuances are also present.

Ch du Merle   map 34
Bordeaux Supérieur
owner: Francis Merlet *area:* 10 ha *cases:* 5,000
grape % R: MER 60% CF 20% CS 20% *other wines:*
Clos des Tuileries (*Lalande-de-Pomerol*)
33910 St-Denis-de-Pile tel: 05 57 84 25 19
fax: 05 57 84 25 19
Reasonably round, meaty and firm Bordeaux Supérieur that undergoes six months' maturing in wood.

Ch Meste-Jean   map 35
Bordeaux, Entre-Deux-Mers Haut-Benauge
owner: Jacques Cailleux *area:* 32 ha *cases:*
16,000, white 3,000 *grape % R:* CS 55% MER 35% CF
10% *grape % W:* SAUV B 45% MUSC 45% SEM 10%
second wines: Ch Haut-La Peyrere; Domaine de la
Croix de Miaille *other wines:* Bordeaux rosé;
Crémant de Bordeaux; Domaine du Broussey
(*Premières Côtes de Bordeaux*)
33760 Escoussans tel: 05 56 23 63 23
fax: 05 56 23 64 21

At their château the Cailleux father and son make a diversity of wines, including red Bordeaux, Entre-Deux-Mers Haut-Benauge, semi-sweet Premières Côtes de Bordeaux and Crémant de Bordeaux. The Ch Meste-Jean, a red Bordeaux matured for eight months in barrel, represents the best quality. This is a wine with usually firm tannins, an aroma dominated by oak (a third of the casks are new each year), and with a pleasing amount of fruit.

Ch La Michelière   map 34
Bordeaux Supérieur
owner: Michel Tobler *area:* 12 ha *cases:* 7,500
grape % R: MER 72% CS 23% CF 5% *second wine:* Ch
Tertre de Cascard (*Bordeaux*) *other wines:*
Bordeaux rosé
33240 St-Romain-la-Virvée tel: 05 57 58 16 39
fax: 05 57 58 15 16
Estate dating from 1972 with its vineyard lying in two communes. Its most successful wine is the Bordeaux Supérieur, aged for a year in oak. This comes across as quite fruity – but also fairly rich in tannin, so that it generally needs to be laid down for four to five years.

Ch Milary   map 34
Bordeaux Supérieur
owner: Christian Moueix *area:* 3.48 ha *cases:*
1,000 *grape % R:* MER 80% CF 20%
33126 Fronsac tel: 05 57 51 78 96
fax: 05 57 51 79 79
At this tiny property Christian Moueix, of Ch Pétrus in Pomerol and other estates, produces a Bordeaux Supérieur of very high quality – velvety, matured in *barriques* for a year, dark-toned and with black fruit.

Ch Mille Secousses   map 47
Bordeaux Supérieur
owner: Philippe Darricarrère *area:* 62 ha *cases:*
30,000 *grape % R:* MER 70% CS 20% CF 10% *second
wine:* Ch Chenu-Lafitte *other châteaux owned:* Ch
de Rider (*Bordeaux Supérieur*); Ch de Mendoce
(*Côtes de Bourg*)
33710 Bourg-sur-Gironde tel: 05 57 68 34 95
fax: 05 57 68 34 91
According to tradition, this elegant château dating from 1831 owes its name to Louis XIV. When he held court at Bourg in 1650 and paid a visit here, the many stones in its mile-long drive gave him *mille secousses*, 'a thousand

Below: Ch Montlau

jolts'. Since the 1992 vintage the quality of the wine has been improving – not in jolts, either, but perceptibly. The stylishly presented Cuvée Classique is worth discovering. It is a properly concentrated, characterful Bordeaux Supérieur combining earthy aspects with black fruit, tannins and oak. Maturing lasts from 6-18 months, depending on the quality of the vintage.

Ch La Mongie   map 34
Bordeaux, Bordeaux Supérieur
owner: Pierre Blouin *area:* 33 ha *cases:* 12,000, white 6,500 *grape % R:* MER 75% CF 15% CS 10% *grape % W:* SAUV B 70% UGNI BLANC 20% COL 10% *second wine:* Ch du Grand Maine *other wines:* Bordeaux rosé
33240 Vérac tel: 05 57 84 37 08
fax: 05 57 74 38 12
The quality of the Bordeaux here can range from excellent to disappointing; the best results generally correspond with the top vintages. The red Cuvée Harmonie has a more consistent standard and spends time in wood. There is also a white version, a pure Sauvignon fermented in new casks. This is a wine that surprises and captivates with its complexity.

Ch du Mont Carlau   map 36
Bordeaux, Entre-Deux-Mers
owner: Jean-Hubert Laville *area:* 15 ha *cases:* 6,700, white 2,000 *grape % R:* MER 40% CS 40% CF 20% *grape % W:* SEM 50% SAUV B 40% *other châteaux owned:* Ch La Gaborie *(Bordeaux, Entre-Deux-Mers)*; Ch Lacombe *(Bordeaux, Entre-Deux-Mers)*; Ch des Tuquets *(Bordeaux, Entre-Deux-Mers)*
33540 St-Félix-de-Foncaude tel: 05 56 71 53 56
fax: 05 56 71 89 42
In the slender red Bordeaux fruity elements are sometimes rather pushed aside by herbaceous ones; but when this is not the case the wine most certainly offers satisfaction. The fresh, stimulating Entre-Deux-Mers offers slightly better quality.

Ch Montlau   map 35
Bordeaux Supérieur, Entre-Deux-Mers
owner: Armand Schuster de Ballwil *area:* 18 ha *cases:* 7,500, white 800 *grape % R:* MER 65% CF 35% *grape % W:* SEM 50% MUSC 40% SAUV B 10% *second wine:* Côtes Montleau *other wines:* Bordeaux rosé; Favory *(Crémant de Bordeaux)*
33420 Moulon tel: 05 57 84 50 71
fax: 05 57 84 64 65
To visit this château is to step back into the Middle Ages, for the courtyard, flanked by two ancient, square towers, evokes the atmosphere of a distant past. Wine has been made at this estate on its high ground since 1473: the present owner, who is Swiss, does so today with energy and skill. His cask-matured Bordeaux Supérieur offers not only woodland scents and berry fruit, but also an elegant firmness; and the lively Entre-Deux-Mers does not lack for fruit.

Ch La Mothe du Barry   map 35
Bordeaux, Entre-Deux-Mers
owner: Joel Duffau *area:* 20 ha *cases:* 10,000, white 2,500 *grape % R:* MER 90% CS 10% *grape % W:* SAUV B 60% SEM 40%
33420 Moulon tel: 05 57 74 93 98
Both character and quality of the red Cuvée Design generally rate enthusiasm. It is a Bordeaux made almost purely from Merlot and

matured in barrels of which a third are new. It is meaty, rich in fruit, nuanced and soundly constructed. This wine has been made since 1988. The standard Bordeaux, too, has considerable class, a velvety and fruity wine, agreeably rounded. The Entre-Deux-Mers white wine is usually a success.

Ch Motte Maucourt   map 35
Bordeaux
owner: Michel & Rémi Villeneuve *area:* 42 ha *cases:* 19,000, white 5,200 *grape % R:* MER 45% CS 45% CF 10% *grape % W:* SAUV B 50% SEM 40% MUSC 10% *second wine:* Ch La Grosse Motte
33760 St-Genis-du-Bois tel: 05 56 71 54 77
fax: 05 56 71 64 23
A vineyard considerably enlarged since 1960, when it covered 7 ha. It is named after a burial mound that once served as a lookout post protecting a pilgrim route; archaeological excavations have been carried out here. The Blanc Sec Bordeaux perhaps tastes somewhat neutral, but the cask-aged version of the red, fragrant with violets, berry fruit and oak, has distinction. The standard red wine tastes rather lighter and fairly round.

Ch Moulin de Launay   map 36
AC Entre-Deux-Mers
owner: Bernard Greffier *area:* 75 ha *cases:* white 44,000 *grape % W:* SEM 40% SAUV B 30% MUSC 20% UGNI BLANC 10%
33790 Soussac tel: 05 56 61 31 51
fax: 05 56 61 40 22
This estate is outstandingly well equipped technically; its Entre-Deux-Mers, made from four grape varieties, represents one of the sure and certain buys in its appellation. Almost always it has a stimulating character, with fresh fruit including gooseberry, grapefruit and pineapple notes; a supple, reasonably full-bodied taste.

Domaine du Moulin de Moustelat
map 36
Bordeaux, Ste-Foy Bordeaux
owner: Robert Barrière *area:* 22 ha *cases:* 9,500, white 3,000 *grape % R:* CS 59% MER 41% *grape % W:* SEM 100% *second wine:* Ch du Petit Montibeau
33890 Pessac-sur-Dordogne tel: 05 57 47 46 77
fax: 05 57 47 48 62
This is Robert Barrière's own estate. He is the man behind the Ste-Foy Bordeaux appellation and the charter of quality drawn up for it. The building and cellars are a former watermill, dating from 1824. Just a tiny part of the vintage is bottled by Barrière himself, and he uses only a part of the best *cuvées* from the best years for his red Ste-Foy Bordeaux. Sample, too, the Agen prunes.

Ch Moulin de Serré   map 34
Bordeaux, Bordeaux Supérieur
owner: J.-François & J.-Jacques Martinez *area:* 30 ha *cases:* 16,500, white 400 *grape % R:* MER 60% CS 20% CF 20% *grape % W:* SAUV B 60% SEM 30% MUSC 10% *second wine:* Ch Gombaud *other wines:* Bordeaux rosé
33910 St-Martin-de-Laye tel: 05 57 69 02 46
fax: 05 57 49 46 10
From the Merlot grape the Bordeaux Supérieur, repeatedly an award winner, gains fruity aromas of cherry, fig and plum, while the Cabernets add some berry fruit and tannins. This wine, which will easily mature for four to five years as a rule, is of reliable quality.

Ch Le Moulin du Roulet   map 36
Bordeaux, Entre-Deux-Mers
owner: Catherine Bonnamy *area:* 10 ha *cases:* 4,000, white 1,000 *grape % R:* MER 40% CS 30% CF 20% MAL 10% *grape % W:* SAUV B 60% SEM 40% *second wine:* La Fleur Roulet
33350 Ste-Radegonde tel: 05 57 40 58 51
The spicy, fruity red Bordeaux is often very enjoyable within two years, but it will usually improve for at least another five. It is given a year in wood before bottling. The estate also delivers an engaging, lightly fruited, succulent Entre-Deux-Mers.

Ch Mousseyron   map 36
Bordeaux
owner: Jacques Larriaut *area:* 20 ha *cases:* 10,000, white 2,500 *grape % R:* CS 50% MER 35% CF 15% *grape % W:* SEM 65% SAUV B 30% MUSC 5% *second wine:* Ch Pujos *other wines:* Bordeaux rosé
33490 St-Pierre-d'Aurillac tel: 05 56 76 44 53
The red wine is a decent Bordeaux, fragrant and meant for early drinking. The rosé is at least as attractive in aroma and taste, and redolent of raspberry and strawberry fruit.

Ch Moutte Blanc   map 18
Bordeaux Supérieur
owner: Josette & Guy Dejean de Bortoli *area:* 1.9 ha *cases:* 1,000 *grape % R:* MER 35% CS 33% PV 32% *second wine:* Galon Bleu du Château Moutte Blanc
33460 Macau tel: 05 57 88 42 36
This estate situated in Macau, in the southern Médoc, generally produces an excellent Bordeaux Supérieur: a complete, lightly spicy, firmly structured wine with vanilla, earthy elements, berry fruit and other nuances. It matures in wood for 18 months, 20% of the *barriques* being new.

Ch Mylord   map 35
Bordeaux, Entre-Deux-Mers
owner: Michel & Alain Large *area:* 54 ha *cases:* 16,500, white 14,500 *grape % R:* MER 60% CF 20% CS 20% *grape % W:* SEM 40% SAUV B 30% MUSC 30%
33420 Grézillac tel: 05 57 84 52 19
fax: 05 57 74 93 95
At this well-maintained property, established in 1763, decent, entirely correct red and white wines are produced. Neither the red Bordeaux nor the Entre-Deux-Mers has tremendous depth of flavour or finesse, but with their fruity aromas and quite lively taste they give much pleasure.

Ch Nardique La Gravière   map 35
Bordeaux Supérieur, Bordeaux, Entre-Deux-Mers
owner: Vignobles Thérèse *area:* 30 ha *cases:* 7,500, white 9,500 *grape % R:* MER 50% CS 30% CF 20% *grape % W:* SAUV B 60% SEM 30% MUSC 10% *second wine:* Ch La Gravière
33670 St-Genès-de-Lombaud tel: 05 56 23 01 37
fax: 05 56 23 25 89
An Entre-Deux-Mers of a good standard is made here, a quite mouthfilling, lively wine of some finesse and with fruit. The Bordeaux Supérieur also deserves notice, a wine that generally lingers well, with its dark aroma – leather and bayleaf – and spicy oak. The red Bordeaux has a fairly energetic character, but is somewhat lighter and more slender than the Bordeaux Supérieur; both these red wines have time in cask, 15 and 12 months respectively. This château is very hospitable: visitors are welcome seven days a week.

Ch Ninon   map 35
Bordeaux, Entre-Deux-Mers
owner: Pierre Roubineau *area:* 28 ha *cases:*
14,500, white 3,750 *grape % R:* MER 60% CS 20% CF
20% *grape % W:* SEM 40% SAUV B 40% MUSC 20%
second wine: Ch Fonjouan *other wines:* Bordeaux
rosé
33420 Grézillac tel: 05 57 84 62 41
Only a very small amount of the production is
bottled and sold at the château itself. One of the
wines is a red Bordeaux matured for six months
in wood; it has black berry fruit and a supple
roundness. A pleasant, stimulating Entre-Deux-
Mers is also made.

Ch La Paillette   map 34
Bordeaux Supérieur
owner: Christian Brasseur *area:* 9.8 ha *cases:*
5,500 *grape % R:* MER 70% CF 30% *second wine:* Ch
de Fonral *other châteaux owned:* Ch Jean Mathieu
(Bordeaux Supérieur)
33500 Libourne tel: 05 57 51 17 31
fax: 05 57 51 33 75
Bordeaux Supérieur with a rather pronounced
taste – earthy tones, sometimes a hint of iron,
prune. Its quality is usually at least correct.

Ch Panchille   map 35
Bordeaux Supérieur
owner: Pascal Sirat *area:* 12 ha *cases:* 7,600
grape % R: MER 70% CF 20% CS 10% *other wines:*
Graves de Vayres; Ch Tour de Queyron *(Graves de
Vayres)*; Bordeaux rosé
33500 Arveyres tel: 05 57 51 57 39
Since the beginning of the 1990s Pascal Sirat
has won a series of medals with his wines. He
makes a delicious Bordeaux Supérieur, meaty
and with a good deal of fruit. Another choice
wine in the range is the Bordeaux rosé. He sells
his Graves de Vayres as Ch Tour de Queyron;
this red wine is given 18 months in oak, as is
the Bordeaux Supérieur.

Ch Pâquerette   map 34
Bordeaux
owner: SARL Dubost *area:* 1 ha *cases:* white 500
grape % W: SAUV B 70% SEM 15% MUSC 15% *other
châteaux owned:* Ch Bossuet *(Bordeaux Supérieur)*;
Ch La Vallière *(Lalande-de-Pomerol)*; Ch Lafleur du
Roy *(Pomerol)*
33500 St-Denis-de-Pile tel: 05 57 51 74 57
fax: 05 57 25 99 95
This dry white Bordeaux shows at best an
average quality, with smooth fruit in the aroma
and a fresh taste.

Ch Paradis Casseuil   map 36
Bordeaux
owner: Ch Rieussec SA *area:* 25 ha *cases:* 10,000,
white 4,000 *grape % R:* MER 50% CS 40% CF 10%
grape % W: SEM 50% SAUV B 30% MUSC 20% *other
châteaux owned:* include Ch Rieussec *(Sauternes)*
33190 Casseuil tel: 05 57 98 14 14
fax: 05 57 98 14 10
This property in the southern corner of the
Entre-Deux-Mers region is managed by the
team from Ch Rieussec in Sauternes, as the two
vineyards belonged to the same owner before
the take-over of Rieussec by Domaines
Rothschild. The red Bordeaux is not oak-aged,
and its dark, slightly spicy aroma is mainly
determined by the Merlot. The white wine is
usually nicely fresh, with elements of
gooseberry and citrus fruit. In the past – as, for
example, in 1985 – the taste has sometimes
been almost semi-sweet.

Above: Ch Pasquet

Below: Ch Petit-Moulin

Ch de Parenchère   map 36
Bordeaux Supérieur
owner: Famille Gazaniol *area:* 61 ha *cases:* 33,500
grape % R: MER 45% CS 40% CF 10% MAL 5% *second
wine:* Cuvée des Fougères
33220 Ligueux tel: 05 57 46 04 17
fax: 05 57 46 42 80
Fine wines from a fine château, which is partly
17th-century. The standard Bordeaux Supérieur
generally has a remarkable fruitiness –
blackcurrant, blackberry, plum, cherry –
combined with a good acidity, tannins, and an
elegant structure. Still more impressive is the
Cuvée Raphaël Gazaniol, named after the man
who bought the estate in 1958: an impressive
wine, complex and voluminous with herbs,
vanilla, spicy oak and mineral notes.

Ch Pascaud   map 34
Bordeaux Supérieur
owner: SCEA Vignobles Avril *area:* 22 ha *cases:*
12,000 *grape % R:* MER 70% CF 30% *other châteaux
owned:* Le Clos de Salles *(Pomerol)*
33133 Galgon tel: 05 57 84 32 11
fax: 05 57 74 38 62
About one-seventh of the vineyard falls within
the appellation, but the whole vintage is sold as
Bordeaux Supérieur. Just under 10% of the
total crop spends a year in barrels, of which
25% are new, to make a *cuvée spéciale*. This
substantial, complete wine has elements of
black cherry, licorice, animal scents, vanilla and

considerable oak. The standard version also has
merit, partly gained from its aroma of red and
black fruit.

Ch Pasquet   map 35
Bordeaux, Bordeaux Supérieur, Entre-Deux-Mers
owner: Vignobles Pernette *area:* 55 ha *cases:*
22,500, white 7,000 *grape % R:* MER 40% CS 40% CF
20% *grape % W:* SEM 60% SAUV B 30% MUSC 10%
second wine: Ch Alexandre
33760 Escoussans tel: 05 56 23 45 27
fax: 05 56 23 64 32
At this estate, which is sited at an altitude of
100 m, the vines grow practically to the front
door of the pale-coloured, meticulously
maintained château. Sémillon is the dominant
grape in the not overly fruity, agreeable Entre-
Deux-Mers; and Cabernets generally provide the
Bordeaux Supérieur with berry fruit and
considerable supple, integrated tannins.

Ch Payard   map 36
Côtes de Bordeaux St-Macaire
owner: Pierre de Musset *area:* 3 ha *cases:* white
700 *grape % W:* SEM 60% SAUV B 30% MUSC 10%
33430 Le Pian tel: 05 56 63 33 81
fax: 05 56 83 51 79
Producer of an interesting dry white Côtes de
Bordeaux St-Macaire, fermented in cask.

Ch Pegneyre   map 35
Bordeaux
owner: Eric Lavie *area:* 52 ha *cases:* 20,300, white
13,000 *grape % R:* CS 48% CF 27% MER 25% *grape
% W:* SEM 55% SAUV B 29% MUSC 12% UGNI BLANC 4%
other wines: Bordeaux rosé
33760 Soulignac tel: 05 56 72 15 66
fax: 05 56 72 17 36
The red Bordeaux is of average quality; the
white version, made from four grape varieties,
is generally of a rather higher standard –
succulent, mouthfilling wine with floral and
fruity elements.

Clos de Péligon   map 35
Bordeaux
owner: Pierre Reynaud *area:* 11.5 ha *cases:* 6,300,
white 300 *grape % R:* MER 67% CS 27% PV 6% *grape
% W:* SEM 72% SAUV B 28% *other wines:* Bordeaux
rosé
33450 St-Loubès tel: 05 56 20 47 52
Estate created in 1964 where all the wines,
including the white and rosé Bordeaux, go into
barrel to mature. The longest spell, 10 months,

is applied to the red wine, which is dominated by dark tones (bayleaf, leather, woodland, coffee), and has quite a firm structure and a most consistent quality.

Ch Penin
map 35

Bordeaux, Bordeaux Supérieur
owner: Patrick Carteyron **area:** 27 ha **cases:** 11,500, white 1,700 **grape % R:** MER 80% CS 20% **grape % W:** SAUV B 80% SEM 20% **other wines:** Bordeaux Clairet & rosé **other châteaux owned:** Ch Grand Clauset (Bordeaux)
33420 Génissac tel: 05 57 24 46 98
fax: 05 57 24 41 99
Penin, on its gravelly soil, is run by an oenologist and produces very good, exceptionally reliable wines. The Bordeaux Clairet has jammy fruit and roundness; the white Bordeaux is a clean wine based on Sauvignon, showing both fruity and floral elements. Maturing in oak – a year in barrels, a third of them new – benefits the Bordeaux Supérieur, a deliciously fruity red wine with a little vanilla and good tannins.

Ch Pessan-St-Hilaire
map 25

Bordeaux Supérieur
owner: Dominique Haverlan **area:** 5 ha **cases:** 2,500 **grape % R:** MER 80% CS 20% **other châteaux owned:** include Vieux Château Gaubert (Graves)
33640 Portets tel: 05 56 67 52 76
fax: 05 56 67 52 76
This estate yields a seductively fragrant Bordeaux Supérieur, creamy and well-structured. The man responsible is Dominique Haverlan, a conscientious wine producer from the Graves. He rented this small estate in 1981, then bought it two years later.

Ch Petit-Freylon
map 35

Bordeaux Supérieur, Bordeaux, Entre-Deux-Mers
owner: Michel Lagrange **area:** 30 ha **cases:** 15,000, white 2,000 **grape % R:** CS 63% MER 31% CF 6% **grape % W:** SAUV B 50% SEM 25% MUSC 25% **second wine:** Ch La Commanderie de St-Genis
33760 St-Genis-du-Bois tel: 05 56 71 54 79
fax: 05 56 71 59 90
The Entre-Deux-Mers and red Bordeaux here are simple, unremarkable wines, but the Bordeaux Supérieur Excellence Lyre has some distinction. This wine, taking its name from the 'lyre' method of training the vines in a V-shape, offers considerable oak and also fruit – particularly berries. Maturing lasts for 12 months, in casks of which a third are new for each vintage.

Ch Petit-Luc
map 35

Bordeaux, Entre-Deux-Mers Haut-Benauge
owner: Guy & Olivier Méhats **area:** 25 ha **cases:** 5,500, white 8,500 **grape % R:** CS 50% MER 30% CF 20% **grape % W:** SAUV B 40% SEM 40% MUSC 20%
33760 St-Pierre-de-Bat tel: 05 56 23 93 33
fax: 05 57 34 40 54
When Guy and Olivier Méhats took in hand the running of this estate in 1978 there were just 8 ha of vines. Wine was relatively unimportant: cattle were raised here, and cereal crops grown. Now the vineyard covers 25 ha and the other activities are in the past. The best of the red wines is the Cuvée Spéciale: it has rather more body and tannin than the sometimes rather herbaceous, slender standard Bordeaux. The white wine is a generally successful Entre-Deux-Mers Haut-Benauge, fermented in stainless steel.

Ch Petit-Moulin
map 35

Bordeaux, Entre-Deux-Mers
owner: Vignobles Signé **area:** 50 ha **cases:** 13,500, white 13,500 **grape % R:** MER 34% CS 33% CF 33% **grape % W:** SEM 60% SAUV B 30% MUSC 10% **other châteaux owned:** Domaine Cheval-Blanc Signé (Bordeaux)
33760 Arbis tel: 05 56 23 93 22
fax: 05 56 23 45 75
The château stands beside a little stream and is a former watermill. It enjoys a sound reputation for its fresh, clean Entre-Deux-Mers – sometimes with a slight carbon dioxide prickle – and its elegantly firm, nicely fruity Bordeaux.

Ch Petit Roc
map 36

Bordeaux, Ste-Foy Bordeaux
owner: Jean-Paul Richard **area:** 11 ha **cases:** 3,000, white 1,750 **grape % R:** MER 50% CS 40% CF 10% **grape % W:** SAUV B 40% SEM 40% MUSC 20% **other wines:** Bordeaux rosé & mousseux
33220 Les Lèves-et-Thoumeyragues
tel: 05 57 41 20 28 fax: 05 57 41 29 95
The family has been making wines here for four generation. Six wines make up the range: the dry white from Sauvignon grapes and the semi-sweet Ste-Foy Bordeaux are two of the best.

Ch Le Peuy-Saincrit
map 34

Bordeaux Supérieur
owner: Bernard Germain **area:** 16 ha **cases:** 7,200, white 2,500 **grape % R:** MER 70% CS 20% CF 10% **grape % W:** SEM 34% SAUV B 33% MUSC 33% **other châteaux owned:** include Ch Charron (Premières Côtes de Blaye)
33240 St-André-de-Cubzac tel: 05 57 42 66 66
fax: 05 57 64 36 20
Maturing in barrels, a third of them new, gives a nice finish to this Bordeaux Supérieur – particularly in the less-good years; but besides its oak the wine also has sufficient fruit (blackberry, cherry), spices and good tannins. The Montalon is a special cuvée, made only in the better years. The Bordeaux Sec, too, has much merit, a complete wine with some depth.

Ch Peyrebon
map 35

Bordeaux, Entre-Deux-Mers
owner: GFA Vignobles Robineau **area:** 15 ha **cases:** 7,200, white 3,300 **grape % R:** MER 80% CS 10% CF 10% **grape % W:** SEM 60% SAUV B 20% MUSC 20% **other châteaux owned:** Ch Roquemont (St-Emilion)

Below: Ch Pierrail

33420 Grézillac tel: 05 57 84 52 26
fax: 05 57 74 97 92
Ch Peyrabon, which is in the north of the Entre-Deux-Mers, yields a firm, dark-toned and somewhat animal-scented red Bordeaux, and a fresh, reasonably expressive Entre-Deux-Mers.

Ch Peyrouley
map 35

Bordeaux
owner: Didier Caminade **area:** 23 ha **cases:** 12,500 **grape % R:** MER 70% CS 15% CS 15%
33420 Génissac tel: 05 57 24 48 37
fax: 05 57 24 40 58
Red Bordeaux from the Dordogne valley, south of Libourne, that is matured in tank. It has considerable tannin as a rule, and a spicy mix of red and black berry fruits.

Ch Picon
map 36

Bordeaux Supérieur
owner: Jean-Claudy Audry **area:** 42 ha **cases:** 23,000 **grape % R:** MER 50% CF 25% CS 25%
33220 Eynesse tel: 05 57 41 01 91
The standard Ch Picon Bordeaux Supérieur often merges bayleaf, black fruit and a herbaceous touch into an agreeable whole, but it can be rather disappointing at times. Quality and reliability increase with Les Graves de Ch Picon, a cuvée spéciale that spends 6-12 months in wood.

Ch Pierrail
map 36

Bordeaux, Bordeaux Supérieur
owner: Jacques Demonchaux **area:** 38 ha **cases:** 22,000, white 2,000 **grape % R:** MER 70% CF 20% CS 10% **grape % W:** SAUV B 70% SAUVIGNON GRIS 30% **second wine:** Ch Haudon **other wines:** Bordeaux rosé
33220 Margueron tel: 05 57 41 21 75
fax: 05 57 41 23 77
The grey, partly ivy-covered château stands in the centre of a magnificent 200-ha estate. Vines grow on about a fifth of the area, with the Merlot predominant. The grapes are fermented in stainless-steel tanks. The red wine, a Bordeaux Supérieur, then goes into oak for a year. Its taste is meaty, with generous fruit, a hint of spice and rounded tannins. Quality is also offered by the fruity, stimulating white wine, a composition of 70% Sauvignon Blanc with the balance made up of the unusual Sauvignon Gris.

Ch Pilet
map 31

Bordeaux

owner: SC Vignobles J. Queyrens & Fils *area:* 60 ha
cases: 19,000, white 12,000 *grape % R:* MER 50%
CS 50% *grape % W:* SEM 93% SAUV B 5% MUSC 2%
other wines: include Ch Pin-Franc-Pilet *(Bordeaux blanc & rosé)*; Ch des Graves du Tich *(Ste-Croix-du-Mont)*; Ch La Massone *(Entre-Deux-Mers)*
33410 Donzac tel: 05 56 62 97 42
fax: 05 56 62 10 15
At this estate various wines are made under a bewildering number of names. Among them is a slender, decent red Bordeaux, a pleasing semi-sweet white Premières Côtes de Bordeaux (Ch du Pin-Franc) and a Ste-Croix-du-Mont (Ch des Graves du Tich). Then there is a Bordeaux rosé, a fruity Bordeaux Sec (Ch Pin-Franc-Pilet), and an Entre-Deux-Mers (Ch La Massone). Only the Ste-Croix-du-Mont goes into cask, for six months.

Ch du Pintey
map 34

Bordeaux Supérieur

owner: René de Coninck *area:* 4.5 ha *cases:* 2,500
grape % R: MER 50% CS 35% CF 15% *other châteaux owned:* Ch Bellevue *(St-Emilion)*; Ch Canon *(Canon-Fronsac)*; Ch Junayme *(Canon-Fronsac)*; Ch Vray Canon Boyer *(Canon-Fronsac)*
33500 Libourne tel: 05 57 51 06 07
fax: 05 57 51 59 61
This estate – one of the oldest in Libourne, and steeped in history – lies where the Barbanne flows into the Isle, not far from the border with Pomerol. Here a correct, not overly expressive Bordeaux Supérieur is made, in which the Cabernet elements are much more noticeable than the Merlot.

Ch Plaisance
map 18

Bordeaux

owner: Jean-Louis Chollet/Famille Tessandier *area:* 10 ha *cases:* 6,000 *grape % R:* MER 70% CS 20% PV 10% *other châteaux owned:* include Ch Maucamps *(Haut-Médoc)*
33460 Macau tel: 05 57 88 07 64
fax: 05 57 88 07 80
This vineyard in the southern Médoc, grubbed up in 1950, was replanted some 40 years later; the first vintage of the new era was the 1993. The wine is made under the supervision of Ch Maucamps, Haut-Médoc, and goes into barrel (20% new oak), for 12-14 months. It is already pleasing – supple, smoothly fruity and clean – but it will undoubtedly gain greater depth as the vines grow older.

Ch Les Planquettes
map 34

Bordeaux, Bordeaux Supérieur

owner: Francis Lagarde *area:* 8 ha *cases:* 2,200,
white 2,200 *grape % R:* MER 50% CS 50% *grape %
W:* SEM 40% SAUV B 40% MUSC 20%
33240 Cubzac-les-Ponts tel: 05 57 58 19 99
fax: 05 57 58 25 90
This estate generally scores highly with its Bordeaux Supérieur. It is a wine with plenty of colour and taste, considerable fruit and a firm constitution. It goes into wood to mature for a year.

Ch Polin
map 35

Bordeaux Supérieur

owner: GAEC La Lande de Taleyran *area:* 11 ha
cases: 6,600 *grape % R:* MER 80% CS 15% CF 5%
other châteaux owned: Ch La Lande de Taleyran *(Bordeaux Supérieur)*; Ch de Jos *(Bordeaux Supérieur)*

33750 Beychac-et-Caillau tel: 05 56 72 98 93
fax: 05 56 72 81 94
Well-made, agreeable Bordeaux Supérieur, without any tremendous concentration but certainly quite fine. Its spell in *barriques*, 20% of them new, lasts a year – giving it a creamy oak note.

Ch Pomirol le Pin
map 31

Bordeaux

owner: Quenehen-Rigout-Collineau Successeurs
area: 10.5 ha *cases:* 10,000, white 1,000 *grape %
R:* MER 60% CS 30% MAL 10% *grape % W:* SAUV B 70%
SEM 30%
33490 Verdelais tel: 05 56 68 08 58
fax: 05 56 62 08 58
The present owners' ancestor bought this property, a family estate that has stayed relatively small in area, in 1780. An important development was the planting of white grapes – 1995 was the first vintage – and the purchase of stainless-steel fermentation tanks specially for them. The red wine is an engaging, sound Bordeaux which often has enough tannin to mature for five years or more in bottle. It is not aged in wood.

Ch du Pontet
map 34

Bordeaux, Bordeaux Supérieur

owner: René Pineaud *area:* 18 ha *cases:* 9,000,
white 600 *grape % R:* MER 70% CF 20% CS 10%
grape % W: SEM 50% MUSC 50%
33240 Vérac tel: 05 57 84 40 69
Rather tannic Bordeaux Supérieur; it spends a short time in cask. Black fruit is there in the background. The Bordeaux Sec sometimes tastes rather commonplace.

Domaine du Pont Rouge
map 8

Bordeaux Supérieur

owner: GFA Ch Tayac/Famille Favin *area:* 10 ha
cases: 5,800 *grape % R:* CS 65% MER 30% CF 5%
other châteaux owned: Ch Tayac *(Margaux)*
33460 Soussans tel: 05 57 88 33 06
fax: 05 57 88 36 06
Bordeaux Supérieur made by the team from Ch Tayac in Margaux. Although not astoundingly great, it is an agreeable table companion nevertheless. The vineyard here will be slightly enlarged.

Right: Ch Queyret-Pouillac

Below: Ch de Rabouchet

Ch Le Porge
map 35

Bordeaux, Bordeaux Supérieur

owner: Pierre Sirac *area:* 20 ha *cases:* 11,500
grape % R: MER 70% CS 25% CF 5% *second wine:* Ch
Haut Bernin *other wines:* Bordeaux rosé
33420 Moulon tel: 05 57 84 63 04
fax: 05 57 74 99 31
In good years Pierre Sirac produces a complete Bordeaux Supérieur, full of spicy oak and berry fruit. He also makes a pleasing rosé.

Ch Pouchaud-Larquey
map 36

Bordeaux, Entre-Deux-Mers

owner: René Piva *area:* 20 ha *cases:* 6,000, white
1,000 *grape % R:* CS 50% MER 40% CF 10% *grape %
W:* SEM 50% SAUV B 45% MUSC 5% *other châteaux
owned:* Ch des Seigneurs de Pommyers *(Bordeaux)*
33190 Morizès tel: 05 56 71 44 97
fax: 05 56 71 44 97
After decades of renting vineyards the Piva family, of Italian origin, bought this estate in 1961. The best wine is the red Bordeaux: lively, firm, succulent and usually with plenty of ripe fruit aromas – cherry, prune, blackberry – and bayleaf and animal notes. The fresh Entre-Deux-Mers also has quality. Both wines, from organically grown grapes, are award-winners.

Ch Le Prieur
map 35

Bordeaux Supérieur, Entre-Deux-Mers

owner: Elie & Elisabeth Garzaro *area:* 23 ha *cases:*
8,000, white 3,500 *grape % R:* MER 70% CF 15%
15% *grape % W:* SAUV B 40% SEM 40% MUSC 20%

second wine: Ch Bel Air Moulard **other wines:**
Bordeaux Clairet; Crémant de Bordeaux **other**
châteaux owned: include Ch Prévost *(Bordeaux,*
Entre-Deux-Mers); Ch Baron Bertin *(Bordeaux*
Supérieur); Vieux Château Ferron *(Pomerol)*
33750 Baron tel: 05 56 30 16 16
fax: 05 56 30 12 63
Vineyard named after a former priory on the
pilgrim route to Compostela. Le Prieur was
bought during the First World War by Paul
Garzaro, born in Paris but with an Italian
father, and is still run by his descendants. One
of the more interesting wines is the cask-aged
Bordeaux Supérieur: fairly firm, and of sound
quality.

Ch La Providence map 18
Bordeaux Supérieur
owner: Elisabeth & Hubert Bouteiller **area:** / ha
cases: 3,000 **grape % R:** CS 60% MER 30% CF 5% PV
5% **other châteaux owned:** include Ch Lanessan
(Haut-Médoc)
33290 Ludon-Médoc tel: 05 57 88 05 20
fax: 05 57 88 05 20
Situated in Ludon, in the southern Médoc, this
estate is the property of Hubert Bouteiller, the
joint owner of Ch Lanessan, among other
estates. La Providence's wine combines power
with finesse, and spends about two years in tank
before bottling.

Ch du Puy map 45
Bordeaux Supérieur
owner: J. & J-P. Amoreau **area:** 11 ha **cases:** 7,000
grape % R: MER 80% CS 20% **second wine:** Ch
Rocher du Puy
33570 St-Cibard tel: 05 57 51 24 28
fax: 05 57 51 31 37
Techniques here are organic in the vineyard,
traditional in the cellar. Thus the Bordeaux
Supérieur spends up to two years in used casks.
The wine is often noteworthy: there can be a
hint of cooked fruit in the aroma, together with
spicy oak and animal notes. Bottle-age makes
the wine velvety.

Ch Puycarpin map 45
Bordeaux Supérieur
owner: CVBG **area:** 14 ha **cases:** 7,500 **grape % R:**
MER 75% CS 20% CF 5% **second wine:** Cabirol
(Bordeaux Supérieur) **other châteaux owned:**
include Ch La Garde *(Pessac-Léognan)*
33350 Belvès-de-Castillon tel: 05 57 47 96 06
The pleasing wine here, which used to be
declared as a Côtes de Castillon, is matured for
a maximum of one year in cask, with red and
black fruit, spice and aspects of oak.

Ch Puyfromage map 45
Bordeaux Supérieur
owner: SCE du Ch Puyfromage/Famille Marque
area: 45 ha **cases:** 21,000 **grape % R:** MER 60% CS
25% CF 15% **second wine:** Vieux Château du
Colombier
33570 St-Cibard tel: 05 56 39 59 04
fax: 05 56 39 20 06
This vineyard falls within two appellations,
Bordeaux Côtes de Francs and Côtes de
Castillon. Not wanting to have to use two labels,
the owners therefore opted for the Bordeaux
Supérieur appellation. The wine is generally
quite rounded, and boasts a lively taste with
succulent fruit and a good balance. There is an
imposing dovecot on the site that dates from
the 12th century and can accommodate around
4,000 birds.

Ch Queyret-Pouillac map 36
Bordeaux Supérieur, Bordeaux, Entre-Deux-Mers
owner: Isabelle & Patrice Chaland **area:** 62 ha
cases: 26,500, white 8,000 **grape % R:** MER 60% CS
20% CF 20% **grape % W:** SEM 48% SAUV B 44% MUSC
8% **other wines:** Bordeaux rosé **other châteaux**
owned: Ch Barbe d'Or *(Bordeaux Supérieur, Entre-*
Deux-Mers)
33790 St-Antoine-du-Queret tel: 05 57 40 50 36
fax: 05 57 40 57 71
After acquiring this old – probably 18th-century
– wine estate in 1982, the present owners
energetically set about renovating it.
Everything was renewed and updated –
vineyard, cellars and château. The largest
production is of a fairly nimble, attractive
Bordeaux Supérieur with blackcurrant and
cherry as its jammy fruit. The dry white
Bordeaux tastes taut and clean, the delicious
Entre-Deux-Mers fresh and fruity, floral and
slightly spicy. Less lively, but more exuberant in
its aroma, is the white Bordeaux *cuvée* Cythère,
made using 12-18 hours' skin contact. A
creditable Bordeaux rosé is also produced.

Ch de Rabouchet map 36
Bordeaux, Ste-Foy Bordeaux
owner: Christian Fournier **area:** 19 ha **cases:**
11,000 **grape % R:** MER 50% CF 25% CS 25%
33220 Pineuilh tel: 05 57 46 46 81
fax: 05 57 46 17 19
Christian Fournier, a builder of cellar
installations, looked at about 100 estates before
deciding to buy this one in 1991. It was in good
condition and offered considerable potential for
quality; and the mainly 19th-century château
was very fine. Since Fournier took over the
wine has simply got better. The best quality is
sold as a red Ste-Foy Bordeaux. The Merlot and
its aromas are totally dominant in this wine – a
lot of black fruit therefore. The taste is meaty
and lively, with a sound setting of oak from 6-
12 months maximum in cask. Fournier wants
eventually to make his Ste-Foy Bordeaux from
99% Merlot grapes.

Ch Le Raït map 36
Bordeaux, Bordeaux Supérieur
owner: Claude Capoul **area:** 18 ha **cases:** 6,500,
white 4,000 **grape % R:** MER 70% CS 30% **grape %**
W: SAUV B 34% SEM 33% MUSC 33% **second wine:**
Domaine Mongenant Billouquet

Below: Ch de Reignac

33220 Les Lèves-et-Thoumeyragues
tel: 05 57 41 22 29 fax: 05 57 41 26 00
The Bordeaux Supérieur, given about 10
months in wood, is generally quite firm in
structure and expressive in character. It has
black fruit in particular, and its tannin gives it a
certain potential for cellaring.

Ch Rauzan Despagne map 35
Bordeaux Supérieur, Bordeaux, Entre-Deux-Mers
owner: Jean Louis Despagne **area:** 40 ha **cases:**
8,000, white 20,000 **grape % R:** MER 50% CS 50%
grape % W: SEM 60% SAUV B 20% MUSC 20% **other**
wines: Bordeaux Clairet **other châteaux owned:** Ch
Bel Air *(Bordeaux, Entre-Deux-Mers)*; Ch Tour de
Mirambeau *(Bordeaux, Entre-Deux-Mers)*
33420 Naujan-et-Postiac tel: 05 57 84 55 08
fax: 05 57 84 57 31
The Jean Louis Despagne team produces a first
class Bordeaux Supérieur at this château. It is a
wine with colour, fruit and substance. Between
6-9 months in wood (25% new barrels), adds an
agreeable contribution of oak. The other wines
are also of a good standard, such as the
nuanced, balanced Entre-Deux-Mers
(containing 33% Sémillon), the Bordeaux Blanc
(60% Sémillon), and the Bordeaux Clairet
(100% Cabernet Sauvignon).

Ch Redon map 35
Bordeaux
owner: GFA de Redon/Vignobles Ducourt **area:** 23
ha **cases:** 8,000, white 5,000 **grape % R:** MER 71%
CF 23% CS 6% **grape % W:** MUSC 54% SAUV B 23% SEM
23% **other châteaux owned:** include Ch La Rose St-
Germain *(Bordeaux)*
33760 Cessac tel: 05 56 23 93 53
fax: 05 56 23 48 78
Quite elegant, reasonably energetic, well-fruited
red Bordeaux, and a fresh, fruity white.

Ch de Reignac map 35
Bordeaux Supérieur
owner: Yves Vatelot **area:** 67 ha **cases:** 33,800
grape % R: MER 60% CS 30% CF 8% MAL 2% **second**
wine: Fleur de Reignac **other wines:** Bordeaux rosé
33450 St-Loubès tel: 05 56 20 41 05
fax: 05 56 68 63 31
When bought by the wealthy businessman Yves
Vatelot in 1989 this estate was selling
exclusively in bulk. Today the wines are retailed
at high prices – the best-quality ones in a fabric

wrapper – and the estate enjoys an excellent reputation. This is due to large-scale investment and to management directed firmly towards quality. The Cuvée Prestige is the best wine: a carefully made Bordeaux Supérieur with colour, power, berry fruit, oak aromas (toast, coffee, vanilla), and good tannins. Around the 17th-century château there is a park, with a stream and a small ornamental lake.

Ch Reindert   map 34
Bordeaux Supérieur
owner: Jean-Bernard Saby *area:* 1.4 ha *cases:* 500 *grape % R:* MER 100% *other châteaux owned:* include Ch Rozier *(St-Emilion)*
33126 St-Aignan tel: 05 57 24 73 03
fax: 05 57 24 67 77
Generous, expressive Bordeaux Supérieur exclusively from Merlot, with black fruit, animal scents, bayleaf. Partly matured in wood.

Ch Le Relais de Cheval Blanc
map 36
Bordeaux, Entre-Deux-Mers
owner: Jacques Chaussie *area:* 25 ha *cases:* 6,000, white 12,000 *grape % R:* CS 34% CF 34% MER 16% MAL 16% *grape % W:* SEM 68% SAUV B 20% MUSC 12% *second wine:* Ch Daliot
33490 St-Germain-de-Grave tel: 05 56 62 99 07
fax: 05 56 23 94 76
This estate, producing exclusively for the firm of Dulong, makes twice as much white as red wine. The best white is the Bordeaux Sec Cuvée Barrique, which is fermented in wood and spends 6-8 months in barrels of which 70% are new. Tropical fruit, oak and vanilla tones contribute to a complex, balanced whole. The red Bordeaux is somewhat less spectacular, but charms with its fruit and suppleness.

Ch Renaissance   map 38
Bordeaux
owner: Gérard Descrambe *area:* 14 ha *cases:* 8,000 *grape % R:* MER 60% CS 20% CF 20% *other wines:* Bordeaux rosé *other châteaux owned:* Ch Barrail des Graves *(St-Emilion)*
33330 St-Sulpice-de-Faleyrens tel: 05 57 74 94 77
fax: 05 57 74 97 49
Red and rosé Bordeaux of a very correct quality, vinified and nurtured in the cellars at Ch Barrail des Graves, St-Emilion. The red wine stays in cask for 6-10 months, and as a rule displays an elegant structure and a reasonable measure of fruit.

Domaine de Ricaud   map 35
Bordeaux, Entre-Deux-Mers Haut-Benauge
owner: Vignobles Chaigne & Fils *area:* 7.3 ha *cases:* white 4,500 *grape % W:* SEM 40% SAUV B 27% MUSC 15% UGNI BLANC 18% *other châteaux owned:* Ch Ballan-Larquette *(Bordeaux, Bordeaux Supérieur)*; Ch Peynaud *(Bordeaux, Bordeaux Supérieur)*
33760 Cantois tel: 05 56 76 46 02
fax: 05 56 76 40 90
Honest white wines – Bordeaux Sec and Entre-Deux-Mers Haut Benauge – without great depth or refinement, but successful as tasty thirst-quenchers.

Ch de Rider   map 47
Bordeaux Supérieur
owner: Philippe Darricarrère *area:* 20 ha *cases:* 10,000 *grape % R:* MER 70% CS 20% CF 10% *other châteaux owned:* Ch de Mendoce *(Côtes de Bourg)*; Ch Mille-Secousses *(Bordeaux Supérieur)*

33710 Bourg-sur-Gironde tel: 05 57 68 34 95
fax: 05 57 68 34 91
Firm, and fairly consistent, style of Bordeaux Supérieur that with its tannins has the potential for bottle-ageing. It is not, however, matured in wood.

Ch Roc de Cayla   map 35
Bordeaux
owner: Jean-Marie Lanoue *area:* 10 ha *cases:* 4,400, white 400 *grape % R:* MER 40% CS 40% CF 10% MAL 10% *grape % W:* SAUV B 80% SEM 20% *other wines:* Bordeaux rosé
33760 Soulignac tel: 05 56 23 91 13
fax: 05 57 34 40 44
Even in the lesser vintages an agreeable, polished red Bordeaux is made here. Its aroma includes some vanilla, from a year maturing in *barriques*, 25% of them new. The Bordeaux Sec is a good straightforward Sauvignon Blanc wine, and the rosé possesses both structure and character.

Ch Roc de Cazade   map 36
Bordeaux
owner: SCEA René & Philippe Cazade *area:* 25 ha *cases:* 9,750, white 3,250 *grape % R:* CS 50% CF 35% MER 10% MAL 5% *grape % W:* SAUV B 70% MUSC 20% SEM 10% *second wine:* Ch Roc La Longuère
33540 Sauveterre-de-Guyenne tel: 05 56 71 50 60
fax: 05 56 71 61 58
After being a member of a cooperative for a long period, this château has since 1991 had its own, modern fermentation equipment. The red wine is fruity and full of character. The white has a fairly generous taste with spicy fruit and a soft acidity. A second name, Ch Roc La Longuère, is also used for these same wines.

Ch Roc Meynard   map 34
Bordeaux Supérieur
owner: Philippe Hermouet *area:* 18 ha *cases:* 10,000 *grape % R:* MER 90% CS 10% *second wine:* Ch Brandeau *(Bordeaux)* *other châteaux owned:* Clos du Roy *(Fronsac)*
33141 Saillans tel: 05 57 74 38 88
fax: 05 57 74 33 47
Bordeaux Supérieur made almost exclusively from Merlot, and generally distinguished by a dark aroma with bayleaf, licorice and leather, some black fruit and solid tannins. A new, modern *cuvier* was installed in 1994, and this has boosted the quality of the wine. Between 1956 and 1980 the estate was a member of a cooperative.

Ch Roquefort   map 35
Bordeaux
owner: Jean Bellanger *area:* 61 ha *cases:* 12,000, white 25,000 *grape % R:* MER 86% CF 14% *grape % W:* SAUV B 57% SEM 25% MUSC 18% *second wine:* Marquis de Hautessey *other wines:* Bordeaux Clairet
33760 Lugasson tel: 05 56 23 97 48
fax: 05 56 23 51 44
The noteworthy features of this property range from 5000BC to 1987AD. There are still traces of the Neolithic culture, including 14 m of a covered avenue – Europe's largest such remains. The château derives its name from a 13th-century fort, of which there are also survivals. The present building, a low, white dwelling with tall windows, was built in the 18th century. It forms the heart of an estate which in 1987 installed modern winemaking equipment. The star of the range here is the

white Cuvée Spéciale, fermented and nurtured in wood. This wine boasts a rich taste with a lot of toast, good acidity, succulent fruit and some spice. Grapefruit, gooseberry and other fruits dominate the aroma of the lively, meaty standard white wine. The red Bordeaux is quite elegant, with adequate tannins, tones of oak and berry fruit. This wine stays in cask for a year.

Ch Roques-Mauriac   map 36
Bordeaux Supérieur
owner: GFA Leclerc *area:* 57 ha *cases:* 25,000 *grape % R:* CF 50% MER 25% CS 25% *other châteaux owned:* Ch Labatut *(Bordeaux Supérieur)*; Ch Lagnet *(Bordeaux Supérieur)*
33350 Doulezon tel: 05 57 40 51 84
fax: 05 57 40 55 48
The Cuvée Hélène has at least as much style as the distinguished 19th-century château. This wine matures for a year in wood, a third of barrels being new. It combines power, grace, character and complexity: red and black fruit, aspects of oak, forest scents and velvety tannins.

Ch La Rose du Pin   map 35
Bordeaux, Entre-Deux-Mers
owner: Vignobles Ducourt *area:* 54 ha *cases:* 19,000, white 11,500 *grape % R:* CS 48% MER 42% CF 10% *grape % W:* SEM 51% SAUV B 23% MUSC 21% UGNI BLANC 5% *other wines:* Bordeaux rosé *other châteaux owned:* include Ch La Rose St-Germain *(Bordeaux)*
33760 Romagne tel: 05 56 23 93 53
fax: 05 56 23 48 78
At this vineyard the Ducourt family produces an energetic and properly fruity red Bordeaux, and a better-than-correct Entre-Deux-Mers.

Ch La Rose-Renève   map 35
Bordeaux, Bordeaux Supérieur
owner: André Bertin *area:* 21 ha *cases:* 11,500 *grape % R:* MER 50% CF 35% CS 10% MAL 5% *second wine:* La Vieille Chapelle Bastoney
33500 Arveyres tel: 05 57 24 81 72
Accessible Bordeaux Supérieur that is ready for drinking after four to five years; its bouquet includes blackcurrant. It sees no wood.

Ch La Rose St-Germain   map 35
Bordeaux
owner: Ducourt & Fils/Vignobles Ducourt *area:* 33 ha *cases:* 12,000, white 6,500 *grape % R:* CS 65% MER 26% CF 8% MAL 1% *grape % W:* SAUV B 61% SEM 34% MUSC 5% *other wines:* Bordeaux rosé *other châteaux owned:* include Ch de Beauregard-Ducourt; Ch Briot; Ch des Combes; Ch La Hargue ; Ch d'Haurets; Ch Larroque; Ch Redon; Ch La Rose du Pin *(all Bordeaux)*
33760 Romagne tel: 05 56 23 93 53
fax: 05 56 23 48 78
This estate, which came to the Ducourt family in 1971 through inheritance, is the birthplace of clean, lively wines. The red is elegant and firm, its taste characterized by black and red berry fruits. The gooseberry fruit of the Sauvignon is clear to taste in the supple, balanced white. The rosé, too, merits attention.

Ch Ruaud   map 36
Bordeaux, Côtes de Bordeaux St-Macaire
owner: Philippe Guignan *area:* 5.6 ha *cases:* 1,400, white 750 *grape % R:* CF 40% MER 30% MAL 30% *grape % W:* SEM 100% *other châteaux owned:* Ch L'Enclos *(Sauternes)*
33490 Le Pian-sur-Garonne tel: 05 56 76 41 69
fax: 05 56 76 41 69

Reliable grower with dry and *moelleux* Côtes de Bordeaux St-Macaire among the range. These are pure Sémillon wines, without oak.

Ch Saincrit   map 34
Bordeaux Supérieur
owner: Jacques & Franck Germain *area:* 12 ha *cases:* 7,500 *grape % R:* MER 80% CS 20% *second wine:* Ch Montalon *(Bordeaux)*
33240 St-André-de-Cubzac tel: 05 57 43 26 77
fax: 05 57 43 28 45
Estate divided off from Ch Le Peuy-Saincrit. It yields a deep-coloured, mellow, substantial Bordeaux Supérieur, pleasingly set off by new oak from 12 months in cask. Besides his *grand vin*, Franck Germain makes a standard version that matures for three months exclusively in used casks. There is also a second wine, which encounters no wood at all.

Ch Saint-Antoine   map 36
Bordeaux
owner: SCE Vignobles Aubert *area:* 110 ha *cases:* 65,000, white 6,500 *grape % R:* MER 70% CF 15% CS 15% *grape % W:* SEM 55% MUSC 45% *second wines:* Ch Haut Mérigot; Ch Tondenac *other châteaux owned:* include Ch Labesse *(Côtes de Castillon)*; Domaine de Musset *(Lalande-de-Pomerol)*; Ch La Couspaude *(St-Emilion)*
33350 St-Antoine-du-Queret tel: 05 57 40 15 76
fax: 05 57 40 10 14
Animal scents, black fruit, firm tannins and considerable oak – from a year in cask (25% new) – are features of the competently made red Bordeaux. There is also a considerably simpler white version.

Ch Sainte-Marie   map 35
Bordeaux Supérieur, Entre-Deux-Mers
owner: Gilles Dupuch *area:* 29 ha *cases:* 8,500, white 8,500 *grape % R:* MER 60% CS 20% CF 20% *grape % W:* SAUV B 50% SEM 35% MUSC 15% *second wine:* Ch Brame-Pan
33760 Targon tel: 05 56 23 00 71
fax: 05 56 23 34 61
At the place where pilgrims used to refresh themselves the Targon watertower now stands, and near it this château. Under the Ch Sainte-Marie name, and also Ch Les Hauts Sainte-Marie, exemplary Entre-Deux-Mers wines are made, aromatic and distinguished. The best quality is represented by the Cuvée Madlys,

fermented in wood. Class is also offered by the red Bordeaux Supérieur: a balanced, cask-aged wine with ageing potential.

Ch Saint-Florin   map 36
Bordeaux, Entre-Deux-Mers
owner: Jean-Marc Jolivet *area:* 54 ha *cases:* 21,000, white 13,000 *grape % R:* MER 50% CS 30% CF 20% *grape % W:* SAUV B 50% MUSC 25% SEM 25% *second wines:* Ch La Coudraie *(Bordeaux)*; Ch Haut Maginet *(Bordeaux)*
33790 Soussac tel: 05 56 61 31 61
fax: 05 56 61 34 87
From this vineyard, doubled in area since 1981, Jean-Marc Jolivet makes a lively red Bordeaux with violets and fruit, including raspberry, in bouquet and taste. Fruit is also present in the agreeable, lively Entre-Deux-Mers with its floral notes. The same qualities are offered with the Ch La Coudraie. The château, where visitors are very welcome, is 19th century.

Ch Saint-Jacques   map 8
Bordeaux Supérieur
owner: Alain Miailhe *area:* 13 ha *cases:* 7,400 *grape % R:* CS 42% MER 35% CF 23% *second wine:* Fort Jaco *other châteaux owned:* Ch Siran *(Margaux)*
33460 Labarde tel: 05 57 88 34 04
fax: 05 57 88 70 05
Exceptionally commendable Bordeaux Supérieur made at Ch Siran, Margaux: fruity, spicy, with good tannins and flattering oak. Maturing lasts 10-12 months, and a third of the casks are new each year.

Ch Saint-Pierre   map 35
Bordeaux, Entre-Deux-Mers
owner: Denis Roumégous *area:* 10.5 ha *cases:* 4,000, white 1,200 *grape % R:* CS 50% MER 40% CF 10% *grape % W:* SEM 60% SAUV B 40% *other wines:* Bordeaux Clairet *other châteaux owned:* Ch de Haux *(Premières Côtes de Bordeaux)*; Ch Gourran *(Premières Côtes de Bordeaux)*
33760 St-Pierre-de-Bat tel: 05 56 23 35 07
fax: 05 56 23 25 29
The red, white and rosé Bordeaux are of a good average quality, made by the team from Ch de Haux in the Premières Côtes de Bordeaux. The best red and white wines carry the name La Mitre du Château Saint-Pierre; they are produced from old vines.

Ch Saint Savet   map 36
Bordeaux, Bordeaux Supérieur
owner: Yves Marceteau *area:* 8 ha *cases:* 8,200, white 200 *grape % R:* MER 64% CS 36% *grape % W:* SEM 100% *other wines:* Bordeaux Clairet
33790 Massugas tel: 05 56 61 36 93
fax: 05 56 61 36 93
A Bordeaux Supérieur matured for 10 months in wood, of decent but not striking quality. Black and red fruit determine its aroma.

Ch Saint-Sulpice   map 35
Bordeaux
owner: Vignobles Pierre & Christophe Dubergé *area:* 35 ha *cases:* 19,000 *grape % R:* MER 70% CS 25% CF 5% *second wine:* Domaine de Guillemin
33450 St-Sulpice-et-Cameyrac tel: 05 56 30 83 06
fax: 05 56 30 20 32
Reasonably firm Bordeaux characterized by its Merlot, with impressions of berry fruit, licorice and forest scents. Mechanically picked grapes. No ageing in wood.

Ch La Salargue   map 35
Bordeaux, Bordeaux Supérieur
owner: Vignobles Bruno Le Roy *area:* 25 ha *cases:* 16,600 *grape % R:* MFR 75% CS 20% CF 5% *other wines:* Bordeaux Clairet
33420 Moulon tel: 05 57 24 48 44
fax: 05 57 24 42 38
Since the 1985 vintage, in cellars near the banks of the Dordogne, the Le Roy family have been making a nuanced Cuvée Prestige with a solid taste. This Bordeaux Supérieur is given six months in cask. The vineyard area is to be increased to 30 ha.

Ch Sarail-la Guillaumière   map 35
Bordeaux Supérieur
owner: Michel Deguillaume *area:* 13.2 ha *cases:* 7,000 *grape % R:* MER 80% CS 20% *other wines:* Vieux Guillaume *(Bordeaux rosé)*
33450 St-Loubès tel: 05 56 20 40 14
fax: 05 56 78 92 07
The property was bought in 1904; the first tractor in St-Loubès arrived here in 1954, stainless-steel fermentation tanks in 1975, barrels in 1982 – energy and drive have long marked the running of this estate. The wine, an elegant Bordeaux Supérieur, has an aroma in which woodland elements of undergrowth, mushrooms (and truffles), plus black fruit, are often combined. Oak-ageing lasts a year.

Domaine du Sarrailley   map 35
Bordeaux Supérieur
owner: Christian Pinaud *area:* 2.3 ha *cases:* 1,250 *grape % R:* MER 80% CF 10% CS 10%
33750 Beychac-et-Caillau tel: 05 56 72 43 81
Bordeaux Supérieur, traditionally matured with about two years in wood, of a decent quality and strongly characterized by Merlot. The estate has been working under this name since 1989.

Ch de Seguin   map 35
Bordeaux, Bordeaux Supérieur
owner: Michael & Gert Carl *area:* 93 ha *cases:* 58,250, white 2,300 *grape % R:* CS 50% MER 45% CF 5% *grape % W:* SAUV B 60% SEM 35% Merlot Blanc 5% *second wines:* Ch Riveret; Ch Haut Blagnac *other wines:* Bordeaux rosé
33360 Lignan-de-Bordeaux tel: 05 56 21 97 84
fax: 05 56 78 34 85
After being taken over in 1985 by the Danish Carl family, owners of the Chris-Wine firm, this estate was totally modernized – both vineyard

Below: Ch Roques-Mauriac

and cellar equipment. Right from 1986, the first vintage the Danes vinified and nurtured themselves, it was clear they were striving for the highest quality. With how much success is obvious from a whole series of medals, and other awards by the dozen. Their Bordeaux Supérieur Cuvée Prestige has repeatedly been picked as the best of its appellation. It is a rich, well-made wine – meaty, with ripe fruit, toasty oak together with vanilla, and an unmistakable finesse. It has a year in wood (20% new casks), which is twice the time for the elegant, spicy, fruity and quite velvety standard Bordeaux Supérieur. The estate also produces a very good, fresh and fruity white Bordeaux, the Sauvignon de Seguin; a prestige version of this; and a delicate, stimulating rosé. The origin of the château goes back to 780AD, when a lodging was built on this site by the Carolingian Count of Seguin.

Ch des Seigneurs de Pommyers
map 36
Bordeaux
owner: Jean-Luc Piva **area:** 8 ha **cases:** 1,400 **grape % R:** MER 60% CS 30% CF 10% **other châteaux owned:** Ch Pouchaud-Larquey (Bordeaux)
33540 St-Félix-de-Foncaude tel: 05 56 71 65 16 fax: 05 56 71 44 97
The Piva family from Piedmont in Italy settled in Entre-Deux-Mers in 1924, and acquired this château 65 years later. It took its name from a medieval castle of which a few parts remain. The vineyard here is organically cultivated and yields a sound Bordeaux that has repeatedly won awards, and is reasonably meaty, with blackcurrant as its fruit.

Ch Senailhac
map 35
Bordeaux
owner: Famille Margnat **area:** 50 ha **cases:** 27,700 **grape % R:** CS 44% MER 43% MAL 12% PV 1% **second wine:** Ch Moulin Desclau
33370 Tresses tel: 05 57 34 13 14 fax: 05 57 34 05 60
Somewhat rustic, earthy wine with mineral and spicy aspects to it, as well as a touch of fruit. It is sold as Bordeaux or Bordeaux Supérieur. This estate has a fine courtyard and two old gateways.

Ch Le Sèpe
map 36
Bordeaux
owner: Marie-Christine Selves **area:** 20 ha **cases:** 10,000, white 2,000 **grape % R:** MER 45% CF 25% CS 25% MAL 5% **grape % W:** SAUV B 70% MUSC 15% SEM 15% **second wine:** Ch Le Brandey **other wines:** Bordeaux rosé
33350 Ste-Radegonde tel: 05 57 40 56 54 fax: 05 57 40 56 54
Venerable estate, its origin going back to the 17th century. Among the wines made here is a very decent red Bordeaux, often combining berry fruit and herbaceous elements in its aroma.

Ch La Serizière
map 35
Bordeaux, Bordeaux Supérieur, Entre-Deux-Mers Haut-Benauge
owner: Gérard Lobre **area:** 40 ha **cases:** 15,000, white 7,000 **grape % R:** CS 40% MER 40% CF 20% **grape % W:** SEM 60% SAUV B 30% MUSC 10% **other wines:** Bordeaux rosé
33760 Ladaux tel: 05 56 23 91 75 fax: 05 57 34 40 72
The traditionally styled Bordeaux Supérieur red and the expressive, floral and fruity Entre-Deux-

Mers Haut-Benauge are the most interesting wines. Casks are not used here.

Ch de Sours
map 35
Bordeaux Supérieur, Bordeaux, Entre-Deux-Mers
owner: Esmé Johnstone & Hugh Ryman **area:** 38 ha **cases:** 12,200, white 3,600 **grape % R:** MER 60% CS 40% **grape % W:** SEM 70% SAUV B 20% MUSC 10% **second wine:** Domaine de Sours **other wines:** Bordeaux rosé **other châteaux owned:** include Ch de la Jaubertie (Bergerac); Ch Vignelaure (Côteaux d'Aix-en-Provence)
33750 St-Quentin-de-Baron tel: 05 57 24 10 81 fax: 05 57 24 10 83
On 1 July 1990 Esmé Johnstone, a former wine merchant from Britain, became the new owner of this estate. He installed modern cellar equipment, went into partnership with Hugh Ryman, the 'flying winemaker', and was also advised by the oenologist Michel Rolland. Maturing casks were installed, both of French and American oak. Only American oak is used for the barrel-fermented Entre-Deux-Mers, a stylish wine in which the oak beautifully complements the rich fruit aromas and fresh acidity. Johnstone works with a mixture of French and American barrels for his red Bordeaux. This has a powerful, mouthfilling taste with appetizing fruit (blackberry, raspberry, elderberry) and firm tannins, rather austere at first. The Bordeaux rosé – made in almost the same quantity as the red – is of the highest quality: delightfully fruity, very lively... perfect of its kind. The vineyard is going to be extended to 50 ha.

Ch Talmont
map 36
Bordeaux
owner: Patrick Mourgues **area:** 167 ha **cases:** 75,000, white 40,000 **grape % R:** CS 76% CF 12% MER 12% **grape % W:** SAUV B 75% SEM 25% **other châteaux owned:** Esclottes
33790 Landerrouat tel: 05 56 61 35 73
Wines made by the cooperative at Landerrouat. The red is not especially powerful in taste, but it has fruit such as raspberry, a touch of acidity and a good balance. The clean-tasting white is usually reasonably aromatic, with floral, some apple, and mineral notes, and offers freshness without any exaggerated acidity.

Ch de Terrefort-Quancard
map 34
Bordeaux, Bordeaux Supérieur
owner: Famille Quancard **area:** 70 ha **cases:** 35,000, white 1,200 **grape % R:** MER 70% CS 22% CF 8% **grape % W:** SAUV B 45% SEM 43% MUSC 12% **second wines:** Clos d'Aubiac; Ch La Tonnelle **other châteaux owned:** include Ch de Paillet-Quancard (Premières Côtes de Bordeaux); Ch Haut-Logat (Haut-Médoc); Ch Cossieu-Coutelin (St-Estèphe); Ch Bel-Air Ortet (St-Estèphe); Ch Faget (St-Estèphe); Ch Tour St Joseph (Haut-Médoc); Ch Pontet (Médoc); Ch Vieux Cardinal Lafaurie (Lalande-de-Pomerol); Ch Canada (Bordeaux Supérieur)
33240 Cubzac-les-Ponts tel: 05 57 43 00 53 fax: 05 57 43 59 87
The de Terrefort family gave this property the first half of its name in the 18th century, but the château was some 200 years old by then. The Quancards have run it in exemplary fashion since the end of the 19th century. The vineyard, on the highest ground in the commune, is mainly planted with black grapes from which a high-quality Bordeaux Supérieur is made. After about five years this wine evolves into an elegant, harmonious whole, with noble oak

tones, black fruit (plum and berries), a touch of tobacco and some spice. The estate also makes Diamant Blanc, an aromatic dry white Bordeaux.

Ch Thieuley
map 35
Bordeaux
owner: Francis Courselle **area:** 60 ha **cases:** 13,300, white 22,400 **grape % R:** MER 60% CS 40% **grape % W:** SAUV B 50% SEM 50% **other wines:** Bordeaux Clairet **other châteaux owned:** Clos Sainte-Anne (Premières Côtes de Bordeaux)
33670 La Sauve Majeure tel: 05 56 23 00 01 fax: 05 56 23 34 37
At the beginning of the 1970s Francis Courselle gave up his career teaching oenology and took over his family's modest wine estate. He then began to make white wine, applying techniques that were modern at the time, such as skin contact. Success was forthcoming and Ch Thieuley became one of the driving forces in bringing prestige and recognition to the Bordeaux Sec appellation. The standard white wine often has a brash bouquet, an aroma of gooseberry, grapefruit, pineapple and various more exotic fruits, a stimulating acidity, good concentration and length. The white Cuvée Francis Courselle offers still more light and shade. This wine is fermented in cask and matured for six months. It emerges with a rich taste, with noble oak from the casks – all of them new – and a succulent, complex mixture of fruit. Red wine of good quality is also made here: softly fruity, rounded, with firmness, elegance, and integrated oak from a year in barrel; and the Bordeaux Clairet is among the better examples of its kind.

Ch Timberlay
map 34
Bordeaux Supérieur
owner: Robert Giraud **area:** 110 ha **cases:** 60,000, white 8,600 **grape % R:** CS 50% MER 35% CF 15% **grape % W:** SEM 60% SAUV B 40% **other châteaux owned:** include Domaine du Cheval Blanc (Bordeaux); Ch Haut-Fourat (Bordeaux); Ch du Cartillon (Haut-Médoc); Clos Larcis (St-Emilion); Ch Villemaurine (St-Emilion); Ch Le Bocage (Bordeaux Supérieur)
33240 St-André-de-Cubzac tel: 05 57 43 01 44 fax: 05 57 43 08 75
A superb estate, the flagship of the wine merchant and grower Robert Giraud. The château goes back to the 14th century; it was totally restored after the Second World War. More than 80% of production consists of red wine, an agreeable Bordeaux Supérieur with a certain vitality, some fruit and creamy vanilla. It spends eight months in wood – 35% of the barrels are renewed each year. Only new barriques are used for fermenting the white Cuvée Prestige. This wine offers considerable oak, which is often to the fore, along with a firm acidity, fruit (including grapefruit), adequate substance and a good length. The ordinary white wine, on the other hand, is unremarkable.

Ch de la Tour
map 35
Bordeaux
owner: Dourthe Frères/Groupe CVBG **area:** 85 ha **cases:** 40,000 **grape % R:** CS 58% MER 42% **second wines:** Ch Lezin; Ch La Vigneraie **other châteaux owned:** include Ch La Garde (Pessac-Léognan); Ch Belgrave (Haut-Médoc)
33370 Salleboeuf tel: 05 56 78 38 24 fax: 05 56 78 38 24

Above: Ch Thieuley

Commendable red wines have been made here under the Bordeaux appellation since the beginning of the 1990s. The accessible, elegant standard wine is not oak-aged, but the Réserve du Château spends up to 18 months in barrels of which about a third are new. It is a wine with considerable nuances, fruit, spices and oak aromas, a decent weight and a certain cellaring potential.

Ch Tour Caillet map 35
Bordeaux Supérieur
owner: Denis Lecourt *area:* 52 ha *cases:* 30,000 *grape % R:* MER 80% CS 20% *other wines:* Bordeaux rosé
33420 Génissac tel: 05 57 24 46 04
fax: 05 57 24 40 18
Some 10% of production here is the Bordeaux Supérieur Cuvée Prestige. This wine, matured for a year in cask, has considerable body, plenty of fruit, and no exaggerated oak tones. The standard Bordeaux Supérieur, a pleasant, fairly light wine, has rather less depth. Some Bordeaux rosé is also made; the Cabernet Sauvignon is its most important grape, while the Merlot dominates in the red wines.

Ch Tour de l'Espérance map 36
Bordeaux Supérieur
owner: GFA Champ d'Auron *area:* 40 ha *cases:* 25,000 *grape % R:* MER 70% CS 30% *second wine:* Ch La Croix d'Auron
33133 Galgon tel: 05 57 74 30 02
fax: 05 57 74 32 22
Pleasant, reasonably concentrated Bordeaux Supérieur from one of the oldest vineyards in the region. No oak-ageing. A lot is exported.

Ch Tour de Mirambeau map 35
Bordeaux, Entre-Deux-Mers
owner: Jean Louis Despagne *area:* 60 ha *cases:* 17,000, white 33,000 *grape % R:* MER 80% CS 20% *grape % W:* SEM 34% SAUV B 33% MUSC 33% *other wines:* Bordeaux Clairet *other châteaux owned:* Ch Bel Air *(Bordeaux, Entre-Deux-Mers)*; Ch Rauzan Despagne *(Bordeaux, Entre-Deux-Mers)*
33420 Naujan-et-Postiac tel: 05 57 84 55 08
fax: 05 57 84 57 31
In a most spectacular manner during the 1980s Jean Louis Despagne made this estate one of the leading producers of dry white Bordeaux. His wines are valued worldwide, and are served by well-known airlines. The standard white

Bordeaux (sold as Entre-Deux-Mers in some countries) could serve as a model of its type: a most expressive wine, with a seductive fruitiness – mango, passion fruit, pear, melon, apple. It has an attractive freshness, elegant structure and a sound balance. With the Cuvée Passion, matured in cask, the standard rises to that of a white Graves or Pessac-Léognan: breadcrust and oak aromas, a substantial, mouthfilling, concentrated taste, and a good deal of fruit. There are also two versions of the red Bordeaux. The standard one is faultless in taste, supple and open, with something of raspberry and cherry. After eight months in cask the red Cuvée Passion is richer, more sumptuous, with integrated tannins, judicious oak and ripe fruit. Nor should the Bordeaux Clairet be overlooked: an exquisite wine, loaded with fruit.

Ch Tour du Moulin du Bric map 36
Bordeaux, Côtes de Bordeaux St-Macaire
owner: Philippe Faure *area:* 25 ha *cases:* 12,000, white 2,600 *grape % R:* CS 50% MER 40% CF 10% *grape % W:* SEM 50% SAUV B 40% MUSC 10% *other wines:* Bordeaux blanc & mousseux
33490 St-André-du-Bois tel: 05 56 76 40 20
fax: 05 56 76 45 29
Although it makes more of its decent red Bordeaux, this estate is best-known for its white Côtes de Bordeaux St-Macaire. There is a dry version of this, which gets six months in wood, and a semi-sweet that gets ten.

Ch Les Tourelles de Bossuet Lagravière map 34
Bordeaux
owner: Vignobles Meyer *area:* 3 ha *cases:* 1,700 *grape % R:* MER 100% *other châteaux owned:* Ch de Bourgueneuf *(Pomerol)*; Clos des Templiers *(Lalande-de-Pomerol)*
33910 St-Denis-de-Pile tel: 05 57 51 16 73
fax: 05 57 25 16 89
No château here, just a small vineyard. The wine is made at Ch de Bourgueneuf, in Pomerol. It is generally a not over-powerful but elegant pure Merlot.

Ch Toutigeac map 35
Bordeaux, Entre-Deux-Mers
owner: P. & M. Mazeau-Hautbois *area:* 40 ha *cases:* 27,500, white 1,250 *grape % R:* CF 60% MER 25% CS 15% *grape % W:* SEM 70% SAUV B 30%

second wines: Ch Pradeau Mazeau; Ch La Loubère; Ch Bellevue *other châteaux owned:* Ch de Hartes *(Bordeaux)*
33760 Targon tel: 05 56 23 90 10
fax: 05 56 23 67 21
Château on the edge of a broad valley: there are delightful views out over its surroundings from the back. Methods here are very modern, with delicious wines the result. The red Bordeaux is a balanced wine, very suitable for drinking young – but still altogether lively after five or six years. Black cherry and berry fruits characterize its aroma. The lively, supple Entre-Deux-Mers also has abundant fruit. Sometimes the same red wine is offered as Ch Pradeau Mazeau.

Ch Le Trébuchet map 36
Bordeaux
owner: Bernard Berger *area:* 34 ha *cases:* 24,600, white 2,800 *grape % R:* CS 40% CF 35% MER 25% *grape % W:* SAUV B 40% SEM 35% COL 20% UGNI BLANC 5% *second wine:* Ch Les Maréchaux *other wines:* Bordeaux Clairet & rosé; Crémant de Bordeaux
33190 Les Esseintes tel: 05 56 71 42 28
fax: 05 56 71 30 15
This château on high ground is said to derive its name from the siege engine that was positioned on this spot during the Hundred Years' War (1337-1453) to attack the fortified village of La Réole. Nowadays, in peaceful and traditional manner, a red *cuvée* is made here and given six months in wood. This wine lingers well, and sometimes rather drily, in the mouth, and is not one of the fruitier Bordeaux. The quite rounded Bordeaux Clairet De Berger is fruity and tastes totally different. One of the other wines made is a Crémant de Bordeaux.

Ch Trincaud map 34
Bordeaux Supérieur
owner: SCEA Entente Janoueix *area:* 14 ha *cases:* 7,000 *grape % R:* MER 60% CF 20% CS 20% *second wine:* Ch Maine-Barreau *other châteaux owned:* Ch Grands Sillons Gabachot *(Pomerol)*; Ch Des Tourelles *(Lalande-de-Pomerol)*; Ch La Bastienne *(Montagne-St-Emilion)*; Ch Petit Clos du Roy *(Montagne-St-Emilion)*
33910 Bonzac tel: 05 57 51 55 44
fax: 05 57 51 83 70
Jammy red and black fruit is often to be found in Ch Trincaud's supple Bordeaux Supérieur, which is of decent quality.

◆
Grape varieties
Main and other permitted varieties for each appellation are given in the appellation fact box at the end of the relevant introduction.

For châteaux, percentages of grapes grown are given as supplied by the château.

Abbreviations: CF Cabernet Franc, COL Colombard, CS Cabernet Sauvignon, MAL Malbec, MER Merlot, MUSC Muscadelle, PV Petit Verdot, SAUV B Sauvignon Blanc, SEM Sémillon

Ugni Blanc is given in full, as are names of less common grapes such as Carmenère, Merlot Blanc and Sauvignon Gris.

Ch Trocard
map 36

Bordeaux Supérieur

owner: Jean-Louis Trocard **area:** 40 ha **cases:** 22,250 **grape % R:** MER 70% CF 15% CS 15% **other wines:** Bordeaux rosé **other châteaux owned:** Ch Les Charmettes *(Bordeaux Supérieur)*; Ch Franc La Rose *(St-Emilion)*; Ch Croix de Rambeau *(Lussac-St-Emilion)*; Clos de la Vieille Eglise *(Pomerol)*; Ch La Croix des Moines *(Lalande-de-Pomerol)*

33570 Les Artigues-de-Lussac tel: 05 57 24 31 16 fax: 05 57 24 33 87

Jean-Louis Trocard, a qualified engineer and a talented, committed winemaker, is one of the great personalities of the region: he has done a lot for the Bordeaux and Bordeaux Supérieur *syndicat*. His Ch Trocard Monrepos comes from a 5-ha plot planted with old Merlot vines. This is a tempting Bordeaux Supérieur, with succulent black fruit, spice, nuances of toast and considerable oak. Maturing lasts a year in casks of which a third are new. There is class, too, in the ordinary Bordeaux Supérieur, an absolutely sound wine with juicy berry fruit, supple tannins and a respectable level of intensity. The Bordeaux rosé is an engaging spring and summer wine. Finally, Trocard offers one, or sometimes two, *cuvées* of an agreeable dry Bordeaux from bought-in white grapes, 60% Sémillon and 40% Sauvignon.

Ch La Tuilerie du Puy
map 36

Bordeaux Supérieur, Entre-Deux-Mers

owner: SCEA Regaud **area:** 55 ha **cases:** 20,000, white 8,000 **grape % R:** CS 40% MER 40% CF 20% **grape % W:** SAUV B 40% SEM 30% MUSC 30% **second wine:** Ch Camerac

33580 Le Puy tel: 05 56 61 61 92 fax: 05 56 61 86 90

This château is a spacious 16th-century *maison de campagne*, contrasting in its venerable age with the modern *cuvier*, full of gleaming fermentation tanks. Below the tanks is the vault where the Bordeaux Supérieur spends a year in cask, and the Entre-Deux-Mers four months. Both of these wines have won dozens of medals since the present owners took over the estate in 1990. The Bordeaux Supérieur is a mouthfilling wine with considerable tannin, and often with a touch of black cherry in its aroma. Smooth fruit and oak, sometimes with a slight hint of bitterness, are features of the fresh white wine.

Ch des Tuquets
map 36

Bordeaux, Entre-Deux-Mers

owner: Jean-Hubert Laville **area:** 35 ha **cases:** 15,800, white 4,200 **grape % R:** MER 40% CS 40% CF 20% **grape % W:** SEM 60% SAUV B 40% **second wine:** Ch Davril **other châteaux owned:** Ch La Gaborie ; Ch Lacombe; Ch du Mont Carlau *(all Bordeaux, Entre-Deux-Mers)*

33540 St-Sulpice-de-Pommiers tel: 05 56 71 53 56 fax: 05 56 71 89 42

Where once the Romans made wine, today Jean-Hubert Laville produces an elegant red Bordeaux with succulent berry fruit, oak, and sometimes a herbaceous hint. His two other wines are a fairly simple, clean, fresh Entre-Deux-Mers, and a correct rosé.

Ch Turcaud
map 35

Bordeaux Supérieur, Bordeaux, Entre-Deux-Mers

owner: EARL Vignobles Robert **area:** 34 ha **cases:** 12,500, white 7,500 **grape % R:** MER 40% CS 40% CF 20% **grape % W:** SEM 50% SAUV B 40% MUSC 10% **second wine:** Ch Moulin de la Grave **other wines:** Bordeaux rosé

33670 La Sauve Majeure tel: 05 56 23 04 41 fax: 05 56 23 35 85

The Turcaud estate, situated between Langoiran and La Sauve, is instantly recognizable by the large umbrella pine near the château, a building that dates from the beginning of the 20th century. Wine is made here with a committed enthusiasm – and with much success. The Entre-Deux-Mers boasts fresh, exotic fruit and a hint of minerals. There is rather more depth and substance in the dry white Bordeaux, which is partly fermented in new casks. This *cuvée bois* has elements of oak as well as of various kinds of fruit (gooseberry, mango, apricot), and there is a good degree of concentration. Nor do the Ch Turcaud red wines disappoint: the Bordeaux has berry fruit, backbone and suppleness. The lively rosé is also to be recommended.

Ch de Valentons Canteloup
map 35

Bordeaux Supérieur

owner: F. Meynard & Fils **area:** 13 ha **cases:** 7,000 **grape % R:** MER 65% CF 20% CS 15% **other wines:** Bordeaux Clairet **other châteaux owned:** Ch Bois-Malot *(Bordeaux Supérieur, Entre-Deux-Mers)*

33450 St-Loubès tel: 05 56 38 94 18 fax: 05 56 38 92 47

Agreeable Bordeaux Supérieur with black and red fruit, and a fresh Bordeaux Clairet. The original 'Domaine' in the name was changed to 'Château' in the 1980s. The owners began a total replanting of the vineyard in 1973.

◆

Map references in this chapter

To find the location of a château in this chapter, note the commune name and the map reference: the communes are shown on maps 34, 35 and 36, which cover the wider Entre-Deux-Mers and the other main zones making Bordeaux and Bordeaux Supérieur wines. Beside each map are grid numbers for the communes. Where châteaux making Bordeaux and Bordeaux Supérieur wines are in other zones, the reference is to that zone's map.

Ch Les Vergnes
map 36

Bordeaux

owner: Univitis **area:** 78 ha **cases:** 25,000, white 16,000 **grape % R:** MER 50% CF 30% CS 20% **grape % W:** SAUV B 43% SEM 36% MUSC 21%

33220 Les Lèves-et-Thoumeyragues tel: 05 57 56 02 02 fax: 05 57 56 02 22

Since 1987 this splendid estate has been run by Univitis, a group of wine cooperatives. For many years before that it had been owned by the family of Maréchal Leclerc de Hautecloque. Attractive wines are produced on a big scale: a decently fruity, supple red Bordeaux and a fairly substantial white that has both fruit and floral aspects in its bouquet and taste. The imposing 19th-century château gives the Univitis group a splendid venue for its receptions.

Ch La Verrière
map 36

Bordeaux, Bordeaux Supérieur, Ste-Foy Bordeaux

owner: André & Jean-Paul Bessette **area:** 32 ha **cases:** 12,500, white 5,500 **grape % R:** MER 50% CF 30% CS 20% **grape % W:** SAUV B 55% SEM 45% **second wine:** Ch La Graula

33790 Landerrouat tel: 05 56 61 36 91 fax: 05 56 61 41 12

Even in lesser vintages the Bordeaux Supérieur is a quite rounded, sometimes almost voluptuous wine with restrained tannins. Usually it is left in tank for a considerable time. The Bordeaux Sec offers a decent quality, and the Bessette brothers also make a semi-sweet Ste-Foy Bordeaux with the yield from 1 ha.

Ch Les Vieilles Tuileries
map 35

Bordeaux, Entre-Deux-Mers

owner: Jean-Michel & Janine Menguin **area:** 60 ha **cases:** 21,500, white 11,000 **grape % R:** CS 40% MER 30% CF 20% MAL 10% **grape % W:** SEM 55% SAUV B 30% MUSC 15% **second wine:** Ch Haut Reygnac **other wines:** Bordeaux rosé **other châteaux owned:** Ch Lenormand *(Premières Côtes de Bordeaux)*

33760 Arbis tel: 05 56 23 61 70 fax: 05 56 23 49 79

Tannin is usually very noticeable in the red wine, which makes this Bordeaux suitable for laying down for some time. Other elements are generally ripe fruit, a herbaceous touch, and aspects of oak. Maturing takes place in casks of which 70% are new, and can last from ten

Below: Summer morning in the Entre-Deux-Mers

months minimum up to two years. Other wines here are an engaging rosé and a succulent, reasonably aromatic Entre-Deux-Mers.

Ch de La Vieille Tour   map 36
Bordeaux Supérieur

owner: Vignobles Boissonneau *area:* 45 ha *cases:* 17,600, white 4,700 *grape % R:* MER 40% CS 35% CF 25% *grape % W:* SAUV B 55% SEM 35% MUSC 10% *second wine:* Ch Moulin de Ferrand *other châteaux owned:* Domaine des Geais *(Côtes du Marmandais)* **33190 St-Michel-de-Lapujade tel: 05 56 61 72 14 fax: 05 56 61 71 01**

Vines have been grown on this land since the mid-12th century. One of the later owners of the property was Jean de Lanne: in about 1600 this poet and educator built a school for the children of his tenants; its foundations can still be seen. The Boissonneau family have owned Ch de La Vieille Tour for more than 150 years now, producing good, sound wines. One of the best is the Réserve Tradition, which matures for a year in wood (25% new barrels). It is a firmly structured Bordeaux Supérieur with nuances of fruit – red and black – earthy notes, and oak. Citrus and tropical fruit are often to be found in the aromatic, lively white Bordeaux.

Vieux Château Lamothe   map 35
Bordeaux

owner: GAEC des Vignobles Latorse *area:* 130 ha *cases:* 52,000, white 12,900 *grape % R:* MER 40% CS 30% CF 30% *grape % W:* SAUV B 60% SEM 40% *second wines:* Ch Gabon; Ch Gabaron; Ch Haut-Riot; Ch Lamothe *other wines:* Bordeaux rosé *other châteaux owned:* include Ch Canteloup *(Premières Côtes de Bordeaux)*; Clos Saint-Vincent *(St-Emilion)* **33670 La Sauve Majeure tel: 05 56 23 92 76 fax: 05 56 23 61 65**

Since 1948 three successive generations of the Latorse family have built an originally small estate into one of the largest in the Entre-Deux-Mers. Vieux Ch Lamothe is the 'flagship' of the various château names they use. Its red Bordeaux is a lively wine with sometimes rather harsh tannins, but at the same time with fruit – cherry and prune, qualities it shares with the rosé. The white version is lively and fresh, qualities it shares with the rosé. The standard rises with a couple of special *cuvées*, both offered under the name of Vignobles Latorse, and both matured for 12-18 months in

new casks. The white wine – called simply 'L' – is very much characterized by vanilla and creamy oak, and is a generous, complex wine meant for drinking soon after bottling. Spicy berry fruit and, again, vanilla and oak, typify the elegant rosé.

Ch Vignol   map 35
Bordeaux Supérieur, Bordeaux, Entre-Deux-Mers

owner: Bernard Doublet *area:* 60 ha *cases:* 32,500, white 6,000 *grape % R:* MER 74% CS 23% CF 3% *grape % W:* SAUV B 50% SEM 40% MUSC 10% *second wine:* Ch Borie de Noaillan *other wines:* Ch Belle Eglise *(Bordeaux Clairet)* *other châteaux owned:* Ch Tour de Calens *(Graves)* **33750 St-Quentin-de-Baron tel: 05 57 24 12 93 fax: 05 57 24 12 83**

Only a very small part of the total vintage is bottled by the owners themselves, but they hope gradually to increase this. And thanks to the reliable quality of the wines – emphasized by the assortment of gold medals won – the number of customers is growing steadily. The Bordeaux Supérieur Cuvée Spéciale spends nine months in oak – 25% new barrels; it generally has a firm taste, is darkly fruity, and lingers nicely with good tannins. Freshness, juicy fruit and floral elements characterize the Entre-Deux-Mers.

Ch Vilotte   map 36
Bordeaux

owner: Yannick Marlotto *area:* 15 ha *cases:* 6,000, white 3,000 *grape % R:* CS 40% CF 30% MER 30% *grape % W:* SAUV B 40% SEM 40% MUSC 10% UGNI BLANC 10% *second wine:* Ch Georges *other wines:* Bordeaux rosé **33540 Cleyrac tel: 05 56 71 83 43 fax: 05 56 71 64 73**

After about six months in casks, 25% of them new annually, the red Bordeaux has an elegant, rounded taste with smooth berry fruit – in good years at least. For wine from a lesser vintage may sometimes lack body and depth. The white wine merits little attention; the rosé on the other hand is often delicious.

Ch Virac   map 36
Bordeaux Supérieur

owner: Trabut-Cussac & Fils *area:* 37.5 ha *cases:* 19,500 *grape % R:* CS 34% CF 33% MER 33% *second wine:* Ch Puy Laborde **33580 Taillecavat tel: 05 56 61 62 66 fax: 05 56 61 62 61**

Well-made Bordeaux Supérieur, often with elements of toast and cocoa in its aroma and taste, as well as berry fruit. The estate dates from 1960.

Ch Vrai Caillou   map 36
Bordeaux, Bordeaux Supérieur, Entre-Deux-Mers

owner: Michel Pommier *area:* 90 ha *cases:* 37,500, white 11,000 *grape % R:* MER 40% CS 30% CF 30% *grape % W:* SEM 40% SAUV B 35% MUSC 25% *second wines:* Ch Jeanguillon; Moulin de Caillou *other châteaux owned:* Ch Darius *(St-Emilion)* **33790 Soussac tel: 05 56 61 31 56 fax: 05 56 61 33 52**

Perfection shines through everything that Michel and Odette Pommier undertake: the 19th-century château and park are immaculately kept, the *cuvier* is spotlessly clean and boasts modern equipment, the small *chai* has both neatness and atmosphere, and this was one of the first Bordeaux estates where mechanical picking made harvesting quick and efficient. Their most notable wine is L'Optimé, a white Bordeaux achieved through skin contact and fermenting in wood. This wine is very much dominated by toast and oak, even up to five years after the vintage, and has a fresh, lively character. The Entre-Deux-Mers is generally rounded, and offers balance and succulent fruit – peach, apple, apricot. Berry fruit from the Cabernet is as a rule clearly present in the Bordeaux Supérieur, often with herbaceous elements and supple tannins.

APPELLATION GRAVES DE VAYRES

APPELLATION GRAVES DE VAYRES

Ch Bacchus   map 35
owner: Grimal & Fils **area:** 30 ha **cases:** 15,500,
white 2,500 **grape % R:** MER 60% CF 25% CS 15%
grape % W: SAUV B 50% SEM 40% MUSC 10%
33870 Vayres tel: 05 57 74 74 61
fax: 05 57 84 92 89
This most vinous name graces a pair of wines: a
supple, mild, somewhat neutral white Graves de
Vayres, and a polished, firm, quite rounded red.

Ch Barre Gentillot   map 35
owner: Yvette Cazenave-Mahé **area:** 39 ha **cases:**
16,000, white 2,000 **grape % R:** MER 70% CF 25%
CS 5% **grape % W:** SEM 100% **other wines:** Ch de
Barre (Bordeaux Supérieur)
33500 Arveyres tel: 05 57 24 80 26
fax: 05 57 24 84 54
Meaty red Graves de Vayres with considerable
body, often deep-coloured and with elements of
licorice, aniseed and bayleaf in its aroma – a
wine that reverberates for a long time in the
mouth. The château itself is a white stone
building, standing between the vineyard and the
tall trees of its park.

Ch Cantelaudette   map 35
owner: Jean-Michel Chatelier **area:** 50 ha **cases:**
20,000, white 15,000 **grape % R:** MER 60% CS 20%
CF 20% **grape % W:** SEM 80% SAUV B 20% **second
wine:** Ch d'Arveyres (Bordeaux Supérieur)
33500 Arveyres tel: 05 57 24 84 71
fax: 05 57 24 83 41
Reasonably firm red Graves de Vayres, likeable
but not offering much real depth, with Merlot
calling the tune. The white tastes smoothly
fresh and decently fruity. The château is a
delightful 1850 chartreuse.

Ch Canteloup   map 35
owner: Jean-Philippe Landreau **area:** 40 ha **cases:**
15,000, white 5,000 **grape % R:** MER 60% CS 40%
grape % W: SAUV B 80% SEM 10% MUSC 10% **second
wine:** Bordeaux Supérieur
33780 Beychac-et-Caillau tel: 05 56 72 97 72
fax: 05 56 72 49 48
This family property, dating from 1948, ranks
among the best of Graves de Vayres. The red
Cuvée Spéciale, given a year in wood (20% new
barrels), is refined, supple, agreeable in taste,
with both succulent ripe fruit and vanilla oak.
The straightforward red Graves de Vayres is as a
rule smooth and generous. A good standard is
also offered by the white Graves de Vayres, a
not-too-dry creation matured in cask and
displaying a pleasing amount of fruit.

Ch La Croix de Bayle   map 35
owner: Philippe Battle-Simon **area:** 10 ha **cases:**
4,000, white 2,500 **grape % R:** CS 70% MER 30%
grape % W: SEM 70% SAUV B 20% MERLOT BLANC 10%
33870 Vayres tel: 05 57 24 57 95
An engaging red Graves de Vayres with a supple
structure, but no really distinct personality. In
the white, Sauvignon usually dominates the
aroma – with gooseberry and asparagus – even
though this variety is in the minority.

Ch Gayat   map 35
owner: Famille Degas **area:** 17 ha **cases:** 4,400,
white 3,000 **grape % R:** MER 44% CS 35% CF 21%
grape % W: SEM 77% SAUV B 13% MUSC 10% **other
châteaux owned:** Ch Haut-Gayat (Graves de Vayres)
33870 Vayres tel: 05 57 87 12 43
fax: 05 57 87 12 61

Estate split off from Ch Haut-Gayat. Here the
red is a slightly rustic Graves de Vayres of
average quality, usually with more licorice and
spices than fruit. The white tastes somewhat
angular and is at best correct.

Ch Haut-Gayat   map 35
owner: Marie-Josée Degas **area:** 13 ha **cases:**
7,200 **grape % R:** MER 50% CS 50% **other châteaux
owned:** Ch Capmartin (Bordeaux Supérieur); Ch Les
Conquêtes (Bordeaux Supérieur); Ch Degas
(Bordeaux); Ch de la Souloire (Bordeaux Supérieur)
33750 St-Germain-du-Puch tel: 05 57 24 52 32
fax: 05 57 24 03 72
An agreeable, supple wine with a slight fatness;
it matures quickly. However, its maturing in
oak is, unfortunately, carried out mainly in used
barrels.

Ch Haut-Mongeat   map 35
owner: Bernard Bouchon **area:** 27 ha **cases:**
15,000, white 1,000 **grape % R:** MER 70% CF 30%
grape % W: SEM 34% MUSC 33% SAUV B 33% **second
wine:** Ch La Croix d'Antonne (Bordeaux; Bordeaux
Supérieur) **other wines:** Bordeaux Supérieur;
Bordeaux Clairet
33420 Génissac tel: 05 57 24 47 55
fax: 05 57 24 41 21
After 18 years of sending the grapes to a
cooperative, in 1987 Bernard Bouchon decided
to make the wine himself – and met with
success. The red Graves de Vayres combines
elements of toast, vanilla, jammy fruit and good
tannins in its aroma. It matures for about a year
in wood (a third of the barriques are new). The
red wine will readily mature in bottle for
around five years as a rule – in contrast to the

fresh white Graves de Vayres, which is best
appreciated in its early youth. The château itself
was built on the foundations of a 16th-century
monastery.

Ch l'Hosanne   map 35
owner: SCEA Chastel-Labat **area:** 12 ha **cases:**
4,800, white 1,200 **grape % R:** MER 80% CF 10% CS
10% **grape % W:** SEM 80% SAUV B 20% **second wine:**
Ch La Croix de l'Hosanne **other wines:** Ch La Croix
de l'Hosanne (Bordeaux Clairet)
33870 Vayres tel: 05 57 74 70 55
fax: 05 57 74 70 36
A year and a half in cask is customary for Ch
l'Hosanne's red Graves de Vayres, a well-made
and succulent wine with fruit and animal
aspects besides the evident oak. The owners –
four wine enthusiasts who took over the estate
in 1988 – also produce a distinguished, quite
substantial white Cuvée Spéciale here, which is
fermented in oak.

Ch Jean Dugay   map 35
owner: GFA Jean-Claude & Nathalie Ballet **area:** 42
ha **cases:** 14,000, white 8,500 **grape % R:** MER
70% CF 15% CS 15% **grape % W:** SAUV B 70% SEM
25% MUSC 5% **other wines:** Ch la Caussade; Ch
Haut-Branda (Bordeaux rosé & blanc)
33870 Vayres tel: 05 57 74 83 17
fax: 05 57 74 83 17
The red Graves de Vayres from this estate,
which was founded at the beginning of the 19th
century, generally develops quickly, and its taste
tends to the velvety. The wine is not aged in
wood.

Ch Juncarret   map 35
owner: Antoine Rouquette **area:** 30 ha **cases:**
11,500, white 7,000 **grape % R:** CF 40% CS 30%
MER 30% **grape % W:** SAUV B 50% MUSC 30% SEM 20%
33870 Vayres tel: 05 57 74 85 23
fax: 05 57 74 81 08
Juncarret is a château with 16th-century
origins and modern equipment. This produces
an aromatic white wine with fruity and floral
elements, and an accessible, fairly light, early-
maturing red.

Left: Signposts point the way to Graves
de Vayres and Entre-Deux-Mers châteaux

Below: The castle of Vayres

Above: Ch Lesparre

Ch du Lau
map 35

owner: Régis Plomby *area:* 15 ha *cases:* 7,000,
white 3,000 *grape % R:* MER 70% CS 20% CF 10%
grape % W: MUSC 40% SEM 40% SAUV B 20%
33500 Arveyres tel: 05 57 51 32 78
fax: 05 57 25 21 00
The celebrated architect Victor Louis is credited
with designing the harmoniously proportioned
château at du Lau in 1762. Harmony is likewise
exhibited by the red Graves de Vayres, a wine
that is matured in wood for 18 months, after
which it has a supple roundness in the mouth
and plentiful vanilla notes. An agreeable wine,
without laying claim to greatness.

Ch Lesparre
map 35

owner: Michel Gonet *area:* 180 ha *cases:* 89,500,
white 19,000 *grape % R:* MER 60% CS 20% CF 20%
grape % W: SEM 70% SAUV B 20% MUSC 10% *second
wines:* Ch Beroy; Ch de Lathibaude; Ch Durand
Bayle *(Bordeaux Supérieur)* *other wines:* Bordeaux
blanc & rosé; Bordeaux Supérieur; Entre-deux-Mers;
Crémant de Bordeaux *other properties owned:*
Champagne Michel Gonet
33750 Beychac-et-Caillau tel: 05 57 24 51 23
fax: 05 57 24 03 99
In 1986 the Gonets, the old Champagne family,
bought this wine estate – with its 180 ha, one
of the largest in Bordeaux – and have proceeded
to make it the leading Graves de Vayres
château. The red wine, a frequent gold medal
winner, contains about 70% Merlot, and is
given 8-12 months in *barriques*, a third of them
new. It is both more complete and more
complex than most comparable wines. Among
its nuances are those of berry fruit, animal
scents, spice and – naturally – oak aromas,
while the tannin provides the wine with
backbone and maturing potential. The
Bordeaux Supérieur, too, is an attractive wine:
supple, with an undertone of fruit and often a
rather higher proportion of Cabernet
Sauvignon. The white Graves de Vayres is one of
the best from the district; it offers depth and
subtle shading, including that of oak from eight
months in cask. Sometimes a *liquoreux* is also
made – more for the love of it than for
economic reasons. This is a wine with
considerable oak, an unobtrusive sweetness and

◆
Information about Graves de Vayres

Details of the appellation are in the
introduction to Entre-Deux-Mers: see page
221. For its location and boundaries,
see map 35.

Châteaux in the Graves de Vayres have the
right to use the appellation Entre-Deux-
Mers for white wines, and the Bordeaux
(white, red & rosé) and Bordeaux Supérieur
(red) appellations.

For further information on the wines of the
Graves de Vayres telephone the Syndicat
on 05 57 74 85 23.

---

apricot for its fruit. That the Gonets also
produce a sparkling Bordeaux (from white
grapes only) rather goes without saying.

Ch Pichon Bellevue
map 35

owner: D. & L. Reclus *area:* 30 ha *cases:* 11,500,
white 7,600 *grape % R:* MER 60% CF 20% CS 20%
grape % W: SEM 50% MUSC 30% SAUV B 20% *second
wine:* Ch Pichon Le Moyne *other wines:* Bordeaux;
Bordeaux rosé .
33870 Vayres tel: 05 57 74 84 08
fax: 05 57 84 95 04
After its creation in 1880 this estate grew
gradually to its present size, and further
expansion is foreseen. The red Graves de Vayres
is a supple, rounded wine with a fairly firm
structure. It sees no wood. The fresh notes of
Sauvignon – sometimes up to 60% of the
grapes – shines through clearly in the white,
both in the bouquet and the fairly slender taste.

Ch Le Tertre
map 35

owner: Pierrette & Christian Labeille *area:* 29 ha
cases: 10,000, white 4,000 *grape % R:* MER 60% CF
30% CS 10% *grape % W:* SEM 50% SAUV B 35% MUSC
15% *other wines:* Bordeaux; Bordeaux rosé;
Crémant de Bordeaux

33870 Vayres tel: 05 57 74 76 91
fax: 05 57 74 87 40
Estate close to the RN89 Bordeaux-Libourne
road that attracts more attention for its wines
than for its architecture. One of the wines goes
into cask: the Cuvée Baron Charles, a red
Graves de Vayres. After 12 months in wood
there emerges a quite generous, supple,
rounded wine, with smooth fruit and nuances
of oak. In quality the ordinary red Graves de
Vayres is correct at least – a standard that the
white version and the Bordeaux rosé usually do
not quite reach.

Ch Toulouze
map 35

owner: Alain Cailley *area:* 10 ha *cases:* 5,500
grape % R: MER 70% CS 25% PV 5% *second wine:*
Prélude de Château Toulouze *other châteaux
owned:* Ch Le Maine Martin *(Bordeaux Supérieur)*
33870 Vayres tel: 05 56 30 85 47
fax: 05 56 30 87 29
This vineyard, created in 1820, was very
prosperous in the 19th century – but by the
1970s all the vines had gone. It was only after
another decade that there was any replanting,
carried out by the present owners. At first
Merlot was the only grape, but the proportion
of it has now been reduced to 70% by the
planting of Cabernet Sauvignon and Petit
Verdot. The red Graves de Vayres almost always
has some fat, some fruit and a pleasing
suppleness. There is no oak-ageing here.

Ch Les Tuileries du Déroc
map 35

owner: Denis Colombier *area:* 13 ha *cases:* 5,000,
white 2,000 *grape % R:* MER 55% CS 35% CF 10%
grape % W: SEM 50% SAUV B 35% MUSC 15% *second
wine:* Ch Montifau
33870 Vayres tel: 05 57 74 71 59
fax: 03 26 54 97 51
Somewhat mineral, spicy and slightly fruity red
Graves de Vayres, and a fresh, clean white. The
château has belonged to the same family for a
number of generations. The present owner, a
qualified oenologist, took over the management
in 1988. He does not mature his wine in casks.

The Right Bank

St-Emilion offers a medieval townscape; the vineyards also seem to have changed little since the town was founded in the 12th century

Viewed from the city of Bordeaux, the Right Bank vineyards are a distant country. Seen from Libourne or St-Emilion, Bordeaux can be a sometimes overweening metropolitan presence. Of course, more unites these two great halves of the Gironde's *vignoble* than divides them: grapes, climate, history. Yet the differences are real. St-Emilion's red wines have a quite distinct personality when compared to those of the Médoc; Pomerol's differ even more. Sweet white wines are virtually unknown here; dry whites are few. The best red-wine *terroirs* are on limestone or even clay: gravel, guarantor of excellence in Médoc and Graves, is rarer. The following pages survey the Right Bank, starting with St-Emilion, its biggest and most important vineyard.

THE RIGHT BANK

The Right Bank vineyards – those lying to the east and north of the Dordogne river and Gironde estuary – fall into clearer focus when their alternative name, the Libournais, is used. The districts of St-Emilion, Pomerol and Fronsac, and the lesser appellations which cluster around them, all look to the town of Libourne as their immediate capital, rather than to the city of Bordeaux itself. Further afield other Right Bank districts, such as Bourg and Blaye to the north, and Castillon and Francs to the east, lie outside the Libourne orbit; though not a few châteaux are linked to the Libournais heartland by ownership and family ties.

Bordeaux holds sway as the administrative centre, but much of the wine commerce of the Right Bank has historically flowed (and still flows) through the ancient river port of Libourne. The Libourne quayside – a broad and rather unkempt band of road and stone beside the Dordogne – is lined with the offices of the *négociants*, the *courtiers* and the château owners who dominate the region. When doing business hereabouts, you may lunch in the medieval charm of St-Emilion or view the vines on the Pomerol plateau, but the work is done in an unassuming office on the Quai du Priourat.

HISTORY OF THE RIGHT BANK WINE TRADE

Libourne owes its existence to the royal rivalries of the Middle Ages, and its long history has much to tell about the wines to this day. It was founded in 1268 by the future King Edward I of England, then lord of Aquitaine, as a fortified town to protect the region against the French. Libourne was planned from the start as a wine port, and until the coming of the railways it held a virtual monopoly in the export of Right Bank wines.

The hilly town of St-Emilion is even older. Its vineyards almost certainly began with the Romans, and in 1199, in the days of the English kings, it became a self-governing town with its own mayor and council, the Jurade, whose wide powers stemmed from a charter granted by King John. These included the regulation of winegrowing and the trade in wine. Disputes with the English crown led to its charter being revoked at least once, but the Jurade survived until the French

Revolution. It was revived in 1948 as a ceremonial body for the promotion of St-Emilion wine. Today the St-Emilion appellation exactly corresponds to the nine parishes listed in King John's charter of 1199, making this one of the world's oldest defined wine districts. For many years the old Jurade fought against the misuse of the St-Emilion name by winegrowers from Bergerac and beyond. In 1742 a group was appointed to go round the *chais*, branding each cask with the town arms and keeping a record book which listed every barrel. Wines not so recorded were refused permission to be sold.

But at that time Libourne's rivalry to Bordeaux as a wine port was diminishing, as the Bordeaux merchants created and exploited the demand for quality red wines in northern Europe – Britain especially. St-Emilion did not have the large estates or the aristocratic landlords of the Médoc: land holdings on the Right Bank typically belonged either to the Church or were farmed by large numbers of small tenants. Thus few châteaux established individual reputations. Despite being closer to Paris, the Libournais was paradoxically isolated, being cut off from Bordeaux by the great rivers, which remained unbridged until the early 19th century. When the railway arrived in 1853, it opened up markets in Paris and the north of France. Slowly, St-Emilion wines became better known there – though the export markets were still dominated by the Médocs. It was not until the 1950s that St-Emilion wines really began to be appreciated in Britain and the United States, though Belgium and the Netherlands had discovered their excellence somewhat earlier.

The other wines of the Right Bank were even less known to the outside world until within living memory – though Fronsac (usually under the name Canon-Fronsac) was well thought of in the 18th century. Pomerol seems to have suffered badly during the medieval wars and languished in obscurity through the period before the French Revolution. Until late in the 19th century Fronsac was considered more important than Pomerol, and many wine merchants and writers bracketed Pomerol with St-Emilion. In 1923 the area attained the appellation, and after the Second World War the fame of its leading growth, Château Pétrus, began to spread until it was accorded unofficial First Growth status – and ever higher prices.

Fronsac, with its attractive hilly landscape, had several handsome châteaux in the 18th century when Pomerol was virtually unknown, and the wines profited

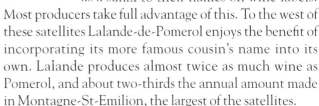
A street in Bourg

from the patronage of Richelieu in the 17th. Its revival in the last two decades of the 20th century was hailed as a new source of good claret, but really only reinstated an area long known in Libourne for quality.

THE APPELLATIONS

St-Emilion is the ceremonial capital of the Right Bank – even older than Libourne, and far more ancient in atmosphere and appearance. It sits on a low ridge of limestone away from, but in sight of, the Dordogne. The vineyards lap right up to the town's walls, and some of the greatest châteaux are a short stroll along country lanes.

St-Emilion is the largest and the most senior appellation of the Libournais. Its production is typically about seven times that of Pomerol, and more than the much bigger (in area) district of Blaye. Its landscape is ruled by the vine. Buildings and roads interrupt the vineyards, but there are no other crops. Pomerol has a monoculture too, but here things are on a much smaller scale. The border between the two appellations is not obvious: but for the signposts it could be one district. The commune boundary follows a small stream – a mere ditch – for a while, but then jinks to follow a road, leaving both banks of the brook in St-Emilion. The northern boundaries of both districts at least are clear: the muddy valley of the Barbanne, a stream which rises east of Puisseguin. Beyond, to the north, both St-Emilion and Pomerol have lesser neighbours, which share some of their prestige through similar names. These so-called satellite districts are sources for much good-value wine, with some châteaux standing out for real quality. Montagne, Lussac, Puisseguin and St-Georges can all add '-St-Emilion' as a suffix to their names on wine labels. Most producers take full advantage of this. To the west of these satellites Lalande-de-Pomerol enjoys the benefit of incorporating its more famous cousin's name into its own. Lalande produces almost twice as much wine as Pomerol, and about two-thirds the annual amount made in Montagne-St-Emilion, the largest of the satellites.

Cross the Isle river west of Libourne and you arrive in the Fronsadais with its two appellations, Fronsac and Canon-Fronsac. Canon is a small enclave whose hilly slopes above the Dordogne provide the finest of settings for many leading vineyards of this district. The Fronsadais is a relatively small area – far smaller than St-Emilion and well below the two Pomerol appellations taken together – but it is currently riding high on the international stage.

In the cellars of Ch Pavie, St-Emilion

Together, these nine form the core of the Right Bank appellations and define the styles of wines made here; but they are surrounded by other ACs to the east and north-west, where leading Libournais producers are spreading their wings and improving the quality of many previously correct but unexciting wines. The first appellation to receive attention was Bordeaux-Côtes de Francs, a small and very attractive district east of the St-Emilion satellites that ends at the *département* boundary. In spite of its small production (even less than Fronsac) it has a number of châteaux which have already obtained a good reputation. To its south is the Côtes de Castillon, a far larger appellation, with both St-Emilion proper and its satellites as neighbours to its west. Here, too, attractive wines are being made.

Purely in terms of size, though, the Right Bank is easily dominated by the two northern appellations Bourg and Blaye, which together produce more than four million cases a year. Côtes de Bourg, on the banks of the Gironde and Dordogne, is by far the smaller, although it has more prestige – partly because its best vineyards are ideally located on hilly riverside slopes. The status of the Blayais, at almost 20,000 hectares one of Bordeaux's largest ACs, suffers somewhat because much of its white wine used to be of mediocre quality and was often made for distillation. Changes are afoot, however, and the white wines show improvement. Of the three Right Bank appellations entitled to produce whites as well as reds (the others being Bourg and Francs), the Blayais is the only one which yields whites in any quantity.

Bourg and Blaye are separated from the other Right Bank wine zones by a broad tract of land: wines here are only entitled to the generic Bordeaux appellations.

THE LANDSCAPES OF THE RIGHT BANK

While the landscape and viticulture of the Médoc and the Graves are built upon gravel, on the Right Bank it is limestone that dictates the shape of the countryside and the sites of the best vineyards. The limestone forms an incomplete (because eroded) top layer over thicker strata of the closely-related sandstone which French geologists call *molasse*. The limestone is in some places obvious, as in St-Emilion; at others it is buried well below the surface. However, it shapes the landscape, which is one of low plateaux bounded by quite steep slopes down to the river valleys of the Dordogne, Gironde and Isle. This is not to say that gravel is absent: the Right Bank underwent the same processes as the Médoc, and the ancient rivers deposited large amounts of gravel on top of the sub-strata. Gravel is important in some localities, such as the north-west of St-Emilion and in Pomerol. The limestone is in places also covered by wind-blown sand, and river valleys have typical alluvial soils.

The best place to see the limestone is St-Emilion, which is both built on and from this honey-coloured stone. The town's jumble of roofs and precipitous streets look down from the head of a valley cut in a long, steep slope. This is the scarp formed by the edge of the limestone plateau. This scarp, or *côte*, provides the site for many of the top châteaux of St-Emilion. Their vineyards lie on the plateau itself and on the slopes where it falls to the Dordogne valley. Under the châteaux you will often see cellars in old subterranean quarries dating from medieval times or earlier.

The limestone *côte* runs on to the west and east of the town: to the east it is discernible as far as the borders of Castillon. To the north, the limestone plateau slopes gently down towards the Isle valley, coming to an end halfway across St-Emilion. The north and north-west of St-Emilion, Pomerol and Lalande-de-Pomerol have gravel and gravel/clay soils on a bedrock of *molasse*.

Further west, limestone is again responsible for the hilly topography of Fronsac, and to the north forms the steep and complex landscapes of Bourg and Blaye. The St-Emilion satellites are on a mixed landscape, with some vineyards well-placed on a limestone plateau and others enjoying less favourable sandy or clay soils.

LIBOURNAIS & RIVE DROITE

37

34   ACs Bordeaux & Bordeaux
       Supérieur
38   St-Emilion
39   St-Emilion
40   Montagne-St-Emilion, Lussac-
       St-Emilion, Puisseguin-St-Emilion
       & St-Georges-St-Emilion
41   Pomerol
42   Pomerol
43   Lalande-de-Pomerol
44   Fronsac & Canon-Fronsac
45   Côtes de Castillon & Bordeaux-
       Côtes de Francs
46   Bourgeais & Blayais
47   Bourgeais & Blayais

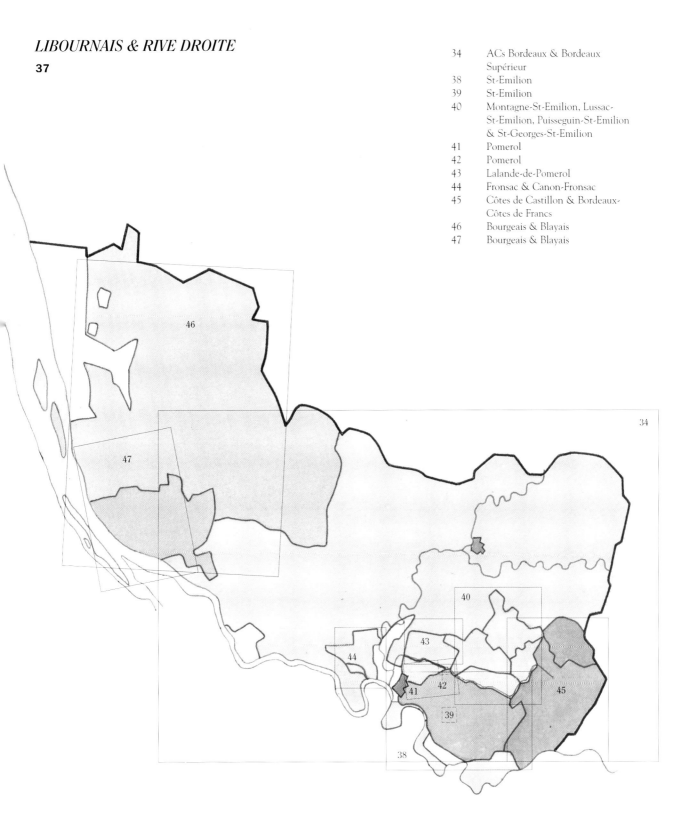

St-Emilion

MICHAEL BROADBENT

It never fails to surprise me how extraordinarily different are the vine-growing districts of Bordeaux: the relatively flat, elongated Médoc following the left bank of the broad Gironde estuary, the undulating mixed farmland, woods and suburbs of the Graves to the south of the City and a positively rural feel to Sauternes.

Then, on the right bank – not of the Gironde estuary, nor of the river Garonne but of the broad, deceptively placid Dordogne – the almost insignificant plateau of Pomerol, leading gently up through the St-Emilion vineyards to the most charming, characterful and attractive little town in the whole of the *département*, St-Emilion itself.

St-Emilion, the town

Incredible really, the contrast between the grimly grey, solidly handsome stone buildings of the vast city of Bordeaux and the warm-coloured stone walls and orange-tiled roofs crammed, higgeldy-piggeldy, either side of the twisting ginnels and the steep narrow streets of St-Emilion. The look, feel and atmosphere of this small fortified town, clinging to its hilltop, is more akin to Provence than Guyenne.

Not surprisingly the town is generally infested with tourists, but don't be put off. The medieval walls, the impressive tower from the top of which senior officers of the Jurade de St-Emilion proclaim the *ban de vendanges* – the official opening of the harvest – and the monolithic church alone are worth a visit.

There is one notable hotel and a number of small restaurants; also, alas, too many little shops competing with each other to sell smart corkscrews and other cellar and dining-table artefacts as well as bottles of wine. The town is entirely focused on its specialist subject – even, it seems to the visitor, to the exclusion of that other French fundamental, food. Where the locals buy provisions – other than the odd baguette – remains a well-hidden mystery; you can, however, discover all about the wines at the ballroom-sized information room, with its giant, light-up map of the area's hundreds of châteaux. The impression is strengthened when one ventures out into the surrounding countryside.

The vineyards, the châteaux and their proprietors

In common with Pomerol, it seems that virtually every bit of land in this fairly substantial district is devoted to the vine. Find one château, look over the wall – or a ditch – and one sees the vines of its neighbour. There is, I think, something very comforting about most of the châteaux themselves. As in Pomerol these are relatively modest in size, although some are minor architectural gems; and they appear to be lived in. At least someone is always in occupation, whether owner, manager or estate staff. Indeed, the impression is one of a large farming community devoted entirely to grape-growing and winemaking: a total contrast to the large, stately but often rather impersonal châteaux of the Médoc with their long history of absentee proprietors – and some of them, in these latter days, the property of large insurance companies and the like.

In St-Emilion there are literally hundreds of wine châteaux, ranging from *grands crus classés* across a bevy of familiar and much admired names to more modest establishments. All seem to be imbued with a more homely feel than elsewhere, and visitors (especially those who give prior notice) are generally warmly welcomed.

Right: the rooftops of St-Emilion

One St-Emilion curiosity, unique in the Gironde, is the practical use of old quarries – some dating back to Roman times. Instead of crudely gouging out stone and leaving vast holes in the landscape, the stone was excavated below ground. The resultant caves, their surprisingly shallow stone roofs supported by monolithic columns, are now used as cellars: cool and slightly damp. These all occur in the higher ground around the town and are well worth a visit. I well recall my first visit to the caves of Clos Fourtet, where condensation produced a thick mist, then seeing bones from an old cemetery piercing the cave roof at Château Beau-Séjour Bécot, and the roots of vines creeping through cracks in those of the cellars at Château Pavie.

ST-EMILION, THE DISTRICT

There are two ways of approaching St-Emilion from Bordeaux, both via Libourne. The first takes the low road which runs parallel to the Dordogne, the D670 – a rather fast, straight and dangerous road heading eastwards towards Castillon: turn sharp left at the hamlet of Bigaroux up to St-Emilion town itself.

The other route – more interesting and less hazardous – crosses Pomerol before going up through the heart of the St-Emilion district directly to the western edge of the town. On the map this road, the D243, is a sort of spine or backbone, traversing roughly 7.5 km from the western boundary of St-Emilion, climbing unobtrusively across the plateau, past the town to the hilly south-east edge of the district.

Stop the car midway and look either side: to your left and right, the north-east and south-west boundaries of the St-Emilion district are a mere 4.5 km apart at this point. The western extremity, behind you, adjoins Pomerol; indeed two of the finest châteaux, Cheval Blanc and Figeac, are only just within the St-Emilion boundary, the vineyards themselves virtually indistinguishable from those of Pomerol.

The Graves de St-Emilion plateau rises gently towards the east and south-east. Then, as can be seen from the contour lines of our maps, the eastern third of the district is quite hilly and appropriately known as the St-Emilion Côtes. 'Graves' is of course a reference to gravel; the Côtes are a limestone plateau and its attendant slopes.

THE WINES

The important thing to note is that only red wine is produced. Quality aside, there are basically two styles of wine made depending on which part of the district the grapes are grown. To the west, on the sandy, gravelly plateau adjacent to Pomerol, elegant, stylish wines are produced: these are epitomized by Château Cheval Blanc, one of the most consistent and delightful of all the great Growths of Bordeaux. Its neighbour Château Figeac also produces wines of high quality: very individual, sometimes idiosyncratic, but often with an unmatched flavour and fragrance due partly to the inclusion of a relatively high percentage of Cabernet Sauvignon grapes.

From the concentration of vineyards on the Côtes come looser-knit, fruity wines: perhaps more rustic, usually sweeter and often quite high in alcohol. They are occasionally referred to as the burgundies of Bordeaux – not without reason, for they are very amenable and relatively quick-maturing. The top Growth in this area is Château Ausone, which, though sharing with Cheval Blanc the highest classification, makes wine of a totally different character: very distinctive, but in some vintages something of an acquired taste.

Overall – First Growths excepted – the common denominator is value for money. The local guild, the Jurade de St-Emilion, is extremely active in promoting their wines, and I find their friendly individuality and unspoiled enthusiasm very contagious. These are wines for drinking, not for speculation or investment.

CLASSIFICATION

Unlike the wines of Pomerol, those of St-Emilion have been classified but, compared to the precision of the 1855 classification of the Gironde – essentially the Médoc – here there is a rather broader-brush approach.

Indeed, unlike the 1855 Classification, St-Emilion's system allows for regular revision. The latest classification is that of 1996: top of the tree are the thirteen *premier grand cru classé* estates of which two, Châteaux Ausone and Cheval Blanc, have the additional distinctive suffix 'A'. The next rung consists of 55 *grand cru classé* châteaux, with a supporting cast of literally hundreds rated *grand cru* – and this is not a classification, but a separate AC (see page 279). To use the words *grand cru*, a château must submit its wine each year to the appellation authorities. It is thus the wine, not the land, which has the classification. Considering that the greatest vineyards in Burgundy are rated *grand cru*, the next best being *premier cru*, one can understand a certain amount of confusion. In St-Emilion they err on the generous side!

SOIL AND VINES

Dominant varieties are Merlot and Cabernet Franc – known here, as in Pomerol, as Bouchet. The Merlot, accounting for over 60 per cent of the vines planted in St-Emilion, ripens early and gives the wine an appealing fleshy fruitiness. A small amount of Cabernet Sauvignon is grown, for example at Château Figeac it makes up 35

Vines wash right up to the walls of St-Emilion

per cent of the vineyard; but generally speaking Cabernet does not ripen well in the higher areas.

What makes St-Emilion so interesting – and its wines so different in character and style – is the extraordinary number of soil types, ranging from the gravel and sand of the sloping plateau to the west to the richer yet stony hillside sites of the south-east.

THE OUTSKIRTS OR SATELLITE DISTRICTS

There are four fairly important districts, all adjoining and lying to the north and north-east: St-Georges-St-Emilion, Montagne-St-Emilion, Lussac-St-Emilion, Puisseguin-St-Emilion. Set on generally rising ground, it is easy to drive into these areas without realizing that one has strayed out of St-Emilion. The wines they produce (red again) are agreeable, reasonably fruity, good value but lacking the finesse of the great Growths and the fragrant charm of those of St-Emilion proper.

Castillon, with a vineyard area which approaches that of St-Emilion, lies to the due east, the two towns being only 10 km apart. All of these districts are described in further chapters.

HISTORY OF ST-EMILION AND ITS WINES

The brief description of St-Emilion, the town, more than hints at its medieval past. The vineyards are in fact far older. Vines were planted and wines made in Roman times, by among others no less than the Latin poet Ausonius after whom Château Ausone is named.

From the 11th century until well beyond the Middle Ages, it was the wines from up the Dordogne rather than around Bordeaux itself that were the most popular and most generally traded. The riverside is still dotted with little ports – no more than jetties and mudbanks now. But the port of St-Emilion, overlooked and guarded by the fortified town itself, played a central role until Libourne rose to prominence, and, in its turn, was displaced by the riverside – this time the Garonne – port of Bordeaux itself.

St-Emilion was one of many important towns in the south-west of France on the medieval pilgrim route to Santiago de Compostela and, it is said, still prides itself on its hospitality.

The emergence of the great First Growths in the late 18th century, with their aristocratic following, was almost exclusively Left Bank, the more homely wines of St-Emilion making little headway throughout the 19th century. And until relatively recently it was less than a handful of châteaux that appeared on the international market, Ausone and Cheval Blanc heading the list then as now. Regarding Cheval Blanc, it is often said that this château first made its resounding reputation with the

St-Emilion's limestone shows in the soil and the roadside walls

admittedly great 1947, but this is not so. Throughout this century Cheval Blanc has been making wine of highly dependable quality, with quite a few star vintages: the 1921 was reputed to be the best of that hot year; 1926, more like a great Burgundy than the real thing – and that magnificent vintage 1929.

And, as mentioned earlier, not far below these heights are a wealth of attractive and reasonably priced reds. Why wait?

VINTAGES

Not surprisingly, as St-Emilion is joined on its western side to Pomerol, vintages follow a similar pattern. Unlike those of Pomerol which were virtually unknown prior to 1945 to the British trade and comfortably off consumers, St-Emilion was a constant source of pleasant and inexpensive wines – save for Ausone, which had the oldest reputation, and Cheval Blanc the most consistent. The same more or less applies to this day. Château Ausone houses an impressive cellar of old vintages of

which I recall a complete, though faded and reduced, 1847. A comprehensive tasting of seventy-six vintages in New Orleans opened up with a perfect 1877: delicate, ideal weight, texture and balance; the 1879 rich, soft; 1894 reflecting a mediocre year; some poor bottles of great vintages like 1900. It seemed to show best in good but otherwise tired vintages like 1911, 1916 and in particular 1918, but also predictably good in the top vintages of the almost unbeatable decade of the 1920s, notably 1921 (particularly successful in this difficult, over-hot year), 1924, 1926, and 1928. Not as good as Cheval Blanc in the admittedly few decent vintages in the 1930s, but some surprisingly fine wartime bottles: 1942, 1943. A disappointing 1945, good 1947, variable 1949 – then, in my opinion, uneven since, and under-performing until very recent vintages.

Cheval Blanc, as I've already said, has been more dependable. The oldest vintage I have tasted is the 1893, so beautiful a wine that my table companion, Jacques Hébrard, now retired, was reduced to tears. The 1908 tasted at the château was also excellent, the 1911 from Rothschild private cellars lean and long, the 1920 at best superb, the 1921 magnificent – the best of that vintage, the 1926 unbelievably rich, the 1929 one of the greatest. It was even good in the 1930s. Then that glorious postwar trio: 1945, the incomparable 1947 (I am almost ashamed to say that I have tasted and drunk this some thirty times since the mid 1950s) – and perfectly reflecting the true quality of every vintage since. The 1966 superbly elegant, 1970 perfection now, 1982 magnificent, 1985 lovely. One could go on...

Figeac is more unpredictable but often more exciting. The oldest tasted was the lovely though faded 1900, a curious 1905, a tart 1906, gentle 1911. Good (but not as good as Cheval Blanc) in the 1920s, dismal in the 1930s, superb in 1947 and 1949, excellent in 1953 and 1955. By the 1960s its high Cabernet Sauvignon content noticeable, particularly in the glorious 1961; excellent 1962, and 1964, beautiful 1966, exciting 1970, uneven 1975, plausible 1976, and good wine in the marvellous decade of the 1980s, particularly the 1989 and 1990.

One of the most consistently well made is Château Canon. I recall an 1892 at a Sunday lunch with Mme. Teysonneau in Bordeaux after checking her cellar. The wine, like an old lady, fragile but with a twinkling eye. Then an unusually good 1937 and the predictable post-war vintages, to date. Its companion on the Côtes, Pavie, was a much less distinguished performer until the mid 1960s. But it really took off in the late 1970s, producing a delicious 1978, good 1981, impressive 1982, excellent 1985 and – subject to vintages – has been an above-par, reliable performer since.

Here is a summary of the best vintages of St-Emilion since 1920: the 1921, 1926, 1928, 1929, 1934, 1937, 1945, 1947, 1949, 1952, 1953, 1955, 1959, 1961, 1964, 1970, 1971, 1976, 1981, 1982, 1985, 1986, 1988, 1989, 1990 – and better in 1993 than the Médocs.

MY PERSONAL FAVOURITES

Unquestionably Château Cheval Blanc for its sheer consistency, beauty and elegance. My favourite vintages here are 1921, 1926, 1929, 1947 of course, 1949, 1966, 1970 and 1971, 1982, 1985, 1988-1990. Next, Château Canon for consistency; for idiosyncratic excitement and character Château Figeac, and the more recent vintages of Château Pavie.

Then, in alphabetical order, Châteaux Beau-Séjour Bécot, Canon la Gaffelière, La Dominique, La Gaffelière, Larmande, Magdelaine and Trotte Vieille.

The steep streets of St-Emilion with, in the distance, the tower from which the start of the vintage is proclaimed

---

THE APPELLATIONS

ST-EMILION AND ST-EMILION GRAND CRU
(red)

Location: Large Right-Bank area slightly south-east of Pomerol; the town of St-Emilion itself approximately 35 km from the centre of Bordeaux. To the north are the other ACs of the St-Emilion jurade, to the east the Côtes de Castillon. St-Emilion Grand Cru is an AC, not a classification. To benefit from this AC, châteaux must apply for the agrément each year and the wine is assessed by the AC authorities.
Area of AC: 7,174 ha
Area under vine: 5,439 ha
Communes: St-Emilion, St-Hippolyte, St-Christophe-des-Bardes, St-Laurent-des-Combes, St-Pey-d'Armens, St-Sulpice-de-Faleyrens, Vignonet, St-Etienne-de-Lisse and a clearly defined part of Libourne.

Average annual production: 2,770,800 cases
Classed growths: 68 (2 premiers grands crus classés 'A', 11 premiers grands crus classés 'B', 55 grands crus classés). With one or two exceptions, all these classed growths are located in the commune of St-Emilion itself.
Others: Approximately 580, including hundreds of unclassified grands crus. Growers must apply annually for the right to use this AC for their wine.
Cooperatives: 1 (c. 210 members)
Main grape varieties: Merlot
Others: Cabernet Franc (Bouchet), Cabernet Sauvignon
Main soil types: Wide variety, including clay-limestone, gravel. The plateau of limestone outcrops in the south, around the town; in the north-west the limestone is overlaid by clay and gravel.

APPELLATION ST-EMILION

Above: Ch Angélus

Above: Ch Ausone

Ch Angélus
map 38/L F8

1er grand cru classé B
owner: Famille de Boüard de Laforest *area:* 26 ha
cases: 10,000 *grape % R:* MER 50% CF 45% CS 5%
second wine: Le Carillon de l'Angélus *other*
châteaux owned: Ch de Francs *(Bordeaux Côtes de
Francs)*
**33330 St-Emilion tel: 05 57 24 71 39
fax: 05 57 24 68 56**

In 1909 Maurice de Boüard de Laforest set
himself up in St-Emilion, having inherited the
Ch Mazerat wine estate. Fifteen years later the
3 ha of neighbouring Angélus were added to it,
and after the Second World War his three sons
decided to market the wine from the two
vineyards as Ch Angélus. Today the quality of
the Angélus wine is in the upper echelons of St-
Emilion, if not of all Bordeaux. This is due to
dynamic, high-quality management, which
began in 1980 and culminated about a decade
later in the building of an ultra-modern
fermentation hall and an impressive cask cellar.
The wine matures for at least 18 months in
barriques; of which 70-100% are new.
Concentration, generosity, body, luscious fruit,
abundant tannins and spicy, smoky, noble oak
have characterized the vintages from 1989.
Angélus is generosity bottled.

Ch de l'Annonciation
map 38/L C8

grand cru
owner: Bruno Callegarin *area:* 4.6 ha *cases:* 2,727
grape % R: MER 34% CF 33% CS 33%
33330 St-Emilion tel: 05 57 51 74 50
Red and black currant fruit – from the large
proportion of Cabernet – and a reasonable
roundness underpinned by oak are the qualities
of this St-Emilion: a decent wine, with a fairly
long finish.

Ch Arnaud de Jacquemeau
map 38/L E7

owner: Denis Dupuy *area:* 4 ha *cases:* 3,900 *grape
% R:* MER 55% CS 25% MAL 15% CF 5%
33330 St-Emilion tel: 05 57 24 73 09
A flavoursome, though not spectacular, wine, its
pleasant bouquet showing elements of fresh
fruit, mint and cloves. This château has been
owned by the same family for five generations.

Ch l'Arrosée
map 38/L G8

grand cru classé
owner: François Rodhain *area:* 10 ha *cases:* 4,250
grape % R: MER 55% CS 30% CF 15%
**33330 St-Emilion
tel: 05 57 24 70 47**
In the 19th century this vineyard belonged to
Pierre Magne, minister and adviser to Napoléon
III; the emperor visited the estate. The château
is beautifully sited on the western part of the
St-Emilion *côte*. During much of the twentieth
century the Ch l'Arrosée wine was vinified at
the nearby cooperative, which resulted in an
unremarkable product. In 1966, however, the
owners started to do their own winemaking
once more – successfully, for today their wine is
a very respected *grand cru classé*. In great years
the vineyard,which is steeply sloping in parts
and boasts a large number of old vines,
produces a concentrated wine, rich in fruit –
black and red currants, plum, cherry – with
spices, vanilla and firm, ripe tannins. Examples
of such years are 1990 and 1994. The wine is a
little less impressive in average vintages, but
still of a high standard even then.

Below: Ch Balestard la Tonnelle

Ch Ausone
map 38/L G9

1er grand cru classé A
owner: Indivision Dubois-Challon-Vauthier *area:* 7.3
ha *cases:* 2,000 *grape % R:* MER 60% CF 40% *other
châteaux owned:* include Ch Belair *(St-Emilion)*; Ch
Moulin Saint-Georges *(St-Emilion)*
33330 St-Emilion tel: 05 57 24 70 26
This château derives its name from the Roman
poet and consul Ausonius, although it is by no
means certain that his villa stood on this site.
The Roman would certainly have enjoyed living
here, however: the château is set on the edge of
a high, vine-clad plateau that gives a splendid
view out over the St-Emilion hills. After a
comparatively poor period from the late 1940s
to the mid-1970s, Ausone's wines rose to the
top again. This was thanks to the arrival in
1975 of a new *régisseur*, Pascal Delbeck, who
made optimum use of this small vineyard with
its many old vines. When young, this St-
Emilion is usually reserved, even introvert, with
substantial tannins: a wine that by definition
needs to mature – usually for 15-20 years. Only
then does it show its true greatness: it is as if a
treasure-house of subtle nuances had been

Above: Ch Béard

opened up: seductive, ripe red or black currants, toast from the oak, exotic spice, mineral aromas. No other St-Emilion has so much Médoc-like style and refinement.

Clos Badon
map 38/L H10

owner: GFA Badon Guérin/Philippe Dugos *area:* 8.5 ha *cases:* 4,400 *grape % R:* MER 52% CF 40% CS 8%
33330 St-Emilion tel: 05 57 24 71 03
fax: 05 57 24 71 03
The standard wine here is usually juicy, somewhat undemanding, with some tannin, but not too much meat or depth. There is more strength, concentration and, in particular, oak in the Ch Badon Vieux Ceps, a specially-selected tenth of the vintage, matured for 15 months in new barrels.

Ch Balestard la Tonnelle
map 38/R E1

grand cru classé
owner: GFA Capdemourlin *area:* 10.6 ha *cases:* 5,000 *grape % R:* MER 65% CF 20% CS 10% MAL 5%
second wine: Chanoine de Balestard *other châteaux owned:* Ch Cap de Mourlin *(St-Emilion)*; Ch Petit-Faurie-de-Soutard *(St-Emilion)*; Ch Roudier *(Montagne-St-Emilion)*
33330 St-Emilion tel: 05 57 74 62 06
fax: 05 57 24 74 35
'A divine nectar, which bears the name of Balestard' is how the 15th-century poet François Villon celebrated this St-Emilion. The history of the estate certainly goes back a long way. 'Tonnelle' was added to the name because of an old round tower on the estate, used nowadays for receptions. The wine is very reliable, and is generally characterized by solid colour and tannins, a full-bodied, muscular taste and aromatic, fruity tones – suggesting black and red fruits; and dark notes of licorice, chocolate and truffle.

Ch Barberousse
map 38/L J10

owner: GAEC J. Puyol & Fils *area:* 7 ha *cases:* 5,000 *grape % R:* MER 70% CF 15% CS 15% *other châteaux owned:* Ch Lamothe Belair *(Bergerac)*
33330 St-Emilion tel: 05 57 24 74 24
fax: 05 57 24 62 77
Solidly-built, sound St-Emilion with dark fruit notes and nicely integrated oak; it matures for a year in cask, a third of them new.

Ch Barrail des Graves
map 38/L K8

owner: Gérard Descrambe *area:* 5.6 ha *cases:* 3,500 *grape % R:* MER 60% CS 40% *other châteaux owned:* Ch Renaissance *(Bordeaux)*
33330 St-Sulpice-de-Faleyrens tel: 05 57 74 94 77
fax: 05 57 74 97 49
This organically-farmed flat vineyard near the Dordogne yields an engaging, middle-range wine with a fruity-cum-animal aroma. Its labels, sometimes drawn by famous cartoonists like Wolinski, tend to be more striking than the wine itself.

Ch du Barry
map 38/L L7

grand cru
owner: Daniel Mouty *area:* 8 ha *cases:* 6,600 *grape % R:* MER 80% CS 20% *second wine:* Ch Tour Renaissance *other châteaux owned:* Ch Haut-Brégnet *(St-Emilion)*; Ch de Mons *(Bordeaux)*; Ch Rambaud *(Bordeaux Supérieur)*; Ch de Barre *(Bordeaux Supérieur)*
33330 St-Sulpice-de-Faleyrens tel: 05 57 84 55 88
fax: 05 57 74 92 99
Superior *grand cru* that derives its quality from its gravel vineyard and the 18 months it spends

Below: Ch Beauséjour

in barrels, 30% of which are bought new for each vintage. Notwithstanding its supple taste, it has ageing potential.

Ch Béard
map 38/R H3

grand cru
owner: Héritiers Goudichaud *area:* 8 ha *cases:* 3,750 *grape % R:* MER 60% CF 25% CS 15%
33330 St-Laurent-des-Combes tel: 05 57 24 72 96
fax: 05 57 24 61 88
A wine with character and class: spices, animal elements, alcohol, good acidity, firm tannins and nicely integrated oak. Matures well. The château dates from 1858.

Ch Beauséjour
map 38/L F8

1er grand cru classé D
owner: Jean-Michel Dubos *area:* 7 ha *cases:* 3,000 *grape % R:* MER 55% CF 30% CS 15% *second wine:* La Croix de Mazerat
33330 St-Emilion tel: 05 57 24 71 61
fax: 05 57 74 48 40
Intensity is the hallmark nowadays of this great St-Emilion; intensity of colour and taste, and mature tannins in its finish. This wine from the heirs of Duffau-Lagarosse seldom offers exuberance, but the nuances are truly and profoundly there: red and black currant fruit, prune, licorice, spice, vanilla and toasty oak. This property used to form a single estate with Beau-Séjour Bécot; the partition took place in 1869 when its owner, M. Ducarpe, divided the vineyard between his two children.

Ch Beau-Séjour Bécot
map 38/L F8

1er grand cru classé B
owner: Gérard & Dominique Bécot *area:* 16.5 ha *cases:* 8,000 *grape % R:* MER 70% CF 24% CS 6% *second wine:* Tournelle des Moines *other châteaux owned:* Ch La Gomerie *(St-Emilion)*; Ch Grand-Pontet *(St-Emilion)*
33330 St-Emilion tel: 05 57 74 46 87
fax: 05 57 24 66 88
The wine from this château is among the élite of St-Emilion. This is due not to the perfectly equipped, modern *cuverie*, nor to the rock cellars or the large proportion of new barrels (a third to a half), but to its intrinsic, faultless quality. That quality continued to improve after Beau-Séjour Bécot was demoted from *premier*

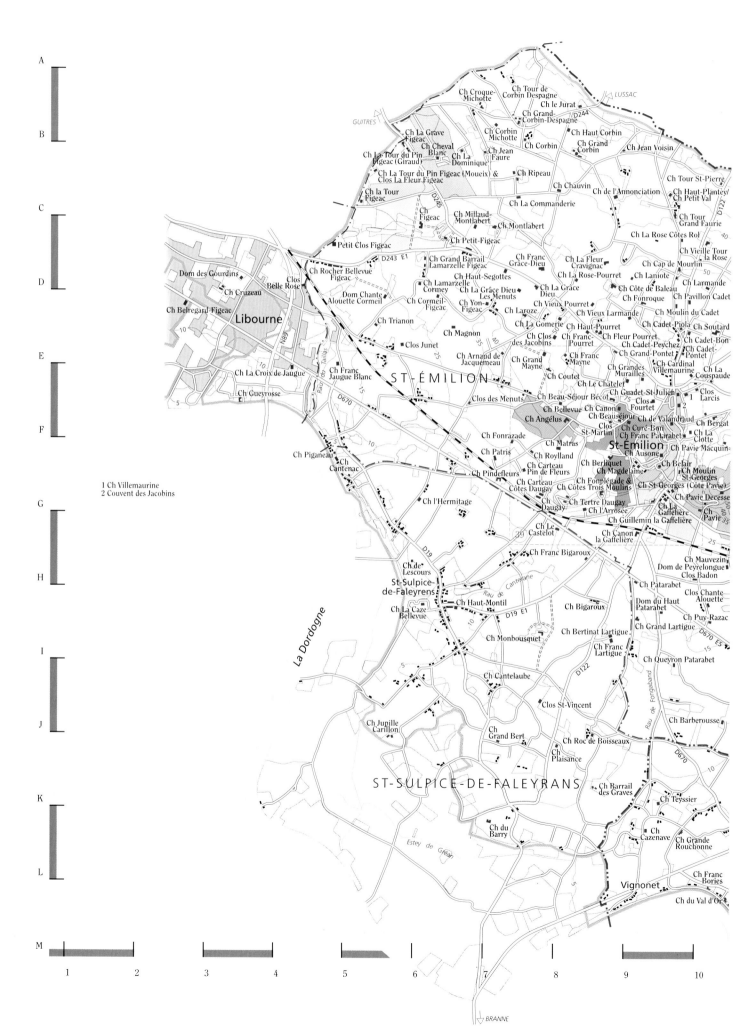

A

B

C

D

E

F

1 Ch Villemaurine
2 Couvent des Jacobins

G

H

I

J

K

L

M

1   2   3   4   5   6   7   8   9   10

GUITRES

LUSSAC

Ch Croque-Michotte
Ch Tour de Corbin Despagne
Ch le Jurat
Ch Grand-Corbin-Despagne
D244
Ch La Grave Figeac
Ch Cheval Blanc
Ch Corbin Michotte
Ch Haut Corbin
Ch Grand Corbin
Ch La Tour du Pin Figeac (Giraud)
Ch La Dominique
Ch Jean Faure
Ch Corbin
Ch Jean Voisin
Ch La Tour du Pin Figeac (Moueix) & Clos La Fleur Figeac
Ch Ripeau
Ch Tour St-Pierre
Ch la Tour Figeac
Ch Chauvin
Ch de l'Annonciation
Ch Haut-Plantey
Ch Petit Val
D122
D245
Ch La Commanderie
Ch Tour Grand Faurie
Ch Figeac
Ch Millaud-Montlabert
Ch Montlabert
Ch La Rose Côtes Rol
40
Petit Clos Figeac
Ch Petit-Figeac
Ch Grand Barrail Lamarzelle Figeac
Ch Franc Grâce-Dieu
Ch La Fleur Cravignac
Ch Cap de Mourlin
Ch Vieille Tour la Rose
D243 E1
D670
Ch Rocher Bellevue Figeac
Ch Haut-Segottes
Ch La Rose-Pourret
Ch Laniote
Ch Larmande
Dom des Gourdins
Clos Belle Rose
Ch Lamarzelle Cormey
Ch La Grâce Dieu
Ch La Grâce Dieu Les Menuts
Ch Côte de Baleau
Ch Fonroque
Ch Pavillon Cadet
Ch Cruzeau
Dom Chante Alouette Cormeil
Ch Cormeil-Figeac
Ch Yon-Figeac
Ch Vieux Pourret
Ch Vieux Larmande
Ch Moulin du Cadet
Ch Belregard-Figeac
Ch Trianon
Ch Laroze
Ch La Gomerie
Ch Haut-Pourret
Ch Cadet-Piola
Ch Soutard
Libourne
Ch Magnon
Ch Clos des Jacobins
Ch Franc-Pourret
Ch Fleur Pourret
Ch Cadet-Bon
Ch Cadet-Peychez
Ch Cadet-Pontet
10
Clos Junet
Ch Arnaud de Jacquemeau
Ch Grand Mayne
Ch Franc Mayne
Ch Grand-Pontet
Ch Grandes Murailles
Ch Cardinal Villemaurine
Ch La Couspaude
25
ST-ÉMILION
Ch Coutet
Ch Le Chatelet
Ch La Croix de Jaugue
Ch Franc Jaugue Blanc
40
Ch Beau-Séjour Bécot
Ch Guadet-St-Julien
Clos Larcis
Ch Gueyrosse
Clos des Menuts
Ch Bellevue
Ch Canon
Clos Fourtet
1   2
5
Ch Angélus
Ch Beauséjour
Ch de Valandraud
Ch Bergat
75
Clos St-Martin
Ch Curé-Bon
Ch Franc Patarabet
Ch La Clotte
Ch Fonrazade
Ch Matras
St-Émilion
Ch Pavie Macquin
Ch Piganeau
Ch Patris
Ch Ausone
Ch Cantenac
Ch Roylland
Ch Berliquet
Ch Belair
Ch Carteau Pin de Fleurs
Ch Magdelaine
Ch Moulin St-Georges
10
Ch Pindefleurs
Ch Carteau Côtes Daugay
Ch Fonplégade &
Ch Côtes Trois Moulins
Ch St-Georges (Côte Pavie)
Ch l'Hermitage
Ch Tertre Daugay
Ch Pavie Decesse
Ch Daugay
Ch l'Arrosée
Ch La Gaffelière
Ch Pavie
50
Ch Le Castelot
39
Ch Guillemin la Gaffelière
35
D19
Ch Canon la Gaffelière
25
Ch Franc Bigaroux
Ch Mauvezin
Ch de Lescours
Dom de Peyrelongue
Clos Badon
St-Sulpice-de-Faleyrens
Rau de Cantelane
Ch Patarabet
Clos Chante Alouette
Ch Haut-Montil
Ch Bigaroux
Dom du Haut Patarabet
Ch La Caze Bellevue
D19 E1
Ch Puy-Razac
Ch Bertinat Lartigue
Ch Grand Lartigue
D670 E5
Ch Monbousquet
Ch Franc Lartigue
Ch Queyron Patarabet
La Dordogne
5
Ch Cantelaube
D122
Rau de Fongaband
Clos St-Vincent
Ch Barberousse
Ch Jupille Carillon
Ch Grand Bert
Ch Roc de Boisseaux
D670
Ch Plaisance
ST-SULPICE-DE-FALEYRANS
Ch Barrail des Graves
Ch Teyssier
10
Ch du Barry
Ch Cazenave
Ch Grande Rouchonne
Estey de Gréan
Ch Franc Bories
Vignonet
5
Ch du Val d'Or
BRANNE

RIVE DROITE

MEDOC

Libourne

Bordeaux

ENTRE-DEUX-
MERS

GRAVES &
SAUTERNES

1:41,700

0   1   2km

N

LUSSAC

Ch Trimoulet

Ch La Fleur
Ch La Rose-
Trimoulet

Ch Laplagnotte-
Bellevue

Ch
Champion

Ch Milon &
Clos de la Cure

Ch Le Loup

Ch Dassault

Ch Rol de
Fombrauge

Clos des
Moines

Ch Faurie de
Souchard

Clos de
l'Oratoire

ST-CHRISTOPHE-DES-BARDES

Ch du Cauze

Ch Petit-Faurie-
de-Soutard
Ch Balestard
la Tonelle

Ch Vieux
Sarpe

St-Christophe-des-
Bardes

Ch Fombrauge

Ch
Grangey

Ch Haut-Sarpe
Clos de Sarpe

Vieux Ch
Pelletan

Ch
Sansonnet

Ch Coudert
Pelletan

Ch Tauzinat
l'Hermitage

Ch Trotte
Vieille

Ch
Rocheyron

Ch de
Cantin

Ch Jacquemineau

Ch Le
Prieuré

Ch Tour
St-Christophe

Ch Laroque

Clos
Labarde

Ch Boutisse

Ch Puyblanquet
Carille

Ch Fleur Cardinale

Ch Haut-Villet

Ch Troplong-
Mondot

Ch Haut-Bruly

Ch Côte
Puyblanquet

Ch Puy-Blanquet

Ch Bellile-Mondotte

Ch Tourans

ST-ETIENNE-DE-LISSE

Ch Mangot

Ch Tour
Baladoz

Ch de Ferrand

Ch Destieux

Ch Tertre
Roteboeuf

Ch de Pressac

Ch Lareis
Ducasse

St-Laurent-des-
Combes

Vieux Ch Haut-Béard

St-Hippolyte

St-Etienne-de-
Lisse

Ch du Calvaire

Ch Faugères

Ch La Clusière

Ch de Candale

Ch Bernateau

Ch Haut
Rocher

Ch Béard

Dom de la
Vieille Eglise

Ch Viramière

Ch Rozier

Dom du
Sable

Ch Lassègue

Ch Lamartre

Ch Paran
Justice

ST-HIPPOLYTE

Ch Franc Pipeau
Descombes

Ch Jacques Blanc

Ch Fleur de
Lisse

Ch du Rocher

Ch
Peyrelongue

Ch
Pipeau

Ch Monlot Capet

Ch Capet-Guillier

ST-LAURENT-
DES-
COMBES

Ch
Piney

Ch Haute Nauve

Ch Bellefont-
Belcier

Ch de
Guilhemmanson

Ch Capet
Duverger

Ch Darius

Ch Rastouillet
Lescure

Ch Billerond

Ch du
Vieux-Guinot

Ch La
Couronne

Ch Juguet

Ch de St-Pey

Ch St-Lô

St-Pey-
d'Armens

Ch La Bonnelle

Ch l'Eglise d'Armens

VIGNONET

Ch la
Boisserie

Ch Bonnet

Ch
Peyrouquet

BERGERAC

ST-PEYS-D'ARMENS

Clos Gerbaud

Ch Hautes-Graves
d'Arthus

Ch Quercy

Ch Vieux
Labarthe

Micouleau

Ch du
Paradis

VILLEFRANCHE-DE-
LONCHAT

Ausone

Angélus

Beau Séjour-Bécot

Belair

Canon

Figeac

Cheval Blanc

La Gaffelière

Magdelaine

Pavie

Beauséjour

Trotte Vieille

Clos Fourtet

La Tour Figeac

Other vineyards

Woods

AC St-Émilion

Rest of vineyards shown
are AC Bordeaux

Commune boundary

Canton boundary

Contour line

status to *grand cru classé* in 1985, until it was at last reinstated in 1996. Generally Beau-Séjour Bécot's wine reveals itself through its fruit – redolent of blackcurrant jam – which is firmly contained in smoky, toasted oak, with a good dose of alcohol and noble tannins. A delightful combination of concentration and complexity.

Ch Belair
map 38/L G9

1er grand cru classé B
owner: Helyett Dubois-Challon *area:* 12.6 ha *cases:* 5,000 *grape % R:* MER 70% CF 30% *other châteaux owned:* Ch Ausone (*St-Emilion*); Ch Tour du Pas St-Georges (*St-Georges-St-Emilion*); Ch Graves de Moustey (*Bordeaux*); Domaine Challon (*Bordeaux*)
33330 St-Emilion tel: 05 57 24 70 94
fax: 05 57 24 67 11

This château is very close to Ausone, on the same limestone hill which forms the crest of the St-Emilion *côte*. What is more, the wine is made by the same team, for the part-owner of Ausone is sole proprietor here. Here, too, the wine has improved in quality since the arrival of *régisseur* Delbeck, albeit less spectacularly. Belair is rather more angular, more austere, leaner than Ausone. Breeding and style are here, however, and rich fruit; you also seem to taste the underlying rock in its coolly mineral undertone. And of course the wood comes into play: the wine spends 18 months maturing in *barriques*, of which half are bought new for each vintage.

Ch Bellecombe
map 38/L

owner: Jean-Marc Carteyron *area:* 3 ha *cases:* 1,450 *grape % R:* MER 90% CF 10% *other châteaux owned:* Ch Haut-Brana (*Bordeaux*)
33330 Vignonet tel: 05 56 78 10 26
fax: 05 56 78 10 26

Fairly rounded wine, usually low in acidity. Distinctive bouquet; a little earthy, but not unpleasant. Matured in wood.

Ch Bellefont-Belcier
map 38/R I1

owner: Jean Labusquière *area:* 12.4 ha *cases:* 6,250 *grape % R:* MER 83% CF 10% CS 7%
33330 St-Laurent-des-Combes tel: 05 57 24 72 16
fax: 05 57 74 45 06

Decent, likeable, particularly dark-toned wine that is firm without being really exciting or having great depth.

Below: Ch Berliquet

Above: Ch Belair

Clos Belle Rose
map 38/L D4

owner: François Faurie *area:* 0.9 ha *cases:* 380 *grape % R:* MER 75% CF 15% CS 9% MAL 1% *second wine:* Domaine de la Jalousie
33500 Libourne tel: 05 57 74 15 57

A miniature vineyard in the town of Libourne itself, close to the swimming pool and surrounded by apartment blocks. In good years the wine is supple and tasty; in great years rounded, decently concentrated and with ripe fruit. Very good for its ordinary St-Emilion status.

Ch Bellevue
map 38/L F8

grand cru classé
owner: Famille de Coninck *area:* 6 ha *cases:* 3,000 *grape % R:* MER 67% CF 16.5% CS 16.5% *other châteaux owned:* Ch Canon (*Canon-Fronsac*); Ch Junayme (*Canon-Fronsac*); Ch Vray Canon Boyer (*Canon-Fronsac*); Ch du Pintey (*Bordeaux Supérieur*)
33330 St-Laurent-des-Combes tel: 05 57 51 06 07
fax: 05 57 51 59 61

This property belonged to the Lacaze family for some three centuries, from 1642, before it was sold to their cousins, the Horeau family. In good vintages its vineyards, which lie on high ground, produce a meaty wine, firmly based on

Above: Ch Bellevue

tannins and with aspects of both black fruits (cherries, prunes) and oak. Nor does this *grand cru classé* disappoint in lesser years – it is simply more elegant then. Each year the owners replace a third to a half of the barrels for the wine's 12-18 months in cask.

Ch Bellile-Mondotte
map 38/R G2

grand cru
owner: GFA Héritiers Escure *area:* 4.5 ha *cases:* 2,500 *grape % R:* MER 60% CF 20% CS 20% *other châteaux owned:* Ch Grand-Pey-Lescours (*St-Emilion*)
33330 St-Emilion tel: 05 57 51 07 59

Agreeable, bold, open wine with not a great deal of fruit, but with tobacco, caramel, and slight impressions of spice.

Ch Belregard-Figeac
map 38/L E2

grand cru
owner: GAEC Pueyo Frères *area:* 4.2 ha *cases:* 2,500 *grape % R:* MER 70% CF 25% CS 5% *second wine:* Ch La Fleur Garderose
33500 Libourne tel: 05 57 51 71 12
fax: 05 57 51 82 88

Normally an expertly-made St-Emilion, with supple tannins, firmness and spicy oak.

Ch Bergat
map 38/L F10

grand cru classé
owner: Indivision Castéja-Preben-Hansen *area:* 4 ha *cases:* 1,500 *grape % R:* MER 55% CF 35% CS 10% *other châteaux owned:* include Ch Trotte Vieille (*St-Emilion*); Ch Batailley (*Pauillac*)
33330 St-Emilion tel: 05 57 24 71 34

Charming wine with a reasonable amount of body, fruit suggesting jam (blackberry, blackcurrants). Since 1990 its quality seems to be rising slightly.

Ch Berliquet
map 38/L G8

grand cru classé
owner: Patrick de Lesquen *area:* 9 ha *cases:* 4,200 *grape % R:* MER 67% CF 25% CS 8% *second wine:* Les Ailes de Berliquet
33330 St-Emilion tel: 05 57 24 70 71
fax: 05 57 24 65 18

Wine from a plateau vineyard which shows discreet notes of red and black fruits, oak, spices – but it is somewhat lacking in fullness, depth, length, and therefore class. It is made under the supervision of the cooperative.

Ch Bernateau — map 38/R H5
grand cru
owner: Régis Lavau *area:* 16.5 ha *cases:* 6,250
grape % R: MER 80% CF 15% CS 5% *second wine:* Ch
Tour Peyronneau
**33330 St-Etienne-de-Lisse tel: 05 57 40 18 19
fax: 05 57 40 27 31**
Estate that has been in the same family for
about two centuries. The wine is solid, with
considerable bayleaves and spices. Due to its
initially rather bitter tannins, it usually requires
some years' bottle-ageing. It spends 6–12
months in barrel.

Ch Bertinat Lartigue — map 38/L I8
owner: Danielle & Richard Dubois *area:* 5.5 ha
cases: 3,000 *grape % R:* MER 80% CS 10% CF 10%
other châteaux owned: include Clos de la Vieille
Eglise *(Côtes de Castillon)*; Vieux Château Gréan
(Bordeaux)
**33330 St-Sulpice-de-Faleyrens tel: 05 57 24 72 75
fax: 05 57 74 45 43**
This belongs to a husband and wife team – both
oenologists. Pure, successful wine, with quite a
lot of fruit and not lacking dark aromas.
Altogether balanced, and uncomplicatedly
delicious. The Ch Orisse du Casse is a superior
version, a *grand cru* made with the best grapes
(70-93% Merlot) from the best plots: at least
half are on gravel. It has 8-18 months in new
oak, sometimes making the wood rather
dominant; without being highly complex, this is
a meaty, firm wine with ageing potential – and
it is also reliable in lesser years.

Ch Bigaroux — map 38/L I8
grand cru
owner: Bernard Dizier *area:* 15 ha *cases:* 8,500
grape % R: MER 70% CF 15% CS 12% MAL 3% *second
wine:* Ch Lartigue Naude *other châteaux owned:* Ch
Haut Durandet *(Bordeaux Supérieur)*
**33330 St-Sulpice-de-Faleyrens tel: 05 57 24 71 97
fax: 05 57 74 45 01**
Estate beside the Libourne-Castillon road which
makes a mellow St-Emilion, a wine with some
style, nuance and roundness to it.

Ch Billerond — map 38/R J3
owner: GFA du Ch Billerond/Famille Robin *area:* 11
ha *cases:* 5,500 *grape % R:* MER 69% CF 21% CS 10%
**33330 St-Hippolyte tel: 05 57 24 70 71
fax: 05 57 24 65 18**

◆ St-Emilion past and present
The St-Emilion Appellation Contrôlée zone
covers nine communes, including St-Emilion
itself and the south-eastern part of
Libourne. This is the zone delineated by the
Jurade in the Middle Ages.

The Libourne portion was once a separate
AC, Sables-St-Emilion. This now-defunct
appellation was withdrawn in 1973. These
vineyards are now within the St-Emilion
appellation.

It used to be commonplace to split St-
Emilion into 'Graves' and 'Côtes' wines, the
former coming from the western, sand and
gravel, side of the appellation.

Until 1936 the 'satellite' communes used
the name St-Emilion: they now have their
own appellations.

A generally balanced wine of average structure,
good-tasting but not very complex. Usually
develops quite quickly. Not aged in wood.
Vinified by the cooperative.

Ch la Boisserie — map 38/R K4
grand cru
owner: Pierrette & Louis Boisserie *area:* 6 ha
cases: 3,540 *grape % R:* MER 80% CF 12% CS 8%
**33330 St-Pey-d'Armens tel: 05 57 24 70 71
fax: 05 57 24 65 18**
Supple, reasonably mouthfilling wine produced
by the cooperative. Short, and a little bitter on
the aftertaste, but otherwise enjoyable.

Ch La Bonnelle — map 38/R K5
grand cru
owner: SCEA des Vignobles Sulzer *area:* 10 ha
cases: 4,800 *grape % R:* MER 70% CF 20% CS 10%
second wine: Ch La Croix Bonnelle
**33330 St-Pey-d'Armens tel: 05 57 47 15 12
fax: 05 57 47 16 83**
The taste is nicely framed by a measure of oak,
but this St-Emilion, which can be enjoyed
readily enough, does not stand out in character
or complexity. This château is associated with
the St-Emilion cooperative.

Ch Bonnet — map 38/R K4
grand cru
owner: Roger Bonnet *area:* 23.5 ha *cases:* 12,000
grape % R: MER 55% CF 27% CS 16% MAL 2% *second
wine:* Ch La Fleur Bonnet *other
wines:* Bordeaux Clairet
**33330 St-Pey-d'Armens tel: 05 57 47 15 23
fax: 05 57 47 12 95**
At this respected family estate a wine full of
flavour on an oak foundation is produced from
vines with an average age of 25 years. The
Réserve du Château brings greater power and
concentration; it spends not the usual 12 or 14
months, but two whole years maturing in cask.

Ch Boutisse — map 38/R G5
owner: Jean-François Carrille *area:* 15 ha *cases:*
7,000 *grape % R:* MER 70% CS 25% CF 5% *second
wine:* Ch Vieux Guadet *other châteaux owned:* Ch
Cardinal Villemaurine *(St-Emilion)*; Ch Caillou Les
Martins *(Lussac)*; Ch de Fussignac *(Bordeaux)*
**33330 St-Christophe-des-Bardes
tel: 05 57 24 74 46 fax: 05 57 24 64 40**
An accessible St-Emilion that usually develops
quickly; there is some velvety fruit here in its
fragrance and taste.

Ch Cadet-Bon — map 38/L E9
grand cru classé
owner: Société Loriene *area:* 6 ha *cases:* 2,500
grape % R: MER 70% CF 30% *second wine:* Ch Vieux
Moulin du Cadet *other châteaux owned:* Ch Curé-
Bon *(St-Emilion)*
**33330 St-Emilion tel: 05 57 74 43 20
fax: 05 57 24 66 41**
Named after the youngest son, the *cadet*, of the
family of Jacques Bon, the mayor said to have
settled just outside the walls of St-Emilion in
1325. Today's owners arrived in 1986: their first
vintages were perhaps somewhat rustic in
character, but after just a few more the standard
rose to that of a *grand cru classé*. Cadet-Bon is
now a gutsy, complete wine, with a good dose of
spicy oak and solid tannins: as *bon* as its name.

Ch Cadet-Peychez — map 38/L E9
owner: GFA Jabiol-Sciard *area:* 2.4 ha *cases:* 1,000
grape % R: MER 70% CF 30% *other châteaux owned:*
Ch Faurie de Souchard *(St-Emilion)*
33330 St-Emilion tel: 05 57 74 43 80
Reasonably aromatic wine, with red berry fruits.
Supple, enjoyable, well made and balanced.

Below: Ch Cadet-Peychez

Below: Ch Canon

Ch Cadet-Piola   map 38/L E9

grand cru classé

owner: Alain Jabiol **area:** 7 ha **cases:** 3,000 **grape % R:** MER 51% CS 28% CF 18% MAL 3% **second wine:** Chevaliers de Malte **other châteaux owned:** Ch de Pasquette *(St-Emilion)*

33330 St-Emilion tel: 05 57 74 47 69

fax: 05 57 74 47 69

This château's nondescript buildings are hidden behind a wall on a 75 m hill. Vaulted cellars have been hewn out of this hill, where bottles of wine lie piled to rest. The wine is full of character and demands patience, because of its solid tannins. With 50% of the casks new, oak aromas are evident; plus dark, spicy elements such as pepper, truffle and licorice.

Ch Cadet-Pontet   map 38/L E9

grand cru

owner: Michel Mérias **area:** 8 ha **cases:** 3,500 **grape % R:** MER 60% CF 30% CS 10% **second wine:** Ch Vieux Pontet

33330 St-Emilion tel: 05 57 24 72 66

fax: 05 57 74 41 21

This usually elegant *grand cru* is quite ready for drinking after four to five years, when it is firm in its alcohol and offers plenty of aroma, somewhat dry tannins and a fairly short finish.

Ch du Calvaire   map 38/R H6

grand cru

owner: Domaines Roland Dumas **area:** 15 ha **cases:** 7,000 **grape % R:** MER 60% CS 30% CF 10% **other châteaux owned:** Ch Larcis Jaumat *(St-Emilion)*; Ch Petit Sicard *(St-Emilion)*; Ch de Christoly *(Côtes de Bourg)*; Ch Lalibarde *(Côtes de Bourg)*; Ch de Mass *(Bordeaux Supérieur)*

33330 St-Etienne-de-Lisse tel: 05 57 43 43 82

fax: 05 57 43 01 89

There are brushwood and other earthy notes in the aroma of this quite full-bodied, very decent St-Emilion *grand cru*.

Ch de Candale   map 38/R H2

grand cru

owner: Jean Dugos **area:** 5 ha **cases:** 2,100 **grape % R:** MER 80% CF 20%

33330 St-Laurent-des-Combes tel: 05 57 24 72 97

fax: 05 57 24 68 31

Pleasant, almost lushly fruity wine in which notes of blackcurrants, chocolate and spices can often be tasted. Weedkillers are entirely banned from this estate.

Ch Canon   map 38/L F8

1er grand cru classé B

owner: Chanel **area:** 18 ha **cases:** 8,800 **grape % R:** MER 55% CF 45% **second wine:** Ch J. Kanon **other châteaux owned:** Ch Rauzan-Ségla *(Margaux)*

33330 St-Emilion tel: 05 57 24 70 79

fax: 05 57 24 68 00

This is not a wine of impressive concentration, but it does have great refinement. Its nuances seem endless and its length is considerable. Its aroma holds fresh red fruits and noble new oak – half of the *barriques* are replaced annually. Justifiably a *premier grand cru classé*, it ranks among the very greatest St-Emilions. The château, where they still work with traditional oak fermentation vats, stands with its vineyard on the St-Emilion plateau, just west of the town. The name comes from *capitaine de corvette* Jacques Kanon, who bought the estate in 1760. In the mid-1990s Ch Canon came into the ownership of the family which also owns Ch Rauzan-Ségla in Margaux.

Above: Ch du Cauze

Ch Canon la Gaffelière   map 38/L H9

grand cru classé

owner: Comtes von Neipperg **area:** 19.5 ha **cases:** 8,000 **grape % R:** MER 55% CF 40% CS 5% **second wine:** Côte Migon la Gaffelière **other châteaux owned:** Ch La Mondotte *(St-Emilion)*; Clos de l'Oratoire *(St-Emilion)*; Ch Haut Lagrange *(Pessac-Léognan)*; Clos Marsalette *(Pessac-Léognan)*

33330 St-Emilion tel: 05 57 24 71 33

fax: 05 57 24 67 95

Considerable sums were spent here after the château was bought in 1971 by the German Count Joseph-Hubert von Neipperg, from Schwaigern in Württemberg. Thus it acquired a new *cuvier*, with stainless-steel fermentation tanks. The count's son Stephan took over in 1985: since then he has brought the estate in brilliant fashion to the upper ranks of the *grands crus classés*. The wine is rich in colour, with toasted, smoky, spicy oak always there in its bouquet, and a combination of fruits – blackcurrants, bilberry, blackberry – together with the dark tones of bay, licorice and cocoa. Its tannins are firm, yet not too aggressive. This elegantly firm, seductive wine shows great charm after just a few years, but has the backbone to go on unfolding for a decade at least.

Ch Cantelaube   map 38/L J7

owner: Maryse Delage **area:** 3.6 ha **cases:** 2,300 **grape % R:** MER 97% CF 3% **other châteaux owned:** Ch Puy Longa *(St-Emilion)*

33330 St-Emilion tel: 05 57 51 98 77

fax: 05 57 51 98 77

Small vineyard yielding a firm St-Emilion with a spicy-earthy aroma and a light touch of oak.

Ch Cantenac   map 38/L G4

grand cru

owner: SCI des Vignobles Brunot **area:** 12 ha **cases:** 5,800 **grape % R:** MER 75% CF 20% CS 5% **other châteaux owned:** Ch Piganeau *(St-Emilion)*; Ch Tour de Grenet *(Lussac-St-Emilion)*; Ch Maledan *(Bordeaux Supérieur)*

33330 St-Emilion tel: 05 57 51 35 22

fax: 05 57 25 19 15

In its taste this wine has an agreeable blend of earthy elements such as truffles, and fruity ones, particularly berries and red and black currants. Often the fairly hard tannins demand bottle-ageing for three to eight years.

Ch de Cantin   map 38/R F5

grand cru

owner: M. Huilizen & Marquis de la Croix Landol **area:** 32.5 ha **cases:** 16,700 **grape % R:** MER 65% CF 21% CS 14% **second wine:** Vieux Ch des Combes

33330 St-Christophe-des-Bardes

tel: 05 57 24 65 73 fax: 05 57 24 65 82

The château here is a former monastery built by the Benedictines in the 17th century, and extended in the 19th. The wine is notable for its often captivating bouquet, with fresh red fruit (strawberry, raspberry), and plenty of new oak. The maturation policy is interesting: the Merlot wine is matured for 12 months in cask, a third of them new; the Cabernet Franc for 6 months; the Cabernet Sauvignon sees no oak. The taste is expansive, with freshness and racy tannins: a wine of character, suitable for laying down. The *cuvée prestige* is Marquis de la Croix Landol.

Ch Cap de Mourlin   map 38/L D9

grand cru classé

owner: GFA Capdemourlin **area:** 14 ha **cases:** 6,000 **grape % R:** MER 60% CF 25% CS 12% MAL 3% **second wine:** Capitan de Mourlin **other châteaux owned:** Ch Balestard la Tonnelle *(St-Emilion)*; Ch Petit-Faurie-de-Soutard *(St-Emilion)*; Ch Roudier *(Montagne-St-Emilion)*

33330 St-Emilion tel: 05 57 74 62 06

fax: 05 57 74 59 34

From 1936 to 1982 this property was divided: there were two estates and two wines of this name. Since being reunited by the Capdemourlin family a single wine has been most expertly produced, not fat – refined, in fact – and quite obviously characterized by the Cabernet Franc.

Ch Capet Duverger   map 38/R I4

grand cru

owner: EARL Héritiers Duverger **area:** 7.7 ha **cases:** 4,460 **grape % R:** MER 64% CF 27% CS 9%

33330 St-Hippolyte tel: 05 57 24 70 71

fax: 05 57 24 65 18

Property belonging to the chairman of the Union des Producteurs cooperative, whose son is an oenologist. The cooperative makes the wine. Animal aromas can predominate in the bouquet, while the taste is fairly full-bodied with a good balance, a certain length, and sometimes slightly bitter tannin in the finish.

Ch Capet-Guillier   map 38/R I3
grand cru
owner: Familles Bouzerand & Galinou **area:** 15.3 ha **cases:** 7,500 **grape % R:** MER 60% CF 30% CS 10% **second wine:** Ch Grands Sables Capet
33330 St-Hippolyte tel: 05 57 24 70 21
fax: 05 57 24 68 96
This estate has belonged to the same family ever since it was separated from Ch Lassègne some two centuries ago. The wine usually has plenty of alcohol; its quality is good, its character rather rustic. Fur, leather and other animal scents are usually to be found, along with jammy fruit and considerable tannin. A pleasant, full-bodied wine.

Ch Cardinal Villemaurine   map 38/L F9
grand cru
owner: Jean-François Carrille **area:** 7 ha **cases:** 3,500 **grape % R:** MER 70% CS 30% **second wine:** Ch Fongaban Bellevue **other châteaux owned:** Ch Boutisse (St-Emilion); Ch Puyblanquet Carille (St-Emilion); Ch Caillou Les Martins (Lussac-St-Emilion); Ch de Fussignac (Bordeaux)
33330 St-Emilion tel: 05 57 24 74 46
fax: 05 57 24 64 40
This is characteristically a fine, creamy wine, provided with smooth tannins, reasonable concentration and elements of coffee and tobacco. Maturing, mainly in used casks, lasts from 6-18 months.

Ch Carteau Côtes Daugay   map 38/L G7
grand cru
owner: Jacques Bertrand **area:** 12.6 ha **cases:** 6,600 **grape % R:** MER 70% CF 25% CS 3% MAL 2% **second wine:** Ch Vieux Lescours **other châteaux owned:** Ch Franc Pipeau Descombes (St-Emilion)
33330 St-Emilion tel: 05 57 24 73 94
fax: 05 57 24 69 07
The nature of the soil here – mainly sand – means that this wine is often low in acidity, especially in good years. It therefore just misses the potential for real greatness. However, Carteau Côtes Daugay stays regularly near the top of the *grands crus*.

Ch Carteau Pin de Fleurs   map 38/L G7
grand cru
owner: Jean-Michel Moueix & Annie-Claude Bion-Moueix **area:** 6 ha **cases:** 3,100 **grape % R:** MER 70% CF 15% CS 15% **other châteaux owned:** include Ch Taillefer (Pomerol)
33330 St-Emilion tel: 05 57 24 78 58
fax: 05 57 24 63 46

A fairly classic wine is made at this vineyard, which is made up of various plots with soils that include sand and iron. It displays spices, leather, tobacco, some rather jam-like fruit, a dash of vanilla, and an adequate length. The estate was formed in 1827.

Ch Le Castelot   map 38/L H8
grand cru
owner: Jean Janoueix **area:** 9 ha **cases:** 5,000 **grape % R:** MER 80% CF 20% **second wine:** Haut Castelot **other châteaux owned:** include Ch Haut-Sarpe (St-Emilion); Ch La Croix (Pomerol)
33330 St-Sulpice-de-Faleyrens tel: 05 57 51 41 86
fax: 05 57 51 76 83
This château owes its name to the 16th-century King Henri IV who, after lodging and dining here, gave permission for the building to be fortified. A slender round tower was also added. The wine here is generally well made, with a rounded, supple, almost sweetish taste, and with licorice and concentration; but at times it fades somewhat quickly, and often rather lacks some acidity and character.

Ch du Cauze   map 38/R E3
grand cru
owner: Bruno Laporte **area:** 20 ha **cases:** 10,000 **grape % R:** MER 90% CF 10%
33330 St-Emilion tel: 05 57 74 62 47
fax: 05 57 74 59 12
The present château arose in the 17th century on the foundations of a medieval castle destroyed during the Hundred Years' War. Since 1986 it has belonged to the Laporte family, from the Montagne-St-Emilion district. They make a round, harmonious wine, with succulent fruit (cherry, blackberry, currant) and a decent depth. Part of the wine matures in barrel, part in tank. The two elements are blended three months before bottling.

Ch La Caze Bellevue   map 38/L I6
owner: Philippe Faure **area:** 7 ha **cases:** 4,000 **grape % R:** MER 80% CF 20%
33330 St-Sulpice-de-Faleyrens tel: 05 57 74 41 85
fax: 05 57 24 62 00
Very accessible wine with mellow fruit, matured mainly in used casks. The estate is of fairly recent date, having been created in 1978.

Ch Cazenave   map 38/L L9
owner: Maxime Champagne **area:** 8.6 ha **cases:** 4,000 **grape % R:** MER 63% CF 29% CS 8%
33330 Vignonet tel: 05 57 24 70 71
fax: 05 57 24 65 18
A correct wine from the cooperative, with a quite long, somewhat bitter finish, good tannin and reasonable structure. Fruit is modestly present.

Ch Champion   map 38/R D2
grand cru
owner: Famille Bourrigaud **area:** 7 ha **cases:** 3,300 **grape % R:** MER 70% CF 15% CS 15% **second wine:** Clos Larguet **other châteaux owned:** Ch Vieux Grand Faurie (St-Emilion)
33330 St-Christophe-des-Bardes tel: 05 57 74 43 98
fax: 05 57 74 41 07
Estate very much geared to the reception of visitors: parties of 15 and upwards can have a meal here, supplied by a caterer. The wine is dark in colour and taste; it matures for a year in tank, followed by a year in barrels, a third of them new.

Clos Chante Alouette   map 38/L I10
grand cru
owner: François Ouzoulias **area:** 3.5 ha **cases:** 1,350 **grape % R:** MER 75% CF 25% **second wine:** Ch Cardinal **other châteaux owned:** Ch Franc-Pourret (St-Emilion); Domaine du Haut-Patarabet (St-Emilion); Ch Grand Ménestrel (Côtes de Castillon)
33330 St-Emilion tel: 05 57 51 07 55
fax: 05 57 25 18 27
The potential for a good St-Emilion seems to be here, but the wine is sometimes not as well made as it might be. Thus the 1990 had good structure, but a not altogether clean bouquet, a slight disagreeable bitterness in the taste, and was not well balanced.

Domaine Chante Alouette Cormeil   map 38/L F5
grand cru
owner: Yves Delol **area:** 10 ha **cases:** 4,500 **grape % R:** MER 60% CF 20% CS 20% **other châteaux owned:** Ch Gueyrosse (St-Emilion)
33330 St-Emilion tel: 05 57 51 02 63
fax: 05 57 51 93 39
Outstanding *grand cru*: ripe fruit, a touch of licorice, some oak, smooth tannin, firm constitution. A creation of Yves Delol (who also owns Ch Gueyrosse), a passionate and expert winemaker.

Ch Le Chatelet   map 38/L F9
grand cru
owner: Hélène Berjal **area:** 5.5 ha **cases:** 2,580 **grape % R:** MER 40% CF 30% CS 30% **second wine:** Saint-Valéry
33330 St-Emilion tel: 05 57 24 70 97
Estate on the limestone plateau, its vineyard bordering Clos Fourtet. This fragrant wine boasts fresh fruit, vanilla, toasted oak and supple tannins.

Ch Chauvin   map 38/L C8
grand cru classé
owner: Béatrice Ondet & Marie-France Février **area:** 12.5 ha **cases:** 6,000 **grape % R:** MER 77% CF 17% CS 6% **second wine:** Chauvin Variation
33330 St-Emilion tel: 05 57 24 76 25
fax: 05 57 74 41 34
The name Chauvin has been on record since 1841, but it has taken more than a century for the vineyard to reach its present extent. Oak tones are dominant in the wine: they are

Below: Ch Le Chatelet

sometimes rather sawdusty, so not integrated. The aroma is distinctly dark – leather, ink, bay, autumn woods – with some fruity aspects as well. Now and again the aftertaste can be disappointing because of dry tannins.

Ch Cheval Blanc
map 38/L C6

1er grand cru classé A

owner: SC Ch Cheval Blanc/Héritiers Fourcaud-Laussac **area:** 36 ha **cases:** 15,000 **grape % R:** CF 57% MER 39% MAL 3% CS 1% **second wine:** Petit Cheval **other châteaux owned:** Ch Laplagnotte-Bellevue (St-Emilion); Ch de Francs (Bordeaux Côtes de Francs)

33330 St-Emilion tel: 05 57 55 55 55
fax: 05 57 55 55 50

The vineyard of this famous *premier grand cru classé* stretches around the château in a rough triangle. It consists of three kinds of soil: sand with clay, gravel with clay, and deep gravel, and it borders on Pomerol. The *cépages* planted depend on the varying soils: Cabernet Franc rather than the Merlot is predominant. The owners, a family numbering around 30 members, have entrusted the management to a very perfectionist team. The greatest care is bestowed on vineyard cultivation, the aim being sound grapes of maximum ripeness at an average yield of not more than around 40 hl/ha. The grapes are picked plot by plot by a Spanish team, then sorted on a slow-moving conveyor belt. After a classic vinification, ageing for 18–20 months takes place in new and not too strongly toasted casks. That Cheval Blanc came into being when Ch l'Evangile in Pomerol was divided up can be tasted in the wine. It has all the generosity of an outstanding Pomerol, sometimes even outdoing it: a Cheval Blanc from a great year is almost decadently opulent. In the sumptuous, velvety-finishing taste there are layers of ripe, black fruit together with elements of cocoa, coffee, tobacco, licorice and spice, all harmoniously set in the aromas of the oak. Petit Cheval, the second wine here, is also of very high quality. Selection for both wines is very strict. Thus no Cheval Blanc was made in 1991, and only half the crop was deemed suitable for Petit Cheval. According to legend, the name Cheval Blanc arose because Henri IV stopped at an inn here to change his white horses.

Below: Ch Cheval Blanc

Ch Clos des Jacobins
map 38/L E7

grand cru classé

owner: Domaines Cordier **area:** 8 ha **cases:** 4,875 **grape % R:** MER 55% CF 40% CS 5% **other châteaux owned:** include Ch La Commanderie (St-Emilion); Ch Haut Corbin (St-Emilion); Ch le Jurat (St-Emilion); Ch Cantemerle (Haut-Médoc); Ch Plagnac (Médoc); Ch Meyney (St-Estèphe); Ch Malagar (Premières Côtes de Bordeaux); Ch Lafaurie-Peyraguey (Sauternes); Ch Sigalas-Rabaud (Sauternes); Ch Le Gardera (Bordeaux Supérieur); Ch Tanesse (Bordeaux)

33330 St-Emilion tel: 05 57 24 70 14
fax: 05 57 24 68 08

Really great concentration is seldom a quality of this *grand cru classé*, but the wine does have a civilized power, nice fruit, dark tones, good oak, and a decent length with usually ripe, supple tannin. Its quality is consistent. Has belonged to Domaines Cordier since 1964.

Ch La Clotte
map 38/L F9

grand cru classé

owner: Héritiers Chailleau **area:** 3.7 ha **cases:** 1,950 **grape % R:** MER 70% CF 30% **second wine:** Clos Bergat Bosson **other wines:** Clairet de Biguey (Bordeaux Clairet)

33330 St-Emilion tel: 05 57 24 66 85

The château has been mentioned in old deeds since the first half of the 18th century. After renting the estate out for two decades to the firm of Jean-Pierre Moueix, the family who own it took over the management in 1989. The wine is of a high standard: a delicious combination of intense fruit, autumnal aromas and noble wood. The casks, a fifth of them new, rest in a cool rock-cut cave of a cellar.

◆
About St-Emilion

The Maison du Vin is located at place Pierre Meyrat, 33330 St-Emilion. Here can be found a map showing the châteaux and a shop selling wines. In summer short introductions to wine tasting and appreciation are held.
Tel 05 57 55 50 55, Fax 05 57 24 65 57.

The Groupement des Premiers Grands Crus Classés de St-Emilion can be contacted at BP15, 33330 St-Emilion.
Tel 05 57 24 69 20

Ch La Clusière
map 38/R H1

grand cru classé

owner: Consorts Valette **area:** 3 ha **cases:** 1,500 **grape % R:** MER 70% CF 20% CS 10% **other châteaux owned:** include Ch Pavie (St-Emilion); Ch Pavie-Decesse (St-Emilion); Ch La Prade (Bordeaux Côtes de Francs)

33330 St-Emilion tel: 05 57 55 43 43
fax: 05 57 24 63 99

Estate with the same owners as nearby Ch Pavie, and situated on the southern flank of the limestone plateau. The wine is generally rather dour, if not severe, due to its ample hard tannins. Only in some of the great years, such as 1990, does succulent, generous fruit break through and this fairly elegant St-Emilion show some richness and charm.

Ch La Commanderie
map 38/L C7

grand cru

owner: Domaines Cordier **area:** 5 ha **cases:** 3,040 **grape % R:** MER 90% CF 10% **other châteaux owned:** include Ch Clos des Jacobins (St-Emilion); Ch Meyney (St-Estèphe)

33330 St-Emilion tel: 05 56 95 53 00
fax: 05 56 95 53 01

Full of taste, and substantial in warm vintages, this wine is drinkable relatively early – and remains so for some years. Ripe fruit together with spices and vanilla characterize the aroma, and the smooth tannins offer grip and structure. Cordier has run this estate since 1988.

Ch Corbin
map 38/L B7

grand cru classé

owner: SC des Domaines Giraud **area:** 12.7 ha **cases:** 6,500 **grape % R:** MER 70% CF 24% MAL 6% **second wine:** Ch Corbin Vieille Tour **other châteaux owned:** Ch Certan-Giraud (Pomerol)

33330 St-Emilion tel: 05 57 74 48 94
fax: 05 57 74 47 18

Since the second half of the 1980s this wine has changed from being traditional, introverted and tannic to something more appealing, less tight. It now also has considerable creamy oak – it spends 12–15 months in cask, a third of them new – and a decent breadth, without having great depth or complexity.

Ch Corbin Michotte
map 38/L B7

grand cru classé

owner: Jean-Noël Boidron **area:** 7 ha **cases:** 3,800 **grape % R:** MER 65% CF 30% CS 5% **other châteaux owned:** include Ch Calon (Montagne-St-Emilion; St-Georges-St-Emilion); Ch Cantelauze (Pomerol)

33330 St-Emilion tel: 05 57 51 64 88
fax: 05 57 51 56 30

In the distant medieval past this estate formed part of the large domain that belonged to the Black Prince. The present buildings, however, date from the 19th century. They have undergone restoration since 1959, when the oenologist Jean-Noël Boidron bought the neglected estate. The wine is notable for its strong, opaque colour, its sumptuous ripe fruit – sweet blackberry, plum – its generosity, and the toast and vanilla from all, or mostly, new casks. A month before picking, the vines' leaves are pruned back so that the grapes get the maximum sun.

Ch Cormeil-Figeac
map 38/L E6

grand cru

owner: Héritiers Moreaud **area:** 10 ha **cases:** 4,000 **grape % R:** MER 70% CF 30% **second wine:** Ch Haut-Cormey **other châteaux owned:** Ch Lamarzelle

Cormey *(St-Emilion)*; Ch Magnan *(St-Emilion)*
33330 St-Emilion tel: 05 57 24 70 53
fax: 05 57 24 68 20
The château here is a sober cellar complex. Its vineyard was separated from the large Figeac estate in 1832. The wine it yields is usually firm, with good keeping potential – although it is usually somewhat smoother than that from Ch Magnan, which has the same owners. Besides its oak, fruit and herbs there can be a slight touch of menthol in the aroma.

Ch Côte de Baleau   map 38/L D8
grand cru
owner: Famille Reiffers *area:* 17.7 ha *cases:* 10,000 *grape % R:* MAL 65% CF 25% CS 10% *second wine:* Ch des Roches Blanches *other châteaux owned:* Ch Grandes Murailles *(St-Emilion)*; Clos St-Martin *(St-Emilion)*
33330 St-Emilion tel: 05 57 24 71 09
fax: 05 57 24 69 72
Justifiably demoted in 1986 from *grand cru classé* to *grand cru*, for even in great years this wine can lack finesse and have a rather dour, angular taste. It sometimes happens, however, that the wine is somewhat smoother, with more fruit: careful selection is essential.

Ch Côte Puyblanquet   map 38/R G6
owner: Christian Bertoni *area:* 10 ha *cases:* 5,000 *grape % R:* MER 70% CF 15% CS 15% *other châteaux owned:* Domaine du Plantey *(Côtes de Castillon)*
33330 St-Etienne-de-Lisse tel: 05 57 40 18 35
Given its *cru*-less status, Côte Puyblanquet is a very successful St-Emilion . Its aroma includes notes of stewed grapes and cherry stones, and in its taste it has soft tannins as well as something chalky. A good balance.

Ch Côtes Trois Moulins   map 38/L G8
grand cru
owner: Madame Armand Moueix *area:* 4 ha *cases:* 2,000 *grape % R:* MER 60% CF 40% *other châteaux owned:* include Ch Taillefer *(Pomerol)*
33330 St-Emilion tel: 05 57 74 43 11
fax: 05 57 74 44 67
Even in lesser years a fairly powerful, full-bodied wine that does not, however, represent the acme of charm or finesse.

Ch Coudert Pelletan   map 38/R F2
owner: Jean Lavau *area:* 6.5 ha *cases:* 3,500 *grape % R:* MER 70% CF 15% CS 15% *second wine:* Ch La Rose Piney *other châteaux owned:* Domaine la Tuque Bel Air *(Côtes de Castillon)*
33330 St-Christophe-des-Bardes tel: 05 57 24 77 30
fax: 05 57 24 66 24
This estate has belonged to the same family since 1858. Each year they replace a third of their barrels; however a special selection of each vintage matures exclusively in the new casks, for at least a year. The resulting wine – look for *vieilli en fûts de chêne neufs* on the label – is usually marked by firm tannins, berry fruit, brushwood notes and, of course, oak.

Ch La Couronne   map 38/R J2
grand cru
owner: Mähler-Besse *area:* 4.3 ha *cases:* 2,500 *grape % R:* MER 60% CF 25% CS 15% *other châteaux owned:* include Ch Bouquey *(St-Emilion)*; Ch d'Arche *(Haut-Médoc)*; Ch Palmer *(Margaux)*; Ch Alfa Bernarde *(Premières Côtes de Blaye)*
33330 St-Hippolyte tel: 05 56 56 04 30
fax: 05 56 56 04 59

Above: Ch Dassault

In 1992, after years of sending its grapes to the cooperative, La Couronne was acquired by Mähler-Besse. This firm built a new, modern cellar, ready by 1994. From that vintage this good, well-balanced *grand cru* was more complex and more interesting than the two previous years. The wine can generally be drunk after just two or three years. The vineyard stretches on either side of the D670 road.

Ch La Couspaude   map 38/L F10
grand cru classé
owner: GFA La Couspaude/Vignobles Aubert *area:* 7 ha *cases:* 3,000 *grape % R:* MER 75% CF 15% CS 10% *second wine:* Junior de la Couspaude *other châteaux owned:* include Ch Saint-Hubert *(St-Emilion)*; Domaine de Musset *(Lalande-de-Pomerol)*
33330 St-Emilion tel: 05 57 40 15 76
fax: 05 57 40 10 14
From this walled vineyard comes a richly-coloured wine displaying abundant vanilla from new oak – 80% of the barrels – and lots of tannin. The oak can often be so dominant that it displaces other elements, the balance is lost and drying out may occur. What La Couspaude awaits is a more controlled use of oak, since all the potential for a really good wine seems to be here.

Ch Coutet   map 38/L F7
grand cru
owner: Jean David-Beaulieu *area:* 12 ha *cases:* 6,000 *grape % R:* MER 45% CF 45% CS 5% MAL 5% *second wine:* Ch Belles-Cimes
33330 St-Emilion tel: 05 57 74 43 21
fax: 05 57 74 40 78
The château is an attractive place, a shaded *chartreuse* in the style of the celebrated architect Victor Louis; it has belonged to the same family since 1806. The vineyard has a relatively high percentage of Cabernets. Interacting with the subsoil, the grapes yield quite a spirited St-Emilion with red and black currant fruit and (at first) taut tannins.

Ch Couvent des Jacobins   map 38/L F9
grand cru classé
owner: Alain Borde *area:* 10 ha *cases:* 4,000 *grape % R:* MER 65% CF 25% CS 10% *second wine:* Ch Beau-Mayne; Ch Beau-Pontet
33330 St-Emilion tel: 05 57 24 70 66
fax: 05 56 24 62 51

In the 13th century the Duke of Lancaster, son of Henry III of England, presented St-Emilion with a new Jacobin monastery. This was to replace an earlier *couvent* that stood outside the town walls and therefore could not be defended. The monks of the Couvent des Jacobins made such good wine that it was served at the English court. Today this former monastery makes a peaceful oasis in busy St-Emilion – and the wine is still of a high standard. Its rounded taste has breeding, with fruit, spices and oak. It is a balanced, complete wine: the only possible criticism is that the oak is sometimes a little dominant.

Ch La Croix de Jaugue   map 38/L F4
owner: Georges Bigaud *area:* 4.5 ha *cases:* 3,000 *grape % R:* MER 85% CF 15%
33500 Libourne tel: 05 57 51 51 29
fax: 05 57 51 29 70
This estate stretches along the Dordogne, in the low-lying south-west part of the appellation. Half the vineyard is on clay, the other half is on a deep bed of gravel. Besides its straightforward St-Emilion, the château makes a *grand cru* of considerably better quality. This wine, Ch La Fleur de Jaugue, matures for at least a year in new barrels. It is a creation of great power and richness of taste, with notes of black and red fruits, bayleaf, brushwood and noble oak aromas – usually an impressive finish, too. This special wine is made only in the good vintage years.

Ch Croque-Michotte   map 38/L B6
grand cru
owner: GFA Geoffrion *area:* 13.7 ha *cases:* 7,500 *grape % R:* MER 75% CF 25%
33330 St-Emilion tel: 05 57 51 13 64
fax: 05 57 51 07 81
Time seems to have stood still at this simple château with its small park full of old trees. Appearances, however, are deceptive, for a battery of stainless-steel tanks stands in the

---

◆
Maps of St-Emilion

Map 38 shows the St-Emilion appellation, and Map 39 shows the Côte in detail, with the vineyards of leading châteaux.

Above: Ch Daugay

cuvier. Croque Michotte wine is characterized by a liberal amount of glycerine; this makes it generous in flavour, while spiciness and jam-like fruit are well to the fore.

Ch Cruzeau   map 38/L E3
grand cru
owner: Famille Luquot **area:** 4.4 ha **cases:** 2,000 **grape % R:** MER 70% CF 30% **other châteaux owned:** Ch Guillot *(Pomerol)*
33500 Libourne tel: 05 57 51 18 95
fax: 05 57 25 10 59
The château was built in the 16th century, the vineyard laid out in 1758. Even in the great years this wine is rather lightly structured, and therefore not destined for keeping. There can be a touch of old oak in the bouquet.

Clos de la Cure   map 38/R D3
grand cru
owner: Christian Bouyer **area:** 6.5 ha **cases:** 3,000 **grape % R:** MER 75% CS 13% CF 12% **other châteaux owned:** Ch Milon *(St-Emilion)*
33330 St-Christophe-des-Bardes tel:
05 57 24 77 18
An extremely reliable *grand cru* is made here, with plenty of fruit, smooth tannin and good concentration.

Ch Curé-Bon   map 38/L F9
grand cru classé
owner: Société Loriene **area:** 4 ha **cases:** 1,800 **grape % R:** MER 70% CF 20% CS 5% MAL 5% **other châteaux owned:** Ch Cadet-Bon *(St-Emilion)*
33330 St-Emilion tel: 05 57 74 43 20
fax: 05 57 24 66 41
Although the Bon family held land on the St-Emilion plateau from the end of the 15th century, it was to be 300 years before any vines were planted – according to legend by the priest, or *curé*, Bon. For decades the estate was called Ch Curé Bon La Madeleine. In 1992 it acquired new owners who, for the present at least, have shortened the name to Curé-Bon. Meaty, supple and at the same time quite elegant wine, with considerable oak and tannin.

Ch Darius   map 38/R J1
grand cru
owner: GFA des Pommiers **area:** 6.7 ha **cases:** 3,000 **grape % R:** MER 50% CF 50% **other châteaux owned:** Ch Vrai Caillou *(Bordeaux Supérieur)*

33330 St-Laurent-des-Combes tel: 05 56 61 31 56
fax: 05 56 61 33 52
Fairly generous, deliciously fruity, meaty wine, with oak elements like vanilla, caramel and fresh toast show on the palate. The colour is often nearly or wholly opaque. Until the 1992 vintage this *grand cru* was sold under the name Ch de Tressan.

Ch Dassault   map 38/R D1
grand cru classé
owner: SARL Ch Dassault **area:** 22.1 ha **cases:** 9,000 **grape % R:** MER 65% CF 30% CS 5% **second wine:** Ch Mérissac
33330 St-Emilion tel: 05 57 24 71 30
fax: 05 57 74 40 33
Marcel Dassault, founder of the aircraft manufacturer – famous for the Mirage – bought this estate in 1953 as a total ruin. It was then called Ch Couprie. The new owner carried out massive restoration work and subsequently gave the estate his own name. A usually amiable, open-knit wine is produced here, with a decent amount of fruit (black cherry, strawberry, plum) and with bayleaf, licorice and toasty, spicy oak.

Ch Daugay   map 38/L G7
grand cru
owner: Christian de Boüard de Laforest **area:** 5.6 ha **cases:** 2,500 **grape % R:** MER 50% CF 48% CS 2%
33330 St-Emilion tel: 05 57 24 78 15
Noble, generous wine with vanilla, fruit, a velvety taste and well-blended tannin. Until 1984 this vineyard belonged to Ch Angélus. Cabernets make up half of the vines.

Ch Destieux   map 38/R G4
grand cru
owner: Christian Dauriac **area:** 13 ha **cases:** 4,800 **grape % R:** MER 66% CF 33% MAL 1%
33330 St-Hippolyte tel: 05 57 24 77 44
fax: 05 57 40 37 42
A sound wine with a sound reputation. Here you have a complete St-Emilion; concentrated, firm, with fruit and tannin. The wine demands at least four years' patience; once ready for drinking, its taste takes on a silky dimension.

Ch La Dominique   map 38/L C6
grand cru classé
owner: Clément Fayat **area:** 22 ha **cases:** 10,000 **grape % R:** MER 80% CF 15% CS 5% **second wine:**

Saint-Paul de Dominique **other châteaux owned:** Ch Clément Pichon *(Haut-Médoc)*; Ch Prieurs de la Commanderie *(Pomerol)*
33330 St-Emilion tel: 05 57 51 31 36
fax: 05 57 51 63 04
This estate's first owner made his fortune in the island of Dominica (now the Dominican Republic), hence the name. The vineyard adjoins Cheval Blanc for nearly a kilometre, and also borders on Pomerol. Since the estate was acquired in 1969 by Clément Fayat, who has invested a great deal in it, the standard of the wine has steadily improved. It is now among the very best *grands crus classés*. Its bouquet shows the extensive use of new barrels – on average 65% a year – and its expansive and almost velvety flavour fills the mouth with impressions of vanilla, fresh toast, spice, meaty fruit and smooth, well-integrated tannins.

Ch l'Eglise d'Armens   map 38/R K4
grand cru
owner: Bertrand Martigue **area:** 3.5 ha **cases:** 1,900 **grape % R:** MER 70% CF 30%
33330 St-Pey-d'Armens tel: 05 57 47 16 45
Nearly all the scattered plots belonging to this small wine estate lie around Bigaroux, a hamlet near St-Emilion. Even in lesser years the wine is firm, harmonious and well-balanced, with a reasonably long aftertaste.

Ch Faugères   map 38/R H7
grand cru
owner: Corinne & Péby Guisez **area:** 20 ha **cases:** 10,000 **grape % R:** MER 70% CF 25% CS 5% **other wines:** Les Roses de Ch Faugères *(Bordeaux rosé)* **other châteaux owned:** Ch Cap de Faugères *(Côtes de Castillon)*
33330 St-Etienne-de-Lisse tel: 05 57 40 34 99
fax: 05 57 40 36 14
In 1987 the film producer Péby Guisez became the owner of this estate and, with his wife Corinne, has energetically breathed new life into it. A spectacular *cuvée* has been built, the 18th-century château on its hill carefully restored, talented advisers taken on for the winemaking. Here are made two wines: the St-Emilion and a Côtes de Castillon *(see Ch Cap de Faugères)*. The St-Emilion is rich and concentrated, with much fresh fruit and considerable oak. The first vintages displayed limited finesse, and were slightly out of balance (too much concentration and oak). Now, however, the balance is struck with increasing

---

◆
Grape varieties

Main and other permitted varieties for each appellation are given in the appellation fact box at the end of the relevant introduction. For châteaux, percentages of grapes grown are given as supplied by the château.

Abbreviations: CF Cabernet Franc, COL Colombard, CS Cabernet Sauvignon, MAL Malbec, MER Merlot, MUSC Muscadelle, PV Petit Verdot, SAUV B Sauvignon Blanc, SÉM Sémillon

Ugni Blanc is not abbreviated, nor are minor varieties such as Carmenère. In St-Emilion, Cabernet Franc is sometimes called Bouchet.

Above: Clos Fourtet

regularity. The soil, clay with limestone, also offers the prospect of high quality. Up to and including the 1992 vintage the wine was sold as Ch Haut Faugères.

Ch Faurie de Souchard map 38/R E1
grand cru classé
owner: GFA Jabiol Sciard *area:* 11 ha *cases:* 5,500 *grape % R:* MER 65% CF 26% CS 9% *other châteaux owned:* Ch Cadet-Peychez *(St-Emilion)*
33330 St-Emilion tel: 05 57 74 43 80
fax: 05 57 74 43 96
Birthplace of a fairly hefty St-Emilion with plenty of well-toasted wood and also fine fruit, including hints of strawberry. However, real depth, intensity and length are usually lacking; and sometimes the wine may contain a minor impurity in the form of volatile acidity. A great battle between the English and French took place here during the Hundred Years' War.

Ch de Ferrand map 38/R G4
grand cru
owner: Famille Bich *area:* 30 ha *cases:* 13,500 *grape % R:* MER 75% CF 15% CS 10% *second wine:* Ch des Grottes
33330 St-Emilion tel: 05 57 74 47 11
fax: 05 57 24 69 08
An estate with a history that goes back for centuries. During the reign of Louis XIV one of its owners had a curious cave system dug out, complete with a well. The industrial magnate Bich, of Bic ballpoints, bought the estate in 1978 and invested heavily in it. A feature of the wine is a slight touch of acidity in aroma and taste. Overall, this St-Emilion is striking for its strength, its tannin – it stays rather hard for a long time – its dark aroma and its great purity. Not a great wine, but a very reliable one.

Ch Figeac map 38/L D6
1er grand cru classé B
owner: Thierry Manoncourt *area:* 40 ha *cases:* 18,000 *grape % R:* CS 35% CF 35% MER 30% *second wine:* La Grange Neuve de Figeac *other châteaux owned:* Ch de Millery *(St-Emilion)*
33330 St-Emilion tel: 05 57 24 72 26
fax: 05 57 74 45 74
Anyone who has had the privilege of being taken around Figeac by its owner, Thierry Manoncourt, will have had something of a geology lecture. He is always eager to explain

Above: Ch Figeac

that this estate is one of the few in St-Emilion with a thick, well-drained layer of gravel in the subsoil – comparable with the top Médoc *crus*. Neighbouring Cheval Blanc, too, has a subsoil partly of *graves*. Figeac, untypically for St-Emilion, has a majority ofCabernets – a big factor in making its wine totally different from that of its higher-ranked arch-rival Cheval Blanc. When mature, it is indeed almost Médoc-like in character. Typical of this *premier grand cru classé* is the early achievement of a velvety elegance; but it has ageing potential as well. Blackcurrant from the Cabernet Sauvignon (35% of the vines) is also present, sometimes with herbaceous elements, and always the best possible oak – all the *barriques* are new. This is not a wine to overwhelm the senses, except perhaps in rich years like 1982, 1985 and 1990, but it does caress them. Possibly Roman in origin, by the 18th century Figeac had grown into a 200-ha manor, the biggest in St-Emilion. It was then divided up in the following century.

Ch La Fleur map 38/R D2
grand cru
owner: Madame Lily Lacoste/Jean-Pierre Moueix *area:* 6.3 ha *cases:* 2,000 *grape % R:* MER 92% CF 8% *other châteaux owned:* include Ch Trotanoy

Below: Ch Fleur Pourret

(Pomerol); Ch Pétrus *(Pomerol)*; Ch de la Dauphine *(Fronsac)*; Ch Magdelaine *(St-Emilion)*
33330 St-Emilion tel: 05 57 51 78 96
fax: 05 57 51 04 29
Property run by Christian Moueix (of Jean-Pierre Moueix), who makes a fine, classic St-Emilion. The wine has ripe tannins, a lively taste, average body, with pleasing hints of both spices and fruit – cherry, currants, plum. Maturing in *barriques*, a quarter of them new, lasts 19–20 months.

Ch Fleur Cardinale map 38/R G7
grand cru
owner: Claude & Alain Asséo *area:* 10 ha *cases:* 4,500 *grape % R:* MER 70% CF 15% CS 15% *second wine:* Ch Bois Cardinal *other châteaux owned:* Ch Guillot Clauzel *(Pomerol)*; Ch Robin *(Côtes do Castillon)*; Domaine de Courteillac *(Bordeaux)*
33330 St-Etienne-de-Lisse tel: 05 57 40 14 05
fax: 05 57 40 28 62
It seems scarcely credible now, but until the beginning of the 1980s wine from this château was sold in bulk to the trade, and its quality was indistinguishable from the ordinary St-Emilions: today this is one of the most respected *grands crus*. Its colour is intense, its aroma conveys spicy oak, licorice, autumnal woods and other such impressions. Its taste holds supple fruit, fine oak, licorice again, firmness; and there is a long, lingering finale. A very sound, balanced St-Emilion with character, backbone and refined tannins.

Ch La Fleur Cravignac map 38/L D8
grand cru
owner: Lucienne Beaupertuis *area:* 7.5 ha *cases:* 3,000 *grape % R:* MER 60% CF 30% CS 10%
33330 St-Emilion tel: 05 57 74 44 01
fax: 05 57 84 56 70
Wine with pleasing roundness and with a good deal of fruit; usually soon ready for drinking. In the 18th century members of the Lavau de Cravignac family were mayors of St-Emilion. The restaurant of the French parliament is a faithful customer for the better vintages.

Clos La Fleur Figeac map 38/L C5
grand cru
owner: Marcel Moueix *area:* 3 ha *cases:* 1,600 *grape % R:* MER 70% CF 30% *other châteaux owned:* include Ch Taillefer *(Pomerol)*

33330 St-Emilion tel: 05 57 55 30 20
fax: 05 57 25 22 14
Clos La Fleur Figeac makes a muscular wine in which the dark Merlot fruit rests on a foundation of tannin and oak.

Ch Fleur de Lisse
map 38/R H6

grand cru

owner: Xavier Minvielle **area:** 9 ha **cases:** 4,500
grape % R: MER 60% CF 37% MAL 3%
33330 St-Etienne-de-Lisse tel: 05 57 40 18 46
fax: 05 57 40 35 74
Unpretentious, but certainly enjoyable, St-Emilion, meant for drinking young. Only since 1995 has this wine been given time in cask.

Ch Fleur Pourret
map 38/L E8

owner: AXA Millésimes **area:** 3 ha **cases:** 1,500
grape % R: MER 60% CF 30% CS 10% **other châteaux
owned:** include Ch Petit-Figeac (St-Emilion); Ch Cantenac-Brown (Margaux); Ch Pichon-Longueville (Pauillac); Ch Petit Village (Pomerol)
33330 St-Emilion tel: 05 57 24 62 61
fax: 05 57 24 68 25
Particularly recommended in great years, for the wine then has unmistakeable class: not too heavy, but a fairly expansive taste with plenty of fruit (cherry, blackcurrants), suppleness and elements of coffee and tobacco, as well as earthy aromas.

Ch Fombrauge
map 38/r f4

grand cru

owner: SA Ch Fombrauge **area:** 52 ha **cases:** 30,000 **grape % R:** MER 70% CF 15% CS 15% **second wine:** Ch Maurens
33330 St-Christophe-des-Bardes tel:
05 57 24 77 12
fax: 05 57 24 66 95
This 17th-century château is named after the winegrower Dumas de Fombrauge, and was originally a monastery. The large vineyard extends over parts of three communities and is among the oldest in St-Emilion. The present consortium of owners of Ch Fombrauge is dominated by Danes – not only a wine merchant and a few hundred private individuals, but also the toy manufacturer Lego with a 10% share. Since 1989 the quality of the wine has shown an upward curve. Its constitution is firm, with solid tannins and a medley of ripe fruits, spices and vanilla (a third of the maturing barrels are new). Rooms and apartments at the estate can be rented.

Ch Fonplégade
map 38/L G8

grand cru classé

owner: Armand Moueix **area:** 18 ha **cases:** 7,500
grape % R: MER 60% CF 35% CS 5% **second wine:** Ch Côtes Trois Moulins **other châteaux owned:** include Ch Moulinet (Pomerol); Ch La Croix Bellevue (Lalande-de-Pomerol)
33330 St-Emilion tel: 05 57 74 43 11
fax: 05 57 74 44 67
Fonplégade is a reference to a fountain and derives from early Christian times. Ch Fonplégade, on its slope, is indeed a very old estate, even though today's château was only built in the mid-19th century. The wine made here is the best from the firm of Armand Moueix. It has finesse and in particular plenty of fruit, including bilberry and blackcurrants. Other attributes of this *grand cru classé* are often notes of cocoa, cinnamon and smoky oak, along with good tannin. It has obvious distinction and usually ages well.

Ch Fonrazade
map 38/L G7

grand cru

owner: Guy Balotte **area:** 15 ha **cases:** 6,500 **grape % R:** MER 75% CS 25% **second wine:** Ch Comte des Cordes
33330 St-Emilion tel: 05 57 24 71 58
fax: 05 57 74 40 87
The Fonrazade land borders on Angélus, but the wines are totally different. This is due in part to a relatively high proportion – 25% – of Cabernet Sauvignon in the Fonrazade vineyard. Wine from this *grand cru* tastes reasonably firm and is fairly traditional in character, with some red and black currant fruit and, when young, rather austere tannins.

Ch Fonroque
map 38/L E9

grand cru classé

owner: Jean-Pierre Moueix **area:** 17.5 ha **cases:** 8,000 **grape % R:** MER 90% CF 10% **other châteaux owned:** include Ch Magdelaine (St-Emilion); Ch Trotanoy (Pomerol); Ch Pétrus (Pomerol); Ch de la Dauphine (Fronsac)
33330 St-Emilion tel: 05 57 51 78 96
fax: 05 57 51 04 29
A stone on the *chai* here bears the date 1756, a silent witness to two and a half centuries of winemaking. The name refers to the rocky subsoil. The firm of Jean-Pierre Moueix here creates a dark-coloured St-Emilion full of character, conservative in style. Its taste usually stays subdued for years because of its tough tannins; its bouquet also needs time to develop. Its quality remains very consistent, but this wine does not get chosen for its depth or refinement.

Clos Fourtet
map 38/L F9

1er grand cru classé B

owner: Simone Noël, André, Lucien & Dominique Lurton **area:** 19 ha **cases:** 9,000 **grape % R:** MER 72% CF 22% CS 6% **second wine:** Domaine de Martialis **other châteaux owned:** include Ch Bonnet (Bordeaux)
33330 St-Emilion tel: 05 57 24 70 90
fax: 05 57 74 46 52
Fourtet's entrance lies opposite the church at St-Emilion. The château, an ivy-covered manor house on the former site of a small fort (a *fourtet*), and the *cuvier* beside it represent only part of the winemaking complex – for three storeys of galleries extend below the ground. Some of these are used to store wine in *barriques*, 80% of them new. There was a period when Clos Fourtet produced a severe, dour wine, but today it has more fruit, more suppleness and more nuances – roasted nuts, vanilla, chocolate, coffee, spice – while firm tannins provide backbone and the potential for ageing. The improvement has been very noticeable since the 1989 vintage.

Ch Franc Bigaroux
map 38/L H8

grand cru

owner: Yves Blanc **area:** 10 ha **cases:** 5,000 **grape % R:** MER 70% CS 20% CF 10%
33330 St-Sulpice-de-Faleyrens tel: 05 57 51 54 73
Organically-farmed vineyard, yielding a St-Emilion with grip and character. The wine usually also offers considerable fruit (red and black currants) and oaky aromas.

◆

Vanished appellations of the Right Bank

Appellation Contrôlée law evolves, and some names have vanished from the list of Right Bank ACs. They may be found on (very) old bottles.

Côtes Canon-Fronsac Superseded by the Canon-Fronsac name in 1964, though it is still legal to add the 'Côtes'.

Côtes de Fronsac Superseded by Fronsac. This AC covered only Fronsac, St-Aignan and Saillans: the present AC (see the relevant chapter) is larger.

Néac Now part of Lalande-de-Pomerol, the commune had its own AC until 1954.

Parsac-St-Emilion The appellation still exists, but no wine is declared: the growers have the right to use Montagne-St-Emilion, and they do.

Sables-St-Emilion A defunct appellation, withdrawn in 1973, which covered the wines from the south-east part of Libourne which are now in AC St-Emilion.

Below: Ch La Grâce Dieu

Ch Franc Bories   map 38/L M10
owner: Gilles Roux & Jean-Claude Arnaud *area:* 9.1 ha *cases:* 5,870 *grape % R:* MER 80% CS 12% CF 8%
33330 Vignonet tel: 05 57 24 70 71
fax: 05 57 24 65 18
Wine vinified by the cooperative, normally with reasonable concentration, fairly ripe tannin, and a fairly long finish with a slight bitter touch. Requires some patience.

Ch Franc Grâce-Dieu   map 38/L D7
grand cru
owner: SEV Fournier *area:* 8.5 ha *cases:* 3,500
grape % R: MER 52% CF 41% CS 7%
33330 St-Emilion tel: 05 57 24 70 79
fax: 05 57 24 68 00
In the Middle Ages this was a Cistercian priory and therefore 'by God's grace' free (*franc*) of taxation. Since 1981 the Fournier family have leased the estate. A firm wine, with a considerable aroma – cherry stone, old wood, animal scents – and body. The aftertaste can sometimes be a little short, rough and bitter. Maturing takes place in used casks from Ch Canon and lasts 10 months.

Ch Franc Jauge Blanc   map 38/L F4
grand cru
owner: Michel Borde *area:* 10.2 ha *cases:* 5,900
grape % R: MER 85% CF 15%
33330 St-Emilion tel: 05 57 24 70 71
fax: 05 57 24 65 18
Pleasant wine with a certain concentration, some fruit; usually well-balanced. Made by the cooperative.

Ch Franc Lartigue   map 38
grand cru
owner: Jean-Pierre Toxé *area:* 7 ha *cases:* 3,750
grape % R: MER 65% CF 35% *other châteaux owned:*
Ch Grande Rouchonne (*St-Emilion*); Ch Bellevue
(*Côtes de Castillon*)
33330 St-Emilion tel: 05 57 40 33 03
fax: 05 57 40 06 05
Pleasing St-Emilion that before bottling matures for an average 15 months in oak, a third of the barrels being new. The wine often has a distinctive bouquet, with elements of orange peel, cocoa and bayleaf. Until well into the 1980s the estate was connected to the cooperative.

Ch Franc Mayne   map 38/L E8
grand cru classé
owner: Georgy Fourcroy *area:* 7 ha *cases:* 3,000
grape % R: MER 70% CS 15% CF 15%
33330 St-Emilion tel: 05 57 24 62 61
fax: 05 57 24 68 25
Château on the limestone plateau, with nearby a former *relais de poste* from the 16th century. AXA Millésimes acquired the estate in 1984, and thereafter the quality of the wine improved significantly. This *grand cru classé* usually has an almost inky colour, a lot of body, succulence and tannin. Apart from its blackfruit, there is often something herbaceous in its aroma. A wine that gives pleasure without being really fine. The property has again been sold in 1996.

Ch Franc Patarabet   map 38/L F9
grand cru
owner: GFA Faure Barraud *area:* 6 ha *cases:* 2,500
grape % R: MER 65% CF 25% CS 10% *second wine:*
Ch Franc
33330 St-Emilion tel: 05 57 24 65 93
fax: 05 57 24 69 05

Above: Ch Grand Mayne

This *grand cru* deserves recommendation, particularly in the great years; it then has more substance and concentration. In lesser years the taste is supple and it is quickly ready for drinking. Maturing in *barriques*, a third of them new, takes place in a cave cellar within the walls of St-Emilion.

Ch Franc Pipeau Descombes
map 38/R I4
grand cru
owner: Jacqueline Bertrand-Descombes *area:* 5.3 ha *cases:* 3,000 *grape % R:* MER 70% CF 25% CS 5% *other châteaux owned:* Ch Carteau Côtes Daugay (*St-Emilion*)
33330 St-Hippolyte tel: 05 57 24 73 94
fax: 05 57 24 69 07
Smooth wine, usually with little acidity, and not much length or nuance. Purity and ripe fruit make it taste uncomplicatedly good.

Ch Franc-Pourret   map 38/L E8
grand cru
owner: François Ouzoulias *area:* 5 ha *cases:* 2,700
grape % R: MER 75% CF 25% *second wine:* Ch Canon Pourret *other châteaux owned:* Clos Chante Alouette (*St-Emilion*); Domaine du Haut-Patarabet (*St-Emilion*); Ch Grand Ménestrel (*Côtes de Castillon*)
33330 St-Emilion tel: 05 57 51 07 55
fax: 05 57 25 18 27
Potential is here in plenty, as is clear from the sound structure of the wine, its smooth tannin and long aftertaste. Sometimes, however, its vinification and upbringing are not the best possible, and it then has a somewhat dusty quality – perhaps due to old barrels.

Ch La Gaffelière   map 38/L G9
1er grand cru classé B
owner: Léo de Malet Roquefort *area:* 22.1 ha
cases: 10,000 *grape % R:* MER 65% CF 30% CS 5%
second wine: Clos la Gaffelière *other châteaux owned:* Ch Tertre Daugay (*St-Emilion*)
33330 St-Emilion tel: 05 57 24 72 15
fax: 05 57 24 65 24
A mosaic from Roman times found near this château depicts a vine tendril, showing that local preoccupations have stayed unchanged since the 4th century AD. The present château is just below Ch Ausone and beside the road into St-Emilion from the south. It acquired its

rather Gothic form in the 17th, 18th and 19th centuries. This is a stylish, elegant wine, seldom very powerful, exuberant or super-concentrated. Its aroma is an alluring blend of ripe red and black currants, with black cherry, spice, vanilla and toasty oak, and it does not lack for tannin.

Clos Gerbaud   map 38/R K5
owner: Patricia Forgeat Chabrol *area:* 12 ha *cases:* 5,800 *grape % R:* MER 65% CS 20% CF 15% *other wines:* Ch Gerbaud (*AC Bordeaux*)
33330 St-Pey-d'Armens tel: 05 57 47 12 39
fax: 05 55 70 47 20
'Quantity does not rhyme with quality' is the motto of the family that has been running this estate for four generations. Not a wine for keeping, it generally has a fairly light, simple structure. But it is aromatic and tastes good – and therefore definitely acceptable, certainly for an unclassified St-Emilion.

Ch La Gomerie   map 38/L E8
grand cru
owner: Gérard & Dominique Bécot *area:* 2.5 ha *cases:* 750 *grape % R:* MER 100% *other châteaux owned:* Ch Beau-Séjour Bécot (*St-Emilion*); Ch Grand-Pontet (*St-Emilion*)
33330 St-Emilion tel: 05 57 74 45 87
fax: 05 57 24 66 85
The Bécot brothers make a *grand cru*, impressive in all respects, from Merlot vines with an average age of 35 years. The time up to and including its malolactic fermentation is spent in all new casks; at the first transfer a quarter of these are replaced, again by new ones. These *barriques* come from eight different coopers. Altogether the wine spends 15-18 months in oak; it is not filtered.

Domaine des Gourdins   map 38/L D3
owner: Héritiers Coudreau *area:* 1.5 ha *cases:* 850
grape % R: MER 60% CF 40% *other châteaux owned:* include Ch La Papeterie (*St-Emilion*); Ch La Cabanne (*Pomerol*); Ch Plincette (*Pomerol*)
33330 St-Emilion tel: 05 57 51 04 09
fax: 05 57 25 13 38
Good use is made of *barriques* for this wine, as is clear from the harmonious presence of vanilla, caramel and oak. Ageing takes place in one-year-old barrels and lasts about 20 months. The wine is aromatic, not particularly concentrated, and usually has a long finish.

Ch La Grâce Dieu　　　map 38/L D7

grand cru

owner: Christian Pauty **area:** 13 ha **cases:** 5,800
grape % R: MER 70% CF 20% CS 10% **second wine:**
Ch Etoile Pourret **other châteaux owned:** Ch
Bouffevent *(Bergerac)*
33330 St-Emilion tel: 05 57 24 71 10
fax: 05 57 24 67 24

A *grand cru* fermented in stainless steel. It
undergoes no oak-ageing, and has an enjoyable,
uncomplicated character. The best years show
reasonable concentration, considerable fruit
and ripe, smooth tannins.

Ch La Grâce Dieu Les Menuts
map 38/L E7

grand cru

owner: Max Pilotte **area:** 13.5 ha **cases:** 6,000
grape % R: MER 60% CF 30% CS 10% **second wine:**
Vieux Domaine des Menuts
33330 St-Emilion tel: 05 57 24 73 10
fax: 05 57 74 40 44

This property, which dates from 1875, has
gradually been enlarged, from very tiny to its
present size, by five succeeding generations.
The wine can be as splendidly complex as its
name, with ripe fruit, such as stewed pears, in
an aroma nicely framed by oak. Smooth
tannin, a hint of licorice and other nuances
can be experienced in the well-concentrated
taste.

Ch Grand Barrail Lamarzelle Figeac
map 38/L D6

grand cru

owner: SCEA Ed. Carrère **area:** 19 ha **cases:** 8,300
grape % R: MER 80% CS 20% **second wine:**
Lamarzelle Figeac **other châteaux owned:** Ch
Cambon la Pelouse *(Haut-Médoc)*
33330 St-Emilion tel: 05 57 24 71 43
fax: 05 57 24 63 44

Mellow wine without great depth, and meant
for drinking relatively young. The modest-
looking château should not be confused with
the splendidly luxurious hotel close by, which
shares its name.

Ch Grand Bert　　　map 38/L K7

grand cru

owner: SCEA Lavigne **area:** 11 ha **cases:** 5,600
grape % R: MER 65% CF 30% CS 5% **other châteaux**
owned: Ch Grand Tuillac *(Côtes de Castillon)*
33330 St-Sulpice-de-Faleyrens tel: 05 57 40 60 09
fax: 05 57 40 66 67

A standard St-Emilion and also – in much more
limited quantity – a *grand cru* are both sold
under the name of this château. Both wines
tend to lack some charm, and often have rather
a high alcohol content. The *grand cru* does
offer some fruit and a touch of oak, and has no
obvious shortcomings, but it is currently below
par for its classification.

Ch Grand Corbin　　　map 38/L C8

grand cru

owner: Société Familiale Alain Giraud **area:** 13.3 ha
cases: 7,000 **grape % R:** MER 68% CF 27% CS 5%
second wine: Tour du Pin Franc
33330 St-Emilion tel: 05 57 24 70 62
fax: 05 57 74 47 18

A wine of sound quality: a full, unctuous,
powerful and long taste, with soft tannins and a
good dose of oak (the latter sometimes a little
too dominant). Grand Corbin rather suggests a
Pomerol wine – which is logical, for the
vineyard lies close to the boundary.

Above: Ch La Grave Figeac

Ch Grand-Corbin-Despagne
map 38/L B7

grand cru

owner: Guy & Gérard Despagne **area:** 26.5 ha
cases: 13,000 **grape % R:** MER 70% CF 25% CS 5%
second wine: Ch Laporte **other châteaux owned:**
Ch Reine Blanche *(St-Emilion)*
33330 St-Emilion tel: 05 57 51 74 04
fax: 05 57 51 29 18

The Despagne family has lived in and around
St-Emilion since 1620 or earlier; the first plots
of Grand-Corbin-Despagne were bought in
1812. The wine is lively, aromatic and
somewhat dry thanks to its tannin, with a fair
amount of oak and occasionally a vague hint of
cooked fruit; there is sometimes a whiff of the
stable plus some coffee and cocoa in its aroma.

Ch Grande Rouchonne　　　map 38/L L9

grand cru

owner: Jean-Pierre Toxé **area:** 3 ha **cases:** 1,600
grape % R: MER 65% CF 35% **other châteaux owned:**
Ch Franc Lartigue *(St-Emilion)*; Ch Bellevue *(Côtes
de Castillon)*
33330 Vignonet tel: 05 57 40 33 03
fax: 05 57 40 06 05

A supple, balanced St-Emilion, usually of
average structure, but a little soft and lacking
in character. Matures for a year in casks of
which a third are new.

Ch Grand Lartigue　　　map 38/L I9

grand cru

owner: Dominique Daudier de Cassini **area:** 7 ha
cases: 3,750 **grape % R:** MER 75% CF 25%
33330 St-Emilion tel: 05 57 24 73 83
fax: 05 57 74 46 93

A *grand cru* of average quality, with sufficient
fruit and tannin. Not oak-aged.

Ch Grand Mayne　　　map 38/L E7

grand cru classé

owner: Jean-Pierre Nony **area:** 19 ha **cases:** 10,000
grape % R: MER 70% CF 25% CS 5% **second wine:**
Les Plantes du Mayne
33330 St-Emilion tel: 05 57 74 42 50
fax: 05 57 24 68 34

Lying partly on the southwest edge of the
limestone plateau, this is an estate where
perfectionism reigns. The wine has everything
in good measure: plenty of colour, bouquet,
concentration, fruit, oak (highly toasted), and

flavour. This opulent whole is usually at its best
when the wine is less than 10-12 years old; after
that it may rather dry out and lose balance.
About three-quarters of the *barriques* are
replaced before each vintage; the wine spends
18 months in them. The outstanding second
wine also contains a lot of oak. The Grand
Mayne château (formerly called Du Mayne or Le
Mayne) was completed in 1767.

Ch Grand-Pontet　　　map 38/L E8

grand cru classé

owner: Famille Pourquet-Bécot **area:** 14 ha **cases:**
6,000 **grape % R:** MER 75% CF 15% CS 10% **second
wine:** Dauphin de Grand-Pontet **other châteaux
owned:** Ch Beau-Séjour Bécot *(St-Emilion)*; Ch La
Gomerie *(St-Emilion)*
33330 St-Emilion tel: 05 57 74 46 87
fax: 05 57 24 66 88

The present owners bought this château from
Barton-Guestier in 1980, after which the quality
improved significantly. A feature of the wine is
its good concentration. Also present in the good
and the great years are plenty of fruit, toasted
oak, richness, and bayleaves and other spices.
The estate came into being through an army
captain, one d'Estieu, who was so charmed by
St-Emilion that he bought land here in 1415.
His family owned Grand-Pontet for 550 years
after that.

Ch Grandes Murailles　　　map 38/L F9

grand cru classé

owner: Famille Reiffers **area:** 2 ha **cases:** 1,000
grape % R: MER 68% CF 32% **other châteaux owned:**
Ch Côte de Baleau *(St-Emilion)*; Clos St-Martin *(St-
Emilion)*
33330 St-Emilion tel: 05 57 24 71 09
fax: 05 57 24 69 72

There is no actual château here. Grandes
Murailles is the remaining wall of a monastery
church, just outside the ramparts of St-
Emilion. The wine from the vineyard in front of
the said wall is made at Ch Côte de Baleau,
which has the same owners. This St-Emilion
has tannin, roundness and oak – too much oak
even, for it displaces the fruit.

Ch Grangey　　　map 38/R F5

grand cru

owner: SCEA du Ch Grangey/F. Arroaz **area:** 6.2 ha
cases: 3,600 **grape % R:** MER 80% CF 20%

33330 St-Christophe-des-Bardes
tel: 05 57 24 70 71 fax: 05 57 24 65 18
Quite a few estate wines from the Union de
Producteurs cooperative are disappointing, but
this one makes a pleasing exception. Even in
less-good years Ch Grangey has a good
structure, a certain finesse, ripe, compact
tannins and a long finish.

Ch La Grave Figeac map 38/L C5
grand cru
owner: Jean-Pierre Clauzel *area:* 6.4 ha *cases:*
3,000 *grape % R:* MER 65% CF 30% CS 5% *second
wine:* Pavillon Figeac
33330 St-Emilion tel: 05 57 51 38 47
fax: 05 57 74 17 18
This property, between Cheval Blanc and La
Conseillante (Pomerol), was acquired by Jean-
Pierre Clauzel in 1993. This former joint-owner
of Ch l'Evangile in Pomerol has managed to
enlarge the 4.3-ha vineyard with the addition of
two plots adjoining Ch Figeac. A balanced wine,
fragrant, fruity – tending to raspberry – with a
touch of vanilla. This is a property worth
following.

Ch Guadet-St-Julien map 38/L F9
grand cru classé
owner: Robert Lignac *area:* 6 ha *cases:* 2,500
grape % R: MER 75% CF 25%

Below: Ch Guadet-St-Julien

33330 St-Emilion tel: 05 57 74 40 04
fax: 05 57 24 63 50
After belonging to the Lacome-Guadet family,
this estate was bought in 1877 by the present
owner's great-grandfather. In that period, too, it
acquired the Guadet-St-Julien name. Elegance
is the key word for the wine produced here.
Even in a sunny year it has no great power or
intensity, but it does possess aroma, some
complexity and finesse. Its bouquet sometimes
has an almost Burgundian mildness, with
caramel and vanilla as well.

Ch Gueyrosse map 38/L F3
grand cru
owner: Yves Delol *area:* 4.5 ha *cases:* 1,600 *grape
% R:* MER 65% CF 20% CS 15% *second wine:*
Domaine Mademoiselle *other châteaux owned:*
Domaine Chante Alouette Cormeil (St-Emilion)
33500 Libourne tel: 05 57 51 93 39
fax: 05 57 51 93 39
Estate by the Dordogne where neither artificial
fertilizer nor weedkiller are used, and where
they still pick the grapes by hand. The château
was built around 1750 and later enlarged.
Unfiltered, fragrant wine, with old-fashioned
firmness, a lot of oak, and strong, lingering
tannins.

Ch Guillemin la Gaffelière map 38/L G9
grand cru
owner: Vignobles Fompérier *area:* 17 ha *cases:*
8,750 *grape % R:* MER 63% CF 25% CS 10% MAL 2%
second wine: Clos Castelot *other châteaux owned:*
Ch Fonds Rondes (Côtes de Castillon)
33330 St-Emilion tel: 05 57 74 46 92
fax: 05 57 74 49 16
A wine that comes from three soil types and
four grape varieties. Of reliable quality, it
beautifully combines strength and complexity.
Depending on the vintage, the wine spends 12-
18 months in oak (one-third new casks).

Ch De Guilnemansoy map 38/R I3
owner: Armande d'Anthouard *area:* 8.3 ha *cases:*
5,370 *grape % R:* MER 68% CF 22% CS 10%
33330 St-Hippolyte tel: 05 57 24 70 71
fax: 05 57 24 65 18
Flavoursome St-Emilion with reasonable
firmness, a measure of finesse and a slightly
bitter aftertaste. Among the better wines from
the St-Emilion cooperative.

Ch Haut Bruly map 38/R G7
owner: Catherine Cante & Didier Minard *area:* 4.4
ha *cases:* 2,850 *grape % R:* MER 70% CF 30%
33330 St-Etienne-de-Lisse tel: 05 57 24 70 71
fax: 05 57 24 65 18
One of the numerous châteaux affiliated to the
cooperative. The wine it makes is not great, but
is quite solid and balanced, sometimes with a
hint of pepper as well as some fruit in its
aroma.

Ch Haut-Cadet map 38
grand cru
owner: Vignobles Rocher-Cap de Rive *area:* 11 ha
cases: 5,800 *grape % R:* MER 34% CF 33%
CS 33% *second wine:* Ch Bragard *other châteaux
owned:* include Ch Cap d'Or (St-Georges-St-
Emilion)
33330 St-Emilion tel: 05 57 40 08 88
fax: 05 57 40 19 93
Sound, accessible St-Emilion in which there are
elements of oak from 18 months in cask,
bayleaf, dried plum, and earthy aromas. Of a
good, consistent quality.

Ch Haut Corbin map 38/L B8
grand cru classé
owner: SMABTP/Domaines Cordier *area:* 6.5 ha
cases: 3,000 *grape % R:* MER 70% CS 20% CF 10%
other châteaux owned: include Ch Clos des
Jacobins (St-Emilion); Ch Cantemerle (Haut-
Médoc)
33330 St-Emilion tel: 05 57 97 02 82
fax: 05 57 97 02 84
Fine, elegantly firm St-Emilion that may
require some time in bottle to lose its initial
toughness. Besides its tannin the wine offers a
decent amount of substance, ripe fruit, dark
notes and spicy oak. Since 1985 it has been
made by Domaines Cordier.

Ch Haute Nauve map 38/R I3
grand cru
owner: Famille Reynier *area:* 8.5 ha *cases:* 4,950
grape % R: MER 60% CF 30% CS 10%
33330 St-Laurent-des-Combes tel: 05 57 24 70 71
fax: 05 57 24 65 18
Decent St-Emilion, usually with an attractive
bouquet, and a not particularly complex or long
aftertaste. From the cooperative.

Ch Hautes-Graves d'Arthus
map 38/R L2
grand cru
owner: Gérard Musset *area:* 10 ha *cases:* 5,650
grape % R: MER 80% CF 10% CS 10% *second wine:*
Ch Moulin des Graves
33330 Vignonet tel: 05 57 84 53 15
fax: 05 57 84 53 15
Bouquet and taste often have a touch of plum
jam and raisins. The wine is smooth in the
mouth at first, but ends rather dourly, with dry
tannin. Its quality is good, its character
somewhat old-fashioned. A St-Emilion that is
worth laying down.

Ch Haut-Montil map 38/L I6
grand cru
owner: Famille Vimeney *area:* 6.7 ha *cases:* 2,500
grape % R: MER 93% CF 7%
33330 St-Sulpice-de-Faleyrens tel: 05 57 24 70 71
fax: 05 57 24 65 18
Fairly open, quite fast-developing wine vinified
by the St-Emilion cooperative. Ch Haut-Montil
has fruit, somewhat dry tannins, and an average
structure.

Domaine du Haut-Patarabet
map 38/L I9
grand cru
owner: François Ouzoulias **area:** 3.5 ha **cases:**
1,350 **grape % R:** MER 75% CF 25% **second wine:** Ch
Tourbadon **other châteaux owned:** include Ch Franc-
Pourret (St-Emilion); Clos Chante Alouette (St-
Emilion); Ch Grand Ménestrel (Côtes de Castillon)
33330 St-Emilion tel: 05 57 51 07 55
fax: 05 57 25 18 27
This St-Emilion, even from good years, has to
be drunk quickly. It is supple, fairly light and
short. Sometimes it has an odd aroma, with not
only old wood but also a hint of tinned sardines.

Ch Haut-Plantey   map 38/L C9
owner: Michel Boutet **area:** 9.4 ha **cases:** 4,400
grape % R: MER 75% CF 20% CS 5% **second wine:** Ch
La Bouygue **other châteaux owned:** Ch Petit Val (St-
Emilion); Ch Vieux Pourret (St-Emilion)
33330 St-Hippolyte tel: 05 57 24 70 86
fax: 05 57 24 68 30
Generous, not really refined wine with a spicy,
dark aroma and considerable oak. The best wine
from Michel Boutet, who owns other châteaux
in this district.

Ch Haut-Pourret   map 38/L E8
grand cru
owner: Serge Mourgout Lepoutre **area:** 3 ha **cases:**
1,500 **grape % R:** MER 60% CF 30% CS 10%
33330 St-Emilion tel: 05 57 74 46 76
Consistent, well-structured wine, supple and
endowed with black fruit. Some oak-ageing.

Ch Haut Rocher   map 38/R H7
grand cru
owner: Jean de Monteil **area:** 9 ha **cases:** 4,000
grape % R: MER 65% CF 20% CS 15% **second wine:**
Pavillon du Haut Rocher **other châteaux owned:** Ch
Bréhat (Côtes de Castillon)
33330 St-Etienne-de-Lisse tel: 05 57 40 18 09
fax: 05 57 40 08 23
Estate that has belonged to the de Monteil
family since the 17th century. The present
owner, Jean de Monteil, studied oenology in
Bordeaux and Burgundy, and makes his wine in
the traditional way. The result is dark in colour,
captivating in its bouquet (mint leaves, fruit,
integrated oak), and has a concentrated taste
without dry tannin. One of the better grands
crus, it also has the potential for ageing.

Below: Ch l'Hermitage

Above: Ch Jean Voisin

Ch Haut-Sarpe   map 38/R F2
grand cru classé
owner: Joseph Janoueix **area:** 11.5 ha **cases:**
5,500 **grape % R:** MER 70% CF 30% **second wine:** Le
Second de Haut-Sarpe **other châteaux owned:**
include Ch Vieux Sarpe; Ch Le Castelot; Ch Haut
Badette (all St-Emilion); Ch La Croix; Ch La Croix St-
Georges; Ch La Croix Toulifaut; Clos des Litanies
(all Pomerol); Ch de Chambrun (Lalande-de-
Pomerol); Ch La Gasparde; Ch Saint-Genès (Côtes
de Castillon); Dom du Galet (Bordeaux Supérieur)
33330 St-Christophe-des-Bardes
tel: 05 57 51 41 86 fax: 05 57 51 76 83
The imposing but unfinished château has since
1930 belonged to the Janoueix family of wine
merchants. They have restored the building
perfectly, an edifice whose central pavilion was
inspired by the Trianon at Versailles. Certainly
in the great years the Haut Sarpe wine now
compels admiration. It is fresh from first taste
to finish, has a sound balance, delicate tannins
and a long aftertaste. In its bouquet, elements
of noble oak, dried fruit and flowers such as
lilac are all there to be discovered.

Ch Haut-Segottes   map 38/L D7
grand cru
owner: Danielle André **area:** 9 ha **cases:** 4,000
grape % R: MER 60% CS 35% CF 5%
33330 St-Emilion tel: 05 57 24 60 98
fax: 05 57 74 47 29
The considerable proportion (35%) of Cabernet
Sauvignon used means that the wine here is at
its most charming in years with really ripe
grapes. Otherwise this grand cru quickly tends
to become slightly stalky and bitter. Wine from
a sunny year is tasty, but without finesse and
with limited staying-power.

Ch Haut-Villet   map 38/R G8
grand cru
owner: Eric Lenormand **area:** 7 ha **cases:** 3,660
grape % R: MER 70% CF 30%
33330 St-Etienne-de-Lisse tel: 05 57 47 97 60
fax: 05 57 47 92 94
This estate, flourishing now, was in rack and
ruin in 1985. Owner Eric Lenormand and some
friends have breathed new life into it – making
grateful use of vines with an average age of 40.
The wine usually has abundant oak and tannin,
against a thin setting of black and red fruits. It

needs to mature over a long period, but if the
fruit is insufficient there is a chance of it drying
out. Around 5% of production is bottled as
Cuvée Pomone, a superior selection.

Ch l'Hermitage   map 38/L G6
grand cru
owner: Véronique Gaboriaud **area:** 4 ha **cases:**
1,400 **grape % R:** MER 100% **other châteaux**
owned: Ch Matras (St-Emilion); Ch Bourseau
(Lalande-de-Pomerol)
33330 St-Emilion tel: 05 57 51 52 39
fax: 05 57 51 70 19
An estate about 90 m up that once belonged to
an archbishop of Bordeaux. The pure Merlot
wine offers a fine combination of animal aromas
(e.g. fur), ripe fruit and oak. In the mouth it is
supple and balanced. A grand cru of quality.

Ch Jacquemineau   map 38/R F4
owner: Jean Rufat **area:** 21 ha **cases:** 10,500
grape % R: CF 50% MER 45% CS 5%
33330 St-Christophe-des-Bardes
tel: 05 57 24 77 71
The grandparents of the present owner bought
this estate, just above Ch Fombrauge, and gave
it the name of a restaurant run by a customer
friend. Cabernet Franc is the most important
grape grown. The wine is therefore fairly
slender and has a supple taste with pleasant
fruit, particularly ripe red and black currants.

Ch Jacques Blanc   map 38/R H4
grand cru
owner: Pierre Chouet **area:** 20 ha **cases:** 10,000
grape % R: MER 70% CF 25% CS 5% **second wine:**
Domaine de Jacques Blanc **other wines:** Clairet de
Pierre (Bordeaux Clairet)
33330 St-Etienne-de-Lisse tel: 05 57 40 18 01
fax: 05 57 40 01 98
Jacques Blanc (1342-1437) was an eminent St-
Emilion alderman (jurat), who also devoted
himself to improving the quality of the local
wine. The estate named after him produces two
grands crus, the Cuvée Aliénor, with 12 months
in used barrels; and the Cuvée du Maître, which
gets 16 months: three cooperages supply one-
third of these barrels new each year. The du
Maître is the better of the two, and besides its
considerable oak and tannin it has a jammy
fruitiness. As a rule it takes at least five years to
develop fully.

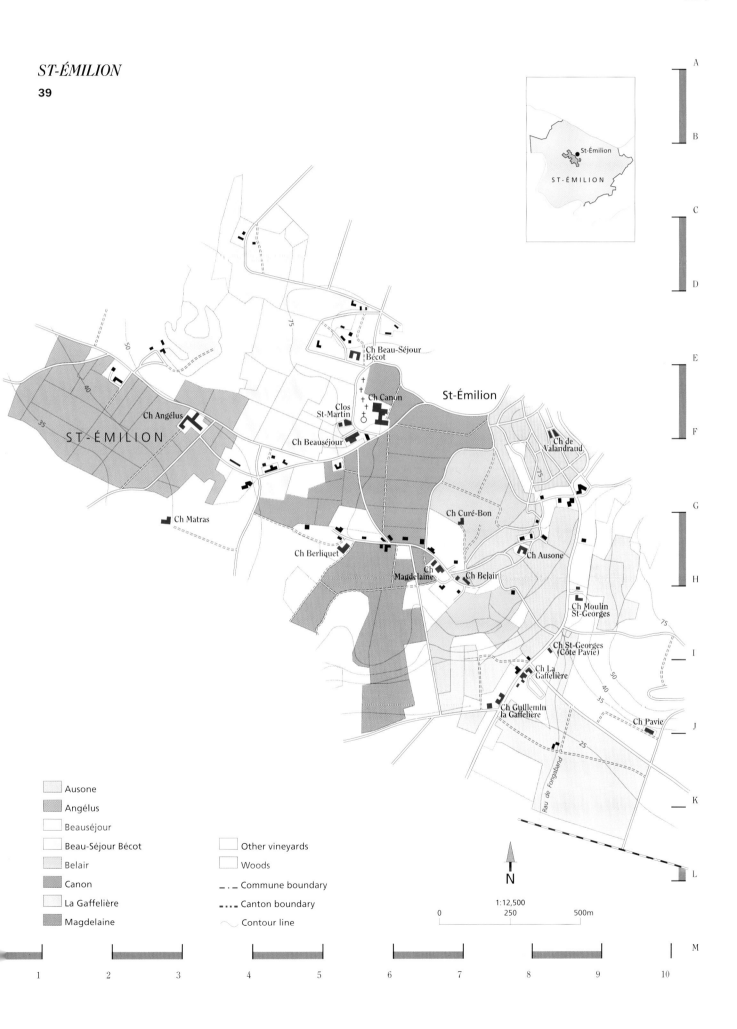

ST-ÉMILION
39

A
B
C
D
E
F
G
H
I
J
K
L
M

St-Émilion

ST-ÉMILION

ST-ÉMILION

Ch Beau-Séjour
Bécot

Ch Canon

Clos
St-Martin

Ch Angélus

Ch Beauséjour

Ch de
Valandraud

Ch Matras

Ch Curé-Bon

Ch Berliquet

Ch Ausone

Ch
Magdelaine

Ch Belair

Ch Moulin
St-Georges

Ch St-Georges
(Côte Pavie)

Ch La
Gaffelière

Ch Guillemin
la Gaffelière

Ch Pavie

Rau de Fongaband

Ausone

Angélus

Beauséjour

Beau-Séjour Bécot

Belair

Canon

La Gaffelière

Magdelaine

Other vineyards

Woods

_ . _ Commune boundary

▪▪▪ Canton boundary

⌒ Contour line

N

1:12,500

0   250   500m

1   2   3   4   5   6   7   8   9   10

Ch Jean Faure   map 38/L C7
grand cru

owner: Michel Amart *area:* 20 ha *cases:* 10,000
grape % R: CF 60% MER 30% MAL 10% *other*
châteaux owned: Ch Montaiguillon *(Montagne-St-Emilion)*
33330 St-Emilion tel: 05 57 51 49 36
Firm tannins and an initial reserve are
properties of the wine made here, not least
because twice as much Cabernet Franc as
Merlot is grown. This atypical St-Emilion is
given 18–24 months in barrels, a quarter of
them new. It is made by an owner who also has
estates in Cognac and Montagne-St-Emilion.

Ch Jean Voisin   map 38/L C8
grand cru

owner: GFA Chassagnoux *area:* 14.2 ha *cases:*
7,000 *grape % R:* MER 66% CS 34% *second wine:*
Cabane Voisin *other châteaux owned:* Ch Renard
(Fronsac)
33330 St-Emilion tel: 05 57 24 70 40
The Cuvée Amédée Chassagnoux is worth
discovering: an attractively nuanced creation
with elements of oak after nine months in
barrel (a third of them new), red and black
fruit, and spice. This wine also has a firm core
of alcohol and tannin.

Ch Juguet   map 38/R J3
grand cru

owner: Maurice Landrodie *area:* 10 ha *cases:*
4,000 *grape % R:* MER 70% CF 20% CS 10% *second*
wine: Ch Gombaud *other wines:* Domaine de Juguet
(AC Bordeaux)
33330 St-Pey-d'Armens tel: 05 57 24 74 10
fax: 05 57 24 66 33
A reasonably concentrated St-Emilion is made
at this estate, which has left the cooperative
and now matures its wine in oak. Ch Juguet
may not have faults, but it does not display
much charm either. Bitter tannins often
dominate the fruit.

Clos Junet   map 38/L E5
owner: Patrick Junet *area:* 1.5 ha *cases:* 790 *grape*
% R: MER 70% CF 30%
33330 St-Emilion tel: 05 57 51 16 39
fax: 05 57 51 16 39
Early-maturing, agreeable, elegantly firm wine
with considerable oak, half the barrels being
new. A tiny vineyard.

Ch Jupille Carillon   map 38/L K5
owner: Régis Visage *area:* 7.1 ha *cases:* 3,500
grape % R: MER 85% CF 15% *other châteaux owned:*
Ch Roc de Troquard *(St-Georges-St-Emilion)*
33330 St-Sulpice-de-Faleyrens
tel: 05 57 24 62 92 fax: 05 57 24 69 40
The wine is supple and firm, but somewhat
lacking in refinement and length. In less good
years Jupille Carillon's aroma may rather
suggest tree bark.

Ch le Jurat   map 38/L B8
grand cru

owner: SMABTP/Domaines Cordier *area:* 7.5 ha
cases: 3,300 *grape % R:* MER 75% CS 25% *other*
châteaux owned: include Ch Cantemerle *(Haut-Médoc)*; Ch Clos des Jacobins *(St-Emilion)*
33330 St-Emilion tel: 05 57 97 02 82
fax: 05 57 97 02 84
Estate run by Cordier and producing a
substantial, juicy St-Emilion, with dark, ripe-fruit aromas, firm build, soft tannins and well-blended oak.

Clos Labarde   map 38/R F2
grand cru

owner: Jacques Bailly *area:* 4.6 ha *cases:* 2,100
grape % R: MER 70% CF 20% CS 10%
33330 St-Laurent-des-Combes tel: 05 57 74 43 39
This estate on the limestone lies not far from
Ch Trotte Vieille, and is rare for St-Emilion in
still having its original walls round it. Its wine
has class: intense colour, and very ripe fruit in
the bouquet which is borne out in the taste,
together with smooth tannins, firmness and
some licorice. Maturing in oak (one-third new
barriques) is kept to eight months.

Ch Lamartre   map 38/R H6
grand cru

owner: Famille Vialard-Patureau *area:* 11.7 ha
cases: 6,500 *grape % R:* MER 83% CF 17%
33330 St-Etienne-de-Lisse tel: 05 57 24 70 71
fax: 05 57 24 65 18
Estate associated with the *cave coopérative*,
which usually supplies a very decent wine. It
has some potential for ageing and a pleasing
fruitiness, without bitter tannin. Sometimes
there can be some stalkiness in the bouquet.

Ch Lamarzelle Cormey   map 38/L D6
grand cru classé

owner: Héritiers Moreaud *area:* 5 ha *cases:* 2,000
grape % R: MER 100% *other châteaux owned:* Ch
Cormeil-Figeac *(St-Emilion)*; Ch Magnan *(St-Emilion)*
33330 St-Emilion tel: 05 57 24 71 43
fax: 05 57 24 63 44
The vineyard has the same owners as the
adjoining Ch Cormeil-Figeac, but is on different
soil: here there are ribbons of clay with sand
beneath. Since 1969 the modest estate has been
replanted entirely with Merlot. The wine tastes
silky, with spice, black fruits, some licorice,
chocolate and subtle oak tones. Usually soon
ready for drinking.

Ch Laniote   map 38/L D9
grand cru classé

owner: Arnaud de la Filolie *area:* 5 ha *cases:* 3,000
grape % R: MER 70% CF 20% CS 10%
33330 St-Emilion tel: 05 57 24 70 80
fax: 05 57 24 60 11
Normally this is a somewhat rustic wine. It has
breeding and tannin, and is made in a
traditional way. Its upbringing consists of 12
months in oak, 25–30% of it new barrels.

Below: Ch Larmande

Ch Laplagnotte-Bellevue   map 38/R D2
grand cru

owner: Henry & Claude de Labarre *area:* 6.1 ha
cases: 2,500 *grape % R:* MER 70% CF 20% CS 10%
second wine: Archange de Laplagnotte-Bellevue
other châteaux owned: include Ch Cheval Blanc *(St-Emilion)*
33330 St-Christophe-des-Bardes
tel: 05 57 24 78 67 fax: 05 57 24 63 62
Since taking over in 1990 the present owners
have devoted great energy to a complete
renovation of this estate. A new *chai* was ready
in 1993, where the wine now spends six months
in barrels, of which half are new. The result is
generous, reasonably concentrated, beautifully
fruity and intended for keeping for a few years.

Clos Larcis   map 38/L F10
grand cru

owner: Robert Giraud *area:* 1 ha *cases:* 450 *grape*
% R: MER 100% *other châteaux owned:* include Ch
Villemaurine *(St-Emilion)*; Ch du Cartillon *(Haut-Médoc)*; Ch Le Bocage *(Bordeaux Supérieur)*; Ch
Timberlay *(Bordeaux Supérieur)*
33330 St-Emilion tel: 05 57 43 01 44
fax: 05 57 43 08 75
Mellow, aromatic, elegant wine with a certain
length, and usually plenty of (new) oak.

Ch Larcis Ducasse   map 38/R H1
grand cru classé

owner: Hélène Gratiot Alphandery *area:* 10.9 ha
cases: 5,000 *grape % R:* MER 65% CF 25% CS 10%
33330 St-Emilion tel: 05 57 24 70 84
Most of the vineyard lies on the slope of the
100-m high plateau south-east of St-Emilion,
and borders on Ch Pavie. The wine made here
suggests a marathon runner: lots of muscle, not
much flesh, and great endurance. In its youth
its toughness can be a shock, but after five to
ten years the tannin begins to fade and other,
more amiable, nuances start to break through.
This *grand cru classé* is at its best in years that
bring it ample fruit, as in 1970 and 1990.

Ch Larmande   map 38/L D10
grand cru classé

owner: GPE La Mondiale *area:* 25 ha *cases:*
12,500 *grape % R:* MER 65% CF 30% CS 5% *second*
wine: Le Cadet de Larmande
33330 St-Emilion tel: 05 57 24 71 41
fax: 05 57 74 42 80

Birthplace of wines of great cachet, usually with a generously filled-out structure. Rich fruit, in the form of blackcurrants, black cherry, plum and prune, is always there, along with a juicy roundness, nicely integrated oak, and supple, firm tannin. Larmande was made great by the Méneret-Capdemourlin family, who acquired the 400-year-old vineyard at the beginning of the 20th century. Late in 1990 the estate went to the insurance company La Mondiale, which further improved the installations, and also endowed the château itself with great style. Half the casks are now replaced annually (previously one-third).

Ch Laroque
map 38/R F4
grand cru classé

Umioii I amilla Uaaumurtin **area:** 9? l"l umrms:
33,000 **grape % R:** MER 80% CF 15% CS 5% **second wine:** Les Tours de Laroque
33330 St-Christophe-des-Bardes
tel: 05 57 24 77 28 fax: 05 57 24 63 65
The château here calls Versailles to mind, for it was built during the 18th century in Louis XIV style. Beside it, St-Emilion's biggest vineyard stretches over 58 ha. Today the wine is of faultless quality, even in less-good years. Its spicy fruit and warm, supple taste has a base of oak and tannin.

Ch Laroze
map 38/L E7
grand cru classé

owner: Famille Meslin **area:** 27 ha **cases:** 13,200 **grape % R:** MER 59% CF 38% CS 3% **second wine:** Clos Yon Figeac
33330 St-Emilion tel: 05 57 51 11 31
fax: 05 57 51 10 36
In 1883 the widow Gurchy combined three small vineyards, calling the result Ch Camus. Two years later the château was built, plus a *cuvier* and a *chai*. With commercial considerations in mind her heir, the wine merchant Maurice Gurchy, changed the name to Laroze in about 1912. It has remained the property of this family. A fairly elegant, balanced wine is produced here, quite firm in taste, although seldom really expansive or sumptuous. There is considerable fruit in its bouquet, varying from raspberry to candied plum, as well as oak. That this well-made wine just slightly lacks class is probably due to the soil: sandy, and not of optimum quality.

Below: Ch Laroze

Ch Lassègue
map 38/R H3
grand cru

owner: GFA Freylon & Fils **area:** 23 ha **cases:** 13,000 **grape % R:** MER 45% CF 35% CS 20% **second wine:** Ch Vignot **other châteaux owned:** Clos Grangeotte Freylon (Bordeaux Supérieur); Ch des Jouailles (Bordeaux Supérieur)
33330 St-Hippolyte tel: 05 57 24 72 83
fax: 05 57 74 48 88
Vineyard largely renewed between 1960 and 1970, when it acquired a high proportion of Cabernets – more than 50%. The wine generally has ripe tannins, and a fairly agreeable taste with elements of autumnal woodland, chocolate, red fruit and spicy oak.

Ch de Lescours
map 38/L H5
Ur ami l ru

owner: Famille Chariol **area:** 21 ha **cases:** 8,300 **grape % R:** MER 80% CF 10% CS 10% **second wine:** La Fleur Lescours; Côtes de Lescours
33330 St-Sulpice-de-Faleyrens tel: 05 57 4 74 75
fax: 05 57 24 68 26
This château has its origins in the 14th century: it was founded in 1341 by Pey de Lascortz, who had been squire to Edward I of England. The wine made here is usually a fairly accessible *grand cru* that, thanks to its suppleness and its lithe tannins, can be drunk in three to five years. Maturing in oak lasts 8-14 months.

Ch Le Loup
map 38/R D4
grand cru

owner: Patrick Garrigue **area:** 6.6 ha **cases:** 3,800 **grape % R:** CF 51% MER 49%
33330 St-Christophe-des-Bardes tel:
05 57 24 70 71
fax: 05 57 24 65 18
Many wines from the Union de Producteurs have a rather strange element in their aroma, suggesting tinned sardines in tomato sauce. However, this wine has a clean aroma, with redcurrants and a hint of rhubarb. The taste is fresh, reasonably structured and harmonious.

Ch Magdelaine
map 38/L G9
1er grand cru classé B

owner: Jean-Pierre Moueix **area:** 10.4 ha **cases:** 5,000 **grape % R:** MER 90% CF 10% **other châteaux owned:** include Ch Trotanoy (Pomerol); Ch Pétrus (Pomerol); Ch de la Dauphine (Fronsac)
33330 St-Emilion tel: 05 57 51 78 96
fax: 05 57 51 04 29
The firm of Jean-Pierre Moueix produces an excellent St-Emilion from vines growing up the slopes and on the great limestone plateau. The vines are 90% Merlot, the largest proportion in any of the *premiers grands crus classés*. When young it is fairly reserved and closed in, but in course of time it becomes more aromatic, more expressive, creamier. Among the nuances there are often prune, ripe – sometimes over-ripe – blackcurrants, chocolate, tobacco, vanilla and oriental spices. The style of the wine changes somewhat in sunny years, becoming more expansive, more opulent. The 1990 vintage exemplified this deliciously.

Ch Magnan
map 38/L E6
grand cru

owner: Héritiers Moreaud **area:** 10 ha **cases:** 4,000 **grape % R:** MER 70% CF 30% **other châteaux owned:** Ch Lamarzelle Cormey (St-Emilion); Ch Cormeil-Figeac (St-Emilion)
33330 St-Emilion tel: 05 57 24 70 53
fax: 05 57 24 68 20

◆
Finding a second wine
To locate a second wine, consult the index which lists all châteaux in the Atlas. Second wines are defined as those made by a château in the same style and colour as its *grand vin*.

Since 1979 the wine has no longer been vinified by the cooperative but by the owners of Ch Cormeil-Figeac. This St-Emilion is a late developer, usually needing five to ten years' maturing. A fresh, at times slightly minty, taste, with spices and a good deal of tannin. Less refined and tougher than Cormeil-Figeac.

Ch Mangot
map 38/R G7
grand cru

owner: Vignobles Jean Petit **area:** 32 ha **cases:** 19,400 **grape % R:** MER 85% CF 10% CS 5% **second wine:** Ch de Lisse **other châteaux owned:** include Ch La Brande (Côtes de Castillon)
33330 St-Etienne-de-Lisse tel: 05 57 40 18 23
fax: 05 57 40 15 97
Somewhat rustic wine, rather dour, a little bitter, with no very long finish – but it is aromatic. A little below par for a *grand cru*.

Ch Matras
map 38/L G8
grand cru classé

owner: Véronique Gaboriaud **area:** 8 ha **cases:** 5,000 **grape % R:** MER 34% CF 33% CS 33% **other châteaux owned:** Ch l'Hermitage (St-Emilion); Ch Bourseau (Lalande-de-Pomerol)
33330 St-Emilion tel: 05 57 51 52 39
fax: 05 57 51 70 19
It could be that this estate derives its name from a soldier of the Hundred Years' War, but there is nothing martial about the wine. It usually tastes mellow, with little acidity and no aggressiveness. This *grand cru classé* has some red fruit, spiciness, well-knit oak and reasonable concentration.

Ch Mauvezin
map 38/L H10
grand cru

owner: Olivier Cassat **area:** 3.5 ha **cases:** 1,500 **grape % R:** MER 50% CF 40% CS 10% **other châteaux owned:** include Ch Grand Gueyrot (St-Emilion); Domaine de Peyrelongue (St-Emilion)
33330 St-Emilion tel: 05 57 24 72 36
fax: 05 57 74 48 54
Small but expanding estate yielding a good, fairly complex, solid wine, yet one with a certain elegance. Alongside ripe fruit and smoky oak, there is something of wet moss and mint in its bouquet.

Clos des Menuts
map 38/L F6
grand cru

owner: SCE Vignobles Rivière **area:** 25 ha **cases:** 12,500 **grape % R:** MER 70% CS 20% CF 10% **other châteaux owned:** include Ch Cheval Brun (St-Emilion); Ch de Beaulieu (Montagne-St-Emilion); Ch Haut-Piquat (Lussac-St-Emilion); Ch de Callac (Graves); Ch de Lavagnac (Bordeaux Supérieur); Ch Saint-Michel (Sauternes)
33350 St-Emilion tel: 05 57 55 59 59
fax: 05 57 55 59 51
A *grand cru* with, in good years, power and a distinctly rustic taste: much leather, tobacco, bayleaf, dry tannins and a touch of bitterness. It has no real complexity and certainly no finesse.

Above: Ch Milon

Ch Millaud-Montlabert   map 38/L D6
grand cru

owner: Claude & Jacqueline Brieux **area:** 4 ha
cases: 1,700 **grape % R:** MER 70% CF 15% CS 15%
second wine: Ch Brieux Chauvin
33330 St-Emilion tel: 05 57 24 71 85
fax: 05 57 24 62 78
Small property that also offers accommodation,
with a few *chambres d'hôtes*. The wine is fairly
round in the mouth at first, but some bitterness
soon follows, and a rather thin finish. Below
grand cru level.

Ch Milon   map 38/R D3
grand cru

owner: Christian Bouyer **area:** 20 ha **cases:** 9,000
grape % R: MER 75% CS 13% CF 12% **other châteaux
owned:** Clos de la Cure *(St-Emilion)*
33330 St-Christophe-des-Bardes tel:
05 57 24 77 18
fax: 05 57 24 64 20
This wine perhaps has a somewhat rustic
bouquet, with animal, stable notes, but usually
has a delicious, very aromatic taste, smooth and
supple, and with reasonable power.

Clos des Moines   map 38/R E5
owner: Jean Menager **area:** 9.5 ha **cases:** 4,000
grape % R: MER 73% CF 21% CS 6% **second wine:** Ch
la Chapelle aux Moines
33330 St-Christophe-des-Bardes tel:
05 57 24 77 02
fax: 05 57 24 60 23
Former Templar property; its name refers to
those soldier-monks. Red fruit – strawberry,
raspberry – can be very noticeable in the taste,
combined with fairly tough tannin and a touch
of fresh acidity. Some oak-ageing began with
the 1995 vintage.

Ch Monbousquet   map 38/L I7
grand cru

owner: Gérard Perse **area:** 32 ha **cases:** 16,500
grape % R: MER 60% CF 30% CS 10% **second wine:**
Ch Caperot; Angelique de Monbousquet
33330 St-Sulpice-de-Faleyrens tel: 05 57 24 67 19
fax: 05 57 74 41 29
There have been many improvements here
since the hypermarket owner Gérard Perse
bought the estate in the early 1990s. This is
true both of work in the vineyard, and of the
vinification and upbringing of the wine. This
now matures solely in new wood in a *chai* with
temperature control. Today this St-Emilion has
an almost decadent character, with sumptuous
fruit – blackberry, raspberry, black currants,
great weight and toasted oak.

Ch Monlot Capet   map 38/R I3
grand cru

owner: Bernard Rivals **area:** 7 ha **cases:** 3,750
grape % R: MER 70% CF 25% CS 5% **second wine:** Ch
Les Dames de Monlot
33330 St-Emilion tel: 05 57 24 62 32
fax: 05 57 24 62 33
Meaty, fairly generous St-Emilion with a lot of
fruit and considerable oak, gained from 18
months in casks of which half are new. The
estate acquired a new owner in 1990.

Ch Montlabert   map 38/L D7
grand cru

owner: SC du Ch Montlabert/Yannick le Menn **area:**
14 ha **cases:** 7,500 **grape % R:** MER 55% CF 32% CS
13% **second wine:** Ch la Croix Montlabert **other
châteaux owned:** Ch Haut Saint Clair *(Puisseguin-
St-Emilion)*; Ch Belair Saint-Georges *(St-Georges-St-
Emilion)*
33330 St-Emilion tel: 05 57 24 70 75
fax: 05 57 74 44 32

◆

**Union de Producteurs de
Saint-Emilion**

The St-Emilion growers' cooperative has
c. 210 members cultivating around
1,000 ha of vineyard.

The wines of around 55 châteaux are made
and marketed by the Union, and the grapes
of many other estates are vinified and
sometimes matured at their winery, with
the wine being returned to the member
for sale.

The Union also markets wines under its own
trademarks or brand names. These include
Royal St-Emilion and Haut Quercus. These
wines are usually rated *grand cru* by the
appellation authorities.

Rather lightly-structured wine, aromatic and
fairly short. Needs to be drunk early. The
vinification is not bad, but the vineyard is on
quite damp soil, near the little Tailhas brook,
where the potential for making great wines is
perhaps lacking.

Ch Moulin du Cadet   map 38/L E9
grand cru classé

owner: Jean-Pierre Moueix **area:** 4.8 ha **cases:**
2,500 **grape % R:** MER 90% CF 10% **other châteaux
owned:** include Ch Magdelaine *(St-Emilion)*; Ch
Trotanoy *(Pomerol)*; Ch Pétrus *(Pomerol)*; Ch de la
Dauphine *(Fronsac)*
33330 St-Emilion tel: 05 57 51 78 96
fax: 05 57 51 04 29
Since the 1989 vintage, wine from this estate
has again been showing *grand cru classé*
quality. Fruit is plentiful, with noble oak
aromas and well-integrated tannins. A pleasing
St-Emilion, made by the J-P Moueix firm.

Ch Moulin Saint-Georges   map 38/L G9
owner: Famille Vauthier **area:** 6.5 ha **cases:** 3,500
grape % R: MER 60% CF 40% **other châteaux owned:**
include Ch Ausone *(St-Emilion)*
33330 St-Emilion tel: 05 57 24 70 26
fax: 05 57 74 47 39
Terraced vineyard on the slope opposite Ch
Ausone. After some ups and downs this wine
has, since 1990, shown a good and consistent
quality. A supple, round St-Emilion with a
somewhat dark, earthy aroma in which fruit is
rather subdued.

Clos de l'Oratoire   map 38/R E1
grand cru classé

owner: SC du Ch Peyreau/Comtes von Neipperg
area: 10.3 ha **cases:** 5,000 **grape % R:** MER 75% CF
25% **other châteaux owned:** include Ch Canon La
Gaffelière *(St-Emilion)*; Ch Peyreau *(St-Emilion)*
33330 St-Emilion tel: 05 57 24 71 33
fax: 05 57 24 67 95
Triangular vineyard near Ch Peyreau with the
same owners as Canon La Gaffelière. A skilfully-
made wine with a lot of concentration, alcohol,
oak (30 to 40% of the *barriques* being new),
and much charm. The 1990 was the first wine
made – or at least matured – by Stephan von
Neipperg, who acquired the estate early in 1991.

Ch du Paradis   map 38/R M1
grand cru

owner: Vignobles Raby Saugeon **area:** 36 ha **cases:**
9,000 **grape % R:** MER 75% CF 20% CS 5% **other
wines:** Ch la Bigarette *(Bordeaux Supérieur)* **other
wines:** Ch Guillemin de Gorre *(Bordeaux Supérieur)*
other châteaux owned: Ch Raby-Jean Voisin *(St-
Emilion)*
33330 Vignonet tel: 05 57 84 53 27
fax: 05 57 84 61 76
The vineyard is less of a paradise than the name
might suggest, for the vines grow on flat land
near the Dordogne, right in the south of the
district. Consequently the wine lacks depth,
concentration and length, although its fruit can
be pleasing. Not of *grand cru* standard.

Ch Paran Justice   map 38/R H6
grand cru

owner: Marie Boutros Toni **area:** 11 ha **cases:**
6,420 **grape % R:** MER 63% CF 33% CS 4%
33330 St-Etienne-de-Lisse tel: 05 57 24 70 71
fax: 05 57 24 65 18
Made by the cooperative, a wine that generally
has some fruit, good tannins, and a decent

Above: Ch Moulin du Cadet

Above: Ch Pavie

quality. It sometimes happens, however, that it has rather too much acidity – perhaps the result of grapes being picked too early. Not matured in cask.

Ch Patarabet map 38/L H9

owner: Eric Bordas *area:* 11 ha *cases:* 5,250 *grape % R:* MER 80% CF 10% CS 10% *second wine:* Domaine de la Palmeraie *(Bordeaux Supérieur)*
33330 St-Emilion tel: 05 57 24 74 73
Low, inconspicuous château by a junction on the Castillon road. Wine from this estate, which was created in 1921, often has a taste rich in extract, with a lot of oak and licorice, and its tannin sticks dry to the teeth. Some fruit is also perceptible. The 1985 vintage was served to the Queen Mother; other vintages have won silver and bronze medals.

Ch Patris map 38/L G7

grand cru
owner: Michel Querre *area:* 12.2 ha *cases:* 6,000 *grape % R:* MER 78% CF 13% CS 9% *second wine:* Ch Grand Gontey *other châteaux owned:* Ch La France *(Médoc)*; Ch Brun Despagne *(Bordeaux Supérieur)*
33330 St-Emilion tel: 05 57 55 51 60
fax: 05 57 55 51 61
In general this is a fine wine, extremely well made and matured for a year in barrels of which 20-40% are of new wood. Firm, soft, aromatic (stewed red and black currants and grapes, licorice, sometimes a flowery element), with oak, vanilla and ample tannin.

Ch Pavie map 38/L G10

1er grand cru classé B
owner: Consorts Valette *area:* 35 ha *cases:* 15,000 *grape % R:* MER 55% CF 25% CS 20% *other châteaux owned:* include Ch Pavie-Decesse *(St-Emilion)*; Ch La Clusière *(St-Emilion)*; Ch La Prade *(Bordeaux Côtes de Francs)*; Abbaye de St Ferme *(Bordeaux)*; Ch de Musset *(Montagne-St-Emilion)*
33330 St-Emilion tel: 05 57 55 43 43
fax: 05 57 24 63 99
The greater part of this vineyard, large for St-Emilion, lies on the south-facing slope of the limestone plateau. The cellar complex stands at the bottom of this slope, the château halfway up; with yet further up a cellar cut in the rock for the barrels – 40% of them new. Pavie wine represents one of the district's sure values. This *premier grand cru classé* is usually a delicious

combination of power and finesse, depth and suppleness with its fruit and oak in balance.

Ch Pavie Decesse map 38/L G10

grand cru classé
owner: Consorts Valette *area:* 9 ha *cases:* 4,000 *grape % R:* MER 60% CF 20% CS 20% *other châteaux owned:* include Ch Pavie *(St-Emilion)*; Ch La Clusière *(St-Emilion)*; Ch La Prade *(Côtes de Francs)*
33330 St-Emilion tel: 05 57 55 43 44
fax: 05 57 24 63 99
Estate set high up on the top of the *côte*, bought in 1971 by the Valette family of nearby Ch Pavie. They have invested a great deal in it, and there's a gradual improvement in wine quality to show for it. Deep colour and abundant tannin are very typical of this *grand cru classé*, so patient bottle-ageing is essential. The better vintages have satisfactory fruit (black currants, black cherry, raspberry), with dark tones and spices. Maturing in oak – a third of the *barriques* are new – adds some vanilla.

Ch Pavie Macquin map 38/L G10

grand cru classé
owner: Famille Corre-Macquin *area:* 15 ha *cases:* 6,500 *grape % R:* MER 70% CF 25% CS 5% *second wine:* Les Chênes de Macquin

Below: Ch Petit-Faurie-de-Soutard

33330 St-Emilion tel: 05 57 24 74 23
fax: 05 57 24 63 78
Since 1990 the vineyard at Pavie Macquin has been organically worked. This has done the standard of the wine no harm: the 1990 was of even better quality than the already impressive 1988 and 1989. Vintages since 1990 also merit praise. Noteworthy qualities of the wine include good – in some vintages impressive – concentration; very pure fruit (notes of cherry, blackberry, raspberry), with smoky oak from *barriques* of which a third are new each year; and well-integrated tannin. Nicolas Thienpont, of Vieux Château Certan (Pomerol) and other estates, is in charge here. Albert Macquin, who gave the property its name, acquired the estate in 1887 and played a great part in the rebirth of the Libournais vineyards after the phylloxera disaster.

Ch Pavillon Cadet map 38/L E9

grand cru
owner: Le Morvan-Leamas *area:* 2.5 ha *cases:* 1,250 *grape % R:* MER 70% CF 30%
33330 St-Emilion tel: 05 56 44 75 11
Remarkably good wine from a small estate: velvety and round, rich in oak, with firm tannin.

Above: Ch Petit Val

Ch Petit Clos Figeac map 38/L D4
grand cru
owner: Guy & Michel Janoueix *area:* 4 ha *cases:* 2,000 *grape % R:* MER 70% CF 15% CS 15% *other châteaux owned:* include Ch Samson *(Pomerol)*; Ch Grate-Cap *(Pomerol)*; Ch Grand Fortin *(St-Emilion)*; Domaine de la Bourrue *(St-Emilion)*
33330 St-Emilion tel: 05 57 51 27 97
fax: 05 57 51 02 74
Vineyard south-west of Ch Figeac yielding a fruity wine, marked by its Merlot, that generally displays firm structure and good tannins. It has one year's ageing in mainly used casks.

Ch Petit-Faurie-de-Soutard
map 38/R E1
grand cru classé
owner: Françoise Capdemourlin/SCE Vignoble Aberlen *area:* 8 ha *cases:* 3,500 *grape % R:* MER 60% CF 30% CS 10% *second wine:* Petit-Faurie-de-Soutard Deuxième *other châteaux owned:* Ch Balestard la Tonnelle *(St-Emilion)*; Ch Cap de Mourlin *(St-Emilion)*; Ch Roudier *(Montagne-St-Emilion)*
33330 St-Emilion tel: 05 57 74 62 06
fax: 05 57 74 59 34
This estate was split off from Ch Soutard in 1850. A reasonably fragrant wine is made here, agreeably fruity as a rule, and also possessing dark, earthy notes. Seldom really generous, but its tannin makes it suitable for ageing in bottle.

Ch Petit-Figeac map 38/L D6
owner: AXA Millésimes *area:* 3 ha *cases:* 1,500 *grape % R:* MER 60% CF 30% CS 10% *other châteaux owned:* include Ch Fleur Pourret *(St-Emilion)*; Ch Cantenac-Brown *(Margaux)*; Ch Pichon-Longueville *(Pauillac)*; Ch Petit Village *(Pomerol)*
33330 St-Emilion tel: 05 57 24 62 61
fax: 05 57 24 68 25
A wine of impeccable quality, generally rich in fruit, but not offering much weight or depth.

Ch Petit Val map 38/L C9
grand cru
owner: Michel Boutet *area:* 9.3 ha *cases:* 4,400 *grape % R:* MER 70% CS 20% CF 10% *other châteaux owned:* Ch Haut Plantey *(St-Emilion)*; Ch Vieux Pourret *(St-Emilion)*
33330 St-Emilion tel: 05 57 24 70 86
fax: 05 57 24 68 30

Certainly no *petit* wine, for it usually boasts roundness, spicy oak, ripe tannins, good fruit and a fine balance.

Ch Peyrelongue map 38/R H1
grand cru
owner: EARL Bouquey & Fils *area:* 12 ha *cases:* 6,000 *grape % R:* MER 70% CF 15% CS 15%
33330 St-Emilion tel: 05 57 24 71 17
fax: 05 57 24 69 24
The Bouquey family, owners of this 1875 château, have lived in St-Emilion for more than three centuries. Peyrelongue is no hail-fellow-well-met kind of wine: its character is rather dour, its taste somewhat angular. But it certainly has quality, together with dark and slightly animal aromas. Matured in cask: 30% new.

Domaine de Peyrelongue
map 38/L H10
grand cru
owner: GFA P. Cassat & Fils *area:* 6 ha *cases:* 2,600 *grape % R:* MER 60% CF 30% CS 10% *other châteaux owned:* include Ch Mauvesin *(St-Emilion)*
33330 St-Emilion tel: 05 57 24 72 36
fax: 05 57 74 48 54
Grand cru made by the Ch Mauvezin team; most of the *barriques* also come from that

Below: Domaine de Peyrelongue

estate. Even in the sunny years the wine is on the fine and fresh side, and has red fruit; but it is without very great power or intensity. Develops quickly.

Ch Peyrouquet map 38/R K5
grand cru
owner: Maurice Cheminade *area:* 18.8 ha *cases:* 10,900 *grape % R:* MER 79% CF 19% CS 2%
33330 St-Pey-d'Armens tel: 05 57 24 70 71
fax: 05 57 24 65 18
A wine with animal aromas and a mellow fruit taste. Less bitter than many other St-Emilions from the cooperative.

Ch Piganeau map 38/L G4
owner: SCI Vignobles Brunot *area:* 3 ha *cases:* 1,300 *grape % R:* MER 75% CF 20% CS 5% *other châteaux owned:* Ch Cantenac *(St-Emilion)*; Ch Tour de Grenet *(Lussac-St-Emilion)*; Ch Maledan *(Bordeaux Supérieur)*
33330 St-Emilion tel: 05 57 51 35 22
fax: 05 57 25 19 15
Firm wine, generally well-balanced. The tannins are usually ripe and there can be stewed fruit in the bouquet, with a touch of mint. Neither great nor particularly long, but sound, savoury and suitable for maturing for some years.

◆ St-Emilion Grand Cru
The term Grand Cru immediately beneath a château name means that the property, although not classified, regularly meets the criteria which entitle it to use the appellation St-Emilion Grand Cru on its label (see appellation information on page 279).

◆ About St-Emilion
The Maison du Vin is located at place Pierre Meyrat, 33330 St-Emilion. Tel 05 57 55 50 55.

The Groupement des Premiers Grands Crus Classés de St-Emilion can be contacted at BP15, 33330 St-Emilion. Tel 05 57 24 69 20.

Above: Ch de Pressac

Ch Pindefleurs
map 38/L G7

grand cru

owner: Micheline Dior *area:* 8.6 ha *cases:* 3,500 *grape % R:* MER 55% CF 45% *second wine:* Clos Lescure

33330 St-Emilion tel: 05 57 24 72 04

Estate at the foot of the slope down from the plateau; it belongs to a member of the Dior family. Partly due to its large proportion of Cabernet Franc, this wine is elegant, fragrant; its fruit is fresh, yet there is also sufficient tannin. Ch Pindefleurs is matured for no less than two full years.

Ch Piney
map 38/R I2

grand cru

owner: Famille Catusseau *area:* 9.6 ha *cases:* 5,570 *grape % R:* MER 57% CF 29% CS 8% MAL 6%

33330 St-Hippolyte tel: 05 57 24 70 71

fax: 05 57 24 65 18

The Union de Producteurs, the St-Emilion cooperative, makes the wines of several dozen individual châteaux. Ch Piney is invariably one of the best: a *grand cru* with ripe fruit and a long finish.

Ch Pipeau
map 38/R I2

grand cru

owner: Famille Mestreguilhem *area:* 35 ha *cases:* 16,600 *grape % R:* MER 80% CS 10% CF 10% *other châteaux owned:* Ch Joinin *(Bordeaux)*

33330 St-Laurent-des-Combes tel: 05 57 24 72 95

fax: 05 57 24 71 25

Superbly-equipped estate in the centre of St-Laurent-des-Combes. An intensely fragrant wine is produced, readily accessible and not very complex. It is soon drinkable – but from a good vintage it has the potential for 10-12 years. Ripe fruit, licorice, bayleaf and oak are present in its aroma.

Ch Plaisance
map 38/L K8

grand cru

owner: Didier Dubois *area:* 8 ha *cases:* 5,000 *grape % R:* MER 75% CS 25%

33330 St-Sulpice-de-Faleyrens tel: 05 57 24 78 85

This estate, established in 1855, generally produces a silky St-Emilion, very open-knit and charming, albeit without much concentration or distinctiveness. 'Pleasing' is the perfect description for it.

Ch de Pressac
map 38/R G6

grand cru

owner: Jacques Pouey *area:* 33 ha *cases:* 13,500 *grape % R:* MER 70% CS 25% MAL 5% *second wine:* Ch Tour de Pressac; Ch Roland *other châteaux owned:* Ch Cadet *(Côtes de Castillon)*

33330 St-Etienne-de-Lisse tel: 05 57 40 18 02

fax: 05 57 40 10 07

Château set on a hill in the east of the appellation, dominating its surroundings and presumably named after the de Pressac family chronicled in the time of the Crusades. The present house dates from the 17th century, and rose on the site of a much larger stronghold which apparently boasted no less than 27 towers. The oldest survival is a gateway in a battlemented wall. The wine has good – occasionally hard – tannins, reasonable oak, and a dark, somewhat animal aroma. Sometimes the vinification is less than immaculate – evidenced by volatile acidity; but the soil here has quality, and the wine can mature over a long period without drying out. There are some interesting old vintages in the cellars.

Ch Le Prieuré
map 38/R F1

grand cru classé

owner: SCE Baronne Guichard *area:* 5.6 ha *cases:* 2,500 *grape % R:* MER 60% CF 30% CS 10% *second wine:* Ch l'Olivier *other châteaux owned:* Ch Vray Croix de Gay *(Pomerol)*; Ch Siaurac *(Lalande-de-Pomerol)*

33330 St-Emilion tel: 05 57 51 64 58

fax: 05 57 51 41 56

A decent, seldom exciting, honourable St-Emilion that in good years has a firm structure, is subtly rounded, with ripe fruit.

Ch Puy-Blanquet
map 38/R G6

grand cru

owner: Roger Jacquet *area:* 23 ha *cases:* 10,800 *grape % R:* MER 60% CF 30% CS 10%

33330 St-Etienne-de-Lisse

tel: 05 57 40 18 18

This wine is generally richer in colour than in taste, although it certainly gives pleasure with its rather supple, ripe red currants and pinch of spice. Tough tannins are also evident. This *grand cru* tastes best from a really great year, for in such vintage it acquires more meat, roundness, fruit and depth.

Ch Puyblanquet Carrille
map 38/R G5

grand cru

owner: Jean-François Carrille *area:* 12 ha *cases:* 6,000 *grape % R:* MER 70% CF 20% CS 10% *second wine:* Ch Boucayery *other châteaux owned:* include Ch Cardinal Villemaurine *(St-Emilion)*

33330 St-Christophe-des-Bardes

tel: 05 57 24 74 46 fax: 05 57 24 64 40

A wine that is usually dark-red, with a lively, spicy and fruity – and also somewhat earthy – firm taste that lingers nicely on the palate. Barrel-ageing lasts 6-12 months; 20% of the casks are new.

Ch Puy-Razac
map 38/L I10

grand cru

owner: Guy Thoilliez *area:* 6 ha *cases:* 2,800 *grape % R:* MER 90% CF 90%

33330 St-Emilion tel: 05 57 24 73 32

No heavyweight: easy, accessible, with a pleasing amount of fruit, but without much nuance or length. For quick consumption. The quality was better in the early 1980s.

Ch Quercy
map 38/R L1

grand cru

owner: Famille Apelbaum-Pidoux *area:* 6 ha *cases:* 2,800 *grape % R:* MER 70% CF 30% *second wine:* Ch Graves de Peyroutas

33330 Vignonet tel: 05 57 84 56 07

fax: 05 57 84 54 82

The small, rather odd château in neo-classical style dates from the end of the 18th century. The name is a reference to *quercus*, the Latin word for oak: there are some ancient oaks in the modest park here. Since 1988 the estate has belonged to the Swiss family Apelbaum-Pidoux, who have been energetically tackling a whole backlog of work. At its best this opaque *grand cru* is mouthfilling, with a distinctly dark, licorice-like aroma, ripe fruit, fine tannins and a judicious amount of oak (one-third of the casks are new for each vintage).

Ch Queyron Patarabet
map 38/L J9

owner: SCEA des Vignobles Itey *area:* 10 ha *cases:* 3,750 *grape % R:* MER 100%

33330 St-Emilion tel: 05 57 24 70 71

fax: 05 57 24 65 18

Wine from the cooperative, with decent fruit and tannin. This pure Merlot wine is far from being the worst St-Emilion from the Union de Producteurs.

Ch Rastouillet Lescure
map 38/R J3

owner: Geneviève Dumery *area:* 8.2 ha *cases:* 5,300 *grape % R:* MER 77% CF 16% CS 7%

33330 St-Hippolyte tel: 05 57 24 70 71

fax: 05 57 24 65 18

A reasonably firm, standard-quality wine, with considerable tannin and some ripe fruit tending towards banana. Vinified by the cooperative.

Ch Ripeau
map 38/L C7

grand cru classé

owner: Françoise de Wilde *area:* 15 ha *cases:* 7,500 *grape % R:* MER 60% CF 30% CS 10% *second wine:* Ch Baradol

33330 St-Emilion tel: 05 57 74 41 41

fax: 05 57 74 41 57

This vineyard dates back at least to 1785, for it appears on the Belleyme map of that date. Françoise de Wilde, who was born at this château, runs the estate and in expert fashion makes an accessible, supple and smooth St-Emilion with an attractive amount of fruit.

Ch Roc de Boisseaux   map 38/L K8
grand cru
owner: Famille Clowez *area:* 8 ha *cases:* 4,200
grape % R: MER 70% CF 15% CS 15% *second wine:*
Ch Mesny de Boisseaux
**33330 St-Sulpice-de-Faleyrens tel: 05 57 74 45 40
fax: 05 57 88 07 00**
This wine does not excel in concentration or
length, but it is well-dbalance, with a varying
measure of fruit and great suppleness. A little
more oak might perhaps make it more
distinguished. The estate was bought in April
1989 by the Clowez family from Calais, who
have installed stainless-steel fermentation vats.

Ch du Rocher   map 38/R H7
grand cru
owner: Baron S. de Montfort *area:* 15 ha *cases:*
6,600 *grape % R:* MER 60% CF 20% CS 20% *second
wine:* Ch Garbillot *other châteaux owned:* Ch
Lagrange Monbadon *(Côtes de Castillon)*
**33330 St-Etienne-de-Lisse tel: 05 57 40 18 20
fax: 05 57 40 37 26**
This ivy-clad château is one of the oldest
buildings in St-Etienne-de-Lisse, and was
named after an earlier family of owners. The
wine has a certain refinement, but it is
sometimes rather dour with fairly high degree
of acidity: it needs ageing to gain suppleness.

Ch Rocher Bellevue Figeac
map 38/L D4
grand cru
owner: Pierre & Charlotte Dutruilh *area:* 7 ha
cases: 3,500 *grape % R:* MER 80% CF 20% *second
wine:* Pavillon la Croix Figeac *other châteaux
owned:* Ch La Croix Figeac Lamarzelle *(St-Emilion)*
**33330 St-Emilion tel: 05 56 81 19 69
fax: 05 56 81 19 69**
Supple wine which quickly becomes silky,
usually of average structure, quite charming
and soon drinkable. Black cherry, black
currants, blackberry and strawberry are among
its nuances, besides some spicy oak and bayleaf.

Ch Rocheyron   map 38/R F4
grand cru
owner: Bernard Oddo *area:* 5.2 ha *cases:* 2,700
grape % R: MER 85% CF 15% *other châteaux owned:*
Ch Roylland *(St-Emilion)*
**33330 St-Emilion tel: 05 57 24 68 27
fax: 05 57 24 65 25**

Below: Ch Ripeau

Above: Ch La Rose-Trimoulet

Grand cru that gives satisfaction, but is not
really deep or concentrated; has some black
fruit and restrained oak tones. It offers
somewhat less class than the same owners' Ch
Roylland.

Ch Rol de Fombrauge   map 38/R E3
grand cru
owner: Francine & Jean-Michel Delloye *area:* 5.5 ha
cases: 3,000 *grape % R:* MER 70% CS 20% CF 10%
second wine: Ch Fleur de Rol *other châteaux
owned:* Ch Terres Mauves *(Côtes de Castillon)*
**33330 St-Christophe-des-Bardes tel:
05 35 86 59 49
fax: 05 35 86 59 49**
This property formed part of Ch Fombrauge
until the beginning of the 20th century. The
'Rol' comes from Role, a local hamlet. It yields
firm, sometimes almost heavy, wine; very sound
and with plenty of oak. Perhaps it does not offer
the utmost refinement, but it is well made. A
third of the casks for maturing are new each
vintage.

Ch Rolland-Maillet   map 38
grand cru
owner: SCEA Fermière des Domaines Rolland *area:*
3.4 ha *cases:* 1,500 *grape % R:* MER 75% CF 25%
other châteaux owned: Ch Fontenil *(Fronsac)*; Ch
Bertineau St-Vincent *(Lalande-de-Pomerol)*; Ch Le
Bon Pasteur *(Pomerol)*
**33500 Pomerol tel: 05 57 51 10 94
fax: 05 57 25 05 54**
Once the long cork has been pulled, an
exquisite wine pours into the glass: muscular,
with luscious fruit, discreet oak and an alluring
generosity.

Ch La Rose Côtes Rol   map 38/L D9
grand cru
owner: Yves Mirande *area:* 9.3 ha *cases:* 3,500
grape % R: MER 65% CF 20% CS 15% *other châteaux
owned:* Ch Roc de Joanin *(Côtes de Castillon)*
**33330 St-Emilion tel: 05 57 24 71 28
fax: 05 57 74 40 42**
A family estate for three generations, where
mechanized grape picking is largely used. Its
wines deserve attention: they often taste and
smell of damp undergrowth and truffles, and in
the aroma there can also be animal elements –
fur, leather – as well as ripe fruit. Smooth and
generous structure.

Ch La Rose-Pourret   map 38/L D8
grand cru
owner: B. et B. Warion *area:* 8 ha *cases:* 4,100
grape % R: MER 75% CF 25%
**33330 St-Emilion tel: 05 57 24 71 13
fax: 05 57 74 43 93**
Firm, richly coloured wine with an aroma
containing elements of candied fruit, earthy
tones and oak. Maturing takes place in wood, a
third of it new barrels, and now lasts a year
instead of 18 months.

Ch La Rose-Trimoulet   map 38/R D1
grand cru
owner: Jean-Claude Brisson *area:* 5 ha *cases:*
2,500 *grape % R:* MER 64% CF 28% CS 8% *other
châteaux owned:* Ch l'Abbaye *(Puisseguin-St-
Emilion)*; Ch La Roseraie du Mont *(Puisseguin-St-
Emilion)*
**33330 St-Emilion tel: 05 57 24 73 24
fax: 05 57 24 67 08**
This estate came into being in 1835 when Jean
Durand bought from Madame Trimoulet the
central part of her property and called it
Domaine Haut-Trimoulet. Its wines won
international medals and acquired an excellent
reputation in Belgium. After the Second World
War the present owner's father changed the
name of the estate to Ch La Rose-Trimoulet.

◆
The St-Emilion classification
Unlike the 1855 Classification, St-Emilion's
system allows for regular revision. The
latest is that of 1996.

At the top of the classification are the
thirteen *premier grand cru classé* estates
of which two, Châteaux Ausone and Cheval
Blanc, have the additional distinctive suffix
'A'. Next come the 55 *grand cru classé*
châteaux.

In St-Emilion, simple *grand cru* is not a
classification, but a separate AC (see page
279). To use the words *grand cru*, a
château must submit its wine for tasting
and analysis each year to the appellation
authorities.

Above: Ch St-Georges (Côte Pavie)

Today the wine has considerable oak – with 50 to 100% of the casks being new – together with notes of spices and black and red currants.

Ch Roylland
map 38/L G7

grand cru

owner: Bernard Oddo **area:** 4.2 ha **cases:** 2,100 **grape % R:** MER 90% CF 10% **other châteaux owned:** Ch Rocheyron (St-Emilion)
33330 St-Emilion tel: 05 57 24 68 27
fax: 05 57 24 65 25
Today a splendid wine is produced here, with a high (90%) Merlot content: there is toasted oak, blackberry jam, cocoa, an elegant firmness, a blackish-red colour. A grand cru with good ageing potential.

Ch Rozier
map 38/R H2

grand cru

owner: Jean-Bernard Saby **area:** 18 ha **cases:** 7,000 **grape % R:** MER 75% CF 20% CS 5% **second wine:** Ch de Monturon **other châteaux owned:** Ch Hauchat (Fronsac); Ch Reindent (Bordeaux Supérieur); Ch Courrière-Rongieras (Lussac-St-Emilion)
33330 St-Laurent-des-Combes tel: 05 57 24 73 03
fax: 05 57 24 67 77
A wine often characterized by spicy oak and tannin, usually modestly fruity. Requires some years to mature. The grapes come from plots in four different communes; the vines have an average age of 40 years.

Domaine du Sable
map 38/R H2

owner: Joël Appollot **area:** 1.1 ha **cases:** 600 **grape % R:** MER 80% CF 10% CS 10% **other châteaux owned:** Clos Haut Troquart (St-Georges-St-Emilion)
33330 St-Christophe-des-Bardes
tel: 05 57 74 61 62 fax: 05 57 74 45 88
Solid wine with a good deal of tannin: it needs time. It can have intense aromas – strawberry jam, ripe fruit, oak, vanilla – plus a touch of pepper in its fairly short finish.

Ch St-Georges (Côte Pavie)
map 38/L G9

grand cru classé

owner: Jacques Masson **area:** 5.5 ha **cases:** 2,500 **grape % R:** MER 80% CS 20%
33330 St-Emilion tel: 05 57 74 44 23
This estate presumably got its name from the chapel built here at the end of the Carolingian period. Foundations of that chapel, Roman coins and other finds were dug up around here in 1875. The property already belonged then to the family who still own it today. The superbly-sited vineyard, between Pavie and La Gaffelière, yields a grand cru classé full of character, with refinement, beautiful fruit, good tannin and a long aftertaste.

Ch Saint-Lô
map 38/R K5

grand cru

owner: Vatana & Fils **area:** 12 ha **cases:** 5,000 **grape % R:** MER 85% CS 15% **second wine:** L'Ermitage de Saint-Lô
33330 St-Pey-d'Armens tel: 05 57 47 14 98
fax: 05 57 47 13 71
Perfectly restored and maintained château with a not especially large vineyard that nevertheless extends into four different communes. The wine has shown increasing quality since the beginning of the 1990s, partly due to being matured in casks – of which half are new – for a maximum 18 months. Worth following.

Clos St-Martin
map 38/L F8

grand cru classé

owner: Famille Reiffers **area:** 1.4 ha **cases:** 700 **grape % R:** MER 67% CF 33% **other châteaux owned:** Ch Côte de Baleau (St-Emilion); Ch Grandes Murailles (St-Emilion)
33330 St-Emilion tel: 05 57 24 71 09
fax: 05 57 24 69 72
Much new oak (from all-new barriques) and toast in the bouquet; a stylish, concentrated taste, very refined, with fruit in plenty and an endless finish. In good years this is a truly great wine, from a minuscule vineyard.

Ch de Saint-Pey
map 38/R K4

owner: Maurice & Pierre Musset **area:** 18 ha **cases:** 9,000 **grape % R:** MER 75% CF 20% CS 5%
33330 St-Pey-d'Armens tel: 05 57 47 15 25
fax: 05 57 47 15 04
This estate has belonged to the Musset family for hundreds of years; part of the château is 17th century. The wine is striking for its deep colour (in less-good years as well), and a meaty, almost creamy taste with dark tones, jam-like fruit and integrated tannin. At its best after four to six years. Usually a very reliable wine, although a technical mistake was made with the 1990 vintage.

Below: Ch Sansonnet

Clos Saint-Vincent
map 38/L J7

grand cru

owner: Michel & Eliane Latorse **area:** 4.6 ha **cases:** 2,500 **grape % R:** MER 60% CS 40% **other châteaux owned:** include Vieux Château Lamothe (Bordeaux); Ch Canteloup (Premières Côtes de Bordeaux)
33330 St-Sulpice-de-Faleyrens tel: 05 57 74 44 80
fax: 05 56 23 92 76
Wine wholly or partly nurtured in new casks with, after 18 months, plenty of wood, tobacco, and luxuriant vanilla, together with licorice, bayleaf, nuts, and at a time a hint of currants, the tannins can be somewhat dry. Generally requires a wait of at least five years.

Ch Sansonnet
map 38/R F1

grand cru

owner: SCEA Robin **area:** 7 ha **cases:** 4,000 **grape % R:** MER 60% CF 20% CS 20% **second wine:** Domaine de la Salle **other châteaux owned:** Ch Doumayne (St-Emilion); Clos Vieux Taillefer (Pomerol)
33330 St-Emilion tel: 05 57 51 03 65
fax: 05 57 25 00 20
Estate comprising one block of land close to Ch Trotte Vieille (so just east of St-Emilion). The wine the Robin family have been making here for four generations is elegant rather than powerful, with a reasonable complexity and a good balance. Oak, herbs and spices chiefly determine its aroma.

Clos de Sarpe
map 38/R F2

grand cru

owner: Jean-Guy Beyney **area:** 4 ha **cases:** 2,000 **grape % R:** MER 80% CF 20%
33330 St-Christophe-des-Bardes
tel: 05 57 24 72 39 fax: 05 57 74 47 54
Real craftsmanship produces a concentrated, well-constructed grand cru wine, always with a good deal of jammy red and black berry fruit. Not oak-aged. Three-quarters of the vines have an average age of around 50 years.

Ch La Serre
map 38/L F10

grand cru classé

owner: Bernard d'Arfeuille **area:** 7 ha **cases:** 3,500 **grape % R:** MER 80% CF 20% **second wine:** Les Menuts de La Serre **other châteaux owned:** Ch La Pointe (Pomerol); Ch Toumalin (Fronsac)
33330 St-Emilion tel: 05 57 24 71 38
fax: 05 57 51 08 15

Above: Clos de Sarpe

La Serre is a 17th-century château built by Romain de Labayme, descendant of a family that included mayors and *parlementaires*. From its vineyard up on the plateau to the east of the town there comes a most distinguished *grand cru classé*, a wine with elements of candied fruit, nicely integrated oak (vanilla, caramel, toast – half the casks are new), and tannins often so mellow that one can hardly taste them. They are certainly there, however, and give the wine a perfect balance and splendid length.

Ch Soutard
map 38/L E10
grand cru classé
owner: Famille des Ligneris **area:** 22 ha **cases:** 10,000 **grape % R:** MER 60% CF 40% **second wine:** Clos de la Tonnelle
33330 St-Emilion tel: 05 57 24 72 23
fax: 05 57 24 66 94
In its youth Soutard's wine is apt to taste rather tight – often even severe – but it has brilliant maturing potential. Soutards from the 1950s and 1960s are among the finest wines you can taste in St-Emilion – to say nothing of the legendary 1947. To an important extent this is due to the nature of the soil, for the grapes grow on one of the highest parts of the limestone plateau. Home of this compact,

Below: Ch La Serre

concentrated *grand cru classé* is a château built around 1775, to which two wings were added in the 19th century.

Ch Tauzinat l'Hermitage
map 38/R F5
grand cru
owner: Bernard Moueix **area:** 9.3 ha **cases:** 5,500 **grape % R:** MER 80% CF 20% **second wine:** Ch Grand Treuil **other châteaux owned:** include Ch Taillefer *(Pomerol)*
33500 St-Christophe-des-Bardes
tel: 05 57 55 30 20 fax: 05 57 25 22 14
From this 1670 château there comes a pleasant, quite lush and supple-tasting charming wine, soon ready for drinking. It is without great depth, but it does offer some dried fruit, tobacco and spices.

Ch Tertre Daugay
map 38/L G8
grand cru classé
owner: Léo de Malet Roquefort **area:** 16 ha **cases:** 7,000 **grape % R:** MER 60% CF 40% **second wine:** Ch de Roquefort **other châteaux owned:** Ch La Gaffelière *(St-Emilion)*
33330 St-Emilion tel: 05 57 24 72 15
fax: 05 57 24 65 24
This estate, which has undergone renewal since 1978, has its *chai* on the southern edge of the

Below: Ch Tertre Daugay

plateau, on the site of a medieval watchtower. The view from here over the Dordogne valley is splendid. The vineyard – a single block of land – lies on the slope of that plateau. In good years the wine has colour, tannin, velvety fruit, firm oak and concentration; but its standard may be noticeably lower in lesser vintages.

Ch Tertre Roteboeuf
map 38/R G2
grand cru
owner: François & Emilie Mitjavile **area:** 5.7 ha **cases:** 2,300 **grape % R:** MER 80% CF 20% **other châteaux owned:** Ch Roc de Cambes *(Côtes de Bourg)*
33330 St-Laurent-des-Combes tel: 05 57 24 70 57
fax: 05 57 74 42 11
The potential of this sloping vineyard on clay and limestone in the east of the appellation was first grasped by François Mitjavile, its owner since the late 1970s. He made fullest use of the natural inheritance of the site here – the *terroir* – by keeping yields low, picking the grapes when on the point of over-ripeness, and then fermenting them, with a period of maceration. Since 1985 Mitjavile has followed this by 18 months' *élevage* in new oak. This method has resulted in almost staggeringly flamboyant wines that are among the best of all St-Emilions. They offer tremendous colour, great vitality, burnt oak, fat layers of fruit, earthy aromas, lush tannins, all adding up to a most concentrated whole.

Ch Teyssier
map 38/L K9
grand cru
owner: Jonathan & Lyn Maltus **area:** 14 ha **cases:** 7,500 **grape % R:** MER 80% CF 20% **second wine:** l'Esprit de Teyssier *(AC Bordeaux)*
33330 Vignonet tel: 05 57 84 64 22
fax: 05 57 84 63 54
Much has changed here since British owners acquired this estate in 1991. In the vineyard the proportion of Merlot has been raised to 80%, the *cuvier* has been equipped with stainless-steel tanks, the capacity of the *chai* doubled to store more casks, a third of them new; and a planned extension means the vineyard will be increased to 26 ha. Although the 1990 was still somewhat below par for a *grand cru*, the quality has been improving since then, with more fruit, better oak, greater concentration. A château worth following.

Ch Tourans
map 38/R G5

grand cru

owner: Vignobles Rocher-Cap de Rive **area:** 12 ha
cases: 7,000 **grape % R:** MER 70% CS 30% **second
wine:** Ch Paradis Sicard **other châteaux owned:**
include Ch Cap d'Or *(St-Georges-St-Emilion)*
**33330 St-Etienne-de-Lisse tel: 05 57 40 08 88
fax: 05 57 40 19 93**

A *grand cru* that benefits from bottle-age, after
its 18 months' maturing in barrels of which a
third are new. It comes across with elements
that include animal tones, black fruit,
considerable oak and firm tannins.

Ch Tour Baladoz
map 38/R G2

grand cru

owner: Jacques de Schepper **area:** 8.1 ha **cases:**
4,150 **grape % R:** MER 80% CF 15% CS 5% **second
wine:** Ch Tour Saint Laurent **other châteaux owned:**
Ch Haut Breton Larigaudière *(Margaux)*; Ch Les
Charmilles *(Bordeaux Supérieur)*
**33330 St-Laurent-des-Combes tel: 05 57 88 94 17
fax: 05 57 88 39 14**

At first, after its foundation in the 19th century,
this estate was called Baladeau. In 1896 this
became Baladoz; its present name arose after a
tower was built on the site in 1911. The wine
has class and character, partly due to a firm
taste with a good balance between fruit and
spicy, smoky oak. As well as herbs and vanilla
the bouquet may hold something reminiscent
of autumn woodlands, undergrowth and moss.
About 60% of the barrels are replaced annually.

Ch Tour de Corbin Despagne
map 38/R B7

owner: Gérard Despagne **area:** 6 ha **cases:** 2,500
grape % R: MER 80% CF 20% **second wine:** Les
Piliers **other wines:** Ch la Rose Figeac *(Pomerol)*;
Ch Maison Blanche *(Montagne-St-Emilion)*
**33330 St-Emilion tel: 05 57 74 62 18
fax: 05 57 74 58 98**

A St-Emilion demanding some patience, usually
with a very clean aroma (fruit such as
blackberry and bilberry), which is followed by a
similarly fruity, round, well-concentrated taste.
The finish can sometimes be a little dry. Made
under the supervision of Ch Maison Blanche, an
estate in Montagne-St-Emilion with the same
owners.

Ch La Tour du Pin Figeac
map 38/L C5

grand cru classé

owner: Giraud-Bélivier **area:** 11 ha **cases:** 5,300
grape % R: MER 75% CF 25% **second wine:** La
Tournelle du Pin Figeac **other wines:** Ch Le Caillou
(Pomerol)
**33330 St-Emilion tel: 05 57 51 63 93
fax: 05 57 51 74 95**

There are two châteaux of this name, on
adjoining sites. Both come from the once much
bigger Figeac estate – and neither of them has
either a tower or a pine tree. This property,
belonging to the Giraud-Béliviers, is slightly
larger than the other one, owned by the Moueix
family. The quality of its wine is on a rising
curve and today has refinement and supple,
very ripe black fruit. The influence of the oak is
not overdone.

Ch La Tour du Pin Figeac
map 38/L C5

grand cru classé

owner: Jean-Michel Moueix **area:** 9 ha **cases:** 4,000
grape % R: MER 70% CF 30% **second wine:** Clos La
Fleur Figeac **other châteaux owned:** include Ch
Taillefer *(Pomerol)*

Above: Ch La Tour du Pin Figeac

**33330 St-Emilion tel: 05 57 74 78 58
fax: 05 57 24 63 46**

A rising standard is also being noticed at the
Moueix portion of La Tour du Pin Figeac *(see
previous entry)*, but the wine made here has a
quite different personality. It offers more power,
fat and extract, plus jammy fruit, and is very
expressive.

Ch la Tour Figeac
map 38/L C5

grand cru classé

owner: Otto Rettenmaier **area:** 13.6 ha **cases:**
6,200 **grape % R:** MER 60% CF 40%
**33330 St-Emilion tel: 05 57 51 77 62
fax: 05 57 25 36 92**

After a number of poor years this wine is back
in form, particularly since the 1994 vintage –
the first from Otto Maximilian Rettenmaier,
who has brought in an American winemaker.
The wine has a Rubenesque voluptuousness,
jammy fruit, fine oak (40% of the casks are
new), and a lengthy finale. This estate was
separated from Ch Figeac around 1880. The
château is a charming, trimly-maintained
chartreuse, with behind it the small tower,
rebuilt in about 1960.

Ch Tour Grand Faurie
map 38/L C9

grand cru

owner: Jean Feytit **area:** 12.7 ha **cases:** 6,000
grape % R: MER 70% CF 30% **second wine:** Clos
Grand Faurie
**33330 St-Emilion tel: 05 57 24 73 75
fax: 05 57 74 46 94**

A warming wine and a frequent prize-winner:
dark-toned, its fruit ripe red and black currants.
Oak shows a quite discreet presence.

Ch Tour St-Christophe
map 38/R F3

grand cru

owner: Gunnar Johannesson **area:** 17 ha **cases:**
8,000 **grape % R:** MER 70% CF 15% CS 15% **other
châteaux owned:** Ch Tour Musset *(Montagne-St-
Emilion)*
**33330 St-Christophe-des-Bardes
tel: 05 57 24 77 15 fax: 05 57 74 43 57**

Usually this is a generous, concentrated St-
Emilion, in a fine setting of wood and its
associated aromas – it matures for a year, a
third of the casks being new. This wine is
generally a success in the lesser years too. It has
won a good number of medals since the 1980s.

◆

Grape varieties: synonyms, oddities and the everyday

Some traditional names are still given
official status in the appellation decrees:

Bouchet St-Emilion name for Cabernet
Franc

Côt or Cot Synonym for Malbec

Pressac St-Emilion name for Malbec

There are also some minor varieties which
figure in the appellation decrees but are
obscure or seldom grown:

Carmenère Red grape considered the
equal of Cabernet Sauvignon in the early
19th century. Susceptible to disease,
therefore now very rare; though still legal in
all Médoc ACs and in the Premières Côtes
de Bordeaux.

Merlot Blanc May be a mutation of Merlot,
or a separate variety. Little is now grown,
but it can be found in the Premières Côtes
de Bordeaux and Entre-Deux-Mers zones.

Ondenc A virtually vanished white grape,
still permitted for the Bordeaux AC.

Mauzac White variety still important
further east; all but gone from Bordeaux,
but still a legal *cépage accessoire* in Entre-
Deux-Mers.

Sauvignon Gris White variety described by
some growers as an old clone, now
reintroduced. Grown in the eastern
Entre-Deux-Mers. Fresh, aromatically
fruity wine.

Some grapes have rather low status but
are still widely grown:

Ugni Blanc White variety, the second most
common in Bordeaux after Sauvignon
Blanc, and the main ingredient of Cognac.
Allowed in generic AC wines.

Colombard White variety common in the
Blayais. White Côtes de Blaye has to be at
least 60% Colombard.

Above: Ch Tour Grand Faurie

Ch Tour Saint-Pierre map 38/L C10
grand cru
owner: Bernard & Jacques Goudineau **area:** 12 ha
cases: 5,000 **grape % R:** MER 80% CS 10% CF 10%
second wine: Domaine de Vachon
33330 St-Emilion tel: 05 57 24 70 23
fax: 05 57 74 42 74
An estate well-known to tourists: it lies close to
the St-Emilion camp-site. The wine has a fairly
rustic character, and there is freshness plus a
reasonable amount of aroma alongside its
suppleness. Of average structure: to be avoided
in lesser years, when acidity can be too high.

Ch Trianon map 38/L E5
owner: Madame Hubert Lecointre **area:** 6.4 ha
cases: 3,750 **grape % R:** MER 70% CF 25% CS 5%
33330 St-Emilion tel: 05 57 51 42 63
Property a few hundred metres south of Ch
Figeac; in the past the Cruse firm was among
those bottling its wine. Today this is a very
decent average St-Emilion, estate-bottled, with
supple roundness and a fair amount of fruit.

Ch Trimoulet map 38/R D1
grand cru
owner: Michel Jean **area:** 17.4 ha **cases:** 9,000
grape % R: MER 60% CF 30% CS 10% **second wine:**
Emilius de Trimoulet **other châteaux owned:** Vieux
Château Negrit (Montagne-St-Emilion)
33330 St-Emilion tel: 05 57 24 70 56
fax: 05 57 74 41 69
Classic, well-constructed St-Emilion with dark
and sometimes also animal notes. It needs to be
given rest. The first time the estate was
mentioned was in 1730, in Jean Trimoulet's
will, when it was divided among his six
children. For the last two centuries the estate
has belonged to the Jean family.

Ch Troplong Mondot map 38/R G1
grand cru classé
owner: Christine Valette **area:** 30 ha **cases:** 14,000
grape % R: MER 80% CF 10% CS 10% **second wine:**
Mondot **other wines:** Rosé de Mondot (AC
Bordeaux)
33330 St-Emilion tel: 05 57 55 32 05
fax: 05 57 55 32 07
Since the 1980s the reputation of this estate has
greatly improved under the inspired and
dedicated direction of Christine Valette. At every
harvest the grapes are rigorously selected –

which means picking by hand. Vinification is
carefully carried out in stainless-steel tanks at a
meticulously controlled temperature, and
maturing takes place in oak *barriques* of which
as a rule 60% are new. The wine is
distinguished by the high degree of extract
(opulent fruit, toasted oak, licorice), combined
with great style. Although the taste quite
quickly takes on a velvety, alluring aspect, the
wine has enough intrinsic strength to last for
10-20 years. The château which makes this
outstanding St-Emilion lies close to the highest
point in the district, and was built in 1745 by
Raymond de Sèze, a lawyer to Louis XIV.

Ch Trotte Vieille map 38/R F1
1er grand cru classé B
owner: Philippe Castéja & Chantal Preben Hansen
area: 10 ha **cases:** 4,750 **grape % R:** MER 50% CF
45% CS 5% **other châteaux owned:** include Ch
Batailley (Pauillac); Ch Bergat (St-Emilion); Ch du
Domaine de l'Eglise (Pomerol)
33330 St-Emilion tel: 05 57 24 71 34
fax: 05 57 87 60 30
According to tradition this modest house was
named after a venerable owner who served her
customers at breakneck speed, *trotte vieille*
here meaning something like 'the galloping

granny'. Since the mid-1980s this estate has
been logging progress with its wine. From
being sound, but not very refined, it has evolved
into a more concentrated, nuanced, and at
times decidedly impressive St-Emilion. Its
aroma can have elements of ripe black fruits,
licorice, coffee and cocoa, while the high
proportion of new casks (half of them each
year) provides added depth.

Ch de Valandraud map 38/L F9
grand cru
owner: Jean-Luc Thunevin & Murielle Andraud **area:**
2.6 ha **cases:** 750 **grape % R:** MER 75% CF 20% MAL
5% **second wine:** Virginie de Valandraud
33330 St-Emilion tel: 05 57 24 65 60
fax: 05 57 24 67 03
Jean-Luc and Murielle Thunevin, who are
involved in a number of wine-shops and
restaurants in St-Emilion, have since 1990
succeeded in putting together a small wine
estate of their own by making no fewer than ten
different purchases in two communes. The
same perseverance has been applied to
producing the best possible wine here: with
success, for in a short time this *grand cru*
acquired superstar status. Its quality is
admirable, thanks to an almost hedonistic,
sumptuous richness of texture, fruit, oak and
other effects. Only new barrels are used for the
maturing period of 18-24 months.

Ch du Val d'Or map 38/L M10
grand cru
owner: Vignobles Bardet **area:** 11 ha **cases:** 5,000
grape % R: MER 85% CF 12% CS 3% **other châteaux
owned:** Ch Lardit (Côtes de Castillon); Ch Rocher
Lideyre (Côtes de Castillon); Ch Pontet-Fumet (St-
Emilion)
33330 Vignonet tel: 05 57 84 53 16
fax: 05 57 74 93 47
A wine with personality, concentration and
strength, it also offers fruit (sometimes tending
to strawberry) and bayleaf – not a St-Emilion
for those liking smooth, accessible wines.

Domaine de la Vieille Eglise
map 38/R H4
grand cru
owner: René Micheau-Maillou & Constant Palatin
area: 13.3 ha **cases:** 6,500 **grape % R:** MER 70% CF
15% CS 15% **second wine:** Ch Marquis de Mons

Below: Ch Tour Saint-Pierre

Above: Ch Troplong Mondot

other châteaux owned: Ch Roquevieille *(Côtes de Castillon)*; Chatain-Pineau *(Lalande-de-Pomerol)*
33330 St-Hippolyte tel: 05 57 24 61 99
fax: 05 57 24 61 99
Very fragrant wine, with fruit (both fresh and preserved), leather, fur, tobacco, and a hint of orange-peel – a wine that despite its sultriness seldom tastes really muscular, and sometimes has some fresh acidity. This engaging, good-quality St-Emilion comes from an estate split off from Ch de Ferrand in 1970.

Ch Vieille Tour la Rose   map 38/L D10
grand cru
owner: Daniel Ybert **area:** 2.8 ha **cases:** 1,200
grape % R: MER 80% CF 15% CS 5% **second wine:** Ch les Polyanthas **other châteaux owned:** Domaine Vieux Taillefer *(Pomerol)*
33330 St-Emilion tel: 05 57 24 73 41
fax: 05 57 74 44 83
Grand cru whose considerable tannin means that it needs to age. Its taste contains notes of red and black currants, plus leather. The wine spends a short time in cask. This small estate has now belonged to three generations of the same family.

Vieux Château Haut-Béard
map 38/R H3
grand cru
owner: Gerard Mayé **area:** 4.5 ha **cases:** 2,000
grape % R: MER 90% CS 10%
33500 St-Laurent-des-Combes tel: 05 57 24 62 71
fax: 05 57 74 94 46
The vines here grow on a well-exposed clay and limestone slope; the Merlot grape predominates. Haut-Béard makes a harmonious wine that is firmly structured, displaying supple fruit and a touch of licorice. A good-tasting St-Emilion, but no high-flyer.

Ch du Vieux-Guinot   map 38/R J4
grand cru
owner: Vignobles Rollet **area:** 10 ha **cases:** 5,600
grape % R: MER 56% CF 27% CS 17% **other châteaux owned:** include Ch Gaillard de la Gorce *(St-Emilion)*
33330 St-Etienne-de-Lisse tel: 05 57 47 15 13
fax: 05 57 47 10 50
Grand cru offering considerable body, with a dark, animal aroma, and at first rather rough tannins.

◆
Neighbouring appellations
The valley of the Barbanne, a stream which runs into the Isle, forms the northern boundary of St-Emilion proper.

Beyond are four appellations collectively known as the St-Emilion 'satellites'. These zones used to label their wine St-Emilion, some using the words 'second cru of St-Emilion', but since 1936 they have had their own ACs.

These are Lussac-St-Emilion, Montagne-St-Emilion, Puisseguin-St-Emilion and St-Georges-St-Emilion. They have their own chapter in the Atlas which follows that on St-Emilion.

To the west of St-Emilion is Pomerol; to the east the Côtes de Castillon.

Some land to the south and south-west of St-Emilion, bordering the Dordogne, is excluded from the appellation as it is too low-lying.

Vieux Château Pelletan   map 38/R F3
grand cru
owner: Marc Magnaudeix **area:** 6.9 ha **cases:** 3,830 **grape % R:** MER 80% CF 20% **second wine:** Ch Tertre de Sarpe **other châteaux owned:** Ch Vieux Larmande *(St-Emilion)*
33330 St-Christophe-des-Bardes
tel: 05 57 24 60 49 fax: 05 57 24 61 91
The property has been run by the same family since 1924. The wine that they make here is notable for its rounded, firm structure, reinforced with tannin, and for its aroma with its balance of animal and licorice notes. It is matured for a year in *barriques* of which 20% are new each year.

Ch Vieux Labarthe   map 38/R L2
owner: Famille Martin **area:** 9.2 ha **cases:** 5,900
grape % R: MER 70% CF 26% CS 4%
33330 Vignonet tel: 05 57 24 70 71
fax: 05 57 24 65 18
An estate that is associated with the Union des Producteurs, the appellation's cooperative. Vieux Labarthe produces a decent, well-structured St-Emilion, which offers mellow fruit and ripe tannins.

Ch Vieux Larmande   map 38/L E9
grand cru
owner: Marc Magnaudeix **area:** 4.3 ha **cases:** 2,300 **grape % R:** MER 75% CF 25% **other châteaux owned:** Vieux Château Pelletan *(St-Emilion)*
33330 St-Emilion tel: 05 57 24 60 49
fax: 05 57 24 61 91
Quite fragrant, fairly lively, sound wine that will readily mature for 5-10 years as a rule. Its aroma is dark with bayleaf, leather, wood scents and licorice. 20% of the casks it is aged in are new each year.

Ch Vieux Pourret   map 38/L E8
grand cru
owner: Michel Boutet **area:** 4.2 ha **cases:** 2,000
grape % R: MER 80% CF 20% **other châteaux owned:** Ch Haut-Plantey *(St-Emilion)*; Ch Petit Val *(St-Emilion)*
33330 St-Emilion tel: 05 57 24 70 86
fax: 05 57 24 68 30
A usually successful wine where oak, fruit and spices are in balance. It also has firm tannins and fills the mouth generously.

Below: Ch Trotte Vieille

Above Ch Villemaurine

Ch Vieux Sarpe
map 38/R E2
grand cru
owner: Jean Janoueix **area:** 7 ha **cases:** 3,500
grape % R: MER 70% CF 20% CS 10% **other châteaux
owned:** include Ch Haut-Sarpe *(St-Emilion)*
**33330 St-Emilion tel: 05 57 51 41 86
fax: 05 57 51 76 83**
Firm, solidly-built St-Emilion from a well-
drained terraced vineyard. It generally takes
nine or ten years for Vieux Sarpe's wine to be
ready for drinking. Besides red fruit it has
considerable oak: each year 30% of the barrels
are new.

Ch Villemaurine
map 38/L F9
grand cru classé
owner: Robert Giraud **area:** 7 ha **cases:** 3,800
grape % R: MER 70% CS 30% **other châteaux
owned:** include Clos Larcis *(St-Emilion)*; Ch du
Cartillon *(Haut-Médoc)*; Ch Timberlay *(Bordeaux
Supérieur)*
**33330 St-Emilion tel: 05 57 74 46 44
fax: 05 57 43 08 75**
The history of Ch Villemaurine goes back to the
8th century AD, when a Moorish force was
encamped just outside St-Emilion. This site
therefore acquired the name *Ville Maure*. The
underground cellar complex here is most
impressive – it is nearly as big as the vineyard
itself, and is used for receptions, conferences
and banquets. There is room for more than
1,500 people. Many Villemaurine vintages have
been characterized by having too much oak
(two thirds of casks are new, and ageing lasts a
year and a half), and too little body and depth to
balance this. The *terroir* is excellent, but is
often not used to full advantage. On the other
hand, in lighter years the wine can sometimes
be amazingly good. Its colour is nearly always
dark and deep.

Ch Viramière
map 38/R H6
grand cru
owner: SCEA des Vignobles Dumon **area:** 11.8 ha
cases: 6,830 **grape % R:** MER 82% CF 15% CS 3%
**33330 St-Etienne-de-Lisse tel: 05 57 24 70 71
fax: 05 57 24 65 18**
Not a top wine, but certainly one of the better
St-Emilions from the Union de Producteurs.
Has decent concentration, fruit, meat and
smooth tannins – even in lesser years.

◆
Grape varieties

Main and other permitted varieties for each
appellation are given in the appellation fact
box at the end of the relevant introduction.

For châteaux, percentages of grapes
grown are given as supplied by the
château.

Abbreviations: CF Cabernet Franc,
COL Colombard, CS Cabernet Sauvignon,
MAL Malbec, MER Merlot, MUSC Muscadelle,
PV Petit Verdot, SAUV B Sauvignon Blanc,
SÉM Sémillon

Ugni Blanc is not abbreviated, nor are
minor varieties such as Carmenère. In St-
Emilion, Cabernet Franc is sometimes
called Bouchet.

Ch La Voûte
map 38
owner: Michel Moreau **area:** 1.5 ha **cases:** 800
grape % R: MER 90% CF 5% CS 5% **other châteaux
owned:** Ch d'Arvouet *(Montagne-St-Emilion)*
**33330 St-Etienne-de-Lisse tel: 05 57 74 56 60
fax: 05 57 74 02 44**
An almost pure Merlot wine, elegant in
character, in which the fruit is as a rule velvety
and abundant.

Ch Yon-Figeac
map 38/L E7
grand cru classé
owner: GFA du Ch Yon Figeac/Vignobles Bernard
Germain **area:** 24.5 ha **cases:** 12,000 **grape % R:**
MER 75% CF 25% **second wine:** Ch Yon Saint Martin
other châteaux owned: include Ch Charron
(Premières Côtes de Blaye); Ch Peyredoulle
(Premières Côtes de Blaye)
**33330 St-Emilion tel: 05 57 64 23 67
fax: 05 57 64 36 20**
Sound, although not highly concentrated, wine:
supple, aromatic and full of flavour. Charred
wood – a third of the casks are new – is always
present, together with related aromas such as
vanilla, cinnamon, coffee and spices. In the
lesser years the oak may be too dominant,
upsetting the balance somewhat.

St-Emilion satellites

To the north-east of St-Emilion itself, across the Barbanne stream, lie four appellations which are allowed to append St-Emilion to their name – Montagne, Lussac, Puisseguin and St-Georges. These outlying areas are a considerable force in their own right: they produce a large quantity of wine the best of which, from one of the finer properties, can be better value and every bit as good as much from their more prestigious neighbour. To the east are the Côtes de Francs and Côtes de Castillon (see page 360), while to the north very similar countryside yields similar wines under the generic Bordeaux appellations (see page 219). See map 37 for the general location and map 40 for the specifics.

These appellations date from 1936. There was a fifth, Parsac; but wines from this former commune have since 1973 been produced under the Montagne-St-Emilion appellation. Of the four, the most prestigious (and the largest) is Montagne, which borders the Barbanne stream, followed closely by Lussac to its north. Puisseguin, which lies to the east of these two, produces roughly half the amount. Very little St-Georges is seen, as most producers with vineyards within this appellation also have the right to use the better-known Montagne appellation.

Unlike St-Emilion with its distinct divide between plateau and hillside, this is an undulating area of valleys and low hills. Soil types vary considerably and reflect those of neighbouring St-Emilion and Pomerol, with a preponderance of clay and limestone. Many of its properties are very small – producing well under 10,000

The church of Montagne-St-Emilion

cases a year – and the local cooperatives are important. Lussac and Puisseguin in fact share the same cooperative, which is located in the village of Puisseguin itself and is responsible for just under a third of the total Lussac production, and well over half that of Puisseguin.

In style the top wines bear a striking similarity to those of St-Emilion itself, and the better examples could easily be considered the equivalent of a St-Emilion *grand cru*. Merlot is the dominant grape variety, followed by Cabernet Franc. These wines are rarely austere; they boast supple flavours and an open, immediately appealing nose. Some of the lesser wines are, however, on the light side, with no real weight or flavours, and in lesser years can appear distinctly dilute. These need to be consumed fairly quickly.

MONTAGNE-ST-EMILION

Changes are taking place at some of the top Montagne estates: vineyards are being enlarged, extensive renovations are taking place in *chai* and *cuvier*, and second wines are appearing. Overall the quality is very good, and the best wines here bear a strong resemblance to a good St-Emilion or even a Pomerol. There are approximately 220 growers making their own wine, and some 30 others are members of the local cooperative. Some estates are quite large, by Libournais standards, and their wines can be found quite widely. Others – which can be just as good – are smaller and only sell direct. Around 30 per cent of the total production is exported: leading markets include the United Kingdom, Germany, the Netherlands and Belgium.

Left: Neat rows of vines lead the eye across the rolling vineyards of the country north of St Emilion

The wines begin to reach maturity at between three and six years, and vary from the light and fairly straightforward to wines in a more concentrated style, but which usually have a fleshy, supple quality and are often quite elegant.

LUSSAC-ST-EMILION

The second most important appellation, Lussac produces only slightly less wine than Montagne. This region of valleys, hillsides and plateaux enjoys a wide variety of soils, varying from clay-limestone hills, a gravel plateau to the west and pure clay in the north. Many of the leading estates, such as Château de Barbe Blanche and Château Haut-Piquat, are on a ridge of relatively high (80 metres plus) ground that runs north-south through the appellation.

As with Montagne-St-Emilion, there are many small properties and the local cooperative is important. Of the approximately 300 growers in the appellation, about 90 belong to the cooperative. These wines are seen abroad and can be found in Denmark, Belgium, Germany and the United Kingdom, among other markets.

The wines are perhaps more rustic in character than those of Montagne, and some have fairly earthy overtones. They can easily be drunk from two to three years after the vintage, though the best wines will last considerably longer in bottle.

PUISSEGUIN-ST-EMILION

This somewhat less-well-known area, which abuts the Côtes de Castillon, produces approximately half the quantity of Montagne. Although the local cooperative is important (some 48 growers are members, while more than 70 make their own wine) some good wines are also made at individual properties, which are starting to build reputations. These wines are exported and can be found mainly in Belgium, Denmark and the Netherlands.

ST-GEORGES-ST-EMILION

Very little wine is made under this appellation, which is dwarfed by surrounding Montagne-St-Emilion. Most wine is produced under the preferred Montagne appellation, although there are old-established estates which continue to use the St-Georges name. These include Châteaux Calon, St Georges and Tour du Pas St Georges.

THE APPELLATIONS

MONTAGNE-ST-EMILION
(red)
Location: *On the right bank of the Dordogne, about 38 km north-east of Bordeaux and 9 east of Libourne, separated from St-Emilion proper to the south by the Barbanne stream and the enclave of St-Georges-St Emilion. To the west lies Lalande-de-Pomerol, to the east the Côtes de Castillon. To the north is Lussac-St-Emilion, to the north-east Puisseguin-St-Emilion.*
Area of AC: *1,960 ha*
Area under vine: *1,550 ha*
Communes: *Montagne*
Average annual production: *940,000 cases*
Classed growths: *None*
Others: *220*
Cooperatives: *1 (c. 30 members)*
Main grape varieties: *Merlot*
Others: *Cabernet Franc, Cabernet Sauvignon*
Main soil types: *Clay-limestone*

LUSSAC-ST-EMILION
(red)
Location: *On the right bank of the Dordogne, some 39 km north-east of Bordeaux and 12 north-east of Libourne. To the south is Montagne-St-Emilion, to the east Puisseguin-St-Emilion and Bordeaux-Côtes de Francs. To the north and west is land covered by the basic*

Bordeaux appellation.
Area of AC: *1,820 ha*
Area under vine: *1,400 ha*
Communes: *Lussac*
Average annual production: *770,000 cases*
Classed growths: *None*
Others: *215*
Cooperatives: *1 (shared with Puisseguin: c. 90 members)*
Main grape varieties: *Merlot*
Others: *Cabernet Franc, Cabernet Sauvignon*
Main soil types: *Clay-gravel in the valleys, sandy clay on the plateaux, clay-limestone on the hillsides*

PUISSEGUIN-ST-EMILION
(red)
Location: *On the right bank of the Dordogne, about 40 km north-east of Bordeaux and 13 east of Libourne. To the north-west lies Lussac-St-Emilion, to the south-west Montagne-St-Emilion. To the east is the Côtes de Castillon.*
Area of AC: *1,038 ha*
Area under vine: *730 ha*
Communes: *Part of the commune of Puisseguin. (The area of the former commune of Monbadon to the east is excluded.)*
Average annual production: *500,000 cases*
Classed growths: *None*

Others: *73*
Cooperatives: *1 (shared with Lussac: c. 48 members)*
Main grape varieties: *Merlot*
Others: *Cabernet Franc, Cabernet Sauvignon*
Main soil types: *Clay-limestone*

ST-GEORGES-ST-EMILION
(red)
Location: *On the right bank of the Dordogne, about 38 km north-east of Bordeaux and 8 km east of Libourne. To the south, beyond the Barbanne stream, lies St-Emilion proper. To the north, west and east it is surrounded by Montagne-St-Emilion.*
Area of AC: *288 ha*
Area under vine: *180 ha*
Communes: *Part of the commune of Montagne*
Average annual production: *90,000 cases*
Classed growths: *None*
Others: *19*
Cooperatives: *None*
Main grape varieties: *Merlot*
Others: *Cabernet Franc, Cabernet Sauvignon, Malbec*
Main soil types: *Clay-limestone*

APPELLATION MONTAGNE-ST-EMILION

Ch d'Arvouet
map 40 L6

owner: Michel Moreau **area:** 3.9 ha **cases:** 1,850
grape % R: MER 75% CF 20% CS 5% **other wines:**
Bordeaux rosé **other châteaux owned:** Ch La Voûte
(St-Emilion)
33570 Montagne tel: 05 57 74 56 60
fax: 05 51 74 02 44

This vineyard, on clay and limestone soil, was
created at the beginning of the 20th century.
Since 1992 the estate has been run by an
industrialist from Brittany, who has started an
extensive renovation programme. The wine
usually has a hint of strawberries in its aroma.
It is also attractive, aromatic and accessible, but
without great concentration, and is sometimes
a little light. It spends between 10 and 12
months maturing in cask.

Ch Les Bardes
map 40 I5

owner: Alain Bonville **area:** 6.5 ha **cases:** 3,000
grape % R: MER 70% CF 30% **other châteaux owned:**
Ch Peyroutas (St-Emilion); Ch Haut-Saint-Georges
(St-Georges-St-Emilion); Ch Marac (Bordeaux
Supérieur)
33570 Montagne tel: 05 57 74 90 03
fax: 05 57 74 90 13

There is no barrel-ageing here, for the owner
wants nothing to obscure the best possible
expression of the grapes and the *terroir* in the
Les Bardes wine. The resultant taste is
characteristically firm, fleshy and supple, with
black fruit flavours.

Ch La Bastidette
map 40 D10

owner: Louis-Gabriel de Jerphanion **area:** 1.1 ha
cases: 650 **grape % R:** MER 70% CF 30% **other**
châteaux owned: Ch Moncets (Lalande-de-Pomerol)
33570 Montagne tel: 05 57 51 19 33
fax: 05 57 51 56 24

Limited production of a supple wine from this
tiny vineyard, with modest amounts of berry
fruit and a hint of oak.

Ch La Bastienne
map 40 J2

owner: SCEA Entente Janoueix **area:** 12 ha **cases:**
6,000 **grape % R:** MER 90% CF 10% **other châteaux**
owned: Ch Trincaud (Bordeaux Supérieur); Ch Petit
Clos du Roy (Montagne-St-Emilion); Ch Grands
Sillons Gabachot (Pomerol); Ch Des Tourelles
(Lalande-de-Pomerol)
33570 Montagne tel: 05 57 51 55 44
fax: 05 57 51 83 70

A wine, made mainly from Merlot, that in the
great years is a dark ruby colour. In the glass it
displays jammy, berry fruits and a touch of oak,
showing its year in cask (25% of the barrels are
new). In a lighter year, however, the quality can
dwindle to the nondescript: thin, without much
depth or fruit.

Ch Bellevue

owner: Robert Gaury **area:** 5 ha **cases:** 3,000
grape % R: MER 90% CF 5% CS 5% **second wine:** Ch
Bellevue St-Martin **other châteaux owned:** Ch Haut-
Bellevue (Lussac-St-Emilion); Ch Bellevue (St-
Georges-St-Emilion)
33570 Montagne tel: 05 57 74 62 24

Wine estate on the boundary between Montagne
and St-Georges, with 90 per cents of its vines
being Merlot. The wine is sinewy and well
provided with tannin, while its taste is marked
by earthy tones and spicy black fruit. It is not
aged in cask. There is also a St-Georges-St-
Emilion, which bears the same name.

Above: Ch Corbin

Ch Bonneau
map 40 K6

owner: Thierry Gouze **area:** 9 ha **cases:** 4,200
grape % R: MER 90% CF 10% **other châteaux owned:**
Ch Hyon La Fleur (St-Emilion)
33570 Montagne tel: 05 57 74 64 27
fax: 05 57 74 51 63

Smooth wine with a reasonably long finale,
black fruit, and usually sound balance. Good
average quality.

Ch Calon
map 40 I4

owner: Jean-Noël Boidron **area:** 36 ha **cases:**
16,000 **grape % R:** MER 70% CF 15% CS 12% MAL 3%
second wine: Ch Fonguillon **other châteaux owned:**
Ch Mayne d'Olivet (Bordeaux blanc); Ch Cantelauze
(Pomerol); Ch Calon (St-Georges-St-Emilion); Ch
Corbin Michotte (St-Emilion)
33570 Montagne tel: 05 57 51 64 88
fax: 05 57 51 56 30

The name of this château may be derived from
the Greek for 'beauty'. The undeniable charms
of the high ground on which it lies have
certainly long been recognized: it boasts the
remains of a Roman granary, and five 15th-
century windmills still stand close by. The
vineyard's history is clearer: the present
owner's ancestors have spent rather more than
300 years creating it. The wine that it yields
spends on average two years maturing in
barrel in a cool rock cellar, after which Ch
Calon is not only of immaculate quality, but of
charming character. This generous wine's
aroma encompasses the oak notes of vanilla,
dark elements – bay, licorice, leather – and
ripe fruit.

Ch Chevalier Saint-Georges
map 40

owner: Guy Appollot **area:** 3 ha **cases:** 1,800
grape % R: MER 80% CF 10% CS 10% **other**
châteaux owned: Clos Trimoulet (St-Emilion)
33330 St-Emilion tel: 05 57 24 71 96
fax: 05 57 74 45 88

Animal aromas and earthy tones form the
bouquet of this fairly full-bodied, supple wine.
Matured in oak for a short time, a third of the
barriques being new.

Ch Corbin
map 40 J3

owner: François Rambeaud **area:** 22 ha **cases:**
9,000 **grape % R:** MER 80% CF 20% **second wine:** La
Clie de Corbin
33570 Montagne tel: 05 57 74 62 41
fax: 05 57 74 55 91

This estate is least 400 years old, and is also
one of the larger properties in Montagne-St-
Emilion. The decent, reasonably fruity and
usually fairly rounded wine undergoes no
barrel-ageing.

Ch Côtes de Bonde
map 40 I5

owner: Philippe Dignac **area:** 12.5 ha **cases:** 7,800
grape % R: CS 65% CF 35% **second wine:** Ch La
Croix du Bailli (St-Emilion) **other châteaux owned:**
Ch Les Grands Sillons (Pomerol)
33570 Montagne tel: 05 57 74 64 52
fax: 05 57 74 55 88

Philippe Dignac's parents bought this estate in
1970. Since taking over the management in
1988 he has extended it by 5 ha, and a
considerable part of the vineyard therefore has
relatively young vines. The wine is honest and
correct, without technical faults – but neither
does it yet have much strength, depth or
character. Not aged in wood.

Ch Coucy
map 40 K7

owner: Héritiers Maureze **area:** 20 ha **cases:**
10,000 **grape % R:** MER 70% CF 20% CS 10% **second**
wine: Ch Baron Ségur **other châteaux owned:** Ch
Puy Arnaud (Côtes de Castillon)
33570 Montagne tel: 05 57 74 62 14
fax: 05 57 74 56 07

Prominent castle that takes its name from an
old English family who settled in the Bordeaux
area. Its origin goes back to the 15th century.
Because of its consistently very decent quality,
this wine usually sells out quickly. It generally
has plenty of fruit, round tannins – the
slightest touch of bitterness to it, a rather
elegant structure and a good balance. Oak-
ageing varies, depending on the vintage: light
years are given no new wood, stronger ones
get up to a third.

Ch La Couronne   map 40 J5
owner: Thomas Thiou **area:** 11.5 ha **cases:** 6,500
grape % R: MER 90% CS 5% CF 5%
33570 Montagne tel: 05 57 74 66 62
The vineyard was bought in 1943 by Edgard
Gineste and reached its present size in 1987,
when he acquired 5 ha on the plateau in front
of the *chai.* In 1994 an enthusiastic new owner,
Thomas Thiou, took over; his firm intention is
to enlarge the estate still further. The wine here
has backbone and ageing potential, and even in
less-good years offers fine, jammy fruit and
good concentration. It is aged for 15 months in
both *barriques* and larger casks.

Ch Croix Beauséjour   map 40 I4
owner: Olivier Laporte **area:** /.5 ha **cases:** 3,750
grape % R: MER 70% MAL 15% CF 7.5% CS 7.5%
33570 Montagne tel: 05 57 74 69 62
fax: 05 57 74 59 21
Two wines are made here: the standard, which
is given no barrel-ageing, and the Cuvée
Prestige, with a year in oak. The straightforward
wine is supple and attractive, with blackberry
and other berry fruit. There is more power in
the Cuvée Prestige, which has considerable
body, with ripe tannins, a dash of vanilla, spices,
dark notes (coffee, licorice), fruit (cherry, plum)
and refined oak.

Ch La Croix de Mouchet   map 40 J7
owner: Primo Grando **area:** 12 ha **cases:** 7,500
grape % R: MER 80% CF 10% CS 10% **other châteaux
owned:** Ch Mouchet *(Puisseguin-St-Emilion)*
33570 Montagne tel: 05 57 74 62 83
fax: 05 57 74 59 61
Pleasant wine, usually with a good amount of
tannin, rounded and with discreet fruit –
tending to blackcurrant, black cherry. Its oak,
from mainly used casks, gives it a somewhat
rustic character.

Ch Faizeau   map 40 H4
owner: Chantal Lebreton & Alain Raynaud **area:**
10 ha **cases:** 5,000 **grape % R:** MER 85% CS 10%
CF 5% **second wine:** Ch Chants de Faizeau
other châteaux owned: Ch La Croix de Gay
(Pomerol)
33570 Montagne tel: 05 57 24 68 94
fax: 05 57 74 15 62

Below: Ch Coucy

Above: The cellars of Ch La Couronne

A new phase in the history of this old property
began in 1989 when the wine from 80-year-old
Merlot vines was vinified, matured and bottled
separately. This Sélection Vieilles Vignes is full
of flavour: expansive in the mouth, with smoky,
toasted oak, nicely integrated tannins and lush
fruit – black cherry, blackberry, plum.

Ch la Fleur   map 40 H2
owner: R. Albert-Richon **area:** 11 ha **cases:** 3,000
grape % R: MER 85% CF 10% CS 5% **second wine:** Ch
Macureau **other châteaux owned:** Ch La Fleur
(Lalande-de-Pomerol); Ch Les Renardières
(Bordeaux Supérieur)
33570 Montagne tel: 05 57 74 02 52
fax: 05 57 74 02 52
The same proprietor owns another château
called La Fleur, in Lalande-de-Pomerol. The
one here in Montagne-St-Emilion yields a
reasonably concentrated wine as a rule, which
can be worth keeping – although it has
sometimes shown a minor flaw in the form of
volatile acidity.

Ch Grand Baril   map 40 F2
owner: Lycée Agro-Viticole **area:** 31 ha **cases:**
15,000 **grape % R:** MER 60% CF 20% CS 20% **second
wine:** Ch Vieux Ferrand **other châteaux owned:** Ch
Réal-Caillou *(Lalande-de-Pomerol)*
33570 Montagne tel: 05 57 51 01 75
fax: 05 57 51 66 13
The Lycée Agro-Viticole in Montagne runs a
couple of its own vineyards, of which this is
one. Grand Baril comes from vines at least 12
years old, and is most professionally made. It
has a firm structure and is fairly concentrated.
In its aroma there is often a suggestion of
pepperiness from the Cabernet Sauvignon,
alongside black fruit from the Merlot. Reliable
in the lesser years.

Ch Haut-Bertin   map 40 I4
owner: GFA des Vignobles Fortin-Belot **area:** 7 ha
cases: 4,000 **grape % R:** MER 70% CS 20% CF 10%
33570 Montagne tel: 05 57 74 64 99
Wine with good intensity, a sometimes rather
earthy bouquet, and an attractive, layered
fruitiness. Its tannins, however, can be
somewhat tough; meaning that the wine often
needs to be kept for at least five years after
vintage. Half of the barrels are replaced each
year, and cask-ageing lasts for 12 months.

Ch Les Hautes Graves   map 40 H2
owner: Famille Gadrat **area:** 2 ha **cases:** 550 **grape
% R:** MER 65% CS 30% MAL 5%
33570 Montagne tel: 05 56 35 00 04
Despite the modest size of this estate, it is made
up of small plots on different types of soil. The
wine has colour, body and tannin, together with
a blend of toasted oak (a quarter of the casks
are new, and the wine matures for 22 months
in them) and fruit – black cherry for example.
The label is by a different artist for every vintage.

Ch Haute Faucherie   map 40 H4
owner: Pierre & André Durand **area:** 6 ha **cases:**
3,500 **grape % R:** CF 80% MER 20% **second wine:** Ch
Vieille Tour Montagne
33570 Montagne tel: 05 57 74 62 02
fax: 05 57 74 53 66
Estate created in 1924, lying close to the
windmills at Calon. The clay and limestone soil
is mainly planted with old Cabernet Franc
vines. Two features usually very much in
evidence in the wine are red fruit and tannin.
Spends a minimal time in wood.

Ch Haut-Goujon   map 40 F1
owner: Henri Garde **area:** 7 ha **cases:** 3,500 **grape
% R:** MER 60% CS 20% CF 15% MAL 5%
33570 Montagne tel: 05 57 51 50 05
fax: 05 57 25 33 93
This property lies nearer to Lalande-de-Pomerol
and Néac than to Montagne. The wine has
substance; a rounded taste with dark, animal
notes is underpinned by firm tannins. Maturing
mainly takes place in vats.

◆

About Montagne-St-Emilion

Information can be obtained from the
Syndicat viticole in the Maison du Vin,
33570 Montagne. Tel 05 57 74 60 13.

Above: Ch Jura-Plaisance

Ch Jura-Plaisance
map **40 J2**

owner: Madame Bernard Delol *area:* 8 ha *cases:*
4,200 *grape % R:* MER 60% CF 40% *second wine:*
Jouvence de Jura-Plaisance
33570 Montagne tel: 05 61 42 83 50
fax: 05 61 59 65 78
This estate lies in the south of the district, not
far from the boundary with the St-Emilion and
Pomerol appellations. From vines with an
average age of 20 years a fragrant, well-vinified
wine is made, with red fruit – like strawberry –
nicely wrapped in oak.

Ch Lestage
map **40 L7**

owner: Famille Boureaud *area:* 8.6 ha *cases:* 5,500
grape % R: MER 85% CS 8% CF 7%
33570 Montagne tel: 05 57 74 63 34
fax: 05 57 74 56 80
At the end of the 19th century Lestage was
regarded as one of the Parsac *premiers crus*. As
well as its ordinary, quite lively, decently fruity
wine, a more serious Montagne-St-Emilion is
produced: the Cuvée Pierre Lavau. This is made
from old vines and matured for one year in
barrel, a third of which are new.

Ch Lys de Maisonneuve
map **40 L7**

owner: Alain Rospars *area:* 6 ha *cases:* 3,000
grape % R: MER 80% CF 20%
33570 Montagne tel: 05 53 04 03 94
fax: 05 53 54 98 73
Two wines are made at this relatively small
property: the standard Cuvée Tradition, with its
pleasing amount of fruit, and the Cuvée
Prestige, matured for 18 months in oak: this
wine has rather more substance and depth.

Ch Maison Blanche
map **40 I2**

owner: Gérard Despagne-Rapin *area:* 30 ha *cases:*
16,000 *grape % R:* MER 70% CF 20% CS 10% *second
wine:* Les Piliers de Maison Blanche *other
châteaux owned:* Ch La Rose Figeac *(Pomerol)*; Ch
Tour de Corbin Despagne *(St-Emilion)*
33570 Montagne tel: 05 57 74 62 18
fax: 05 57 74 58 98
The 18th-century château, with its white walls
and blue roof, is surrounded by a park and a 30-
ha vineyard. A very good, sturdy Montagne-St-
Emilion is made here, a wine with jammy fruit
– especially blackcurrant – and spicy oak. The

Louis Rapin is a premium *cuvée:* solid in
colour, with fine tannins, a rich, spicy taste with
plenty of berry fruit, a touch of chocolate and
distinct vanilla notes. It is limited to 10,000
bottles a year at most.

Ch de Maison Neuve
map **40 H4**

owner: Michel Coudroy *area:* 40 ha *cases:*
25,000 *grape % R:* MER 80% CF 20% *second wine:*
Cuvée Madame du Château de Maison Neuve
other châteaux owned: Ch Haut-Tropchaud
(Pomerol); Ch La Faurie Maison Neuve *(Lalande-
de-Pomerol)*
33570 Montagne tel: 05 57 74 62 23
fax: 05 57 74 64 18
Supple, meaty, slightly rustic wine with a lot of
concentration in good years, and at times a
rather dry aftertaste. Mint, spices and small
black berry fruits are frequently present in the
aroma. If the wine is from a lesser year
herbaceous elements may turn up, as a result of
Cabernet not fully ripe. There is also a special
version, called Prestige du Ch Maison Neuve.
This is oak-matured in *barriques* of which one-
quarter to one-third are new. The owners, the
Coudroy family, have been making wine since
the 16th century.

Below: Ch Montaiguillon

Ch des Moines
map **40 I4**

owner: Vignobles Raymond Tapon *area:* 19 ha
cases: 7,000 *grape % R:* MER 70% CF 20% CS 10%
second wine: Ch Fleur des Moines *other wines:* Ch
Gay-Moulin *other châteaux owned:* Ch Lafleur
Vachon *(St-Emilion)*; Ch La Croix St-Jean *(Lalande-de-
Pomerol)*; Ch Bellevue les Hugons *(Bordeaux
Supérieur; Bordeaux blanc)*
33570 Montagne tel: 05 57 74 61 20
fax: 05 57 24 69 32
The great-grandmother of today's owner bought
this estate towards the end of the 19th century.
It owes its origin and name to Cistercian
monks, who cultivated grapes here in the 17th
century. The wine has some tannin, oak and
fresh red fruit, and can usually be drunk early -
that is to say within about five years. Ch Gay-
Moulin, a wine dominated by Cabernets, is
made from 5 ha here. This is only made in years
when there are enough fully-ripe Cabernet
grapes (not, therefore, in 1991 or 1992). The
wine tastes fairly slender, with berry fruit.

Ch Montaiguillon
map **40 J2**

owner: Roger Amart *area:* 28 ha *cases:* 15,000
grape % R: MER 40% CF 30% CS 30%
33570 Montagne tel: 05 57 74 62 34
fax: 05 57 74 59 07
An unusual balance of grape varieties here: 60%
of the vines are Cabernets. Nevertheless the
wine is seldom really harsh. Even in its youth it
tastes quite supple, with fruit suggesting red or
black currants, plum, cherry; and enough
alcohol and tannin to give it ageing potential. It
matures for a year in *barriques* of which one-
third are bought new for each vintage.

◆
Grape varieties
Percentages of grapes grown are given as
supplied by the château. The abbreviations
used are:

CF Cabernet Franc, COL Colombard,
CS Cabernet Sauvignon, MAL Malbec,
MER Merlot, MUSC Muscadelle, PV Petit
Verdot, SAUV B Sauvignon Blanc,
SEM Sémillon

MONTAGNE-, LUSSAC, PUISSEGUIN- & ST-GEORGES-ST-ÉMILION

40

Vineyards
Woods
AC St-Georges-St-Emilion
AC Montagne-St-Emilion
AC Lussac-St-Emilion
AC Puisseguin-St-Emilion
Commune boundary
Canton boundary
Contour line

1:54,000
0   1   2km

Above: Ch Petit Clos du Roy

Above: Ch Plaisance

Ch Moulin Blanc La Chapelle
map 40 I7
owner: Gilles Mérias *area:* 4 ha *cases:* 2,500
grape % R: CF 50% CS 32% MER 18% *other wines:*
Ch Coq Rouge
33570 Lussac tel: 05 57 74 50 27
fax: 05 57 74 58 88
Modest property where the wine often tastes
more exciting than it smells. Reasonably full-
bodied, it soon becomes ready for drinking –
within five years.

Ch de Musset
map 40 L6
owner: Patrick Valette *area:* 7.5 ha *cases:* 4,800
grape % R: MER 70% CS 20% CF 10% *second wine:*
Domaine du Petit Musset *other châteaux owned:*
include Ch Pavie *(St-Emilion)*; Ch La Prade
(Bordeaux Côtes de Francs)
33570 Parsac tel: 05 57 74 40 10
fax: 05 57 24 63 99
Patrick Valette, of Ch Pavie in St-Emilion and
other properties, leased this estate in 1991 –
since when the quality of its wine has improved.
This is partly due to strict selection – with, as a
consequence, the appearance of a second wine.
Half of the casks used for maturing come from
St-Emilion *grands crus classés*. Ch de Musset is
a substantial concentrated Montagne-St-
Emilion with good firm tannins and ripe berry
fruit. The château is among the district's finest,
and below its notable 18th-century hall there is
a vaulted cellar for the casks.

Ch La Papeterie
map 40 J1
owner: Jean-Pierre Estager *area:* 10 ha *cases:*
5,000 *grape % R:* MER 70% CF 30% *other châteaux*
owned: Domaine de Gachet *(Lalande-de-Pomerol)*;
Domaine des Gourdins *(St-Emilion)*; Domaine de
Compostelle *(Pomerol)*; Ch Plincette *(Pomerol)*; Ch
La Cabanne *(Pomerol)*; Ch Haut-Maillet *(Pomerol)*
33570 Montagne tel: 05 57 51 04 09
fax: 05 57 25 13 38
Until 1920 this estate belonged to the Pomerol
appellation. Today the wine still has much of
the character of a Pomerol. Its aroma is
determined by generous Merlot fruit and animal
notes. Often this is a relatively rich wine, with
good tannins, great length, and unmistakeable
class.

Ch Petit Clos du Roy
map 40 I3
owner: SCEA Entente Janoueix *area:* 20 ha *cases:*
10,000 *grape % R:* MER 80% CF 20% *second wine:*
Ch Chanteclerc; Ch Bychaud *other châteaux*
owned: Ch La Bastienne *(Montagne-St-Emilion)*; Ch
Grands Sillons Gabachot *(Pomerol)*; Ch Des
Tourelles *(Lalande-de-Pomerol)*; Ch Trincaud
(Bordeaux Supérieur)
33500 Libourne tel: 05 57 51 55 44
fax: 05 57 51 83 70
The château here is an 18th-century *chartreuse*
with a terrace and a small park. The winery
premises have been built on to it. In good
vintages the taste can become almost corpulent,
and when mature the wine emerges velvety,
with impressions of oak, animal elements and
mellow fruit.

Ch Plaisance
map 40 J1
owner: Les Celliers de Bordeaux Benauge/Famille
Ducourt *area:* 17.2 ha *cases:* 10,900 *grape % R:*
MER 57% CF 35% CS 8% *second wine:* Ch de Branne
other châteaux owned: include Ch de Beauregard
(Bordeaux); Ch La Rose St-Germain *(Bordeaux)*
33570 Montagne tel: 05 56 23 93 53
fax: 05 56 23 48 78

◆

Quantities

Figures are as supplied by the châteaux.

Area of vineyard: given in hectares,
abbreviated to ha. Châteaux are asked to
specify vineyards in production, and to
exclude from their answers those owned
but unplanted, and to advise when
extensions are planned.

Production: given in cases of 12 bottles,
each of 0.75 litres. A case is thus 9 litres.
A hectolitre is 100 litres or just over 11
cases.

Yield per hectare: to obtain this, multiply
the 'cases' figure by 9, to give litres, then
divide by 100, to give hectolitres. Then
divide the result by the area in hectares.

A really enjoyable wine: supple, with good fruit,
a touch of bayleaf and oak that suggests vanilla.
The wine matures for a year in cask; one-third
of them are new barrels.

Ch Puy Rigaud
map 40 K7
owner: Guy & Dany Desplat *area:* 4.5 ha *cases:*
1,500 *grape % R:* MER 80% CS 10% CF 10% *second*
wine: Ch Naguet *other châteaux owned:* Ch Grand
Rigaud *(Puisseguin-St-Emilion)*; Ch La Clide *(St-
Emilion)*
33570 Puisseguin tel: 05 57 74 61 10
fax: 05 57 74 58 30
Guy Desplat understands his trade, and very
reliable wine is the result. The Puy Rigaud has
freshness without acidity, a medium structure,
good tannins and some red fruit. In the lesser
years, too, it is usually very successful. The
wine rather resembles that from Ch Grand
Rigaud, Puisseguin-St-Emilion; the two
vineyards adjoin.

Ch Roudier
map 40 K5
owner: GFA Capdemourlin *area:* 30 ha *cases:*
15,000 *grape % R:* MER 60% CF 25% CS 15% *second*
wine: Cap de Roudier *other châteaux owned:* Ch
Petit-Faurie-de-Soutard *(St-Emilion)*; Ch Cap de
Mourlin *(St-Emilion)*; Ch Balestard la Tonnelle *(St-
Emilion)*
33570 Montagne tel: 05 57 74 62 06
fax: 05 57 74 59 34
The wine here is made by the Capdemourlin
family, owners of some renowned *grands crus*
classés in St-Emilion. In quality Roudier can
hold its own with many St-Emilions: aromatic,
splendidly concentrated, with great finesse, firm
tannins and *fruits confits*. One of the top wines
in its district; beautifuly balanced, too.

Ch St Jacques Calon
map 40 I4
owner: Paul Maule *area:* 9 ha *cases:* 5,000 *grape*
% R: MER 66% CF 34%
33570 Montagne tel: 05 41 43 67 51
fax: 05 41 43 09 26
Estate on the hill at Calon where the wines are
of better than average quality. The best is the
1er Vin, which spends 6-12 months in cask –
100% new – after at least 18 months in tank. Its
aroma is defined by red and black fruit, earthy
notes and aspects of oak, while the solid, ripe
tannins guarantee its potential for maturing.

Above: Windmills at Ch St Jacques Calon

Ch Samion
map 40

owner: Vignobles Rocher-Cap de Rive **area:** 4 ha
cases: 2,200 **grape % R:** MER 50% CF 33% CS 17%
second wine: Saint Paul de Montagne **other
châteaux owned:** include Ch Cap d'Or (St-Georges)
33570 Montagne tel: 05 57 40 08 88
fax: 05 57 40 19 93
Aged in oak for a year: quite meaty, rounded,
with a dash of aniseed and earthy aromas. A most
reliable wine – as is shown by its many awards.

Ch Teyssier
map 40 J7

owner: GFA du Ch Teyssier/Groupe CVBG **area:** 40
ha **cases:** 20,000 **grape % R:** MER 60% CF 20% CS
20% **second wine:** Ch Puybonnet **other wines:**
Puisseguin-St-Emilion **other châteaux owned:**
include Ch Belgrave (Haut-Médoc); Ch La Garde
(Pessac-Léognan); Ch de la Tour (Bordeaux)
33570 Montagne tel: 05 57 74 63 11
fax: 05 57 74 63 11
That half the barrels are replaced each year can
clearly be tasted in this wine: it has a vanilla
aroma suggesting toast, together with aromatic
fruit, a smooth suppleness and a firm
constitution. A Médoc firm, CVBG (Dourthe),
runs this extensive estate.

Below: Ch Vieux Bonneau

Ch Tour Musset
map 40 L6

owner: Gunnar Johannesson **area:** 30 ha **cases:**
15,000 **grape % R:** MER 70% CF 15% CS 15% **other
châteaux owned:** Ch Tour St-Christophe (St-Emilion)
33570 Montagne tel: 05 57 24 77 15
fax: 05 57 74 43 57
This property is situated in the former Parsac
commune, joined to Montagne in 1972. Merlot
is the main grape and this, combined with the
clay and limestone soil, gives a usually
aromatic, supple wine that pleasingly fills the
mouth with smooth fruit.

Ch Vieux Bonneau
map 40 K6

owner: Alain Despagne **area:** 13 ha **cases:** 5,000
grape % R: MER 80% CF 10% CS 10% **other châteaux
owned:** Ch Jamard Belcour (Lussac-St-Emilion); Ch
Lafourcoud-Bellevue (Bordeaux Supérieur)
33570 Montagne tel: 05 57 74 60 72
fax: 05 57 74 58 22
No assertive, overbearing wine this, but
civilized; balanced and expertly made. Its aroma
often has elements of ripe fruits, licorice, spices
and cocoa. Its oak is due to eight months' cask-
maturing – 20% new barrels.

Vieux Château Birot
map 40 K8

owner: Jean-Loup Robin **area:** 4.5 ha **cases:** 2,500
grape % R: MER 50% CS 50% **other châteaux owned:**
Ch Sansonnet (St-Emilion); Ch Gontet-Robin
(Puisseguin-St-Emilion)
33570 Puisseguin tel: 05 57 24 76 29
fax: 05 57 51 86 19
Smooth and well-balanced, sometimes with
wild strawberry as the fruit note: an engaging,
somewhat short wine that undergoes no barrel-
ageing. The proportion of Cabernet Sauvignon
is relatively high - one half, in fact.

Vieux Château Calon
map 40 I4

owner: Yves Gros **area:** 7 ha **cases:** 3,500 **grape %
R:** MER 80% CF 20% **other châteaux owned:** Ch
Grange-Neuve (Pomerol)
33570 Montagne tel: 05 57 74 63 87
fax: 05 57 25 36 14
Animal scents sometimes dominate the
powerful bouquet here – scents of fur, leather,
even of a stable. But the wine also has ripe fruit
– blackberry, bilberry. Vintages from lesser
years become ready for drinking quite soon. In
the great vintages it comes across as a classic
wine for laying down: concentrated, firm and

rich in tannin. Vieux Ch Calon owes its class in
part to the son of the proprietor, the graduate
oenologist Jean-Marie Gros.

Vieux Château Rocher Corbin
map 40 H4

owner: SCE du Ch Rocher Corbin/Famille Durand
area: 9.5 ha **cases:** 5,000 **grape % R:** MER 85% CF
10% CS 5%
33570 Montagne tel: 05 57 74 55 12
fax: 05 57 74 53 15
A wine with (as a rule) plenty of colour, good
intensity and a fairly supple taste. Correct – or
better – in quality. No oak.

Vieux Château Saint André
map 40

owner: Jean-Claude Berrouët **area:** 6.4 ha **cases:**
3,200 **grape % R:** MER 75% CF 25% **other châteaux
owned:** Ch Samion (Lalande-de-Pomerol)
33570 Montagne tel: 05 57 51 78 96
fax: 05 57 51 79 79
Absolutely delightful and also extraordinarily
reliable wine from the oenologist Jean-Claude
Berrouët, well-known in Libourne and
responsible for the Jean-Pierre Moueix estates.
The Montagne-St-Emilion offers a blend of
dark, earthy tones with red and black berry
fruits. It is mouthfilling and harmonious.

Ch Vieux Moulins de Chéreau
map 40 H5

owner: Max Silvestrini **area:** 5.4 ha **cases:** 3,000
grape % R: MER 65% CS 20% CF 15% **second wine:**
Ch La Croix de Chéreau **other châteaux owned:**
Domaine de la Pointe (Pomerol); Ch Chéreau
(Lussac-St-Emilion)
33570 Montagne tel: 05 57 74 50 76
fax: 05 57 74 53 22
There is hardly any de-stalking of the grapes at
this estate. To avoid any subsequent 'green'
taste in the wine, the grapes are picked as ripe
as possible here. Impressions of forest floor,
animal notes, red and black currants, cherry,
are all interwoven into a quite generous taste.
This is a wine of a high standard – and one
which has personality.

APPELLATION LUSSAC-ST-EMILION

Ch de Barbe Blanche   map 40/F7
owner: Crédit Foncier *area:* 28 ha *cases:* 15,800
grape % R: MER 85% CS 15% *second wine:* Ch La
Tour-Ségur *other châteaux owned:* Ch Bastor-
Lamontagne *(Sauternes);* Ch Saint Robert *(Graves);*
Ch Beauregard *(Pomerol)*
33570 Lussac tel: 05 56 63 27 66
fax: 05 56 76 87 03
In medieval times, wines from this estate were
served at the English court – and, as the labels
declare, one of the past owners was Henri IV,
king of France and Navarre. It was in his day,
the end of the 16th century, that the château
acquired its strange name which might, or
might not, refer to the royal beard.... In more
recent times, the present owners, Crédit
Foncier, bought Barbe Blanche in 1985. A
delightful wine is made here, with the flavours
of black and red berry fruits, animal notes and
vanilla, plus backbone and a supple roundness.
The Cuvée Henri IV shows even more class; a
complex ensemble largely, and sometimes
exclusively, made from Merlot and matured in
new *barriques.*

Ch Bel-Air   map 40/E7
owner: Jean-Noël Roi *area:* 20.5 ha *cases:* 10,000
grape % R: MER 70% CF 15% CS 15% *second wine:*
Ch La Gravette
33570 Lussac tel: 05 57 74 60 40
fax: 05 57 74 52 11
A low, white limestone 18th-century château
with a later winery complex adjoining it. An
agreeable, fairly quick-developing wine is
produced here. Oak-aged for six months, Bel-
Air emerges quite full of colour and taste, and
rather traditional in character. A long series of
awards demonstrate its sound qualities.

Ch de Bellevue   map 40/J4
owner: Charles Chatenoud *area:* 11.9 ha *cases:*
5,000 *grape % R:* MER 90% CF 5% CS 5%
33570 Lussac tel: 05 57 74 60 25
fax: 05 57 74 53 69
Red berry fruits are plentiful in the aroma of
this mouthfilling wine. Half the barrels in
which it is matured for between four and six
months are replaced annually, giving this wine
spicy oak with a suggestion of vanilla, along
with some well-integrated tannins.

Above: Ch les Couzins

Ch de Bordes   map 40/F4
owner: EARL Vignobles Paul Bordes *area:* 10 ha
cases: 5,000 *grape % R:* MER 100% *other
châteaux owned:* Ch Lafaurie *(Puisseguin-St-
Emilion);* Ch des Huguets *(Bordeaux Supérieur)*
33570 Les Artigues-de-Lussac
tel: 05 57 24 33 66
fax: 05 57 24 30 42
A pure Merlot wine with vigour, sweet, lush
fruit, fine tannins and a noble oak-and-vanilla
aroma. With a year spent in new *barriques,* this
wine's upbringing has class.

Ch Caillou Les Martins   map 40
owner: Jean-François Carrille *area:* 8 ha
cases: 4,000 *grape % R:* MER 70% CS 30%
second wine: Ch Pilot Les Martins *other
châteaux owned:* Ch de Fussignac *(Bordeaux);*
Ch Cardinal Villemaurine *(St-Emilion);* Ch Boutisse
(St-Emilion)
33570 Lussac tel: 05 57 24 74 46
fax: 05 57 24 64 40
Creditable wine, marked more by earthy tones
and soft black fruit than by oak: a clear
expression of Merlot.

Ch Cap de Merle   map 40/D5
owner: EARL Vins Bel *area:* 14 ha *cases:* 8,300
grape % R: MER 60% CF 40%
33570 Lussac tel: 05 57 51 00 88
fax: 05 57 51 65 70
Since 1966 this vineyard has grown from 3 ha
to 14; and the quality has grown likewise: the
wine now tastes very correct, supple and juicy.
In its dark aroma there is an undertone of berry
fruits, often combined with freshness from the
generous 40% Cabernet Franc. No oak-ageing.

Ch du Courlat   map 40/G8
owner: Pierre Bourotte *area:* 17 ha *cases:* 8,300
grape % R: MER 70% CF 20% CS 10% *second wine:*
Les Echevins
33570 Lussac tel: 05 57 51 62 17
fax: 05 57 51 28 28
A firm, clean, interesting Lussac-St-Emilion is
most expertly made here, on an estate first
mentioned in 1748. It flatters the senses with
impressions of spicy oak (one-third new
barrels), notes of both dried and fresh ripe fruit,
and licorice together with bay. Its structure and
tannin make it suitable for laying down.

Ch Courrière-Rongiéras   map 40/H7
owner: Jean-Bernard Saby *area:* 1.2 ha *cases:* 600
grape % R: MER 100% *other châteaux owned:*
include Ch Rozier *(St-Emilion)*
33570 Lussac tel: 05 57 24 73 03
fax: 05 57 24 67 77
Minuscule property – but not so the wine it
makes. It is broad-shouldered, with a velvety,
rich taste that can have elements of chocolate,
toffee and toasted oak.

Ch les Couzins   map 40/E7
owner: Robert Seize *area:* 21.6 ha *cases:* 12,500
grape % R: MER 75% CS 15% CF 10%
33570 Lussac tel: 05 57 74 60 67
fax: 05 57 74 55 60
Richly coloured, thoroughly sound wine from
an immaculately maintained estate. Even in
moderate years this Lussac-St-Emilion has
gratifyingly ample body, while both bouquet
and taste often have dark (cocoa) and animal
(leather) aspects. It gives great pleasure after
a couple of years' bottle-age.

Below: Ch de Bellevue

Above: Ch La Govinière

Above: Ch de la Grenière

Ch Croix de Rambeau map 40/F4
owner: Jean-Louis Trocard *area:* 8 ha *cases:* 4,500
grape % R: MER 80% CF 10% CS 10% *other châteaux owned:* include Ch Trocard *(Bordeaux Supérieur)*
33570 Lussac tel: 05 57 24 31 16
fax: 05 57 24 33 87
Oak (one-third new casks each vintage) is clearly there to be tasted in this elegantly firm wine. Its fruit is raspberry, blackberry, cherry (and cherry stones). A sound, charming product that can be drunk within five years.

Ch La Govinière map 40/F7
owner: Jean-Claude Charpentier *area:* 6.5 ha *cases:* 3,200 *grape % R:* MER 65% CS 20% CF 15% *other châteaux owned:* Ch Haut-Jamard *(Lussac-St-Emilion)*
33570 Lussac tel: 05 57 74 51 28
fax: 05 57 74 57 72
What is bottled here goes principally to French private buyers. Neat, sometimes rather austere wine, with mainly berry fruit.

Ch de la Grenière map 40/D7
owner: Jean-Pierre Dubreuil *area:* 10 ha *cases:* 4,200 *grape % R:* MER 55% CS 30% CF 15% *other châteaux owned:* Ch Haut-La Grenière *(Lussac-St-Emilion)*
33570 Lussac tel: 05 57 74 64 96
fax: 05 57 74 56 28
The best wine made at this 17th-century *chartreuse* is the Cuvée de la Chartreuse. It is matured for at least 15 months in cask, of which a third are new. Its taste is rich and full, with silky tannins, style and fine nuances – fruit, vanilla, toast, caramel. The regular wine, too, is of a good standard, with an attractive, blackcurranty fruitiness.

Ch Haut-Jamard map 40/F7
owner: Jean-Claude Charpentier *area:* 5 ha *cases:* 2,500 *grape % R:* MER 80% CS 15% CF 5% *other châteaux owned:* Ch La Govinière *(Lussac-St-Emilion)*
33570 Lussac tel: 05 57 74 51 28
fax: 05 57 74 57 72
The oak-aged special *cuvée*, with its muscular structure, is worth discovering. It has been produced at this traditionally-run estate since

1992; and new *barriques* only have been used here since 1994. The ordinary wine, of average quality, shows its supple taste early on.

Ch Haut-La Grenière map 40/D79
owner: Jean-Pierre Dubreuil *area:* 5 ha *cases:* 2,500 *grape % R:* MER 58% CS 30% CS 12% *other châteaux owned:* Ch de la Grenière *(Lussac-St-Emilion)*
33570 Lussac tel: 05 57 74 64 96
fax: 05 57 74 56 28
Related to Ch de la Grenière, but from a separate vineyard. This wine is somewhat more rustic, less polished than La Grenière's offering, but nevertheless gives satisfaction after a few years' bottle-age. It has berry fruits and tannin, and is not aged in cask.

Ch Haut-Piquat map 40/H6
owner: Jean-Pierre Rivière *area:* 33 ha *cases:* 20,000 *grape % R:* MER 70% CS 20% CF 10% *other châteaux owned:* include Clos des Menuts *(St-Emilion)*; Ch de Beaulieu *(Montagne-St-Emilion)*
33570 Lussac tel: 05 57 55 59 59
fax: 05 57 55 59 51
This is a sizeable estate that produces a mouthfilling, classic wine full of character; a little rustic, perhaps, but of good quality.

◆

About Lussac-, Puisseguin- & St-Georges-St-Emilion

Information on the wines of Lussac can be obtained from the Syndicat viticole which is located in the Maison du Vin,
33570 Lussac.
Tel 05 57 74 50 35.

Information about the wines of Puisseguin can be obtained from the Maison du Vin,
33570 Puisseguin.
Tel 05 57 74 50 62.

Information on the wines of St-Georges can be obtained from the Syndicat viticole, St-Georges, 33570 Lussac-St-Emilion.
Tel 05 57 51 64 88.

Clos les Hauts Martins
map 40/D7
owner: Hugues Jaume *area:* 7.5 ha *cases:* 3,750 *grape % R:* CF 34% CS 33% MER 33%
33570 Lussac tel: 05 57 74 54 03
The Clos les Hauts Martins estate has been gradually enlarged and improved by a family of returning colonists from Algeria. Considerable investments have been made – especially between 1987 and 1992. Cabernets predominate in the vineyard, and this shows in the wine. Worth following.

Ch Lion Perruchon map 40/G8
owner: Maguy & Jean-Pierre Thézard *area:* 10 ha *cases:* 5,000 *grape % R:* MER 65% CF 35%
33570 Lussac tel: 05 57 74 64 71
fax: 05 57 74 58 39
An accessible, juicy wine, pleasantly fruity (cherry, raspberry). No great depth here, or complexity, but Lion Perruchon is certainly agreeable. Has been awarded various medals at the Paris *concours*. Weedkiller is barred from the vineyard, which laps around the 16th-century house.

Below: Ch Haut-Piquat

Above: Ch de Lussac

Above: Ch Vieux Busquet

Ch de Lussac
map 40/H7

owner: Olivier Roussel *area:* 25 ha *cases:* 12,500
grape % R: MER 80% CF 20%
33570 Lussac tel: 05 57 74 65 55
This is a wine with a fairly lush, rich and juicy taste, combined with smooth tannins. Fig, plum, cherry, herbs and cocoa can be subtly present – but not oak: there is no barrel-ageing at this estate.

Ch Mayne Blanc
map 40/E7

owner: Jean Boncheau *area:* 15 ha *cases:* 7,500
grape % R: MER 60% CS 30% CF 10% *other wines:*
Roseraie de Mayne *(Bordeaux Clairet)* *other*
châteaux owned: Ch Julien *(Bordeaux)*
33570 Lussac tel: 05 57 74 60 56
fax: 05 57 74 51 77
Hospitable, rose-bedecked château where two Lussac-St-Emilions are produced. The standard one is made from relatively young vines and has an accessible character: a supple taste, and pleasantly fruity. The fruit becomes jam-like in the Cuvée St-Vincent, which is made from vines that average 40 years old, and brought up entirely in new *barriques*. This *cuvée* naturally has plenty of oak and vanilla, and is a powerfully concentrated wine.

Below: Ch Mayne Blanc

Ch du Moulin Noir
map 40/H7

owner: Indivision Tessandier *area:* 12 ha *cases:*
6,000 *grape % R:* MER 65% CF 35% *other wines:*
Montagne-St-Emilion *other châteaux owned:* include
Ch Maucamps *(Haut-Médoc)*; Ch Barreyre *(Bordeaux Supérieur)*
33570 Lussac tel: 05 57 88 07 64
fax: 05 57 88 07 00
Considerable investment took place in 1989 when this estate was acquired by the Ambrosia group, based in Macau in the Médoc. Thus the 1990 vintage was made in new stainless-steel tanks. Cask-maturing followed, a quarter of them new. A smooth, and at the same time firm, wine; alluring with its fruit (blackcurrant, plum, fig), its dark tones (as of bayleaf), its noble oak and its well-knit tannin.

Ch des Rochers
map 40/C4

owner: Jean-Marie Rousseau *area:* 2.8 ha *cases:*
1,800 *grape % R:* MER 100% *other châteaux owned:* Ch La Borderie-Mondésir *(Lalande-de-Pomerol)*; Ch Haut-Sorillon *(Bordeaux Supérieur)*
33570 Lussac tel: 05 57 49 06 10
fax: 05 57 49 38 96
Pure, cask-matured Merlot wine of impeccable quality. Solidly put together and usually with the potential to mature for at least five years.

Ch de Tabuteau
map 40/F6

owner: Vignobles J. Bessou *area:* 20 ha *cases:*
11,000 *grape % R:* MER 70% CF 15% CS 15% *other châteaux owned:* Ch Durand-Laplagne *(Puisseguin-St-Emilion)*; Ch Cap de Merle *(Bordeaux Supérieur)*
33570 Lussac tel: 05 57 74 63 07
fax: 05 57 74 59 58
This estate in the north of the appellation delivers a substantial, aromatic wine – one with both the earthy tones of autumn woodland and red fruit such as strawberry and raspberry. Has no contact with oak.

Ch Tour de Grenet
map 40/F6

owner: SCI des Vignobles Brunot *area:* 33 ha
cases: 15,000 *grape % R:* MER 75% CF 20% CS 5%
other châteaux owned: Ch Cantenac *(St-Emilion)*
33570 Lussac tel: 05 57 51 35 22
fax: 05 57 25 19 15
The tower in question is an austere erection up on a vine-covered hill. It dates from the 19th century, when the estate still belonged to the

Neighbouring appellations
Lussac is the northernmost of the four satellites. Further north still is land with the generic Bordeaux ACs. To the south-west of Lussac is Montagne, to the south-east, Puisseguin. St-Georges forms an enclave within Montagne. To the east of Puisseguin are the Côtes de Francs and Castillon.

AC Parsac-St-Emilion
This, the fifth satellite, still exists, but no wine is declared: the growers have the right to use Montagne-St-Emilion, and they do.

abbey of Faize. From this elevated vineyard, the highest in the district, the Brunot and Roskam-Brunot families make a very creditable, supple wine that shows its charm early on, and with some discreet oak to it.

Ch Vieux Busquet
map 40/D5

owner: Michel Pinaud *area:* 15 ha *cases:* 7,500
grape % R: MER 80% CS 15% CF 5% *second wine:*
Ch Les Graves de Julien *(Bordeaux)*
33570 Lussac tel: 05 57 74 64 94
fax: 05 57 74 64 94
Smooth, fairly substantial wine, with fruit in good years, as well as a deep colour. It has no cask-ageing.

Vieux Château Chambeau
map 40/H9

owner: Jean-Michel Biehler *area:* 32.5 ha *cases:*
16,800 *grape % R:* MER 65% CF 35% *second wine:*
La Fleur Chambeau *other châteaux owned:* Ch Branda *(Puisseguin-St-Emilion)*
33570 Lussac tel: 05 57 74 62 55
fax: 05 57 74 57 33
In this Lussac, with its foundation of good tannin and toasted oak, there is also rich, ripe fruit to be tasted – it adds up to an exceptionally attractive whole. Normally it gains from about five years in the cellar.

APPELLATION PUISSEGUIN-ST-EMILION

Ch L'Abbaye
map 40/J8

owner: J.-C. Brisson **area:** 6 ha **cases:** 3,000 **grape % R:** MER 75% CF 10% CS 10% MAL 5% **other châteaux owned:** Ch La Rose-Trimoulet (St-Emilion); Ch La Roseraie du Mont (Puisseguin-St-Emilion) **33570 Puisseguin tel: 05 57 24 73 24 fax: 05 57 24 68 07**
A gentle limestone hill with many oyster fossils forms the highest part of this vineyard. The traditionally-made wine, which is matured at Ch La Rose-Trimoulet, St-Emilion, is of a good average quality.

Ch de l'Anglais
map 40/J9

owner: GFA du Ch de l'Anglais/Jean-Pierre Marsant **area:** 3.2 ha **cases:** 1,200 **grape % R:** MER 70% CF 20% CS 10% **other châteaux owned:** Ch Vieux Barrail (Côtes de Castillon) **33330 St-Emilion tel: 05 57 24 61 79 fax: 05 57 74 44 00**
Small estate that for a decade was affiliated to the cooperative; but under its new owner it has, since 1990, been making its own wine again. This is very agreeable, with ripe fruit and a pleasing finish. Its quality improved still further with the 1994 and 1995 vintages. The wine spends about a year in cask. Worth following.

Ch Bel-Air
map 40/J8

owner: Adoue Frères **area:** 16 ha **cases:** 10,000 **grape % R:** MER 75% CF 20% CS 5% **second wine:** Ch Hautes-Roches **33570 Puisseguin tel: 05 57 74 51 82 fax: 05 57 74 59 94**
In its youth this wine is quite often on the austere side, but fruit is discernible. Needs to mature for a few years. Bel-Air has been making a Cuvée Spéciale since 1994: in contrast to the standard wine, this has some 10 months in oak.

Ch Branda
map 40/H9

owner: SC Ch Branda/Jean-Michel Biehler **area:** 5.5 ha **cases:** 2,500 **grape % R:** MER 65% CF 35% **other châteaux owned:** Vieux Château Chambeau (Lussac-St-Emilion) **33570 Puisseguin tel: 05 57 74 62 55 fax: 05 57 74 57 33**
Consistent, generous wine with touches of fruit and spicy oak. Fermented in stainless steel, it then has a year in oak (one-third new barrels).

Below: Ch de l'Anglais

Ch Chêne-Vieux
map 40/K8

owner: SCE Y. Foucard & Fils **area:** 11 ha **cases:** 6,600 **grape % R:** MER 65% CS 20% MAL 10% CF 5% **other châteaux owned:** Ch de Musset (Lalande-de-Pomerol) **33570 Puisseguin tel: 05 57 74 63 15 fax: 05 57 25 36 45**
Aroma and taste call up associations of autumn woodlands. Pleasant, firm, meaty flavour, but without great depth.

Ch Durand-Laplagne
map 40/I9

owner: Vignobles J. Bessou **area:** 14 ha **cases:** 8,800 **grape % R:** MER 70% CF 15% CS 15% **second wine:** Ch Marsauda **other châteaux owned:** Ch de Tabuteau (Lussac-St-Emilion); Ch Cap de Merle (Bordeaux Supérieur) **33570 Puisseguin tel: 05 57 74 63 07 fax: 05 57 74 59 58**
Wine estate on clay and limestone soil, saved from anonymity by the present owner. The wine gives impressions of dark berry fruits, and has a rounded, open-knit taste. The Cuvée Sélection offers more dimension and spiciness. This wine goes into barriques, a fifth of them new, to mature for a year.

Ch Fongaban
map 40/J10

owner: G. Taïx **area:** 7 ha **cases:** 3,000 **grape % R:** MER 80% CS 20% **33570 Puisseguin tel: 05 57 74 54 07 fax: 05 57 74 50 97**
Mouthfilling wine, characteristically displaying supple tannins, a cherryish aroma and a touch of oak with vanilla.

Ch Grand Rigaud
map 40/K7

owner: Guy & Dany Desplat **area:** 7 ha **cases:** 3,000 **grape % R:** MER 80% CF 10% CS 10% **other châteaux owned:** Ch Puy Rigaud (Montagne-St-Emilion); Ch La Clide (St-Emilion) **33570 Puisseguin tel: 05 57 74 61 10 fax: 05 57 74 58 30**
Ch Grand Rigaud has the same owner as Ch Puy Rigaud, across the commune border in Montagne-St-Emilion. The two estates adjoin, and their wines show similarities. Grand Rigaud is a well made, reliable, powerful and supple wine, and has enough tannin to be laid down for a few years.

Below: Ch Bel-Air

Ch Guibot la Fourvieille
map 40/H10

owner: Henri Bourlon **area:** 41 ha **cases:** 23,000 **grape % R:** MER 70% CF 20% CS 10% **second wine:** Ch Guibeau **other châteaux owned:** Ch des Laurets (Puisseguin-St-Emilion); Ch les Barails (Côtes de Castillon) **33570 Puisseguin tel: 05 57 74 63 29 fax: 05 57 74 58 52**
Two old pillars mark the entrance to this well-equipped estate. Its wine usually has strength, good tannin, decent concentration, ripe fruit and some oak. The superior cuvée, Sélection Henri Bourlon, is named after the owner.

Ch Guillotin
map 40/J8

owner: Jean Michel Moritz **area:** 5 ha **cases:** 2,500 **grape % R:** MER 80% CF 15% CS 5% **second wine:** Plainier de Guillotin **33570 Puisseguin tel: 05 57 74 60 82 fax: 05 57 74 54 16**
An engaging wine that requires a few years' patience because of its tannin. This château has belonged to the same family for several generations.

Ch Haut-Bernat
map 40/J9

owner: Dominique Bessineau **area:** 5.5 ha **cases:** 2,200 **grape % R:** MER 85% CS 15% **other châteaux owned:** Ch Côte Monpezat (Côtes de Castillon) **33370 Puisseguin tel: 05 57 47 96 04 fax: 05 57 47 90 82**
Expressive wine with a bouquet that can offer nuances of toasted oak (50% of the casks are new), spices, red and black berries, and something exotic such as ginger. Oak can sometimes overwhelm the other elements. Quite substantial.

Ch Haut Saint Clair
map 40/K10

owner: SCEA Ch Haut Saint Clair/Yannick le Menn **area:** 4 ha **cases:** 2,083 **grape % R:** MER 65% CF 25% CS 10% **second wine:** Cuvée Moulin Saint Clair **other châteaux owned:** Ch Belair St-Georges (St-Georges-St-Emilion); Ch Montlabert (St-Emilion) **33570 Puisseguin tel: 05 57 74 66 82 fax: 05 57 74 51 50**
Modest estate on the edge of a limestone plateau that has been making its mark since the end of the 1980s. A sound wine, full of character, with plenty of tannin. Still higher

Below: Ch Durand-Laplagne

Above: Ch des Laurets

quality is shown by the Cuvée Moulin St-Clair, a special selection that is given 8-14 months in cask, a third of which are new.

Ch Lafaurie
map 40/I9

owner: EARL Vignobles Paul Bordes *area:* 10 ha *cases:* 5,000 *grape % R:* MER 60% CF 20% CS 20% *second wine:* Ch des Huguets *(Bordeaux Supérieur; Bordeaux rosé) other châteaux owned:* Ch de Bordes *(Lussac-St-Emilion)*
33570 Puisseguin tel: 05 57 24 33 66
fax: 05 57 24 30 42
Full-bodied, juicy wine that regularly wins medals and has fine tannins, spicy oak, and dark aromas, earthy and truffle-like.

Ch des Laurets
map 40/K8

owner: SA Ch des Laurets/Henri Bourlon *area:* 81 ha *cases:* 45,000 *grape % R:* MER 80% CF 15% CS 5% *second wine:* Ch Maison Rose; Ch La Rochette; Métairie de Grangeneuve *(Montagne-St-Emilion)*; Manoir de Villebout *(Montagne-St-Emilion) other wines:* Montagne-St-Emilion *other châteaux owned:* Ch Guibot la Fourvieille *(Puisseguin-St-Emilion)*; Ch les Barrails *(Côtes de Castillon)*
33570 Puisseguin tel: 05 57 74 63 40
fax: 05 57 74 65 34
The extensive vineyard of this fine 19th-century château yields a Montagne-St-Emilion as well as a Puisseguin-St-Emilion. The two wines are sometimes hard to tell apart. The vintages are marketed under various names, chiefly by the firm of Jean-Pierre Moueix. The present owners bought this large estate in 1995 and have since made considerable investments in both *cuvier* and the vineyard, planting a further 5 ha or so. There was a period when the wine had fruit, but rather lacked depth; a real improvement in quality may now be expected. Near the château stands a ruined castle, almost 700 years old.

Ch Mouchet
map 40/J7

owner: Primo Grando *area:* 6 ha *cases:* 3,000 *grape % R:* MER 75% CS 15% CF 10% *other châteaux owned:* Ch La Croix de Mouchet *(Montagne-St-Emilion)*
33570 Montagne tel: 05 57 74 62 83
fax: 05 57 74 59 61
The wine here is akin to that from Ch La Croix de Mouchet, so it has roundness, discreet, soft fruit, dark notes, considerable tannin, and a somewhat rustic note to its oak.

Ch du Moulin
map 40/I9

owner: Guy & Jean-Claude Chanet *area:* 12 ha *cases:* 6,000 *grape % R:* MER 80% CS 10% CF 10% *second wine:* Ch Puy de Boissac *other wines:* Domaine Galvesses Grand Moine *(Lalande-de-Pomerol)*
33570 Puisseguin tel: 05 57 74 60 85
fax: 05 57 74 59 90
After about four years in bottle this wine generally acquires a supple, agreeable taste with mellow, dark and fruity tones. The château takes its name from a sail-less windmill in the grounds.

Ch Rigaud
map 40/K7

owner: J. Taïx *area:* 8 ha *cases:* 4,000 *grape % R:* MER 80% CF 20% *second wine:* Ch La Chesnaie
33570 Puisseguin tel: 05 57 74 63 35
fax: 05 57 74 50 97
Thanks to its tannin this wine has backbone, combined with fruit and oak. Maturing lasts 12 months in barrels of which one-fifth are replaced each year.

Ch Roc de Bernon
map 40/J9

owner: Jean-Marie Lénier *area:* 14 ha *cases:* 7,000 *grape % R:* MER 80% CS 10% CF 10% *second wine:* Ch Champs de Durand

Below: Ch Teyssier

33570 Puisseguin tel: 05 57 74 53 42
fax: 05 57 74 53 42
A generally easy Puisseguin, soon ready for drinking, with smooth tannins and little complexity. Part of the vineyard stretches over the district's highest clay and limestone plateau.

Ch Roc de Boissac
map 40/I8

owner: SCI de Boissac *area:* 35 ha *cases:* 16,000 *grape % R:* MER 75% CF 15% CS 10% *second wine:* Ch La Millerie *other châteaux owned:* Ch Le Grand Bos *(Lussac-St-Emilion)*
33570 Puisseguin tel: 05 57 74 61 22
fax: 05 57 74 59 54
A vineyard that is large for the district and has belonged to the same family for nearly two centuries. The château, built on a slope, has impressive cellars in the rock beneath it, where the wine matures for a year in oak, 30% of it new barrels. A genial wine that offers oak alongside its cherry-like fruit.

Ch de Roques
map 40/H9

owner: Michel Sublett *area:* 34 ha *cases:* 15,000 *grape % R:* MER 65% CF 32% CS 3% *second wine:* Ch La France de Roques
33570 Puisseguin tel: 05 57 74 69 56
fax: 05 57 74 58 80
This estate named after Jean de Roques, comrade-in-arms of Henri IV, is about the same size as it was four centuries ago. This château produces an accessible wine that demands little patience (the memory of the watery 1990 is beginning to fade). There is an atmospheric rock cellar here; Ch de Roques also has a few rooms to let, and a restaurant for parties and functions.

Ch Soleil
map 40/K8

owner: Jean Soleil *area:* 20 ha *cases:* 9,000 *grape % R:* MER 70% CF 15% CS 15% *second wine:* Rayon de Soleil *other wines:* Ch le Mayne
33570 Puisseguin tel: 05 57 74 63 46
fax: 05 57 74 50 66
One of the better wines of the appellation. It deserves attention for its concentration, its jammy fruit, its roundness and its balancing dose of oak. Jean Soleil, the owner, is stringently selective: thus the whole 1991 vintage was brought out as a second wine.

Ch Teyssier
map 40/J7

owner: GFA du Ch Teyssier/Groupe CVBG *area:* 40 ha *cases:* 20,000 *grape % R:* MER 60% CF 20% CS 20% *second wine:* Ch Puybonnet *(Montagne-St-Emilion) other wines:* Montagne-St-Emilion *other châteaux owned:* include Ch Belgrave *(Haut-Médoc)*; Ch La Garde *(Pessac-Léognan)*; Ch de la Tour *(Bordeaux)*
33570 Puisseguin tel: 05 57 74 63 11
This is the same estate as the one described under Montagne-St-Emilion; but the Puisseguin wine is rather different. Its oak, for example, is often less prominent. The wine is very well made, balanced, has a structure that is at least adequate, and demands time to open up.

APPELLATION ST-GEORGES-ST-EMILION

Ch Belair St-Georges map 40/J3
owner: Yannick le Menn & Nadine Pocci *area:* 10 ha
cases: 5,000 *grape % R:* MER 70% CF 15% CS 15%
second wine: Ch Belair Montaiguillon *other chateaux owned:* Ch Haut Saint Clair *(Puisseguin-St-Emilion);* Ch Montlabert *(St-Emilion)*
33570 Montagne tel: 05 57 74 65 40
fax: 05 57 74 51 50
Fairly firm wine with adequate tannins that are rather angular when young. Its aroma displays both chocolate and fruit (black cherry) notes, plus a hint of spices. Worth keeping a few years.

Ch Bellonne Saint Georges map 40/K3
owner: Denis Corre-Macquin *area:* 35 ha *cases:* 17,500 *grape % R:* MER 60% CS 20% CF 20% *second wine:* Ch Macquin St Georges; Domaine de Maisonneuve *other chateaux owned:* Ch Grand Moulin *(Montagne-St-Emilion)*
33570 Montagne tel: 05 57 74 64 66
fax: 05 57 74 55 47
This estate is where Albert Macquin began the restoration of the vineyards around Libourne after the phylloxera disaster: in 1885 he grafted the first French vines onto American rootstocks. The wine usually has a lively taste with weight and backbone; oak is clearly evident, and sufficient tannin as well.

Ch Calon map 40/J2
owner: Jean-Noël Boidron *area:* 5.5 ha *cases:* 3,500 *grape % R:* MER 80% CF 10% CS 9% MAL 1%
second wine: Ch Les Abeilles *other chateaux owned:* include Ch Calon *(Montagne-St-Emilion);* Ch Corbin Michotte *(St-Emilion*
33570 Montagne tel: 05 57 51 64 88
fax: 05 57 51 56 30
This vineyard adjoins Ch Calon in Montagne-St-Emilion. It shares the same owner, and the wine is made in the same – that is to say meticulous – way. Usually it has just a little more intensity, depth and length than the Montagne. Black berry fruit is there in plenty, combined with spicy elements , a hint of oak and vanilla. Very consistent high quality.

Ch Cap d'Or map 40
owner: Vignobles Rocher-Cap de Rive *area:* 16 ha *cases:* 12,500 *grape % R:* MER 70% CS 30% *second wine:* La Croix de Thomas *other chateaux owned:*

include Ch Tourans *(St-Emilion);* Ch Vieux Coutelin *(St-Estèphe);* Ch Grand Jour *(Côtes de Bourg);* Ch Samion *(Montagne St-Emilion)*
33570 Montagne tel: 05 57 40 08 88
fax: 05 57 40 19 93
Blackberry is often clearly present in the aroma of this succulent, firm wine. Licorice and forest scents are also there, along with oak and vanilla from its year maturing in cask.

Ch Le Roc de Troquard map 40/J3
owner: Régis Visage *area:* 3.1 ha *cases:* 1,500 *grape % R:* MER 85% CF 15% *other châteaux owned:* Ch Jupille Carillon *(St-Emilion)*
33570 Montagne tel: 05 57 24 62 92
fax: 05 57 24 69 40
Fairly reserved but mouthfilling wine, from a small family vineyard where the vines grow on heavy clay and limestone soil. No cask-ageing.

Ch Saint-André Corbin map 40/J3
owner: SCEA du Priourat *area:* 19 ha *cases:* 8,000 *grape % R:* MER 70% CF 30%
33570 Montagne tel: 05 57 51 00 48
fax: 05 57 25 22 56
Excavations suggest that the present château is on the site where in the 4th century AD, the Villa Luccanius stood. Here the Roman consul Ausonius lived and wrote about his own wine. Today the wine is still worthy of note: the estate yields a good, well-endowed St-Georges-St-Emilion with modest fruit and soft tannins.

Ch St Georges map 40/K4
owner: Georges Desbois *area:* 45 ha *cases:* 25,000 *grape % R:* MER 60% CS 20% CF 20% *second wine:* Ch Puy St Georges
33570 Montagne tel: 05 57 74 62 11
fax: 05 57 74 58 62
The château is in palatial style, and was built in 1770 by the architect Victor Louis. Four round corner towers flank the symmetrical structure of a main building and two wings. The wine here might be described as suitably princely. It has generosity, strength, jammy fruit, spices, breeding and – in good years – an iron constitution. The noble tones of oak are due to at least 16 months in cask (50% new barrels). With its 45 ha, Ch St Georges is by far the largest estate in the appellation.

Ch Tour du Pas St Georges map 40/K4
owner: Helyett Dubois-Challon *area:* 15 ha *cases:* 6,000 *grape % R:* MER 65% CF 20% CS 15% *second wine:* Le Sablier; St-Georges-St-Emilion *other châteaux owned:* Ch Ausone *(St-Emilion);* Ch Belair *(St-Emilion)*
33570 Montagne tel: 05 57 24 70 94
fax: 05 57 24 67 11
Since 1885 this estate has belonged to the Dubois-Challon family, owners of châteaux Ausone and Belair in St-Emilion. It goes without saying that here, too, the wine is made with a great feeling for perfection, albeit in a less expensive way: only a fifth of the barrels are new. This wine has style and elegance. It is firm, with fruit that includes prune, and with a certain potential for ageing. Two striking contemporary sculptures in wood stand by the cellar entrance.

Ch Troquart map 40/J3
owner: GFA Ch Troquart/Famille Marcès *area:* 5.3 ha *cases:* 2,000 *grape % R:* MER 70% CF 13% CS 12% MAL 5%
33570 Montagne tel: 05 57 74 62 45
fax: 05 57 74 56 20
This estate works in a craftsmanlike way, and little of the wine is exported. The wine is fairly muscular, with a taste that suggests berry fruits and licorice. It matures in *barriques* of which 15% are new, and generally calls for about five years' cellaring.

Ch Vieux Guillou map 40/J3
owner: Jean-Paul Menguy *area:* 12 ha *cases:* 6,500 *grape % R:* MER 70% CF 20% CS 8% MAL 2%
33570 Montagne tel: 05 57 74 62 09
An estate more than four centuries old, looking out across the St-Emilion plateau. The wine, made from four grape varieties, is accessible and undemanding, without great depth – but it does have fruit.

Below: Ch Belair St-Georges

Below: Ch St Georges

POMEROL

MICHAEL BROADBENT

The wines of Pomerol, all red incidentally, are currently very fashionable – and one can see why. They tend to be richly-coloured, full of fruit, fleshy and (dare I say it) more obvious, less subtle than their equivalents in the Médoc. In short they come closer to the New World gold-medal, 100-point wines beloved of the pundits, and are consequently more amenable and acceptable to the novice. Also, rather conveniently, they tend to develop more quickly than their counterparts in the Médoc. Having said this, the average quality of Pomerols is high: dependable, extremely drinkable.

The production of wine in this relatively small and compact district is limited by the modest average size of the vineyards. The combination of strong international demand for wines in limited supply results, quite naturally, in disproportionately high prices.

It is fair to say that the wine of Château Pétrus sets the pace. Small – its vineyard area one-seventh that of Lafite in Pauillac – and producing well-made wine of undoubtedly high quality, Pétrus was the first to achieve stratospheric prices. But within only the past year or so, even Pétrus has been upstaged in price by Le Pin. A glance at the relative size of the vineyards gives at least a partial explanation. Partial, because if the wine made in a tiny vineyard is of poor or even indifferent quality it will not, I am glad to say, hit the jackpot. Very small but very good, as at Le Pin, is the right combination!

Pursuing the subject of price and quality, my own personal view is simply to leave the market to sort itself out. If an oriental collector wishes to corner the market in the 1982 – or any other vintage – of Le Pin, then let him do so. When the excitement blows over and he decides to resell, the bubble might well have burst. It might seem unfair and undemocratic to make available the rarest wines in the world only to the seriously rich; but how else? Drawing lots? Bottling it all in miniatures? Queuing up at the cellar door for a meagre allowance which, in due course, would encourage local brokers to behave like ticket touts at Wimbledon? In that other great French wine region, Burgundy, the wines of Domaine de la Romanée-Conti face the same situation, the price of Romanée-Conti itself reflecting not just the quality but the size of the vineyard, only a fraction larger than that of Le Pin.

THE WINE, ITS STYLE AND APPEAL

If the foregoing sounded cynical let me hasten to put the wines of Pomerol into perspective. The majority are decently made, delicious and fairly reasonably priced.

Broadly, there are two styles of wine: the first is deeply coloured, firm, fairly tannic reds whose weight and shape are nearer to those from the Médoc than from neighbouring St-Emilion; the other is paler in colour, lighter in weight – altogether more amenable, easy, and relatively quick-maturing. These are usually from grapes grown on the lighter sandy soils but, as always, not only the vintage but the aim of the proprietor has a bearing.

On the whole, Pomerols tend to be sweeter, their richness and extract masking a tannic content that in the wines of the Médoc would be more obvious, more laid bare and perhaps more bitter when young. And, at their best, the wines of Pomerol have a wonderful texture, suave and silky. To achieve this, Pomerol's patchwork of little properties has an advantage. Because of their relatively small size, the vineyards are more manageable: the proprietor is unusually well-placed to choose the optimum moment to pick. Having assessed the ripeness and balance of the grapes, he will be in a position to harvest them quickly. Let me give you an example. The

Ripe Merlot grapes and roses offer a metaphor of Pomerol's opulence

bakingly hot summer of 1982 was followed by an equally hot early September. The grapes – particularly the early-developing Merlot – were exceptionally ripe, with a very high sugar content. Christian Moueix, part-owner and manager of Château Pétrus, is keen on flying and keeps a close watch on the weather. The reports he was getting one mid-September day were that it was due to break at the weekend. So, having satisfied himself that his grapes were ready on the Friday, he sent in 140 pickers who managed to harvest the entire crop in ten hours. Now, 140 pickers would take some three to three and a half *weeks* to pick the crop at, say, Château Léoville Las Cases in the Médoc, not merely due to the size of the vineyard but because of the ripening times of the different grapes. The risk of the weather changing half way through the harvest is very real – and, indeed, this often happens.

So, in short, the vineyard owner in Pomerol has a considerable advantage at vintage time – though he too can of course be let down by a sudden change of weather. There is a downside: the disadvantage of owning a neat little vineyard is that the quantity of wine is limited, so quality is crucial to justify a compensatingly high price.

THE LANDSCAPE, SOIL AND GRAPE VARIETIES

Pomerol, on reflection, seems to have more peculiarities than the other major districts. To begin with it is a relatively small, compact area: a gently tilted square in shape, almost exactly two miles from east to west and from north to south. Virtually the entire surface area of this flat, slightly sloping plateau is devoted to vines: roughly 800 ha under vine, one-seventh of the area of St-Emilion. Merlot dominates, supported by Cabernet Franc (known locally as Bouchet) and, at some châteaux, a little Cabernet Sauvignon. All are grown on a gravelly soil, with clay on the upper, eastern side, sand to the west.

There are no really grand châteaux, just a few rather charming old houses adjoining their own *chais* and vineyards. Pétrus itself is modest in the extreme: just a small neat complex to house the presses, vats and first- and second-year *barriques*. In short, little space is wasted.

Despite theoretically helpful signs, this is a singularly confusing area to visit, and it is often hard to discern which vines belong to which château. Vineyards seem to be continuous, divided by a ditch, possibly a small wall... often by nothing at all. To make matters

worse, there is no centre; even villages scarcely exist – just a scattering of hamlets and buildings joined by a haphazard criss-crossing of minor roads. And yet, and yet, what superb wines can emerge from these small properties!

LIBOURNE AND THE POMEROL DISTRICT

If Pomerol's vineyards have a mundane, indeed rather unexciting look, the same cannot be said of Libourne – a charming old town. Quite large, crammed with narrow geometric streets, at its centre a handsome market square, its riverside protected by medieval bastions. In Libourne one can feel the presence of the English, who for some 300 years occupied – indeed owned – all of south-west France. Yet it is very French: the well-proportioned stone buildings, the shops, an unmistakeable atmosphere.

Libourne is the door to Pomerol. A good place to stay; not a bad place to eat. Once a hair-raisingly dangerous drive from Bordeaux, the three-lane highway inviting head-on collisions, most of the route is now dual carriageway and, traffic permitting, a speedy half-hour drive. Avoid the centre if your plan is to drive straight to the vineyards. Take the road towards the town, not the new bypass that swings around it to the east. Cross the bridge over the Dordogne, and immediately take the inner ring road right, looking out for the railway station and the signs to Pomerol. The vines start at the north-east outskirts of the town, and continue to the border with St-Emilion – the destination of most visitors after solicitously doffing their caps at the great names en route: Pétrus, Trotanoy, Vieux Château Certan, La Conseillante and the like.

Left: Ch Lafleur. Above: Pomerol church

It is hard to say how many châteaux are lived in by the vineyard proprietors, or who will be there to greet one after a knock at the door. At most, however, a genuinely interested visitor will be able to visit the *chai* and, perhaps, to taste the young wine in cask. As always, an introduction is advisable where possible. In the case of Pétrus and other châteaux owned by the ubiquitous Moueix family, a preliminary call must be made to their very modest office on the riverside *quai* in Libourne.

THE TRADE IN POMEROL'S WINES

At the opening of this chapter I explained some of the reasons for the current vogue for the wines of Pomerol.

When did this upsurge of interest take place, and why did it not happen before? The answer lies in the history and organization of the wine trade. Prior to the 1960s, the UK wine trade was dominated by family firms, wine merchants with close personal relations not only with their customers but with their suppliers, the importers who in turn dealt on a sole-agency basis with the major *négociants*, then the 'merchant princes' of Bordeaux. The *négoce* tended to specialize in the better-known châteaux of the Médoc: the First Growths for the top of the market; good middle-class wines such as Calon-Ségur, Lynch-Bages, Gruaud-Larose and Talbot for the professional classes – châteaux with familiar names that made enough wine to match a regular healthy demand. The vineyards of Pomerol were too small, unknown, unfamiliar in name and in style to interest these buyers. The Belgian and Dutch markets were different. Always closer to Burgundy than to Bordeaux, their connoisseurs appreciated the richer style of Pomerol. Much was imported in cask, to be bottled not only by merchants but in the cellars of private houses. The turning-point came with the immediate post-war vintages, in particular 1945, 1947 and 1949. Some superlative wines were made and caught the attention of a handful of connoisseurs, both English and Bordelais. These included Edouard Cruse and his London agent Jack Rutherford, and the wine merchants Harry Waugh and Ronald Avery. It was also in 1945 that the shrewd, far-sighted Jean-Pierre Moueix became exclusive distributor of Pétrus; he took a direct interest in 1964, subsequently carving an influential niche in the market for Pomerol and acquiring a stake in vineyards which have now become world-famous. However, these wines thoroughly deserve their reputation and, even if some are now destined only for rich men's cellars, there are so many others to provide immense pleasure, to drink, to keep.

VINTAGES

Such old vintages I have come across have been from European cellars, the oldest being the 1893 Pétrus: a hefty, chocolaty wine. I also noted a 1900 Pomerol bottled in Leith, its bouquet fragrant despite decay and pungency; a decadently opulent 1908, and a deep, murky 1917 – admittedly vintages that would be tired whatever the provenance. The decade of the 1920s was as successful for the wines of Pomerol as the more widely

Oil heaters protect the vines from spring frost at Ch Pétrus

Of the next decade, 1950 quite good, notably Le Gay; 1952, as in St-Emilion, on the whole better than the Left Bank; 1953 lovely (but I prefer the best Médocs); 1955 good, notably Vieux Château Certan, also good in 1959 – in that year Pétrus was great. 1961 stellar: Pétrus again, also l'Evangile, Le Gay and the splendid Latour à Pomerol and Trotanoy – but a disappointing Gazin; 1962s as under-appreciated as elsewhere; 1964s once good, mainly tiring; 1966 far healthier. The late 1960s rarely seen, thank goodness; 1970 good, 1971 excellent – particularly La Conseillante, Le Gay, La Fleur-Pétrus and Trotanoy; my own top 1971 is La Grave Trigant de Boisset.

My opinion of mid-to late-1970s red Bordeaux is one of fading illusions if not disillusion – though the 1979 Pomerols were impressive as (to move into the next decade) were and are the 1981s. 1982 produced blockbusters, 1983 more charm (my first experience of Le Pin was a half-bottle brought to Christie's in April 1984! 'Very exotic', I noted). Pomerol is Merlot country and, alas, in 1984 that grape variety was destroyed by the weather, so we pass on to the pleasant 1985s, the firmer, finer 1986s and 1988s, and the opulent 1989s.

Short of weather disasters the small Pomerol vineyards have an advantage over the larger, multi-cépage Médocs in most vintages: the early to mid 1990s being no exception. But, apart from the dependable workhorses La Pointe and de Sales, the best-known names are distinctly over-fashionable, over-expensive.

PERSONAL FAVOURITES

I would be churlish to deny Pétrus its supreme position, not to mention other lovely wines of the Moueix 'stable', notably La Fleur-Pétrus and Trotanoy. (At a tasting of all the First Growths of the great post-war vintages, I privately awarded full marks (20/20) to each vintage of Pétrus – and even a somewhat exaggerated 21/20 for its 1947.) Of the rest I have always regarded highly the dependable – deservedly expensive – La Conseillante, also Vieux Château Certan. The latest (apart from Le Pin – which, I am happy to report, is good) to gain star status is l'Eglise-Clinet. But where does one stop?

known Médocs: 1921 Pétrus perfection; the year 1924 had a good reputation but Nenin (the oldest of this château tasted) variable; 1926 good, 1928 excellent, particularly Trotanoy. 1929 was renowned, though the Pétrus I tasted was described by someone as 'like a farmer with mud on his boots'. L'Enclos was more typical: rich, fleshy. 1934s were good, 1937s variable, now astringent. The war vintages were not bad but it was that great post-war trio that made everyone sit up. The first I tasted was the magnificent 1945 Gazin but the now almost priceless classic is Pétrus, not only of that year but also the 1947 and 1949 (Certan and La Conseillante also impressive).

THE APPELLATION

POMEROL (red)

Location: *On the right bank of the Dordogne. To the north it is limited by the Barbanne stream, beyond which lies Lalande-de-Pomerol, and to the east by St-Emilion. Its southern limit is the Libourne-Bergerac railway line and the town of Libourne, and to the west the D910 Libourne-Angoulême road.*
Area of AC: *975 ha*
Area under vine: *785 ha*
Communes: *Pomerol and a clearly defined part of Libourne*

Average annual production: *367,000 cases*
Classed growths: *None; the wines of Pomerol have never been classified*
Others: *Roughly 185, including several international stars*
Cooperatives: *None*
Main grape varieties: *Merlot*
Others: *Cabernet Franc (Bouchet), Cabernet Sauvignon*
Main soil types: *Clay-gravel on the central plateau, becoming increasingly sandy at the outer edges of the appellation*

APPELLATION POMEROL

Clos Beauregard
map 41 E6

owner: Héritiers Marcel Moueix **area:** 5 ha **cases:** 1,900 **grape % R:** MER 60% CS 30% CF 10% **other châteaux owned:** include Ch Taillefer *(Pomerol)*
33500 Pomerol tel: 05 57 55 30 20
fax: 05 57 25 22 14
This vineyard was separated from Beauregard in 1935, and bought by Antoine Moueix. A muscular, balanced wine that lingers on the palate and can have a delicious aroma of red and black berry fruit, as well as plenty of tannin.

Ch Beauregard
map 41 E8

owner: Crédit Foncier de France **area:** 17 ha **cases:** 7,000 **grape % R:** MER 60% CF 30% CS 10% **second wine:** Le Benjamin de Beauregard **other châteaux owned:** Ch de Barbe Blanche *(Lussac-St-Emilion)*; Ch Saint Robert *(Graves)*; Ch Bastor-Lamontagne *(Sauternes)*
33500 Pomerol tel: 05 57 51 13 36
fax: 05 57 25 09 55
The 18th-century château of Beauregard has wide steps sweeping up to a terrace, flanked by small towers, and was designed by a pupil of Victor Louis. It all made such an impression on one American architect that you will find a copy at Port Washington, Long Island. For a long time Beauregard wine was rather slender, and modest in its nuances. Since the end of the 1980s, however, the standard has risen greatly. The quality improved again after Crédit Foncier took over the estate in 1991. Selection became more stringent than ever before: the whole 1991 vintage was sold as a second wine. Starting with the 1993 vintage Beauregard has been most impressive: a solid Pomerol, with mellow fruit and an almost creamy structure; oak is nobly present. This has continued in subsequent vintages – including the superb, concentrated 1994, with its ample, berry fruit.

Ch Bel-Air
map 41 I4

owner: Jean Sudrat **area:** 13 ha **cases:** 5,500 **grape % R:** MER 95% CS 5% **other châteaux owned:** Ch Beauséjour *(Fronsac)*
33500 Pomerol tel: 05 57 51 02 45
Sturdy and very correct Pomerol, with some roundness. This estate, predominantly Merlot, has belonged to the Sudrat family since 1914.

Ch Bellegrave
map 41 L5

owner: Jean-Marie Bouldy **area:** 7 ha **cases:** 3,500 **grape % R:** MER 70% CF 25% CS 5% **second wine:** Ch des Jacobins **other châteaux owned:** Ch Matignon *(St-Emilion)*
33500 Pomerol tel: 05 57 51 20 47
fax: 05 57 51 23 14
Half of the casks for maturing are generally replaced each year, so that in its youth this traditionally-made wine has a noticeable aroma of oak and vanilla (ageing lasts 12-16 months). This substantial Pomerol acquires smoothness and balance after some five years as a rule. 'Bellegrave' is a reference to the gravel topsoil in the vineyard.

Ch Bonalgue
map 41 J7

owner: Pierre Bourotte SA **area:** 6.5 ha **cases:** 2,750 **grape % R:** MER 80% CF 20% **second wine:** Ch Burgrave **other châteaux owned:** Clos du Clocher *(Pomerol)*; Ch du Courlat *(Lussac-St-Emilion)*; Ch Les Hauts-Conseillants *(Lalande-de-Pomerol)*
33500 Libourne tel: 05 57 51 62 17
fax: 05 57 51 28 28

In good years this is a strongly structured Pomerol combining the dark tones of truffles, leather, coffee and cedar with the generous, spicy fruit of black cherry and prune. Oak is unmistakeably there, without being intrusively dominant. In ordinary years the wine is rather slighter and more supple. The château was built around 1815 by a captain from Napoléon's army: hence the bas-reliefs with regimental flags and weapons.

Ch Le Bon Pasteur
map 41 C4

owner: SCEA des Domaines Rolland **area:** 7 ha **cases:** 3,500 **grape % R:** MER 75% CF 25% **other wines:** Ch Fontenil *(Fronsac)*; Ch Rolland-Maillet *(St-Emilion)*, Ch Bertineau St-Vincent *(Lalande de Pomerol)*
33500 Pomerol tel: 05 57 51 10 94
fax: 05 57 25 05 54
Since 1978 this modest property has been run by Michel Rolland, one of the most renowned oenologists in Bordeaux, if not the whole of France. He makes a formidable Pomerol, among the best in the appellation. The wine has solid colour and a fleshy, almost opulent taste, generous with delicious fruit (plum, cherry), and is underpinned by smoky, toasted, spicy oak. Rolland uses 70-100% new oak for each vintage, with a maturing period that ranges from 12-18 months.

Ch de Bourgueneuf
map 41 I4

owner: Vignobles Meyer **area:** 4.7 ha **cases:** 2,400 **grape % R:** MER 60% CF 30% CS 10% **second wine:** Domaine de Bourg-Neuf **other châteaux owned:** include Clos de Templiers *(Lalande-de-Pomerol)*; Les Tournelles de Bossuet La Gravière *(Bordeaux)*
33500 Pomerol tel: 05 57 51 16 73
fax: 05 57 25 16 89
Somewhat rustic, rounded Pomerol, usually with agreeable fruit and reasonable substance – but less as a rule than its neighbour Bourgneuf-Vayron. Maturing lasts a year and generally half of the barrels are new.

Ch Bourgneuf-Vayron
map 41 I5

owner: Xavier Vayron **area:** 9 ha **cases:** 4,750 **grape % R:** MER 90% CF 10%
33500 Pomerol tel: 05 57 51 42 03
fax: 05 57 25 01 40

Below: Ch Bourgneuf-Vayron

A wine that nearly always excels in its strength and concentration, but sometimes lacks a little refinement. Dominant animal aromas along with fine oak, vanilla and jammy fruit.

Ch La Cabanne
map 41 H4

owner: Jean-Pierre Estager **area:** 10 ha **cases:** 5,000 **grape % R:** MER 92% CF 8% **second wine:** Domaine de Compostelle **other châteaux owned:** Ch Plincette *(Pomerol)*; Ch Haut-Maillet *(Pomerol)*; Domaine de Gachet *(Lalande-de-Pomerol)*; Domaine des Gourdins *(St-Emilion)*; Ch La Papeterie *(Montagne-St-Emilion)*
33500 Pomerol tel: 05 57 51 04 09
fax: 05 57 25 13 38
In great years a powerful wine, filling the mouth with lingering tannin and earthy aromas. Its structure becomes lighter, more supple and accessible in normal vintages. Some 40% of the maturing casks are new each year.

Ch Le Caillou
map 41 G7

owner: Giraud-Bélivier **area:** 7 ha **cases:** 3,300 **grape % R:** MER 75% CF 25% **second wine:** La Fleur Lacombe; Domaine de Lacombe **other wines:** Ch La Tour du Pin Figeac *(St-Emilion)*
33500 Pomerol tel: 05 57 51 06 10
fax: 05 57 51 74 95
After about five years in bottle this Pomerol does not reveal great power, but the flavour is good, with a certain finesse. The finish may include some dry tannin; the bouquet some licorice, old oak, red fruit and bilberry.

Ch Cantelauze
map 41 F2

owner: Jean-Noël Boidron **area:** 0.7 ha **cases:** 300 **grape % R:** MER 90% CF 10% **other châteaux owned:** Ch Mayne d'Olivet *(Bordeaux)*; Ch Calon *(St-Georges-St-Emilion; Montagne-St-Emilion)*; Ch Corbin Michotte *(St-Emilion)*
33500 Pomerol tel: 05 57 51 64 88
fax: 05 57 51 56 30
Very skilfully made wine: generous, dark-toned, clean, succulent and with smoky oak. Spends 20 months maturing entirely in new *barriques*. Production is minuscule.

Ch Certan de May de Certan
map 41 E5

owner: Odette Barreau-Badar **area:** 5 ha **cases:** 2,000 **grape % R:** MER 70% CF 25% CS 5% **other châteaux owned:** Ch Poitou *(Lussac-St-Emilion)*; Ch Grand Sorillon *(Bordeaux Supérieur)*
33500 Pomerol tel: 05 57 51 41 53
fax: 05 57 51 88 51
The estate takes its name from a Scottish family who established themselves in Pomerol in the 16th or 17th century. The property became known as Vieux Ch Certan *(see below)*, but it was split up after the 1848 revolution. The smaller part remained with the Certan de May family and at first was called Petit-Certan. The

---

◆
About Pomerol

Information on the wines of Pomerol can be obtained from the Syndicat, which is in the heart of the village of Pomerol at the Maison du Syndicat viticole de Pomerol, 33500 Pomerol. Tel 05 57 25 06 88.

Above: Vieux Château Certan

Above: Ch La Conseillante

modesty of the estate contrasts with the greatness of its wine. Particularly on the palate it is among the best in the district: heaps of soft fruit, velvety tannins, reined-in power, endless length – and it has splendid oak from maturing in casks of which half are new.

Ch Certan-Giraud map 41 E4
owner: SC des Domaines Giraud *area:* 7.5 ha *cases:* 4,550 *grape % R:* MER 79% CF 21% *other châteaux owned:* Ch Corbin *(St-Emilion)*
33500 Pomerol tel: 05 57 74 48 94
fax: 05 57 74 47 18
Distinguished wine, with power and finesse in balance. It also has great amounts of smooth tannin and a long finish. Noble oak – usually all casks are new – provides a suitable framework.

Ch Clinet map 41 G3
owner: GAN *area:* 9 ha *cases:* 3,500 *grape % R:* MER 75% CS 15% CF 10% *second wine:* Fleur de Clinet *other châteaux owned:* include Ch La Croix du Casse *(Pomerol)*; Ch Jonqueyres *(Bordeaux)*
33500 Pomerol tel: 05 56 68 55 88
fax: 05 56 30 11 45
A superb Pomerol is created here, often from grapes picked extremely late. The wine spends at least 24 months in *barriques*, all of them new; it is rich, exceptionally intense, complex, lingering and full of fruit – blackcurrants – plum, blackberry, black cherry.

Clos du Clocher map 41 F7
owner: Madame Vve Audy *area:* 6 ha *cases:* 3,000 *grape % R:* MER 70% CF 30% *second wine:* Ch Monregard La Croix *other châteaux owned:* Ch de Brondeau *(Bordeaux Supérieur)*
33500 Pomerol tel: 05 57 51 62 17
fax: 05 57 51 28 28
This is often a full-bodied, almost fat, but none too compact wine, possessing fine fruit and a truffle-like, earthy aroma. Oak, from the 50% new casks, is prominent and sometimes even slightly sawdusty.

◆
Finding a second wine
To locate a second wine, consult the index which lists all the châteaux covered in this Atlas.

Ch La Commanderie map 41 G8
owner: Marie-Hélène Dé *area:* 6 ha *cases:* 3,000 *grape % R:* MER 86% CS 12% CF 2% *second wine:* Ch Haut Manoir; Le Priourat
33500 Pomerol tel: 05 57 51 79 03
The name refers to a *commanderie* of the powerful military and religious order of the Knights of St John of Jerusalem, established here in the 13th century. A Maltese cross from that time is still to be seen on the estate. Well-made, harmonious wine that is not particularly concentrated, and at times somewhat short. It develops rather quickly, having matured for two years in oak (50% new barrels).

Ch La Conseillante map 41 D6
owner: Famille Nicolas *area:* 12 ha *cases:* 5,000 *grape % R:* MER 65% CS 30% MAL 5%
33500 Pomerol tel: 05 57 51 15 32
fax: 05 57 51 42 39
This is generally a refined Pomerol, very aromatic, with a sound balance between fruit and oak, and an almost silky texture. In the 1970s its quality was rather inconsistent, but today La Conseillante is again among the best Pomerols. In principle new barrels are now used every year, and the wine spends 20 months in them. The unpretentious 18th-century château borders on the St-Emilion vineyard of Ch Cheval Blanc, and since 1874 it has belonged to the Nicolas family. The estate has the motto *Faire peu, mais faire bon.*

Ch La Croix map 41 F7
owner: Famille Joseph Janoueix *area:* 10 ha *cases:* 4,500 *grape % R:* MER 70% CF 20% CS 10% *second wine:* Ch Le Gabachot *other châteaux owned:* include Ch La Croix St-Georges *(Pomerol)*; Ch Haut-Sarpe *(St-Emilion)*
33500 Pomerol tel: 05 57 51 41 86
fax: 05 57 51 76 83
This château, restored in 18th-century style, takes its name from a stone crucifix by the vineyard. One illustrious owner was Jean de Sèze, an enterprising winegrower and lawyer to Louis XVI. The wine usually has power and substance, with the animal aromas of leather and musk, considerable oak from at least 14 months in cask (30-50% new), candied fruit, and quite mature, elegant tannins. Has rather more refinement than La Croix St-Georges, also made by the Janoueix family.

Ch La Croix de Gay map 41 F3
owner: Noël Raynaud *area:* 12 ha *cases:* 7,000 *grape % R:* MER 80% CS 10% CF 10% *other châteaux owned:* Ch Faizeau *(Montagne-St-Emilion)*
33500 Pomerol tel: 05 57 51 19 05
fax: 05 57 74 15 62
A wine that treads on the heels of the leaders. Cedar, spicy oak, ripe fruit and bayleaf are often found in its aroma, and its taste is rich in oak, meaty, powerful and smooth, yet with some freshness. A very good wine that sometimes just lacks a little finesse to be truly great. A superior selection is brought out, in good years only, under the Ch La Fleur de Gay label. A decadent wine, pure Merlot, it is matured entirely in new barrels. Production is 800-1,000 cases a year.

Ch La Croix du Casse map 41 H9
owner: GAN *area:* 9 ha *cases:* 4,500 *grape % R:* MER 70% CF 30% *other châteaux owned:* include Ch Clinet *(Pomerol)*; Ch Jonqueyres *(Bordeaux Supérieur)*
33500 Pomerol tel: 05 56 68 55 88
fax: 05 56 30 11 45
Unfiltered and un-fined wine that owes its clarity to 24-27 months in oak cask, half of them new as a rule. This Pomerol has good colour, and its oak and tannin blend beautifully into a velvety, rounded taste very characteristic of its *appellation*.

Ch La Croix St-Georges map 41 F6
owner: Famille Joseph Janoueix *area:* 5 ha *cases:* 2,700 *grape % R:* MER 95% CF 5% *second wine:* Le Gabachot *other châteaux owned:* include Ch La Croix *(Pomerol)*; Ch Haut-Sarpe *(St-Emilion)*
33500 Pomerol tel: 05 57 51 41 86
fax: 05 57 51 76 83
Very powerful, mouthfilling wine, firmly packed in its tannin. Warm, animal aromas of leather and roast game, a touch of fruit; of limited finesse. Fairly consistent quality.

Ch La Croix-Toulifaut map 41 E8
owner: Jean-François Janoueix *area:* 1.8 ha *cases:* 830 *grape % R:* MER 100% *other châteaux owned:* include Ch La Croix *(Pomerol)*
33500 Libourne tel: 05 57 51 41 86
fax: 05 57 51 76 83
This wine is a frequent medal winner on account of its meaty, quite stylish taste, strongly dominated by oak – all casks are new.

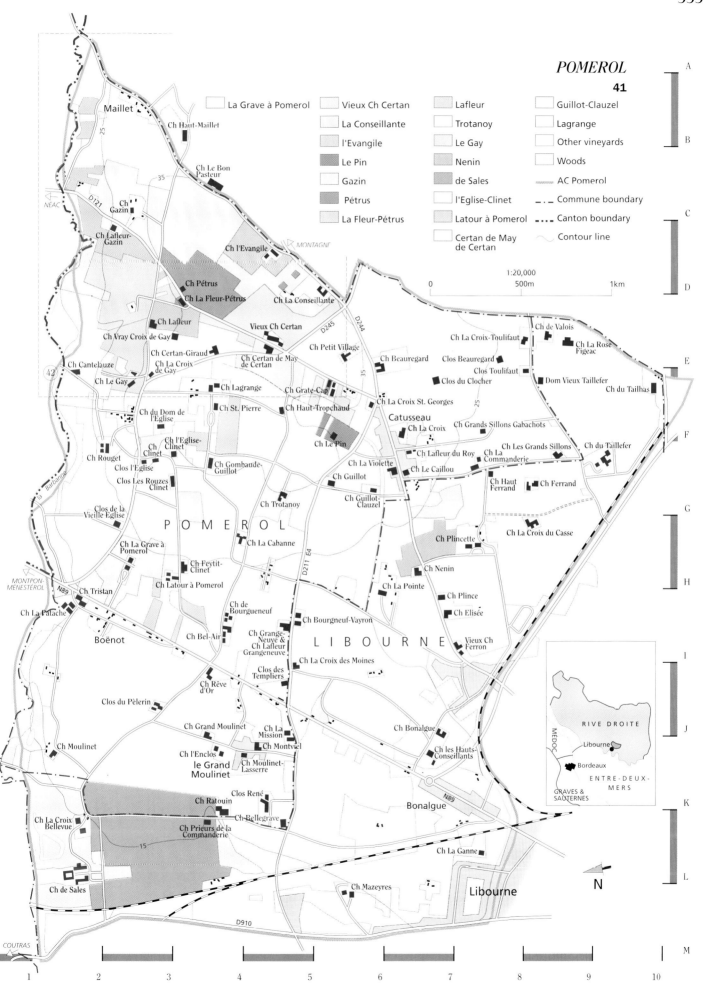

POMEROL

41

La Grave à Pomerol
Vieux Ch Certan
Lafleur
Guillot-Clauzel
La Conseillante
Trotanoy
Lagrange
l'Evangile
Le Gay
Other vineyards
Le Pin
Nenin
Woods
Gazin
de Sales
AC Pomerol
Pétrus
l'Eglise-Clinet
Commune boundary
La Fleur-Pétrus
Latour à Pomerol
Canton boundary
Certan de May
de Certan
Contour line

1:20,000

0   500m   1km

RIVE DROITE

MÉDOC

Libourne

Bordeaux

ENTRE-DEUX-MERS

GRAVES & SAUTERNES

N

Above: Ch l'Eglise-Clinet

Clos l'Eglise
map 41 G3

owner: Sylviane Garcan-Cathiard *area:* 6 ha *cases:* 2,800 *grape % R:* MER 57% CF 36% CS 7% *other châteaux owned:* Ch Haut-Bergey *(Pessac-Léognan)*
33500 Pomerol tel: 05 57 51 20 24
fax: 05 57 51 59 62
This vineyard has a relatively large proportion of Cabernet (43%), so the wine is at its best in years when both this variety and the Merlot become fully ripe. Then a perfumed, complete and balanced Pomerol emerges, with backbone and a meaty taste without being fat.

Ch du Domaine de l'Eglise
map 41 F3

owner: Indivision Castéja-Preben-Hansen *area:* 7 ha *cases:* 3,500 *grape % R:* MER 90% CF 10% *other châteaux owned:* include Ch Trotte Vieille *(St-Emilion)*; Ch Batailley *(Pauillac)*
33500 Pomerol tel: 05 56 00 00 70
fax: 05 56 52 29 54
The quality here has improved considerably since the end of the 1980s: the wine now has more extract and volume. As well as blackberry and blackcurrant fruit, its aroma also holds the vanilla and toast of new oak (50% of the barrels). The next step should be towards even more concentration and complexity.

Ch l'Eglise-Clinet
map 41 G4

owner: Denis Durantou *area:* 6 ha *cases:* 2,000 *grape % R:* MER 80% CF 20% *second wine:* La Petite Eglise
33500 Pomerol tel: 05 57 25 99 00
fax: 05 57 25 21 96
A distinguished Pomerol that derives its class both from some plots of very old vines, and from careful winemaking followed by a controlled use of oak. Its taste is often velvety, with a creamy roundness, great refinement, a reasonable intensity, and tones of both jammy fruit and of darker elements, cocoa among them.

Ch Elisée
map 41 I7

owner: Pierre-Etienne Garzaro *area:* 2 ha *cases:* 800 *grape % R:* MER 90% CF 5% PV 5% *other châteaux owned:* include Vieux Château Ferron *(Pomerol)*; Ch Le Prieur *(Bordeaux)*
33500 Libourne tel: 05 56 30 16 16
fax: 05 56 30 12 63
For this wine at least half of the maturing casks are new each year. Oak and related elements such as vanilla and coffee are thus prominent, as well as black fruits. The taste has a generous, typically Pomerol roundness.

Ch l'Enclos
map 41 K4

owner: GFA du Château l'Enclos/Hugues Weydert *area:* 9.5 ha *cases:* 4,200 *grape % R:* MER 82% CF 17% MAL 1% *other châteaux owned:* Domaine du Chapelain *(Lalande-de-Pomerol)*
33500 Pomerol tel: 05 57 51 04 62
Not a Pomerol notable for its finesse, but one that is nearly always a joy to taste. Its seductive fruitiness – plum and fig – and some spice make it well balanced. The simple château was built in 1898 on the foundations of a much older house.

Ch l'Evangile
map 41 D5

owner: Domaines Barons de Rothschild *area:* 14.1 ha *cases:* 5,000 *grape % R:* MER 78% CF 22% *second wine:* Blason de l'Evangile *other châteaux owned:* include Ch Lafite Rothschild *(Pauillac)*; Ch Rieussec *(Sauternes)*
33500 Pomerol tel: 05 57 51 15 30
fax: 05 57 51 45 78
This estate has a perfect vineyard made up of different soil types – pure gravel, clay, sand. Its potential has been increasingly realized since Domaines Barons de Rothschild, of Ch Lafite Rothschild and elsewhere, acquired a majority

Below: Ch Feytit-Clinet

shareholding in 1990. The wine that it produces is an exceptionally harmonious Pomerol, redolent of red and black summer fruits and the subtle aroma of spring flowers, with integrated oak, mineral elements, a touch of licorice and bayleaf. It is a brilliant, athletic wine, at once concentrated and refined. The vines lie on the Pomerol border, between those of Ch Pétrus and Ch La Conseillante, and those of Ch Cheval Blanc in St-Emilion.

Ch Ferrand
map 41 G9

owner: Henry Gasparoux *area:* 11 ha *cases:* 5,500 *grape % R:* CF 60% MER 40% *other châteaux owned:* Ch Haut Ferrand *(Pomerol)*
33500 Libourne tel: 05 57 51 21 67
fax: 05 57 25 01 41
Ferrand produces a fairly slender, supple and pleasantly fruity Pomerol, made principally from Cabernet Franc grapes. It also has some smoky oak – a third of the barrels in which it matures for 18 months are new.

Ch Feytit-Clinet
map 41 H4

owner: Michel Chasseuil/Jean-Pierre Moueix *area:* 7 ha *cases:* 2,500 *grape % R:* MER 75% CF 25% *second wine:* Cuvée Mary Domergue *other châteaux owned:* include Ch Trotanoy *(Pomerol)*; Ch Pétrus *(Pomerol)*; Ch Magdelaine *(St-Emilion)*; Ch de la Dauphine *(Fronsac)*
33500 Pomerol tel: 05 49 05 28 29
fax: 05 49 05 22 48
Not a wine with the power of a great Pomerol, but it tastes good, is balanced, and made with skill. Some oak is there on nose and taste, and sometimes violets as well. The estate is managed by the Jean-Pierre Moueix firm.

Ch La Fleur-Pétrus
map 41 D4

owner: Jean-Pierre Moueix *area:* 13.5 ha *cases:* 6,500 *grape % R:* MER 90% CF 10% *other châteaux owned:* include Ch Trotanoy *(Pomerol)*; Ch Pétrus *(Pomerol)*; Ch Magdelaine *(St-Emilion)*; Ch de la Dauphine *(Fronsac)*
33500 Pomerol tel: 05 57 51 78 96
fax: 05 57 51 79 79
A distinguished Pomerol; finer and more complex than most, and at the same time rather less rounded and smooth. When fully mature it is satiny yet firm, with modest fruit and a good level of oak. A narrow road divides this vineyard from that of the starry Pétrus and the châteaux are a few yards apart.

Above: Ch Le Gay

Above: Ch La Grave à Pomerol

Ch La Ganne
map 41 L8

owner: Paul & Michel Dubois *area:* 4 ha *cases:* 1,600 *grape % R:* MER 80% CF 20% *second wine:* Vieux Château Brun *other châteaux owned:* Ch Georges de Guestres *(Bordeaux Supérieur)*

33500 Libourne tel: 05 57 51 18 24

fax: 05 57 51 62 20

The same family has been making wine here for four generations. The wine is traditional in style, dark-toned and well endowed with tannin. It is matured for a year in casks (one-third of them new), after which it needs to develop for a considerable time in bottle.

Ch Le Gay
map 41 F3

owner: Marie Robin *area:* 5.2 ha *cases:* 2,000 *grape % R:* MER 60% CS 40% *other châteaux owned:* Ch Lafleur *(Pomerol)*

33500 Pomerol tel: 05 57 51 12 43

In the great years this modest vineyard produces a sturdy, mouthfilling, stunningly fruity Pomerol with plenty of tannin, which demands considerable time before its charms unfold. In light vintages there is sometimes a relatively sharp decline in quality.

Ch Gazin
map 41 C3

owner: Nicolas de Bailliencourt *area:* 26 ha *cases:* 10,000 *grape % R:* MER 80% CF 15% CS 5% *second wine:* l'Hospitalet de Gazin

33500 Pomerol tel: 05 57 51 07 05

fax: 05 57 51 69 96

After a weak period, interest is again being shown in Gazin's wine. Winemaking here is technically proficient, and maturing takes place in markedly charred casks, 30% of them new. It is a Pomerol that speaks loudly of (for example) coffee beans, animal aromas, chocolate, tar, spices and ripe fruit, along with racy tannins and a fair amount of alcohol. Perhaps real finesse is still lacking, but Gazin's quality still improves.

Ch Gombaude-Guillot
map 41 G4

owner: GFA Château Gombaude-Guillot/Famille Laval *area:* 7 ha *cases:* 2,500 *grape % R:* MER 67% CF 30% MAL 3% *second wine:* Cadet de Gombaude

33500 Pomerol tel: 05 57 51 17 40

fax: 05 57 51 16 89

Hefty Pomerol with massive, rather dry tannins and some licorice. A real powerhouse of a wine. A cask-aged *cuvée* is also produced from this

perfectly maintained vineyard. This offers somewhat more richness and breadth, and in it can be tasted jammy fruit, bayleaf, berry fruits and raisins.

Ch Grand Moulinet
map 41 J4

owner: Ollet-Fourreau & Fils *area:* 0.9 ha *cases:* 400 *grape % R:* MER 90% CF 10% *other châteaux owned:* Ch Haut-Surget *(Lalande-de-Pomerol)*

33500 Néac tel: 05 57 55 30 20

fax: 05 57 25 22 14

Given the production level here, *grand* seems rather an exaggeration. Oak is discreetly noticeable in the wine, an accessible if seldom full-bodied or very powerful Pomerol.

Ch Grands Sillons Gabachot
map 41 F8

owner: SCEA Entente Janoueix *area:* 4 ha *cases:* 2,000 *grape % R:* MER 70% CS 20% MAL 10% *other châteaux owned:* Ch Des Tourelles *(Lalande-de-Pomerol)*; Ch La Bastienne *(Montagne-St-Emilion)*; Ch Petit Clos du Roy *(Montagne-St-Emilion)*; Ch Trincaud *(Bordeaux Supérieur)*

33500 Libourne tel: 05 57 51 55 44

fax: 05 57 51 83 70

The château is an elegant *chartreuse*, approached by a double flight of steps. The vineyard lies in the south of the district, between those of Beauregard and Taillefer, with a good number of old vines. The wine offers a good measure of substance, tannin and oak – only new casks are used.

Ch les Grands Sillons
map 41 G9

owner: Philippe Dignac *area:* 2.9 ha *cases:* 1,500 *grape % R:* MER 70% CS 17% CF 7% MAL 6% *other châteaux owned:* Ch Côtes de Bonde *(Montagne-St-Emilion)*

33500 Pomerol tel: 05 57 74 64 52

fax: 05 57 74 55 88

Aromatic, with forest scents, fungi, old oak, but with not much fruit, or concentration. Supple, good-tasting, reasonably firm wine, but without a distinct character of its own. Sometimes has dry tannin in a short finish.

Ch Grange-Neuve
map 41 I5

owner: SCE Gros & Fils/Yves Gros *area:* 7 ha *cases:* 2,500 *grape % R:* MER 95% CF 5% *second wine:* La Fleur des Ormes *other châteaux owned:* Vieux Château Calon *(Montagne-St-Emilion)*

33500 Pomerol tel: 05 57 51 23 03

fax: 05 57 25 36 14

In good years the oenologist Jean-Marie Gros makes a muscular, warm, classic Pomerol one can chew on. Licorice root and cherry stones are among its nuances. A third of the maturing barrels are new.

Ch Grate-Cap
map 41 F6

owner: Guy & Michel Janoueix *area:* 7.4 ha *cases:* 5,000 *grape % R:* MER 70% CF 15% CS 15% *other châteaux owned:* include Ch Samson *(Pomerol)*; Ch Grand Fortin *(St-Emilion)*; Domaine de la Bourrue *(St-Emilion)*; Ch Petit Clos Figeac *(St-Emilion)*

33500 Pomerol tel: 05 57 51 27 97

fax: 05 57 51 02 74

A robust type of Pomerol of average quality. Little new wood.

Ch La Grave à Pomerol
map 41 H3

owner: Christian Moueix *area:* 8.4 ha *cases:* 3,500 *grape % R:* MER 85% CF 15% *other châteaux owned:* include Ch Trotanoy *(Pomerol)*; Ch Pétrus *(Pomerol)*; Ch Magdelaine *(St-Emilion)*; Ch de la Dauphine *(Fronsac)*

33500 Pomerol tel: 05 57 51 78 96

fax: 05 57 51 79 79

Creamy, full-bodied, sometimes strikingly smooth wine with velvety tannin and much fruit. A long finish, and flawless harmony. For a long time the estate was called Ch La Grave Trigant de Boisset: the last three words still appear in small type on the labels. Christian Moueix has been the owner since 1971.

Ch Guillot
map 41 G6

owner: Famille Luquot *area:* 4.7 ha *cases:* 2,300 *grape % R:* MER 70% CF 30% *other châteaux owned:* Ch Cruzeau *(St-Emilion)*

33500 Pomerol tel: 05 57 51 18 95

fax: 05 57 25 10 59

This estate lies near the church at Pomerol. Its wine is honest and generous, if not of the greatest finesse. A firm nucleus of alcohol, oak and crusty bread marks its aroma (a third of the barrels are new), together with animal scents and herbs.

Ch Guillot-Clauzel
map 41 G6

owner: Paul Clauzel/Stéphane Asséo *area:* 1.7 ha *cases:* 600 *grape % R:* MER 60% CF 40% *second wine:* Ch Graves Guillot *other châteaux owned:* include Dom de Courteillan *(Bordeaux)*

33500 Pomerol tel: 05 57 51 14 09

fax: 05 57 51 57 66

Concentrated, mouthfilling, velvet Pomerol in which jammy fruit and toasted oak contend for dominance. Very limited production, which goes to those in the know.

Ch Haut Ferrand
map 41 G8

owner: Henry Gasparoux *area:* 4.5 ha *cases:* 2,000 *grape % R:* MER 60% CF 40% *other châteaux owned:* Ch Ferrand *(Pomerol)*

33500 Libourne tel: 05 57 51 21 67

fax: 05 57 25 01 41

With a third of the maturing casks being new, there is as a rule good and ample wood in the bouquet, but in its taste this is a somewhat rustic, solid Pomerol lacking real class.

Ch Haut-Maillet
map 41 B4

owner: Héritier Delteil/Jean-Pierre Estager *area:* 5 ha *cases:* 2,500 *grape % R:* MER 70% CF 30% *other châteaux owned:* Ch La Cabanne *(Pomerol)*; Ch Plincette *(Pomerol)*; Domaine de Gachet *(Lalande-de Pomerol)*; Domaine des Gourdins *(St-Emilion)*; Ch La Papeterie *(St-Emilion)*

Above: Ch Latour à Pomerol

33500 Pomerol tel: 05 57 51 04 09
fax: 05 57 25 13 38
Ch Haut-Maillet's vineyard was created about a century ago, with plots bordering on those of l'Evangile, La Fleur-Pétrus and Gazin. This is an attractive, well-concentrated Pomerol, full of flavour, with some licorice in its long aftertaste. A generous aroma, nobly oaked – 30% of the barrels are new.

Ch Haut-Tropchaud   map 41 F5
owner: Michel Coudroy *area:* 2.1 ha *cases:* 800 *grape % R:* MER 90% CF 10% *other châteaux owned:* include Ch de Maison Neuve *(Montagne-St-Emilion)*; Ch La Faurie Maison Neuve *(Lalande-de-Pomerol)*
33500 Pomerol tel: 05 57 74 62 23
fax: 05 57 74 64 18
A pretty minimal yield, and pretty maximum quality. This is a concentrated, generous wine with a great deal of fruit (blackberry, blackcurrant, cherry), a pinch of spices and flattering oak.

Ch Lafleur   map 41 E3
owner: Marie Robin/Jacques Guinaudeau *area:* 4.5 ha *cases:* 1,250 *grape % R:* MER 50% CF 50% *second wine:* Pensées de Lafleur *other châteaux owned:* Ch Le Gay *(Pomerol)*; Ch Grand Village *(Bordeaux Supérieur)*
33500 Pomerol tel: 05 57 84 44 03
fax: 05 57 84 83 31
Thanks to perfect soil conditions, old vines and rigorous selection, this is usually a spectacular Pomerol, firmly ensconced right at the top. The vineyard is just across the road from Pétrus, on the Pomerol plateau. Lafleur's concentration is almost extreme, as is its amazing, richly nuanced aroma. Generally this wine only begins to blossom after a decade, like a great Médoc. Rare and costly.

Ch Lafleur du Roy   map 41 G3
owner: SARL Dubost *area:* 4 ha *cases:* 1,800 *grape % R:* MER 80% CF 10% CS 10% *other châteaux owned:* include Ch La Vallière *(Lalande-de-Pomerol)*; Ch Pâquerette *(Bordeaux)*; Ch Bossuet *(Bordeaux Supérieur)*
33500 Pomerol tel: 05 57 51 74 57
fax: 05 57 25 99 95
Small estate, in existence since 1958, that makes an agreeable, fresh, quite firm and taut Pomerol, with a decent amount of tannin. Relatively consistent in quality.

Above: Ch Moulinet

Ch Lafleur-Gazin   map 41 D3
owner: Famille Delfour/Jean-Pierre Moueix *area:* 7.8 ha *cases:* 3,000 *grape % R:* MER 80% CF 20% *other châteaux owned:* include Ch Trotanoy *(Pomerol)*; Ch Pétrus *(Pomerol)*; Ch Magdelaine *(St-Emilion)*; Ch de la Dauphine *(Fronsac)*
33500 Pomerol tel: 05 57 51 78 96
fax: 05 57 51 79 79
At this château, which is run by Jean-Pierre Moueix, a dark, expansive wine is produced – a wine with generosity, oak and vanilla (thanks to 20 months in barrels of which a fifth are new), ripe berry fruit, some spiciness and an impeccable quality: *très Pomerol*.

Ch Lafleur Grangeneuve   map 41 I5
owner: C. Estager *area:* 4 ha *cases:* 1,800 *grape % R:* MER 85% CF 15%
33500 Néac tel: 05 57 51 35 09
fax: 05 56 20 14 20
Classic Pomerol which seldom becomes absolutely smooth as butter, but it does offer fruit, both dried and jammy, as well as spicy oak. The vines have an average age of 30 years.

Ch Lagrange   map 41 F4
owner: Jean-Pierre Moueix *area:* 8.5 ha *cases:* 3,500 *grape % R:* MER 95% CF 5% *second wine:*

Below: Ch Nenin

Ch Perrucheau *other châteaux owned:* include Ch Trotanoy *(Pomerol)*; Ch Pétrus *(Pomerol)*; Ch Magdelaine *(St-Emilion)*; Ch de la Dauphine *(Fronsac)*
33500 Pomerol tel: 05 57 51 78 96
fax: 05 57 51 79 79
Very reliable wine from the Pomerol plateau, 95% Merlot. Solid in structure, it tends more to tannin than to a creamy generousness. Earthy aroma, with something in it of nuts and tobacco. Of modest finesse; mostly used casks.

Ch Latour à Pomerol   map 41 H3
owner: Lily Lacoste/Jean-Pierre Moueix *area:* 7.9 ha *cases:* 3,000 *grape % R:* MER 90% CF 10% *other châteaux owned:* include Ch Trotanoy *(Pomerol)*; Ch Pétrus *(Pomerol)*; Ch Magdelaine *(St-Emilion)*; Ch de la Dauphine *(Fronsac)*
33500 Pomerol tel: 05 57 51 78 96
fax: 05 57 51 79 79
One former owner of this late 19th-century château was Mme Edmond Loubat, who at the time also owned Ch Pétrus. The wine has a very full-bodied, exceptionally generous taste – velvety in the mouth, but also possessing so much integrated tannin that it is able to mature over a long period. Classic, truffle-like aroma, with an undertone of concentrated, ripe fruit. It might perhaps have more class with a little more new wood; the present quota is a third.

Clos des Litanies   map 41
owner: J. Janoueix *area:* 0.8 ha *cases:* 400 *grape % R:* MER 100% *other châteaux owned:* include Ch La Croix *(Pomerol)*; Ch Haut-Sarpe *(St-Emilion)*
33500 Pomerol tel: 05 57 51 41 86
fax: 05 57 51 76 83
Merlot wine from a micro-estate, nurtured in new *barriques*. Hefty taste, with smoky oak, ripe fruit and good tannins.

Ch Mazeyres   map 41 M6
owner: Caisse de Retraites de la Société Générale *area:* 19.7 ha *cases:* 5,000 *grape % R:* MER 80% CF 20% *second wine:* Ch l'Hermitage Mazeyres
33500 Pomerol tel: 05 57 51 00 48
fax: 05 57 25 22 56
This estate was taken over by its present owner in 1989, then acquired a new director in 1992. The new team has since carried through a number of changes that have led to an improvement in quality. The wine has become

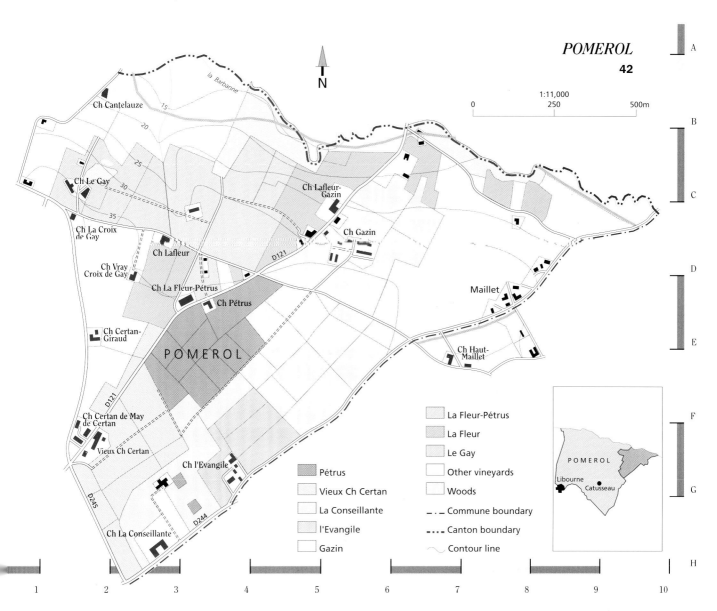

POMEROL
42

1:11,000

0   250   500m

La Fleur-Pétrus

La Fleur

Le Gay

Other vineyards

Woods

Pétrus

Vieux Ch Certan

La Conseillante

l'Evangile

Gazin

_._. Commune boundary

.... Canton boundary

Contour line

POMEROL

Libourne   Catusseau

---

less dry in its finish, and acquired rather greater refinement on the fairly elegant palate with its red fruit and good oak. Mazeyres lies just outside Libourne and was built in *Directoire* style on the site of a Roman villa (some fine pottery has been found here). The *chai* is in a former 16th-century monastery.

Ch Montviel
map 41 K5

owner: Yves & Catherine Péré-Vergé **area:** 5 ha **cases:** 2,000 **grape % R:** MER 60% CF 30% CS 10% **second wine:** Ch Bellevue **other châteaux owned:** Domaine de Montviel (Lalande-de-Pomerol)
33500 Pomerol tel: 05 57 51 87 92
fax: 05 21 38 06 23
Sound, supple and flavoursome Pomerol which matures luxuriously in all-new casks, but nevertheless does not quite have the strength, depth and class to be really impressive.

Ch Moulinet
map 41 K2

owner: GFA du Domaine de Moulinet/Antoine Moueix & Fils **area:** 18 ha **cases:** 7,500 **grape % R:** MER 70% CF 20% CS 10% **second wine:** La Grange Chatelière **other châteaux owned:** include Ch Taillefer (Pomerol); Ch La Croix Bellevue (Lalande-de-Pomerol); Ch Fonplégade (St-Emilion)

33500 Pomerol tel: 05 57 55 30 20
fax: 05 57 25 22 14
In general this is an elegant wine, not overly powerful, and with both smooth tannin and a long aftertaste. The vineyard lies on the north side of Pomerol. In the park a stone with a Maltese cross stands as silent witness to Ch Moulinet's long history.

Ch Moulinet-Lasserre
map 41 K5

owner: Jean-Marie Garde **area:** 5 ha **cases:** 2,500 **grape % R:** MER 60% CF 30% CS 10% **other châteaux owned:** Clos René (Pomerol); Ch La Mission (Lalande-de-Pomerol)
33500 Pomerol tel: 05 57 51 10 41
fax: 05 57 51 16 28
Warm and rounded Pomerol, usually delightfully smooth and very accessible, if without a great deal of power or length. Forest and animal aromas, plus some oak.

Ch Nenin
map 41 H7

owner: François Despujol **area:** 25 ha **cases:** 11,000 **grape % R:** MER 70% CF 20% CS 10% **second wine:** Saint-Roch de Nenin
33500 Pomerol tel: 05 57 51 00 01
fax: 05 57 51 77 47

This is one of the largest Pomerol properties. The 25-ha vineyard spreads out around a 19th-century château set in a fine park. The potential for a great wine is there, but until recently it was only sporadically realized (in 1975, for example). Starting with 1994 there have been considerably better wines, of great intensity, much power, firm tannins and good fruit. This is due to investment in the *cuvier*, where stainless-steel tanks now stand, and in the *chai*, where 30% of the barrels are new each year.

Ch La Patache
map 41 I2

owner: GFA de La Diligence **area:** 2.2 ha **cases:** 1,000 **grape % R:** MER 70% CF 30% **other châteaux owned:** l'Enclos de Viaud (Lalande-de-Pomerol)
33500 Pomerol tel: 05 57 24 70 86
fax: 05 57 24 68 30
La Patache's small estate is spread over various sites, from which it produces a powerful, traditional Pomerol of a decent standard.

Clos du Pèlerin
map 41 J3

owner: Norbert & Josette Egreteau **area:** 3 ha **cases:** 1,300 **grape % R:** MER 80% CF 10% CS 10% **other châteaux owned:** Ch de la Maréchaude (Lalande-de-Pomerol)

Above: Ch Pétrus

Above: Ch Plince

**33500 Pomerol tel: 05 57 74 03 66
fax: 05 57 25 06 17**
According to tradition, Clos du Pèlerin was founded by a pilgrim who settled in Pomerol. Its wine offers earthy, woodland notes, considerable oak, and has plenty of structure.

Ch Petit Village   map 41 E6
owner: Axa Millésimes *area:* 11 ha *cases:* 4,000 *grape % R:* MER 80% CF 10% CS 10% *other châteaux owned:* include Ch Cantenac-Brown *(Margaux)*; Ch Pichon-Longueville *(Pauillac)*; Ch Suduiraut *(Sauternes)*
**33500 Pomerol tel: 05 57 24 62 61
fax: 05 57 24 68 25**
This château, with its triangular vineyard, has belonged to AXA Millésimes since 1989. After tasting Petit Village, King Leopold of the Belgians is supposed to have exclaimed: 'Take away that *petit*, for this is truly a great wine'. It is indeed one of the best from the district: a powerful, expansive wine with thick, almost sweet fruit, smoky toasted oak and ample, well-integrated tannins. This Pomerol matures for 15 months in cask, 40% of them new.

Ch Pétrus   map 41 E4
owner: Lily Lacoste/Famille Loubat & Jean-Pierre Moueix *area:* 11.4 ha *cases:* 4,500 *grape % R:* MER 95% CF 5% *other châteaux owned:* include Ch Trotanoy *(Pomerol)*; Ch Magdelaine *(St-Emilion)*; Ch de la Dauphine *(Fronsac)*
**33500 Pomerol tel: 05 57 51 78 96
fax: 05 57 51 79 79**
With its turquoise shutters and a garden mainly under grass, this unassuming château close to the road would not lead the visitor to suppose that one of the world's most legendary, most expensive red wines is made here. But the Pétrus secret lies largely below, not above, the ground. The vineyard, on the highest part of Pomerol, has soil that is not only rich in clay, but is also well-drained. The Merlot – 95% of the vines – does perfectly here. The human factor plays a part as well: few wine estates are worked with such an obsessive concern for detail. Pétrus is in all respects a masterpiece of a wine that overwhelms the senses with its creamy strength, its unbelievable concentration, the richness of its aroma (syrupy fruit, spices, truffles, chocolate, coffee, tobacco, the wood of new casks), its solid tannins and its well-nigh everlasting finish. Since even at

Pétrus – the property of the Lacoste, Loubat and Moueix families – nature cannot be controlled, not all vintages are equally sensational: as was shown in 1984 and 1987, for example. But more often than not, drinking this wine is an exceptional privilege.

Ch Le Pin   map 41 F6
owner: Jacques Thienpont *area:* 2 ha *cases:* 600 *grape % R:* MER 92% CF 8% *other châteaux owned:* Vieux Château Certan *(Pomerol)*; Ch Labégorce Zédé *(Margaux)*
**33500 Pomerol tel: 05 57 51 33 99
fax: 05 57 25 35 08**
Very expensive and rare Pomerol, cheered by many and criticized by some – particularly for its sometimes dominant aromas of charred oak, toast and vanilla. Neither does it achieve the class of less-costly Pomerols, such as Ch Trotanoy. In its favour are an opulent, decadent taste, with generous black and red berry fruits, and smooth, firm tannins. The first vintage was the 1979, when the Thienpont family bought Le Pin. Before that the wine had been sold in bulk to a merchant.

Ch Plince   map 41 I7
owner: SCEV Moreau *area:* 8.3 ha *cases:* 3,500 *grape % R:* MER 68% CF 24% CS 8%
**33500 Libourne tel: 05 57 51 20 24
fax: 05 57 51 59 62**
Despite only modest use of new casks – one in five, with a 15-month maturing period – oaky elements such as vanilla and breadcrust are obvious in this wine as a rule. Generally it is a well-filled, aromatic, decent Pomerol, without great acidity. A fine drive between old plane trees leads to the 19th-century château.

Ch Plincette   map 41 H8
owner: Héritier Coudreau/Jean-Pierre Estager *area:* 2 ha *cases:* 1,000 *grape % R:* MER 70% CF 30% *other châteaux owned:* Domaine de Gachet *(Lalande-de-Pomerol)*; Domaine des Gourdins *(St-Emilion)*; Ch La Papeterie *(Montagne-St-Emilion)*; Ch Haut-Maillet *(Pomerol)*; Ch La Cabanne *(Pomerol)*
**33500 Pomerol tel: 05 57 51 04 09
fax: 05 57 25 13 38**
This modest estate, leased by Jean-Pierre Estager, delivers a rounded, smooth, aromatic Pomerol. Skilfully made, but it lacks a little power and length. An attractive element of oak in the bouquet.

Ch La Pointe   map 41 I6
owner: Bernard d'Arfeuille *area:* 22 ha *cases:* 10,000 *grape % R:* MER 75% CF 25% *second wine:* Ch La Pointe Riffat *other châteaux owned:* Ch La Serre *(St-Emilion)*; Ch Toumalin *(Canon-Fronsac)*
**33500 Pomerol tel: 05 57 51 02 11
fax: 05 57 51 42 33**
This château, set in parkland, is just outside Libourne. Built in the *Directoire* style, it has a splendid tiled hall. It takes its name from the shape of one of the vineyard plots. The wine produced here is generally of medium build, and has an accessible, supple, sometimes almost fat taste. It is pleasing and velvety in the mouth, with sweet fruit and integrated oak – around one-third of the maturing *barriques* are new each year. This is an attractive Pomerol, of above average quality.

Ch Prieurs de la Commanderie
map 41 L4
owner: Clément Fayat *area:* 4 ha *cases:* 2,000 *grape % R:* MER 80% CF 20% *second wine:* Ch André *other châteaux owned:* Ch Clément Pichon *(Haut-Médoc)*; Ch La Dominique *(St-Emilion)*
**33500 Pomerol tel: 05 57 51 31 36
fax: 05 57 51 63 04**
Since 1984 this estate has belonged to Clément Fayat, as do Ch La Dominique in St-Emilion and other properties. The wine normally has considerable wood, from 40-50% new barrels, yet does not quite have the substance, backbone, balance or charm to be really impressive. But then, sometimes, this Pomerol rises above the limits of its status – as in 1994.

Ch Ratouin   map 41 L4
owner: Serge Ratouin *area:* 2 ha *cases:* 800 *grape % R:* MER 80% CF 20% *other châteaux owned:* Domaine des Sabines *(Lalande-de-Pomerol)*
**33500 Pomerol tel: 05 57 51 47 92
fax: 05 57 51 47 92**
Robust, dark-toned, rather old-fashioned wine that spends at least a year in casks, a fifth new.

Clos René   map 41 K5
owner: Pierre Lasserre *area:* 12 ha *cases:* 6,000 *grape % R:* MER 60% CF 30% MAL 10% *other châteaux owned:* Ch La Mission *(Lalande-de-Pomerol)*; Ch Moulinet-Lasserre *(Pomerol)*
**33500 Pomerol tel: 05 57 51 10 41
fax: 05 57 51 16 28**

Above: Ch Rouget

From this white château dating from 1880 comes one of the best wines west of the RN89 road. Clos René generally provides good ripe fruit, noble oak (a quarter of the *barriques* are new), smooth tannins, a flawless balance and plenty of bouquet. Offers more class and substance than the same owner's Ch Moulinet-Lasserre.

Ch Rêve d'Or   map 41 J4

owner: Maurice Vigier **area:** 7 ha **cases:** 3,000 **grape % R:** MER 80% CF 20% **second wine:** Ch du Mayne **other châteaux owned:** Ch La Croix Blanche *(Lalande-de-Pomerol)*
33500 Pomerol tel: 05 57 51 11 92
fax: 05 57 51 87 70
Meaty, reasonably powerful Pomerol conveying impressions that include oak (about 30% of barrels are new), animal aromas, jammy fruit (sometimes including raspberry) and mature tannin. Reliable.

Ch La Rose Figeac   map 41 E9

owner: Gérard Despagne-Rapin **area:** 5 ha **cases:** 2,000 **grape % R:** MER 85% CF 10% CS 5% **other châteaux owned:** Ch Tour de Corbin Despagne *(St-Emilion)*; Ch Maison Blanche *(Montagne-St-Emilion)*
33500 Pomerol tel: 05 57 74 62 18
fax: 05 57 74 58 98
Firm, generous wine with spicy oak in its bouquet from all-new casks, as well as forest aromas, bayleaf and blackberry and blackcurrant fruits. The same elements are to be found in the long-lasting flavour with its ample, but integrated, tannin. One of the district's better wines.

Ch Rouget
map 41 G3
owner: Société Grands Vins Pomerol **area:** 16 ha **cases:** 6,500 **grape % R:** MER 85% CF 15% **second wine:** Vieux Château des Templiers
33500 Pomerol tel: 05 57 51 05 85
fax: 05 57 51 05 85
Estate on the northern border of Pomerol, with a château built around 1750. The potential of the excellent *terroir* seems to have been fully realized only since the arrival of a new owner in 1993. Thus half of the barrels are now replaced each year. The wine offers elements of toasted oak, fresh, red fruit, a reasonable to good level of concentration, and sound, smooth tannins which provides ageing potential.

Clos Les Rouzes Clinet   map 41 G3

owner: EARL du Clos Les Rouzes Clinet/Bosc & Jollivet **area:** 2.4 ha **cases:** 1,800 **grape % R:** MER 80% CF 15% CS 5%
33500 Pomerol tel: 05 57 51 31 77
The various plots belonging to this property lie at the heart of Pomerol, and have been cultivated by the same family for a century and a half. They produce a costly wine, mainly from old vines, that is generous as well as rich in tannin. It spends 12-14 months in oak; a quarter of the barrels for each vintage are new.

Ch St Pierre   map 41 F4

owner: Famille de Lavaux **area:** 3 ha **cases:** 1,500 **grape % R:** MER 65% CF 20% CS 15% **other châteaux owned:** include Ch des Bordes *(Pomerol)*; Ch Haut Cloquet *(Pomerol)*; Ch La Renaissance *(Pomerol)*; Clos du Vieux Plateau Certan *(Pomerol)*; Ch Martinet *(St-Emilion)*
33500 Pomerol tel: 05 57 51 06 07
fax: 05 57 51 59 61
Likeable, somewhat slender Pomerol, usually with decent tannin and fresh berry fruit. A third of the *barriques* are new.

Ch de Sales   map 41 L2

owner: Bruno de Lambert **area:** 47.5 ha **cases:** 20,000 **grape % R:** MER 70% CF 15% CS 15% **second wine:** Ch Chantalouette
33500 Libourne tel: 05 57 51 04 92
fax: 05 57 25 23 91
With 47.5 ha, this is by far the biggest Pomerol vineyard – and its château, close to the Barbanne stream, one of the most impressive. It has stood since at least the mid-16th century, and was remodelled in the two centuries following. Normally Ch de Sales produces stylish, fairly light, refined wines that can mature very well. But sometimes, as in 1990, a more solid, concentrated type of Pomerol with low acidity emerges. New oak is never used.

Ch du Tailhas   map 41 F10

owner: SC Nebout & Fils **area:** 10.5 ha **cases:** 5,000 **grape % R:** MER 70% CS 15% CF 15% **second wine:** Ch La Garenne
33500 Pomerol tel: 05 57 51 26 02
fax: 05 57 25 17 70
Generally a fairly rounded Pomerol, of low acidity and therefore somewhat flat. Half of the casks are replaced each year. In a letter dated

June 7, 1289 Edward I, King of England and Duke of Aquitaine, stipulated that the border between St-Emilion and Pomerol should be the little Tailhayat stream, from which this château takes its name.

Ch Taillefer   map 41 G10

owner: Antoine Moueix & Fils/Bernard Moueix **area:** 11.5 ha **cases:** 7,000 **grape % R:** MER 75% CF 25% **second wine:** Ch Fontmarty **other châteaux owned:** include Clos Beauregard *(Pomerol)*; Ch Moulinet *(Pomerol)*; Clos Sainte-Anne *(Pomerol)*; Ch Tauzinat l'Hermitage *(St-Emilion)*; Ch Côtes Trois Moulins *(St-Emilion)*; Clos La Fleur Figeac *(St-Emilion)*; Clos Toulifaut *(Pomerol)*; Ch La Tour du Pin Figeac *(St-Emilion)*; Ch Fonplégade *(St-Emilion)*; Ch La Croix du Moulin *(Lalande-de-Pomerol)*; Ch La Croix Bellevue *(Lalande-de-Pomerol)*
33500 Libourne tel: 05 57 55 30 20
fax: 05 57 25 22 14
At best this is a clean, reasonably concentrated wine with a fairly slender, but seldom generous profile. It displays considerable tough tannins, forest aromas, fruit and oak – one-third new maturing casks. Antoine Moueix bought this Libourne estate in 1923, and the business bearing his name has its headquarters here.

Clos Toulifaut   map 41 F9

owner: Héritiers Marcel Moueix/Antoine Moueix & Fils **area:** 7 ha **cases:** 4,000 **grape % R:** MER 60% CF 30% CS 10% **other châteaux owned:** include Ch Taillefer *(Pomerol)*
33500 Pomerol tel: 05 57 51 50 63
fax: 05 57 25 22 14
A property Antoine Moueix acquired in 1930. Here a moderately rounded wine for keeping is made; it needs time to lose its initial reserve.

◆

Neighbouring appellations

To the east is St-Emilion: parts of the commune of Libourne, to the south, have the St-Emilion AC. To the north, beyond the Barbanne valley, is Lalande-de-Pomerol. To the west of Pomerol is the valley of the Isle, beyond which are Fronsac and Canon-Fronsac.

Below: Ch St Pierre

Above: Ch Taillefer

Ch Tristan
map 41 I2

owner: SCE Cascarret *area:* 3 ha *cases:* 1,000
grape % R: MER 50% CS 25% CF 25% *second wine:*
Ch Feythit La Grave *other wines:* Ch La Gravière
(Lalande-de-Pomerol)
33500 Pomerol tel: 05 57 51 04 54
fax: 05 57 51 24 22
With its high proportion of Cabernet (half the
vines), this is an atypical Pomerol – but one of
steady quality. In its youth the generous dose of
tannin makes it reserved, and even austere; but
smoothness breaks through with the years.
Fruit and oak are discreetly present.

Ch Trotanoy
map 41 G5

owner: Jean-Pierre Moueix *area:* 8 ha *cases:* 2,500
grape % R: MER 90% CF 10% *other châteaux owned:*
include Ch Pétrus *(Pomerol)*; Ch La Grave à Pomerol
(Pomerol); Ch Lafleur-Gazin *(Pomerol)*; Ch Lagrange
(Pomerol); Ch Feytit-Clinet *(Pomerol)*; Ch Latour à
Pomerol *(Pomerol)*; Ch Magdelaine *(St-Emilion)*; Ch
La Fleur *(St-Emilion)*; Ch Fonroque *(St-Emilion)*; Ch
Moulin du Cadet *(St-Emilion)*; Ch Canon *(Canon-
Fronsac)*; Ch Canon-Moueix *(Canon-Fronsac)*; Ch
Canon de Brem *(Canon-Fronsac)*; Ch Charlemagne
(Canon-Fronsac); Ch de la Dauphine *(Fronsac)*; Ch
Milary *(Bordeaux Supérieur)*
33500 Pomerol tel: 05 57 51 78 96
fax: 05 57 51 79 79
The vineyard of this renowned property, owned
by Jean-Pierre Moueix since 1953, consists
partly of gravel, partly of clay. The gravel
becomes hard in drought, the clay slippery in
rain. Hence the name: Trotanoy is supposed to
come from *trop ennoye*, 'too difficult to work'.
In successful form – certain 1980s vintages
were disappointing – Trotanoy is one of the very
best Pomerols. The wine then has an opaque
colour and a complex, intense aroma with
charred oak (from the one-third new barrels),
nuts, animal scents, cocoa, black cherry and
ripe plum. The taste is rounded and rich in
extract; at once strong and fine, with velvety
fruit, spices and nicely integrated tannins.

Ch de Valois
map 41 E9

owner: SCEA des Vignobles Leydet *area:* 7.5 ha
cases: 3,500 *grape % R:* MER 75% CF 13% CS 10%
MAL 2% *second wine:* Ch La Croix St. Vincent *other
wines:* Ch Leydet-Figeac *(St-Emilion)*
33500 Pomerol tel: 05 57 51 19 77
fax: 05 57 51 00 62

Above: Vieux Château Certan

A wine with mellow fruit, considerable oak (a
quarter of the casks are new) and a mouthfilling character. It is, however, somewhat
limited in nuances and length. The vineyard
was separated in 1862 from the Figeac estate –
large at that time – and acquired its present
name in 1886.

Clos de la Vieille Eglise
map 41 H3

owner: Jean-Louis Trocard *area:* 1.5 ha *cases:* 750
grape % R: MER 90% CF 10% *other châteaux owned:*
include Ch Trocard *(Bordeaux Supérieur)*
33500 Pomerol tel: 05 57 24 31 56
fax: 05 57 24 33 87
A well-concentrated, firm, but not refined
Pomerol that sometimes has rather too much
wood – 60% of the *barriques* are new.

Vieux Château Certan
map 41 E5

owner: Famille Thienpont *area:* 13.5 ha *cases:*
5,000 *grape % R:* MER 60% CF 30% CS 10% *second
wine:* La Gravette de Certan *other châteaux
owned:* include Ch Le Pin *(Pomerol)*; Ch Labégorce
Zédé *(Margaux)*; Ch Puygueraud *(Bordeaux Côtes de
Francs)*
33500 Pomerol tel: 05 57 51 17 33
fax: 05 57 25 35 08
This distinguished estate was bought in 1924 by
the Belgian wine merchant Georges Thienpont,
whose descendants have gone on to manage it
with energy and commitment. The wine is
classic in character, with both a stylish grace
and considerable toasted oak – one-half to two-
thirds new barrels – plus fine tannins. Within
this classic package all kinds of nuances may be
found: caramel, toffee, black berry fruits, a
mixture of spices. In great years Vieux Château
Certan is a delightful wine, full of character –
one that will mature beautifully. The bottles can
be recognized from afar by their pink capsules.

Vieux Château Ferron
map 41 I8

owner: Pierre-Etienne Garzaro *area:* 2 ha *cases:*
1,100 *grape % R:* MER 90% CF 10% *second wine:*
Clos des Amandiers *other châteaux owned:* include
Ch Elisée *(Pomerol)*; Ch Le Prieur *(Bordeaux)*
33500 Libourne tel: 05 56 30 16 16
fax: 05 56 30 12 63
Good, fairly substantial, aromatic Pomerol, a
little rustic and sometimes a trifle short in its
aftertaste. Matures in casks of which at least
half are new. Since 1988 made by the Garzaro
family from Entre-deux-Mers.

Clos du Vieux Plateau Certan
map 41

owner: Famille de Lavaux *area:* 0.5 ha *cases:* 200
grape % R: MER 100% *other châteaux owned:*
include Ch St Pierre *(Pomerol)*; Ch Martinet *(St-
Emilion)*
33500 Pomerol tel: 05 57 24 80 69
fax: 05 57 51 59 61
Microscopically small estate yielding a pure
Merlot wine with plenty of new oak, black berry
fruit, cocoa and tannin.

Domaine Vieux Taillefer
map 41 F9

owner: Daniel Ybert *area:* 0.5 ha *cases:* 200 *grape
% R:* MER 80% CF 20% *other châteaux owned:*
include Ch Vieille Tour La Rose *(St-Emilion)*
33500 Pomerol tel: 05 57 24 73 41
fax: 05 57 74 44 83
An average 2,400 bottles a year are made here of
a velvety, classic Pomerol, dark in tone and with
subtle oak.

Ch La Violette
map 41 G7

owner: Jean Servant *area:* 4 ha *cases:* 2,300
grape % R: MER 80% CF 20% *second wine:* Ch
Pavillon la Violette *other châteaux owned:* Ch
l'Eglise *(Montagne-St-Emilion)*; Ch Les Templiers
(Lalande-de-Pomerol)
33500 Pomerol tel: 05 57 51 70 27
fax: 05 57 51 60 34
This is often a perfumed and elegant Pomerol
that does indeed have something of violets in its
bouquet. Oak is usually there also, as are
velvety impressions that include cherry, plum
and licorice.

Ch Vray Croix de Gay
map 41 E4

owner: SCE Baronne Guichard *area:* 4 ha *cases:*
1,300 *grape % R:* MER 80% CF 15% CS 5% *other
châteaux owned:* Ch Siaurac *(Lalande-de-Pomerol)*;
Ch Le Prieuré *(St-Emilion)*
33500 Pomerol tel: 05 57 51 64 58
fax: 05 57 51 41 56
A less-well-known Pomerol that in quality
ranges from correct to good. With many old
vines and a good subsoil, it generally boasts a
decent intensity of taste. However, sometimes
the wine lacks finesse, and its tannins are
rather too overwhelming.

LALANDE-DE-POMEROL

North of Pomerol, across the gentle Barbanne stream, lies Lalande-de-Pomerol. Lalande enjoys roughly the same kind of relationship to Pomerol as the satellites do to St-Emilion – very much that of a junior cousin. However, wine has been made here for well over 1,000 years by the Romans, then the monks and the Knights of St-John.

The AC covers two communes, separated by the N89. West of this *route nationale* is Lalande; east is the commune of Néac. It is Néac rather than Lalande which lies closest to the Pomerol plateau, immediately south across the Barbanne. Some (although by no means all) of the better properties lie here where the soil has the highest clay content, very well suited to the predominant Merlot grape. Other top estates can be found on the western side of the appellation in Lalande itself, where the soil is lighter.

Soil types are much more diverse than those of Pomerol. The lightest are found towards the west, in the commune of Lalande. The further west, the sandier it

becomes. In the north and north-east, gravel becomes increasingly important, but it is towards the east that the clay also found in Pomerol appears, sometimes mixed with gravel. Estates are generally very small – 4 ha is the average – and it is rare indeed to find anything over 20 hectares. Surprisingly, in view of these small sizes, there is no cooperative. Some very good wines are made here. Like Pomerol, there is no formal classification. Pomerol, however, has an unwritten hierarchy: here there is none. A handful do make consistently good wines, easily equal to the lesser Pomerols, sometimes even better. At their best, these wines are supple and graceful, with attractive plummy fruit, and age well in bottle for five years or more. Rarely are they austere even when very young – although some producers add to their wine's potential lifespan by using a percentage of new oak, which may make them appear somewhat restrained until they have spent a few years in bottle. With age, they take on some of the fleshy, slightly decadent character of a Pomerol.

THE APPELLATION

LALANDE-DE-POMEROL
(red)
Location: On the right bank of the Dordogne, 30 km north-east of Bordeaux. To the south is Pomerol; to the east and north-east Montagne-St-Emilion; to the north is AC Bordeaux land; to the west the Isle valley.
Area of AC: 1,334 ha
Area under vine: 1,000 ha
Communes: Lalande-de-Pomerol, Néac

Average annual production: 600,000 cases
Classed growths: None
Others: 210
Cooperatives: None
Main grape varieties: Merlot
Others: Cabernet Franc (Bouchet), Cabernet Sauvignon
Main soil types: Sand in the west, more gravel in the north and north-east, more clay in the east

APPELLATION LALANDE-DE-POMEROL

Ch de Bel-Air
map 43 K6

owner: Jean-Pierre Musset *area:* 15 ha *cases:* 7,000 *grape % R:* MER 75% CF 20% CS 5% *second wine:* Ch Decats
33500 Lalande-de-Pomerol tel: 05 57 51 40 07 fax: 05 57 74 17 43
This estate lies to the south of the village of Lalande-de-Pomerol itself, on a plateau that slopes down to the little Barbanne stream. The wine is classical in character, one of the district's dependable buys. It offers substance, tannin, meatiness, fruit and good oak. The soil with its sand, clay and traces of iron provides low acidity, but nevertheless the wine has ageing potential.

Ch Belles-Graves
map 43 G8

owner: GFA Theallet-Piton *area:* 14 ha *cases:* 6,500 *grape % R:* MER 80% CF 20%
33500 Néac tel: 05 57 51 09 61 fax: 05 57 51 01 41
Estate with slopes well exposed to the south. This, together with efficient vinification, gives a full-bodied, lively wine of unmistakeable class. It has plenty of oak and tannin, but can taste splendid after just five years.

Ch Bertineau St-Vincent

owner: SCEA des Domaines Rolland *area:* 5.6 ha *cases:* 2,700 *grape % R:* MER 75% CF 25% *other châteaux owned:* Ch Rolland-Maillet *(St-Emilion);* Ch Le Bon Pasteur *(Pomerol);* Ch Fontenil *(Fronsac)*
33500 Lalande-de-Pomerol tel: 05 57 51 10 94 fax: 05 57 25 05 54
This is a wine of outstanding quality, which is in fact vinified at Ch Le Bon Pasteur in Pomerol. Juicy, firm and velvety in the mouth, it has a relatively elegant structure, displaying notes of black fruit and oak, as well as smooth tannins.

Domaine Bois de Laborde
map 43 J3

owner: Joseph Callegarin *area:* 0.8 ha *cases:* 330 *grape % R:* MER 50% CS 50%
33500 Lalande-de-Pomerol tel: 05 57 51 34 05
Good, somewhat old-fashioned wine, often with some ripe fruit. A tiny vineyard.

Ch la Borderie-Mondésir
map 43 J4

owner: Vignobles Rousseau *area:* 2.1 ha *cases:* 1,100 *grape % R:* MER 75% CS 25% *other châteaux owned:* Ch des Rochers *(Lussac-St-Emilion);* Ch Haut-Sorillon *(Bordeaux Supérieur)*
33500 Lalande-de-Pomerol tel: 05 57 49 06 10 fax: 05 57 49 38 96
The motto of the Rousseau family states 'our aim is to make wines that please with their quality'. And they succeed nicely: the wine has freshness, berry fruit, dark elements, some oak and a rather elegant structure.

Ch Bourseau
map 43 J5

owner: Véronique Gaboriaud *area:* 10 ha *cases:* 4,000 *grape % R:* MER 70% CS 20% CF 10% *second wine:* Ch Croix de Bourseau *other châteaux owned:* Ch l'Hermitage *(St-Emilion);* Ch Matras *(St-Emilion)*
33500 Lalande-de-Pomerol tel: 05 57 51 52 39 fax: 05 57 51 70 19
Usually a wine with a mellow aroma, plenty of oak (a third of the casks are new each year; maturing takes 12-18 months) and a creamy taste. Ch Bourseau may not quite have the character to be truly great, but is very successful nevertheless.

Above: Ch Bourseau

Ch Canon-Chaigneau
map 43 C8

owner: SCEA Marin-Audra *area:* 21 ha *cases:* 11,000 *grape % R:* MER 60% CF 25% CS 10% MAL 5% *second wine:* Ch Tour Chaigneau; Ch Tour Canon *other châteaux owned:* Moulin de Fontmurée *(Montagne-St-Emilion);* Ch Tour de Blanchon *(Lussac-St-Emilion);* Ch La Croizille *(St-Emilion)*
33500 Néac tel: 05 57 24 69 13 fax: 05 57 24 69 11
At the beginning of the 15th century this estate was cultivated by monks; today it is the Marin family. Selection is rigorous: there was no Canon-Chaigneau in 1991. In its aroma the wine has something of forest earth and undergrowth, together with black and red fruits. Oak, too, can be detected. Its tannins are often substantial, so this wine needs to mature – certainly for five years.

Ch de Chambrun
map 43 D8

owner: Jean-Philippe Janoueix *area:* 1.5 ha *cases:* 800 *grape % R:* MER 90% CF 10% *other châteaux owned:* include Ch Haut-Sarpe *(St-Emilion);* Ch La Croix *(Pomerol)*
33500 Néac tel: 05 57 51 41 86 fax: 05 57 51 76 83
High quality is the order of the day at this recently-created miniature estate: for instance the use of all-new barrels. A velvety, smoothly fruity wine in a toasted-oak setting.

Ch Chatain Pineau
map 43

owner: René Micheau-Maillou *area:* 5.5 ha *cases:* 3,200 *grape % R:* MER 75% CF 20% CS 5% *second wine:* Ch le Jard
33500 Néac tel: 05 57 24 61 99 fax: 05 57 24 61 99
The family owning this estate started by leasing it in 1934; they bought it in 1987. Good, slightly rustic wine; spicy, warm, concentrated.

Ch Chevrol Bel Air
map 43 E8

owner: SCEA Pradier *area:* 15 ha *cases:* 6,500 *grape % R:* MER 45% CF 45% CS 10% *other châteaux owned:* Dom Mont du Pressoir *(Bordeaux Supérieur)*
33500 Néac tel: 05 57 51 10 23 fax: 05 57 51 65 65
Mid-range wine, with reasonable fruit, from the centre of the Néac district. Not oak-aged.

Above: Ch Bourseau: the *chai*

Ch de la Commanderie
map 43 G4

owner: SCEA Lafon *area:* 22 ha *cases:* 11,000 *grape % R:* MER 75.5% CF 18% CS 3.5% MAL 3% *second wine:* Ch du Grand Bois
33500 Lalande-de-Pomerol tel: 05 57 51 05 20
This nicely maintained château makes a firm, pleasantly robust wine with impressions of jammy fruit (blackberry, prune), earthy notes such as truffles and autumn woods, plus coffee, caramel and spices. This wine is given no barrel ageing.

Ch La Croix Bellevue
map 41 L2

owner: GFA du Domaine de Moulinet/Famille A. Moueix *area:* 8 ha *cases:* 4,000 *grape % R:* CS 70% MER 30% *other châteaux owned:* include Ch Moulinet *(Pomerol);* Ch Côtes Trois Moulins *(St-Emilion);* Ch Fonplégade *(St-Emilion)*
33500 Lalande-de-Pomerol tel: 05 57 74 43 11 fax: 05 57 74 44 67
An a typical Lalande-de-Pomerol, mainly from Cabernet grapes, quite slender and made with care by Armand Moueix, the *négociant*. Matures in *barriques* of which a third are new.

Below: Ch Canon-Chaigneau shows that names can change

Ch La Croix des Moines
map 41 J5

owner: Jean-Louis Trocard **area:** 8 ha **cases:** 4,500 **grape % R:** MER 80% CS 10% CF 10% **other châteaux owned:** include Ch Trocard (Bordeaux Supérieur); Ch Tour de Marchesseau (Lalande-de-Pomerol)

33500 Lalande-de-Pomerol tel: 05 57 24 31 16
fax: 05 57 24 33 87

Animal and woodland scents, spices and some oak are often displayed by this wine's nose. Its flavour is racy and strong, with plenty of tannin in sunny years.

Ch la Croix St-André
map 43 E8

owner: Famille Carayon **area:** 16.5 ha **cases:** 8,400 **grape % R:** MER 80% CS 20% **second wine:** Ch La Croix Saint Louis **other châteaux owned:** Ch Pétrarque (Fronsac); Ch Chabiran (Bordeaux Supérieur)

33500 Néac tel: 05 57 51 08 36
fax: 05 57 25 93 44

An exemplary wine is produced here – one that can match many a Pomerol. It is generous, powerful, and very concentrated. Many famous personalities from the world of literature, films, stage and politics are among its faithful customers. One client was pianist Artur Rubinstein (1887-1982), to whose memory the 1982 vintage was dedicated.

Ch La Croix St-Jean
map 43 B6

owner: Vignoble Raymond Tapon **area:** 1.3 ha **cases:** 750 **grape % R:** MER 80% CF 20% **other châteaux owned:** include Ch des Moines (Montagne-St-Emilion); Ch Lafleur Vachon (St-Emilion)

33500 Néac tel: 05 57 74 61 20
fax: 05 57 24 69 32

Fairly rustic, dark-toned wine for keeping. Cask ageing can vary from 6-18 months.

Clos de l'Eglise
map 43 J5

owner: Famille Paul Berry **area:** 9.9 ha **cases:** 4,500 **grape % R:** MER 60% CF 20% CS 15% MAL 5% **second wine:** Clos des Grands Moines

33500 Lalande-de-Pomerol tel: 05 57 51 40 25
fax: 05 57 74 17 13

Estate with modern equipment producing a fragrant Lalande-de-Pomerol that becomes velvety afer a few years in bottle. It does not come into contact with wood.

Below: Ch Chevrol Bel Air

Above: Ch Garraud

Ch de l'Evéché
map 43 G5

owner: Indivision Chaumet **area:** 10.1 ha **cases:** 5,400 **grape % R:** MER 60% CS 20% CF 20% **second wine:** Ch Vieux Duché **other châteaux owned:** include Ch Moulin de Salles (Lalande-de-Pomerol)

33500 Lalande-de-Pomerol tel: 05 57 25 50 12
fax: 05 57 25 51 48

This wine, which is not oak-aged, can produce a round, almost buttery-fat taste. In some years, though, the Cabernet in it predominates and tannin comes to the fore, together with somewhat herbaceous elements.

Ch La Faurie Maison Neuve
map 40

owner: Michel Coudroy **area:** 5.6 ha **cases:** 2,000 **grape % R:** MER 80% CS 20% **other châteaux owned:** include Ch de Maison Neuve (Montagne-St-Emilion)

33570 Montagne tel: 05 57 74 62 23
fax: 05 57 74 64 18

Wine made by a producer from Montagne-St-Emilion, and matured in casks of which one-third are new. Black fruits, oak and a touch of licorice can often be detected. Supple tannins soon make pleasant drinking of it.

Ch La Fleur Saint Georges
map 43 E6

owner: AGF **area:** 17 ha **cases:** 10,000 **grape % R:** MER 70% CF 30% **second wine:** Ch du Rosaire **other châteaux owned:** include Ch Larose-Trintaudon (Haut-Médoc); Ch La Tourette (Pauillac)

33500 Néac tel: 05 56 59 41 72
fax: 05 56 59 93 22

Property belonging to the French AGF insurance company with an ultra-modern cuvier at its disposal. A flawless, meaty, fragrant wine is produced. Oak-ageing is 12-15 months; in principle a third of the casks are new.

Domaine de Gachet
map 43 C9

owner: Jean-Pierre Estager **area:** 1 ha **cases:** 500 **grape % R:** MER 70% CF 30% **other châteaux owned:** Ch Haut-Maillet (Pomerol); Ch La Cabanne (Pomerol); Domaine des Gourdins (St-Emilion); Ch La Papeterie (Montagne-St-Emilion); Ch Plincette (Pomerol)

33500 Néac tel: 05 57 51 04 09
fax: 05 57 25 13 38

Intensely fragrant, powerful wine; mouth-filling, with a lot of smooth tannin, and some licorice in the finale: a true Pomerol style. The quality is high. Oak is well used, with 20 months' maturing in year-old barriques.

Ch Garraud
map 43 E5

owner: Jean-Marc Nony **area:** 32 ha **cases:** 13,000 **grape % R:** MER 60% CF 30% CS 10% **second wine:** Ch Graves de Garraud; Ch Treytins

33500 Néac tel: 05 57 55 58 58
fax: 05 57 25 13 43

A former 18th-century hunting lodge that acquired a vineyard around 1850. It came into the possession of the Nony family about 80 years later. The quality of the wine has been on the rise since the 1988 vintage, partly due to considerable investment in the cellars. Today the wine has firmness and elegance. Soft fruit, bayleaf and spicy oak mark the aroma.

Ch Grand Ormeau
map 43 H6

owner: Jean-Claude Beton **area:** 11.5 ha **cases:** 4,800 **grape % R:** MER 65% CF 25% CS 10% **second wine:** Chevalier d'Haurange

33500 Lalande-de-Pomerol tel: 05 57 25 30 20
fax: 05 57 25 22 80

Grand Ormeau's second wine is called Chevalier d'Haurange, a play on the word *orange*: In 1987 château was bought by Jean-Claude Beton, who made the soft drink Orangina famous. He paid FF 12 million for the estate, then invested a further FF 8 million. Very concentrated, full-bodied, if not sensual, in the mouth, the wine shows a lot of oak (40% of the *barriques* are new), although it does not offer real finesse.

Domaine du Grand Ormeau   map 43 H6
owner: Jean-Paul Garde *area:* 16 ha *cases:* 8,000 *grape % R:* MER 80% CS 10% CF 10% *second wine:* Ch Fleur des Ormes *other châteaux owned:* Ch la Truffe *(Pomerol)*; Vieux Château Goujon *(Montagne-St-Emilion)*; Ch Laulan *(Bordeaux Côtes de Francs)*
33500 Néac tel: 05 57 51 40 43
fax: 05 57 25 19 02
Old family estate whose wine is striking for its beautifully integrated tannins, its almost over-ripe black fruit and its aimiable character. Cask-ageing is employed in strictly controlled doses.

Ch Graves des Annereaux   map 43 M4
owner: Paul Boujut *area:* 7 ha *cases:* 3,300 *grape % R:* MER 60% CF 25% CS 15%
33500 Lalande-de-Pomerol tel: 05 57 51 22 45
fax: 05 57 74 04 63
Fairly generous wine from grapes of maximum ripeness, picked as late as possible. Not cask-aged. Has won quite a few awards.

Ch Haut-Chaigneau   map 43 C8
owner: J. & A. Chatonnet *area:* 20 ha *cases:* 10,000 *grape % R:* MER 70% CF 15% CS 15% *second wines:* Ch Tour Saint-André; Ch La Croix Chaigneau *other wines:* Le Grand Rosé de Haut-Chaigneau *(Bordeaux rosé)*; Les Perles de Haut-Chaigneau *(Crémant de Bordeaux)*
33500 Néac tel: 05 57 74 62 25
fax: 05 57 74 51 04
In good years a solid, well-structured Lalande is made at this estate, which originated in the 12th century. Besides nuances of leather, bayleaf and cocoa there is fruit here, as well as considerable oak – at least a year is spent in barrels, a quarter of which are new. New cellar equipment came into use in 1994, which further raised the standard of the wine. Guests are stylishly received here, and the barrels occupy a fine vaulted *chai*. The Haut-Chaigneau name is also associated with an AC Bordeaux and a Crémant de Bordeaux, both rosés.

Ch Haut-Châtain   map 43 D8
owner: Héritiers Rivière *area:* 15.4 ha *cases:* 6,000 *grape % R:* MER 80% CF 10% CS 10% *second wine:* Ch la Rose Châtain *other châteaux owned:* Ch Lacoste-Châtain *(Montagne-St-Emilion)*; Domaine du Châtain *(Bordeaux Supérieur)*
33500 Néac tel: 05 57 25 98 48
fax: 05 57 25 95 45
Since 1912 this estate has been passed form generation to generation throught the female line. Clay soil in the vineyard gives the wine strength, and gravel imparts finesse. In addition, this Lalande-de-Pomerol often has jammy fruit and firm tannin. Depending on its vintage it can be drunk after 5-10 years.

Ch Haut-Goujon   map 43 G5
owner: Henri Garde *area:* 8.5 ha *cases:* 4,750 *grape % R:* MER 60% CS 20% CF 20% *other wines:* Montagne-St-Emilion
33500 Lalande-de-Pomerol tel: 05 57 51 50 05
fax: 05 57 25 33 93

Above: Ch Haut-Chaigneau

Berry fruit and animal scents often show in the aroma of this fairly expansive wine. It matures in *barriques* of which about a third are new.

Ch les Hauts-Conseillants   map 41 K7
owner: Pierre Bourotte *area:* 10 ha *cases:* 5,000 *grape % R:* MER 70% CF 20% CS 10% *other châteaux owned:* Ch Bonalgue *(Pomerol)*; Ch du Courlat *(Lussac-St-Emilion)*
33500 Néac tel: 05 57 51 62 17
fax: 05 57 51 28 28
Classic, concentrated, creamy wine, generous of nature and with liberal oak – it has 18 months in cask (50% new wood). Bouquet and taste contain notes of truffles and other fungi, bayleaf, spices and soft black fruit. The vineyard lies partly in Néac, partly in Lalande-de-Pomerol.

Ch Haut-Surget   map 43 F7
owner: Jean-Pierre Fourreau *area:* 23 ha *cases:* 11,100 *grape % R:* MER 70% CF 15% CS 15% *second wine:* Ch la Fleur-Vauzelle *other wines:* Ch Grand Moulinet *(Pomerol)*
33500 Néac tel: 05 57 51 28 68
fax: 05 57 51 91 79
The vineyards here are picked by hand, and the grapes are then also sorted by hand on a table. The result of this care is a Lalande that is

Below: Ch Moncets

About Lalande-de-Pomerol

Information on the wines of Lalande-de-Pomerol can be obtained from the Syndicat viticole which is located in the centre of Lalande opposite the church.

The postal address is Cidex 36 BP 17, 33500 Lalande-de-Pomerol.

Tel 05 57 25 21 60.

◆

Néac

The commune of Néac used to have its own appellation, but it was incorporated into Lalande-de-Pomerol in 1954.

creamy, very Pomerol-like – and sometimes impressively good. Among its nuances there may be fresh toast (the wine matures for nine months in barrels of which one-third are new), fruit and cherry stones.

Clos de l'Hermitage   map 43
owner: Vignobles Bertin *area:* 3.1 ha *cases:* 1,500 *grape % R:* MER 80% CF 20% *second wine:* Domaine de Picardan *(Bordeaux Supérieur)* *other châteaux owned:* Ch Cardinal *(St-Emilion)*; Ch Dallau *(Bordeaux Supérieur)*
33500 Néac tel: 05 57 84 21 17
fax: 05 57 84 29 44
Wine, characterized by its Merlot, that doesn't require much waiting for, and in principle at least is given no barrel-ageing.

Ch La Mission   map 41 J5
owner: Pierre Lasserre & Jean-Marie Garde *area:* 1.7 ha *cases:* 800 *grape % R:* MER 60% CF 30% MAL 10% *other châteaux owned:* Clos René *(Pomerol)*; Ch Moulinet-Lasserre *(Pomerol)*
33500 Lalande-de-Pomerol tel: 05 57 51 10 41
fax: 05 57 51 16 28
Nuanced, muscular wine with integrated tannins and considerable oak – a quarter of the *barriques* are new. A very good Lalande-de-Pomerol, beautifully balanced. La Mission is vinified by the team from Clos René, Pomerol.

LALANDE-DE-POMEROL

43

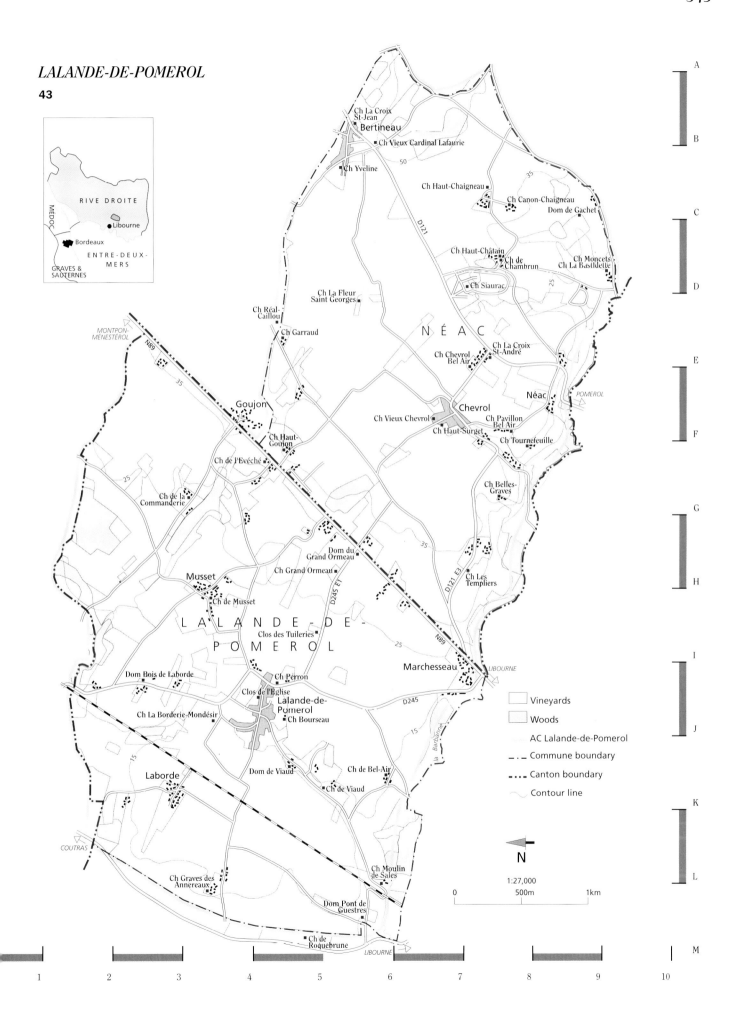

RIVE DROITE

MÉDOC

● Libourne

■ Bordeaux

ENTRE-DEUX-MERS

GRAVES & SAUTERNES

Ch La Croix St-Jean
Bertineau
■ Ch Vieux Cardinal Lafaurie

50

■ Ch Yveline

Ch Haut-Chaigneau ■

35

Ch Canon-Chaigneau ■
Dom de Gachet

Ch Haut-Châtain

25

Ch Moncets
Ch La Bastidette

Ch de Chambrun

Ch Siaurac ■

N É A C

Ch La Fleur Saint Georges

Ch Réal-Caillou

Ch Garraud

Ch La Croix St-André

Ch Chevrol Bel Air

MONTPON-MÉNESTÉROL

N89

35

Néac

POMEROL

Goujon

Chevrol

Ch Vieux Chevrol
Ch Haut-Surget

Ch Pavillon Bel Air

Ch Haut-Goujon

Ch Tournefeuille

Ch de l'Evêché

25

Ch de la Commanderie

Ch Belles-Graves

G

35

Dom du Grand Ormeau

Ch Grand Ormeau

D245 E1

Ch Les Templiers

D121 E3

Musset

Ch de Musset

L A L A N D E - D E - POMEROL

Clos des Tuileries

25

N89

Marchesseau

LIBOURNE

Dom Bois de Laborde

Ch Perron

Clos de l'Eglise

Lalande-de-Pomerol

Ch La Borderie-Mondésir

Ch Bourseau

D245

15

Laborde

Dom de Viaud

Ch de Bel-Air

Ch de Viaud

la Barbanne

COUTRAS

Ch Moulin de Sales

15

N

Ch Graves des Annereaux

Dom Pont de Guestres

1:27,000

0   500m   1km

Ch de Roquebrune

LIBOURNE

□ Vineyards
□ Woods
─ AC Lalande-de-Pomerol
─·─ Commune boundary
··· Canton boundary
◡ Contour line

A B C D E F G H I J K L M

1 2 3 4 5 6 7 8 9 10

Ch Moncets
map 43 D10

owner: L.G. & E. de Jerphanion *area:* 18.5 ha
cases: 10,000 *grape % R:* MER 60% CF 30% CS 10%
second wine: Ch Gardour *other châteaux owned:*
Ch La Bastidette *(Montagne-St-Emilion)*
33500 Néac tel: 05 57 51 19 33
fax: 05 57 51 56 24
At this white château, with its twin turrets, a
usually attractive wine is produced; it soon
becomes supple, and conveys discreet
impressions of fruit and oak.

Ch Moulin de Sales
map 43 L6

owner: A. Chaumet *area:* 9.6 ha *cases:* 5,000
grape % R: MER 70% CF 15% CS 15% *second wine:*
Ch l'Ancestral
33500 Lalande-de-Pomerol tel: 05 57 25 50 12
fax: 05 57 25 51 48
Reliable wine, supple in the lesser years,
reserved and fairly rich in tannin in the good or
great ones. Besides elements of oak (from the
20% of new casks), this Lalande-de-Pomerol
often displays earthy and fruity notes. The
château has been the property of the same
family since 1863.

Ch de Musset
map 43 I4

owner: SCE Y. Foucard & Fils *area:* 24 ha *cases:*
10,000 *grape % R:* MER 70% CS 15% CF 10% MAL 5%
other châteaux owned: Ch Chêne-Vieux *(Puisseguin-
St-Emilion)*
33500 Lalande-de-Pomerol tel: 05 57 51 11 40
fax: 05 57 25 36 45
In this wine, which is usually suitable for
laying down, intelligent use has been made of
oak (a fifth of the casks are new). The tannins
are smooth, the taste offers refinement and
length, and there is an immaculate balance. In
short, it has class.

Ch Pavillon Bel Air
map 43 F8

owner: Jean-François & Dominique Quenin *area:* 7
ha *cases:* 3,000 *grape % R:* MER 60% CF 40%
second wine: Ch Les Longées
33500 Néac tel: 05 57 51 82 26
This vineyard, created in 1952, acquired new
owners in 1994 who have chosen quality as
their policy. Modern technology is combined
with craftsmanlike values – such as maturing
for a year in *barriques*, of which a third are new
for each vintage. The first results are most
encouraging. Worth watching.

Below: Ch Siaurac

Ch Perron
map 43 J5

owner: Michel-Pierre Massouie *area:* 15 ha *cases:*
6,600 *grape % R:* MER 80% CS 10% CF 10% *second
wine:* Ch Pierrefitte; Clos de Malte *other châteaux
owned:* Ch La Valette *(Lalande-de-Pomerol)*; Ch
Thibert *(Bordeaux Supérieur)*
33500 Lalande-de-Pomerol tel: 05 57 51 35 97
fax: 05 57 51 13 37
Mouthfilling wine that often lingers beautifully
in the mouth, offering nuances of bayleaf,
licorice, plum and, quite distinctly, oak – about
a third of the barrels being new. The château is
17th-century.

Domaine Pont de Guestres
map 43 M6

owner: Rémy Rousselot *area:* 3.5 ha *cases:* 1,750
grape % R: MER 80% CF 20% *second wine:* Ch au
Pont de Guitres; Ch Lavergne *other châteaux
owned:* Ch Les Roches de Ferrand *(Fronsac)*
33126 St-Aignan tel: 05 57 24 95 16
fax: 05 57 24 91 44
The main wine here is pure Merlot: usually with
considerable fruit, it is harmonious and spicy,
with oak influences and strong, supple tannins.
Maturing in *barriques*, a third of them new, can
last anything from 6-18 months.

Ch Réal-Caillou
map 43 E5

owner: Lycée Agricole de Libourne-Montagne *area:*
31 ha *cases:* 17,000 *grape % R:* MER 60% CF 25%
CS 15% *other châteaux owned:* Ch Grand Baril
(Montagne-St-Emilion)
33500 Lalande-de-Pomerol tel: 05 57 51 01 75
fax: 05 57 51 66 13
Property belonging to the French state and run
by the Lycée Agricole de Libourne-Montagne, in
Montagne. The wine is nursed along in casks,
often with half of them new. It has supple
tannins, a solid structure and nuances both of
fruit – berries, cherries – and licorice. Nearly
three-quarters of production goes to private
French customers.

Ch de Roquebrune
map 43 M5

owner: Claude Guinjard *area:* 3 ha *cases:* 1,000
grape % R: MER 75% CS 25% *second wine:* Sablot
de Roquebrune *(Bordeaux Supérieur)*
33500 Lalande-de-Pomerol tel: 05 57 51 44 54
fax: 05 57 51 44 54
Well-structured, meaty wine that is often rich
in tannin, traditional in style. A dark aroma and
a short stay in wood.

Above: Ch Perron

Ch Samion
map 43

owner: Jean-Claude Berrouët *area:* 0.4 ha *cases:*
150 *grape % R:* MER 100% *other châteaux owned:*
Vieux Château Saint André *(Montagne-St-Emilion)*
33500 Lalande-de-Pomerol tel: 05 57 51 75 55
fax: 05 57 25 13 30
Delicious, pure Merlot wine: satiny, rich in
fruit, generous and with refined tannins.
Unfortunately only 150 cases a year.

Ch Siaurac
map 43 D8

owner: Olivier Guichard *area:* 33 ha *cases:* 15,000
grape % R: MER 60% CF 35% CS 5% *other châteaux
owned:* Ch Le Prieuré *(St-Emilion)*; Ch Vray Croix de
Gay *(Pomerol)*
33500 Néac tel: 05 57 51 64 58
fax: 05 57 51 41 56
At this imposing château in its parkland setting,
an expansive, substantial, characteristic but
perhaps a shade old-fashioned Lalande is made;
it is perfumed and generally has ample fruit.
Aged in *barriques*, 25% of them new, for a year.

Clos des Templiers
map 41 J5

owner: Vignobles Meyer *area:* 11 ha *cases:* 5,500
grape % R: CS 60% MER 40% *other châteaux owned:*
include Ch de Bourgueneuf *(Pomerol)*
33500 Lalande-de-Pomerol tel: 05 57 51 16 73
fax: 05 57 25 16 89
Well-made wine, but not quite having the
structure to join the highest class. Charming
after just 3-5 years, despite the unusually high
proportion of Cabernets. Matures for at least a
year in wood; a quarter of the casks are new.

Ch Les Templiers
map 43 H8

owner: Jean Servant *area:* 7 ha *cases:* 3,300
grape % R: MER 80% CF 20% *second wine:* Ch
Teysson *other châteaux owned:* Ch l'Eglise
(Montagne-St-Emilion); Ch La Violette *(Pomerol)*
33500 Néac tel: 05 57 51 70 27
fax: 05 57 51 60 34
Very characteristic Lalande-de-Pomerol,
perfumed, accessible, with impressions of forest
soil, fungi, spices, coffee, caramel and some
discreet fruit. Solid rather than fine and
elegant.

Ch Tour de Marchesseau
map 43

owner: Jean-Louis Trocard *area:* 5 ha *cases:* 3,000
grape % R: MER 90% CS 5% CF 5% *other châteaux
owned:* include Ch Trocard *(Bordeaux Supérieur)*; Ch
La Croix des Moines *(Lalande-de-Pomerol)*
33500 Lalande-de-Pomerol tel: 05 57 24 31 16
fax: 05 57 24 33 87
Aromatic wine from gravel soil; normally supple
but without great concentration or substance.
Can also be very acceptable in the poorer years.
A minimum use of new barrels.

◆
Finding a château
To locate a château from its name alone, use the index/gazetteer, which will provide a page and a map reference. When the name and appellation are known consult the relevant Directory pages. When the commune is known, but not the AC, consult the index by commune, which lists châteaux under the commune name.

Ch Des Tourelles   map 43

owner: SCEA Entente Janoueix *area:* 18 ha *cases:* 9,000 *grape % R:* MER 60% CF 20% CS 20% *other châteaux owned:* Ch Grands Sillons Gabachot *(Pomerol)*; Ch La Bastienne *(Montagne-St-Emilion)*; Ch Petit Clos du Roy *(Montagne-St-Emilion)*; Ch Trincaud *(Bordeaux Supérieur)*
33500 Libourne tel: 05 57 51 55 44
fax: 05 57 51 83 70
Reasonably broad wine tending towards the rustic. Earthy, dark tones such as undergrowth, bayleaf and leather mark the aroma, together with spicy oak.

Ch Tournefeuille   map 43 G8

owner: GFA Sautarel *area:* 16 ha *cases:* 5,000 *grape % R:* MER 75% CF 15% CS 10% *second wine:* Ch du Bourg
33500 Néac tel: 05 57 51 18 61
fax: 05 57 51 00 04
The château and cellars here are set above a splendidly situated south-facing vineyard. The soil has great quality, being made up of clay and gravel. It yields a slightly spicy wine on a sound base of well integrated tannins, suitably contained by oak. Tournefeuille remains in its barrels – a quarter of them new – for as long as two years.

Clos des Tuileries   map 43 I5

owner: Francis Merlet *area:* 2 ha *cases:* 1,000 *grape % R:* MER 80% CF 20% *other châteaux owned:* Ch du Merle *(Bordeaux Supérieur)*
33500 Lalande-de-Pomerol tel: 05 57 84 25 19
fax: 05 57 84 25 19
An often muscular Lalande-de-Pomerol, ample in its alcohol and not demanding too much

Below: Ch Tournefeuille

Above: Ch Vieux Chevrol

patience. It spends a short time – six months – in casks of which a third are new. Bouquet and taste are frequently rather autumnal, with forest and mushroomy, animal aromas.

Ch La Vallière   map 43

owner: SARL Dubost *area:* 1 ha *cases:* 500 *grape % R:* MER 70% CF 15% CS 15% *other châteaux owned:* Ch Lafleur du Roy *(Pomerol)*; Ch Pâquerette *(Bordeaux)*; Ch Bossuet *(Bordeaux Supérieur)*
33500 Lalande-de-Pomerol tel: 05 57 51 74 57
fax: 05 57 25 99 95
This hard-to-find wine is of average structure; not great – but attractive.

Domaine de Viaud   map 43 K5

owner: GFA Vignobles Marius Bielle *area:* 14 ha *cases:* 5,000 *grape % R:* MER 85% CF 15% *other châteaux owned:* Ch Bellevue Montaigu *(Fronsac)*
33500 Lalande-de-Pomerol tel: 05 57 51 06 12
fax: 05 57 25 10 14
Property sited halfway between the railway line and the N89 road. Its Lalande-de-Pomerol is fairly classic in character, combining a certain elegance with firm tannins. Black fruit, animal aromas and spices determine the bouquet. Domaine de Viaud's wine spends 18 months in barrels, of which 20-25% are new.

Ch de Viaud   map 43 K6

owner: SCEA du Château de Viaud *area:* 19 ha *cases:* 9,000 *grape % R:* MER 85% CF 10% CS 5% *second wine:* Ch du Grand Chambellan; Dames de Viaud
33500 Lalande-de-Pomerol tel: 05 57 51 17 86
fax: 05 57 51 79 77

Wine estate resurrected by a dynamic group of investors in 1986, and fitted out with modern cellar equipment three years later. A mouth-filling and at the same time very civilized Lalande-de-Pomerol, rich in fruit and showing good oak – three months' ageing, and 50% of the casks are new.

Ch Vieux Cardinal Lafaurie
map 43 B6
owner: Famille Quancard *area:* 5 ha *cases:* 2,500 *grape % R:* MER 65% CF 25% CS 10% *other châteaux owned:* include Ch de Terrefort-Quancard *(Bordeaux Supérieur)*; Ch de Paillet-Quancard *(Premières Côtes de Bordeaux)*
33500 Néac tel: 05 56 33 80 60
fax: 05 56 33 80 64
This vineyard has a history going back to the 12th century. More recently, the Quancard family bought it in 1978. The wine often tastes meaty, without being enormous, with jammy fruit and restrained oak; very pleasant.

Ch Vieux Chevrol   map 43 F7

owner: Jean-Pierre Champseix *area:* 20 ha *cases:* 10,000 *grape % R:* MER 70% CF 15% CS 15% *second wine:* Ch la Rose Vosel
33500 Néac tel: 05 57 51 09 80
fax: 05 57 25 35 05
Even in great years this is a fairly light wine with some jam-like fruit, spice and earthy tones. It matures not in the usual 225-litre *barriques* – but in 600-litre *demi-muids*, for 12-18 months.

Ch Yveline   map 43 C6

owner: Christian Durand *area:* 6.5 ha *cases:* 2,800 *grape % R:* MER 80% CS 20% *other wines:* Ch la Chapelle *(Montagne-St-Emilion)*
33500 Néac tel: 05 57 51 62 40
fax: 05 57 51 68 30
The warmth and roundness of the Merlot are unmistakeably present in this wine, along with tannin and a smooth freshness. No oak.

FRONSAC AND CANON-FRONSAC

To the west of Pomerol and St-Emilion, just north-west of the quayside town of Libourne, lie the other vineyards of the Libournais, Fronsac and Canon-Fronsac. Neatly ensconced in the angle between the wide and stately Dordogne and one of its tributary rivers, the Isle, this charming, verdant area takes its names from the two *canons* or hills which dominate the countryside: the Canon itself, which is 61 metres in height, and the 76-metre Tertre de Fronsac, atop of which sits the Château de Fronsac.

With its 1,341 hectares divided between the two appellations (959 in Fronsac and 382 in Canon-Fronsac) the area is very similar in size to Lalande-de-Pomerol – although considerably larger than Pomerol itself. Though the ACs are heavily influenced by the proximity of the two rivers, it is interesting to note that land bordering the Isle, on the eastern flank of the area, lies outside the appellations, while the vines that run down to the shores of the Dordogne are straight AC Bordeaux.

Less than 20 years ago, this was one of the most obscure corners of Bordeaux, totally dwarfed by neighbouring St-Emilion and Pomerol and the giants of the Left Bank. Even as recently as ten years ago, no-one other than a committed Bordeaux-ophile would have been able to locate it on a map with any confidence. How things have changed. Investors (including foreigners) and top *négociants* are now seriously committed to this area and its future, with the result that the best wines of

the Fronsadais currently rank as some of the most fashionable and sought-after in the world, and the future status of this area seems assured.

It would be wrong to say, however, that this area had no high-profile existence until the recent upsurge of interest and investment, led by the prestigious firm of Jean-Pierre Moueix, the Libourne *négociants*. In fact the Fronsadais has an extremely interesting and varied history: Charlemagne built a fortress here, on the site which is now Château de Carles in the northernmost part of the area, and in the 17th century Cardinal Richelieu bought land here and introduced the wines to the Court of Versailles. In the 18th century these wines enjoyed a very strong reputation, often eclipsing prices fetched by other Libournais wines.

SITES, SOILS AND CHÂTEAUX

The Fronsadais is roughly triangular in shape, its broad southern base gradually tapering off to a north-easterly point. It spreads over seven communes, of which six are allowed to produce wines under the Fronsac appellation. A small part of the Fronsac commune itself also has the right to the Canon-Fronsac appellation, as does the seventh commune, St-Michel-de-Fronsac. They are both situated in the southern section of the Fronsadais, just to the north of the D670. Soil types range from the rich alluvium (not AC land) down by the rivers, to limestone and clay-limestone for some of the best sites. With the mitigating presence

Early spring in the Fronsadais: the Dordogne is running bank-high

of two rivers and its hilly slopes, the Fronsac area is well protected from potentially damaging spring frosts.

Although this is essentially an area of modest farmhouses, some very attractive châteaux, like de la Dauphine and the hugely impressive de la Rivière (one of Bordeaux's most riveting sights when seen from the D670 road), testify to the area's rich and extensive history. Vineyards can be extremely small though, and production tiny: one of the leading properties of the Canon-Fronsac, Château Canon (owned by Christian Moueix) makes less than 1,000 cases annually.

STYLE AND STATUS

Like Pomerol, the wines of the Fronsadais have never been classified. However, they differ from those of neighbouring Pomerol in two ways. First, whereas in Pomerol the track record is sufficiently long for there to be a pretty accurate unwritten classification, the same is not true here. Until the early 1970s, when outsiders first started taking an interest, this was a somewhat backward area producing wines which were frequently of very doubtful quality, often quite harsh and tannic and short on fruit. Secondly, although Pomerol enjoys a basic quality level which makes the wines universally reliable, in the Fronsadais this is not yet the case: it is essential to know who owns which château and how the wines are made in order to avoid disappointment. Although the smaller, hillier Canon-Fronsac generally produces the finest wines, a well-made straight Fronsac from a good winemaker can be less expensive and better quality than a Canon-Fronsac from an indifferent producer. Nor are older vintages necessarily that reliable, and they should be bought with care. Even if quality is acceptable, in an area where so much change is occurring these older wines are not necessarily a good indicator of the style of wine currently being produced at the same property.

As with Pomerol and St-Emilion, Merlot is the dominant grape variety. Some producers, like Haut

Long views are a feature of this countryside: here a rain-squall sweeps up the river valley

Lariveau and du Pavillon, make a pure Merlot wine but most prefer to include some Cabernet Franc and Cabernet Sauvignon in the blend. Some châteaux actually use a fairly high percentage of the latter variety – which is virtually unheard of in Pomerol – resulting in a wine with more tannin and structure. This is certainly true in châteaux like La Croix-Gandineau and Mazeris-Bellevue: Both have 35 per cent of Cabernet Sauvignon in the blend. New oak is also an important component, especially in the prestige *cuvées* which quite a number of properties produce – again something which is almost unknown in Pomerol, where most producers make just a single wine.

At their worst, the wines of Fronsac can be unmemorable: decidedly light and lean, with high acidity and a distinctly hard edge. However, at their best they can be superb, and will easily last for 20 years or more. Although fairly rich and tannic, the tannin is usually well-integrated and the wine has an appealing fleshy texture.

There is just one cooperative for the area, located at Lugon. Its approximately 240 members tend to own land in the Fronsac appellation rather than in Canon-Fronsac. In the Fronsac there are about 100 growers making their own wines; the far smaller Canon-Fronsac boasts no fewer than 55 growers.

THE APPELLATIONS

FRONSAC
(red)

Location: *On the right bank of the Dordogne, 25 km north-east of Bordeaux. To the east beyond the River Isle are Pomerol and St-Emilion. To the north and west is a large area of land covered by the straight Bordeaux AC.*
Area of AC: *959 ha*
Area under vine: *830 ha*
Communes: *Fronsac, La Rivière, Saillans, St-Aignan, St-Germain-la-Rivière, plus precisely defined parcels of Galgon*
Average annual production: *530,000 cases*
Classed growths: *None*
Others: *100*
Cooperatives: *1 (for both Fronsac and Canon-Fronsac: c. 240 members)*
Main grape varieties: *Merlot*
Others: *Cabernet Franc, Cabernet Sauvignon*
Main soil types: *Clay-limestone*

CANON-FRONSAC
(red)

Location: *On the right bank of the Dordogne, 25 km north-east of Bordeaux. To the north-west, north and east it is surrounded by the Fronsac appellation. To the south is land covered by the basic Bordeaux appellations.*
Area of AC: *382 ha*
Area under vine: *300 ha*
Communes: *Clearly defined parcels of St-Michel-de-Fronsac and Fronsac*
Average annual production: *180,000 cases*
Classed growths: *None*
Others: *55*
Cooperatives: *1 (for both Fronsac and Canon-Fronsac: c. 240 members)*
Main grape varieties: *Merlot*
Others: *Cabernet Franc, Cabernet Sauvignon*
Main soil types: *Clay-limestone*

APPELLATION FRONSAC

Ch Arnauton
map 44 H9

owner: Jean-Pierre Hérail **area:** 24 ha **cases:**
13,000 **grape % R:** MER 80% CS 10% CF 10% **second
wine:** Ch Montahut; Ch La Vieille Eglise **other
châteaux owned:** Ch Pierron *(Buzet)*
33126 Fronsac tel: 05 57 51 31 32
fax: 05 57 25 33 25
This château regularly wins medals with its
Fronsac. The wine is of a very decent quality,
especially in the great years, with firm,
sometimes rather harsh tannins then. In the
lesser years the wine is not so structured.
Maturing in oak lasts an average six months,
and each year 50% of the casks are new.
Arnauton is in the middle of the quality range.

Ch Beauséjour
map 44 E9

owner: Famille Sudrat **area:** 22 ha **cases:** 13,000
grape % R: MER 80% CF 10% CS 10% **second wine:**
Ch Faure-Beauséjour **other châteaux owned:** Ch
Bel-Air *(Pomerol)*
33141 Saillans tel: 05 57 51 02 45
At its best this is a succulent, quite lively wine
with a decent amount of fruit and a fleshy
structure. But it can happen that in lesser years
this Fronsac has rather high acidity and tastes
quite hard. Check the vintage.

Ch Bourdieu La Valade
map 44 M8

owner: Alain Roux **area:** 12 ha **cases:** 6,000 **grape
% R:** MER 65% CF 30% MAL 5% **second wine:** Ch La
Cornelle **other châteaux owned:** Ch Capet Bégaud
(Canon-Fronsac); Ch Chêne de Gombeau *(Canon-
Fronsac)*; Ch Coustolle *(Canon-Fronsac)*
33126 Fronsac tel: 05 57 51 31 25
fax: 05 57 74 00 32
A generally good Fronsac with freshness, earthy
and spicy elements, a firm structure and some
discreet wood from a year in cask, 20% of them
new. The château was once a hunting lodge for
Cardinal Richelieu.

Ch La Brande
map 44 C9

owner: Béraud Pierre **area:** 18 ha **cases:** 9,000
grape % R: MER 75% CF 20% CS 5% **second wines:**
Ch La Brande *(Bordeaux Supérieur)* **other wines:**
Bordeaux, Bordeaux rosé
33141 Saillans tel: 05 57 74 36 38
fax: 05 57 74 38 46
An estate belonging to the same family since
1750, and very hospitably disposed. There is a
large room where some 60 visitors can be
received, and tasting courses are held. The
simplest Fronsac here carries the château name
and is a fairly elegant, slightly spicy wine that
usually develops quickly. The prestige *cuvée*,
called Ch Moulin de Reynaud, has more class
and character. This is given two years in barrels,
a quarter of them new, and is a firm, dark-toned
wine with animal aromas, vanilla and some
jam-like black fruit. Other wines made are a
Bordeaux Supérieur and a Bordeaux rosé, both
sold under the Ch La Brande name.

Ch du Breuil
map 44 I5

owner: Celse Campaner **area:** 7 ha **cases:** 2,500
grape % R: MER 80% CS 20%
33126 La Rivière tel: 05 57 24 97 37
fax: 05 57 24 97 37
The standard wine, tending towards the rustic,
has six months in cask, the *cuvée prestige* a
year; a quarter of the barrels are new. The *cuvée*
has a firm structure, as well as nuances of
tobacco and berries.

Above: Ch de Carles

Ch Canevault
map 44 F2

owner: Jean-Pierre Chaudet **area:** 10 ha **cases:**
4,500 **grape % R:** MER 50% CF 30% CS 15% MAL 5%
other wines: Ch Vieux Bômale *(Bordeaux Supérieur)*
33240 Lugon tel: 05 57 74 35 97
fax: 05 57 84 31 72
An estate that changed hands in 1987 and has
since been renovated. Underground galleries
house wine in wood (half of the casks are new
each year) and bottle. Only 2 ha out of the 10
yield Fronsac – an engaging wine with berry
fruit, a certain elegance and considerable
tannin. This is worth following. The larger part
of the estate produces Bordeaux Supérieur.
Besides fresh fruit this wine often has a slightly
herbaceous touch, but is pleasingly supple.

Ch Capet
map 44 H8

owner: Michel & Francine Soulas **area:** 4 ha **cases:**
2,000 **grape % R:** MER 60% CF 30% MAL 5% CS 5%
other châteaux owned: Ch Perron la Croix *(Canon-
Fronsac)*
33126 Fronsac tel: 05 57 51 77 09
Very correct Fronsac with fresh fruit; it does
not as a rule demand great patience. No
weedkillers or pesticides are used.

Ch Cardeneau
map 44 E9

owner: Jean-Noël Hervé **area:** 5 ha **cases:** 2,000
grape % R: MER 70% CF 20% CS 10% **second wine:**
Fronsac Générique **other châteaux owned:** Ch
Moulin Haut-Laroque *(Fronsac)*
33141 Saillans tel: 05 57 74 35 43
fax: 05 57 84 31 84
The aroma of this often deep-coloured wine
usually has a touch of plum, with some berry
fruit. The wine is generally concentrated,
without being very expansive or fat. Oak-ageing
is with a light touch: a fifth to a third of the
casks are new. This is a Fronsac to trust.

Ch de Carles
map 44 E10

owner: Antoine Chastenet de Castaing & Stéphane
Droulers **area:** 20 ha **cases:** 9,550 **grape % R:** MER
65% CF 30% MAL 5%
33141 Saillans tel: 05 57 84 32 03
fax: 05 57 84 31 91
The origins of this château go back at least to
the early 15th century, when it rose on a site
where Charlemagne once set up camp. The
building, flanked by towers, stands on a hill

above the river Isle and is classified as a historic
monument. The wine has a seductive,
sometimes almost silky fruitiness – blackberry,
blackcurrant, cherry – together with the darker
tones of cocoa and oak (20% of casks are new).
Tannins are sometimes conspicuous. The *cuvée
prestige*, Haut de Carles, is better still.

Ch Castagnac
map 44 C3

owner: Bernard Coudert **area:** 35 ha **cases:** 20,600
grape % R: MER 95% CF 3% CS 2% **second wine:** Ch
Rossignol; Ch Coudert-Mauvezin *(Bordeaux)*
33141 Villegouge tel: 05 57 84 44 07
fax: 05 57 84 47 96
In 1990 this estate left the local cooperative.
The emphasis here is on Bordeaux and
Bordeaux Supérieur. Just 5% of the area yields a
very decent Fronsac, which is not oak-aged.

Ch La Croix
map 44 I9

owner: Michel Dorneau **area:** 11 ha **cases:** 5,500
grape % R: MER 70% CF 25% CS 5% **second wine:** Ch
la Rose Chevrol **other châteaux owned:** Ch Roullet
(Canon-Fronsac); Ch Pontus *(Fronsac)*; Ch Haut Gros
Bonnet *(Canon-Fronsac)*
33126 Fronsac tel: 05 57 51 31 28
fax: 05 57 74 08 88
A Fronsac from an old family estate. Sometimes
it can give great pleasure, but it can also be
disappointing, with a lean and superficial taste.

Ch La Croix-Gandineau
map 44 I9

owner: Solange Frappier-Bouyge **area:** 7.5 ha
cases: 3,500 **grape % R:** MER 60% CS 35% MAL 5%
other châteaux owned: Ch Haut Panet *(Canon-
Fronsac)*; Clos Lagrave *(Lalande-de-Pomerol)*
33126 Fronsac tel: 05 57 51 30 38
fax: 05 57 51 81 18
In good years this is usually a succulent,
charming wine with ripe fruit; it is quite
rounded, and the balance is also sound.

Ch La Croix-Laroque
map 44 I9

owner: Guy Morin **area:** 10 ha **cases:** 5,000 **grape
% R:** MER 70% CF 20% CS 10% **second wine:** Ch La
Croix Sainte-Anne *(Bordeaux Supérieur)* **other wines:**
Ch La Croix Sainte-Anne *(Bordeaux rosé)*
33126 Fronsac tel: 05 57 51 24 33
fax: 05 57 51 64 23
Shirts and trophies from the world of cycling
are much in evidence at this estate: since 1984
it has been owned by Guy Morin, the Tour de

France rider – and his Fronsac, too, has sinew and staying power. In quality it comes somewhere in the middle of the field. Tradition governs its nurture, with 15-18 months in oak.

Ch Dalem
map 44 E9

owner: Michel Rullier *area:* 14.5 ha *cases:* 7,000 *grape % R:* MER 85% CF 10% CS 5% *second wine:* Ch La Longua *other châteaux owned:* Ch de La Huste *(Fronsac)*
33141 Saillans tel: 05 57 84 34 18
fax: 05 57 74 39 85
A splendid view from this white, 18th-century château on its hilltop, and an excellent Fronsac in its cellar. It is rich in fruit (especially blackcurrant), low in acidity, smoothly meaty in taste and characterized by its tannin and oak, both nicely integrated. Up to a third of the casks are replaced here each year.

Ch de la Dauphine
map 44 K9

owner: Jean-Pierre Moueix *area:* 10 ha *cases:* 5,000 *grape % R:* MER 70% CF 30% *other châteaux owned:* include Ch Trotanoy *(Pomerol)*; Ch Pétrus *(Pomerol)*; Ch Canon de Brem *(Canon-Fronsac)*; Ch Magdelaine *(St-Emilion)*
33126 Fronsac tel: 05 57 51 78 96
fax: 05 57 51 79 79
Unmistakeably a wine of class. In good years it offers a richly full, creamy structure, spice, very ripe fruit – blackcurrant, black cherry – a firm nucleus of alcohol (about 13.5%), good tannins and hints of oak: from 20-25% of the casks are new. However, this standard is not always reached. The château in its sizeable park was built by Victor Louis, and since 1985 has belonged to Jean-Pierre Moueix.

Ch Fontenil
map 44 E9

owner: Michel & Dany Rolland *area:* 8.5 ha *cases:* 4,000 *grape % R:* MER 85% CS 15% *second wine:* Tilet Rouge *other châteaux owned:* Ch Rolland-Maillet *(St-Emilion)*; Ch Bertineau St-Vincent *(Lalande-de-Pomerol)*; Ch Le Bon Pasteur *(Pomerol)*
33141 Saillans tel: 05 57 51 10 94
fax: 05 57 25 05 54
One of the stars of Fronsac: a wine that compels admiration for its usually dense colour and its taste – lively, rich in extract, fruit and oak (at least 30% of the casks are new). Michel and Dany Rolland bought the estate in 1986, and since then have extended it by about a third.

Below: Ch de la Dauphine

Above: Ch de Fronsac

Ch du Fort Pontus
map 44 I9

owner: François de Lavaux *area:* 4 ha *cases:* 2,000 *grape % R:* MER 75% CS 25% *other châteaux owned:* include Ch Martinet *(St-Emilion)*; Clos du Vieux Plateau Certan *(Pomerol)*
33126 Fronsac tel: 05 57 24 80 69
fax: 05 57 51 59 61
The substantial, rectangular château was built around 1850 by the family who owned Ch La Conseillante in Pomerol and other properties. A usually very successful wine is produced here with meticulous care: quite generous and with good tannins, candied black fruit and spicy elements. This Fronsac is given six months in oak by means of a rotational system. The owner intends to at least double the vineyard area.

Ch de Fronsac
map 44 K10

owner: Paul Sevrin *area:* 8 ha *cases:* 4,000 *grape % R:* MER 90% CF 10%
33126 Fronsac tel: 05 57 51 27 46
fax: 05 57 51 65 45
The château occupies a site rich in history – the top of the Tertre de Fronsac, a hill dominating the landscape round about and the River Dordogne nearby. The present building is a reconstruction: the château was destroyed by fire in 1993. Other châteaux had stood on the Tertre de Fronsac in the past, and before them the site was occupied by a Roman fort. Today the wine has a charming character thanks to succulent, jammy fruit, agreeable tannins, some spice, and sometimes animal aromas as well. The number of new ageing *barriques* and the time the wine spends in them vary greatly from year to year.

Ch Gagnard
map 44 J9

owner: SC Vignobles Bouyge-Barthe *area:* 11 ha *cases:* 5,500 *grape % R:* MER 70% CS 15% CF 15% *second wine:* Domaine du Haut Manoir *other wines:* Ch du Moustier *(Bordeaux)* *other châteaux owned:* Clos Toumalin *(Canon-Fronsac)*; Domaine Petit Moulin *(Lalande-de-Pomerol)*
33126 Fronsac tel: 05 57 51 42 99
fax: 05 57 51 10 83
Somewhat rustic wine for keeping, of variable quality. At its best in sunny years, when the Cabernets – 30% of the vines – reach maximum ripeness.

Ch La Grave
map 44 L9

owner: Paul Barre *area:* 4.2 ha *cases:* 1,600 *grape % R:* MER 60% CS 30% CF 10% *second wine:* Esterling *other châteaux owned:* Ch La Fleur Cailleau *(Canon-Fronsac)*
33126 Fronsac tel: 05 57 51 31 11
fax: 05 57 25 08 61
The vineyard to this estate lies between the Fronsac church and the Dordogne; it is organically cultivated. The wine is usually very pure, with elements of licorice, bayleaves, spices, berry fruit, all of this enriched by oak – a quarter of the casks are new. The styles of the 13th, 15th and 18th centuries can all be seen in the château.

Ch Hauchat
map 44 H6

owner: Jean-Bernard Saby *area:* 6.5 ha *cases:* 3,000 *grape % R:* MER 86% CF 14% *other châteaux owned:* include Ch Rozier *(St-Emilion)*
33126 St-Aignan tel: 05 57 24 73 03
fax: 05 57 24 67 77
Partly barrel-aged, relatively light Fronsac. Fairly dry, acidic and austere in the past, but nowadays more supple and agreeable.

Ch Haut Lariveau
map 44 I7

owner: B. & G. Hubau *area:* 4.7 ha *cases:* 2,000 *grape % R:* MER 100% *second wine:* Le Moulin de Lariveau *other châteaux owned:* Ch Moulin Pey-Labrie *(Canon-Fronsac)*, Ch Des Combes *(Canon-Fronsac)*
33126 St-Michel-de-Fronsac tel: 05 57 51 14 37
fax: 05 57 51 53 45
This château rose on the foundations of a building belonging to the hospital of La-Riveau, founded in the 12th century by the Order of St John of Jerusalem. The 100% Merlot wine has an ample structure, plenty of aroma (stewed fruit), a smooth acidity, refined tannins and integrated oak, 30% of the casks being new.

Ch de La Huste
map 44 E9

owner: Michel Rullier *area:* 3.5 ha *cases:* 2,000 *grape % R:* MER 85% CF 10% CS 5% *other châteaux owned:* Ch Dalem *(Fronsac)*
33141 Saillans tel: 05 57 84 34 18
fax: 05 57 74 39 85
From a sloping vineyard a very typical Fronsac is produced – aromatic, with dried black fruit, licorice, earthy and animal elements, and reasonable tannin. It matures for 15 months in used barrels.

Ch Jeandeman
map 44 G8

owner: Jean-Marie Roy-Trocard *area:* 25 ha *cases:* 13,000 *grape % R:* MER 80% CF 15% CS 5% *second wine:* Tonnelle du Roy *other châteaux owned:* Ch Laborde *(Lalande-de-Pomerol)*
33126 Fronsac tel: 05 57 74 30 52
fax: 05 57 74 39 96
Château named after a Fleming or Dutchman where an attractive, firm, but seldom heavy or fat Fronsac is made. It is soon ready for drinking; however, it can also be matured for a few years. Bouquet and taste have jammy fruit together with earthy and forest tones, and some spice. Not aged in oak.

Ch Labory
map 44 F9

owner: Henri Trocard *area:* 7 ha *cases:* 5,000 *grape % R:* MER 90% CS 5% MAL 5% *second wine:* Ch Barbey
33141 Saillans tel: 05 57 84 37 35
Documents show that the Trocard family has owned this vineyard since 1628. An elegantly

Above: Ch Lagüe

Above: Ch Mayne-Vieil

firm Fronsac is made here, with a strong Merlot character. It conveys impressions of ripe fruit, often with a hint of cocoa and bayleaf. Oak is absent: there is no ageing in cask.

Ch Lagüe   map 44 K9
owner: Françoise Roux *area:* 8 ha *cases:* 3,000 *grape % R:* MER 80% CF 20% *second wine:* Ch Capet-Lagüe *other châteaux owned:* Ch Vincent *(Fronsac)*; Ch Vrai Canon Bouché *(Canon-Fronsac)*
33126 Fronsac tel: 05 57 51 24 68
The château stands imposingly on a 62-metre hill and offers a delightful panoramic view over Libourne and the surrounding landscape. It was here that Louis François Duplessis, Marshal of France and Duke of Richelieu, held his rather exuberant festivities from 1746 onwards. The wine matures for at least a year, with 30% of the barrels new, and so combines spicy oak with fresh fruit, tannin (sometimes rather dry), and an often muscular body. Its quality is in the middle range.

Ch Laroche Pipeau   map 44 I4
owner: Jean Grima *area:* 4 ha *cases:* 2,000 *grape % R:* MER 90% CF 10%
33126 La Rivière tel: 05 57 24 90 69
fax: 05 57 24 90 61
In general a nicely fruity, quickly-developing Fronsac. This is a rounded wine with discreet oak and a good balance.

Ch Magondeau   map 44 F10
owner: SCEV du Château Magondeau/Famille Goujon *area:* 16 ha *cases:* 8,000 *grape % R:* MER 70% CS 15% CF 15%
33141 Saillans tel: 05 57 84 32 02
fax: 05 57 84 39 51
Estate run by the same family since 1882. The standard Fronsac usually combines firm tannins with gutsy fruit, especially blackcurrant. The special *cuvée* Ch Magondeau Beau-Site is more complex, and matures for six months in new casks.

Ch Mayne-Vieil   map 44 B9
owner: Famille Sèze *area:* 41 ha *cases:* 25,000 *grape % R:* MER 90% CF 10% *second wine:* Ch Moine-Martin *other châteaux owned:* Ch Buisson-Redon *(Bordeaux)*; Ch Charmail *(Haut-Médoc)*
33133 Galgon tel: 05 57 74 30 06
fax: 05 57 84 39 33

Extensive vineyard on a wide plateau, around an 1860 *chartreuse*. There is nearly always a herbaceous note in the wine, sometimes quite slight, at other times distinct, although the proportion of Cabernet is very limited. The taste is medium in structure, has an undertone of fruit (raspberry, black cherry), and licorice and bayleaves may also be found. This generally appealing wine is ready fairly quickly.

Ch Moulin des Tonnelles   map 44 G6
owner: Jean-Pierre Artiguevieille *area:* 13.6 ha *cases:* 6,000 *grape % R:* MER 90% CF 10%
33126 St-Aignan tel: 05 57 24 95 10
fax: 05 57 24 91 58
The remains of old windmills not only appear on the labels here, but also in the vineyard of this 150-year-old estate. A fairly traditional Fronsac is produced, showing a strong Merlot character and not aged in cask. In aroma and taste animal notes mingle with soft black fruit, and the solid tannins require time to soften. Since 1985 the wine has won an uninterrupted string of gold, silver and bronze medals.

Ch Moulin Haut-Laroque   map 44 F8
owner: Jean-Noël Hervé *area:* 15 ha *cases:* 5,500 *grape % R:* MER 65% CF 20% CS 10% MAL 5% *second wine:* Ch Hervé Laroque *other châteaux owned:* Ch Carnedeau *(Fronsac)*
33141 Saillans tel: 05 57 84 32 07
fax: 05 57 84 31 84
A consistently good, top-quality wine is made here from selected grapes, hand-picked and in perfect condition. It usually fills the mouth stylishly and generously, the fruit conveying very ripe cherry, blackberry, plum. The total effect is completed by firm yet elegant tannins, licorice, vanilla, and oak from the 15 months to nearly two years in barrels, a third of them new.

Ch Plain-Point   map 44 F6
owner: Pierre & Michel Aroldi *area:* 30 ha *cases:* 20,700 *grape % R:* MER 80% CS 10% CF 10% *second wine:* Cuvée La Métairie du Château Plain-Point *other wines:* Ch Angelique *(Bordeaux)* *other châteaux owned:* Ch Fon de Sergay *(Bordeaux)*
33126 St-Aignan tel: 05 57 24 96 55
fax: 05 57 24 91 64
Today the wine from this 16th-century château, resplendent on its hilltop, has a pleasing measure of fruit as well as supple tannins.

Ch Pontus   map 44 I9
owner: Michel Dorneau *area:* 9.8 ha *cases:* 5,555 *grape % R:* MER 69% CS 31% *other châteaux owned:* Ch Haut Gros Bonnet *(Canon-Fronsac)*; Ch La Croix *(Fronsac)*
33126 Fronsac tel: 05 57 51 31 28
fax: 05 57 74 08 88
The relatively large amount of Cabernet in the vineyard is clear from the taste: a somewhat slender structure, berry fruits in the aroma, and the tannin making a duly lasting impression. The Merlot gives some dark aspects; its oak is not excessive. In quality this wine falls between correct and good.

Ch Puy Guilhem   map 44 E9
owner: SCEA Château Puy Guilhem/Jean-François Enixon *area:* 11 ha *cases:* 6,000 *grape % R:* MER 90% CF 10% *second wine:* Ch Puy Saint Vincent
33141 Saillans tel: 05 57 84 32 08
fax: 05 57 74 36 45
Estate on high ground, with a fine view. Its wine nearly always makes an impact with its sometimes rather dry tannin. It is a fairly elegant and complete creation, in which a touch of spice can be detected as well as black fruit. The property changed hands in 1995.

Ch Renard   map 44 H4
owner: Xavier Chassagnoux *area:* 7 ha *cases:* 3,700 *grape % R:* MER 85% CF 10% MAL 5% *other châteaux owned:* Ch Virecourt *(Bordeaux Supérieur)*; Ch Jean Voisin *(St-Emilion)*
33126 La Rivière tel: 05 57 24 96 37
This 18th-century château in *Directoire* style is at the foot of the hill crowned by Ch de la Rivière. About a third of the production is the special Ch Renard Mondésir *cuvée* with which the estate has been making its name in recent years. This charming wine has succulent black fruit, a fleshy taste, and a firm base of supple tannins and noble oak – 30-50% of the casks are new. The standard wine is less notable.

Ch Richotey   map 44 H6
owner: Yves Pontalier *area:* 13 ha *cases:* 6,500 *grape % R:* MER 70% CF 20% CS 10% *other wines:* Domaine des Vieilles Souches *(Bordeaux Supérieur)* *other châteaux owned:* Ch de la Galocheyre *(Bordeaux)*
33126 St-Michel-de-Fronsac tel: 05 57 24 96 57
fax: 05 57 24 91 41
The standard Fronsac is not always inspiring, but the *cuvée prestige*, produced in very modest quantities, is generally a good wine. It has both black fruit and quite firm tannins, and a clear oak tone. A considerable part of the total vintage is sold through one particular firm.

Ch de la Rivière   map 44 G4
owner: Jean Leprince *area:* 53 ha *cases:* 28,000 *grape % R:* MER 65% CS 15% CF 12% MAL 8% *second wine:* Prince de la Rivière *(Bordeaux Supérieur)* *other wines:* Prince de la Rivière *(Bordeaux Clairet; Graves)*
33126 La Rivière tel: 05 57 55 56 56
fax: 05 57 24 94 39
Fronsac's most imposing château: a group of buildings from around 1560, its salient features being the square towers, gallery, courtyard with fountain and steps, the splendid view across the Dordogne, and 8 ha of cellars in former stone quarries. The wine is a formidable Fronsac: powerful, solid, earthy, spicy, and endowed with jammy fruit and good oak. It ages well, but would benefit from a little more finesse.

Ch Les Roches de Ferrand   map 44 H6
owner: Rémy Rousselot **area:** 11 ha **cases:** 5,800
grape % R: MER 80% CF 15% CS 5% **second wine:** Ch
Vray Houchat; Ch Saint Rémi **other châteaux
owned:** include Domaine Pont de Guestres
(Lalande-de-Pomerol)
**33126 St-Aignan tel: 05 57 24 95 16
fax: 05 57 24 31 91**
Fairly open-knit wine, meant for drinking
within a few years. Ripe, preserved fruit, round
and with subtle oak, but little depth. The
greater part is sold as a second or third wine.

Ch Rouet   map 44 F4
owner: Patrick Danglade **area:** 12 ha **cases:** 5,750
grape % R: MER 75% CF 20% CS 5% **second wine:** Ch
Chevalier de la Garde; Ch Capailley
**33240 St-Germain-de-la-Rivière tel: 05 57 84 40 24
fax: 05 56 50 85 07**
Wine of an average structure, and often even
elegant. It generally shows quite a lot of oak
from maturing 15 months in barrels (5% of
them new); also considerable tannin, forest
aromas, black berry fruit and a slightly bitter
touch. The château home of this good Fronsac
is a classic 18th-century building, with a park
and cellars dug into the rock.

Ch Roumagnac La Maréchale
map 44 I5
owner: Pierre Dumeynieu **area:** 4.9 ha **cases:**
2,500 **grape % R:** MER 90% CF 10%
**33126 La Rivière tel: 05 57 24 98 48
fax: 05 57 24 90 44**
Classic, carefully made and matured wine that
demands patience. Black cherry, bitter
chocolate, spicy oak and autumnal scents are
among the aromas often noted.

Ch La Rousselle   map 44 H5
owner: Jacques & Viviane Davau **area:** 3.5 ha
cases: 1,800 **grape % R:** MER 60% CS 30% CF 10%
**33126 La Rivière tel: 05 57 24 96 73
fax: 05 57 24 91 05**
An estate reborn: since 1971 it has been totally
renovated. Some of the vines grow on very
calcareous soil. The 1986 vintage was the first
from the new *cuvier* with its stainless-steel
tanks; from that year on the wine has won
regular awards. It generally offers fruit (ripe
blackcurrant), notes of coffee and bayleaf, solid
tannin, and oak from casks (one- third new).

Clos du Roy   map 44 F8
owner: Philippe Hermouet **area:** 22 ha **cases:**
11,000 **grape % R:** MER 90% CS 10% **other wines:**
Ch Roc Meynard *(Bordeaux Supérieur)*
**33141 Saillans tel: 05 57 74 38 88
fax: 05 57 74 33 47**
After taking over this estate in 1987 from his
wife's family, Philippe Hermouet more or less
doubled the vineyard area. In 1994 he built a
new *cuvier* with tanks of stainless steel. A
subsequent project could be the introduction of
barrel-ageing. At present the wine is spicy and
quite fruity, with dark notes. Worth following.

Ch Tour du Moulin   map 44 F8
owner: Josette Dupuch **area:** 6 ha **cases:** 3,000
grape % R: MER 85% CF 7.5% CS 7.5% **second wine:**
Cuvée du Grand Père
**33141 Saillans tel: 05 56 35 10 23
fax: 05 57 74 34 26**
Since the disappointing 1990 vintage better
wines have been produced, wines with a dark-
red colour, jam-like black and red fruits, and a

Above: Ch La Vieille Cure

reasonably broad structure. Depth can still be
lacking, a result of relatively young vines – 5
out of the 6 ha were replanted from 1987 to
1994. Oak-ageing lasts at least a year, a fifth of
the casks being new. A château worth following.

Ch Les Trois Croix   map 44 F8
owner: Michèle Guillou-Kérédan **area:** 13.7 ha
cases: 8,500 **grape % R:** MER 80% CF 20% **second
wine:** Ch Lamolière
**33126 Fronsac tel: 05 57 84 32 09
fax: 05 57 84 34 03**
Château on high ground with land in three
parishes, Fronsac, Saillans and St-Aignan –
hence the name referring to their three church
towers. The taste of the wine is generally
supple, meaty and thoroughly fruity. Truffles
and other earthy elements are sometimes also
found. Not aged in wood.

Ch La Valade   map 44 H8
owner: Bernard Roux **area:** 22 ha **cases:** 11,000
grape % R: MER 80% CF 20% **second wine:** Ch
Chante Alouette
**33126 Fronsac tel: 05 57 24 96 71
fax: 05 57 24 91 16**
Fairly slender Fronsac of a correct quality that
may lack substance and also fruit. Its spicy oak
results from 18 months in used *barriques*.

Ch La Vieille Croix   map 44 E9
owner: SCEA de La Vieille Croix/I. Dupuy & R.
Vironneau **area:** 13 ha **cases:** 5,560 **grape % R:**
MER 80% CF 10% CS 10% **other châteaux owned:**
Clos Lormenat *(Bordeaux Supérieur)*
**33141 Saillans tel: 05 57 74 30 50
fax: 05 57 84 30 96**
The standard Fronsac is well made and has a
generous, likeable character. Besides earthy
elements and some bayleaves it has conspicuous
jammy fruit. Oak is barely perceptible – in
contrast to the Cuvée DM, which spends a year
in entirely new casks.

Ch La Vieille Cure   map 44 F9
owner: Colin C. Ferenbach **area:** 19 ha **cases:**
8,000 **grape % R:** MER 80% CF 15% CS 5% **second
wine:** Ch Coutreau
**33141 Saillans tel: 05 57 84 32 05
fax: 05 57 74 39 83**
An estate that since 1986 has belonged to
Americans, who have invested a great deal in

cellar equipment and an ultra-modern *chai*
with temperature control. There has also been
much new planting, and the vineyard area is to
be more than doubled. With its generally quite
generous, accessible, exceptionally drinkable
nature, this wine is now among the best from
Fronsac. It contains elements of spice, cherry,
blackberry, bayleaf, vanilla and cedarwood, and
tannins abound. This charming Fronsac is *élevé*
in barrels of which 30% are new.

Ch Villars   map 44 E8
owner: Jean-Claude Gaudrie **area:** 29.5 ha **cases:**
15,000 **grape % R:** MER 70% CF 20% CS 10% **second
wine:** Ch Moulin Haut Villars; Ch Malvat
**33141 Saillans tel: 05 57 84 32 17
fax: 05 57 84 31 25**
An excellent Fronsac is produced here in a
highly expert manner from vines 25 to 50 years
old; it is matured for a year in cask, a maximum
of 40% of them new. Besides noble, toast-like
oak its generally deep, concentrated taste has a
good deal of fruit (cherry, blackcurrant,
raspberry), a hint of bitter chocolate and fine
tannins. Six generations of the same family
have been active at this estate.

Ch Vincent   map 44 G7
owner: Françoise Roux **area:** 10 ha **cases:** 3,500
grape % R: MER 80% CF 20% **other châteaux owned:**
Ch Lagüe *(Fronsac)*; Ch Vrai Canon Bouché *(Canon-
Fronsac)*
**33126 St-Aignan tel: 05 57 51 24 68
fax: 05 57 25 98 67**
As its vineyard is spread over plots in four
districts, this château produces both a Fronsac
and a Canon-Fronsac. These represent three-
fifths and two-fifths of the output respectively.
There is little or no distinction between them.
The Canon-Fronsac is intended mainly for
private customers. The wine is fairly rich in
tannin, slightly spicy, firm, and shows both
animal and earthy aromas.

FRONSAC & CANON-FRONSAC
44

1:33,350

0   1km

N

Vineyards

Woods

—— AC Canon-Fronsac

—— AC Fronsac

–·–· Commune boundary

···· Canton boundary

⌒ Contour line

APPELLATION CANON-FRONSAC

Above: Ch Barrabaque

Ch Barrabaque
map 44 J8

owner: Bernard Noël **area:** 9 ha **cases:** 5,000
grape % R: MER 70% CF 20% CS 10% **second wine:** B
de Barrabaque **other wines:** B de Barrabaque
(Bordeaux Clairet)
33126 Fronsac tel: 05 57 51 31 79
fax: 05 57 25 32 83
Of the four wines produced here, Ch
Barrabaque Prestige is the star. This Canon-
Fronsac is matured in *barriques* of which 30-
50% are new, and usually has massive colour,
much berry fruit, bayleaf and other herbs and
spices, some cocoa, a slight touch of bitterness
and nicely integrated, not-too-intense, elegant
tannins. The standard Ch Barrabaque is rather
less concentrated, but also shows quality. The
château stands on a hill, gazing out over the
Dordogne.

Ch Belloy
map 44 J7

owner: GAF Bardibel-Travers **area:** 6.9 ha **cases:**
3,807 **grape % R:** MER 60% CF 40% **second wine:**
Pavillon de Belloy **other châteaux owned:** Ch
Queyreau de Haut (Canon-Fronsac); Ch Bardineau
(Bordeaux Supérieur)
33126 Fronsac tel: 05 57 24 98 05
fax: 05 57 24 97 79
Somewhat rustic wine with an earthy
undertone, some fruit and a respectably long
finish. Contains a lot of Cabernet Franc. Not
aged in cask.

Ch Caillou
map 44 J8

owner: Eric Vareille **area:** 2.7 ha **cases:** 1,550
grape % R: MER 50% CF 50% **other châteaux owned:**
Ch Pey Labrie (Canon-Fronsac)
33126 Fronsac tel: 05 57 51 65 17
Small estate producing a decent but
unremarkable Canon-Fronsac. The proportion
of Cabernet Franc – half of the vines – is
unusually high. Given hardly any oak-ageing.

Ch Canon
map 44 K6

owner: Christian Moueix **area:** 1.2 ha **cases:** 500
grape % R: MER 95% CF 5% **other châteaux owned:**
include Ch de la Dauphine (Fronsac); Ch Canon de
Brem (Canon-Fronsac); Ch Trotanoy (Pomerol); Ch
Pétrus (Pomerol); Ch Magdelaine (St-Emilion)
33126 Fronsac tel: 05 57 51 78 96
fax: 05 57 51 79 79

Above: Ch Canon-Moueix

In good years a distinguished, lively and subtly-
nuanced wine, harmoniously framed by its oak
– 25% of the barrels are new. Often among the
best of Canon-Fronsac. Since 1971 this tiny
estate has belonged to Christian Moueix.

Ch Canon
map 44 K6

owner: Henriette Horeau/Famille de Coninck **area:**
10 ha **cases:** 5,800 **grape % R:** MER 90% CF 5% CS
5% **other wines:** Ch Canon Lange (Canon-Fronsac)
other châteaux owned: Ch Junayme (Canon-
Fronsac); Ch Vray Canon Boyer (Canon-Fronsac); Ch
Bellevue (St-Emilion); Ch du Pintey (Bordeaux
Supérieur)
33126 St-Michel-de-Fronsac tel: 05 57 51 06 07
fax: 05 57 51 59 61
Although it is not the last word in refinement,
this wine does have depth and, in the course of
time, develops elegance. This is due in part to
very old vines on a steep slope. As a rule it can
easily mature for a decade.

Ch Canon de Brem
map 44 K9

owner: Jean-Pierre Moueix **area:** 4.7 ha **cases:**
2,000 **grape % R:** MER 65% CF 35% **other châteaux
owned:** include Ch Canon (Canon-Fronsac); Ch de la

Below: Ch Cassagne Haut-Canon

Dauphine (Fronsac); Ch Trotanoy (Pomerol); Ch
Pétrus (Pomerol); Ch Magdelaine (St-Emilion)
33126 Fronsac tel: 05 57 51 78 96
fax: 05 57 51 79 79
Generally an aristocratic, stylish Canon-Fronsac
showing good balance between its ripe fruit,
oak (25% of the casks are new), dark tones and
firm tannins.

Ch Canon Feydieu
map 44

owner: Michel Ponty **area:** 0.5 ha **cases:** 250 **grape
% R:** MER 100% **other châteaux owned:** Ch Grand-
Renouil (Canon-Fronsac); Ch du Pavillon (Canon-
Fronsac); Clos Virolle (Bordeaux)
33126 Fronsac tel: 05 57 51 29 57
fax: 05 57 74 08 47
A pure Merlot wine of high standard. Matured
in oak: a quarter of the barrels here are new.
Tiny production from a half-acre vineyard – this
Canon-Fronsac is a well-kept secret.

Ch Canon-Moueix
map 44 K9

owner: Jean-Pierre Moueix **area:** 4 ha **cases:** 2,000
grape % R: MER 90% CF 10% **other châteaux owned:**
include Ch Canon de Brem (Canon-Fronsac); Ch de
la Dauphine (Fronsac); Ch Trotanoy (Pomerol); Ch
Pétrus (Pomerol); Ch Magdelaine (St-Emilion)
33126 Fronsac tel: 05 57 51 78 96
fax: 05 57 51 79 79
Quite generous wine that is firm, but develops
more quickly than Christian Moueix's Ch Canon
or Ch Canon de Brem. In its aroma there are

◆
Grape varieties

Main and other permitted varieties for each
appellation are given in the appellation fact
box at the end of the relevant introduction.

For châteaux, percentages of grapes grown
are given as supplied by the château.

Abbreviations: CF Cabernet Franc,
COL Colombard, CS Cabernet Sauvignon,
MAL Malbec, MER Merlot, MUSC Muscadelle,
PV Petit Verdot, SAUV B Sauvignon Blanc,
SÉM Sémillon. Ugni Blanc is
not abbreviated

Above: Ch Des Combes Canon

Above: Ch Coustolle

the earthy tones of fungi and the smooth, fruity ones of cherry. A quarter of the maturing casks are new each year. The Canon-Moueix estate was formerly known as Pichelèbre.

Ch Capet Bégaud   map 44 H8
owner: Alain Roux *area:* 4 ha *cases:* 2,000 *grape % R:* MER 80% CS 20% *second wine:* Ch Sorbier *other châteaux owned:* Ch Chêne de Gombeau *(Canon-Fronsac);* Ch Coustolle *(Canon-Fronsac);* Ch Bourdieu La Valade *(Fronsac)*
**33126 Fronsac tel: 05 57 51 31 25
fax: 05 57 74 00 32**
Wine that is usually ready for drinking after about five years. By then it possesses considerable charm, with ripe, succulent fruit and a modest dose of oak: generally it displays fine balance.

Ch Cassagne Haut-Canon   map 44 J7
owner: Jean-Jacques Dubois *area:* 13 ha *cases:* 6,000 *grape % R:* MER 70% CF 25% CS 5%
**33126 St-Michel-de-Fronsac tel: 05 57 51 63 98
fax: 05 57 51 62 20**
Estate created at the end of the 19th century, whose château stands amid some venerable oaks ('Cassagne' is a reference to them). The standard wine usually tastes meaty, with animal aromas as well as those of bayleaves and blackberry fruit, and also adequate tannins. More colour, power, concentration, berry fruit and breeding is offered by the renowned La Truffière *cuvée*, an autumnal Canon-Fronsac that also contains a higher proportion of Cabernet Sauvignon – 20% instead of around 5%. What is more, a third of the *barriques* for La Truffière are bought new each year.

Ch Charlemagne   map 44 K9
owner: Jean-Pierre Moueix *area:* 14 ha *cases:* 5,000 *grape % R:* MER 70% CF 25% CS 5% *second wine:* Ch Bodet *other châteaux owned:* include Ch de la Dauphine *(Fronsac);* Ch Trotanoy *(Pomerol);* Ch Pétrus *(Pomerol);* Ch Magdelaine *(St-Emilion)*
**33126 Fronsac tel: 05 57 51 78 96
fax: 05 57 51 79 79**
Jean-Pierre Moueix acquired this old and charming château in the mid-1990s. The new owners changed the name from Ch Bodet – the

original title is now used for the second wine. Charlemagne, which is made partly from very old vines, is characterised by Merlot, and has considerable fruit. In its rather elegant, not voluminous taste, there are notes of bayleaves, spices, oak and chocolate. The wine spends 18 months maturing ing in wood; a quarter of the barrels are new.

Ch Chêne de Gombeau   map 44
owner: Alain Roux *area:* 4 ha *cases:* 2,000 *grape % R:* MER 80% CF 20% *second wine:* Ch Tour de Gombeau *other châteaux owned:* Ch Capet Bégaud *(Canon-Fronsac);* Ch Coustolle *(Canon-Fronsac);* Ch Bourdieu La Valade *(Fronsac)*
**33126 Fronsac tel: 05 57 51 31 25
fax: 05 57 74 00 32**
Not the foremost wine from Alain Roux, but a supple creation that does not require too long a wait. After a year's barrel-ageing its quality is correct.

Ch Des Combes Canon   map 44 K7
owner: B. & G. Hubau *area:* 3.5 ha *cases:* 1,650 *grape % R:* MER 100% *other châteaux owned:* Ch Moulin Pey-Labrie *(Canon-Fronsac);* Ch Haut Lariveau *(Fronsac)*
**33126 St-Michel-de-Fronsac tel: 05 57 51 14 37
fax: 05 57 51 53 45**
The Hubau family, of Moulin Pey-Labrie and other châteaux, took over this modest vineyard in the spring of 1995, subsequently producing a generous, pure Merlot wine of very good quality. Ageing in wood lasts from 12-18 months. One- to two-thirds of the *barriques* are replaced for each vintage.

Ch Coustolle   map 44 H8
owner: Alain Roux *area:* 20 ha *cases:* 10,000 *grape % R:* MER 60% CF 30% MAL 10% *other châteaux owned:* Ch Capet Bégaud *(Canon-Fronsac);* Ch Chêne de Gombeau *(Canon-Fronsac);* Ch Bourdieu La Valade *(Fronsac)*
**33126 Fronsac tel: 05 57 51 31 25
fax: 05 57 74 00 32**
Aromatic wine, with woodland and animal scents, and a modest amount of fruit. It is reasonably concentrated at its best, but often somewhat lacking in body; 20% of the maturing casks are renewed each year.

Ch La Fleur Cailleau   map 44
owner: Paul Barre *area:* 4.4 ha *cases:* 1,250 *grape % R:* MER 90% CF 10% *other châteaux owned:* Ch La Grave *(Fronsac)*
**33126 Fronsac tel: 05 57 51 31 11
fax: 05 57 25 08 61**
Very accessible, creamy, flavoursome wine in a characteristically open style. It offers power, jammy blackcurrant and cherry fruit, ripe tannins, some oak (a third of the barrels are new), and a good length. This estate dates from 1982 and is cultivated organically.

Ch du Gazin   map 44 I6
owner: Henri Robert *area:* 30 ha *cases:* 17,440 *grape % R:* MER 70% CS 20% MAL 10% *other wines:* Fronsac
**33126 St-Michel-de-Fronsac tel: 05 57 24 95 82
fax: 05 57 24 92 09**
Fairly supple and as a rule agreeably fruity wine, with an animal aroma and no oak.

◆

Vanished appellations

Appellation Contrôlée law evolves, and some names have vanished. They may be found on (very) old bottles.

Côtes Canon-Fronsac Superseded by the Canon-Fronsac name in 1964, though it is still legal to use the 'Côtes'.

Côtes de Fronsac Superseded by Fronsac. This AC covered only Fronsac, St-Aignan and Saillans: the present AC is larger.

Néac Now part of Lalande-de-Pomerol, the commune had its own AC until 1954.

Parsac-St-Emilion The appellation still exists, but no wine is declared: the growers have the right to use Montagne-St-Emilion, and they do.

Sables-St-Emilion A defunct AC, withdrawn in 1973, which covered the wines from the south-east part of the Libourne commune. These are now AC St-Emilion.

Ch Grand Renouil map 44 J7

owner: Michel Ponty **area:** 5.5 ha **cases:** 2,600, white 300 **grape % R:** MER 100% **grape % W:** SAUV B 50% SEM 50% **second wine:** Ch Petit Renouil **other wines:** Blanc de Grand Renouil (Bordeaux) **other châteaux owned:** Ch du Pavillon (Canon-Fronsac); Ch Canon Feydieu (Canon-Fronsac); Clos Virolle (Bordeaux)

33126 St-Michel-de-Fronsac tel: 05 57 51 29 57 fax: 05 57 74 08 47

A well-built wine, among the leaders in Canon-Fronsac: full-bodied, powerful, creamy, with good tannins, generous fruit, vanilla and toasty oak. Merlot is the only grape used, and the year-long maturing takes place in barriques, 25% of these being new. About 300 cases a year of a notable white Bordeaux, Blanc de Grand Renouil, are also made here.

Ch Haut Ballet map 44 J6

owner: Famille Fournial **area:** 3.5 ha **cases:** 1,700 **grape % R:** MER 95% CF 5% **second wine:** Domaine du Calvaire (Fronsac) **other châteaux owned:** include Ch de la Capelle (St-Emilion)

33126 St-Michel-de-Fronsac tel: 05 57 68 00 56 fax: 05 57 68 03 22

At its best this Canon-Fronsac is a reasonably fruity and well-constructed wine that is properly ready for drinking in two or three years. This quality is not always achieved; less-good vintages can sometimes have a rather herbaceous aroma and taste.

Ch Haut Gros Bonnet map 44

owner: Michel Dorneau **area:** 4 ha **cases:** 2,200 **grape % R:** MER 77% CS 23% **other châteaux owned:** Ch Roullet (Canon-Fronsac); Ch La Croix (Fronsac); Ch Pontus (Fronsac)

33126 Fronsac tel: 05 57 51 31 28 fax: 05 57 74 08 88

A Canon-Fronsac with berry fruit, good oak (30% of the casks are new), and an agreeable roundness. Has somewhat more class than Ch Pontus, a Fronsac from the same owner.

Ch Haut-Mazeris map 44 I7

owner: Marie-Christine Ubald-Bocquet & André Bleynie **area:** 11 ha **cases:** 6,700 **grape % R:** MER 66% CS 17% CF 17% **second wine:** Ch Fond-Gazan **other wines:** Ch Haut-Mazeris (Fronsac)

33126 St-Michel-de-Fronsac tel: 01 53 77 28 38 fax: 01 53 77 28 30

A Fronsac and a Canon-Fronsac are both made here, but the latter has the better reputation. It is a sound, often award-winning wine with the potential to mature: firm, spicy and fruity in the mouth, with smooth tannins and some discreet oak.

Ch Haut Panet map 44 I9

owner: Solange Frappier-Bouyge **area:** 4.1 ha **cases:** 2,000 **grape % R:** CS 50% MER 48% MAL 2% **other châteaux owned:** Ch La Croix Gandineau (Fronsac); Clos Lagrave (Lalande-de-Pomerol)

33126 Fronsac tel: 05 57 51 30 38 fax: 05 57 51 81 18

Quite lively and nuanced Canon-Fronsac, supple and lingering – but sometimes dry and bitter. The vintages tasted showed fluctuations in quality: this middle-range wine needs to be chosen with care.

Ch Junayme map 44 K7

owner: René de Coninck **area:** 16 ha **cases:** 8,000 **grape % R:** MER 80% CF 15% CS 5% **second wine:** Ch La Tour Canon **other châteaux owned:** Ch Canon

Above: Ch La Roche Gaby

(Canon-Fronsac); Ch Vray Canon Boyer (Canon-Fronsac); Ch du Pintey (Bordeaux Supérieur); Ch Bellevue (St-Emilion)

33126 Fronsac tel: 05 57 51 06 07 fax: 05 57 51 59 61

This graceful château on a hill is surrounded by a well-wooded park and dates from the 19th century. A good, reasonably stylish wine is made here; it perhaps lacks some concentration and length.

Ch La Marche-Canon map 44 K7

owner: Eric Julien/Vignobles Germain **area:** 5 ha **cases:** 2,500 **grape % R:** MER 90% CS 10% **other châteaux owned:** include Ch Lamarche (Bordeaux Supérieur); Ch Charron (Premières Côtes de Bordeaux)

33126 Fronsac tel: 05 57 64 23 67 fax: 05 57 64 36 20

A Canon-Fronsac that generally offers distinct blackcurrant and other berry fruits, juicy, supple and with considerable oak (a third of the casks are new). Since the 1992 vintage a special cuvée called the Candelaire has been bottled. This comes only from old vines and is matured longer in cask. (A point to note is that the château name is spelt Lamarche Canon on the Candelaire labels).

Below: Ch du Gazin

Below: Ch Haut-Mazeris

Ch Mausse map 44 J7

owner: Guy Janoueix **area:** 8 ha **cases:** 4,000 **grape % R:** MER 60% CF 25% CS 15% **other châteaux owned:** Ch Samson (Pomerol); Ch Grand Fortin (Montagne-St-Emilion); Domaine de la Bourrue (St-Emilion); Ch Petit Clos Figeac (St-Emilion)

33126 St-Michel-de-Fronsac tel: 05 57 51 27 97 fax: 05 57 51 02 74

Potential here for a good, earthy, decently fruity wine; but so far it has only appeared sporadically.

Ch Mazeris map 44 I7

owner: Christian de Cournuaud **area:** 15 ha **cases:** 7,000 **grape % R:** MER 85% CF 15%

33126 St-Michel-de-Fronsac tel: 05 57 24 96 93 fax: 05 57 24 98 25

In the same family since 1800. Their seductive wine is wrapped in a velvet cloak of berry fruit. Its tannins are supple and the maturing is sensibly handled, with 16 months in cask (20% new). Since the 1994 vintage a very limited special selection, the La Part des Anges cuvée, has been produced from vines 40-80 years old.

Ch Mazeris-Bellevue map 44 I7

owner: Jacques Bussier **area:** 11 ha **cases:** 5,000 **grape % R:** MER 45% CS 35% CF 15% MAL 5%

33126 St-Michel-de-Fronsac tel: 05 57 24 98 19 fax: 05 57 24 90 32

◆

About Fronsac and Canon-Fronsac

Information on the wines of the Fronsac and Canon-Fronsac appellations can be obtained from the Maison du Vin, BP 7, 33126 Fronsac. Tel 05 57 51 80 51.

◆

Communes

AC Fronsac covers the communes of Fronsac, La Rivière, Saillans, St-Aignan, St-Germain-la-Rivière and parts of Galgon.

AC Canon-Fronsac covers defined parts of the communes of St-Michel-de-Fronsac and Fronsac.

See map 44

In good years dark in colour, aroma and taste, Mazeris-Bellevue is a wine with a firm core of alcohol and spice. Tannin is never lacking, and it can be very strongly evident thanks to the large proportion – a half – of Cabernets. The wine therefore usually needs to be kept for it to acquire some roundness. The fruit is mainly berries; oak plays a subordinate role. The estate was created in 1848 by an ancestor of the present owner.

Ch Moulin Pey-Labrie   map 44 I8
owner: B. & G. Hubau *area:* 6.7 ha *cases:* 2,750 *grape % R:* MER 70% CS 20% CF 10% *second wine:* Ch Moulin *other châteaux owned:* Ch Haut Lariveau *(Fronsac);* Ch Des Combes Canon *(Canon-Fronsac)*
33126 Fronsac tel: 05 57 51 14 37
fax: 05 57 51 53 45
Licorice, generous fruit – berries, plums – spicy oak and refined tannins are among the characteristic nuances of this excellent, powerful Canon-Fronsac. At least a third to a half of each vintage is sold as a second wine: selection is strict. Many of the *barriques* – from 33% up to 65% – are new each year.

Ch du Pavillon   map 44 K8
owner: Michel Ponty *area:* 4.1 ha *cases:* 2,000 *grape % R:* MER 100% *second wine:* Ch Les Menuts Gros Bonnet *other châteaux owned:* Ch Canon Feydieu *(Canon-Fronsac);* Ch Grand-Renouil *(Canon-Fronsac);* Clos Virolle *(Bordeaux)*
33126 Fronsac tel: 05 57 51 29 57
fax: 05 57 74 08 47
Wine produced solely from Merlot grapes: lively, deeply fruity, meatily rounded, lightly spicy – and in good years it lingers long in the mouth. Matured for a year in casks, (25% are new barrels). A Canon-Fronsac with class.

Ch Perron la Croix   map 44 H9
owner: Francine Soulas *area:* 0.3 ha *cases:* 130 *grape % R:* MER 70% CS 30% *other châteaux owned:* Ch Capet *(Fronsac)*
33126 Fronsac tel: 05 57 51 77 09 tel:
05 57 51 77 09
Supple wine, rounded rather than deep. Only 130 cases are made a year.

Ch Pey Labrie   map 44 J8
owner: Eric Vareille *area:* 7.5 ha *cases:* 3,950 *grape % R:* MER 75% CF 15% CS 10% *other wines:* Bouquet des Roches *(Fronsac)* *other châteaux owned:* Ch Caillou *(Canon-Fronsac)*

◆
Neighbouring appellations

Fronsac and Canon-Fronsac are bordered to the west and north by land holding the generic Bordeaux appellations. Some châteaux in Fronsac also own land in these areas and make wines declared as Bordeaux or Bordeaux Supérieur.

To the east and south, the river plains of the Isle and Dordogne have small areas of Bordeaux AC land, but are mostly not vineyard. Beyond the Isle to the east lies Pomerol.

Across the Dordogne to the south is the appellation of Graves de Vayres, where both red and white wines are made. Beyond this is the Entre-Deux-Mers AC.

Above: Ch Mazeris-Bellevue

33126 Fronsac tel: 05 57 51 65 17 tel:
05 57 51 65 17
Estate on high ground, with views all around. Its wine was being praised as early as 1807. Today this Canon-Fronsac has a respectably solid, but not corpulent taste in which dark aromas keep company with ripe fruit and a pinch of spice. Generally the wine is only bottled after two and a half years, having spent that time in both tanks and used casks.

Ch La Roche Gaby   map 44 J9
owner: Marie-Madeleine Frouin *area:* 9.3 ha *cases:* 4,500 *grape % R:* MER 83% CF 17% *second wine:* Ch Gaby
33126 Fronsac tel: 05 57 51 24 97
fax: 05 57 25 18 99
Rather rustic Canon-Fronsac in which tart tannins, earthy tones and a slight fruitiness are the foremost elements.

Ch Roullet   map 44
owner: Michel Dorneau *area:* 2.6 ha *cases:* 1,450 *grape % R:* MER 77% CS 23% *other châteaux owned:* Ch Haut Gros Bonnet *(Canon-Fronsac);* Ch Pontus *(Fronsac);* Ch La Croix *(Fronsac)*
33126 Fronsac tel: 05 57 51 31 28
fax: 05 57 74 08 88
Soon ready for drinking as a rule, this is a quite elegant Canon-Fronsac with its generous fruit (fig, cherry) well-balanced by spicy oak – 30% of the barrels are new. At times the finish has something dusty about it.

Ch Toumalin   map 44 I8
owner: Bernard d'Arfeuille *area:* 8 ha *cases:* 4,000 *grape % R:* MER 75% CF 25% *other châteaux owned:* Ch Tessendey *(Fronsac);* Ch La Serre *(St-Emilion);* Ch La Pointe *(Pomerol)*
33126 Fronsac tel: 05 57 51 17 57
fax: 05 57 51 08 15
Complete, solidly-structured wine with, in particular, autumnal aromas and firm tannins. Matures well. Oak-aged (25% new barrels).

Ch Vrai Canon Bouché   map 44 K7
owner: Françoise Roux *area:* 13 ha *cases:* 5,000 *grape % R:* MER 80% CF 20% *second wine:* Ch Roc de Canon *other châteaux owned:* Ch Vincent *(Canon-Fronsac);* Ch Lagüe *(Fronsac)*
33126 Fronsac tel: 05 57 51 24 68
fax: 05 57 25 98 67

Above: Ch Pey Labrie

Very old and gravelly vineyard with vast underground stone quarries beneath, where the wine is put to mature. The black fruit in the bouquet and in the full-bodied taste is almost jam-like. Some spice is also present. Since 1990 the estate has also carried a *cuvée prestige*, strongly characterized by oak in its youth.

Ch Vray Canon Boyer   map 44 K6
owner: Famille de Coninck *area:* 8.5 ha *cases:* 4,550 *grape % R:* MER 90% CF 5% CS 5% *other châteaux owned:* Ch Canon *(Canon-Fronsac);* Ch Junayme *(Canon-Fronsac);* Ch Bellevue *(St-Emilion);* Ch du Pintey *(Bordeaux Supérieur)*
33126 St-Michel-de-Fronsac tel: 05 57 51 06 07
fax: 05 57 51 59 61
Sound, racy wine that perhaps is no longer up to the standard it once reached, but one that nevertheless offers enjoyment with its supple taste and tannins. Its finish sometimes has a slightly bitter touch to it.

Côtes de Castillon and Côtes de Francs

The Côtes de Castillon appellation takes its name from the pretty town of Castillon-la-Bataille, which lies on the north bank of the Dordogne at the eastern gateway to the Bordeaux region. It was here in July 1453 that an historic battle, won by the French, put an end to the Hundred Years' War and three centuries of English ownership of Aquitaine. Each summer a re-enactment takes place using 100 horses and 600 local actors dressed in the costume of the times.

This is one of Bordeaux's newest appellations, and one which is gaining in status. Until 1989, these wines were produced as Bordeaux Supérieur Côtes de Castillon. Indeed, until the 1920s they were known as 'St-Emilionnais' or 'près St-Emilion' – the 100-metre-high vineyards lie along the slopes that stretch eastwards from St-Emilion. Enclosing hills provide shelter and a gentle climate, and the vines face mainly south-west, looking out towards the Dordogne valley. It is a fairly large area, with an average annual production roughly just over half that of St-Emilion. The vast majority of the properties are small – less than twenty hectares in size – and the local cooperative is important: it vinifies about 15 per cent of total production and has around 150 members. Some 250 properties make and market their own wine.

Like St-Emilion and its satellites, this is red wine country only. The dominant variety is Merlot and although some of the wines can be quite soft and supple, there is also a slightly more austere style of wine with more structure and power: this requires time in bottle to mellow. The softer wines can be very approachable in youth and good from a couple of years after the vintage; the more austere style requires longer. Wines from top châteaux in warm vintages can age for six to eight years.

Bordeaux-Côtes de Francs

This small, picturesque area to the north of the Côtes de Castillon has emerged since the mid-1980s as one to watch. It produces some very well-made, serious wines, mostly red but with a little white too. It was the Thienpont family, owners of Vieux Château Certan in Pomerol, who first saw its potential back in the early 1980s. They produce Puygueraud and Les Charmes-Godard, two of the area's leading wines, among others. Since the Thienponts' pioneering work, more Right-Bank producers have become involved in the area and now make some of the top wines, including de Francs and La Prade.

This compact area enjoys a warm climate with low average rainfall and is very well suited to winegrowing. Its clay-limestone soil is similar to that found in other Right-Bank appellations. The style of the red wines is not dissimilar to the better ones of the Côtes de Castillon – quite full-bodied and powerful, with a certain supple elegance. They have good ageing potential: up to eight years from warm vintages. The white wines made at the leading properties like de Francs and Les Charmes-Godard are treated very seriously indeed, with some ageing in new oak: they, too, can gain from bottle-age. However, quantities are small and they can be quite difficult to find.

The area boasts one cooperative with some 30 members, and a further 30 estates make and market their own wine.

The feudal castle of Monbadon was completed in 1331

THE APPELLATIONS

CÔTES DE CASTILLON
(red)
Location: *On the right bank of the Dordogne, 40 km east of Bordeaux. To the west lies St-Emilion, north is Bordeaux-Côtes de Francs. South lies the Dordogne river. To the east is the département of the Dordogne.*
Area of AC: *4,854 ha*
Area under vine: *3,000 ha*
Communes: *Belvès-de-Castillon, Castillon-la-Bataille, Gardegan-et-Tourtirac, Ste-Colombe, St-Genès-de-Castillon, St-Magne-de-Castillon, Les Salles-de-Castillon, St-Philippe-d'Aiguille, plus a part of Puisseguin corresponding to the former commune of Monbadon*
Average annual production: *1,600,000 cases*
Classed growths: *None*
Others: *250*
Cooperatives: *1 (c. 150 members)*
Main grape varieties: *Merlot*
Others: *Cabernet Franc, Cabernet Sauvignon, Malbec*
Main soil types: *Hard limestone in the north, clay-limestone on the hillsides, gravel on the banks of the Dordogne*

BORDEAUX-CÔTES DE FRANCS
(red, dry and semi-sweet white)
Location: *On the right bank of the Dordogne, some 47 km east of Bordeaux. To the west are the St-Emilion satellites of Lussac and Puisseguin; to the south is the Côtes de Castillon. Beyond its northern boundary is a large stretch of land covered by the Bordeaux AC and to the east is the départemental boundary of the Dordogne.*
Area of AC: *895 ha*
Area under vine: *450 ha*
Communes: *Francs, St-Cibard, Tayac*
Average annual production: *220,000 cases (90% red; 10% white)*
Classed growths: *None*
Others: *30*
Cooperatives: *1 (c. 30 members)*
Main grape varieties: *Merlot*
Others: *Red: Cabernet Franc, Cabernet Sauvignon. White: Sémillon, Muscadelle, Sauvignon*
Main soil types: *Clay-limestone*

APPELLATION CÔTES DE CASTILLON

Above: Ch d'Aiguilhe

Ch d'Aiguilhe
map 45 G5

owner: Famille Raventós i Blanc *area:* 36 ha *cases:* 20,000 *grape % R:* MER 80% CS 10% CF 10% *second wine:* Ch Fourtanet *other wines:* La Rose d'Aiguilhe *(Bordeaux rosé)*
33350 St-Philippe-d'Aiguilhe tel: 05 57 40 60 10 fax: 05 57 40 63 56
The castle is a large, overgrown ruin with a 16th-century dovecot, but the cellars have extremely modern equipment. This is due to the Raventós i Blanc family from Catalonia, who bought this estate at the end of the 1980s. The wine is characterized by an elegant firmness, considerable toasty oak (a third of the casks are new), and a good concentration and balance. This is one of the better Côtes de Castillons. It begins to be ready for drinking after about five years.

Ch Les Arpents du Bourg-Dieu
map 45 F4

owner: Philippe Mounet *area:* 5.3 ha *cases:* 3,000 *grape % R:* MER 70% CS 15% CF 15% *other châteaux owned:* Ch Fayan *(Puisseguin-St-Emilion)*
33570 Puisseguin tel: 05 57 74 63 49 fax: 05 57 74 54 73
In good years this is a reasonably full-bodied wine with a bouquet that shows elements of spice, oak and fruit. Its taste is supple, but at times lacks a little breeding and depth. About two-thirds of the casks for maturing are new each year. A summer art exhibition is held at the château, which has belonged to the Mounet family since 1986.

Ch Arthus/Clos de La Vieille Eglise
map 45 J3

owner: Danielle & Richard Dubois *area:* 9.3 ha *cases:* 4,500 *grape % R:* MER 90% CS 10% *other wines:* Vieux Gréan *(Côtes de Castillon)* *other châteaux owned:* Ch Bertinat Lartigue *(St-Emilion)*
33330 St-Sulpice-de-Faleyrens tel: 05 57 24 72 75
The energetic oenologists Richard and Danielle Dubois work 9.3 ha in Côtes de Castillon, and from them make three wines. The best of these – if not the best of all the wines from this district – is the Arthus, a special selection made from at least 70% Merlot, from old vines on hillside vineyards. This wine offers power

without aggressiveness, much ripe fruit and a wealth of integrated, noble tannins. Ageing takes place in new *barriques*, and the yield is from 10-15,000 bottles a year. Slightly less rich, but with great charm, is the mouthfilling Clos de La Vieille Eglise, which has some oak. The Vieux Gréan offers a more average quality. This is given no ageing in cask and is meant for early drinking.

Ch Belcier
map 45 F8

owner: MACIF *area:* 52 ha *cases:* 32,500 *grape % R:* MER 60% CF 35% MAL 5% *second wine:* Ch de Monreceuil *other wines:* Fleurs de Belcier *(Bordeaux rosé)*
33350 Les Salles-de-Castillon tel: 05 57 40 62 90 fax: 05 57 40 64 25
Château dating from around 1780, built to receive the king by François de Belcier, one of his counsellors. The monarch, however, never arrived. A full-bodied, creamy style, with jammy, candied fruit, and noble, nicely integrated oak are characteristics of the wine. It is one of the best from the district, a creation that shows refinement as well as concentration.

Ch Bellevue
map 45 I5

owner: Jean-Pierre Toxé *area:* 10 ha *cases:* 6,100 *grape % R:* MER 60% CF 40% *other châteaux owned:* Ch Pillebois *(Côtes de Castillon)*; Ch Franc Lartigue *(St-Emilion)*; Ch Grande Rouchonne *(St-Emilion)*
33350 St-Magne-de-Castillon tel: 05 57 40 33 03 fax: 05 57 40 06 05
The best wine here is the Vieilles Vignes launched in 1994. This represents about a sixth of the total quantity and matures for about a year in used barrels. It has just that little extra depth and power compared with the standard wine. The latter has an agreeable aroma and taste, with fruit and spice, but can sometimes be on the light side.

Ch Blanzac
map 45 K5

owner: Bernard Depons *area:* 18 ha *cases:* 11,000 *grape % R:* MER 65% CF 35%
33350 St-Magne-de-Castillon tel: 05 57 40 11 89 fax: 05 57 40 35 29
A wine that's usually successful even in the lesser years, with a good deal of fruit – plum, blackberry, blackcurrant – and a supple taste

Below: Ch Belcier

nicely framed in oak. The cask-aged Cuvée Prestige offers rather more concentration and nuance, including vanilla. This estate is graced by an 18th-century *chartreuse*.

Ch du Bois
map 45 J3

owner: SEV Vignobles Lenne-Mourgues *area:* 22 ha *cases:* 12,000 *grape % R:* MER 60% CS 20% CF 17% MAL 3% *second wine:* Ch de Colombe *other châteaux owned:* Ch Le Bois du Loup *(St-Emilion)*; Ch Bois de l'Or *(St-Emilion)*
33350 St-Magne-de-Castillon tel: 05 57 40 07 87 fax: 05 57 40 30 59
The château, a 14th-century country house, was acquired halfway through the 20th century by the family of the present owners. The wine, which has a clean, very supple taste, undergoes a minimum of cask-ageing.

Clos du Bois Joli
map 40

owner: Michel Berny *area:* 2.1 ha *cases:* 1,000 *grape % R:* MER 95% CS 5%
33570 Puisseguin tel: 05 57 74 62 69 fax: 05 57 74 64 54
Accessible, meaty wine dominated by Merlot. Not aged in oak.

Ch La Brande
map 45 I3

owner: Vignobles Jean Petit *area:* 14 ha *cases:* 8,300 *grape % R:* MER 60% CF 30% CS 10% *other châteaux owned:* Ch Briand *(Côtes de Castillon)*; Ch Mangot *(St-Emilion)*
33350 Belvès-de-Castillon tel: 05 57 40 18 23 fax: 05 57 40 15 97
A new generation of the Petit family has been running this property since 1990, and a great deal of renewal and renovation has been carried out in the vineyard and cellars. The wine is good, reliable, middle-of-the-range, with a dark aroma, and is not aged in wood.

Ch Brandeau
map 45 G8

owner: Andréa Gray & Anthony King *area:* 9.4 ha *cases:* 5,000 *grape % R:* MER 75% CF 23% CS 2% *second wine:* Ch Marceloup
33350 Les Salles-de-Castillon tel: 05 57 40 65 48 fax: 05 57 40 65 65
For many years this wine was made by a cooperative, but since the 1989 vintage it has been vinified at the estate. Not matured in cask,

Above: Ch Castegens

it is a wine with an accessible, mellow, fresh-fruit taste. No pesticides or weedkillers are allowed in the vineyard.

Ch Brehat
map 45 J2

owner: Jean de Monteil *area:* 5.3 ha *cases:* 2,000 *grape % R:* MER 65% CS 20% CF 15% *second wine:* Bag in box (10 l.) *other châteaux owned:* Ch Haut-Rocher *(St-Emilion)*
33350 St-Magne-de-Castillon tel: 05 57 40 18 09
fax: 05 57 40 08 23
Modest property where a quite firm wine is made from 35-year-old vines. It has something of berry fruit in its aroma. With its short spell in wood, there are only discreet notes of oak and vanilla.

Ch Briand
map 45 I3

owner: Vignobles Jean Petit *area:* 8.5 ha *cases:* 4,580 *grape % R:* CF 65% MER 30% CS 5% *second wine:* Ch Chante Grive *other châteaux owned:* Ch La Brande *(Côtes de Castillon)*; Ch Mangot *(St-Emilion)*
33350 Ste-Colombe tel: 05 57 40 18 23
fax: 05 57 40 15 97
With its high Cabernet Franc content (two-thirds of the vines here) this is a fairly slender, supple Côtes de Castillon, with berry fruit. Not aged in cask.

Ch Cantegrive
map 45 E5

owner: Doyard Frères *area:* 17 ha *cases:* 10,500 *grape % R:* MER 65% CS 20% CF 15% *other wines:* Bordeaux Clairet *other châteaux owned:* include Ch Gasquerie *(Bordeaux-Côtes de Francs)*
33570 Monbadon tel: 05 26 52 14 74
fax: 05 26 52 24 02
The Doyard brothers, who also own a vineyard in the Champagne village of Vertus, make four different wines here. The best is the Cuvée de l'An 1453. Selected grapes are used for this, and the wine matures for 10 months in new barrels. It is a very generous creation: creamy, firm, expansive in the mouth, and well provided with ripe fruit. The standard version, too, is very creditable and is aged in casks, a quarter of them new. The two other wines are a Bordeaux Clairet, and a red Côtes de Francs called Ch Gasquerie.

Above: Ch de Chainchon

Ch Cap de Faugères
map 45 J3

owner: Corinne & Peby Guisez *area:* 26 ha *cases:* 13,000 *grape % R:* MER 50% CF 38% CS 12% *other wines:* Les Roses de Ch Faugères *(Bordeaux rosé)* *other châteaux owned:* Ch-Faugères *(St-Emilion)*
33350 Ste-Colombe tel: 05 57 40 34 99
fax: 05 57 40 36 14
Since the French film magnate Guisez bought this estate and the adjoining Ch Faugères in St-Emilion, there has been large-scale investment: the cellar equipment is not now inferior to that of many a Médoc *cru classé*. And the wine – with 50% new wood, and concentrated, racy tannin – has more class and character than many St-Emilions. Also worth discovering is the agreeably fruity Bordeaux rosé.

Domaine de la Caresse
map 45 J3

owner: Jean Blanc *area:* 15 ha *cases:* 10,000 *grape % R:* MER 60% CS 20% CF 20% *second wine:* Ch Fauroux *other châteaux owned:* Ch Grands-Champs *(St-Emilion)*
33350 St-Magne-de-Castillon tel: 05 57 40 07 59
fax: 05 57 40 07 59
A university-trained winemaker makes a wine that can usually boast considerable substance, and a pleasing aroma with both black fruit and oak. A Côtes de Castillon to gratify the senses.

Ch Castegens
map 45 J6

owner: Jean-Louis de Fontenoy *area:* 26 ha *cases:* 12,500 *grape % R:* MER 65% CF 30% CS 5% *second wine:* Ch Peyfol
33350 Belvès-de-Castillon tel: 05 57 47 96 07
fax: 05 57 47 91 61
The battle of Castillon is re-enacted every year close to this ancient castle with its quartet of towers. The Cuvée Spéciale is the best wine here: it has six months' oak-ageing in the castle cellars, followed by about a year's bottle age. This is a firm Côtes de Castillon, one that can be laid down. The standard wine also merits attention.

Ch de Chainchon
map 45 K7

owner: André Erésue *area:* 22 ha *cases:* 10,000 *grape % R:* MER 70% CF 20% CS 10% *second wine:* Ch Les Martinelles

33350 Castillon-la-Bataille tel: 05 57 40 14 78
fax: 05 57 40 25 45
A wine that is supple in the mouth, and without an excessive amount of tannin. For the rest, its taste has a pleasant freshness and obvious fruit. This Côtes de Castillon is not aged in cask, but is given 18 month in vats in the Château's cellar before bottling.

Ch Chinchon la Bataille
map 45 K6

owner: Union de Producteurs St-Pey-de-Castets *area:* 18.5 ha *cases:* 9,000 *grape % R:* MER 57% CF 27% CS 16%
33350 Castillon-la-Bataille tel: 05 57 40 52 07
fax: 05 57 40 57 17
Not a really concentrated wine – not even in the great vintages   but it does have ripe fruit, and taken as a whole it is a tasty mouthful. Bottled by the Castillon-la-Bataille cooperative. The estate is, as its name suggests, on the site of the 1453 battle.

Ch La Clarière Laithwaite
map 45 I4

owner: Société France Ecosse de Vente Directe *area:* 3.4 ha *cases:* 2,000 *grape % R:* MER 70% CS 20% CF 10%
33350 Ste-Colombe tel: 05 57 47 95 14
fax: 05 57 47 94 47
Estate created by the English wine merchant Tony Laithwaite, in the village where he worked as a student in 1965. At this small property the *modus operandi* is very quality-conscious, with fresh egg white for clarifying, and oak-maturing in casks of which 25% are new. The greater part of the production goes to subscribing members of a wine club, Les Confrères de la Clarière. The wine has backbone, breeding, suppleness, class.

Ch Côte Montpezat
map 45 J5

owner: Dominique Bessineau *area:* 30 ha *cases:* 18,000 *grape % R:* MER 80% CF 20% *second wine:* Ch de Brousse *other châteaux owned:* Ch Haut-Bernat *(Puisseguin-St-Emilion)*
33350 Belvès-de-Castillon tel: 05 57 47 96 04
fax: 05 57 47 90 82
Although a great deal of modernization has been carried out since the present owner bought this estate in 1989, some reminders of the past, such as a medieval well, remain intact. The château itself was built at the beginning of

Below: Ch Côte Montpezat

the 17th century. Côte Monpezat wine is usually aromatic, mouthfilling and very concentrated. Of the barrels used for its maturation, 30% are new. One of the stars of the district.

Ch La Croix Bigorre
map 45 H3
owner: Joël-Dominique Fritegotto *area:* 21 ha *cases:* 11,000 *grape % R:* MER 75% CF 20% CS 5% *second wine:* Ch La Croix Bigorre (*Bordeaux*)
33350 St-Genès-de-Castillon tel: 05 57 47 94 08
Appealing, very supple wine of standard quality. The better vintages – such as 1989, 1990 or 1994 – are preferable, since only in such auspicious years is the wine oak-matured, in (used) *barriques*.

Ch La Croix de Louis
map 45 J7
owner: Denis Pallaro *area:* 10.5 ha *cases:* 5,500 *grape % R:* MER 60% CF 35% CS 5% *second wine:* Fleur Pérouillac
33350 Castillon-la-Bataille tel: 05 57 40 13 93 fax: 05 57 40 15 36
Estate created in 1981, when it covered 5 ha. The cellar has modern equipment and the wine is matured in cask (a quarter are new oak). A most decent wine, very drinkable when young, but with the backbone to age for some years.

Ch de l'Estang
map 45 G4
owner: Christophe Bocquillon *area:* 25 ha *cases:* 13,650, white 150 *grape % R:* MER 71% CF 19% CS

Above: Ch de Lescaneaut

Left: Ch de Pitray

Above right: Ch des Faures

9% MAL 1% *grape % W:* SAUV B 100% *other wines:* Bordeaux Clairet, Bordeaux blanc
33350 St-Genès-de-Castillon tel: 05 57 47 91 81 fax: 05 57 47 92 13
Well-made wine, flavoursome and balanced, but with no claim to greatness. The château has a very modern *cuvier* and a fine *chai* for its casks, a third of them new. The quality seems to be improving; worth following.

Ch des Faures
map 45 D6
owner: Roland Mas *area:* 15 ha *cases:* 10,000 *grape % R:* MER 80% CS 15% CF 5%
33570 Monbadon tel: 05 57 40 61 07 fax: 05 57 40 64 87
Wine estate dating from 1970 and producing a rather rustic Côtes de Castillon: firm, spicy, with licorice and black cherry.

Ch Ferrasse
map 45 J6
owner: Vignobles Massarin *area:* 30 ha *cases:* 17,000 *grape % R:* MER 70% CS 15% CF 15% *second wine:* Ch Terre Blanche
33350 Castillon-la-Bataille tel: 05 57 40 06 12
Behind the label with its delightful watercolour there is an attractive, open wine with berry fruit and suppleness. The Massarin family acquired the estate in 1954.

Ch Flojague
map 45 H5
owner: Bruno Aymen de Lageard *area:* 4 ha *cases:* 2,000 *grape % R:* MER 70% CF 25% MAL 5%
33350 St-Genès-de-Castillon tel: 05 57 47 95 47 fax: 05 57 47 90 19
Fairly earthy and slightly spicy wine with a firm structure. No oak. Some vines date from 1905.

Ch Fongaban
map 45 E4
owner: Famille Taïx *area:* 34 ha *cases:* 25,000 *grape % R:* MER 80% CF 20%
33570 Monbadon tel: 05 57 74 54 07 fax: 05 57 74 50 97
Somewhat rustic wine that is ready to be enjoyed after about four or five years. Not cask-aged, and with a slightly spicy aroma. In 1940 this vineyard covered 8 ha; today it is about four times as large.

Ch Fontbaude
map 45 K3
owner: GAEC Sabate *area:* 12 ha *cases:* 7,000 *grape % R:* MER 60% CF 30% CS 10% *other wines:* Rosé de Fontbaude (*Bordeaux rosé*)
33350 St-Magne-de-Castillon tel: 05 57 40 06 58 fax: 05 57 40 26 54
At this family estate the supple, reasonably full-bodied standard wine is not matured in *barriques*. The Cuvée Spéciale is – for 12 months – with a third of the casks new. The Spéciale is made only in the better years, and represents about one-tenth of the production. It is a wine more likely to be chosen for its power and tannin than for its depth and refinement.

Ch La Fourquerie
map 45 K1
owner: Vignobles Rollet *area:* 6 ha *cases:* 3,750 *grape % R:* MER 59% CF 34% CS 7% *other châteaux owned:* include Ch Grand Tertre (*Côtes de Castillon*); Ch Fourney (*St-Emilion*); Ch du Vieux-Guinot (*St-Emilion*)
33350 Gardegan-et-Tourtirac tel: 05 57 47 15 13 fax: 05 57 47 10 50
A frequent prizewinner, this Côtes de Castillon is from an estate that has belonged to the Rollet family for more than six decades. It is a wine that usually offers a hint of ripe blackberry and notes of both licorice and bayleaf. It is not given any barrel-ageing, and is ready quite soon.

Below: Ch Flojague

CÔTES DE CASTILLON &
CÔTES DE FRANCS

45

Ch Grand Tuillac
map **45 F6**

owner: SCEA Lavigne *area:* 22 ha *cases:* 12,000
grape % R: MER 65% CF 30% CS 5% *second wine:* Ch
Longues Reys *other châteaux owned:* Ch Grand
Bert *(St-Emilion)*
**33350 St-Philippe-d'Aiguilhe tel: 05 57 40 60 09
fax: 05 57 40 66 67**
About half of the total estate is planted with
vines, and the vineyard lies on the highest slope
of the Côtes de Castillon. There can be
considerable fruit – such as raspberry – in the
aroma of the Cuvée Elégance, while the taste
holds a reasonable intensity, smooth tannins
and – on account of the alcohol – a sometimes
rather burnt aftertaste. This special *cuvée* is
significantly better than the standard wine.

Ch Grimon
map **45 F6**

owner: Gilbert Dubois *area:* 5 ha *cases:* 3,000
grape % R: MER 60% CF 35% MAL 5%
**33350 St-Philippe-d'Aiguilhe tel: 05 57 40 65 19
fax: 05 57 40 64 25**
Agreeable, accessible wine: juicy, with elements
of cherry, blackcurrant, bitter chocolate and a
touch of oak – from 8-10 months in cask, 10%
of them new. A well-made Côtes de Castillon,
this, with a certain depth. The estate took shape
between 1981 and 1985.

Ch Les Hauts-de-Granges
map **45 F7**

owner: L. Vincent-Dalloz *area:* 19 ha *cases:* 10,000
grape % R: MER 65% CS 25% CF 10% *other châteaux
owned:* Ch du Vieux Chêne *(Bordeaux-Côtes de
Francs)*
**33350 Les Salles-de-Castillon tel: 05 57 40 62 20
fax: 05 57 40 64 79**
Very old estate situated where agriculture was
already being practised in Roman times. A
quarter of the vintage, comprising the Cuvée
Réserve, is nurtured for a year in casks of which
a third are new. The wine tends to the rustic,
and has some vanilla, tones of licorice and
bayleaf, a little jammy fruit and an adequate
firmness. Not without merit.

Ch Lagrange-Monbadon
map **45 E5**

owner: Baron S. de Montfort *area:* 25 ha *cases:*
12,500 *grape % R:* MER 60% CS 40% *other
châteaux owned:* Ch du Rocher *(St-Emilion)*
**33570 Monbadon tel: 05 57 40 18 20
fax: 05 57 40 37 26**
The present château lies at the foot of a
medieval fortress that has belonged to the same
family since 1330. The wine contains a
relatively high proportion of Cabernet
Sauvignon (40%), and besides its suppleness
offers jammy fruit, a hint of bayleaf – and
sometimes a slightly bitter touch.

Ch Lamartine
map **45 G6**

owner: Gilbert Gourrand & Fils *area:* 17 ha *cases:*
8,300 *grape % R:* MER 65% CF 25% CS 10%
**33350 St-Philippe-d'Aiguilhe tel: 05 57 40 60 46
fax: 05 57 40 66 01**
The château takes its name from a hamlet
where the famous poet and historian Alphonse
de Lamartine is reputed to have stayed. The
wine has an open style and a sometimes almost
mild, elegant, fruity taste. It is meant for
drinking early: prose, perhaps, rather than
poetry.

Ch Lapeyronie
map **45 J4**

owner: Jean-Frédéric Lapeyronie/Alfred Charrier
area: 8 ha *cases:* 2,100 *grape % R:* MER 70% CF
15% CS 15% *second wine:* Ch La Font Du Jeu *other*

châteaux owned: Vignoble d'Alfred *(Bordeaux-Côtes
de Francs)*
**33350 Ste-Colombe tel: 05 57 40 19 27
fax: 05 57 40 14 38**
Generous, smoky oak is characteristic of the
aroma of this very good Côtes de Castillon, for
it is wood-aged for a year in 50-70% new
barrels. The wine also boasts considerable fruit,
as well as a touch of spice. The vineyard lies
600 m from the boundary with St-Emilion, on a
southwest-facing slope.

Ch Lardit
map **45 H6**

owner: Vignobles Bardet *area:* 12 ha *cases:* 6,000
grape % R: MER 80% CF 15% CS 5% *other châteaux
owned:* Ch Rocher Lideyre *(Côtes de Castillon)*; Ch
du Val d'Or *(St-Emilion)*
**33330 Ste-Colombe tel: 05 57 84 53 16
fax: 05 57 74 93 47**
This wine has a fairly traditional character, is
quite powerful, with some soft, spicy fruit, and
occasionally a slight bitterness in its finish.
Fermented in stainless-steel tanks; no ageing in
cask. The vineyard here is to be enlarged by
50%.

Ch de Lescaneaut
map **45 M4**

owner: François Faytout-Garamond *area:* 12 ha
cases: 6,000 *grape % R:* MER 80% CF 20%
**33350 St-Magne-de-Castillon tel: 05 57 40 14 91
fax: 05 57 40 21 08**
Côtes de Castillon made from two grape
varieties, with a somewhat rustic character and
modest fruit. Not oak-matured, it usually calls
for a few years' patience. The château acquired
its present form between 1704 and 1875.

Ch Paret-Beauséjour
map **45 H5**

owner: Philippe Fauché *area:* 25 ha *cases:* 15,000
grape % R: MER 75% CF 20% CS 5% *second wine:* Ch
La Nauge
33350 St-Genès-de-Castillon tel: 05 57 47 99 78
Decent Côtes de Castillon, with a fairly slender
structure coupled with some red fruit, such as
raspberry. Not outstanding. The estate has
belonged to the same family since 1850.

Ch Les Parres
map **45 J8**

owner: Francis Laurent *area:* 6 ha *cases:* 3,200
grape % R: MER 65% CF 13% CS 12% MAL 10%
second wine: Ch Haut-Giraudon
33350 St-Magne-de-Castillon tel: 05 53 58 67 21
The Laurents, a family of millers, acquired this
modest estate after the French Revolution, and
grew corn here until the beginning of the 20th
century. The wine is usually flavoursome,
reasonably full-bodied, and with something of a
woodland scent. Unfortunately, there can also

◆
About Castillon & Francs

Information on the wines of the Côtes de
Castillon can be obtained from the Syndicat
viticole at 6, allée de la République, 33350
Castillon-la-Bataille.
Tel 05 57 40 00 88.

Information on the wines of the Côtes de
Francs can be obtained from the Syndicat
viticole, c/o Château Lauriol,
33570 St-Cibard.
Tel 05 57 40 61 04.

---

be an inconvenient aroma of burnt rubber as
well, as in the 1993 vintage. Maturing – in tank,
not cask – lasts from one to two years.

Ch Peyrou
map **45 J2**

owner: Catherine Papon-Nouvel *area:* 5 ha *cases:*
2,900 *grape % R:* MER 80% CF 20%
**33350 St-Magne-de-Castillon tel: 05 57 24 72 05
fax: 05 57 74 40 03**
Small estate with vines that average around 40
years of age. The grapes are carefully vinified in
a modern *cuvier*, after which the wine spends
some time in cask. Its constitution is firm, with
rich, jammy fruit – plum and blackcurrant –
and spice, ripe tannins, toasted oak and a fine
length. Reliable in the lesser years as well.

Ch de Pitray
map **45 H6**

owner: Madame de Boigne *area:* 30 ha *cases:*
16,000 *grape % R:* MER 70% CF 28% MAL 2%
**33350 Gardegan-et-Tourtirac tel: 05 57 40 63 38
fax: 05 57 40 66 24**
The Pitray vineyard has limestone in its subsoil
and spreads out over the Gardegan plateau,
around a château built in neo-Renaissance style
in 1868. Here a delicious wine full of character
is produced: rounded, with masses of fruit and
succulent, ripe tannins. In the distant past Ch
de Pitray belonged to the famous Ségur family,
of Ch Calon-Ségur in St-Estèphe and other
estates.

Ch des Plantanes
map **45 K2**

owner: Jean-Pierre Hibert *area:* 10 ha *cases:* 5,000
grape % R: MER 60% CF 25% CS 15%
33350 St-Magne-de-Castillon tel: 05 57 40 33 13
In the same family for a century. The wine is
not really deep or complex, but it offers enough
fruit, some spice and bayleaf, to make it an
agreeable table companion.

Ch Poupille
map **45 J5**

owner: Jean-Marie & Philippe Carille *area:* 10.7 ha
cases: 5,650 *grape % R:* MER 85% CS 10% CF 5%
other châteaux owned: Ch Haut-Cardinal *(St-
Emilion)*; Ch Robin des Moines *(St-Emilion)*
**33350 Ste-Colombe tel: 05 57 74 43 03
fax: 05 57 74 45 12**
Poupille is an impressive, Pomerol-like special
cuvée, dominated by Merlot, with great potency,
integrated tannins, dark aromas and nuances of
both fruit and oak. The standard Ch Poupille is
more open and meant for quicker consumption.
Black cherry and blackcurrant are the fruit
notes most often found in this well-made wine.

Ch Puy Arnaud
map **45 I5**

owner: Héritiers Maurèze *area:* 5 ha *cases:* 2,500
grape % R: MER 85% CF 10% CS 5% *second wine:* Ch
Bastille *other châteaux owned:* Ch Coucy
(Montagne-St-Emilion)
**33350 Belvès-de-Castillon tel: 05 57 74 62 14
fax: 05 57 74 56 07**
In its aroma this wine is usually pleasant and
open, with a suggestion of black cherry. In the
mouth, however, it tends towards the rustic,
with a certain austerity and a slightly bitter
touch. About a third of the maturing barrels are
replaced each year.

Ch Robin
map **45 J6**

owner: Société Lurkcroft/Stéphane Asséo *area:*
12.8 ha *cases:* 6,400 *grape % R:* MER 65% CS 35%
second wine: Ch La Fleur de Robin *other châteaux
owned:* include Domaine de Courteillac *(Bordeaux
Supérieur)*

Above: Ch Robin

Above: Ch Terrasson

33350 Belvès-de-Castillon tel: 05 57 40 55 65 fax: 05 57 40 58 07
Elegant Côtes de Castillon that offers a flavoursome interplay of fresh fruit (cherry, raspberry, blackcurrant), spice, licorice and vanilla oak. A third of the maturing casks are new. The present owners bought Ch Robin in 1992.

Ch Roc de Joanin
map 45 F5
owner: Yves Mirande *area:* 4.5 ha *cases:* 2,000 *grape % R:* MER 65% CF 20% CS 15% *other châteaux owned:* Ch La Rose Côtes Rol *(St-Emilion)*
33350 St-Philippe-d'Aiguilhe tel: 05 57 24 71 28 fax: 05 57 74 40 42
A small estate offering pleasing, harmonious, open wine, with delicious fruit notes (strawberry, cherry); it is quite meaty, with good tannins.

Ch Rocher Bellevue
map 45 K4
owner: Vignobles Rocher-Cap de Rive *area:* 15 ha *cases:* 10,800 *grape % R:* MER 60% CF 27% CS 13% *second wines:* La Palène; Coutet Saint-Magne *other châteaux owned:* include Ch Cap d'Or *(St-Georges-St-Emilion)*
33350 St-Magne-de-Castillon tel: 05 57 40 08 88 fax: 05 57 40 19 93
This is a dark-coloured Côtes de Castillon, a wine with a good taste and grip, with candied, jammy black fruit and some discreet oak from 10-12 months in cask.

Ch Roquevieille
map 45 F6
owner: Jean-Pierre Palatin *area:* 11.5 ha *cases:* 5,800 *grape % R:* MER 70% CF 15% CS 15%
33350 St-Philippe-d'Aiguilhe tel: 05 57 74 47 11 fax: 05 57 24 69 08
The vineyard is sited close to the highest point in the Côtes de Castillon appellation. The wine it yields conveys impressions of spicy oak, animal scents, and the earthy elements of an autumn wood – and fruit is not lacking. Oak-matured for a short time (one-third new casks).

Ch La Rose Fayan
map 45 F8
owner: Daniel & Christiane Brückner *area:* 8.2 ha *cases:* 4,400 *grape % R:* MER 40% CS 38% CF 22%
33350 Les Salles-de-Castillon tel: 05 57 24 72 25 fax: 05 57 24 66 27
A Swiss couple replanted this vineyard between 1981 and 1991. Since '91 they have been

producing an attractive wine dominated by berry fruit. Besides some roundness it generally has a good deal of tannin from the Cabernet Sauvignon. No wood ageing

Ch Saint-Jean-Baron
map 45
owner: Renée & Benoît Fabaron *area:* 3.4 ha *cases:* 7,700 *grape % R:* MER 85% CF 10% CS 5% *other châteaux owned:* Ch Baron Lestrade *(Bordeaux Supérieur)*
33350 St-Magne-de-Castillon tel: 05 57 84 50 82
The greater part of the production from this small estate consists of the oak-aged Cuvée Spéciale, matured in 25% new barrels; a firm, rounded wine, sometimes an award winner.

Ch de Saint-Philippe
map 45 F6
owner: Philippe & Henri Bécheau *area:* 21 ha *cases:* 10,500 *grape % R:* MER 70% CF 20% CS 10% *second wine:* Ch de Génis *other châteaux owned:* Ch Haut Lalande *(Bordeaux-Côtes de Francs)*
33350 St-Philippe-d'Aiguilhe tel: 05 57 40 60 21 fax: 05 57 40 62 28
The vineyard belonging to this white château with its modern cellars was entirely reorganized from 1970 onwards. The wine has a fairly traditional personality, with an aroma that has more dark, earthy tones than fruity ones. The Cuvée Helmina has a year in mainly used casks.

Ch Terrasson
map 45 E6
owner: Christophe Lavau *area:* 14 ha *cases:* 8,800 *grape % R:* MER 80% CF 10% CS 10% *other wines:* Ch Terrasson *(Bordeaux-Côtes de Francs) other châteaux owned:* Domaine de Lagardette *(Côtes de Castillon)*
33570 Monbadon tel: 05 57 40 60 55 fax: 05 57 40 63 45
Under the same name this château produces both a Côtes de Castillon and a Côtes de Francs – with a much smaller quantity of the latter, from just 1.5 ha. Red fruit is often present in the supple Côtes de Castillon, with its tannins. The standard rises and the concentration increases with the Cuvée Prévenche, which spends a year in oak (one-third new barrels).

Ch Tour d'Horable
map 45 K6
owner: Jean-Albert Faytout *area:* 16 ha *cases:* 7,000 *grape % R:* MER 75% CF 25% *second wine:* Ch Lucas *other châteaux owned:* Ch la Rigordie *(Puisseguin-St-Emilion)*

33350 Castillon-la-Bataille tel: 05 57 40 04 98 fax: 05 57 40 04 98
Côtes de Castillon produced from vines on average 35 years old, reasonably full-bodied in taste and with jammy fruit.

Ch la Treille des Girondins
map 45 L3
owner: Alain Goumaud *area:* 19 ha *cases:* 11,000 *grape % R:* MER 60% CF 25% CS 15% *second wines:* Ch Grand Mézières; Ch Sablay
33350 St-Magne-de-Castillon tel: 05 57 40 05 38 fax: 05 57 40 26 60
Most reliable estate yielding a Côtes de Castillon that is rounded in the mouth and develops a supple taste and sufficient concentration. There is slight oak present. The influence of the casks is more prominent in the Cuvée Prestige des Girondins, which goes into *barriques* of which 30% are new. The name of the château refers to a bloody episode during the French Revolution, when the last three Girondins - adherents of the moderate Revolutionary party - were killed here.

Ch Vernon
map 45 G5
owner: Christian Lavie *area:* 9 ha *cases:* 5,500 *grape % R:* MER 50% CF 40% CS 10%
33350 St-Philippe-d'Aiguilhe tel: 05 57 40 61 47 fax: 05 57 40 61 47
Vineyard with a relatively large proportion of Cabernet, which besides its decent standard wine also produces the Réserve Prestige. This possesses a fair concentration, reasonably firm tannins, an adequate measure of berry fruit and oak from 12 months in cask – a third of these are new. At the end of the 19th century successful experiments in grafting to counter the phylloxera louse were carried out at this estate.

Vieux Château Champs de Mars
map 45 F7
owner: Régis Moro *area:* 17 ha *cases:* 9,500 *grape % R:* MER 80% CF 15% CS 5% *second wine:* Ch Puy Landry *other châteaux owned:* Ch Pelan-Bellevue *(Bordeaux-Côtes de Francs)*
33350 St-Philippe-d'Aiguilhe tel: 05 57 40 63 49
This wine often has tremendous concentration, partly thanks to the very old vines - some of them planted in 1902. In some years tannins can be massively and rather drily present, so that balanced development may prove difficult. Among the layers and nuances are those of charred oak (a third of the casks are new), animal aromas, vanilla, caramel, and jammy blackberry fruit.

APPELLATION BORDEAUX-CÔTES DE FRANCS

Ch Les Charmes-Godard   map 45 D7
owner: GFA Charmes-Godard/Famille Thienpont
area: 6.3 ha *cases:* 2,500, white 900 *grape % R:*
MER 70% CF 30% *grape % W:* SEM 60% MUSC 20%
SAUV B 20% *second wine:* Lauriol *other châteaux*
owned: include Ch Laclaverie (*Bordeaux-Côtes de*
Francs); Ch Puygueraud (*Bordeaux-Côtes de Francs*);
Vieux Château Certan (*Pomerol*)
33570 St-Cibard tel: 05 57 40 63 76
fax: 05 57 40 66 08
This modest property was bought in 1988 by
the Thienpont family, owners of Ch Puygueraud
and other estates. At first its wine was sold
under a brand name. Since the beginning of the
1990s, however, it has had the status of château
wine. In a good year the red wine has a fine,
juicy taste with unctuous, jammy fruit (cherry,
plum), attractive tannins and integrated oak.
The white is fermented in wood (50% new
casks), and has fresh, apple-like fruit,
considerable oak and an average structure.

Ch de Francs   map 45 C7
owner: Hébrard-de Boüard de Laforest *area:* 27 ha
cases: 10,000, white 400 *grape % R:* MER 60% CF
40% *grape % W:* SAUV B 50% SEM 50% *second*
wines: Ch Rozier; Ch Les Douves de Francs *other*
châteaux owned: Ch Cheval Blanc (*St-Emilion*); Ch
l'Angélus (*St-Emilion*)
33570 Francs tel: 05 57 40 65 91
fax: 05 57 40 63 04
During English rule in Aquitaine this was an
important stronghold, sheltering some 300
soldiers. Only a small part of the medieval
building remains, but even this is quite
sizeable. Since 1985 the château, cellars and
vineyard have been renovated by Hubert de
Boüard and Dominique Hébrard, of Ch
l'Angélus and Ch Cheval Blanc in St-Emilion
respectively, who are the co-owners. Their red
wine is among the best in the district: full-
bodied, seductive, with jammy fruit and fine,
supple tannins. The white wine is given a
privileged start in life in new casks and has a
nut- and toast-like aroma in which exotic fruit
can also be discerned.

Ch de Garonneau   map 45 D7
owner: EARL Roussille *area:* 20 ha *cases:* 7,500
grape % R: MER 60% CS 25% CF 15%
33570 St-Cibard tel: 05 57 40 60 74
fax: 05 57 40 60 74
A correct red Côtes de Francs, rounded and
provided with tannin; it matures in wood for
just a short period.

Ch Haut Rozier   map 45 C7
owner: René Laporte *area:* 8.4 ha *cases:* 4,700
grape % R: MER 75% CF 15% CS 10%
33570 Tayac tel: 05 57 40 63 05
In good years this is a splendid wine: intense
bouquet (bayleaf, licorice, black fruits), meaty,
juicy taste that bears out the aromas, and a
sound balance. From a less-successful vintage
the wine will taste lighter and more supple. Not
wood-aged.

Ch Laclaverie   map 45 D7
owner: Nicolas Thienpont *area:* 10 ha *cases:* 3,750
grape % R: MER 50% CS 25% CF 25% *second wine:*
Lauriol *other châteaux owned:* include Ch Les
Charmes-Godard (*Bordeaux-Côtes de Francs*); Ch
Puygueraud (*Bordeaux-Côtes de Francs*); Vieux
Château Certan (*Pomerol*)

33570 St-Cibard tel: 05 57 40 63 76
fax: 05 57 40 66 08
An estate dominated by a 15th-century tower,
and restored in stages by Georges Thienpont
and his son Nicolas. Their first vintage was
1985. The wine is balanced, does not call for too
much patience, and has a lovely, quite elegant,
taste that can have elements of licorice, spicy
oak, chocolate and blackcurrant.

Ch Marsau   map 45 C8
owner: Jean-Marie & Sylvie Chadronnier *area:* 9.5
ha *cases:* 4,500 *grape % R:* MER 85% CF 15%
33570 Francs tel: 05 57 40 67 23
fax: 05 56 02 26 41
An estate reborn through the efforts of the wine
merchant Jean-Marie Chadronnier, whose first
vintage was 1994. Marsau characteristics are a
fine creaminess, mature and smooth tannins,
nuances of currants and other fruit, of herbs
and spices, such as bayleaf, and a fine length.
The wine spends a year in barrels, half new.

Ch Moulin la Pitié   map 45 D6
owner: Dominique Clerjaud *area:* 10.5 ha *cases:*
5,300 *grape % R:* MER 60% CS 30% CF 10%
33570 St-Cibard tel: 05 57 40 62 38
The many old vines here give the wine a very
intense colour, almost black, and a taste in
which concentration, velvetiness and finesse are
deliciously combined. In addition Moulin la
Pitié has considerable fruit – cherry, fig,
blackcurrant, raisin. There is no oak-ageing.

Ch La Prade   map 45 E6
owner: Patrick Valette *area:* 4.5 ha *cases:* 2,200
grape % R: MER 80% CS 10% CF 10% *other châteaux*
owned: include Ch Pavie (*St-Emilion*); Ch de Musset
(*Montagne-St-Emilion*)
33570 St-Cibard tel: 05 57 74 40 10
fax: 05 57 24 63 99
A wine produced by Patrick Valette, of Ch Pavie,
St-Emilion. It is full of character, with firm
tannins, interesting nuances, juicy fruit: a
flavoursome creation.

Ch Puyanché   map 45 D7
owner: Joseph Arbo *area:* 31.5 ha *cases:* 16,000,
white 400 *grape % R:* MER 80% CS 10% CF 8% MAL
2% *grape % W:* SEM 55% SAUV B 40% MUSC 5% *other*
châteaux owned: Ch Haut des Coines (*Bordeaux*
Supérieur)
33570 Francs tel: 05 57 40 65 77
Estate that broke away from the cooperative in
about 1990. It was named after Armance
Puanché, a hard-working grower who started
cultivating vines here at the beginning of the
20th century. A small but increasing part of the
vintage is bottled at the château itself. The red
is of a very decent quality, with fruit and oak;
the white, which is also cask-aged, is expressive,
soft and fresh.

Ch Puygueraud   map 45 E6
owner: Georges Thienpont *area:* 30 ha *cases:*
15,000 *grape % R:* MER 55% CF 30% CS 15% *second*
wine: Clos des Bories *other châteaux owned:*
include Ch Les Charmes-Godard (*Bordeaux-Côtes de*
Francs); Ch Laclaverie (*Bordeaux-Côtes de Francs*);
Vieux Château Certan (*Pomerol*)
33570 St-Cibard tel: 05 57 40 61 04
fax: 05 57 40 66 07
The rise of Côtes de Francs as a wine district is
to a great extent due to the efforts of the

Thienpont family at Ch Puygueraud. Replanting
began in 1979, and the first wine was launched
in 1983. This vintage was so good that it put
Côtes de Francs on the wine map for the first
time; soon several winegrowers from St-
Emilion were investing in the district.
Puygueraud has stayed at the top. It is a Côtes
de Francs of an often amazing complexity, at
once rich and lively, with jammy fruit and great
potential for ageing. Oak maturing usually lasts
for 16 months; each year a quarter of the
barriques are new.

Ch Les Rivaux   map 45 B6
owner: Gérard Marighetto *area:* 7.4 ha *cases:*
2,500 *grape % R:* MER 50% CS 25% CF 25%
33570 Tayac tel: 05 57 40 62 65
fax: 05 57 40 64 58
After changing hands in 1972 this vineyard was
entirely replanted. Since 1982 picking has been
mechanized; there is no maturing in cask. The
wine is of moderate quality, and would benefit
from having more depth and concentration. For
drinking young.

Ch du Vieux Chêne   map 45 E6
owner: GFA L. Vincent-Dalloz *area:* 3.8 ha *cases:*
1,850 *grape % R:* MER 100% *other châteaux*
owned: Ch Les Hauts de Granges (*Côtes de*
Castillon)
33570 St-Cibard tel: 05 57 40 62 20
fax: 05 57 40 64 79
A wine that one would choose not for its
strength or its nuances, but for its supple fruit,
its freshness and clean flavours.

Vignoble d'Alfred   map 45 B5
owner: Alfred Charrier *area:* 1.5 ha *cases:* 700
grape % R: MER 40% CF 30% CS 30% *other châteaux*
owned: Ch Lapeyronie (*Côtes de Castillon*)
33350 Ste-Colombe tel: 05 57 40 19 27
fax: 05 57 40 14 38
Miniature estate where since 1993 the wine has
been made by the talented Jean-Frédéric
Lapeyronie, of Ch Lapeyronie, Côtes de
Castillon. Delightful wine marked by its
Cabernets: velvety, firm and aromatic, with
noble oak elements.

Below: Ch Puygueraud

BOURG AND BLAYE

These two areas taken together make more wine than the top six Médoc ACs, and more than St-Emilion. Located on the Right Bank, the Bourgeais faces Margaux across the Gironde estuary, while the riverside section of the vast Blayais area – Bordeaux's most northern appellation – is closer to St-Julien. They are separated from the other leading Right-Bank areas, the Libournais vineyards to the south-east, by a large tract of land which has the basic generic Bordeaux and Bordeaux Supérieur appellations.

Of the two, the Blayais is by far the larger area: at 60,000 hectares, much of it devoted to general agriculture rather than vines, it easily dwarfs the Bourgeais. From the historically important port of Blaye, some 50 kilometres downstream from Bordeaux, the area fans out to the east and north as far as the *département* of the Charente-Maritime, famed for the production of Cognac.

Tucked under the Blayais' southern wing, next to the Gironde estuary, is the much more compact area of the Bourgeais. The town of Bourg itself is opposite the Bec d'Ambès, at the confluence of the Gironde and Dordogne, and many of the vineyards, spread across the crests of three hills, look out over these rivers.

This is fairly high and hilly countryside – locally the Côtes de Bourg is known as 'the Switzerland of the Gironde' – and one of the loftiest points of the Gironde *département* is at Berson (65 metres) near the Blaye/Bourg boundary. The wide range of soils and aspects includes some good south-facing sites on limestone, or sometimes clay-limestone.

Until quite recently the Blaye vineyards in particular were very important for white wine production, much of which was distilled. Today, however, only a little white wine is made under these appellations – roughly ten per cent in the Blayais and less than a minuscule one per cent in the Bourgeais. These white wines can be very good, especially those containing a high percentage of Sauvignon, which have fresh, flowery aromas and good grip on the palate.

This is red wine country, though, and in spite of their difference in size the two areas produce roughly the same amount under their respective specific appellations – some two million cases a year. This similarity is explained by the fact that a large percentage of Blayais land is devoted to the production of generic Bordeaux and Bordeaux Supérieur wines.

The styles of red wine made in these two areas vary from those with a certain rustic charm – highly coloured, powerful and with red fruits to the fore, which are best drunk within a couple of years of the vintage – to the more elegant and creamy, with greater finesse and staying power. A high percentage of these wines – which can often be very good value and are worth seeking out – never leave the borders of France, but leading export markets include Belgium, Germany, Holland, Denmark and the UK.

THE BLAYAIS
These vineyards are spread across an impressive 41 communes, yet only 4,000 hectares are planted with vines which are permitted in one or other of the Blayais

appellations. There are actually three tiers of appellations here, and the main distinction between them – unusually for Bordeaux – is neither land nor method of production, but grape varieties. This is especially true for the white wines.

The basic appellation is the AC Blaye or Blayais, which can be used (although it rarely is) for both red and white wines. A very wide range of grape varieties is permitted. The next tier is the Côtes de Blaye, which is limited to white wine only and which, since the 1995 vintage, has to include at least 60 per cent Colombard in the blend. Some white wine is now also being produced under the Premières Côtes de Blaye appellation: the blend must be made up of at least 70 per cent of either Sauvignon Blanc, Sémillon or Muscadelle, although Sauvignon Blanc is usually the preferred variety these days. The major usage of the Premières Côtes de Blaye appellation, however, is still for the red wines produced in this area, which account for some 90 per cent of the total production. The major grape variety is Merlot, followed by Cabernet Sauvignon and Cabernet Franc.

Some of the Blayais estates are quite large in size – about 20 hectares – and there are six cooperatives, each with around a hundred members.

BOURG

The Bourg vineyards cover almost 4,000 hectares located within a single canton (an arrangement unique in Bordeaux) and are spread throughout 15 communes. There is just one appellation here: Côtes de Bourg, devoted essentially to the production of red wine, but also permitted for white. Although the alternative names Bourg or Bourgeais were used in the past, it is very doubtful that you would now see them on a label.

There are a few great domaines in this area, but most of the estates are small, family-run affairs. Cooperatives are important, and the four main ones (Gauriac, Lansac, Pugnac and Tauriac) are responsible for about a quarter of the total production.

There has been a recent upsurge in interest in Côtes de Bourg, with winemakers from other Bordeaux areas searching out favoured corners with the best sites and microclimates: this is an area to watch. Some of the riverside vineyards are very attractively placed and the local climate is one of the warmest in the Gironde. Bourg's historic importance may return.

Bourg is an attractive port on the lower Dordogne, with views across to the Médoc

---

THE APPELLATIONS

CÔTES DE BOURG (red and dry white)

Location: 30 km north of Bordeaux on the right banks of the Dordogne and Gironde rivers. To the north and east is Blaye.
Area of AC: 7,017 ha
Area under vine: 3,727 ha
Communes: All lie within a single canton (the only appellation to do so): Bayon, Bourg, Comps, Gauriac, Lansac, Mombrier, Prignac-et-Marcamps, a part of Pugnac, St-Ciers-de-Canesse, St-Seurin-de-Bourg, St-Trojan, Samonac, Tauriac, Teuillac, Villeneuve
Average annual production: 2,200,000 cases (less than 1% is white)
Classed growths: None   **Others:** 310
Cooperatives: 4 (c. 300 members)
Main grape varieties: Red: Merlot, Cabernet Franc, Cabernet Sauvignon
Others: Red: Malbec; White: Sémillon, Sauvignon, Muscadelle
Main soil types: Diverse: alluvia, limestone, sandy-clayey gravel, clay-limestone

PREMIÈRES CÔTES DE BLAYE INCLUDING CÔTES DE BLAYE AND BLAYE/BLAYAIS (red and dry white)

Location: On the right bank of the Gironde estuary, about 50 km from Bordeaux. To the south is the Côtes de Bourg and to the east a large area of land covered by the Bordeaux AC. All three ACs cover the same area. Premières Côtes de Blaye and Blaye/Blayais are for red and white. Côtes de Blaye is white. Premières Côtes de Blaye has stricter conditions on viticulture and (for reds) yield.
Area of AC: 19,665 ha
Area under vine: 4,000 ha
Communes: 41, in three cantons. Canton of Blaye: Berson, Blaye, Campugnan, Cartelègue, Cars, Fours, Mazion, Plassac, St-Androny, St-Genès-de-Blaye, St-Martin-Lacaussade, St-Paul, St-Seurin-de-Cursac. Canton of St-Savin: Cavignac, Cézac, Civrac-de-Blaye, Cubnezais, Donnezac, Générac, Laruscade, Marcenais, Marsas, St-Christoly-de-Blaye, St-Girons-d'Aiguevives, St-Mariens, St-Savin, St-Vivien-de-Blaye, St-Yzan-de-Soudiac, Saugon. Canton of St-Ciers-sur-Gironde: Anglade, Braud-et-St-Louis, Etauliers, Eyrans, Marcillac, Pleine-Selve, Reignac, St-Aubin-de-Blaye, St-Caprais-de-Blaye, St-Ciers-sur-Gironde, St-Palais. Also part of the commune of Pugnac, in the Canton of Bourg, which corresponds to the former commune of Lafosse
Average annual production: 2,200,000 cases (90% red; 10% white, including Côtes de Blaye and Blaye/Blayais)
Classed growths: None   **Others:** 520
Cooperatives: 6 (c. 600 members)
Main grape varieties: Red: Merlot; White: Sauvignon, Sémillon, Muscadelle, Colombard (for Côtes de Blaye)
Others: Red: Cabernets Sauvignon & Franc, Malbec White: Ugni Blanc
Main soil types: Clay-limestone, clay-gravel, sandy clay

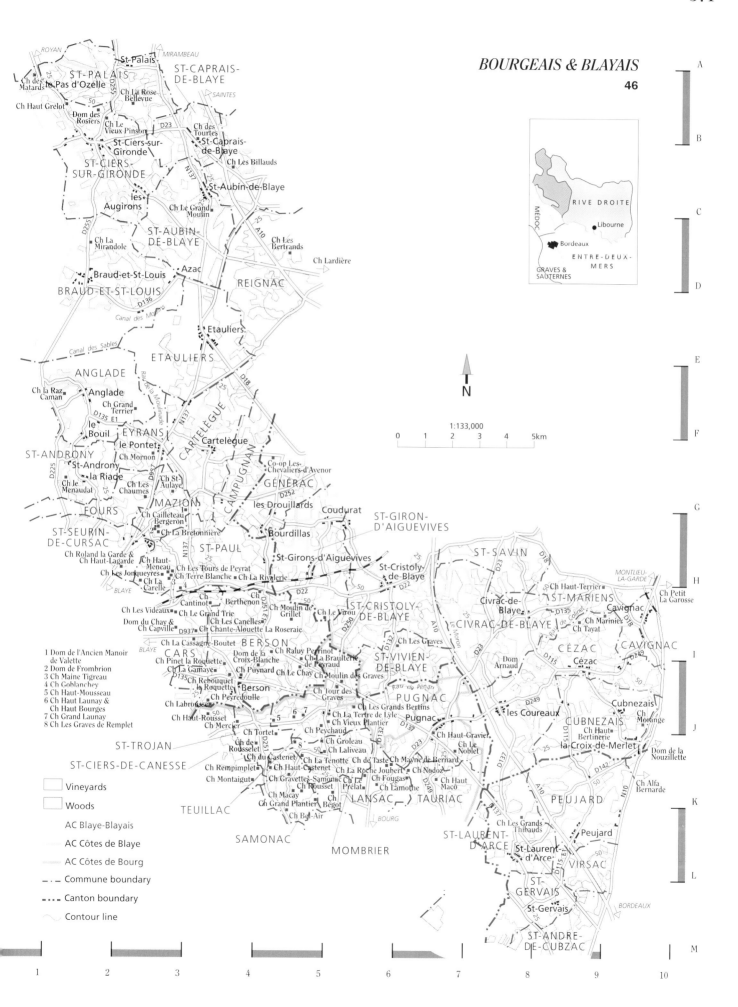

BOURGEAIS & BLAYAIS
46

ROYAN
St-Palais
MIRAMBEAU
St-Palais
ST-PALAIS
ST-CAPRAIS-DE-BLAYE
Ch des Matards
le Pas d'Ozelle
Ch La Rose Bellevue
SAINTES
Ch Haut Grelot
Dom des Rosiers
Ch Le Vieux Pinson
D23
Ch des Tourtes
St-Ciers-sur-Gironde
St-Caprais-de-Blaye
ST-CIERS-SUR-GIRONDE
N137
Ch Les Billauds
les Augirons
St-Aubin-de-Blaye
Ch Le Grand Moulin
A10
Ch La Mirandole
ST-AUBIN-DE-BLAYE
Ch Les Bertrands
D225
Braud-et-St-Louis
Azac
Ch Lardière
BRAUD-ET-ST-LOUIS
REIGNAC
D136
Canal des Moulins
Etauliers
Canal des Sables
ETAULIERS
ANGLADE
Ch la Raz Caman
Anglade
Rau de la Moulinade
D18
Ch Grand Terrier
le Bouil
D135 E1
EYRANS
CARTELÈGUE
N137
Cartelègue
ST-ANDRONY
le Pontet
Ch Mornon
CAMPUGNAN
Co-op Les-Chevaliers-d'Avenor
D997
St-Androny
la Riade
Ch St-Aulaye
GÉNÉRAC
Ch Le Menaudat
D225
Ch Les Chaumes
D252
les Drouillards
Coudurat
ST-GIRON-D'AIGUEVIVES
FOURS
MAZION
Ch Cailleteau Bergeron
Bourdillas
ST-SEURIN-DE-CURSAC
2
Ch La Bretonnière
ST-PAUL
St-Girons-d'Aiguevives
ST-SAVIN
D22
D18
Ch Roland la Garde &
Ch Haut-Lagarde
Ch Haut-Meneau
Ch Les Tours de Peyrat
St-Cristoly-de-Blaye
MONTLIEU-LA-GARDE
BLAYE
Ch Les Jonqueyres
Ch Terre Blanche
Ch La Rivalerie
50
D22
Ch Haut-Terrier
Ch Petit La Garosse
Ch La Carelle
4
Ch Cantinot
Berthenon
Ch Moulin de Grillet
ST-CRISTOLY-DE-BLAYE
Civrac-de-Blaye
ST-MARIENS
Cavignac
Ch Les Videaux
D251 E
Ch Le Virou
D250
Ch Haut-Terrier
D135
Ch Marinier
Ch Le Grand Trie
Ch Les Canelles
Ch Les Graves
CIVRAC-DE-BLAYE
Ch Tayat
Dom du Chay &
Ch Capville
D937
Ch Chante-Alouette La Roseraie
D132
CÉZAC
CAVIGNAC
D249
Ch La Cassagne-Boutet
BERSON
Ch Raluy Perrinot
ST-VIVIEN-DE-BLAYE
Cézac
1 Dom de l'Ancien Manoir de Valette
Dom de la Croix-Blanche
Ch La Braulterie de Peyraud
Dom Arnaud
2 Dom de Frombrion
CARS
Ch Pinet la Roquette
D115
3 Ch Maine Tigreau
Ch La Gamaye
Ch Puynard
Ch Le Chay
Ch Moulin des Graves
Rau de Pénan
D115
Cubnezais
4 Ch Goblanchey
D135
Ch Rebouquet la Roquette
PUGNAC
5 Ch Haut-Mousseau
Berson
Ch Tour des Graves
D249
6 Ch Haut Launay & Ch Haut Bourges
Ch Peyredoulle
7
Ch Les Grands Bertins
les Coureaux
CUBNEZAIS
Ch Morange
7 Grand Launay
Ch Labrousset
5
6
Ch La Tertre de Lyle
Ch Haut Bertinerie
8 Ch Les Graves de Remplet
Ch Haut-Rousset
Ch Vieux Plantier
Pugnac
la-Croix-de-Merlet
Ch Mercier
Ch Peychaud
D137
Dom de la Nouzillette
ST-TROJAN
Ch Tortet
Ch Groleau
Ch Haut-Gravier
D115 E
Ch de Rousselet
8
50
Ch Le Noblet
D142
ST-CIERS-DE-CANESSE
Ch du Castenet
Ch Laliveau
D23
Ch Alfa Bernarde
Ch Rempimplet
Ch Haut-Castenet
Ch La Tenotte
Ch de Taste
Ch Mayne de Bernard
Ch Nodoz
A10
Ch Montaigut
Ch Gravettes-Samonac
Ch La Roche Joubert
Ch Haut Maco
PEUJARD
N10
Ch Rousset
Ch Prélat
Ch Fougas
Ch Macay
Ch Lamothe
Vineyards
Ch Grand Plantier
Ch Bégot
LANSAC
TAURIAC
Woods
Ch Bel-Air
N137
Ch Les Grands Thibauds
AC Blaye-Blayais
TEUILLAC
BOURG
ST-LAURENT-D'ARCE
Peujard
AC Côtes de Blaye
SAMONAC
St-Laurent-d'Arce
AC Côtes de Bourg
MOMBRIER
VIRSAC
Commune boundary
ST-GERVAIS
Canton boundary
St-Gervais
BORDEAUX
Contour line
ST-ANDRÉ-DE-CUBZAC

RIVE DROITE
MÉDOC
Libourne
Bordeaux
ENTRE-DEUX-MERS
GRAVES & SAUTERNES

N

1:133,000
0 1 2 3 4 5km

A B C D E F G H I J K L M
1 2 3 4 5 6 7 8 9 10

APPELLATION CÔTES DE BOURG

Clos Alphonse Dubreuil

owner: Isabelle & Pascal Montaut *area:* 0.5 ha
cases: 200 *grape % R:* CS 70% MER 30% *other
châteaux owned:* Ch Les Jonqueyres *(Premières
Côtes de Blaye)*
33710 Gauriac tel: 05 57 42 34 88
fax: 05 57 42 93 80
Microscopic production of a generally very
concentrated wine, well sustained by oak: half
the casks are new each year.

Ch de Barbe   map 47 G3

owner: Sovivi *area:* 64 ha *cases:* 38,000 *grape %
R:* MER 60% CS 30% CF 10% *second wine:* Ch
Brivazac; Chapelle de Barbe *(Bordeaux);* Chapelle
de Brivazac *(Bordeaux) other châteaux owned:*
include Ch La Nerthe *(Châteauneuf-du-Pape)*
33710 Villeneuve-de-Blaye tel: 05 56 64 80 51
fax: 05 56 64 94 10
The splendid château was built at the end of the
18th century, on the foundations of a medieval
castle. The cellar complex, too, is impressive. In
good years the wine, a frequent award-winner,
tastes virile and energetic: dark-toned, with some
cocoa and a slightly animal aroma. In lesser
years it is somewhat lighter and more elegant.

Ch Beauguérit   map 47 J7

owner: Richard Porcher *area:* 7.5 ha *cases:* 4,500
grape % R: MER 50% CS 40% MAL 10% *other
châteaux owned:* Ch Guionne *(Côtes de Bourg)*
33710 Lansac tel: 05 57 68 42 17
fax: 05 57 68 29 61
Sound, traditionally made wine, usually supple
and ready for drinking quite early. There is no
barrel-ageing. Since 1972 the château has
belonged to the Porcher family, who also own
Ch Guionne in Lansac.

Ch Bégot   map 46 K6

owner: Alain Gracia *area:* 16 ha *cases:* 8,750
grape % R: MER 70% CS 20% MAL 10%
33710 Lansac tel: 05 57 68 42 14
fax: 05 57 68 29 90
Since the Gracia family took over this solid-
looking *maison bourgeoise* in 1976, their
investment has included a new barrel cellar. At
present about a third of the production consists
of the Cuvée Prestige, which is matured for 12-
14 months in *barriques* of which a third are
new each year. The standard wine is reasonably
firm, with in sunny years ripe, jammy red fruit
with sweet pepper and other nuances. This is a
very correct Côtes de Bourg, with some
potential for ageing.

Ch Belair-Coubet   map 47 G4

owner: Vignobles A. Faure *area:* 23 ha *cases:*
11,500 *grape % R:* MER 65% CS 35% *second wine:*
Ch du Bois de Tau; Ch Jansenant *other châteaux
owned:* Ch Labardonne *(Bordeaux)*
33710 St-Ciers-de-Canesse tel: 05 57 64 90 06
fax: 05 57 64 90 61
A near-opaque colour characterizes the Cuvée
Spéciale which, thanks to the vanilla from the
oak barrels, has an almost mild taste – a taste,
however, in which toast, spices and red fruits
are not lacking. The standard wine is somewhat
more rustic, although it can have supple fruit,
as well as darker, more animal aspects.

Ch du Bousquet   map 47 K7

owner: SC du Château du Bousquet/Castel Frères
area: 62 ha *cases:* 34,000 *grape % R:* CS 50% MER

Above: Ch du Bousquet

50% *other châteaux owned:* include Ch d'Arcins
(Haut-Médoc); Ch Barreyres *(Haut-Médoc);* Ch
Ferrande *(Graves)*
33710 Bourg-sur-Gironde tel: 05 57 68 40 53
This large estate yields a balanced, but
sometimes rather light, Côtes de Bourg; one
that is not intended to be laid down for a long
period. Cherry, spice and bayleaf can all be
present in the aroma, with some oak as well.
The quality of the wine improves in years when
the weather has been sunnier.

Ch Le Breuil   map 47 I4

owner: GAEC Doyen & Fils *area:* 18 ha *cases:*
9,000 *grape % R:* MER 75% CS 20% MAL 5%
33710 Bayon-sur-Gironde tel: 05 57 64 80 10
fax: 05 57 64 93 75
This château stands only 500 m from the
Gironde, on the first line of hills above its
banks. An agreeable, rounded red wine is made
here, with the flavours of berry fruits.

Ch Brûlesécaille   map 47 K8

owner: Rodet *area:* 25 ha *cases:* 12,000 *grape %
R:* MER 48% CS 26% CF 22% MAL 4% *second wine:* Ch
La Gravière
33710 Tauriac tel: 05 57 68 40 31
fax: 05 57 68 21 27

◆

About Côtes de Bourg

The Syndicat viticole for the Côtes de
Bourg is located at 1, place de l'Eperon,
33710 Bourg-sur-Gironde.
Tel 05 57 68 46 47.

◆

Maps of the area

The Bourgeais and Blayeais appellation
areas are covered by maps 46 and 47. The
latter covers the riverside zone – mostly
the Côtes de Bourg, with some parts of
Blaye – in greater detail.

The whole Right Bank zone, including
Bourg and Blaye, is covered by
map 37.

This château, encircled by its vines, has
belonged to the same family since 1924 and is
among the most renowned in the district. From
this high site, with its splendid view, it yields
wines that are practically always a success for
their particular vintage – with charred oak and
vanilla, cherry and blackcurrant in the aroma.
These elements are also there in the taste,
which has character along with a certain
concentration. Maturing lasts a year at most, in
casks of which a quarter are new. The name
Brûlesécaille is said to come from French
brûler and Latin *secare*: a reference to the
burning and pruning of vines.

Ch de la Brunette   map 47 M10

owner: SCEA Lagarde Père & Fils *area:* 4.1 ha
cases: 2,200 *grape % R:* MER 70% CS 15% MAL 15%
33340 Prignac-et-Marcamps tel: 05 57 43 58 23
fax: 05 57 43 01 21
This is one of the lesser-known properties in the
Côtes de Bourg AC because no wine was made
here from 1976 to 1989. Production has re-
started now, with very pleasing results: the wine
offers a lively, supple, fruity taste, and is ready
for drinking relatively quickly. No oak-ageing
here so far.

Ch Bujan   map 47 H4

owner: Pascal Méli *area:* 15 ha *cases:* 8,000 *grape
% R:* MER 60% CS 30% MAL 10% *second wine:* Ch
Tertre Bujan; Ch Sartre Bujan
33710 Gauriac tel: 05 57 64 86 56
fax: 05 57 64 93 96
Gold and silver medals are among the evidence
for the high quality of Bujan wine.

Ch Caruel   map 47 J5

owner: Jacqueline Auduteau & ses Enfants *area:* 18
ha *cases:* 10,800 *grape % R:* MER 45% CS 25% CF
15% MAL 15% *other châteaux owned:* Ch Bellevue
(Côtes de Bourg); Ch Saint-Paulin *(Bordeaux)*
33710 Bourg-sur-Gironde tel: 05 57 68 43 07
In the 18th century Charles Auduteau, a miller,
decided to become a *vigneron*, and converted
his cornfields into a vineyard. The estate has
remained in his family ever since. Here the
Auduteaus live, in a château built between 1800
and 1830; it offers a delightful view out over the
Dordogne, and produces a delightful wine. It is

Above: Ch La Croix-Davids

Above: Ch Eyquem

meaty, fills the mouth and lingers well; the aroma combines ripe fruit (blackcurrant and other berries) with a touch of spice. No oak is involved at Ch Caruel: the wine here is both fermented and matured in tanks of concrete and stainless steel.

Ch Le Clos du Notaire   map 47 K5
owner: Roland Charbonnier *area:* 22 ha *cases:* 12,000, white 750 *grape % R:* MER 65% CS 30% MAL 5% *grape % W:* SAUV B 75% SEM 25% *second wine:* Ch Baron Bellevue *other wines:* Bordeaux blanc & rosé, Crémant de Bordeaux
33710 Bourg-sur-Gironde tel: 05 57 68 44 36 fax: 05 57 68 32 87
In the 15th century the buildings of this renowned estate formed part of the abbey of Camillac. During the 19th, various of its owners were lawyers, and one of these devised the name Cru des Notaires. The quality can be outstanding in the great years, fleshy and darkly aromatic – but sometimes rather dried out, especially in its finish, in the lesser ones. Clos du Notaire matures for an average 12 months in casks, half of them new.

Ch Colbert   map 47 I5
owner: Famille Duwer *area:* 19 ha *cases:* 10,000 *grape % R:* MER 55% CS 30% CF 10% MAL 5% *second wine:* Ch Berthou
33710 Comps tel: 05 57 64 95 04
The standard wine is perhaps rather rustic, but the oak-aged Cuvée Prestige has the cold ash and pipe tobacco aroma sometimes very typical of Côtes de Bourg. There are also spicy undertones present in this generally deep-red wine. The small Neo-Gothic, Disney-esque castle was built around 1880 after the owner at that time received a considerable sum in reward for an invention – a ship that would remain afloat thanks to its use of empty wine casks as buoyancy aids. It was called the *Colbert*.

Ch Conilh Haute-Libarde   map 47 J6
owner: Domaines Bernier *area:* 5.5 ha *cases:* 3,600 *grape % R:* MER 70% CS 20% MAL 10% *other châteaux owned:* Vieux Domaine de Taste (*Côtes de Bourg*)
33710 Bourg-sur-Gironde tel: 05 57 68 46 46 fax: 05 57 68 36 09

The black fruit of the Merlot is usually to be found in plenty in this supple wine, which does not come in contact with wood. The château is a fine 18th-century building on a high hill dominating Bourg-sur-Gironde and the river.

Ch La Croix-Davids   map 47 J7
owner: Didier Meneuvrier *area:* 37 ha *cases:* 20,500, white 500 *grape % R:* CF 55% MER 45% *grape % W:* SEM 70% SAUV B 30% *second wine:* La Mission des Davids
33710 Bourg-sur-Gironde tel: 05 57 63 40 05 fax: 05 57 63 24 82
As its name indicates, this estate had a religious origin: it was a Lazarist monastery dating back to the Romanesque period. After the French Revolution a large house was built here in the style of that time, and then the vineyard was extended. Today, a fifth of the vintage spends a year maturing in barrels of which 30% are new. The Cabernet Franc grape makes the largest contribution to the wine, which is dark-toned in both aroma and taste, and often gives impressions of tobacco.

Ch La Croix de Millorit   map 47 J4
owner: GAEC Jaubert *area:* 25 ha *cases:* 10,000 *grape % R:* MER 40% CS 20% CF 20% MAL 20% *second wine:* Ch Jaubert *other wines:* Ch La Croix (*Bordeaux rosé*) *other châteaux owned:* Ch Peyrefaure (*Côtes de Bourg*); Ch Civrac (*Côtes de Bourg*)
33710 Bayon-sur-Gironde tel: 05 57 64 84 13 fax: 05 57 64 94 11
This estate was bought in 1959 by the Jaubert family, who had returned from Algeria, and were among the first in the area to sell bottled wine. This Côtes de Bourg is somewhat rustic in character, and seldom really powerful. In its aroma, coffee, caramel and spices are more noticeable than juicy fruit.

Ch Croûte-Charlus   map 47 K7
owner: Guy Sicard *area:* 10 ha *cases:* 5,500 *grape % R:* MER 50% CS 40% MAL 10% *second wine:* Ch Croûte-Charlus (*Bordeaux Supérieur*)
33710 Bourg-sur-Gironde tel: 05 57 68 42 87
Wine that has repeatedly won awards, with a firm constitution and supple taste. It usually matures for 18 months in oak.

Ch Croûte Courpon   map 47 L8
owner: Jean-Paul Morin *area:* 7.4 ha *cases:* 3,500 *grape % R:* MER 38% CS 29% CF 20% MAL 13% *second wine:* Le Puits de Raynaud (*Bordeaux Supérieur*)
33710 Bourg-sur-Gironde tel: 05 57 68 42 81
This château, built on the site of a medieval monastery, has belonged to the same family for several generations. Casks are not used here — 'because we prefer the taste of grapes to that of wood'. The wine contains 13% Malbec, a relatively large proportion; it conveys impressions of herbs, spices, and a touch of ripe blackcurrant with other berry fruits.

Ch Eyquem   map 47 J4
owner: Vignobles Bayle-Carreau *area:* 30 ha *cases:* 19,000 *grape % R:* MER 70% CS 25% MAL 5% *second wine:* Ch Tour d'Eyquem *other châteaux owned:* Ch La Carelle (*Premières Côtes de Blaye*); Ch Barbé (*Premières Côtes de Blaye*); Ch Pardaillan (*Premières Côtes de Blaye*)
33710 Bayon-sur-Gironde tel: 05 57 64 32 43 fax: 05 57 64 22 74
Château dating from the 17th century that was the summer residence of Louis Eyquem, a relative of Michel Eyquem de Montagne, the king's counsellor in the Guyenne *parlement*. Claude Carreau and his wife bought the château and its vineyard in 1976, then carried through some drastic changes and renovations. This often deep-coloured, rustic, dark-toned wine matures for 12-15 months in used *barriques*, and it can usually be drunk quite quickly.

Ch Falfas   map 47 I5
owner: John & Véronique Cochran *area:* 22 ha *cases:* 10,000 *grape % R:* MER 55% CS 25% MAL 15% CF 5% *second wine:* Ch de Beychade
33710 Bayon-sur-Gironde tel: 05 57 64 80 41 fax: 05 57 64 93 24
Falfas is a former hunting lodge that acquired its present Louis XIII appearance in the 17th century. The château derives its name from Gaillard de Falfas, chairman of the Guyenne *parlement*, whose family owned it late in the 17th century. The present proprietors took over in 1988 and cultivate their vineyard organically. Falfas' wine is often characterized by an opaque

Above: Ch Falfas

Above: Ch De la Grave

colour and a full-bodied, lingering taste with ripe blackcurrant and blackberry fruit; cherry and plum may also be there along with leather and bayleaf. Besides the standard wine, which is matured in oak for 18 months, there is a special *cuvée*, Ch Falfas Le Chevalier. This is made from old vines, and spends 24 months in new wood. Usually the Chevaliercontains a lot of Cabernet Sauvignon, which gives the wine its markedly blackcurrant aroma. Its colour is dense, its concentration great, and its sometimes slightly dry finish lasts in the mouth for several minutes.

Ch Fougas
map **46 K7**
owner: GFA Château Fougas/Famille Béchet *area:* 11 ha *cases:* 5,500 *grape %:* MER 50% CF 25% CS 25%
33710 Lansac tel: 05 57 68 42 15
fax: 05 57 68 28 59
Although its quality fluctuates, Ch Fougas from a good year is an extremely agreeable wine: fragrant, supple, reasonably fruity, floral, and with integrated tones of oak and vanilla (after 12 months in barrels of which a third are new each year). The more expensive Maldoror *cuvée* is rather more nuanced, with somewhat more

Below: Ch Les Grands Thibauds

class. Since 1983 the owners of this estate have been leasing out vines to nearly 200 private individuals: these enthusiasts sometimes come along to help with the harvest.

Ch Grand-Jour
map **47 L10**
owner: Vignobles Rocher-Cap de Rive *area:* 98 ha *cases:* 66,500 *grape % R:* MER 70% CS 30% *second wine:* Terres Vieilles *(Bordeaux);* Ch Le Mugron *(Bordeaux Supérieur) other châteaux owned:* include Ch Cap d'Or *(St-Georges-St-Emilion)*
33710 Prignac-et-Marcamps tel: 05 57 40 08 88
fax: 05 57 40 19 93
Wine that has won gold and silver medals; it is generally meaty in the mouth and has fresh black fruit, a hint of chocolate and some oak, from 10-12 months in *barriques*. Besides this Côtes de Bourg, the estate also produces a significantly greater amount of Bordeaux Supérieur. Grand-Jour's fine château, riding high on its hill, was built at the end of the 17th century.

Ch Grand Launay
map **46 J5**
owner: Michel Cosyns *area:* 26.8 ha *cases:* 16,500, white 500 *grape % R:* MER 60% CS 30% CF 5% MAL 5% *grape % W:* SAUV B 100% *second wine:* Ch Les Hermats
33710 Teuillac tel: 05 57 64 39 03
fax: 05 57 64 22 32
An enthusiastically run family estate that used to form part of a much bigger property. Sometimes the wine is weak – the 1990, for example, which lacked depth and was short-lived – but more often it is successful, as numerous medals and other distinctions bear witness. The standard wine is accessible, with fruit, cocoa, and elegance. The Réserve Lion Noir *cuvée*, in which vanilla and oak mingle happily with ripe black and red fruits, offers more breadth and power; it matures for a year in casks, a third of them new.

Ch Les Grands Bertins
map **46 J6**
owner: Arlette Dupont *area:* 7 ha *cases:* 4,200 *grape % R:* MER 60% CS 25% MAL 15%
33710 Teuillac
tel: 05 57 64 38 00
Les Grands Bertins is generally a fairly light Côtes de Bourg, matured for 18 months in tanks rather than barrels.

◆
Quantities
Figures are as supplied by the châteaux.

Area of vineyard: given in hectares, abbreviated to ha. Châteaux are asked to specify vineyards in production, and to exclude from their answers those owned but unplanted, and to advise when extensions are planned.

Production: given in cases of 12 bottles, each of 0.75 litres. A case is thus 9 litres. A hectolitre is 100 litres or just over 11 cases.

Yield per hectare: to calculate a property's yield in hectolitres per hectare (hl/ha), multiply the 'cases' figure by 9, to give production in litres, then divide by 100, to give hectolitres. Then divide the result by the area in hectares.

Ch Les Grands Thibauds
map **46 L8**
owner: Daniel Plantey *area:* 18 ha *cases:* 9,500 *grape % R:* MER 70% CS 15% MAL 15% *second wine:* Ch St-Laurent *other châteaux owned:* include Clos de la Baronnerie *(Premières Côtes de Blaye)*
33240 St-Laurent-d'Arce tel: 05 57 43 08 37
Correct, smooth wine, on the rustic side, which gives vague impressions of chocolate combined with blackcurrant. Cask-ageing lasts 10-12 months.

Ch De la Grave
map **47 J6**
owner: Philippe Bassereau *area:* 45 ha *cases:* 20,000 *grape % R:* MER 70% CS 20% MAL 10% *second wine:* Ch Maine d'Arman *other châteaux owned:* Ch La Croix de Bel-Air *(Côtes de Bourg)*
33710 Bourg-sur-Gironde tel: 05 57 68 41 49
fax: 05 57 68 99 26
Photogenic château restored in Louis XIII style in about 1835. It stands above a romantic valley, and the owners have a collection of turtledoves in large aviaries. The classically made and matured wine – eight months in *barriques*, a third of them new – has an energetic, reasonably full-bodied taste with elements of toast and oak. Very reliable.

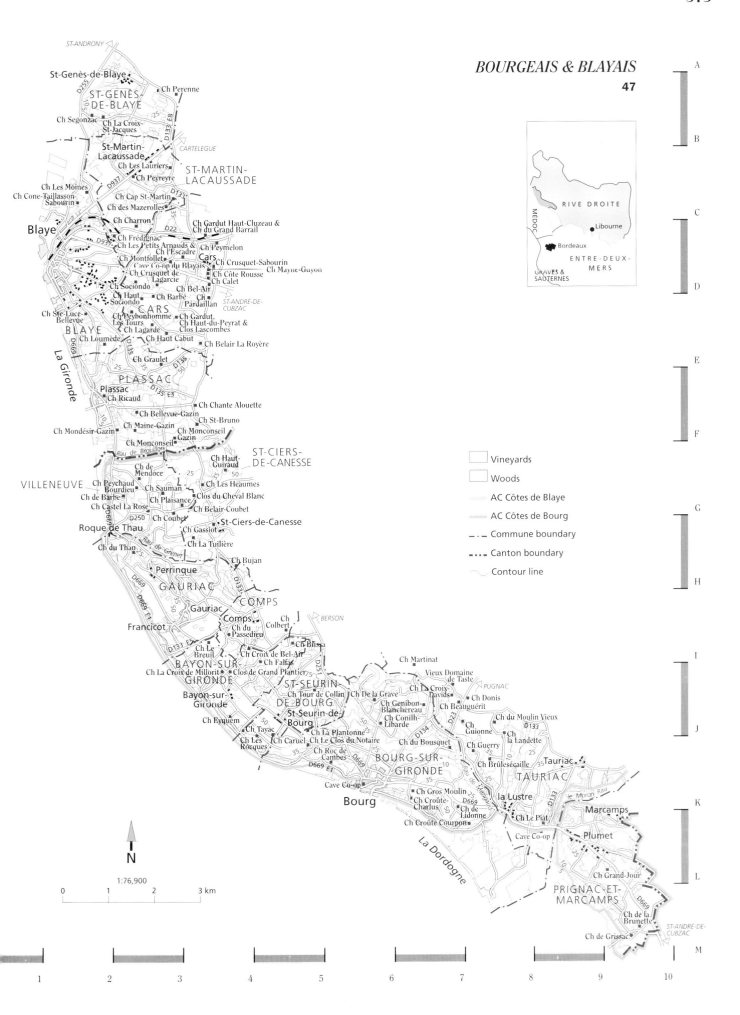

ST-ANDRONY

St-Genès-de-Blaye

ST-GENÈS-
DE-BLAYE

Ch Perenne

Ch Segonzac   Ch La Croix-
St-Jacques

St-Martin-
Lacaussade   CARTELEGUE

Ch Les Lauriers

Ch Peyreyre   ST-MARTIN-
LACAUSSADE

Ch Les Moines
Ch Cone-Taillasson-   Ch Cap St-Martin
Sabourin
Ch des Mazerolles

Ch Charron   Ch Gardut Haut-Cluzeau &
Ch du Grand Barrail

Blaye   Ch Frédignac
Ch Les Petits Arnauds &   Ch Peymelon
Ch l'Escadre
Ch Montfollet   Cars
Cave Co-op du Blayais   Ch Crusquet-Sabourin
Ch Crusquet de   Ch Mayne-Guyon
Lagarcie   Ch Côte Rousse
Ch Calet
Ch Sociondo   Ch Bel-Air
Ch Haut   Ch Barbé
Sociondo   Ch Pardaillan
ST-ANDRÉ-DE-
Ch Peybonhomme   Ch Gardut,   CUBZAC
Ch Ste-Luce-   Les Tours   Ch Haut-du-Peyrat &
Bellevue   Ch Lagarde   Clos Lascombes
BLAYE   Ch Loumède   Ch Haut Cabut
Ch Belair La Royère

Ch Graulet

La Gironde   PLASSAC

Plassac
Ch Ricaud   Ch Chante Alouette

Ch Bellevue-Gazin
Ch St-Bruno
Ch Maine-Gazin
Ch Mondésir-Gazin   Ch Monconseil
Gazin
Ch Monconseil   ST-CIERS-
DE-CANESSE
Rau de Brouillon   Ch Haut-
Guiraud
Ch de
VILLENEUVE   Mendoce   Ch Les Héaumes
Ch Peychaud
Bourdieu   Ch Sauman
Ch de Barbe   Clos du Cheval Blanc
Ch Plaisance
Ch Castel La Rose   Ch Belair-Coubet
Ch Coubet
Roque de Thau   Ch Gassiot   St-Ciers-de-Canesse
Ch La Tuilière
Ch du Thau
Rau de Grenet
Ch Bujan
Perrinque

GAURIAC   COMPS   BERSON

Gauriac   Comps   Ch
Colbert
Ch du
Francicot   Passedieu   Ch Blissa
Ch Le
Breuil   Ch Croix de Bel-Air   Ch Martinat
BAYON-SUR-   Ch Falfas
Ch La Croix de Millorit   Clos de Grand Plantier   Vieux Domaine
GIRONDE   de Taste
ST-SEURIN-   PUGNAC
Bayon-sur-   DE-BOURG   Ch Tour de Collin   Ch De la Grave
Gironde   Ch Croix   Ch Donis
St-Seurin-de-   Davids
Ch Eyquem   Ch Génibon-   Ch Beauguérit
Bourg   Blanchereau
Ch La Plantonne   Ch Conilh-   Ch du Moulin Vieux
Ch Tayac   Libarde
Ch Caruel   Ch Le Clos du Notaire   Ch du Bousquet
Ch Les   Ch   Ch
Rocques   Ch Roc de   Guionne   la Landette
Cambes   BOURG-SUR-   Ch Guerry
GIRONDE   Ch Brûlesécaille   Tauriac
Cave Co-op   Ch Gros Moulin   la Lustre   TAURIAC   Marcamps
Ch Croûte-   Ch de
Charlus   Lidonne
Bourg   Ch Le Piat   Plumet
Ch Croûte Courpon   Cave Co-op
La Dordogne   Ch Grand-Jour

N   PRIGNAC-ET-
1:76,900   MARCAMPS
0   1   2   3 km   Ch de la
Brunette   ST-ANDRÉ-DE-
Ch de Grissac   CUBZAC

Vineyards

Woods

AC Côtes de Blaye

AC Côtes de Bourg

Commune boundary

Canton boundary

Contour line

RIVE DROITE

Libourne

Bordeaux

ENTRE-DEUX-
MERS

MEDOC

GRAVES &
SAUTERNES

A   B   C   D   E   F   G   H   I   J   K   L   M

1   2   3   4   5   6   7   8   9   10

Above: Ch de Grissac

Ch Gravettes-Samonac   map 46 K5
owner: Gérard Giresse **area:** 25 ha **cases:** 15,000 **grape % R:** MER 70% CS 15% CF 15% **second wine:** Ch Thuillac
33710 Samonac tel: 05 57 68 21 16
fax: 05 57 68 36 43
When Gérard Giresse took over this estate from his parents in 1985 he was able to more than double the vineyard area with land belonging to his wife. He also installed stainless-steel fermentation tanks. The wine is a good Côtes de Bourg that lingers well, with its smooth tannins and some toast. Its aroma is dominated by dark and animal tones. Sometimes a superior version is brought out; it receives more ageing in oak – all of it is matured in cask rather than the 30% of the standard wine – and is more nuanced. It is sold with a numbered label.

Ch de Grissac   map 47 M10
owner: GFA du Château de Grissac/Bernadette Cottavoz **area:** 25 ha **cases:** 15,000 **grape % R:** MER 65% CS 30% MAL 5% **second wine:** Ch Mayne de Grissac (Bordeaux Supérieur)
33710 Prignac-et-Marcamps tel: 05 57 43 01 17
fax: 05 57 43 01 17
The château here was built in 1652 on the site of a medieval fortress. De Grissac produces a fairly round, solidly-built wine; a superior version is oak-aged.

Ch Groleau   map 46 K5
owner: Didier Raboutet **area:** 18 ha **cases:** 8,000 **grape % R:** MER 70% CS 25% CF 5% **other châteaux owned:** Ch Le Chay (Premières Côtes de Blaye)
33710 Mombrier tel: 05 57 64 39 50
fax: 05 57 64 25 08
A wine of an average, honourable quality, matured for a year in casks; a quarter of the barrels are new. It becomes ready for drinking relatively early.

Ch Gros Moulin   map 47 K7
owner: Jacques Eymas **area:** 34 ha **cases:** 17,000 **grape % R:** MER 60% CS 30% MAL 10% **second wine:** Ch Croûte-Mallard
33710 Bourg-sur-Gironde tel: 05 57 68 41 56
fax: 05 57 68 21 26
The wine from this estate, founded in 1757, perhaps lacks some intensity and excitement, but it nevertheless offers a pleasant, aromatic

medley of bayleaf, spice, plum and cherry. In the 1980s the maximum time spent in cask was increased from three to nine months.

Ch Guerry   map 47 K8
owner: Betrand De Rivoyre **area:** 23 ha **cases:** 12,000 **grape % R:** MER 50% CS 30% MAL 20% **other châteaux owned:** include Ch Fourcas-Hosten (Listrac-Médoc)
33710 Tauriac tel: 05 57 68 20 78
fax: 05 57 68 41 31
Guerry's château sits high on its hilltop; Guerry's wine sits high among the top wines of the district.

Ch Guiet
owner: Stéphane Heurlier **area:** 9.5 ha **cases:** 5,400 **grape % R:** MER 70% CS 30% **other châteaux owned:** Ch La Bretonnière (Premières Côtes de Blaye)
33390 Mazion tel: 05 57 64 59 23
fax: 05 57 64 59 23
Pleasant, well-made wine which displays a juicy roundness and, in particular, black fruit. No wood is used here.

Below: Ch Guionne

Ch Guionne   map 47 J7
owner: Richard Porcher **area:** 14 ha **cases:** 8,600 **grape % R:** MER 50% CS 45% MAL 5% **other wines:** Bordeaux rosé **other châteaux owned:** Ch Beauguérit (Côtes de Bourg)
33710 Lansac tel: 05 57 68 42 17
fax: 05 57 68 29 61
Estate set in the heart of the Côtes de Bourg, its clay and limestone vineyard facing south. The highest quality here is represented by the Cuvée Bois Neuf, which has potential for ageing. However, the standard wine also merits attention: a stimulating, elegantly firm taste with berry fruit and suppleness.

Ch Haut-Castenet   map 46 K5
owner: Michel Adouin **area:** 10 ha **cases:** 6,200 **grape % R:** MER 50% CS 20% CF 20% MAL 10%
33710 Samonac tel: 05 57 64 35 97
There is something of tobacco and cold ash in the aroma, together with some fruit and a modest dose of tannin. Haut-Castanet's wine gains in both concentration and substance in sunny years.

Ch Haut-Gravier   map 46 J7
owner: Francis Petit **area:** 11 ha **cases:** 5,500 **grape % R:** MER 80% CS 20%
33710 Pugnac tel: 05 57 68 81 01
fax: 05 57 68 83 17
This is a barrel-aged wine, vinified and matured by the cooperative at Pugnac. Characteristically it displays dark berry fruits, supple tannins, some toast and vanilla.

Ch Haut-Guiraud   map 47 G4
owner: Christophe Bonnet **area:** 35 ha **cases:** 15,500 **grape % R:** MER 70% CS 30% **other châteaux owned:** Ch Castaing (Côtes de Bourg); Ch Guiraud-Grimard (Côtes de Bourg)
33710 St-Ciers-de-Canesse
tel: 05 57 64 91 39 fax: 05 57 64 88 05
The present vineyard, with its delightful view out across the Gironde, has been gradually enlarged by the family that owns it: succeeding generations have been buying additional plots since 1856. In 1957 it was in fact doubled in size. As well as the very honourable standard Côtes de Bourg made here, there is a special cuvée which is aged for a year in wood, a third of the barrels being new. This is sound, supple, mouthfilling wine with some distinction, endowed with both vanilla and fruit, including red and black currants.

♦
Grape varieties

Main and other permitted varieties for each appellation are given in the appellation fact box at the end of the relevant introduction. For châteaux, percentages of grapes grown are given as supplied by the château.

The abbreviations used are:
CF Cabernet Franc,
COL Colombard, CS Cabernet Sauvignon,
MAL Malbec, MER Merlot, MUSC Muscadelle,
PV Petit Verdot, SAUV B Sauvignon Blanc,
SEM Sémillon

Ugni Blanc is not abbreviated, nor are rarer varieties such as Merlot Blanc and Carmenère.

Above: Ch Lamothe

Ch Haut Macô
map 46 K7

owner: Bernard & Jean Mallet *area:* 49 ha *cases:* 26,000 *grape % R:* MER 50% CS 50% *second wine:* Ch Robert *other wines:* Domaine de Lilotte *(Bordeaux)*; Le Clairet de Haut Macô *(Bordeaux Clairet)*

33710 Tauriac tel: 05 57 68 81 26

fax: 05 57 68 91 97

One of the best wines of the district, the Cuvée Jean Bernard, matures in the semicircular cellar at this château. After spending 8-12 months in new *barriques* it is full-bodied and firm in taste: dark-toned, with wood, fresh toast and cocoa on a foundation of tannin. The standard wine is more elegant; its fruit (blackcurrant, blackberry) clearly comes from the Cabernet Sauvignon.

Ch Haut-Mousseau
map 46 J5

owner: Dominique Briolais *area:* 33 ha *cases:* 18,000 *grape % R:* MER 60% CS 40% *other châteaux owned:* Ch Terrefort-Bellegrave *(Médoc)*; Ch Pontac Gadet *(Côtes de Bourg)*

33710 Teuillac tel: 05 57 64 34 38

fax: 05 57 64 31 73

Production here has increased sevenfold since 1978 and is sold direct to over 10,000 customers, mainly French. Thanks to its structure and tannin, the wine will age well. In both aroma and taste there are in particular elements of leather, bayleaf and oak, with hints of game and pepper, and some fruit. Besides the standard wine there is a Cuvée Prestige.

Ch Haut-Rousset
map 46 J4

owner: Joël Grellier *area:* 42 ha *cases:* 25,000 *grape % R:* MER 80% CS 20% *second wine:* Ch La Renardière *other châteaux owned:* Ch Terre Blanche *(Premières Côtes de Blaye)*

33710 St-Ciers-de-Canesse tel: 05 57 64 92 45

fax: 05 57 64 89 27

◆

Bordeaux & Bordeaux Supérieur

Many estates within and close to the Bourgeais use these generic appellations. For the adjoining areas see map 34.

Above: Ch Macay

Machines pick the grapes here, but maturing is traditional: 8-10 months in oak (one-sixth new casks). Much Merlot gives it juicy fruit, with a roundness and an often licorice aroma. There are plans to enlarge the vineyard by 10 ha.

Ch Les Heaumes
map 47 G4

owner: Max Robin *area:* 18 ha *cases:* 10,000 *grape % R:* MER 70% CF 20% CS 5% MAL 5% *second wine:* Ch Graveyrou *other châteaux owned:* Ch Gazin-Montaigu *(Premières Côtes de Blaye)*

33710 St-Ciers-de-Canesse tel: 05 57 64 92 11

The Robin family has been making wine here since the 17th century. That experience can be tasted in the wine, which after a long spell in cask comes across pleasingly, with supple roundness and considerable substance.

Ch Laliveau
map 46 K6

owner: Geneviève Durand *area:* 6.8 ha *cases:* 3,600 *grape % R:* MER 34% CS 33% MAL 33%

33710 Mombrier tel: 05 57 64 33 00

A Côtes de Bourg of classic style is produced from this estate, with rounded tannins, animal aromas, fruit and a hint of spicy oak.

Below: Ch de Mendoce

Ch Lamothe
map 46 K6

owner: Anne Pousse & Michel Pessonnier *area:* 23 ha *cases:* 10,000 *grape % R:* MER 60% CS 30% MAL 10% *second wine:* Ch Lamothe-Joubert

33710 Lansac tel: 05 57 68 41 07

fax: 05 57 68 46 62

This château dates from the mid-19th century, and has been in the hands of the same family since 1900. Pleasant wine, not the utmost in refinement, but certainly it offers berry fruit. There is also a Grande Réserve. In contrast to the standard wine, this is aged for a year in casks, 25% of them new.

Ch la Landette
map 47 J8

owner: Guy & Sylvie Bardeau *area:* 10 ha *cases:* 6,000, white 100 *grape % R:* MER 50% CS 25% MAL 25% *grape % W:* SAUV B 100% *other wines:* Bordeaux rosé

33710 Tauriac tel: 05 57 68 35 38

fax: 05 57 68 35 38

Four wines are made here, including a white Côtes de Bourg and a Bordeaux rosé. The red Côtes de Bourg, oak-aged and reasonably rounded, merits attention. It is given a year in cask and has a somewhat rustic character.

Ch de Lidonne
map 47 K7

owner: Famille Audoire *area:* 18 ha *cases:* 11,000 *grape % R:* MER 60% CS 30% MAL 10%

33710 Bourg-sur-Gironde tel: 05 57 68 47 52

In the 15th century this wine estate was run by a religious order who made communion wine and offered shelter and hospitality to pilgrims – the name comes from *lit donné*, literally 'given bed'. The *chai* stands in the shade of four centuries-old cedars, and it is here that the wine spends at least 18 months in tanks. This Côtes de Bourg is apt to be rather closed in its youth, with austere tannins, but its charm increases after four to six years in bottle.

Ch Macay
map 46 K5

owner: Eric & Bernard Latouche *area:* 25 ha *cases:* 13,000 *grape % R:* MER 65% CF 15% CS 10% MAL 10% *second wine:* Les Forges de Macay; Ch Samonac

33710 Samonac tel: 05 57 68 41 50

fax: 05 57 68 35 23

Above: Ch Nodoz

Estate named after a Scottish officer, and now dynamically run by two brothers: in 1987 they built a completely new cellar. Wine from Macay (pronounced *Macaille*) lingers beautifully on the palate and is firm without being fat or too full-bodied. Its fresh fruit usually tends towards blackcurrant. For its year-long maturing a quarter of the casks are new each vintage.

Ch Martinat   map 47 J7
owner: SCEV Marsaux-Donze **area:** 9 ha **cases:** 4,700 **grape % R:** MER 70% CF 30% **other châteaux owned:** Ch Grand Chemin *(Côtes de Bourg)*; Ch Les Donats *(Premières Côtes de Blaye)*
33710 Lansac tel: 05 57 68 34 98
fax: 05 57 68 35 39
Taken over by new owners in 1994, who immediately made some improvements. The quality of their first vintages makes this an estate worth watching. The wine matures for a year in barrels, a third of them new.

Ch de Mendoce   map 47 G3
owner: Philippe Darricarrère **area:** 14.8 ha **cases:** 7,000 **grape % R:** MER 70% CS 20% CF 5% MAL 5% **other châteaux owned:** Ch Mille-Secousses *(Bordeaux Supérieur)*; Ch de Rider *(Bordeaux Supérieur)*
33710 Villeneuve tel: 05 57 68 34 95
fax: 05 57 68 34 91
This château is one of the rare surviving examples of the Gironde's 15th- and 16th-century rural architecture. The stately building of light-coloured stone is flanked by *towers* with loopholes and stands in a broad park. On its north side there is a very old *pigeonnier* or dovecote. Mendoce wine is characteristically supple and meant for drinking within three years. The Cuvée Spéciale is matured in cask for 18 months, and has more depth to offer.

Ch Mercier   map 46 J4
owner: Philippe & Martine Chéty **area:** 23 ha **cases:** 10,500, white 900 **grape % R:** MER 40% CS 30% CF 20% MAL 10% **grape % W:** SAUV B 60% SEM 20% MUSC 20% **second wine:** Ch Marguerite de Fonneuve **other wines:** Bordeaux rosé **other châteaux owned:** Ch La Cottière *(Côtes de Bourg)*
33710 St-Trojan tel: 05 57 64 92 34
fax: 05 57 64 83 37
With its deep, opaque colour, its smoky and toast-like aroma, which also offers sweet pepper

and cocoa, Mercier's becomingly fruity Cuvée Prestige is a very superior Côtes de Bourg. The Chéty family gives it a year in barrels of which a third are new. No wood touches the ordinary red wine, but this supple creation can also be delightful. Ch Mercier, which has belonged to the same family for a dozen generations, is one of the few estates where a really attractive white Côtes de Bourg is produced.

Ch Montaigut   map 46 K4
owner: François de Pardieu **area:** 31 ha **cases:** 15,000, white 500 **grape % R:** MER 65% CS 15% CF 15% MAL 5% **grape % W:** SAUV B 60% SEM 20% MUSC 20% **second wine:** Ch Peyrolan **other wines:** Bordeaux rosé
33710 St-Ciers-de-Canesse tel: 05 57 64 92 49
fax: 05 57 64 94 20
The name Montaigut comes from an owner at the beginning of the 20th century, but the château was already several decades old by then. Between 1962 and 1975, the vineyard was considerably enlarged by the purchase of further small plots. Since 1976 the estate has belonged to François de Pardieu, a passionate producer who makes a wine dark in colour and taste, with an undertone of blackberry fruits. The quality rises further with the Vieilles Vignes

Below: Ch Roc de Cambes

(with its special, stylish label), which has plenty of fruit, good oak, noble tannins and a long finish. Ch Montaigut also produces an appealing white wine.

Ch Moulin des Graves   map 46 J6
owner: Jean Bost **area:** 10 ha **cases:** 4,000, white 1,600 **grape % R:** MER 70% CS 20% MAL 10% **grape % W:** SAUV B 100%
33710 Teuillac tel: 05 57 64 30 58
Sympathetic, traditionally made red wine, reasonably round, but seldom very fruity. On the other hand there is plenty of fruit (tropical notes in particular) in the white Côtes de Bourg, which shows some oak influence. It comes purely from Sauvignon vines, some over 85 years old.

Ch du Moulin Vieux   map 47 J8
owner: Jean-Pierre Gorphe **area:** 16 ha **cases:** 7,600 **grape % R:** MER 50% CF 45% MAL 5% **second wine:** Ch du Moulin Vieux *(Bordeaux)*
33710 Tauriac tel: 05 57 68 26 21
fax: 05 57 68 23 75
Although the standard wine perhaps lacks some concentration, the Sélection du Propriétaire has considerably more to offer: more strength, more aroma (fruit, spices, oak), more tannin. A grain mill once stood on the site of this estate – hence the name.

Ch Noblet   map 46 K7
owner: Bernard Pommier **area:** 20.5 ha **cases:** 10,300 **grape % R:** MER 55% CS 45%
33710 Pugnac tel: 05 57 68 81 01
fax: 05 57 68 83 17
Likeable, supple and usually decently fruity creation from the cooperative at Pugnac.

◆
About Bourg

In contrast to neighbouring Blaye, Bourg has only one appellation, and 99% of the wine it produces is red. The Côtes de Bourg AC covers all or part of 15 communes in the canton of Bourg.

To the east and north is Blaye; to the south-east, land covered by the generic Bordeaux appellations.

Above: Ch Les Rocques

Ch Nodoz
map 46 K7
owner: Magdeleine Frères *area:* 40 ha *cases:*
20,000 *grape % R:* MER 60% CS 25% CF 15% *second
wine:* Ch Galau
33710 Tauriac tel: 05 57 68 41 03
Wine lovers can have an almost blind faith in
this exemplary estate, even in the lesser years.
The wine practically always has a firm, almost
robust taste with the breeding, fruit and tannin
of the Cabernet Sauvignon, and a fair range of
other nuances. The Cuvée Prestige also offers a
considerable dose of toasty oak. Ch Nodoz was
formerly affiliated to the Tauriac cooperative.

Ch Peychaud
map 46 J5
owner: Bernard Germain *area:* 29 ha *cases:*
17,500 *grape % R:* MER 60% CS 40% *other
châteaux owned:* include Ch Charron (*Premières
Côtes de Blaye*); Ch Peyredoulle (*Premières Côtes
de Blaye*); Ch Yon-Figeac (*St-Emilion*)
33710 Teuillac tel: 05 57 42 66 66
fax: 05 57 64 36 20
The private estate of a well-known wine
merchant from the Blaye district. The wine
generally is a good commercial product:
smooth, supple and reasonably concentrated,
without being very expressive. It is at its best in
the good or great vintages, however, when the
Cabernet Sauvignon ripens fully and impart its
blackcurrant aroma to the wine, without
conferring any bitterness.

Ch Le Piat
map 47 L9
owner: Françoise Lisse *area:* 10 ha *cases:* 5,500
grape % R: MER 80% CS 10% CF 5% MAL 5%
33710 Tauriac tel: 05 57 68 41 12
fax: 05 57 68 36 31
The showpiece of the Tauriac cooperative. The
château with its long façade, built in Louis
XIV's reign, stands on a hill directly opposite
this *cave*. The wine receives 12 months' ageing
in casks, a sixth of them new, and is a delicious
composition with aspects of toast, oak and
vanilla, ripe blackcurrant and cocoa.

Ch Roc de Cambes
map 47 K6
owner: François & Emilie Mitjavile *area:* 9.6 ha
cases: 4,000 *second wine:* Domaine de Cambes
(*Bordeaux*) *other châteaux owned:* Ch Le Tertre
Roteboeuf (*St-Emilion*)

◆
Finding a château
To locate a château from its name alone,
use the index/gazetteer, which will provide
the page and map reference. When the
name and appellation are known, consult
the Directory pages of the relevant chapter.
When the commune is known, but not the
appellation, consult the index by commune:
this lists châteaux in the Atlas under the
commune name.

Second wines and other wines made by an
estate are listed in the index, as are
special *cuvées* when the name used does
not make clear the connection with the
parent château.

33710 Bourg-sur-Gironde tel: 05 57 68 25 58
fax: 05 57 68 35 97
Indisputably the star of the Côtes de Bourg. The
wine comes from vines with an average age of
35 years; they grow in a natural amphitheatre
stretching down to the Dordogne. Night frosts
hardly ever occur here. The potential of this
vineyard has been grasped and realized by
François Mitjavile, whose first vintage was in
1988. Mitjavile had earlier won fame at Ch Le
Tertre Roteboeuf in St-Emilion. With grapes
nearly always picked very late, this talented
grower is able to create a Côtes de Bourg that is
not only brimful of fruit (blackcurrant, cherry,
plum), but also has good oak in its rich,
expansive, almost creamy taste, plus noble,
lingering tannins. Half of the casks used for the
18 months' maturing are new.

Ch Les Rocques
map 47 J5
owner: Feillon Frères & Fils *area:* 15 ha *cases:*
8,000 *grape % R:* MER 70% CS 15% CF 10% MAL 5%
second wine: Ch Haut Barateau *other châteaux
owned:* Ch Saint-Ignan (*Bordeaux Supérieur*); Ch
Barbanson (*Bordeaux Supérieur*)
33710 St-Seurin-de-Bourg tel: 05 57 68 42 82
fax: 05 57 68 36 25
The Les Rocques estate is a single block of land,
run by three generations of the same family. In
good years it is a meaty wine, nicely fruity and

---

with adequate tannins. It is oak-aged for a
relatively short period, spending 6-8 months in
cask. Visitors to this château always enjoy the
splendid view across the river.

Ch de Rousselet
map 46 K5
owner: Francis Sou *area:* 10 ha *cases:* 4,700
grape % R: MER 60% CS 15% CF 15% MAL 10%
second wine: Ch la Chapelle St-Loup
33710 St-Trojan tel: 05 57 64 32 18
fax: 05 57 64 32 18
This estate creates an enjoyable Côtes de Bourg
from vines with an average age of 25 years.
Besides red and black berry fruit, the wine
offers earthy notes, plus some oak and vanilla.
Its maturing in *barriques* – 20% of them new –
lasts for a year.

Ch Rousset
map 46 K5
owner: Jean Teisseire *area:* 23 ha *cases:* 13,200
grape % R: MER 47% CS 38% MAL 10% CF 5% *second
wine:* Ch Les Aubarèdes; Ch l'Ebraude
33710 Samonac tel: 05 57 68 46 34
fax: 05 57 68 36 18
This former *maison noble*, first mentioned in
the 17th century, stands resplendent on the
highest point in the Samonac district,
dominating its vineyard to the south. The
standard wine is of a decent quality, but the
Grande Réserve has wider horizons. It matures
for 12-18 months in *barriques*, a third of them
new; this adds spicy oak and vanilla overtones
to the notes of berry fruit. It also has more
tannin than its stablemate.

Ch Sauman
map 47 G3
owner: SCEA des Vignobles Braud *area:* 24 ha
cases: 14,300 *grape % R:* MER 75% CS 20% MAL 5%
second wine: Domaine Moulin de Mendoce
33710 Villeneuve tel: 05 57 42 16 64
fax: 05 57 42 93 00
The standard wine has a sombre red colour, a
bouquet with dark and spicy elements, and a
juicy, supple, somewhat rustic taste without any
astringency. The Cuvée Particulière has more to
it, not only because it is aged in cask, but also
because it is meatier, has a longer finish and an
aroma that often contains plenty of licorice and
some chocolate.

Ch de Taste
map 46 K6
owner: Jean-Paul Martin *area:* 15 ha *cases:* 8,000
grape % R: MER 50% CS 20% CF 20% MAL 10%
33710 Lansac tel: 05 57 68 40 34
In 1983 this estate left the Tauriac *cave
coopérative*, so new winemaking facilities had
to be put in. The resulting wine, which is clean
and firm, offers a harmonious blend of fruit,
spice and tannin.

Ch Tayac
map 47 J4
owner: Pierre Saturny & Fils *area:* 30 ha *cases:*
15,000 *grape % R:* MER 50% CS 45% CF 5% *second
wine:* Clos du Pain de Sucre; Ch Haut Tayac *other
châteaux owned:* Ch La Joncarde (*Côtes de Bourg*)
33710 St-Seurin-de-Bourg tel: 05 57 68 40 60
fax: 05 57 68 29 93
A 17th-century château near the river; in the
great years its wines are among the foremost
from the Côtes de Bourg. The Cuvée Réservée
has plenty of colour and tannin, with berry fruit
and a strong constitution. The Cuvée Prestige
contains more Cabernet – 80% instead of 50%
— and is somewhat richer, more intense. In
average or lesser years the quality drops to
ordinarily good or correct. Rubis du Prince

Above: Ch Tayac

Noir, a pleasant, pure Merlot wine, is also made here at Ch Tayac. This spends its 18-24 months' maturing in used *barriques* and vats.

Ch La Tenotte   map 46 K5
owner: Michel Elie *area:* 5.2 ha *cases:* 2,700 *grape % R:* MER 63% MAL 26% CF 7% CS 4% *other châteaux owned:* Ch Sociondo *(Premières Côtes de Blaye)*
33370 Mombrier tel: 05 57 42 14 49
fax: 05 57 42 12 39
Château on a gravel hill, run since 1990 by the owners of Ch Sociondo (Premières Côtes de Blaye). Aromatic, supple wine with a pleasing amount of fruit. Briefly cask-aged.

Ch Tour de Collin   map 47 J5
owner: Denis Levraud *area:* 15 ha *cases:* 7,500 *grape % R:* MER 60% CS 30% MAL 10% *second wine:* Ch Prieuré La Libarde *other châteaux owned:* Ch Laurensanne *(Côtes de Bourg)*; Ch Gontier *(Premières Côtes de Blaye)*
33710 St-Seurin-de-Bourg tel: 05 57 68 46 26
fax: 05 57 68 37 16
This wine not only has a good deal of oak, toast and vanilla, but also great charm and some ageing potential. It spends 8-12 months in cask (a third are new). The château had earlier careers as a flour mill and an observation post.

Ch Tour des Graves   map 46 J6
owner: Arnaud Frères *area:* 16 ha *cases:* 6,500, white 1,500 *grape % R:* MER 65% CS 25% CF 5% MAL 5% *grape % W:* SAUV B 100% *second wine:* Ch Les Aubastons *(Bordeaux)*
33710 Teuillac tel: 05 57 64 32 02
fax: 05 57 64 23 94
This estate yields a worthy, supple red wine for drinking young, and a decent white from Sauvignon grapes. The ordinary red Côtes de Bourg is rather modest, but the prestige *cuvée* labelled *vieilli en fûts de chêne* matures for a year in cask, has more aroma and has won several prizes.

Ch La Tuilière   map 47 H4
owner: Philippe Estournet *area:* 15 ha *cases:* 8,000 *grape % R:* MER 60% CS 35% MAL 5%
33710 St-Ciers-de-Canesse tel: 05 57 64 80 90
fax: 05 57 64 89 97
The present owners bought the La Tuilière estate in 1991, with the 1989 and 1990 vintages still in the cellar. The latest vintages show a change in style: from being on the rustic side, the wine has become rather fruitier and more velvety, while retaining the foundation of fine tannin. Worth watching.

Vieux Domaine de Taste   map 47 J7
owner: Domaines Bernier *area:* 8.8 ha *cases:* 4,500, white 1,600 *grape % R:* MER 60% CS 20% CF 15% MAL 5% *grape % W:* SAUV B 40% MUSC 25% SEM 20% COL 15% *second wine:* Ch La Croix de Taste *other wines:* Bordeaux blanc *other châteaux owned:* Ch Conilh Haute-Libarde *(Côtes de Bourg)*
33710 Lansac tel: 05 57 68 46 46
fax: 05 57 68 36 09
This family property is situated on a clay and limestone plateau, near the 12th-century church at Lansac. The domaine's wine, which sees no oak, is usually slender in its makeup, and soon becomes supple enough to drink. Besides this red Côtes de Bourg the estate also produces a white AC Bordeaux.

Below: Vineyards of Vieux Domaine de Taste

APPELLATION BLAYE

Above: Domaine de l'Ancien Manoir de Valette

Ch Alfa Bernarde   map 46 K10
owner: Mähler-Besse *area:* 14.1 ha *cases:* 7,800,
white 1,700 *grape % R:* MER 60% CS 30% CF 10%
grape % W: SAUV B 50% SEM 40% COL 10% *second
wine:* Ch de Seize *(Bordeaux)* *other châteaux
owned:* include Ch d'Arche *(Haut-Médoc)*; Ch Palmer
(Margaux); Ch La Couronne *(St-Emilion)*
33620 Marsas tel: 05 56 56 04 30
fax: 05 56 56 04 59
Since 1989 this estate has belonged to the
Bordeaux *négociant* firm of Mähler-Besse,
which has considerably enlarged the originally
very small vineyard. The red wine tastes light,
fruity and supple; the aromatic white Côtes de
Blaye is redolent of Sauvignon Blanc.

Domaine de l'Ancien Manoir de
Valette   map 46 G4
owner: Jean Ferchaud *area:* 16 ha *cases:* 8,500,
white 1,200 *grape % R:* MER 70% CF 25% MAL 5%
grape % W: COL 50% UGNI BLANC 40% SEM 10%
33390 Mazion tel: 05 57 42 18 69
Red is the more important wine here, both in
quantity and quality. Since it spends a lengthy
period – two years – in cask (25% new barrels),
oak elements such as aniseed, licorice and

Below: Ch Barbé

spices dominate the aroma, while the aftertaste
can be somewhat dry. The estate goes back to
the 16th century, when the Genouillacs, a
military family, farmed an extensive property
here. More recently, the present owner's family
took over in 1918.

Domaine Arnaud   map 46 J8
owner: Dominique Arnaud *area:* 30 ha *cases:*
15,500, white 2,800 *grape % R:* MER 60% CS 35% CF
5% *grape % W:* SAUV B 50% UGNI BLANC 50% *second
wine:* Ch Les Sacquerelles *other wines:* Bordeaux
rosé & blanc
33920 St-Christoly-de-Blaye tel: 05 57 42 48 24
fax: 05 57 42 40 15
In recent years the proportion of Merlot grapes
used in Domaine Arnaud has risen from 40 to
60%, so that the originally rather light wine has
now gained more body.

Ch Barbé   map 47 E3
owner: Vignobles Bayle-Carreau *area:* 25 ha *cases:*
16,000 *grape % R:* MER 70% CS 25% MAL 5% *other
châteaux owned:* Ch Eyquem *(Côtes de Bourg)*; Ch
La Carelle *(Premières Côtes de Blaye)*; Ch
Pardaillan *(Premières Côtes de Blaye)*
33390 Cars tel: 05 57 64 32 43
fax: 05 57 64 22 74
This estate derives its name from a M. Barbé,
the official responsible for the citadel at Blaye
and for the Dordogne riverbanks in the 18th
century. The château, in *Directoire* style, was
built after the French Revolution. Its red wine
spends 12-15 months in cask, has no great
depth, and can be drunk quite young.

Ch La Bergère
owner: Michelle & Dominique Brimaud *area:* 32 ha
cases: 20,000, white 1,350 *grape % R:* MER 70% CS
30% *grape % W:* SEM 50% SAUV B 50% *second wine:*
Ch Tour de la Motte
33390 Mazion tel: 05 57 64 63 53
fax: 05 46 49 63 20
About a tenth of the vintage here is selected for
maturing in cask. This wood-aged red
Premières Côtes de Blaye has good intensity; its
dark-toned taste, which has a lot of Merlot in it,
is underpinned by a reasonable amount of oak
and tannin. La Bergère therefore has the
potential for ageing.

Ch Berthenon   map 46 I5
owner: Henri Ponz *area:* 25 ha *cases:* 12,500,
white 1,500 *grape % R:* MER 60% CS 40% *grape %
W:* SAUV B 60% SEM 40%
33390 St-Paul-de-Blaye tel: 05 57 42 52 24
Both the red and the white wines from this
château regularly win awards. Where the
vintage allows, the black grapes are picked in a
very ripe condition, and are macerated for a
long time after fermenting. The wine therefore
has considerable colour, substance and tannin,
with an agreeable fruitiness. The white Côtes de
Blaye is mainly from Sauvignon grapes and
tastes best when young.

Ch Les Bertrands   map 46 D5
owner: Jean-Pierre Dubois *area:* 73 ha *cases:*
32,500, white 6,500 *grape % R:* MER 60% CS 35% CF
5% *grape % W:* SAUV B 72% MUSC 14% COL 7% UGNI
BLANC 7% *second wine:* Ch de Cor-Bugeaud
(Bordeaux)
33860 Reignac tel: 05 57 32 40 27
fax: 05 57 32 41 36
The same family has been busy here for nine
generations. The red wine from this
meticulously maintained property comes in two
forms: a decent standard bottling and a Cuvée
Prestige matured for a year in casks, of which
one-fifth are new. This wine offers a fairly
stimulating character with pleasant berry fruit,
an elegant structure and nicely integrated
toasted oak. Since 1995 the estate has been
giving its firm, fresh white Premières Côtes de
Blaye four months in *barriques*, so it has rather
gained in stature.

Ch Les Billauds   map 46 C4
owner: Jean-Claude Plisson *area:* 11 ha *cases:*
4,400, white 3,000 *grape % R:* MER 60% CS 30% CF
10% *grape % W:* SAUV B 70% MUSC 30%
33860 Marcillac tel: 05 57 32 77 57
fax: 05 57 32 95 27
Renowned estate with a château built in 1890
by Henri Vergez, mayor of Marcillac, who also
created the vineyard. At the beginning of the
20th century its wines were already winning
medals – as they still do today. The words *vieilli
en fût de chêne* appear on the label of the best
red, a delightful, meaty wine that conveys
impressions of toast, vanilla oak, ripe fruit and
darker notes. The white Premières Côtes de
Blaye has a Sauvignon aroma, with gooseberry
and exotic fruit, and a taste that is fresh without
being thin.

Ch La Braulterie de Peyraud
map 46 I5
owner: Familles David & Migne *area:* 15 ha *cases:*
6,000, white 1,500 *grape % R:* MER 75% CS 20% MAL
5% *grape % W:* SAUV B 90% SEM 10% *second wine:*
Ch Morisset; Ch Les Graves David *other wines:*
Bordeaux rosé *other châteaux owned:* Domaine
Les Cailloux de Blais *(Côtes de Bourg)*
33390 Berson tel: 05 57 64 39 51
fax: 05 57 64 23 60
Here in Berson, 5 km from Blaye, two families
expertly produce some pleasing wines. The
ordinary red is supple and of an average quality;
and after a perhaps less successful interlude the
red Cuvée Prestige is beginning to achieve a
rather higher standard – and especially a better
balance. Balance is also generally apparent in
the refreshing white Côtes de Blaye, which is
95% from Sauvignon grapes.

Above: Ch La Cassagne-Boutet

Above: Ch Chante Alouette

Ch La Bretonnière map 46 H3

owner: Stéphane Heurlier *area:* 10 ha *cases:*
5,200, white 800 *grape % R:* MER 70% CS 30%
grape % W: SAUVIGNON GRIS 70% SEM 20% SAUV B 10%
other wines: Bordeaux Clairet *other châteaux*
owned: Ch Guiet *(Côtes de Bourg)*
33390 Mazion tel: 05 57 64 59 23
fax: 05 57 64 59 23
In 1982 this somewhat neglected estate gained
a new owner, who is rejuvenating it. This has
raised the quality of the wine from poor to
satisfactory – and further improvement seems
likely. A fine Bordeaux Clairet is produced here,
and the vineyard is to be increased by 3 ha.

Ch Cailleteau Bergeron map 46 H3

owner: Dartier & Fils *area:* 30 ha *cases:* 15,300,
white 1,200 *grape % R:* MER 80% CS 10% CF 10%
grape % W: UGNI BLANC 100%
33390 Mazion tel: 05 57 42 11 10
fax: 05 57 42 37 72
The ageing of the red Cuvée Prestige isn't
lengthy – about three months – but takes place
in new casks. Besides its oak aroma this
Premières Côtes de Blaye has a supple
roundness, considerable tannin and spicy fruit.

Ch Cap Saint-Martin map 47 C3

owner: SCEA des Vignobles Ardoin *area:* 9 ha
cases: 4,500 *grape % R:* MER 90% CS 10% *other*
châteaux owned: Ch Mazerolles-Benoît, Ch Les
Rousseaux *(both Premières Côtes de Blaye)*
33390 St-Martin-Lacaussade tel: 05 57 42 13 29
The present owner's great-grandfather began by
buying a few plots with vines in 1904; later he
enlarged the property, taking in for good
measure an 1856 *maison bourgeoise.* Thus the
origins of Ch Cap Saint-Martin, a vineyard sited
quite high up. It yields a sometimes agreeable,
sometimes rather dry red wine that is soon
ready for drinking; the proportion of Merlot is
no less than 90%. The wine spends six months
in barrels of which a third are new.

Ch Capville map 46 I3

owner: Janick Beneteau *area:* 9 ha *cases:* 4,500
grape % R: MER 70% CS 20% MAL 10% *other*
châteaux owned: Domaine du Chay *(Premières
Côtes de Blaye)*
33390 Cars tel: 05 57 64 44 41
fax: 05 57 64 42 84

Traditionally-styled red wine, with some Malbec
in it, and no lack of fruit or oak. The quality of
the casks perhaps leaves something to be
desired, resulting in a somewhat dry, bitter
element in the finish.

Ch La Cassagne-Boutet map 46 I4

owner: Marie-Louise Mirieu de Labarre *area:* 10.2
ha *cases:* 4,000 *grape % R:* MER 65% CS 25% MAL
5% CF 5% *second wine:* Allendy de La Cassagne
33390 Cars tel: 05 57 42 80 84
fax: 05 57 42 17 62
One of the oldest properties in Cars, with a
château dating from the end of the 17th
century. The wine, often richly coloured,
usually takes on an agreeable smoothness after
just a few years. Its aroma frequently has a
touch of prune as well as oak elements. The
reliable quality is partly due to stringent
selection: on average half the vintage is sold as
a second wine.

Ch Chante Alouette map 47 F4

owner: Georges Lorteaud *area:* 25 ha *cases:*
13,000, white 1,200 *grape % R:* MER 60% CF 20%
MAL 20% *grape % W:* SAUV B 50% SEM 25% UGNI BLANC
25% *second wine:* Ch La Chapelle du Couvent
33390 Plassac tel: 05 57 42 16 38

Below: Ch Charron

The view here is glorious, the wine sound. Most
of it – 70% — is matured in new casks, which
gives it plenty of oak. Jammy fruit is also there
as a rule, together with quite a firm structure.
Needs patience.

Ch Chante-Alouette La Roseraie
map 46 I4

owner: SCE Viticole Sigogneaud-Voyer *area:* 30 ha
cases: 20,000 *grape % R:* MER 65% CS 25% CF 6%
MAL 4% *second wine:* Ch Le Rimensac
33390 Cars tel: 05 57 64 36 09
fax: 05 57 64 22 82
Property run by four generations of the same
family. Restrained, correct red wine, which does
not undergo cask-ageing. The greater part of
the vintage is bottled on-site for a *négociant.*

Ch Charron map 47 D3

owner: Bernard Germain/Vignobles Germain *area:*
25 ha *cases:* 13,000, white 2,500 *grape % R:* MER
90% CS 10% *grape % W:* SEM 70% SAUV B 30% *other*
châteaux owned: include Ch Labrousse *(Premières
Côtes de Blaye)*; Ch Peyredoulle *(Premières Côtes
de Blaye)*; Ch Yon-Figeac *(St-Emilion)*; Ch Lamarche
(Bordeaux Supérieur); Ch La Marche-Canon *(Canon-
Fronsac)*; Ch Peychaud *(Côtes de Bourg)*; Ch Le
Peuy-Saincrit *(Bordeaux Supérieur)*

Above: Ch Les Chaumes

**33390 St-Martin-Lacaussade tel: 05 57 42 66 66
fax: 05 57 64 36 20**
With its exemplary red and white wines, Charron is gradually working its way to the top in the district. Its standard wines are praiseworthy; even more so the special Les Gruppes *cuvées*. In the red version, fruit and oak balance each other beautifully, and the wine properly fills the mouth. The white Acacia, a Côtes de Blaye fermented in cask, has an attractive bouquet with enticing nuances of blossom, fruit and toast; it needs time before the oak is well integrated with the other elements.

Ch Les Chaumes   map 46 G3
owner: Pierre Parmentier **area:** 23 ha **cases:** 11,000 **grape % R:** CS 50% MER 40% MAL 10%
second wine: Ch Les Joualles
**33390 Fours tel: 05 57 42 18 44
fax: 05 57 42 83 93**
An estate that concentrates entirely on red wine. Fairly traditional in character, the wine contains a relatively high proportion of Cabernet. This gives it breeding, berry fruit and tannin, while oak maturation confers smoothness and some extra aroma. However, the rather dry finish hints that the period in cask is sometimes a little on the long side. In the château building itself, Les Chaumes' owners have a *chartreuse* as home.

◆
About the Blayais
There are three appellations in this large district. AC Blaye or Blayais is the most basic, but it is little used. It can be red or white, and a wide range of grapes is permitted. Côtes de Blaye is for white wines only. Premières Côtes de Blaye is for red and white wines, though most wines made are red. Grape varieties must be chosen from a restricted list.

Information about the Blayais wines can be obtained from the Syndicat viticole des Côtes de Blaye, which is located at 11, cours Vauban, 33390 Blaye. Tel 05 57 42 91 19.

Domaine du Chay   map 46 I3
owner: Guy & Janick Beneteau **area:** 20 ha **cases:** 11,500 **grape % R:** MER 70% MAL 20% CS 10% **other châteaux owned:** Ch Capville *(Premières Côtes de Blaye)*
33390 Cars tel: 05 57 42 15 24
The red wine here seldom tastes really full-bodied – though not too light either. Its quality is very reliable: fresh currant fruit, a touch of spicy oak, juicy, tempered tannins.

Ch Le Chay   map 46 J5
owner: Didier Raboutet **area:** 18 ha **cases:** 8,000 **grape % R:** MER 70% CS 20% CF 10% **other châteaux owned:** Ch Groleau *(Côtes de Bourg)*
**33390 Berson tel: 05 57 64 39 50
fax: 05 57 64 25 08**
Somewhat rustic red Premières Côtes de Blaye. A quarter of the casks are replaced each year.

Ch Cone-Taillasson Sabourin   map 47 C2
owner: Sabourin Frères **area:** 9 ha **cases:** 5,500 **grape % R:** MER 55% CS 35% CF 10% **other châteaux owned:** Ch Lemoine-Lafon-Rochet *(Haut-Médoc)*; Ch Crusquet-Sabourin *(Premières Côtes de Blaye)*
**33390 Blaye tel: 05 57 42 15 27
fax: 05 57 42 05 47**

Below: Ch Crusquet-de Largarcie

A fine *chartreuse*, bigger than most, with an imposing double set of steps at the front. The 18th-century painter Jean Joseph Taillasson lived here; the second part of the name comes from the family who have owned the estate since 1902. The red wine here is relatively finely structured and owes its supple juiciness to a high percentage of Merlot.

Ch La Croix-Saint-Jacques   map 47 B2
owner: Jacques Collard **area:** 16 ha **cases:** 7,500, white 600 **grape % R:** MER 60% CS 25% CF 10% MAL 5% **grape % W:** UGNI BLANC 95% SEM 5%
33390 St-Genès-de-Blaye tel: 05 57 42 16 83
The best wine here is a cask-aged red Premières Côtes de Blaye of a sound colour and meaty taste. Its fruit, however, is often rather edged aside by the oak, which shows in such associated aromas as vanilla.

Ch Crusquet-de Lagarcie   map 47 D3
owner: GFA Philippe de Lagarcie **area:** 22 ha **cases:** 12,500, white 1,200 **grape % R:** MER 70% CS 30% **grape % W:** SEM 50% SAUV B 40% Ugni Blanc 10%
second wine: Ch Les Princesses de Lagarcie **other wines:** Clos des Rudel *(Blayais)* **other châteaux owned:** Ch le Cône-Taillasson-de-Lagarcie *(Premières Côtes de Blaye)*; Ch Touzignan *(Premières Côtes de Blaye)*
**33390 Cars tel: 05 57 42 15 21
fax: 05 57 42 90 87**
The wine begins its life in an impressive *cuverie* with traditional wooden fermenting vats. The wine stays in these for about three weeks, so that a great deal of colour and tannin is extracted from the grapeskins. The quality of the wine fluctuates. At its best, red Crusquet-de Lagarcie has a firm constitution, ripe fruit, oak and adequate tannins, which endow it with a certain potential for ageing.

Ch Crusquet-Sabourin   map 47 D4
owner: Sabourin Frères **area:** 20 ha **cases:** 12,000 **grape % R:** MER 50% CS 50% **other châteaux owned:** Ch Lemoine-Lafon-Rochet *(Haut-Médoc)*; Ch Cone-Taillasson Sabourin *(Premières Côtes de Blaye)*
**33390 Cars tel: 05 57 42 15 27
fax: 05 57 42 05 47**
In the mid-1960s this estate was separated from Ch Crusquet-de Lagarcie and passed to the Sabourins, a family who had been making wine since 1760. The red Premières Côtes de Blaye usually has firmness, mature tannins and some jammy fruit; the taste is pleasing, but is often a little lacking in spirit and refinement. Ageing in cask lasts 12-18 months.

Ch l'Escadre   map 47 D4
owner: Jean-Marie Carreau **area:** 32 ha **cases:** 20,000 **grape % R:** MER 70% CS 20% MAL 10%
second wine: Ch l'Amiral de l'Escadre; Ch la Croix Saint-Pierre **other châteaux owned:** Ch Les Petits Arnauds *(Premières Côtes de Blaye)*
**33390 Cars tel: 05 57 42 36 57
fax: 05 57 42 14 02**
The name apparently comes from a sea captain who described the various plots of his vineyard as his 'squadron'. The red wine should generally be drunk within three to four years. There is no great personality to it, but it does have a supple, rounded quality and a reasonably firm taste.

Ch Frédignac   map 47 D3
owner: Michel l'Amouller **area:** 15.5 ha **cases:** 6,000, white 400 **grape % R:** MER 72% CS 15% CF 9% MAL 4% **grape % W:** SEM 75% SAUV B 25%

33390 St-Martin-Lacaussade tel: 05 57 42 24 93 fax: 05 57 42 00 64

Frédignac's barrel-aged *cuvée* is their most interesting wine: a dark-toned, reasonably mouthfilling red that does not lack for fruit. Until 1984 a cooperative processed the grapes.

Ch Gardut   map 47 E3

owner: Patrick Revaire *area:* 10 ha *cases:* 5,000 *grape % R:* MER 75% CS 25% *second wine:* Vieux Ch Valentin *other châteaux owned:* Clos Lascombes, Ch Haut-du-Peyrat *(both Premières Côtes de Blaye)*

33390 Cars tel: 05 57 42 20 35 fax: 05 57 42 12 84

Clean, slender red Premières Côtes de Blaye with fresh fruit and abundant tannin in youth: very characteristic of its appellation, in fact.

Ch Gardut Haut-Cluzeau   map 47 D4

owner: Denis Lafon *area:* 5 ha *cases:* 3,000 *grape % R:* MER 80% MAL 10% CS 10% *other châteaux owned:* include Ch du Grand Barrail, Ch Cavalier *(both Premières Côtes de Blaye)*

33390 Cars tel: 05 57 42 33 04 fax: 05 57 42 08 92

A wine estate that since 1971 has belonged to Denis Lafon, of Ch du Grand Barrail and other properties. Light and likeable red wine, with some nuances of fruit, cocoa and spices.

Ch Goblangey   map 46 I3

owner: Michel Planteur *area:* 17 ha *cases:* 7,700, white 1,250 *grape % R:* MER 50% CS 30% CF 10% MAL 10% *grape % W:* SAUV B 85% COL 15% *other wines:* Bordeaux blanc & rosé

33390 St-Paul-de-Blaye tel: 05 57 42 88 54

Under the tiles of the long white *chai* the red wine matures for 8-14 months in barrels of which a third are new. The aroma is at times somewhat herbaceous, the quality middling. The pale-coloured Bordeaux blanc tastes fresh, but not sensationally fruity.

Ch du Grand Barrail   map 47 D4

owner: Denis Lafon *area:* 28 ha *cases:* 15,000, white 1,200 *grape % R:* MER 65% CS 30% MAL 5% *grape % W:* SAUV B 80% SEM 20% *second wine:* Ch du Cavalier *other châteaux owned:* include Ch Gardut Haut-Cluzeau *(Premières Côtes de Blaye)*; Ch Graulet *(Premières Côtes de Blaye)*

33390 Cars tel: 05 57 42 33 04 fax: 05 57 42 08 92

In good years the red wine offers a relatively rich taste with impressions of spice, cherries in brandy, blackcurrant, bayleaf, licorice and oak – in the cask-aged version. The standard red is lighter and resembles the one from Ch Gardut Haut-Cluzeau (in the same ownership). Also interesting is the expressive Blayais Sauvignon M. P., a white which undergoes skin contact before fermentation.

Ch Le Grand Moulin   map 46 C4

owner: Jean-François Réaud *area:* 25 ha *cases:* 7,000, white 2,000 *grape % R:* MER 65% CS 25% CF 10% *grape % W:* SAUV B 100% *second wine:* Ch Les Aubiers *(Bordeaux rosé; AC Bordeaux blanc)*

33820 St-Aubin-de-Blaye tel: 05 57 32 62 06 fax: 05 57 32 73 73

The château is a stately grey country house from the beginning of the 20th century; the cellar installations from the end of it. The red Cuvée Particulière is an elegant wine, very deep in colour and with berry fruit. Half the barrels used are new and maturing lasts one year, so the oak is nicely integrated. There is also a

special *cuvée* of the white Premières Côtes de Blaye. Called Elégance, this is a pure Sauvignon wine: bracingly fresh, with fruit and discreet notes of oak.

Ch Grand Terrier   map 46 F3

owner: Névéol & Fils *area:* 12 ha *cases:* 5,500, white 300 *grape % R:* MER 75% CF 23% MAL 2% *grape % W:* MUSC 50% SAUV B 25% SEM 25%

33390 Anglade tel: 05 57 64 55 13 fax: 05 57 64 59 71

Owned a family who have been cultivating vines for several generations. They make a decent red wine with berry fruit and, in its youth, some toughness. The white is a fairly simple Blayais.

Ch Graulet   map 47 E3

owner: GFA Château Graulet/Denis Lafon *area:* 30 ha *cases:* 17,500, white 1,200 *grape % R:* MER 50% MAL 30% CS 20% *grape % W:* SAUV B 34% SEM 33% MUSC 33% *second wine:* Ch Vieux Brignon *other châteaux owned:* include Ch du Grand Barrail *(Premières Côtes de Blaye)*

33390 Plassac tel: 05 57 42 33 04 fax: 05 57 42 08 92

Acquired by new – Swedish – owners in 1991. The red wine is usually characterized by a hint of spicy oak, fresh berry fruit, a slender structure and adequate tannins.

Ch Les Graves   map 46 I7

owner: Jean-Pierre Pauvif *area:* 17 ha *cases:* 4,000, white 1,000 *grape % R:* MER 70% CS 20% MAL 10% *grape % W:* SAUV B 60% MUSC 20% SEM 10% COL 10% *second wine:* Ch La Grave Julien

33920 St-Vivien-de-Blaye tel: 05 57 42 47 37 fax: 05 57 42 55 89

The red Cuvée Prestige represents this château's highest quality. It usually holds substantial oak flavours of toast and vanilla, with the dark notes of cocoa and bayleaf balanced by its black cherry and blackcurrant fruit – this fairly meaty wine lingers nicely on the palate, with mature tannins. It is pleasingly ready for drinking within a few years. The white Sauvignon, a Côtes de Blaye, is on the other hand fresh and light, with floral and fruity notes including gooseberry.

Ch Haut Bertinerie   map 46 J10

owner: Daniel Bantegnies & Fils *area:* 45 ha *cases:* 26,930, white 5,900 *grape % R:* MER 45% CS 45% CF 10% *grape % W:* SAUV B 95% SEM 2% COL 2% MUSC 1%

Below: Ch Largarde

second wine: Ch Bertinerie; Ch Manon la Lagune *other wine:* Bordeaux Clairet

33620 Cubnezais tel: 05 57 68 70 74 fax: 05 57 60 01 03

Haut Bertinerie is reckoned to be the unofficial *grand cru* of the Premières Côtes de Blaye – and justifiably so, for the red wine made here is of top quality. It is cossetted with 12 months' maturing in new oak; the grapes come from vines with an average age of 40 years. In this way a rich, classical taste with both depth of flavour and length of finish emerges. In its complex aroma there are elements of noble oak – vanilla, toast, cinnamon, licorice – and fruit that is jammy with cherry, fig, plum. The white Haut Bertinerie is also exceptional: a Sauvignon of stature, with a certain amount of ageing potential. There is even a remarkable barrel-fermented Bordeaux Clairet. The slightly less spectacular wines, red, white and rosé, use the Ch Bertinerie label – but these, too, are of exemplary quality and represent exceptional value for money. A striking feature is that much of the vineyard is planted *en lyre*: the vines are trained in V-form. This gives them more sun – and means they have to be picked by hand.

Ch Haut-du-Peyrat   map 47 E3

owner: Patrick Revaire *area:* 10 ha *cases:* 5,000 *grape % R:* MER 75% CS 20% CF 5% *second wine:* Vieux Château Valentin *other wines:* Bordeaux blanc *other châteaux owned:* Ch Gardut, Clos Lascombes *(both Premières Côtes de Blaye)*

33390 Cars tel: 05 57 42 20 35 fax: 05 57 42 12 84

An estate that has been on an upswing since the mid-1980s. In bouquet and taste the red cask-aged wine generally offers considerable oak, with toast and vanilla – sometimes even too much in the lesser years. Cherry fruit is also discernible to a greater or lesser degree.

Ch Haut Grelot   map 46 B2

owner: Joël Bonneau *area:* 41 ha *cases:* 15,500, white 6,000 *grape % R:* MER 70% CS 30% *grape % W:* SAUV B 60% SEM 30% COL 10% *other wines:* Bordeaux blanc *other wines:* Bordeaux Supérieur

33820 St-Ciers-sur-Gironde tel: 05 57 32 65 98 fax: 05 57 32 71 81

Since 1992 this estate has produced a *barrique*-matured red Premières Côtes de Blaye. This has an accessible taste, with cedarwood, grip, supple tannins and nice fruit – cherry, blackcurrant – as well as a touch of bayleaf. The standard red wine also has much merit, and the white Côtes de Blaye plenty of fresh acidity.

Ch Haut Sociondo — map 47 E3

owner: Famille Martinaud **area:** 16 ha **cases:** 9,500 **grape % R:** MER 70% CS 20% MAL 10%
33390 Cars tel: 05 57 42 03 22
The red wine made here has been gaining attention once again since the beginning of the 1990s. It is a substantial, supple Premières Côtes de Blaye, ready for drinking quite early, and with a fair dash of fruit.

Ch Haut-Terrier — map 46 I10

owner: Bernard Denéchaud **area:** 40 ha **cases:** 18,000, white 7,700 **grape % R:** MER 80% CS 20% **grape % W:** COL 60% SAUV B 20% MUSC 20% **second wine:** Ch Bel-Enclos
33620 St-Mariens tel: 05 57 68 53 54
fax: 05 57 68 16 87
The vineyard here consists of various plots with curious names such as 'Champagne' and 'l'Enclos de la Guillotine'. Serious and enthusiastic work put in here makes wines of good quality. One proof of this is the red wine with *vieilli en barriques neuves* on its label, which is robust but also displays charm and a lively fruitiness. Exciting tropical fruit is generously present in the Colombard-dominated white Côtes de Blaye, which is fermented at low temperature.

Ch Les Jonqueyres — map 46 H3

owner: Pascal Montaut **area:** 8.7 ha **cases:** 4,400 **grape % R:** MER 90% CS 5% MAL 5% **second wine:** Domaine de Courgeau **other châteaux owned:** Clos Alphonse Dubreuil *(Côtes de Bourg)*
33390 St-Paul-de-Blaye tel: 05 57 42 34 88
fax: 05 57 42 93 80
Belongs among the elite of the appellation on account of a red wine with a very consistently high quality: solid colour, a substantial taste, toasty oak, an alluring roundness, splendid fruit. Half of the *barriques* used for the 12-16 months' ageing of the wine are new. The vineyard, set in a natural amphitheatre, is to be enlarged by 4 ha within the foreseeable future.

Ch Labrousse — map 46 J4

owner: Jacques Chardat/Vignobles Germain **area:** 21 ha **cases:** 10,500, white 2,200 **grape % R:** MER 90% CS 10% **grape % W:** SEM 80% SAUV B 20% **second wine:** Ch Lacaussade Saint-Martin **other châteaux owned:** include Ch Charron *(Premières Côtes de Blaye)*
33390 St-Martin-Lacaussade tel: 05 57 42 66 66
fax: 05 57 64 36 20
A not-too-slender, darkly fruity red wine that also has some oak and spices – including a touch of aniseed. The juicy, crisp, fruity white Sauvignon Premières Côtes de Blaye is sold as Ch Lacaussade Saint-Martin.

Ch Lagarde — map 47 E3

owner: Hans Gertsch & Fils **area:** 4 ha **cases:** 1,000 **grape % R:** MER 75% MAL 25% **other wines:** Chapelle Lagarde **other wines:** Bordeaux rosé
33390 Cars tel: 05 57 42 91 56
fax: 05 57 42 91 56
This estate has been totally renovated by its Swiss owners since 1990. In the Middle Ages it offered shelter to pilgrims. The vineyard is very small, but will be more than doubled in the coming years. An unusual combination of

grapes here – just Merlot and Malbec – means the wine can be drunk quite soon. In a good year it has a reasonable amount of fruit, while the colour is deep and the taste meaty. Toasty oak is to be found, through the use of second-hand casks from a celebrated Pomerol or St-Emilion *cru;* the wine stays in these for a year.

Ch Lardière — map 46 D6

owner: René Bernard **area:** 20 ha **cases:** 6,650, white 5,550 **grape % R:** MER 50% CS 50% **grape % W:** SAUV B 60% COL 20% SEM 10% MUSC 10% **second wine:** Domaine Renaissance
33860 Marcillac tel: 05 57 32 41 38
fax: 05 57 32 41 13
Estate with many different products: its range includes sparkling wines and Bordeaux *fine.* Normally its red wine forms a harmonious whole of ripe fruit, dark aromas, smoky oak and round tannins. Its white Côtes de Blaye verges on the generous, and is quite fresh and rich in fruit.

Clos Lascombes — map 47 E3

owner: Patrick Revaire **area:** 2.7 ha **cases:** 1,000 **grape % R:** MER 100% **other châteaux owned:** Ch Gardut *(Premières Côtes de Blaye);* Ch Haut-du-Peyrat *(Premières Côtes de Blaye)*
33390 Cars tel: 05 57 42 20 35
fax: 05 57 42 12 84
Tiny property where the first vintage was in 1991. The red wine matures for a year in new oak, and has decent concentration, tannin, modest fruit and dark aromas. It demands some time in bottle to allow it to find its balance.

Ch Loumède — map 47 E2

owner: Famille Raynaud **area:** 18 ha **cases:** 11,000 **grape % R:** MER 50% CS 35% MAL 15% **second wine:** Ch Les Aublines; Ch Pré-Videau
33390 Blaye tel: 05 57 42 16 39
fax: 05 57 42 25 30
The house and winemaking buildings of this château form a complex that amounts to a hamlet. Since 1962 the Raynauds, who returned from Algeria, have been the owners. The wine is traditionally made, and therefore matured in oak barrels. The result is equally traditional: good red Bordeaux with plenty of oak, jammy fruit (blackberry, cherry, blackcurrant) and with a backbone of firm tannins.

Ch Maine-Gazin — map 47 F3

owner: Sylvie Laffargue **area:** 8 ha **cases:** 4,000 **grape % R:** MER 95% CS 5%
33390 Plassac tel: 05 57 64 23 67
fax: 05 57 64 36 20
After a change of ownership in 1989 the quality of the wine improved greatly. The red Premières Côtes de Blaye is a delightful composition of red and black fruits, and oak with vanilla. Generally a third of the casks in which the wine matures for 12-15 months are new.

Ch Maine Tigreau — map 46 H3

owner: Danielle & Jean-Pierre Auduberteau **area:** 13 ha **cases:** 8,300 **grape % R:** MER 70% CF 12% CS 12% MAL 6% **second wine:** Ch Cassame
33390 St-Paul-de-Blaye tel: 05 57 42 04 28
fax: 05 57 42 85 40
Run by the same family for four generations – and each generation has carried out improvements. Thus in 1987 the present lady owner renovated the *chai.* Elegant red wine, smooth in style, with juicy fruit: a table companion full of charm.

Ch Marinier — map 46 I10

owner: Thierry Cotet **area:** 27 ha **cases:** 12,000, white 4,000 **grape % R:** MER 80% CS 20% **grape % W:** SAUV B 100% **second wine:** Domaine de Marinier
33620 Cézac tel: 05 57 68 63 13
fax: 05 57 68 18 08
Excellent red Cuvée Prestige: a well-deserved epithet for the dense colour, the concentration, the red and black berry fruit, the smoky oak and the firm structure. The white, which is fermented in new casks, is also well worth recommending: an aromatic, prize-winning wine entirely from Sauvignon Blanc.

Ch des Matards — map 46 B1

owner: Terrigeol & Fils **area:** 27 ha **cases:** 8,000, white 6,000 **grape % R:** MER 75% CS 25% **grape % W:** SAUV B 70% COL 20% MUSC 10% **second wine:** Ch Beaudry **other wines:** Domaine de la Margotterie *(Pineau des Charentes)*
33820 St-Ciers-sur-Gironde tel: 05 57 32 61 96
fax: 05 57 32 79 21
Matards, on the borders of the Gironde and Charente-Maritime *départements,* makes a reasonably rounded, quite powerful and enjoyable red wine. The dry whites are not to be neglected either: the château produces a fresh Sauvignon with 20% Colombard and the barrel-fermented Cuvée Quentin from Sauvignon Blanc and about 10% Muscadelle. The vineyard across the *départemental* boundary is the Domaine de la Margotterie; it yields Pineau des Charentes.

Ch Mazerolles — map 47 C3

owner: Guy Valleau **area:** 10 ha **cases:** 5,500 **grape % R:** MER 80% CS 15% MAL 5%
33390 St-Martin-Lacaussade tel: 05 57 42 18 61
Not very exuberant, but certainly an agreeable red wine meant for drinking young. It is matured in cask and has won occasional awards.

Ch le Menaudat — map 46 G2

owner: Madame Edouard Cruse **area:** 15 ha **cases:** 10,000 **grape % R:** MER 65% CS 30% MAL 5% **second wine:** Ch les Favières
33390 St-Androny tel: 05 56 65 20 08
fax: 05 57 64 40 29
The red wine made here tastes best in its youth, when its fruit is still vigorous; after four to five years this Premières Côtes de Blaye can become rather lacklustre. Starting with the 1994 vintage, some of the wine is now matured in cask. The same family has owned this château for around 150 years.

Ch Les Millards — map 46 D2

owner: M. Michel Courpon **area:** 14 ha **cases:** 7,500, white 1,300 **grape % R:** MER 70% CS 30% **grape % W:** SAUV B 100% **other châteaux owned:** Ch Maine La Gaillarde *(Côtes de Bourg)*
33390 St-Vivien-de-Blaye tel: 05 57 42 53 21
The red wine is no high flyer, but slips down pleasantly; for fruit it has cherry, plum and blackcurrant.

Ch La Mirandole — map 46 D2

owner: Paul Berjon **area:** 10 ha **cases:** 4,500, white 900 **grape % R:** MER 70% MAL 15% CF 10% CS 5% **grape % W:** SAUV B 100%
33820 Braud-et-St-Louis tel: 05 57 32 61 47
fax: 05 57 32 61 47
For a couple of decades now the vines here have been grown organically, without weedkillers or the like. The red wine is of decent quality, with fruit in its aroma, plus some oak and tannin.

Above: Ch Monconseil Gazin

Above: Ch Peybonhomme Les Tours

Ch Les Moines   map 47 C2
owner: Alain Carreau *area:* 20 ha *cases:* 10,500
grape % R: MER 70% CS 20% MAL 10% *second wine:*
Ch La Grange
33390 Blaye tel: 05 57 42 12 91
Renowned red wine that has repeatedly won
distinctions. Les Moines is well composed, with
creaminess, tannin, freshness and attractive
fruit – blackcurrant and cherry.

Ch Monconseil Gazin   map 47 F3
owner: Jean-Michel Baudet *area:* 35 ha *cases:*
16,000 *grape % R:* MER 60% CS 30% MAL 10%
second wine: Ch Le Roc *other châteaux owned:* Ch
Ricaud *(Premières Côtes de Blaye)*
33390 Plassac tel: 05 57 42 16 63
fax: 05 57 42 31 22
Charlemagne is said to have come across a
vineyard here that the Romans had laid out. In
the 16th century a château was built, of which
some parts – such as the imposing crenellated
gateway – still remain. A long series of medals
confirms the sound quality of the red. It is a
dark-toned wine, with considerable tannin; it
matures in *barriques* and then demands some
years of patience. In 1994 the Baudet family
celebrated their centenary as the owners of
Monconseil Gazin.

Ch Mondésir-Gazin   map 47 F3
owner: Marc Pasquet *area:* 9.5 ha *cases:* 4,000
grape % R: CS 30% MER 60% MAL 10% *other*
châteaux owned: Ch Haut-Mondésir *(Côtes de*
Bourg)
33390 Plassac tel: 05 57 42 29 80
fax: 05 57 42 84 86
Unfiltered, cask-aged red wine with body, ripe
tannins and plenty of toasty oak (which
sometimes lingers rather drily). This is a
serious Premières Côtes de Blaye that has the
stamina to age well. Since 1990 the estate has
had a new and very committed owner who was
trained at châteaux such as Haut-Marbuzet (St-
Estèphe), among others.

Ch Morange   map 46 J10
owner: Alain Routurier *area:* 5 ha *cases:* 2,000
grape % R: MER 65% CS 30% CF 5% *second wine:* Ch
des Nauves *(Bordeaux)*
33620 Marsas tel: 05 57 68 71 35
fax: 05 57 68 03 22

A qualified oenologist attends the birth of Ch
Morange's exclusively red wine: an immaculate
Premières Côtes de Blaye with a slender,
pleasing taste and reasonable fruit.

Ch Mornon   map 46 G3
owner: Serge Birot *area:* 14 ha *cases:* 6,700 *grape*
% R: MER 70% CS 25% MAL 5% *grape % W:* SAUV B
100% *second wine:* Domaine de Mornon *other*
wines: Domaine de Mornon *(Bordeaux rosé)*
33390 Eyrans tel: 05 57 64 71 62
The red Premières Côtes de Blaye here
sometimes carries a curious label, with
drawings of a monk and a knight. The wine
itself is less striking: a good average quality,
friendly character, fresh and fruity, it makes a
harmonious impression.

Ch Moulin de Grillet   map 46 I5
owner: GAEC Glémet & Fils *area:* 28 ha *cases:*
15,000 *grape % R:* MER 65% CS 35%
33390 Berson tel: 05 57 64 34 47
A property, passed from father to son, that has
gradually been enlarged from an original 8 ha
to its present 28. In good years the red wine has
a fairly meaty taste; its character is somewhat
rustic, with elements of oak, aniseed, licorice
and bayleaf.

Below: Ch Perenne

Domaine de la Nouzillette   map 46 K10
owner: N. & P. Catherinaud *area:* 20 ha *cases:*
7,000, white 4,100 *grape % R:* MER 60% CS 30% CF
10% *grape % W:* COL 40% SAUV B 30% SEM 20% MUSC
10% *second wine:* Ch Moulin Borgne *other wines:*
Bordeaux rosé *other wines:* Crémant de Bordeaux
33620 Marcenais tel: 05 57 68 70 25
fax: 05 57 68 09 12
Estate at the south of the district, run by the
same family since the beginning of the 19th
century. An extensive range is produced, not
only still wines but also two Crémants and a
Bordeaux *fine*. The most attractive red wine, the
Premières Côtes de Blaye, is aged in new casks.
The oak does not dominate, usually being well
integrated with the other elements such as
berry fruits. Even in sunny years this is not a
really full-bodied wine. The very pleasant
standard red wine is more supple, if a little less
concentrated in taste. The white Côtes de Blaye
does not reach the same level.

Ch Perenne   map 47 B3
owner: Château Perenne I/S *area:* 90 ha *cases:*
37,600, white 500 *grape % R:* MER 54% CS 44% CF
1% MAL 1% *grape % W:* COL 100% *second wine:* Ch
St-Genès; Ch La Girouette *other châteaux owned:*
Ch Le Ruisseau de Grillet *(Premières Côtes de*
Blaye); Ch Prieuré *(Premières Côtes de Blaye)*
33390 St-Genès-de-Blaye tel: 05 57 42 18 25
fax: 05 57 42 15 86
Small château dating from 1871 that belonged
to the Morin family until the mid-1970s, when
it passed to the Oudinot Champagne house. In
1989 Oudinot sold it to a Danish group. The red
wine typically has a fairly elegant structure. Its
aroma is a smooth combination of berry fruits,
herbaceous elements such as sweet peppers, a
hint of spice and some oak. There is some
concentration in the Cuvée Prestige, which has
been made since 1993.

Ch Petit La Garosse   map 46 H10
owner: Jean-Paul Clavé *area:* 14 ha *cases:* 7,500
grape % R: MER 65% CS 25% CF 10% *second wine:*
Ch Le Bizon *(Bordeaux; AC Bordeaux Clairet)*
33620 Laruscade tel: 05 57 68 67 20
fax: 05 57 68 17 04
The present owner has invested heavily here. In
1992 he put in a battery of new stainless-steel
tanks (keeping a few concrete *cuves*); then the

chai was completely renovated. From 1995 onwards, part of the red wine has been matured in cask. In short, this estate is worth watching.

Ch Les Petits Arnauds   map 47 D4
owner: George Carreau *area:* 28 ha *cases:* 15,000 *grape % R:* MER 75% CS 25% *second wine:* Ch Moulin des Arnauds; Ch Clairac *other châteaux owned:* Ch l'Escadre *(Premières Côtes de Blaye)*
33390 Cars tel: 05 57 42 36 57
fax: 05 57 42 14 02
Well-known wine estate whose red wine, however, does not have a wholly enthusiastic reception. Sometimes it is praised for its balance, its well-integrated tannins and the sun-drenched taste of its fruit; but some criticize it for its rapid development and its somewhat dry, at times rather burning, finish.

Ch Peybonhomme Les Tours
map 47 E3
owner: Vignobles Bossuet-Hubert *area:* 58 ha *cases:* 25,000 *grape % R:* MER 65% CF 15% CS 15% MAL 5% *second wine:* Ch Le Thil
33390 Cars tel: 05 57 42 11 95
fax: 05 57 42 38 15
This estate up above Blaye can be recognized from afar by its two towers: a round, crenellated keep and a detached square tower with embrasures, dating from Huguenot times. Red wine from an average vintage is pleasant, with a slight bitter touch, a fairly light structure, and blackcurrant and cherry fruit. The better vintages are characterized by more power and tannin. Maturing lasts 8-12 months in barrels (a third are new), and gives this Premières Côtes de Blaye elements of spicy, aniseedy oak.

◆
ACs Bordeaux & Bordeaux Supérieur
These are the basic generic ACs that cover the entire Bordeaux *vignoble*. Many estates in the Blayais use these appellations as well as, or instead of, the Blaye ones. Châteaux using just Bordeaux generic ACs are covered in the chapter on AC Bordeaux and Entre-Deux-Mers.

Below: Ch Peyredouelle

Above: Ch Peyreyre

Ch Peymelon   map 47 D4
owner: SCE Chapard-Tuffreau *area:* 21 ha *cases:* 10,000, white 500 *grape % R:* MER 80% CS 20% *grape % W:* SAUV B 100% *second wine:* Ch Bristeau *other wines:* Les Petits *(Bordeaux Supérieur)*
33390 Cars tel: 05 57 42 19 09
fax: 05 57 42 00 73
Supple red wine, fairly elegant, with a smooth acidity. Lacks obvious fruit, which goes to make it rather old-fashioned in style.

Ch Peyredoulle   map 46 J4
owner: Bernard Germain *area:* 19 ha *cases:* 11,000 *grape % R:* MER 90% CS 10% *other châteaux owned:* include Ch Charron *(Premières Côtes de Blaye)*; Ch Yon-Figeac *(St-Emilion)*
33390 Berson tel: 05 57 42 66 66
fax: 05 57 64 36 20
Pleasant red wine that at its best has ample fruit (black cherries, currants, berries), is supported by oak, and has a harmonious aftertaste. In poorer years the tannins may sometimes be rather desiccating and bitter. This château once belonged to the Italian philosopher Pic de la Mirandole; since 1976 it has been run by the Germain family of wine merchants and growers.

Below: Ch la Raz Caman

Ch Peyreyre   map 47 C3
owner: Michel Trinque *area:* 20 ha *cases:* 11,000, white 1,200 *grape % R:* MER 65% CS 25 CF 5% MAL 5% *grape % W:* SAUV B 100% *second wine:* Ch La Cassidouce
33390 St-Martin-Lacaussade tel: 05 57 42 18 57
fax: 05 57 42 94 17
Traditional, if not rustic, red Premières Côtes de Blaye with considerable dark, spicy old oak, tannin and a fairly dry finish. At this château, which dates from 1762, a pleasant, refreshing white wine is also made, exclusively from Sauvignon Blanc.

Ch Pinet la Roquette   map 46 J4
owner: Monique & Daniel Orlianges *area:* 6 ha *cases:* 3,125, white 300 *grape % R:* MER 70% CS 25% MAL 5% *grape % W:* SEM 60% SAUV B 40% *other wine:* Bordeaux rosé
33390 Berson tel: 05 57 64 37 80
fax: 05 57 64 23 57
The red wine is matured for a year in *barriques* of which a quarter are new. Oak is present in the aroma but in a controlled way, for juicy fruit can usually be detected as well. A smoothly fresh white Premières Côtes de Blaye and a mellow, fruity Bordeaux rosé complete the picture.

Ch la Raz Caman   map 46 F2
owner: Jean-François Pommeraud *area:* 33 ha *cases:* 17,000, white 1,500 *grape % R:* MER 60% CS 35% CF 4% MAL 1% *grape % W:* SAUV B 80% Ugni Blanc 20% *second wine:* Ch Caman
33390 Anglade tel: 05 57 64 41 82
fax: 05 57 64 41 77
This estate goes back to the beginning of the 17th century, when it was a *maison noble*. It acquired its name later from the *chevalier* la Raz Caman. A delightful red is made here, a wine with complexity and character. This usually offers stimulating, plentiful fruit with masses of blackcurrant, together with toasty oak – from a year in casks of which a third are new – and the spicy dark aspects of leather and resin. Strict selection is the secret: the larger part of the vintage is sold as a second wine.

Ch Rebouquet la Roquette   map 46 J4
owner: Jean-Francis Braud *area:* 12 ha *cases:* 5,800, white 1,000 *grape % R:* MER 60% CS 30% MAL 10% *grape % W:* COL 60% SAUV B 40%

**33390 Berson tel: 05 57 42 82 49
fax: 05 57 42 08 07**
Rebouquet la Roquette makes a lively red
Premières Côtes de Blaye that has some toasted
oak as well as body and fruit – a charmer.
Tropical and other fruits are to be found in the
bouquet of the refreshing Sauvignon white.

Ch La Rivalerie   map 46 H4
owner: Georges Gillibert **area:** 35 ha **cases:**
19,000, white 1,000 **grape % R:** CS 65% MER 30% CF
5% **grape % W:** SAUV B 55% SEM 45% **other wines:**
Bordeaux rosé
**33390 St-Paul-de-Blaye tel: 05 57 42 18 84
fax: 05 57 42 14 27**
After being abandoned in 1956 after the
devastating frost of that year, this estate was
brought back to life in 1972 by three
winegrowers. They opted for a relatively high
proportion – 65% – of Cabernet Sauvignon.
This was a wise decision, to judge by a long
series of awards for their red wine. When nature
has been helpful, this wine has a dark colour
and a taste with finesse, berry fruit and tannin;
oak plays a subordinate role. If the Cabernets
are less than fully ripe, then a significantly
lighter wine results, which may rather lack
fruit, juice, and depth. The white Premières
Côtes de Blaye is lively, fairly expressive, and
meant for early drinking.

Ch Roland la Garde   map 46 H3
owner: Bruno Martin **area:** 25.5 ha **cases:** 15,000
grape % R: MER 80% CS 20% **other wines:** Ch Moulin
de Pey-Long (Bordeaux rosé)
**33390 St-Seurin-de-Cursac tel: 05 57 42 32 29
fax: 05 57 42 01 86**
Supple wine that does not startle you with its
greatness but, with its fresh fruit and elegantly
rounded taste, makes an agreeable mouthful.
The Prestige – about a quarter of production –
offers more depth. According to tradition
Roland, Charlemagne's nephew, hurled his
spear into the Gironde from the hills near St-
Seurin-de-Cursac.

Ch La Rose Bellevue   map 46 B3
owner: Jean-Pierre Eymas **area:** 25 ha **cases:**
13,000 **grape % R:** MER 70% CS 20% CF 10%
**33820 St-Palais tel: 05 57 32 66 54
fax: 05 57 32 78 78**
La Rose Bellevue has been gradually enlarged
through three generations. In its bouquet and
taste the red wine characteristically has an
alluring aroma of black and red berry fruit,
together with smoky oak and tannin. Has
repeatedly won awards.

Domaine des Rosiers   map 46 B2
owner: Christian Blanchet **area:** 15.5 ha
cases: 6,500, white 1,800 **grape % R:** MER 70%
CF 30% **grape % W:** SAUV B 80% MUSC 20%

◆
Neighbouring appellations
The south-western border of the Blayais is
with the Gironde and the Côtes de Bourg.
To the north, an area of *palus* land is
excluded from the AC, and to the north-
east and east the border follows that of the
Gironde *département*. Vineyards beyond
this frontier are in Cognac.

Above: Ch Segonzac

**33820 St-Ciers-sur-Gironde tel: 05 57 32 75 97
fax: 05 57 32 78 37**
The white Premières Côtes de Blaye spends
eight months in new casks. Besides its oak the
wine offers a lot of citrus and tropical fruit, as
well as floral elements and good acidity.
Alongside the fairly accessible, rounded
standard red wine there is also a cask-aged
version which matures for 18 months.

Ch Saint-Aulaye   map 46 G3
owner: James & Huguette Berneaud **area:** 26 ha
cases: 12,000, white 1,800 **grape % R:** MER 70% CS
29% MAL 1% **grape % W:** UGNI BLANC 67% SAUV B 33%
second wine: Ch Cazeau-Morin
33390 Mazion tel: 05 57 42 11 14
Respectable red Premières Côtes de Blaye in
which toast, oak, vanilla and dark, somewhat
animal, aromas are perceptible.

Ch Segonzac   map 44 B2
owner: Jacob Marmet **area:** 31 ha **cases:** 19,000
grape % R: MER 60% CS 20% CF 10% MAL 10%
second wine: Tonnellerie du Château Segonzac
**33390 St-Genès-de-Blaye tel: 05 57 42 18 16
fax: 05 57 42 24 80**
Splendid château in a neatly rectangular park,
on a hill surrounded by vines. Since 1990 it has
belonged to a Swiss owner who has carried out
the necessary improvements, so that from 1991
the quality of the wine improved notably. The
cask-aged *cuvée* is particularly worth tasting.
Behind its colourful label lurks an impeccable
wine, with plenty of bouquet, mature, jammy
fruit, fine tannins and rich, creamy vanilla. The
standard wine also deserves attention. This, too,
is of high quality, but tastes more supple and
somewhat lighter.

Ch Sociondo   map 47 D3
owner: Michel Elie **area:** 9.9 ha **cases:** 5,000 **grape
% R:** MER 63% CS 27% CF 10% **second wine:** l'Ecuyer
de Sociondo **other châteaux owned:** Ch La Tenotte
(Côtes de Bourg)
**33390 Cars tel: 05 57 42 12 49
fax: 05 57 42 12 39**
Technically a very expertly made, lively red wine
with straightforward fruit notes (blackcurrant,
blackberry), some tannin – and, in particular,
great elegance. The château is notable for its
17th-century stone gateway, and there is also an
old chapel on the estate.

Ch Tayat   map 46 I9
owner: Bernard Favereaud **area:** 30 ha **cases:**
16,000, white 1,000 **grape % R:** MER 60% CS 30% CF
10% **grape % W:** SAUV B 70% SEM 30% **second wine:**
Domaine de la Baconne (Bordeaux)
**33620 Cézac tel: 05 57 68 62 10
fax: 05 57 68 15 07**
Even in lesser years this family estate, where
the fifth generation is now in charge, makes a
firm red wine with pleasing, mainly fruity
nuances and a hint of oak. The spirited white
Côtes de Blaye is also very good in its category.

Ch des Tourtes   map 46 B4
owner: Philippe Raguenot **area:** 35 ha **cases:**
10,300, white 5,700 **grape % R:** MER 65% CS 30% CF
5% **grape % W:** SAUV B 80% SEM 10% COL 10% **other
wines:** Philippe Raguenot (Bordeaux rosé;
Premières Côtes de Blaye)
**33820 St-Caprais-de-Blaye tel: 05 57 32 65 15
fax: 05 57 32 99 38**
From old legal documents it has been possible
to trace this estate back to the time of Louis
XIV. At its best the red Premières Côtes de Blaye
is a good average-quality wine, but it can
sometimes rather lack fruit, depth and length.
The standard rises with the Philippe Raguenot
cuvée, named after the owner: a cask-matured
wine made from half Merlot and half Cabernet
Sauvignon. This has more substance and needs
bottle age to get the initially dominant oak into
balance. The comparable white wine, a Côtes de
Blaye, is from Sauvignon Blanc fermented in
new barrels and is full in its taste, with much
toasted oak. The standard white is more
accessible and fresher.

Ch Le Vieux Pinson   map 46 B2
owner: Philippe Latté **area:** 8 ha **cases:** 1,300,
white 4,250 **grape % R:** MER 80% CS 20% **grape %
W:** SAUV B 50% COL 25% UGNI BLANC 25%
**33820 St-Ciers-sur-Gironde tel: 05 57 32 94 10
fax: 05 57 32 78 42**
Vineyard in existence from at least 1830, and
directed since 1991 by a new generation of the
family who own it. As a consequence both the
quantity of bottled wines has increased, and the
quality improved – particularly the red
Premières Côtes de Blaye. Barrels are not yet
used. Worth following.

Ch Le Virou   map 46 I6
owner: SCEA du Château Le Virou/Bernard Bessède
area: 63 ha **cases:** 40,000 **grape % R:** MER 50% CS
30% CF 20% **second wine:** Ch Prieuré d'Aiguevives
**33920 St-Girons-d'Aiguevives tel: 05 57 43 43 82
fax: 05 57 43 01 89**
Extensive estate on the site of a former
monastery. Bought in 1984 by the Tari family,
then the owners of Ch Giscours, Margaux, and
other properties, it was acquired by a *négociant*
in 1991. He began a programme of renovation,
and the vineyard is to be increased by 15 ha. So
far the red wine has been agreeably fruity with
dark notes, but otherwise rather light and
limited in personality.

Classifications

1855 CLASSIFICATION OF THE RED WINES OF THE GIRONDE

Premiers Crus:
Haut-Brion
Lafite Rothschild
Latour
Margaux
Mouton Rothschild
Seconds Crus:
Brane-Cantenac
Cos d'Estournele
Ducru-Beaucaillou
Durfort-Vivens
Gruaud-Larose
Lascombes
Léoville-Barton
Léoville-Las-Cases
Léoville Poyferré
Montrose
Pichon Longueville
Pichon Longueville Comtesse de Lalande
Rauzan-Gassies
Rauzan-Ségla
Troisièmes Crus:
Boyd-Cantenac
Calon-Ségur
Cantenac-Brown
Desmirail
Ferrière
Giscours
d'Issan
Kirwan
Lagrange
La Lagune
Langoa-Barton
Malescot St-Exupéry
Marquis d'Alesme Becker
Palmer
Quatrièmes Crus:
Beychevelle
Branaire
Duhart-Milon
Lafon-Rochet
Marquis de Terme
Pouget
Prieuré-Lichine
St-Pierre
Talbot
La Tour Carnet
Cinquièmes Crus:
d'Armailhac
Batailley
Belgrave
Camensac
Cantemerle
Clerc Milon
Cos Labory
Croizet-Bages
Dauzac
Grand-Puy Ducasse
Grand-Puy-Lacoste
Haut-Bages Libéral
Haut-Batailley
Lynch-Bages
Lynch-Moussas
Pédesclaux
Pontet-Canet
du Tertre

1959 CLASSIFICATION OF THE RED AND WHITE WINES OF THE GRAVES

Premier Cru Classé:
Haut-Brion
Crus Classés, red wines:
Bouscaut
Carbonnieux
Domaine de Chevalier
de Fieuzal
Haut-Bailly
Latour-Haut-Brion
Malartic-Lagravière
La Mission-Haut-Brion
Olivier
Pape Clément
Smith Haut Lafitte
La Tour Martillac
Crus Classés, White wines:
Bouscaut
Carbonnieux
Domaine de Chevalier
Couhins
Couhins-Lurton
Laville Haut Brion
Malartic-Lagravière
Olivier
La Tour Martillac

1855 CLASSIFICATION OF THE WHITE WINES OF THE GIRONDE

Premier Cru Supérieur:
d'Yquem
Premiers Crus Classés:
Climens
Clos Haut-Peyraguey
Coutet
Guiraud
Lafaurie-Peyraguey
Rabaud-Promis
de Rayne-Vigneau
Rieussec
Sigalas-Rabaud
Suduiraut
La Tour Blanche
Deuxièmes Crus Classés:
d'Arche
Broustet
Caillou
Doisy-Daëne
Doisy-Dubroca
Doisy-Védrines
Filhot
Lamothe
Lamothe Guignard
de Malle
Myrat
Nairac
Romer du Hayot
Suau

1996 CLASSIFICATION OF THE WINES OF ST-EMILION

Premiers Grands Crus Classés:
A: Ausone
A: Cheval Blanc
l'Angélus
Beau-Séjour Bécot
Beauséjour
Belair
Canon
Figeac
Clos Fourtet
La Gaffelière
Magdelaine
Pavie
Trotte Vieille
Grands Crus Classés:
l'Arrosée
Balestard-la-Tonnelle
Bellevue
Bergat
Berliquet
Cadet-Bon
Cadet-Piola
Canon la Gaffelière
Cap de Mourlin
Chauvin
Clos des Jacobins
Clos St Martin
La Clotte
La Clusière
Corbin
Corbin-Michotte
La Couspade
Curé-Bon
Dassault
La Dominique
Faurie de Souchard
Fonplégade
Fonroque
Franc-Mayne
Grand Mayne
Grand Pontet
Grandes Murailles
Guadet-St Julien
Haut-Corbin
Haut Sarpe
Couvent des Jacobins
Lamarzelle
Laniote
Larcis Ducasse
Larmande
Laroque
Laroze
Matras
Moulin du Cadet
Clos de l'Oratoire
Pavie Decesse
Pavie Macquin
Petit-Faurie-de-Soutard
Le Prieuré
Ripeau
St-Georges (Côte Pavie)
La Serre
Soutard
Tertre Daugay
La Tour-Figeac
Tour-du-Pin-Figeac (Giraud-Bélivier)
Tour-du-Pin-Figeac (Moueix)
Troplong-Mondot
Villemaurine
Yon-Figeac

1996 MEMBERSHIP OF THE SYNDICATE OF CRUS BOURGEOIS OF THE MÉDOC

AC Médoc:
Bégadan: des Bertins, de By, des Cabans, Caillous de By, La Clare, La Gorre, Greysac, Haut-Peyrillat, Laffitte Laujac, Lalande Robin, Laujac, du Monthil, Moulin de la Roque, Patache d'Aux, Plagnac, Rollan de By, La Roque de By, La Tour de By, Vieux Robin, Vieux Château Landon
Blaignan: Blaignan, Canteloup, La Cardonne, La Gorce, Grivière, Haut-Myles, Lalande d'Auvion, Normandin, Pontey, Prieure, Ramafort, Rose de France, des Tourelles, Tour Haut-Caussan
Civrac-en-Médoc: Bournac, la Chandellière, d'Escurac, de Panigon
Couqueques: de Conques, Les Moines, Les Ormes Sorbet
Jau-Dignac-et-Loirac: Fergraves, Gravelongue, Haut Brisey, Lacombe Noaillac, Listran, Moulin de Noaillac, Nausicaa, Noaillac, La Pirouette, Saint-Aubin, Segue-Longue, Sestignan, Les Traverses
Lesparre-Médoc: Preuillac, Vernous
Ordonnac: de la Croix, Fontis, Gallais Bellevue, Goudy La Cardonne, Lassalle, Pey-Martin, Potensac, Taffard de Blaignan, Terre Rouge
Prignac-en-Médoc: Chantelys, La Fontaine de L'Aubier, Haut-Garin, Hourbanon, Lafon
Queyrac: Carcanieux
St-Christoly: Le Boscq, Les Grands Chênes, Guiraud-Peyrebrune, Haut-Canteloup, du Moulin, Moulin de Castillon, Les Mourlanes, du Perier, Saint Bonnet, Tour Blanche, La Valière
St-Germain-d'Esteuil: Brie-Caillou, Castera, Hauterive
St-Yzans-de-Médoc: des Brousteras, La Croix du Chevalier, Haut-Maurac, Lestruelle, Loudenne, Mazails, La Mothe, Moulin de Bel-Air, Le Plantey, Quintaine-Mazails, La Ribaud, Sigognac, Les Tuileries
Valeyrac: Bellegrave, Bellerive, Bellevue, Le Bourdieu, Sipian, Le Temple, Valeyrac
Vensac: Comtesse de Gombaud, David, de Taste
AC Haut-Médoc:
Arcins: d'Arcins, Arnauld, Barreyres, Tour Bellevue, Tour du Mayne, Tour-du-Roc
Arsac: Le Monteil d'Arsac
Avensan: Citran, Meyre, Moulins de Citran, de Villegeorge
Blanquefort: Magnol, St Ahon
Cissac: Abiet, du Breuil, Le Chêne, Cissac, Hanteillan, Haut-Logat, Laborde, Lamothe-Cissac, Landat, de Martiny, Moulin du Breuil, Puy Castéra, La Tonnelle, Tour du Mirail, Tour St Joseph, de Villambis
Cussac-Fort-Médoc: Aney, d'Arvigny, Beaumont, Bel Air, Fort de Vauban, Julien, Lamothe Bergeron, du Moulin Rouge, du Raux, Romefort, Tour du Haut-Moulin
Lamarque: du Cartillon, de Lamarque, Malescasse
Le Pian: Barthez, Laffitte-Canteloup, Lemoine-Nexon, de Malleret, Sénéjac
Le Taillan: La Dame Blanche, du Taillan
Ludon: d'Agassac, d'Arche
Parempuyre: Clément-Pichon
Macau: Cambon la Pelouse, Dasvin-Bel-Air, Maucamps
St-Laurent-Medoc: Balac, Barateau, Caronne Ste Gemme, Labat, Lagrave-Genestra, Larose-Mascard, Larose-Perganson, Larose Sieujan, Larose-Trintaudon
St-Sauveur: Fonpiqueyre, Fontesteau, Fournas Bernadotte, La Grave, Haut-Laborde, Haut-Madrac, Hourtin-Ducasse, Lieujean, Liversan, Peyrabon, Peyrahaut, Ramage La Batisse, Tourteran
St-Seurin-de-Cadourne: d'Aurilhac, Bel Orme Tronquoy de Lalande, Bonneau-Livran, Charmail, Coufran, Dilhac, La Fagotte, Grand Moulin, Lartigue De Brochon, Lestage Simon, Marquis de Cadourne, Muret, Perselan, Plantey De La Croix, Pontoise Cabarrus, Puy-Medulli, La Rose Marechale, St-Paul, Sénilhac, Sociando-Mallet, Soudars, Troupian, Verdignan
Vertheuil: de l'Abbaye, Le Bourdieu Vertheuil, La Graviere, Haut-Vignoble Du Parc, le Meyniou, Reysson, Le Souley-Ste Croix
AC Moulis-en-Médoc: Anthonic, Biston-Brillette, Brillette, Caroline, Chasse-Spleen, Chemin Royal, Duplessis , Dutruch Grand Poujeaux, Franquet Grand Poujeaux, Malmaison, Maucaillou, Moulin à Vent, Moulin de St-Vincent, Moulis, Poujeaux, La Salle de Poujeaux
AC Listrac-Médoc: La Bécade, Bellevue-Lafont, Cantegric, Cap Léon Veyrin, Clarke, de Corde, L'Ermitage, Fonréaud, Fourcas Dupré, Fourcas Hosten, Fourcas Loubaney, Les Hauts Marcieux, Lafon, Lalande, La Lauzette, Lestage, Liouner, Mayne Lalande, Moulin de Laborde, Peyredon Lagravette, Peyre-Lebade, Reverdi, Sansarot-Dupré, Sémeillan Mazeau
AC St-Estèphe: Andron Blanquet, Beau-Site, Beau-Site Haut Vignoble, Canteloup, Capbern Gasqueton, Chambert-Marbuzet, La Commanderie, Coutelin-Merville, Le Crock, Domeyne, Haut-Baradieu, Haut-Beauséjour, Haut Coteau, Haut-Marbuzet, Les Hauts de Pez, La Haye, Lavillotte, Lilian Ladouys, Mac Carthy, de Marbuzet, Meyney, Morin, les Ormes de Pez, Phélan-Ségur, Pomys, La Rousselière, St-Estèphe, St-Roch, Ségur de Cabanac, Tour du Haut Vignoble, Tour de Marbuzet, Tour de Pez, Tour des Termes, Tronquoy-Lalande
AC Pauillac: Artigues, Belle Rose, Bernadotte, Chanteclerc-Milon, Colombier-Monpelou, La Fleur Milon, Fonbadet, Haut-Bages Monpelou, Pibran, du Plantey
AC St-Julien-Beychevelle: La Bridane, du Glana, Moulin de la Rose, Moulin-Riche, Sirène, Terrey-Gros-Cailloux
AC Margaux: d'Arsac, Deyrem Valentin, La Gurgue, Haut-Breton Larigaudière, Labégorce, Labégorce-Zédé, Larruau, Marsac Séguineau, Martinens, Monbrison, Paveil de Luze, Pontet-Chappaz, Tayac, La Tour de Mons

1997 MEMBERSHIP OF THE SYNDICATE OF CRUS ARTISANS OF THE MÉDOC

AC Médoc:
Bégadan: Lolan, Panigon
Blaignan: Blaignan
Civrac-en-Médoc: La Tessonnière
Couqueques: La Croix du Breuil, L'Hermitage, Vieux Serestin
Gaillan: Gadet-Terrefort
Jau-Dignac-et-Loirac: Les Graves de Loirac, Jeanton
Lesparre-Médoc: Larieux
Ordonnac: Lagardieu
St-Christoly: Cantegric
St-Germain-d'Esteuil: Baudens
St-Yzans-de-Médoc: Bois de Roc, Clair Moulin, Guillaume, Terre Feu
Valeyrac: Lalande de Villeneuve
Vensac: Les Trieux
Vertheuil: des Moulins
AC Haut-Médoc:
Arcins: Tour Bellegrave
Avensan: Semonlon
Cissac: d'Osmond, Tour Bel Air
Cussac-Fort-Médoc: de Coudot, de Lauga, Micalet, du Moulin, Tour du Goua, Viallet-Nouhant
Lamarque: Haut Bellevue, Vieux Gabarrey
Le Pian: Louens
Le Taillan: Graveyron Monlun
Ludon: Dom. Grand Lafont
Macau: Guittot Fellonneau
St-Laurent-Médoc: Le Bouscat, Devise D'Ardilly
St-Estèphe: Dom. du Vatican
St-Sauveur: La Fon Du Berger, Laroze Labatisse
St-Seurin-de-Cadourne: Haut-Bregat
Vertheuil: Ferré, Lesquireau-Desse, La Marsaudrie
AC Moulis-en-Médoc: Lagorce Bernadas
AC Listrac-Médoc: Gobinaud, Tourilles
AC St-Estèphe: La Peyre
AC Pauillac: Béhèré
AC St-Julien-Beychevelle: Capdet
AC Margaux: les Baraillots, Clos de Bigos, Gassies du Vieux Bourg, Les Graviers, Moulin de Tricot, Tayac Plaisance, Les Vimières

Index & Gazetteer of châteaux & wines

This index lists all châteaux with entries in the Atlas, and also acts as a gazetteer to those with map references (*in italics*). Thus Ch d'Arsac is on map 8 (left), grid square M7, and its entry is on p40.

The index also lists second wines, special *cuvées* and other wines mentioned in main entries, when these have names which differ from the parent château. These show the name of the château in whose entry they appear *in italics*. An index of châteaux by commune follows the main index: see p399. Use this to find which château are in a given commune.

1er Vin *St Jacques Calon*
Abbaye, L' *40 J8* ... 323
Abbaye, de l' *Reysson*
Abbaye de St Ferme *36* ... 222
Abeille de Fieuzal, l' *de Fieuzal*
Abeilles, Les *Calon* ... 325
Abeilley, Clos l' *de Rayne-Vigneau*
Abzac, d' *34* ... 222
Acacia *Charron*
Accabailles de Barréjats *Cru Barréjats*
Agassac, d' *18 F7* ... 106
Aiguilhe, d' *45 G5* ... 362
Aiguilhe, La Rose d' *d'Aiguilhe*
Ailes de Berliquet, Les *Berliquet*
Ailes de Paloumey, Les *Paloumey*
Aillan *Lavillotte*
Albert Duran *Beauregard Ducasse*
Albertine Payri *Beauregard Ducasse*
Alex *Plaisance*
Alexandre *35* ... 222
Alexandre *Pasquet*
Alfa Bernarde *46 K10* ... 381
Aliénor *Jacques Blanc*
Allegret *35* ... 222
Allendy de La Cassagne *La Cassagne-Boutet*
Alphonse Dubreuil, Clos *46* ... 372
Amandiers, Clos des *Vieux Ch Ferron*
Amédée Chassagnoux *Jean Voisin*
Amiral de Beychevelle *Beychevelle*
Amiral de l'Escadre, l' *l'Escadre*
An 1453, l' *Cantegrive*
Anaïs Damien *Brondelle*
Ancestral, l' *Moulin de Sales*
Ancien Manoir de Valette, Dom. de l' *46 G4* ... 381
Ancres, Les *de Jayle*
Andoyse du Hayot *Romer du Hayot*
André *Prieurs de la Commanderie*
Andron Blanquet *15 J5* ... 83
Aney *19 F6* ... 106
Aney d'Arnaussan *Aney*
Angelique *Plain-Point*
Angelique de Monbousquet *Monbousquet*
Angélus *38/L F8* ... 280
Anglais, de l' *40 J9* ... 323
Angludet, d' *8/R I3* ... 40
Anniche *32/R G6* ... 196
Annonciation, de l' *38/L C8* ... 280
Antholien *Domaine de Courteillac*
Anthonic *17 G7* ... 99
Antognan *Saint Paul*
Aôst, l' *de Villambis*
Archambeau, d' *26/L G6* ... 155
Archange de Laplagnotte-Bellevue *Laplagnotte-Bellevue*
Arche, d' *18 E7* ... 106
Arche, d' *27/R K3* ... 176
Arcins, d' *19 K7* ... 106
Ardennes, d' *26/L G6* ... 155
Ardilles, Les *Les Mangons*
Ardilleys, Dom. des *d'Osmond*
Argent, Aile d' *Mouton Rothschild*
Argenteyre, l' *22/R I5* ... 126
Argilas le Pape, d' *27/L H8* ... 176
Armailhac, d' *12/L G7* ... 67
Armajan des Ormes, d' *27/L E4* ... 176
Armens, d' *Bonnet* ... 285
Arnaud de Jacquemeau *38/L E7* ... 280
Arnaud, Dom. *46 J8* ... 381
Arnauld *19 K7* ... 106
Arnaussan, d' *Aney*
Arnauton *44 H9* ... 351

Arpents du Bourg-Dieu, Les *45 F4* ... 362
Arras, Des *34* ... 222
Arricaud, d' *26/L H6* ... 155
Arromans, Les *35* ... 222
Arrosée, l' *38/L G8* ... 280
Arroucats, des *31/R L6* ... 216
Arthus/Clos de La Vieille Eglise *45 J3* ... 362
Artigue de Sénéjac *Sénéjac*
Artigues *Plantey*
Artigues Arnaud *Grand-Puy Ducasse*
Artiste, de l' *de Lisennes*
Arveyres, d' *Cantelaudette*
Arvigny, d' *Beaumont*
Arvouet, d' *40 L6* ... 314
Au Grand Paris *36* ... 241
Aubarèdes, Les *Rousset*
Aubastons, Les *Tour des Graves*
Aubiac, Clos d' *de Terrefort-Quancard*
Aubiers, Les *Le Grand Moulin* ... 384
Aublines, Les *Loumède*
Aubrade, de L' *Jamin*
Aubrade, De l' *36* ... 222
Aurilhac, d' *21/R J6* ... 106
Ausone *38/L G9* ... 280
Avensan, d' *Métria*
B de Barrabaque *Barrabaque*
Bacchus *35* ... 266
Baconne, Dom. de la *Tayat*
Badon, Clos *38/L H10* ... 281
Badon Vieux Ceps *Clos Badon*
Bahans de Haut-Brion, Le *Haut-Brion*
Balac *20 K6* ... 106
Balan, de *36* ... 222
Balardin, Dom. du *Malescot St-Exupéry*
Balestard la Tonnelle *38/R E1* ... 281
Balestard, de *35* ... 222
Balirac *Le Temple*
Ballan-Larquette *36* ... 222
Balot *31/R K2* ... 196
Baradol *Ripeau*
Baragan *de Marsan*
Barail Beaulieu, Le *35* ... 223
Barateau *20 L8* ... 106
Barauderie, La *Croix Grand Barail*
Barbazan *36* ... 223
Barbé *47 E3* ... 381
Barbe Blanche, de *40 F7* ... 320
Barbe, de *47 G3* ... 372
Barberousse *38/L J10* ... 281
Barbey *Labory*
Bardes, Les *40 I5* ... 314
Bardey *Bardins*
Bardins *23/R C4* ... 143
Bardis *Verdus*
Bardonne, La *34* ... 223
Baret *23/R B1* ... 143
Barjuneau Chauvin, Dom. de *28/R M5* ... 176
Baron Bellevue *Le Clos du Notaire*
Baron Bertin *35* ... 223
Baron Charles *Le Tertre*
Baron d'Estours *Tour Saint-Fort*
Baron de Brane, Le *Brane-Cantenac*
Baron La Mouline *Baron Bertin*
Baron Ségur *Coucy*
Baron Villeneuve de Cantemerle *Cantemerle*
Barrabaque *44 J8* ... 356
Barrail, du *35* ... 223

Barrail de Franc *Bétoule*
Barrail de Guillon *27* ... 223
Barrail des Graves *38/L K8* ... 281
Barrailh, du *des Gravières*
Barraillots, les *8/L F10* ... 40
Barre, de *Barre Gentillot*
Barre Gentillot *35* ... 266
Barreyre *32/R H8* ... 196
Barreyre *18* ... 223
Barreyres *19 J9* ... 107
Barry, du *38/L L7* ... 281
Barthez *de Malleret*
Bastian *36* ... 223
Bastide de Siran, La *Siran*
Bastidette, La *43 D10* ... 314
Bastienne, La *40 J2* ... 314
Bastille *Puy Arnaud*
Bastor-Lamontagne *27/L G8* ... 176
Batailley *12/R H7* ... 67
Bauduc *35* ... 223
Bavolier, Dom. de *32/L J6* ... 196
Béard *38/R H3* ... 281
Beau Rivage Laguens, de *32* ... 224
Beau Site Monprimblanc *Balot*
Beau Village *Grand Village*
Beau-Mayne *Couvent des Jacobins*
Beau-Pontet *Couvent des Jacobins*
Beau-Séjour Bécot *38/L F8* ... 281
Beau-Site *15 D5* ... 83
Beau-Site Haut-Vignoble *15 D5* ... 83
Beauchamps, Dom. de *de l'Eglise*
Beaudry *des Matards*
Beaufresque *34* ... 224
Beauguérit *47 J7* ... 372
Beaulieu Bergey *36* ... 224
Beaulieu, de *34* ... 224
Beaulieu, de *36* ... 224
Beaumont *19 G5* ... 107
Beauregard *41 E6* ... 331
Beauregard Ducasse *26/R J6* ... 155
Beauregard, Clos *41 E8* ... 331
Beauregard-Ducourt, de *35* ... 224
Beauséjour *38/L F8* ... 281
Beauséjour *44 E9* ... 351
Beauval *35* ... 224
Bec en Sabot, Le *de France*
Bécade, La *Fourcas Loubaney*
Bécasse, La *12/R E3* ... 67
Béchereau *34* ... 224
Béchereau *27/L L9* ... 176
Bégot *46 K6* ... 372
Bel Air *20 E7* ... 107
Bel Air *35* ... 224
Bel Air *36* ... 224
Bel Air *31/R L5* ... 216
Bel-Air *40 E7* ... 320
Bel-Air *40 J8* ... 323
Bel-Air *41 I4* ... 331
Bel-Air, de *43 K6* ... 342
Bel Air Moulard *Le Prieur*
Bel Air-Marquis de Pomereu *Bel-Air Marquis d'Aligre*
Bel-Air l'Espérance *35* ... 225
Bel-Air Lagrave *17 E9* ... 99
Bel-Air Marquis d'Aligre *8/L F7* ... 40
Bel-Air Ortet *15 F7* ... 83
Belair *38/L G9* ... 284
Belair Montaiguillon *Belair St-Georges*
Belair-Coubet *47 G4* ... 372
Belcier *45 F8* ... 362
Belgrave *20 L10* ... 107
Bel-Enclos *Haut-Terrier*
Bel Orme Tronquoy de Lalande *21/R J9* ... 107
Belle Eglise *Vignol*
Belle Ile *8* ... 225
Belle Rose *12/L E6* ... 67
Belle Rose, Clos *38/L D4* ... 284
Belle-Croix *de Haut-Calens*
Belle-Garde *35* ... 225
Bellecombe *38/L* ... 284
Bellefont, de *Le Tuquet*

Bellefont-Belcier *38/R I1* ... 284
Bellegarde *Siran*
Bellegrave *22/R G7* ... 126
Bellegrave *41 L5* ... 331
Bellegrave Van der Voort *12/R D5* ... 67
Bellerive *22/R G9* ... 126
Belles-Cimes *Coutet* ... 289
Belles-Graves *43 G8* ... 342
Bellevue *22/R G8* ... 126
Bellevue *38/L F8* ... 284
Bellevue ... 314
Bellevue *45 I5* ... 362
Bellevue *Montviel*
Bellevue *Toutigeac*
Bellevue, Clos *31/R I2* ... 196
Bellevue, de *40 H6* ... 320
Bellevue Canteranne *Haut-Bellevue*
Bellevue Favereau *Haut-Favereau*
Bellevue Jos *35* ... 225
Bellevue La Mongie *35* ... 225
Bellevue Laffont *Fourcas Dupré*
Bellevue Lagravette *Rose Ste-Croix*
Bellevue St-Martin *Bellevue* ... 314
Bellile-Mondotte *38/R G2* ... 284
Belliquet *Haut-Guérin*
Belloc, de *Ferran*
Bellonne Saint Georges *40 K3* ... 325
Belloy *44 J7* ... 356
Belon *25/L I4* ... 155
Belregard-Figeac *38/L E2* ... 284
Bénillan *Lalande d'Auvion*
Benjamin de Beauregard, Le *Beauregard*
Bequet *Rabaud-Promis*
Berbec de *des Coulinats*
Bergat *38/L F10* ... 284
Bergat Bosson, Clos *La Clotte*
Berger *25/R* ... 155
Berger, De *Le Trébuchet*
Bergère, La ... 381
Bergieu, Le *La Closerie du Grand Poujeaux*
Berliquet *38/L G8* ... 284
Bernadotte *20 I8* ... 67
Bernat, Le *Dom. du Calvaire*
Bernateau *38/R H5* ... 285
Bernèdes, Les *Vieux Ch Landon*
Bernet, Le *21/R J9* ... 126
Bernones *19 F7* ... 107
Beroy *Lesparre*
Berthault Brillette *Brillette*
Berthenon *46 I5* ... 381
Berthou *Colbert*
Bertin, de *35* ... 225
Bertinat Lartigue *38/L I8* ... 285
Bertineau St-Vincent ... 342
Bertinerie *Haut Bertinerie*
Bertrand *de l'Escaley*
Bertrande, la *31/R G2* ... 196
Bertrands, les *46 D5* ... 381
Bessan *Saint-Marc* ... 188
Bétoule *34* ... 225
Beychade, de *Falfas*
Beychevelle *10 I8* ... 55
Biac, du *32/R K6* ... 196
Biarnès *35* ... 225
Bibian Tigana *17 F5* ... 94
Bichon Cassignols *25/L E5* ... 155
Bigarette, la *du Paradis*
Bigarnon, Dom. de *Léoville Las Cases*
Bigaroux *38/L I8* ... 285
Billauds, Les *46 C4* ... 381
Billerond *38/R J3* ... 285
Biré *18* ... 225
Birot, de *31/L J8* ... 196
Birot, Dom. de *35* ... 225
Biscarets, du *la Bertrande*
Biston-Brillette *17 H7* ... 99
Bizelles, Dom. des *34* ... 228
Bizon, Le *Petit La Garosse*
Blagnac *Hanteillan*
Blaignan *21/R G3* ... 126
Blancherie, La *25/L F5* ... 155
Blanchet *36* ... 228

Blancherie-Peyret, la *La Blancherie*
Blanquerie, La *36* ... 228
Blanzac *45 K5* ... 362
Blason de l'Evangile *l'Evangile*
Blason de Pomys, Le *Pomys*
Blassan, de *34* ... 228
Blayac *21/L G5* ... 126
Blayais *Haut-Boisron*
Bocage, Le *34* ... 228
Bodet *Charlemagne*
Bois, du *45 J3* ... 362
Bois Cardinal *Fleur Cardinale*
Bois de Favereau *Haut-Favereau*
Bois de Laborde, Dom. *43 J3* ... 342
Bois de Lunier *Vieux Robin*
Bois de Roc *21/R F6* ... 126
Bois de Roche *Terrefort*
Bois du Monteil *Martinens*
Bois Joli, Clos du *40* ... 362
Bois Noir *34* ... 228
Bois Redon *de Cornemps*
Bois-Cardon *Le Bourdieu*
Bois-Malot *35* ... 228
Bois Sacrée *Le Luc-Regula*
Boisgrand, Dom *Ségur*
Boisserie, la *38/R K4* ... 285
Bon Dieu des Vignes *de Chantegrive*
Bon Jouan *36* ... 228
Bon Pasteur, Le *Bertineau St-Vincent*
Bon Pasteur, Le *41 C4* ... 331
Bonalgue *41 J7* ... 331
Bonhoste, de *36* ... 228
Bonnat, Le *25/L I10* ... 155
Bonneau *40 K6* ... 314
Bonneau-Livran *Sociando-Mallet*
Bonnelle, La *38/R K5* ... 285
Bonnet *35* ... 228
Bonnet *38/R K4* ... 285
Bordenave, Dom. de *36* ... 229
Borderie-Mondésir, la *43 J4* ... 342
Borderon, Le *Larrivaux*
Bordes, de *40 F4* ... 320
Borie de l'Anglais *Dom. du Calvaire*
Borie de Noaillan *Vignol*
Bories, Clos des *Puygueraud*
Bory Rollet, Le *36* ... 229
Bos, Le *Camus*
Bos, Le *35* ... 229
Boscq, Le *15 C6* ... 83
Boscq, Le *21/R B6* ... 126
Bosquet *35* ... 229
Bossuet *34* ... 229
Botte, La *46* ... 229
Bouade, La *29 E6* ... 176
Boucayery *Puyblanquet Carrille*
Bougan *des Arroucats*
Bouilh, du *34* ... 229
Bouillerot, Dom. de *35* ... 229
Bouquet de Monbrison *Monbrison*
Bouquet des Roches *Pey Labrie*
Bourbon La Chapelle *Castera*
Bourbon, Clos *31/R I4* ... 197
Bourdicotte *36* ... 229
Bourdieu, Dom. du *Haut Mallet*
Bourdieu, Le *Haut Mallet*
Bourdieu, Le *22/R H8* ... 126
Bourdieu La Valade *44 M8* ... 351
Bourdieu Vertheuil, Le *20 D6* ... 107
Bourdillot, Le *25/R E4* ... 156
Bourdon *Piot-David*
Bourg, du *Tournefeuille*
Bourg-Neuf, Dom. de *de Bourgueneuf*
Bourgelat, Clos *26/L C8* ... 156
Bourgneuf-Vayron *41 I5* ... 331
Bourgueneuf, de *41 I4* ... 331
Bourguette, La *36* ... 230
Bournac *21/R E2* ... 128
Bourseau *43 J5* ... 342
Bouscat, Le *35* ... 230
Bouscat, Le *20 L8* ... 128
Bouscaut *23/R E4* ... 143

Bousquet *Pouyanne*
Bousquet, du *47 K7* 372
Bouteilley, Dom. de
 32/R D7 197
Boutillon *36* 230
Boutisse *38/R G5* 285
Bouygue, La *Haut-Plantey*
Bouzigues, les *36* 230
Boyd-Cantenac *8/R H3* 40
Bragard *Haut-Cadet*
Brame-Pan *Sainte-Marie*
Bran de Compostelle *35* 230
Branaire *10 I7* 55
Branas Grand Poujeaux
 17 F9 99
Branda *40 H9* 323
Brande, La *44 C9* 351
Brande, La *45 I3* 362
Brande-Bergère *34* 230
Brandeau *45 G8* 362
Brandeau *Roc Meynard*
Brandey, Le *Le Sèpe*
Brandille, Dom. de la *34* 230
Brane-Cantenac *8/R H2* 40
Braneyre, Cru de *d'Arche* 176
Branne, de *Plaisance* 318
Brannens *Magence*
Brassens-Guiteronde *Guiteronde du Hayot*
Braulterie de Peyraud, La
 46 I5 381
Brehat *45 J2* 363
Breillan *Dillon*
Brethous *32/L I5* 197
Bretonnière, La *46 H3* 382
Breuil, du *44 I5* 351
Breuil, du *20 F7* 107
Breuil, Le *47 I4* 372
Breuil Renaissance, Le
 21/R C2 128
Breuilh *Le Temple*
Briand *45 I3* 363
Bridane, La *10 E7* 55
Bridoire *Launay*
Bridoire-Bellevue *Launay*
Brie-Caillou *21* 128
Brieux Chauvin *Millaud-Montlabert*
Brillette *17 G7* 99
Briot *35* 230
Bristeau *Peymelon*
Brivazac *de Barbe*
Brondeau, de *35* 230
Brondelle *26/R G6* 156
Brousse, de *Côte Montpezat*
Broussey, Dom. de *Meste-Jean*
Broustaret, du *31/L G9* 197
Brousteras, des *21/R E7* 128
Broustet *29 H6* 177
Brown *23/L* 143
Brown-Lamartine *8* 230
Brown-Lamartine *Cantenac-Brown*
Bru, du *36* 230
Brûlésécaille *47 K8* 372
Brulières de Beychevelle *Beychevelle*
Brun Despagne *35* 231
Brunette, de la *47 M10* 372
Bujan *47 H4* 372
Burayre *35* 231
Burdigala *de l'Emigré*
Burdigala *Coulac*
Burgrave *Bonalgue*
Butte de Cazevert *35* 231
By, de *22/R I10* 128
By, Dom. de *Greysac*
Bychaud *Petit Clos du Roy*
Cabane Voisin *Jean Voisin*
Cabanne, La *41 H4* 331
Cabannes, des *35* 231
Cabannieux *25/R F3* 156
Cabans, des *22/R J8* 128
Cabirol *Puycarpin*
Cablanc *36* 231
Cabos *Joinin*
Caderie, La *Dom. de Birot*
Cadet de Gombaude *Gombaude-Guillot*

Cadet de Larmande, Le *Larmande*
Cadet La Vieille France *La Vieille France*
Cadet-Bon *38/L E9* 285
Cadet-Peychez *38/L E9* 285
Cadet-Piola *38/L E9* 286
Cadet-Pontet *38/L E9* 286
Cadillac-Branda *34* 231
Cadillac Lesgourgues *Cadillac-Branda*
Caillavet, de *31/L E4* 197
Cailleteau Bergeron *46 H3* 382
Caillou *29 J3* 177
Caillou *44 J8* 356
Caillou, du *26/L D9* 156
Caillou, Le *41 G7* 331
Caillou, Le *La Tour du Pin Figeac*
Caillou Blanc *Talbot*
Caillou Les Martins *40* 320
Cailloux de By *La Tour de By*
Cailloux, Dom. des *35* 231
Callac, de *26/L F7* 156
Calmeilh *Belle Ile*
Calon *40 I4* 314
Calon *40 J2* 325
Calon-Ségur *15 D6* 83
Calvaire, Dom. du *Haut Ballet*
Calvaire, Dom. du *34* 231
Calvaire, du *38/R H6* 286
Calvimont, de *de Cérons*
Camail *32/R J3* 197
Caman *la Raz Caman*
Camarsac, de *35* 231
Camarset *25/L* 156
Cambes, Dom. de *Roc de Cambes*
Cambon la Pelouse *18 C6* 108
Camensac *20 M9* 108
Camerac *La Tuilerie du Puy*
Camperos *Closiot*
Camperos *Guiteronde du Hayot*
Camus *26/R F7* 156
Canada *34* 231
Candale, de *d'Issan*
Candale, de *38/R H2* 286
Candelaire *La Marche-Canon*
Candelley *36* 231
Canet *35* 232
Canevault *44 F2* 351
Canon *38/L F8* 286
Canon *44 K6* 356
Canon de Brem *44 K9* 356
Canon Feydieu *44* 356
Canon la Gaffelière
 38/L H9 286
Canon Lange *Canon* 356
Canon Pourret *Franc-Pourret*
Canon-Chaigneau *43 C8* 342
Canon-Moueix *44 K9* 356
Cantebau *Couhins-Lurton*
Cantegric *21/R C6* 128
Cantegric *Liounier*
Cantegrive *45 E5* 363
Cantelaube *38/L J7* 286
Cantelaudette *35* 266
Cantelaudette, Dom. de *Mathereau*
Cantelauze *41 F2* 331
Canteloudette *35* 232
Canteloup *32/L G4* 197
Canteloup *35* 266
Canteloup *La Gorce*
Cantelys *23/R J2* 143
Cantemerle *18 D6* 108
Cantenac *38/L G4* 286
Cantenac-Brown *8/L G10* 41
Cantin, de *38/R F5* 286
Canuet *Cantenac-Brown*
Cap Blanc *Gantonet*
Cap de Faugères *45 J3* 363
Cap de Haut *19 H8* 108
Cap de Merle *40 D5* 320
Cap de Mourlin *38/L D9* 286
Cap d'Or *40* 325
Cap de Roudier *Roudier*
Cap Léon Veyrin *17 B5* 94
Cap Saint-Martin *47 C3* 382

Cap-de-Haut-Maucaillou *Maucaillou*
Capailley *Rouet*
Capbern Gasqueton *15 E8* 83
Capbern Grand Village *Capbern Gasqueton*
Capdeville, Dom. de *Gobinaud*
Capelle, La *35* 232
Capella *La Capelle*
Caperot *Monbousquet*
Capet *44 H8* 351
Capet Bégaud *44 H8* 357
Capet Duverger *38/R I4* 286
Capet-Guillier *38/R I3* 287
Capet-Lagüe *Lagüe*
Capitan de Mourlin *Cap de Mourlin*
Cappes, de *36* 232
Capucins, Clos des *Fayau*
Capville *46 I3* 382
Carbon d'Artigues *26/L G5* 156
Carbonnieux, Dom. de
 27/L K8 177
Carbonnieux *23/R E1* 143
Carcanieux *22/R J3* 128
Cardaillan, de *De Malle*
Cardeneau *44 E9* 351
Cardinal *Clos Chante Alouette*
Cardinal Villemaurine *38/L F9* 287
Cardonne, La *21/R H1* 128
Cardus *La Cardonne*
Caresse, Dom. de la
 45 J3 363
Carignan *32/L E4* 197
Carillon de l'Angélus, Le *Angélus*
Carles, de *44 E10* 351
Carmes Haut-Brion, Les *24* 143
Carmes, Le Clos des *Les Carmes Haut-Brion*
Carnedeau *Moulin Haut-Laroque*
Caroline *17 H4* 99
Caroline *de Chantegrive*
Carolle, de *de Roquetaillade La Grange*
Caronne Ste Gemme
 19 D2 108
Carpia, du *36* 232
Carsin *31?L H7* 197
Carte Blanche *Le Livey*
Carte Noire *Le Livey*
Carteau Côtes Daugay
 38/L G7 287
Carteau Pin de Fleurs
 38/L G7 287
Cartillon, du *19 H7* 108
Cartujac, Dom. de- *20 M6* 108
Caruel *47 J5* 372
Cassagne Haut-Canon
 44 J7 357
Cassagne-Boutet, La *46 I4* 382
Cassame *Maine Tigreau*
Cassidouce, La *Peyreyre*
Cassiot, de *de Rouillac*
Castagnac *44 C3* 351
Castagney, Le *Terrey-Gros-Cailloux*
Castaing, Dom *10 H6* 55
Castegens *45 J6* 363
Castel Vieilh La Salle *35* 232
Castelbruck *Haut Breton Larigaudière*
Castelnau de Suduiraut *Suduirant*
Castelneau, de *35* 232
Castelot, Clos *Guillemin la Gaffelière*
Castelot, Le *38/L H8* 287
Castenet-Greffier *36* 232
Castera *21/R J3* 128
Castéra, du *25/R F6* 157
Catherine de France *Sainte-Catherine*
Caulet *Haut-Mayne*
Caussade, la *Jean Dugay*
Cauze, du *38/R E3* 287
Cavalier, du *du Grand Barrail*
Cayla *31/L H7* 198
Cazalis *36* 232
Caze Bellevue, La *38/L I6* 287

Cazeau *35* 232
Cazeau Vieil *Peyredon Lagravette*
Cazeau-Morin *Saint-Aulaye*
Cazenave *38/L L9* 287
Cazenove, de *8* 232
Cérons, de *26/L B9* 157
Certan de May de Certan
 41 E5 331
Certan-Giraud *41 E4* 332
Chabiran *34* 232
Chainchon, de *45 K7* 363
Chalet de Germignan, Dom
 18 J2 108
Chambert-Marbuzet *15 J8* 84
Chambrun, de *43 D8* 342
Champ de la Rose *Launay*
Champion *38/R D2* 287
Champs de Durand *Roc de Bernon*
Chandellière, La *21/R E2* 129
Chano *20 E6* 110
Chanoine de Balestard *Balestard la Tonnelle*
Chantalouette *de Sales*
Chante Alouette *47 F4* 382
Chante Alouette *La Valade*
Chante Alouette Cormeil, Dom.
 38/L E5 287
Chante Alouette, Clos
 38/L I10 287
Chante Grive *Briand*
Chante-Alouette La Roseraie
 46 I4 382
Chantecler Milon *La Fleur Milon*
Chanteclerc *Petit Clos du Roy*
Chantegrive, de *25/R H7* 157
Chanteloiseau *31* 232
Chantélys *21/L H10* 129
Chants de Faizeau *Faizeau*
Chapelains, des *36* 232
Chapelle, Dom. de la *Le Maine Martin*
Chapelle, la *Yveline*
Chapelle aux Moines, la *Clos des Moines*
Chapelle d'Escurac, la *d'Escurac*
Chapelle de Bages, La *Haut-Bages Libéral*
Chapelle de Barbe *de Barbe*
Chapelle de Brivazac *de Barbe*
Chapelle de La Mission Haut-Brion, La *La Mission Haut-Brion*
Chapelle de Lafaurie, La *Lafaurie-Peyraguey*
Chapelle du Couvent, La *Chante Alouette*
Chapelle Lagarde *Lagarde*
Chapelle Maillard, La *36* 233
Chapelle Maracan *36* 233
Chapelle St-Loup, la *de Rousselet*
Chapelles, Dom. des *34* 233
Charlemagne *357*
Charmail *21/R K9* 110
Charmant *8/L D9* 41
Charmant, Clos *Charmant*
Charme Labory *Cos Labory*
Charmes de Kirwan, Les *Kirwan*
Charmes de Liversan, Les *Liversan*
Charmes-Godard, Les
 45 D7 368
Charmettes, Les *34* 233
Charmilles, Les *Médouc*
Charmilles, Les *18* 233
Charron *47 D3* 382
Charron, du *35* 233
Chartreuse, de la *de la Grenière*
Chartreuse, de la *Saint-Amand*
Chartreuse de Ch Coutet, La
 Coutet 177
Chartreuse d'Hosten *Fourcas Hosten*
Chasse-Spleen *17 F9* 99
Chassière, La *34* 233
Chastelet, Dom. de
 32/L J7 198

Chataignier, Le *Lassime*
Chatain Pineau *342*
Chatelet, Le *38/L F9* 287
Chaumes, Les *46 G3* 383
Chaumont, Clos *32/R G5* 198
Chauvin *38/L C8* 287
Chauvin Variation *Chauvin*
Chaÿ, Dom. du *31* 214
Chay, Dom. du *46 I3* 383
Chay, Le *46 J5* 383
Chec, Le *25/L F6* 157
Chelivette, de *32/R C6* 198
Chemin Royal *17 H4* 100
Chêne, Le *La Tonnelle*
Chêne de Gombeau *44* 357
Chêne Noir, Le *Les Grands Chênes*
Chêne-Vieux *40 K8* 323
Chênes de Macquin, Les *Pavie Macquin*
Chênevert *Picque Caillou*
Chenu-Lartte *Mille Secousses*
Cheret-Pitres *25/R C5* 157
Chesnaie, La *Rigaud*
Cheval Blanc *38/L C6* 288
Cheval Blanc, Dom. de *34* 233
Cheval-Blanc Signé, Dom. de
 35 233
Chevalier, Dom. de *23/L I2* 146
Chevalier, Dom. de *Dom. de la Solitude*
Chevalier Coutelin *Vieux Coutelin*
Chevalier d'Haurange *Grand Ormeau*
Chevalier de la Garde *Rouet*
Chevalier de Lamalétie *Duplessy*
Chevalier de Malle *De Malle*
Chevalier de Reignac *la Bertrande*
Chevalier Saint-Georges
 40 314
Chevaliers de Malte *Cadet-Piola*
Chevrol Bel Air *43 E8* 342
Chèze, La *31/L D3* 198
Chinchon la Bataille *45 K6* 363
Cinquet, Cru du *La Tour Blanche*
Cissac *20 F6* 110
Citran *17 H8* 110
Civrac-Lagrange *Grand Bourdieu*
CL, Cuvée *Cazalis*
Clairac *Les Petits Arnauds*
Clairbore *Arnauld*
Clairefont, de *Prieuré-Lichine*
Clairet de Ballan *Ballan-Larquette*
Clairet de Biguey *La Clotte*
Clairet d'une Nuit *Le Parvis de Dom. Tapiau*
Clairet de Pierre *Jacques Blanc*
Clare, La *22/L I9* 129
Clarière Laithwaite, La
 45 I4 363
Clarke *17 GG* 94
Classique *Mille Secousses*
Clauzet *15 H5* 84
Clément Pichon *18 H7* 110
Clerc Milon *12/L G5* 67
Clie de Corbin, La *Corbin* 314
Climens *29 K4* 177
Clinet *41 G3* 332
Clocher, Clos du *41 F7* 332
Clocher, Cru du *Caillou*
Clos Delord, du *35* 235
Clos du Notaire, Le *47 K5* 373
Closerie, de la *du Juge*
Closerie de Camensac, La *Camensac*
Closerie de Fourcas-Loubaney, La *Fourcas Loubaney*
Closerie de Malescasse, La *Malescasse*
Closerie du Grand Poujeaux, La
 17 E9 100
Closiot *29 K7* 177
Clotte, La *38/L F9* 288
Clusière, La *38/R H1* 288
Cluzel *32/L F1* 198
Clyde, la *32/R K4* 198
Colbert *47 I5* 373

Colbert Cannet Saint Ahon
Colin Lamothe Clos des Confréries
Collin du Pin Clos Chaumont
Colombe, de du Bois
Colombier, du de Chelivette
Colombier, Le Balac
Colombier de Bardis Verdus
Colombier de Ch Brown, Le Brown
Colombier-Monpelou 12/L E8 70
Colombine, Dom. de la 34 233
Colome Peylande 19 E6 110
Combes, des 35 233
Combes Canon, Des 44 K7 357
Commanderie, de la 43 G4 342
Commanderie, la 15 I5 84
Commanderie, la 35 234
Commanderie, La 38/L C7 288
Commanderie, La 41 G8 332
Compostelle, Dom. de La Cabanne
Commanderie de Queyret, La 36 234
Commanderie de St-Genis, La Petit-Freylon
Comte de L'Escart L'Escart
Comte des Cordes Fonrazade
Comtesse Adèle Malromé
Comtesse de Gombault de Taste 136
Comtesse de Laubès Le Bos
Comtesse de Laubès Laubès
Comtesse du Parc 20 C8 110
Cone-Taillasson Sabourin 47 C2 383
Confréries, Clos des 35 234
Conilh Haute-Libarde 47 J6 373
Connétable Talbot Talbot
Conques, de Les Ormes Sorbet
Conseillante, La 41 D6 332
Conseiller, Le 34 234
Constantin Melin
Coq Rouge Moulin Blanc La Chapelle
Coqs, de Haut Mouleyre
Coqs, de Le Bos
Coqs, de Laubès
Coquillas de France
Cor-Bugeaud, de Les Bertrands
Corbin 38/L B7 288
Corbin 40 J3 314
Corbin Michotte 38/L B7 288
Corbin Vieille Tour Corbin 288
Cordeillan-Bages 12/R D4 70
Cormeil-Figeac 38/L E6 288
Corneillan Martinens
Cornelle, La Bourdieu La Valade
Cornemps, de 34 234
Cos d'Estournel 15 K7 84
Cos Labory 15 K6 84
Cossieu-Coutelin 15 84
Côte de Baleau 38/L D8 289
Côte Migon la Gaffelière Canon la Gaffelière
Côte Montpezat 45 J5 363
Côte Puyblanquet 38/R G6 289
Coteau, Le 8/L L9 41
Coteaux Verts, Les Côtes des Caris
Côtes de Bonde 40 I5 314
Côtes de Lescours de Lescours
Côtes des Caris 36 234
Côtes Montleau Montlau
Côtes Trois Moulins 38/L G8 289
Côtes Trois Moulins Fonplégade
Coucheroy de Rochemorin
Coucy 40 K7 314
Coudert Pelletan 38/R F2 289
Coudert-Mauvezin Castagnac
Coudraie, La Saint-Florin
Coufran 21/R H9 111
Couhins 23/R C3 146
Couhins-Lurton 23/R C2 146
Coulac 31/R L4 216
Coulinats, des 31/R L6 216
Couloumey-le Tuquet Le Tuquet

Courgeau, Dom. de Les Jonqueyres
Courlat, du 40 G8 320
Courneau, du Haut Breton Larigaudière
Couronne, La 40 J5 315
Couronne, La 38/R J2 289
Couronneau 36 234
Courrière-Rongiéras 40 H7 320
Courros, du 36 234
Coursou 36 235
Courteillac, Dom. de 36 235
Courtey 36 235
Courtiade Peyvergès, La 36 235
Couspaude, La 38/L F10 289
Coustaut Magneau
Coustolle 44 H8 357
Coutelin-Merville 15 I3 84
Coutet 29 J6 177
Coutet 38/L F7 289
Coutet Saint-Magne Rocher Bellevue
Coutreau La Vieille Cure
Coutreau Haut-Garriga
Couvent des Jacobins 38/L F9 289
Couzins, les 40 E7 320
Coy, du 27/R I3 178
Crabitan, Clos de Crabitan-Bellevue
Crabitan-Bellevue 31/R K5 216
Crain, de 35 235
Creste, La Bichon Cassignols
Crock, Le 15 J7 84
Croisière, La Justa
Croix, de la 21/R H4 129
Croix, Dom. de la Mazarin
Croix, La Ducru-Beaucaillou
Croix, La La Croix de Millorit
Croix, La 26/R F7 157
Croix, La 41 F7 332
Croix, La 44 I9 351
Croix Beaurivage La Joye
Croix Beauséjour 40 I4 315
Croix Bellevue, La 41 L2 342
Croix Bigorre, La 45 H3 364
Croix Bonnelle, La La Bonnelle
Croix Chaigneau, La Haut-Chaigneau
Croix d'Antonne, La Haut-Mongeat
Croix d'Auron, La Tour de l'Espérance
Croix de Bayle, La 35 266
Croix de Bourseau Bourseau
Croix de Cabaleyran Le Trale
Croix de Calens de Haut-Calens
Croix de Chéreau, La Vieux Moulins de Chéreau
Croix de Chouteau Dom. du Calvaire
Croix de Gay, La 41 F3 332
Croix de Jaugue, La 38/L F4 289
Croix de l'Hosanne, La l'Hosanne
Croix de Laborde Reverdi
Croix de Louis, La 45 J7 364
Croix de Mazerat, La Beauséjour 281
Croix de Miaille, Dom. de la Meste-Jean
Croix de Millorit, La 47 J4 373
Croix de Monthil du Monthil
Croix de Mouchet, La 40 J7 315
Croix de Moussas Fontesteau
Croix de Rambeau 40 F4 321
Croix de Roche, La 34 235
Croix de Taste, La Vieux Dom. de Taste
Croix de Terrefort Haut Bastor
Croix de Thomas, La Cap d'Or
Croix des Bommes Haut-Sorillon
Croix des Moines, La 41 J5 343
Croix du Bailli, La Côtes de Bonde
Croix du Casse, La 41 H9 332
Croix du Chevalier, La Sigognac
Croix Grand Barail 34 235

Croix Landon, La La Gorre
Croix Lugagnac, La de Lugagnac
Croix Margantot, La Haut-Logat
Croix Montlabert, la Montlabert
Croix Saint Pey, La Brondelle
Croix Saint-Louis, La la Croix St-André
Croix Saint-Pierre, la l'Escadre
Croix Sainte-Anne, La La Croix-Laroque
Croix St-André, la 43 E8 343
Croix St-Estèphe, la Le Crock
Croix St-Georges, La 41 F6 332
Croix St-Jean, la 43 B6 343
Croix St. Vincent, La de Valois
Croix-Bouey, La 31/R L8 198
Croix-Davids, La 47 J7 373
Croix-Gandineau, La 44 I9 351
Croix-Laroque, La 44 I9 351
Croix-Saint-Jacques. La 47 B2 383
Croix-Toulifaut, La 41 E8 332
Croizet-Bages 12/R E3 70
Croque-Michotte 38/L B6 289
Cros, du 31/R L3 214
Cros Bois et Tradition, Le du Cros
Croûte Courpon 47 L8 373
Croûte-Charlus 47 K7 373
Croûte-Mallard Gros Moulin
Cru Barréjats 29 J3 176
Cru Champon 31 214
Cru Claverie/Dom. du Petit de l'Eglise 27/R B3 177
Cru d'Arche Pugneau 27/L H10 176
Cru Peyraguey 27/L I9 178
Crusquet de Lagarcie 47 D3 383
Crusquet-Sabourin 47 D4 383
Cruzeau 38/L E3 290
Cruzeau, de 23/R M6 146
Curcier, de Cabannieux
Cure, Clos de la 38/R D3 290
Curé-Bon 38/L F9 290
Cure-Bourse, Dom. de Durfort-Vivens
Cythère Queyret-Pouillac
Cyprès de Climens, Les Climens
Cypres, au La Prioulette
Cyprien Lagrave Paran
Dalem 44 E9 352
Daliot Le Relais de Cheval Blanc
Dallau 34 235
Damase 34 235
Damazac, Dom. de La Capelle
Dame Blanche, La du Taillan
Damis, de Beaulieu Bergey
Darius 38/R J1 290
Dartigue Gamage
Darzac Fondarzac
Dassault 38/R D1 290
Dasvin-Bel-Air 18 C7 111
Daubrin La Peyrère
Daugay 38/L G7 290
Dauphin de Bel-Air Lagrave, Le Bel-Air Lagrave
Dauphin de Grand-Pontet Grand-Pontet
Dauphin du Ch Guiraud, Le Guiraud
Dauphiné Rondillon 31/R I3 214
Dauphine, de la 44 K9 352
Dauzac 8/R I7 41
David 22/L G9 129
Davril des Tuquets
Decats de Bel-Air
Decorde 17 G3 111
Decorde Séméillan Mazeau
Degas 35 235
Delayat Hourbanon
Delmond Laville 183
Delord Montjouan
Demoiselles Hostens-Picant
Demoiselles de Braneyre, Les Vieux Braneyre
Demoiselles, Clos des 17 H4 94

Desclan Loupiac-Gaudiet
Desclaux, Clos 35 235
Design La Mothe du Barry
Desmirail 8/R G4 41
Destieux 38/R G4 290
Detey Métria
Devise d'Ardilley 20 L7 111
Devise de Lilian, La Lilian-Ladouys
Deyrem Valentin 8/L C9 41
Diane de Belgrave Belgrave
Diamant Blanc de Terrefort-Quancard
Dilhac Senilhac
Dillon 18 I5 111
DM, Cuvée La Vieille Croix
Doisy-Daëne 29 J5 178
Doisy-Dubroca 29 J5 178
Doisy-Védrines 29 L6 178
Dom. de l'Eglise, du 41 F3 334
Domeyne 15 E7 86
Dominante, La 34 238
Dominique, La 38/L C6 290
Donjon de Lamarque de Lamarque
Douley Lagarosse
Douve de Romefort, La Meyre
Douves de Carnet, Les La Tour Carnet
Douves de Francs, Les de Francs
Dubois Claverie 36 238
Dubory Launay
Duc d'Arnauton 29 J5 157
Duc Decazes La Grave
Ducasse Roûmieu-Lacoste
Ducasse Beauregard Ducasse
Ducla 36 238
Ducluzeau 17 H2 94
Ducru-Beaucaillou 10 H8 55
Dudon 29 I6 178
Dudon 32/R K1 198
Duhart-Milon 12/R C1 70
Duhau-Laplace Nouret
Duluc Branaire
Duplessis Hauchecorne 17 H6 100
Duplessy 32/L H5 198
Durand Bayle Lesparre
Durand-Laplagne 40 I9 323
Durfort-Vivens 8/L F1 41
Dutruch Grand Poujeaux 17 F9 100
Duverger 26/L J5 157
Ebraude, l' Rousset
Echevins, Les du Courlat
Ecuyer de Sociondo, l' Sociondo
Edouard de Chantegrive
Eglise d'Armens, l' 38/R K4 290
Eglise, Clos de l' 43 J5 343
Eglise, Clos l' 41 G3 334
Eglise, Clos L' Plince
Eglise, de l' 32/R K7 199
Eglise-Clinet, l' 41 G4 334
Egmont d'Arche 106
Elégance Grand Tuillac
Elégance Le Grand Moulin
Elisée 41 I7 334
Emigré, de l' 26/L C9 157
Emilius de Trimoulet Trimoulet
Emotion La Freynelle
Enclos du Banneret, l' Paveil de Luze
Enclos, Cuvée de l' Lamouroux/Grand Enclos du Ch de Cérons
Enclos, L' 36 238
Enclos, l' 41 K4 334
Ermitage de Chasse Spleen, L' Chasse-Spleen
Ermitage de Saint-Lô, L' Saint-Lô
Ermitage, l' Reverdi
Ermitage, l' 27/L F4 178
Escadre, L' 47 D4 383
Escaley, de l' 31/R K5 216
Escart, L' 35 238
Esclade, Dom. de l' Carsin
Escot, l' 21/L J6 129
Escurac, d' 21/L D5 129
Espérance, Cru de l' Larruau
Esplanade, de l' Plaisance

Esprit de Chevalier l' Dom. de Chevalier
Esprit de Teyssier l' Teyssier 306
Estagne, l' Loudenne
Estang, de l' 45 G4 364
Esteau, d' 20 H5 111
Esterling La Grave 352
Estève, d' Haut Nadeau
Estrémade, Dom. de l' Rabaud-Promis
Etoile Pourret La Grâce Dieu
Evangile, l' 41 D5 334
Evéché, de l' 43 G5 343
Excellence Lyre Petit-Freylon
Expérience Ducla
Extravagance, l' Doisy-Daëne
Eyquem 47 J4 373
Eyrans, d' 23/R J10 146
Fagotte, La d'Aurilhac
Faise, de 34 238
Faizeau 40 H4 315
Falfas 47 J3 373
Falfas Le Chevalier Falfas
Fargues, de 27/R D4 179
Farluret 29 L5 179
Fauconnin Haut-Grignon
Faugères 38/R H7 290
Faure-Beauséjour Beauséjour 351
Faures, des 45 D6 364
Faures, les 36 238
Faurie de Souchard 38/R E1 291
Faurie Maison Neuve, La 343
Fauroux Dom. de la Caresse
Favereau 36 238
Favière, La 34 238
Favières, les le Menaudat
Favory Montlau
Fayau 31/L H5 199
Fayon Labatut-Bouchard
Ferbos du Mayne 163
Ferme d'Angludet, La d'Angludet
Fernon 26/R F6 157
Ferran 23/R K6 146
Ferrand 41 G9 334
Ferrand, de 38/R G4 291
Ferrande 25/R D2 160
Ferrasse 45 J6 364
Ferrière 8/R E1 42
Feythit La Grave Tristan
Feytit-Clinet 41 H4 334
Fief de Cantelande Lieujean
Fiefs de Lagrange, Les Lagrange 58
Fieuzal, de 23/L K5 148
Fifteen Barons du Ch de Portets de Portets
Figeac 38/L D6 291
Filhot 27/R K6 179
Fillon, Clos de Joumes-Fillon
Fleur, La 38/R D2 291
Fleur, la 40 H2 315
Fleur Baudron, La Haut-Colas-Nouet
Fleur Bonnet, La Bonnet 285
Fleur Cailleau, La La Grave
Fleur Cailleau, La 44 357
Fleur Cardinale 38/R G7 291
Fleur Chambeau, La Vieux Ch Chambeau
Fleur Cravignac, La 38/L D8 291
Fleur de By Rollan de By
Fleur de Clinet Clinet
Fleur de Courteillac, Dom. La Dom. de Courteillac
Fleur de Cros du Cros
Fleur de Gay, La La Croix de Gay
Fleur de Jaugue, La La Croix de Jaugue
Fleur de Lisse 38/R H6 292
Fleur de Reignac de Reignac
Fleur de Robin, La Robin
Fleur de Rol Rol de Fombrauge
Fleur des Jouailles, La des Jouailles
Fleur des Moines des Moines
Fleur des Ormes Dom. du Grand Ormeau

Fleur des Ormes, La *Grange-Neuve*
Fleur Figeac, Clos La
  38/L C5 291
Fleur Figeac, Clos La *La Tour du Pin Figeac*
Fleur Frimont, La *Bosquet*
Fleur Garderose, La *Belregard-Figeac*
Fleur Jonquet, La *25/R H4* 160
Fleur Lacombe, La *Le Caillou*
Fleur Lescours, La *de Lescours*
Fleur Milon, La *12/L F5* 70
Fleur Pérouillac *La Croix de Louis*
Fleur Peyrabon, La *Peyrabon*
Fleur Pourret *38/L E8* 292
Fleur Roulet, La *Le Moulin du Roulet*
Fleur Saint Georges, La
  43 E6 343
Fleur-Bécade, la *Fourcas Loubaney*
Fleur-Carney, Dom. de La *Le Conseiller*
Fleur-Pétrus, La *41 D4* 334
Fleur-Vauzelle, la *Haut-Surget*
Fleuron Blanc *Loubens*
Fleurs de Belcier *Belcier*
Fleurs de Graville, Les *Roûmieu-Lacoste*
Flojague *45 H5* 364
Florestan *Plaisance* 209
Floridène, Clos *26/L H8* 160
Florimond *Dom. Florimond-La-Brède*
Florimond-La-Brède, Dom.
  46 238
Florys, Cuvée *Grand Village*
Fombrauge *38/R F4* 292
Fon Du Berger, La *19 J8* 111
Fonbadet *12/R D6* 70
Fonchereau *35* 239
Fond-Gazan *Haut-Mazeris*
Fondarzac *35* 239
Fonfroide *36* 239
Fongaban *40 J10* 323
Fongaban *45 E4* 364
Fongaban Bellevue *Cardinal Villemaurine*
Fonguillon *Calon* 314
Fonjouan *Ninon*
Fonpigueyre *Liversan*
Fonplégade *38/L G8* 292
Fonral, de *La Paillette*
Fonrazade *38/L G7* 292
Fonréaud *17 H4* 94
Fonroque *38/L E9* 292
Fonsèche *Lamothe-Cissac*
Font Bonnet *Blayac*
Font Du Jeu, La *Lapeyronie*
Font Neuve, La *22/R H4* 129
Fontaine, Clos *Cru Claverie / Dom. du Petit de l'Eglise*
Fontaine de l'Aubier *Lafon* 131
Fontaine Royale *Fonréaud*
Fontanelle *Tour-du-Roc*
Fontanille, Dom. de la *du Payre / Clos du Monastère de Broussey*
Fontarney *Desmirail*
Fontbaude *45 K3* 364
Fontebride *Haut-Bergeron*
Fontenil *44 E9* 352
Fontenil *Le Bon Pasteur*
Fontenille, de *35* 239
Fontesteau *20 G5* 111
Fontmarty *Taillefer*
Forêt Saint-Hilaire, La *Ducla*
Forêt, La *32/L J7* 199
Forges de Macay, Les *Macay*
Fort de Vauban *19 H7* 111
Fort Jaco *Saint-Jacques*
Fort Pontus, du *44 I9* 352
Fortin *Dom. du Chaÿ*
Forts de Latour, Les *Latour*
Fosselongue *35* 239
Fougas *46 K7* 374
Fougères, Cuvée des *de Parenchère*

Fougères, des *25/L F5* 160
Fougey *Barreyres*
Fourcas Dupré *17 D4* 96
Fourcas Hosten *17 F4* 96
Fourcas Loubaney *17 C4* 96
Fourcas, du *17 E4* 96
Fournas Bernadotte *19 I8* 111
Fourquerie, La *45 K1* 364
Fourtanet *d'Aiguilhe*
Fourtet, Clos *38/L F9* 292
Franc *Franc Patarabet*
Franc Bigaroux *38/L H8* 292
Franc Bories *38/L M10* 293
Franc Grâce-Dieu *38/L D7* 293
Franc Jaugue Blanc
  38/L F4 293
Franc La Cour *36* 239
Franc Lartigue *38* 293
Franc Mayne *38/L E8* 293
Franc Patarabet *38/L F9* 293
Franc Pipeau Descombes
  38/R I4 293
Franc-Pourret *38/L E8* 293
France, de *23/L J5* 148
France, La *21/R F1* 129
France, La *35* 239
France de Roques, La *de Roques*
Francis Courselle *Thieuley*
Francs, de *45 C7* 368
Frank Phélan *Phélan-Ségur*
Franquet Grand Poujeaux
  17 E8 100
Frappe-Peyrot *Mazarin*
Frédignac *47 D3* 383
Frégent, Dom. de *Le Maine Martin*
Frère *32/R H7* 199
Freychère, La *de la Grande Chapelle*
Freynelle, La *35* 239
Frimont, de *36* 239
Fronsac *du Gazin*
Fronsac, de *44 K10* 352
Frontenac *36* 240
Fuie-St Bonnet, la *La Tour St Bonnet*
Fussignac, de *34* 240
Fussignac Le Cofour *de Fussignac*
G Ch Guiraud *Guiraud*
Gabachot, Le *La Croix* 332
Gabachot, Le *La Croix St-Georges*
Gabaron *Vieux Ch Lamothe*
Gabon *Vieux Ch Lamothe*
Gaborie, La *35* 240
Gaby *La Roche Gaby*
Gachet, Dom. de *43 C9* 343
Gadet Terrefort *22/L E1* 129
Gaffelière, Clos la *La Gaffelière*
Gaffelière, La *38/L G9* 293
Gagnard *44 J9* 352
Gaillardon *Justa*
Gaillat, du *26/R E6* 160
Galau *Nodoz*
Galet, Dom. du *34* 240
Galeteau *Le Gardera*
Galets de Couhenne *La Lauzette*
Galiane, La *8/L C8* 42
Gallais-Bellevue *Potensac*
Galland *17 E8* 100
Galland-Dast *32/L J8* 199
Gallies *Dudon* 178
Galon Bleu du Ch Moutte Blanc *Moutte Blanc*
Galop d'Essai du Clos Bourbon *Clos Bourbon*
Galvesses Grand Moine, Dom *du Moulin*
Gamage *36* 240
Ganga Cata *de France*
Ganne, La *41 L8* 335
Gantonet *36* 240
Garance, la *Rahoul*
Garbillot *du Rocher*
Garde, La *23/R K5* 148
Garde de la Clyde *la Clyde*
Gardera, Le *32* 240
Gardour *Moncets*
Gardut *47 E3* 384

Gardut Haut-Cluzeau *47 D4* 384
Garenne, Clos de la *du Grand Moëys*
Garenne, La *du Tailhas*
Garonneau, de *45 D7* 368
Garosse, Dom. de la *du Bouilh*
Garraud *43 E5* 343
Garreau *de Ricaud*
Garricq, La *17* 100
Gartieux, Dom. des *Pichon Longueville Comtesse de Lalande*
Gascon, du *Dom. du Noble*
Gassies *32/L H2* 199
Gatine, Dom. de la *du Grand Moëys*
Gaury Balette *36* 240
Gauthier *46* 240
Gauthier *Chantélys*
Gay, Le *35* 240
Gay, Le *41 F3* 335
Gay-Moulin *des Moines*
Gayat *35* 266
Gazaniol *de Parenchère*
Gazelles, Les *34* 240
Gazin *41 C3* 335
Gazin, du *44 I6* 357
Gazin Roquencourt *23/L H4* 148
Gemme de Rayne Vigneau *de Rayne-Vigneau*
Génis, de *Saint-Philippe*
Génisson *31/R G6* 199
Gentilhomme, du *La Clare*
Georges *Vilotte*
Georges de Guestres *31* 240
Gerbaud *Clos Gerbaud*
Gerbaud, Clos *38/R K5* 293
Germignan, de *Dom. Chalet de Germignan*
Gilette *27/L D4* 179
Giraudot *Cazeau*
Girondins *la Treille des Girondins*
Gironville, de *18 D6* 112
Gironville, Duc de *de Gironville*
Girouette, La *Perenne*
Giscours *8/R J5* 42
Glana, du *10 H7* 56
Gloria *10 H7* 56
Gobinaud *17 C7* 96
Goblangey *46 I3* 384
Goffreteau *Candeley*
Gombaud *Juguet*
Gombaud *Moulin de Serré*
Gombaude-Guillot *41 G4* 335
Gomerie, La *38/L E8* 293
Gonbères, Dom. du *Castéra*
Gondats, des *Marquis de Terme*
Gontrie, La *32/L J9* 199
Gorce, de *32/L K6* 199
Gorce, La *21/R F4* 130
Gorre, La *21/R C2* 130
Goudy La Cardonne *Potensac*
Goulefaisan *Tour Marcillanet*
Goumin *Bonnet* 228
Gourdins, Dom. des
  38/L D3 293
Gourran *32/R J8* 202
Goutey-Lagravière *31/R J4* 216
Govinère, La *40 F7* 321
Grâce Dieu, La *38/L D7* 294
Grâce Dieu Les Menuts, La
  38/L E7 294
Grâce d'Ormon, Dom. de la *Pontac Monplaisir*
Grand Abord, du *25/R E4* 160
Grand Baril *40 F2* 315
Grand Barrail Lamarzelle Figeac
  38/L D6 294
Grand Barrail, du *47 D4* 384
Grand Bern, du *de Marsan*
Grand Bert *38/L K7* 294
Grand Bireau *35* 240
Grand Bois, du *de la Commanderie*
Grand Bos, du *25/L F10* 160
Grand Bourdieu *25/L E9* 160
Grand Canyon *Colombier-Monpelou*

Grand Chambellan, du *de Viaud*
Grand Chemin, Le *34* 240
Grand Clapeau Olivier
  18 H4 112
Grand Claret *La Grange Clinet*
Grand Clauset *35* 241
Grand Corbin *38/L C8* 294
Grand Courbian *l'Argenteyre*
Grand Donnezac *36* 241
Grand Faurie, Clos *Tour Grand Faurie*
Grand Ferrand, du *36* 241
Grand Gontey *Patris*
Grand Jauga *Farluret*
Grand Jour *32/R D7* 202
Grand Lafont, Dom *18 D7* 112
Grand Lartigue *38/L I9* 294
Grand Launay *46 J5* 374
Grand Maine, du *La Mongie*
Grand Mayne *38/L E7* 294
Grand Mazerou *la Treille des Girondins*
Grand Moëys, du *31/L D1* 202
Grand Monteil *35* 241
Grand Moulin *21/R J7* 112
Grand Moulin, Le *46 C4* 384
Grand Moulinet *41 J4* 335
Grand Moulinet *Haut-Surget*
Grand Ormeau *43 H6* 343
Grand Ormeau, Dom. du
  43 H6 344
Grand Parc, du *Léoville Las Cases*
Grand Père, Cuvée du *Tour du Moulin*
Grand Perreau *Labourdette*
Grand Peyruchet *31/R I1* 214
Grand Plantier, du
  31/R J4 202
Grand Pré, Le *Loubens*
Grand Puch, du *35* 241
Grand Queyron, Le *la Commanderie* 234
Grand Renouil *44 J7* 358
Grand Rigaud *40 K7* 323
Grand Soussans *Tayac* 49
Grand Terrier *46 F3* 384
Grand Treuil *Tauzinat l'Hermitage*
Grand Tuillac *45 F6* 366
Grand Verdus, Le *35* 241
Grand Verger d'Agassac, Le *d'Agassac*
Grand Village *34* 242
Grand-Corbin-Despagne *38/L B7* 294
Grand-Duroc-Milon *12/L I4* 71
Grand-Jean *35* 241
Grand-Jour *47 L10* 374
Grand-Pontet *38/L E8* 294
Grand-Puy Ducasse
  12/L C10 71
Grand-Puy-Lacoste *12/R G3* 71
Grande Chapelle, de la *34* 241
Grande Rouchonne
  38/L L9 294
Grandes Bornes, Les *36* 241
Grandes Murailles *38/L F9* 294
Grandis *21/R J9* 112
Grandmaison, Dom. de
  23 E8 148
Grands Bertins, Les *46 J6* 374
Grands Cèdres de Sipian, Les *Sipian*
Grands Chênes, Les
  21/R C6 130
Grands Jays, Les *34* 241
Grands Moines, Clos des *Clos de l'Eglise*
Grands Sables Capet *Capet-Guillier*
Grands Sillons Gabachot
  41 F8 335
Grands Sillons, les *41 G9* 335
Grands Thibauds, Les
  46 L8 374
Grange, La *Les Moines*
Grange Brûlée, Dom. de la
  35 242

Grange Chatelière, La *Moulinet*
Grange Clinet, La *32/R J1* 202
Grange du Roy, Dom. de la
  36 242
Grange Neuve de Figeac, La *Figeac*
Grange-Neuve *41 I5* 335
Grange-Vieille, Clos de la
  21/R C6 130
Grangeneuve, de *Hostens-Picant*
Granges, des *35* 242
Granges de Gazin, Les *Gazin Roquencourt*
Grangeotte-Freylon, Clos *des Joualles*
Granges des Doms. Edmond de Rothschild, Les *Clarke*
Granges des Doms. Rothschild, Les *Malmaison*
Granges des Doms. Rothschild, Les *Peyre-Lebade*
Grangey *38/R F5* 294
Granins *Granins Grand Poujeaux*
Granins Grand Poujeaux
  17 E9 100
Grate-Cap *41 F6* 335
Graula, La *La Verrière*
Graulet *47 E3* 384
Grava, Dom. de *31* 242
Grava, du *36* 242
Grava-Lacoste *Lamourette*
Gravaillas, de *26/L C8* 160
Gravas *29 J5* 179
Grave à Pomerol, La *41 H3* 335
Grave Figeac, La *38/L C5* 295
Grave Julien, La *Les Graves*
Grave Martillac, La *La Tour Martillac*
Grave Singalier la *des Gravières*
  161
Grave, De la *47 J6* 374
Grave, Dom. La *Dom. La Grave*
Grave, Dom. de la *35* 242
Grave, Dom. La *25/R E4* 161
Grave, La *31/R K6* 216
Grave, La *34* 242
Grave, La *44 L9* 352
Gravelière, La *36* 242
Gravelongue *Sestignan*
Graves David, Les *La Braulterie de Peyraud*
Graves de Bossuet *Bossuet*
Graves de Garraud *Garraud*
Graves de Julien, Les *Vieux Busquet*
Graves de Laulan *Laulan Ducos*
Graves de Matiou, Les *Puy Bardens*
Graves de Peyroutas *Quercy*
Graves de Vayres *Panchille*
Graves des Annereaux
  43 M4 344
Graves du Tich, des *Pilet*
Graves Guillot *Guillot-Clauzel*
Graves, Le *46 I7* 384
Gravette de Certan, La *Vieux Ch Certan*
Gravette, La *Bel-Air* 320
Gravettes-Samonac *46 K5* 376
Graveyron *25/R E4* 161
Graveyron *Biston-Brillette*
Graveyron La France *44* 242
Graveyrou *Les Heaumes*
Gravière Grand Poujeaux, La *Dutruch Grand Poujeaux*
Gravière, La *Brûlesécaille*
Gravière, La *Nardique La Gravière*
Gravière, La *le Meynieu*
Gravière, La *Tristan*
Gravières de Marsac *Marsac Séguineau*
Gravières, des *25/R E4* 161
Grèche, Dom. de la *du Broustaret*
Grenière, de la *40 D7* 321
Grenons, Les *Castenet-Greffier*
Gressier Grand Poujeaux
  17 E9 100
Greteau *36* 242

Greysac 22/R I10 130
Grimon 45 F6 366
Grimont 32/L L5 202
Grissac, de 47 M10 376
Grivet, Clos 23/R 148
Grivière 21/R G2 130
Groleau 46 K5 376
Grolet Laborie
Gros Moulin 47 K7 376
Grosse Motte, La Motte Maucourt
Grossombre 35 243
Grottes, des de Ferrand 291
Gruaud-Larose 10 I5 56
Gruppes, Les Charron
Guadet-St-Julien 38/L F9 295
Guérin, Clos de de Guérin
Guérin, de 35 243
Guérin-Jacquet 25/R E4 161
Guerry 47 K8 376
Gueydon La Croix 157
Gueydon, de Berger
Gueyrosse 38/L F3 295
Guibeau Guibot la Fourvieille
Guibon Bonnet 228
Guibot la Fourvieille 40 H10 323
Guichot 36 243
Guiet 46 376
Guilhem de Fargues de Fargues
Guilhem de Rey l'Ermitage
Guillemin, Dom. de Saint-Sulpice
Guillemin de Gorre du Paradis
Guillemin la Gaffelière 38/L G9 295
Guillon Ferrande
Guillot 41 G6 335
Guillot Gantonet
Guillot-Clauzel 41 G6 335
Guillot-Clauzel Dom. de Courteillac
Guillotin 40 J8 323
Guilnemansoy, De 38/R I3 295
Guionne 42 J7 376
Guiraud 27/R J4 179
Guiraud Peyrebrune Tour Blanche
Guirauton Magneau
Guiteronde du Hayot 29 J3 182
Gurgue, La 8/R E1 42
Guyney Martinens
Hanteillan 20 E8 112
Hargue, La 35 243
Harmonie La Mongie
Hartes, de 35 243
Hauchat 44 H6 352
Haudon Pierrail
Hauret Lalande, Dom. du 26/L 161
Haurets, d' 35 243
Haut Ballet 44 J6 358
Haut Barateau Les Rocques 379
Haut Bastor 35 243
Haut Bernin Le Porge
Haut Bertinerie 384
Haut Blagnac de Seguin
Haut Bourdieu 34 243
Haut Breton Larigaudière 8/L C7 42
Haut Brisey 22/R G3 130
Haut Bruly 38/R G7 295
Haut Cantelaudette, Dom. du 35 243
Haut Cantonnet 36 243
Haut Carras du Junca
Haut Castelot Le Castelot
Haut Corbin 38/L B8 295
Haut Coteau 15 C5 86
Haut de Carles de Carles
Haut de Domy Lafargue
Haut de Plaignac Plagnac
Haut Desarnaud Beaulieu Bergey
Haut du Puy 20 112
Haut Faugères Faugères
Haut Ferrand 41 G8 335
Haut Goutey 31/R J4 202
Haut Graveyron Lestrille
Haut Grelot 46 B2 384
Haut Gros Bonnet 44 358
Haut Guillebot 35 244

Haut la Gravière Laffitte-Carcasset
Haut Lafitte de Beau Rivage Laguens
Haut Lagrange 23/L I9 149
Haut Lariveau 44 I7 352
Haut Lestiac de Lestiac
Haut Macô 46 K7 377
Haut Maginet Saint-Florin
Haut Mallet 35 244
Haut Manoir La Commanderie 332
Haut Manoir, Dom. du Gagnard
Haut Maurin 31 244
Haut Mayne Caillou 177
Haut Mayne, Dom. du des Mailles
Haut Mérigot Saint-Antoine
Haut Migot Cabannieux
Haut Mouleyre 31/L G7 202
Haut Nadeau 36 244
Haut Padarnac Pédesclaux
Haut Panet 44 I9 358
Haut Picot des Cabans
Haut Plantey 21/R F6 131
Haut Pougnan 36 244
Haut Reygnac 35 245
Haut Reygnac Les Vieilles Tuileries
Haut Rian 31/L I5 202
Haut Rocher 38/R H7 296
Haut Rouargue Blanchet
Haut Rozier 45 C7 368
Haut Saint Clair 40 K10 323
Haut Saint Pey 36 245
Haut Saint Vincent Mayne d'Imbert
Haut Sociondo 47 E3 385
Haut Tayac Tayac 379
Haut Tucot La Courtiade Peyvergès
Haut-Bages Averous Lynch-Bages
Haut-Bages Libéral 12/R D6 71
Haut-Bages Monpelou 12/R C1 72
Haut-Bailly 23/L G9 149
Haut-Bana Le Breuil Renaissance
Haut-Baradieu 15 G3 86
Haut-Barry La Favière
Haut-Barry Haut-Sorillon
Haut-Batailley 12/R H8 72
Haut-Beauséjour 15 E7 86
Haut-Bellevue 19 I8 112
Haut-Bergeron 27/L H7 182
Haut-Bergey 23/L H5 149
Haut-Bernat 40 J9 323
Haut-Bertin 40 I4 315
Haut-Beychevelle Gloria 10 H7 56
Haut-Boisron 46 243
Haut-Bommes Clos Haut-Peyraguey
Haut-Branda Jean Dugay
Haut-Brion 24 149
Haut-Cadet 38 295
Haut-Calens, de 25/L C10 161
Haut-Castenet 46 K5 376
Haut-Castenet Castenet-Greffier
Haut-Chaigneau 43 C8 344
Haut-Chardon Dom. Florimond-La-Brède
Haut-Châtain 43 D8 344
Haut-Claverie 27/R F5 182
Haut-Colas-Nouet 34 243
Haut-Cormey Cormeil-Figeac
Haut-Coutelin 15 H5 86
Haut-du-Peyrat 47 E3 384
Haut-Favereau 36 244
Haut-Franquet 17 E9 101
Haut-Gardère 23/L K6 149
Haut-Garriga 35 244
Haut-Gayat 35 266
Haut-Germineau Mauros
Haut-Giraudon Les Parres
Haut-Gouat 20 C5 112
Haut-Goujon 40 F1 315
Haut-Goujon 43 G5 344
Haut-Gravat 22/R E3 130

Haut-Graveyron 35 244
Haut-Gravier 46 J7 376
Haut-Greyzeau 32/R D6 202
Haut-Grignon 22/R G7 130
Haut-Guérin 35 244
Haut-Guiraud 47 G4 376
Haut-Jamard 40 F7 321
Haut-La Grenière 40 D7 321
Haut-La Peyrere Meste-Jean
Haut-Lamothe 25/L C10 161
Haut-Logat 20 F6 112
Haut-Madrac Lynch-Moussas
Haut-Maillet 41 B4 335
Haut-Marbuzet 15 J8 86
Haut-Mardan Tanesse
Haut-Marmont Les Grandes Bornes
Haut-Maurac 21/R E7 131
Haut-Mayne 26/L C8 161
Haut-Mazeris 44 I7 358
Haut-Mazières 35 244
Haut-Médoc du Prieuré, Le Prieuré-Lichine
Haut-Meillac 34 244
Haut-Mondain du Barrail
Haut-Mongeat 35 266
Haut-Montil 38/L I6 295
Haut-Morin de Caillavet
Haut-Mourleaux 36 244
Haut-Mousseau 46 J5 377
Haut-Nouchet 23/R L5 149
Haut-Paradie Galland
Haut-Patarabet, Dom. du 38/L I9 296
Haut-Peyraguey, Clos 27/R K2 182
Haut-Peyredoule Dom. Florimond-La-Brède
Haut-Peyrillat La Gorre
Haut-Pineuilh Frontenac
Haut-Piquat 40 H6 321
Haut-Plantade 23/L H5 149
Haut-Plantey 38/L C9 296
Haut-Pourret 38/L E8 296
Haut-Rigaleau 36 245
Haut-Riot Vieux Ch Lamothe
Haut-Roquefort Anniche
Haut-Rousset 46 J4 377
Haut-Saint-Romain 34 245
Haut-Sarpe 38/R F2 296
Haut-Segottes 38/L D7 296
Haut-Selve 25/L H9 161
Haut-Sorillon 34 245
Haut-Surget 43 F7 344
Haut-Terrier 46 I10 385
Haut-Toutifaut La Commanderie de Queyret
Haut-Tropchaud 41 F5 336
Haut-Vigneau 23/R L2 149
Haut-Villet 38/R G8 296
Haute Brande 36 244
Haute Faucherie 40 315
Haute Nauve 38/R I3 295
Hautegrave-Tris du Fourcas
Hauterive 21/R L3 130
Hautes-Graves d'Arthus 38/R L2 295
Hautes Graves, Les 40 H2 315
Hautes Graves de By de By
Hautes Gravilles de Panigon, Les de Panigon
Hautes-Roches Bel-Air 323
Hautesserre du Périer
Hautmont, du Millet
Hauts de Cluzel, Les Cluzel
Hauts de Martet, Les Martet
Hauts de Palette, Les 31/L J9 202
Hauts de Perey, Les Gaury Balette
Hauts de Pez, Les Tour de Pez
Hauts de Plaisance, Les Pontoise Cabarrus
Hauts de Pontet, Les Pontet-Canet
Hauts de Ricaud de Ricaud
Hauts de Savignac, Les Damase
Hauts de Smith, Les Smith Haut Lafitte
Hauts du Tertre, Les du Tertre

Hauts Marcieux, Les Lafon 97
Hauts Martins, Clos les 40 D7 321
Hauts Sainte-Marie, Les Sainte-Marie
Hauts-Conseillants, les 41 K7 344
Hauts-de-Granges, Les 45 F7 366
Haux, de 32/R H7 203
Haye, La 15 I5 86
Heaumes, Les 47 G4 377
Hélène Roques-Mauriac
Helmina de Saint-Philippe
Henri Bourlon Guibot la Fourvieille
Henry de France 32/L K7 203
Henri IV de Barbe Blanche
Héreteyre, l' Tour de Pez
Héritage Brun Despagne
Hermats, Les Grand Launay
Hermitage, l' 38/L G6 296
Hermitage, Clos de l' 344
Hermitage Mazeyres, l' Mazeyres
Hervé Laroque Moulin Haut-Laroque
Heyrisson, L' 35 245
Hez, Clos du 26 161
Holden Puy Castéra
Hortevie 10 H7 56
Hosanne, l' 35 266
Hospital, de l' 25/R E4 161
Hospitalet de Gazin, l' Gazin
Hoste-Blanc, L' 35 245
Hostens-Picant 36 245
Houissant 15 H6 88
Hountic Lagorce Bernadas
Hourbanon 21/L H9 131
Hourcade, La 22/R E3 131
Houringue, La 18 D5 114
Huguets, des 34 245
Huguets, des Lafaurie
Huste, de La 44 E9 352
If, de l' du Mont
Ile Margaux, Dom. de l' 8 245
Illot, Rosé de l' La Chassière
Isis La Tour Blanche
Issan, d' 8/R F3 42
Jabastas, de 35 246
Jacobins, Clos des 38/L E7 288
Jacobins, des Bellegrave 331
Jacquemineau 38/R F4 296
Jacques Blanc 38/R H4 296
Jacques Blanc, Dom. de Jacques Blanc
Jacques le Haut Mont-Joye
Jalgue, La 36 246
Jalousie, Dom. de la Clos Belle Rose
Jamin 36 246
Jamin De l'Aubrade
Jansenant Belair-Coubet
Jard, le Chatain Pineau
Jaubert La Croix de Millorit
Jaugaret, Dom. du 10 H6 58
Jauguet Courtey
Jayle, de 36 246
Jean, Clos 31/R J3 214
Jean Bernard Haut Macô
Jean Dugay 35 266
Jean Faure 38/L C7 298
Jean Fontenille Rondillon
Jean Fonthenille Clos Jean
Jean Gervais 25/R E4 162
Jean Mathieu 34 246
Jean Médeville Fayau
Jean Voisin 38/L C8 298
Jeandeman 44 G8 352
Jeanguillon Vrai Caillou
Jeantieu, Dom. de 36 246
Jeanton 22/R F7 131
Jésuites, Les 31/R M8 203
Joffre du Grand Ferrand
Joinin 35 246
Jonchet 32/L J8 203
Jonquet, J. de La Fleur Jonquet
Jonquet, Rosé de La Fleur Jonquet

Jonqueyres, Les 46 H3 385
Jossème de Bertin
Jouailles, des 36 246
Jouailles, Dom. des du Grand Moëys
Jouailles, Les Les Chaumes
Joumes-Fillon 36 246
Jouvence de Jura-Plaisance Jura-Plaisance
Joye, La 34 246
Juge, du 31/L I9 203
Juge, du Fayau
Juguet 38/R J3 298
Juguet, Dom. de Juguet
Julien Cap Léon Veyrin
Julien Magneau
Junayme 44 K7 358
Junca, du 20 G7 114
Juncarret 35 266
Junet, Clos 38/L E5 298
Junior de la Couspaude La Couspaude
Jupille Carillon 38/L K5 298
Jura-Plaisance 40 J2 316
Jurat, le 38/L B8 298
Justa 36 246
Justices, Dom. des Les Justices
Justices, Les 27/L E2 182
Kanon, J. Canon
Kirwan 8/R H3 43
L Vieux Ch Lamothe
Labadie 21/L C10 131
Labarde Dauzac
Labarde, Clos 38/R F2 298
Labastide Landat
Labastide Dauzac Dauzac
Labat Caronne Ste Gemme
Labatut 36 246
Labatut, Dom. de Mestrepeyrot
Labatut-Bouchard 31/R K9 203
Labégorce 8/L D9 43
Labégorce Zédé 8/L D9 43
Laborde Hanteillan
Laborde, Clos de La Chassière
Laborde, de 35 246
Laborie 31/R L6 216
Labory 44 F9 352
Labory de Tayac Tayac 49
Labourdette 36 246
Labrousse 46 J4 385
Lacaussade, Clos de Franquet Grand Poujeaux
Lacaussade Saint-Martin Labrousse
Lachesnaye 19 C5 114
Laclaverie 45 D7 368
Lacombe 35 247
Lacombe Noaillac 22/R F3 131
Lacombe, Dom. de Le Caillou
Lacoste-Borie Grand-Puy-Lacoste
Lacour Jacquet 19 E6 114
Lady Langoa Langoa Barton
Lafargue 23/R J3 149
Lafaurie 40 I9 324
Lafaurie-Peyraguey 27/R J1 182
Laffitte-Carcasset 15 G6 88
Laffitte Laujac 21/L B6 131
Lafite Monteil Grand Monteil
Lafite Rothschild 12/L H3 72
Lafleur 41 E3 336
Lafleur du Roy 41 G3 336
Lafleur Grangeneuve 41 I5 336
Lafleur-Gazin 41 D3 336
Lafon 17 D7 97
Lafon 21/L H9 131
Lafon 27/R I2 182
Lafon-Laroze Raymond-Lafon
Lafon-Rochet 15 K5 88
Lafont-Fourcat 36 247
Lagarde 47 E3 385
Lagarenne 36 247
Lagarère de Marsan
Lagarosse 32/R J3 204
Lage, de 35 247
Lagnet 36 247
Lagorce 32/R I6 204
Lagorce Bernadas 17 K1 101

Lagorce du Ch La Mouline, Dom. de *La Mouline*
Lagrange *10 H2* 58
Lagrange *25/R F6* 162
Lagrange *36* 247
Lagrange *41 F4* 336
Lagrange les Tours *34* 247
Lagrange-Monbadon *45 E5* 366
Lagrave Paran *36* 247
Lagrave-Genestra *Caronne Ste Gemme*
Lagüe *44 K9* 353
Lagune, La *18 E6* 114
Lagupeau *Beauregard Ducasse*
Lahon, Dom. de *35* 248
Lalande *10 H7* 58
Lalande *17 H2* 97
Lalande d'Auvion *21/R G2* 131
Lalande de Balestard *de Balestard*
Lalande-Borie *10 H6* 58
Lalande Camail *Camail*
Lalande de Gravelongue *22/R F3* 132
Lalande Méric *Anniche*
Lalande Robin *Vieux Ch Robin*
Laliveau *46 K6* 377
Lamarche *44* 248
Lamarque *31/R L4* 216
Lamarque, de *19 H7* 114
Lamartine *45 G6* 366
Lamartre *38/R H6* 298
Lamarzelle Cormey *38/L D6* 298
Lamarzelle Figeac *Grand Barrail Lamarzelle Figeac*
Lamolière *Les Trois Croix*
Lamothe *27/R L4* 182
Lamothe *35* 248
Lamothe *46 K6* 377
Lamothe *de Plassan*
Lamothe *Vieux Ch Lamothe*
Lamothe, Clos *25/R D4* 162
Lamothe Bergeron *19 E7* 114
Lamothe Chaveau *Clos Lamothe*
Lamothe de Haux *32/R H5* 204
Lamothe Guignard *27/R L4* 182
Lamothe Pontac *René Georges*
Lamothe-Barrau *Lamothe-Gaillard*
Lamothe-Cissac *20 F6* 115
Lamothe-Gaillard *34* 248
Lamothe-Joubert *Lamothe* 377
Lamothe-Vincent *Lamothe*
Lamourette *27/R M1* 183
Lamouroux/Grand Enclos du Ch de Cérons *26/L C9* 162
Landat *20 E6* 115
Lande de Taleyran, La *35* 248
Landereau *35* 248
Landette, la *47 J8* 377
Landiras, de *26/L G3* 162
Landotte, La *Tour Haut-Caussan*
Lanessan *19 C4* 115
Lange *27/L K8* 183
Langoa Barton *10 G7* 58
Langoiran *32/R K7* 204
Laniote *38/L D9* 298
Lannes, des *de Paillet-Quancard*
Lapeyrere *Les Hauts de Palette*
Lapeyronie *45 J4* 366
Lapiey *Peyrabon*
Lapinesse *Villefranche*
Laplagnotte-Bellevue *38/R D2* 298
Laporte *Grand-Corbin-Despagne*
Larcis, Clos *38/L F10* 298
Larcis Ducasse *38/R H1* 298
Lardière 385
Lardit *45 H6* 366
Large-Malartic *Canet*
Larguet, Clos *Champion*
Laribotte *27/L F4* 183
Larmande *38/L D10* 298
Laroche *32/R K1* 204
Laroche Belair *Laroche*
Laroche Pipeau *44 I4* 353
Larode-Bonvil *Marac*

Laronde Desormes *36* 248
Laroque *38/R F4* 299
Laroque *Le Coteau*
Larose Saint-Laurent *Larose-Trintaudon*
Larose St-Genès *Listran*
Larose-Trintaudon *20 K9* 115
Laroze *38/L E7* 299
Larrivaux Vicomtesse de Carheil *20 E7* 115
Larrivet, Dom. de *Larrivet-Haut-Brion*
Larrivet-Haut-Brion *23/L G8* 149
Larroque *36* 248
Larruau *8/R E1* 43
Lartigue *35* 248
Lartigue de Brochon *Sociando-Mallet*
Lartigue Naude *Bigaroux*
Lascombes *8/L F10* 43
Lascombes, Clos *47 E3* 385
Lassalle *Potensac*
Lassalle, Dom. de *Kirwan*
Lassègue *38/R H3* 299
Lassime *36* 248
Lassus *22/R I9* 132
Lathibaude, de *Lesparre*
Laton *Laborie*
Latour *12/R C8* 72
Latour à Pomerol *41 H3* 336
Latour Camblanes *32/L I5* 204
Latour-Laguens *36* 248
Latrezotte *29 L5* 183
Lattes, Les *Carcanieux*
Lau, du *35* 267
Laubertine, Dom. de *34* 249
Laubès *35* 249
Lauga, de *19 E6* 115
Laulan Ducos *22/R G3* 132
Launay *36* 249
Laurès *Martinon*
Laurets, des *40 K8* 324
Lauriers de Boyrein, les *Le Pavillon de Boyrein*
Lauriol *Laclaverie*
Lauriol *Les Charmes-Godard*
Lauzac-Desclaux *35* 249
Lauzac-Desclaux *Clos Desclaux*
Lauzette, la *17 C7* 97
Laveline *La Clare*
Lavergne *Dom. Pont de Guestres*
Laville *27/L G5* 183
Laville *35* 249
Laville Haut-Brion *24* 150
Lavillotte *15 F2* 88
Lebrevigne, Dom. de *des Brousteras*
Léhoul *26/R F6* 162
Lemoine-Lafon-Rochet *18 E7* 115
Lenormand *31/R F1* 204
Léon *Carignan*
Léoville Barton *10 G7* 58
Léoville Las Cases *10 E7* 59
Léoville Poyferré *10 E7* 59
Lepine *31/R L4* 217
Lescale *36* 249
Lescaneaut, de *45 M4* 366
Lescours, de *38/L H5* 299
Lescure, Clos *Pindefleurs*
Lesparre *35* 267
Lespault *23/R L2* 150
Lespault *de Gorce*
Lestage *17 G5* 97
Lestage *40 L7* 316
Lestage-Darquier *17 E9* 101
Lestage Simon *21/R J8* 115
Lestey Noir *La Capelle*
Lestiac, de *32/R K7* 204
Lestiac, de *de Marsan*
Lestillon *des Granges*
Lestrille *35* 249
Lestrille Capmartin *Lestrille*
Letaillanet *Bois de Roc*
Letourt *Hauterive*
Levant, du *Liot*

Leydet-Figeac *de Valois*
Lezardière, de La *35* 250
Lezin *de la Tour*
Lézongars *31/L G4* 204
Licorne de Duplessis, La *Duplessis Hauchecorne*
Lidonne, de *47 K7* 377
Lieujean *20 I8* 116
Ligassonne *32/R K7* 204
Lilian-Ladouys *15 J4* 88
Lilotte, Dom. de *Haut Macô*
Limagère, de la *Haut-Lamothe*
Limbourg *Pontac Monplaisir*
Linas *18* 250
Lion Beaulieu *35* 250
Lion de Saint Marc, Le *Saint-Marc*
Lion Perruchon *40 G8* 321
Liot *29 K4* 183
Liotin *de Lage*
Lionnier *17 F2* 97
Lisennes, de *35* 250
Lisse, de *Mangot*
Listran *22/R E4* 132
Litanies, Clos des 336
Liversan *20 H7* 116
Livey, Le *36* 250
Livran *21/R K2* 132
Loiseau *34* 250
Loiseau, Clos de *Loiseau*
Longées, Les *Pavillon Bel Air*
Longua, La *Dalem*
Longues Reys *Grand Tuillac*
Lorient *35* 250
Losiot, Clos *Fort de Vauban*
Loubens *31/R L5* 217
Loubère, La *Toutigeac*
Loudenne *21/R G9* 132
Louis Rapin *Maison Blanche*
Loumède *47 E2* 385
Loup, Le *38/R D4* 299
Loupiac-Gaudiet *31/R K2* 214
Loustalot *Clos Jean*
Loustalot *Rondillon*
Lousteau-Vieil *31/R L6* 217
Lousteauneuf *22/R H7* 133
Louvière, L de *La Louvière*
Louvière, La *23/L F9* 150
Loyac *Malescot St-Exupéry*
Luc-Regula, Le *36* 250
Lucas *Tour d'Horable*
Lucat, de *du Peyrat*
Lucques, des *Millet*
Lucques, Dom. des *25/R D4* 163
Ludeman La Côte *26/R E6* 163
Ludeman les Cèdres *Pont de Brion*
Ludon Pomiès Agassac *La Lagune*
Lugagnac, de *36* 251
Lussac, de *40 H7* 321
Lutet *Lamarche*
Lynch-Bages *12/R D3* 74
Lynch-Moussas *12/R L5* 74
Lyne, de 251
Lys de Maisonneuve *40* 316

M de Malle *De Malle*
Mac Carthy *15 J8* 88
Macalan *32/R C5* 204
Macay *46 K5* 377
Macquin St Georges *Bellonne Saint Georges*
Macureau *la Fleur* 315
Madame *Coutet*
Mademoiselle, Dom. *Gueyrosse*
Mademoiselle de Calon *Calon-Ségur*
Mademoiselle de St Marc *La Tour Blanche*
Madlys *Sainte-Marie*
Madran 251
Magdelaine *38/L G9* 299
Magence *26/R E8* 163
Magence-Maragnac *Magence*
Magens, des *de Gravaillas*
Magnan *38/L E6* 299
Magneau *25/L G5* 163
Magnol *18 K6* 116

Magnotte, la *Bellevue* 126
Magondeau *44 F10* 353
Magondeau Beau-Site *Magondeau*
Mahon-Laville *Laville*
Maillard *32* 251
Mailles, des *31/R L6* 217
Maine, du *26/R G7* 163
Maine-Barail, Du *du Maine*
Maine-Barreau *Trincaud*
Maine Bonnet *de Respide*
Maine d'Arman *De la Grave*
Maine-Gazin 385
Maine Martin, Le *35* 251
Maine Tigreau *46 H3* 385
Maison Blanche *40 I2* 316
Maison Blanche *Tour de Corbin Despagne*
Maison Neuve, de *40 H4* 316
Maison Noble Saint-Martin *36* 251
Maison Rose *des Laurets*
Maisonneuve, Dom. de *Bellonne Saint Georges*
du Maître *Jacques Blanc*
Majureau-Sercillan *34* 251
Majureaux, Clos les *Ludeman La Côte*
Maldoror *Fougas*
Malagar *31/R K8* 204
Malartic-Lagravière *23/L I6* 150
Malbec Lartigue *Mayne Lalande*
Maledan *35* 251
Malène *Au Grand Paris*
Malescasse *19 I8* 116
Malescot St-Exupéry *8/R F1* 43
Maleterre *Haut-Franquet*
Malherbes, de *32/L G3* 205
Malinay, Le *Anthonic*
Malle, De *27/L E8* 183
Malleret, de *18 F5* 116
Malmaison *17 G6* 101
Malromé *36* 251
Malte, Clos de *Perron*
Malvat *Villars*
Mangons, Les *36* 251
Mangot *38/R G7* 299
Manoir, Cru du *de Chelivette*
Manoir de Villebout *des Laurets*
Manon la Lagune *Haut Bertinerie*
Manos *32/R G6* 205
Marac *36* 251
Maracan *Chapelle Maracan*
Maragnac *Magence*
Marbuzet *15 J8* 88
Marceloup *Brandeau*
Marche de Vernous, La *Vernous*
Marche-Canon, La *44 K7* 358
Marches de Castelnau, Les *de Castelnau*
Marcieuses, Les *Gobinaud*
Marcisseau *34* 251
Maréchaux, Les *Le Trébuchet*
Margaux *8/R E2* 46
Margès *Pouyanne*
Margotterie, Dom. de la *des Matards*
Marguerite de Fonneuve *Mercier*
Marianotte, Dom. de la *Bouscaut*
Marie *La Vieille France*
Marie-Claire *Renon*
Marinier *46 I10* 385
Marjolaine, de *Dom. de Bordenave*
Marot *36* 254
Marquis, Clos du *Léoville Las Cases*
Marquis d'Alesme Becker *8/R F1* 46
Marquis de Brassane *Hauterive*
Marquis de Cadourne *Soudars*
Marquis de Calon *Calon-Ségur*
Marquis de la Croix Landol *de Cantin*
Marquis de Hautessey *Roquefort*
Marquis de Lalande *Lalande* 58
Marquis de Mons *Dom. de la Vieille Eglise*
Marquis de Terme *8/R F1* 46

Marquise d'Alesme *Marquis d'Alesme Becker*
Marsac Séguineau *8/L C9* 46
Marsalette, Clos *23/R L4* 150
Marsan, de *32/R K8* 205
Marsau *45 C8* 368
Marsauda *Durand-Laplagne*
Martet *36* 254
Martialis, Dom. de *Clos Fourtet*
Martillac *Loupiac-Gaudiet*
Martinat *47 J7* 378
Martindoit *32/R H7* 205
Martinelles, Les *de Chainchon*
Martinens *8/L G9* 46
Martinon *35* 254
Martinot *Haut Guillebot*
Martouret *35* 254
Mary Domergue, Cuvée *Feytit-Clinet*
Massone, La *Pilet*
Matards, des *46 B1* 385
Mathereau *32/R C6* 205
Matras *38/L G8* 299
Maubert *Suau* 211
Maucaillou *17 D9* 101
Maucaillou, Dom. de *17 D9* 97
Maucaillou Felletin *17* 116
Maucamps *18 C7* 116
Maugey, Clos *Dom. de Bavolier*
Maujan, de *Smith Haut Lafitte*
Maurac *Le Trale*
Maurac-Major *Grandis*
Maurandes, les *Laulan Ducos*
Mauras *27/L L8* 183
Maurens *Fombrauge*
Maurian *Maurian de Prade*
Maurian de Prade *18 H5* 116
Maurin, Dom. de *Haut Maurin*
Maurin des Mottes *Haut Maurin*
Mauros *35* 254
Mausse *44 J7* 358
Mauves, de *25/R I8* 163
Mauvesin *17 J4* 102
Mauvezin *38/L H10* 299
May, Clos de *Maucamps*
Mayne Blanc *40 E7* 322
Mayne d'Imbert *25/R I8* 163
Mayne de Coutureau *25/R I8* 163
Mayne de Grissac *de Grissac*
Mayne des Carmes *Rieussec*
Mayne Lalande *17 H2* 97
Mayne Lévêque *de Chantegrive*
Mayne Pompon *du Mayne* 183
Mayne, du *26/R G7* 163
Mayne, du *29 H7* 183
Mayne, du *Rêve d'Or*
Mayne, du *Lange*
Mayne, Le *36* 254
Mayne, le *Soleil*
Mayne-Vieil *44 B9* 353
Mazails *21/R D8* 133
Mazarin *31/R K3* 214
Mazeris *44 I7* 358
Mazeris-Bellevue *44 I7* 358
Mazerolles *47 C3* 385
Mazeyres *41 M6* 336
Méaume *34* 254
Médouc *31/R L5* 217
Médulli, Les *La Hourcade*
Meillac *34* 254
Melin *32/R J2* 205
Melin Cadet Courreau *Melin*
Mémoires *31/R L8* 214
Menate *Ménota*
Menaudat, le *46 G2* 385
Mendoce, de *47 G3* 378
Ménota *29 H6* 184
Menuts, Clos des *38/L F6* 299
Menuts Gros Bonnet, Les *du Pavillon* 359
Menuts de La Serre, Les *La Serre*
Mercier *46 J4* 378
Mercier *Mont-Joye*
Mercier, Clos *La Bouade*
Mérissac *Dassault*
Merle Blanc, Le *Clarke*
Merle, du *31/R I3* 215

Merle, du *34* 254
Merlet, Dom. de *23/L G9* 150
Merville *Coutelin-Merville*
Mesny de Boisseaux *Roc de Boisseaux*
Messire de Fontesteau *Fontesteau*
Meste-Jean *35* 254
Mestrepeyrot *31/R K4* 205
Métairie de Grangeneuve *des Laurets*
Métairie du Ch Plain-Point, Cuvée La *Plain-Point*
Métria *17* 116
Meulière, de la *32/L F6* 205
Meyney *15 G8* 89
Meynieu, le *20 D7* 116
Meyre *17 K6* 118
Micalet *19 F6* 118
Michelière, La *34* 254
Milan, Dom. du *Haut-Nouchet*
Milary *34* 254
Millards, Les 385
Millaud-Montlabert *38/L D6* 300
Mille Secousses *47* 254
Millerie, La *Roc de Boissac*
Millet *25/R E5* 163
Milon *38/R D3* 300
Mingets, Dom. des *Villefranche*
Mingot *Rondillon*
Mirandole, La *46 D2* 385
Mission, La *41 J5* 344
Mission des Davids, La *La Croix-Davids*
Mission Haut-Brion, La *24* 150
Moine, Dom. du *Lagarenne*
Moine-Martin *Mayne-Vieil*
Moines, Clos des *38/R E5* 300
Moines, des *40 I4* 316
Moines, des *Lagarenne*
Moines, Les *21/R D4* 133
Moines, Les *47 C2* 386
Monbousquet *38/L I7* 300
Monbrison *8/R L1* 46
Moncets *43 D10* 346
Monconseil Gazin *47 F3* 386
Mondésir-Gazin *47 F3* 386
Mondiet *Graveyron*
Mondion, Dom. de *Dom. de la Grange Brûlée*
Mondot *Troplong Mondot*
Monet *27/L E3* 184
Mongenan *25/R E5* 163
Mongenant Billouquet, Dom *Le Raît*
Mongie, La *34* 255
Monlot Capet *38/R I3* 300
Monlot, Les Dames de *Monlot Capet*
Monreceuil, de *Belcier*
Monregard La Croix *Clos du Clocher*
Monrepos, Dom. de *de Faise*
Mont Carlau, du *36* 255
Mont, du *31/R K5* 217
Mont-Joye *29 H4* 184
Montagne de Mauvesin, La *Mauvesin* 102
Montahut *Arnauton*
Montaiguillon *40 J2* 316
Montaigut *46 K4* 378
Montalon *Le Peuy-Saincrit*
Montalon *Saincrit*
Monteil *Dubois Claverie*
Monteil, Le *d'Arsac*
Montet *Haut Guillebot*
Monthil, du *22/R I7* 133
Montifau *Les Tuileries du Déroc*
Montignac, Clos de *Pierre de Montignay*
Montjouan *32/L G1* 208
Montlabert *38/L D7* 300
Montlau *35* 255
Montrose *15 H9* 89
Monturon, de *Rozier*
Montviel *41 K5* 337
Morange 386
Morin *15 C5* 89

Morisset *La Braulterie de Peyraud*
Mornon *46 G3* 386
Mornon, Dom. de *Mornon*
Morton *Millet*
Mothe, La *Grand Moulin*
Mothe du Barry, La *35* 255
Motte de Clément Pichon, La *Clément Pichon*
Motte Maucourt *35* 255
Mouchet *40 J7* 324
Moulin *Moulin Pey-Labrie*
Moulin, du *40 I9* 324
Moulin, du *Saint Bonnet*
Moulin, du *Grand Peyruchet*
Moulin, Clos du *La Peyre*
Moulin Blanc La Chapelle *40 I7* 318
Moulin Borgne *Dom. de la Nouzillette*
Moulin de Bel Air *21* 133
Moulin de Bel Air *Les Tuileries*
Moulin de Brion *Les Moines* 133
Moulin de Caillou *Vrai Caillou*
Moulin de Duhart *Duhart-Milon*
Moulin de Ferrand *de La Vieille Tour*
Moulin de Ferregrave *Laulan Ducos*
Moulin de Grillet *46 I5* 386
Moulin de Jos, Dom. du *Haut-Garriga*
Moulin de la Bridane *La Bridane*
Moulin de la Grave *Turcaud*
Moulin de la Roque *La Tour de By*
Moulin de la Rose *10 H7* 60
Moulin de la Tonnelle *du Bouilh*
Moulin de Laborde *Fourcas Loubaney*
Moulin de Laborde *Gantonet*
Moulin de Lariveau, Le *Haut Lariveau*
Moulin de Launay *36* 255
Moulin de Ludon, Le *La Lagune*
Moulin de Mare *de Chantegrive*
Moulin de Mendoce, Dom *Sauman*
Moulin de Moustelat, Dom. du *36* 255
Moulin de Pey-Long *Roland la Garde*
Moulin de Pillardot *Bourdicotte*
Moulin de Poujeaux *Franquet Grand Poujeaux*
Moulin de Raymond *Laville* 249
Moulin de Reynaud *La Brande*
Moulin de Saint Vincent *Moulin à Vent*
Moulin de Sales *43 L6* 346
Moulin de Serré *34* 255
Moulin de T. *Talbot*
Moulin de Tricot *8/L L9* 48
Moulin des Arnauds *Les Petits Arnauds*
Moulin des Graves *46 J6* 378
Moulin des Graves *Hautes-Graves d'Arthus*
Moulin des Tonnelles *44 G6* 353
Moulin Desclau *Senailhac*
Moulin du Bourg *du Fourcas*
Moulin du Breuil *du Breuil* 107
Moulin du Cadet *38/L E9* 300
Moulin du Cartillon *du Cartillon*
Moulin du Prieur *Butte de Cazevert*
Moulin du Roulet, Le *36* 255
Moulin Haut Villars *Villars*
Moulin Haut-Laroque *44 F8* 353
Moulin la Pitié *45 D6* 368
Moulin Noir, du *40 H7* 322
Moulin Pey-Labrie *44 I8* 359
Moulin Riche *Léoville Poyferré*
Moulin Rouge, du *19 E6* 118
Moulin Saint Clair, Cuvée *Haut Saint Clair*
Moulin Saint Hubert *Lacombe*
Moulin Saint-Georges *38/L G9* 300

Moulin à Vent *17 I4* 102
Moulin Vieux, Dom. du *du Merle* 215
Moulin Vieux, du *47 J8* 378
Mouline, La *17 H4* 102
Mouline de Labégorce, La *Labégorce*
Moulinet *41 K2* 337
Moulinet-Lasserre *41 K5* 337
Mouliney *Grand Moulin* 112
Moulins de Ch-Cazalis, Les *Cazalis*
Moulins de Citran *Citran*
Mourlet *d'Archambeau*
Mousseyron *36* 255
Moustier, du *Gagnard*
Mouton Rothschild *12/L G5* 74
Moutte Blanc *18* 255
Mugron, Le *Grand-Jour*
Murailles de Ch-Cablanc, Les *Cablanc*
Musset, La *41 I2* 318
Musset, de *43 I4* 346
Mylord *35* 255
Myon de l'Enclos *17 H2* 102
Myrat *29 I4* 184
Naguet *Puy Rigaud*
Nairac *29 F7* 184
Nardique La Gravière *35* 255
Naudin Larchey *La Garde*
Nauge, La *Paret-Beauséjour*
Nausicaa *Haut Brisey*
Nauves, des *Morange*
Negre Pey *Haut-Rigaleau*
Nenin *41 H7* 337
Nère, La *31/R K3* 215
Ninon *35* 256
Ninon *Martinon*
Noaillac *22/R F2* 133
Noble, Dom. du *31/R I3* 215
Noblet *46 K7* 378
Nodoz *46 K7* 379
Notaires, Cru des *Le Clos du Notaire*
Notton *Brane-Cantenac*
Nougueys, des *Haut Coteau*
Noulet de Crain
Nouret *21/L C8* 133
Nouzillette, Dom. de la 386
Ogier de Gourgue *32/L J9* 208
Olivia *Lassime*
Olivier *23/L D7* 150
Olivier, l' *Le Prieuré*
Optimé, L' *Vrai Caillou`*
Oratoire, Clos de l' *38/R E1* 300
Oratoire de Chasse-Spleen, L' *Chasse-Spleen*
Orisse du Casse *Bertinat Lartigue*
Orleac, d' *des Arroucats*
Ormeau, L' *Brie-Caillou*
Ormes, des *d'Armajan des Ormes*
Ormes de Lagrange, Les *Lagrange les Tours*
Ormes de Pez, les *15 E5* 89
Ormes Sorbet, Les *21/R D4* 133
Osiris *La Tour Blanche*
Osmond, d' *20 F6* 118
Osmose Sec *Melin*
Pagodes de Cos, Les *Cos d'Estournel*
Paillet-Quancard, de *31/L I4* 208
Paillette, La *34* 256
Pain de Sucre, Clos du *Tayac* 379
Palène, La *Rocher Bellevue*
Palette, de *Les Hauts de Palette*
Palmer *8/R F2* 48
Palmeraie, Dom. de la *Patarabet*
Palombes de Noaillac, Les *Noaillac*
Paloumey *18 D5* 118
Panchille *35* 256
Panigon, de *21/L C7* 133
Pape, Le *23/R G1* 150
Pape Clément *23/L C4* 150
Papeterie, La *40 J1* 318

Papin *Dom. de la Grange Brûlée*
Pâquerette *34* 256
Paradis, du *38/R M1* 300
Paradis Casseuil *36* 256
Paradis Sicard *Tourans*
Paran Justice *38/R H6* 300
Parde de Haut-Bailly, La *Haut-Bailly*
Parenchère, de *36* 256
Paret-Beauséjour *45 H5* 366
Parres, Les *45 J8* 366
Part des Anges, La *Mazeris*
Parvis de Dom. Tapiau, Le *32/L I5* 208
Pascaud *34* 256
Pascaud-Villefranche *29 K7* 184
Pascot *32/L H2* 208
Pasquet *35* 256
Passion *Bel Air*
Passion *Domaine de Bouillerot*
Passion *Tour de Mirambeau*
Patache, La *41 I2* 337
Patache d'Aux *22/R J8* 133
Patarabet *38/L H9* 301
Patris *38/L G7* 301
Paveil de Luze *8/L C5* 48
Pavie *38/L G10* 301
Pavie Decesse *38/L G10* 301
Pavie Macquin *38/L G10* 301
Pavillon Bel Air *43 F8* 346
Pavillon Blanc du Ch Margaux *Margaux*
Pavillon Cadet *38/L E9* 301
Pavillon de Belloy *Belloy*
Pavillon de Boyrein, Le *26/R H3* 64
Pavillon des Connétables *Léoville Poyferré*
Pavillon du Ch Léhoul *Léhoul*
Pavillon du Haut Rocher *Haut Rocher*
Pavillon Figeac *La Grave Figeac*
Pavillon la Croix Figeac *Rocher Bellevue Figeac*
Pavillon la Violette *La Violette*
Pavillon Rouge du Ch Margaux *Margaux*
Pavillon, du *31/R L4* 218
Pavillon, du *44 K8* 359
Pavillons de Saint-Estèphe *Beau-Site*
Payard *36* 256
Payre, du/Monastère de Broussey, Clos du *31/L G6* 208
Pédesclaux *12/L E6* 76
Pegneyre *35* 256
Pèlerin, Clos du *41 J3* 337
Pelet *Lartigue*
Péligon, Clos de *35* 256
Penin *35* 257
Pensées de Lafleur *Lafleur*
Pérac *Sansarot-Dupré*
Perenne *47 B3* 386
Perguerie, La *Lamarque*
Périer, du *21/R C6* 134
Perin de Naudine, Dom. *25/R D2* 164
Perles de Haut-Chaigneau, Les *Haut-Chaigneau*
Pernaud *29 K7* 184
Perron *43 J5* 346
Perron la Croix *44 H9* 359
Perrucheau *Lagrange* 336
Pessan *25/R D4* 164
Pessan-St-Hilaire *25* 257
Petit Bocq *15 C6*
Petit Caillou Blanc *Picque Caillou*
Petit Cheval *Cheval Blanc*
Petit Clos du Roy *40 I3* 318
Petit Clos Figeac *38/L D4* 302
Petit La Garosse 386
Petit Montibeau, du *Dom. du Moulin de Moustelat*
Petit Mouton de Mouton Rothschild, Le *Mouton Rothschild*

Petit Musset, Dom. du *de Musset* 318
Petit Renouil *Grand Renouil*
Petit Roc *36* 257
Petit Val *38/L C9* 302
Petit Village *41 E6* 338
Petit-Faurie-de-Soutard *38/R E1* 302
Petit-Faurie-de-Soutard Deuxième *Petit-Faurie-de-Soutard*
Petit-Figeac *38/L D6* 302
Petit-Freylon *35* 257
Petit-Luc *35* 257
Petit-Moulin *35* 257
Petite Chardonne, La *Dom. Florimond-La-Brède*
Petite Culotte, La *Lacombe*
Petite Eglise, La *l'Eglise-Clinet*
Petits, Les *Peymelon*
Petits Arnauds, Les *47 D4* 387
Pétrarque *Chabiran*
Pétrus *41 E4* 338
Peuy-Saincrit, Le *34* 257
Pey, Le *21/L C9* 134
Pey Barrail *Le Pey*
Pey de Lalo *La Rose St Germain* 135
Pey la Rose *12* 76
Pey Labrie *44 J8* 359
Pey-Arnaud *Pernaud*
Pey-Baron, Dom. de *20 M6* 118
Peybonhomme Les Tours *47 E3* 387
Peybrun *31/R J4* 208
Peychaud *46 J5* 379
Peyfol *Castegens*
Peymartin *Gloria*
Peymelon *47 D4* 387
Peyrabon *20 H7* 118
Peyrarey *Dom. de Bouteilley*
Peyrat, du *31/L C5* 208
Peyre, La *15 I4* 89
Peyre-Lebade *17 F6* 98
Peyrebon *35* 257
Peyredon Lagravette *17 E8* 97
Peyredoulle *46 J4* 387
Peyrelongue *38/R H1* 302
Peyrelongue, Dom. de *38/L H10* 302
Peyrère, La *31/R L5* 218
Peyreyre *47 C3* 387
Peyrolan *Montaigut*
Peyrot-Marges *31/R J4* 21
Peyrou *45 J2* 366
Peyrouley *35* 257
Peyrouquet *38/R K5* 302
Peyruche, La *32/R J6* 209
Peyvigneau *Bel-Air Lagrave*
Pez, de *15 F5* 89
Phélan-Ségur *15 E8* 89
Philippe Raguenot *des Tourtes*
Piada *29 J7* 184
Piada-Lalanda *Piada*
Piat, Le *47 L9* 379
Piaut *Simon*
Pibran *12/L G9* 76
Pic, de *32/R J5* 209
Picardan, Dom. de *Dallau*
Picardan, Dom. de *Clos de l'Hermitage*
Pichon Bellevue *35* 267
Pichon Le Moyne *Pichon Bellevue*
Pichon Longueville Comtesse de Lalande *12/R D7* 77
Pichon-Longueville *12/R D7* 76
Picon *36* 257
Picourneau *Le Bourdieu Vertheuil*
Picque Caillou *24* 151
Pierbone *Peyrabon*
Pierrail *36* 257
Pierre Bibian *Bibian Tigana*
Pierre Lavau *Lestage*
Pierre de Montignac *21/L E7* 134
Pierrefitte *Perron*
Piganeau *38/L G4* 302
Pigotte Terre Feu, La *21* 134
Pilet *31* 258

Piliers, Les *Tour de Corbin Despagne*
Piliers de Maison Blanche, Les *Maison Blanche*
Pilot Les Martins *Caillou Les Martins*
Pin, du *des Cèdres*
Pin, Le *41 F6* 338
Pin-Franc-Pilet *Pilet*
Pindefleurs *38/L G7* 303
Pineau du Rey *Filhot*
Pinet la Roquette *46 J4* 387
Piney *38/R I2* 303
Pintey, du *34* 258
Piot-David *29 J7* 184
Pipeau *38/R I2* 303
Piras, du *du Grand Moëys*
Pitray, de *45 H6* 366
Plagnac *21/L C9* 134
Plain-Point *44 F6* 353
Planier de Guillouin *Guillouin*
Plaisance *31/L D3* 209
Plaisance *18* 258
Plaisance *38/L K8* 303
Plaisance *40 J1* 318
Plaisance St. Lambert *Batailley*
Planquettes, Les *34* 258
Plantanes, des *45 K2* 366
Plantat *25/L J5* 164
Plantes du Mayne, Les *Grand Mayne*
Plantey *12/R I1* 77
Plantey de la Croix *Verdignan*
Plantey de Lieujean *La Fon Du Berger*
Plantiers du Haut-Brion, Les *Haut-Brion*
Plassan, de *32/R J4* 209
Plégat-La Gravière *du Grand Bos*
Plince *41 I7* 338
Plincette *41 H8* 338
Pointe, La *41 I6* 338
Pointe Riffat, La *La Pointe*
Polin *35* 258
Polyanthas, les *Vieille Tour la Rose*
Pomeys *17 J3* 102
Pomirol le Pin *31* 258
Pommerie, La *Madran*
Pomone *Haut-Villet*
Pomys *15 I6* 90
Poncet *31/R G1* 209
Poncet *La Freynelle*
Poncet-Deville *Saint-Robert*
Pont de Brion *26/R E7* 164
Pont de Guestres, Dom. *43 M6* 346
Pont de Guitres, au *Dom. Pont de Guestres*
Pont Rouge, Dom. du *8* 258
Pontac Lynch *8/R F3* 48
Pontac Monplaisir *23/R* 151
Pontac-Phénix *Pontac Lynch*
Ponteilh-Monplaisir *Haut-Bergey*
Pontet *21/R G2* 134
Pontet, du *34* 258
Pontet Caillou *Le Bourdillot*
Pontet-Barrail *Labadie*
Pontet-Canet *12/L H7* 77
Pontet-Chappaz *8/L L10* 48
Pontet-Coussan *Pontet*
Pontoise Cabarrus *21/R K9* 118
Pontus *44 I9* 353
Porge, Le *35* 258
Port du Roy *de Portets*
Portail, de *d'Arricaud*
Portets, de *25/R D3* 164
Potensac *21/R H3* 134
Pouchaud-Larquey *36* 258
Pouget *8/R H3* 48
Poujeaux *17 E9* 102
Poupille *45 J5* 366
Pouyanne *26/L J5* 165
Prade, La *45 E6* 368
Pradeau Mazeau *Toutigeac*
Pré-Videau *Loumède*
Prélude de Ch Toulouze *Toulouze*
Pressac *de Beau Rivage Laguens*
Pressac, de *38/R G6* 303

Prestige de Jonchet *Jonchet*
Preuillac *21/L H10* 134
Prévenche *Terrasson*
Prieur, Le *35* 258
Prieur de Meyney *Meyney*
Prieuré, Le *38/R F1* 303
Prieuré d'Aiguevives *Le Virou*
Prieuré La Libarde *Tour de Collin*
Prieuré les Tours *Millet*
Prieuré, de *Lézongars*
Prieuré-Lichine *8/R G3* 48
Prieurs de la Commanderie *41 L4* 338
Primat, Dom. de *17 J8* 118
Prince de la Rivière *de la Rivière*
Princesses de Lagarcie, Les *Crusquet-de Lagarcie*
Prioulette, La *31/R K9* 209
Prioulette, La *Mayne de Coutureau*
Pilourat, Le *Lu Commanderie* 332
Private Réserve *Kirwan*
Priverat *d'Escot*
Proche-Pontet *19 I8* 118
Prost *29 F7* 184
Providence, La *18* 259
Pucelle, de la *Plantat*
Puits de Raynaud, Le *Croûte Courpon*
Pujos *Mousseyron*
Puy, du *45* 259
Puy Arnaud *45 I5* 366
Puy Bardens *32/L K8* 209
Puy Castéra *20 F8* 118
Puy de Boissac *du Moulin*
Puy Guilhem *44 E9* 353
Puy la Rose *12* 77
Puy Laborde *Virac*
Puy Landry *Vieux Ch Champs de Mars*
Puy Rigaud *40 K7* 318
Puy Saint Vincent *Puy Guilhem*
Puy St Georges *St George*
Puy-Blanquet *38/R G6* 303
Puy-Marceau *Landereau*
Puy-Razac *38/L I10* 303
Puyanché *45 D7* 368
Puyblanquet Carrille *38/R G5* 303
Puybonnet *Teyssier* 319
Puycarpin *45* 259
Puyfromage *45* 259
Puygueraud *45 E6* 368
Puyjalon *Jean Gervais*
Quentin *des Matards*
Quentin, de *de Cruzeau*
Quercy *38/R L1* 303
Queyret-Pouillac *36* 259
Queyron Patarabet *38/L J9* 303
Quinsac *La France* 239
Quintaine Mazails *Haut-Maurac*
R de Rieussec *Rieussec*
Rabaud-Promis *27/L J9* 186
Rabouchet, de *36* 259
Rahoul *25/R E4* 165
Raït, Le *36* 259
Ramafort *21/R G2* 134
Ramage La Batisse *20 H7* 118
Rambal, de *de Malherbes*
Rame, La *31/R L6* 218
Raphaël *de Parenchère*
Rastouillet Lescure *38/R J3* 303
Ratouin *41 L4* 338
Raux, du *19 F7* 119
Rauzan Despagne *35* 259
Rauzan-Gassies *8/R F1* 49
Rauzan-Ségla *8/R F1* 49
Raymond-Lafon *27/R I1* 186
Rayne-Vigneau, de *27/R K1* 186
Rayon de Soleil *Soleil*
Raz Caman, la *46 F2* 387
Réal-Caillou *43 E5* 346
Rebouquet la Roquette *46 J4* 387

Redon *35* 259
Reflets du Ch Cissac *Cissac*
Reignac, de *35* 259
Reindert *34* 260
Relais de Cheval Blanc, Le *36* 260
Relais de Patache d'Aux, Le *Patache d'Aux*
Reléou *Grand Bireau*
Remparts de Bastor, Les *Bastor-Lamontagne*
Remparts de Dudon *Dudon* 198
Remparts de Ferrière, Les *Ferrière*
Renaissance *38* 260
Renaissance, Dom *Lardière*
Renard *44 H4* 353
Renardière, La *Haut-Rousset*
René, Clos *41 K5* 338
René Georges *22/R F4* 135
Renon *32/R J4* 260
Renon, Clos *Millet*
Réserve JR *Des Arras*
Réserve d'O du Ch Olivier *Olivier*
Réserve de la Comtesse *Pichon Longueville Comtesse de Lalande*
Réserve de Marquis d'Evry de *Lamarque*
Réserve du Général, La *Palmer*
Réserve Lion Noir *Grand Launay*
Réserve du Marquis de Sorans *Cap de Haut*
Respide, Dame de *Respide-Médeville*
Respide, de *26/R F7* 165
Respide-Médeville *26/R D4* 165
Rêve d'Or *41 J4* 339
Reverdi *17 C5* 98
Reynon *31/L I8* 209
Reys, Dom. du *25/L F8* 165
Reysse, Le *Lassus*
Reysson *20 C6* 119
Ricaud, de *31/R H2* 210
Ricaud, Dom. de *36* 260
Richeterre *La Tour de Mons*
Richotey *44 H6* 353
Rider, de *47* 260
Rieussec *27/R G3* 186
Rigaud *40 K7* 324
Rimensac, Le *Chante-Alouette La Roseraie*
Ripeau *38/L C7* 303
Riquette, Dom. de la *Simon*
Rivalerie, La *46 H4* 388
Rivaux, Les *45 B6* 368
Riveret *de Seguin*
Rivière, de la *44 G4* 353
Rivière, La *27/R L1* 186
Robert *Haut Macô*
Robin *45 J6* 366
Robin *Dom. de Courteillac*
Roc, Le *Monconseil Gazin*
Roc de Bernon *40 J9* 324
Roc de Boissac *40 I8* 324
Roc de Boisseaux *38/L K8* 304
Roc de Cambes *47 K6* 379
Roc de Canon *Vrai Canon Bouché*
Roc de Cayla *35* 260
Roc de Cazade *36* 260
Roc de Joanin *45 F5* 367
Roc de Troquard, Le *40 J3* 325
Roc La Longuère *Roc de Cazade*
Roc Meynard *34* 260
Roc Meynard *Clos du Roy*
Roc-Taillade *de la Croix*
Rocard *Saint-Amand*
Roche Gaby, La *44 J9* 359
Rochemorin, de *23/R I3* 151
Rocher, du *38/R H7* 304
Rocher Bellevue *45 K4* 367
Rocher Bellevue Figeac *38/L D4* 304
Rocher du Puy *du Puy*
Rocher du Tuquet *Le Tuquet*
Rocher Lideyre *Lardit*
Rochers, des *20 C4* 322
Roches, des *du Cros*

Roches Blanches, des *Côte de Baleau*
Roches de Ferrand, Les *44 H6* 354
Rochette, La *des Laurets*
Rocheyron *38/R F4* 304
Rocques, Les *31* 215
Rocques, Les *47 J5* 379
Rocs, des *Beaulieu Bergey*
Rocs de Damis, Les *Beaulieu Bergey*
Rode, la *Le Grand Verdus*
Rol de Fombrauge *38/R E3* 304
Roland *de Pressac*
Roland la Garde *46 H3* 388
Rollan de By *22/R I10* 135
Rolland, de *29 I9* 186
Rolland-Maillet *38* 304
Romefort *Lamothe Bergeron*
Romer du Hayot *27/L E8* 186
Rondillon *31/R J3* 215
Rondillon Loubat *Rondillon*
Roque de By, La *La Tour de By*
Roquebert *32/L L7* 210
Roquebert, Dom. de *Dom. de la Grave*
Roquebrune *32/L G5* 210
Roquebrune, de *43 M5* 346
Roquefort *35* 260
Roquefort, de *Tertre Daugay*
Roquegrave *22/R H9* 135
Roques, de *40 H9* 324
Roques-Mauriac *36* 260
Roquetaillade, de *26/R J4* 165
Roquetaillade La Grange, de *26/R J4* 165
Roquetaillade le Bernet, de *de Roquetaillade La Grange*
Roquevieille *45 F6* 367
Rosaire, du *La Fleur Saint Georges*
Rose Bellevue, La *46 B3* 388
Rose Castenet, La *Castenet-Greffier*
Rose Châtain, la *Haut-Châtain*
Rose Chevrol, la *La Croix* 351
Rose Côtes Rol, La *38/L D9* 304
Rose Coulon, La *Dom. des Lucques*
Rose du Pin, La *35* 260
Rose du Pont *22/R I5* 135
Rose Fayan, La *45 F8* 367
Rose Figeac, La *41 E9* 339
Rose Figeac, la *Tour de Corbin Despagne*
Rose Garamey, La *Livran*
Rose Laurent, La *Belle Ile*
Rose MacCarthy, La *Haut-Marbuzet*
Rose Maréchale, La *Coufran*
Rose Noaillac, la *Noaillac*
Rose Piney, La *Coudert Pelletan*
Rose Saint-Bonnet, La *Saint-Christoly*
Rose St Germain, La *21/R I2* 135
Rose St-Germain, La *35* 260
Rose Ste-Croix *17 F4* 98
Rose Vosel, la *Vieux Chevrol*
Rose-Pourret, La *38/L D8* 304
Rose-Renève, La *35* 260
Rose-Trimoulet, La *38/R D1* 304
Roseé de Bacchus, La *Dom. du Haut Cantelaudette*
Roseraie de Mayne *Mayne Blanc*
Roses de Ch Faugères, Les *Cap de Faugères*
Rosier *Loupiac-Gaudiet*
Rosiers, Dom. des *46 B2* 388
Rossignol *Castagnac*
Roudier *40 K5* 318
Rouet *44 F4* 354
Rouget *41 G3* 339
Rouillac, de *23/L D6* 151
Roullet *44* 359

Roumagnac La Maréchale *44 I5* 354
Roumieu *29 K5* 188
Roumieu *29 H7* 188
Roûmieu-Lacoste *29 K4* 188
Rouquette, de *Dauphiné Rondillon*
Rousselet, de *46 K5* 379
Rousselle, La *44 H5* 354
Rousset *46 K5* 379
Roustit, Dom. *31/R K7* 218
Rouzes Clinct, Clos Les *41 G3* 339
Roy, Clos du *44 F8* 354
Roy, Clos du *Piada*
Roylland *38/L G7* 305
Rozier *38/R H2* 305
Rozier *de Francs*
Ruat *Ruat Petit Poujeaux*
Ruat Petit Poujeaux *17 H6* 102
Ruaud *36* 260
Ruban Bleu du Ch d'Arsac *d'Arsac*
Rubis du Prince Noir *Tayac*
Rudel, Clos des *Crusquet-de Lagarcie*
Sablay *la Treille des Girondins*
Sable, Dom. du *38/R H2* 305
Sablier, Le *Tour du Pas St Georges*
Sablot de Roquebrune *de Roquebrune*
Sacquerelles, Les *Dom. Arnaud*
Sadran-Quancard, de *de Paillet-Quancard*
Saincrit *34* 261
Saint Ahon *18 I5* 119
Saint Bonnet *21/R B5* 135
Saint Corbian *Tour des Termes*
Saint Estèphe *15 I5* 90
Saint Germain *du Grand Puch*
Saint Mathieu *Le Grand Chemin*
Saint Paul *21/R K9* 119
Saint Paul de Montagne *Samion* 319
Saint Pierre en l'Isle *Saint-Aubin*
Saint Rémi *Les Roches de Ferrand*
Saint Roch *Andron Blanquet*
Saint Savet *36* 261
St-Vincent *Mayne Blanc*
Saint-Agrèves *26/L G5* 165
Saint-Amand *27/L J9* 188
Saint-André Corbin *40 J3* 325
Saint-Antoine *36* 261
Saint-Aubin *22/R F10* 135
Saint-Aulaye *46 G3* 388
Saint-Benoît *21* 135
Saint-Christoly *21/R B6* 135
Saint-Christophe *21/R C7* 135
Saint-Cricq *du Caillou*
Saint-Estèphe de Calon la Chapelle *Calon-Ségur*
Saint-Florin *36* 261
Saint-Jacques *8* 261
Saint-Jean-Baron *367*
Saint-Lô *38/R K5* 305
Saint-Marc *8/L E8* 49
Saint-Marc *29 G6* 188
Saint-Ourens *32/R J8* 210
Saint-Paul de Dominique *La Dominique*
Saint-Pey, de *38/R K4* 305
Saint-Philippe, de *45 F6* 367
Saint-Pierre *10 I7* 60
Saint-Pierre *35* 261
Saint-Robert *26/L G9* 168
Saint-Roch de Nenin *Nenin*
Saint-Romans *Barrcyrc*
Saint-Seurin *Charmail*
Saint-Sulpice *35* 261
Saint-Valéry *Le Chatelet*
Saint-Vincent, Clos *38/L J7* 305
Sainte Anne, Dom *Haut Mallet*
Sainte-Anne, Clos *31/L F4* 210
Sainte-Catherine *31/L G3* 210
Sainte-Gemme, de *19 C6* 119
Sainte-Hélène, de *De Malle*
Sainte-Marie *35* 261

Salargue, La *35* 261
Sales, de *41 L2* 339
Salle de Pez, La *de Pez*
Salle de Poujeaux, La *Poujeaux*
Salle du Courros, La *du Courros*
Salle, Dom. de la *Sansonnet*
Samion *40* 319
Samion 346
Samonac *Macay*
Sansaric, de *25/R D2* 168
Sansarot-Dupré *17 E4* 98
Sansonnet *38/R F1* 305
Sarail-la Guillaumière *35* 261
Sarget de Gruaud Larose *Gruaud-Larose*
Sarpe, Clos de *38/R F2* 305
Sarrailley, Dom. du *35* 261
Sartre, le *23/L L4* 151
Sartre Bujan *Bujan*
Sauman *47 G3* 379
Saumey, La *La Font Neuve*
Sauvetat *Fonchereau*
Sauvignon M.P. *du Grand Barrail*
Sec de Rayne Vigneau, Le *de Rayne-Vigneau*
Second de Durfort *Durfort-Vivens*
Second de Floridène, Le *Clos Floridène*
Ségla *Rauzan-Ségla*
Segonnes *Lascombes*
Segonzac *47 B2* 388
Seguin *23/L C6* 151
Seguin, de *35* 261
Ségur *18 F7* 119
Ségur, de *Brousset*
Ségur de Cabanac *15 D9* 90
Ségur du Cros *du Cros*
Ségur Fillon *Ségur*
Seigneurs de Pommyers, des *36* 262
Seignouret, de *de Castelneau*
Seize, de *Alfa Bernarde*
Sémeillan Mazeau *17 G3* 98
Semonlon *17 F2* 119
Senailhac *35* 262
Sénéjac *18 F2* 119
Senilhac *21/R J6* 120
Sens, de *32/L G5* 210
Sèpe, Le *36* 262
Sercillan *Majureau-Sercillan*
Serizière, La *35* 262
Serre, la *38/L F10* 305
Sestignan *22/R F3* 135
Seuil, Dom. du *du Seuil*
Seuil, du *26/L B9* 168
Siaurac *43 D8* 346
Sigalas-Rabaud *27/L J10* 188
Sigognac *21/R E5* 135
Sillage de Malartic, Le *Malartic-Lagravière*
Simon *29 I7* 188
Simon Carretey *Gravas*
Sipian *22/R H7* 135
Siran *8/R H6* 49
Sirène *du Glana*
Sirène de Giscours, La *Giscours*
Sissan *32/L H8* 211
Smith Haut Lafitte *23/R F3* 151
Sociando-Mallet *21/R K10* 120
Sociondo *47 D3* 388
Soleil *40 K8* 324
Solitude, Dom. de la *23/R L2* 152
Sorbier *Capet Bégaud*
Soudars *21/R I9* 120
Souley-Ste Croix, Le *20 B6* 120
Sours, de *35* 262
Sours, Dom. de *de Sours*
Soussans *Deyrem Valentin*
Soutard *38/L E10* 306
St Georges *40 K4* 325
St Jacques *Génisson*
St Jacques Calon *40 I4* 318
St Mambert Bellevue *12/R C6* 77
St Pierre *41 F4* 339
St-Genès *Perenne*
St-Georges (Côte Pavie) *38/L G9* 305

St-Jean-des-Graves *30 K4* 168
St-Laurent *Les Grands Thibauds*
St-Martin, Clos *38/L F8* 305
St-Michel *29 I2* 188
Sterlines *Loupiac-Gaudiet*
Suau *29 G8* 188
Suau *31/L F5* 211
Suduirant *27/L H9* 189
Tabuteau, de *40 F6* 322
Taffard de Blaignan *21/R H3* 135
Tailhas, du *41 F10* 339
Taillan, du *18 K3* 120
Taillefer *41 G10* 339
Talbot *10 F5* 60
Talmont *36* 262
Tanesse *32/R K7* 211
Tarey, Le *31/R I2* 215
Taste, de *22/L G9* 136
Taste, de *46 K6* 379
Tastère, La *Le Livey*
Tauzinat l'Hermitage *38/R F5* 306
Tayac *8/L C6* 49
Tayac *47 J4* 379
Tayac la Rauza *Tayac* 49
Tayac Plaisance *8/L B6* 50
Tayat *388*
Temple, Le *22/R H7* 136
Templey, Le *Grand-Jean*
Templiers, Clos des *41 J5* 346
Templiers, Les *43 H8* 346
Tenotte, La *46 K5* 380
Ternefat *Terrefort*
Terrasse, La *Belle Ile*
Terrasses de Taffar, Les *Taffard de Blaignan*
Terrasson *45 E6* 367
Terre Blanche *Les Tuileries*
Terre Blanche *Ferrasse*
Terre Brune de St. Paul *Saint Paul*
Terre Rouge *de la Croix*
Terrefort *31/R H2* 215
Terrefort *Lescalle*
Terrefort, Clos *Balot*
Terrefort-Quancard, de *34* 262
Terres Vieilles *Grand-Jour*
Terrey-Gros-Cailloux *10 H6* 60
Tertre, du *8/L K10* 50
Tertre, Le *35* 267
Tertre Bujan *Bujan*
Tertre Daugay *38/L G8* 306
Tertre de Cascard *La Michelière*
Tertre de La Veine, Clos du *Haut Bourdieu*
Tertre de Sarpe *Vieux Ch Pelletan*
Tertre Roteboeuf *38/R G2* 306
Teychon, Dom. de *Lagrange*
Teyssier *38/L K9* 306
Teyssier *40* 319
Teyssier *40 J7* 324
Teyssier *Bel Air* 224
Teysson *Les Templiers*
Thibaut-Ducasse *de l'Hospital*
Thieuley *35* 262
Thil, Le *Peybonhomme Les Tours*
Thil Comte Clary, Le *23/R F2* 152
Thuillac *Gravettes-Samonac*
Tilet Rouge *Fontenil*
Timberlay *34* 262
Tondenac *Saint-Antoine*
Tonnelle, Clos de la *Soutard*
Tonnelle, La *20 F6* 120
Tonnelle, La *de Terrefort-Quancard*
Tonnelle de Cazalis, La *Cazalis*
Tonnelle du Roy *Jeandeman*
Tonnellerie du Ch Segonzac *Segonzac*
Toulifaut, Clos *41 F9* 339
Toulouze *35* 267
Toumalin *44 I8* 359
Tour, de la *35* 262
Tour Baladoz *38/R G2* 307
Tour Baron de Gascq *de Portets*
Tour Bellegrave *19* 120
Tour Bellevue *Barreyres*

Tour Bicheau *25/R E4* 168
Tour Blanche *21/R C6* 136
Tour Blanche, La *27/R L3* 189
Tour Caillet *35* 263
Tour Canon *Canon-Chaigneau*
Tour Canon, La *Junayme*
Tour Carelot *Métria*
Tour Carnet, La *20 M9* 120
Tour Chaigneau *Canon-Chaigneau*
Tour d'Aspic, La *Haut-Batailley*
Tour d'Eyquem *Eyquem*
Tour d'Horable *45 K6* 367
Tour de Bessan, La *8/L C7* 50
Tour de Buch *Labourdette*
Tour de By, La *22/R I3* 136
Tour de Calens *25/L D9* 168
Tour de Cluchon *Jean Gervais*
Tour de Collin *47 J5* 380
Tour de Corbin Despagne *38/R B7* 307
Tour de Gombeau *Chêne de Gombeau*
Tour de Grenet *40 F6* 322
Tour de l'Espérance *36* 263
Tour de Langoiran *Langoiran*
Tour de la Motte *La Bergère*
Tour de Marbuzet *15 J8* 90
Tour de Marchesseau *346*
Tour de Mirambeau *35* 263
Tour de Mons, La *8/L B8* 50
Tour de Pez *15 E4* 90
Tour de Pic *de Pic*
Tour de Pressac *de Pressac*
Tour de Queyron *Panchille*
Tour des Graves *46 J6* 380
Tour des Termes *15 D5* 91
Tour du Haut Moulin *19 H7* 120
Tour du Mayne *d'Arcins*
Tour du Mirail *20 F6* 120
Tour du Moulin *354*
Tour du Moulin du Bric *36* 263
Tour du Palais *La Mouline*
Tour du Pas St Georges *40 K4* 325
Tour du Pin Figeac, La *38/L C5* 307
Tour du Pin Figeac, La *Le Caillou*
Tour du Pin Franc *Grand Corbin*
Tour Figeac, la *38/L C5* 307
Tour Grand Faurie *38/L C9* 307
Tour Haut-Brion, La *24* 152
Tour Haut-Caussan *21/R G2* 136
Tour Léognan, La *Carbonnieux*
Tour Marcillanet *20 L6* 121
Tour Martillac, La *23/R K5* 152
Tour Massac, La *Pouget*
Tour Musset *40 L6* 319
Tour Peyronneau *Bernateau*
Tour Pomys *Houissant*
Tour Renaissance *du Barry*
Tour Saint Laurent *Tour Baladoz*
Tour Saint Paul *Grimont*
Tour Saint Vincent *La France*
Tour Saint-André *Haut-Chaigneau*
Tour Saint-Fort *15 G3* 91
Tour Saint-Pierre *38/L C10* 308
Tour St Bonnet, La *21/R B4* 136
Tour St Joseph *20 F6* 121
Tour St-Christophe *38/R F3* 307
Tour-Camail *la Clyde*
Tour-Chapoux *La Commanderie de Queyret*
Tour-Clanet *du Bouilh*
Tour-du-Roc *19 K7* 121
Tour-Ségur, La *de Barbe Blanche*
Tourans *38/R G5* 307
Tourbadon *Dom. du Haut-Patarabet*
Tourelles, Des *347*
Tourelles, Les *Haut Bastor*
Tourelles de Bossuet Lagravière, Les *34* 263
Tourelles de Lamothe, Les *Lamothe* 182

Tourelles de Longueville, Les *Pichon-Longueville*
Tourette, La *20 K9* 77
Tournefeuille *43 G8* 347
Tournelle des Moines *Beau-Séjour Bécot*
Tournelle du Pin Figeac, La *La Tour du Pin Figeac*
Tours, des *Loubens*
Tours de Beaumont, Les *Beaumont*
Tours de Laroque, Les *Laroque*
Tours de Malle *De Malle*
Tourteran *Ramage La Batisse*
Tourtes, des *46 B4* 388
Toutigeac *35* 263
Trale, Le *21/R K1* 121
Traverses, les *Lacombe Noaillac*
Trébuchet, Le *36* 263
Tréhon, Le *22/R I6* 136
Treille des Girondins, la *45 L3* 367
Treilles de Vauban, Les *Fort de Vauban*
Tretin, Le *Haut-Gravat*
Tressan, de *Darius*
Treytins *Garraud*
Trianon *38/L E5* 308
Tricot d'Arsac *Pontet-Chappaz*
Trimoulet *38/R D1* 308
Trincaud *34* 263
Tristan *I2* 340
Trocard *36* 264
Trocard Monrepos *Trocard*
Trois Hectares, Les *Bauduc*
Trois Clochers, Doms. des *32/R H7* 211
Trois Croix, Les *44 F8* 354
Trois Moulins *Cambon la Pelouse*
Tronquoy de Sainte-Anne *Tronquoy-Lalande*
Tronquoy-Lalande *15 G7* 91
Troplong Mondot *38/R G1* 308
Troquart *40 J3* 325
Trotanoy *41 G5* 340
Trotte Vieille *38/R F1* 308
Truffière, La *Cassagne Haut-Canon*
Troupian *Lestage Simon*
Tuilerie, La *d'Ardennes*
Tuilerie du Puy, La *36* 264
Tuileries, Clos des *43 I5* 347
Tuileries, Clos des *du Merle* 254
Tuileries, Les *21/R F6* 136
Tuileries du Déroc, Les *35* 267
Tuilière, La *47 H4* 380
Tuquet, Le *25/L D9* 169
Tuquets, des *36* 264
Turcaud *35* 264
Vachon, Dom. de *Tour Saint-Pierre*
Val d'Or, du *38/L M10* 308
Val d'Or, du *Lardit*
Valade, La *44 H8* 354
Valandraud, de *38/L F9* 308
Valdor, de *de l'Emigré*
Valentin *Deyrem Valentin*
Valentin *Peybrun*
Valentons Canteloup, de *35* 264
Vallière, La *347*
Valois, de *41 E9* 340
Valoux *Bouscaut*
Valrose *Belle Ile*
Vatican, Dom. du *20* 121
Ventouse *du Grand Ferrand*
Verdignan *21/R I9* 121
Verdun, du *Sipian*
Verdus *21/R K9* 121
Vergnes, Dom. de *Mongenan*
Vergnes, Les *36* 264
Vernon *45 G5* 367
Vernous *21/L I8* 137
Verrière, La *36* 264
Viaud, de *43 K6* 347
Viaud, Dom. de *43 K5* 347
Vic, Dom. du *du Payre/Clos du Monastère de Broussey*

Vicomtesse, la *Laffitte-Carcasset*
Victoria *Saint-Agrèves*
Victoria *Le Bourdieu Vertheuil*
Vie, La *du Taillan*
Vieille Chapelle Bastoney, La *La Rose-Renève*
Vieille Croix, La *44 E9* 354
Vieille Cure, La *44 F9* 354
Vieille Eglise, Clos de la *41 H3* 340
Vieille Eglise, Dom. de la *38/R H4* 308
Vieille Eglise, La *Arnauton*
Vieille France, La *25/R E3* 169
Vieille Tour *31/L H8* 211
Vieille Tour la Rose *38/L D10* 309
Vieille Tour Montagne *Haute Faucherie*
Vieille Tour, de La *36* 265
Vieilles Souches, Dom. des *Richotey*
Vieilles Tuileries, Les *35* 264
Vieux Bômale *Canevault*
Vieux Bonneau *40 K6* 319
Vieux Braneyre *20 F5* 121
Vieux Brignon *Graulet*
Vieux Busquet *40 D5* 322
Vieux Cardinal Lafaurie *43 B6* 347
Vieux Ch. Birot *40 K8* 319
Vieux Ch. Brun *La Ganne*
Vieux Ch. Calon *40 I4* 319
Vieux Ch. Certan *41 E5* 340
Vieux Ch. Chambeau *40 H9* 322
Vieux Ch. Champs de Mars *45 F7* 367
Vieux Ch. des Combes *de Cantin*
Vieux Ch. des Templiers *Rouget*
Vieux Ch. du Colombier *Puyfromage*
Vieux Ch. Ferron *41 I8* 340
Vieux Ch. Gaubert *25/R E4* 169
Vieux Ch. Haut-Béard *38/R H3* 309
Vieux Ch. Lamothe *35* 265
Vieux Ch. Landon *21/R C2* 137
Vieux Ch. Pelletan *38/R F3* 309
Vieux Ch. Rocher Corbin *40 H4* 319
Vieux Ch. Saint André *40* 319
Vieux Ch. Valentin *Gardut*
Vieux Ch. Valentin *Haut-du-Peyrat*
Vieux Chêne, du *45 E6* 368
Vieux Chênes, Les *21/R C6* 137
Vieux Chevrol *43 F7* 347
Vieux Coutelin *15 I3* 91
Vieux Dom. des Menuts *La Grâce Dieu Les Menuts*
Vieux Dom. de Taste *47 J7* 380
Vieux Dominique *Bois Noir*
Vieux Duché de *l'Evêché*
Vieux l'Estage *Domaine des Cailloux*
Vieux Ferrand *Grand Baril*
Vieux Gabiran *La Blanquerie*
Vieux Gréan *Arthus/Clos de La Vieille Eglise*
Vieux Grenet *Haut-Sorillon*
Vieux Guadet *Boutisse*
Vieux Guillaume *Sarail-la Guillaumière*
Vieux Guillou *40 J3* 325
Vieux Labarthe *38/R L2* 309
Vieux Larmande *38/L E9* 309
Vieux Lescours *Carteau Côtes Daugay*
Vieux Moulin *17 F4* 98
Vieux Moulin Cazeaux *31R I3* 215
Vieux Moulin du Cadet *Cadet-Bon*
Vieux Moulins de Chéreau *40 H5* 319
Vieux Pignon *La Chandellière*

Vieux Pinson, Le *46 B2* 388
Vieux Plateau Certan, Clos du *41* 340
Vieux Pontet *Cadet-Pontet*
Vieux Pourret *38/L E8* 309
Vieux Prézat *Pontet*
Vieux Robin *22/R I9* 137
Vieux Sarpe *38/R E2* 310
Vieux Taillefer, Dom. *41 F9* 340
Vieux-Guinot, du *38/R J4* 309
Vigneau, de *Poncet*
Vigneraie, La *de la Tour*
Vignes de Saint Sauveur, Les *Barateau*
Vignoble d'Alfred *45 B5* 368
Vignobles Latorse *Vieux Ch Lamothe*
Vignol *35* 265
Vignol *Tour de Calens*
Vignot *Lassègue*
Villa Bel Air *25/L I8* 169
Villambis, de *20 G5* 121
Villars *44 E8* 354
Villefranche *29 L7* 189
Villegeorge, de *17 K9* 121
Villemaurine *38/L F9* 310
Vilotte *36* 265
Vimières Le Tronquéra, les *12 H7* 50
Vincent *44 G7* 354
Vinésimes *Fontesteau*
Violette, La *41 G7* 340
Virac *36* 265
Viramière *38/R H6* 310
Virelade *25/R H7* 169
Virginie de Valandraud *de Valandraud*
Virou, Le *46 I6* 388
Vivier, Le *Grivière*
Voûte, La *38/R* 310
Vrai Caillou *36* 265
Vrai Canon Bouché *44 K7* 359
Vray Canon Boyer *44 K6* 359
Vray Croix de Gay *41 E4* 340
Vray Houchat *Les Roches de Ferrand*
Ygrec *d'Yquem*
Yon Figeac, Clos *Laroze*
Yon Saint Martin *Yon-Figeac*
Yon-Figeac *38/L E7* 310
Yquem, d' *27/R I2* 189
Yveline *43 C6* 347
Z de Zédé *Labégorce Zédé*
Zédé, Dom *Labégorce Zédé*

CHÂTEAUX BY COMMUNES

Consult this index to find châteaux in the atlas listed by their commune. Châteaux in communes with their own appellation, such as Montagne, or which share a major appellation, such as Soussans with the Margaux AC, are not listed if the châteaux use that AC. For lists of these estates consult the directory pages.

Abzac d'Abzac, de Beaulieu Haut-Sorillon
Anglade Grand Terrier, la Raz Caman
Arbanats du Castéra, Lagrange
Arbis Dom de Cheval-Blanc Signé, Haut Reygnac, Petit-Moulin, Les Vieilles Tuileries
Arcins d'Arcins, Arnauld, Barreyres, Tour Bellegrave, Tour-du-Roc
Arsac *see AC Margaux p40*
Artigues-près-Bordeaux Le Gay
Arveyres Barre Gentillot, de Brondeau, Burayre, Cantelaudette, La Capelle, du Lau, Panchille, La Rose-Renève
Auriolles Castenet-Greffier
Auros Bastian
Avensan Citran
Métria, Meyre, Dom de Primat, Semonlon, de Villegeorge
Baron Baron Bertin, de Crain, Le Prieur
Barsac *see ACs Barsac & Sauternes p176*
Baurech de Beau Rivage Laguens, Dudon, Laroch, Melin
Bayon-sur-Gironde Le Breuil, La Croix de Millorit, Eyquem, Falfas
Beautiran de Haut-Calens, Haut-Lamothe, Tour de Calens, Le Tuquet
Bégadan l'Argenteyre, le Bernet, Le Breuil Renaissance, de By, des Cabans, La Clare, La Font Neuve, La Gorre, Greysac, Labadie, Laffitte Laujac, Lassus, Laujac, du Monthil, Patache d'Aux, Le Pey, Plagnac, Rollan de By, Rose du Pont, La Tour de By, Vieux Ch Landon, Vieux Ch Robin
Béguey de Birot, Les Hauts de Palette, Reynon
Belvès-de-Castillon La Brande, Castegens, Côte Montpezat, Puy Arnaud, Puycarpin, Robin
Berson La Braulterie de Peyraud, Le Chay, Dom Florimond-La-Brède, Moulin de Grillet, Peyredoulle, Pinet la Roquette, Rebouquet la Roquette
Beychac-et-Caillau Canteloup, Fosselongue, La France, Dom de la Grave, La Lande de Taleyran, Lesparre, Polin, Dom du Sarrailley
Blaignan Blaignan, La Cardonne, La France, La Gorce, Grivière, Lalande d'Auvion, La Pigotte Terre Feu, Pontet, Ramafort, Tour Haut-Caussan
Blanquefort Dillon, Grand Clapeau Olivier, Linas, Magnol, Saint Ahon
Blasimon Bel Air
Blaye Cone-Taillasson Sabourin, Loumède, Les Moines
Bommes *see ACs Barsac & Sauternes p176*
Bonzac La Grave, Trincaud
Bouliac Cluzel, Montjouan
Bourg-sur-Gironde du Bousquet, Caruel, Le Clos du Notaire, Conilh Haute-Libarde, La Croix-Davids, Croûte Courpon, Croûte-Charlus, De la Grave, Gros Moulin, de Lidonne, Mille Secousses, de Rider, Roc de Cambes
Braud-et-St-Louis La Mirandole
Budos Duverger, Pouyanne
Cadaujac Bardins, Bouscaut
Cadillac Fayau, Greteau, du Juge, Justa
Cadillac-en-Fronsadais Le Bocage, Cadillac-Branda, La Chassière
Camarsac de Camarsac
Cambes La Forêt, Galland-Dast, Henry de France, Jonchet, Puy Bardens
Camblanes-et-Meynac Dom de Bavolier, Brethous, Latour Camblanes, Le Parvis de Dom Tapiau, Sissan
Camiran Les Faures
Campugnan La Botte
Canéjan de Rouillac, Seguin
Cantenac *see AC Margaux p40*
Cantois de Bertin, Dom de Ricaud
Capian de Caillavet, La Chèze, du Grand Moëys, Lagrange, Martindoit, du Peyrat, Plaisance, Clos Sainte-Anne, Suau
Caplong Dubois Claverie
Cardan Haut Mouleyre, du Payre/Clos du Monastère de Broussey
Carignan-de-Bordeaux Carignan
Cars Barbé, Capville, La Cassagne-Boutet, Chante-Alouette La Roseraie, Dom du Chay, Crusquet-de Lagarcie, Crusquet-Sabourin, l'Escadre, Gardut Haut-Cluzeau, Gardut, du Grand Barrail, Haut Sociondo, Haut-du-Peyrat, Lagarde, Clos Lascombes, Les Petits Arnauds, Peybonhomme Les Tours, Peymelon, Sociondo
Casseuil La Courtiade Peyvergès, Paradis Casseuil
Castelnau-de-Médoc Mauvesin
Castelviel Castel Vieilh La Salle, de Guérin
Castillon-de-Castets du Carpia
Castillon-la-Bataille de Chainchon, Chinchon la Bataille, La Croix de Louis, Ferrasse, Tour d'Horable
Castres Ferrande, du Grand Bos, Dom Perin de Naudine
Caudrot Dom de Bordenave
Cazaugitat Bourdicotte, Au Grand Paris
Cénac Duplessy, de la Meulière, Roquebrune
Cérons
See ACs Graves, Graves Supérieures & Cérons p155
Cessac Briot, Redon
Cézac Marinier, Tayat
Cissac-Médoc du Breuil Chano, Cissac, Hanteillan, Haut du Puy, Haut-Logat, Lamothe-Cissac, Landat, Larrivaux, d'Osmond, Puy Castéra, La Tonnelle, Tour St Joseph, Tour du Mirail, Vieux Braneyre, de Villambis
Civrac-de-Blaye Gauthier
Civrac-en-Médoc Bournac, La Chandellière, d'Escurac, Haut Plantey, Nouret, de Panigon, Pierre de Montignac
Cleyrac Vilotte
Coimères Larroque
Comps Colbert
Coubeyrac Fonfroide, La Jalgue
Couquèques Les Ormes Sorbet
Créon Bauduc
Cubnezais Haut Bertinerie
Cubzac-les-Ponts Canada, Lagrange les Tours, Les Planquettes, de Terrefort-Quancard
Cussac-Fort-Médoc Aney, Beaumont, Bel Air, Bernones, Colome Peylande, Fort de Vauban, Lachesnaye, Lacour Jacquet, Lamothe Bergeron, Lanessan, de Lauga, Micalet, du Moulin Rouge, du Raux, de Sainte-Gemme, Tour du Haut Moulin
Daignac La Freynelle, de Laborde
Dardenac Grossombre
Daubèze de Lage
Donzac Haut Maurin, Pilet
Doulezon Labatut, Lagnet, Roques-Mauriac
Escoussans Le Bos, Laubès, Meste-Jean, Pasquet
Espiet de La Lezardière
Eynesse Martet, Picon
Eyrans Mornon
Fargues *see ACs Barsac & Sauternes p176*
Flaujagues Barbazan
Fours Les Chaumes
Francs de Francs, Marsau, Puyanché
Fronsac *See AC Fronsac p 351*
Frontenac Bran de Compostelle
Gabarnac Haut Goutey, Mestrepeyrot, Peybrun, Peyrot-Marges
Gaillan-en-Médoc Blayac, Gadet Terrefort
Galgon Chabiran, La Croix de Roche, Mayne-Vieil, Pascaud, Tour de l'Espérance
Gardegan La Fourquerie
Gardegan-et-Tourtirac de Pitray
Gauriac Clos Alphonse Dubreuil, Belle Ile, Bujan
Génissac Belle-Garde, Bellevue La Mongie, Brun Despagne, Grand Clauset, Haut-Guérin, Haut-Mongeat, Penin, Peyrouley, Tour Caillet
Gironde-sur-Dropt Bosquet, Dom de Bouillerot, de Frimont
Gornac Cazeau, Lacombe, Martinon
Gours Bétoule, Haut-Meillac
Grézillac Bellevue Jos, Bonnet, Haut-Garriga, Mylord, Ninon, Peyrebon
Guillac Canet Mauros
Haux Anniche, Clos Chaumont, Frère, du Grava, de Haux, Lagorce, Lamothe de Haux, Manos, Doms des Trois Clochers
Illats d'Archambeau, d'Ardennes, de Callac, Dom du Hauret Lalande
Izon de Jabastas
Jau-Dignac-et-Loirac Haut Brisey, Haut-Gravat, La Hourcade, Lacombe Noaillac, Lalande de Gravelongue, Laulan Ducos, Listran, Noaillac, René Georges, Saint-Aubin, Sestignan
Juillac Le Bory Rollet
La Lande-de-Fronsac Lagarenne, Loiseau
La Réole Le Luc-Regula
La Rivière du Breuil, Laroche Pipeau, Renard, de la Rivière, Roumagnac La Maréchale, La Rousselle
La Roquille Franc La Cour
La Sauve Majeure Allegret, de Fontenille, Thieuley, Turcaud, Vieux Ch Lamothe
Labarde Dauzac, Giscours, Saint-Jacques, Siran
Labrède Bichon Cassignols, La Blancherie, Le Chec, des Fougères, Magneau
Ladaux des Combes, La Gaborie, La Hargue, d'Haurets, La Serizière
Lalande-de-Pomerol *See AC Lalande-de-Pomerol p 342*
Lamarque Cap de Haut du Cartillon, Haut-Bellevue, de Lamarque, Malescasse, Maucaillou Felletin, les Vimières Le Tronquéra
Landerrouat Talmont, La Verrière
Landerrouet-sur-Ségur Lassime
Landiras d'Arricaud, Carbon d'Artigues, de Landiras, Saint-Agrèves
Langoiran Barreyre, du Biac, de l'Eglise, Le Gardera, Gourran, Langoiran, Ligassonne, La Peyruche, Saint-Ourens, Tanesse
Langon Brondelle, Camus, La Croix, Cru Claverie/Dom du Petit de l'Eglise, Fernon, du Gaillat, Léhoul, Ludeman La Côte, du Maine, Pont de Brion
Lansac Beauguérit, Bégot, Fougas, Guionne, Lamothe, Martinat, de Taste, Vieux Dom de Taste
Lapouyade La Bardonne
Laroque Vieille Tour
Laruscade Petit La Garosse
Latresne Clos Desclaux Gassies, Lauzac-Desclaux, de Malherbes, Pascot
Le Pian-sur-Garonne Fayard
Le Pian-Médoc de Malleret, Maurian de Prade, Sénéjac
Le Pian-sur-Garonne La Gravelière, Ruaud
Le Pout Le Barail Beaulien
Le Puy La Tuilerie du Puy
Le Taillan-Médoc Dom Chalet de Germignan, du Taillan
Le Tourne de Pic
Léognan *See AC Pessac-Léognan p143*
Les Artigues-de-Lussac Béchereau, de Bordes, Dom des Chapelles, Les Charmettes, Dom de la Colombine, de Faise, Les Grands Jays, Haut-Colas-Nouet, des Huguets, Trocard
Les Billaux Georges de Guestres
Les Eglisottes-et-Chalaures Brande-Bergère
Les Esseintes Le Trébuchet
Les Lèves-et-Thoumeyragues Haut-Mourleaux, Hostens-Picant, Petit Roc, Le Raït, Les Vergnes
Les Salles-de-Castillon Belcier, Brandeau, Les Hauts-de-Granges, La Rose Fayan
Lesparre d'Escot, Les Moines, Preuillac, Le Tréhon, Vernous
Lestiac-sur-Garonne de Lestiac, de Marsan
Libourne Clos Belle Rose, Belregard-Figeac, Bonalgue, La Croix de Jaugue, La Croix-Toulifaut, Cruzeau, Elisée, Ferrand, Dom du Galet, La Ganne, Grand Sillons Gabachot, Gueyrosse, Haut Ferrand, Jean Mathieu, La Paillette, Petit Clos du Roy, du Pintey, Plince, de Sales, Taillefer, Tour Des Tourelles, Vieux Ch Ferron
Lignan-de-Bordeaux de Seguin
Ligueux Couronneau, de Parenchère
Listrac-Médoc *See AC Listrac-Médoc p94*
Loupès Lartigue, Maledan
Loupiac *see AC Loupiac p214*
Ludon-Médoc d'Agassac, d'Arche, La Bessane, La Garricq, Dom Grand Lafont, La Lagune, Lemoine-Lafon-Rochet, Paloumey, La Providence
Lugaignac Haut Guillebot
Lugasson Le Bouscat, Canteloudette, Roquefort
Lugon de Blassan, Canevault, Le Conseiller, de la Grande Chapelle
Lussac *See AC Lussac-St-Emilion p320*
Macau Barreyre, Biré, Cambon la Pelouse, Cantemerle, de Cazenove, Les Charmilles, Dasvin-Bel-Air, de Gironville, La Houringue, Laronde Desormes, Lescalle, Maucamps, Moutte Blanc, Plaisance
Maransin Bois Noir, Croix Grand Barail, Méaume
Marcenais Dom de la Nouzillette
Marcillac Les Billauds, Lardière
Margaux *see AC Margaux p40 and Dom de l'Ile Margaux*
Margueron Pierrail
Marsas Alfa Bernarde, Morange
Martillac Cantelys, Ferran, La Garde, Clos Grivet, Haut-Nouchet, Haut-Vigneau, Lafargue, Lespault, de Rochemorin, Smith Haut Lafitte, Dom de la Solitude, La Tour Martillac
Martres la Commanderie
Massugas Blanchet, Haut-Rigaleau, Saint Savet
Mauriac Gaury Balette
Mazères Beauregard Ducasse, de Roquetaillade La Grange, de Roquetaillade
Mazion Dom de l'Ancien Manoir de Valette, La Bergère, La Bretonnière, Cailleteau Bergeron, Guiet, Saint-Aulaye
Mérignac Picque Caillou
Mérignas La Blanquerie
Mesterrieux Boutillon
Mombrier Groleau, Laliveau, La Tenotte
Monbadon Cantegrive, des Faures, Fongaban, Lagrange-Monbadon, Terrasson

Monprimblanc Balot, du Grand Plantier

Montagne See AC *Montagne-St-Emilion p314*

Montignac Lamothe

Montussan Fonchereau

Morizès Pouchaud-Larquey

Mouillac Grand Village

Mouliets-et-Villemartin Chapelle Maracan, Les Grandes Bornes

Moulis-en-Médoc See AC *Moulis en-Médoc p99*

Moulon Les Arromans, Montlau, La Mothe du Barry, Le Porge, La Salargue

Mourens du Barrail

Naujan-et-Postiac Bel Air, Butte de Cazevert, Fondarzac, Grand Bireau, Lion Beaulieu, Rauzan Despagne, Tour de Mirambeau

Néac See AC *Lalande-de-Pomerol p342*

Nérigean Martouret

Omet la Bertrande, Poncet

Ordonnac de la Croix, Potensac, Taffard de Blaignan

Paillet Clos Bourbon, des Cèdres, de Paillet-Quancard, Sainte-Catherine

Parempuyre Clément Pichon, Ségur

Pauillac See AC *Pauillac p67*

Pellegrue Bon Jouan, Favereau, Haut-Favereau, de Lugagnac

Pessac See AC *Pessac-Léognan p143*

Pessac-sur-Dordogne Coursou, Dom du Moulin de Moustelat

Petit-Palais-et-Cornemps Dom du Calvaire, de Cornemps, de Fussignac

Pineuilh Frontenac, de Rabouchet

Plassac Chante Alouette, Graulet, Maine-Gazin, Monconseil Gazin, Mondésir-Gazin

Podensac de Chantegrive, de Mauves, Mayne d'Imbert

Pomerol See AC *Pomerol p331*

Portets Berger, Cabannieux, Cheret-Pitres, La Fleur Jonquet, du Grand Abord, Grand Bourdieu, Dom La Grave, Graveyron, des Gravières, Guérin-Jacquet, de l'Hospital, Jean Gervais, Clos Lamothe, Dom des Lucques, Millet, Monet, Mongenan, Pessan, Pessan-St-Hilaire, de Portets, Rahoul, de Sansaric, Tour Bicheau, La Vieille France, Vieux Ch Gaubert

Preignac d'Argilas le Pape, d'Armajan des Ormes, Bastor-Lamontagne, Cru d'Arche Pugneau, Cru Peyraguey, l'Ermitage, Gilette, Haut-Bergeron, Les Justices, Laribotte, Laville, De Malle, Saint-Amand, Suduiraut

Prignac-en-Médoc Chantélys, Hourbanon, Lafon

Prignac-et-Marcamps de la Brunette, Grand-Jour, de Grissac

Pugnac Haut-Gravier, Noblet

Puisseguin See AC *Puisseguin-St-Emilion p323*

Pujols-sur-Ciron Barréjats, Clos Floridène, Clos du Hez, St-Jean-des-Graves, Saint-Robert

Pujols-sur-Dordogne Cazalis, Dom de la Grange du Roy, Lafont-Fourcat, Marac

Queyrac Carcanieux

Quinsac Dom de Chastelet, de Gorce, Grimont, Roquebert

Rauzan du Charron, des Granges, Haut-Mazières, L'Heyrisson, Joinin

Reignac Les Bertrands, Haut-Boisron

Rimons De l'Aubrade, Haute Brande, Jamin

Rions du Broustaret, Carsin, Cayla, Haut Rian

Roaillan Le Pavillon de Boyrein, de Respide

Romagne Dom des Cailloux, La Rose du Pin, La Rose St-Germain

Ruch Dom de Courteillac, des Joualles

Sadirac Le Grand Verdus, L'Hoste-Blanc, Landereau

Saillans Beauséjour, La Brande, Cardeneau, de Carles, Dalem, Fontenil, de La Huste, Labory, Magondeau, Moulin Haut-Laroque, Puy Guilhem, Roc Meynard, Clos du Roy, Tour du Moulin, La Vieille Croix, La Vieille Cure, Villars

Saint-Caprais Ogier de Gourgue, Le Sens

Salignac Dom de Laubertrie, Majureau-Sercillan

Salleboeuf Grand Monteil de la Tour

Samonac Gravettes-Samonac, Haut-Castenet, Macay, Rousset

Sauternes See AC *Sauternes & Barsac p146*

Sauveterre-de-Guyenne Abbaye de St Ferme, de Beaulieu, du Grand Ferrand, Roc de Cazade

Savignac-de-l'Isle Dom des Bizelles, Damase

Soulignac Grand-Jean, Haut Mallet, Pegneyre, Roc de Cayla

Soussac Launay, Marot, Moulin de Launay, Saint-Florin, Vrai Caillou

Soussans See AC *Margaux p40*

St-Aignan Moulin des Tonnelles, Plain-Point, Dom Pont de Guestres, Reindert, Les Roches de Ferrand, Vincent

St-André-de-Cubzac du Bouilh, Dom de Cheval Blanc, La Joye, Le Peuy-Saincrit, Saincrit, Timberlay

St-André-du-Bois de Cappes, Dom de Jeantieu, Lagrave Paran, Malromé, Tour du Moulin du Bric

St-André-et-Appelles des Chapelains, Côtes des Caris

St-Androny le Menaudat

St-Antoine-du-Queret Candelley, La Commanderie de Queyret, Guichot, Queyret-Pouillac, Saint-Antoine

St-Aubin-de-Blaye Le Grand Moulin

St-Avit-St-Nazaire du Bru, Haut Cantonnet

St-Brice Haut Bastor

St-Caprais-de-Blaye des Tourtes

St-Caprais-de-Bordeaux Canteloup, La Gontrie, La Grange Clinet

St-Christoly-de-Blaye Dom Arnaud, Saint-Christoly

St-Christoly-Médoc Le Boscq, Cantegric, Les Grands Chênes, Clos de la Grange-Vieille, du Périer, Saint Bonnet, Saint-Christophe, Tour Blanche, La Tour St Bonnet

St-Christophe-des-Bardes Boutisse, de Cantin, Champion, Coudert Pelletan, Clos de la Cure, Fombrauge, Grangey, Haut-Sarpe, Jacquemineau, Laplagnotte-Bellevue, Laroque, Le Loup, Milon, Clos des Moines, Puyblanquet Carrille, Rol de Fombrauge, Dom du Sable, Clos de Sarpe, Tauzinat l'Hermitage, Tour St-Christophe, Vieux Ch Pelletan

St-Cibard Les Charmes-Godard, de Garonneau, Laclaverie, Moulin la Pitié, La Prade, du Puy, Puyfromage, Puygueraud, du Vieux Chêne

St-Ciers-d'Abzac Lamothe-Gaillard

St-Ciers-de-Canesse Belair-Coubet, Haut-Guiraud, Haut-Rousset, Les Heaumes, Montaigut, La Tuilière

St-Ciers-sur-Gironde Haut Grelot,

des Matards, Dom des Rosiers, Le Vieux Pinson

St-Denis-de-Pile Bossuet, Dom de la Brandille, Dallau, La Dominante, Les Gazelles, du Merle, Pâquerette, Les Tourelles de Bossuet Lagravière

Ste-Colombe Briand Cap de Faugères, La Clarière Laithwaite, Lapeyronie, Lardit, Poupille, Vignoble d'Alfred

Ste-Croix-du-Mont See AC *Ste-Croix-du-Mont p214*

Ste-Eulalie de Chelivette, Macalan, Mathereau

Ste-Foy-la-Grande L'Enclos, Les Mangons

Ste-Foy-la-Longue de Balan, Beaulieu Bergey

Ste-Gemme les Bouzigues

St-Emilion See AC *St-Emilion p280*

Ste-Radegonde Gantonet, Le Moulin du Roulet, Le Sèpe

St-Estèphe See AC *St-Estèphe p83*

Ste-Terre Beaufresque, de Lyne, Marcisseau

St-Etienne-de-Lisse Bernateau, du Calvaire, Côte Puyblanquet, Faugères, Fleur Cardinale, Fleur de Lisse, Haut Bruly, Haut Rocher, Haut-Villet, Jacques Blanc, Lamartre, Mangot, Paran Justice, de Pressac, Puy-Blanquet, du Rocher, Tourans, du Vieux-Guinot, Viramière, La Voûte

St-Exupéry Ducla

St-Félix-de-Foncaude du Mont Carlau, des Seigneurs de Pommyers

St-Genès-de-Blaye La Croix-Saint-Jacques, Perenne, Segonzac

St-Genès-de-Castillon La Croix Bigorre, de l'Estang, Flojague, Paret-Beauséjour

St-Genès-de-Lombaud Biarnès, Haut Pougnan, Nardique La Gravière

St-Genis-du-Bois Motte Maucourt, Petit-Freylon

St-Germain-de-Grave Génisson, Le Relais de Cheval Blanc

St-Germain-de-la-Rivière Rouet

St-Germain-d'Esteuil Brie-Caillou, Castera, Hauterive, Livran, La Rose St Germain

St-Germain-du-Puch Clos des Confréries, Degas, du Grand Puch, Haut-Gayat, Haut-Graveyron, Lestrille

St-Gervais Des Arras

St-Girons-d'Aiguevives Le Virou

St-Hippolyte Billerond, Capet Duverger, Capet-Guillier, La Couronne, Destieux, Franc Pipeau Descombes, De Guilnemansoy, Haut-Plantey, Lassègue, Piney, Rastouillet Lescure, Dom de la Vieille Eglise

St-Jean-de-Blaignac de Bonhoste

St-Julien-Beychevelle See AC *St-Julien p55*

St-Laurent-d'Arce Les Grands Thibauds, Haut Bourdieu

St-Laurent-des-Combes Béard, Bellefont-Belcier, Bellevue, de Candale, Darius, Haute Nauve, Clos Labarde, Pipeau, Rozier, Tertre Roteboeuf, Tour Baladoz, Vieux Ch Haut-Béard

St-Laurent-du-Bois Ballan-Larquette, Joumes-Fillon

St-Laurent-Médoc Balac, Barateau, Belgrave, Le Bouscat, Camensac, Caronne Ste Gemme, Dom de Cartujac, Devise d'Ardilley, Larose-Trintaudon, Dom de Pey-Baron, La Tour Carnet, Tour Marcillanet, La Tourette

St-Léon de Castelneau

St-Loubès Bois-Malot, L'Escart,

Dom du Haut Cantelaudette, Dom de Lahon, Lorient, Clos de Péligon, de Reignac, Sarail-la Guillaumière, de Valentons Canteloup

St-Louis-de-Montferrand Madran

St-Magne-de-Castillon Bellevue, Blanzac, du Bois, Brehat, Dom de la Caresse, Fontbaude, de Lescaneaut, Les Parres, Peyrou, des Plantanes, Rocher Bellevue, Saint-Jean-Baron, la Treille des Girondins

St-Maixant La Croix-Bouey, Les Jésuites, Labatut-Bouchard, Malagar, Mayne de Coutureau, Mémoires, La Prioulette

St-Mariens Haut-Terrier

St-Martial Courtey

St-Martin-de-Laye Moulin de Serré

St-Martin-de-Sescas de Jayle

St-Martin-du-Bois Dom de Birot

St-Martin-du-Puy Latour-Laguens, Maison Noble Saint-Martin

St-Martin-Lacaussade Cap Saint-Martin, Charron, Frédignac, Labrousse, Mazerolles, Peyreyre

St-Médard-d'Eyrans de Cruzeau, d'Eyrans

St-Michel-de-Fronsac See AC *Canon-Fronsac p356*

St-Michel-de-Lapujade de La Vieille Tour

St-Morillon Belon Camarset, Plantat, Villa Bel Air

St-Palais La Rose Bellevue

St-Paul-de-Blaye Berthenon, Goblangey, Les Jonqueyres, Maine Tigreau, La Rivalerie

St-Pey-d'Armens la Boisserie, La Bonnelle, Bonnet, l'Eglise d'Armens, Clos Gerbaud, Juguet, Peyrouquet, Saint-Lô, de Saint-Pey

St-Pey-de-Castets Cablanc, Gamage, Haut Saint Pey

St-Philippe-d'Aiguilhe d'Aiguilhe, Grand Tuillac, Grimon, Lamartine, Roc de Joanin, Roquevieille, de Saint-Philippe, Vernon, Vieux Ch Champs de Mars

St-Philippe-du-Seignal La Bourguette

St-Pierre-d'Aurillac Le Livey, Mousseyron

St-Pierre-de-Bat Petit-Luc, Saint-Pierre

St-Pierre-de-Mons Magence

St-Quentin-de-Baron de Balestard, de Sours, Vignol

St-Quentin-de-Caplong La Chapelle Maillard, Le Mayne

St-Romain-la-Virvée Haut-Saint-Romain, Meillac, La Michelière

St-Sauveur d'Esteau, La Fon Du Berger, Fontesteau, Fournas Bernadotte, du Junca, Lieujean, Liversan, Peyrabon, Proche-Pontet, Ramage La Batisse

St-Selve Le Bonnat, Haut-Selve, Dom du Reys

St-Seurin-de-Bourg Les Rocques, Tayac, Tour de Collin

St-Seurin-de-Cadourne d'Aurilhac, Bel Orme Tronquoy de Lalande, Charmail, Coufran, Grand Moulin, Grandis, Lestage Simon, Pontoise Cabarrus, Saint Paul, Senihhal, Sociando-Mallet, Soudars, Le Trale, Verdignan, Verdus

St-Seurin-de-Cursac Roland la Garde

St-Seurin-sur-l'Isle La Favière

St-Sulpice-de-Faleyrens Arthus/Clos de La Vieille Eglise, Barrail des Graves, du Barry, Bertinat Lartigue, Bigaroux, Le Castelot, La Caze Bellevue, Franc Bigaroux, Grand

Bert, Haut-Montil, Jupille Carilloy, de Lescours, Monbousquet, Plaisance, Renaissance, Roc de Boisseaux, Clos Saint-Vincent

St-Sulpice-de-Pommiers Labourdette, des Tuquets

St-Sulpice-et-Cameyrac Beauval, Laville, Le Maine Martin, Saint-Sulpice

St-Trojan Mercier, de Rousselet

St-Vincent-de-Paul Dom de la Grange Brûlée

St-Vincent-de-Pertignas du Courros, Grand Donnezac

St-Vivien-de-Blaye Les Graves, Les Millards

St-Yzans-de-Médoc Bois de Roc, des Brousteras, Haut-Maurac, Loudenne, Mazails, Moulin de Bel Air, Saint-Benoît, Sigognac, Les Tuileries

Tabanac Camail, la Clyde, Lagarosse, de Plassan, Renon

Taillecavat Virac, **Talence** Laville Haut-Brion, La Mission Haut-Brion, La Tour Haut-Brion

Targon Alexandre, de Beauregard-Ducourt, Bel-Air l'Espérance, des Cabannes, de Hartes, Sainte-Marie, Toutigeac

Tauriac Brûlesécaille, Guerry, Haut Macô, la Landette, du Moulin Vieux, Nodoz, Le Piat

Tayac Haut Rozier, Les Rivaux

Teuillac Grand Launay, Les Grands Bertins, Haut-Mousseau, Moulin des Graves, Peychaud, Tour des Graves

Toulenne Respide-Médeville

Tresses du Clos Delord, de Lisennes, Senailhac

Valeyrac Bellegrave, Bellerive, Bellevue, Le Bourdieu, Haut-Grignon, Jeanton, Lousteauneuf, Roquegrave, Sipian, Le Temple, Les Vieux Chênes

Vayres Bacchus, La Croix de Bayle, Gayat, l'Hosanne, Jean Dugay, Juncarret, Pichon Bellevue, Le Tertre, Toulouze, Les Tuileries du Déroc

Vensac David, de Taste

Vérac La Mongie, du Pontet

Verdelais Chanteloiseau, Dom de Grava, Pomirol le Pin

Vertheuil Le Bourdieu Vertheuil, Comtesse du Parc, Haut-Gouat, le Meynieu, Reysson, Le Souley-Ste Croix

Vignonet Bellecombe, Cazenave, Franc Bories, Grande Rouchonne, Hautes-Graves d'Arthus, du Paradis, Quercy, Teyssier, du Val d'Or, Vieux Labarthe

Villegouge Castagnac

Villenave-de-Rions Lenormand, Lézongars

Villenave-d'Ornon Baret, Couhins, Couhins-Lurton, Pontac Monplaisir

Villeneuve de Mendoce, Sauman

Villeneuve-de-Barbe de Barbe

Virelade Le Bourdillot, Virelade

Virsac Le Grand Chemin

Yvrac Dom de Bouteilley, Grand Jour, Haut-Greyzeau, Maillard